PSYCHOLOGICAL TESTING

AND ASSESSMENT

Second Edition

PSYCHOLOGICAL TESTING AND ASSESSMENT

An Introduction to

Tests and Measurement

Second Edition

Ronald Jay Cohen
St. John's University

Mark E. Swerdlik
Illinois State University

Douglas K. Smith
University of Wisconsin

Mayfield Publishing Company
Mountain View, California

Library of Congress Cataloging-in-Publication Data

Cohen, Ronald Jay.
    Psychological testing and assessment ; an introduction to tests &
measurement / Ronald Jay Cohen, Mark E. Swerdlik, Douglas K. Smith.
    —2nd ed.
        p.   cm.
    Rev. ed. of: Psychological testing / Ronald Jay Cohen . . .
[et al.], c1988.
    Includes bibliographical references and index.
    ISBN 0-87484-983-7
    1. Psychological tests.   I. Swerdlik, Mark E.   II. Smith, Douglas K.
III. Cohen, Ronald Jay. Psychological testing.   IV. Title.
    [DNLM: 1. Psychological Tests.   BF 176 C878p]
BF176.P777   1991
150′.28′7—dc20
DNLM/DLC
for Library of Congress   91-38912
                                                                                                  CIP

Manufactured in the United States of America

10 9 8 7 6 5 4

Mayfield Publishing Company
1240 Villa Street
Mountain View, California 94041

Sponsoring editor, Franklin C. Graham; production editor, Sharon Montooth; text designer, Hal Lockwood; cover designer, Cynthia Bogue; cover artist, Gunner Kullenberg; illustrator, Linda McVay. The text was set in 10/12 Bembo by G&S Typesetters, Inc. and printed on 45# Penntech Penn Plus by R. R. Donnelley & Sons Co.

Photo and illustration credits appear on page 885.

This book is dedicated to:

Edith and Harold Cohen
Susan R. Cohen
Barbara Cohen-Pavlo
Alan Cohen
Edna and Al Swerdlik
Peggy, Jenny, and Danny Swerdlik
Julie Smith
Beth and Claude Smith, and
Sheena

Brief
Contents

Contents

PART 2

THE SCIENCE OF PSYCHOLOGICAL MEASUREMENT

Chapter 6
Validity   **158**

Chapter 7
Test Development   **194**

—— PART 3 ——
THE ASSESSMENT OF INTELLIGENCE

Chapter 8
Intelligence and Its Measurement: An Overview   231

Chapter 9
Tests of Intelligence   276

Chapter 10
Educational Assessment   **324**

Chapter 11
Preschool Intelligence and Ability Assessment   **376**

—— PART 4 ——

PERSONALITY ASSESSMENT

Chapter 14
Other Methods of Assessing Personality and Behavior   483

— PART 5 —
TESTING AND ASSESSMENT IN ACTION

Chapter 20
Computer–Assisted Psychological Assessment   707

Preface

IT IS WITH a sense of pride that we present the second edition of this textbook. While endeavoring to maintain the clarity, comprehensiveness, and scholarship of the first edition, this volume has been thoroughly updated. There is a new chapter on preschool measures, a new chapter on computer-assisted psychological assessment, and expanded coverage of behavioral measures, child abuse evaluation, and marital and family assessment. Subsequent to the publication of our first edition, many important new tests such as the WISC-III and the MMPI-2 were published. Our coverage of these and other tests continues to be designed not only to acquaint readers with them, but to integrate facts about their structure, scoring, and interpretation into a more global framework for understanding measurement theory, practice, and issues.

Our expanded discussion of the distinction between the terms *psychological testing* and *psychological assessment* takes cognizance of the differences between them in contemporary usage. For decades, the term "psychological testing" has been widely used to refer to an exceptionally broad range of evaluative enterprises—too broad a range according to the many current contributors to the professional literature who view "testing" to be a subset of "assessment." In accordance with what we view to be a reasonable distinction between these two terms, the main title used in the previous edition (*Psychological Testing*) has been modified to better reflect the way these terms are used in the 1990's—hence, our new title, *Psychological Testing and Assessment.*

Many of the professors who were kind enough to write us about some aspect of the first edition will find the fruit of their labor in these pages. In response to requests to shift our coverage of legal/ethical matters to an earlier point in the book, this material is now presented in Chapter 2. The appendix for more detailed coverage of factor analysis, and the chapter on consumer assessment—two innovations in our previous work that were received enthusiastically—have been retained. In an effort to satisfy the technical demands of our most rigorous reviewers, individual words, phrases, and sentences were rewritten as many times as necessary.

The seven objectives outlined in the first edition of this book remain relatively unchanged in the present edition. It remains our intention to

1. provide a thorough, state-of-the-art, and readable description of basic measurement concepts at a level of technical complexity sufficient to equip students to understand technical terms in professional journals, test manuals, and test reports;

2. present up-to-date, reasonably detailed and well-balanced discussion of various issues in measurement ranging from the issue of heritability in intelligence, to general legal/ethical issues, to administration, scoring, and interpretation concerns with respect to computer-assisted psychological assessment;
3. blend theoretical and applied material in a way so as to provide the student with both a rationale for, and a hands-on feel of, the assessment process;
4. provide ample case illustrations of the wide range of "real world" contexts in which psychological testing and assessment occurs, including clinical, counseling, neuropsychological, educational, industrial-organizational, and consumer contexts;
5. provide an historical perspective on measurement complete with biographical material on many important contributors such as Alfred Binet, David Wechsler, Hermann Rorschach, Henry Murray, David Rappaport, and Lauretta Bender;
6. to excite genuine interest in the field of testing and assessment by writing with warmth, even occasional humor, and liberally illustrating with relevant material; and
7. to impart a sense of the authors' belief in and respect for the psychological assessment enterprise balanced by a healthy and realistic degree of self-criticism and an eye towards the challenges that still lie ahead.

We would like to express our appreciation to Louis H. Primavera of St. John's University, Dennis Cannon of Indiana University/Purdue University, Ft. Wayne, Michael Lambert of Brigham Young University, Terry G. Newell of California State University, Fresno, and Louis Snellgrove of Lambuth College for their thoughtful reviews and commentary on preliminary drafts of the second edition manuscript. Special thanks also to Kevin L. Moreland for his assistance in the preparation of the chapter on computer-assisted psychological assessment, and to David W. Stewart for his assistance in the preparation of the consumer assessment chapter.

In the pages that follow, one of the concepts to be discussed in the psychometric sense is that of error. But here we make reference to that concept in its non-psychometric, everyday meaning when we note that the responsibility for any error in this book rests with the authors and not with any of the people who were kind enough to provide us with assistance.

January 1992

Ronald Jay Cohen
Chestnut Ridge, New York

PART

1

AN OVERVIEW

Chapter 1

Psychological Testing

and Assessment

MEASUREMENT IS ONE thing we all seem to take for granted; we're quite accustomed to measuring the commodities of daily life in different units—gas by the gallon, milk by the quart, and so forth. In the study of psychological testing and assessment, however, we cannot afford to take measurement for granted. Measuring psychological variables is so complex that a variety of skills and knowledge must be brought to bear on every measurement made. If we look at the history of a familiar variable, such as distance measurements, we can better appreciate the complexity involved in measuring psychological variables.

The first tools used to measure distance were probably stones, branches, or parts of the measurer's own body. A measure of distance used throughout the world at one time was a *cubit,* defined as the length between an adult's elbow and the outstretched middle finger. If "standardization" were required, the length of some body part (such as a cubit, a foot, a palm, or a finger) of a royal personage could be used. An Egyptian "royal cubit," for example, is equal in length to seven palms—and presumably was "standardized" on a pharaoh with incredibly long arms. A measure of distance employed in England was a barleycorn, a unit equal to the width of a grain of barley (approximately one-third of an inch). Although we might chuckle at the thought of ordering a tuxedo in barleycorns or having a gown tailored in units of royal cubits, in fact the standard measure of length in America—the foot—is based on the length of an English king's foot.

Figure 1–1 *"One for the Road"—But How Much Is "One"?* Alcoholism researchers and educators speak of something called a "standard drink" in their studies of all types of alcohol consumption. What is supposed to be standard in a "standard drink" is a fixed amount of ethanol (one of the constituents of alcohol). But national differences exist with respect to standard drink units. In the United States, the standard drink unit most commonly employed in alcohol research and education is one that is about equivalent to what you might find in a typical U.S. drink of beer, wine, or spirits: one-half a U.S. fluid ounce of pure ethanol. In Canada, however, a standard drink is one that has a somewhat greater concentration of ethanol than you will find in a U.S. standard drink—this based on a customary serving of whiskey dispensed in Canadian bars. The standard in the United Kingdom has fluctuated between 8 and 10 grams of pure ethanol, a unit that has less ethanol by volume than either the American or Canadian standard. If all this sounds a little confusing to you, you're in good company; after analyzing 125 published studies that employed "standard drinks," Turner (1990) questioned the comparability of the various measures used on numerous grounds. Subsequent researchers have "pulled no punches" in their description of the state of research involving "standard drinks":

> The current situation in alcohol education and research is analogous to conditions following the collapse of the Tower of Babel. We speak in a plethora of different tongues, and our progress is impeded by the absence of a common language for understanding each other. (Miller, Heather, & Hall, 1991, p. 46)

So much for taking measurement for granted!

The worldwide standardization of distance measures occurred relatively recently in history. Not until 1875 did 17 nations ratify a treaty at the Convention of the Meter stipulating that a particular platinum bar, stored in a vault at the International Bureau of Weights and Measures in France, was to be the standard for the meter. As late as 1960, 38 countries represented at a conference on weights and measures redefined an international meter as "1,650,763.73 vacuum wavelengths of monochromatic orange light emitted by krypton atom of mass 86." The platinum bar idea was a lot simpler. The inch, as used in the United States and England, was also redefined to be equal in measurement to 2.54 centimeters (whereas it had previously been 2.54005 centimeters in the United States and 2.5399956 centimeters in England).

All fields of human endeavor use measurement in some form, and each field has its own set of measuring tools and measuring units. If you're recently engaged or thinking about becoming engaged, you may have obtained an education on a unit of measure called the *carat*. If you've been shopping for a computer, you may have learned something about a unit of measurement called a *byte*. And if you're in need of an air conditioner, you'll no doubt want to know about the Btu (British thermal unit). Other units of measurement you may or may not be familiar with include a mile (land), a mile (nautical), a ton (long), a ton (short), a hertz, a henry, miles per hour, cycles per second, and candela per square meter. Professionals in the fields that employ these units (as well as various tools to obtain measurements) know the potential uses, benefits, and limitations of the measuring tools they use and the measurements they make. So, too, it is incumbent upon the user or potential user of psychological measurements to have a working familiarity with the tools used in such measurement and the theoretical underpinnings of the enterprise.

USES OF TEST AND ASSESSMENT DATA

Educational Settings

From your own experience you are probably no stranger to the many types of tests administered in the classroom. You will recall that you have taken achievement tests—some constructed by the teacher, and others nationally standardized (for example, the Iowa Tests). You may have taken tests designed to assess your ability, aptitude, and/or interest with respect to a particular occupation or course of study. During at least one point in your career as a student, you have also probably taken a group-administered test of intelligence, now also referred to as a *school ability test*. Such tests are frequently administered, in part, to help identify children who may not be achieving at a level commensurate with their capability. In cases where appropriate, further evaluation with more specialized instruments may follow to assess the need for special education intervention. *Public Law 94–142*, now referred to as the *Individuals with Disabilities Education Act* (IDEA) mandates that appropriate educational programs be made available to individuals with disabilities between the ages of 3 and 21 who require special education. *Public Law 99–457*, specifies that services be delivered to preschoolers with disabilities (birth to age 2) and encourages services to at-risk infants, toddlers, and their families.

Tests are often used in educational settings to diagnose learning and/or behavior problems and to establish eligibility for special education programs. Individually administered intelligence and achievement measures are most often used for diagnostic purposes and are generally administered by school psychologists, psychoeducational diagnosticians, or similarly trained professionals. Interviews, behavioral observation, self-report scales, and behavior checklists are also widely used in educational settings.

In recent years we have witnessed the birth of a new type of achievement test: a certification of education. Particularly at the high school level, students in some areas of the country are being evaluated at the end of their course of study to determine if they indeed have acquired the minimal knowledge and skills expected of a high school graduate. Students unable to pass this certification test receive a certificate of attendance as opposed to a high school diploma. Needless to say, the cutting score (that is, the dividing line between passing and failing) on such a test is one with momentous consequences, and its determination must be made only by persons with a very sound technical knowledge of tests and measurement.

Another type of test administered in educational settings is that used for educational selection; many colleges and universities require scores on standardized tests such as the Scholastic Aptitude Test (SAT) or the Graduate Record Examination (GRE) as part of the undergraduate or graduate school admission process. Foreign applicants to North American universities may be required to take a standardized test of English proficiency as part of their admission application.

We will note here that few, if any, universities rely solely on standardized test scores in making admissions decisions. Typically, such decisions are based on an assessment of a number of factors ranging from grade-point average to letters of recommendation to written statements by the applicant to extracurricular interests and activities. To fulfill affirmative action requirements, variables such as ethnic background and gender may sometimes enter into the admission decision as well. Our coverage of psychological testing and assessment in educational settings appears in Chapter 10.

Counseling Settings

The use of assessment in a counseling context may occur in environments as diverse as a school, a prison, or a government or privately owned institution. Regardless of where it is done, assessment is typically undertaken to identify various strengths or weaknesses, with the ultimate objective being an improvement in the assessee's adjustment, productivity, and/or general quality of life. Measures of social and academic skills or abilities and measures of personality, interest, attitudes, and values are among the many types of tests that a counselor might administer to a client. Objectives in testing for counseling purposes vary with stage of life and particular situation; questions to be answered range from "How can this child work and play better with other children?" to "What career is the client best suited for?" to "What activities are recommended for retirement?" Since the test taker is in many instances the primary recipient and user of the data from a test administered by a counselor, it is imperative that either (1) a well-trained counselor fully explain the test results or (2) the results of the test be readily interpreta-

Table 1–1

A Scale to Measure College Students' "Hassles"

A new test designed to measure the "hassles," or everyday stressors in life, may one day be in use in college counseling centers. The authors of the Inventory of College Students' Recent Life Experiences (ICSRLE) noted that "because of the peculiarities of the college experience (e.g., dealing with professors, teaching assistants, exams, and term papers), it is often desirable to develop special measures for this population in the area of stress" (Kohn, Lafreniere, & Gurevich, 1990). If the number and quality of hassles in life are indeed predictive of adverse physical and mental health, as some have concluded (Burks & Martin, 1983; De Longis et al., 1982; Eckenrode, 1984; Kanner, Coyne, Schaefer, & Lazarus, 1981; Monroe, 1983; Weinberger, Hiner, & Tierney, 1987), it would seem important to have a scale to gauge hassles. Indeed, a test called the Hassles Scale (Kanner et al., 1981) was developed about a decade prior to the ICSRLE. However, Kohn et al. (1990, p. 620) argue that the Hassles Scale is "contaminated by items and a format which imply distressed physical and mental responses to stress as well as exposure to daily hassles." By contrast, they argue that their ICSRLE is an uncontaminated measure that measures only hassles—nothing more, nothing less. Here are the administration instructions and a few sample items from the ICSRLE:

Following is a list of experiences which many students have some time or other. Please indicate for each experience how much it has been a part of your life *over the past month.* Put a "1" in the space provided next to an experience if it was *not at all part* of your life over the past month (e.g., "trouble with mother in law—1"); "2" for an experience which was *only slightly* part of your life over that time; "3" for an experience which was *distinctly* part of your life; and "4" for an experience which was *very much* part of your life over the past month.

Intensity of Experience over Past Month
1 = *not at all* part of my life
2 = *only slightly* part of my life
3 = *distinctly* part of my life
4 = *very much* part of my life

1. Conflicts with boyfriend's/girlfriend's/spouse's family   _____
2. Being let down or disappointed by friends   _____
3. Conflict with professor(s)   _____
4. Social rejection   _____
5. Too many things to do at once   _____
6. Being taken for granted   _____
7. Financial conflicts with family members   _____
8. Having your trust betrayed by a friend   _____

Will the ISCRLE make it onto the shelves of counseling centers throughout North America? The answer to that depends on whether or not it is ultimately judged to be a "good test." Now, you might ask, "What constitutes a 'good test'?" Keep reading.

ble by test takers themselves via easy-to-follow instructions. It is also incumbent upon the interpreter of counseling tests to "consider whether learning experiences leading to the development of preferences and competencies have been stereotyped by expectations of behaviors considered appropriate for females and males, for racial and ethnic minorities, based on socioeconomic status, or for people with handicapping conditions" (*Standards*, 1985, p. 56).

Clinical Settings

Tests and other methods of assessment (such as interviews, case studies, and be-havioral observation) are widely used in clinical settings such as inpatient and outpatient clinics; public, private, and military hospitals; private-practice consult-ing rooms; and other institutions (such as schools) to screen for or diagnose be-havior problems. Situations that might raise the need for tests and other tools of clinical assessment include the following:

- A private psychotherapy patient wishes to be evaluated to see if the assess-ment can provide any nonobvious clues regarding his maladjustment.
- A school psychologist clinically evaluates a child experiencing learning difficulties to determine if her problem lies in a deficit of ability, a problem of adjustment, a discrepancy between teaching techniques being employed and the child's favored receptive and expressive modalities, or some com-bination of such factors.
- A psychotherapy researcher uses assessment procedures in order to deter-mine if a particular method of psychotherapy is effective in treating a par-ticular problem.
- A psychologist/consultant retained by an insurance company is called on to give an opinion as to the reality of a patient's psychological problems; is the patient really experiencing such problems or malingering?
- A court-appointed psychologist is asked to give an opinion as to a defen-dant's competency to stand trial.
- A prison psychologist is called on to given an opinion as to how rehabili-tated a prisoner convicted for a violent crime is.

The tests employed in clinical settings may be intelligence tests, personality tests, neuropsychological tests, or other specialized instruments, depending on the presenting or suspected problem area. The hallmark of testing in clinical set-tings is that the test or measurement technique is employed with only one indi-vidual at a time; group testing can be used only for screening at best—identifying those individuals who require further diagnostic evaluation. In Chapter 15 (Clini-cal and Counseling Assessment) and elsewhere, we will look at the nature, uses, and benefits of clinical assessment as well as some of its problematic issues.

Business Settings

In the business world, psychological tests and measurement are used extensively in such areas as employee selection. As we will see in Chapter 18, personnel psy-chologists use tests and measurement procedures to assess whatever knowledge or skills an employer needs to have assessed—be it the ability of a prospective air traffic controller to sustain attention to detail for hours on end or the ability of a prospective military officer to lead others. A wide range of achievement, ap-titude, interest, motivational, and other tests may be used not only in the decision to hire but also in related decisions regarding promotions, transfer, performance and/or job satisfaction, and eligibility for further training. Engineering psychol-ogists also employ a variety of existing and specially devised tests to help people at home and in the workplace, in part by designing ergonomically efficient consumer and industrial products—products ranging from office furniture to space-ship cockpit layout.[1]

Consumer psychologists help corporate America in the development, marketing, and sale of products. Using tests as well as other techniques, psychologists who specialize in this area may be involved in "taking the pulse" of the consumers—helping to predict the public's receptivity to a new product, a new brand, or a new advertising or marketing campaign. "What type of advertising will appeal to which type of individual?"—tests of attitudes and values have proved to be one valuable source of information to consumer psychologists and marketing professionals who endeavor to answer such questions. Tests and measurement in consumer psychology are the subject of Chapter 19.

Other Settings

Testing and assessment procedures are used in many other areas. Obtaining professional credentials is one such area; tests are used at the entry level (and beyond) for most professions. Before they are legally entitled to practice medicine, physicians must pass an examination. Law school graduates cannot hold themselves out to the public as attorneys until they pass their state's bar examination. Psychologists, too, must pass an examination entitling them to present themselves to the public as psychologists. And just as physicians can take further training and a test indicating that they are "board certified" in a particular area, so can psychologists specializing in certain areas be evaluated for a diploma from the American Board of Professional Psychology to recognize excellence in the practice of psychology.

Measurement may play an important part in program evaluation—be it a large-scale governmental program or a small-scale privately funded one. Is the program working? How can the program be improved? Are funds being spent in the areas where they ought to be spent? These are the types of general questions that tests and measurement procedures used in program evaluation are designed to answer.

Psychological assessment plays a valuable role in the process of psychological theory building; tests and measures may be employed in basic research to confirm or disprove hypotheses derived from behavioral theories. Tests, interviews, and other tools of assessment may be used to learn more about the organization of psychological traits and serve as vehicles by which new traits can be identified.

The courts rely on psychological test data and related expert testimony as one source of information to help answer important questions such as "Is this convict competent to be executed?" "Is this parent competent to take custody of the child?" and "Did this defendant know right from wrong at the time the crimi-

---

1. "Ergonomically efficient"? An *erg* is a unit of work and *ergonomics* is the study of work; more specifically in the present context, it is the relationship between people and tools of work. Among other endeavors, engineering psychologists are involved in designing things so that we can see, hear, reach, or generally use them better. For example, it was through extensive research by engineering psychologists that the division of letters and numbers that appears on a telephone was derived. Interested in obtaining a firsthand look at the kind of work engineering psychologists do? Take a moment to look through journals like *Ergonomics, Applied Ergonomics,* and *Man-Environment Systems* next time you're in your university library.

nal act was committed?" Issues such as these are covered in the forensic psychology section of Chapter 15.

Issues about testing people with disabling conditions have become increasingly prominent in recent years, and our survey of these issues as well as a glimpse at specialized measurement procedures used in this area appears in Chapter 17. In Chapter 16 we detail some of the methods used by neuropsychologists to help in the diagnosis and treatment of neuropsychological deficits.

TESTING AND ASSESSMENT

The development of an intelligence test in the early twentieth century that was designed to help place Paris schoolchildren in appropriate classes was a catalyst to the field of psychological testing like none before it in contemporary history; more than an object of lay curiosity or the stuff of experiments reported in academic journals, psychological test data were being applied in the hope of positively influencing lives. In the decades that followed, thousands of tests purporting to measure a variety of psychological variables would be developed and administered worldwide. A great impetus was given to the testing movement by the two world wars; group tests of intelligence and adjustment were successfully used to quickly screen large numbers of military recruits.

The heyday of psychological testing was the 1950s and early 1960s. Then, the prevailing philosophy in most mental health facilities was—as it remains in some quarters today—that an individual could be adequately evaluated if administered a variety of psychological tests (such as, at a minimum, a test of intelligence, a test of personality, and a test of neurological functioning). Corporate America, as well as many government agencies, also embraced psychological testing, and a potpourri of instruments and procedures were employed in decisions regarding the hiring, firing, and general utilization of personnel. But as psychological test use mushroomed, so did public concern about the use to which test data were being put. Because the test items and their scoring and interpretation were all typically confidential—if not shrouded, at least in the public eye, in mystery—many individuals compelled by an employer or prospective employer to sit for psychological tests were understandably apprehensive. Further, there was no guarantee that test takers would ever be given any feedback as to how they performed on the tests or the criteria on which their performance was being judged. Were the tests valid for the purpose for which they were being used? Was the constitutional right of privacy being violated by the widespread use of psychological tests? These are the kinds of questions that the courts began to grapple with. Public scrutiny of psychological testing reached its zenith in 1965, with probing congressional hearings (see Amrine, 1965).

Against a backdrop of mounting legal challenges to, and public concern about, psychological testing, many psychologists were compelled to look anew at the tools (and methods) of their profession. Beyond mere instruments of measurement, psychological tests began to be viewed as the tools of a highly trained examiner. This view is typified in the writing of Sundberg and Tyler (1962):

> The truth of the matter is that *tests are tools*. In the hands of a capable and
> creative person they can be used with remarkable outcomes. In the hands of

a fool or an unscrupulous person they become pseudoscientific perversion. (p. 131)

In later years, others would seek to refine the meaning of the term "psychological testing" by distinguishing the tools that may be used in an evaluative process (such as psychological tests) from the evaluative process itself. For example, in their text *Psychological Assessment,* Maloney and Ward (1976) conceptualized *psychological assessment* as a problem-solving process, ever variable in nature as a result of many different factors, beginning with the reason the assessment is being undertaken. Different tools of evaluation—psychological tests among them—may be marshaled in the process of assessment depending on the particular objectives, people, and circumstances involved, as well as other variables unique to the particular situation. By contrast *psychological testing* was seen as much narrower in scope, referring only to "the process of administering, scoring, and interpreting psychological tests" (Maloney & Ward, 1976, p. 9). Testing was also seen as differing from assessment because the process is "test-controlled"; decisions and/or predictions are made solely or largely on the basis of test scores. The examiner is more key to the process of assessment, in which decisions and/or predictions are made on the basis of many possible sources of data (including tests). Maloney and Ward also distinguished "testing" from "assessment" in terms of their respective objectives. In testing, a typical objective is to measure the magnitude of some psychological trait (for example, a trait related to intelligence or personality). In assessment, the typical objective is to answer a specific referral-for-assessment question. "Assessment" could also be distinguished from "testing" in other ways:

> [Testing] could take place without being directed at answering a specific referral question and even without the tester actually seeing the client or testee. For example, tests could be (and often are) administered in groups and then scored and interpreted for a variety of purposes. (p. 9)

> . . . while psychometric tests usually just add up the number of correct answers or the number of certain types of responses or performances with little if any regard for the how or mechanics of such content, clinical assessment is often far more interested in *how* the individual processes rather than the results of what he processes. The two operations, in fact, serve very different goals and purposes. (p. 39)

Regarding the collection of psychological assessment data, Maloney and Ward (1976) urged that far beyond the use of psychological tests alone, "Literally, any method the examiner can use to make relevant observations is appropriate" (p. 7). Some sixteen years later, we read of a "revolution" (Roberts & Magrab, 1991, p. 144) occurring in the assessment and treatment of children, a community-based, interdisciplinary, family-centered model that clearly emphasizes "assessment" (in the sense that Maloney and Ward had used that term) while deemphasizing "testing." Roberts and Magrab (1991) described their approach as follows:[2]

---

2. Roberts and Magrab (1991) used the term "assessment" in much the same way that Maloney and Ward (1976) did. However, Roberts and Magrab raise the question of how "ecologically valid" an

Assessment in this model does not emphasize stable traits but attempts to understand a problem in the larger ecological framework in which it occurs. For assessment to be ecologically valid, a broad range of information must be collected and new methods may be required to obtain the necessary information. These methods could include routine visits to the home and the community or naturalistic observations. (p. 145) . . .

Although standardized assessment procedures are very valuable in gaining insight into the developmental status of a child, they may not provide all the answers. Seeing the child in his or her natural environment may give valuable clues into styles of learning, additional skills, and interactional patterns in the family. (p. 146)

A former president of the American Psychological Association (APA) and expert in the area of psychological testing and assessment, Joseph D. Matarazzo, has added his voice to those who see value in a semantic distinction between "testing" and "assessment." This distinction was the subject of his presidential address delivered at the 1990 APA annual meeting, in which he stated:

Competent practitioners in psychology learn from clinician role models during apprenticeship training and from their own subsequent experiences that, objective psychological *testing* and clinically sanctioned and licensed psychological *assessment* are vastly different, even though assessment usually includes testing. Personnel technicians, elementary school teachers, and high school counselors monitoring, respectively, a group administration of the Otis Classification Tests, Iowa Tests of Educational Development, or College Entrance Examination Board's Scholastic Aptitude Tests (SAT) . . . are involved in psychological *testing,* an activity that has little or no continuing relationship or legally defined responsibility between examinee and examiner. Psychological *assessment,* however, is engaged in by a clinician and a patient in a one-to-one relationship and has statutorily defined or implied professional responsibilities. With the exception of those examiners involved in litigation, the typical psychological examination carried out by the clinical psychologist is geared specifically to the benefit and needs of the particular patient, determined from a careful reading of the patient's hospital chart or, in the case of an outpatient, from a telephone call or letter of referral. (Matarazzo, 1990, p. 1000)

As for the key role of the examiner in the process of assessment, Matarazzo (1990) echoed the observations of Sundberg and Tyler (1962):

In the hands of a good clinician, the results of an examination of intelligence or personality, correlated with information from the person's history, are as useful as analogous information would be in the hands of a good surgeon, internist, accountant, or plumber. In the hands of a fool—whether psychol-

---

assessment is—according to them, how valid the assessment is with respect to "the larger ecological framework in which it occurs." As we will see in the chapter that deals with the concept of validity (Chapter 6), psychologists have traditionally spoken of different types of validity, but "ecological validity" has not been one of them. Perhaps the type of validity that comes closest to the sense of "validity in the grand scheme of things" is what is referred to as construct validity. Think about this question again after you complete Chapter 6. You may also wish to consider whether a new type of validity measurement, one of "ecological validity," is needed—and, if so, how one might go about measuring it.

ogist, physician, physicist, elementary school teacher, college admissions officer, surgeon, or plumber—such data are tools for potential harm. (Matarazzo, 1990, p. 1001)

The authors cited above—Matarazzo (1990), Roberts and Magrab (1991), and Maloney and Ward (1976)—limited the scope of "psychological assessment" to clinical settings. But why not extend the testing/assessment distinction to personnel decision making—indeed, all possible settings in which evaluations of a psychological nature are made? A historical precedent exists for doing so. During World War II, the United States Office of Strategic Services (OSS) employed a variety of procedures and measurement tools—psychological tests among them— for the purpose of selecting military personnel for highly specialized positions involving spying, espionage, intelligence gathering, and the like. As summarized in *Assessment of Men* (OSS, 1948) and elsewhere (Murray & MacKinnon, 1946), the assessment data generated were subjected to thoughtful integration and evaluation by the highly trained assessment center staff. The OSS model of using an innovative variety of evaluative tools, with the data derived from the evaluations analyzed by highly trained assessors, would later inspire what is now referred to as the "assessment center" approach to personnel evaluation (Bray, 1982).

The semantic distinction that many have proposed between the terms "psychological testing" and "psychological assessment" has, like many semantic changes, been relatively slow in becoming integrated into everyday parlance; in practice, the two terms tend to be used almost interchangeably. It is also true that the dividing line between "testing" and "assessment" is not always clear; this is especially the case if "test" and "testing" are construed in a very broad sense. Consider, in this context, the activities described in Table 1–2.

Admittedly, the line between what constitutes "testing" and what constitutes "assessment" is not always as straightforward as we might like it to be. However, by acknowledging that such ambiguity exists, we can work toward sharpening our definition and use of these terms; denying or ignoring their distinctiveness provides no hope of a satisfactory remedy. For our purposes, we will define *psychological assessment* as "the gathering and integration of psychology-related data for the purpose of making a psychological evaluation, accomplished through the use of tools such as tests, interviews, case studies, behavioral observation, and specially designed apparatuses and measurement procedures."

Tools in the Assessment Process

The test A *test* may be defined simply as a measuring device or procedure. When the word *test* is prefaced with a modifier, what is being referred to is a measuring device or procedure designed to measure a variable related to that modifier. Consider, for example, the term *medical test,* which refers to a measuring device or procedure designed to measure some variable related to the practice of medicine (including a wide range of tools and procedures such as X-rays, blood tests, and testing of reflexes). In a like manner, the term *psychological test* refers to a measuring device or procedure designed to measure variables related to psychology (for example, intelligence, personality, aptitude, interests, attitudes, and values). And whereas a medical test might involve the analysis of a sample of blood,

Table 1-2

"Psychological Testing" or "Psychological Assessment"?

From your own understanding of the distinction between "testing" and "assessment," how would you classify each of these activities? Why?

An undergraduate student and part-time test proctor administers the Miller Analogies Test (MAT) to a group of students in the university's counseling center.

A man suffers neurological loss caused by an on-the-job accident that he claims was the result of the negligence of his employer. A court refers the man to a neuropsychologist to evaluate the extent of the loss, if any. The neuropsychologist administers a battery of psychological tests and submits a written report of the findings to the court.

A man suffers neurological loss caused by an on-the-job accident that he claims was the result of the negligence of his employer. A court refers the man to a neuropsychologist to evaluate the extent of the loss, if any. The neuropsychologist seeks out and obtains case study material in an effort to evaluate the man's neuropsychological intactness prior to the date of the accident. The neuropsychologist interviews the man with respect to observations made from the case study material, as well as related matters. A series of tests to determine the nature and extent of any impairment are administered, and a report of the findings is submitted to the court.

An experimental psychologist devises and uses a "tongue taste dispenser" apparatus to investigate aspects of the perception of taste in humans. After experiencing each of ten different tastes, subjects are asked to describe verbally each of the taste sensations.

A comparative psychologist uses the "tongue taste dispenser" to investigate taste perception in chimpanzees. After experiencing each of the ten different tastes, a group of trained raters rate each subject for positive or negative effect, as indicated by facial expression.

A social psychologist studies the phenomenon of obedience to authority by means of an apparatus that leads research subjects to believe that they will dispense electric shocks to other research subjects upon the experimenter's commands.

A psychologist exploring alternative definitions of "intelligence" studies the "street smarts" of adolescent subjects by means of in-school, in-home, and on-the-street observation and evaluation of subjects' interactions.

A personality psychologist seeks an answer to the question "Do people with eating disorders have distorted images of their body?" by studying a sample of patients who have eating disorders and a matched sample of subjects who do not. The methodology of the study calls for the administration of paper-and-pencil tests of body image distortion, as well as interviews with family members, friends, and other associates of the subjects.

A personnel psychologist evaluates a candidate's suitability for a position as the manager of a multimillion-dollar mutual fund by interviewing the candidate, evaluating the candidate's employment history and record and letters of reference, and reviewing the candidate's record of civic involvement and recreational interests.

An auto manufacturer pondering whether to name its latest model car "Exacta" refers this question to a consumer psychologist. The consumer psychologist administers a specially devised series of tests to a sample of people who have expressed interest in purchasing a car within the next month. This series is made up of a word-association test (subjects are asked to say the first thing that comes into their mind when they hear the word "Exacta" as well as other automobile-related words), figure drawings (people are

Table 1-2 (*continued*)

13

PSYCHOLOGICAL
TESTING AND
ASSESSMENT

asked to draw and then explain the picture of the car they envision when they hear that the car is called an "Exacta"), and a picture/story-telling test in which they are asked to make up a story upon being exposed to pictures involving "Exacta" in various types of situations.

A graduate research assistant proctors a computer administration of two tests: one that is a general measure of personality and another that surveys vocational interests. Immediately after the administration of the two tests, the computer scores the answer sheets and spews out a written narrative that summarizes the results, integrates and analyzes the findings from the two tests, and makes recommendations of possible vocational pursuits on the basis of the findings.

Although the semantic border between "testing" and "assessment" may appear clear, it can quickly become blurry, and people may differ as to whether some of the vignettes cited above illustrate instances of "psychological testing" or "psychological assessment."

of tissue, or the like, a psychological test almost always involves the analysis—in the broadest sense of the word—of a sample of behavior. The behavior sample could range from responses to a pencil-and-paper questionnaire to oral responses to questions to performance of some task. The behavior sample could be elicited by the stimulus of the test itself or could be naturally occurring behavior (under observation). The term *psychological testing* can be defined as "the process of measuring psychology-related variables by means of devices or procedures designed to obtain a sample of behavior."

Psychological tests may differ on a number of variables such as content, format, administration procedures, scoring and interpretation procedures, and psychometric or technical quality. The *content* of the test will of course vary with the focus of the particular test. But even two psychological tests purporting to measure the same construct—for example, "personality"—may differ widely in item content because of factors such as the test developer's definition of personality and the theoretical orientation of the test (that is, items on a psychoanalytically oriented personality test may have little resemblance to those on an existentially oriented personality test, yet both are "personality tests"). *Format* pertains to the plan, organization, arrangement, and layout of test items as well as to related considerations such as time limits. Variables related to *administration* may overlap to some extent with format variables. Is the test self-administered or examiner-administered? If examiner-administered, does the examiner merely proctor the test, or does the examiner require specialized training to properly administer the test? Such questions may be raised with respect to administration procedures.

Psychological tests differ widely in terms of *scoring and interpretation guidelines*. Some tests are designed to be scored by test takers themselves, others are designed to be scored only by a trained examiner, and still others may be scored only by a computer. Some tests, such as most tests of intelligence, come complete with test manuals that are very explicit not only about scoring criteria but also about the nature of the interpretations that can be made from the calculated score. Other tests, such as the Rorschach Inkblots Test (discussed in Chapter 13),

are sold with no manual; the purchaser buys the stimulus materials and then selects and uses one of many available guides for administration, scoring, and
interpretation.

Tests differ with respect to their *technical or psychometric quality*. At this point
suffice it to say that a good test measures what it purports to measure in a consistent way and that if two tests purport to measure the exact same (identically defined) construct, the test that measures the construct better is the better (that is,
the technically superior or more psychometrically sound) instrument. We have
more to say about what constitutes a "good test" later in this chapter, and all of
Part 2 is concerned with issues related to the psychometric quality of a test. Let's
also note here that it is easier to identify a "good test" than to identify a "good
assessment process." A developing body of knowledge and a proving ground of
experience have yielded methodologies with which tests can be evaluated for psychometric soundness. However, it is generally more difficult to evaluate the
soundness of an assessment procedure because there are typically many more
variables involved. Unlike a test, which may be designed to measure a particular
trait, psychological assessment is undertaken in an effort to provide more information relevant to specific questions or issues, and the nature of the tools used
and the procedures followed will vary accordingly. Because of the diversity of
assessors' backgrounds, it is conceivable that two assessors might use entirely different sets of tools and procedures to answer any given assessment question. Can
one approach to assessment be more valid than the other? Yes. But determining
the answer to that question with a fair amount of certainty can sometimes be an
ambitious undertaking. As Maloney and Ward (1976, p. 4) put it: "We do have
ways of assessing test-as-tools efficiency. On the other hand, it is much more
difficult to determine the efficiency of the process of psychological assessment,
primarily because there is much less agreement on what this process is or what it
entails."

The interview   Another widely used tool in the process of psychological assessment is the *interview*—a word that may conjure images of face-to-face talk.
But an interview as a tool of psychological assessment involves more than talk. If
the interview is being conducted face to face, the interviewer will probably be
noting nonverbal as well as verbal behavior. (Is the interviewee dressed appropriately? Is the interviewee sitting with a clenched fist? With inordinately sweaty
palms? Are the interviewee's affective facial expressions appropriate in terms of
what is being said? Does the interviewee make good eye contact?) A face-to-face
interview need not necessarily even involve any speech if the interviewee is deaf
or suffering from a hearing impairment; the entire interview might be conducted
in sign language. An interview can be conducted over the telephone, in which
case the interviewer might make inferences regarding the content of what is said
as a function of changes in the interviewee's voice quality. An interview of sorts
could also conceivably be conducted via other electronic media, with an interviewer at one computer terminal and an interviewee at another terminal. In its
broadest sense, then, we can define an interview as a method of gathering information through direct, reciprocal communication. (See Figure 1–2.)

The interview is a very popular information-gathering tool not only in psychology but in virtually all other fields as well. To appreciate just how widespread

Figure 1–2 *Different Interviewers Have Different Interview Styles.* Focusing on three
or four of the people above who you feel you know something about, what words would
you use to describe the differences between them as interviewers? By the way, in case you
are wondering, pictured above from left to right are (top row) Johnny Carson, Barbara
Walters, and Ed Bradley; (second row) Joan Rivers, Louis Rukeyser (ask your professor if
you don't know who he is), and Oprah Winfrey; (third row) Dan Rather, Mike Wallace,
and the senior author of this book, Ronald Jay Cohen.

interviewing is, try to recall the last time you went through a day without being
exposed to an interview on television, radio, in the print media, or somewhere
else. In psychology as in other professions, there are different types of interviews.
For example, in Chapter 15 you will be introduced to one specialized type of
clinical interview called the *mental status examination*. Another variety of interview
is one that is conducted while the interviewee is in an altered state of consciousness. For example, interviews conducted under hypnosis (Hoffman, 1985) or

while the interviewee is under the influence of a drug such as sodium amytal (Pellegrini & Putman, 1984) are sometimes undertaken in an effort to obtain more information than might otherwise be obtained.

A stress interview, as its name implies, is one in which the interviewee is purposely placed in some stressful situation. The stress might take almost any form: seating the interviewee on a wobbly chair, repeatedly interrupting the interviewee, encouraging the interviewee to partake of greasy "finger food" without providing napkins, or giving the interviewee instructions that are impossible to execute. Rarely used, stress interviews may have application in specialized employment settings where it is critical to sample and evaluate a candidate's effectiveness in dealing with stress. During World War II, stress interviews were employed to help select intelligence agents.

The form any interview takes depends on many factors, including the purpose and objectives of the interview (clinical evaluation? evaluation for employment? evaluation for admission to some specialized program?), time or other limitations or restrictions, and the anticipated ability (or willingness) of the interviewee to respond. Interviewers themselves vary widely with respect to variables such as their pacing of interviews, the extent to which they attempt to develop (and succeed in developing) a rapport with their interviewees, and the extent to which they convey genuineness, empathy, and a sense of humor.

The case study   Also referred to as a *case history,* the case study is, in essence, a compilation of biographical data from as many relevant sources as the compiler can find (such as records, parents, siblings, teachers, friends, employers, and, of course, the subject of the study). The focus of the case study will vary as a function of the purpose of the assessment. If a job applicant is being evaluated, the case study will focus on aspects of the applicant's previous employment such as duties and responsibilities, level of performance, interpersonal relations skills, and salary history. Perhaps most typically, the case history is a tool used in clinical settings as an aid in developing a treatment plan. Here the case study data may include, at a minimum, synopses of available reports by doctors and hospitals and information concerning the patient's early as well as current adjustment. Case history data provide a useful framework for integrating new information about a patient.

Behavioral observation   "To the extent that it is practically feasible, direct observation of behavior frequently proves the most clinically useful of all assessment procedures" (Goldfried & Davison, 1976, p. 44). Behavioral observation has indeed proved to be a very useful assessment procedure, particularly in institutional settings such as schools, hospitals, prisons, and group homes. Using published or self-constructed behavioral checklists such as the one shown in Figure 1–4, staff professionals can observe firsthand the behavior of the person under observation and design interventions accordingly. In a school situation, for example, behavioral observation on the playground of a culturally different child suspected of having linguistic problems might reveal that the child does have English language skills but is unwilling—for reasons of shyness, cultural upbringing, or whatever—to demonstrate these abilities to an adult.

Despite the potential usefulness of behavioral observation in settings ranging from the private practitioner's consulting room to the interior of a manned rocket on a space mission, it tends to be used infrequently outside institutional settings.

Figure 1–3 *Case Study Material.* Just as family photographs and albums, as well as other memorabilia, including letters and other correspondence, films, videotapes, audiotapes, and personal collections of valued items or mementos, may supply sources of information to a biographer writing a biography, such items may yield insights to a psychologist writing a case study.

For private practitioners, it is economically unfeasible to spend hours out of the consulting room engaged in behavioral observation. And as for behavioral scientists observing, firsthand, space crew members in flight—that must await NASA's acceptance of behavioral scientists as crew members (Jones, 1984).

Other tools Numerous other types of tools are available for specialized assessment applications. Ordinary blood pressure or body temperature readings may become tools of assessment in a psychological study, especially if analyzed with measures of stress or other psychological variables (see, for example, McCubbin et al., 1991; Ussher & Wilding, 1991). Biofeedback equipment is useful in obtaining measures of bodily reactions (such as muscular tension or galvanic skin response) to various sorts of stimuli. An instrument called a penile plethysmograph, which gauges male sexual arousal, has found application in sexual therapy programs with normal males experiencing sexual difficulties as well as in the treatment of sexual offenders. Impaired ability to identify odors is not uncommon in disorders such as Alzheimer's disease and Down's syndrome, in which the central nervous system (CNS) may be affected. Tests such as the University of Pennsylvania Smell Identification Test (UPSIT) have been helpful in assessing the extent of olfactory deficit in these and other diseases where there is suspected CNS involvement, such as acquired immunodeficiency syndrome (AIDS)

Figure 1–4 *The Taking-Out-the-Garbage Checklist.* Deinstitutionalization and the placement of children and adult psychiatric patients into community-based facilities has created a need for behavioral checklists by which the facility staff can gauge the progress of developmentally disabled individuals. Rudimentary skills necessary for independent living—such as taking out the garbage—are tracked via checklists such as the one below. This checklist came from the "Housekeeping Skills" section of a book of behavioral checklists, with other sections such as "Personal Management," "Kitchen Skills," "Street Safety," "Travel Training," "Leisure Skills," and "Community Skills." (Source: Roth & Hermus, 1980, p. 89)

BEHAVIORAL PROGRAMMING SCALE

Name of Client: **Instructor:**   **Date:**

EMPTYING GARBAGE

LRO	SRO Behavior			Daily Recordings					
		M	T	W	Th	Fri	Weekly total	Criteria met? (Yes = +, No = −)	
1	**Removing Garbage**	//////	//////	//////	//////	//////		
	A. Goes to garbage can.							
	B. Takes full bag from garbage can.							
2	**Disposing of Garbage**	//////	//////	//////	//////	//////		
	C. Takes bag of garbage to trash can.							
	D. Opens trash can.							
	E. Places garbage in trash can.							
	F. Closes trash can.							
3	**Lining Can with New Bag**	//////	//////	//////	//////	//////		
	G. Goes to closet.							
	H. Takes new garbage bag.							
	I. Takes bag to garbage can.							
	J. Places bag in can.							
	K. Pushes bag into can.							
	L. Overlaps bag top over can top.							

LRO = Long-range behavior objective
SRO = Short-range behavior objective
   Enter "1" through "7" in appropriate box to indicate client's level of skill. Criterion is met when a score of "7" is achieved four times out of five for two consecutive trial periods.

(Brody, Serby, Etienne, & Kalkstein, 1991). The UPSIT test taker is sequentially exposed to 40 scratch-and-sniff odors and asked to identify each odor from a four-item word list.

There has been no shortage of innovation on the part of psychologists in devising measurement tools, or adapting existing tools, for use in psychological measurement. In any additional courses in psychology you may take—abnormal, social, developmental, experimental, or whatever—you may marvel at the many ingenious ways psychologists have devised to measure variables of interest. Consider, for example, the apparatus illustrated in Figure 1–5.

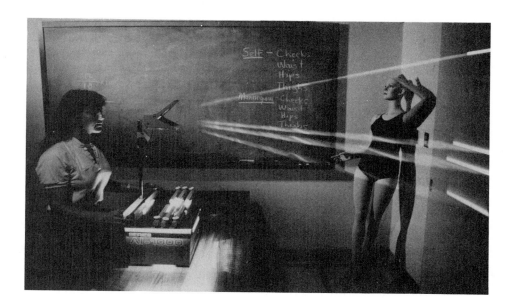

Figure 1–5 *Measuring Body Image Distortion in Persons with Eating Disorders.* People with eating disorders such as anorexia nervosa (characterized by maintenance of below-average body weight and a preoccupation with remaining very thin) and bulimia nervosa (also known as "binge-purge syndrome") frequently exhibit evidence of body image distortion when interviewed; they tend to see themselves as heavier than they really are (Bruch, 1962; Cash & Brown, 1987; Garner, Garfinkel, Stancer, & Moldofsky, 1976; Slade, 1985). But just how distorted is one's image of one's own body? To address that question a number of measuring devices and procedures have been devised, ranging from paper-and-pencil questionnaires to adjustable calipers to imaging techniques that employ photographs, mirrors, or video recorders (Garner & Garfinkel, 1981; Gleghorn, Penner, Powers, & Schulman, 1987; Lindholm & Wilson, 1988; Ruff & Barrios, 1986).
An apparatus called the adjustable light beam apparatus (ALBA), developed by Thompson and Thompson (1986) and described in a number of studies by J. Kevin Thompson and his associates (Thompson & Spana, 1988; Thompson, 1990; Penner, Thompson, & Coovert, 1991), is one of the tools that have been developed as aids to assess body image distortion. The procedure entails the removal of any bulky clothing, so that the assessee is in usual street clothes when the measurements are taken. The use of the ALBA is explained and, after practice with it, assessees adjust four beams of light to reflect what they believe to be the width of their cheeks, waist, hips, and thighs. A measure of the accuracy—or the distortion—of the estimate is obtained by dividing the estimated width by the actual width. The resulting ratio is then multiplied by 100 to yield a percentage of over- or under-estimation of body size.

THE WHO, WHAT, AND WHERE
OF PSYCHOLOGICAL TESTING

Who Are the Parties?

It may be said that the endeavor of psychological testing involves a minimum of three parties: the test developer, the test user, and the test taker. We should also point out that, in a broader sense, another party to the test situation is society as a whole; testing—be it individual testing in a private practitioner's office or a government-sponsored nationally administered group test—affects individual lives and ultimately the quality of life. As pointed out elsewhere:

> Educational and psychological testing involves and significantly affects individuals, institutions, and society as a whole. The individuals affected include students, parents, teachers, educational administrators, job applicants, employees, patients, supervisors, executives, and evaluators. The institutions affected include schools, colleges, business, industry, and government agencies. Individuals and institutions benefit when testing helps them achieve their goals. Society, in turn, benefits when the achievement of individual and institutional goals contributes to the general good. (*Standards,* 1985, p. 1)

Some of the other roles in the process of psychological testing include the test marketer, the test sponsor, the test administrator (examiner), the test scorer, and the interpreter of test results. Once a test developer independently creates a test, the test must either be sold to a commercial test publisher or marketed directly to its potential users (such as clinicians or school boards). Sometimes a test is developed under the auspices of a test publisher or an institution that, in effect, acts as the test's sponsor. If an institution sponsors the development of a test and then wishes to use the test for its own purposes, the test sponsor is also a test user. In addition to the not mutually exclusive roles of test administrator, test scorer, and test interpreter, we might add one other individual to our list: the test reviewer. Published reviews play an important role in decisions regarding the use of a particular test.

The test developer The test developer creates the test. As we will see in Chapter 7, certain steps are common to the development of a test regardless of whether the test is to be standardized and published or is simply designed for classroom use. Publications such as *Standards for Educational and Psychological Testing* (1985) attempt to serve—and ethically should serve—as a source of guidelines for the development of any new test. The test developer may or may not assume other roles vis-à-vis the test, including the following: test publisher, test marketer, test sponsor, test user, test administrator, test scorer, and test results interpreter.

The number of psychological tests developed and made available to test users burgeons with every passing year. The next time you're in your university library, go to the journals and pick, at random, a half dozen or so psychology-related publications. Look through the articles in each of the journals; we think the chances are good that you will find at least one reference to some newly developed psychological test. The authors of this book performed a similar task; we looked through psychology journals that happened to be on the shelves whenever we made one of our frequent trips to the library to do research for this book. Interestingly, we found many references to new tests (or at least tests that were new to us), and a partial listing of these tests appears in Table 1–3.

The American Psychological Association has estimated that upwards of 20,000 new psychological tests are developed each year. *Why?* Many psychologists who develop tests seem to feel that they can aid clinicians in their therapy-related decisions or counseling psychologists in their responsibilities to their clients or researchers in testing a specific hypothesis or evaluating the effectiveness of a particular program. Given that the business of psychological testing has become big business, the promise of financial remuneration may in some instances be motivating as well.[3]

The test user Tests, like any tools, can be used properly or abused. No matter how psychometrically sound a test is, the purpose of the test will be defeated if the user does not in every respect follow the recommendations for test use that appear in the test's manual (if the test, in fact, has a test manual). The results of a testing can be made questionable at best if the recommendations of the test manual are compromised at any point in the process—from test administration to test scoring to test results interpretation.

The test user has ethical obligations that must be fulfilled even before any test taker is exposed to the test. For example, the test must be stored in a way that reasonably ensures that its specific contents will not be made known to test takers in advance—leaving open the possibilities of irregularities later. Note that we used the term *specific contents* in describing what must be secured from test takers in advance of the test. In the case of some specific types of tests, mostly tests of achievement, acquainting the test taker with the general type of questions the test will contain helps to lift the veil of mystery that may surround a test and minimize the associated test anxiety (see, for example, the booklets prepared for prospective Scholastic Aptitude Test or Graduate Record Examination examinees). With some types of tests, such as intelligence tests and projective tests of personality, such pretest descriptions of the test materials would not be advisable because the resulting data might be biased. Another obligation of the test user prior to the test's administration is to ensure that a prepared and suitably trained person administers the test properly. The test administrator (or examiner) must be familiar with the test materials and procedures and have at the test site all of the materials needed to properly administer the test—a sufficient supply of test protocols and other supplies, a stopwatch, if necessary, and so forth.[4] The test examiner

---

3. Test publishers do not publicize their earnings, and exact, up-to-date figures are hard to come by. However, to provide the reader with an idea of the extent to which psychological and educational testing is indeed "big business," consider a sampling of the revenues earned by just a few of the many psychological and educational test publishers in the mid-1970s. Kohn (1975) reported that one test publisher, Harcourt Brace Jovanovich, had approximately $21 million in sales in 1974. For that same year, Kohn reported that the measurement and guidance division of Houghton Mifflin recorded sales of approximately $5.5 million, the American College Testing Program had sales of approximately $11 million, and Educational Testing Service had sales of approximately $54 million.
4. *Protocol* in everyday usage refers to diplomatic etiquette. A less common usage of the word is as a synonym for the first copy or rough draft of a treaty or other official document prior to its ratification. This second meaning comes closer to the way the word is used with reference to psychological tests, as a noun referring to the form or sheet on which the test taker's responses have been entered.

The Standards for Educational and Psychological Testing

standards for educational and psychological testing

American Educational Research Association
American Psychological Association
National Council on Measurement in Education

Standards for Educational and Psychological Testing (1985) was prepared by a joint committee of the American Educational Research Association (AERA), the American Psychological Association (APA), and the National Council on Measurement in Education (NCME). The origins of this publication can be traced to the work of an American Psychological Association committee chaired by Lee Cronbach between 1950 and 1954. In March of 1954, that committee issued a document entitled *Technical Recommendations for Psychological Tests and Diagnostic Techniques*. One year later, a document called *Technical Recommendations for Achievement Tests* was developed by committees from the AERA and the National Council on Measurements Used in Education (an organization that subsequently abbreviated its name to the National Council on Measurement in Education). In late 1963, an eight-person committee composed of members from each of these three organizations worked to develop a document published in 1966 by the American Psychological Association and entitled *Standards for Educational and Psychological Tests and Manuals*. The committee members were John W. French (Co-chair, APA), William B. Michael (Co-chair, AERA-NCME), Oscar K. Buros, Herbert S. Conrad, Lee J. Cronbach, Max D. Englehart, J. Raymond Gerberich, and Willard G. Warrington. The *Standards* underwent revision in 1974 and again, most recently, in 1985.

An indispensable reference work for professional users and developers of psychological and educational tests, this publication is divided into four parts, which cover standards for (1) test construction and evaluation, (2) test use, (3) "particular applications" (that is, testing linguistic minorities and testing people who have handicapping conditions), and (4) administrative procedures. Its objective is "to provide criteria for the evaluation of tests, testing practices, and the effects of test use. Although the evaluation of the appropriateness of a test or application should depend heavily on professional judgment, the *Standards* can provide a frame of reference to assure that relevant issues are addressed" (p. 2).

Earlier editions of this work used terms such

as "desirable," "very desirable," and "essential" to classify the relative importance of the various guidelines. The guidelines in the latest edition are categorized as being of either primary or secondary importance, "in part to avoid the troublesome distinction between desirable and highly desirable and to avoid the label 'essential' . . . Importance is viewed largely as a function of the potential impact that the testing process has on individuals, institutions, and society" (p. 2). *Primary standards* are defined as "those that should be met by all tests before their operational use and in all test uses, unless a sound professional reason is available to show why it is not necessary, or technically feasible, to do so in a particular case." *Secondary standards* are "desirable as goals but are likely to be beyond reasonable expectation in many situations." A third category, *conditional*, takes cognizance of the fact that standards may vary in importance as a function of their application; a particular standard may be primary in one situation but secondary in another. Following are examples of each of these three types of standards, drawn from the section on testing people with disabling conditions (p. 79):

People who modify tests for individuals with disabilities should have available to them psychometric expertise for so doing. In addition, they should have available to them knowledge of the effects of various disabling conditions on test performance, acquired either from their own training or experience or from close consultation with disabled individuals or those thoroughly familiar with such individuals. (*Primary*)

Empirical procedures should be used whenever possible to establish time limits for modified forms of timed tests rather than simply allowing handicapped test takers a multiple of the standard time. Fatigue should be investigated as a potentially important factor when time limits are extended. (*Secondary*)

Forms of tests that are modified for people who have various handicapping conditions should generally be pilot tested on people who are similarly handicapped to check the appropriateness and feasibility of the modifications. (*Conditional*)

The authors of the *Standards* remind us, however, that the "categories in which standards are placed should be viewed as imperfect. Where testing has a limited role in a larger assessment procedure (e.g., tests conducted by a clinical, industrial, or school psychologist), some primary standards, especially those dealing with documentation, should be considered as having a secondary designation" (p. 3).

The 1985 edition of the *Standards* contains more guidelines related to all aspects of test use than did previous editions. It is emphasized throughout that "test users should have a sound technical and professional basis for their actions, much of which can be derived from research done by test developers and publishers. In selecting a test, a potential user should depend heavily upon the developer's research documentation that is clearly related to the intended application. Although the test developer should supply the needed information, the ultimate responsibility for appropriate test use lies with the user" (p. 3).

Table 1–3

Have You Heard of These Tests?

In leafing through recent volumes of various psychology journals, we were struck by the variety of subject matter on which tests are available. We had not heard of many of these tests, and we list them here only to provide you with a sampling of the variety of new tests being developed. We've listed the tests by subject and next to the name of the test is the reference citation for where we happened to have found it. Let us emphasize that the citation is simply a reference to where we saw the article; the authors of the article are *not* necessarily the authors of the test.

Subject	*Test*
Anger	Spielberger Anger Expression Scale (Knight, Chisholm, Paulin, & Waal-Manning, 1988)
	Anger Control Inventory (Hoshmand & Austin, 1987)
Anhedonia	Physical Anhedonia Scale (Peterson & Knudson, 1983)
	Revised Social Anhedonia Scale (Mishlove & Chapman, 1985)
Body image avoidance	Body Image Avoidance Questionnaire (Rosen, Srebnik, Saltzberg, & Wendt, 1991)
Bonding	Therapeutic Bond Scales (Saunders, Howard, & Orlinsky, 1989)
Bulimia	BULIT (bulimia test; Smith & Thelen, 1984; Thelen, Farmer, Wonderlich, & Smith, 1991)
Burnout	Maslach Burnout Inventory (Gold, 1984)
Child abuse potential	Child Abuse Potential Inventory (Milner, 1989)
Combat exposure	Combat Exposure Scale (Lund, Foy, Sipprelle, & Strachan, 1984)
Computers	Computer Attitude Scale (Loyd & Loyd, 1985)
Death-related concerns	Threat Index (Moore & Neimeyer, 1991)
Depression	Depressive Experiences Questionnaire (Klein, 1989)
	Depression Coping Questionnaire (Kleinke, 1988)
Dysfunctional attitudes	Dysfunctional Attitude Scale (Oliver & Baumgart, 1985)
Eating disorders and dieting beliefs	Dieting Beliefs Scale (Stotland & Zuroff, 1990)
	Eating Disorders Inventory (Rosen, Silberg, & Gross, 1988)
Family environment	Family Environment Scale (Oliver, May, & Handel, 1988)
Fears	Agrophobic Cognitions Questionnaire (Chambless, Caputo, Bright, & Gallagher, 1984)
	Goldfarb Fear of Fat Scale (Goldfarb, Dykens, & Gerrard, 1985)
	Social Phobic and Anxiety Inventory (Turner, Beidel, Dancu, & Stanley, 1989)
	Fear of Negative Evaluation Questionnaire (Davison, Feldman, & Osborn, 1984)
Guilt	Hostility-Guilt Inventory (Kolko, Kazdin, & Meyer, 1985)
Hopelessness	Hopelessness Scale (Holden & Fekken, 1988)
Hysteria	Hysteroid-Obsessoid Questionnaire (Weeks, 1985)
Insomnia	Assessment of Insomnia (Spielman, 1986)
Intimacy	The Intimacy Attitude Scale—Revised (Amidon, Kumar, & Treadwell, 1983)
Loneliness	The Loneliness Rating Scale (Scalise, Ginter, & Gerstein, 1984)
Malingering	Structured Interview of Reported Symptoms (Rogers, Gillis, Dickens, & Bagby, 1991)

Table 1–3 (*continued*) 25

Marital adjustment	Marital Adjustment Test (O'Farrell, Cutter, & Floyd, 1985)
	Spousal Conflict Arousal Scale (Seymour & Lessne, 1984)
Physical concerns	Body Cathexis Scale (Jupp, 1983)
	Body Elimination Attitude Scale (Templer, King, Brooner, & Corgiat, 1984)
	Menstrual Symptom Questionnaire (Nelson, Sigmon, Amodei, & Jarrett, 1984)
Psychological-mindedness	Psychological Mindedness Assessment Procedure (McCallum & Piper, 1990)
Psychotherapy alliance	California Psychotherapy Alliance Scales (Gaston, 1991)
Psychotherapy evaluation	Child Evaluation Inventory (Kazdin, Esveldt-Dawson, French, & Unis, 1987)
Self-concept	Academic Self-Concept Scale (Reynolds, 1988)
Self-consciousness	Self-Consciousness Scales (Burnkrant & Page, 1984)
Self-efficacy	Generalized Self-Efficacy Scale (Selby, 1984)
Self-righteousness	Self-Righteousness Scales (Falbo & Belk, 1985)
Self-statements	Social Interaction Self-Statement Test (Zweig & Brown, 1985)
Sexual assault symptoms	Sexual Assault Symptom Scale (Ruch, Gartrell, Amedeo, & Coyne, 1991)
Sexual interaction/ satisfaction	Sexual Interaction Inventory (LoPiccolo, Heiman, Hogan, & Roberts, 1985)
	Sexual Arousability Index (Anderson, Broffitt, Karlsson, & Turnquist, 1989)
	Golombok-Rust Inventory of Sexual Satisfaction (Rust & Golombok, 1985)
Social support	The Significant Others Scale (Power, Champion, & Aris, 1988)
Social tension	Test of Negative Social Exchange (TENSE) (Ruehlman & Karoly, 1991)
Statistics	Attitudes Towards Statistics Scale (Wise, 1985)
	Mathematics Anxiety Rating Scale (Levitt & Hutton, 1984)
Stress	Daily Stress Inventory (Brantley, Dietz, McKnight, & Jones, 1988)
Suicide	Scale for Suicide Ideation (Beck, Steer, & Ranieri, 1988)
	Aftermath of Suicide Instrument (Spence, Goldney, & Moffitt, 1984)
Unpleasant events	Unpleasant Events Schedule (Lewinsohn, Mermelstein, Alexander, & MacPhillamy, 1985)
	Pain Assessment Questionnaire (Sturmey, Newton, & Ghadiali, 1988)
	Dental Visit Satisfaction Scale (Corah, O'Shea, Pace, & Seyrek, 1984)
Women as managers	Women as Managers Scales (WAMS) (Crino, White, & Looney, 1985)
Miscellaneous	Autonomic Nervous System Response Inventory (Waters, 1984)
	Satisfaction with Life Scale (Diener, Emmons, Larsen, & Griffin, 1985)
	Scale of Attitudes Towards the Treatment of Animals (Bowd, 1984)
	Autonomic Nervous System Response Inventory (Waters, 1984)

Figure 1–6 *Less-Than-Optimal Testing Conditions.* In 1917, new Army recruits sat on the floor as they were administered the first group tests of intelligence—not ideal testing conditions by current standards.

must also ensure that the room the test will be conducted in is suitable and conducive to the testing (see Figure 1–6). To the extent that it is possible, distracting conditions such as excessive noise, heat, cold, interruptions, glaring sunlight, crowding, inadequate ventilation, and so forth should be avoided. Even a badly scratched or graffiti-grooved writing surface on a desk can act as a contaminating influence on the test administration; if the writing surface is not reasonably smooth, the written productions made on it may in some instances lead a test scorer to suspect that the examinee had a tremor or some type of perceptual-motor deficit. In short, if the test is a standardized one, it is the obligation of the test administrator to see that reasonable testing conditions prevail during the test administration; if for any reason these conditions did not prevail during an administration of the test (for instance, there was a fire drill or a real fire), an accounting of such unusual conditions should be enclosed with the test record.

Especially in one-on-one or small-group testing, rapport between the examiner and examinee is important. In the context of the testing situation, *rapport* may be defined as a working relationship between the examiner and the examinee. Such a working relationship can sometimes be achieved with a few words of "small talk" when examiner and examinee are introduced. If appropriate, some words regarding the nature of the test as well as why it is important for examinees to do their best may also be helpful. In other instances, as with the case of a frightened child, the achievement of rapport might involve more elaborate techniques such as engaging the child in play or some other activity until the child is deemed to have acclimated to the examiner and the surroundings. It is important that attempts to establish rapport with the test taker not compromise any rules of the test's standardized administration instructions.

Evidence exists to support the view that examiners themselves may have an effect on test results. Whether the examiner is familiar or a stranger (Sacks, 1952; Tsudzuki, Hata, & Kuze, 1957), whether the examiner is present or absent (Bernstein, 1956), and the general manner of the examiner (Wickes, 1956; Exner 1966; Masling, 1959) are some factors that may influence performance on ability as well as personality tests (see also Cohen, 1965; Masling, 1960; Kirchner, 1966). In assessing children's abilities, the effect of examiner sex, race, and experience has been examined with a mixed pattern of results (Lutey & Copeland, 1982). Whereas some studies have indicated that students receive higher scores from female rather than male examiners (e.g., Back & Dana, 1977; Gillingham, 1970; Samuel, 1977), others have found that the key variable is whether the examiner and student are of the same or opposite sex. For example, Smith, May, and Lebovitz (1966) and Cieutat (1965) found that students perform better with examiners of the opposite sex, but Pedersen, Shinedling, and Johnson (1968) found that students perform better with examiners of the same sex. Examiner race and experience have been examined in a number of studies, and reviews of these studies have concluded that these variables have little effect on student performance (Sattler & Gwynne, 1982; Sattler, 1988).

The test taker   Test takers approach an assessment situation in different ways, and test users must be sensitive to the diversity of possible responses to a testing situation. On the day of test administration, test takers may vary on a continuum with respect to numerous variables, including:

- The amount of test anxiety they are experiencing and the degree to which that test anxiety might significantly affect the test results.
- Their capacity and willingness to cooperate with the examiner or to comprehend written test instructions.
- The amount of physical pain or emotional distress being experienced.
- The amount of physical discomfort brought on by not having had enough to eat, having had too much to eat, or other physical conditions.
- The extent to which they are alert and wide awake as opposed to "nodding out."
- The extent to which they are predisposed to agreeing or disagreeing when presented with stimulus statements.
- The extent to which they have received prior coaching.
- The importance they may attribute to portraying themselves in a good—or bad—light.
- The extent to which they are, for lack of a better term, "lucky" and can "beat the odds" on a multiple-choice achievement test (despite the fact that they may not have learned the subject matter).

What Is a "Good Test"?

In everyday language, psychologists and other professionals as well as lay people may use words such as "good" and "bad" in describing a test. But what constitutes a "good"—or a "bad"—test? From a practical standpoint, some considerations that immediately come to mind include the clarity of the instructions for administering the test as well as the clarity of the guidelines for interpreting the test results. Also from a practical standpoint, we might say that it would be a plus if a test offers economy in the time it takes to administer, score, and interpret it. But in addition to such practical considerations, other technical concepts can be brought to bear on the question, concepts such as *reliability, validity,* and *norms.* We now introduce these concepts while noting that a more detailed presentation of them as well as other technical terms related to the development, administration, scoring, and interpretation of tests appears in succeeding chapters of this book, particularly in Part 2.

Reliability   A good test, or more generally, a good measuring tool or instrument is *reliable.* As we will explain in Chapter 5, devoted entirely to the concept of reliability, the criterion of reliability has to do with the *consistency* of the measuring tool, the precision with which the test measures. In theory, the perfectly reliable measuring tool consistently measures in the same way. For example, to determine if a digital scale was a reliable measuring tool, we might take repeated measures of the same standard weight, such as a one-pound gold bar. If the scale repeatedly indicated that the gold bar weighed one pound, we would say that the scale was a reliable measuring instrument. But suppose we weighed the bar ten times and six of those times the scale registered one pound, on two occasions the bar weighed in at a fraction of an ounce less than a pound, and on two other occasions it weighed in at a fraction of an ounce more than a pound . . . would the scale still be considered a reliable instrument?

Whether we are measuring gold bars, behavior, or anything else, unreliable measurement is a problem to avoid: we want to be reasonably certain that the measuring tool or test we are using will yield the same numerical measurement every time we observe the same thing under the same conditions. Psychological tests, like other tests and instruments, are reliable to varying degrees. Specific procedures for making determinations as to the reliability of an instrument will be introduced in Chapter 5, as will the various types of reliability.

Validity   A good test is a *valid* test, and a test is considered to be valid if it in fact measures what it purports to measure. A test of reaction time is a valid test if it truly measures reaction time. A test of intelligence is a valid test if it truly measures intelligence. A potential problem, however, is that while there is little controversy about the definition of a term such as "reaction time," there may be a lot of controversy about the definition of "intelligence." You can see that one basis for attacking the validity of a particular test might be the definition of whatever that test purports to measure; a test creator's conception of what constitutes "intelligence" might be different from yours, and on that basis you may claim that the test is "invalid."

Just as a test can be discussed with respect to various types of reliability, a test can be discussed with respect to various types of validity. These types will be introduced and explained in Chapter 6.

Norms   A good test is a test that contains *norms* or normative data. Simply stated, norms provide us with a standard with which we can compare the results of measurement; a test can provide us with a sample of behavior, but it is normative information that gives meaning to that behavioral sample. To illustrate this point, what if you were told that Joan got a score of 72 on the "Smith Anxiety Test" and John scored 92 on the same test; what could you conclude? The answer is you could conclude nothing at all. You would need to know a lot more about the test—its reliability, its validity, and its norms. The norms would tell us how Joan and John scored relative to other people like themselves. We might find that both Joan and John scored in the average range, or that one scored below average and one above, and so on. The point here is that test scores cannot be interpreted in a vacuum. A complete test manual includes normative information. It describes people who were tested with the instrument (the norm group) and gives their scores. Typically the norm group is representative of the people who would be taking the test. Thus, for example, if our hypothetical "Smith Anxiety Test" was designed for use with college freshmen, the norm group would ideally be composed of college freshmen. A detailed discussion of various types of norms is the subject of Chapter 4. In Chapter 7 we take a "soup-to-nuts" look at the process of test development—from the moment the idea is born to the time when number 2 pencils are being distributed.

Reference Sources for Test Information

Many reference sources exist for learning more about published tests. These sources vary with respect to detail; some merely provide descriptions of a test, whereas others provide very technical information regarding reliability, validity, norm sample, and other such matters. The following discussion lists some sources for information about tests.

Test Catalogues   Perhaps one of the most readily accessible sources of information about a test is a catalogue distributed by the publisher of the test. Since most test publishers make available catalogues of their offerings, this source of test information can be tapped by a simple telephone call or note. As you might expect, however, publishers' catalogues usually contain only a brief description of a test and seldom contain the kind of detailed technical information that a prospective user of the test might require. Further, remember that the objective of the catalogue is to sell the test; expect any quotations from reviews critical of a test to be excluded from the description. An exhaustive listing of psychological tests and test publishers can be found in the popular reference work *The Tenth Mental Measurements Yearbook* (Conoley & Kramer, 1989) and in *The Supplement to the Tenth Mental Measurements Yearbook* (Kramer & Conoley, 1990) and *Test Critiques,* Volumes I–VII (Keyser & Sweetland, 1988).

Test Manuals   Much more detailed information concerning the development of a particular test, the normative sample, the test's reliability and validity, and other such information should be found in the manual for the test itself. The chances are good that somewhere within your university (be it the library or the counseling center), a collection of popular psychological test manuals is maintained. If not, most test publishers are willing to sell a test manual by itself, sometimes within some sort of "sampler" kit. In the near future, we can expect to find more books available on tests and other instruments of assessment. This is because the book-publishing arm of the American Psychological Association has launched an aggressive campaign to disseminate more test-related information.

Test Reviews   Objective reviews of published tests can be found in a number of sources, including professional journals. Perhaps the most comprehensive and authoritative compilation of test reviews is *The Mental Measurements Yearbook* (*MMY*), whose first edition was published in 1938. Authored by Oscar Krisen Buros, the first *MMY* was approximately four hundred pages in length. As the number of tests made available by commercial publishers has mushroomed, the number of pages in this reference work has grown. Buros died in 1978 but the work he began lives on at the Buros Institute of Mental Measurements at the Department of Educational Psychology of the University of Nebraska–Lincoln. Over a thousand pages long, *The Tenth Mental Measurements Yearbook* (Conoley & Kramer, 1989) contains information on 396 commercially published tests (with reviews prepared by 303 professional reviewers). Also included is a publishers' directory with a list of test offerings. From test-publisher catalogues, journal articles, and other less formal means (such as tips from a faculty member or reviewer), the staff of the institute monitors the market of commercially available tests and selects certain new and revised tests for review. Between-edition reviews of new and revised tests are accessible through an on-line computer service; as soon as a review received by the institute receives its editorial stamp of approval, it is entered into a computer and is available to anyone with access to it. In addition, a supplement is published in alternate years. *The Supplement to the Tenth Mental Measurements Yearbook* (Kramer & Conoley, 1990), for example, contains 183 test reviews of 98 commercially available instruments and serves "as a bridge between the publication of the *Tenth Mental Measurements Yearbook* in 1989 and the forthcoming publication of the *Eleventh Mental Measurements Yearbook*" (Kramer & Conoley, 1990, p. ix).

In addition to the *MMY,* The University of Nebraska Press distributes a number of other publications from the Buros Institute of Mental Measurements, including *Tests in Print II* (Buros, 1974) and *Tests in Print III* (Mitchell, 1983). *Tests in Print* is essentially an index to tests, test reviews, and literature on tests (including cross-references to the *MMY*). Individual monographs containing information from the *MMY* on a specific area such as personality tests, intelligence tests, vocational tests, mathematics tests, social studies tests, science tests, foreign language tests, English tests, and reading tests are also published by the institute. *Test Critiques,* Volumes I–VII (Keyser & Sweetland, 1988) reviews approximately 720 tests. Each review is divided into four parts: a description of the test, the practical applications and uses of the test, technical aspects of the test (normative data, reliability and validity information), and the reviewer's critique of the test.

Test reviews can also be found in a number of other reference works. Critical reviews of a select listing of tests can be found in *Measuring Human Behavior* (Lake, Miles, & Earle, 1973). For reviews of measures used in the fields of personality and social psychology, *Measures of Social Psychological Attitudes* (Robinson & Shaver, 1973) can be most useful. Brief and relatively nonevaluative summaries of various tests are contained in *A Sourcebook for Mental Health Measures* (Comrey, Backer, & Glaser, 1973). *Measures for Psychological Assessment* (Chun, Cobb, & French, 1975) and *Tests and Measurements in Child Development: A Handbook* (Johnson & Bommarito, 1971) are both noteworthy because they contain reviews

Figure 1-7 *The Most Frequently Used Psychological Tests.* Test use varies according to a number of interrelated variables such as setting, population served, and objectives of the testing (see, for example, Lubin, Larsen, Matarazzo, & Seever, 1985; Piotrowski & Lubin, 1990). A school psychologist testing children for classroom ability, a clinical psychologist testing adult outpatients on adjustment-related questions, and a neuropsychologist testing adult inpatients to determine the extent of neurological injury, for example, will all require various kinds of assessment instruments.

Below we summarize some of the findings from four surveys of psychological test use, each one reporting on the most frequently used psychological test in a particular type of setting. Smith (1985) surveyed a national sample of practicing school psychologists; his findings are reported under the heading School. Under the heading Private Practice are the Harrison, Kaufman, Hickman, and Kaufman (1988) findings; they surveyed a sample of American Psychological Association members who regularly assessed adults. The findings under the heading Outpatient are from a study of trends in outpatient testing (Piotrowski & Keller, 1989). Under the heading Inpatient are the findings from a study of psychological testing practices in acute care inpatient settings (Sweeney, Clarkin, & Fitzgibbon, 1987). Abbreviations for many of the tests appear within the grid, and a key to the abbreviations appears below it. The tests include intelligence tests (WISC-R, WAIS-R, WPPSI, Stanford-Binet, Shipley Hartford Institute of Living Scale), achievement tests (PIAT, WRAT-R, Woodcock-Johnson Achievement), personality tests (MMPI, Rorschach, TAT, Sentence Completion, DAP, HFD, H-T-P, Figure Drawings), specialized ability tests (Wechsler Memory Scale, Bender-Gestalt, VMI), and other tests such as the Beck Depression Inventory and the Strong-Campbell Interest Inventory. You probably are not familiar with many of these tests right now . . . but you will be.

What are the most popular psychological tests? Keeping in mind that the answer varies by setting, it seems fair to say that, overall, tests such as the MMPI, the Wechsler intelligence scales (for adults and children), the Bender-Gestalt, the Rorschach, and the TAT are among the most widely used.

Frequently Used Psychological Tests

	School	Private Practice	Outpatient	Inpatient
		Setting		
1.	WISC–R	WAIS-R/WAIS	MMPI	MMPI
2.	Bender-Gestalt	MMPI	WAIS-R	Rorschach
3.	WRAT	Rorschach	Bender-Gestalt	WAIS-R/WISC-R
4.	VMI	WRAT-R/WRAT	WISC-R/WPPSI	TAT
5.	PIAT	TAT	HFD	Bender-Gestalt
6.	TAT	Strong Campbell	Sentence Completion	Figure Drawings
7.	Stanford-Binet	Sentence Completion	H-T-P	Sentence Completion
8.	W-J Achievement	Vineland	Rorschach	Wechsler Memory Scale
9.	WAIS-R	Bender-Gestalt	TAT	Shipley-Hartford
10.	Rorschach	DAP	WRAT	Beck Depression Inventory

Abbreviations: DAP: Draw A Person Test; HFD: Human Figure Drawing; H-T-P: House, Tree, Person Drawings; MMPI: Minnesota Multiphasic Personality Inventory; PIAT: Peabody Individual Achievement Test; TAT: Thematic Apperception Test; VMI: Developmental Test of Visual Motor Integration; WAIS: Wechsler Adult Intelligence Scale; WAIS-R: Wechsler Adult Intelligence Scale—Revised; WISC-R: Wechsler Intelligence Scale for Children—Revised; WPPSI-R: Wechsler Preschool and Primary Scale of Intelligence Scale for Children—Revised; WRAT: Wide Range Achievement Test; WRAT-R: Wide Range Achievement Test—Revised; W-J Achievement: Woodcock-Johnson Achievement Scale.

of many unpublished as well as published tests. Test reviews also appear in various journals and in publications distributed by various special-interest organizations. As an example of the latter, the Washington, D.C.–based organization Teachers of English to Speakers of Other Languages (TESOL) publishes a review of English-language proficiency tests (Alderson, Krahnke, & Stansfield, 1987).

Although the format of test reviews may vary, certain dimensions are usually addressed: purpose of the test, age range, administration time, number of forms, scores that are produced, adequacy of the normative sample, evidence of reliability, and evidence of validity. Such information should be available in the test's technical manual. A sample review is presented in Table 1–4.

To gain some hands-on familiarity with these various sources of test information, try this exercise: select any one test from those listed on pages 24 and 25 and see if you can locate at least two published reviews of it. On the basis of those reviews, would you recommend that the test be used for its intended purpose? Why? Be prepared for your next class period to share your experience and questions regarding the process of such test-related library research.

Our overview of psychological testing and assessment continues in the following chapter with a look backward—the better to appreciate this enterprise in its historical and social context. Some of the legal and ethical considerations in testing will also be introduced.

Table 1–4

A Sample Test Review

Test reviews written by one of this book's authors (M.E.S.) can be found in the ninth and tenth editions of the Mental Measurements Yearbook. *One such review, this one of a test called Otis-Lennon School Ability Test (Swerdlik, 1992) is presented here for illustrative purposes.*

Review of the Otis-Lennon School Ability Test, Sixth Edition by MARK E. SWERDLIK, Professor of Psychology, Illinois State University, Normal, IL:

The Sixth Edition of the Otis-Lennon School Ability Test (OLSAT) represents the most recent in a series that began over a half century ago with the publication of the Otis Group Intelligence Scale. The Otis Group Intelligence Scale had its roots in the original Binet Scale. The earlier versions of the OLSAT, growing out of the original Otis Group Intelligence Scale, have included the Self-Administering Tests of Mental Ability, Quick Scoring Mental Ability Tests, Otis Mental Ability Test, and in 1979, the fifth revision of the test was renamed the School Ability Test. The use of the term School Ability to replace Mental Ability was intended to "discharge overinterpretation of the nature of the ability assessed."

A number of changes from the Fifth Edition have been implemented. These include all new items; levels designated from A through G; two additional levels that include separate tests for Kindergarten through grade 3; Level D (grade 3) administered as a separate level; and both Verbal and Nonverbal part scores.

The OLSAT series is a multilevel test designed for use in Kindergarten through grade 12. The test includes seven levels and one form. Test materials are labeled Form 1. Form 2 is to be developed but is not yet available.

Uses of the test. The major purpose of the OLSAT is to "assess examinees' ability to cope with school learning tasks, to suggest their possible placement for school learning functions, and to evaluate their achievement in relation to the talents they bring to school learning situations." The basis of the OLSAT is that "to learn new things, students must be

Table 1–4 (*continued*)

able to perceive accurately, to recognize and recall what has been perceived, to think logically, to understand relationships, to abstract from a set of particulars, and to apply generalizations to new and different contexts." Specific cautions against any possible misuses of the test such as educational placement based solely on the scores yielded from this group test are not specified.

    Test Construction. Twenty-one different item types are organized into five clusters. The major types of items were used in earlier editions of the series and reflect the objective of a broad sampling of reasoning tasks. For Levels A—C (grades K—2) the cluster of Verbal Comprehension includes the item type Following Directions. Verbal Reasoning includes Aural Reasoning and Arithmetic Reasoning. The cluster of Pictorial Reasoning is composed of Picture Classification, Picture Analogies, and Picture Series (K only). Figural Reasoning includes the item types of Figural Classification, Figural Analogies, Pattern Matrix, and Figural Series. Quantitative reasoning is not included at grades K—2. Level D does not include all of the item formats of the upper levels but rather item types from both the upper and lower levels. For Levels D—G (grades 3—12), the additional Verbal Comprehension item types include Antonyms, Sentence Completion, and Sentence Arrangement. Verbal Reasoning includes Logical Selection, Word/Letter Matrix, Verbal Analogies, Verbal Classification, and Inference (Levels E—G only). Quantitative Reasoning is briefly sampled (seven items) at grade 3, and more extensively tapped at Levels E—G including item types of Number Series, Numeric Inference, and Number Matrix. Pictorial Reasoning item types are not included at Levels D—G.

    Equal numbers of verbal and nonverbal items are included at each level. The classification of an item as verbal or nonverbal "hinges upon whether understanding of the English language is requisite to answering the items."

    The OLSAT went through an extensive test development process. This process included 50 free-lance item writers initially submitting a total of 4,000 items. A thorough editorial review process was accomplished.

    The test specifications for the OLSAT included an equal number of verbal and nonverbal items within each of the levels and appropriate coverage of the item types specified above. Four parallel forms were constructed at each of the three lower levels, and five parallel forms at each of the four upper levels. Items were eliminated that did not meet specifications.

    Word and reading levels at each of the grade levels (Levels D and above) were checked. A final count of number of words at each vocabulary level according to EDL Core Vocabularies is presented. The count indicated that most of the word levels are below the recommended grades for the test level. Although the authors suggest these word levels insure the items are measuring reasoning skills and not reading ability, at each level there are words above the recommended level of the test. In addition, no data are presented relative to the difficulty level of the vocabulary of the items presented orally on the lower levels of the test.

    Special attention was also paid to racial, ethnic, and gender balance of the content of the items. This included use of proper names, pronouns, pictures, activities, and implied status. However, no specific information as to criteria used to select items was provided. In addition to new items, each form of the new test included a core of items from corresponding levels of Form R of the Fifth Edition. The purpose of this set of items was to equate the tryout forms to one another and to place the new items and items from the previous edition on a common scale of difficulty.

    National item tryout occurred in February 1987, with approximately 35,000 students from 65 schools across the United States. School systems were included in the national item tryout based on a stratified random sampling of socioeconomic status based on a composite measure of the median family income in thousands of dollars plus the percentage of adults in the community over 25 years of age with a high school diploma, average school district enrollment per grade, and geographic region. Specific information relative

(Continues)

Table 1–4 (*continued*)

to the exact composition of the sample used for national tryouts was not provided in the Technical Manual.

Specific attention to eliminating item bias related to gender, socioeconomic status, ethnic, cultural, or regional groups was also a part of the test development process. The initial focus was on a content analysis approach using an extensive editorial review process focusing on whether the items depicted differences in activities, emotions, occupations, or personality attributes. This was accomplished throughout the test development process with the items reviewed and revised by editors and psychologists. In addition, items were reviewed by a separate panel of "prominent educator[s]; several having been outspoken critics of tests as being biased against minorities" representing various minority groups, including a representative who was a strong advocate of women's rights and one representing rural areas. Teachers participating in the national item tryout were also asked to note the inappropriateness of any item.

In addition to a focus on the content of the items, statistical analyses for differential performance of various groups were conducted. Separate analyses were conducted for males, females, Blacks, Whites, and Hispanics. Items that showed significant differences for the five groups were targeted to be dropped from the final form. No specific information is provided regarding the number of items that were dropped or revised on the basis of these analyses.

A brief discussion of only one paragraph on the theoretical framework for the OLSAT is presented. The framework presented is that of the Hierarchical Theory of Human Abilities of Vernon and Burt. Spearman's general cognitive ability (g) factor is divided into two broad factors corresponding to "verbal-educational" and "practical-mechanical" abilities with the OLSAT designed to assess only the verbal-educational. These two broad factors are divided into a number of minor groups including verbal or numerical which are further divided into the specific factors or tasks involved in reasoning. The authors point out that the OLSAT does not assess all of the abilities considered to be "verbal-educational" but only a subpart of them. In addition, responding to much of the criticism surrounding IQ tests, the authors indicate that all of the tests are "considered to be measures of learned or developed abilities in the broadest sense. Performance on the samples of tasks included in the tests reflects a complex interaction of genetic and environmental factors influencing the ability to deal with the abstract manipulation of the verbal, numerical, and figural symbol systems of our culture." Although the test user is referred to Vernon's text, *The Structure of Human Abilities,* the brief discussion presented in the Technical Manual does not facilitate or provide a greater understanding on how to interpret the results of the OLSAT. It is unclear how this theory guided test development.

Administration and scoring. Levels A—B were created for younger children. The tests at these levels are dictated. Items are organized into three sections in a format that allows examinees to become familiar with the item types and not get discouraged. Items do not increase in difficulty but are spiraled by difficulty levels with harder items cushioned by easier ones. Level C, appropriate for grade 2 students, is identical in format to Levels A and B. However, the first two parts of Level C are self-administered with the remaining parts dictated. Levels D—G are entirely self-administered. Level D includes self-administered classification sections with figural and verbal items that are spiraled by difficulty levels similar to Levels A—C. Other items are arranged in a spiral omnibus format similar to Levels E—G. For Levels E–G, the spiral omnibus format is rotated throughout the test according to item type and difficulty. Items are not grouped.

Both hand- and machine-scoring formats are available. Levels E–G have separate answer sheets, whereas examinees at the lower levels (grades K—3) mark their responses directly in the test booklet for use on reflective scanners. At the lower levels, the spaces in which the examinees place their responses are quite small.

Each level of the OLSAT includes separate Directions for Administering that provides an overview of the OLSAT, general instructions regarding the process of test administration, and specific directions for administering the test. Each level of the hand-scorable test booklets also has an accompanying Class Record that provides a mechanism to summarize

Table 1–4 (continued)

35

PSYCHOLOGICAL
TESTING AND
ASSESSMENT

class performance on the OLSAT. It facilitates the analysis of the performance of individual students and the class as a whole. The Score Record is located on the back of each of the hand-scorable test booklets and is a form for summarizing each student's performance. It can also be used to provide test results to parents.

For Levels A—C, special markers are available that assist children's focus on the test question the teacher dictates. Test takers move the marker down from row to row in the test booklet. The use of the markers reduces the child's chance of getting lost or distracted.

The OLSAT administration instructions are clear, concise, and easy to follow. No specific training in test administration is required. Directions encourage students not to guess blindly. Although the authors suggest that ample time is given to complete the entire test, no data are presented to support the claim that the test is a power test.

The degree to which coaching and practice result in improvements in test scores is an issue frequently discussed regarding the use of individual and group intelligence tests. No information or data are presented relating to this issue. Practice tests are available for each level of the OLSAT. Each level includes one sample item for each new item type. Test takers are free to ask questions regarding the rationale for the correct responses for the sample items.

The Practice Test assists test takers in becoming familiar with the types of questions that are included on the actual test and the way they are to mark their responses. According to the authors, the practice test will allow students to "learn to recognize row finders, to use a marker, to follow a row across the page from left to right, to mark their answers properly, and to change their answers when necessary." Practice tests must be ordered separately and it is recommended they be administered one week prior to the regular test administration. The practice tests provide more opportunity than the sample items, which are part of the actual OLSAT, to practice test format and become familiar with the testing process thereby reducing or eliminating the effect of test-taking skills on test performance.

Hand-scorable record booklets and scoring keys are available. Directions are presented in sufficient detail and clarity to maximize the accuracy of scoring. Directions are clear and easy to follow.

The OLSAT manuals provide little information on interpretation. This is limiting to the test user and increases the likelihood of inappropriate uses of the test. No specific cautions regarding test use are included in the manual.

Types of scores. The OLSAT yields a number of derived scores including School Ability Indexes (SAI), which are normalized standard scores with a mean of 100 and a standard deviation of 16. SAIs for Total scores and verbal and nonverbal part scores are provided. The SAIs seem very much like IQ scores and are somewhat ambiguous as to their meaning. In addition to SAIs, percentile ranks, stanines, and Normal Curve Equivalents useful for interpolating and averaging are provided. The scaled score system of the OLSAT provides a continuous scale that allows comparison of performance of students taking different levels of the test. The scaled scores are appropriate for comparing scores from different levels of the test, for studying changes in performance over time, and for testing out of level.

The manual includes a discussion of the advantages and limitations of each of the scores. According to the authors, the total score represents the best overall indicator of school-learning ability. Although the authors indicated that a higher verbal or nonverbal part score could suggest a student's greater proficiency with one type of content than another, instructional implications of this discrepancy are not addressed in any of the manuals.

Normative data. A separate Norms Booklet is available for each level of the OLSAT. The booklet contains information about the various derived scores yielded by the test, the meanings of these scores, norm tables, and basic statistical data relating to the tests. The instructions for hand scoring are also located in these Norms Booklets. In addition to separate booklets for each level of the test, a Multilevel Norms Booklet is also available. This

(Continues)

Table 1–4 (*continued*)

booklet includes norms for all ages and grades for all levels of the OLSAT. It also provides information about the types and meanings of the various derived scores yielded. This booklet might be especially useful for out-of-level testing.

A Technical Manual provides statistical data and information about the test development and norming process. Needed information about the norm group including the year in which it was collected and sampling design are included. Norms are provided for both age and grade and were developed on the basis of data collected in both the fall and spring standardization programs.

The standardization sample was selected to approximate the school district composition of the United States. The population characteristics of school districts on which the sample was stratified included socioeconomic status, urbanicity, geographic region, ethnicity, plus Catholic and other nonpublic schools. A stratified random sampling technique was utilized within each state. The spring standardization consisted of "approximately" 175,000 students from 1,000 school districts in 48 states and the District of Columbia with another 11,200 in the equating programs. The fall standardization consisted of "approximately" 135,000 students. The spring sample closely approximated the 1980 census.

Approximately 20% of the spring and 30% of the fall standardization invitations were accepted. No data are provided regarding the frequency and magnitude of sampling bias if a selected school elected not to participate in the standardization and a second, third, or fourth school was selected as a replacement.

The authors state that a Verbal/Nonverbal score difference "may . . . be indicative of some student's greater proficiency with one type of content than with the other." They go on to say that because students' ability to learn in the educational setting is dependent upon proficiency in both verbal and nonverbal reasoning abilities, it is recommended that the Total Score is the best overall indicator of a student's learning ability. The manual does not include an adequate explanation of the meaning of the verbal and nonverbal part scores.

Reliability. Internal consistency estimates (Kuder–Richardson Formula 20 and 21) of reliability are presented for both age and grade. The estimates were calculated on the large number of cases included in the standardization sample. Raw score Standard Errors of Estimate and means and standard deviations are provided for the Total, Verbal, and Nonverbal scores, and for the clusters across all levels of the OLSAT. The authors also explain the meaning of the standard error of measurement. For all scores, internal consistency estimates of reliability for the Total, Verbal, and Nonverbal scores range from the low .70s to low .90s across all grade levels suggesting the OLSAT is an internally consistent and homogeneous measure of general ability. The authors point out that, as expected, due to the fewer number of test items in the clusters as compared to the other scores, the reliability estimates for these clusters are lower with one as low as .24 and some in the .60s. No estimates of the stability of scores are provided.

Validity. Separate sections of the Technical Manual are devoted to the content, criterion-related, and construct validity evidence for the OLSAT.

Overall, the amount of validity data presented in the Technical Manual is quite adequate. However, validity evidence for the different uses of the OLSAT and for the interpretation of verbal/nonverbal differences are not specifically presented. These deficiencies deserve attention.

Summary of concerns. Despite many positive features, the OLSAT developers should attend to continuing improvement of the instrument.

1. Although plans call for the availability of alternate forms for the Sixth Edition, none are available at the time of publication.
2. The levels administered orally (Levels A and B and part of C) can be considered qualitatively different from the other levels because of the content of the items and the nature of the tasks are different. The orally administered items take more time to administer and must be given in more than one sitting. Test performance on these levels can also be influenced by the variations in the timing and fluency of the speech by the examiner. These issues were not addressed by the authors.

Table 1–4 (*continued*)

37

PSYCHOLOGICAL
TESTING AND
ASSESSMENT

3. Satisfactory internal consistency reliability data are presented but no data relating to the stability of OLSAT scores are reported.

4. Standard Errors of Measurement are provided to aid in interpretation of scores. However, differences in SEMs based on ability level are not provided.

5. Limited information is presented on what the OLSAT actually measures, and the instructional relevance of the verbal and nonverbal part scores is not discussed. Although validity data are presented that suggest the OLSAT measures similar abilities to other group-administered achievement tests, it is unclear what unique aspects are captured by the OLSAT.

6. Cautions about possible misuse of test scores or overinterpretation of the test results are also not provided.

If the test user accepts the limitations associated with group-administered school ability tests and accepts its use as only a screening instrument, the OLSAT represents a technically adequate test with a variety of strengths.

Chapter 2

Historical, Legal, and
Ethical Considerations

CONSIDER A WORLD without tests.

"Great!" might be your initial response. Upon reconsideration, however, you may conclude that a world without tests would be more of a nightmare than a dream. In a world without tests virtually anyone, qualified or not, could present himself or herself to the public as an airline pilot, a surgeon, or a bridge builder. In a world without tests, some teacher could have seen to it that you were placed into a class for the developmentally disabled simply because, in the teacher's sole and arbitrary judgment, that is where you belonged. When you begin to think of the many critical decisions that are made on the basis of tests, you can appreciate the need for them—and be thankful that such decisions are being made on the basis of tests as opposed to simple human judgment, nepotism, or the like. But the effectiveness of even the best test depends in large part on the extent to which the test is used with proficiency and in accordance with prescribed ethical and legal standards.

In this chapter we look at some of the legal and ethical issues surrounding the use of psychological tests. We begin by placing the enterprise of psychological testing and assessment in historical context.

The uniqueness of individuals is one of the most fundamental characteristic facts of life. . . . At all periods of human history men have observed and described differences between individuals. . . . But educators, politicians, and administrators have felt a need for some way of organizing or systematizing the many-faceted complexity of individual differences. (Tyler, 1965, p. 3)

The societal need for "organizing" and "systematizing" has historically manifested itself in terms of such varied questions as "Who is a witch?" "Who is schizophrenic?" and "Who is qualified?" The nature of the specific questions asked has shifted with societal concerns. The methods used to determine the answers have varied throughout history as a function of factors such as intellectual sophistication and religious preoccupation. Palmistry, podoscopy, astrology, and phrenology, among other pursuits, have had proponents who argued that the best means of understanding and predicting human behavior was through the study of the palms, the feet, the stars, bumps on the head, tea leaves, and so on. Amidst this wide array of competing points of view, it might help us to determine where the roots of modern-day psychological testing and assessment lie. We begin our brief historical survey in antiquity for academic purposes, though it was really not until the nineteenth century or so that the identifiable roots of modern-day testing were manifest.

Antiquity to the Nineteenth Century

According to historian Philip DuBois (1966, 1970), a primitive form of proficiency testing existed in China as early as 2200 B.C. Little is known about this Chinese testing program other than that it involved some form of examination of public officials by the Chinese Emperor every third year. Much more is known about the civil service examinations extant in China beginning during the Chan dynasty in 1115 B.C. and ending in the year 1905, when a reform measure abolished the system. For three thousand years, the open and competitive system of examinations that prevailed in China provided for evaluation of proficiency in areas such as music, archery, horsemanship, writing, and arithmetic. Proficiency was also examined with respect to skill in the rites and ceremonies of public and social life, civil law, military affairs, agriculture, revenue, and geography.

There were three required examinations, the first of which was administered in principal cities throughout the Empire. Candidates, all male, composed a poem and wrote on an assigned theme while confined for a day and a night in a small abode used for the test administration (see Figure 2–1). The number of people who "passed" on the basis of their eloquence and penmanship was only between 1% and 7% of all the applicants. Every third year all men fortunate enough to have passed the first test were given a second and more rigorous test that required three days and three nights of testing. Penmanship did not count at this level, and official scribes copied the exams before they were submitted to evaluators. As Martin (1870) noted, the official scribe was used to copy the written exam so that "the examiners may have no clew [sic] to its author and no temptation to render a

Figure 2–1 *Testing Booths in China.* Unlike exams for a position with the U.S. Postal Service, testing in China went on for days, and examinees occasionally died of the strain in these hundreds of civil service examination "cubicles" in Nanking. This photograph was taken about 20 years after the cessation of such testing in 1905.

biased judgment." The 1–3% of the examinees who passed this second test were admitted to a third examination in the Empire's capital, Peking, where approximately 3% became eligible for public office.

The historical significance of this type of testing program is that thousands of years ago there existed a civilization that evidenced concern for some of the same basic principles of psychometrics that we are concerned with today.[1] Modern readers might note with fascination that activities such as archery and horsemanship were included among the tests, but keep in mind that the test users of the day felt that civil servants should be proficient in these skills; stated another way, the tests were content-valid. In a period of history when nepotism was no doubt rampant, we can look with admiration to a society where employment was based on open competitive examinations.

Some primitive thoughts about the assessment of personality are evident in early Greco-Roman writings. For example, the Greek physician Hippocrates (460–377 B.C.) advanced the notion that individual differences in temperament were due to the balance of four fluids ("humors" as he referred to them) known to be in the body: blood, phlegm, black bile, and yellow bile. Considering that Hippocrates lived at a time when exorcism was the treatment of choice for aberrant

---

1. *Psychometrics* is a plural noun that may be defined as the science of psychological measurement, a word that is synonymous with *psychometry*. Variants of these words include the adjective "psychometric" and the nouns "psychometrist" and "psychometrician." In common usage, a *psychometrist* is a person, usually with a master's degree, who is qualified to administer specific tests. A *psychometrician* is a Ph.D. psychologist who specializes in the areas of quantitative psychology, individual differences, and theories of mental testing.

behavior, the humoral theory represented an important first step in drawing attention away from the supernatural and to the body as a point of focus.

In the *Republic*, Plato (427–347 B.C.) suggested that people should work at jobs consistent with their abilities and endowments, a notion perfectly in accord with the philosophy of modern employment testing. Claudius Galenus (A.D. 131–205), commonly known as Galen, designed experiments to prove that it was the brain and not the heart (as many had believed) that was the seat of the intellect. Indeed, historians place the beginning of the Middle Ages, or "Dark Ages," in history at about the time of Galen's death; interest in individual differences, medicine, and philosophy were subjugated to interest in religion. The reading of the works of philosophers such as Plato was banned.

Christianity was established as the state religion by A.D. 313 and "psychology texts" of the day dutifully reflected church doctrines. For example, in the *Confessions,* St. Augustine (354–430) discussed topics such as perception, creativity, and self-control while making the point that little could be gained by asking questions about these phenomena since only God could provide such knowledge. By the time of the Middle Ages, "medical practice" was by and large the province of the clergy, and cures were attempted through methods such as prayer, potions, and magic. In 1265, St. Thomas Aquinas (1225–1274) argued that the notion of a thinking/reasoning capacity in people should be replaced with the notion of an immortal soul.

In a religion-dominated society in which all natural catastrophes (such as earthquakes, floods, and epidemics) were viewed as the work of the devil, persons who seemed different from the rest (that is, those whose behavior seemed unnatural) were viewed as being in league with Satan. Had a manual for diagnosing behavior disorders existed at the time, persons "diagnosed" to be "in league with Satan" might have fallen into one of two subdiagnostic types: "voluntary league" or "involuntary league" (the former being viewed as the more severe pathology). Included among the many signs and symptoms deemed to betray demonic possession were a kind of squint (the "evil eye"), being cross-eyed, and failing to bleed when pricked. The great need for society to answer the question "Who is possessed?" was reflected in the form of a 1484 papal bull asking the clergy's assistance in identifying evil. Two Dominican monks who responded to the bull, Heinrich Kraemer and Johann Sprenger, wrote an influential treatise on how to identify, try, and dispose of those who threatened the Christian way of life (see Figure 2–2). The sixteenth and seventeenth centuries witnessed innumerable witch hunts, witch trials, and witch executions in Europe as well as in the newly colonized America.

The Renaissance witnessed a rebirth of interest in philosophy and the nature of humanity. Some raised their voices against the clergy's view of abnormal behavior even though doing so placed them in jeopardy: they could be accused of being in league with the devil. Johann Weyer, a German physician, published a book in the mid-sixteenth century which argued that those accused of being witches were probably suffering from a mental or physical disorder. One clergyman reacted to Weyer's book with an accusation: "Recently Satan went to a Sabbath attired as a great prince, and told the assembled witches that they need not worry since, thanks to Weyer and his followers, the affairs of the Devil were brilliantly progressing" (Castiglioni, 1946, p. 253). However, by the seventeenth century, some clergymen were beginning to acknowledge the existence of mental disease. At this point the pendulum began to swing away from a religion-dominated view of people to a more philosophical and scientific view.

Many philosophers of the seventeenth, eighteenth, and nineteenth centuries touched in their writings on ideas that later behavioral scientists would research or expand on in theoretical formulations. The French philosopher and mathematician René Descartes (1596–1650) grappled with the question of how mental and physical processes are related. The "British empiricists," as they are called, John Locke, George Berkeley, David Hume, and David Hartley all made important philosophical contributions. In *An Essay Concerning Human Understanding*, Locke (1690) expressed the view that all knowledge comes from experience, a view elaborated on in works such as Berkeley's *A Treatise Concerning the Principles of Human Knowledge* (1710), Hume's *A Treatise on Human Nature* (1739), and Hartley's *Observations on Man, his Frame, his Duty, and his Expectations* (1749).

Another Englishman, James Mill, would argue in *Analysis of the Phenomena of the Human Mind* (1829) that the structure of mental life consists of sensations and ideas—an idea that the later group of psychologists who are referred to as

---

Figure 2–2 *Some "Diagnostic" Techniques of a (thankfully) Bygone Era.*

In the Middle Ages, a popular "diagnostic manual" of the day was a book called *Malleus Malificarum* (translated *The Hammer of Witches*). The book was divided into three parts. Part I affirmed the existence of witches and argued that those who did not accept that fact were either mistaken or heretics. Part II detailed some telltale signs of collusion with the devil. Part III was replete with suggestions on how to "examine" witches—usually by torturing them until they confessed. Also in Part III were guidelines on disposing of witches once a confession had been extracted; setting the individual on fire, hanging, and mutilations were some of the options discussed.

Two "assessment techniques" used to determine whether an individual was in league with the devil are illustrated by these nineteenth-century engravings. The procedure illustrated at left entailed stripping the accused, tying her hand-to-foot, and throwing her into the water; if the woman floated, it constituted "proof" that the accused was indeed a witch. Other such evidence might come from an "interview" conducted in a manner illustrated by the engraving at right; the interviewee was in essence tortured into a confession while on a rack.

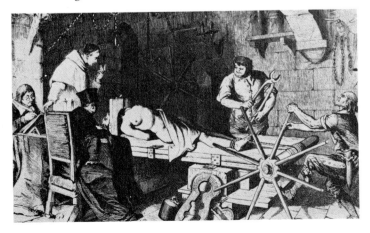

"structuralists" would experimentally explore. In Germany, philosopher Gott-fried Leibniz (1646–1716) hypothesized that there exist perceptions below the threshold of awareness, which he called "petites perceptions"—a notion similar to what Freud would refer to as the "subconscious." A student of Leibniz, Christian von Wolff, published books entitled *Psychologia Empirica* (1732) and *Psychologia Rationalis* (1734), which popularized some of the views of his mentor. Lapoint (1972) tells us that it was Wolff who first suggested that a subject called "psychology" should be conceived as a possibility and it was also Wolff who first conceived of psychometry as a science.

The Nineteenth Century

A thorough review of the many landmark events that occurred during the nineteenth century is beyond our scope, and the interested reader is referred to texts on history and systems in psychology. Below we outline some of the critically important contributions made by a few of the scientists of the day.

In 1859, a book entitled *On the Origin of Species by Means of Natural Selection* by Charles Darwin (1809–1882) was published. In this important, far-reaching work, Darwin argued that chance variation in species would be selected or rejected for survival by Nature according to adaptivity and survival value. The case was made that humans had descended from the ape as a result of such chance genetic variations. This revolutionary notion aroused interest, admiration, and a good deal of enmity—the latter primarily from members of the religious community who interpreted Darwin's ideas as an affront to the biblical account of creation as written in *Genesis*. An account of a debate that took place at Oxford University between Thomas Huxley and Bishop Wilberforce conveys the strident tone of the controversy:

> Wilberforce asked Huxley whether it was through his grandmother or his grandfather that he claimed descent from an ape, thus phrasing the central issue in terms every man could understand. Huxley replied that an ape would be preferable to the Bishop as an ancestor, and with that the battle began. (Miller, 1962, p. 129)

Of primary importance to the field of psychology is the fact that the notion of an evolutionary link between human beings and animals conferred a new scientific respectability on experimentation with animals. It also raised questions about how animals and humans compare with respect to states of consciousness—questions that would beg for answers in laboratories of future behavioral scientists.[2]

Darwin's work kindled interest in research in heredity in his half cousin, Francis Galton (1822–1911), an extremely influential figure in the history of psychological testing (see Figure 2–3).[3] Galton's initial work on inheritance was done with sweet peas, in part because there tended to be fewer variations among the

---

2. A tangential note: The influence of Darwin's thinking is also apparent in the theory of personality formulated by Sigmund Freud. From a Darwinian perspective, it would be the strongest persons with the most "efficient" sex drives that would have been most responsible for contributing to the human gene pool. In this context, Freud's notion of the primary importance of instinctual sexual and aggressive urges can better be understood.
3. The reader so inclined is urged to read one of the many volumes that have been written on this highly influential, brilliant, and colorful historical figure (such as Forrest, 1974).

Figure 2–3 *Sir Francis Galton (1822–1911).*

It is probably not an overstatement to assert that Sir Francis Galton was one of the world's greatest scientists. While this brilliant man's interests spanned a wide variety of areas (ranging from fashion to fingerprints to an experimental investigation of the efficacy of prayer) and his writings made contributions in many fields of human endeavor, we focus on those contributions that pertain to the field of psychological testing and assessment.

Galton was the ninth and last child in a large, wealthy, and influential British family. Galton's father was a banker and at his insistence young Galton took up the study of medicine—study that Galton abandoned soon after his father's death. After travel, an award from the Royal Geographic Society for his account of his exploration of southern Africa, the publication of a guide for explorers, and the invention of some new instruments, including a teletype printer and instruments for charting weather, Galton's attention turned to the work of his half cousin Charles Darwin. Galton was intrigued with the implications of Darwin's theory of evolution, and he became increasingly intrigued—particularly with the social implications of the theory—as he grew older. Galton's (1869) study of heredity and genius pioneered the use of the statistical concept of correlation—a concept most integral to testing. Galton's scientific study of genetics led him to formulate various ways of measuring people, and he described these in his 1883 book, *Inquiries into Human Faculty and Its Development.* Some of the measurement techniques devised by Galton to gauge aspects of human perception included a tool to measure visual discrimination ability (referred to as the Galton bar), a whistle designed for use in measuring auditory discrimination of pitch, and

a set of blocks that were similar in appearance but varied in weight in order to measure weight discrimination ability. Also included among the assessment instruments was a questionnaire—not a very revolutionary instrument by contemporary standards but certainly among the first formally used in psychological research when Galton introduced it.

At the International Health Exhibition in London (1884–1885) Galton exhibited the laboratory tools designed to measure people—his "anthropometric laboratory." After the Exhibition closed, the laboratory was reconstructed at London's Science Museum in South Kensington where it continued in operation for six years. During its total period of operation, over 9,000 people had measurements taken on 17 variables—leaving a mass of data that was still being analyzed long after Galton's death in 1911.

Much of Galton's work was used in support of the argument that genius ran in families and that the

birth of more eminent people should be encouraged while the birth of the less eminent (and in Darwinian terms, "less fit") should be discouraged. Though he did not completely overlook the effect of environment on intelligence, Galton tended to minimize it— perhaps, as Schultz (1969) has suggested, because "he considered his own education for the most part a waste of time" (p. 92).

In general, Galton is perhaps best remembered for his systematic investigation of individual differences between people— an area of inquiry that has been referred to as a glaring "blind spot" in the field of psychology as it existed before Galton (Murphy, 1949). Despite views on the role of heredity and environment that in today's world would at best be highly controversial, we cannot deny that Galton was a great thinker of his day. As others (such as Flugel & West, 1964) have noted, one would be hard put to name another scientist who was so brilliant and versatile.

peas in a single pod. In this work with peas Galton pioneered the use of a statistical concept central to psychological experimentation and testing: the coefficient of correlation. Although Karl Pearson (1857–1936) developed the product-moment correlation technique, the roots of this technique can be traced directly to the work of Galton:

> Galton weighed and measured the diameter of the mother and daughter peas. By studying the various generations of peas he was able to set up his first regression line. . . . These experiments led to an improvement for gardeners who fertilized peas. The results of his work, *Typical Laws of Heredity,* were first presented at the Royal Institute in 1877. Galton had discerned, from his data, that the coefficient of regression for the offspring on a midparent is double what it is for the midparent on the offspring. He had determined this without any knowledge of the bivariate distribution, its two means, and without knowing the difference between correlation and regression. All of this would later be unravelled by Karl Pearson. (Magnello & Spies, 1984)

From heredity in peas Galton's interest turned to heredity in humans and various ways of measuring aspects of people and their abilities. At an exhibition in London in 1884, Galton displayed his Anthropometric Laboratory where, for three or four pence (depending on whether you were already registered or not), you could be measured on variables such as the following:

- Height (standing)
- Height (sitting)
- Arm span
- Weight
- Breathing capacity
- Strength of pull
- Strength of squeeze
- Swiftness of blow
- Keenness of sight
- Memory of form
- Discrimination of color
- Steadiness of hand

Through his own efforts and his urging of educational institutions to keep anthropometric records on their students, Galton was instrumental in launching widespread interest in developing a body of psychological assessment-related data. It would remain for the Frenchman Alfred Binet to "turn the corner," as it were, and fully enter the realm of making assessments of a cognitive nature (such as assessments of memory or judgment) as opposed to assessments of variables related to perceptual acuity, muscular strength, and the like. Before briefly reviewing Binet's work here (and reviewing it in greater detail in Part 3), we examine the historical contribution to psychological testing of one of the founders of experimental psychology, Wilhelm Wundt.

The first experimental psychology laboratory was founded at the University of Leipzig in Germany by Wilhelm Max Wundt (1832–1920), a medical doctor whose title at the university was Professor of Philosophy. Wundt and his students tried to formulate a general description of human abilities with respect to variables such as reaction time, perception, and attention span. Stated another way, the focus at Leipzig was not on how individuals differed, but on how individuals were the same. In fact, individual differences were viewed by Wundt as a frustrating source of error in experimentation. In his experimentation, Wundt attempted to control all extraneous variables in an effort to reduce error to a minimum. But regardless of whether the focus is on similarities between people (as it was in Wundt's laboratory) or on differences between people (as is the focus of attention for the psychological assessor), the practice of attempting to control extraneous variables lives on in psychological testing: standardized conditions are routinely used to help ensure that differences in scores are the result of true differences among individuals.

In spite of the prevailing research orientation that focused on how people tended to be the same, one of Wundt's students at Leipzig, an American named James McKeen Cattell, managed to complete a doctoral dissertation that dealt with individual differences (specifically, individual differences in reaction time) (Figure 2–4). After receiving his doctoral degree from Leipzig, Cattell returned home to the states, and taught at Bryn Mawr and then at the University of Penn-

Figure 2–4 *The Cattells: James McKeen and daughter, Psyche.*

James McKeen Cattell
(1860–1944)

Psyche Cattell
(1893–1989)

The psychologist who coined the term "mental test," James McKeen Cattell, has often been mistakenly credited (along with another psychologist, Raymond B. Cattell— no relation) with the authorship of a measure of infant intelligence called the Cattell Infant Intelligence Scale (CIIS). Actually, it was Psyche, the third of seven children of Cattell and his wife,

Josephine Owen, who created the CIIS. From 1919 through 1921, Psyche assisted her famous father in statistical analyses for the third edition of *American Men of Science*. In 1927 she earned a doctor of education degree at Harvard. In 1931 she adopted a son, becoming one of the first unmarried women to do so (Sokal, 1991). Later in the decade she adopted a daughter.

Her book *The Measurement of Intelligence in Infants and Young Children* was published in 1940, and it was in that book that the CIIS was introduced. Later in her career she would author a popular book, *Raising Children with Love and Limits,* which represented a reaction against the permissiveness being advocated by child-rearing authorities such as Benjamin Spock.

sylvania before leaving for Europe to teach at Cambridge. At Cambridge, Cattell came in contact with Francis Galton, whom Cattell later described as "the greatest man I have known" (Roback, 1961, p. 96).

Inspired by his contact with Galton, Cattell returned to the University of Pennsylvania in 1888 and coined the term "mental test" in an 1890 publication. Boring (1950, p. 283) has noted that "Cattell more than any other person was in this fashion responsible for getting mental testing underway in America, and it is plain that his motivation was similar to Galton's and that he was influenced, or at least reinforced by Galton." Cattell went on to accept the position as professor and chairman of the psychology department at Columbia University and for the 26 years he was there not only trained many psychologists but also founded a number of publications (such as *Psychological Review, Science,* and *American Men of Science*). In 1921 Cattell was instrumental in founding the Psychological Corporation, which named 20 of the country's leading psychologists as its directors. The goal of the corporation was the "advancement of psychology and the promotion of the useful applications of psychology." Originally, the corporation's stock was held by 170 psychologists. Today the Psychological Corporation is still very active in providing psychological test-related services to the profession and to the public.

Other students of Wundt at Leipzig included Charles Spearman, Victor Henri, Emil Kraepelin, E. B. Titchener, G. Stanley Hall, and Lightner Witmer. Spearman is credited with being the originator of the psychometric concept of test reliability. Victor Henri is the Frenchman who would collaborate with Alfred Binet on papers suggesting how mental tests could be used to measure higher mental processes (for example, Binet & Henri, 1895a, 1895b, 1895c). Psychiatrist Emil Kraepelin was an early experimenter with the word association technique as a formal test (Kraepelin, 1892), and he measured the effect of a number of different variables (such as drugs, alcohol, tea, hunger, fatigue) on word associations. Kraepelin (1895) also devised tests (mainly of an arithmetic nature) to measure practice effects, memory, and susceptibility to fatigue. Wundt's disciple, the Englishman E. B. Titchener, brought the Leipzig school of thought to America at Cornell University, where he set up a psychological laboratory. Massachusetts-born G. Stanley Hall was a Leipzig alumnus who set up a psychological laboratory at Johns Hopkins University, founded the first American psychology journal (*American Journal of Psychology*), and on December 27, 1892, became the first president of the then-26-member American Psychological Association. Lightner Witmer received his Ph.D. from Leipzig and went on to succeed Cattell as director of the psychology laboratory at the University of Pennsylvania. In March 1896, Witmer was challenged by a public school teacher to provide a solution in the case of a "chronic bad speller" (see Brotemarkle, 1947). Later that year Witmer founded the first psychological clinic in the United States at the University of Pennsylvania. In 1907 Witmer founded the journal *Psychological Clinic* with the first article entitled "Clinical Psychology" (Witmer, 1907). Witmer has been cited as the "little known founder of clinical psychology" (McReynolds, 1987).

The Twentieth Century

The early 1900s witnessed the birth of the first formal tests of intelligence. As such tests were welcomed into various cultures throughout the world, the testing movement began to gain momentum. As we will see in the rest of this section, there was initially great receptivity throughout the world to instruments that could purportedly measure mental characteristics—intelligence at first and a wide range of other characteristics (such as those related to personality, interests, attitudes, and values) later.

The measurement of intelligence   Much of the nineteenth-century testing that could be described as psychological in nature involved the measurement of sensory abilities, reaction time, and the like. One person who had a vision of broadening testing to include the measurement of cognitive abilities was Alfred Binet (1857–1911). As early as 1895, Binet and his colleague Henri would publish several articles in which they argued for the measurement of abilities such as memory and social comprehension. Ten years later, Binet and collaborator Théodore Simon would publish a 30-item "measuring scale of intelligence" designed to help identify mentally retarded Paris schoolchildren (Binet & Simon, 1905). The Binet test would go through many revisions and translations—and in the process launch both the intelligence testing movement and the clinical testing movement. This point has been made by Pintner (1931):

> Although clinical psychology proper dates back at least to the last decade of the nineteenth century, it is undoubtedly true that the Binet scale was the one most potent factor in its development and expansion. Shortly after the first work with the Scale in the institutions for the feebleminded, we find psychological testing of all kinds spreading rapidly to juvenile courts, reformatories, prisons, children's homes, and schools. The psychological clinic did not and does not depend upon the Binet scale, but it is unquestionably true that the appearance of the Binet Scale acted as a tremendous stimulus to this type of work.

In 1939 David Wechsler, a clinical psychologist at Bellevue Hospital in New York City, introduced a test designed to measure adult intelligence—defined as "the aggregate or global capacity of the individual to act purposefully, to think rationally, and to deal effectively with his environment" (p. 3). The test, originally called the Wechsler-Bellevue Intelligence Scale, subsequently underwent revision and was renamed the Wechsler Adult Intelligence Scale (WAIS). Later, an "R" (for revision) was added to the name of a further revised version of the test, resulting in the present name, the Wechsler Adult Intelligence Scale (WAIS-R). In Part 3, "The Assessment of Intelligence," we will examine in greater detail Wechsler's definition of intelligence as it was reflected in the series of adults', children's, and young children's intelligence tests that bear his name.

A natural outgrowth of the individually administered intelligence test devised by Binet was the *group* intelligence test. Group intelligence tests came into being in this country in response to the military's need for an efficient method of screening the intellectual ability of World War I recruits. Because of military manpower needs during World War II, psychologists were enlisted into government service in order to develop, administer, and interpret group psychological test data. Psychologists returning from military service brought back with them a wealth of applied testing skills that would be useful not only in government service but also in settings as diverse as private industry, hospitals, and schools.

Figure 2–5 *Welcome to America!* Immigrants coming to America via Ellis Island were greeted not only by the Statue of Liberty but also by immigration officials ready to evaluate them with respect to physical, mental, and other variables. Here, a block design test, one measure of intelligence, is administered to a would-be American. Presuming the uniformed examiner is not a psychologist, the photo is also useful as a historic, pictorial illustration of the difference between "psychological testing" and "psychological assessment"; individual psychological testing, and not psychological assessment, is what appears to be going on here.

Immigrants who failed physical, mental, or other tests were returned to their country of origin at the expense of the shipping company that had brought them. Critics would later charge that at least some of the immigrants who had fared poorly on mental tests were sent away from our shores not because they were indeed mentally deficient but simply because they did not understand English well enough to execute instructions. Additionally, the criterion against which these immigrants from many lands were being evaluated was questioned: who served as the standardization sample, and how appropriate was that sample for this application?

The measurement of personality   The general receptivity to tests of intellectual ability spurred the development of a number of other types of tests (Garrett & Schneck, 1933; Pintner, 1931), including tests of personality. Only eight years after the publication of Binet's scale, the field of psychology was being criticized for being too test-oriented (Sylvester, 1913). By the late 1930s approximately four thousand different psychological tests were in print (Buros, 1938), and "clinical psychology" was synonymous with mental testing. As Tulchin (1939, p. 125) observed, "By the very nature of his early work and interest the psychologist easily became identified with mental tests" (see also Institute for Juvenile Research, 1937, p. 81).

World War I brought with it not only the need to screen the intellectual functioning of recruits but also the need to screen for personality problems. A government Committee on Emotional Fitness chaired by psychologist Robert S. Woodworth was assigned the task of developing a measure of adjustment and emotional stability that could be administered quickly and efficiently to groups of recruits. The committee developed several experimental versions of what in essence were paper-and-pencil psychiatric interviews. To disguise the true purpose of the test, the questionnaire was labeled and referred to as a Personal Data Sheet. Draftees and other test takers (volunteers) were asked to indicate "Yes" or "No" to a series of questions that probed the existence of various kinds of psychopathology. For example, one of the questions on the test was "Are you troubled with the idea that people are watching you on the street?"

The Personal Data Sheet developed by Woodworth and his colleagues never went beyond the experimental stages, for the armistice ending the war preceded the final form of the test. After the war, Woodworth developed a personality test for civilian use that was based on the Personal Data Sheet and called it the Woodworth Psychoneurotic Inventory. This inventory was the first widely used self-report test of personality—a method of assessment that would soon be employed in a long line of succeeding personality tests (for instance, the Humm-Wadsworth Temperament Scale, the Bernreuter Personality Inventory, the Edwards Personal Preference Schedule, and the Mooney Problem Checklist). Personality tests that employ self-report methodologies have both advantages and disadvantages. On the one hand, the person answering the question is—assuming sound judgment and insight—among the people best qualified to provide the most accurate answers. On the other hand, the person may possess neither good judgment nor good insight. And regardless of judgment or insight, respondents might be unwilling to reveal anything that could place them in a negative light. A need existed for personality tests that did not rely heavily on a respondent's self-report.

One type of test that provided a means of drawing inferences about personality without relying on self-report was the projective test. As we will see in Chapter 13, the projective test is one in which an individual is assumed to "project" onto some ambiguous stimulus his or her own unique needs, fears, hopes, and motivation. The ambiguous stimulus might be an inkblot, a drawing, a photograph, or something else. Perhaps the best known of all projective tests is the Rorschach Inkblots developed by the Swiss psychiatrist Hermann Rorschach. But note that as early as 1895, Alfred Binet had suggested the use of inkblots as a way of studying personality. Others, using their own inkblots with various kinds of administration instructions and scoring criteria, experimented with this personality assessment method (Dearborn, 1897, 1898; Sharp, 1899; Kirkpatrick, 1900; Pyle, 1913; Bartlett, 1916; Parsons, 1917). The use of pictures as projective stimuli was popularized in the late 1930s by Henry A. Murray and his colleagues at the Harvard Psychological Clinic (see Figure 2–6).

In addition to projective tests, other alternatives to reliance on self-report for personality assessment have been—and continually are being—developed. A sampling of these instruments, some additional historical observations, and a general discussion of personality assessment appear in Part 4. Students desirous of more detailed background in the history of psychological testing and measurement are referred to texts (such as Thorndike, 1990; Wainer, 1990; DuBois, 1970;

Boring, 1950), review articles (such as Guilford, 1985; Lewis, 1986), and specialized journals (such as *Journal of the History of the Behavioral Sciences*) that focus on this area.

Measurement in various settings   Like the development of the parent field of psychology, the development of psychological measurement can be traced along

---

Figure 2–6   *Henry A. Murray (1893–1988).*

Born in New York City, Henry A. Murray had an impressive collection of initials after his name by 1927; he earned an A.B. (with a major in history) from Harvard in 1915, an M.D. from Columbia in 1919, an M.A. in biology from Columbia in 1920, and a Ph.D. from Cambridge in 1927. Murray (1940, pp. 152–153) reminisced about his budding fascination with the mental life of others, including his colleagues and medical patients at Columbia:

> During my fourth year at the College of Physicians and Surgeons, while waiting for calls to deliver babies in Hell's Kitchen, I completed a modest study of 25 of my classmates, in which 40 anthropometric measures were later correlated with 30 traits.
>
> . . . Later, as an interne [sic] in a hospital, I spent more time than was considered proper for a surgeon, inquisitively seeking psychogenic factors in my patients. Whatever I succeeded in doing for them—the dope fiend, the sword-swallower, the prostitute, the gangster— was more than repaid when, after leaving the hospital, they took me through their haunts in the underworld. This was psychology in the rough, but at least it prepared me to recognize the similarity between downtown doings and uptown dreams. . . . But it was Jung's book, *Psychological Types,* which . . . started me off in earnest toward psychology. There were

besides this, another book, a woman, some German music and several other fructifying influences that made me feel and think at once, instead of separately.

In 1925 Murray visited with Carl Jung in Zurich. He wrote that "we talked for hours, sailing down the lake and smoking before the hearth of his Faustian retreat." Murray was profoundly affected by that meeting: he said that he had *experienced* the unconscious and it was then that he decided to pursue depth psychology as a career. He advised others to do the same type of thing with someone they respect:

Take your mysteries, your knottiest dilemmas, to a fit exponent of a system and judge the latter by its power to order and illumine your whole being. The Harvard Psychological Clinic had been founded by Morton Prince and it was at Prince's invitation that Murray came to the clinic as an instructor. In 1937, Murray was made the director of the clinic—one that was fast gaining a reputation for being an exciting, stimulating, innovative place to work. In 1938 Murray and his collaborators at the clinic published the now classic *Explorations in Personality,* a work that described, among other techniques, the Thematic Apperception Test (to be discussed in Chapter 12).

In 1943, Murray left Harvard for a position in the Army Medical Corps to help with the war effort. He established and directed the Office of Strategic Services, an agency charged in part with selecting men for James Bond–like tasks during the war (see OSS, *Assessment of Men,* 1948). In 1947 Murray returned to Harvard, where he lectured part time and helped establish the Psychological Clinic Annex in 1949. In 1962 Murray became emeritus professor at Harvard and after that earned the Distinguished Scientific Contribution Award from the American Psychological Association and the Gold Medal Award for lifetime achievement from the American Psychological Foundation. Murray died of pneumonia on June 23, 1988, at the age of 95.

two distinct threads: the academic and the applied. In the tradition of Galton, Wundt, and other scholars, psychological testing and assessment are practiced today in university psychology laboratories as a means of furthering knowledge about the nature of the human experience: knowledge about intelligence, abilities, potential, personality, creativity, interests, attitudes, values, neuropsychological processes—the list goes on.

There is also a very strong applied tradition—one that dates back in modern times to the work of people like Binet (and in ancient times to China and the administration of competitive civil service examinations). Which child should be placed in which class? Who of these military recruits should be rejected on the basis of intellectual or personality problems? Which person is best suited for the job? Society requires answers to questions such as these, and psychological tests and measures used in a competent manner can help provide answers. In addition to being used skillfully, tests must also be used ethically and in accordance with the law. We now survey some of the legal and ethical considerations attendant upon the use of psychological tests.

LEGAL AND ETHICAL CONSIDERATIONS

A society's laws are rules that individuals must obey for the good of the society as a whole—or rules thought to be for the good of society as a whole. Some laws are and have been relatively uncontroversial. For example, the law that mandates driving on the right side of the road has been neither a subject of debate, nor a source of emotional soul-searching, nor a stimulus to civil disobedience. For safety and the common good, most people are willing to relinquish their freedom to drive anywhere on the road they might please. But what about laws pertaining to abortion? to busing? to capital punishment? to euthanasia? to "deprogramming" of religious cult members? to affirmative action in employment? Exactly how laws regulating matters such as these should be written and interpreted are issues of heated controversy—as are some of the laws that pertain to psychological measurement.

Whereas a body of laws is a body of rules, a body of ethics is a body of principles of "right," "proper," or "good" conduct. Thus, for example, an ethic of the Old West was "Never shoot 'em in the back." Two well-known principles subscribed to by the seafaring set are "Women and children leave first in an emergency" and "A captain goes down with his ship."[4] The ethics of journalism dictate that reporters present all sides of a controversial issue. A research principle is that the scientist should never "fudge" data (that is, all data must be reported accurately). What kinds of ethical guidelines do you think should govern the professional behavior of psychologists involved in psychological testing and assessment? The answer to this question is important; to the extent that a code of ethics is recognized and accepted by members of a profession, it defines the standard of care expected by members of that profession.

---

4. We leave the problem of what to do when the captain of the ship is a woman to some future volume on seafaring ethics.

Members of the public and members of the profession have at times in recent history been on "different sides of the fence" with respect to issues of ethics and law. We now trace some concerns of the public and the profession.

The Concerns of the Public

The enterprise of psychological testing has never been very well understood by the public. Even today, it is unfortunate that we may hear statements symptomatic of misunderstanding with regard to tests (for example, "The only thing tests measure is the ability to take tests."). Possible consequences of public misunderstanding include fear and, in the extreme, hysteria—not to mention legislation, litigation, and administrative regulations. Recent decades have witnessed periods of heightened public concern regarding psychological tests—some of it justified, some of it not.

Perhaps the first time the American public evidenced widespread concern about psychological testing came in the aftermath of World War I. At that time, various professionals (as well as nonprofessionals) sought to adapt group tests developed by the military (such as the Army Alpha and Beta tests) for civilian use in schools and industry. As noted by Haney (1981), many articles in the periodical literature of the early 1920s reflected discomfort with the burgeoning testing industry. Representative of this discomfort were articles by Walter Lippmann in the popular *New Republic* magazine, such as "The Abuse of Tests" in November 1922 and "The Mental Age of Americans" in October 1922. In the latter article Lippmann asserted, among other things, that an intelligence test amounted to a "vain effort to discount training and knowledge." The renowned Stanford psychologist Lewis Terman attempted to respond to Lippmann's sensational and misleading remarks in the same magazine. However, because the issues were complex and the forum of the debate was a lay magazine, Terman was the loser in the eyes of the readership. As Cronbach (1975, p. 12) observed, Terman had "tried to play the same game and was hopelessly overmatched."

The 1930s witnessed a boom in the number of published standardized tests. Oscar Buros had the idea to publish a bibliography of available tests called *Educational, Psychological and Personality Tests of 1933 and 1934,* and this was the first edition of what later came to be known as the *Mental Measurements Yearbook.* This first edition contained only 44 pages; the second edition published later in the decade (Buros, 1938) contained nearly ten times as many pages and listed several thousand tests. Haney (1981) observed that the periodical literature in the 1930s was generally "far freer of criticisms of testing" than was that of the 1920s.

The widespread military testing that took place during the 1940s as a result of World War II did not appear to arouse as much popular interest as did the testing that had been undertaken during World War I. The periodical literature was relatively free of articles dealing with psychological testing until the 1960s, when considerable media attention was focused on gifted children. Perhaps the greatest stimulus to that attention was an event that occurred in the Soviet Union on October 4, 1957; on that day the Russians launched into space a satellite they called Sputnik—and the race to space was on. About a year after the Russian launch, Congress passed the National Defense Education Act, which provided federal money to local schools for the purpose of ability and aptitude testing; a rush was on to identify gifted and academically talented students.

The subsequent proliferation of large-scale testing programs in the schools combined with the increasing use of ability as well as personality tests in government, military, and business employment selection led to renewed widespread public concern about the efficacy of psychological tests. This concern was reflected in magazine articles such as "Testing: Can Everyone be Pigeonholed?" (*Newsweek*, July 20, 1959) and "What the Tests Do Not Test" (*New York Times Magazine*, October 2, 1960) and in books such as *The Brain Watchers* (Gross, 1962), *They Shall Not Pass* (Black, 1963), and *The Tyranny of Testing* (Hoffman, 1962)—books described by one authority in the field of psychological testing as "sensational books . . . [that] have added to the confusion" (Anastasi, 1968, p. 548).[5] The upshot of the heightened public concern was Congressional hearings on the subject of testing (see the November 1965 special issue of *American Psychologist*).

In 1969 widespread media attention was accorded the publication of an article in the prestigious *Harvard Educational Review*, and once again public concerns with respect to testing were aroused. The article was entitled "How Much Can We Boost IQ and Scholastic Achievement?" and its author, Arthur Jensen, argued that "genetic factors are strongly implicated in the average Negro–white intelligence difference" (1969, p. 82). An outpouring of public and professional attention to nature versus nurture issues regarding intelligence served to focus attention on the instruments used to gauge intellectual differences—instruments we commonly refer to as intelligence tests. The United States Select Committee on Equal Education Opportunity, in preparation for hearings on the matter of the relationships between intelligence, genetics, and environment, compiled a document of over 600 pages called *Environment, Intelligence and Scholastic Achievement* (1972). However, according to Haney (1981), the hearings "were canceled because they promised to be too controversial" (p. 1026).

The 1970s also witnessed the rise of what has come to be known as the "minimum competency" testing movement. Grass-roots support for the idea that high school graduates should have, at the very least, "minimal competencies" in areas such as reading, writing, and arithmetic has resulted in legislation in some jurisdictions providing that if such minimal competencies cannot be demonstrated on a test, a student may be denied a high school diploma (Lerner, 1981). Other legislation affecting testing and assessment in the 1970s included the Family Education Rights and Privacy Act (1974), which, among other things, mandates that parents and eligible students be given access to school records. Additionally, the act formally granted parents and students the right to challenge findings in those records in a hearing.

In the 1980s we saw the enactment by some states of what are known as "truth-in-testing" laws. This type of law mandates the disclosure of questions and answers of postsecondary and professional school admission tests within 30

---

5. Hoffman's (1962) book has been cited as raising some important questions regarding the value of standardized, multiple-choice questions in educational settings. Hoffman argued that these tests tap the variable of quickness or facility as it relates to intelligence and might therefore discriminate against the "deep, brooding" thinker. One might well wonder how well "deep, brooding" thinkers such as Kant and Spinoza would have performed on a standardized, multiple-choice examination such as the SAT: would they have labored over the meaning of the questions while other test takers simply took the questions in stride? This particular concern is a legitimate one and one that psychologists as well as educators still debate.

days of the publication of test scores. One objective of this type of law is to aid test takers in learning the criteria by which they are being judged. Another objective is to achieve greater public accountability on the part of the developers of such standardized tests. Other provisions of a truth-in-testing law may touch on matters such as disclosure of (1) a description of the test's purpose and its subject matter, (2) the knowledge and skills the test purports to measure, (3) procedures for ensuring accuracy in scoring as well as procedures for notifying test takers of errors in scoring, and (4) procedures for ensuring the test taker's confidentiality.

In reaction to the enactment of a truth-in-testing law in New York, some organizations such as the Association of American Medical Colleges (AAMC) and the American Dental Association announced that they would no longer administer the tests they publish—tests required for admission to most American medical and dental schools—in New York State. These and other test developers have argued that it is essential that they be able to keep the items they use on such tests secret since (1) there is a limited item pool and (2) the cost of developing an entirely new set of items for each succeeding administration of a test would be prohibitive.

The Concerns of the Profession

As early as 1895, the infant American Psychological Association (APA) had formed its first committee on mental measurement, a committee charged with investigating various aspects of the new practice of standardized testing. Another APA committee on measurements was formed in 1906 to further study the issues and problems attendant upon test standardization. In 1916 and again in 1921, symposia dealing with various issues surrounding the burgeoning uses of tests were sponsored (*Mentality tests,* 1916; *Intelligence and its measurement,* 1921) and in 1923 an APA committee recommended that nonpsychologists' use of tests be monitored. However, that recommendation was voted down by the APA membership. Not until 1954 did the Association publish its *Technical Recommendations for Psychological Tests and Diagnostic Tests,* a document that set forth testing standards and technical recommendations. The objective of preparing and publishing the *Recommendations* was stated as follows:

> The essential principle that sets the tone of this document is that a test manual should carry information sufficient to enable any qualified user to make sound judgments regarding the usefulness and interpretation of the test. (APA, 1954, p. 2)

The following year, another professional organization, the National Educational Association (working in collaboration with the National Council on Measurements Used in Education—now known as the National Council on Measurement) published its *Technical Recommendations for Achievement Tests.*[6] Collaboration between these professional organizations led to the development of testing standards (as summarized in the Chapter 1 Close-up).

Paralleling APA's ongoing concerns regarding the ethics of psychological

---

6. For a more detailed description of these documents and their impact on the practice of testing, the interested reader is referred to Novick (1981).

Table 2-1

Legislation, Litigation, and Administrative Regulations

A sampling of legislation, court decisions, and administrative regulations that have an impact on the practice of psychological testing follows.

Legislation

Americans with Disabilities Act of 1990

This law defines a disability as a condition that "substantially limits" a "major life activity." The law bans discrimination in employment, transportation, public accommodations, and telecommunications on the basis of physical or mental disability. Its provisions apply to business, transportation systems, commercial establishments, and telephone companies and require that reasonable accommodation be made to allow disabled workers to perform their duties; additionally, facilities must be accessible to individuals with physical disabilities. Implementation of the act will likely result in changes in job selection and placement procedures. Although "reasonable accommodations" for the disabled individual have not been defined, they may include modified work schedules, restructuring of jobs to minimize the worker's disability, and modification of training materials. For example, if reading or vision skills are not essential for performing one's duties, training materials will be modified so that they do not emphasize these skills. Similarly, testing procedures and materials must be designed to measure the skills essential to the particular job, rather than reflecting the effect of the person's handicap. The use of paper-and-pencil tests as a selection procedure would not be appropriate if such skills are unrelated to the job and the applicant's performance would reflect his or her handicap. It is the responsibility of employers to determine the essential functions of the job and to develop selection procedures reflective of the skills necessary to perform the job. Issues in personnel selection are discussed in greater detail in Chapter 18.

Title VII of the Civil Rights Act of 1964

This law, also referred to as the Equal Employment Opportunity Act, provides for nondiscrimination in employment by reason of race, color, religion, sex, or national origin. An amendment to it stipulates that it is permissible to "give and to act upon the results of any professionally developed ability test provided that such test, its administration or action upon the results is not designed, intended, or used to discriminate because of race, color, religion, sex, or national origin." The Equal Employment Opportunity Commission was established by this act with a mandate to enforce the nondiscrimination require-

ment. Some of the guidelines set forth by this commission are listed in the later section, "Administrative Regulations."

Public Law 94-142

Also referred to as the Education for All Handicapped Children Act, this law was enacted in 1977. The law mandated that all children with suspected mental or physical handicaps must be identified through the use of screening instruments. Once identified, the children must be evaluated by a professional team qualified to determine what each individual child's special educational needs are. The school must then institute an educational program designed to meet these special needs, and the child must be reevaluated periodically to assess progress. On October 30, 1990, President George Bush signed into law the *Education of the Handicapped Act, Amendments of 1990*. The Amendments changed the name of the law to *Individuals with Disabilities Education Act,* and replaced the term "handicapped" with the term "disabilities" throughout the act.

Minimum Competency Legislation

Numerous states have enacted what are referred to as minimum competency testing programs—formal testing programs designed to be used in decisions regarding various aspects of students' education (such as award of diplomas, grade promotions, and identification of areas needed for remedial instruction).

Truth-in-Testing Legislation

This type of legislation is designed to provide examinees with the right to gain access to the questions and answers given on various kinds of examinations in order for them to know the basis on which they are being judged. Another objective of such legislation is to make test publishers more accountable to the public by mandating that information relevant to a test's development and psychometric soundness be kept on file. This type of legislation, as variously written in different states, might provide for the right of examinees' privacy to be upheld and the right of examinees to be informed of the intended uses of the test results.

Table 2–1 (*continued*)

Litigation

Hobson v. Hansen (1967)

As a result of the 1954 case of *Brown v. Board of Education,* schools are required to desegregate. Possibly as a means of circumventing *Brown,* some school systems instituted testing programs designed to group children of the same ability in the same classes. Since many black children were deemed to have similar—supposedly inadequate—abilities, they were to be grouped in lower track classes. At issue in *Hobson* was whether or not an ability tracking system violated the Fourteenth Amendment (the equal protection clause) of the Constitution. The Supreme Court held that "mere classification . . . does not of itself deprive a group of equal protection." However, because the tests in use at such school systems "are standardized primarily on and are relevant to a white middle class group of students, they produce inaccurate and misleading test scores when given to lower class Negro students," the ability tracking system as it existed at that time was therefore to be abolished.

Diana v. State Board of Education (1970)

Children with Spanish surnames in California constituted approximately 18% of the total pupil population and nearly 33% of the population of classes for the educable mentally retarded (EMR). *Diana* was initiated in an attempt to remedy the perceived problem of having a disproportionate number of Mexican-American pupils in EMR classes. The basis for the EMR classification had been test scores on the Wechsler Intelligence Scale for Children or on the Stanford-Binet Intelligence Scale. The plaintiffs asserted that (1) the tests were culturally biased in favor of white students who composed the standardization sample, and (2) successful performance on the tests relied heavily on English verbal skills and therefore discriminated against Spanish-speaking children. The plaintiffs presented evidence that when nine Spanish-speaking children were tested in Spanish, eight of the nine scored at or above the established cutoff score for EMR placement.

The following provisions of the *Diana* court's determination were incorporated into the California Education Code: (1) there should be no socioeconomic, racial, or ethnic disproportions in EMR classes; (2) all IQ test scores used for EMR placement would be administered in the language the pupil is most fluent in; (3) a child who scored higher than two standard deviations below the mean on a nonverbal test or subtest could not be classified as EMR unless recommended unanimously in writing by an admissions committee that considered all relevant in-

formation; (4) an EMR placement would require a comprehensive evaluation by a certified school psychologist based on an intelligence test and on data from a developmental history, from an educational evaluation, and from measures of adaptive behavior; and (5) an EMR placement would require written parental consent.

Larry P. v. Riles (1979)

Like *Diana,* *Larry P.* is a California case that alleged discrimination in the assignment of children to EMR classes; whereas *Diana* involved Hispanic children, *Larry P.* involved blacks. The suit was brought with supporting evidence from the Bay Area Association of Black Psychologists; this group retested six children using the same intelligence test they had previously taken but with a rewording of some of the items that, in the psychologists' opinion, were more reflective of the children's cultural background. Scores as a function of such retesting ranged from 17 to 38 points higher than the initial scores obtained by school psychologists, and all six children scored above the cutoff for EMR placement.

The court enjoined the defendant California State Department of Education "from utilizing, permitting the use of, or approving the use of any standardized tests . . . for the identification of black EMR children or their placement into EMR classes without first securing approval by this court." In effect, the judge would be the arbiter or who was to be placed in which class. The case of *Larry P.* began in 1972 and was concluded in 1979 at which time the court ruled that intelligence tests were "racially and culturally biased" and have a "discriminatory impact on black children." It was held that the use of intelligence tests such as the Wechsler tests and the Stanford-Binet for the purpose of determining whether blacks should be placed in EMR classes was unconstitutional. The litigation resulted in a moratorium on the use of intelligence tests in making EMR placements. The decision was appealed but upheld in 1984 by the United States Court of Appeals for the Ninth Circuit. In 1986, the California judge who made the 1979 ruling reaffirmed it by stating flatly and "in no uncertain terms . . . that schools in that state may not use I.Q. tests to assess black children for placement in special education classes" (Landers, 1986, p. 18).

Griggs v. Duke Power Company (1971)

Black employees of a private power company brought suit against their employer and challenged the legal-

(Continues)

Table 2-1 (continued)

ity of using criteria such as a high school diploma and satisfactory scores on the Wonderlic Personnel Test and the Bennett Mechanical Comprehension Test to hire and promote personnel. The suit claimed that the use of such tests for these purposes was in violation of Title VII of the Civil Rights Act of 1964, which prohibited discrimination in employment on the basis of race, religion, sex, or national origin. In a 1971 ruling, the Supreme Court found in favor of the plaintiffs, interpreting Title VII as outlawing "not only overt discrimination but also practices that are fair in form, but discriminatory in operation." The plaintiffs had introduced evidence that the criteria had a disproportionate impact on minorities. The court held that the employer bore the burden of demonstrating that "any given requirement had a manifest relationship to the employment in question." In short, "broad and general testing devices" were faulted, and tests that "fairly measure the knowledge or skills required by a particular job" were mandated. The court ruled that employment tests must "measure the person for the job and not the person in the abstract."

Albemarle Paper Company v. Moody (1976)

In *Griggs,* the Supreme Court stated in essence that tests must be job-related. In *Albemarle Paper Company,* the Court delved deeper into the question of what constitutes a job-related test. The case involved an industrial psychologist employed by a paper mill. The psychologist routinely administered a general ability test as a condition of employment—a practice that was challenged as discriminatory. The psychol-

ogist argued that the test was valid for the purpose that it was being used for, because scores on this test could be shown to relate in the predicted direction with job-related criteria such as supervisors' judgments of competence. The United States District Court found the procedure to be sufficiently job-related to be considered valid. However, the decision of that court was reversed on appeal. Unlawful discrimination was held to have existed irrespective of the paper mill's "good intent or absence of discriminatory intent."

Debra P. v. Turlington (1981)

Suit was brought against Florida's Commissioner of Education (Turlington) by ten black students after they had been denied high school diplomas; the students had failed a statewide test of minimal competency (which in this instance was essentially a literacy test). The plaintiffs argued that if the minimal competency test were to be sanctioned, 20 percent of the black high school seniors in Florida would be denied high school diplomas as compared to only 2 percent of the white population of high school seniors. In 1979 a federal judge ruled that the minimal competency testing program in Florida was unconstitutional and that it perpetuated the effects of past discrimination; a moratorium on such testing was ordered. In 1981, the United States Court of Appeals affirmed the lower court's ruling, holding that such a program violated the equal protection clause of the Constitution since it punished black students for prior discrimination in schooling.

Administrative Regulation

The Equal Employment Opportunity Commission (EEOC) was created as a result of Title VII of the Civil Rights Act of 1964 and was charged with enforcement duties. Through executive action, EEOC's authority was later strengthened as was the authority of other administrative agencies that dealt with issues related to equal employment opportunities. Since its creation, EEOC has published sets of guidelines concerning standards to be met in constructing and using employment tests. Other agencies, such as the Civil Service Commission, the Department of Labor, and the Justice Department, have also published guidelines on employment practices designed to eliminate discrimination. In 1978, these four agencies jointly published the *Uniform Guidelines on Employee*

Selection Procedures, a document that was hailed by the American Psychological Assocation Testing Committee as "a major step forward" (Novick, 1981). One sample guideline is as follows:

The use of any test which adversely affects hiring, promotion, transfer or any other employment or membership opportunity of classes protected by Title VII constitutes discrimination unless (a) the test has been validated and evidences a high degree of utility as hereinafter described, and (b) the person giving or acting upon the results of the particular test can demonstrate that alternative suitable hiring, transfer or promotion procedures are unavailable for . . . use.

testing were concerns about general ethics in the field of psychology. In 1953 APA published its *Ethical Standards of Psychologists,* a culmination of the work of many APA committees that had been established over the years to study ethical standards and practices for various types of professional and scientific activities. APA published a *Casebook on Ethical Standards of Psychologists* (1967) and a revised edition, *Casebook on Ethical Principles of Psychologists* (1987), to provide examples of the types of cases brought before the APA Ethics Committee. APA periodically updates its *Ethical Principles of Psychologists* (see, for example, APA, 1981; APA, 1990).

Through the years, numerous other publications of the American Psychological Association have reflected the organization's deep concern for maintenance of high professional standards and the welfare of people who take psychological tests. A partial listing of some APA publications that reflect this concern and that deal directly or indirectly with the subject of testing is summarized in Table 2–2.

The National Association of School Psychologists (NASP) has also established professional standards for its members. Its *Principles for Professional Ethics,* adopted in 1984, provides guidance in the selection, use, and interpretation of psychological tests and assessment procedures.

Who should be privy to psychological test data? Who should be able to purchase psychological test materials? Who is qualified to administer, score, and interpret psychological tests? What level of expertise in psychometrics is required in order to be qualified to administer which type of test? A consideration of these important questions follows.

Test-user qualifications   Should anyone be allowed to purchase and use psychological test materials? If not, who should be permitted to use psychological tests? Psychologists have a long history of grappling with these most difficult questions. As early as 1950, an APA Committee on Ethical Standards for Psychology published a report called *Ethical Standards for the Distribution of Psychological Tests and Diagnostic Aids.* This report defined three "levels" of tests in terms of

Table 2–2

Some APA Publications Bearing on Psychological Testing

Standards for Educational and Psychological Tests and Manuals (1966)
Standards for Educational and Psychological Tests (1974)
Standards for Educational and Psychological Testing (1985)
Standards for Providers of Psychological Services (APA, 1977)
Specialty Guidelines for the Delivery of Services by Clinical Psychologists (APA, 1981a)
Specialty Guidelines for the Delivery of Services by Counseling Psychologists (APA, 1981b)
Specialty Guidelines for the Delivery of Services by Industrial/Organizational Psychologists (APA, 1981c)
Specialty Guidelines for the Delivery of Services by School Psychologists (APA, 1981d)
Ethical Principles of Psychologists (APA, 1981e)
Principles for the Validation and Use of Personnel Selection Procedures (APA, 1980)
Automated Test Scoring and Interpretation Practices (APA, 1966)
Guidelines for Computer-Based Tests and Interpretations (APA, 1986)

the degree to which the test's use required knowledge of testing and the subject matter of psychology:

Level A. Tests or aids that can adequately be administered, scored, and interpreted with the aid of the manual and a general orientation to the kind of institution or organization in which one is working (e.g., achievement or proficiency tests).

Level B. Tests or aids that require some technical knowledge of test construction and use, and of supporting psychological and educational fields such as statistics, individual differences, psychology of adjustment, personnel psychology, and guidance (e.g., aptitude tests, adjustment inventories applicable to normal populations).

Level C. Tests and aids that require substantial understanding of testing and supporting psychological fields, together with supervised experience in the use of these devices (e.g., projective tests, individual mental tests).

The report, which also included descriptions of the general levels of training corresponding to each of the three levels of tests, was reprinted in APA's *Ethical Standards of Psychologists* (1953) and cited in APA's *Standards for Educational and Psychological Tests and Manuals* (1966), though it was omitted from mention in the two editions of the *Standards* that followed. Although many test publishers continue to use this three-level classification, some do not. The current edition of the *Standards* (1985) says that "Responsibility for test use should be assumed or delegated only to those individuals who have the training and experience necessary to handle this responsibility in a professional and technically adequate manner" (p. 42). Likewise, NASP's *Principles for Professional Ethics* (1984) includes one principle which states that school psychologists "offer only those services which are within their individual area of training and experience" (p. 3) and one that emphasizes "the use of valid and reliable instruments and techniques that are applicable and appropriate for the student" (p. 4).

APA's *Ethical Principles of Psychologists* (1981a) lists two principles that have a bearing on questions concerning test-user qualifications; Principle 2 states that psychologists "only provide services and only use techniques for which they are qualified by training and experience," and Principle 8 holds that psychologists "strive to ensure that the results of assessments and their interpretations are not misused by others." The application of these principles is illustrated by the following case from APA's *Casebook on Ethical Principles of Psychologists* (1987):

A psychologist was hired by the fire department of a large suburban county to set up a procedure for selecting new hires from among the many applicants for firefighter positions. As part of the selection process the psychologist established, she used a computerized MMPI program that had proved useful in selecting candidates for firefighter positions. A year later, as a result of severe budget cutbacks, the fire department found it necessary to dispense with the psychologist's services and asked her to allow the department to continue to use the MMPI program. The psychologist was also asked to release all previous assessment results to the department and to train a nonprofessional to administer and interpret the program. The psychologist wrote to the Ethics Committee to ask if it would be ethical for her to comply with the fire department's requests.

assessments to persons not trained to interpret them would violate Principle 8.e. (scoring and interpretation services) of the *Ethical Principles*.

Despite the publication of ethical guidelines and standards, the situation regarding the issue of test-user qualifications might legitimately be described as chaotic. As Moreland (1986, p. 3) observed, "At present, qualification policies are as plentiful as test publishers." Moreland went on to point out that at least part of the problem lies in the fact that "test users" in no way constitute a homogeneous group; "test users can be found in virtually every walk of life. The owner of the clothing store where I buy my suits tests all prospective employees" (p. 3).

In an effort to remedy the situation, the American Psychological Association, the American Educational Research Association, the National Council on Measurement in Education, and two dozen or so test publishers have banded together and established the Joint Committee on Testing Practices (JCTP). In 1988 the *Code of Fair Testing Practices in Education* was developed by the group. The *Code* delineates the obligations of both test developers and test users in four broad areas: (1) developing/selecting tests, (2) interpreting scores, (3) striving for fairness, and (4) informing test takers. The *Code* is directed primarily at professionally developed tests such as those sold by commercial test publishers or used in formally administered testing programs. The roles of test developers and test users are addressed separately. Test users are defined as those "who select tests, commission test development services, or make decisions on the basis of test scores." Test developers are those "who actually construct tests as well as those who set policies for particular testing programs" (p. 10). The *Code* has been endorsed by a number of test publishers, including the American College Testing Program, The College Board, Educational Testing Service, Psychological Corporation, and Riverside Publishing Company. The *Code* (see Table 2–3) is intended to be consistent with the *Standards for Educational and Psychological Testing* (1985) and is designed to be understood by the general public.

Testing members of cultural and linguistic minorities   America has a well-earned reputation for being a "melting pot," and a number of U.S. citizens and residents do not speak English as their native tongue. For the individual whose English-language skills are limited, any test—be it an intelligence test, an employment test, or a test of music appreciation—can amount, in essence, to a test of proficiency in the English language. When an individual with limited language skills in English is to be tested, a threefold dilemma arises: (1) the problem of transforming the test into an equivalent form understandable to the test taker, (2) the problem of comprehending and scoring the test taker's responses, and (3) the problem of meaningfully interpreting test data.

This issue is illustrated by the following case from APA's *Casebook on Ethical Principles of Psychologists* (1987):

A psychologist in a large metropolitan school district contacted the Ethics Office for an opinion about the suitability of a testing and placement program in the school system about which he was concerned. The district based its placement decisions for entering students on the Wechsler Intelligence Scale for Children–Revised (WISC-R). His concern was that the test

Table 2–3

Code of Fair Testing Practices in Education

A   Developing/Selecting Appropriate Tests*

Test developers should provide the information that test users need to select appropriate tests.

Test Developers Should:

1. Define what each test measures and what the test should be used for. Describe the population(s) for which the test is appropriate.
2. Accurately represent the characteristics, usefulness, and limitations of tests for their intended purposes.
3. Explain relevant measurement concepts as necessary for clarity at the level of detail that is appropriate for the intended audience(s).
4. Describe the process of test development. Explain how the content and skills to be tested were selected.
5. Provide evidence that the test meets its intended purpose(s).
6. Provide either representative samples or complete copies of test questions, directions, answer sheets, manuals, and score reports to qualified users.
7. Indicate the nature of the evidence obtained concerning the appropriateness of each test for groups of different racial, ethnic, or linguistic backgrounds who are likely to be tested.
8. Identify and publish any specialized skills needed to administer each test and to interpret scores correctly.

Test users should select tests that meet the purpose for which they are to be used and that are appropriate for the intended test-taking populations.

Test Users Should:

1. First define the purpose for testing and the population to be tested. Then, select a test for that purpose and that population based on a thorough review of the available information.
2. Investigate potentially useful sources of information, in addition to test scores, to corroborate the information provided by tests.
3. Read the materials provided by test developers and avoid using tests for which unclear or incomplete information is provided.
4. Become familiar with how and when the test was developed and tried out.
5. Read independent evaluations of a test and of possible alternative measures. Look for evidence required to support the claims of test developers.
6. Examine specimen sets, disclosed tests or samples of questions, directions, answer sheets, manuals, and score reports before selecting a test.
7. Ascertain whether the test content and norms group(s) or comparison group(s) are appropriate for the intended test takers.
8. Select and use only those tests for which the skills needed to administer the test and interpret scores correctly are available.

B   Interpreting Scores

Test developers should help users interpret scores correctly.

Test Developers Should:

9. Provide timely and easily understood score reports that describe test performance clearly and accurately. Also explain the meaning and limitations of reported scores.
10. Describe the population(s) represented by any norms or comparison group(s), the dates the data were gathered, and the process used to select the samples of test takers.
11. Warn users to avoid specific, reasonably anticipated misuses of test scores.
12. Provide information that will help users follow reasonable procedures for setting passing scores when it is appropriate to use such scores with the test.

Test users should interpret scores correctly.

Test Users Should:

9. Obtain information about the scale used for reporting scores, the characteristics of any norms or comparison group(s), and the limitations of the scores.
10. Interpret scores taking into account any major differences between the norms or comparison groups and the actual test takers. Also take into account any differences in test administration practices or familiarity with the specific questions in the test.
11. Avoid using tests for purposes not specifically recommended by the test developer unless evidence is obtained to support the intended use.

Table 2–3 (*continued*)

13. Provide information that will help users gather evidence to show that the test is meeting its intended purpose(s).

12. Explain how any passing scores were set and gather evidence to support the appropriateness of the scores.
13. Obtain evidence to help show that the test is meeting its intended purpose(s).

	C	Striving for Fairness

Test developers should strive to make tests that are as fair as possible for test takers of different races, gender, ethnic backgrounds, or handicapping conditions.

Test Developers Should:

14. Review and revise test questions and related materials to avoid potentially insensitive content or language.
15. Investigate the performance of test takers of different races, gender, and ethnic backgrounds when samples of sufficient size are available. Enact procedures that help to ensure that differences in performance are related primarily to the skills under assessment rather than to irrelevant factors.
16. When feasible, make appropriately modified forms of tests or administration procedures available for test takers with handicapping conditions. Warn test users of potential problems in using standard norms with modified tests or administration procedures that result in non-comparable scores.

Test users should select tests that have been developed in ways that attempt to make them as fair as possible for test takers of different races, gender, ethnic backgrounds, or handicapping conditions.

Test Users Should:

14. Evaluate the procedures used by test developers to avoid potentially insensitive content or language.
15. Review the performance of test takers of different races, gender, and ethnic backgrounds when samples of sufficient size are available. Evaluate the extent to which performance differences may have been caused by inappropriate characteristics of the test.
16. When necessary and feasible, use appropriately modified forms of tests or administration procedures for test takers with handicapping conditions. Interpret standard norms with care in the light of the modifications that were made.

	D	Informing Test Takers

Under some circumstances, test developers have direct communication with test takers. Under other circumstances, test users communicate directly with test takers. Whichever group communicates directly with test takers should provide the information described below.

Test Developers or Test Users Should:

17. When a test is optional, provide test takers or their parents/guardians with information to help them judge whether the test should be taken, or if an available alternative to the test should be used.
18. Provide test takers the information they need to be familiar with the coverage of the test, the types of question formats, the directions, and appropriate test-taking strategies. Strive to make such information equally available to all test takers.

Under some circumstances, test developers have direct control of tests and test scores. Under other circumstances test users have such control. Whichever group has direct control of tests and test scores should take the steps described below.

Test Developers or Test Users Should:

19. Provide test takers or their parents/guardians with information about rights test takers may have to obtain copies of tests and completed answer sheets, retake tests, have tests rescored, or cancel scores.
20. Tell test takers or their parents/guardians how long scores will be kept on file and indicate to whom and under what circumstances test scores will or will not be released.
21. Describe the procedures that test takers or their parents/guardians may use to register complaints and have problems resolved.

*Many of the statements in the Code refer to the selection of existing tests. However, in customized testing programs test developers are engaged to construct new tests. In those situations, the test development process should be designed to help ensure that the completed tests will be in compliance with the Code.

was used to assess and place newly arrived immigrant Puerto Rican children, who lacked any fluency in the English language and for whom there were no appropriate norms. As a result, many children were labeled mentally retarded and placed in special education classes. The Ethics Committee sent a letter to the psychologist to the effect that this kind of test usage could be seen as a violation of Principle 8.c (reporting assessment results) because of the inappropriateness of the norms and the language difficulties. When apprised of this difficulty the school stopped using the WISC-R with non–English speaking children and accepted the psychologist's offer to help them devise an alternative and more appropriate placement program.

Professional guidelines in this area suggest that if a test developed and standardized on English-speaking people is to be translated into another language, precautions must be taken to ensure that the translation is indeed an equivalent form; merely translating word for word is not satisfactory because some words may have very different connotations, difficulty levels, and/or word frequencies in the other language. If the testing is to be conducted in a language other than English, the examiner should ideally have had special training in administering the test in that language. The reliability and validity of a translated test should be established *for the specific group* the test is to be used with. Thus, for example, if an English-language test designed for use in this country is translated into Spanish, its reliability and validity should be established separately with each of the various Spanish-speaking groups of test takers with whom it might be used (such as Mexicans, Puerto Ricans, and Guatemalans).

Obvious exceptions to these cautions are tests that have been designed expressly to assess proficiency in the English language. However, even here, a word of caution is in order. An orally administered test of English proficiency should not be construed as representative of written proficiency (and vice versa). Additionally, examiners must ideally be knowledgeable about relevant aspects of the culture from which the people they test come. For example, a child may present as noncommunicative and having only minimal language skills when verbally examined; this finding may be due to the fact that the child is from a culture where elders are revered, where children speak to adults only when they are spoken to and then only in as short a phrase as possible.

In addition to linguistic barriers, the contents of tests from a particular culture are typically laden with items and material—some obvious, some very subtle—that draw heavily from that culture; test performance may, at least in part, reflect not only whatever variables the test purports to measure but also one additional variable—the degree to which the test taker has assimilated the culture. On the one hand, it is possible to view this state of affairs and say "this is the way it should be; tests devised within a particular culture necessarily should be imbued with and reflective of that culture." On the other hand, the fact that it is difficult if not impossible to devise truly culture-free tests has been a source of frustration to many members of linguistic and cultural minorities.

Testing people with disabilities Difficulties analogous to those concerning test takers from linguistic and cultural minorities are present when the testing of people with disabling conditions is undertaken. Specifically, these difficulties may include (1) transforming the test into a form that can be taken by the test taker,

(2) transforming the responses of the test taker so that they are scorable, and (3) meaningfully interpreting the test data.

The nature of the transformation of the test into a form ready for administration to the individual with disabling conditions will, of course, depend on the nature of the disability. If, for example, the test taker is blind or visually impaired, the test will have to be transformed into braille or large-type print. In turn, the format for responding to test items will have to be appropriately modified. And if the materials of a test to be transformed contain pictures or other artwork, professional judgment and discretion will be necessary in decisions related to the omission of such materials or the development of oral descriptions of them. One question underlying all such decisions is "What effect will such transformations have on the reliability and validity of the findings?"

Answers to questions like this one are simply not known at this point in time; precious little research designed to answer such questions has been undertaken. Some tests, particularly group-administered tests, may not be amenable at all to administration to people with particular disabilities (or, for that matter, to people from linguistic or cultural minorities). In all phases of testing people with disabling conditions, from setting up the location of the testing with special furniture if need be, to test administration, to test interpretation, reasonable decision making for testing is required. The present authors recommend that, in instances where standardized test conditions have been modified, all such modifications be noted in the record of the tests and considered in the interpretation of test results. Chapter 17 deals with the issues involved in testing people with disabling conditions.

Computerized test administration, scoring, and interpretation The widespread availability of relatively inexpensive computers has had a great impact on the field of psychological testing. An ever-growing number of psychological tests can be purchased on disks, and their administration, scoring, and interpretation are as simple as pressing keys on a keyboard. In many respects, the relative simplicity, convenience, and range of potential testing activities that computer technology brings to the testing industry have been a great boon. Test users have under one roof the means by which they can quickly administer, score, and interpret a wide range of tests. Additionally, they own the technology that allows them to administer complex tests of eye-hand coordination, reaction time, and other abilities (McCullough, 1990). However, if the burgeoning computer-assisted testing industry looks, at first blush, rosy, a more careful look reveals a welter of thorns.

The availability of psychological tests that can be administered, scored, and interpreted by computer may be a temptation to the public. Employers who currently use personnel psychologists to screen prospective employees, for example, might well believe it to be more efficient and economical to have psychological testing done by computer and supervised by a clerical worker. This raises the question of access to psychological tests—on disk or otherwise. Who should have access? Why?

Another question—this one a step backward from the access question—involves the issue of the soundness of the test software itself. If the test is a computer version of a paper-and-pencil test, how does one know whether the two versions of the test are indeed equivalent? If the test contains a program for providing a narrative interpretation of the test results, how does one know that the interpretation is valid? What other possible "thorns" can you envision around the "rose" of computerized psychological testing? In Chapter 20 we will explore these issues in greater detail.

The Rights of Test Takers

As prescribed by the *Standards* (1985), some of the rights test users accord to test takers are as follows: the right of informed consent to testing, the right to be informed of test findings, the right not to have privacy invaded, the right to the least stigmatizing label, and the right to have findings held confidential.

The right of informed consent to testing   Test takers have a right to know why they are being tested, how the test data will be used, and what, if any, information will be released to whom. The disclosure of such information must, of course, be in language the test taker can understand. Thus, for a test taker as young as 2 or 3 years of age or a mentally retarded individual with limited language ability, a disclosure prior to testing might be worded as follows: "I'm going to ask you to try to do some things so that I can see what you know how to do and what things you could use some more help with" (*Standards*, 1985, p. 85). If a test taker is incapable of providing an informed consent to testing, such consent may be obtained from a parent or legal representative. Ideally, the consent should be written as opposed to oral in nature, and the written form should specify (1) the general purpose of the testing, (2) the specific reason it is being undertaken in the present case, and (3) the general type of instruments to be administered. Many school districts now routinely send home such forms prior to testing children. Such forms typically include the option to have the child assessed privately if the parent so desires. In instances where testing is legally mandated (as in a court-ordered situation), obtaining informed consent to test may be considered to be more of a courtesy (undertaken in part for reasons of establishing good rapport) than a necessity.

One "gray area" with respect to the test taker's right of fully informed consent prior to testing involves research and experimental situations wherein the examiner's complete disclosure of all facts pertinent to the testing (including the experimenter's hypothesis and so forth) might irrevocably contaminate the test data. In such instances, professional discretion is in order; test takers might be given a minimum amount of information before the testing (for example, "This testing is being undertaken as part of an experiment on obedience to authority. . . .") with a full and complete disclosure and debriefing made after the testing.

The right to be informed of test findings   In a bygone era, the inclination of many psychological assessors, particularly many clinicians, was to tell test takers as little as possible about the nature of their performance on a particular test or test battery and in no case to disclose diagnostic conclusions that could arouse anxiety and/or precipitate a crisis. This orientation was reflected in at least one authoritative text where testers were advised to keep feedback superficial and focus only on "positive" findings so that the examinee would leave the test session feeling "pleased and satisfied" (Klopfer, Ainsworth, Klopfer, & Holt, 1954, p. 15). But all of that has changed, and realistic feedback to examinees is not only ethically and legally mandated, but may be useful from a therapeutic perspective as well (see Berg, 1985).

Test takers have a right to be informed, in terms that they can understand, of the nature of the findings with respect to a test that they took. They are also entitled to know what recommendations are being made as a consequence of the test data. Conversely, if for any reason test results or findings (or recommendations made on the basis of test data) are being voided for any reason (such as irregularities found to have been in evidence), test takers have a right to know that, as well.

Because of the possibility of untoward consequences as a result of providing individuals with feedback about themselves—their ability, their lack of ability, their personality, their values—the communication of results of a psychological test is a most important part of the test process. With sensitivity to the situation, the test user will inform the test taker (and/or the parent or legal representative) of the purpose of the test, the meaning of the score relative to those of other test takers, and the possible limitations and margins of error of the test. And regardless of whether such reporting is done in person or in writing, a qualified psychologist should ideally be available to answer any further questions test takers (or their parents) have about the test scores. Further, the resource of counseling should ideally be available for test takers who become distraught at learning how they scored on a particular test.

The right not to have privacy invaded The concept of privacy "recognizes the freedom of the individual to pick and choose for himself the time, circumstances, and particularly the extent to which he wishes to share or withhold from others his attitudes, beliefs, behavior, and opinions" (Shah, 1969, p. 57). When people in court proceedings "take the fifth" and refuse to answer a question put to them on the grounds that the answer might be self-incriminating, they are asserting a right of privacy provided by the Fifth Amendment to the Constitution. The information withheld in such a manner is referred to as *privileged* information, information that is protected by law from disclosure in a legal proceeding. State statutes have extended the concept of privileged information to parties who communicate with each other in the context of certain relationships, including the lawyer-client relationship, the doctor-patient relationship, the priest-penitent relationship, and the husband-wife relationship. In most states privilege is also accorded to the psychologist-client relationship. The law extends privileged communication to parties in these relationships because it has been deemed that these parties' right to privacy serves a greater public interest than would be served by having their communications vulnerable to revelation during legal proceedings. Stated another way, it is for society's good if people feel confident that they can talk freely to their attorneys, clergy, physicians, psychologists, and spouses. Professionals such as psychologists who are parties to such special relationships have a legal and ethical duty to keep their clients' communications confidential. Distinguishing the term "confidentiality" from the term "privilege," Jagim, Wittman, and Noll (1978, p. 459) pointed out that whereas "confidentiality concerns matters of communication outside the courtroom, privilege protects clients from disclosure in judicial proceedings."

Privilege is not absolute; there are occasions when a court can deem the disclosure of certain information necessary and can order the disclosure of that information. Should the psychologist or other professional so ordered refuse to make the ordered disclosure, he or she does so under the threat of going to jail and/or being fined. Note also that the privilege in the psychologist–client relationship belongs to the client; the competent client can direct the psychologist to disclose information to some third party (such as an attorney or an insurance carrier), and the psychologist is obligated to make the disclosure. In some rare instances, the psychologist may be ethically (if not legally) compelled to disclose information if that information will prevent harm to either the client or some endangered third party. An illustrative case would be the situation where a client details a plan to commit suicide or homicide. In such an instance, the psychologist would be legally and ethically compelled to take reasonable action to prevent such an occurrence—the preservation of life being deemed an objective more important than the nonrevelation of privileged and confidential communications. The guiding principle here was set forth in the 1981 revision of APA's *Ethical Principles of Psychologists:*

> Psychologists have a primary obligation to respect the confidentiality of information obtained from persons in the course of their work as psychologists. They reveal such information to others only with the consent of the person or the person's legal representative, except in those unusual circumstances in which not to do so would result in clear danger to the person or to others.

Of course, determining when there exists one of "those unusual circumstances . . . which . . . would result in clear danger to the person or to others" is no easy matter. Further, a wrong judgment on the part of the clinician might lead to premature disclosure of confidential information and untoward consequences for not only the examinee and the examiner but the profession as well. A landmark court case that set forth the principle that "protective privilege ends where the public peril begins" was the 1974 case *Tarasoff v. Regents of University of California.* In that case, a therapy patient had made known to his psychologist his intention to kill an unnamed but readily identifiable girl two months prior to the murder. The court in *Tarasoff* held that the therapist had a duty to warn the endangered girl of her peril. More recently, the *Tarasoff* precedent was adopted and expanded upon by the Vermont Supreme Court in *Peck v. the Counseling Service of Addison County, Inc.* (Stone, 1986). A 1983 United States Court of Appeals (9th Circuit) decision in *Jablonski v. United States* placed a burden upon mental health professionals of being able to predict violent behavior even if no threat of violence had been made; key here was the matching of the profile of the intended victim with the profile of prior victims. In the 1987 Washington, D.C., case of *White v. United States,* the United States Court of Appeals (D.C. Circuit) found a hospital negligent for failing to adequately confine a patient to the hospital grounds. Dwayne White, a psychiatric patient who had been found not guilty by reason of insanity in a preceding case, had been granted privileges that permitted him free access to the hospital grounds for 12 hours a day. White left the grounds through one of three open exits and then repeatedly stabbed his wife, Genoa White, with a pair of scissors. Ms. White survived and brought suit against the hospital and its staff. A more complete discussion of the complex issues involved in duty to warn–

type cases can be found elsewhere (for example, Cohen, 1979a, Cohen & Mariano, 1982; Winslade, 1986; Meyers, 1986; Smith & Meyer, 1987).

The Supreme Court of the United States ruled in *Pennsylvania v. Ritchie* (1987) that states may be required to breach confidentiality in the interest of assisting in a criminal defense. The case involved the right of George Ritchie, a man charged with sexually assaulting his daughter, to obtain records from a State of Pennsylvania youth agency—records he sought to employ in his defense. The state agency refused to forward the records, claiming the information in them was privileged. The Supreme Court ruled that Ritchie had a right to have the records reviewed by the trial court judge *in camera* (in private), and the trial court judge would then determine if the records were material to the trial.

The right to the least stigmatizing label Standard number 16.6 of the *Standards* reads: "When score reporting includes assigning individuals to categories, the categories chosen should be based on carefully selected criteria. The least stigmatizing labels, consistent with accurate reporting, should always be assigned."

To better appreciate the need for this standard, consider the case of Jo Ann Iverson.[7] Jo Ann was 9 years old and suffering from claustrophobia when her mother brought her to a state hospital in Blackfoot, Idaho, for a psychological evaluation. Arden Frandsen, a psychologist employed part-time at the hospital, conducted an evaluation of Jo Ann, during the course of which he administered a Stanford-Binet Intelligence test. In his report, Frandsen classified Jo Ann as "feeble-minded, at the high-grade moron level of general mental ability." Following a request from Jo Ann's school guidance counselor, a copy of the psychological report was forwarded to the school—and embarrassing rumors concerning Jo Ann's mental condition began to circulate.

Jo Ann's mother, Carmel Iverson, brought a libel (defamation) suit against Frandsen on behalf of her daughter.[8] Mrs. Iverson lost the lawsuit, the court ruling in part that the psychological evaluation "was a professional report made by a public servant in good faith, representing his best judgment. . . ." But while Mrs. Iverson did not prevail in her lawsuit, we can certainly sympathize with her anguish at the thought of her daughter going through life with a label such as "high-grade moron"—this despite the fact that the psychologist had probably merely copied that designation from the test manual. We would also add that, in retrospect, it might have been possible to prevail in a suit against the guidance counselor for breach of confidentiality, since there appeared to be uncontested testimony that it was from the guidance counselor's office that rumors concerning Jo Ann first emanated.

The right to have findings held confidential Test takers have a right to have their test results held confidential and be released only to third parties who have a legitimate need for access to these records—and such release must also be contingent on the informed consent of the test taker. Whereas the term "confiden-

---

7. See *Iverson v. Frandsen,* 237 F.2d 898 (Idaho, 1956) or consult Cohen (1979a, pp. 149–150).
8. An interesting though tangential aspect of this case was the argument advanced by Iverson that she had brought her child in for claustrophobia and, given that fact, the administration of an intelligence test was unauthorized and beyond the scope of the consultation. However, the defendant proved to the satisfaction of the court that the administration of the Stanford-Binet was necessary in order to determine if Jo Ann had the mental capacity to respond to psychotherapy.

What Constitutes Malpractice?

. . . the Ancients measured facial beauty by the **millihelen,** *a unit equal to that necessary to launch one ship . . .*

While learning about theory and practice in psychology, undergraduate—as well as many graduate—students spend little time, if any, learning about what constitutes *mal*practice in the field of psychology. As we delve deeper into theory and practice in psychological measurement, some discussion about the subject of malpractice seems appropriate. The institution of a malpractice suit against a practicing psychologist can quickly become a very expensive, time-consuming, and worrisome affair. Psychologists engaged in the practice of testing and assessment, in contrast to psychologists who are primarily engaged in practices such as teaching and research, are particularly exposed to the possibility of litigation. This is so because the assessor may frequently have occasion to write a psychological test report that is adverse to the interest of the assessee—a report that, if allowed to let stand, could be used to deny the assessee something that he or she wants (for example, a report that could be used to deny employment, child custody, or release from a mental hospital). A person referred or sent to a psychologist for the specific purpose of psychological assessment may perceive the psychologist more as an adversary than as a helping professional, this in contrast to the situation with respect to the psychotherapist/psychologist who is typically not looked upon as an adversary. If an individual learns that the findings of the "adversary" psychologist will be used in some way counter to his or her perceived interest, one tack taken is to challenge the findings by challenging the competence of the psychologist.

MALPRACTICE IN THE SCHEMA OF THE LAW

All individuals in society have a duty to conduct themselves in a reasonable way—the way any other ordinary and reasonable person would conduct themselves in the same or similar circumstances. If a person behaves in some way that fails to live up to this "reasonable person" standard, that person is said to be *negligent*. Professionals, such as physicians and psychologists, can be held not only to the "reasonable person" standard, but also to a "reasonable professional" standard. Legally this means that when acting in their professional capacity, professionals must act in a way that any other reasonable person in their profession would act under the same or similar circumstance. If a professional unintentionally fails to meet this standard in his or her actions, the word *malpractice* applies; malpractice refers to negligence in the execution of professional duties. If the professional is a physician, one speaks of medical malpractice; a lawyer—legal malpractice; a psychologist—psychological malpractice, and so forth. As illustrated in Figure 1 and Table 1, malpractice is technically an unintentional tort. A *tort,* for our purposes, can be defined as a "legal wrong." As shown in Table 1, a tort can be either intentional or unintentional in nature. In a technical sense, then, if a professional, say a psychologist, *intentionally* acted in a way that was inconsistent with the way

any ordinary and reasonable psychologist would have acted under the same or similar circumstances, it would be incorrect to speak of "malpractice"; a broader term, *professional liability,* would be appropriate. Still, in common parlance, the term "malpractice" is used to refer to intentional as well as unintentional acts for which a professional could potentially be held liable.

Statutory law is law written by legislative bodies and administrative agencies. *Common law,* also called "judge-made law," is law that has evolved from rulings and interpretations made by judges. *Criminal law* covers acts offensive to society in general (such as murder, extortion, or failing to signal for a left turn) and only the government—not a private citizen—can bring a criminal action. *Civil law* covers acts that may be offensive to particular individuals under particular circumstances (such as property-line disputes, fee disputes, or disputes arising from malfeasance in dry cleaning). In both criminal and civil disputes, defendants are presumed to be blameless until proven

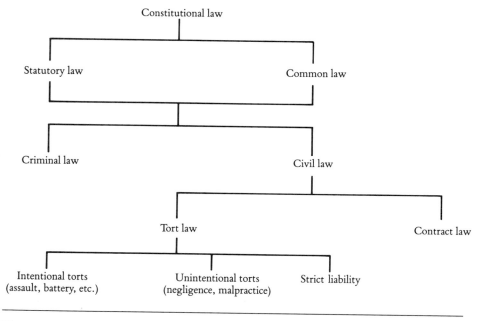

Figure 1 *The Place of Malpractice within the Law. (Source: Cohen & Mariano, 1982)*

What Constitutes Malpractice? (continued)

Table 1

Some Intentional and Unintentional Torts

Intentional	Unintentional (negligence)

Torts to person
  Battery
  Assault
  False imprisonment
	Negligence based on duty of due care
	  Breach of duty of due care (malpractice),
	    including special affirmative duties to
	    prevent harm
	  Duty to prevent suicide
	  Duty to prevent assault to third parties

Torts to property
  Trespass to land
  Trespass to chattels
  Conversion of chattels
	Other
	  Negligent misrepresentation
	  Negligent causing of emotional distress
	  Negligent invasion of privacy

Other
  Intentional or fraudulent misrepresentation (deceit)
  Intentional causing of emotional distress
  Intentional invasion of privacy
  Malicious prosecution
  Abuse of the process of law	

Source: Cohen (1979a)

to be blameable. In criminal actions, the defendant is said to be innocent until proven guilty and guilt must be proven beyond "a reasonable doubt." In civil actions the defendant is said to have incurred *liability* or accountability for his or her actions, if such liability was proven by "the preponderance of the evidence." The "reasonable doubt" standard is higher than that of the "preponderance of the evidence" standard.

THE ELEMENTS OF MALPRACTICE

It is the burden of the plaintiff in a malpractice action against a psychologist to prove the following three things:

1. A professional relationship (such as "doctor-patient" relationship) existed between the plaintiff and the defendant, and the professional therefore had a duty of due care.
2. The duty of due care was breached.
3. As a result of the breach the plaintiff suffered some damage.

Whether or not a professional relationship existed between two parties and whether or not the plaintiff was owed a duty of due care is usually not a matter of dispute. There are, however, exceptions. In one case cited by Cohen (1983b), *O'Neill v. Montefiore Hospital,* a question before the court was whether or not a doctor-patient relationship had been established as a result of a telephone call. The patient in that case had reported to a hospital emergency room in the early hours of the morning seeking treatment for chest pain. While in the emergency room he was overheard to say to a doctor on the telephone who told him to come back at 8:00 A.M., "Well I could be dead by 8 o'clock." The patient returned home by foot, and while being helped to disrobe by his wife, fell to the floor and died. A question before the court in that case was whether or not the doctor on the telephone owed the patient a duty of due care. In *Rainer v. Grossman,* a medical school professor who expressed an opinion regarding the treatment of a patient at a professional conference was sued for malpractice after a physician acted on the advice. The *Rainer* court did not, however, find the professor liable, writing in part:

> As a teacher of doctors, defendant used as a teaching vehicle cases presented to him by his pupils. It is conceded that his opinion became part of the total information upon which one of those pupils, Dr. Rainer, drew in giving advice to his patient.
>
> Presumably every professor or instructor in a professional school hopes, expects or foresees that his students will absorb and apply in their own careers at least some of the information he imparts. Does he thereby assume a duty of care and potential liability to those persons who may ultimately become the clients or patients of those students? We think not.

Once it is established that a professional relationship and a duty of care existed, the plaintiff in a malpractice action must prove that the duty was breached. In many instances, the proof of the breach will require the testimony of someone in the field, an expert witness, to testify that the professional acted in a manner that was substandard to the way any ordinary and reasonable professional in the field would have acted under the same or similar circumstances. There are certain kinds of situations, however, that will not require the testimony of an expert. In *Steinke v. Bell,* for example, a dentist who had extracted the wrong tooth argued that the plaintiff could not recover unless expert testimony regarding the applicable standard of care was presented. The court disagreed:

> We think laymen, looking at this case in the light of their common knowledge and experience, can say that a dentist engaged to remove a lower left second molar is not acting with the care and skill normal to the average member of the profession, if, in so doing, he extracts or causes to come out an upper right lateral incisor.

Another type of case that would not require expert testimony is that where the court invokes the doctrine *res ipsa loquitur* (the act speaks for itself): but for malpractice, the damage would not have occurred. An example of such a case is *Rodriguez v. State*. A profoundly retarded 5-year-old resident of a state hospital who was physically incapable of sitting, standing, or even crawling on her own was discovered by her mother to have a fracture in her leg. Suit was brought against the hospital by the mother and she recovered under the doctrine of *res ipsa loquitur*; but for the hospital's malpractice, the girl could not have had her leg fractured.

The plaintiff in a malpractice action must also prove that the breach of the duty was the direct cause of some damage, loss, or injury. "Causation" in the legal sense is a complicated concept: suffice it to say that it is sometimes quite difficult to prove. It may also be quite difficult to prove damage, loss, or injury especially when the injury claimed is emotional in nature. Still, in recent years, an increasingly liberal trend on the part of courts in allowing for emotional-type injuries has been observed. In *Chavez v. Southern Pacific Transportation*, for example, a Mexican-American railroad worker was awarded $1,300,000 after suffering a back injury that healed after nine months but left him depressed; the plaintiff had argued that the depression was intensified due to his "machismo" cultural background. The plaintiff in *Samms v. Eccles* was awarded damages as a result of the emotional distress she suffered as a result of the plaintiff exposing himself to her and propositioning her. Note that the term *damages* in the plural refers to monetary compensation for loss. Damages may be *compensatory* in nature to compensate for a loss or *punitive,* the latter type reserved to punish an individual for some reckless, wanton, or heinous action or failure to act.

Our treatment of the subject of malpractice has of necessity been brief and simplified. For a more in-depth yet equally well written discussion of this subject see *Malpractice: A Guide for Mental Health Professionals* (Cohen, 1979b) or Cohen (1983b).

tiality" was once thought of solely as a matter of professional ethics, it is now true that "case law, statutes, and licensing regulations in many states have given this standard of conduct legal status as well. For example, a practitioner is legally liable for breach of confidentiality" (Swoboda, Elwork, Sales, & Levine, 1978, p. 449).

Test users must take reasonable precautions to safeguard test records. If these data are stored in a filing cabinet, the cabinet should be locked and preferably made of steel. If these data are stored in a computer, electronic safeguards must be taken to ensure only authorized access. We might also mention here that it is not a good idea for individuals and institutions to store records *in perpetuity*. Rather, the test-using individual or institution should have a reasonable policy covering (1) the storage of test data—when, if at any time, these records will be deemed to be outdated, invalid, and/or useful only from an academic perspective, and (2) the conditions under which requests for release of records to a third party would be entertained.

Having explored some of the historical, legal, and ethical considerations of psychological testing and assessment, our attention now turns to some of the more technical, "nuts and bolts" considerations. Many important questions—such as "Is this a valid test?" "Is this a valid item?" and "How does this test or item compare to that test or item?"—can be answered only with reference to the statistical tools used to answer such questions. For many undergraduate students—as well as all too many graduate students—gaining mastery over statistical tools is viewed as a kind of rite of passage to a satisfactory course grade. If that is the way you regard learning about statistics in psychological measurement, we suggest that you modify your thinking: read Part 2 of our text with the objective of truly learning and understanding the material presented, and ask a lot of questions in class about any of the material you find difficult. As documented by Matarazzo (1990), even practicing clinicians find that they must return to their texts to restudy statistical and related concepts in order to respond satisfactorily to courtroom challenges: "Inasmuch as increasing numbers of attorneys are becoming familiar with the psychometric properties of psychological tools, it is incumbent upon psychologist-clinicians to be at least as familiar as are they with the strengths and weaknesses of the instruments currently used in psychological assessment" (p. 1016). The present authors would extend that sage advice beyond clinicians, to any psychologist who has occasion to use any test or assessment procedure in a professional capacity.

Our study begins with a refresher course in some basic statistical concepts. From there, it's on to an explanation of the term "norms" as it is used in psychological measurement. A concept discussed in Chapter 4 that you will find key to your understanding of everything from how tests are developed to how tests are interpreted is the concept of correlation. Professionals who use psychological tests and measurement procedures may speak of how "psychometrically sound" a test or procedure is; by that, they are often referring to reliability or validity in the psychometric sense—terms that you will be well acquainted with after reading Chapters 5 and 6. Finally, in Chapter 7 we describe aspects of the construction of a test, from initial idea to final form; you may be surprised to learn about some of the kinds of steps in between.

THE SCIENCE OF PHYCHOLOGICAL MEASUREMENT

Chapter 3

A Statistics Refresher

FROM THE RED-PENCIL number circled at the top of your first spelling test to the computer printout of your college entrance examination scores, tests and test scores touch your life. They seem to reach out from the paper and shake your hand when you do well and punch you in the face when you do poorly. They can point you toward or away from a particular school or curriculum. They can help you to identify strengths and weaknesses in your physical and mental abilities. They can accompany you on job interviews and influence a job or career choice.

In your role as a student (as well as in other roles such as job applicant), the nature of your relationship to various tests has probably been primarily that of a test taker. But as a psychologist, teacher, researcher, or business person, the primary nature of your relationship with tests could well be that of a user—the person who breathes life and meaning into test scores by applying the knowledge and skill needed to interpret them appropriately. You may also one day find yourself creating a test (whether in a classroom or business setting) and then having the additional responsibility of developing a framework for reasonably interpreting data derived from an administration of your test. An understanding of the theory underlying test use and principles of test score interpretation is essential to the prospective test user.

Test scores are frequently expressed as numbers, and statistical tools are used to describe, make inferences, and draw conclusions about numbers.[1] In this statistics refresher, we cover scales of measurement, tabular and graphic presentations of data, measures of central tendency, measures of variability, and standard scores. If these statistics-related terms look painfully familiar to you, we ask your indulgence and also ask you to keep in mind that overlearning is the key to retention. However, if these terms look painfully unfamiliar, we urge you to get hold of—and spend ample time reviewing—a good elementary statistics text. The brief review of statistical concepts that follows is designed only to supplement an introductory course in statistics.

SCALES OF MEASUREMENT

Measurement is the act of assigning numbers or symbols to characteristics of objects (people, events—whatever) according to rules. The rules used in assigning numbers are guidelines for representing the magnitude (or other characteristic) of the object being measured. An example of a measurement rule is "Assign the number 12 to all lengths that are exactly the same length as a 12-inch ruler." A *scale* is a set of numbers (or other symbols) whose properties model empirical properties of the objects to which the numbers are assigned. Various types of scales exist. One way of labeling a scale is to label it with reference to the type of variable being measured. Thus a scale used to measure a continuous variable might be referred to as a "continuous scale," while a scale used to measure a discrete variable might be referred to as a "discrete scale." If, for example, research subjects were to be categorized as being either female or male, the categorization scale would be said to be discrete in nature because it would not be meaningful to categorize a subject as anything other than a female or a male.[2] By contrast, a continuous scale exists when it is possible theoretically to divide any of the values of the scale. A distinction must be made, however, between what is theoretically possible and what is practically desirable; the units into which a continuous scale will actually be divided may depend on the purpose of the measurement. Thus, although it may be theoretically possible to divide measurements of length into millimeters or even micrometers, it may be impractical to do so if the purpose of the measurement is to install Venetian blinds.

Measurement using continuous scales always involves some error. For example, the length of the window you measured to be exactly 35.5 inches could, in reality, be 35.7 inches; it's just that your measuring scale is conveniently marked off in more gross gradations of measurement. Most scales used in psychological testing are continuous in nature and can therefore be expected to contain error. A consideration of sources of error in testing appears in the Close-up (as well as elsewhere in this book), but the point here is that error will arise from the mere

---

1. Of course, a test score may be expressed in other forms such as in a letter grade or a pass/fail designation. Unless stated otherwise, terms such as "test score," "test data," "test results," and "test scores" will be used throughout this book in reference to numeric descriptions of test performance.
2. The authors acknowledge that if all females were labeled "1" and all males were labeled "2," some people, most visibly some popular rock stars, might seem to qualify as a 1.5. Regardless, all cases on a discrete scale must lie on a point on the scale, and it is theoretically impossible for a case to lie between two points on the scale.

use of a continuous scale; the number or score used to characterize the trait being measured on a continuous scale should be thought of as an approximation of the "real" number. Thus, for example, a score of 25 on some test of anxiety should not be thought of as a precise measure of anxiety but rather as an approximation of the "real" anxiety score had the measuring instrument been calibrated to yield such a score (that is, perhaps the score of 25 is an approximation for a "real" score of 24.7 or 25.44). In contrast to numbers or scores used to characterize traits in continuous scales, the numbers or scores used in dichotomous scales are presumed to be exact.

Measurement can be further categorized with respect to the amount of quan-

---

Close-up

Error of Measurement and the True Score Model

To help you understand the concept of *error* in measurement, see page 90 and the example of the job applicant Kathy and the word processing scores she achieved on seven different occasions. If you were the company's personnel director and you looked at these seven scores, you might logically ask "Which of these scores is the best measure of Kathy's 'true' word processing ability?" or, stated more succinctly, "Which is her 'true' score?"

The "true" answer to the question posed above is that we cannot say with absolute certainty from the data we have exactly what Kathy's true word processing ability is—*but,* we can make an educated guess. Our educated guess would be that her true word processing ability is equal to the mean of the distribution of her word processing scores plus or minus a number of points accounted for by *error* in the measurement process. "Error" in the measurement process can be thought of as any factor entering into the process that is not directly relevant to whatever it is that is being measured. If Kathy had the misfortune on one occasion of drawing a word processor that had not been properly serviced and was of lesser quality than the other word processors she had been tested on, this is an example of "error" entering into the testing process. If there was excessive noise in the room on a testing occasion, if Kathy wasn't feeling well, if light bulbs blew . . . the list could go on, but the point is that any number of factors other than an individual's ability can enter into the process of measuring that ability. We can try to reduce error in a testing situation such as Kathy's by making certain, to the extent that it is possible, that all typewriters used are functioning equally well, that the test room is free of excessive noise and has adequate lighting, and so forth. However, we can never entirely eliminate "error." The best we can do is estimate how much error entered into a particular test score and then intelligently interpret the score with that information.

The tool used to estimate or infer how far observed scores deviate from "true" scores is a statistic called the *standard error of measurement*. In the case of Mary and her IBMM word processing scores, the standard error of measurement would be equal to the standard deviation of the observed scores. In practice, few developers of tests designed for use on a widespread basis would investigate the magnitude of error with respect to a single test taker; more typically, an average standard error of measurement is calculated for a sample of the population on which the test is designed for use. More detailed information on the nature and computation of the standard error of measurement will appear in Chapter 5. As we will see, measures of reliability assist us in making inferences about the proportion of the total variance of test scores attributable to error variance.

titative information the assigned numbers possess. It is generally agreed that there are four different levels or scales of measurement. Numbers at different levels or scales of measurement convey different kinds of information. In testing and in research in general, it is important to know which scales of measurement are being employed, for the kind of scale will be one factor in determining which statistical manipulations of the data would or would not be appropriate.[3]

The French word for black is *noir* (pronounced "n'wăre"). We bring this up here only to call attention to the fact that this French word is a useful acronym for remembering the four levels or scales of measurement; each letter in *noir* is the first letter of each of the succeedingly more rigorous levels. *N* stands for "nominal," *o* for "ordinal," *i* for "interval," and *r* for "ratio scales."

Nominal Scales

Nominal scales are the simplest form of measurement. These scales involve classification or categorization based on one or more distinguishing characteristics where all objects must be placed into mutually exclusive and exhaustive categories (see Figure 3–1). For example, people may be characterized by gender in a study designed to compare performance of men and women on some test. In such a study all males might be labeled "Men," "1," "B," or some other symbol and all females might be labeled "Women," "2," or "A." In the specialty area of clinical psychology, one often-used nominal scale is the American Psychiatric Association's *Diagnostic and Statistical Manual of Mental Disorders III—Revised* (often referred to simply as *DSM III-R*). Each disorder listed in the manual has its own number assigned to it. Thus, for example, the number 303.00 identifies alcohol intoxication and the number 307.00 identifies stuttering. But these numbers are used exclusively for classification purposes and cannot be meaningfully added, subtracted, ranked, or averaged (the number 305 does *not* equal an intoxicated stutterer).

Arithmetic operations that can legitimately be performed with nominal data include counting for the purpose of determining how many cases fall into each category and some consequential determination of proportion or percentages.[4] Suppose, for example, that one Friday night at midnight a research psychologist visited the Omega chapter of the Mu Delta Phi (MDP) sorority and psychologically evaluated the 50 sisters in residence for psychopathology. The psychologist diagnosed five of the MDP sisters as manic-depressive, ten as intoxicated, two as paranoid schizophrenic, and one as an antisocial personality. Stated with reference to *DSM III-R*, we could say that 10% of the membership was 296.41 (5/50 = .10), 20% was 303.00 (10/50 = .20), 4% was 295.31 (2/50 = .04), and 2% was 301.70 (1/50

---

3. For the purposes of our statistics refresher, we present what Nunnally (1978) called the "fundamentalist" view of measurement scales—a view that "holds that 1. there are distinct types of measurement scales into which all possible measures of attributes can be classified, 2. each measure has some 'real' characteristics that permit its proper classification, and 3. once a measure is classified, the classification specifies the types of mathematical analyses that can be employed with the measure." (p. 24). Yet Nunnally (Chapter 1) and others have argued that alternatives to the "fundamentalist" view may also be viable.

4. Nominal data may be also be analyzed by means of nonparametric statistical techniques, log linear modeling, and other techniques (see Gokhale & Kullback, 1978), discussion of which is beyond the scope of our "refresher."

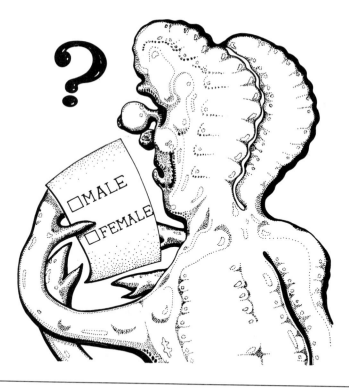

Figure 3–1 *Check One.* A nominal scale with an incomplete set of categories may lead to improper classification and erroneous data.

= .02). It can be seen that these *DSM III-R* numbers are useful only for classification purposes; they in no way represent amounts of anything. Numbers that *do* represent an amount can be found in ordinal, interval, and ratio scales.

Ordinal Scales

Like nominal scales, ordinal scales permit classification. However, in addition to classification, rank-ordering on some characteristic is also permissible with ordinal scales. Judges may rank-order beauty pageant contestants on presentation in a swimsuit; wine connoisseurs may rank-order Chablis on variables such as taste, smell, and "bouquet"; and students may rank-order textbooks with respect to clarity of writing style. If, for example, the wine connoisseurs were asked to judge five wines on taste, they might assign the best wine a "1" and their least favorite a "5" or vice versa (the best being assigned a "5" and the least favorite a "1"). Another characteristic of ordinal scales is—as you might expect—that they have no absolute zero point; without units, zero is without meaning. In the case of the wines, for example, it is presumed that all of the wines have some taste and no wine has absolutely no taste.

When using ordinal scales, no implications are made about how much greater one ranking is than another. Although a ranking has been made, the nature of the units of measurement that went into the ranking is not typically known. What are the units of measurement that enter into the judgment of a beauty contest? All we can say in such instances is that we have a ranking; it would be meaningless to say in the case of the beauty contest, for example, that the contestant ranked "second runner-up" is twice as beautiful as the contestant ranked "fourth runner-up."

Interval Scales

In addition to the features of nominal and ordinal scales, interval scales contain equal intervals between numbers; each unit on the scale is exactly equal to any other unit on the scale. As with ordinal scales, interval scales contain no absolute zero point. As an illustration of interval scales, consider the measurement of temperature. On the Fahrenheit thermometer the difference between 20 degrees and 40 degrees is the same as the difference between 75 degrees and 95 degrees. Additionally, zero degrees Fahrenheit is not indicative of the complete absence of temperature. Because there is no absolute zero point on the Fahrenheit scale, it would not be meaningful to make statements in terms of ratios; while we can say that the difference between 20 and 40 degrees Fahrenheit is the same as the number of degrees difference as 75 and 95 degrees Fahrenheit, we cannot accurately say that 40 degrees is twice as hot as 20 degrees.

Ratio Scales

In addition to having all of the properties of nominal, ordinal, and interval measurement, a ratio scale has a true zero point. All mathematical operations can meaningfully be performed on ratio scales because there exist equal intervals between the numbers on the scale as well as a true or absolute zero point.[5] The measurement of distance is typically accomplished using ratio scales; 12 inches is twice 6 inches and 0 distance between two points is a possibility. A ratio scale for measuring temperature, the Kelvin scale, has at its zero point the temperature at which molecular activity ceases. Statements such as "20 degrees is twice as warm (or half as cold) as 10 degrees" are legitimate with reference to such a scale because equal intervals do exist.

Ratio-level measurement scales abound in the physical and biological sciences but are few and far between in psychological measurement. The ordinal level of measurement is most frequently used in psychology. As Kerlinger (1973, p. 439) put it, "Intelligence, aptitude, and personality test scores are, *basically and strictly speaking,* ordinal. They indicate with more or less accuracy not the amount of intelligence, aptitude, and personality traits of individuals, but rather the rank-order positions of the individuals." Kerlinger allowed that "most psychological and educational scales approximate interval equality fairly well," though he cautioned that if ordinal measurements were treated as if they were interval measure-

---

5. Note that the distinction between ordinal scales and interval scales is the result of the empirical observations on which numerical assignments are based. The difference between interval and ratio scales seems more closely related to theoretical considerations related to the attribute being measured. It has been suggested that another useful scale of measurement lies between the interval and ratio level of measurement (Narens & Luce, 1986).

ments, the test user must "be constantly alert to the possibility of *gross* inequality of intervals" (pp. 440–441).

Regardless of the scale or level of measurement inherent in a particular test, the data from that test must be placed in a manageable, interpretable form. One way this can be accomplished is by describing the test results in terms of statistics such as the mean or average. Another way to place the data in readable form is to place them in a table or illustrate them in a graph. Our statistics refresher continues with a review of the various ways test data can be described.

DESCRIBING DATA

Suppose you have magically changed places with the professor teaching this course and you have just administered an examination that consists of 100 multiple-choice items (where one point is awarded for each correct answer). The scores for the 25 students enrolled in your class could theoretically range from 0 (none correct) to 100 (all correct). Assume it is the day after the examination and you are sitting in your office with the data listed in Table 3–1. One task at hand is to communicate the test results to your class in a way that will best assist each

Table 3-1

Data from Your
Measurement Course Test

Student	Score (number correct)
Judy	78
Joe	67
David	69
Miriam	63
Valerie	85
Diane	72
Henry	92
Gertrude	67
Paula	94
Martha	62
Bill	61
Homer	44
Robert	66
Michael	87
Brandon	76
Mary	83
"Mousey"	42
Barbara	82
John	84
Donna	51
Uriah	69
Leroy	61
Ronald	96
Vinnie	73
Patty	79

individual student in understanding how he or she performed on the test in comparison to all of the other test takers in the class. How do you accomplish this objective?

Frequency Distributions

You might begin by setting up a distribution of the raw scores; rather than a helter-skelter listing of all of the raw data, a distribution will aid you in comparing the performance of one student to another. One way the scores could be distributed is by the frequency with which they occur. In a *frequency distribution* all the possible scores are listed alongside the number of times each score occurred. The scores might be listed in tabular or graphic form. Table 3–2 lists the frequency of occurrence of each score in one column and the score itself in the other column.

Before we see how these data would look in graphic form, we should note that there exists another kind of frequency distribution, a *grouped frequency distribution,* which further summarizes the data. In a grouped frequency distribution, test-score intervals, also called "class intervals," replace the actual test scores. The number of class intervals used and the size or "width" of each class interval (that is, the range of test scores contained in each and every class interval) will be a matter left for you to decide as regards the data in need of summarizing; the width that most conveniently summarizes the data will be best. But how do you decide?

In *Exploratory Data Analysis,* Tukey (1977) introduced one type of data analysis technique called *stem-and-leaf display,* which may be a useful reference for persons seeking a set of formal ground rules by which to set class intervals. Because this technique can get quite complicated (especially when there are lots of "stems" or "leaves"), readers interested in a detailed presentation of this statistical technique are referred to Tukey (1977). In most instances, a decision as to the size of a class interval in a grouped frequency distribution is made on the basis of convenience and with the knowledge that virtually any decision will represent a trade-off; a convenient, easy-to-read summary of the data is the trade-off for the loss of detail. To what extent must the data be summarized? How important is detail? These types of questions must be reckoned with in arriving at a determination as to the size of the class interval. In the grouped frequency distribution in Table 3–3, the test scores have been grouped—simply on the basis of a judgment concerning the need for convenience in reading the data as opposed to the need for detail—into 12 class intervals with each class interval being equal to 5 points.[6] The highest class interval (95 to 99) and the lowest class interval (40 to 44) are referred to respectively as the upper and lower limits of the distribution.

Frequency distributions of test scores can also be illustrated graphically. A *graph* is a diagram or chart composed of lines, points, bars, or other symbols that describe the data being measured. With a good graph, the place of a single score in

---

6. Technically, each number on such a scale would be viewed as ranging from as much as 0.5 below it, to as much as 0.5 above it. For example, the "true" but hypothetical width of the class interval ranging from 95–99 would be the difference between 99.5 and 94.5 or 5. The true upper and lower limits of the class intervals presented in the table would respectively be 99.5 and 39.5.

Table 3–2	
Frequency Distribution of Scores from Your Test	
Score	*f (frequency)*
96	1
94	1
92	1
87	1
85	1
84	1
83	1
82	1
79	1
78	1
76	1
73	1
72	1
69	2
67	2
66	1
63	1
62	1
61	2
51	1
44	1
42	1

Table 3–3	
A Grouped Frequency Distribution	
Class interval	*Frequency*
95–99	1
90–94	2
85–89	2
80–84	3
75–79	3
70–74	2
65–69	5
60–64	4
55–59	0
50–54	1
45–49	0
40–44	2

relation to a distribution of test scores can easily be grasped by a casual "eyeball-ing" of the data. Three kinds of graphs used to illustrate frequency distributions are the *histogram*, the *frequency polygon*, and the *bar graph* (see Figure 3–2). A his-togram is a graph with vertical lines drawn at the true limits of each test score (or class interval) forming a series of contiguous rectangles. It is customary for the test scores (either the single scores or the midpoints of the class intervals) to be placed along the graph's horizontal axis (also referred to as the abscissa or *X*-axis) and numbers indicative of the frequency of occurrence along the graph's vertical axis (also referred to as the ordinate or *Y*-axis). In a bar graph, numbers indicative of frequency also appear on the *Y*-axis while reference to some categorization (such as Yes/No/Maybe, Male/Female, and so forth) appears on the *X*-axis; here the rectangular bars typically are not contiguous. Data illustrated in a frequency polygon are expressed by a continuous line connecting the points where test scores or class intervals (as indicated on the *X*-axis) meet frequencies (as indicated on the *Y*-axis). As illustrated in Figure 3–3, graphs may obscure or distort infor-mation as well as convey it.

Frequency distributions of test scores may assume any of a number of differ-ent shapes (see Figure 3–4)—this due to a variety of factors including the vari-able(s) being researched, the measurement technique(s), and the sampling procedures. The "normal" or "bell-shaped" curve is of particular interest to us and it is discussed in greater detail later in this chapter.

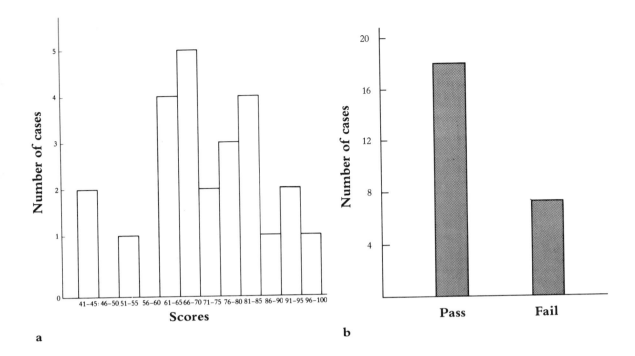

a

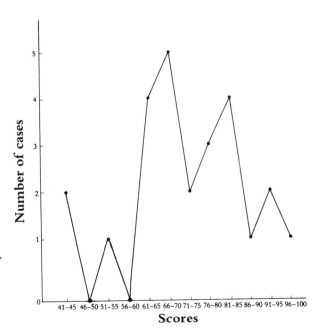

c

Figure 3–2 *Graphic Illustrations of Data from Table 3–3.*

A histogram (a), a bar graph (b), and a frequency polygon (c) all may be used to graphically convey information about test performance. Of course, the labeling of the bar graph and the specific nature of the data conveyed by it depend on the variables of interest; in (b) the variable of interest is the number of students who passed the test (assuming for the purpose of this illustration that a raw score of 65 or higher had been arbitrarily designated in advance to be a passing grade).

Returning to the question posed earlier—the one in which you are playing the role of instructor and must communicate the test results to your students— which type of graph would best serve your purpose? Why?

As we continue our review of descriptive statistics, you may wish to return to your role of professor and formulate your response to challenging related questions such as "Which measure(s) of central tendency shall I use to convey this information?" and "Which measure(s) of variability would convey the information best?"

Figure 3-3 *Consumer (of graphed data) Beware!*

"One picture is worth a thousand words" and one purpose of representing data in graphic form is to convey information at a glance. However, although two graphs may be accurate with respect to the data they represent, their pictures—and the impression drawn from a glance at them—may be vastly different. As an example, consider the following hypothetical scenario involving a hamburger restaurant chain we'll call "The Charred House."

The Charred House chain serves very charbroiled, microscopically thin hamburgers formed in the shape of little, triangular houses. In the ten-year period since its founding in 1978, the company has sold on average, 100 million burgers per year. On the chain's tenth anniversary, The Charred House distributes a press release proudly announcing, "Over a Billion Served."

Reporters from two business-type publications set out to research and write a feature article on this hamburger restaurant chain. Working solely from sales figures as compiled from annual reports to the shareholders, Reporter 1 focuses her story on the differences in yearly sales. Her article is titled "A Billion Served—But Charred House Sales Fluctuate From Year ro Year" and the graph that was printed alongside the article is reprinted here.

Quite a different picture of the company emerges from Reporter 2's story, titled "A Billion Served—And The Charred House Sales Are as Steady as Ever." The latter story is based on a diligent analysis of comparable data for the same number of hamburger chains in the same areas of the country over the same time period. While researching the story, Reporter 2 learned that yearly fluctuations in sales is common to the entire in-

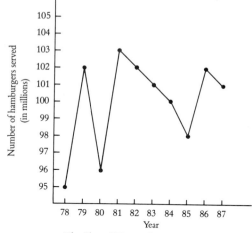

The Charred House sales over a 10-year period

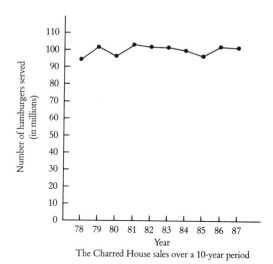

The Charred House sales over a 10-year period

dustry and that the annual fluctuations observed in the Charred House figures were—relative to other chains—insignificant. The graph that accompanied his story is also illustrated here.

Look closely at the frequency polygons that accompanied each story. Although both are accurate insofar as they are based on the correct numbers, the impression

they are likely to leave is quite different.

Incidentally, custom dictates that the intersection of the two axes of a frequency polygon be at 0; the fact that this custom is violated in the graph accompanying Reporter 1's story should serve as a warning to evaluate the pictorial representation of the data all the more critically.

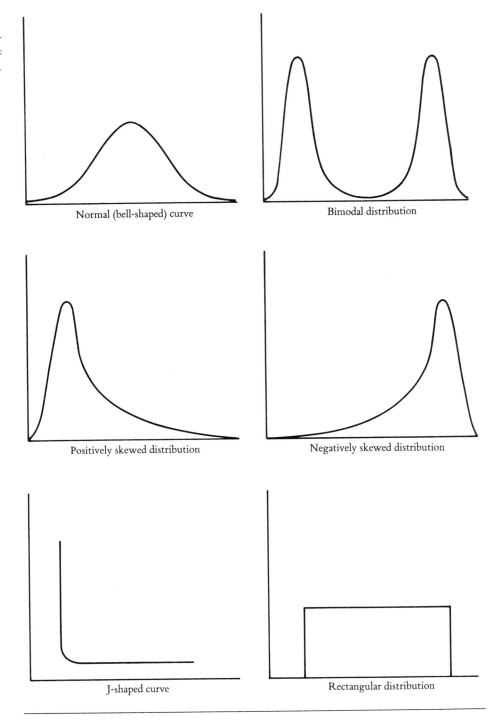

Figure 3-4 *Shapes Frequency Distributions Can Take.*

Distributions can be conveniently described in terms of characteristics such as their central tendency, variability, skewness, and kurtosis.

Measures of Central Tendency

Measures of central tendency are indices of the central value or location of a frequency distribution. The center of a distribution can be defined in different ways. Perhaps the most commonly used measure of central tendency is the *arithmetic mean,* referred to in everyday language as the "average." The mean takes into account the actual mathematical size of every score. In special instances, such as when there are only a few scores and one or two of the scores are extreme in relation to the remaining ones, a measure of central tendency other than the mean may be desirable. Other measures of central tendency we review include the *median* and the *mode.* Note that in the formulas that follow, the standard statistical shorthand called "summation notation" (*summation* meaning "the sum of") is used. The Greek uppercase letter *sigma,* Σ, is the symbol used to signify "sum"; if X represents a test score, then the symbol $\Sigma\ X$ means "add all the test scores."

The arithmetic mean   The *arithmetic mean,* denoted by the symbol $\bar{X}$ (pronounced "X bar") is equal to the sum of the observations (or test scores in this case) divided by the number of observations. Symbolically written, the formula for the arithmetic mean is $\bar{X} = \Sigma\ X/n$, where n equals the number of observations or test scores. The arithmetic mean is typically the most appropriate measure of central tendency for interval or ratio data when the distributions are believed to be approximately normal. An arithmetic mean can also be computed from a frequency distribution. The formula for doing this is

$$\bar{X} = \frac{\Sigma\ fX}{n}$$

where $\Sigma\ fX$ means "multiply the frequency of each score by its corresponding score and sum."

As we explain certain concepts, we will urge you to get involved with the subject matter by doing more than merely reading. Your learning of this subject matter may be facilitated if you get actively involved in it, if you transcend the role of "observer" and become more of a "participant/observer." Take a few minutes now to use the two arithmetic mean formulas we've just discussed to compute the arithmetic mean for your examination data (contained in Table 3–1).

The median   The *median,* defined as the middle score in a distribution, is another commonly used measure of central tendency. As an example, you can determine the median of a distribution of scores by ordering the scores in a list by magnitude—in either ascending or descending order. When the total number of scores ordered is an odd number, the median will be the score that is exactly in the middle, with one-half of the remaining scores lying above it and the other half of the remaining scores lying below it. When the total number of scores ordered is an even number, the median can be calculated by determining the arithmetic mean of the two middle scores. For example, suppose that ten people took a preemployment word-processing test at the "IBMM Corporation" and obtained the following scores, presented here in descending order:

66
65
61
59
53
52
41
36
35
32

The median in these data would be computed by obtaining the average (that is, the arithmetic mean) of the two middle scores, 53 and 52 (which would be equal to 52.5).

The median is an appropriate measure of central tendency for ordinal, interval, and ratio data, especially if data are highly skewed. Suppose the IBMM Corporation has a requirement that all of its clerks be able to do word processing at a rate of 50 words per minute (with total accuracy). And suppose the personnel office of this company has a policy of testing job applicants' word-processing speed on seven different days before making any determination as to employment. The word-processing scores in words per minute for one applicant, "Kathy," follow. If you were the personnel officer, would you hire her?

52   55   39   56   35   50   54

If you were to obtain the arithmetic mean for this distribution of scores, the resulting figure is below 50. Thus, if the company's policy was to routinely take an average of word processing-test scores and reject people whose average score did not meet the minimum of 50 words per minute, Kathy would have to be dismissed from further consideration. However, if you as the personnel officer had some discretion, you might have used the median and not the mean as the preferred measure of central tendency in this situation. You would have then grouped these scores from highest to lowest and located the middle score in the distribution:[7]

35
39
50
52   (the middle score)
54
55
56

---

7. Consult an appropriate statistics text for specialized formulas used to calculate the median with a large, unwieldy group of scores (that is, a group of scores so large it would be impractical merely to order them in ascending order and locate the middle score), to calculate the median of a grouped frequency distribution, or to calculate the median of a distribution where various scores are identical.

If Kathy's resume looked good in all respects, if the company needed to hire clerks immediately, or for any other good reason, a decision to hire Kathy could be justified by the use of the median as the measure of central tendency—in this case, as a measure of Kathy's word processing ability. The median may well be the most appropriate measure to use with such a distribution of scores. On the days when Kathy's score was in the thirties, she may not have been feeling well, the word processor used for the test may not have been operating properly, or other factors could have influenced the score. Technically, while the mean is the preferred measure of central tendency for symmetrical distributions, the median is the preferred measure for skewed distributions.

The mode   The most frequently occurring score in a distribution of scores is the *mode*.[8] As an example, determine the mode for the following scores obtained on the IBMM test by another applicant for a clerk's position, "Bruce":

43   46   45   51   42   44   51

The most frequently occurring score in this distribution of scores is 51. Again, if you were the personnel officer, would you hire Bruce? If your hiring guideline dictated that you use the arithmetic mean, you would definitely not hire Bruce since his mean performance falls below 50 words per minute. But even if you had the leeway to use another measure of central tendency, you still might not hire him; even a casual look at these data indicates that Bruce's typical performance would fall below the level required by the company.

Distributions that contain a tie for the designation as "most frequently occurring score" can have more than one mode. Consider the following scores—arranged in no particular order—obtained by 20 students on the final exam of a new trade school called the "Home Study School of Elvis Presley Impersonators":

51   49   51   50   52   52   53   38   17   66
33   44   73   13   21   91   87   92   47   3

The distribution of these scores is said to be "bimodal" because it contains two scores (51 and 52) that occur with the highest frequency (a frequency of two). Except for use with nominal data, the mode tends not to be a very commonly used measure of central tendency. Unlike the arithmetic mean, which has to be calculated, the value of the modal score is not calculated—one simply counts and determines which score occurs most frequently. Because the mode is arrived at in this manner, the modal score may be a totally atypical score—one at an extreme end of the distribution—but nonetheless one that occurs with the greatest frequency. In fact, it is theoretically possible for a bimodal distribution to have two modes that each fall at the high or low end of the distribution—thus violating our expectation that a measure of central tendency should be indicative of a point at the middle of the distribution.

Despite the fact that the mode is not calculated and despite the fact that the mode is not necessarily a unique point in a distribution (a distribution can have

8. If adjacent scores occur equally often and more often than other scores, custom dictates that the mode be referred to as the "average."

two, three, or even more modes), the mode can be useful in conveying certain types of information. For example, suppose you wanted an estimate of the number of journal articles published by clinical psychologists in the United States in the last year. To arrive at this figure, you might total the number of journal articles accepted for publication by each clinical psychologist in the United States, divide by the number of psychologists, and arrive at the arithmetic mean—an indication of the average number of journal articles published. Whatever that number would be, we can say with certainty that it would be more than the mode: it is well known that most clinical psychologists do not write journal articles; therefore, the mode for publications by clinical psychologists in any given year is zero. The mode in this instance provides useful information in addition to the mean because it tells us that no matter what the figure is for the average number of publications, the fact remains that most clinicians do not publish.

Because the mode is not in a true sense calculated, it is a nominal statistic and could not legitimately be used in further calculations. The median is a statistic that takes into account the order of scores and is, itself, ordinal in nature. The mean is the most stable and generally the most useful measure of central tendency, and it is an interval statistic.

Variability

Variability is an indication of how scores in a distribution are scattered or dispersed. As Figure 3–5 illustrates, two or more distributions of test scores can have the same mean, though differences in the scatter or dispersion of scores around the mean can be wide. In both distributions A and B, test scores could range from 0 to 100. In distribution A, we see that the mean score was 50 and the remaining scores were normally distributed around the mean. In distribution B, the mean was also 50, though few if any people scored higher than 60 or lower than 40.

Statistics that describe the amount of variation in a distribution include the range, the interquartile range, the semi-interquartile range, the standard deviation, and the variance.

The range   The *range* of a distribution is equal to the difference between the highest and the lowest scores. We could describe distribution B of Figure 3–5, for example, as having a range of 20 if we knew that the highest score in this distribution was 60 and the lowest score was 40 (60 − 40 = 20). With respect to distribution A, if we knew that the lowest score was 0 and the highest score was 100, the range would be equal to 100 − 0, or 100. The range is the simplest measure of variability to compute but it is also of limited use; one extreme score can radically alter the value of the range, since the range is based entirely on the value of the two extreme scores. Suppose, for example, that there was one score in distribution B equal to 90. The range of this distribution would now be equal to 90 − 40, or 50. Yet in looking at the data in the graph for distribution B, it is clear that the vast majority of scores tend to be between 40 and 60.

As a descriptive statistic of variation, the range provides a quick but gross

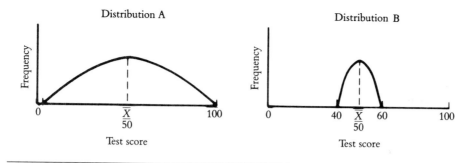

Figure 3–5 *Two Distributions with Differences in Variability.*

description of the spread of scores. Better measures include the *interquartile range* and the *semi-interquartile range*.

The interquartile and semi-interquartile range A distribution of test scores (or any other data for that matter) can be divided into four parts such that 25 percent of the test scores occur in each quarter. As illustrated in Figure 3–6, the dividing points between the four quarters in the distribution are referred to as the *quartiles;* there are three of them and they are respectively labeled "Q_1," "Q_2," and "Q_3." Note that "quartile" refers to a specific point while "quarter" refers to an interval; an individual score may, for example, fall *at* the third quartile or *in* the third quarter (but *not* "in" the third quartile or "at" the third quarter). It should not come as a surprise to you that Q_2 and the median are exactly the same. And just as the median is the midpoint in a distribution of scores, so quartiles Q_1 and Q_3 are "quarter-points" in a distribution of scores (and there exist technical formulas for determining the exact value of these points). The *interquartile range* is equal to the difference between Q_3 and Q_1 and, like the median, it is an ordinal statistic. A related measure of variability is the *semi-interquartile range,* which is equal to the interquartile range divided by two. Knowledge of the relative distances of Q_1 and Q_3 from Q_2 (the median) provides the seasoned test interpreter with immediate information as to the shape of the distribution of scores. In a perfectly symmetrical distribution, Q_1 and Q_3 will be exactly the same distance from the median. If these distances are unequal there will be a lack of symmetry ("skewness"—discussed later in this chapter).

The average deviation Another tool that could conceivably be used to describe the amount of variability that exists in a distribution is the *average deviation,* or *AD* for short. Its formula is

$$AD = \frac{\Sigma \, |x|}{n}$$

The lowercase, italicized "x" in the formula signifies a score's deviation from the mean; it is obtained by subtracting the mean from the score $(X - \text{mean}) = x$. The bars on each side of x indicate that you must use the absolute value of the devia-

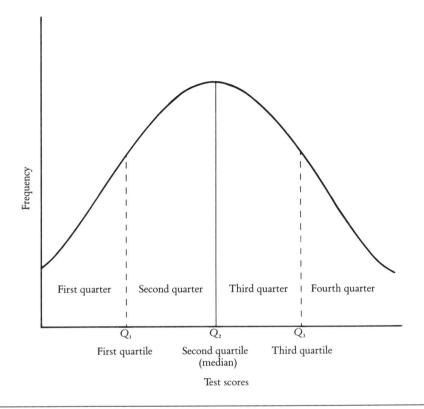

Figure 3–6 *A Quartered Distribution.*

tion score (ignoring the positive or negative sign and treating all deviation scores as positive). All of the deviation scores are then summed and divided by the total number of scores (*n*) to arrive at the average deviation. As an exercise, compute the average deviation for the following distribution of test scores:

$$85 \quad 100 \quad 90 \quad 95 \quad 80$$

Begin by calculating the arithmetic mean. Next obtain the absolute value of each of the five deviation scores and sum them (and note what would happen if you did not ignore algebraic signs—all of the deviation scores would sum to 0). Divide the sum of the deviation scores by the number of measurements (5). Did you obtain an *AD* of 6? The *AD* tells us that each of the five scores in this distribution varied, on average, 6 points from the mean.

The *AD* is a very rarely used statistic since the arbitrary discarding of algebraic signs renders it a useless measure with respect to any further operations. An understanding of how the *AD* is arrived at, however, is useful in understanding another much more widely used statistic, the standard deviation.

The standard deviation   The *standard deviation* is a measure of variability that is equal to the square root of the average squared deviations about the mean. We could define a standard deviation more succinctly by saying simply that it is equal to the square root of the variance—and of course you remember from your statistics course how "variance" is defined. If the definition has slipped your mind, the *variance.* is equal to the arithmetic mean of the squares of the differences between the scores in a distribution and their mean.

In computing the average deviation, the problem of the sum of all deviation scores around the mean equaling zero was solved by employing only the absolute value of the deviation scores. In computing the standard deviation, the same problem is dealt with in a different way; instead of using the absolute value of each of the deviation scores, each score is squared; thus, the sign of the negative deviations becomes positive when these deviations are squared. Since all of the deviation scores are squared, we know that before we are finished with our calculations, we must go back and obtain the square root of whatever number we reach. The formula used to calculate the variance (s^2) using deviation scores is

$$s^2 = \frac{\Sigma \, x^2}{n}$$

Simply stated, the variance is calculated by squaring and summing all of the deviation scores and dividing by the total number of scores. The variance can also be computed from raw scores by first calculating the summation of the raw scores squared, dividing by the number of scores, and then subtracting the mean squared:

$$s^2 = \frac{\Sigma \, X^2}{n} - \bar{X}^2$$

The variance is a widely used measure in psychological research. To make meaningful interpretations, the test score distribution should be approximately normal, which means that the greatest frequency of scores occurs near the arithmetic mean and correspondingly fewer and fewer scores relative to the mean occur on both sides of it as scores differ from the mean.

For some "hands-on" experience with—as well as a sense of mastery of—the concepts of variance and standard deviation, why not allot the next 10 or 15 minutes or so to computing the standard deviation for the test scores originally contained in Table 3–1? Use both formulas to verify that they produce the same results.

Using deviation scores, your calculations should look similar to these:

$$s^2 = \frac{\Sigma \, x^2}{n}$$

$$s^2 = \frac{\Sigma \, (X - \text{mean})^2}{n}$$

$$s^2 = \frac{\Sigma \, [(78 - 72.12)^2 + (67 - 72.12)^2 + \cdots (79 - 72.12)^2]}{25}$$

$$s^2 = \frac{4972.64}{25}$$

$$s^2 = 198.91$$

Using the raw-scores formula, your calculations should look similar to these:

$$s^2 = \frac{\Sigma\, X^2}{n} - \bar{X}^2$$

$$s^2 = \frac{\Sigma\, [(78)^2 + (67)^2 + \cdots (79)^2]}{25} - 5201.29$$

$$s^2 = \frac{135005}{25} - 5201.29$$

$$s^2 = 5400.20 - 5201.29$$

$$s^2 = 198.91$$

In both cases, the standard deviation is the square root of the variance (s^2). According to our calculations, the standard deviation of the test scores is 14.10. If $s = 14.10$, one standard deviation unit is approximately equal to 14 units of measurement, or with reference to our example and rounded to a whole number, 14 test-score points. The test data did not provide a good normal curve approximation; rather they were positively "skewed," a concept we will review shortly. Some things you need to know about test-score interpretation when the scores are *not* skewed—that is, when the test scores are approximately normal in distribution—are presented later in the section Area Under the Normal Curve.

The symbol for standard deviation has variously been represented as s, S, SD, and the lowercase Greek letter sigma (σ). One custom—the one we adhere to—has it that s refers to the sample standard deviation while σ refers to the population standard deviation. The number of observations in the sample is n and the denominator $n - 1$ is sometimes used to calculate what is referred to as an "unbiased estimate" of the population value—it's actually only *less* biased (see Hopkins & Glass, 1978). Unless n is 10 or less, the use of n or $n - 1$ tends not to make a meaningful difference.

But whether the denominator is more properly n or $n - 1$ has been something of a matter of debate. Lindgren (1983) has argued for the use of $n - 1$, in part because this denominator tends to make correlation formulas simpler. By contrast, most texts recommend the use of $n - 1$ only when the data constitute a sample; n is preferable when the data constitute a population. For Lindgren (1983), it matters not whether the data are from a sample or a population. Perhaps the most reasonable convention—and the one we will follow—is to use n when either the population has been assessed (as we might legitimately assume it has when dealing with the examination scores of one class of students—including all of the people about whom we're going to make inferences) or no inferences to the population are intended. $\bar{X}$ represents a sample mean, M (mu) a population mean. The formula for the population standard deviation is

$$\sigma = \sqrt{\frac{\Sigma\, (X - M)^2}{N}}$$

The standard deviation is a very useful measure of variation since each individual score's distance from the mean of the distribution is employed in its computation. This statistic, devised by Karl Pearson in the course of his work in the area of correlation, has become a widely used measure in the field of testing not only because of its utility as an indicator of degree of dispersion but also because of its use in a number of other statistical formulas (for example, the computation of "standard scores," which is discussed later).

Skewness

Distributions can be characterized in terms of their *skewness,* or the nature and extent to which symmetry is absent. Skewness is an indication of how the measurements in a distribution are distributed. A distribution is said to be skewed positively when relatively few of the scores fall at the positive end of the distribution. Results from an examination that are positively skewed may indicate that the test was too difficult; more items that were easier would have been desirable in order to discriminate better at the lower end of the distribution of test scores. A distribution is said to be skewed negatively when relatively few of the scores fall at the negative end of the distribution. Results from an examination that are negatively skewed may indicate that the test was too easy; in such an instance, more items of a higher level of difficulty would have been desirable so that better discrimination between scores could have been made with respect to the upper end of the distribution of scores.

Experience in teaching measurement courses has indicated to the authors that the term "skewed" carries with it negative implications for many students, perhaps because of an association with abnormality—given that a skewed distribution deviates from a "normal" distribution. However, the presence or absence of symmetry in a distribution (skewness) is simply one characteristic by which a distribution can be described, and skewness is not in and of itself bad (or good). We might expect a distribution of household income in dollars to be skewed negatively if samples such as Beverly Hills residents or Harvard Law School graduates were employed—because of the clustering that could be expected at the higher end of possible household incomes. A hypothetical "Marine Corps Endurance Test" used to screen male applicants might consistently yield positively skewed distributions; its built-in difficulty level would be designed to guarantee that only a few would "pass"—consistent with the advertised objective that the Corps isn't seeking "a lot of good men" but rather only "a few good men." A test purporting to measure abilities that are assumed to be normally distributed in the population would be expected to yield distributions that are also approximately normal in distribution. If testing with such an instrument using samples from the general population repeatedly yielded skewed distributions, the assumptions made by such a test would have to be reconsidered.

Various formulas exist for measuring skewness. One way of gauging the skewness of a distribution is through examination of the relative distances of quartiles from the median. In a positively skewed distribution, $Q_3 - Q_2$ will be greater than the distance of $Q_2 - Q_1$. In a negatively skewed distribution, $Q_3 - Q_2$ will be less than the distance of $Q_2 - Q_1$. In a distribution that is symmetrical, the distances from Q_1 and Q_3 to the median are the same.

Kurtosis

The term testing professionals use to refer to the steepness of a distribution in its center is *kurtosis,* and the descriptive suffix *kurtic* is added to either *platy, lepto,* or

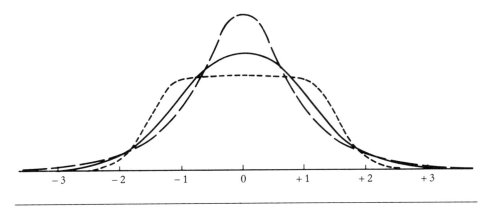

Figure 3–7 *The Kurtosis of Curves.*

meso to describe the peakedness/flatness of three general types of curves (see Figure 3–7). Distributions are generally described as being either "platykurtic" (relatively flat), "leptokurtic" (relatively peaked), or—somewhere in the middle— "mesokurtic." Although many methods exist for measuring kurtosis, the subject of kurtosis—including technical matters related to its measurement and interpretation—is still a matter of controversy among measurement specialists.

THE NORMAL CURVE

Development of the concept of a normal curve began in the middle of the eighteenth century with the work of Abraham DeMoivre and, later, Pierre Simon de Laplace. At the beginning of the nineteenth century, Karl Friedrich Gauss made some substantial contributions to the normal curve concept with his work on his "theory of errors" (work that resulted in a statistical technique known as the method of least squares). In the early nineteenth century, the normal curve was referred to as the Laplace–Gaussian curve. It was Karl Pearson who first referred to this curve as the "normal curve," perhaps in an effort to be diplomatic and avoid international questions of priority. Diplomacy aside, referring to the curve as "normal" instead of assigning someone's name to it created some confusion at the time, especially since many wondered aloud whether all other curves should be thought of as "abnormal." Somehow, the name "normal curve" stuck—though don't be surprised if you're sitting at some scientific meeting one day and you hear this distribution or curve referred to as "Gaussian" in nature.

Theoretically, the normal curve is a bell-shaped, smooth, mathematically defined curve highest at the center and then gradually tapered on both sides ap-
proaching the X-axis *asymptotically* (meaning that it approaches, but never
touches, the axis). In theory, the distribution of the normal curve ranges from
negative infinity to positive infinity. The curve is perfectly symmetrical, with no
skewness, so if you "folded" it in half at the mean, one side would lie exactly on
top of the other. Because it is symmetrical, the mean, median, and mode all have
the same exact value. Many psychological tests will yield approximately normal
distributions, especially when administered to large numbers of subjects though
few, if any, will yield precisely normal distributions (Micceri, 1989). As a general
rule—with ample exceptions—the larger the sample size and the wider the range
of abilities measured by a particular test, the closer the curve will approximate the
theoretical normal curve. As an illustration of this, consult Thorndike et al. (1927)
and you will find distributions of scores that very closely approximate normal
curves; the distributions are composites of intelligence test scores of large numbers of student test takers (29,000 in total).

Area Under the Normal Curve

The normal curve can be conveniently divided into areas defined in standard deviation units. A hypothetical distribution of "National Spelling Test" scores with
a mean of 50 and a standard deviation of 15 is illustrated in Figure 3–8. In this
example, a score equal to 1 standard deviation above the mean would be equal to
65 ($\bar{X} + 1\ s = 50 + 15 = 65$). Before reading on, take a minute or two to calculate

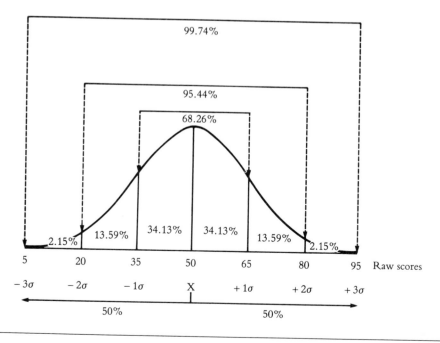

Figure 3–8   *Area under the Normal Curve.*

what a score exactly at 3 standard deviations below the mean would be equal to. How about a score exactly at 3 standard deviations above the mean? Were your answers 5 and 95, respectively? The graph tells us that 99.74% of all scores in these normally distributed spelling test data lie between ±3 standard deviations. Stated another way, 99.74% of all spelling test scores lie between 5 and 95. This graph also illustrates other characteristics true of all normal distributions:

- 50% of the scores occur above the mean, and 50% of the scores occur below the mean.
- Approximately 34% of all scores occur between the mean and 1 standard deviation above the mean.
- Approximately 34% of all scores occur between the mean and 1 standard deviation below the mean.
- Approximately 68% of all scores occur between the mean and ±1 standard deviation.
- Approximately 95% of all scores occur between the mean and ±2 standard deviations.

Knowledge of the areas under the normal curve can be quite useful to the interpreter of test data. If, for example, you know that some high school student's score on a national, well-reputed spelling test was more than 3 standard deviations above the mean, it's a good bet that that student would know how to spell words like "asymptotic" and "leptokurtic."

STANDARD SCORES

Simply stated, a *standard score* is a raw score that has been converted from one scale into another scale—the latter typically being one that is more widely used and interpretable—that has some arbitrarily set mean and standard deviation. Raw scores may be converted to standard scores because standard scores are more readily interpretable than raw scores, whether the raw scores are on the same test or on different tests. With a standard score, the position of a test taker's performance relative to other test takers is readily apparent. Different types of systems for standard scores exist, each unique as regards its respective mean and standard deviations. One type of standard score scale has been referred to as the "zero plus or minus one" scale because it has a mean set at zero and a standard deviation set at one. Raw scores converted into standard scores on the "zero plus or minus one scale" are more popularly referred to as z scores.

z Scores

A z score is equal to the difference between a particular raw score and the mean divided by the standard deviation. In essence, a z score expresses a score in terms of the number of standard deviation units the raw score is below or above the mean of the distribution. Using an example from the normally distributed "National Spelling Test" data in Figure 3–8, we can convert a raw score of 65 to a z score using the following formula:

$$z = \frac{X - \bar{X}}{s} = \frac{65 - 50}{15} = \frac{15}{15} = 1$$

In this test a raw score of 65 is equal to a z score of $+1$. Knowing simply that someone obtained a raw score of 65 on a spelling test conveys virtually no usable information because information about the context of this score is lacking. However, knowing that someone obtained a z score of 1 on a spelling test provides context and meaning to the score; drawing on our knowledge of areas under the normal curve, for example, we would know that only about 16% of the other test takers obtained higher scores.

Standard scores provide a convenient way to compare various raw scores within and between tests. It helps us little to know, for example, that Crystal's raw score on the "Main Street Reading Test" was 24 and that her raw score on the "Main Street Arithmetic Test" was 42. It would be more informative and helpful to know that the z score Crystal achieved on the reading test was 1.32 and the z score she achieved on the arithmetic test was -0.75. From just these data we know that, although her raw arithmetic score was higher than her raw reading score, she did perform better on the reading test. An interpretation of exactly how much better she performed could be obtained by reference to tables detailing distances under the normal curve (and the resulting percentage of cases that could be expected to fall above or below a particular standard deviation point, or z score).

T Scores

If the scale used in the computation of z scores is called a "zero plus or minus one" scale, then the scale used in the computation of T scores is called a "fifty plus or minus ten" scale: a scale that has a mean set at 50 and a standard deviation set at 10. Devised by W. A. McCall (1922, 1939) and named a T score in honor of his professor E. L. Thorndike, this standard score system is composed of a scale that ranges from 5 standard deviations below the mean to 5 standard deviations above the mean. Thus, for example, a raw score that fell exactly at 5 standard deviations below the mean would be equal to a T score of 0, a raw score that fell at the mean would be equal to a T of 50, and a raw score that fell at a point that was 5 standard deviations above the mean would be equal to a T of 100. An advantage in using T scores is that none of the scores is negative. By contrast, in a z score distribution, scores can be positive and negative, making further computation cumbersome in some instances.

Other Standard Scores

Numerous other standard scoring systems exist. Researchers during World War II developed a standard score with a mean of 5 and a standard deviation of approximately 2. Divided into nine units, the scale was christened a *stanine,* deriving from a contraction of the words "*sta*ndard" and "*nine.*" This scale was subsequently refined statistically (see Kaiser, 1958). Raw scores on tests such as the Scholastic Aptitude Test (SAT) and the Graduate Record Examination (GRE) are converted to standard scores such that the resulting distribution has a mean of 500 and a standard deviation of 100. If the letter A is used to represent a standard score from a college or graduate school admissions test whose distribution has a mean of 500 and a standard deviation of 100, then the following is true:

$$(A = 600) = (z = 1) = (T = 60)$$

The relationship of z, T, and A scores to each other in a normal distribution is illustrated in Figure 3–9.

Another kind of standard score that you may be familiar with is the "deviation intelligence quotient" (or "deviation IQ" or simply "IQ" for short). If you are not familiar with this type of score, rest assured that after studying Part 3 of this text you will be. For most IQ tests, the distribution of raw scores will be converted to IQ scores, whose distribution typically has a mean set at 100 and a standard deviation set at 15 (note that we say "typically" because there is some variation in standard scoring systems depending on the test used). We will have a lot more to say about deviation IQs (as well as their predecessor, *ratio IQs*) in Part 3. We will also see that each of the individual subtests of the Wechsler set of intelligence tests is a standard score itself, with a mean set at 10 and a standard deviation set at 3.

Standard scores converted from raw scores may involve either *linear* or *non-linear transformations*. A standard score obtained by a linear transformation is one that retains a direct numerical relationship to the original raw score, and the mag-

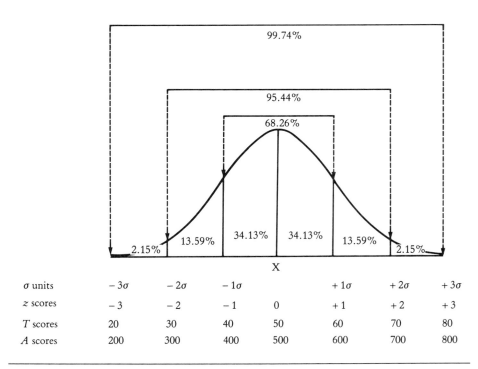

σ units	-3σ	-2σ	-1σ		$+1\sigma$	$+2\sigma$	$+3\sigma$
z scores	-3	-2	-1	0	$+1$	$+2$	$+3$
T scores	20	30	40	50	60	70	80
A scores	200	300	400	500	600	700	800

Figure 3–9 *Some Standard Score Equivalents.*

nitude of differences between such standard scores exactly parallels the differences between corresponding raw scores. Sometimes a standard score such as a z score may undergo more than one linear transformation; for example, the creators of the SAT did a second linear transformation on their data to convert z scores into a new scale that has a mean of 500 and a standard deviation of 100. A *nonlinear* transformation may be required when the data under consideration are not normally distributed and comparisons to normal distributions need to be made. When such a nonlinear transformation is done, the original distribution is said to have been "normalized."

Normalized standard scores   A test developer interested in developing an instrument that yields a normal distribution of scores may find that, even after very large samples have been tested with the instrument, skewed distributions result. If the test developer is intent on having scores on this test be distributed normally, the distribution can be "normalized." Conceptually, "normalizing" a distribution involves "stretching" the skewed curve into a shape of a normal curve and creating a corresponding scale of standard scores—a scale that is technically referred to as a *normalized standard score scale*.

Normalization of a skewed distribution of scores may also be desirable for purposes of comparability. One of the primary advantages of a standard score on one test is that it can readily be compared to a standard score on another test. However, comparison of standard scores is appropriate only when the distributions from which they derived are the same—and in most instances they are the same because the two distributions are approximately normal. But if, for example, distribution A was normal and distribution B was highly skewed, z scores in these respective distributions would represent different amounts of area subsumed under the curve. A z score of -1 with respect to normally distributed data tells us, among other things, that about 84% of the scores in this distribution were higher than this score. A z score of -1 with respect to data that were very positively skewed might mean, for example, that only 62% of the scores were higher.

For test developers intent on creating tests that yield normally distributed measurements, it is generally preferable to "fine-tune" the difficulty level of the test (and/or other factors) so that the resulting distribution will approximate the normal curve—as opposed to trying to normalize skewed distributions. This is true because there are technical cautions to be observed before attempting normalization (for instance, transformations should be made only when there is good reason to believe that the test sample was large and representative enough and the failure to obtain normally distributed scores was due to the measuring instrument). In situations where the distribution is not perfectly normal but closely approximates normal—a common enough situation—normalization is not typically conducted, since the normalized standard score (derived from a nonlinear transformation) will closely approximate the standard score (derived from a linear transformation). Further, the score derived from a nonlinear transformation will be limited with respect to additional computations that can legitimately be performed with it, while the score derived from the linear transformation will not.

And speaking of transformations, it's about time to make one to Chapter 4. It may be helpful at this time to review this statistics refresher to make certain that you indeed feel "refreshed." Apply what you have learned about frequency distributions, graphing frequency distributions, measures of central tendency, measures of variability, and the normal curve and standard scores to the question posed on page 84. . . . How would you communicate the data from Table 3–1 to the class? Which type of frequency distribution might you use? Which type of graph? Which measure of central tendency? Which measure of variability? Might reference to a normal curve or to standard scores be helpful? Why or why not?[9]

Come to the next class session prepared with your thoughts on the answers to these questions—as well as your own questions regarding any of the material that could still stand a bit more explanation. We will be building on your knowledge of basic statistical principles in the chapters to come and it is important that such building be on a rock-solid foundation.

---

9. A detailed, step-by-step illustration of the computation of each of various statistics for these data appears in Cohen (1992), the companion workbook to this text.

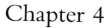

Chapter 4

Norms, Correlation,

and Regression

A POPULARLY HELD notion is that "the crazies come out of the woodwork when the moon is full." Is there really a correlation between the occurrence of a full moon and "lunacy"? While the popular belief that such a correlation exists finds support in some published studies, scrutiny of the methods used to analyze and interpret the data has raised a number of questions. Rotton and Kelly (1985) carefully reviewed over three dozen published studies addressed to the "lunacy" question and concluded that phases of the moon could account for no more than 1 percent of the variance in "lunatic"-related behavior such as homicides and other criminal offenses, crisis calls, and mental hospital admissions. Rotton and Kelly suggested that alleged relations between the moon and lunacy found to exist by other researchers were due at least in part to inappropriate statistical analyses.

An understanding of the concept of correlation is basic to the study of psychology and essential in the study of psychological testing. Our statistics refresher continues with a review of correlation and regression, preceded by discussion of another essential subject area in psychological testing: norms.

NORMS

Each year thousands of college-bound students, with "number 2" pencil firmly in hand, blacken thousands of little grids on college entrance examination answer forms. After months of anticipation, the mail brings a computer-generated statement with the test scores. Typically enclosed with the scores is a booklet or leaflet explaining how the scores should be interpreted. Students are advised to judge their own individual performance in comparison to the performance of some other group of students that took the test—a *normative sample* (also variously referred to as a *norm group*, a *reference group*, or a *standardization sample*).

Like the tests used to aid colleges in making entry decisions, many other carefully researched tests have been administered to people who are typical with respect to some characteristic(s) of the people for whom the particular test was designed. A test administration to this representative sample of test takers yields a distribution (or distributions) of scores. This distribution of scores, in raw or more typically in converted score form, is referred to as the *norms* for the test: data that will be used to place into context the score of any individual test taker relative to the scores of the standardization sample.

Norm in the singular is frequently used in practice to refer to some measure of central tendency with respect to the standardization sample. For example, "Sylvester scored 600 on the quantitative portion of the SAT and the norm is 500." Knowing that the standard deviation for this particular test is equal to 100 and armed with a little knowledge about areas under the normal curve, we would know that Sylvester outperformed approximately 84% of the standardization sample on the quantitative portion of the SAT.

The Normative or Standardization Sample

The process of administering a test to a representative sample of test takers for the purpose of establishing norms is referred to as "standardizing a test." A test is said to be *standardized* when it has clearly specified procedures for administration and scoring—including normative data. But how are norms obtained? And on whom? In the process of developing a test, a test developer has targeted some defined group as the "population" for which the test is designed for use. This population is the complete universe or set of individuals with at least one common, observable characteristic. The common observable characteristic might be anything ranging from "high school seniors who aspire to go to college" to "the 16 boys and girls in Mrs. Smith's day care center," to "all housewives with primary responsibility for household shopping who have purchased over-the-counter headache remedies within the last two months." To obtain a distribution of scores, the test developer could have the test administered to every person in the targeted population; and if the total targeted population consists of something like "the 16 boys and girls in Mrs. Smith's day care center," there would be no problem. However, with tests developed for use with large or wide-ranging populations, it is usually impossible, impractical, or simply too expensive to administer the test to everyone; nor is it necessary.

The test developer can obtain a distribution of test responses by administering the test to a *sample* of the population—a portion of the universe of people deemed to be representative of the whole population. The size of the sample could be as small as one person, though as the size of the sample approaches the size of the population, possible sources of error as a result of insufficient sample size diminish.

Subgroups within a defined population may differ with respect to some characteristics, and it is sometimes essential to have these differences proportionately represented in the sample. Thus, for example, if you devised a "Public Opinion Test" and you wanted to sample the opinions of Manhattan residents with this instrument, it would be desirable to include in your sample people representing different subgroups or layers (or "strata") of the population, such as blacks, whites, Asians, other nonwhites, males, females, the poor, the middle class, the rich, professional people, business people, office workers, skilled and unskilled laborers, the unemployed, homemakers, Catholics, Jews, members of other religions, and so forth—all in proportion to the occurrence of these strata in the population of people who reside on the island of Manhattan. Such sampling, referred to as *stratified sampling,* would help prevent sampling bias and ultimately aid in the interpretation of the findings. If such sampling were random in nature (that is, if every member of the population had the same chance of being included in the sample), then the procedure would be referred to as *stratified-random sampling.*

Two other types of sampling procedures that we will briefly mention are called *purposive sampling* and *incidental sampling.* If we arbitrarily select some sample because we believe it to be representative of the population, the sample we have selected is referred to as "purposive." Manufacturers of products frequently use purposive sampling when they test the appeal of a new product in one city or market and then make assumptions about how that product would sell nationally. For example, the manufacturer might test a product in a market such as Cleveland because, on the basis of experience with this particular product, "how goes Cleveland goes the nation." The danger in using such a purposive sample is that the sample, in this case Cleveland residents, may no longer be representative of the nation or may simply not be representative of national preferences with regard to the particular product being test-marketed.

Another type of sample, and an all-too-frequently used type, is called an *incidental sample.* When the authors think of this type of sample, we think of the old joke about the drunk searching for some money he lost under the lamppost; he may not have lost it there, but he's searching for it there simply because that's where the light is. Like the drunk searching for money under the lamppost, a researcher may sometimes employ a sample that is not necessarily the most appropriate, but rather the most convenient. Unlike the drunk, we hope, the researcher employing this type of sample is not doing it as a result of poor judgment, but because of other factors (such as budgetary limitations or situational constraints). An incidental sample (also referred to as a *convenience sample*) is one that is convenient or available for use. You may have personally been a party to incidental sampling if you have ever been placed in a subject pool for experimentation with introductory psychology students. It's not that the students in such subject pools are necessarily the most appropriate subjects for the experiments, but that they are the most available. Generalization of findings made with respect to incidental samples must be made with caution.

Having obtained a sample, the test developer administers the test and then describes the resulting data in terms of descriptive statistics that include measures of central tendency and variability. The statistical findings for the standardization sample, as well as a precise description of the sample used to "norm" the test, are essential. As stated in the *Standards for Educational and Psychological Testing,*

"Norms that are presented should refer to clearly described groups. These groups should be the ones with whom users of the test will ordinarily wish to compare the people who are tested" (1985, p. 33). This standard (number 4.3) continues: "Test publishers should also encourage the development of local norms by test users when the published norms are insufficient for particular test users."[1] In a similar vein, the *Code of Fair Testing Practices in Education* (1988, p. 3) encourages test developers to "Describe the population(s) represented by any norms or comparison group(s), the dates the data were gathered, and the process used to select the samples of test takers."

In practice, the preciseness of the descriptions of the standardization sample varies widely. Not surprisingly, test authors wish to present their tests in the most favorable light possible, and shortcomings in the standardization procedure (or elsewhere in the process of the test's development) may be given short shrift or totally overlooked. Sometimes the sample may be scrupulously defined, but the generalizability of the norms to a particular group or individual is questionable. For example, a test carefully normed on school-age children who reside within the Los Angeles school district may be relevant only to some lesser degree to school-age children who reside within the Dubuque, Iowa, school district. How many children in the standardization sample were English speaking? How many were of Hispanic origin? How does the elementary school curriculum in Los Angeles differ from the curriculum in Dubuque? These are the types of questions that must be raised before the Los Angeles norms are judged to be generalizable to the children of Dubuque. Test manuals sometimes supply prospective test users with guidelines for establishing local norms—one of many different ways norms can be categorized.

Types of Norms

Some of the many different ways we can classify norms are as follows: age norms, grade norms, national norms, national anchor norms, local norms, norms from a fixed reference group, subgroup norms, and percentile norms. We begin with a detailed explanation of the term *percentile* because the norms for many tests are expressed as *percentile norms* (the raw data from a test's standardization sample converted to percentile form).

Percentiles Like the word "impeach," "percentile" is one of those words that most people believe they understand, yet many—perhaps most—are not really aware of its true definition. By way of arriving at a definition and understanding of what a percentile is, let's build on what we already have learned about how a distribution can be divided up. In our discussion of the median, we saw that a distribution could be divided into quartiles where the median was the second quartile (Q_2), the point at which 50% of the scores fell at or below and the remaining 50% fell above. Instead of dividing a distribution of scores into quartiles, we might wish to divide the distribution into *deciles,* or 10 equal parts. Alternatively, we could divide a distribution into 100 equal parts—100 *percentiles.* In

---

1. "Local norms" will be discussed later in this chapter.

such a distribution the xth percentile is equal to the score at or below which x scores fall. Thus the 15th percentile is the score at or below which 15% of the scores in the distribution fall: the 99th percentile is the score at or below which 99% of the scores in the distribution fall. If 99% of a particular standardization sample answered fewer than 47 questions on a test correctly, then we could say that a raw score of 47 corresponds to the 99th percentile on this test. It can be seen that a percentile is a ranking that conveys information about the relative position of a score within a distribution of scores. As an example, refer back to the test data that appeared in Table 3–1 and let's focus on Valerie. Valerie achieved a raw score of 85 on the test; this places her score at the 80th percentile.

A *percentile* is a raw score that has been converted into something else—an expression of the percentage of people whose score falls below a particular raw score. A more familiar description of test performance, the concept of *percentage correct*, must be distinguished from the concept of a percentile; the two are different. Whereas a percentile is a converted score that refers to a percentage of test takers, "percentage correct" as this term is colloquially used refers to the distribution of raw scores—specifically, the number of items that were answered correctly multiplied by 100 and divided by the total number of items.

Because percentiles are easily calculated and easily grasped (once you have a little experience with them), they are a popular way of organizing test data—be it data from the standardization sample or otherwise. Additionally, percentiles are very adaptable for use with a wide range of tests, whether they are tests of ability, personality, interests, or whatever. A problem with using percentiles with normally distributed scores is the fact that real differences between raw scores may be minimized near the ends of the distribution and exaggerated in the middle of the distribution (and this distortion problem may even be worse with highly skewed data). In the normal distribution, the highest frequency of raw scores occurs in the middle. This being the case, the differences between all those scores that cluster in the middle might in reality be quite small, yet even the smallest difference will appear as differences in percentiles. The reverse is true at the extremes of the distributions, where differences between raw scores may be great, though we would have no way of knowing that from the relatively small differences in percentiles.

Age norms   Also referred to as *age-equivalent scores, age norms* indicate the average performance of different samples of test takers who were at various ages at the time the test was administered. If the measurement under consideration is height in inches, for example, we know that children's "scores" (that is, heights) will gradually increase at various rates as a function of age up to their middle to late teens.

Carefully constructed age norm tables for physical characteristics such as height enjoy widespread acceptance and are virtually noncontroversial. This is not the case, however, with respect to age norm tables for psychological characteristics such as intelligence. Suppose you created the "National Intelligence Test" (NIT) and designed it for use with children between the ages of 5 and 14. And let's say that you obtained NIT norms using large, nationally representative, random samples of 5-year-olds, 6-year-olds—all the way through to 14-year-olds. Your standardization sample data tell you that the average 6-year-old obtains a raw score of, say, 30 on your test, while the average 12-year-old obtains a raw score of 60. In the course of examining your data you note that one 12-year-old, Adolf, scored 30 on your test. You also find that one 6-year-old, Anna, obtained a raw score of 60. Is it legitimate for you to make statements like "Adolf has a mental age of 6 and Anna has a mental age of 12"?

As we will see in the material dealing specifically with intelligence testing, for many years psychologists have made statements like those referring to "mental ages" of test takers. The child of any chronological age whose performance on a valid test of intellectual ability indicated that he or she had intellectual ability similar to that of the average child of some other age was said to have the "mental

Figure 4–1 *"We're Number 1!"*

Like other cheerleading squads in colleges throughout the country, and not unlike the sports fans you see unfurling banners at virtually every kind of televised athletic event, these exuberant leaders of cheer are indicating that their team is "Number 1." The next time you see the "Number 1" sign, you might give some thought to whether reference is being made to current standing among competitors where "1" is best, to a wish for such standing, or to something else—such as a current percentile ranking (in which case such a statement could be interpreted as "99% of our competition is ranked higher than us"). The point here is that while we usually think of first place as best, when it comes to percentiles, the reverse is true: the higher the number, the better (and a claim like "We're 99th" could be quite impressive). By the way, this photo was snapped during half-time at a collegiate football game in October 1987. It is with proper sadness that we report that despite brilliant, inspiring efforts of the cheerleaders (including cheers involving death-defying acrobatics), their team lost and in so doing added yet another game to what was already a new college football record for most consecutive games lost. Oh well, there's always next season to be Number 1 in the standings and basketball, and soccer, and fencing, and academics, and . . .

age" of the norm group in which his or her test score fell. The reasoning here was that irrespective of chronological age, children with the same "mental age" could be expected to read the same level of material, solve the same kinds of math problems, reason with a similar level of judgment, and so forth. But some have complained that the concept of "mental age" is too broad and that while a 6-year-old might, for example, perform intellectually like a 12-year-old, the 6-year-old might not be very similar at all to the average 12-year-old socially, psychologically, and otherwise. In addition to such intuitive considerations, the "mental age" concept has also been criticized on technical grounds.[2]

Grade norms Designed to indicate the average test performance of test takers in a given grade, *grade norms* are developed by administering the test to representative samples of children over a range of consecutive grade levels (such as first through sixth grade). Next, the mean or median score for children at each grade level is computed. Because the school year typically runs from September to June—ten months—fractions in the mean or median are easily expressed as decimals. Thus, for example, a sixth-grader performing exactly at the average on a grade-normed test administered during the fourth month of the school year (December) would achieve a grade-equivalent score of 6.4. Like age norms, grade norms have widespread application with children of elementary school age, the thought here being that children learn and develop in ways that are in some aspects predictable (though they do so at varying rates—rates that can in some way be gauged in terms of age and/or grade equivalency scores).

Suppose Raoul is in grade 12 but his score on a grade-normed spelling test is 6. Does this mean that Raoul has the same spelling abilities as the average sixth-grader? The answer is no: accurately interpreted, all this finding means is that Raoul and a hypothetically average sixth-grader answered the same fraction of items correctly on that test. Grade norms do not provide information as to the content or type of items that a student could or could not answer correctly. Perhaps the primary use of grade norms is as a convenient, readily understandable gauge of how one student's performance compares to that of fellow students in the same grade.

Because of the ease with which they may be misinterpreted, some experts in testing have called for a moratorium on the use of grade-equivalent (as well as age-equivalent) scores and reliance on other types of scales. Writing in 1970, Cronbach described age and grade norms as "archaic." He argued that "grade conversions should never be used in reporting on a pupil or a class, or in research. Standard scores or percentiles or raw scores serve better. Age conversions are also likely to be misinterpreted" (p. 98). Another—most obvious—drawback to using grade norms is that they are useful only with respect to years and months of

2. For many years, IQ (intelligence quotient) scores on tests such as the Stanford-Binet were calculated by dividing "mental age" (as indicated by the test) by chronological age. The quotient would then be multiplied by 100 to eliminate the fraction. The distribution of IQ scores had a mean set at 100 and a standard deviation of approximately 16. A child of 12 with a "mental age" of 12 had an IQ of 100 ($12/12 \times 100 = 100$). The technical problem here is that IQ standard deviations were not constant with age; at one age, an IQ of 116 might be indicative of performance at 1 standard deviation above the mean, while at another age an IQ of 121 might be indicative of performance at 1 standard deviation above the mean.

schooling completed (and have little or no applicability to children who are not yet in school or out of school). Age norms are also limited in this regard since, for many tests, the value of such norms is limited with an adult population.[3]

National norms   As the name implies, a *national norm* is derived from a standardization sample that was nationally representative of the population. In the fields of psychology and education, for example, national norms may be obtained through the testing of large numbers of students representative of different variables of interest such as socioeconomic strata, geographical location (such as North, East, South, West, Midwest), and different types of communities within the various parts of the country (such as rural, urban, suburban). Norms would typically be obtained for every grade to which the test sought to be applicable, and other factors related to the representativeness of the school itself might be criteria for inclusion in or exclusion from the standardization sample. For example, is the school the student attends publicly funded, privately funded, religiously oriented, military-oriented, or something else? How representative are the pupil-teacher ratios in the schools under consideration? Does the school have a library and, if so, how many books are in it? These are only a sample of the types of questions that could be raised in assembling a standardization sample to be used in the establishment of national norms; the precise nature of the questions asked will depend on whom the test is designed for and what it is designed to do. Since norms from different tests all represented as "national" in nature may have "nationally representative" standardization samples that differ in many important respects, it is always a good idea to check the manual of the tests under consideration to see exactly how comparable the tests are; the greater the differences in standardization sample among these tests, the more the comparability of one student's scores on each of these tests is strained.

National anchor norms   Even the most casual survey of catalogues from various test publishers will reveal that, with respect to almost any human characteristic or ability, there exist many different tests purporting to measure the characteristic or ability. There exist dozens of tests, for example, that purport to measure reading. Suppose we select one reading test designed for use in grades 3 to 6, which—for the purposes of this hypothetical example—we call "The Best Reading Test" (BRT), because we feel it to be "the best" in terms of such factors as the national representativeness of its standardization sample and its reliability and validity. Suppose further that we now want to be able to compare findings obtained on other national reading tests designed for use with grades 3 to 6 (such as the "XYZ Reading Test") with the BRT. A typical question in this regard might be, "I have reading scores for these children on the XYZ Test and I would like to know what these scores would be equivalent to on the BRT." An equivalency table for scores on the two tests or *national anchor norms* could provide the answer; just as an anchor provides some stability to a vessel, so "national anchor

3. But age norms in tests standardized with adult populations can be expected to rise in future years. With the "graying of America," there is increased interest in performance on various types of psychological tests as a function of advancing age. Already, we are beginning to see more and more age-specific norms in the adult age range in the area of neuropsychological assessment.

norms" provide some stability to test scores by "anchoring" them to other test scores.

The method by which such equivalency tables or national anchor norms are established typically begins with the computation of percentile norms for each of the tests to be compared. Using what has been referred to as the *equipercentile method,* the equivalency of scores on different tests is calculated with reference to corresponding percentile scores. Thus if the 96th percentile corresponds to a score of 69 on the "BRT," and if the 96th percentile corresponds to a score of 14 on the "XYZ," we can say that a BRT score of 69 is equivalent to an XYZ score of 14. We should note that the national anchor norms for our hypothetical BRT and XYZ tests must have been obtained on the same sample—each member of the sample took both tests and the equivalency tables were then calculated on the basis of these data. Although national anchor norms provide an indication of the equivalency of scores on various tests, it would be a mistake, due to technical considerations, to treat these equivalencies as precise equalities (Angoff, 1964, 1966, 1971).

Subgroup norms   A standardization sample can be segmented by any of the criteria initially used in selecting subjects for the sample, and *subgroup norms* for any of these more narrowly defined groups can be developed. Thus, for example, suppose criteria used in selecting children for inclusion in the "XYZ Reading Test" standardization sample were age, educational level, socioeconomic level, region, community type, and "handedness" (whether the child was right-handed or left-handed). The test manual or a supplement to it might report normative information by each of these subgroups. A community school board member might find the regional norms to be most interesting, while a psychologist doing exploratory research in the area of brain lateralization and reading scores might find the handedness norms most useful.

Local norms   Typically developed by test users themselves, *local norms* provide normative information with respect to the local population's performance on some test. A local company personnel director might find some nationally standardized test useful in making selection decisions, but might deem the norms published in the test manual to be far afield from local job applicants' score distributions. Individual high schools may wish to develop their own school norms (local norms) for student scores on some examination that is administered statewide. A school guidance center may find that locally derived norms for a particular test—say, a survey of personal values—are more useful in counseling students than the national norms printed in the manual.

Fixed Reference Group Scoring Systems

Norms provide a context for interpreting the meaning of a test score. Another type of aid in providing a context for interpretation is what has been called a *fixed reference group scoring system.* Here, the distribution of scores obtained on the test from one group of test takers—referred to as the "fixed reference group"—is used as the basis for the calculation of test scores for future administrations of the test. Perhaps the test most familiar to college students that exemplifies the use of a fixed reference group scoring system is the SAT. This test was first administered in 1926 and its norms then based on the mean and standard deviation of the people who took the test at the time. With passing years, more colleges—as well as a variety of different kinds of colleges—became members of the College Board (the sponsoring organization for the test). It soon became evident that SAT scores tended to vary somewhat as a function of the time of year the test was administered. In an effort to ensure perpetual comparability and continuity of scores, the custom of norming the SAT with respect to the group of test takers who had taken a given administration of the test was abandoned in 1941.

The distribution of scores from the 11,000 people who took the SAT in 1941 was immortalized as a standard to be used in the conversion of raw scores on future administrations of the test. The scores obtained by this "fixed reference group" of 1941 paralleled successive administrations of the test; a score of 500 on the SAT corresponds to the mean obtained by the 1941 sample, a score of 400 corresponds to a score that is one standard deviation below the 1941 mean, and so forth. A highly simplistic—though possibly enlightening—concrete example may help in illustrating the meaning of "fixed reference group" and how that concept is used in practice. Say John took the SAT in 1941 and answered 50 items correctly on a particular scale. And let's say Mary took the test in 1942 and, just like John, answered 50 items correctly on the same scale. While John and Mary may have both achieved the same raw score, they would not necessarily both achieve the same scaled score. If, for example, the 1942 version of the test under discussion was judged to be somewhat easier than the 1941 version, scaled scores for the 1942 test takers would be calibrated downward so that scores achieved in 1942 would be comparable to scores earned in 1941. The statistical procedures that are used to equate scores from one administration to the next are technically sophisticated, and the interested reader is urged to consult Donlon (1984) for a detailed, yet readable description of the process.

Test items common to each new version of the SAT and each previous version of it are employed in a procedure (called *anchoring*) that permits the conversion of raw scores on the new version of the test into what are technically referred to as "fixed reference group scores." Like other fixed reference group scores, SAT scores are most typically interpreted with respect to local norms. Thus, for example, admissions offices of colleges typically rely on their own independently collected norms to make selection decisions (focusing perhaps on variables such as SAT scores for those who successfully completed their program versus scores for dropouts, number of available places, and so on). Conceptually, the idea of a "fixed reference group" seems analogous to the idea of a "fixed reference foot"— the foot of the English king that also became immortalized as a measurement standard (Angoff, 1962).

Norm-Referenced versus Criterion-Referenced Interpretation

One way to derive meaning from test scores is to view the test score in the context of a distribution of test scores. *Norm-referenced* interpretations of test scores do just that; they provide a vehicle for interpreting the meaning of a test score in comparison to the score achieved on the same test by other people. To state it another way, the results of a norm-referenced test describe test performance in terms of the test taker's relative standing among others along some continuum.

Another way in which meaning can be interpreted from a test score has to do simply with the question of whether the test score meets or fails to meet some criterion or standard. A community might legislate as a standard, for example, a minimum requirement of sixth-grade reading ability for eligibility to receive a high school diploma; a student must be able to demonstrate at least sixth-grade reading-level ability on some test as one requirement for the award of a high school diploma. Assuming a reading test of unchallenged validity is being employed, the people responsible for evaluating the results of the reading test will probably not concern themselves very much with where individual test-taker scores fall in relation to the mean or to other scores; all they are interested in is whether or not sixth-grade reading ability has been demonstrated. The interpretation of test scores derived from this administration of the reading test would be said to be *criterion-referenced* because the interpretation of the score is made with respect to some standard or criterion.

What we are referring to as "criterion-referenced" tests have been variously referred to as "domain-" or "content-referenced" tests because the focus of interest in not on individual scores in relation to other people's scores, but on scores in relation to a particular content area or domain.[4] Generally speaking, it can be said that criterion-referenced interpretations provide information about what people can do, whereas norm-referenced interpretations provide information about how people have done in relation to other people. Criterion-referenced tests are frequently used to gauge achievement or mastery (and are sometimes referred to as *mastery tests* in this context). "Has this flight trainee mastered the material she needs to be an airline pilot?" This is the type of question that an airline personnel office might have to address with a test of mastery (that is, a criterion-referenced test). If a standard, or criterion, for passing on a hypothetical "Airline Pilot Test" (APT) has been set at 85% correct, then trainees who score 84% correct or less will not pass; it matters not whether they scored 84% or they scored 42%. Conversely, trainees who score 85% or better on the test will pass regardless if they scored 85% or 100%; all who score 85% or better are said to have mastered the skills and knowledge necessary to be an airline pilot. Taking this example one step further, another airline might find it useful to set up three categories of findings based on criterion-referenced interpretation of test scores:

85% or better correct = pass
75% or better correct = retest after two-month refresher course
74% or less = fail

How should cutoff scores in mastery testing be determined? How many test items and what kinds of test items are needed to demonstrate mastery in a given field? The answers to these and related questions could be the subject of a text in itself; they have been tackled in various ways ranging from empirical analyses (for

4. While acknowledging that "content-referenced" interpretations can be referred to as "criterion-referenced" interpretations, the 1974 edition of *Standards* also noted a technical distinction between interpretations referred to as "criterion-" and "content-referenced": "*Content-referenced* interpretations are those where the score is directly interpreted in terms of performance at each point on the achievement continuum being measured. *Criterion-referenced* interpretations are those where the score is directly interpreted in terms of performance at any given point on the continuum of an *external* variable. An external criterion variable might be grade averages or levels of job performance" (p. 19; footnote in original omitted).

example, Panell & Laabs, 1979) to applications of decision theory (Glaser & Nitko, 1971) and Bayesian prediction techniques (Ferguson & Novick, 1973).

The criterion-referenced approach has enjoyed widespread acceptance in the field of computer-assisted education programs where mastery of segments of materials is assessed before the program user can proceed to the next level of material. This approach is also utilized in educational assessment to determine if students have mastered basic academic skills, including reading and arithmetic. The criterion-referenced approach is the basis for curriculum-based assessment. Critics of the criterion-referenced approach argue that if it is strictly followed, potentially important information about an individual's performance relative to other test takers is lost. Another criticism is that while this approach may have value with respect to the assessment of mastery of basic knowledge and/or skills, it has little or no meaningful application at the upper end of the knowledge/skill continuum. To state this last point another way: although it might be meaningful to use criterion-oriented tests to see if pupils have mastered basic reading, writing, and arithmetic, the value of such tests would be at best questionable in gauging the progress of an advanced doctoral-level student in his or her area of specialization; stand-alone originality and brilliant analytic ability are not the stuff of which criterion-oriented tests are made. By contrast, brilliance and superior abilities are recognizable in tests that employ norm-referenced interpretations; they're the scores you see all the way to the right, near the third standard deviation, or the tenth decile or the one-hundredth percentile.

Before leaving our comparison of norm- and criterion-referenced testing, let's note that all testing is in reality normative—even if the scores are as criterion-referenced as "pass/fail" in nature. Even in a pass/fail score there is an inherent acknowledgment that a continuum of abilities exists—it's just that some dichotomizing cutoff point has been applied.

We now proceed to a discussion of another one of those words that—along with "impeach" and "percentile"—would easily make a national list of "Frequently Used but Little Understood Terminology." The word is *correlation*—a word that enjoys widespread confusion with the concept of causation. Let's state at the outset that correlation is *not* synonymous with causation. But what does correlation mean? Read on.

CORRELATION

Central to psychological testing and assessment is finding out how some things (such as traits, abilities, or interests) are related to other things (such as behavior). A *coefficient of correlation* is the number that provides us with an index of the strength of the relationship between two things. An understanding of the concept of correlation and an ability to compute a coefficient of correlation is therefore central to the study of tests and measurement.

The Concept of Correlation

Simply stated, *correlation* is an expression of the degree and direction of correspondence between two things; a coefficient of correlation (r) expresses a linear relationship between two (and only two) variables. It reflects the degree of concomitant variation between variable *X* and variable *Y*. The *coefficient of correlation* is the numerical index that expresses this relationship; it tells us the extent to which *X* and *Y* are "co-related."

The meaning of a correlation coefficient is interpreted by its sign (positive or negative—indicative of a positive or negative correlation) and by its magnitude (the greater its absolute value, the greater the degree of relatedness). A correlation coefficient can range in value from +1 to −1. If a correlation coefficient is +1 or −1 this means that the relationship between the two variables is perfect—without "error" in the statistical sense. Here, "error" refers to variability or imprecision of measurement and not to a mistake. Perfect correlations in psychological work— or other work for that matter—are difficult to find (just as perfection in almost anything tends to be difficult if not impossible to find). If a correlation is zero, then no relationship exists between the two variables. If two variables simultaneously increase or simultaneously decrease together, then these two variables could be said to be *positively* (or "directly") correlated. The height and weight of normal, healthy children ranging in age from birth to 10 years of age tends to be positively or directly correlated; as children get older, their height and weight generally increase simultaneously. A positive correlation also exists when two variables simultaneously decrease (for example, the less preparation a student does for an examination, the lower the score on the examination). A *negative* (or "inverse") correlation occurs when one variable increases while the other variable decreases. For example, there tends to be an inverse relationship between the number of miles on your car's odometer (mileage indicator) and the number of dollars a used car dealer is willing to give you on a trade-in allowance; all other things being equal, as the mileage increases, the number of dollars offered as a trade-in decreases.

As we stated in our introduction to this topic, "correlation" is often confused with "causation." It must be emphasized that a correlation coefficient is merely an index of the relationship between two variables, *not* an index of the causal relationship between two variables. If you were told, for example, that from birth to age 5 there is a high positive correlation between hat size and measurable intelligence, would it be appropriate to conclude that hat size causes intelligence? Of course not; this is a time of maturation in *all* areas, including development in cognitive and motor abilities as well as growth in physical size. Thus while intellectual development parallels physical development in these years and while it is true that a relationship clearly exists between physical and mental growth, it is not necessarily a causal relationship.

Although correlation does not imply causation, there *is* an implication of prediction. Stated another way, if we know that there is a high correlation between *X* and *Y*, we should be able to predict—with various degrees of accuracy, depending on other factors—the value of one of these variables if we know the value of the other. We will return to this point about predictability later in this chapter in the section Regression.

The Pearson *r*

The *Pearson product-moment correlation*, also referred to as the *Pearson correlation coefficient* and simply as the "Pearson *r*," is the most widely used of several alternative measures of correlation. It can be the statistical tool of choice when the relationship between the variables is linear and when the two variables being correlated are continuous (that is, they can theoretically take any value). Other correlational techniques can be employed with data that are discontinuous and where the relationship is nonlinear. The formula for the Pearson r takes into account the relativity of each test score's position (or, stated more broadly, each measurement's position) with respect to the mean of its distribution of scores.

Figure 4–2   *Why* r *Is Referred to as "Product-Moment Correlation"*

A *moment* is a relatively brief, indefinite, time interval—according to one usage of that word. In the language of physics, *moment* refers to the product of a quantity and its perpendicular distance from a reference point. In the language of statistics, a *moment* is the expected value of a positive integral power of a random variable. In psychometric parlance, the word *moment* is used to describe a deviation about a mean of a distribution.

Now consider the word *deviate*. Individual deviations about the mean of a distribution are referred to as *deviates*. In psychometric parlance, deviates are referred to as the "first moments" of the distribution. The "second moments" of the distribution are the moments squared. The "third moments" of the distribution are the moments cubed, and so forth.

The computation of the Pearson r in one of its many formulas entails multiplying corresponding standard scores on two measures. One way of conceptualizing standard scores is as "the first moments of a distribution"—this because standard scores are deviates about a mean of zero. A formula that entails the multiplication of two corresponding standard scores can therefore be conceptualized as one that entails the computation of the *product* of corresponding *moments*. Because r is the average product of the first moments of two distributions, it may well have been referred to in terms such as "product-of-moments correlation," "average-product-of-first-moments correlation," or "average-product-of-corresponding-moments correlation." The simpler *product-moment correlation* is the term commonly used to refer to r.

YOU STANDARD SCORES ARE A BUNCH OF
DEVIATES ABOUT A MEAN OF **ZERO**!

A number of formulas can be used to calculate a Pearson r. One formula necessitates converting each raw score to a standard score and then multiplying each pair of standard scores. A mean for the sum of the products is calculated and that mean is the value of the Pearson r. Even from this simple verbal conceptualization of what a Pearson r is, it can be seen that the sign of the resulting r would be a function of the sign and the magnitude of the standard scores being used; if, for example, there were all negative standard score values for all measurements of X along with corresponding negative standard score values for all Y scores, the resulting r would be positive (since the product of two negative values is positive). Similarly, if all of the standard score values in the equation were positive, the resulting correlation would also be positive. However, if all of the standard score values for X were positive and all of the standard score values for Y were negative, an inverse relationship would exist and a negative correlation would result. A zero or near-zero correlation could result when some cross products are positive and some are negative.

The formula used to calculate a Pearson r from raw scores is as follows:

$$r = \frac{\Sigma\,(X - \bar{X})(Y - \bar{Y})}{\sqrt{[\Sigma\,(X - \bar{X})^2][\Sigma\,(Y - \bar{Y})^2]}}$$

This formula can and has been simplified for "shortcut" purposes. One such shortcut formula is a deviation formula employing "little x," or x in place of $X - \bar{X}$, and "little y," or y in place of $Y - \bar{Y}$:

$$r = \frac{\Sigma\,xy}{\sqrt{(\Sigma\,x^2)(\Sigma\,y^2)}}$$

Another formula for calculating a Pearson r is as follows:

$$r = \frac{N\,\Sigma\,xy - (\Sigma\,X)(\Sigma\,Y)}{(\sqrt{N\,\Sigma\,x^2 - (\Sigma\,x)^2})(\sqrt{N\,\Sigma\,Y^2 - (\Sigma\,Y)^2}}$$

Although this formula looks more complicated than the previous deviation formula, it is easier to use. N represents the number of paired scores; $\Sigma\,xy$ is the sum of the product of the paired x and y scores; $\Sigma\,x$ is the sum of the x scores; $\Sigma\,y$ is the sum of the y scores; $\Sigma\,x^2$ is the sum of the squared x scores and $\Sigma\,y^2$ is the sum of the squared y scores. Similar results are obtained with the use of each formula.

The next logical question concerns what to do with the number obtained for the value of r. The answer is that you ask even more questions, such as "Is this number statistically significant given the size and nature of the sample?" or "Could this result have occurred by chance?" Tables of significance for Pearson r—tables that are probably in the back of your old statistics textbook—will need to be consulted at this point. In those tables you will find, for example, that a Pearson r of .899 with an $N = 10$ is significant at the .01 level. You will recall from your statistics course that "significant at the .01 level" tells you, with reference to these data, that a correlation such as this could have been expected to occur by chance alone less than one time or less in a hundred. You will also recall that significance at either the .01 level or the (somewhat less rigorous) .05 level—meaning that result could have been expected to occur by chance alone five times

Pearson, Galton, Correlation, and Regression

In reading about the development of a correlation coefficient, you may have asked yourself certain questions like "Why is the correlation coefficient abbreviated as *r*?" or "If Galton is credited with developing correlation, why do they call it a Pearson *r*?"

For the answers to these questions let's go back to the year 1873, when one question of interest to English scientists was whether or not the general physique for Englishmen was stable. In the course of studies addressed to that point, Galton developed several statistical techniques. His interest in being able to describe the rank of each subject in contrast to the rank of every other subject led him to the development of the concept of a median—the point at which 50 percent of the sample falls above and below. Because physical measurements from generation to generation in humans had not been made, much of Galton's initial experimentation involved work with plants. He briefly experimented with the cress and then went on to the sweet pea. Galton examined the diameter and weight of mother and daughter sweet pea seeds and through tables and graphs constructed ways of examining their relationship. Karl Pearson later recollected that these tables and graphs were the early precursors to more familiar correlation tables and scatterplots.

In an 1877 paper entitled "Typical Laws of Heredity," Galton presented his findings along with formulas for a phenomenon he labled "reversion"—and abbreviated by reference to the first initial *r*. The *r* commonly used today to denote "correlation" is a statistical descendant of the *r* Sir Francis Galton used to describe what he called "reversion" (which has subsequently come to be referred to as "regression"). Galton

Karl Pearson and his Daughter.

had observed that the mother pea's magnitude of deviation from the population mean differed from the daughter pea's magnitude of deviation from the population mean. Although it was generally true that the larger the mother sweet pea, the larger the daughter, there was also some "reversion" in size toward the average ancestral type.

In 1884 Galton fulfilled a dream by setting up his "Anthropometric Laboratory" at the International Health Exhibition in South Kensington, England. One of the traits Galton was interested in measuring was "stature" (that is, height), specifically the stature of fathers and sons. During the course of the one-year Exhibition, approximately nine thousand people went through the doors of Galton's Laboratory. Even at that time, Galton was aware that the father did not contribute solely to that characteristic in his son; Galton described the contribution of the father to the son's height as a "partial" contribution—other ancestral or genetic factors were operative as well. In a paper read by Galton at a scientific meeting on December 5, 1888, he discussed his findings regarding what he referred to as "co-relation":

> . . . co-relation must be the consequence of the variations of the two organs being partly due to common causes. If they were wholly due to common causes, the co-relation would be perfect, as is approximately the case with the symmetrically disposed parts of the body. If they were in no respect due to common causes, the co-relation would be nil. Between these two extremes are an endless number of intermediate cases and it will be shown how the closeness of co-relation in any particular case admits of being expressed by a single number.

Note that Galton took account of positive or direct correlation and the case where no correlation exists; however, he did not take account of the concept of negative or inverse correlation. At the time, Galton thought that two variables could be correlated only if they were positively or directly related (Magnello & Spies, 1984).

In examining the heights of parents in relation to their children, Galton noted, among other things, that very tall parents did not necessarily have very tall children and very short parents did not necessarily have very short children; the correlation between height of parents and the height of their children is not perfect. Rather, there was a tendency for the offspring's height to deviate less from their population mean than the parents' height deviated from their population mean. Galton conceptualized this finding regarding the reversion of heights of offspring back to the general population mean in what he called a "law of ancestral heredity."

Galton felt that a numerical index of the strength of the reversion or regression phenomenon could be obtained by calculating the slope for the *regression line*—the line of best fit through all of the points in the scatterplot. The numerical index of the strength of the reversion or regression is the "coefficient of regression" (symbolized by the letter r). But as a result of the work of Galton's contemporary, Karl Pearson, we have now come to view what Galton labeled r to be a measure of the slope (b) of a regression line. Pearson developed an alternative formula for Galton's r, and it is the latter r (the Pearson r) that has become the most-used measure of correlation.

The heights of parents (X) and their children (Y) expressed in standard scores (so as to place them on a common measuring scale) show a correlation of about .50. From your knowledge of coefficients of determination, you know that 25% of the variance (r^2 or $.5^2$) can be attributed to the X factor (height of parent) and the remaining 75% must be attributed to other factors (such as height of ancestors, nutrition, or chance).

or less in a hundred—provides a basis to conclude with confidence that a correlation does indeed exist.

The value obtained for the coefficient of correlation can be further interpreted by deriving from it what is called a *coefficient of determination* or r^2. The coefficient of determination is an indication of how much of the variance can be explained by the X and the Y variable. The calculation of r^2 is quite easy; simply square the correlation coefficient, multiply by 100, and express the result equal to the percentage of the variance accounted for. If, for example, you calculated an r to be .9, then r^2 would be equal to .81; the remaining variance, equal to $100 (1 - r^2)$, or 19%, could presumably be accounted for by chance, error, or otherwise unmeasured or unexplainable factors. In an interesting but somewhat technical article, Ozer (1985) cautioned that both the interpretation of an effect size as well as the actual estimation of a coefficient of determination must be made with scrupulous regard to the assumptions operative in the particular case; evaluating effect size solely in terms of variance accounted for may lead to interpretations that underestimate the magnitude of a relation.

Other Correlation Coefficients

The Pearson r enjoys such widespread use and acceptance as an index of correlation that if for some reason it is not used in calculating a correlation coefficient, mention must be made of the statistic that was used. There are times when, because of the nature of the data or the size of the sample other correlation coefficients can be employed. The correlation coefficients referred to as the Spearman rho, the point-biserial r, and the phi coefficient are actually special cases of the Pearson r. The formulas used to calculate each of these statistics appear to be different from each other and from the formula used to calculate r, but such differences are due entirely to the type of data for which each statistic is applicable. The mathematical rationale is the same in calculating r, the Spearman rho, the point-biserial r, and the phi coefficient, and all four statistics are "product-moment" correlation measures. By contrast, the biserial r and the tetrachoric r are not measures of product-moment correlation. Rather, they are used in special circumstances to estimate product-moment correlation. What circumstances? This and related questions are addressed as we further explore correlation.

The Spearman rho   Charles Spearman, a British psychologist, developed what has been variously called a "rank-order correlation coefficient," a "rank-difference correlation coefficient," or simply, Spearman's rho (see Figure 4–3). This coefficient of correlation is frequently used when the sample size is small (fewer than 30 pairs of measurements) and especially when both sets of measurements are in ordinal (or rank-order) form. Special tables are used to determine if an obtained rho coefficient is or is not significant.[5]

---

5. Another ranking method of correlation is embodied in a correlation coefficient with another Greek letter name: the *tau* (τ). It is also referred to as "Kendall's tau" and use of this coefficient rests on no special assumptions. Interested readers are invited to consult Kendall (1948) for a detailed discussion of its development and applications.

The biserial r A biserial coefficient of correlation, also known as the biserial r and denoted by the symbol r_b, is appropriate when the two variables to be correlated are continuous in nature but one of the two has arbitrarily been dichotomized. An example of an arbitrarily dichotomized variable is a test score that has been characterized as being at either the "pass" or "fail" level. Thus, for example, if one wanted to look at the relationship between entry-level students' scores on a hypothetical "Computer Programmer Aptitude Test" and performance on their final examination in terms of whether they passed or failed, the appropriate correlation coefficient to compute would be r_b. The biserial r is an approximation of the Pearson r and so the requirements for the use of a Pearson r must be met (for example, the relationship of the variables must be linear). Two additional assumptions regarding the two variables' respective distributions of measurements must be met. The distribution for the continuous variable should be unimodal and generally symmetrical (though not necessarily normal). The distribution of measurements from which the dichotomized values were dichotomized must be normal (in our example, the distribution of scores by students who ultimately passed or failed the final examination in Computer Programming School must be normal). If either of these requirements is not met, r_b will be meaningless and may

Figure 4–3 *Charles Spearman (1863–1945).*

Charles Spearman has earned a place in any history of psychology not only because he developed the Spearman *rho* statistic but also because of his involvement in developing what was at one time referred to as the "Spearman-Brown prophecy formula." As if that weren't enough, Spearman also has the distinction of being the person on whom many statisticians confer the title "father of factor analysis." With all of these accomplishments in the field of statistics you might conclude that numbers were his first love—a reasonable but incorrect conclusion. Spearman loved most of the philosophical aspects of psychology and his chief research work was in the area of intelligence—as we will see when we run across his name again in Part 3. He regretted not being able to become immersed in the field of psychology sooner than he did, saying of the time he spent in the military, "As for these almost wasted years, I have since mourned them as bitterly as ever Tiberius did for his lost legions" (Spearman, 1930–1936, Vol. 1).

Spearman received his doctorate at Leipzig and went on to obtain an instructorship—there called a "readership"—in experimental psychology at the University of London. He worked at that institution until his retirement, when he was succeeded as Grote Professor of Philosophy by Professor of Psychology Cyril Burt (a now controversial figure in the history of psychology since the veracity of his data was called into question). Spearman was fairly moderate when it came to statistical versus more intuitive approaches to the subject matter of psychology. He summed up the psychology of his day in the following way: "At one extreme, statistical zealots have accumulated masses of figures that remain psychologically senseless. At the other extreme, no less ardent typologists have been evolving an abundance of psychological ideas with little or no genuine evidence as to their truth" (Spearman, 1930–1936, Vol 2).

even be calculated to have a value that is higher than $+1$ or lower than -1, this because the assumptions underlying its use have been violated.

Point-biserial correlation A point-biserial r, denoted by r_{pbi}, is a correlation coefficient designed for use with a variable that is continuous in nature and another variable that is a true—not an arbitrary—dichotomy. Examples of true dichotomies are categorizations such as male/female, living/dead, and living in Buffalo/not living in Buffalo. Sometimes researchers may also use r_{pbi} with dichotomies that are not so well-defined and "true" as those we've listed. For example, correlations employing a point-biserial coefficient of correlation wherein the dichotomous category was one like "drug abuser/non−drug abuser" or "normal color vision/color blind" have appeared in the research literature. The rule appears to be that if the dichotomy is "reasonably discontinuous," r_{pbi} is appropriate. An advantage r_{pbi} has over r_b is that its use does not carry with it the requirement that the distribution of the dichotomous variable be normal.

Tetrachoric correlation Denoted by the symbol r_t, the tetrachoric r is used when the two variables to be correlated have each been arbitrarily reduced to a dichotomy. Two assumptions underlying the use of r_t are that the X and Y variables be linearly related and each of their respective distributions be normally distributed. Many statisticians would add that a tetrachoric coefficient of correlation should be used only with large samples ($N = 300$ or more) if its accuracy is to be relied on.

The phi coefficient A coefficient of correlation designed for use with variables that are true dichotomies is the phi coefficient, denoted by the Greek letter phi (ϕ). As we will see in the section of Chapter 7 entitled Item Analysis, the phi

Table 4–1

Summary of Correlation Coefficient Types

Correlation coefficient	Conditions for appropriate use
Pearson r	both variables are continuous and linearly related
Spearman rho	small sample size
	measurements are ordinal or rank-order
Biserial (r_b)	variables are continuous but one has been dichotomized (the other must be unimodal and symmetrical)
	dichotomized variable must be based on a normal distribution
	linear relationship between variables
Point-biserial (r_{pbi})	one variable that is continuous and one variable that is a true dichotomy
Tetrachoric (r_t)	both variables have been arbitrarily reduced to a dichotomy
	original distributions must be linearly related and normally distributed
Phi (ϕ)	both variables are true dichotomies

coefficient—as well as other correlation coefficients—has special application in studying the degree to which a test item correctly distinguishes between groups of examinees with respect to what the test purports to measure.

Graphic Representations of Correlation

One type of graphic description of correlation is called a *scatterplot* or *scatter diagram*. A scatterplot is a simple graphing of the coordinate points for values of the *X* variable (placed along the graph's horizontal axis) and the *Y* variable (placed along the graph's vertical axis). Scatterplots are useful because they provide a quick indication of the direction and magnitude of the relationship, if any, between the two variables. Figures 4–4 and 4–5 offer a quick course in "eyeballing" the nature and degree of correlation by means of scatterplots. In distinguishing positive from negative correlations, note the direction of the curve. And in estimating the strength of magnitude of the correlation, note the degree to which the coordinate values form a straight line.

Scatterplots are useful in revealing the presence of curvilinearity in a relationship. Remember that a Pearson *r* should only be used if the relationship between the variables is linear; if the graph does not appear to take the form of a straight line, the chances are good that the relationship is not linear (see Figure 4–6). When the relationship is nonlinear, other statistical tools and techniques may be employed.[6] If even after graphing the data a question remains concerning the linearity of the correlation, a statistic called *eta squared* (η^2) can be used to compute the exact degree of curvilinearity.

A graph also makes the spotting of scores relatively easy. An *outlier* is an extremely atypical point located at a relatively long distance—an "outlying" distance—from the rest of the coordinate points in a scatterplot (Figure 4–7). Outliers stimulate interpreters of test data to speculate about the reason for the atypical score. For example, the professor interpreting midterm examination data correlated with study time might wonder about Curly's performance on the test; Curly studied for ten hours and achieved a score of only 57. Was this "outlier" due to some situational emotional strain? Poor learning skills or study habits? Or was it simply reflective of using a very small sample? If the sample size were larger, perhaps more low-scorers who put in large amounts of study time would have been identified. Sometimes an outlier can provide a hint regarding some deficiency in the testing or scoring procedures.

Before leaving the subject of graphic representations of correlation, we should point out that the interpreter of such data needs to know, among other things, if the range of scores has been restricted in any way. To understand why this is the case, look at Figure 4–8. Let's say that graph A describes the relationship between Public University entrance test scores for 600 applicants (all of whom were later admitted) and their grade-point averages at the end of the first

---

6. The specific statistic to be employed will depend at least in part on the suspected reason for the nonlinearity. For example, if it is believed that the nonlinearity is due to one distribution being highly skewed because of a poor measuring instrument, the skewed distribution may be statistically normalized and the result may be a correction of the curvilinearity.

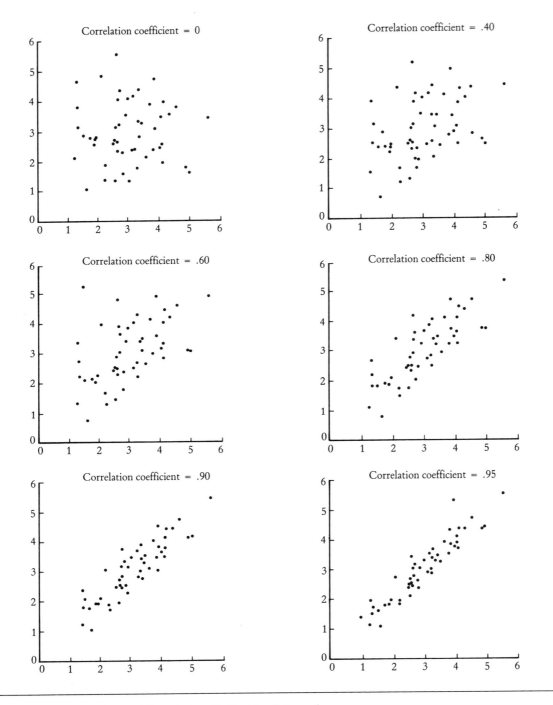

Figure 4–4 *Scatterplots and Correlations for Positive Values of* r.

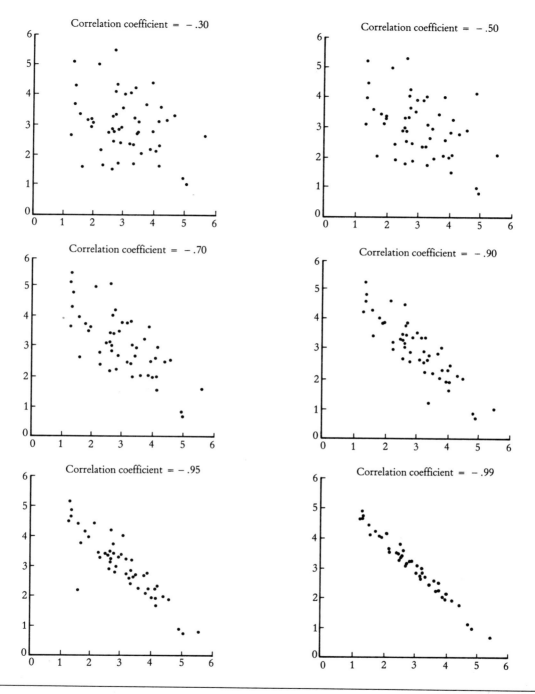

Figure 4–5 *Scatterplots and Correlations for Negative Values of* r.

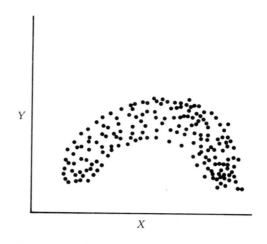

Figure 4-6 *A Scatterplot Showing a Nonlinear Correlation.*

semester. The scatterplot indicates that the relationship between entrance test scores and grade-point average is both linear and positive. But what if the admissions officer had accepted only the applications of the students who subsequently scored within the top 40 with respect to grade-point average? To a trained eye, this scatterplot (graph B) appears to indicate a correlation much less strong than that indicated in graph A—an effect attributable exclusively to the restriction of range.

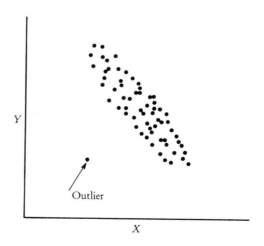

Figure 4-7 *Scatterplot Showing an Outlier.*

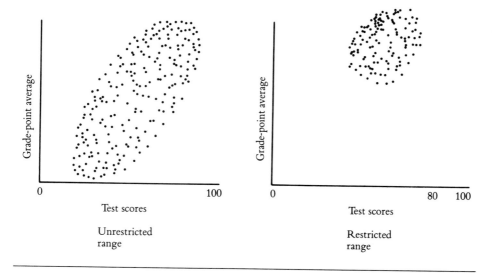

Figure 4–8   *Two Scatterplots Illustrating Unrestricted and Restricted Ranges.*

REGRESSION

In everyday language, the word "regression" is synonymous with "reversion to some previous state." In the language of statistics, "regression" is also a word that describes a kind of reversion—a reversion to the mean.

Defined broadly, *regression* is the analysis of relationships among variables. A *regression equation* contains one independent variable (X) and one dependent variable (Y). An equation that contains more than one independent variable is a *multiple regression equation* (briefly discussed later). If you create a scatterplot of linearly related variables, the *regression line* is the "line of best fit"—the graphic representation of an ongoing mean of the points in the scatterplot. The regression line is not only the "line of best fit," but it also might be called the "line of best prediction"; from this line, predictions can be made concerning what value of X will correspond to what value of Y (and vice versa). The primary use of a regression equation in testing is to predict one score or other variable when only one variable is known. The higher the correlation between the variables to begin with, the greater the accuracy—and the less the error—of prediction.

Does the following equation look familiar?

$$Y = a + bX$$

In high school algebra you were probably taught that this is the equation for a straight line. It's also the equation for a regression line. In the formula, a and b are *regression coefficients*; b is equal to the slope of the regression line, and a (also referred to as "the intercept") is a constant. The value of a and b can be determined from raw data by simple algebraic calculations. Other equations exist for calculating the line of best fit as well; but, regardless of the equation used, the line of best fit is the line fitted to the points in the scatterplot such that the sum of the squared vertical distances of the points from the line will be smaller than for any other straight line drawn through the points. The following equation for a regression line tells you that for each whole unit X changes, the predicted value of Y (or $\hat{Y}$— pronounced "Y hat") changes only one-half of a unit:

$$\hat{Y} = 0 + .5X$$

The corresponding value of Y for a given value of X can also be estimated graphically as illustrated in Figure 4–9. A line is drawn from the appropriate point on the horizontal axis (that is, the given X value) up to the regression line. Directly from the point where the drawn line meets the regression line, another line is drawn across to the Y-axis. The value of Y is equal to the value of Y at the point where this second line intersects the Y-axis. Because the regression line is a kind of mean, an index of deviation of points about that mean can be calculated, and that index is called a *standard error of estimate;* the margin of error inherent in the prediction can be estimated by the calculation of a standard error of estimate. As r increases, the standard error of estimate decreases.

Multiple regression   Suppose a dean at the "De Sade School of Dentistry" wished to predict what type of grade–point average an applicant might have after the first year at De Sade. The dean accumulated a wealth of data from prior years

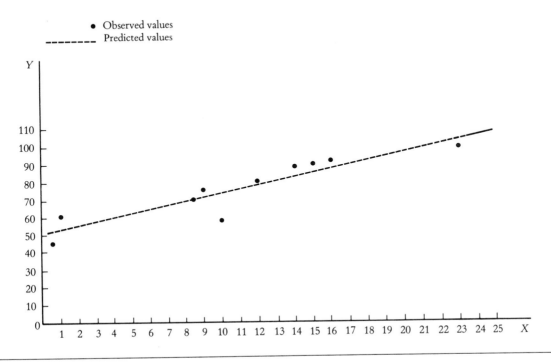

Figure 4–9   *Graphic Estimation of* **Y** *from* **X** *from a Regression Line.* The equation for this regression line is $Y = 50.12 + 1.613X$; for each unit increase in X, the predicted value of Y would increase by $1.613X$.

such as scores on college entrance examinations and end-of-first-year grade-point average. The dean attempted to solve the prediction problem with a regression equation where X equalled the score on a dental college admissions test and Y equalled the grade-point average at the end of the first year of dental school. But suppose that, after trying that regression formula, the dean suspects that prediction will be enhanced if another test score—say, a score on a test of fine motor skills—is also used as a predictor of dental school success. Such a use of more than one score to predict to some criterion score would necessitate the use of a *multiple regression* equation.

The presentation and discussion of multiple regression equations is not necessary for our purposes (and they are available to the interested reader in almost any psychological statistics text). What is important conceptually is that the multiple regression equation takes into account two things: (1) the correlation between the two or more scores and the criterion and (2) the intercorrelation between the two scores themselves (in this case, the correlation between dental college admissions test scores and scores on the test used to measure fine motor skills). The better a score from a given test (or other measure such as grade-point average) correlates with the criterion, the more weight that score is given in the multiple regression equation. When a number of test scores are being used to predict a criterion, it may in some instances also be useful to weight more heavily scores from those tests that are known to have little correlation with other predictor measurements, yet high correlation with the criterion.

In using the technique of multiple regression, it is not necessarily true that the more predictors you use, the greater the prediction accuracy. In our example, if the De Sade dean observed that the two predictor variables (dental school admission test scores and scores on the test of fine motor skills) were highly correlated with each other and that each of these scores correlated about the same with the criterion, the dean might revert to using only one predictor since nothing was gained by the addition of the second predictor.

In the remainder of Part 2, we build on your knowledge of correlation and regression as we see how these statistical techniques are integrally involved in the computation of coefficients of reliability and validity as well as methods of test development and item analysis.

Chapter 5

Reliability

IN EVERYDAY CONVERSATION, "reliability" is a synonym for dependability or consistency—as in "the reliable train that you can set your watch by" or "the reliable friend who is always there if you are in need." In the language of statistics, *reliability* refers, broadly speaking, to the attribute of consistency in measurement (though we will see shortly that there are various types of reliability). And whereas in everyday conversation "reliability" always connotes something that is positively valued, "reliability" in the strict statistical sense merely connotes something that is consistent—not necessarily consistently good or bad, but simply consistent.

It is important for us as users of tests and consumers of information about tests to know how reliable tests and other measurement procedures are. But reliability is seldom an all-or-none matter; there are degrees of reliability and ways of measuring those degrees. A *reliability coefficient* is an index of reliability. More technically, it is a proportion that indicates the ratio between the "true" score on a test and the total variance. In this chapter, we explore different kinds of reliability coefficients, including those for measuring "test-retest reliability," "alternate-form reliability," "split-half reliability," and "inter-scorer reliability." We begin with a more detailed look at the concept of reliability in general.

THE CONCEPT OF RELIABILITY

To better understand a concept related to the consistency of a measuring instrument, let's begin by asking why test scores vary. We know from our discussion of the "true score model" in Chapter 3 that a test score on a test of ability may vary because of (1) the "true" ability of the test taker or (2) other factors ranging from unwanted influences on the test situation (such as noise from a construction site outside) to chance.[1] If we use X to represent an observed score, E to represent an error score (a score due to random, irrelevant influences on the test—anything except what the test is measuring), and T to represent a true score (part of the observed score not affected by error), then the observed score equals the true score plus the error score, or

$$X = T + E$$

A statistic useful in describing sources of test score variability is the variance (σ^2)—the standard deviation squared. This statistic is useful because it can be broken into components. Variance from true differences is called *true variance,* and variance from irrelevant, random sources is called *error variance.* If σ^2 represents the total variance, σ_{tr}^2 represents the true variance, and σ_e^2 represents error variance, then the relationship of the variances can be expressed as

$$\sigma^2 = \sigma_{tr}^2 + \sigma_e^2$$

In this equation, the total variance in an observed distribution of test scores (σ^2) equals the sum of the true variance (σ_{tr}^2) plus the error variance (σ_e^2). The term *reliability* refers to the proportion of the total variance attributed to true variance. The greater the proportion of the total variance attributed to true variance, the more reliable the test. Since true differences are assumed to be stable, they are presumed to yield consistent scores on repeated administrations of the same test (as well as on equivalent forms of tests and equivalent halves of tests). Because error variance may increase or decrease a test score by varying amounts, consistency of the test score—and thus the reliability—would be affected. Note that a systematic source of error would *not* affect score consistency. If a measuring instrument, such as a weight scale, consistently underweighed everyone who stepped on it by five pounds, then the relative standings of the people would remain unchanged (even though the weights themselves would consistently vary from the true weight by five pounds). A scale underweighing all comers by five pounds is analogous to a constant being subtracted from (or added to) every test score. It is a systematic error source that does not change the variability of the distribution nor affect reliability.

---

1. For illustration purposes, tests of ability are frequently used. However, it must be understood that unless stated otherwise, the principles to which we refer with respect to ability tests also hold true with respect to other types of tests such as tests for personality. Thus, according to the true score model, it is also true that the magnitude of the presence of a certain psychological trait (such as extraversion) as measured by testing with a test of extraversion will be due to (1) the "true" amount of extraversion and (2) other factors.

Sources of Error Variance

As we have intimated, error variance is everything in addition to true variance that makes up a test score. Error variance can come "from anywhere," but in the following discussion we limit our focus to sources of error variance during the development of a test and selection of items, test administration, and test scoring and interpretation.

Test construction   One source of variance during test construction is called *item sampling* or *content sampling*, a term that refers to variation among items within a test, as well as to variation among items between tests. Consider two or more tests designed to measure almost anything (such as knowledge, skill, or personality attributes); although there may be some overlap, differences in the way the items are worded and differences in the exact content sampled are sure to be found. Each of us has probably walked into an achievement test setting, thinking "I hope they ask this question" or "I hope they don't ask that question." With luck, only the questions we wanted to be asked appeared on the examination. In such situations some test takers achieve higher scores on one test than they would on another test purporting to measure the same thing, simply because of the specific content sampled on the first test, the way the items were worded, and so on. The extent to which a test taker's score is affected solely by the content sampled on the test as well as the way the content is sampled (the way in which the item is constructed) is a source of error variance. With reference to what is referred to as the domain sampling model (discussed later in this chapter), Nunnally (1978) reminds us to be particularly careful in examining the assumptions we make when we consider error variance inherent in the administration of two alternative forms of a test:

> The model envisions an actual sampling of items from a hypothetical domain, but in practice items are composed rather than drawn from a hat. For example, two spelling tests independently composed by two persons might emphasize different kinds of words. Then the correlation between the two tests might be less than would be predicted from the average correlation among the items within each test. Similarly, alternative forms of a measure of attitudes toward the United Nations might be systematically different in content, and consequently the correlation between the two forms would be less than that predicted by the domain-sampling model. (p. 228)

We have more to say about technical aspects of item selection with respect to test construction in Chapter 7.

Test administration   Sources of error variance that occur during test administration may influence the test taker's attention or motivation; thus, the test taker's reactions to these influences are the source of one kind of error variance. Examples of untoward influences operative during administration of a test include factors related to the test environment: the room temperature, the level of lighting, and the amount of ventilation and noise, for instance. A relentless fly may develop a tenacious attraction to an examinee's face. A wad of gum on the seat of the chair makes itself known only after the test taker sits down on it; the list goes on. Other environment-related variables include the instrument used to enter responses (such as a pencil with a broken point or a pen that has dried up) and the writing surface (which may be riddled with hearts carved into it—the legacy of past years' students who felt compelled to express their lifelong devotion to someone whom they by now have probably long forgotten).

Other potential sources of error variance during test administration include test-taker variables such as degree of physical discomfort, amount of sleep the night before, the degree of test anxiety present, the extent of pressing emotional problems, or the effects of drugs. A test taker may, for whatever reason, make a mistake in entering a test response. For example, the examinee may blacken a "b" grid when the blackening of the "d" grid had been intended. An examinee might read a test question such as "Which is not a factor that prevents measurements from being exactly replicable?" and mistakenly read, "Which is a factor that prevents measurements from being exactly replicable?" One carelessly skipped question on a long list of multiple-choice grid-type questions could result in subsequent test responses being "out of sync"; thus, for example, the test taker might respond to the eighteenth item but blacken the grid for the seventeenth item—this because the twelfth item was inadvertently skipped. With respect to the administration of alternate forms of a test, formal learning experiences, casual life experiences, therapy, illness, and other such events that may have occurred in the period intervening between test administration may also be sources of examinee-related error variance.

Examiner-related variables that are potential sources of error variance include the presence or absence of an examiner, the examiner's physical appearance and demeanor, and the professionalism the examiner brings to the test situation. Some examiners in some testing situations may knowingly or unwittingly depart from the procedure prescribed for a particular test. On an oral examination, some examiners might unwittingly provide clues by posing questions that emphasize various words, or they may unwittingly convey feedback concerning the correctness of a response through behavior such as throat clearing, eye movements, or facial expressions.

Test scoring and interpretation   The advent of computer scoring and the burgeoning reliance on objective, computer-scorable items, has virtually eliminated error variance due to scorer differences in many tests, ranging from standardized college entrance examinations to classroom quizzes. However, not all tests can be scored from grids blackened by number 2 pencils. Individually administered intelligence tests, some tests of personality, tests of creativity, various behavioral measures, and countless other tests still require hand scoring by someone well trained in testing. Manuals for individual intelligence tests tend to be very explicit about scoring criteria lest examinees' IQs vary as a function of who is doing the testing and scoring. In some tests of personality, examinees are asked to supply open-ended responses to stimuli such as pictures, words, sentences, and inkblots, and it is the examiner who must then "score" (or perhaps more appropriately, "assess") the responses. In one test of creativity, examinees might be given the task of creating as many things as they can out of a set of blocks. For a behavioral measure of social skills in an inpatient psychiatric service, the scorers or raters might be asked to rate patients with respect to the variable of "social-relatedness." Such a behavioral measure might require the rater to check "Yes" or "No" to items like "Patient says 'Good morning' to at least two staff members."

You can appreciate that, as soon as a psychological test uses anything but objective-type items amenable to reliable computer scoring, the scorer or scoring system becomes a source of error variance. To state this another way: if there is judgment involved in scoring, the scorer (or rater) can be a source of error variance. Indeed, despite very rigorous scoring criteria set forth in many of the better-known tests of intelligence, examiner/scorers will occasionally still be confronted by situations where an examinee's response lies in a "gray area." The element of subjectivity in scoring may be present to a much greater degree in the administration of certain non-objective-type personality tests and certain academic tests (such as essay examinations) and even in behavioral observation. Consider the case of two observers given the task of rating one psychiatric inpatient on the variable of social-relatedness. On an item that asks simply whether two staff members were greeted in the morning, one rater might judge the patient's eye contact and mumbling of something to two staff members to qualify as a "Yes" response, while another observer might feel strongly that a "No" response to the item is appropriate. Such problems in scoring agreement can be addressed through rigorous training designed to make the consistency—or reliability—of various scorers as near perfect as can be.

Given the numerous and varied sources of error inherent in a testing situation, there is good news and bad news. The bad news is that even with the greatest minds and the highest-speed computers, we will never be able to know what the "true" value of a given reliability coefficient is.[2] The good news is that we have ways of estimating the value of reliability coefficients. We now discuss four kinds of reliability estimates: test-retest reliability estimates, parallel-forms (and alternate-forms) reliability estimates, split-half reliability estimates, and inter-scorer reliability estimates.

TYPES OF RELIABILITY ESTIMATES

Test-Retest Reliability Estimates

A ruler made from the highest quality steel can be a very reliable instrument of measurement; every time you measure something that is exactly 12 inches in length, for example, your ruler will tell you that what you are measuring is exactly 12 inches in length. The reliability of this instrument of measurement may also be said to be stable over time; whether you measure the 12 inches today, tomorrow, or next year, the ruler is still going to measure 12 inches as 12 inches. By contrast, a ruler constructed of putty might be a very unreliable instrument of measurement. One minute it could measure some known 12-inch standard as 12 inches, the next minute it could measure it as 14 inches, and a week later it could

---

2. In this context, Stanley's (1971) caution that a *true score* is "not the ultimate fact in the book of the recording angel" (p. 361) seems relevant.

measure it as 18 inches. One way of estimating the reliability of a measuring instrument is by using the same instrument to measure the same thing at two points in time. In the language of psychological testing, this approach to reliability evaluation is called the "test-retest method" and the result of such an evaluation is an estimate of "test-retest reliability."

Test-retest reliability is an estimate of reliability obtained by correlating pairs of scores from the same person (or people) on two different administrations of the same test. The test-retest measure is appropriate when evaluating the reliability of a test that purports to measure something that is relatively stable over time (such as a personality trait presumed to manifest itself consistently over time). If the characteristic being measured is assumed to fluctuate over time, there would be little sense in assessing the reliability of the test using the test-retest method; insignificant correlations between scores obtained on the two administrations of the test would be found and this insignificance would be due to real changes in whatever is being measured (rather than to factors inherent in the measuring instrument).

As time passes, people change; they may learn new things, they may forget some things, they may acquire new skills, they may lose some skills, and so on. In this context, it is generally the case—though there are exceptions—that as the time interval between administrations of the same test increases, the correlation between the scores obtained on each testing decreases (see Table 5–1). To state

Table 5–1

Test-Retest Reliability and the Passage of Time

Test-retest reliability tends to decrease as the test-retest interval of time increases. As an example, consider the average test-retest reliabilities reported in the manual for the California Occupational System. With a one-week interval between test administrations, the median coefficient of reliability was equal to .88. With a one-year interval, the median coefficient of reliability dropped to .66. Below, coefficients of reliability for individual subtests are presented for intervals of one week and one year.

	One-week interval (n = 113)	One-year interval (n = 182)
Science (professional)	.90	.61
Science (skilled)	.84	.52
Technical (professional)	.91	.76
Technical (skilled)	.87	.69
Outdoor	.89	.66
Business (professional)	.89	.63
Business (skilled)	.85	.53
Clerical	.81	.62
Linguistic (professional)	.89	.69
Linguistic (skilled)	.86	.62
Aesthetic (professional)	.88	.74
Aesthetic (skilled)	.91	.76
Service (professional)	.89	.72
Service (skilled)	.84	.66
Median reliability	.88	.66

this another way: the passage of time can be a source of error variance; the longer the time that passes, the more likely the reliability coefficient will be lower. When the interval between testing is greater than six months, the estimate of test-retest reliability is often referred to as the *coefficient of stability*. An estimate of test-retest reliability from a math test might be low if the test takers took a math tutorial before the second test was administered. An estimate of test-retest reliability from a personality profile might be low if the test taker either suffered some emotional trauma or received counseling during the intervening period. A low estimate of test-retest reliability may be found even when the interval between testings is relatively brief—this if the tests happen to be conducted during a time of great developmental change with respect to the variables the test was designed to assess. An evaluation of a test-retest reliability coefficient must therefore extend beyond the significance of the obtained coefficient; it must extend to a consideration of possible intervening factors between test administrations (such as, Was this child given a math tutorial? Did this person suffer great trauma?) if proper conclusions about the reliability of the measuring instrument are to be made.

An estimate of test-retest reliability may be most appropriate in gauging the reliability of tests that employ as outcome measures reaction time or perceptual judgments (such as discriminations of brightness, loudness, or taste). However, even in measuring variables such as these and even when the time period between the two administrations of the test is relatively small, note that various factors (like experience, practice, memory, fatigue, and motivation) may be operative and render confounded an obtained measure of reliability.

Before considering other forms of reliability, let us emphasize that measurement is a process—in some cases, a most dynamic process—not a tangible entity. Thus, although we may make reference to a number as the summary statement of the reliability of individual tools of measurement, any such index of reliability can only meaningfully be interpreted in the context of the process of measurement—the unique circumstances surrounding the use of the ruler, test, or other measuring instrument in a particular application or situation.

Parallel-Forms and Alternate-Forms Reliability Estimates

If you have ever taken a makeup examination in which the questions on the makeup were not all the same as on the test initially given, you have had experience with different forms of a test. And if you have ever wondered whether the two forms of the test were really equivalent, you have wondered about the *alternate-forms* reliability of the test. The degree of the relationship between various forms of a test can be evaluated by means of an *alternate-forms* or *parallel-forms* coefficient of reliability, which is often referred to as the *coefficient of equivalence*.

"Alternate" forms and "parallel" forms are terms sometimes used interchangeably, though there is a technical difference between them (see Allen & Yen, 1979). *Parallel forms* of a test exist when for each form of the test, the means and variances of observed test scores are equal. In theory, the means of scores obtained on parallel forms correlate equally with the "true score." More practically, scores obtained on parallel tests correlate equally with other measures. *Alternate forms* are simply different versions of a test that have been constructed so as to be parallel. Although they do not meet the requirements for the legitimate designation of "parallel," alternate forms of a test are typically designed to be equivalent with respect to variables such as content and level of difficulty.

Estimates of alternate- and parallel-forms reliability are similar to an estimate of test-retest reliability in two ways: (1) two test administrations with the same group are required and (2) test scores may be affected by factors such as motivation, fatigue, or intervening events like practice, learning, or therapy. However, an additional source of error variance—item sampling—is inherent in the computation of an alternate- or parallel-forms reliability coefficient; test takers may do better or worse on a specific form of the test, not as a function of their "true" ability, but simply because of the particular items that were selected for inclusion in the test.[3] Another potential disadvantage of an alternate test form is financial in nature; it is typically time-consuming and expensive to develop alternate or parallel test forms—just think of all that might be involved in getting the same people to sit for repeated administrations of an experimental test! A primary advantage of using an alternate or parallel form of a test is that the effect of memory for the content of a previously administered form of the test is minimized.

Certain traits are presumed to be relatively stable in people over time, and we would expect tests measuring those traits—alternate forms, parallel forms, or otherwise—to reflect that stability. As Nunnally (1978, p. 235) put it, "If a measure is intended to represent the *relatively enduring* status of a trait in people, it would need to remain stable over the period in which scores were employed for that purpose" (emphasis in the original). As an example, we expect that there will be—and in fact there is—a reasonable degree of stability in scores on intelligence tests. Conversely, we might expect there to be relatively little stability in scores obtained on a measure of state or current level of anxiety; the level of anxiety experienced by the test taker could be expected to vary from hour to hour—let alone day to day, week to week, or month to month. In discussing temporal stability of test scores, Nunnally (1978) addressed a concern of critics:

> Some have accused measurement specialists of assuming that psychological traits remain largely stable throughout life and, thus, that very little can be done to improve people. Such a philosophy is not at all necessary for the theory of measurement error. The theory would hold as well if people changed markedly in their characteristics from day to day; but if that occurred, it would make chaos out of efforts to formulate practical decisions about people and to find general principles of human behavior. People do change, but in most traits they change slowly enough to allow valid uses of psychological measures in daily life and in research investigations. (pp. 235–236)

An estimate of the reliability of a test can be obtained without developing an alternate form of the test and without having to administer the test twice to the same people; such an assessment entails the scrutiny of the individual items that make up the test and their relation to each other. Because this type of reliability estimate is obtained not through comparison with data from an alternate form

---

3. According to the classical true score model, the effect of such factors on test scores are indeed presumed to be measurement error. There are alternative models in which the effect of such factors on fluctuating test scores would not be considered error (Atkinson, 1981).

and not through a test-retest procedure but rather through an examination of the items of the test, it is referred to as an "internal-consistency" estimate of reliability or as an estimate of "inter-item consistency." Our focus now shifts to such types of reliability estimates, beginning with the "split-half" estimate.

Split-Half Reliability Estimates

An estimate of *split-half reliability* is obtained by correlating two pairs of scores obtained from equivalent halves of a single test administered once. It is a useful measure of reliability when it is impractical or undesirable to assess reliability with two tests or to have two test administrations (due to factors such as time or expense). The computation of a coefficient of split-half reliability generally entails three steps, each listed below and then explained further:

Step 1. Divide the test into equivalent halves.
Step 2. Compute a Pearson *r* between scores on the two halves of the test.
Step 3. Adjust the half-test reliability using the Spearman-Brown formula.

You may have heard the saying that "there's more than one way to skin a cat." A corollary to that bit of wisdom could be that "there are some ways you should never skin a cat." An analogous bit of wisdom when it comes to calculating split-half reliability coefficients is: "there's more than one way to split a test," or "there are some ways you should never split a test." Simply dividing the test in half is not recommended, since this procedure would probably spuriously raise or lower the reliability coefficient (because of factors such as differential fatigue for the first versus the second part of test, differential amounts of test anxiety operative, and differences in item difficulty as a function of placement in the test).[4] One acceptable way to split a test is to randomly assign items to one or the other half of the test. A second acceptable way is to assign odd-numbered items to one half of the test and even-numbered items to the other half (yielding an estimate that is also referred to as "odd-even reliability").[5] A third way is to divide the test by content so that each half of the test contains items equivalent with respect to content and difficulty. In general, a primary objective in splitting a test in half for the purpose of obtaining a split-half reliability estimate is to create what might be termed "mini-parallel-forms," with each half equal to the other—or as equal as humanly possible—in format, stylistic, statistical, and related aspects.

Step 2 in the procedure entails the computation of a Pearson *r,* which requires little explanation at this point. However, the third step requires the use of the Spearman-Brown formula, which we discuss in the following section.

---

4. A trusted colleague and reviewer of this book, Louis H. Primavera, informs us that in one widely used computer analysis program (SPSS-X), a split-half reliability coefficient is calculated by correlating the total from the first half of the items with that of the second half of the items. Primavera has contacted the developers of the program about this matter.
5. One precaution here: with respect to a group of items on an achievement test that deals with a single problem, it is usually desirable to assign the whole group of items to one half of the test. Otherwise—if part of the group were in one half and another part in the other half—the similarity of the half scores would be spuriously inflated; a single error in understanding, for example, might affect items in both halves of the test.

The Spearman-Brown formula   Use of the Spearman-Brown formula to estimate internal consistency reliability from a correlation of two halves of a test is a specific application of a more general formula that allows a test developer or user to estimate the reliability of a test that is lengthened or shortened by any number of items. Because the reliability of a test is affected by its length, a formula is necessary for estimating the reliability of a test that has been shortened or lengthened. The general Spearman-Brown (r_{SB}) formula is:

$$r_{SB} = \frac{nr_{xy}}{1 + (n - 1)r_{xy}}$$

where r_{SB} is equal to the reliability adjusted by the Spearman-Brown formula, r_{xy} is equal to the Pearson r in the original-length test, and n is equal to the number of items in the revised version divided by the number of items in the original version.

By determining the reliability of one-half of a test, a test developer can then use the Spearman-Brown formula to estimate the reliability of a whole test. Because a whole test is two times longer than half the test, n becomes 2 in the Spearman-Brown formula for the adjustment of split-half reliability. The symbol r_{hh} stands for the Pearson r of scores in the two half tests:

$$r_{SB} = \frac{2r_{hh}}{1 + r_{hh}}$$

It is generally—though definitely not always—true that reliability increases as test length increases, providing that the additional items are equivalent with respect to the content and the range of difficulty of the original items. Estimates of reliability based on consideration of the entire test will therefore tend to be higher than those based on half of a test. Table 5–2 shows half-test correlations presented alongside adjusted reliability estimates for the whole test. You can see that all of the adjusted correlations are higher than the unadjusted correlations— this because Spearman-Brown estimates are based on a test that is twice as long as the original half-test. If we were to calculate the Spearman-Brown adjustment using the data from the kindergarten pupils, we would learn that a half-test reliability of .718 can be estimated to be equivalent to a whole-test reliability of .836.

Table 5–2

Odd-Even Reliability Coefficients before
and after the Spearman-Brown Adjustment*

Grade	Half-test correlation (unadjusted r)	Whole-test estimate
K	.718	.836
1	.807	.893
2	.777	.875

*for scores on a test of mental ability

If test developers or users wish to shorten a test, the Spearman-Brown formula may be used to estimate the effect of the shortening on the test's reliability. Reduction in test size for the purpose of reducing test administration time is a common practice in situations where the test administrator may have only limited time with the test taker (such as a consumer research situation) or in situations where boredom or fatigue could produce responses of questionable meaningfulness.

A Spearman-Brown formula could also be used to determine the number of items needed in order to attain a desired level of reliability. In adding items to increase test reliability to a desired level, the rule is that the new items must be equivalent in terms of content and difficulty so that the longer test still measures what the original test measured. If the reliability of the original test is relatively low, it may be impractical to increase the number of items to reach an acceptable level of reliability. Another alternative would be to abandon this relatively unreliable instrument and locate—or develop—a suitable alternative. It also might be a possibility that the reliability of the instrument could be raised in some way (for example, by creating new items, clarifying the test's instructions, or simplifying the scoring rules).

Internal-consistency estimates of reliability, such as that obtained by use of the Spearman-Brown formula, are inappropriate for measuing the reliability of heterogeneous tests and speed tests—the internal consistency of such tests will tend to appear lower by assessment with other measures.

Other Methods of Estimating Internal Consistency

In addition to the Spearman-Brown formula, other methods in wide use to estimate internal consistency reliability include formulas developed by Kuder and Richardson (1937) and Cronbach (1951). *Inter-item consistency* is a term that refers to the degree of correlation between all of the items on a scale; it is an internal reliability measure based on response consistency to individual test items. A measure of inter-item consistency is calculated from a single administration of a single form of a test. An index of inter-item consistency is, in turn, useful in assessing the *homogeneity* of the test. Tests are said to be *homogeneous* if they contain items that measure a single trait. As an adjective used to describe test items, *homogeneity* (derived from the Greek words *homos* meaning "same" and *genous* meaning "kind") refers to the degree to which a test measures a single factor or, stated another way, the extent to which items in a scale are unifactorial.

In contrast to test homogeneity is the concept of test *heterogeneity,* a term that refers to the degree to which a test measures different factors. A *nonhomogeneous* or *heterogeneous* test is composed of items that measure more than one trait. A test that assesses knowledge of only color television repair skills could be expected to be more homogeneous in content than a test of electronic repair; the former test assesses only one area and the latter assesses several, such as knowledge not only of television but also of radios, typewriters, videorecorders, compact disc players, and so forth. The more homogeneous a test is, the more it will have inter-item consistency; since the test would be sampling a relatively narrow content area, it would contain more inter-item consistency. A person who is skilled in color television repair might be somewhat familiar with the repair of other electronic devices such as radios and televisions, but would probably know virtually nothing about videorecorders or compact disc players. Thus there would be less inter-item consistency in this test of general repair ability than in a test designed to assess only color television repair knowledge and skills.

Test homogeneity is desirable because it allows relatively straightforward test-score interpretation. Test takers with the same score on a homogeneous test probably have similar abilities in the area tested. Test takers with the same score on a more heterogeneous test may have quite different abilities. But although a homogeneous test is desirable because it so readily lends itself to clear interpretation, it is often an insufficient tool for measuring multifaceted variables of the psychological variety (such as intelligence or personality). One way to circumvent this potential source of difficulty has been to administer a series of homogeneous tests, each designed to measure some component of a heterogeneous variable.[6] In addition to some of the random influences that can affect reliability measures, error variance in a measure of inter-item consistency comes from two sources: (1) item sampling and (2) the heterogeneity of the content area. The more heterogeneous the content area sampled, then the lower will be the inter-item consistency.

The Kuder-Richardson formulas Dissatisfaction with existing split-half methods of estimating reliability compelled G. Frederic Kuder and M. W. Richardson (1937; Richardson & Kuder, 1939) to develop their own measures for estimating reliability. The most widely known of the many formulas they collaborated on is their Kuder-Richardson formula 20 or "KR-20" (so named because it was the twentieth formula developed in a series). In the instance where test items are highly homogeneous, KR-20 and split-half reliability estimates will be similar. However, KR-20 is the statistic of choice for determining the inter-item consistency of dichotomous items, primarily those items that can be scored right or wrong (such as multiple-choice items). If test items are more heterogeneous, KR-20 will yield lower reliability estimates than the split-half method. Table 5–3 shows items on a heterogeneous test.

Now, only if you've taken a careful look at Table 5–3, and with absolutely no other information, answer this question: Assuming the difficulty level of all the items on the test to be about the same, would you expect a split-half (odd-even) estimate of reliability to be fairly high or low? How might you suspect the KR-20 reliability estimate to compare to the odd-even estimate of reliability—would it be higher or lower?

We might guess that since the content areas sampled for the 18 items from this "Hypothetical Electronics Repair Test" are ordered in a manner whereby odd and even items tap the same content area, the odd-even reliability estimate will probably be quite high. With respect to a reasonable guess concerning the KR-20 reliability estimate, due to the great heterogeneity of content areas when taken as a whole, it could reasonably be predicted that the KR-20 estimate of reliability will be lower than the odd-even one. Look now at the data in Table 5–4. If the

---

6. As we will see in Chapter 15 (as well as in the other chapters of Part 5), it is seldom that important decisions are made on the basis of one test only. Psychologists frequently rely on what is called a *test battery*—a selected assortment of tests and assessment procedures (such as an interview) in the process of evaluation. A test battery may or may not be composed of homogeneous tests.

variance of the number of correct items (σ^2) is equal to 5.26, and $\Sigma\, pq$ is equal to 3,975, then KR-20 is equal to what? The following formula may be used:

$$r_{\text{kr}20} = \left(\frac{k}{k-1}\right)\left(1 - \frac{\Sigma\, pq}{\sigma^2}\right)$$

where $r_{\text{kr}20}$ stands for the Kuder-Richardson formula 20 reliability coefficient, k is the number of test items, σ^2 is the variance of total test scores, p is the proportion of test takers who pass the item, q is the proportion of people who fail the item, and $\Sigma\, pq$ is the sum of the pq products over all items.

An approximation of KR-20 can be obtained by the use of the twenty-first formula in the series developed by Kuder and Richardson, a formula known—you guessed it—as "KR-21." KR-21 may be used if there is reason to believe that all of the test items have approximately the same degree of difficulty—an assumption, we should add, that is seldom justified. Formula KR-21 tends to be outdated in an era of calculators and computers since it was used as an approximation of KR-20 that required less computation. Another formula once used in the measurement of internal-consistency reliability and now for the most part outdated was a statistic you may see referred to in some texts as the Rulon formula (Rulon, 1939).

Though numerous modifications of Kuder-Richardson formulas have been proposed through the years (for example, Horst, 1953; Cliff, 1984), perhaps the one variant of the KR-20 formula that has received the most acceptance to date is a statistic called "coefficient alpha," sometimes referred to as *coefficient α-20* (α being the Greek letter *alpha* and "20" referring to KR-20).

Table 5–3	
Content Areas Sampled for 18 Items of the "Hypothetical Electronics Repair Test" (HERT)	
Item number	Content area
1	Color television
2	Color television
3	Black and white television
4	Black and white television
5	Radio
6	Radio
7	Videorecorder
8	Videorecorder
9	Typewriter
10	Typewriter
11	Compact disc
12	Compact disc
13	Stereo receiver
14	Stereo receiver
15	Turntable
16	Turntable
17	Microwave
18	Microwave

Table 5–4	
"HERT" Scores for 20 Test Takers	
Item number	Number of test takers correct
1	14
2	12
3	9
4	18
5	8
6	5
7	6
8	9
9	10
10	10
11	8
12	6
13	15
14	9
15	12
16	12
17	14
18	7

Coefficient alpha Developed by Cronbach (1951) and subsequently elaborated on by others (such as Novick & Lewis, 1967; Kaiser & Michael, 1975), *coefficient alpha* may be thought of as the mean of all possible—the "good" along with the "bad"—split-half correlations, corrected by the Spearman-Brown formula. As we have noted above, KR-20 is appropriately used on tests with dichotomous items. Coefficient alpha may also be used on tests with dichotomous items. Additionally, coefficient alpha is appropriate for use on tests containing non-dichotomous items: items that can individually be scored along a range of values. Examples of such tests include opinion and attitude polls, where a range of possible alternatives are presented; essay tests; and short-answer tests, where partial credit can be given. The formula for coefficient alpha is

$$r_\alpha = \left(\frac{k}{k-1}\right)\left(1 - \frac{\Sigma\, \sigma_i^2}{\sigma^2}\right)$$

where r_α is coefficient alpha, k is the number of items, σ_i^2 is the variance of one item, $\Sigma\, \sigma_i^2$ is the sum of variances of each item, and σ^2 is the variance of the total test scores. In the age of computers and programmable calculators, few of the people who would have occasion to calculate this statistic would undertake the rather laborious calculations by hand—and the number of people who would prefer "the old-fashioned way" could reasonably be presumed to dwindle as the number of items on the test rises. Today, perhaps because of the ready availability of computers (mainframe to laptop), coefficient alpha is the preferred statistic for obtaining an estimate of internal consistency reliability (Keith & Reynolds, 1990). In fact, it is the statistic that is calculated under the reliability program of the Statistical Package for the Social Sciences (SPSS-X), a set of statistical software that is widely used in academia.

Measures of Inter-Scorer Reliability

For many, if not all, situations in which we are in some way being evaluated, we usually would like to believe that no matter who is doing the evaluating, we would be evaluated in the same way.[7] For example, if the instructor of this course were to evaluate your knowledge of the subject matter by means of an essay test, you would like to think that the grade you would receive on the essay test would be the same whether it was graded by your professor or any other professor who teaches this course. If you take a road test for a driver's license, you would like to believe that whether you pass or fail is solely a matter of your performance behind the wheel and not a function of who is sitting in the passenger's seat. Unfortunately, in some types of tests under some conditions, the score is sometimes more a function of the scorer than anything else. This was demonstrated back in 1912 when researchers presented one pupil's English composition to a convention of teachers, and volunteers graded the papers—with grades that ranged from a low of 50% to a high of 98% (Starch & Elliott, 1912).

---

7. We say "usually" because exceptions in real-life situations do exist. Thus, for example, if you go on a job interview and the employer/interviewer is your father, you might reasonably expect that the nature of the evaluation you receive would *not* be the same were the evaluator to be someone else.

Variously referred to as "scorer reliability," "judge reliability," "observer reliability," and "inter-rater reliability," *inter-scorer reliability* refers to the degree of agreement or consistency that exists between two or more "scorers" (or "judges" or "raters"). Reference to levels of inter-scorer reliability for a particular test may be published (either in the test's manual or elsewhere) and if the reliability coefficient is very high, the prospective test user knows that with sufficient training, test scores can be derived in a systematic, consistent way by various scorers. A responsible test developer who is unable to create a test that can be scored with a reasonable degree of consistency by trained scorers will go "back to the drawing board" to discover the reason for this problem (such as lack of clarity in scoring criteria) and then remedy it (for example, by rewriting the scoring criteria section of the manual to include clearly written scoring rules along with specific examples). One review of the literature on training raters to make performance ratings suggests that lectures to raters on scoring rules are not as effective in promoting inter-rater consistency as is providing raters with the opportunity for group discussion along with practice exercises and feedback (Smith, 1986). Perhaps the simplest way of determining the degree of consistency that exists between scorers in the scoring of a test is to calculate a coefficient of correlation (which would in this instance be synonymous with a coefficient of inter-scorer reliability). Assuming, for example, that a 30-item test of reaction time was administered to one subject and scored by two scorers, the inter-scorer reliability would be equal to the value of the Spearman-Brown corrected correlation coefficient obtained with respect to 30 pairs of scores. If the reliability coefficient were found to be, say, .90, this would mean that 90% of the variance in the scores assigned by the raters stemmed from true differences in the subject's reaction time while 10% could be attributed to factors other than the subject's reaction time (that is, error). In many cases, more than two scorers are used in such reliability studies—sometimes as many as a dozen may be used. In such instances, scorers are treated as items, and coefficient alpha is the statistic that would be used to provide the reliability estimate. Another approach to obtaining an estimate of reliability is to use the kappa statistic.

The kappa statistic A statistic called *kappa* was initially designed for use in the case where scorers make ratings using nominal scales of measurement (Cohen, 1960). The kappa statistic was subsequently modfied by Fliess (1971) for use with multiple scorers (and readers interested in the computational formula for this statistic should consult that source). The kappa statistic has generally been received quite well as a measure of inter-scorer reliability (Hartmann, 1977), though there are special instances where it may be appropriate to use kappa in a modified form (Conger, 1985) or to use another measure such as Yule's *Y* (see Spitznagel & Helzer, 1985).

USING AND INTERPRETING A COEFFICIENT OF RELIABILITY

We have seen that with respect to the test itself, there are basically three approaches to the estimation of reliability: (1) test-retest, (2) alternate or parallel forms, and (3) internal or inter-item consistency. The method or methods employed will depend on a number of factors—primary among them the purpose of obtaining a measure of reliability and the way that measure will be used.

The Purpose of the Reliability Coefficient

How repeatable are repeated measurements—with the same form of a test or alternate forms of a test—over short intervals of time? over long intervals? These are some of the types of questions we seek to answer with reference to a coefficient of reliability. If a specific test of employee performance is designed for use at various points in time over the course of the employment period, it would be reasonable to expect that the test demonstrate reliability across time—in which case knowledge of the instrument's test-retest reliability would be essential. For a test designed for a single administration only, an estimate of internal consistency would be the coefficient computed. If the purpose of determining reliability is to analyze the error variance into its component parts, then a number of reliability coefficients will have to be computed. Table 5–5 summarizes the various types of reliability discussed in this chapter; Figure 5–1 illustrates associated sources of error variance.

The Nature of the Test

Closely related to considerations concerning the purpose and use of a reliability coefficient are considerations concerning the nature of the test itself. Included here are considerations such as whether (1) the test items are homogeneous or heterogeneous in nature; (2) the characteristic, ability, or trait being measured by the test is presumed to be dynamic or static; (3) the range of test scores is or is not restricted; (4) the test is a speed or power test; and (5) the test is or is not criterion-referenced. We now discuss each of these considerations.

Table 5–5

Summary of Reliability Types

Type of reliability	Number of testing sessions	Number of test forms	Source(s) of error variance	Statistical procedure(s)
Test-retest	2	1	Time interval	Pearson r
Alternate-form (with time interval)	2	2	Time interval Item sampling	Pearson r
Alternate-form (consecutive administrations)	1	2	Item sampling	Pearson r
Split-half	1	1	Item sampling	Pearson r between equivalent test halves Spearman-Brown adjustment
Inter-item consistency	1	1	Item sampling Test heterogeneity	Kuder-Richardson for dichotomous items; coefficient alpha for multi-point items
Scorer	1	1	Scorer differences	Pearson r or percent agreement or Kappa coefficient

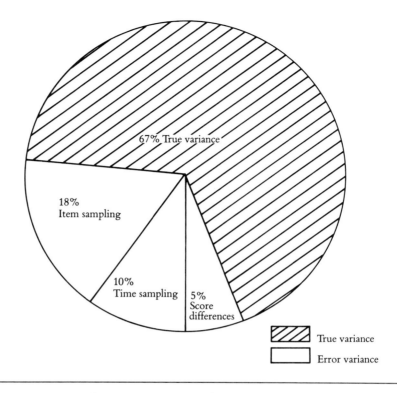

Figure 5–1 *Sources of Variance in a Hypothetical Test.*

Homogeneity versus heterogeneity of test items   If the test is homogeneous in items (that is, if it is functionally uniform throughout because it is designed to measure one factor such as one ability or one trait), it would be reasonable to expect a high degree of internal consistency. If the test is heterogeneous in items, an estimate of internal consistency might be low relative to a—more appropriate—estimate of test-retest reliability.

Dynamic versus static characteristics   Whether what is being measured by the test is *dynamic* or *static* is also a consideration in obtaining an estimate of reliability. Dynamic characteristics are presumed to be ever-changing as a function of situational and cognitive experiences. If, for example, one were to take hourly measurements of the dynamic characteristic of anxiety as manifested in a stockbroker throughout a business day, one might find the measured level of this characteristic to change from hour to hour (with the change possibly even related to the magnitude of the Dow Jones index). Since the "true" amount of anxiety presumed to exist would vary with each assessment, a test-retest measure would be of little help in gauging the reliability of the measuring instrument—the best estimate of reliability could be obtained from an internal-consistency measure. Contrast this situation to one in which hourly assessments of this same stockbroker are made on a characteristic that is not dynamic in nature but presumed to be relatively unchanging or static (such as intelligence). In this instance, obtained measurement would not be expected to vary significantly as a function of time, and either the test-retest or alternate-forms method would be appropriate.

Restriction or inflation of range   In using and interpreting a coefficient of reliability, the issue variously referred to as "restriction of range" or "restriction of variance" (or, conversely, as "inflation of range" or "inflation of variance") is essentially one of sampling of the variances employed in a correlational analysis. If the variance of either variable in a correlational analysis is restricted by the sampling procedure used, then the resulting correlation coefficient tends to be lower. If the variance of either variable in a correlational analysis is inflated by the sampling procedure, then the resulting correlation coefficient tends to be higher. Also of critical importance is whether or not the range of variances employed is appropriate to the objective of the correlational analysis. Consider in the latter context, for example, a published educational test designed for use with children in grades 1 through 6. Ideally, the manual for this test should contain not one reliability value covering all of the test takers in grades 1 through 6, but reliability values for test takers at each grade level. A corporate personnel officer who employs a certain screening test in the hiring process must maintain reliability data with respect to scores achieved by job applicants—as opposed to hired employees—if the range of measurements is not to be restricted (this because the people that were hired typically scored higher on the test than any comparable group of applicants).

Speed versus power tests   When a time limit is long enough to allow test takers to attempt all items and if some items are so difficult that no test taker is able to obtain a perfect score, then the test is referred to as a *power* test. By contrast, a *speed* test generally contains items of uniform level of difficulty (typically uniformly low) so that when given generous time limits, all test takers should be able to complete all of the test items correctly. In practice, however, the time limit on a speed test is established so that few if any of the test takers will be able to complete the entire test. Score differences on a speed test are therefore based on performance speed since items attempted tend to be correct. A reliability estimate of a speed test should be based on performance from two independent testing periods using one of the following: (1) test-retest reliability, (2) alternate-form reliability, or (3) split-half reliability from two, separately timed half tests. If a split-half procedure is used, the obtained reliability coefficient is for a half test and should be adjusted using the Spearman-Brown formula.

It would be inappropriate to estimate the reliability of a speed test using a single administration with a single time limit. It would also be inappropriate to estimate the reliability of a speed test using either odd-even splits or the Kuder-Richardson formula; using any of these estimates would yield spuriously high coefficients of reliability. A measure of the reliability of a speed test should provide a measure of the consistency of response speed. If a test taker completes 82 of 100 items in a speed test (and the items are all correct), odd-even reliability procedures might place 41 correct responses in the "even" half and 41 correct responses in the "odd" half, yielding a correlation of 1.00—a value that would be virtually useless to us as test users or developers, since it tells us nothing about response consistency. A Kuder-Richardson reliability coefficient would yield a similar coefficient. Recall that KR-20 reliability is based on the proportion of test takers correct (p) and the proportion of test takers incorrect (q) on each item. In the case of a speed test, it is conceivable that p would equal 1.0 and q would equal 0 for many of the items. Toward the end of the test—when many items would not even be attempted due to the time limit being imposed—p might equal 0 and q might equal 1.0. For many, if not a majority, of the items then, the summation of pq would equal or approximate 0. When 0 is substituted in the KR-20 formula for $\Sigma\ pq$, the reliability coefficient is 1.0 (a meaningless coefficient in this instance).

Criterion-referenced tests In Chapter 4 we presented the differences between norm-referenced and criterion-referenced testing and noted that the latter is designed to provide an indication of where a test taker stands with respect to some criterion such as an educational or vocational objective. Unlike norm-referenced tests, criterion-referenced tests tend to contain material that has been mastered in hierarchical fashion; the would-be pilot masters on-ground skills before attempting to master in-flight skills. Scores on criterion-referenced tests tend to be interpreted in "pass/fail" (or, more accurately, "master/failed-to-master") terms, and any scrutiny of performance on individual items tends to be for diagnostic (and remedial) purposes. Traditional techniques of estimating reliability employ measures based on total test scores. In test-retest reliability, a reliability estimate is based on the correlation between the total scores on two administrations of the same test. In alternate-form reliability, a reliability estimate is based on the correlation between the two total scores on the two forms. In split-half reliability, a reliability estimate is based on the correlation between scores on two halves of the test and then adjusted using the Spearman-Brown formula to obtain a reliability estimate of the whole test. These traditional procedures of estimating reliability are inappropriate for use with criterion-referenced tests. To understand why, recall that reliability is defined as the proportion of total variance (σ^2) attributable to true variance (σ_{tr}^2). Total variance in a test score distribution equals the sum of the true variance plus the error variance (σ_e^2):

$$\sigma^2 = \sigma_{tr}^2 + \sigma_e^2$$

A measure of reliability, therefore, depends on the variability of the test scores: how different the scores are from one another. In criterion-referenced testing and particularly in mastery testing, individual differences between examinees on total test scores may be minimal; the key issue is not the test scores in comparison to the other test scores but simply if a certain criterion score has been obtained. As individual differences (and the variability) decrease, a traditional measure of reliability would also decrease (regardless of the stability of individual performance). Traditional ways of estimating reliability are therefore not always appropriate for criterion-referenced tests, though there may be instances in which traditional estimates can be adopted (such as the case where the same test is used at different stages in some program—training, therapy, or the like—and variability in scores could reasonably be expected; see Ebel, 1973). For a presentation of statistical techniques applicable to the assessment of the reliability of criterion-referenced tests, the interested reader is referred to Hambleton and Jurgensen (1990), Hambleton and Novick (1973), Millman (1974, 1979), Lord (1978), Panell and Laabs (1979), and Subkoviak (1980).

Regardless of the method used to calculate a reliability coefficient, the interpretation of the coefficient must be relativistic. We have previously noted, for example, that the length of the test can affect the size of a reliability coefficient; in general, the coefficient of reliability tends to increase as the number of test items increases. But beyond consideration of factors such as test length, the range of measurements, dynamic versus static nature of measured characteristics, and so forth, there is a very basic consideration concerning the theory of measurement to which the prospective test developer or user subscribes. Thus far (and throughout this book unless specifically stated otherwise) the model we have been assumed to be operative is the "true score" or "classical" model—the most widely used and accepted model in the psychometric literature today. However, our discussion of reliability and the interpretation of reliability coefficients would be incomplete if we did not at least acquaint the reader with an alternative to the true score model.

Historically, the true score model of the reliability of measurement enjoyed a virtually unchallenged reign of acceptance from the early 1900s through the 1940s. The 1950s saw the development of an alternative theoretical model, one referred to as the *domain sampling theory* originally and as *generalizability theory* in one of its many modified forms (see the Close-up). As set forth by Tryon (1957) the theory of domain sampling rebels against the concept of a "true" score existing with respect to the measurement of psychological constructs (in the same way that a "true" score might exist with respect to measurement in the physical sciences). Whereas those who subscribe to true score theory seek to estimate the portion of a test score that is attributable to "error," proponents of domain sampling theory seek to estimate the extent to which specific sources of variation under defined conditions are contributing to the test score. In the latter model, a test's reliability is conceived of as an objective measure of how precisely the test score assesses the domain from which the test draws a sample (Thorndike, 1985). A *domain* of behavior—or the universe of items that could conceivably measure that behavior—can be thought of as a hypothetical construct: one that shares certain characteristics with (and is measured by) the sample of items that make up the test. In theory, the items in the domain are thought to have the same means and variances of those in the test that samples from the domain. Of the three types of estimates of reliability, measures of internal consistency are perhaps the most compatible with domain sampling theory.[8]

RELIABILITY AND INDIVIDUAL SCORES

The reliability coefficient helps the test developer build an adequate measuring instrument, and it helps the test user select a suitable test. However, the usefulness of the reliability coefficient does not end with test construction and selection. By employing the reliability coefficient in the formula for the standard error of mea-

---

8. Generalizability theory may also be viewed as an extension of true score theory wherein the concept of a universe score replaces that of a true score (see Shavelson, Webb, & Rowley, 1989).

Cronbach's Generalizability Theory

Lee J. Cronbach (1970) and his colleagues (Cronbach, Gleser, Nanda, & Rajaratnam, 1972) developed what they called a "theory of generalizability for scores and profiles." Essentially this theory provides alternative ways of estimating the respective amounts of variance contributed by all possible sources of variance that are operative in a given testing situation. Building on classical true score theory, Cronbach and his colleagues carefully detail the conditions of interest under which a particular test score was obtained and then refer to this detailed description as the "universe." Numerous different aspects of a test's universe, referred to as "facets" (such as the number of items in the test, the amount of training the test scorers have had, and the purpose of the test administration) are included in the description of the universe. According to the theory, given the exact same conditions in the universe, the exact same test score should be obtained.

Analogous to a "true score" in the classical true score model, generalizability has its "universe score," the expected value of a score across all of the scores that could have possibly been obtained within the same universe of observations. Cronbach (1970) put it this way:

"What is Mary's typing ability?" This must be interpreted as, "What would Mary's score be if a large number of measurements were collected and averaged?" The particular test score Mary earned is just one out of a *universe* of possible observations, any of which the investigator would be willing to base his conclusion or decision on. If one of these scores is as acceptable as the next, then the mean, called the *universe score* and symbolized here by M_p (mean for person p), would be the most appropriate statement of Mary's performance in the type of situation the test represents.

The universe is a collection of possible measures "of the same kind," but the limits of the collection are determined by the investigator's purpose. If he needs to know Mary's typing ability on May 5 (for example, so that he can plot a learning curve that includes one point for that day), the universe would include observations on that day and on that day only. He probably does want to generalize over passages, testers, and scorers—that is to say, he would like to know Mary's ability on May 5 without reference to any particular passage, tester, or scorer. . . .

The person will ordinarily have a different universe score for each universe. Mary's universe score covering tests on May 5 will not agree perfectly with her universe score for the whole month of May. . . . Some testers call the average over a large number of comparable observations a "true score"; e.g., "Mary's true typing rate on 3-minute tests."

Lee J. Cronbach

Instead, we speak of a "universe score" to emphasize that what score is desired depends on the universe being considered. For any measure there are many "true scores," each corresponding to a different universe.

When we use a single observation as if it represented the universe, we are generalizing. We generalize over scorers, over selections typed, perhaps over days. If the observed scores from a procedure agree closely with the universe score, we can say that the observation is "accurate," or "reliable," or "generalizable." And since the observations then also agree with each other, we say that they are "consistent" and "have little error variance." To have so many terms is confusing, but not seriously so. The term most often used in the literature is "reliability." The author prefers "generalizability" because that term immediately implies "generalization to what?" . . . There is a different degree of generalizability for each universe. The older methods of analysis do not separate the sources of variation. They deal with a single source of variance, or leave two or more sources entangled. (pp. 153–154)

Cronbach, Gleser, Nanda, and Rajaratnam (1972) urge test developers and publishers to put generalizability theory into practice by executing what they refer to as a *generalizability study* during the development of a test—that study to be followed by what they call a *decision study*. A generalizability study is designed to determine how generalizable scores from a particular test are to situations that involve the administration of the same test but under different conditions. From statistical procedures that involve, among other operations, the estimation of the contributing variances of different facets of the universe, *coefficients of generalizability* are computed (the exact number of coefficients to be computed will depend on the number of facets being examined

in the study). A coefficient of generalizability is in generalizability theory what a reliability coefficient is in classical true score theory.

The generalizability coefficients are then put to use in the step Cronbach et al. recommend subsequent to the generalizability study—the decision study. Here, the conditions of a test's administration and the accuracy of the decisions that can be reached as a function of a specific administration of a test are carefully studied. When it comes to the decisions psychologists are called on to make, Cronbach (1970) strongly believes that there is little room for error:

The decision that a student has completed a course or that a patient is ready for termination of therapy must not be seriously influenced by chance errors, temporary variations in performance, or the tester's choice of questions. An erroneous favorable decision may be irreversible and may harm the person or the community. Even when reversible, an erroneous unfavorable decision is unjust, disrupts the person's morale, and perhaps retards his development. Research, too, requires dependable measurement. An experiment is not very informative if an observed difference could be accounted for by chance variation. Large error variance is likely to mask a scientifically important outcome. Taking a better measure improves the sensitivity of an experiment in the same way that increasing the number of subjects does. (p. 152)

One of the important contributions generalizability theory makes is its strong reminder to us that a test's reliability is not something that statically resides within the test; the reliability of a test is very much a function of the circumstances under which the test is developed, administered, and interpreted. Critical to the accurate interpretation of a test score is an understanding of each of the individual sources of variance that contributed to the test score.

surement, the test user now has another descriptive statistic useful in test interpretation, this one useful in describing the amount of error in a test or a measure.

The Standard Error of Measurement

The standard deviation of a theoretically normal distribution of test scores obtained by one person on equivalent tests is called the *standard error of measurement*. Also referred to as the *standard error of a score* and denoted by the symbol σ_{meas}, the standard error of measurement is an index of the extent to which one individual's scores vary over tests presumed to be parallel. In accordance with the true score model, an obtained test score represents one point in the theoretical distribution of scores the test taker could have obtained. Further, the test user has no way of knowing the test taker's "true score." However, if the standard deviation for the distribution of test scores is known (or can be calculated) and if an estimate of the reliability of the test is known (or can be calculated), an estimate of the standard error of a particular score (that is, the standard error of measurement) can be determined through the use of the following formula:

$$\sigma_{meas} = \sigma\sqrt{1 - r}$$

where σ_{meas} is equal to the standard error of measurement, σ is equal to the standard deviation of test scores by the group of test takers, and r is equal to the reliability coefficient of the test.

If, for example, a spelling test has a reliability coefficient of .84 and a standard deviation of 10, then:

$$\sigma_{meas} = 10\sqrt{1 - .84} = 4$$

Thus, one standard error ($1\sigma_{meas}$) of measurement is equal to 4 test points; two standard errors of measurement would be equal to 8 test points, and so forth. Because a large number of scores by an individual on equivalent tests would tend to be normally distributed, the standard error of measurement could be used in the same manner as a standard deviation—stating the percentage of scores most likely to fall within the stated limits for an individual. If one individual took a large number of equivalent tests, then

- 68% of the scores would be expected to occur within $\pm 1\sigma_{meas}$
- 95% of the scores would be expected to occur within $\pm 2\sigma_{meas}$
- 99.7% of the scores would be expected to occur within $\pm 3\sigma_{meas}$

If a student achieved a score of 50 on one spelling test and if that test had a reliability coefficient of .84 with a standard error of measurement equal to 4, then the following assumptions could be made regarding the student's future performance on equivalent tests:

- 68% of the scores would occur within $50 \pm 1(4)$ or $50 \pm 1\sigma_{meas}$
- 95% of the scores would occur within $50 \pm 2(4)$ or $50 \pm 2\sigma_{meas}$
- 99.7% of the scores would occur within $50 \pm 3(4)$ or $50 \pm 3\sigma_{meas}$

Converting σ_{meas} to test-score points, we could say further that

- 68% of the scores would occur within 50 ± 4
- 95% of the scores would occur within 50 ± 8
- 99.7% of the scores would occur within 50 ± 12

And converting plus-or-minus test-score points to the score interval we could say that

- 68% of the scores would occur between 46 and 54
- 95% of the scores would occur between 42 and 58
- 99.7% of the scores would occur between 38 and 62

The percentage of scores occurring within a score interval is referred to as a *confidence level*. That is, a test user could state with 95% confidence that Jim's score on a single test is likely to occur between 42 and 58. Stated differently, given a series of equivalent tests, Jim's true score is likely to occur within $\pm 2\sigma_{meas}$ of his obtained score in 95% of the cases.

The standard error of measurement, like the reliability coefficient, is one way of expressing test reliability. The smaller the σ_{meas}, the more reliable the test will be; as r increases, the σ_{meas} decreases. For example, when a reliability coefficient equals .67 and σ equals 15, the standard error of measurement equals 9:

$$\sigma_{meas} = 15\sqrt{1 - .67} = 9$$

With a reliability coefficient equal to .95 and σ still equal to 15, the standard error of measurement decreases to 3:

$$\sigma_{meas} = 15\sqrt{1 - .95} = 3$$

In practice, the standard error of measurement is most frequently used in the interpretation of individual test scores as opposed to comparing scores between tests. This is understandable since the standard error of measurement is expressed in units of the test's score, and units between tests may (and often do) vary—as in the case of trying to compare scores on a word processing test with scores on a filing test. The standard error of measurement is often abbreviated as SEM or SEm.

The Standard Error of the Difference Between Two Scores

Error related to any of the number of possible variables operative in a testing situation (such as item sampling, test taker's physical or mental state, and the test environment) can contribute to a change in a score achieved on the same test (or a parallel test) from one administration of the test to the next. Of course "true" differences in whatever is being measured can also be responsible for changes in test scores over succeeding administrations of the test—and indeed we would hope this to be the case if we were testing, for example, to see if intervening psychotherapy had any effect on the mental state of a patient. The *standard error of the difference between two scores* is a statistical measure that can aid a test user in determining how large a difference should be before it is considered statistically significant. As you are probably aware from your course in statistics, custom in the field of psychology dictates that if the probability is more than 5% that the difference occurred by chance, then for all intents and purposes it is presumed that there was no difference. A more rigorous standard is the 1% standard; by this criterion, no statistically significant difference would be deemed to exist unless the observed difference could have occurred by chance alone less than one time in a hundred.

The standard error of the difference between two scores can be the appropriate statistical tool to address three types of questions:

1. How did this individual's performance on test 1 compare to his/her performance on test 2?
2. How did this individual's performance on test 1 compare to someone else's performance on test 1?
3. How did this individual's performance on test 1 compare to someone else's performance on test 2?

As you might have expected, when comparing scores achieved on the different tests, it is essential that the scores be converted to the same scale. The formula for the standard error of the difference between two scores is

$$\sigma_{diff} = \sqrt{\sigma_{1\,meas}^2 + \sigma_{2\,meas}^2}$$

where σ_{diff} is the standard error of the difference between two scores, $\sigma_{1\,meas}^2$ is the squared standard error of measurement for test 1, and $\sigma_{2\,meas}^2$ is the squared standard error of measurement for test 2. Substituting reliability coefficients for the standard errors of measurement of the separate scores, the formula becomes

$$\sigma_{diff} = \sigma\sqrt{2 - r_1 - r_2}$$

where r_1 is the reliability coefficient of test 1, r_2 is the reliability coefficient of test 2, and σ is the standard deviation—both tests having the same standard deviation since they would have had to have been on the same scale (or converted to the same scale) before a comparison could be made.

The standard error of the difference between two scores is larger than the standard error of measurement for either score alone because the former is affected by measurement error in both scores. To find how large a score difference is needed in order to be considered significantly different, determine σ_{diff} using the formula given and multiply σ_{diff} by a factor of 1.96. The rounded product represents the number of points there should be between two scores in order for there to be significance at the .05 level.

As an illustration of the use of the standard error of the difference between two scores, consider the situation of a corporate personnel manager who is seeking a highly responsible person for the position of vice president of safety. The personnel officer in this hypothetical situation decides to use a new published test called the "Safety-Mindedness Test" (S-MT) to screen applicants for the position. After placing an ad in the employment section of the local newspaper, the personnel officer tests 100 applicants for the position, using the S-MT. The personnel officer narrows the search for the vice president to the two highest scorers on the S-MT: Moe, who scored 125, and Larry, who scored 134. Assuming the measured reliability of this test to be .92 and its standard deviation to be 14, should the personnel officer conclude that Larry performed significantly better than Moe? No, this assumption cannot legitimately be made. Whether or not a significant difference exists between these two scores can be determined by use of the formula for σ_{diff}:

$$\sigma_{diff} = 14\sqrt{2 - .92 - .92} = 14\sqrt{.16} = 5.6$$

Note that in this formula the two test reliability coefficients are the same because the two scores we are comparing are derived from the same test. Our calculations indicate that the two scores must differ by at least 11 points ($5.6 \times 1.96 = 10.976$ rounded to 11) in order to be statistically significant at the .05 level. It can therefore be said that Larry did not score significantly higher than Moe on the S-MT. The personnel officer in this example would have to resort to other means to decide whether Moe, Larry, or someone else would be the best candidate for the position.

As a postscript to the example above, suppose Larry got the job primarily on the basis of data from our hypothetical S-MT. And let's further suppose that it soon became all too clear that Larry turned out to be the hands-down, absolute worst vice president of safety that the company had ever seen. Larry spent much of his time playing practical jokes on fellow corporate officers, and he spent many of his off-hours engaged in his favorite pastime: flagpole sitting. The personnel officer might then have very good reason to question how well the instrument called the "Safety-Mindedness Test" truly measured "safety-mindedness." Or, to put it another way, the personnel officer might question the *validity* of the test. Not coincidentally, the subject of test *validity* is taken up in the next chapter.

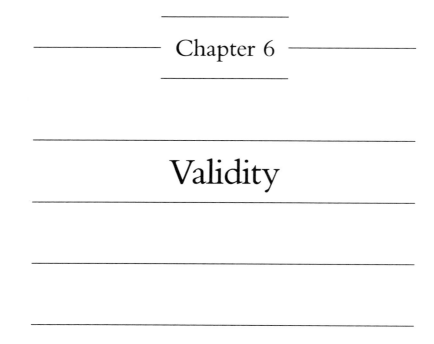

Chapter 6

Validity

IN EVERYDAY LANGUAGE, we speak of something as being *valid* if it is sound, meaningful, or well-grounded on principles or evidence (for example, a valid theory, a valid argument, or a valid reason). In legal terminology, lawyers speak of something as being valid if it is "executed with the proper formalities" (Black, 1979) such as a valid contract and a valid will. In each of these instances, someone makes a judgment based on evidence as to the meaningfulness or veracity of something. Similarly, in the language of psychological assessment, *validity* is a term used in conjunction with the meaningfulness of a test score—what the test score truly means.

THE CONCEPT OF VALIDITY

Stated succinctly, the word *validity* as applied to a test refers to a judgment concerning how well a test does in fact measure what it purports to measure. More specifically, it is a judgment based on evidence about the appropriateness of inferences drawn from test scores.[1] An *inference* is a logical result or deduction in a

---

1. The word *test* is used in this chapter and throughout the book in the broadest possible sense; it may therefore also apply to measurement procedures and processes that would not, strictly speaking, colloquially be referred to as "tests."

reasoning process. Characterizations of the validity of tests and test scores are frequently phrased in terms such as "acceptable" or "weak"—such terms reflecting a judgment about how adequately the attribute the test was designed to measure is actually measured (for example, how adequately the score on a ninth-grade algebra test represents knowledge and facility with ninth-grade algebra and how adequately a score on a measure of job satisfaction actually reflects level of job satisfaction). Inherent in a judgment of validity is a judgment of usefulness; in fact, Nunnally (1978, p. 86) defined validity in terms of how "useful scientifically" an instrument of measurement is.

Validation is the process of gathering and evaluating validity evidence. Both the test developer and the test user may play a role in the validation of a test for a specific purpose. It is the test developer's responsibility to supply validity evidence in the test manual. Because test scores may be valid for measuring achievement or for predicting success in one type of environment and not in another, the test developer will ideally report validity evidence based on test scores obtained in a variety of settings (such as different grade levels, schools, hospitals, or work situations). The prudent test user selects a particular published test on the basis of a careful evaluation of the psychometric soundness of the instrument—a consideration of the reliability and validity evidence. Additionally, it may sometimes be appropriate for test users to conduct their own validation studies with their own groups of test takers. Such "local" validation studies are a necessity in instances where the test user plans to alter in some way the format, instructions, language, or content of the test (such as changing the test from written form to braille form). Local validation studies would also be appropriate in instances where the test will be used with a population of test takers that differs from the population on which the test was standardized.

How does one go about evaluating the validity of a test? A prerequisite to addressing this question is the development of a more precise conceptualization of validity. One way of conceptualizing validity has been with respect to the following three-category taxonomy:

Content validity
Criterion-related validity
Construct validity

This view of validity—referred to by Guion (1980) as the *trinitarian* view—is clearly the prevailing one in the field of psychology today and has been at least since the 1950s. Accordingly, answers to questions about methods for determining the validity of a test tend to be couched in terms such as content validation strategies, criterion-related validation strategies, and construct validation strategies. There are also references to other categories such as "predictive validity" and "concurrent validity," but these two terms tend to be collapsed under the more general category of criterion-related validity.

Within the context of the three-category taxonomy, the validity of a test may be evaluated by (1) scrutinizing its content, (2) relating scores obtained on the test to other test scores or other measures, and (3) executing a comprehensive analysis of not only how scores on the test relate to other test scores and measures, but also how they can be understood within some theoretical framework for understanding the construct the test was designed to measure. These three approaches to validity assessment are not mutually exclusive; each should be thought of as one type of evidence that, with others, contributes to a judgment concerning the validity of the test. All three types of validity evidence contribute to a unified picture of a test's validity, though a test user may not need to know about all three types of validity evidence; depending on the use to which a test is being put, one or another of these three types of validity evidence may not be as relevant as the next. For example, a personnel officer using a particular test in an applicant selection process might be very interested in content and criterion-related validity but not be particularly interested in construct validity. Let us also note at the outset that while the three-category taxonomy of validity is widely accepted, it is not "gospel" and has its critics (see, for example, Landy, 1986). We will return to this point in the section on validity in employment testing in Chapter 18.

Face Validity

The concept of *face validity* relates more to what a test appears to measure than to what the test actually measures. Face validity is a judgment concerning how relevant the test items appear to be. Stated another way, if a test definitely appears to measure what it purports to measure "on the face of it," it could be said to be high in face validity. A paper-and-pencil personality test labeled "The Introversion/ Extraversion Test" with items that ask respondents whether they have acted in an introverted on extraverted way in particular situations will be perceived as a highly *face-valid* test by the respondents. On the other hand, a personality test in which respondents are asked about a variety of inkblots may generally be perceived as a test with low face validity; no doubt many respondents would wonder how on earth what they said they saw in the inkblots really had anything at all to do with personality.

In contrast to judgments concerning the reliability of a test and in contrast to judgments concerning the content, construct, or criterion-related validity of a test, judgments concerning the face validity of a test are frequently thought of from the perspective of the test taker as opposed to the test user.[2] A test may in reality be very relevant and useful in a particular context, but if it is not perceived as such, negative consequences (ranging all the way from a negative test-taking attitude to a lawsuit) may result. Suppose, for example, you wish to hire a researcher for an entry-level position in an advertising agency. One of the skills required for the position is the ability to calculate percentages. The two sample items below are both designed to measure this skill. If you were in the process of developing a screening test for job applicants, which of these two items do you think you would use? Why?

> Item A—Twelve-year-old Billy was asked to help his teacher take inventory of the school supplies in stock at the end of the school term. Among the supplies were 150 boxes of chalk, including 80 boxes of yellow chalk, 20 boxes of blue chalk, and 50 boxes of white chalk. What percentage of the boxes contained blue chalk?

---

2. It is conceivable that the lack of face validity could contribute to a lack of confidence with respect to the perceived effectiveness of the test—with a consequential decrease in the test taker's motivation to do his or her best.

Item B—A market researcher for a beer client in an advertising agency interviewed 150 consumers who reported drinking a light beer at least once a week. Each consumer was shown a television commercial and asked to identify one element in the commercial they found most appealing. Of the 150 consumers, 80 said they preferred the sports action, 20 said they preferred the shots of beer overflowing the mug, and 50 said they preferred the shots of hero sandwiches. What percentage of the consumers preferred the shots of beer overflowing the mug?

Although each of these items could be presumed to require an identical level of mathematical ability, item B would clearly carry with it greater face validity in the context of an advertising agency's screening test; it appears more job-related than item A.

The face validity of a test—the mere appearance of validity—is not an acceptable basis for interpretive inferences from test scores (*Standards*, 1974, p. 26), and this type of validity is not discussed in the section on validity in the 1985 revision of the *Standards*. Still, face validity is important to the extent that it may influence motivational levels (or other factors) from the perspective of the test taker. From the perspective of the test user, face validity may also be important as it contributes (or fails to contribute) to users' confidence in the test. It can therefore be concluded that face validity may have "p.r. (public relations) value" for both test takers and test users.

CONTENT VALIDITY

Content validity refers to a judgment concerning how adequately a test samples behavior representative of the universe of behavior the test was designed to sample. For example, the universe of behavior referred to as "assertive" is very wide-ranging. A content-valid paper-and-pencil test of assertiveness would be one that is adequately representative of these wide-ranging situations. We might expect that such a test would contain items sampling from hypothetical situations at home (such as whether the respondent has difficulty in making her or his views known to fellow family members), on the job (such as whether the respondent has difficulty in asking subordinates to do what is required of them), and in social situations (such as whether the respondent would send back a steak not done to order in a fancy restaurant).

With respect to educational achievement tests, it is customary to consider a test a content-valid measure when the proportion of material covered by the test approximates the proportion of material covered in the course. A final exam in introductory statistics would be considered content-valid if the proportion and type of introductory statistics problems on the test approximated the proportion and type of introductory statistics problems presented in the course; performance on the test represents performance from the hypothetical universe of introductory statistics problems.

The early stages of a test being developed for use in the classroom—be it one classroom or those throughout the state or nation—typically entail research exploring the universe of possible instructional objectives for the course. Included among the many possible sources of information on such objectives are course syllabi, course texts, teachers who teach the course, specialists who develop curricula, and professors and supervisors who train teachers in the particular subject area. From the pooled information (along with the judgment of the test developer) a blueprint for the structure of the test will emerge—a blueprint representing the culmination of efforts designed to adequately sample the universe of content areas that could conceivably be sampled in such a test.[3]

For an employment test to be content-valid, the content of the test must be a representative sample of the job-related skills required for employment. One technique frequently used in "blueprinting" the content areas to be covered in certain types of employment tests is observation: the test developer will observe successful veterans on that job, note the behaviors necessary for success on the job, and design the test to include a representative sample of those behaviors. These same workers (as well as their supervisors and others) may subsequently be called on to act as experts or judges in rating the degree to which the content of the test is a representative sample of the required job-related skills. What follows is one method for quantifying the degree of agreement between such raters.

The Quantification of Content Validity

Lawshe (1975) proposed a simple formula for quantifying the degree of consensus by asking a panel of experts to determine the content validity of an employment test. The method can be applied to other situations requiring a panel of experts to render some judgment. Each panel member is given several items and is asked to respond to the following question for each item:

Is the skill or knowledge measured by this item:

- essential
- useful but not essential
- not necessary

to the performance of the job? Responses by the panelists are pooled, and the number of people indicating "essential" for each item is counted. According to Lawshe, any item has some degree of content validity if more than 50% of the panelists perceive the skill or knowledge measured by the item to be essential. The more panelists who perceive the item as essential (beyond 50%), the greater the degree of its content validity. Using these assumptions, Lawshe developed a formula called the *content validity ratio:*

$$CVR = \frac{n_e - N/2}{N/2}$$

where CVR = content validity ratio, n_e = number of panelists indicating "essential," and N = total number of panelists. Assuming a panel consists of ten experts, the following three examples illustrate the meaning of the CVR when it is negative, zero, and positive.

---

3. The application of the concept of "blueprint" and of "blueprinting" is of course not limited to achievement tests; blueprinting may be used in the design of a personality test, an attitude measure—any test—sometimes employing the judgments of experts in the field.

1. *Negative CVR:* When fewer than half the panelists indicate "essential," the *CVR* is negative. Assume four of ten panelists indicated "essential":

$$CVR = \frac{4 - (10/2)}{10/2} = -0.2$$

2. *Zero CVR:* When exactly half of the panelists indicate "essential," the *CVR* is zero:

$$CVR = \frac{5 - (10/2)}{10/2} = .00$$

3. *Positive CVR:* When more than half but not all the panelists indicate "essential," the *CVR* ranges between .00 and .99. Assume nine of ten indicated "essential":

$$CVR = \frac{9 - (10/2)}{10/2} = .80$$

In validating a test, the content validity ratio is calculated for each item. The items for which agreement could have occurred by chance are eliminated. Table 6–1 shows the minimum *CVR* values needed for significance at the .05 level. In the case where there are ten panelists, an item would need a minimum *CVR* of .62 for significance at the .05 level. In our third example (the one in which nine of ten panelists agreed), the *CVR* of .80 is significant; the item would therefore be retained. We now turn our attention from an index of validity derived from looking at the test itself to an index of validity derived from an examination of how scores on the test are related to something other than the test itself—some criterion.

Table 6–1

Minimum Values of the Content Validity Ratio for Significance at p = .05 (one-tailed test)

Number of panelists	Minimum value
5	.99
6	.99
7	.99
8	.78
9	.75
10	.62
11	.59
12	.56
13	.54
14	.51
15	.49
20	.42
25	.37
30	.33
35	.31
40	.29

Source: Lawshe (1975).

CRITERION-RELATED VALIDITY

Criterion-related validity is a judgment regarding how adequately a test score can be used to infer an individual's most probable standing on some measure of interest—the measure of interest being the criterion. Two types of validity evidence are subsumed under the heading "criterion-related validity." *Concurrent validity* refers to the form of criterion-related validity that is an index of the degree to which a test score is related to some criterion measure obtained at the same time (concurrently). *Predictive validity* refers to the form of criterion-related validity that is an index of the degree to which a test score predicts some criterion measure. Before we discuss each of these types of validity evidence in detail, it seems appropriate to raise (and answer) an important question.

What Is a Criterion?

A dictionary-type definition of *criterion* is "a standard or test on which a judgment or decision can be based." In the language of tests and measurement and specifically in the context of criterion-related validity, a criterion may be broadly defined as the standard against which a test or test score is evaluated. Operationally, a criterion can be most anything: from "pilot performance in flying a Boeing 767" to "grade on examination in Advanced Hairweaving" to "number of days spent in psychiatric hospitalization." In short, there are no hard-and-fast rules for what constitutes a criterion; it can be a specific behavior or group of behaviors, a test score, an amount of time, a rating, a psychiatric diagnosis, a training cost, an index of absenteeism, an index of alcohol intoxication, and so on. But while a criterion can be almost anything, it ideally is reliable, relevant, valid, and uncontaminated.

Characteristics of a criterion   Like test scores, the criterion scores should be reliable. The reliability of the criterion and the reliability of the test each limit the magnitude of the validity coefficient according to the following theoretical relationship:

$$r_{xy} \leq \sqrt{(r_{xx})(r_{yy})}$$

Here, r_{xy} is the validity coefficient (the correlation between the test and the criterion), r_{xx} is the test reliability, and r_{yy} is the criterion reliability. The formula is read as follows: The validity coefficient is less than or equal to the square root of the test's reliability coefficient multiplied by the criterion's reliability coefficient.

An adequate criterion is also relevant. We would expect, for example, that a test purporting to tell us something about an individual's aptitude for a career in psychology had been validated using some sort of criterion involving data obtained from psychologists.

An adequate criterion measure must also be valid for the purpose for which it is being used. If one test (X) is being used as the criterion to validate a second test (Y), then evidence should exist that test X is valid. If the criterion used is a rating made by a judge or a panel, then evidence should exist that the rating is valid. If, for example, a test manual for a diagnostic test of personality reported that the test had been validated using a criterion of "diagnoses made by a blue ribbon panel of psychodiagnosticians," the test user might wish to probe further—either by reading on in the manual or writing the test publisher—regarding variables such as (1) the specific definitions of diagnostic terms and categories, (2) the precise nature of the background, training, and experience of the "blue ribbon panel," and (3) the nature and extent of panel members' extra-test contact with the diagnosed subjects.

Ideally, a criterion is also uncontaminated. *Criterion contamination* is the term applied to a situation where the criterion measure itself has been based, at least in part, on predictor measures. Suppose that we just completed a study of how accurately a test called the MMPI predicted psychiatric diagnosis in the psychiatric population of the Minnesota state hospital system. In this study, the predictor is the MMPI, and the criterion is the psychiatric diagnosis that exists in the patient's record. Let's suppose further that, while we are in the process of analyzing our data, someone informs us that the diagnosis for every patient in the Minnesota state hospital system was determined, at least in part, by an MMPI test score. Should we still proceed with our analysis? The answer, of course, is no; since the predictor measure has "contaminated" the criterion measure, it would be of little value to find, in essence, that the predictor can indeed predict itself.

Concurrent Validity

If test scores are obtained at about the same point in time that the criterion measures are obtained, measures of the relationship between the test scores and the criterion provide evidence of *concurrent validity*. Statements of concurrent validity indicate the extent to which test scores may be used to estimate an individual's present standing on a criterion. If, for example, scores (or classifications) made on the basis of a psychodiagnostic test were to be validated against a criterion of already diagnosed psychiatric patients, the process would be one of concurrent validation. In general, once the validity of the inference from the test scores is established, the test may provide a faster, less expensive way to offer a diagnosis or classification decision. A test with satisfactorily demonstrated concurrent validity may therefore be very appealing to prospective users since it holds out the potential of savings in terms of money and professional time; what administrator, for example, wouldn't prefer to use an inexpensive paper-and-pencil test if he or she could obtain the same results with this test as through the use of highly trained mental health personnel (who might more efficiently and valuably be spending their time doing other things, such as conducting research or therapy)?

Sometimes the concurrent validity of a particular test (we'll call it "Test A" for the purposes of this example) is explored with respect to how it compares to another test (one we'll call "Test B"). In such studies, prior research has satisfactorily demonstrated the validity of Test B, and the question of interest becomes "How well does Test A compare to Test B?" Here, Test B is used as what is referred to as the "validating criterion." In some studies, Test A is either a brand new test, or a test being used for some new purpose, perhaps with a new population. In the example of a concurrent validity study that follows, a group of researchers explored whether a test that had been validated for use with adults could be used with children.

The Beck Depression Inventory (BDI; Beck, Rush, & Shaw, 1979) is a 21-item, self-report measure that is widely used by clinicians and researchers as an aid to quantifying the severity of depressive symptoms. First introduced in 1961 and subsequently revised, the BDI has undergone extensive study of its validity in numerous investigations using adult subjects. But is the BDI valid for use with outpatient adolescents? And more specifically, can the BDI successfully differentiate depressed from nondepressed patients in a population of adolescent outpatients? These were the questions for which Ambrosini, Metz, Bianchi, Rabinovich, & Undie (1991) sought answers. Diagnoses generated from the concurrent administration of an instrument previously validated for use with adolescents (the Kiddie-Schedule for Affective Disorders and Schizophrenia) were used as the criterion validators. The findings suggested that the BDI is valid for use with adolescents.

We now turn our attention to another form of criterion validity, one in which the criterion measure is obtained not concurrently but rather at some future time.

Predictive Validity

Test scores may be obtained at one point in time and the criterion measures obtained at a future time—after some intervening event has taken place (such as training, experience, therapy, medication, or simply the passage of time). Measures of the relationship between the test scores and a criterion measure obtained at a future point in time provide an indication of the *predictive validity* of the test (that is, how accurately scores on the test predict to some criterion measure). Measures of the relationship between college admissions tests and freshman grade-point average, for example, provide evidence of the predictive validity of the admissions tests.

In settings where tests might be employed, such as a personnel agency, a college admissions office, or a warden's office, a test's high predictive validity can be a very useful aid to decision makers who must select successful students, productive workers, or convicts who are good parole risks. Whether a test result is valuable in making a decision depends on how well the test results improve selection decisions over those decisions made without knowledge of test results. In an industrial setting where volume turnout is important, if the use of a personnel selection test can have the effect of enhancing productivity to even a small degree, the enhanced productivity will pay off year after year and may translate into millions of dollars of increased revenue. And in a clinical context, no price could be placed on a test that has the effect of saving more lives from suicide or homicide if the test could provide predictive accuracy over and above existing tests with respect to such acts. Unfortunately, the difficulties inherent in developing such tests are numerous and multifaceted (see Murphy, 1984; Mulvey & Lidz, 1984; Petrie & Chamberlain, 1985).

Judgments of criterion-related validity, whether concurrent or predictive, are based on two types of statistical evidence: the validity coefficient and expectancy data.

The validity coefficient   The *validity coefficient* is a correlation coefficient that provides a measure of the relationship between test scores and scores on the criterion measure. The correlation coefficient computed from a score (or classification) on a psychodiagnostic test and the criterion score (or classification) assigned by psychodiagnosticians is one example of a validity coefficient. Typically, the

Pearson correlation coefficient is used to determine the validity between the two measures. However, depending on variables such as the type of data, the sample size, and the shape of the distribution, other correlation coefficients could be used. For example, in examining self-rankings of performance on some job with rankings made by job supervisors, the formula for the Spearman rho rank-order correlation would be employed.

Like the reliability coefficient and other correlational measures, the validity coefficient is affected by restriction or inflation of range. And as in other correlational studies, a key issue is whether or not the range of variances employed is appropriate to the objective of the correlational analysis; it may not be in situations where, for example, attrition in the number of subjects has occurred over the course of the analysis. To illustrate, suppose that a clinical psychologist working in the psychiatric emergency room of a municipal hospital has developed a new test called "The Very Brief Psychodiagnostic Classification Test" (VBPCI). The psychologist hypothesizes that a patient's score or classification on this (hypothetical) test will be predictive of the diagnosis on the patient's chart seven days from the day it was administered. Since the test takes only a minute or two to administer—it is indeed *very* brief—all people who present themselves at (or who are brought to) the psychiatric emergency room are administered the test as part of a validation study. The study runs for one month, at the end of which time a statistically significant validity coefficient describing the relationship between VBPCI score and the criterion diagnosis is computed. Should the psychologist immediately proceed to a test publisher's office, VBPCI in hand?

Not necessarily—at least not until the effects of attrition, if any, in the sample, have been analyzed. The impressive VBPCI findings might well be an artifact of such attrition, and the findings might more accurately be interpreted as reflecting the fact that the VBPCI is an accurate predictor of psychiatric diagnosis for conditions in the middle range of psychopathology only; one may not be able to tell from the design of this study how well a predictor the VBPCI is at extreme ranges. Here's why: if the municipal hospital psychiatric emergency room the study was conducted in is typical of others, the least disordered patients will have been discharged after a day or two—and they therefore will be eliminated from the sample. Attrition of the sample can be expected to occur not only with respect to the least disordered patients, but at the other extreme as well; many of the severely disordered patients will have been transferred to a state hospital before seven days from the time of their initial admission. Because the data for the remaining subjects represent only the middle range of the wide range of psychodiagnostic types that could be encountered in a psychiatric emergency room, the reported measure of the VBPCI's validity is spuriously inflated.[4]

The problem of restricted range can occur through a self-selection process in the sample employed for the validation study. Thus, for example, if the test purports to measure something as technical and/or dangerous as "oil barge firefighting aptitude," it may well be that the only people who reply to an ad for the

---

4. A more detailed discussion—complete with illustrative scatterplots—of the influence on correlation coefficients of (1) restriction of range and (2) combining data from different groups, can be found in Allen and Yen (1979, pp. 34–36).

position of oil barge firefighter are people who actually are highly qualified for the position; hence, you would expect the range of the distribution of scores on some test of "oil barge firefighting aptitude" to be restricted. For less technical or dangerous positions, a self-selection factor might be operative if the test developer selects a group of newly hired employees to test (with the expectation that criterion measures will be available for this group at some subsequent date). However, because the newly hired employees have probably already passed some sort of evaluation—however formal or informal—in the process of being hired, there is a good chance that ability to do the job among this group will be higher than ability to do the job among a random sample of ordinary job applicants. Consequently, scores on the criterion measure that is later administered will tend to be higher than scores on the criterion measure obtained from a random sample of ordinary job applicants; stated another way, the low-end scores will be restricted in range.

While it is the responsibility of the test developer to report validation data in the test manual, it is the responsibility of test users to carefully read the description of the validation study and evaluate the suitability of the test for their specific purposes. What were the characteristics of the sample used in the validation study? How matched are these characteristics to the people for whom an administration of the test is being contemplated? Are some subtests of a test more appropriate for a specific test purpose than the entire test is?

How high should a validity coefficient be in order for a user or test developer to infer that the test is valid? There are no rules for determining the acceptable level of a validity coefficient. Essentially, the validity coefficient should be high enough to result in the identification and differentiation of test takers with respect to target attribute(s), such as employees who are likely to be more productive, police officers who are less likely to misuse their weapons, and students who are more likely to be successful in a particular course of study.

Expectancy data Expectancy data provide a source of information that can be used in evaluating the criterion-related validity of a test. Using a score obtained on some test(s) or measure(s), expectancy tables illustrate the likelihood that the test taker will score within some interval of scores on a criterion measure—an interval that may be seen as "passing," "acceptable," and so on. If the criterion scores can be dichotomized (for example, satisfactory/unsatisfactory, pass/fail, or at above average/below average), then the data on a group of test takers' performances with respect to some dichotomous criterion measure can be placed into expectancy table form. An expectancy chart shows the percentage of people within specified test-score intervals who subsequently were placed in either of the dichotomized categories of the criterion (for example, placed in "passed" category or "failed" category). An expectancy table may be created from a scatterplot according to the steps listed in Figure 6–1. An expectancy table showing the relationship between scores on a subtest of the Differential Aptitude Tests (DAT) and course grades in American history for eleventh-grade boys is presented in Table 6–2. You can see that, of the students who scored between 40 and 60, 83% scored 80 or above in their American history course.

To illustrate how an expectancy chart might be used by a corporate personnel office, suppose that on the basis of various test scores and personal interviews,

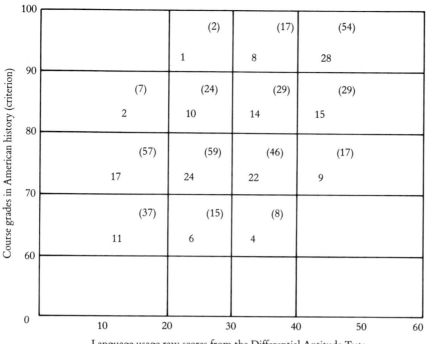

( ) percentage of points per cell

Figure 6–1 *Seven Steps to an Expectancy Table.*

1. Draw a scatterplot such that each point in the plot represents a particular test score–criterion score combination.
2. Draw grid lines in such a way as to summarize the number of people who scored within a particular interval.
3. Count the number of points in each cell (n_i) as shown in the figure.
4. Count the total number of points within each vertical interval (N_v). This number represents the number of people scoring within a particular test score interval.
5. Convert each cell frequency to a percentage (n_i/N_v). This represents the percentage of people obtaining a particular test score–criterion score combination. Write the percentages in the cells. Enclose the percentages in parentheses to distinguish them from the frequencies.
6. On a separate sheet, create table headings and subheadings and copy the percentages into the appropriate cell tables as shown in Table 6-2. Be careful to put the percentages in the correct cell tables. (Note that it's easy to make a mistake at this stage because the percentages of people within particular score intervals are written horizontally in the table and vertically in the scatterplot.)
7. If desired, write the number and percentage of cases per test-score interval. If the number of cases in any one cell is very small, it is more likely to fluctuate in subsequent charts. If cell sizes are small, the user could create fewer cells or accumulate data over several years.

Table 6–2

DAT Language Usage Subtest Scores and American History Grade for 171 Eleventh-Grade Boys (Showing Percentage of Students Obtaining Course Grades in the Interval Shown)

	Course grade interval				Cases per test-score interval	
Test score	0–69	70–79	80–89	90–100	N_v	%
40 and above		17	29	54	52	100
30–39	8	46	29	17	48	100
20–29	15	59	24	2	41	100
below 20	37	57	7		30	101*

*Total sums to more than 100% due to rounding.

personnel experts rated all applicants for a manual labor position that entailed piecework as "excellent," "very good," "average," "below average," and "poor." In this example, then, the "test score" is actually a rating made by personnel experts on the basis of a number of test scores and a personal interview. Let's further suppose that because of a severe labor scarcity at the time, all the applicants were hired (a dream-come-true for a researcher interested in conducting a validation study with respect to the validity of the assessment procedure). Floor supervisors who were blind with respect to the composite score obtained by the newly hired workers provided the criterion measure in this validation study; specifically, they provided ratings of each employee's performance—"satisfactory" or "unsatisfactory." Figure 6–2 is the resulting expectancy chart (or graphic representation of an expectancy table). It can be seen that of all applicants originally rated "excellent," 94% were rated "satisfactory" on the job. By contrast, among applicants originally rated "poor," only 17% were rated "satisfactory" on the job. In gen-

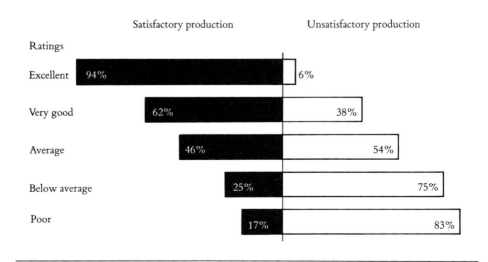

Figure 6–2 *Test Ratings and Job Performance.* (Source: The Psychological Corporation)

eral, this expectancy chart tells us that the higher the initial rating, the greater the probability of job success. Stated another way, it tells us that the lower the initial rating, the greater the probability of job failure. The company experimenting with such a rating system could reasonably expect to improve its productivity by using this rating system. Specifically, job applicants who obtained ratings of "average" or higher would be the only applicants hired.

Tables that could be used as an aid for personnel directors in their decision-making chores were published by H. C. Taylor and J. T. Russell in the *Journal of Applied Psychology* in 1939. Referred to by the names of their authors, the Taylor-Russell tables provide an estimate of the extent to which inclusion of a particular test in the selection system will actually improve selection. More specifically, the tables provide an estimate of the percentage of employees hired by the use of a particular test who will be successful at their jobs, given different combinations of three variables: the test's validity, the selection ratio used, and the percentage of people currently employed in the vacant position who are considered successful. The value assigned for the test's validity is the computed validity coefficient. The selection ratio is a numerical value that reflects the relationship between the number of people to be hired and the number of people available to be hired (for instance, if there are 50 positions and 100 applicants, the selection ratio is 50/100, or .50). The third variable, percentage of employees currently employed in the vacant position who are considered successful, is an indication of the personnel office's current "batting average" using whatever techniques it is currently using. If, for example, a firm employs 25 computer programmers and 20 are considered successful, the percent successful using current hiring techniques would be 80%. With knowledge of the validity coefficient of a particular test (such as a "Computer Programmer Skills Test") along with the selection ratio, reference to the Taylor-Russell tables would provide the personnel officer with an estimate of how much using the test would improve selection over existing methods.

One limitation inherent in the use of the Taylor-Russell tables is that the relationship between the predictor (the test) and the criterion (rating of performance on the job) must be linear. If, for example, there is some point at which job performance levels off, no matter how high the score on the test gets, use of the Taylor-Russell tables would be inappropriate. Another limitation inherent in the use of the Taylor-Russell tables is the potential problem of having to identify a criterion score that separates "successful" from "unsuccessful" employees. This problem was avoided in an alternative set of tables (Naylor & Shine, 1965) that provide an indication of the difference in average criterion scores for the selected as compared with the original group. Use of the Naylor-Shine tables entails obtaining the difference between the means of the selected and unselected groups in order to obtain an index of what the test (or other tool of assessment) is adding to already established procedures. Both the Taylor-Russell and the Naylor-Shine tables can assist in judging the utility of a particular test, the former in terms of determining the increase over current procedures and the latter in terms of the increase in average score on some criterion measure. With both tables, the validity coefficient used must be one obtained by concurrent validation procedures—a fact that should not be surprising since it is obtained with respect to current employees hired by the selection process in effect at the time of the study.

If hiring decisions were made solely on the basis of variables such as the validity of an employment test and the prevailing selection ratio, then tables such as those offered by Taylor and Russell and Naylor and Shine would be in wide use today. The fact is that many other kinds of variables might well enter into hiring decisions (for example, minority status, general physical and/or mental health of applicant, or drug use by applicant). Given that many variables may enter into a hiring—or other—decision, of what use is a given test in the decision process? After publication of the Taylor-Russell tables, a number of articles probing ways to determine how appropriate the use of a given test is with respect to different types of assessment procedures began to appear (Brogden, 1946, 1949; Smith, 1948), and a literature dealing with "test utility theory" began to grow. Also during this period, statisticians such as Wald (1947, 1950) were involved in identifying statistical rules for developing a sequential analysis of a problem that would lead to an optimal decision; "decision theory" had been born, and it would be applied to answering questions about the utility of psychological tests.

Decision theory and test utility   Perhaps the most oft-cited application of statistical decision theory to the field of psychological testing is Cronbach and Gleser's *Psychological Tests and Personnel Decisions,* though other work in this area (not so comprehensive as Cronbach and Gleser's) was published subsequently (for example, Dunnette, 1963; Mahoney & England, 1965; Rorer, Hoffman, LaForge, & Hsieh, 1966; Darlington & Stauffer, 1966). The idea of applying statistical decision theory to questions of test utility was conceptually appealing and promising, and an authoritative textbook of the day reflects the great enthusiasm with which this marriage of enterprises was greeted:

> The basic decision-theory approach to selection and placement . . . has a number of advantages over the more classical approach based upon the correlation model. . . . There is no question but that it is a more general and better model for handling this kind of decision task, and we predict that in the future problems of selection and placement will be treated in this context more frequently—perhaps to the eventual exclusion of the more stereotyped correlational model. (Blum & Naylor, 1968, p. 58)

Stated generally, Cronbach and Gleser (1965) presented (1) a classification of decision problems (for an example of their work in this area, see Table 6–3), (2) various selection strategies ranging from single-stage processes to sequential analyses, (3) a quantitative analysis of the relationship between test utility, the selection ratio, cost of the testing program, and expected value of the outcome, and (4) a recommendation that in some instances job requirements be tailored to the applicant's ability instead of the other way around (a concept they refer to as "adaptive treatment").

Before we illustrate decision theory in action, let us briefly—and somewhat loosely—define five terms frequently encountered in discussions of decision theory as applied to psychological testing and measurement: "base rate," "hit rate," "miss rate," "false positive," and "false negative."

A *base rate* may be defined as the extent to which a particular characteristic or attribute exists in the population (expressed as a proportion). A *hit rate* may be defined as the proportion of people a test accurately identifies as possessing a particular characteristic or attribute (for example, the proportion of people accurately predicted to be able to perform graduate-school-level work or the number of patients accurately diagnosed as having a brain tumor). A *miss rate* may be de-

Table 6–3

Addressing a Personnel Decision Problem

If you had a personnel decision problem you might begin by asking yourself the following questions. Your answer to each of these six pairs of questions will result in the identification of the specific type of personnel decision problem with which you are dealing—one of 64 (or 2 to the sixth power) possible types of personnel decision problems identified by the authors of these questions, Cronbach and Gleser (1965):

1. (a) Are the benefits obtained from a decision evaluated in the same way for each person? (or)
   (b) Are different values used in deciding about each person?
2. (a) Is the decision about each person made independently? (or)
   (b) Are decisions about various persons interrelated?
3. (a) Is each individual assigned to just one of the available treatments [jobs]? (or)
   (b) May each individual be assigned to multiple treatments?
4. (a) Is one of the allowable treatments "reject" [that is, is this a selection situation]? (or)
   (b) Are all persons retained in the institution [a placement decision]?
5. (a) Is the information used in univariate form? (or)
   (b) Is it in multivariate form?
6. (a) Are decisions final? (or)
   (b) May one decide to obtain further information prior to final decisions?

fined as the proportion of people the test fails to identify as having—or not having—a particular characteristic or attribute; a *miss* amounts to an inaccurate prediction. The category of "misses" may be further subdivided. A *false positive* is a miss wherein the test predicted that the test taker did possess the particular characteristic or attribute being measured. A *false negative* is a miss wherein the test predicted that the test taker did not possess the particular characteristic or attribute being measured.

Suppose you developed a measurement procedure you called the "Vapor Test" (VT), which was designed to determine if alive-and-well subjects are indeed breathing. The procedure for the VT entails having the examiner hold a mirror under the subject's nose and mouth for a minute or so and observing if the subject's breath fogs the mirror. Let's say that 100 introductory psychology students are administered the VT and it is concluded that 89 were, in fact, breathing (while 11 are deemed, on the basis of the VT, not to be breathing). Is the VT a good test? Obviously not. Since the base rate is 100% of the (alive and well) population, we really don't even need a test to measure the characteristic "breathing"—and if for some reason we did need a measurement procedure, we probably wouldn't use one that was inaccurate in approximately 11% of the cases. A test is obviously of no value if the hit rate is higher *without* using it; one measure of the value of a test lies in the extent to which its use improves on the hit rate that exists without its use.

As a simple illustration of decision theory applied to testing, suppose a test is administered to a group of 100 job applicants and some cutoff score is applied to distinguish applicants who will be hired (applicants judged to have "passed" the test) from applicants whose employment application will be rejected (applicants judged to have "failed" the test). And let's further suppose that some criterion measure will be applied some time later in order to ascertain whether the newly hired person worked out—whether the newly hired person was considered a success or a failure at the job. In such a situation, if the test is a perfect predictor (if its validity coefficient is equal to 1), two distinct types of outcomes can be identified: (1) some applicants will score at or above the cutoff score on the test and be successful at the job or (2) some applicants will score below the cutoff score and would not have been successful at the job. But since few, if any, employment tests are perfect predictors, two other types of outcomes are also possible: (3) some applicants will score at or above the cutoff score, be hired, and fail at the job (the criterion), and (4) some applicants who scored below the cutoff score and were not hired could have been successful at the job. People who fall into group 3 could be categorized as "false positives" while those who fall into group 4 might be categorized as "false negatives."

Without resorting to any formulas or tables, logic alone tells us that if the selection ratio is, say, 90% (nine out of ten applicants will be hired), the cutting score will probably be set lower than if the selection ratio is 5% (only five of the 100 applicants will be hired). Further, if the selection ratio is 90%, it is a good bet that the number of "false positives" (people hired who will fail on the criterion measure) will be greater than in a case where the selection ratio is 5%. Conversely, if the selection ratio is only 5%, it is a good bet that the number of "false negatives" (people not hired who could have succeeded on the criterion measure) will be greater than in a case where the selection ratio is 90%. Decision theory provides guidelines for setting optimal cutting scores. In setting such scores, the relative seriousness of making false positive or false negative selection decisions is frequently taken into account. Thus, for example, it is a prudent policy for an airline personnel office to set cutoff scores on tests for pilots that might result in a false negative (a pilot who is truly qualified being rejected) as opposed to a cutoff score that would allow a false positive (the hiring of a pilot who is, in reality, unqualified).

In the hands of highly skilled and dedicated—not to mention, highly financed—researchers, principles of decision theory applied to problems of test utility have led to some enlightening and impressive findings. For example, Schmidt, Hunter, McKenzie, and Muldrow (1979) demonstrated in dollars and cents how the utility of a company's selection program (and the validity coefficient of the tests used in that program) can play a critical role in the profitability of the company. Focusing on one employer's population of computer programmers, these researchers asked supervisors to rate, in dollars, the value of "good," "average," and "poor" programmers. This information was used in conjunction with other information, including these facts: (1) each year the employer hired 600 new programmers, (2) the average programmer remained on the job for about ten years, (3) the Programmer Aptitude Test currently in use as part of the hiring process had a validity coefficient of .76, (4) it cost about $10 per applicant to administer the test, and (5) the employer currently had in excess of 4,000 programmers in its employ.

Schmidt et al. (1979) made a number of calculations using different values for some of the variables. For example, knowing that some of the tests previously used in the hiring process had validity coefficients ranging from .00 to .50, they varied the value of the test's validity coefficient (along with other factors such as different selection ratios that had been in effect) and examined the relative efficiency of the various conditions. Among their findings was the fact that the existing selection ratio and selection process provided a great gain in efficiency over a previous situation (when the selection ratio was 5% and the validity coefficient of the test used in hiring was equal to .50)—a gain equal to almost $6 million per year (and multiplied over, say, ten years, that's $60 million). The existing selection ratio and selection process provided an even greater gain in efficiency over a previously existing situation in which the test had no validity at all and the selection ratio was .80; here, in one year, the gain in efficiency was estimated to be equal to over $97 million.

By the way, the employer in the study above was the United States government. Hunter and Schmidt (1981) applied the same type of analysis to the national work force and made a compelling argument with respect to the critical relationship between valid tests and measurement procedures and our national productivity. In a subsequent study, Schmidt, Hunter, and their colleagues found that substantial increases in work output or reductions in payroll costs would result from using valid measures of cognitive ability as opposed to nontest procedures (such as evaluations of education; see Schmidt, Hunter, Outerbridge, & Trattner, 1986).

The question of why more employers aren't using methodologies based on decision theory in their hiring practices may be raised at this point. The answer lies in the complexity of their application. Statistically elegant and highly rational expositions of decision theory as applied to questions of test utility tend to be extremely complex (Guion, 1967; Dunnette & Borman, 1979) and vulnerable to challenge at a number of points (such as how validity data are actually compiled and criterion measures used; see Algera, Jansen, Roe, & Vign, 1984). For example, it is difficult at best to estimate with accuracy a standard deviation, in dollars, of performance of a particular job. Thus while decision theory approaches to assessment held—and still do hold—great promise, their complexity in application has prevented that great promise from being fulfilled. For an expanded discussion on this subject, the interested reader is referred to Wiggins (1973).

CONSTRUCT VALIDITY

Construct validity refers to a judgment about the appropriateness of inferences drawn from test scores regarding individual standings on a certain kind of variable called a construct. A *construct* is an informed, scientific idea "constructed" to describe or explain behavior. "Intelligence" is a construct that may be invoked to describe why a student performs well in school. "Anxiety" is a construct that may be invoked to describe why a psychiatric patient paces the floor. Other examples of constructs are "job satisfaction," "personality," "bigotry," "clerical aptitude," "depression," "motivation," "self-esteem," "emotional adjustment," "potential dangerousness," "creativity," and "mechanical comprehension." They are all unobservable, presupposed (underlying) traits that a test developer may invoke to describe test behavior or criterion performance. The researcher investigating a test's construct validity must formulate hypotheses about the expected behavior of high scorers and low scorers on the test. From these hypotheses arises a tentative theory about the nature of the construct the test was designed to measure. If the test is a valid measure of the construct, the high scorers and low scorers will behave as predicted by the theory. If high scorers and low scorers on the test do not behave as predicted, the investigator will need to reexamine hypotheses made about the construct (and/or reexamine the nature of the construct itself). One possible reason for obtaining results contrary to those that would have been predicted by the theory is that the test simply is not a valid measure of the construct. An alternative explanation could lie in the theory that generated hypotheses about the construct—perhaps that theory needs to be reexamined. Perhaps the reason for the contrary finding can be traced to the incorrect inclusion in the experimental design of a particular statistical procedure or the incorrect execution of the procedure. Thus while confirming evidence contributes to a judgment that the test is indeed a valid measure of some construct, contrary evidence—on the bright side—provides a stimulus for the discovery of new facets of the construct and/or alternative ways to measure it.

Increasingly, construct validity has been viewed as the unifying concept for all validity evidence; all types of validity evidence, including content and criterion-related, are seen as a form of construct validity. A group of validity coefficients for a given test when considered individually can be interpreted with respect to the test's criterion-related validity; collectively, however, these coefficients have bearing on the construct validity of the test (Guion, 1980).

Evidence of Construct Validity

A number of procedures may be used to provide different kinds of evidence that a test has construct validity. The various techniques of construct validation may provide evidence, for example, that:

- The test is homogeneous, measuring a single construct.
- Test scores correlate with scores on other tests in accordance with what would be predicted from a theory that covers the manifestation of the construct in question.
- Test scores increase or decrease as a function of age or the passage of time as theoretically predicted.
- Test scores obtained subsequent to some event or the mere passage of time (that is, posttest scores) differ from pretest scores as theoretically predicted.
- Test scores obtained by people from distinct groups vary as predicted by theory.

A brief discussion of each type of construct validity evidence and the procedures used to obtain it follows.

Evidence of homogeneity *Homogeneity,* also referred to as *internal consistency,* generally refers to how well a test measures a single concept. A test developer can increase the homogeneity of an instrument in several ways. If, for example, the test contains a series of subtests that all contribute to the total score (for example, a test of academic achievement with subtests in areas such as mathematics, spelling, reading comprehension), the Pearson r could be used to correlate average subtest scores with average total test score. Subtests that in the test developer's judgment do not correlate very well with the test as a whole might have to be reconstructed (or eliminated) lest the test not measure the construct "academic achievement." Correlations between subtest scores and total test score are generally reported in the test manual as evidence of homogeneity.

One way a test developer can improve the homogeneity of a test containing items that are scored dichotomously (for example, "right" or "wrong") is by eliminating those items that do not show significant point-biserial correlation coefficients with another (continuous) variable. If all test items show significant, positive correlations with total test scores, and high scorers on the test tend to pass each item more than low scorers, then each item is probably measuring the same construct as the total test, thereby contributing to test homogeneity.

The homogeneity of a test in which items are scored on a multipoint scale can also be improved. For example, some attitude and opinion questionnaires require respondents to indicate level of agreement with specific statements by responding, for example, "strongly agree," "agree," "disagree," or "strongly disagree." Each response is then assigned a numerical score, and items that do not show significant Spearman rank-order correlation coefficients are eliminated. If all test items show significant, positive correlations with total test scores, then each item is most likely measuring the same construct that the test as a whole is measuring (and thereby contributing to the test's homogeneity). Coefficient alpha may also be used in estimating the heterogeneity of a test composed of multiple-choice items (Novick & Lewis, 1967).

A case study illustrating how a test's homogeneity can be improved can be found with reference to the Marital Satisfaction Scale (Roach, Frazier, & Bowden, 1981), an instrument designed to assess various aspects of married people's attitudes toward their marital relationship. The scale contains an approximately equal number of items expressing positive and negative sentiments with respect to marriage (for example, "My life would seem empty without my marriage" and "My marriage has 'smothered' my personality"). In one stage of the development of this test, subjects indicated how much they agreed or disagreed with the various sentiments in each of 73 items by marking a five-point scale that ranged from "strongly agree" to "strongly disagree." Based on the correlations between item scores and total score, the test developers elected to retain 48 items with correlation coefficients greater than .50, thus creating a more homogeneous instrument. We will continue to use the Marital Satisfaction Scale to illustrate the different types of procedures used to obtain the various kinds of evidence for the construct validity of a test.

In addition to correlational measures of test homogeneity, let us also mention an item-analysis procedure that entails focusing on the relationship between test takers' scores on individual items and their score on the entire test. Each item is examined with respect to how high scorers versus low scorers on the test responded to it. If it is an academic test and high scorers on the entire test for some reason tended to get that particular item wrong while low scorers on the test as a whole tended to get the item right, the item is obviously not a good one (and should be eliminated in the interest of test homogeneity, among other things). If the test is one of, say, marital satisfaction and individuals who score high on the test as a whole respond to a particular item in a way that would indicate that they are not satisfied (while people who tend not to be satisfied respond to the item in a way that would indicate that they are satisfied), then again the item should probably be eliminated or at least reexamined for its clarity.

While test homogeneity is desirable because it assures us that all of the items on the test tend to be measuring the same thing, it is not the "be-all and end-all" with respect to construct validity. Knowing that a test is homogeneous contributes no information about how the construct being measured relates to other constructs. It is therefore important that evidence of a test's homogeneity be reported along with other evidence of construct validity.

Evidence of changes with age The nature of some constructs is such that changes in them would be expected to occur over time. "Reading ability," for example, tends to increase dramatically year by year from age 6 to the early teens. If a test score purports to be a measure of a construct that could be expected to change over the course of time, it too should show the same progressive changes with age if the test score is to be considered a valid measure of the construct. We would expect, for example, that if children in grades 6, 7, 8, and 9 sat for a test of eighth-grade reading skills, the total number of items scored as correct from all of the test protocols would increase as a function of the higher grade level of the test takers.

Some constructs lend themselves more readily to predictions concerning changes over time than other constructs do. Thus, while we may be able to predict, for example, that a gifted child's scores on a test of reading skills will increase over the course of the test taker's years of elementary and secondary education, we may not be able to predict with such confidence how a newlywed couple will score through the years on a test of marital satisfaction. This fact does not relegate a construct such as "marital satisfaction" to any less stature than "reading ability"; rather, it simply means that measures of "marital satisfaction" may be less stable over time and/or more vulnerable to situational events (such as in-laws coming to visit and refusing to leave for three months) than is "reading ability" in specific instances. It must also be kept in mind that evidence of change over time, like evidence of test homogeneity, does not in itself provide information about how the construct relates to other constructs.

Evidence of pretest/posttest changes Evidence showing that test scores change as a result of some experience between a pretest and posttest can be evidence of construct validity. Some of the more typical intervening experiences responsible for changes in test scores are formal education, a course of therapy or medication, and on-the-job experience. Of course, depending on the construct being measured, almost any intervening life experience could be predicted to show changes in score from pretest to posttest (for example, reading an inspirational book, watching a TV talk show, undergoing surgery, visiting Haiti, or the mere passage of time).

Returning to our example regarding the use of the Marital Satisfaction Scale, one investigator cited in Roach, Frazier, & Bowden (1981) compared scores on that instrument before and after a sex therapy treatment program. Scores showed a significant change between pretest and posttest. A second posttest given eight weeks later showed that scores remained stable (suggesting the instrument was reliable) while the pretest/posttest measures were still significantly different. Such changes in scores in the predicted direction after the treatment program contribute to evidence of the construct validity for this test, which purports to measure the construct "marital satisfaction." Conversely, we would expect a decline in marital satisfaction scores if a pretest were administered to a sample of couples shortly after they took their nuptial vows and a posttest was administered shortly after members of the couples first consulted their respective divorce attorneys (employing for the purposes of the experimental group in this study only couples who consulted divorce attorneys). In designing such pretest/posttest research, a control group should ideally be included as a means of ruling out alternative explanations of the findings. Thus, with reference to the two examples above, simultaneous testing of a matched group of couples who did not undergo sex therapy and simultaneous testing of a matched group of couples who did not consult divorce attorneys would be advisable. In both instances, there would presumably be no reason to expect any significant changes in the test scores of these two control groups.

Evidence from distinct groups Also referred to as the method of contrasted groups, one way of providing evidence for the validity of a test is to demonstrate that scores on the test vary in a predictable way as a function of membership in some group. The rationale here is that if a test is a valid measure of a particular construct, then test scores from groups of people who would be presumed to differ with respect to that construct should have correspondingly different test scores. It would be reasonable to expect that on a test designed to measure depression (wherein the higher the test score, the more depressed the test taker is presumed to be), individuals psychiatrically hospitalized for depression should score higher than a random sample of fans at the local baseball stadium. Suppose it was your intention to provide construct validity evidence for the Marital Satisfaction Scale by means of showing differences in scores between distinct groups; how might you go about doing that?

Roach, Frazier, and Bowden (1981) proceeded by identifying two groups of married couples, one relatively satisfied in their marriage, the other not so satisfied. The groups were identified by means of ratings by peers and by professional marriage counsellors. A *t*-test on the difference between mean score on the test was significant ($p<.01$)—evidence to support the notion that the Marital Satisfaction Scale is indeed a valid measure of the construct "marital satisfaction."

In a bygone era, another way test developers created distinct groups was, to put it bluntly, by deception. For example, if it had been predicted that more of the construct would be exhibited on the test in question if the subject was made to feel highly anxious, an experimental situation might be designed to make the subject feel highly anxious. Virtually any feeling state (such as low self-esteem or impotence) the theory called for could be induced by an experimental scenario that typically involved giving the research subject some misinformation or false feedback. However, given the ethical constraints of contemporary psychologists combined with the fact that academic institutions and other sponsors of research tend not to condone deception in human research, the method of obtaining distinct groups by creating them through the dissemination of deceptive information is seldom employed.

Convergent evidence Evidence for the construct validity of a particular test may "converge" from a number of sources, such as other tests or measures designed to assess the same (or a similar) construct. Thus if scores on the test undergoing construct validation tend to correlate highly in the predicted direction with scores on older, more established, and already validated tests designed to measure the same (or a similar) construct, this would be an example of convergent evidence.[5]

Convergent evidence for validity may come not only from correlations with tests purporting to measure an identical construct, but also from correlations with measures purporting to measure related constructs. Consider, for example, a new test designed to measure the construct "test anxiety." Generally speaking, we might expect high positive correlations between this new test and older, more established measures of test anxiety. However, we might also expect more moderate correlations between this new test and measures of general anxiety.

Roach, Frazier, and Bowden (1981) provided convergent evidence of the construct validity of the Marital Satisfaction Scale by computing a validity coeffi-

---

5. Data indicating that a test measures the same construct as other tests purporting to measure the same construct are also referred to as *convergent validity*. One question that may be raised at this juncture concerns the necessity for the new test if it simply duplicates existing tests that measure the same construct. The answer, generally speaking, is a claim that the new test has some advantage over the more established test (for example, it is shorter and can be administered in less time without significant loss in reliability or validity, or it examines the construct being assessed in a more up-to-date way).

Close-up

The Multitrait-Multimethod Matrix

"Multitrait" means "two or more traits" and "multimethod" means "two or more methods." The multitrait-multimethod matrix (Campbell & Fiske, 1959) is the matrix or table that results from correlating variables (traits) within and between methods. Values for any number of traits (such as aggressiveness or extraversion) as obtained by various methods (such as behavioral observation or a projective test) are inserted into the table, and the resulting matrix of correlations provides insight with respect to both the convergent and discriminant validity of the methods used. Table 1 provides a preview of the basic structure of the matrix when measures of three traits have been obtained by the use of three methods.

Let's suppose you have developed a test you wish to validate that purports to measure the trait

"job satisfaction" (JS). Your test is a paper-and-pencil, self-report measure of satisfaction in the workplace. Using the multitrait-multimethod design, you would need to examine at least one other variable. You select marital satisfaction (MS) as a second trait to examine. "For good measure," you add a third trait to the experimental design: self-satisfaction (SS), a trait you define as the comfort and satisfaction one has with oneself alone, including personal comfort and satisfaction with level of academic, financial, and social achievement. If strong correlations were found to exist between measures of JS, MS, and SS, you might conclude that all three of these measures were actually measuring the same thing, a construct you might call "general life satisfaction." Alternatively, moderate correlations among these traits as assessed by the instruments

cient between scores on it and scores on the Marital Adjustment Test (Locke & Wallace, 1959). The validity coefficient of .79 provided additional evidence of the construct validity of the instrument.

Discriminant evidence   A validity coefficient showing little (that is, a statistically insignificant) relationship between test scores and/or other variables with which scores on the test being construct-validated should *not* theoretically be correlated provides *discriminant evidence* of construct validity (also referred to as "discriminant validity"). In the course of developing the Marital Satisfaction Scale (MSS), scores on that instrument were correlated with scores on the Marlowe-Crowne Social Desirability Scale (Crowne & Marlowe, 1964). Roach, Frazier, and Bowden (1981) hypothesized that high correlations between these two instruments would suggest that respondents were probably not answering entirely honestly to items on the MSS but were instead responding in socially desirable ways. But the correlation between the MSS and the social desirability measure did not prove to be significant, and the test developers concluded that social desirability could be ruled out as a primary factor in explaining the meaning of MSS test scores.

In 1959 an experimental design useful for examining both convergent and discriminant validity evidence appeared in the pages of *Psychological Bulletin*. In the Close-up for this chapter, we provide a barebones summary of this rather

you are using would suggest that while all three may be components of general satisfaction, each also contributes something unique; each represents a viable trait separate and distinct from the others.

As illustrated in Table 2, the three methods you have elected to use are (1) a self-report rating scale, (2) a spouse rating scale, and (3) a peer questionnaire; each of the three types of satisfaction traits we are interested in will be assessed by each one of these methods. This means, for example, that a measure of "self-satisfaction" will be obtained not only by the subject himself or herself, but also by the subject's spouse (that is, how self-satisfied the spouse believes the subject to be) and by a peer of the subject.

The data required for insertion into the matrix include the following: reliability coefficients, va-

lidity coefficients, correlations between the different traits measured by the same method, and correlations between different traits measured by the different methods. In Table 3, along the diagonal we have labeled **a,** are the reliability coefficients for the three traits measured by the same method. Focusing on this part of the matrix we can see that the reliability coefficient of the self-report job satisfaction scale is .98; the reliability coefficient of the self-report marital satisfaction is .94, the reliability of self-satisfaction as measured by the peer questionnaire is .88, and so on. The reliability coefficients will typically be the highest values reported in the matrix.

Another part of the matrix contains correlations between different traits using the same method; it is highlighted in Table 4 in the solid triangles labeled **b.** If tests are actually measuring

The Multitrait-Multimethod Matrix (continued)

Table 1

***Basic Structure of a Multitrait-Multimethod Matrix
for Three Traits Assessed by Three Methods***

	Method 1			Method 2			Method 3		
	Trait 1	Trait 2	Trait 3	Trait 1	Trait 2	Trait 3	Trait 1	Trait 2	Trait 3
Method 1									
Trait 1	.								
Trait 2	.	.							
Trait 3	.	.	.						
Method 2									
Trait 1	.	.	.	.					
Trait 2	.	.	.	.	.				
Trait 3	.	.	.	.	.	.			
Method 3									
Trait 1	.	.	.	.	.	.	.		
Trait 2	.	.	.	.	.	.	.	.	
Trait 3	.	.	.	.	.	.	.	.	.

Table 2

***A Multitrait-Multimethod Matrix for Three Measures
of Satisfaction Assessed by Three Different Methods***

	Self-report			Spouse rating scale			Peer questionnaire		
	JS	MS	SS	JS	MS	SS	JS	MS	SS
Self-report									
JS	.								
MS	.	.							
SS	.	.	.						
Spouse rating scale									
JS	.	.	.	.					
MS	.	.	.	.	.				
SS	.	.	.	.	.	.			
Peer questionnaire									
JS	.	.	.	.	.	.	.		
MS	.	.	.	.	.	.	.	.	
SS	.	.	.	.	.	.	.	.	.

Table 3

Multitrait-Multimethod Matrix with Reliability Coefficients Inserted

	Self-report			Spouse rating scale			Peer questionnaire		
	JS	MS	SS	JS	MS	SS	JS	MS	SS
Self-report									
JS	**a** .98								
MS	.	.94							
SS	.	.	.96						
Spouse rating scale									
JS	.	.	.	**a** .92					
MS	.	.	.	.	.89				
SS	.	.	.	.	.	.86			
Peer questionnaire									
JS	.	.	.	.	.	.	**a** .80		
MS	.	.	.	.	.	.	.	.85	
SS	.	.	.	.	.	.	.	.	.88

Table 4

Multitrait-Multimethod Matrix, with Correlations Between Different Traits Using the Same Methods Highlighted

	Self-report			Spouse rating scale			Peer questionnaire		
	JS	MS	SS	JS	MS	SS	JS	MS	SS
Self-report									
JS	.								
MS	**b** .50	.							
SS	.42	.59	.						
Spouse rating scale									
JS	.	.	.	.					
MS	.	.	.	**b** .40	.				
SS	.	.	.	.60	.52	.			
Peer questionnaire									
JS	.	.	.	.	.	.	.		
MS	.	.	.	.	.	.	**b** .10	.	
SS	.	.	.	.	.	.	.50	.46	.

The Multitrait-Multimethod Matrix (continued)

different constructs, these correlations should be relatively low. Self-report measures of marital satisfaction and job satisfaction correlate .50—a fact that suggests that while they are measuring something in common, they are also both contributing unique information as well. Much the same could be said about the self-satisfaction measures, which also seem to fall in the .40 to .60 range.

A third part of the matrix contains the validity coefficients—designated in Table 5 along the **c** diagonals. Here we see the correlations between the same trait using different methods. For example, the validity coefficient between job satisfaction by self-report and job satisfaction by spouse rating is .65; the validity coefficient between marital satisfaction by spouse rating and marital satisfaction by peer questionnaire is .72.

As illustrated in Table 6 a fourth component of the matrix contains correlations between different traits using different methods (**d** triangles). The value of these correlation coefficients will be among the lowest in the matrix if

evidence of construct validity is deemed to be present.

The complete multitrait-multimethod matrix is presented in Table 7. For satisfactory evidence of construct validity, the validity coefficients (representing correlations between the same traits using different methods) in the **c** diagonal should be higher than correlations between different traits, same methods (**b** triangles); they should also be higher than correlations between different traits, different methods (**d** triangles). If job satisfaction correlated with marital satisfaction using different methods (validity coefficients), it should be higher than job satisfaction correlated with marital satisfaction by the same method. If the correlation between self-report job and marital satisfaction were higher than job satisfaction by self-report correlated with job satisfaction by peer questionnaire, one could assume that the scores on self-report were affected substantially by some other factor common to the method (such as desire to respond in a socially desirable way).

Table 5

Multitrait-Multimethod Matrix with Validity Coefficients
for the Same Trait Assessed by Different Methods

	Self-report			Spouse rating scale			Peer questionnaire		
	JS	MS	SS	JS	MS	SS	JS	MS	SS
Self-report									
JS	.								
MS	.	.							
SS	.	.	.						
Spouse rating scale									
JS	**c** .65	.		.					
MS	.	.61	.	.	.				
SS	.	.	.66	.	.	.			
Peer questionnaire									
JS	**c** .59	.		**c** .69	.		.		
MS	.	.55	.	.	.72	.	.	.	
SS	.	.	.58	.	.	.68	.	.	.

Table 6

Multitrait-Multimethod Matrix with Correlations for Different Traits Assessed by Different Methods

	Self-report			Spouse rating scale			Peer questionnaire		
	JS	MS	SS	JS	MS	SS	JS	MS	SS
Self-report									
JS	.								
MS	.	.							
SS	.	.	.						
Spouse rating scale									
JS	.	d .10	.15	.					
MS	d .02	.	.18	.	.				
SS	.04	.10	.	.	.	.			
Peer questionnaire									
JS	.	d .08	.11	.	d .00	.04	.		
MS	d .01	.	.09	d .00	.	.02	.	.	
SS	.06	.11	.	.02	.05	.	.	.	.

Table 7

A Sample Multitrait-Multimethod Matrix

	Self-report			Spouse rating scale			Peer questionnaire		
	JS	MS	SS	JS	MS	SS	JS	MS	SS
Self-report									
JS	a .98								
MS	b .50	.94							
SS	.42	.59	.96						
Spouse rating scale									
JS	c .65	d .10	.15	a .92					
MS	d .02	.61	.18	b .40	.89				
SS	.04	.10	.66	.60	.52	.86			
Peer questionnaire									
JS	c .59	d .08	.11	c .69	d .00	.04	a .80		
MS	d .01	.55	.09	d .00	.72	.02	b .10	.85	
SS	.06	.11	.58	.02	.05	.68	.50	.46	.88

lengthy journal article that describes the technically complex, but highly useful multitrait-multimethod matrix.[6]

Factor analysis Both convergent and discriminant evidence of construct validity can be obtained by the use of *factor analysis*. "Factor analysis" is a term used to describe a class of mathematical procedures designed to identify *factors* or—in the case of psychological test data—to identify the specific variables that are presumed to influence or explain test performance. It is, in essence, a data reduction method in which several sets of scores and the correlations between them are mathematically considered; its purpose is to identify the factor or factors that are presumed to cause the test scores to correlate.

A new test purporting to measure bulimia, for example, can be factor-analyzed with other known measures of bulimia, as well as with other kinds of measures (such as measures of intelligence, self-esteem, general anxiety, anorexia, or perfectionism). High factor loadings by the new test on a "bulimia factor" would provide convergent evidence of construct validity. Moderate to low factor loadings by the new test with respect to measures of other eating disorders such as anorexia would provide discriminant evidence of construct validity. A *factor loading* has been explained by Tyler (1965, p. 44) as "a sort of metaphor. Each test is thought of as a vehicle carrying a certain amount of one or more of the abilities. Another way of explaining it is that the loading of a certain factor in a certain test shows us the extent to which this factor determines the scores individuals make on the test."

Factor-analytic procedures may involve technical procedures so complex that few contemporary researchers would attempt to routinely conduct one without the aid of a prepackaged computer program. But while the actual data analysis has become work for computers, humans still tend to be very much involved in the *naming* of factors once the computer has identified them. Thus, for example, if a factor analysis identified a common factor being measured by two hypothetical instruments, a "Bulimia Test" and an "Anorexia Test," a question concerning what to name this factor would arise. One factor analyst looking at the data and the items of each test might christen the common factor an "Eating Disorder Factor." Another factor analyst examining exactly the same materials might label the common factor a "Body Weight Preoccupation Factor." A third analyst might name the factor a "Self-Perception Disorder Factor," and so forth. The point here is that the naming of factors that emerge from a factor analysis tends not to be a matter of mathematical skill; it is more a matter of precision in verbal abstraction.[7] We will come across reference to factor analysis again in the following chapter on test development and a brief, readable description of what it is, how it's used, and why you need to know about it appears in Appendix B. Be-

---

6. For an interesting, "real-life" application of the multitrait-multimethod technique, see Meier's (1984) examination of the validity of the construct "burnout." In a subsequent construct validity study, Meier (1991) used an alternative to the multitrait-multimethod matrix to examine another construct: "occupational stress."

7. No specific rules for labeling factors exist; factor analysts can only be expected to make their best judgment concerning what name accurately communicates the meaning of the factor.

yond those discussions, the reader interested in obtaining more detailed information on this statistical tool is referred to books devoted to its explanation (such as Gorsuch, 1974).

VALIDITY AND TEST BIAS

Our discussion of test validity would be incomplete without mention of the topic of test bias. In the eyes of many lay people, questions concerning the validity of a test are intimately tied to questions concerning the fair use of a test and the issue of test bias. Let us hasten to point out that issues of validity, fairness in the use of a test, and test bias are three separate issues. It is possible for a valid test to be used fairly or unfairly. It is even possible for a test that is biased to be used fairly or unfairly. To see why, an understanding of test bias and related terminology is necessary.

The Definition of "Test Bias"

The term *bias* as applied to tests may be defined as a factor inherent within a test that systematically prevents accurate, impartial measurement. If the test in question were a "flip-coin test" (FCT), the FCT would be considered to be biased if the "instrument" (the coin) were weighted so that either heads or tails would appear more frequently than it would by chance alone. If the test in question were an intelligence test, the test would be considered to be biased if it were constructed so that people who had brown eyes consistently and systematically obtained higher scores than people with green eyes—assuming, of course, that in reality people with brown eyes are not generally more intelligent than people with green eyes. "Systematic" is a key word in our definition of test bias. We have previously looked at sources of *random* or chance variation in test scores; *bias,* however, implies *systematic* variation.

To illustrate, let's suppose we need to hire 50 secretaries, and so we place an ad in the newspaper. In response to the ad, 200 people reply, including 100 people who happen to have brown eyes and 100 people who happen to have green eyes. Each of the 200 applicants is individually administered a hypothetical test we will call the "Test of Secretarial Skills" (TSS). Logic tells us that eye color is probably not a relevant variable with respect to performing the duties of a secretary; we would therefore have no reason to believe that green-eyed people are better secretaries than brown-eyed people or vice versa. We therefore might reasonably expect that after the tests have been scored and the selection process has been completed, an approximately equivalent amount of brown-eyed and green-eyed people would have been hired (that is, approximately 25 brown-eyed people and 25 green-eyed people). But what if, in the end, it turned out that 48 green-eyed people were hired and only two brown-eyed people were hired? Is this evidence that the TSS is a biased test?

Although the answer to this question seems simple on the face of it—"Yes the test is biased because they should have hired 25 and 25!"—a truly responsible answer to this question would entail statistically "troubleshooting" the test and the entire selection procedure (see Berk, 1982). To begin with, the following three characteristics of the regression lines (see Figure 6–3) used to predict success on the criterion would have to be scrutinized: (1) the slope, (2) the intercept, (3) the error of estimate. And because these three features of regression are functions of two other statistics (the validity coefficient and the reliability coefficient for both the test and the criterion) that could vary with respect to the two groups in question, there exists a total of five characteristics that must be statistically examined. A test of significance could indicate that our brown-eyed and green-eyed groups are the same or different with respect to any of these five characteristics. This binary choice (that is, same or different) taken to the fifth power (meaning that there are five ways that the two groups could conceivably differ) means that a comprehensive "troubleshooting" would entail examination of a total of 32 ($2^5 = 32$) possible ways the test could be found to be biased.

If, for example, a test systematically underpredicts or overpredicts the performance of members of a particular group (such as people with green eyes) with respect to a criterion (such as supervisory rating), there exists what is referred to as *intercept bias*—a term taken from the point where the regression line intersects the Y-axis. If a test systematically yields significantly different validity coefficients for members of different groups, there exists what is referred to as *slope bias*—so named since the slope of one group's regression line is different in a statistically significant way from the regression line of another group. One reason some tests have been found to be biased has more to do with the design of the research study than the design of the test; if there are too few test takers in one of the groups (such as the minority group—literally), this methodological problem will make it appear as if the test is biased when in fact it may not be. A situation in which a test may justifiably be deemed biased is one in which some portion of its variance stems from some factor(s) irrelevant to performance on the criterion measure; as a consequence, one group of test takers will systematically perform

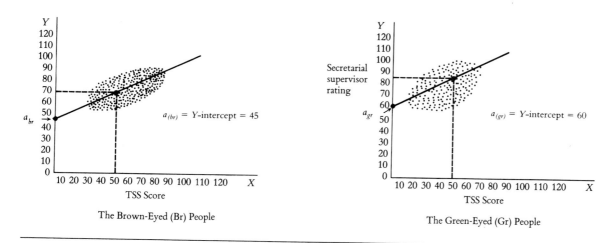

Figure 6–3 *TSS Scores and Supervisor Ratings for Two Groups.* Note the different points of the Y-intercept corresponding to a TSS score of 50 for the green-eyed and brown-eyed test takers. If the TSS were an unbiased test, any given score on it would correspond to exactly the same criterion score for both groups.

differently from another. Prevention (during test development) is the best cure for test bias though a procedure called "estimated true score transformations" represents one of many available *post hoc* remedies (Mueller, 1949; see also Reynolds & Brown, 1984).[8]

differently from another. Prevention (during test development) is the best cure for test bias though a procedure called "estimated true score transformations" represents one of many available *post hoc* remedies (Mueller, 1949; see also Reynolds & Brown, 1984).[8]

Let us for the moment turn our attention away from the test and focus on the supervisory ratings that are at the heart of the criterion ("satisfactory" or "unsatisfactory" evaluation of performance). Is it possible for systematic error to exist in ratings? Yes it is, and a discussion of this variety of bias follows.

Rating error   A *rating* is a numerical or verbal judgment (or both) that places a person or attribute along a continuum identified by a scale of numerical and/or word descriptors called a *rating scale* (for example, a supervisor rates a worker on a scale of productivity, or a psychiatric patient rates himself or herself on the degree of depression being experienced). Simply stated, a *rating error* is a judgment resulting from the intentional or unintentional misuse of a rating scale. Thus, for example, a *leniency error* (also referred to as a *generosity error*) is, as its name implies, an error in rating that arises due to the tendency on the part of the rater to be lenient in marking. From your own experience during course registration, you might be aware that a section of a particular course will fill very quickly if the section is being taught by a professor who has a reputation for committing leniency errors when it comes to end-of-term grading. At the other extreme from a leniency error in rating is a *severity error.* Movie critics who pan just about everything they review may be guilty of severity errors (assuming that these critics review a wide range of movies that might consensually be viewed as good and bad). Another type of error might be referred to as a *central tendency error.* Here, the rater, for whatever reason, exhibits a general and systematic reluctance to giving ratings at either the most positive or negative extreme and so all ratings tend to cluster in the middle of the rating continuum. One way to overcome what might be called "restriction of range rating errors" (central tendency, leniency, severity errors) is to use *rankings,* a procedure that requires the rater to compare individuals against one another instead of against an absolute scale. Now the rater is forced to select first, second, third choices and so forth.

A *halo effect* refers to the fact that, for some raters, some ratees can do no wrong. More specifically, a halo effect may also be defined as a tendency to give a particular ratee a higher rating than he or she objectively deserves based on the rater's failure to discriminate among conceptually distinct and potentially independent aspects of a ratee's behavior. To give a (very) hypothetical example, suppose Frank Sinatra consented to write and deliver a speech on multivariate analysis. His speech would probably earn much higher all-around ratings if given before the founding chapter of the Frank Sinatra Fan Club than if delivered before and rated by the membership of, say, the Royal Statistical Society (even in the unlikely event that the members of each group were equally savvy with respect to multivariate analysis).

8. Lest the student think that there is something not quite right about transforming data under such circumstances, we would add that even though "transformation" is synonymous with "change," the change referred to here is merely a change in form—not meaning. Data may be transformed to place them in a more useful form, not to change their meaning.

Criterion data may also be influenced by the rater's knowledge of the ratee's race or sex (Landy & Farr, 1980). Males have been shown to receive more favorable evaluations than females in traditionally masculine occupations. Except in highly integrated situations, ratees tend to receive higher ratings from raters of the same race (Landy & Farr, 1980). Returning to our TSS situation, a particular rater may have had particularly great—or particularly distressing—prior experiences with green-eyed (or brown-eyed) people and be making extraordinarily high (or low) ratings on that irrational basis.

Training programs to familiarize raters with common rating errors and sources of rater bias have shown promise in reducing rating errors and increasing measures of reliability and validity. Lecture, role playing, discussion, use of videotaped feedback, and computer simulation of different situations are some of the many techniques that could be brought to bear in a training program designed to increase inter-rater reliability.

Bias, tests, and the federal courts   "How good are federal judges in detecting differences in item difficulty on intelligence tests for ethnic groups?" This was the intriguing question raised by Sattler (1991) in an article titled with this same question. Sattler's inquiry was spurred by two conflicting judgments made in two different federal courts regarding allegations of bias in individually administered intelligence tests. In the 1979 California case of *Larry P. et al. v. Wilson Riles et al.,* individual intelligence tests were found to be biased against black children. In the 1980 Illinois case of *Parents in Action on Special Education (PASE) v. Joseph P. Hannon,* individual intelligence tests were not found to be culturally biased. Both judges had reached their decision regarding the weight of the evidence on the basis of personal inspection of test items and on the testimony of expert witnesses. Although their final judgments differed, both judges had expressed the opinion that certain items on the Wechsler Intelligence Scale for Children (WISC), and on the revised version of this test, the WISC-R, were biased. According to Sattler (1991, p. 125), "A reading of the two judges' opinion briefs suggests that the term 'biased' was used in the sense of 'too difficult' or 'too hard,' and thus these items were biased from the judges' point of view." Sattler (1991) reviewed the literature on the issue of bias in WISC and WISC-R items, and reported on his investigation of the comparative difficulty of 25 selected items from these tests. Twelve of the 25 items were found to be significantly more difficult for the black children than for the white children. Of these 12 items, six had been cited by the two judges—yielding an accuracy hit rate which was no better than chance for the judges attempting to judge the comparative difficulty of intelligence-test items.

One question that consideration of these cases brings to the fore is: "If members of one ethnic group consistently score significantly lower than members of another ethnic group on a particular test, is the test necessarily biased?"

For members of the lay public—and perhaps some federal judges as well—the answer to the latter question is "Yes" (Reschley & Grimes, 1990; Reynolds & Kaiser, 1990a, 1990b). Underlying the opinion that differences among groups on ability tests represents bias in the test is the assumption that there is no reason to expect differences in level of performance on various tasks by various groups of people. Accordingly, any test demonstrating such differences is deemed to be biased. But just as there is no reason to believe that differences in performance exist between groups, there is no reason for deciding in advance that no differences exist (Reynolds & Kaiser, 1990a, 1990b).

The Definition of "Fairness" as Applied to Tests

As difficult and complex as it is to define *bias,* it is a "piece of cake" when compared to the difficulty encountered in searching for a definition of *fairness.* Though the definition of "bias" in the statistical sense may be technically complex, it is after all a definable mathematical entity as applied to a test. By contrast, issues of fairness tend to be rooted in moral/philosophical questions regarding the use of test data—questions that cannot be answered with mathematical preciseness or conceptualized in terms of statistical probabilities. Apart from the patently obvious unfair use of tests—situations that any reasonable person would consider unfair (for instance, the misuse of psychological tests in some countries to detain, even imprison)—what constitutes a "fair" and an "unfair" use of tests is a matter left to parties such as the test developer (in the test manual's usage guidelines), the test user (in the way the test is actually used in practice), and society (in the form of legislation, judicial decisions, and administrative regulations).[9] Although a definition of fairness as applied to testing eludes any simple definition, Ghiselli, Campbell, and Zedeck (1981) offered the following: "In general fairness refers to whether a difference in mean predictor scores between two groups represents a useful distinction for society, relative to a decision that must be made, or whether the difference represents a bias that is irrelevant to the objectives at hand." (p. 320)

Although fairness as applied to tests is at best difficult to address, it is possible to address some rather common misunderstandings regarding what are sometimes perceived as "unfair" or even "biased" tests. Some tests, for example, have been termed "unfair" because they discriminate between groups of people;[10] the reasoning here goes that while differences may exist between individuals, all people are created equal and any differences found between groups of people on any psychological trait must be an artifact of the "unfair" or "biased" test. Because this position is so rooted in faith as opposed to scientific evidence—it in fact flies in the face of scientific evidence—it is virtually impossible to refute; one either believes it or doesn't. While we would all like to believe that people are equal in every way and are capable of rising to the same heights given equal opportunity, a more realistic view would appear to be that each person is capable of fulfilling a personal potential. We all differ in so many ways—individually and as groups—with respect to physical traits, that one would be hard put to believe that

---

9. In the latter context, you may wish to consult an interesting review article by Russell (1984) that provides an overview of federal fair-employment legislation, administrative guidelines, and court cases that relate to issues such as the "fairness" of personnel selection practices involving the use of training as a criterion.

10. The verb *discriminate* here is used in the psychometric sense, meaning, "to show a statistically significant difference between individuals or groups with respect to measurement." The great difference between this statistical, scientific definition and other colloquial definitions (such as "to treat differently and/or unfairly because of group membership") must be kept firmly in mind in discussions of bias and fairness.

psychological differences found to exist between individuals—and groups of individuals—are purely a function of inadequate tests. Again, although a test is not inherently unfair or biased simply because it is a tool by which group differences are found, the *use* of the test data can, like the use of any data, be unfair.

Another misunderstanding regarding what constitutes an unfair or unbiased test is the idea that it is unfair to administer to a particular population a standardized test that did not include members of that population in the standardization sample. In fact, it may well be unfair but whether it is or not must be determined by statistical or other means; the sheer fact that no members of a particular group were included in the standardization sample does *not*, in and of itself, invalidate the test for use with that group. Consider in this context a test we will call "The 7-Year Itch Test" (7-YIT). Initially designed to explore whether husbands really do become "itchy" (read "restless") after seven years of marriage, this hypothetical test of marital restlessness was originally standardized in the 1960s on a large sample of men who had been married for seven years. But in the 1990s, the test is being used not only to assess how "itchy" men get after seven years of marriage, but women as well. Suppose that a couple married seven years, Bob and Carole, take the 7-YIT and are informed that they each scored at the 95th percentile in marital "itchiness." We can conclude that their 7-YIT scores are higher than 95% of the men who take the test. We would have no basis on these data alone, however, to draw any comparisons between Bob and Carole and other couples with respect to 7-YIT performance, nor any basis for conclusions about Carole's "itchiness" relative to other women who have also been married seven years.

A final source of misunderstanding is that concerned with the complex problem of remedying situations where bias or unfair test usage has been found to occur. In the area of selection for jobs, positions in universities and professional schools, and the like, courts across the country have caused the institution of systems that in principle are designed to compensate for prior unfair practices. Systems such as *quotas* (wherein a preset proportion of members of a particular group must be selected regardless of their standing with respect to other applicants) make selection of the best-qualified applicants on the basis of test scores a consideration secondary to the social benefit anticipated as a result of instituting a quota system. Hunter and Schmidt (1976) have raised some important considerations in this regard:

> In college selection, for example, the poor risk blacks who are admitted by a quota are more likely to fail than the higher scoring whites who were rejected because of the quota. Thus, in situations where low criterion performance carries a considerable penalty being selected on the basis of quotas is a mixed blessing.
>
> If lowered performance is met by increased rates of expulsion or firing, then the institution is relatively unaffected but (1) the quotas are undone and (2) there is considerable anguish for those selected who didn't make it. On the other hand, if the institution tries to adjust to the candidates selected by the quotas, there may be great cost and inefficiency. Finally, there is the one other problem which academic institutions must face. Quotas will inevitably lower the average performance of graduating seniors, and hence lower the prestige of the school. Similar considerations apply in the case of the employment setting. In both cases, the effects of these changes on the

broader society must also be considered. These effects are difficult to assess, but they may be quite significant. (p. 1069)

Hunter and Schmidt also described a related consideration with respect to the institution of a quota system in one company wherein the company "deliberately reduced its entrance standards so as to hire more blacks. However, these people could not then pass the internal promotion tests and hence accumulated in the lowest level jobs in the organization. The government then took them to court for discriminatory promotion policies!" (p. 1069).

An additional consideration with respect to quota and quotalike systems has to do with the feelings of "minority applicants who are selected under a quota system but who also would have been selected under unqualified individualism and must therefore pay the price, in lowered prestige and self-esteem, of the over-all lower average performance of minority selectees, which is due mostly to the lower performance of those minority selectees who were accepted in preference to better qualified but rejected majority applicants" (Jensen, 1980, p. 398).

If performance differences between identified groups of people on a particular test are found to consistently occur and such performance differences are found to have an adverse impact on one or more of the groups, some "hard" questions will no doubt have to be dealt with if the test is to continue to be used: What steps can be taken to eliminate (or at least minimize) the adverse impact? What is the value to the organization doing the testing and to society as a whole with respect to (1) continuing to use the test in the way it has been used in the past, or, (2) modifying the way the test has been used in the past? And, of course, there is the bottom-line, multifaceted, and difficult-to-answer question: "What constitutes a fair use of a test?" Once some consensus as to the fair use of a test has been agreed to, the matter moves from the abstract province of morals and philosophy to the more mundane matter of instituting the agreed-on policy via clearcut guidelines for test use, the calibration of cutoff scores on the criterion measure, and so forth.

In the meantime our use of tests is guided by state and federal rules, regulations, and legislation, as well as by the ethical standards of our professional organizations. Tests that are used should be technically adequate, show appropriate evidence of reliability and validity, and be administered and interpreted carefully so that individuals are not unduly penalized on the basis of disabling conditions, language differences, or related factors. Within the school setting, test results must be used in a way that provides maximal educational opportunities, in no way adversely impacting or restricting such opportunities.

Our discussion of issues of test fairness and test bias may seem to have brought us some distance from the cut-and-dried, relatively nonemotional subject of test validity. However, the complex issues accompanying discussions of test validity, including issues of fairness and bias, must be wrestled with by us all. For further consideration of the philosophical issues involved, the interested student is referred to the solitude of his or her own thought and the "reading" of his or her own conscience.

Chapter 7

Test Development

ALL TESTS ARE not created equal. The creation of a "good test" is not a matter of chance; it is the product of the thoughtful and sound application of established principles of test construction. In this chapter we explore the basics of test development and examine in detail the processes by which tests are constructed. While we focus on tests of the published, standardized variety, much of what we have to say also applies to "custom-made" tests (for example, teacher-made for classroom use and researcher-made for a particular study); and, in fact, the last section of this chapter deals exclusively with special considerations in custom-designing a test.

You can think of the process of developing a test as occurring in five stages:

test conceptualization
test construction
test tryout
item analysis
test revision

Briefly, once the idea for a test is conceived (test conceptualization), items for the test are drafted (test construction). This "first draft" of the test is then tried out on a group of sample test takers (test tryout). Once the data from the tryout are in, test takers' performance on the test as a whole and on each of the test's

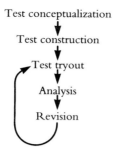

Test conceptualization

Test construction

Test tryout

Analysis

Revision

Figure 7–1 *The Test Development Process.*

items will be analyzed. Statistical procedures collectively referred to as "item analysis" will be employed to assist in making judgments about which items are good as they are, which items may need to be revised, and which items should be discarded. The analysis of the test's items may include analyses of item reliability, item validity, item discrimination, and—depending on the type of test it is—item difficulty level. On the basis of the item analysis and related considerations a revision or "second draft" of the test will be created. This revised version of the test will now be tried out on a new sample of test takers, the result will be analyzed, the test will be further revised if necessary—and so it goes (Figure 7–1). A detailed description of each step in the test development process follows.

TEST CONCEPTUALIZATION

The beginnings of any published test can probably be traced to thoughts—"self-talk" in behavioral terms. The test developer says to himself or herself something like: "There ought to be a test designed to measure [fill in the blank] in [such and such] way." The stimulus for such a thought could be almost anything. A review of the available literature on existing tests designed to measure a particular construct might indicate that such tests leave much to be desired in terms of psychometric soundness—and the would-be test developer thinks he or she can do better. The emergence to prominence of some social phenomenon or pattern of behavior might serve as the stimulus for the development of a new test. If, for example, celibacy were to become a widely practiced lifestyle, we might witness the development of "celibacy tests," tests that might measure variables like " reasons for adopting this lifestyle," "commitment to this lifestyle," "degree of celibacy by specific behaviors." The analogy in medicine is straightforward; once a new disease (such as acquired immune deficiency syndrome [AIDS], Legionnaire's disease, or toxic shock syndrome) comes to the attention of medical researchers, they attempt to develop diagnostic tests to assess its presence or absence as well as the severity of its manifestation in the body. The development of a new test may be a response to a need to assess level of mastery in relatively new professions (such as computer programming or financial planning).

Regardless of the stimulus for developing the new test, the prospective test developer must at some point confront a number of important questions if the test is to be published by a reputable publisher and taken seriously by potential test users. A partial listing of the questions to be dealt with includes:

- *What is the objective of the test?* How is this objective the same as or different from existing tests designed to measure the same thing? How will the objective(s) be met?
- *Is there really a need for this test?* Are there other tests that purport to measure the same thing? In what ways will the proposed test be better than existing tests? Will it be more reliable? More valid? More comprehensive? Take less time to administer? How might this not be better than the other tests? Who would use this test and why?
- *Who would need to take this test?* Who would need the data derived from an administration of it? Why?
- *What content area should the test cover?* How and why is this different from the content of existing similar tests?
- *How will the test be administered?* Will the test be individually administered or group administered, or should it be amenable for both individual and group administration? What differences will exist between the individually administered version and the group-administered version? Will the test be designed for computer administration? How might differences between different versions of the test be reflected in test scores?
- *What is the ideal item format for this test?* Why?
- *Should more than one form of the test be developed?* Why?
- *What special training will be required of test users in terms of administering or interpreting the test?* What background and qualifications will a prospective user of data derived from an administration of this test need to have? What restrictions, if any, should be placed on distributors of the test and on the test's usage?
- *What types of responses will be required by test takers?* What "real world" behaviors would be anticipated to correlate with these responses? Why will scores on this test be important?

Depending on the nature of the test and the specific question asked, the task of answering such questions may require activity ranging from simple logic, to literature reviews, to experimentation, to "soul-searching." Once the test has been conceived, however, the process of test construction begins.

TEST CONSTRUCTION

Scaling

We have previously defined *measurement* as "the assignment of numbers according to rules" and noted that *scales* are the rules of measurement. *Scaling* may be defined as the process of setting rules for assigning numbers in measurement. Stated another way, scaling refers to the process by which a measuring device is designed and "calibrated," the way numbers (or other indices)—scale values—are assigned to different amounts of the trait, attribute, or characteristic being measured.

From a historical perspective, the prolific L. L. Thurstone may be credited with being at the forefront of efforts to develop methodologically sound scaling techniques. His 1925 article in the *Journal of Educational Psychology* entitled "A Method of Scaling Psychological and Educational Tests" was a thoughtful, pioneering essay that introduced, among other things, the notion of "absolute scaling"—a procedure for obtaining a measure of item difficulty across different samples of test takers who vary in ability. Two years later, his influential paper on the "law of comparative judgment" (Thurstone, 1927) was published. Of this law and of Thurstone, Nunnally (1978) wrote:

> The author had the privilege of sitting in Thurstone's classroom when he stated in effect that the law of comparative judgment was his proudest achievement—this coming from a man for whom the word *genius* would not be inappropriate. Hundreds of journal articles and numerous books (e.g., Bock and Jones, 1968) have been written in large measure about empirical studies employing the law of comparative judgment or about theoretical issues relating to it. Derivations relating to the law are difficult for some students to understand, and the law is held almost in a sanctum of reverence by some specialists in psychometrics. In the end, however, the law is very simple. It consists of converting percentages of responses "greater than" into corresponding deviates on the normal curve. The mass of material that has been written about the topic concerns the underlying logic of making this transformation, the psychophysical methods that can be employed for gathering data, the mathematical techniques that can be applied to hundreds of special cases, and applications to very unusual situations. (pp. 60–61)

Thurstone's adaptation of scaling methods used in psychophysical research to the study of attitudes and values (see Thurstone & Chave, 1929; Thurstone, 1959) served as a model for generations of attitude researchers to come. More detailed discussion of Thurstone's contributions in the area of scaling can be found in Bock and Jones (1968) and in Chapter 15 of this book.

Types of scales   In common parlance, *scales* are instruments used to measure something. These instruments may be categorized by various typologies as a function of different characteristics. For example, we may refer to a scale used for weighing variously as "a type of instrument used to measure weight," or "a type of tool used to convert the pressure a stimulus exerts into a number representing ounces (pounds, tons—whatever)," or "an instrument of the variety that yields ratio-level measurement." Of course such typologies are not mutually exclusive; a scale is a ratio-level instrument of measurement that converts a stimulus of pressure into a number representing units of weight.

In the field of psychological testing, *scales* may also be conceived of as "instruments used to measure something"—that "something" typically being a psychological trait, characteristic, or attribute. Further, it is meaningful to speak of different types of scales as a function of various characteristics. We have seen, for example, that scales can be meaningfully categorized along a continuum of level of measurement; here we make reference to nominal scales, ordinal scales, interval scales, and ratio scales. But we might also characterize scales in other ways. If the test taker's performance on a test as a function of age is of critical interest, then the test might be referred to as an "age scale." If the test taker's performance on a test as a function of grade is of critical interest, then the test might be referred to as a "grade scale." If all raw scores on the test are to be transformed into scores that can range from 1 to 9, then the test might be referred to as a "stanine scale." If the focus of interest with respect to a particular test is primarily on the level of measurement it permits, the test may be referred to as a nominal, ordinal, interval, or ratio scale. Additionally, a scale might be referred to in other ways, such as unidimensional versus multidimensional, and comparative versus categorical. The meaning of referring to scales in these different ways will become clear as we discuss different methods of scale development.

Test developers design a measurement method (that is, scale a test) in the manner they believe is optimally suited to the way they have conceptualized measurement of the target trait(s). There is no one method of scaling; scaling may be accomplished in various ways. There is also no best type of scale; whether a scale to be developed should be nominal, ordinal, interval, or ratio in nature will depend in part on variables such as the objectives of the scale and the mathematical legitimacy of the manipulations and transformations of the resulting data. In this context, recall from Chapter 3 that few statistical procedures may be employed with nominal scales, while all statistical procedures may be employed with ratio scales. Many scholarly volumes have been written on the subject of scaling alone (for example, Torgerson, 1958; Gulliksen & Messick, 1960; Maranell, 1974), and our treatment should be thought of as only a very brief overview of some general principles. More detailed and technical expositions of this topic can be found not only in the books specifically devoted to it, but in others as well (such as Chapters 2 and 10 in Guilford, 1954a; Chapter 2 in Nunnally, 1978; Chapter 8 in Allen & Yen, 1979).

Scaling methods Speaking generally, a test taker is presumed to have more or less of the characteristic measured by a (valid) test as a function of the test score; the higher or lower the score, the more or less of the characteristic he or she presumably possesses. But how are numbers assigned to test responses?

Let's illustrate the answer to that question with one method—one of many possible methods—that could be used to develop a scale. Suppose you wish to develop a "Depth of Hypnosis Scale" (DHS) whereby the higher a subject scores on the test, the deeper the subject is presumed to be in a hypnotic trance. You make an arbitrary decision that two of the requirements for this test are that it be brief and easily administered. In the interest of simplicity (for *both* your test and our example), you make a preliminary decision that there will be ten items on this test and that possible scores on this test will range from 0 to 10, with a score of 0 indicating a nonhypnotized state and a score of 10 indicating a most deep hypnotic state.

The next step is to assemble an item pool, consisting perhaps of 20 or so possible items from which you will ultimately select the ten items that you feel measure the construct. One way to assemble this item pool is to enlist the aid of a number of expert hypnotists and instruct each to compose a list of ten behaviors that, from their experience, represent ten indicators of depth of hypnosis in ascending order. By examining where there is a consensus between the experts and by resolving discrepancies between the judgments of the experts (by methods such as interviewing the experts or researching the literature), a scale will begin to emerge. You might find that some items on that scale, each scored Yes or No (with one point assigned for each "Yes" answer), are as follows (in ascending order, as given by the experts):

1. Subject does not obey any commands at all.
2. Subject obeys simple command that his or her eyelids are "stuck to-gether" and, in fact, is unable to open eyes.
5. Subject responds to suggestion of positive hallucination (such as "there is a white elephant in the room").
6. Subject responds to suggestion of negative hallucination (such as "there is no one else in the room but you and me"—when the room is actually filled with people).
10. Suggestion of analgesia (inability to experience pain) is strong enough to sustain patient through major surgery without administration of anesthesia.

Some points about the DHS and the method used to derive it are useful in shedding light on scales and scaling methods in general. The DHS is an ordinal scale because the different "depths" are more than merely named (as would be the case in nominal measurement); they are ranked. Yet the interval level of measure-ment is not reached by the DHS, since it is not necessarily the case that equal intervals exist between points on the scale. Ordinal scales such as the DHS can be obtained by numerous methods, such as through the use of *sorting techniques* whereby the people doing the ranking (usually referred to as the "judges" or "raters") sort a pile of cards with respect to the degree to which a particular trait is reflected by what is printed on the card. For example, one way a sorting tech-nique might be used in the construction of a scale to measure "attractiveness of a popular soft-drink container from the perspective of male college students" would be to have cards made up depicting a drawing or a photo of a container with one design feature (such as color, shape, or script) varied on each card. An appropriate sampling of male respondents would be instructed to sort the cards from "least attractive" to "most attractive."[1] Sorting techniques can also be used to obtain nominal scales. For this purpose, subjects would be instructed to sort the cards (or objects or whatever) into mutually exclusive categories, each cate-gory then being assigned a number and/or a name. Sorting tasks may even be used to obtain interval scales—or scales that are at least presumed to be equal. The *method of equal-appearing intervals* was first described by Thurstone (1929), and an example of the steps one might follow in executing it to develop an attitude scale—say, one concerned with attitude toward gun control—are as follows:

1. Collect as many statements as possible reflecting all the pros and cons of the gun control issue (such as "The Bill of Rights assures the right of people to bear arms" and "Gun control advocates have misinterpreted the section of the Bill of Rights that says people have a right to bear arms").

1. What constitutes an "appropriate sampling" varies as a function of the reason the scale is being developed. We can envision such a "physical attractiveness" scale being developed for use by com-panies like advertising agencies, which—in the regular course of their work—must maintain cur-rent information on what the general public (or some particular segment thereof) considers to be attractive."

2. Acknowledged experts on the issue of gun control are asked to judge each item as to the favorability it reflects toward gun control (that is, favorability toward the idea of restrictive legislation with respect to the sale, ownership, and use of firearms). Specifically, each judge rates each statement and sorts it into one of, say, nine categories ranging from "extremely favorable" to gun control to "extremely unfavorable." Judges are cautioned to focus in their ratings only on the perceived favorability of the statement and *not* on their own views of the matter; to the extent that it is possible, judges are asked to set aside their own views in conducting these ratings. Judges are further instructed to sort the statements *as if* the subjective distance between each attitude is equal.

3. A mean and a standard deviation are computed for each item. Suppose, for example, that 15 judges rated 100 or so items with respect to nine degrees of favorability toward gun control, ranging from 1 (extremely favorable) to 9 (extremely unfavorable). Focusing on just one of these items, suppose five of the judges rated it 1, five of the judges rated it 2, and five of the judges rated it 3. Averaging the 1, 2, and the 3 for each of the five judges we compute a mean favorability rating of 2 (with a standard deviation equal to .816 in this instance).

4. Items are selected or rejected for inclusion in the final scale based in part on their mean and standard deviation. It should be clear that the larger the standard deviation, the more disagreement there was between the judges. Typically, a user of this method will set in advance a cutoff point for the value of the standard deviation of a prospective item: beyond that point the item will be discarded. The criteria for selection to be included in the final scale will include (1) the mean rating, (2) the standard deviation, (3) the degree to which the item contributes to a comprehensive measurement of the variable in question, and (4) the degree of confidence the test developer has that the items have indeed been sorted into equal intervals (see Thurstone, 1929).

5. The scale is now ready for administration to subjects. The exact way the scale is used may differ as a function of the objectives of the test situation; most typically, the subjects are asked to select those statements that best characterize their own attitudes toward the subject—in this case, gun control. The scale values of the items endorsed are summed and this summation is equal to the subject's "score" on the test.

The method of equal-appearing intervals is an example of a scaling method of the *direct estimation* variety. In contrast to other methods that involve *indirect estimation,* there is no need to transform the subject's responses into some other scales. Direct estimation techniques exist for ratio scales, but we do not discuss them since they are so seldom used in psychology and education.

Another way we might categorize the method of equal-appearing intervals is as a *unidimensional* scale, a scale where it is presumed that there is one and only one dimension underlying the phenomenon being studied. If, for example, there were more than one dimension underlying a score on the gun control scale, we wouldn't know whether a particularly low score on this test reflected very favorable attitudes toward gun control or something else. When there is more than one dimension under study, *multidimensional* scaling procedures can be used to identify these dimensions. Finally, by way of description, we can also describe the scaling procedure for gun-control attitudes as *categorical* in nature as opposed to *comparative* in nature. *Categorical scaling* procedures entail placing stimuli into one of two or more alternative categories that differ quantitatively with respect to some continuum. *Comparative scaling* entails judgments of a stimulus in comparison to every other stimulus on the scale—such as would be the case if subjects were asked to rank each of the items on the gun-control attitudes survey in terms of the strength with which they agree.

In addition to sorting methods, another method used to derive ordinal scales is called the *method of paired comparisons*. Here, judges are asked to compare pairs of stimuli (such as two photos, two objects, or two sounds) and decide which of the two has more of the trait being scaled; the higher scale value will go to whichever of the two stimuli is deemed to have more of the trait in question in over 50 percent of the comparisons. *Rating scales* constitute another class of methods by which ordinal scales may be obtained. A rating scale may take various forms but in general it can be defined as a grouping of words, statements, or symbols on which judgments concerning the strength of a particular trait are indicated. As our example shows, rating scales may be designed for self-assessment, "other-assessment," or assessment of stimuli:[2]

> *Rating Scale Item A*
> I believe I would like the work of a lighthouse keeper.
> True   False   (circle one)
>
> *Rating Scale Item B*
> Please rate the employee on ability to cooperate and get along with fellow employees:
> Excellent ____ / ____ / ____ / ____ / ____ / ____ / ____ / Unsatisfactory
>
> *Rating Scale Item C*
> How did you feel about what you just saw on television?

One type of rating scale that is relatively easy to construct yet usually reliable is a *summative scale* or *Likert scale* (Likert, 1932). Typically employed to scale people with respect to their attitudes, each item on a Likert scale presents the test taker with five alternative responses, usually—though not necessarily—on an agree/disagree or approve/disapprove type of continuum. An example:

---

2. "Smiley" faces as those illustrated have been used in social-psychological and consumer research with very young children in lieu of words such as "positive," "neutral," and "negative."

The Catholic Church should take a more liberal stand on the issue of abortion.

Do you:

| Strongly Approve | Approve | Undecided | Disapprove | Strongly Disapprove |

Likert (1932) experimented with different weightings of the five categories illustrated but concluded that a simple weight of 1 for endorsement of items at one extreme to a weight of 5 for endorsement of items at the other extreme worked well. Because the final score is obtained by summing the appropriate scale value for each item, scales of this variety are referred to as "summative scales."

If a test purports to measure attitude toward the church, it is only logical that each item on the test should, indeed, measure attitude toward the church; stated another way, homogeneity of test items would be a desirable feature of such a test. Although Guttman scales have been used in various ways since their introduction, this scaling procedure was originally introduced as a method of ensuring test homogeneity (Guttman, 1944, 1947). Stated succinctly, a Guttman scale in attitude measurement would be one where items move sequentially from weaker to stronger expressions of the attitude, and it is presumed that all respondents who agree with stronger statements of the attitude will agree with milder statements. For example, consider the following statements A through D, reflecting attitudes toward the general area of adoption. Mentally consider whether you agree or disagree with each statement as you read:

A. If the woman in a mature, responsible, financially secure, loving married couple is infertile, then the couple should have the right to contract with a surrogate mother to bear the father's child.

B. If a mature, responsible, financially secure married couple is infertile, then they have a right to adopt a child.

C. If a mature, responsible, financially secure, loving married couple is having difficulty conceiving a child, then they have the right to seek medical intervention.

D. All mature, responsible, financially secure married couples have a right to have children.

If this were a perfect Guttman scale, all test takers who agree with item A (the most extreme position) should also agree with items B, C, and D, which appear to represent progressively less extreme positions. All test takers who do not agree with item A but who do agree with item B should also agree with items C and D, and so forth. Guttman scales are created by administering a number of items to a target group of people and then analyzing the findings—a procedure called "scalogram analysis"—with the object being to obtain an arrangement of items such as that for the attitudes toward adoption. While this procedure holds great intuitive appeal, it has drawn severe criticism for its impracticality, among other things (see Nunnally, 1978). Despite such criticisms, Guttman scales have found application in a variety of settings. One application of this type of scaling, for example, is in the study of *purchase intent*, a concept in consumer psychology that relates to an inferred level of motivation to engage in buying behavior—

based on many variables such as verbal/nonverbal behavior, advertising exposure, and market conditions.

Writing Items

In the grand scheme of test construction, considerations related to the actual writing of the test's items go hand in hand with scaling considerations. Three questions that the prospective test developer/item writer faces immediately are:

- What range of content should the items cover?
- Which of the many different types of item formats should be employed?
- How many items should be written?

When devising a standardized test using a multiple-choice-item format, it is usually advisable for the number of items written for the "first draft" of a standardized test to contain approximately twice the number of items that the final version of the test will contain.[3] If, for example, a test called "American History: 1940 to 1980" was to have 30 questions in its final version, it would be useful to have as many as 60 items—items that comprehensively sample the domain of the test—in the "item pool" (the "reservoir" or "well" from which items on the final version of the test will be drawn or discarded). Because approximately half of these items will be eliminated in the test's final version, the test developer needs to ensure that the final version of the test also contains items that adequately sample the domain. Thus if all the questions on the Persian Gulf War from the original 60 items were determined to be poorly written items, it would be incumbent on the test developer to either rewrite items sampling this period or create new items—and then subject the rewritten or new items to tryout as well. Of course, the number of planned forms of the test is another consideration here; multiply the number of items required in the pool for one form of the test by the number of forms planned.

Considerations related to variables such as the purpose of the test and the number of examinees to be tested at one time enter into decisions regarding the format of the test. Thus, for example, if the purpose of a test is to screen large numbers of military recruits for minimal intellectual ability, a constructed response format, such as one including essay items, would be impractical. Preferable would be a test format wherein an examinee must select one of many alternative answers—a selected-response format. Selected-response formats facilitate automated scoring and can readily accommodate a large number of examinees.

The rest of this section takes an in-depth look at the selected-response format as well as other test-item formats.

Item Formats As noted, the *selected-response item format* presents the examinee with a choice of answers and requires selection of one alternative. If the test is one

---

3. Common sense and the practical demands for the situation may dictate that fewer items be written for the first draft of a test. If, for example, the final draft were to contain 1,000 items, it could be an undue burden to attempt to create an item pool of 2,000 items. Further, if the test developer was a very knowledgeable and capable item writer, it might be necessary to create only about 1,200 items for the item pool.

of achievement, the examinee's task is to select the correct (that is, the "keyed") answer. If the test is one designed to measure the strength of a particular trait, the examinees' task may be to select the alternative that best answers the question with respect to themselves. For the sake of simplicity, we'll confine our examples to achievement tests, though the reader may wish to mentally substitute other appropriate terms for words such as "correct"; such substitutions might apply to personality or other types of tests that are not achievement tests.

Three types of selected-response item formats are multiple-choice, matching, and true-false items. As illustrated by item A in the following example, a multiple-choice item has three elements: (1) a stem, (2) a correct alternative or option, and (3) several incorrect alternatives or options variously referred to as "distractors" or "foils":

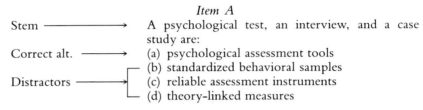

Item A

Stem ⟶ A psychological test, an interview, and a case study are:
Correct alt. ⟶ (a) psychological assessment tools
Distractors ⟶ (b) standardized behavioral samples
(c) reliable assessment instruments
(d) theory-linked measures

Now consider Item B:

Item B
A good multiple-choice item in an achievement test:
(a) has one correct alternative
(b) has alternatives that are grammatically parallel
(c) has alternatives of similar length
(d) has alternatives that fit grammatically with the stem
(e) includes as much as possible of the item in the stem to avoid unnecessary repetition
(f) avoids ridiculous distractors
(g) is not excessively long
(h) all of the above
(i) none of the above

If you answered "h" to item B, you are correct. In the process of going through the list of alternatives, it may have occurred to you that item B violated many of the rules it set forth!

A matching item is a variant of a multiple-choice item. The examinee is presented with two columns of responses and the task is to determine which response from one column "goes with" which response from the other. An example follows:

Match the following actors' names with their roles by writing the appropriate number next to the letter.[4]

---

4. For the record, the answers to this matching question are as follows: A-4, B-1, C-6, D-5, E-10, F-8, G-11, H-9, I-2, J-7, and K-3. In case you are wondering, Julie Andrews played Victor (as well as Victoria) in *Victor/Victoria*. Paul Newman played Luke in *Cool Hand Luke*.

_____	A. Sylvester Stallone	1. Topper
_____	B. Leo G. Carroll	2. Victor
_____	C. Ernest Borgnine	3. Arthur
_____	D. Cliff Robertson	4. Rocky
_____	E. Dustin Hoffman	5. Charly
_____	F. Christopher Reeve	6. Marty
_____	G. Barbra Streisand	7. Luke
_____	H. Robin Williams	8. Superman
_____	I. Julie Andrews	9. Popeye
_____	J. Paul Newman	10. Tootsie
_____	K. Dudley Moore	11. Yentl

A true-false item is another of the selected-response variety, this one in the form of a sentence that requires the examinee to indicate whether the statement is or is not a fact. A good true-false item contains a single idea, is not excessively long, and is not subject to debate; that is, it is indeed either true or false.

Like multiple-choice items, true-false items have the advantage of being readily applicable to a wide range of subject areas. Also like multiple-choice items, acceptable levels of item reliability can be achieved with true-false items. True-false items need not contain a list of distractor alternatives as multiple-choice items must, and therefore true-false items tend to be easier to write than multiple-choice items. A disadvantage of true-false items is that the probability of obtaining a correct response purely on the basis of chance (guessing) on any one item is .5 or 50% (as compared to .25 or 25% on a four-alternative multiple-choice question).[5]

An alternative to a selected-response format is a *constructed-response format*— one that requires the examinee to supply or to create the correct answer (as opposed to merely selecting it). Three types of constructed-response items are the completion item, the short answer, and the essay. A completion item requires the examinee to provide a word or phrase that completes a sentence, as in the following example:

The standard deviation is generally considered the most useful measure of _____.

A good completion item should be worded so that the correct answer is specific. Completion items that can be correctly answered in many ways can lead to scoring problems. The correct completion for the item above is *variability*. An alternative way of writing this item would be as a short answer item:

What descriptive statistic is generally considered the most useful measure of variability? _____

A good short answer item is written clearly enough so that the test taker can indeed respond succinctly—with a "short answer." There are no hard-and-fast

---

5. We note in passing, however, that while the probability of guessing correctly on an individual true-false item on the basis of chance alone may be .5, the probability of guessing correctly on a *sequence* of true-false items decreases as the number of items increases. The probability of guessing correctly on two such items is equal to $.5^2$ or 25%. The probability of guessing correctly on ten such items is equal to $.5^{10}$ or .001; there is therefore a one-in-a-thousand chance that a test taker would guess correctly on ten true-false items on the basis of chance alone.

definitions of how short an answer must be to be considered a "short answer"—a word, a term, a sentence, or a paragraph—though beyond a paragraph or two, the item might more properly be referred to as an *essay item*. An example follows:

> Compare and contrast definitions and techniques of classical and operant conditioning. Include examples of how principles of each have been applied in clinical as well as educational settings.

An essay is a useful type of item when the test developer wants the examinee to demonstrate a depth of knowledge about a single topic. In contrast to selected-response items and constructed-response items such as the short answer or completion items, the essay question not only permits the restating of learned material, but also allows for the creative integration and expression of the material in the test taker's own words. It can also be appreciated that the skills tapped by essay-type items are different from those tapped by items of the true-false and matching genre; whereas an essay requires recall, organization, planning, and writing ability, the other types of items require only recognition. Drawbacks with respect to essay items as compared to short-answer items may include a more limited area of coverage relative to the amount of testing time and a degree of subjectivity in the scoring.

TEST TRYOUT

Having created a pool of items from which the final version of the test will be developed, the test developer's next step is to try out the test. The test should be tried out on people like the people for whom the test was designed. Thus, for example, if a test is designed to aid in decisions regarding the selection of corporate employees with management potential at a certain level, it would be appropriate to try out the test on corporate employees at the targeted level—and inappropriate to try out the test on introductory psychology students.

Equally important as questions concerning *whom* the test should be tried out on are questions regarding *how many* people the test should be tried out on. While there are no hard-and-fast rules here, some have recommended that there be no fewer than five subjects, and preferably as many as ten subjects, for every one item on the test. In general, the more subjects in the tryout the better; all other things being equal, ten subjects per test item is better than five because of the lessening of the role of chance in subsequent analyses of the data, particularly in factor analysis. A definite risk in using too few subjects during test tryout comes during factor analysis of the findings, when what we might call "phantom factors"—nonexistent factors that are actually artifacts of the small sample size—may emerge.

The test tryout should be executed under conditions that are as identical as possible to the conditions under which the standardized test will be administered. This means that all instructions, and everything from the time limits allotted for completing the test, to the "atmosphere" at the test site, should be as similar as possible. As Nunnally (1978, p. 279) so aptly phrased it, "If items for a personality inventory are being administered in an atmosphere that encourages frankness and the eventual test is to be administered in an atmosphere where subjects will be reluctant to say bad things about themselves, the item analysis will tell a faulty story." In general, the test developer endeavors to ensure that differences in response to the test's items are due in fact to the items—not to extraneous factors.

What Is a "Good" Item?

Before reading on, pick up a piece of scrap paper and just jot down—using logic and common sense—what you believe the criteria of a good test item are. After you've done that, compare what you've written to the following discussion.

In the same sense that we can speak of a good test as being reliable and valid, we can speak of a good test item as being reliable and valid. Further, a good test item helps to discriminate test takers; a good test item is one that high scorers on the test as a whole get right. An item that high scorers on the test as a whole do not get right is probably not a good item. We may also describe a good test item as one that low scorers on the test as a whole get wrong; an item that low scorers on the test as a whole get right may not be a good item.

How does a test developer identify "good" items? There are quantitative approaches to answering this question—the subject of most of the rest of this chapter—and qualitative approaches as well. An example of one qualitative approach would take the form of what could be called a "think aloud" test administration. On a one-to-one basis, examiners sit down with examinees and ask them to "think aloud"—to verbally express what they are thinking as they respond to each of the items. If the test is one designed to measure achievement, such verbalizations will be useful in assessing not only if certain students (such as low or high scorers on previous examinations) are misinterpreting a particular item, but also *why* they are misinterpreting the item. If the test is one designed to measure some aspect of personality, say self-esteem, a "think aloud" procedure might similarly yield valuable insights into the way test takers in general—as well as members of preidentified groups—perceive, interpret, and respond to the items. Another qualitative method is a small group discussion in which group members discuss the test as a whole as well as individual items. The membership of the group may be people who have taken the test or people who have administered, scored, or interpreted the test, or a group of experts in a particular area—the membership of the group to be determined by the needs and interests of the test developer.

After the first draft of the test has been administered to a representative group of examinees, it remains for the test developer to analyze test scores and responses to individual items. The different types of statistical scrutiny that the test data can potentially undergo at this point are referred to collectively as "item analysis." Note that while "item analysis" tends to be regarded as a quantitative endeavor, it may also be, as we have illustrated above, qualitative.

ITEM ANALYSIS

Statistical procedures used to analyze items may become quite complex, and our treatment of this subject should be thought of only as introductory. We briefly survey some procedures typically used by test developers in their efforts to select the best items from a pool of tryout items. The student should understand that the criteria for the "best" items may differ as a function of the test developer's objectives. Thus, for example, one test developer might deem the "best" items to be those that optimally contribute to the internal reliability of the test. Another test developer might wish to design a test with the highest possible criterion-related validity—and select items accordingly. Among the tools test developers might employ to analyze and select items will be an index of an item's difficulty, an item-validity index, an item-reliability index, and an index of the item's discrimination. Brief coverage of each of these statistics appears in this section. For a more in-depth treatment, the interested reader is referred to Gulliksen (1950).

In the interest of simplifying our discussion and clearly illustrating the concepts presented, assume that you are the author of 100 items for a ninth-grade-level American History Test (AHT) and that this 100-item (draft) test has been administered to 100 ninth-graders. Hoping in the long run to standardize the test and have it distributed by a commercial test publisher, you have a more immediate, short-term goal—to select the 50 best of the 100 items you originally created. How might that short-term goal be achieved? As we will see, the answer lies in item-analysis procedures. Before elaborating on those procedures, however, we once again remind and invite students to apply the following material—making "translations" in phraseology when appropriate—to tests other than achievement tests, such as tests of personality.

Item-Difficulty Index

Suppose every examinee got item 1 of the test correct. Can we say that item 1 is a good item? What if no one got item 1 correct? In either case, item 1 is not a good item. If everyone gets the item right, the item is too easy. If everyone gets the item wrong, the item is too difficult. Just as the test as a whole is designed to provide an index of degree of knowledge about American history, so each individual item on the test should be "passed" (scored as correct) or "failed" (scored as incorrect) on the basis of test takers' differential knowledge of American history.[6]

An index of an item's difficulty is obtained by calculating the proportion of the total number of test takers who got the item right. A lowercase, italicized p (p) is used to denote item difficulty, and a subscript refers to the item number (p_1 is read "item-difficulty index for item 1"). The value of an item-difficulty index can theoretically range from 0 (if no one got the item right) to 1 (if everyone got the item right). If 50 of the 100 examinees got item 2 right, then the item-difficulty index for this item would be equal to 50 divided by 100 or .5 ($p_2 = .5$). If 75 of the examinees got item 3 right, p_3 would be equal to .75, and we could say that item 3 was easier than item 2. Note that the larger the item-difficulty index, the easier the item. Since p refers to the percent of people passing an item, the higher the p for an item, the easier the item. The statistic referred to as an item-difficulty index in the context of achievement testing, may be referred to as an

---

6. An exception here may be a "give-away" item—typically inserted near the beginning of a test—to spur motivation and a positive test-taking attitude (particularly on the part of test-anxious test takers). In general, however, if an item analysis suggests that a particular item is too easy or too difficult, the item must either be rewritten or discarded.

item-endorsement index in other contexts, such as personality testing. Here, the statistic provides not a measure of the percent of people passing the item, but a measure of the percent of people who said "yes" to, agreed with, or otherwise "endorsed" the item.

An index of the difficulty of the "average" test item for a particular test can be calculated by averaging the item-difficulty indices for all the test's items (that is, summing the item difficulty indices for all test items and dividing by the total number of items on the test). For maximum discrimination among the abilities of the test takers, the optimal average item difficulty is approximately .5, with individual items on the test ranging in difficulty from about .3 to .8. Note, however, that the possible effect of guessing must be taken into account when considering items of the selected-response variety; here the optimal average item difficulty is usually the midpoint between 1.00 and the chance success proportion (defined as the probability of answering correctly by random guessing). In a true-false item, the probability of guessing correctly on the basis of chance alone is 1/2, or .50. Therefore, the optimal item difficulty is halfway between .50 and 1.00, or .75. In general, the midpoint representing the optimal item difficulty is obtained by summing the chance success proportion and 1.00 and then dividing the sum by 2, or:

$$.50 + 1.00 = 1.5$$

$$\frac{1.5}{2} = .75$$

For a five-option multiple-choice item, the probability of guessing correctly on any one item on the basis of chance alone is equal to 1/5, or .20. The optimal item difficulty is therefore .60:

$$.20 + 1.00 = 1.20$$

$$\frac{1.20}{2} = .60$$

Item-Validity Index

The item-validity index can be calculated once the following two statistics are known:

- the item-score standard deviation
- the point-biserial correlation between the item score and the criterion score

The item-score standard deviation of item 1 (denoted by the symbol s_1) can be calculated using the index of the item's difficulty (p_1) in the following formula:

$$s_1 = \sqrt{p_1(1 - p_1)}$$

The point-biserial correlation between the score on item 1 and a score on the criterion measure (denoted by the symbol r_{1C}) is multiplied by item 1's item-score standard deviation (s_1), and the product is equal to an index of an item's validity ($s_1 r_{1C}$). The calculation of the item-validity index will be important when the test developer's goal is to maximize the criterion-related validity of the test. A visual representation of the best items on a test (if the objective is to maximize criterion-

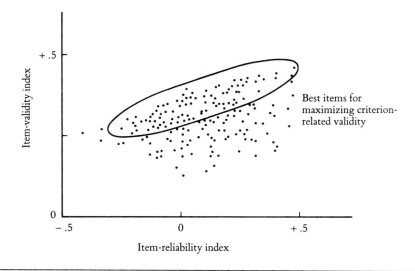

Figure 7–2 *Maximizing Criterion-Related Validity.* (Source: Allen & Yen, 1979)

related validity) can be achieved by a plotting of each item's item–validity index and item–reliability index (see Figure 7–2).

Item-Reliability Index

The item reliability index provides an indication of the internal consistency of a test (Figure 7–3); the higher this index, the greater the test's internal consistency.

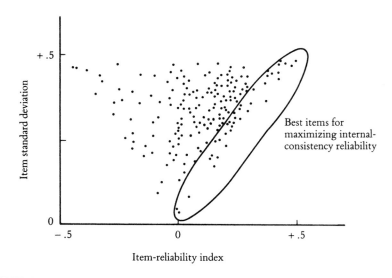

Figure 7–3 *Maximizing Internal-Consistency Reliability.* (Source: Allen & Yen, 1979)

This index is equal to the product of the item-score standard deviation (s) and the point-biserial correlation (r) between the item score and the total test score.

Factor analysis and inter-item consistency   A statistical tool useful in determining whether items on a test appear to be measuring the same thing(s) is the technique of factor analysis (mentioned in Chapter 6 and discussed in greater detail in Appendix B). Through the judicious use of factor analysis, items that do not "load on" the factor that they were written to tap (that is, items that do not appear to be measuring what they were designed to measure) can be revised or eliminated. If too many items appear to be tapping a particular area, the weakest of such items can be eliminated. Additionally, factor analysis can be useful in the test interpretation process especially when comparing the constellation of responses to the items from two or more groups. Thus, for example, if a particular personality test is administered to two groups of hospitalized psychiatric patients (each group with a different diagnosis), the same items may be found to load on different factors in the two groups. Such information will compel the responsible test developer to revise or eliminate certain items from the test or to describe the differential findings in the test manual.

Item-Discrimination Index

Measures of item discrimination indicate how adequately an item separates or discriminates between high scorers and low scorers on an entire test. In this context, a multiple-choice item on an achievement test that (1) most of the high scores get right and (2) most of the low scorers get wrong is usually a good item. If most of the high scorers fail a particular item, then it is possible that these test takers may be making an alternative interpretation of a response intended to serve as a distractor. In such a case, the test developer would do well to interview the examinees in order to understand better the basis for the choice and then appropriately revise (or eliminate) the item. Common sense dictates that an item on an achievement test is not doing its job if it is answered correctly by respondents who understand the subject matter least. Similarly, an item on a test purporting to measure a particular personality trait is not doing its job if responses to it indicate that people who, for example, score very low on the test as a whole (indicating the absence or low level of the trait in question), tend to score very high on the item (indicating that they are very high on the trait in question—contrary to what the test as a whole indicates).

There are many measures of item discrimination, and the choice of methods depends on the nature of the data. If the test developer wants to correlate one true dichotomous variable with one continuous variable, then the point-biserial correlation (another form of the Pearson product-moment correlation) is the appropriate measure. However, when the dichotomous variable has been created from an underlying distribution that is in reality a continuous distribution (such as achievement test data that for the sake of convenience have been converted into two categories—pass and fail), the biserial correlation would be more appropriate. If a measure of the relationship between two true dichotomous variables is desired, another form of the Pearson product-moment correlation, the phi coefficient, is used. And when both variables have been created from an underlying continuous distribution, then the tetrachoric correlation is used.[7]

The *item-discrimination index* is a measure of item discrimination symbolized by a lowercase, italicized letter d (*d*). This estimate of item discrimination, in essence, compares performance on a particular item with performance in the upper and lower regions of a distribution of continuous test scores. The optimal boundary lines to demarcate what we are referring to as the "upper" and "lower" areas of a distribution of scores are scores within the upper and lower 27% of the distribution of scores—provided the distribution is normal (Kelley, 1939). As the distribution of test scores becomes more platykurtic (flat), the optimal boundary line for defining "upper" and "lower" gets larger and approaches 33% (Cureton, 1957). Allen and Yen (1979, p. 122) assure us that "for most applications, any percentage between 25 and 33 will yield similar estimates."

The item-discrimination index is a measure of the difference between the proportion of high scorers answering an item correctly and the proportion of low scorers answering the item correctly; the higher the value of *d*, the greater the number of high scorers answering the item correctly. A negative *d* value on a particular item is a "red flag" because it indicates a situation where low-scoring examinees are more likely to answer the item correctly than high scoring examinees. This situation calls for some action such as revision or elimination of the item.

Assume a teacher gave a test to 119 people and isolated the upper (*U*) and lower (*L*) 27% of the test papers (with a total of 32 papers in each group). Data and item-discrimination indices for items 1 through 5 are presented in Table 7–1. Note that 20 test takers in the *U* group answered item 1 correctly and 16 test takers in the *L* group answered item 1 correctly. With an item-discrimination index equal to .13, item 1 is probably a reasonable item because more members of the *U* than of the *L* group answered it correctly. The higher the value of *d*, the more adequately the item discriminates the higher-scoring from the lower-scoring test takers. For this reason, item 2 is a better item than item 1; its item-discrimination index is .63. The highest possible value of *d* is +1.00—this in the case where all members of the *U* group answer the item correctly and all members

---

7. Nunnally (1978) provided what he himself described as a "scathing denunciation" (p. 137) of the point-biserial *r* and the tetrachoric *r*; the reasons provided were numerous, but for our purposes we will say that the strict assumptions inherent in the use of these statistics are rarely met.

Table 7–1

Item-Discrimination Indices for Five Hypothetical Items

Item	U	L	U − L	n	d (U − L/n)
1	20	16	4	32	.13
2	30	10	20	32	.63
3	32	0	32	32	1.00
4	20	20	0	32	0.00
5	0	32	−32	32	−1.00

of the L group answer the item incorrectly. In a situation where the same proportion of members of the U and L group pass the item, the item is not discriminating between test takers at all, and d, appropriately enough, would be equal to 0. The lowest value that an index of item discrimination can take is −1. A d equal to −1 is a test developer's nightmare; it indicates a situation where all the members of the U group fail the item and all the members of the L group pass it. On the face of it, such an item is the worst possible type of item and is in dire need of revision or elimination. However, it is possible that the test developer might learn or discover something new about the construct being measured if he or she takes the time to try to uncover the reason for this unanticipated finding.

Analysis of item alternatives The quality of each alternative within a multiple-choice item can be readily assessed with reference to the comparative performance of upper and lower scorers. No formulas or statistics are really necessary here; by charting the number of test takers in the U and L groups who chose each alternative, the test developer can get an idea of the effectiveness of a distractor by means of a simple "eyeball test." For purposes of illustration, let's analyze responses to five items on a hypothetical test, assuming that there were 32 scores in the upper level (U) of the distribution and 32 scores in the lower level (L) of the distribution. Let's begin by looking at the pattern of responses to item 1 (where ★ denotes the correct alternative):

	Alternatives				
Item 1	★a	b	c	d	e
U	24	3	2	0	3
L	10	5	6	6	5

The response pattern to item 1 indicates that the item is a good one. More members of the U than of the L group answered the item correctly, and each of the distractors attracted some test takers.

Item 2	a	b	c	d	★e
U	2	13	3	2	12
L	6	7	5	7	7

Item 2 signals a situation in which a relatively large number of members of the U group chose a particular distractor choice (in this case, "b"). This item could probably be improved upon revision, preferably one made after an interview with some or all of the U students who chose "b."

Item 3	a	b	★c	d	e
U	0	0	32	0	0
L	3	2	22	2	3

Item 3 indicates a most desirable pattern of test-taker response. All members of the U group answered the item correctly, and each distractor attracted one or more members of the L group.

Item 4	a	★b	c	d	e
U	5	15	0	5	7
L	4	5	4	4	15

Item 4 is more difficult than item 3—fewer examinees answered it correctly. Still, this item provides useful information in terms of discrimination because it effectively discriminates higher-scoring from lower-scoring examinees. For some reason, one of the alternatives ("e") was particularly effective—perhaps too effective—as a distractor to students in the low-scoring group. The test developer may wish to further explore why this was the case.

	a	b	c	★d	e
Item 5					
U	14	0	0	5	13
L	7	0	0	16	9

Item 5 is a poor item because more members of the L as opposed to the U group answered the item correctly. Furthermore, none of the examinees chose the "b" or "c" distractors.

Item-Characteristic Curves

A graphic representation of item difficulty and discrimination can be made in an *item-characteristic curve* (ICC). As shown in Figure 7–4, an ICC is a graph on which ability is plotted on the horizontal axis while probability of correct response is plotted on the vertical axis.[8] Note that the extent to which an item discriminates high- from low-scoring examinees is apparent from the slope of the curve; the steeper the slope, the greater the item discrimination. Also note that if the slope is positive, more high-scorers are getting the item correct than low-scorers while if the slope is negative, the reverse is true. Now focus on the item-characteristic curve for item (a); do you think this is a good item? The answer is that it is not a good item; the probability of a test taker responding correctly—responding in a way that is keyed as correct on the test's answer key—is high for test takers of low ability and low for test takers of high ability. What about item (b); is that a good item? Again, the answer is no. The curve tells us that test takers of moderate ability have the highest probability of answering this item correctly; test takers with the greatest amount of ability—as well as their counterparts at the other end of the ability spectrum—are unlikely to respond correctly to this item. Item (b) may be one of those items where people who "know too much" or "think too much" are likely to respond incorrectly to the item.

Item (c) is a good item; the probability of responding correctly to it increases with ability. What about item (d)? This item-characteristic curve profiles an item that discriminates at only one point on the continuum of ability; the probability is very high that all test takers at or above this point will respond correctly to the item. We can also say that the probability of an incorrect response is very high for test takers who fall below that particular point in ability. An item such as (d) has excellent discriminative ability and would be useful in a test designed, for example, to select applicants on the basis of some cutting score. However, such an

---

8. In the interest of simplicity, we have omitted scale values for the axes. The vertical axis in such a graph lists probability of correct response in values ranging from 0 to 1. Values for the horizontal axis, which we have simply labeled "ability," are derived from data on the proportion of test takers at different levels of ability who respond correctly to the item. In other sources you may find the vertical axis of an item-characteristic curve labeled something like "proportion of examinees who respond correctly to the item" and the horizontal axis labeled "total test score."

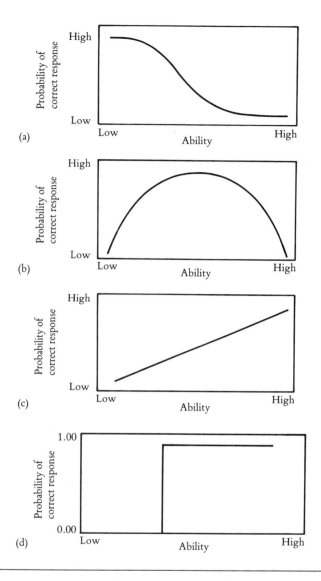

(a)

(b)

(c)

(d)

Figure 7–4 *Some Sample Item-Characteristic Curves.* (Source: Ghiselli, Campbell, & Zedeck, 1981)

item might not be desirable in a test designed to provide detailed information on test-taker ability across all ability levels—as might be the case, for example, in a diagnostic reading or arithmetic test.

Latent-trait models   A test is typically designed to provide an estimate of the amount of knowledge or ability (or strength of a particular trait) possessed by the test taker. The variable on which performance on the test is presumed to depend—

be it knowledge, ability, a personality trait, or something else—is never directly measurable itself; an estimate of the amount of the variable is obtained through the test. According to a *latent-trait model* of measurement, this underlying, unobservable, variable—this latent trait—is unidimensional. Presumably, all of the items on a test are measuring this trait. It is further presumed that how well each item is accomplishing this objective can be determined by reference to the item-characteristic curve. In contrast to classical "true score" test theory in which no assumptions are made about the frequency distribution of test scores, inherent in latent-trait models are assumptions regarding the probability of the occurrence of a particular observed score in test takers with a particular true score. As Allen & Yen (1979, p. 240) put it, "Latent-trait theories propose models that describe how the latent trait influences performance on each test item. Unlike test scores or true scores, latent traits theoretically can take on values from $-\infty$ to $+\infty$ [minus to plus infinity]."

The applicability of latent-trait models to psychological tests has been questioned by some theoreticians. It has been argued, for example, that the assumption of test unidimensionality is violated when many psychological tests are considered. It has been further argued that even the same item on a psychological test may be tapping different abilities from the same test taker depending on the life experiences of the test taker. Despite lingering theoretical questions, latent-trait models appear to be playing an increasingly dominant role in the design and development of new tests and testing programs. More detailed discussion of the various types of latent-trait models (also referred to as *item-response theory* in some of the literature) can be found in various sources (such as Hambleton, 1988, 1979; Hambleton & Cook, 1977; Lord, 1980; Lord & Novick, 1968; Weiss & Davison, 1981; Wright & Stone, 1979).

Other Considerations in Item Analysis

Guessing   Guessing on responses to personality and related psychological tests is not thought of as a great problem; although it may sometimes be difficult to choose the most appropriate alternative on a selected-response format personality test (particularly one with forced-choice items), the presumption is that the test taker does indeed make the best choice. In the area of achievement testing, however, the problem of how to handle test-taker guessing is one that has eluded any universally acceptable solution. It is true that a number of different procedures purporting to be corrections for guessing have been published, but none has proven to be entirely satisfactory. The reason is that the problem of guessing is more complex than it first appears. To understand why, consider the following three criteria that any correction for guessing must meet as well as the interacting problems that must be addressed:

1. A correction for guessing must take cognizance of the fact that when a respondent guesses at an answer on an achievement test, the guess is not typically made on a totally random basis. It is more reasonable to assume

that the test taker's guess is based on some knowledge of the subject matter and the ability to rule out one or more of the distractor alternatives. However, the individual test taker's amount of knowledge of the subject matter will vary from one item to the next.

2. A correction for guessing must also deal with the problem of omitted items. Sometimes instead of guessing, the test taker will simply omit a response to an item. Should the omitted item be scored "wrong"? Should the omitted item be excluded from the item analysis? Should the omitted item be scored as if the test taker had made a random guess? Exactly how should the omitted item be handled?

3. Just as some people may be luckier than others in front of a Las Vegas slot machine, so some test takers may be luckier than others with respect to guessing on a particular test. Any correction for guessing may seriously underestimate or overestimate the effects of guessing for "lucky" and "unlucky" test takers.

A number of different solutions to the problem of guessing have been proposed. In addition to proposed interventions at the level of test scoring through the use of corrections for guessing (referred to as *formula scores*), intervention has also been proposed at the level of test instructions: test takers may be instructed not to omit any item and to guess when in doubt. To date, no solution to the problem of guessing has been deemed to be entirely satisfactory. The responsible test developer addresses the problem of guessing by including in the test manual (1) explicit instructions regarding this point to be conveyed to examinees, and (2) specific instructions for dealing with omitted items in the test protocol.

Item fairness   Item-characteristic curves provide one tool for identifying which items are to be considered fair and which may be biased. If an item is to be considered *fair* to two or more groups of test takers (who differ as a group with respect to some characteristic such as race, sex, or age), the item-characteristic curves for the two groups should not be significantly different. Conversely, if an item-characteristic curve for one group shows significant differences from the item-characteristic curve obtained by another group—this group differing only on some test-irrelevant characteristic—the item can be said to be *biased* in the statistical sense:

> The essential rationale of this ICC criterion of item bias is that any persons showing the same ability as measured by the whole test should have the same probability of passing any given item that measures that ability, regardless of the person's race, social class, sex, or any other background characteristics. In other words, the same proportion of persons from each group should pass any given item of the test, provided that the persons all earned the same total score on the test. (Jensen, 1980, p. 444)

A statistical determination of a biased item requires the use of an appropriate measure to test the null hypothesis of no differences between the item-characteristic curves of the two groups. Items that show significant differences in item-characteristic curves should either be revised or eliminated from the test. If a relatively large number of items biased in favor of one group coexist with approximately the same number of items biased in favor of another group, it cannot be claimed that the test measures the same abilities in the two groups—this despite the fact that overall test scores between the individuals in the two groups may not be significantly different (Jensen, 1980).

Analysis of item-characteristic curves represents only one way of detecting item bias. Ironson and Subkoviak (1979) evaluated different methods for detecting item bias across different groups, including differences in item difficulty, item discrimination, item-characteristic curves, and the distribution of incorrect responses. These investigators concluded that the choice of item-analysis method does indeed affect determinations of item bias. Camilli & Shepard (1985) reported on the development of a computer program to aid in the detection of biased items on ability tests; a "biased item" was defined in the program as an item that favors one particular group of examinees in relation to another when differences in group ability are controlled.

Speeded tests Item analyses of tests taken under speeded conditions yield misleading or uninterpretable results; the more toward the end of the test an item is, the more difficult it may appear to be—this simply because a test taker may not have reached it! Similarly, measures of item discrimination may be artificially high for late-appearing items because examinees who know the material better may work faster and would be more likely to answer the later items. Thus, items appearing late in a speeded test are more likely to show positive item-total correlations because of the select group of examinees reaching those items. One obvious solution to the problem is to restrict the item analysis of items on a speeded test only to the items completed by the test taker. However, this solution is *not* recommended for at least three reasons: (1) item analyses of the later items would be based on a progressively smaller number of test takers, yielding progressively more unreliable results; (2) if the more knowledgeable examinees reach the later items, part of the analysis is based on all test takers and part of the analysis is based on a selected sample; and (3) because the more knowledgeable test takers are more likely to score correctly, their performance will make items occurring toward the end of the test appear easier than they might in reality be.

An example drawn from the research literature serves to illustrate the effects of a speeded test on item score–total score correlations. Wesman (1949) administered the same test to comparable groups of female nursing school applicants. One group took the test under speeded conditions, and the other group took the same test with generous time limits (power condition). The results showed that for items appearing toward the beginning of the test, there were no real differences under speed and power conditions. For items appearing late in the test, the item-total correlations were lower under the speed condition.

If speed is not an important element of the ability being measured by the test and because speed produces misleading information about item performance, the test developer should ideally administer the test to be item-analyzed with generous time limits to complete the test. Once the item analysis is completed, norms should be established using the speed conditions intended when the test is used in actual practice.

TEST REVISION

On the basis of the item analysis, some items from the original item pool will be eliminated, others will be rewritten, and the net result will be a test that better meets the objectives of the test developer in terms of variables such as item difficulty, item discrimination, item reliability, and item validity. The next step in the test development process will be an administration of the revised test under standardized conditions to a second appropriate sample from the population of examinees for whom the test will be intended for use. On the basis of an item analysis of data derived from this administration of the second draft of the test, the test developer may deem the test to be in its finished form—in which case the test's norms may be developed from the data, and the test will be said to have been "standardized" on this (second) sample.

Standardization can be viewed as "the process employed to introduce objectivity and uniformity into test administration, scoring and interpretation" (Robertson, 1990, p. 75). The standardization sample represents the groups of individuals with whom examinees' performance will be compared. For norm-referenced tests it is important that this sample be representative of the population on those variables that might affect performance. Ability tests, for example, are developed so that the standardization group is representative of the population on such characteristics as age, gender, geographic region, type of community, ethnic group, and parent education. The latest available census data are usually utilized to ensure that the standardization sample closely matches the population on these demographic characteristics.

In those instances in which the item analysis of the data for a test administration indicates, for any reason, that the test is not yet in finished form, the steps of revision and item analysis are repeated until the test is satisfactory and standardization can occur. Once the items of the test have been finalized, professional test development procedures dictate that conclusions about the test's validity await what is called a *cross-validation* of findings.

Cross-validation The term *cross-validation* refers to a revalidation of a test on a sample of test takers other than the ones on whom test performance was originally found to be a valid predictor of some criterion. It is to be expected that items selected for the final version of the test (in part because of their high correlations with a criterion measure) will have smaller item validities when administered to a second sample of test takers—this due to the operation of chance factors. The decrease in item validities that inevitably occurs after cross-validation of findings is referred to as *validity shrinkage*. Such shrinkage is to be expected and is viewed as an integral part of the test development process. Further, such shrinkage is infinitely preferable to a scenario wherein (spuriously) high item validities are published in a test manual as a result of the inappropriate use of the identical sample of test takers for test standardization and cross-validation of findings; users of such a test will in all likelihood be let down by the lower-than-expected validity of such a test when the test is administered to a sample of test takers (other than members of the standardization group). The test manual accompanying commercially prepared tests should outline the test development procedures utilized. Reliability information, including test-retest reliability and internal consistency estimates, should be reported along with evidence of the test's validity. Detailed information on the development of commercial tests can be found in Robertson (1990).

Close-up

Anatomy of the Development of a Test: The Personality Research Form

Test author Douglas N. Jackson afforded readers an "inside look" at the way his test, the Personality Research Form (PRF), was created in his detailed account of the sequential system used. According to Jackson (1970), the PRF was developed in the hope that "by a careful application of modern conceptions of personality and of psychometric theory and computer technology more rigorous and more valid assessment of important personality characteristics would result" (p. 62). More specifically, Jackson viewed four interrelated principles as essential to the development of the PRF (as well as other tests of personality). He described them as follows:

1. The importance of psychological theory (see Loevinger, 1957; Cronbach & Meehl, 1955)
2. The necessity for suppressing response style (for example, suppressing the tendency to respond in socially desirable ways or the tendency to respond nonpurposively or randomly) (see Jackson & Messick, 1958)
3. The importance of scale homogeneity and scale generalizability
4. The importance of fostering convergent and discriminant validity

Jackson (1970) labeled the four major stages in the development of the PRF as follows:

I. The substantive definition of personality scale content
II. A sequential strategy in scale construction
III. The appraisal of the structural component of validity

IV. Evaluation of the external component of validity.

In abbreviated, simplified fashion, each stage is described below.

STAGE I: THE SUBSTANTIVE DEFINITION OF PERSONALITY SCALE CONTENT

A. The Choice of Appropriate Constructs

Jackson (1970) advises that "The first step in constructing a personality test is to decide what to measure" (p. 66). If, for example, a test or scale within a test is to measure "aggressiveness," a clear definition of this construct must be arrived at; do we mean physical aggression? verbal aggression? overt aggression? covert aggression? all of these? The answers to these and related questions will depend on variables such as the objectives of the test and the "costs" involved—the latter term referring to factors such as the length of the test and time it will take to administer the test (see Cronbach & Gleser, 1965). An additional consideration in selecting a construct for measurement concerns how much is already known about it: "It is easier to prepare large numbers of items for dimensions whose correlates are well established" (Jackson, 1970, p. 67). The PRF was based on personality variables conceptualized and defined by Henry Murray and his colleagues (Murray, 1938). To help lay the foundation for items to be written that will be high in validity, mutually exclusive definitions of each personality variable had to be de-

Many students who take a course in psychological testing will themselves have occasion sòme time in the future to design a test; the test need not be one of the standardized variety but might be one designed for use in classrooms, research laboratories, or corporate offices. For this reason, we now complement our con-

rived if they did not already exist (for example, "exhibition" had to be distinguished from "need for social recognition").

B. The Development of Substantively Defined Item Sets

Jackson (1970, p. 67) described this step as "the most difficult of all—the creation and editing of the item pool of some three thousand items, comprising the set from which PRF scales were finally developed." He went on to describe the evaluation and editing of each item with respect to the following criteria:

- their conformity to the definition of the scale for which they were written
- the adequacy of the negative instances of the trait
- their clarity and freedom from ambiguity
- their judged freedom from extreme levels of desirability bias
- their judged discriminating power and popularity levels when administered to appropriate populations
- their judged freedom from various forms of content bias and their representativeness as a set
- the degree to which they conformed to the definition of the scale for which they were written as well as their "fortuitous convergence with irrelevant constructs, particularly those which were to be included in the PRF" (p. 68).

C. A Multidimensional Scaling Evaluation of Substantive Item Selection

The empirical value of rational judgment methods used in item selection was demonstrated by means of a technique called "multidimensional successive intervals scaling" (see Torgerson, 1958). Through the use of judges' ratings of descriptions of hypothetical people, information was obtained with respect to (1) the number of dimensions along which items were perceived to differ and (2) the scale value of each stimulus on each of the dimensions.

D. Empirical Evaluation of Homogeneity of Postulated Item Content

An empirical evaluation of the structured properties of the set of theoretically defined items was undertaken by means of the administration of provisional scales to an approximately equal amount of male and female university students. Estimates of item reliability were obtained through the use of the KR-20 formula; the median reliability was found to be .925 with the highest reliability estimate being .94 for six of the scales: Aggression, Endurance, Exhibition, Harmavoidance, Order, and Social Recognition. Interestingly, the lowest reliability estimate (.80) was obtained for the scale called "Defendence." Of this finding Jackson (1970, pp. 71–72) wrote: "This is not at all surprising, since defensive people might be less willing to admit defensiveness consistently."

Anatomy of the Development of a Test:
The Personality Research Form (continued)

II. A SEQUENTIAL STRATEGY IN SCALE CONSTRUCTION

Responses to each of the items on the provisional PRF underwent a computerized item analysis to determine if the item would be retained or rejected. Some of the criteria employed at this stage of the test development process follow:

- Infrequently endorsed items—or items that almost everyone would endorse—were to be eliminated since they reveal little about respondents. Stated a bit more technically, they will fail to appreciably add to the reliability and validity of the test due to their small variances. Further, such items have been found to elicit stylistic tendencies to respond deviantly or nonpurposively. For these reasons, items with a p value of either below .05 or above .95 were eliminated. An obvious exception to this rule would be items deliberately selected for use in the "Infrequency" scale—a scale designed to detect nonpurposive or random responding and related response styles. A sample item on this scale might be one like "I have visited the Republic of Samoa during the past year."
- If an item correlated higher with any content-scale total score other than the one it was written for, the item was eliminated—a method of helping to ensure convergent and discriminant validity.
- An evaluation was made as to the degree to which the item elicited tendencies to respond desirably. This was accomplished, at least in part, by evaluating each item's correlation with a desirability scale.
- An evaluation was made of the item's saturation as indicated by the magnitude of its correlation with the total scale.
- An evaluation was made of the item's content saturation in relation to its desirability bias as indicated by a specially devised Differential Reliability Index.

- Items were assigned to parallel forms of the test on the basis of item and scale statistical properties. The rigor with which this process was executed can be seen graphically in Figure 1.
- Each item was subjected to a final substantive review designed to evaluate its generalizability and its representativeness with respect to scale content.

III. THE APPRAISAL OF THE STRUCTURED COMPONENT OF VALIDITY

Steps were taken to ensure that optimal levels of homogeneity existed—homogeneity attributable to the test's content as opposed to response style or other variables.

IV. EVALUATION OF THE EXTERNAL COMPONENT OF VALIDITY

Paid volunteers who lived in Stanford University housing and who all were "well acquainted with one another" served as the sample for the validity study. Jackson (1970, p. 88) informs us that each subject sat for a four-hour assessment battery including two forms of the PRF, a set of behavior ratings of 20 variables relevant to the 20 PRF content scales, and 600 adjectives measuring the same 20 traits relevant to each of the 20 scales. Subjects responded true or false to each of the 600 adjectives as self-descriptive, and later judged the desirability of each of them in other people. This latter task was included to appraise the hypothesis that a person's point of view about the desirability of a trait would tell us something valid about his own personality (Jackson, 1964; Stricker, Messick, & Jackson, 1968).

An examination of correlations between PRF scales and appropriate criterion measures revealed that there was substantial convergent and discriminant validity associated with PRF scales.

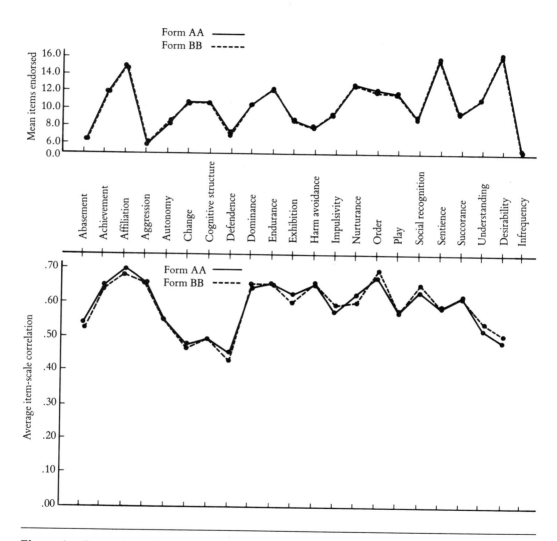

Figure 1 *Comparison of Parallel Forms.* (Source: Jackson, 1970, p. 84)

siderations of standardized-test development with some additional considerations of what we are calling "custom-made" tests.

General Considerations

Let's state the obvious at the outset: custom-made tests necessarily share many of the characteristics of a test designed for more widespread distribution. Specifically, these characteristics include those related to planning, scoring, and interpretation. The prospective test writer must pose and then answer many of the same questions listed early in this chapter with respect to variables such as the objectives, content coverage, length, difficulty level (of items and reading level), reliability, and validity of the test. Regardless of whether the test is to be administered to one person or one thousand people, all rules of good item writing apply; items must be written clearly and unambiguously. Ideally, designers of custom-made tests will call on one or more colleagues for a critique of the first draft of the test. The first administration of the test will serve as an occasion for item analysis and test revision. For future administrations of the same test—and future revisions—it will be useful to create and maintain an item file with notes on the performance of test takers on each of the test's items.

Scoring and grading   As a student, an area of testing that is of no small concern to you is probably test scoring and grading. It may be of some comfort to you to know that issues with regard to test scoring and grading have also been a matter of concern on the other side of the desk; while many a student has agonized about getting a particular grade on a test, many a teacher has agonized about assigning a particular grade. Focusing on the context of a classroom test situation, two questions that arise are (1) How many categories of scoring should be used? (2) How many students should get each grade?

Assume a teacher has administered and scored the 100-item achievement test to 100 students. What should the teacher do with the resulting 10,000 (100 students X 100 items) pieces of raw data? One thing the teacher must do is decide how many categories the scores will be placed into. Is performance on this test best reflected by placement of scores into 2 categories (pass/fail)? 3 categories (pass/fail/honors)? 5 categories (A-B-C-D-F)? 15 categories (A through F with pluses and minuses)? 100 categories (a percentile system)? or something else?

Related to questions concerning the number of categories to choose are questions concerning the assignment of grades; how many students should get which grade? In certain kinds of testing situations, the answer to this question is straightforward. For example, if it has been determined that the test will be scored on a pass/fail basis and if passing is dependent on knowing all of the subject matter of the test, then test takers who know less than all of the subject matter of the test will receive a failing grade. New postal clerks may be required to learn the street boundaries of all of the zip codes within their particular territories; a perfect score (that is, all items correct) may constitute a passing grade on a test of street boundaries, while anything less than a perfect score may be considered a failing score. In most test situations, however, the question of how many students should get which grade is not so straightforward.

Returning to the example of the 100-item achievement test administered to 100 students, one school of thought on grading is based on the presumption that

Table 7–2

225

Standard score value on normal curve	% Cases	Grade
1.5 to 2.5 (or above)	7	A
0.5 to 1.5	24	B
−0.5 to +0.5	38	C
−1.5 to −.05	24	D
−2.5 (or below) to −1.5	7	F

The Normal Curve and Test Grades (n = 100)

knowledge of the test's subject matter is normally distributed within the population of test takers. Thus, grades on the test should be normally distributed as well, and if a five-point (A through F) grading system is to be used, the normal curve would need to be split into five parts; the grade assigned to each test paper would then correspond to the number of scores that fall within each of the five ranges (see Table 7–2).

While such a solution has intuitive appeal, it is not necessarily the best solution in every case. The scorer must decide how desirable it will be to make it a rule that the bottom 7 percent of the class will fail a test. Answers to this and other difficult questions relating to the grading of achievement (as well as other) tests must be made not haphazardly but deliberately and with sound judgment. Perhaps most importantly, the grading system for a custom-made test must be devised with an eye toward the use the test scores will ultimately be put to; are the scores being used to make fine diagnostic judgments? Will the scores be used to provide meaningful feedback to students? to counselors? to parents of children in the lower grades? What does the evaluator really require from the scoring system? What action will result as a function of the assignment of a particular test score (for example, Will the decision to place a child in a special class hinge in whole or in part on the test score?) Should the scoring of a test (or a battery of tests) vary with each of the subtests and/or with time in the sequence that the test is administered? Would it be beneficial, in terms of lessening test anxiety and increasing test-taker motivation, to have more liberal scoring and grading near the beginning of the test or test battery? These are some types of questions that must be addressed when a developer of a custom-made test undertakes to develop a scoring and/or grading system.

The Oral Test

One special category of custom-made test is the *oral test*. While the oral test will never become extinct, it has been pushed closer and closer to extinction with the advent of test-scoring machines and inexpensive computers (complete with accompanying programs that are capable not only of scoring tests but of executing functions such as item analysis and factor analysis as well). The oral test prevails not only because of its tradition and ceremony (for example, the oral defense of a doctoral dissertation) but also because of its unique advantages in an assessment situation.

An oral examination can provide very detailed diagnostic information as the interviewer probes the examinee with as many follow-up questions as is deemed appropriate. In addition to assessment of the knowledge of the content area, an oral examination provides a sampling of the examinees' ability to spontaneously organize, plan, and present their thoughts—an ability that is deemed to be key in certain managerial and executive positions. An oral examination provides the examiners with a glimpse of the demeanor and the affect with which the examinee is responding. Thus, for example, a police officer up for promotion who orally responds to a question regarding law-enforcement ethics will no doubt be evaluated not only for what is said, but also for the way it is said; does the police officer seem to be paying "lip service" to the correct response "according to the book" or does the response appear to be delivered with sincerity? Like any constructed-response as opposed to selected-response format, the oral examination also provides a forum for the examinee to display unique attributes and gifts that may complement—or bias (depending on which way you look at it)—a response (for example, creativity or a good sense of humor).

Paralleling the many advantages of the oral test are their many disadvantages. Perhaps the most obvious is the great amount of time it takes to individually administer, score, and interpret each test separately. There would also appear to be a good deal more subjectivity inherent in the process of scoring and interpretation than there would be in other forms of testing. And related to the increased subjectivity is the great difficulty in attempting to standardize an oral test. While it may, in theory at least, be possible to standardize an oral test, it may not in practice be desirable to do so, since many of the unique advantages of this type of test will be lost in the process (that is, it is usually the case that items or questions that follow up on some initial, prewritten questions are based not on a script, but on the examinee's response to the initial question). Because most oral tests are not standardized, questions of fairness to individual examinees can arise much more frequently than would be expected from the administration of items of the written, objective short-answer variety. The number of sources of variance in the oral test situation rises dramatically as compared to the objective, written examination due to factors related to the examinee (such as amount of test anxiety or the content of the response) and the examiner (such as knowledge, ability, and judgment). Some examinees may be at a disadvantage simply because their "evaluation apprehension" is heightened to a point where their functioning is actually impaired; stuttering, stammering, and responses that make the examinees look as if English is their second language (when it isn't) are not uncommon when anxiety reaches a high level. Unfortunately, such functioning could be evident irrespective of whether the examinee knows the correct or best answer.

The prospective developer of an oral test must be sensitive to the unique benefits and liabilities of this assessment method and use it accordingly. It is a good idea to include, at a minimum, a provision for audiotaping (or videotaping) an oral examination so that some record of it is retained for future reference if necessary.[9] One of the ideal uses for this method of testing is a situation in which

---

9. The user of such techniques needs to be aware of the possibility that videotaping, audiotaping, and related observational methods (such as observation of the interview by others through a one-way mirror) may in some way affect the conduct of the interview. Zinberg (1985) has pointed out that such observational techniques may change the social uniqueness of the situation or in some instances affect the interviewer's concentration.

the criterion the test is designed to predict closely parallels the test situation itself. Thus, for example, a law firm might assess a new associate's readiness to handle a particular type of trial by providing the lawyer with a standard fact situation and then staging a mock trial. The lawyer's knowledge, demeanor, verbal skills, and related abilities would then be assessed and diagnostically critiqued. Similar types of "oral examinations" of the role-playing variety have been used in other professions such as psychology, where such techniques are useful in evaluating a clinician's ability to make diagnostic judgments, conduct psychotherapy, and present research findings.

Part

3

The Assessment of

Intelligence

Chapter 8

Intelligence and Its
Measurement: An
Overview

SUPPOSE THAT YOU received in your mail a request from your local school board. The board was writing you because its members had heard of your keen interest and abilities in the area of psychological assessment. The letter requests your assistance in identifying "slow" children who might require and profit from a special education program. Putting aside for the moment the possibility that the board had been given your name in error, and imagining further that you were indeed quite eager to participate in such a venture, how do you proceed?

In October 1904, Alfred Binet was faced with a similar question. At that time, the Minister of Public Instruction for the Paris schools appointed Binet and three other members of a child study group to which Binet belonged (called "La Société") to a "Ministerial Commission for the Abnormal." The Commission's mandate was to study ways in which mentally retarded youngsters could be identified. Proceeding on the assumption that the difference between the retarded and normal children had to do with intelligence—an assumption that was not so commonplace then as it is today—Binet and a collaborator (Théodore Simon) developed a 30-item test of intelligence designed to be administered to one child at a time. That test, published in 1905, is the ancestor of all formal tests of intelligence that have since appeared.

In this chapter, we will examine a sampling of the many ways "intelligence" has been defined and measured. More detailed discussion of specific individual

231

and group tests of intelligence follows in Chapter 9. Psychological measurement in educational settings is the subject of Chapter 10, and Chapter 11 is devoted entirely to assessment of preschool children. We begin with a question that must of necessity precede consideration of any issues related to the measurement of intelligence.

WHAT IS INTELLIGENCE?

Before reading on, take a piece of scrap paper and jot down your own definition of the word "intelligence." How does your definition compare to those written by the experts we cite? In comparing your definition to the many different ones that follow, you may come to the conclusion, as did Neisser (1979), that because of the nature of intelligence, "intelligence" cannot be explicitly defined. Drawing on the work of Rosch (1978) and Wittgenstein (1953) in the area of concept formation and categorization, Neisser points out that for certain categories of things, no single prototype exists. As an example, consider the word *game;* no sharp boundary separates games from nongames, many categories of "game" exist, and there is no single feature that all games have in common. According to Neisser, concept formation and categorization are organized around prototypes, and it is possible to imagine prototypes that we have not in reality encountered. Neisser argues further that "the ideally intelligent person is one such imaginary prototype" (p. 220). Neisser's description of the intelligent person as an "imaginary prototype" does *not* imply that intelligence does not exist or that the concept lacks utility or even that intelligence cannot be measured. Rather Neisser's essay speaks to the difficulty in defining a multifaceted construct.

Research conducted by Robert Sternberg and his associates at Yale University (Sternberg, 1981; Sternberg et al., 1981; Sternberg, 1982) was designed to shed light on questions such as "What does 'intelligence' mean to lay people?" and "How does the lay person's definition differ from that of the research psychologist?" The researchers asked a total of 476 people from the New Haven, Connecticut, area to respond to a questionnaire or participate in a personal interview. Students, commuters, supermarket shoppers, people who answered newspaper advertisements, and people randomly selected from the phone book were asked for their views of intelligence. They were asked to list the behaviors considered to be characteristic of "intelligence," "academic intelligence," "everyday intelligence," and "unintelligence." After a list of various behaviors characterizing intelligence was generated, 28 nonpsychologists in the New Haven area were asked to rate on a scale of 1 (low) to 9 (high) how characteristic each of the behaviors was for the ideal "intelligent" person, the ideal "academically intelligent" person, and the ideal "everyday intelligent" person. The views of 140 doctoral-level research psychologists who were experts in the area of intelligence were also solicited.[1]

All people polled had definite ideas about what intelligence (or the lack of it) was. For the nonpsychologists, the behaviors most commonly associated with in-

---

1. All such experts were themselves involved in research on intelligence in major university and research centers around the United States.

telligence were "reasons logically and well," "reads widely," "displays common sense," "keeps an open mind," and "reads with high comprehension." Leading the list of most frequently mentioned behaviors associated with "unintelligence" were "does not tolerate diversity of views," "does not display curiosity," and "behaves with insufficient consideration of others."

Sternberg and his colleagues grouped the list of 250 behaviors characterizing intelligence and unintelligence into subsets that were most strongly related to each other in order to make these results more understandable. The analysis indicated that the nonpsychologists and experts conceived of intelligence in general as practical problem-solving ability (such as "listens to all sides of an argument"), verbal ability ("displays a good vocabulary"), and social competence ("is on time for appointments"). Each specific type of intelligence was characterized by various descriptors. "Academic intelligence" included verbal ability, problem-solving ability, and social competence, as well as specific behaviors associated with acquiring academic skills (such as "studying hard"). "Everyday intelligence" included practical problem-solving ability, social competence, character, and interest in learning and culture. In general, the researchers found a surprising degree of similarity between the experts and lay people's conceptions of intelligence. With respect to academic intelligence, however, the experts tended to stress motivation ("is persistent," "highly dedicated and motivated in chosen pursuits") as a critical component, whereas lay people stressed the interpersonal and social aspects of intelligence ("sensitivity to other people's needs and desires," "is frank and honest with self and others").

In another study (Siegler & Richards, 1980), subjects (students enrolled in college developmental psychology classes) were asked to list behavior associated with intelligence in infancy, childhood, and adulthood. Perhaps not surprisingly, different conceptions of intelligence as a function of developmental stage were noted. In infancy, intelligence was associated with physical coordination, awareness of people, verbal output, and attachment. In childhood, verbal facility, understanding, and characteristics of learning were most often listed. Verbal facility, use of logic, and problem solving were most frequently associated with adult intelligence.

A study conducted with first-, third-, and sixth-graders (Yussen & Kane, 1980) suggested that children as young as first grade also have notions about intelligence. Younger children's conceptions tended to emphasize interpersonal skills (acting nice, being helpful, being polite) while older children emphasized academic skills (being good at reading).

From what you have read so far, you can see that lay people have rather diverse conceptions of what "intelligence" means. And, as we will see, psychologists too have traditionally had—and continue to have—differing views as to its meaning.

The 1921 Symposium

In a symposium published in the *Journal of Educational Psychology* in 1921, seventeen of the country's leading psychologists addressed the following questions: (1) What is intelligence? (2) How can it best be measured in group tests? and (3) What should the next steps in the research be? No two psychologists agreed (see Thorndike et al., 1921). Six years later, Spearman (1927, p. 14) would observe that, "In truth, intelligence has become . . . a word with so many meanings that finally it has none." And decades after the symposium was first held, Wesman (1968, p. 267) concluded that there appeared to be "no more general agreement as to the nature of intelligence or the most valid means of measuring intelligence today than was the case 50 years ago."

As Neisser (1979) observed, while the *Journal* felt that the symposium would generate vigorous discussion, it generated more heat than light and led to a general increase in exasperation with discussion on the subject. Symptomatic of that exasperation was an unfortunate statement by a historian of psychology and—nonpsychometrician—experimental psychologist, Edwin G. Boring (1923, p. 5), who attempted to quell the argument by pronouncing that "Intelligence is what the tests test." Although such a view is not entirely devoid of merit (see Neisser, 1979, p. 225), it is an unsatisfactory, incomplete, and circular definition. What some other behavioral scientists think about the meaning of the term "intelligence" follows.

Francis Galton

Sir Francis Galton advanced the intuitively appealing hypothesis that the most intelligent persons were those equipped with the best sensory abilities, for it is through the senses that one comes to know the world. In his book, *Inquiries Into Human Faculty and Development,* Galton (1883, p. 27) wrote, "The only information that reaches us concerning outward events appears to pass through the avenues of our senses; and the more perceptive the senses are of difference, the larger is the field upon which our judgment and intelligence can act." Following this logic, tests of visual acuity or hearing ability were generally thought of as tests of "intelligence." Viewed in this context we can appreciate the great efforts Galton expended in obtaining measurements of these and related variables.

Not all scientists of the day agreed with Galton's views. Among the dissenters was the Frenchman, Alfred Binet.

Alfred Binet

Although Alfred Binet (Figure 8–1) never provided an explicit definition of intelligence, as early as 1890, he wrote that the components of intelligence included reasoning, judgment, memory, and the power of abstraction (Varon, 1936). In a paper critical of Galton's approach to intellectual assessment, Binet called for more complex measurements of intellectual ability (Binet & Henri, 1895). Unlike Galton, Binet was motivated by the very demanding and challenging task of developing and recommending a procedure for identifying intellectually limited Parisian schoolchildren who could not benefit from a regular instructional program and required special educational experiences. Whereas Galton and his colleagues viewed intelligence as a number of distinct processes or abilities that could only be assessed by separate tests, Binet argued that when one solves a particular problem, the distinct abilities used cannot be separated, but rather interact together to produce the solution. For example, memory and concentration interact together when a subject is asked to reiterate digits presented orally. When analyzing a subject's response to such a task, it is difficult to determine the relative contribution of memory and concentration to the successful solution. This difficulty is the reason that Binet called for more complex measurements of intellectual ability that included a focus on measuring "general mental ability," the pervasive component that plays a role in all intelligent behavior.

Consistent with present-day beliefs concerning the assessment of intelligence, Binet also acknowledged that an intelligence test could provide only a *sample* of all of an individual's intelligent behaviors. Further, Binet wrote that the purpose of an intelligence test was to classify, not measure:

> I have not sought in the above lines to sketch a method of measuring, in the physical sense of the word, but only a method of classification of individuals. The procedures which I have indicated will, if perfected, come to classify a person before or after such another person, or such another series of persons; but I do not believe that one may measure one of the intellectual aptitudes in the sense that one measures a length or a capacity. Thus, when a person studied can retain seven figures after a single audition, one can class him, from the point of his memory for figures, after the individual who retains eight figures under the same conditions, and before those who retain six. It is a classification, not a measurement . . . we do not measure, we classify. (Binet, quoted in Varon, 1936, p. 41)

Figure 8–1 *Alfred Binet (1857–1911).*

Born in Nice, France, to a family where both his father and his grandfather were physicians, young Alfred was also expected to take up medicine as his calling. It is believed, however, that a childhood exposure to a cadaver by his father pushed the young Binet away from medicine and into law school instead. Binet was a lawyer by age 21 but because of his family's wealth felt no necessity to practice law. Binet spent much of his time in the library, reading psychology books among other things. In 1880 Binet himself published a psychology-related article, though it was subsequently criticized as having been plagiarized. Binet's interest was caught for a while by the subject of "animal magnetism"—hypnosis—and he published numerous papers detailing how magnets could change emotions, influence perceptions,

Alfred Binet with his two daughters.

and accomplish all sorts of other things—things that hypnosis is known to be able to accomplish.

To Binet's embarrassment, his findings would be shown to have been an artifact of poor experimental methodology.

In 1894 Binet earned a doctorate in natural science from the Sorbonne. His doctoral dissertation concerned the correlation between insects' physiology and behavior. In 1899, while he was director of the physiological psychology laboratory at the Sorbonne, Binet took into his employ a 26-year-old physician named Théodore Simon. The association was to be of historic significance. Given impetus by Binet's growing dedication to finding a way of identifying and then properly educating the slow child, the Binet-Simon test of intelligence would be published in 1905—a test that most historians view as the launching stimulus for the testing movement.

In Chapter 9, we examine in detail the test that is a direct descendant of Binet's early work in the area of intelligence testing. We also examine in detail the work of David Wechsler, another renowned psychologist whose name is closely identified with intelligence testing.

David Wechsler

David Wechsler's conceptualization of "intelligence" can perhaps best be summed up in his own words:

> Intelligence, operationally defined, is the aggregate or global capacity of the individual to act purposefully, to think rationally and to deal effectively with his environment. It is aggregate or global because it is composed of elements or abilities which, though not entirely independent, are qualitatively differentiable. By measurement of these abilities, we ultimately evaluate intelligence. But intelligence is not identical with the mere sum of these abilities, however inclusive. . . . The only way we can evaluate it quantitatively is by the measurement of the various aspects of these abilities. (Wechsler, 1958, p. 7)

Elsewhere Wechsler added that there are "nonintellective" factors that must be taken into account when assessing intelligence. Included among these factors are "capabilities more of the nature of connative, affective, or personality traits (which) include such traits as drive, persistence, and goal awareness (as well as) an individual's potential to perceive and respond to social, moral and aesthetic values" (Wechsler, 1975, p. 136). Thus, Wechsler viewed intelligence tests as "dynamic, clinical instruments" (Kaufman, 1990). Binet also had observed that a comprehensive study of intelligence involved the study of personality as well.

Jean Piaget

Since the early 1960s, the theoretical research of the Swiss developmental psychologist Jean Piaget (1954, 1971) has received increasing attention. Piaget's research focused on the development of cognition in children: how children think, how they understand themselves and the world around them, and how they reason and solve problems. For Piaget, intelligence may be conceived of as a kind of evolving biological adaptation to the outside world; as cognitive skills are gained, adaptation (at a symbolic level) increases; mental trial-and-error replaces actual physical trial-and-error. Yet, according to Piaget, the process of cognitive development is thought to occur neither solely through maturation, nor solely through learning; it is as a consequence of interaction with the environment that psychological structures become reorganized. Piaget carefully described four stages of cognitive development through which he theorized all of us pass during our lifetimes. Although individuals can move through these stages at different rates and ages, he believed that their order was unchangeable. Piaget viewed the unfolding of these stages of cognitive development as the result of the interaction of biological factors and learning.

According to this theory, biological aspects of mental development are governed by inherent maturational mechanisms. As individual stages are reached and passed through, the child is also having experiences within the environment.

Each new experience, according to Piaget, requires some form of cognitive organization or reorganization in a mental structure called a *schema*. More specifically, Piaget used the term "schema" to refer to an organized action or mental structure that, when applied to the world, leads to knowing or understanding. Infants are born with several simple *schemata* (the plural for schema), including sucking and grasping. Learning initially about the world by grasping and by putting almost anything in their mouths, infants use these schemata to understand and appreciate their world. As the infant grows older, schemata become more complicated and are tied less to overt action than to mental transformations. For example, when you add a series of numbers, you are transforming numbers mentally to reach your answer. Infants, children, and adults continue to apply schemata to objects and events in order to understand their world. Our schemata are constantly being adjusted to fit the characteristics of the world we live in.

Piaget hypothesized that the individual learns through the two basic mental operations of *assimilation* (actively organizing new information so that it fits in with what already is perceived and thought) and *accommodation* (changing what is already perceived or thought to fit in with new information). For example, a child who sees a butterfly and calls it a bird has *assimilated* the idea of butterfly into an already-existing mental structure, bird. However, when the new concept of "butterfly," separate from "bird," has additionally been formed, the mental operation of *accommodation* has been employed. Piaget also stressed the importance of physical activities and social peer interaction in promoting a disequilibrium that represents the process by which mental structures change. Disequilibrium causes the individual to discover new information, perceptions, and communication skills.

The four periods of cognitive development, each representing a more complex form of cognitive organization, are outlined in Table 8–1. The stages range from the sensorimotor period wherein infants' thoughts are dominated by their perceptions, to the formal operations period wherein an individual has the ability to construct theories and make logical deductions without the need for direct experience.

A major thread running through the theories of Binet, Wechsler, and Piaget is the concept of *interactionism*. Interactionism refers to the complex concept by which heredity and environment are presumed to interact to influence the development of one's intelligence. Tackling the nature of intelligence from a somewhat different perspective is a group of theorists we will refer to collectively as "the factor analysts."

The Factor Analysts

As we have already seen, factor analysis refers to a group of statistical techniques designed to determine if underlying relationships between sets of variables (or test scores) exist. Factor-analytic theories of intelligence tend to fall into two main schools of thought that can be categorized as a "general" school and a "multiple-factor" school. The general theory of intelligence postulates the existence of a general intellectual ability that is partially tapped by all intellectual activities and numerous specific aptitudes. According to the multiple-factor viewpoint, an individual's intellect is composed of many independent abilities or faculties such as verbal, mechanical, artistic, and mathematical faculties.

As early as 1904, the influential British psychologist Charles Spearman (see p. 123) proposed a theory of the "universal unity of the intellective function," which was based on the observation that all intelligence tests correlated to a greater or lesser degree with each other. Spearman (1927) hypothesized that the proportion of the variance that the tests had in common accounted for a general (or g) factor of intelligence. The remaining portions of the variance were either accounted for by some specific (s) component of this general factor or by error (e). This "two-factor theory of intelligence," as it was later called, is graphically illustrated in Figure

Table 8–1

Piaget's Stages of Cognitive Development

Stage	Age span	Characteristics of thought
Sensorimotor period	Birth–2 years of age	Child develops ability to exhibit goal-directed, intentional behavior; develops the capacity to coordinate and integrate input from the five senses; acquires the capacity to recognize the world and its objects as permanent entities (that is, the infant develops "object permanency").
Preoperational period	2–6 years of age	Child's understanding of concepts is based largely on what is seen; the child's comprehension of a situation, event, or object is typically based on a single, usually the most obvious, perceptual aspect of the stimulus; thought is irreversible (child focuses on static states of reality and cannot understand relations between states; for example, child believes the quantities of a set of beads changes if the beads are pushed together or spread apart); animistic thinking (attributing human qualities to nonhuman objects and events).
Concrete operations period	7–12 years of age	Reversibility of thought now appears; conservation of thought (certain attributes of the world remain stable despite some modification in appearance); part-whole problems and serial ordering tasks can now be solved (able to put ideas in rank order); can only deal with relationships and things with which he or she has had direct experience; able to look at more than one aspect of a problem and able to clearly differentiate between present and historical time.
Formal operations period	12 years of age and older	Increased capacity for abstraction and to deal with ideas independent of his or her own experience; greater capacity to generate hypotheses and test them in a systematic fashion ("if-then" statements, more alternatives); able to think about several variables acting together and their combined effects; can evaluate own thought; applies learning to new problems in a deductive way.

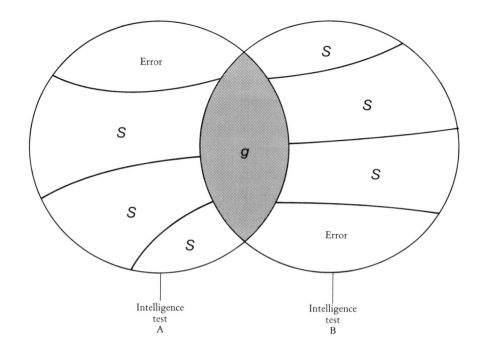

Figure 8–2 *Spearman's Two-Factor Theory of Intelligence.* Here, *g* stands for a general intelligence factor and *s* stands for a specific factor of intelligence (specific to a single intellectual activity only).

8–2. Tests that correlated highly with other intelligence tests were thought to be highly saturated with the *g* factor. Those tests with no *g* factor were not considered to assess intelligence or cognition, but rather were viewed as tests of pure sensory, motor, or personality traits.

Spearman (1927) conceived of the basis of the *g* factor as some type of general electrochemical mental energy available to the brain for problem solving. In addition, it was associated with facility in thinking of one's own experience and in making observations and extracting principles. It was *g* rather than *s* that was assumed to afford the best prediction of overall intelligence. Abstract-reasoning problems were thought to be the best measures of *g* in formal tests. As Spearman and his students continued their research, they acknowledged the existence of an "intermediate" class of factors common to a group of activities but not to all. This class of factors, called *group factors,* is not so general as *g* nor so specific as *s*. Examples of these broad group factors include linguistic, mechanical, and arithmetical abilities.

E. L. Thorndike (1874–1949), a pioneer in the area of psychometrics, conceived of intelligence as a large number of interconnected intellectual elements, each representing a distinct ability. He advanced a theory that is known today as the "multifactor theory of intelligence" (Thorndike, Lay, & Dean, 1909; Thorndike et al., 1921) in which he identified three clusters of intelligence, including social intelligence (dealing with people), concrete intelligence (dealing with objects), and abstract intelligence (dealing with verbal and mathematical symbols). In addition, Thorndike incorporated a general (*g*) mental ability factor as part of his theory. He defined *g* as the total number of modifiable neural connections available in the brain, which he called "bonds." A person's ability to learn, according to Thorndike, is determined by the number and speed of the "bonds" that are brought to bear on a problem.

Louis L. Thurstone, another pioneer in the development of factor analysis, conceived of intelligence as being composed of distinct abilities called primary mental abilities (PMAs): verbal meaning, perceptual speed, reasoning, number facility, rote memory, word fluency, and spatial relations. Thurstone (1938) developed and published the Primary Mental Abilities Test, which consisted of separate tests—each designed to measure only one PMA. Although Thurstone's original theory did not include a general mental ability factor (*g*), he found that his primary mental abilities correlated moderately with each other. This finding led Thurstone to acknowledge the existence of second-order factors that are fewer in number than primary factors. These factors were labeled by Vernon (1950) as "V:ed," representing verbal-educational aptitudes, and K:m, representing spatial, mechanical, and "practical" aptitudes. Thurstone subsequently came to believe that it is impossible to develop a test in the cognitive domain if it does not at least partially tap *g*.

Raymond B. Cattell, another factor analyst, proposed an innovative theory of the structure of intelligence that has special significance and application to the issue of cultural bias in mental testing (Cattell, 1971). Cattell's major contribution has been his two-factor theory of intelligence, the two factors being "fluid intelligence" and "crystallized intelligence." The abilities that make up *fluid intelligence* are nonverbal, relatively culture-free, and independent of specific instruction (such as memory for digits). *Crystallized intelligence* includes acquired skills and knowledge that are very much dependent on exposure to a particular culture as well as formal and informal education (vocabulary, for example). Retrieval of information and application of general knowledge are frequently tapped as part of crystallized intelligence. Cattell's theory of the structure of intelligence stresses that crystallized intelligence develops through the use of fluid intelligence and that the two are highly correlated—and very highly correlated among school-age children who share similar experiences such as a common culture, language, and schooling.

Unlike the other theorists discussed, the American theoretician and factor analyst J. P. Guilford has argued that there exists no general mental ability factor (*g*) in intelligence. Guilford (1967) proposed as an alternative a "three-dimensional structure of intellect model" whereby all mental activities could be classified and explained. According to this model, a mental activity can be classified according to (1) its operation (cognition, memory, divergent thinking, convergent thinking, and evaluation), (2) its content (figural, symbolic, semantic, and behavioral), and (3) the product resulting from the mental operation (units, classes, relations, systems, transformations, and implications). This leads to 120 possible separate ability factors (5 operations × 4 content × 6 products; see Figure 8–3). Thus, for example, a word fluency task (for example, "name all the words that have the letter *a* in them") would be classified as a divergent thinking (operation), symbolic (content) unit (mental operation).

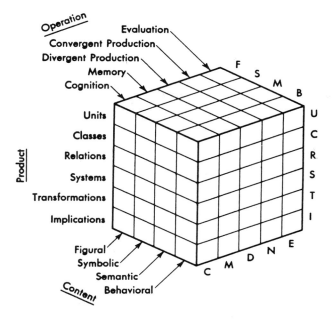

Figure 8–3 *Guilford's Model of the Structure of Intellect.*

Guilford has attempted to develop tests that can be used to individually measure the separate ability factors; the tests are expressly designed to minimize factors from correlating (and hence are designed to prevent *g* from occurring). Some have criticized this approach for its lack of a central factor (Eysenck, 1967; McNemar, 1964), while others have sought to shift focus to the "process of intelligent thinking" (Lohman, 1989, p. 535). Despite efforts to minimize the saturation of *g* in specific tests of mental ability, individual tests tapping each of the 120 separate ability factors have not yet been developed.

A de-emphasis, if not elimination, of the concept of *g* can also be found in the writing of others. Concluding a study of highly talented individuals, Commons (1985) wondered aloud whether there might not exist 800,000 or more intellectual abilities. And likening human abilities to the free-floating swarms of clouds of the Milky Way on a clear night, Horn (1988) asked, "Is there genuine order in this throng, or can one at least impose an order that will not do great injustice to the complexity and still enable one to organize thinking and talking about it?" (p. 645). Citing the Commons estimate regarding the number of different human abilities that may exist, Horn further speculated:

> when one realizes that humans develop new abilities as circumstances change (as when printing, the slide rule, video games, and other such inventions enter a culture), it is not difficult to see that humans do indeed display a myriad of abilities. When one realizes, also, that every human possesses billions of neurons that can be arranged in other billions of ways, and each arrangement can support a different pattern of abilities, then again

it is not difficult to suppose that 800,000 abilities could be an underestimate of the number of different specific abilities humans possess. (p. 646)

If we, in fact, conceptualize the range of human abilities as a kind of Milky Way, an intriguing problem arises for the factor analyst: where and how to draw the lines of commonality (see Figure 8–4). Acknowledging that "a small number of common-factor concepts can help describe and understand this Milky Way," Horn (1988) grappled with the many alternative means by which that feat could be accomplished.

The Information-Processing View

Another approach to conceptualizing intelligence derives from the work of the Russian neuropsychologist, Aleksandr Luria (1966a, 1966b, 1970, 1973, 1980).

Figure 8–4 *Where to draw the lines?*

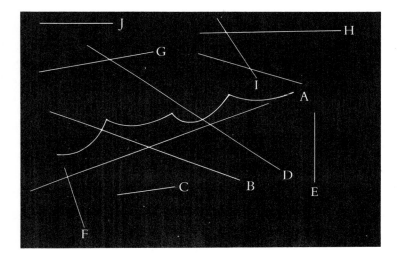

As Horn (1988) has observed, some might look at the welter of stars in the galaxy—each representing a human ability for the sake of this example—and say there is no possible way to draw order. Others may impose order only with respect to relatively few of the many potential "lines" of abilities that could be drawn (such as the lines A, D, E, and J), concluding, as Carroll (1985, p. 9) did, that "there exist only a relatively small number of identifi-

able, replicable abilities." Other people may draw the lines elsewhere, using any of the several available systems of factor analysis—statistical tools used to identify, describe, and understand common factors. Yet factor-analytic techniques will not fully take into account all available information about the data (Thurstone, 1947), such as how human abilities are unique, yet different from each other.

The concept of "general intelli-

gence," usually abbreviated as *g,* is thought to cut across many, if not all, of the lines of common factors between abilities. But a problem arises when one contemplates where and how the "*g*-line" should be drawn. And as we will see in our study of various tests, general intelligence is not only referred to in different tests by different terms (such as "IQ," "general conceptual ability," and "general cognitive ability"), but conceived of as being composed of different abilities. Because different tests of intelligence conceive of *g* differently, the question arises, "Does a true *g* exist?" Though the concept of *g* is very much alive and well in mainstream psychology, voices of discontent have been heard. Horn (1988, p. 680), for example, has argued that "different intelligences can be distinguished even in early childhood, partly because they stem from separate genetic determiners and partly because they stem from separate environmental determiners" and that "the trend of the future is away from further study of very broad concepts of intelligence and toward the study of somewhat less broad abilities—separate intelligences."

This approach focuses on the mechanisms by which information is processed; *how* information is processed, rather than *what* is processed. Two basic types of information-processing styles, "simultaneous" and "successive," have been distinguished (Das, Kirby, & Jarman, 1975; Luria, 1966a, 1966b). In *simultaneous* (also referred to as *parallel*) *processing,* information is integrated all at one time. In *successive* (also referred to as *sequential*) processing, each bit of information is individually processed in sequential fashion. As its name implies, sequential processing is logical and analytic in nature; piece-by-piece and one-piece-after-the-other, information is arranged and rearranged so that it makes sense. When you try to anticipate who the murderer is while watching a mystery movie, your thinking could be characterized as sequential in nature; you are constantly integrating bits of information that will lead you to a solution of the problem of "Whodunnit?" Memorizing a telephone number or learning the spelling of a new word is typical of the types of tasks that involve acquisition of information through successive processing.

By contrast, simultaneous processing may be described as synthesized in nature; information is integrated and synthesized at once and as a whole. As you stand before and appreciate a painting in an art museum, the "information" conveyed by the painting is processed in a manner that, at least for most of us, could reasonably be described as simultaneous—art critics and connoisseurs may be exceptions to this general rule. Tasks that involve the simultaneous mental representations of images or information, as is typical in map reading and in thinking about relationships between things, involve simultaneous processing (see Figure 8–5).

Some tests, such as the Kaufman Assessment Battery for Children (Kaufman & Kaufman, 1983), which will be discussed in Chapter 10, rely heavily on this concept of a distinction between successive and simultaneous information processing. The strong influence of an information-processing perspective is also evident in the work of others (Das, 1972; Das, Kirby, & Jarman, 1975; Naglieri & Das, 1988; Naglieri, 1989, 1990) who have developed a "PASS" model of intellectual functioning—"PASS" being an acronym for Planning, Attention, Simultaneous, and Successive. Within this model, *planning* refers to strategy development for problem solving, *attention* (also referred to as *arousal*) refers to receptivity to information, and *simultaneous* and *successive* refer to the type of information processing employed. Proponents of the PASS model have argued that existing tests of intelligence do not adequately assess planning.

Our consideration of the nature of intelligence continues with a brief overview of the types of ways intelligence is measured at various developmental stages.

MEASURING INTELLIGENCE

The measurement of intelligence entails sampling an examinee's performance on different types of tests and tasks as a function of developmental level. At all developmental levels the intellectual assessment process also provides a standardized situation from which the examinee's approach to the various tasks can be closely observed: an opportunity for assessment in itself, and one that can have great

Figure 8–5 *Successive and Simultaneous Processing.* Successive and simultaneous processing are two different, sometimes complementary, styles of information processing; each is represented below and on the opposite page. We would expect that party invitation "A" and the seminar outline labeled "B" are both processed successively, whereas the other forms of the invitation and the outline are each processed simultaneously. In which form would you prefer to receive the directions to the party? the seminar outline? Why?

Party Invitation "A"

Come to Jennifer's Surprise
Birthday Party!

When: July 4th, 8:00 P.M.
Where: Mel's Bowl-A-Rama
         & Pizza, Flushing,
         New York

Directions: From Manhattan:
Take the Midtown Tunnel to the
   Long Island Expressway-East.
Get off at the "Flushing" exit.
You will come to a blinking
   yellow light, which is the intersection of Sheena Boulevard.
Make left at light and go under the
   Long Island Expressway.
Proceed on Sheena Boulevard
   about 3 miles and you will go
   over railroad tracks.
Make the sharp right that comes
   up immediately after going over
   the railroad tracks; you are now
   on Dead Man's Curve.
Be prepared to make a quick,
   sharp left—a very sharp left—
   which takes you under Sheena
   Boulevard, and then down an
   extremely steep hill.
At the bottom of the hill you will
   come to a "Stop" sign. On the
   opposite corner is an abandoned
   gas station. Mel's is two doors
   down from the gas station, right
   next to the pawn shop at 1313
   Mockingbird Lane. Please be
   prompt and don't park near the
   entranceway, because we want
   Jennifer to be surprised! Park in
   the clearing in the woods behind
   the pawn shop.

Party Invitation "B"

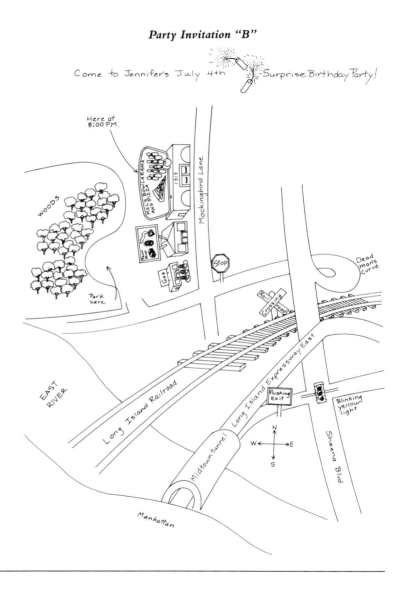

244

Figure 8–5 *(continued)*

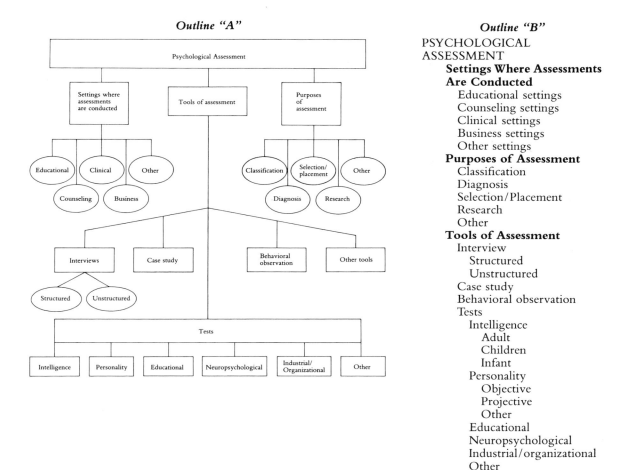

Outline "A"

Outline "B"

PSYCHOLOGICAL
ASSESSMENT
    **Settings Where Assessments
    Are Conducted**
        Educational settings
        Counseling settings
        Clinical settings
        Business settings
        Other settings
    Purposes of Assessment
        Classification
        Diagnosis
        Selection/Placement
        Research
        Other
    Tools of Assessment
        Interview
            Structured
            Unstructured
        Case study
        Behavioral observation
        Tests
            Intelligence
                Adult
                Children
                Infant
            Personality
                Objective
                Projective
                Other
            Educational
            Neuropsychological
            Industrial/organizational
            Other
        Other tools of assessment

clinical utility. Using data from the administration of an intelligence test and other tests, behavioral observation during testing, and other sources, the clinician can obtain a well-rounded picture of the problem areas (as well as strengths) of the examinee. A brief, general overview of the types of tasks involved in intelligence testing follows.

Measuring Intelligence in Infancy

In infancy (the period from birth through 18 months), intellectual assessment consists primarily of measurement of sensory-motor development. This includes, for example, the measurement of nonverbal, motor responses such as turning over, lifting of the head, sitting up, following a moving object with the eyes, gestural imitation, and reaching for a group of objects. Typically, measures of infant intelligence also rely to a great degree on information obtained from a structured interview with the examinee's parents.

The examiner who attempts to assess the intellectual and related abilities of infants must be skillful in establishing and maintaining rapport with examinees who do not yet know the meaning of words like "cooperation" and "patience." A more detailed look at some instruments used to measure the intellectual ability of infants appears in Chapter 11.

Measuring the Intelligence of Children

Whereas the assessment of intelligence in infancy primarily involves evaluation of sensory-motor development, the focus of evaluation in the older child shifts to verbal and performance abilities. More specifically, the child may be called on during the course of a test to perform tasks designed to yield a measure of general fund of information, vocabulary, social judgment, language, reasoning, numerical concepts, auditory and visual memory, attention, concentration, and spatial visualization. The administration of many of the items may be preceded, as prescribed by the test manual, with "teaching items" designed to provide the examinee with practice in what is required by a particular item.[2] In a bygone era, many intelligence tests were scored and interpreted with reference to the concept of "mental age" (see the Close-up).

Especially when individually administered by a trained professional, the tests afford the examiner a unique opportunity to observe the child's reactions to success, failure, frustration, and his or her general approach to problem solving and the test situation. Keen observation of the child's verbal and nonverbal behavior during the testing can yield a wealth of insights that in many cases will help to clarify ambiguities that arise in the test data. The tests may be extremely useful in bringing to light hitherto unidentified assets or deficits and may have value not only in general class placement, but in individual tailoring of teaching agendas.

A list of the most frequently administered children's intelligence tests would include individually administered tests such as the Wechsler Intelligence Scale for Children—III, the Wechsler Preschool and Primary Scale of Intelligence—Revised, the Kaufman Assessment Battery for Children, the Stanford-Binet Intelligence Scale: Fourth Edition, and a group test called the Otis-Lennon School Ability Test. All of these tests will be discussed in the coming chapters. In Chapter 10, we will focus on, among other things, a "new breed" of intelligence test for children, the psychoeducational test battery. Integrated into such tests is not only coverage of many of the abilities tapped in more traditional intelligence tests, but measures of more school-related ability and achievement as well.

Measuring the Intelligence of Adults

According to Wechsler (1958, p. 7), adult intelligence scales should assess the individual's global capacity to act purposefully, think rationally, and deal effectively with the environment and should tap such abilities as retention of general information, social judgment, quantitative reasoning, and expressive language and memory. The specific types of tasks used to reach these objectives on the Wechsler scale for adults are the same as many of the tasks used with children.

One issue here has to do with the distinction between skill application and skill acquisition. During childhood and adolescence, intelligence is considered in the context of skill acquisition and learning potential (such as the learning of reading, writing, and arithmetic), while during adulthood a more relevant area of focus might be skill application. Wesman (1968) argued that the areas in which adults have learned are not tapped on conventional intelligence tests. Some have also questioned the extent to which some of the tasks used in the assessment of adult intelligence engage the motivation of adults in the same way that they engage the motivation of children (Marquette, 1976). Schaie (1978) has pointed out that while novelty in a task may be important as a motivator for the young child, this may not be the case for adults.

The purpose of intelligence testing with adults differs in some respects from the purpose of intelligence testing with children. Tests of intelligence are seldom administered to adults for purposes of educational placement. Rather, they are generally administered to obtain some measure of potential along with clinically relevant information (Harrison, Kaufman, Hickman, & Kaufman, 1988).

Publishers of intelligence tests have made available series of tests that can be used through a period that not quite—but almost—spans "cradle to grave." The Wechsler series of tests, for example, includes a preschool measure, a children's measure, and an adult measure. The current edition of the Stanford-Binet has an age range of 2 years to adulthood. The current revision of the Woodcock-Johnson Psychoeducational Battery has an age range of 2½ years to 84 years. The Kaufman Assessment Battery for Children, combined with its sister test, the Kaufman Adolescent and Adult Intelligence Scale, has an age range of 2½ years through 75 years.

Measuring the Intelligence of Special Populations

Measuring the intelligence of disabled or exceptional individuals is an important part of evaluating their overall strengths and deficits in order to provide a basis for designing intervention. When administering and interpreting tests of cognitive functioning as part of a full evaluation, the examiner attempts to explain the effects of the individual's ability on all aspects of his or her growth and development and to design an intervention strategy that will enhance the examinee's growth and development. It is often important to include in a full evaluation tests designed specifically for and standardized on a particular special population. This is necessary because of the comparatively lower performance and decreased validity of tests developed for the nondisabled when used with an individual with a particular disabling condition. These lower scores are due to a variety of factors, including the differences in the life experiences of the two groups and the fact that the tests often require skills (motor, visual, auditory, or language) that the disabled individual may lack.

Although it is important to be sensitive to the effects of a test designed for and standardized on the nondisabled on the performance of the disabled, as part of a full evaluation it is often important to also compare the performance of exceptional individuals with their nondisabled peers. It is the nondisabled who set the standards in the world at large and into whose social group the exceptional individual may want to move as a functioning member. More specifically, how the disabled individual compares with nondisabled peers may be critical in determining whether the exceptional individual can compete in a particular educational, recreational, or work setting. To meet this critical aspect of the evaluation, test developers and users have modified standardized tests in a number of ways to meet the needs of exceptional individuals. These modifications include adapting test stimuli and mode of responding to make the tests more response-fair and, therefore, more valid.

Hearing-impaired individuals often cannot respond to the verbal directions included as part of most conventional tests and/or cannot respond verbally because of the severe language deficits that often accompany hearing loss. For the hearing-impaired, directions, test stimuli, and the subject's responses are often pantomimed. The visually impaired often require modifications such as enlarged test stimuli (enlarged print, for example) or the presentation of test stimuli by

---

Close-up

The Concept of Mental Age

Have you ever found yourself telling someone something like, "You're acting like a two-year-old?" Such statements reflect the great intuitive appeal the concept of "mental age" holds—the idea that someone can behave in a way that is more typical of a person who is either younger or older. Perhaps the first reference to "mental age" in the scholarly literature was made by Esquirol (1838), who observed that an idiot—one diagnostic classification of mental retardation of the day—was incapable of learning at the same rate as other people of the same age. Duncan and Millard (1866) and Down (1887) were referring to mental age when they suggested that to increase one's understanding of mentally retarded children, it would be helpful to compare their behavior and abilities to younger children—a practice that has continued long after such a recommendation was first made (Goodman, 1978). Another early reference to the concept of mental age came when a psychiatrist, Hall (1848), testi-

fied during a murder trial that it was his professional opinion that the defendant in the trial had the knowledge of a 3-year-old.

The first use of the mental-age concept in a test was in 1877 when S. E. Chaille published an infant test in the *New Orleans Medical and Surgical Journal*. This infant test included items arranged according to age level. The assignment of particular age levels was made by determining the levels at which the tests were commonly passed. It was Alfred Binet, however, who refined the mental-age concept—first referring to it as "mental level"—made it more concrete in definition, and popularized it. Terman and Merrill (1960, p. 5) remind us that "One of Binet's basic assumptions of the original scale was that a person is thought of as normal if he can do the things persons of his age normally do, retarded if his test performance corresponds to the performance of persons younger than himself, and accelerated if his performance exceeds that of

tactile-kinesthetic perception. There are also a number of specifically designed intelligence tests for the visually impaired and hearing-impaired. Individuals with motor impairments reflected in their speech or body movement resulting from stroke, cerebral palsy, or other disease may require modification such as using their eye movements for indicating responses, modifying written tasks to require an oral response, or presenting test items in an oral multiple-choice format. In the assessment of mental retardation, state and federal law dictate the use of supplementary adaptive behavior measures or measures of social competency assessment techniques (measures that we cover in Chapter 17). Items on these scales might assess adaptive behavior in a number of areas, including self-help eating (skills such as drinking from a cup, using a spoon to eat), locomotion (walking, going about town), self-direction (use of money, looking after one's own health), and communication (comprehension of instructions, use of telephone, use of mail, enjoyment of reading).

Some have argued that because of cultural influences in the assessment of intelligence, the identification of mental retardation requires the adoption of assessment practices other than reliance on conventional IQ tests. One such comprehensive assessment model is Mercer's System of Multicultural Pluralistic Assessment (SOMPA) and this will be covered in Chapter 10.

persons his own age." The mental-age concept brought to Binet's test a readily comprehensible "yardstick" by which the examinee's intellectual functioning could be gauged, a yardstick that no doubt also served to stir professional—as well as popular—interest in the test.

In his 1916 revision to the Binet-Simon scale, Terman had attempted to provide standards of intellectual performance for average American-born children from age 3 to young adulthood, which was assumed, on the basis of available information for purposes of the scale, to be age 16. Tests were arranged in order of difficulty by age levels. The intellectual ability of an individual, determined by performance on the scale, was judged by comparison with the standards of performance for normal children of different ages (Terman & Merrill, 1960, p. 5).

Similar to the infant tests that had been developed by Chaille, this placement of items at various age levels had been determined by calculat-

ing the age level at which the majority of normal children in the standardization sample passed the particular item.

The first step in the calculation of an individual's mental age entailed finding the sum of the total number of mental age credits assigned to test items passed (including all items that were below the established basal age but presumed to be passed). As illustrated in Table 1, the "mental age" for a test taker was the "ceiling" (or highest) age level passed by the examinee. Sam's chronological age (CA) at the time of testing was 4 years 6 months. His performance on the test earned him a mental age (MA) score of 5 years 2 months. A conversion table in the manual might, for example, indicate that this mental age was equal to an intelligence quotient (IQ) of 115. But what is an "IQ?"

Soon after Binet's death in 1911, Stern (1914) introduced the notion of a "mental quotient," suggesting that the index of intellectual func-

The Concept of Mental Age (continued)

tioning derived from the Binet-Simon test could be expressed as the ratio of the test taker's mental age to his or her chronological age—and then multiplied by 100 for the sake of convenience and to eliminate decimals:

$$\text{mental quotient} = \frac{\text{mental age}}{\text{chronological age}} \times 100$$

Thus, if a child earned a mental-age equivalent exactly equal to his or her chronological age, his or her mental quotient would be equal to 100.

Lewis Terman (1916) employed Stern's notion of a mental quotient but renamed it, referring to it as a ratio intelligence quotient. Had Terman not renamed this concept, it is possible that the term "MQ" (for "mental quotient") and not "IQ" would be in common usage today. But regardless of whether it is called an "IQ" or an "MQ," the important point here is that the "Q" refers to a quotient; one is referring here to a number derived from the ratio of mental age to chronological age.

The concepts of mental age and ratio IQ were not without their critics. For example, L. L. Thurstone (1926) attacked the mental-age concept as ambiguous, and he urged test users as well as test developers to abandon its usage. In place of the concept of mental age, Thurstone advocated percentile scores or standard scores based on the mean and standard deviation of raw scores of the normative group within each level.

David Wechsler was among those psychometrists who agreed with Thurstone. In the intelligence tests that Wechsler developed, the concept of mental age was completely abandoned. Wechsler argued that the intelligence level of, say, an 18-year-old retarded adult with a calculated mental age of 9 was qualitatively quite different from that of a 7-year-old with a calculated mental age of 9—yet both would be described in mental age terminology as "9 years." Wechsler also pointed to conceptual difficulties inherent in the ratio IQ concept. For example, a 5-year-old with a mental age of 6 and a 10-year-old with a mental age of 12 would both have an

Table 1

A Sample Summary Sheet for the Calculation of a Mental Age
SUMMARY OF INTELLIGENCE TEST DATA FOR "SAM"
Date of testing *June 15, 1961*

Test Level	Year	Month
2		
2-6		
3		
3-6		
4		
4-6	4	6
5		4
6		4
7		0
8		
9		
10		
11		
12		
13		
14		
Average Adult		
Superior Adult 1		
Superior Adult 2		
Superior Adult 3		
TOTAL	4	14
CA	4	6
MA	5	2
IQ	115	

IQ calculated to be 120, yet one child would be two years advanced in mental age whereas the other would only be one year advanced in mental age. Wechsler also noted that the concept of mental age has little utility in describing adult functioning, as "mental age" ceases to be very meaningful beyond certain ages; is a 28-year-old apt to have more intellectual ability than a 29-year-old, for example? A test developer would be hard put to develop an intelligence test where mean scores on the test would increase with age at the ages, for example, of 20, 25, 30, 35, and 40. Here it must also be pointed out that because growth in intellectual abilities is disproportionately rapid in the first few years of life and through early childhood, it would appear to be a mistake to equate the 16-year-old with a calculated mental age of 14 to the 4-year-old with a calculated mental age of 2; although both individuals' calculated mental ages are exactly two years behind their chronological ages, the degree of overall impairment is probably much greater in the 4-year-old.

As an alternative to the ratio IQ, Wechsler proposed what he called a "deviation IQ"—a measure to describe how much an individual's intellectual ability deviates from the average performance of others of approximately the same chronological age. Initially devising a test to measure adult intelligence, Wechsler (1939) culled the standardization sample's data and constructed tables so that the person who scored just at the average level for his or her age group (for example, 20 to 24 years of age) would receive an IQ of 100. The standard deviation was set at 15 points, meaning, for example, that IQs ranging from 85 to 115 would also be considered to be within the normal range on Wechsler tests. With the development of Wechsler's tests for children,

IQs were obtained by comparing the child's performance to the average performance of those of his or her age.

In contrast to previous editions of the Stanford-Binet, the third (1960) edition of this test no longer expressed test takers' performance in terms of a ratio IQ but, like the Wechsler scales, expressed performance in terms of a deviation IQ. Terman and Merrill (1960) noted that the deviation IQs avoided the inadequacies of the ratio IQs in that,

(a) a given IQ now indicates the same relative ability at different ages, (b) a subject's IQ score, ignoring errors of measurement, remains the same from one age to another unless there is a change in ability level, and (c) a given change in IQ indicates the same amount of change in relative standing regardless of the ability level of the subject. Basically, the revised IQ is a standard score with a mean of 100 and a standard deviation of 16. (pp. 27–28)

Although the 1960 revision of the Stanford-Binet yielded a deviation IQ, it remained an age scale with the "guiding principle . . . [having been] to secure an arrangement of tests that makes the average mental age that the scale gives agree closely with chronological age" (Terman & Merrill, 1960, p. 25). By 1972, the concept of mental age as defined in the 1972 restandardization of the 1960 test had changed; here the mental age was tantamount to a raw score and was not indicative of the average performance of the average child at the same chronological age. By 1986 and the publication of the fourth edition of the Stanford-Binet, the concept of mental age had essentially become a term of historic interest rather than practical value.

The gifted Tests of intelligence are widely used as an aid in the identification of members of special populations at all points in the possible range of human abilities—including that group of exceptional people we collectively refer to as "the gifted." But who are these people and how do psychological tests help us to identify them?

Gifted people have been described in many ways. Witty (1940, p. 516) succinctly described the gifted individual as "one whose performance is consistently remarkable in any positively valued area." Public Law 95-561 defined giftedness a little less broadly and with reference to specific areas such as intellectual ability, creative thinking, leadership ability, and visual and performing arts (see Table 8–2).

Studies of gifted children have yielded a number of findings, many of which are summarized in Table 8–3. The most extensive study of the gifted was undertaken in 1921 by Lewis M. Terman at Stanford University. Using the 1916 edition of the Stanford-Binet, Terman and colleagues began the longitudinal research project by identifying 1,528 children (with an average age of 11) whose IQ of 140 or over placed them within the top 1 percent in the country in intellectual functioning. Terman followed these gifted children for the remainder of his own life, taking measures of physical and social development, achievement, character traits, books read, and recreational interests. Also included were interviews with parents, teachers, and the subjects themselves. Terman first published some of his findings four years after the study had begun (Terman, 1925) though others have continued to collect data and analyze them (for example, Sears, 1977). The early results from the study served to dispel many of the myths and stereotypes that

---

Table 8–2

"Giftedness" as Defined by Public Law 95-561

Intellectual Ability—The child possessing general intellectual ability is consistently superior to other children in the school to the extent that he or she needs and can profit from specially planned educational services beyond those normally provided by the standard school program.

Creative Thinking—The creative thinking child is that child who consistently engages in divergent thinking that results in unconventional responses to conventional tasks to the extent that he or she needs and can profit from specially planned educational services beyond those normally provided by the standard school program.

Leadership Ability—The child possessing leadership ability is that child who not only assumes leadership roles, but also is accepted by others as a leader to the extent that he or she needs and can profit from specially planned educational services beyond those normally provided by the standard school program.

Visual and Performing Arts Ability—The child possessing visual and performing arts ability is that child who, by virtue of consistently outstanding aesthetic production in graphic arts, sculpture, music, or dance, needs and can profit from specially planned educational services beyond those normally provided by the standard school program.

Specific Ability Aptitude—The child possessing a specific ability aptitude is that child who has an aptitude in a specific area such as mechanical aptitude or psychomotor ability that is consistently superior to the aptitudes of other children in the school to the extent that he or she needs and can profit from specially planned educational services beyond those normally provided by the standard school program.

existed with respect to the gifted—myths such as "early ripe, early rot" and "genius and insanity go hand in hand." In general, the gifted tended to maintain their superior intellectual ability. Further, they tended to have lower mortality rates and were in general in better physical and mental health than were their nongifted counterparts. They tended to hold moderate political and social views, were successful in educational and vocational pursuits, and committed less crime than did the nongifted.

How are gifted people identified? Intelligence tests are widely used for this purpose, though as you might expect from what you have read so far in this chapter, the definition of "gifted" may change as a function of the particular test used. Models of intelligence range from the unidimensional, as in Spearman's (1927) g, to the multidimensional—3 dimensions according to Sternberg's (1985) triarchic theory, and 120 according to Guilford (1967; Meeker & Meeker, 1973; Comrey, Michael, & Fruchter, 1988). Tests in the Wechsler series of tests (as well as other intelligence tests) yield two primary factors: a verbal factor and a performance factor. The verbal and performance scores taken together yield what is known as a full scale score—interpreted by professionals to reflect g, and colloquially referred to as "IQ." In some programs designed to identify gifted children, a cutoff point for a (high) IQ on a Wechsler test is established for the criterion used to define giftedness. This practice is questionable because it obscures (1) superior performance on individual subtests if the record as a whole is not superior, (2) a significant discrepancy, if one exists between the verbal and performance scores, and (3) the fact that each of the subtests administered does not contribute equally to g; stating this latter point in the language of factor analysis, the various subtests

Table 8–3

Characteristics of Gifted Children

1. Superior physique as demonstrated by above-average height, weight, coordination, endurance, and general health.
2. Longer attention span.
3. Learns rapidly, easily, and with less repetition.
4. Learns to read sooner and continues to read at a consistently more advanced level.
5. More mature in the ability to express himself or herself through the various communicative skills.
6. Reaches higher levels of attentiveness to his or her environment.
7. Asks more questions and really wants to know the causes and reasons for things.
8. Likes to study some subjects that are difficult because he or she enjoys the learning.
9. Spends time beyond the ordinary assignments or schedule on things that are of interest to him or her.
10. Knows about many things of which other children are unaware.
11. Is able to adapt learning to various situations somewhat unrelated in orientation.
12. Reasons out more problems since he or she recognizes relationships and comprehends meanings.
13. Analyzes quickly mechanical problems, puzzles, and trick questions.
14. Shows a high degree of originality and often uses good but unusual methods or ideas.
15. Possesses one or more special talents.
16. Is more adept in analyzing his or her own abilities, limitations, and problems.
17. Performs with more poise and can take charge of the situation.
18. Evaluates facts and arguments critically.
19. Has more emotional stability.
20. Can judge the abilities of others.
21. Has diverse, spontaneous, and frequently self-directed interests.

Source: French (1964)

"load" differentially on *g*. In one study that employed gifted students as subjects, Malone, Brownstein, von Brock, and Shaywitz (1991) cautioned that their findings might be colored by what is called a *ceiling effect*. Some of the subtests apparently had "too low a ceiling" to accurately gauge the gifted student's ability and a greater range of items at the high end of the difficulty continuum would have been preferable. One practical implication of Malone et al.'s (1991) findings was that "the use of the overall IQ score to classify students as gifted, or as a criterion for acceptance into special advanced programs, may contribute to the lack of recognition of the ability of some students" (p. 26).

Identification of the gifted should ideally be made not simply on the basis of an intelligence test but also on the basis of the goals of the program for which the test for giftedness is being conducted. Thus, for example, if an assessment program is undertaken to identify gifted writers, common sense indicates that a component of that assessment program should be a writing sample taken from the examinee and evaluated by an authority in the area. It is true, however, that the single most effective—and most frequently used—instrument for identifying gifted children is an intelligence test. Traditionally, the individual intelligence test of choice has been the Stanford-Binet because it has a higher ceiling than do most other individual intelligence tests. However, use of the current version of the Stanford-Binet for such purposes has not yet been established; the test's "ceiling" may have been lowered (Gridley, 1990). School systems screening for candidates for gifted programs might employ a group test for the sake of economy. A group test frequently employed for this purpose is the Otis-Lennon Group Ability Test. In order to screen for special abilities or aptitudes, tests such as the Differential Aptitude Test or Guilford et al.'s, (1974) Structure of Intellect (SOI) test may be administered. Creativity might be assessed through the use of the SOI, through personality and biographical inventories (Davis, 1989), or through other measures of creative thinking.

Numerous other assessment techniques may be pressed into use to identify gifted people. Nominating techniques whereby people such as parents, teachers, and peers answer questions such as "Who has the most leadership ability?" "Who has the most original ideas?" and "Who would you most like to help you with this project?" may be employed. It must be noted that not all teachers can accurately identify gifted children in their classes. The gifted child may be a misbehaving child in the classroom, and this misbehavior may be due to boredom with the low level of the material being presented. The gifted child may ask questions of or make comments to the teacher that the teacher either doesn't understand or misconstrues as "smart alec" in nature. Thus, although teacher nomination is a widely used method of identifying gifted children, it is not necessarily the most reliable one (French, 1964; Gallagher, 1966; Tuttle & Becker, 1980; Jacobs, 1970). Clark (1988) outlines specific behaviors that gifted children may display in the classroom (see Table 8–4). Parents are probably better judges than are teachers; however, there is some evidence suggesting that parents tend to be quite conservative when assessing their children's abilities (Mandell & Fiscus, 1981).

Behavior rating scales such as Clark's (1979) Rating Scale for the Identification of Gifted Children may provide a useful adjunct to instruments used in identifying gifted children (see Figure 8–6). The case-study method in which information from home, school, and other sources is collected and integrated

Table 8–4

Classroom Behaviors That May Indicate Giftedness

Cognitive Giftedness
  Asks a lot of questions
  Has lots of information on many things
  Becomes unusually upset at injustices
  Seems interested in and concerned about social or political problems
  Refuses to drill on spelling, math facts, flash cards, or handwriting
  Criticizes others for dumb ideas
  Becomes impatient if work is not "perfect"
  Completes only part of an assignment or project and then takes off in a new direction
  Sticks to a subject long after the class has gone on to other things
  Daydreams
  Likes solving puzzles and problems
  Loves metaphors and abstract ideas
  Loves debating issues

Academic Giftedness
  Shows unusual ability in some areas
  Enjoys meeting or talking with experts in the fields
  Gets math answers correct but finds it difficult to tell you how
  Invents new, obscure systems and codes

Creative Giftedness
  Tries to do things in different, unusual, imaginative ways
  Enjoys new routines or spontaneous activities
  Loves variety and novelty
  Loves controversial and unusual questions
  Seems never to proceed sequentially

Giftedness in Leadership Ability
  Organizes and leads group activities
  Enjoys taking risks
  Seems cocky, self-assured
  Enjoys decision making
  Synthesizes ideas and information from a lot of different sources

Giftedness in Performing Arts
  Seems to pick up skills in the arts without instruction
  Invents new techniques
  Sees minute detail in products or performances
  Has high sensory sensitivity

Source: Clark (1988)

provides an excellent basis on which to make a determination of giftedness. Included in the case study are not only formal psychological test data, but also the results of sociometric techniques (such as nominating techniques), if available, and any autobiographical material that is available—statements of interests and aspirations that have been recorded. A complete assessment of the gifted child will contain not only adequate documentation of the giftedness, but also a report on any "islets of difficulty" that may exist with respect to physical, psychological, social, or academic functioning.

Figure 8–6 *Excerpts from Rating Scale for the Identification of Gifted Students. (Clark, 1979)*

Social Development

Check the column that best describes this child's social development.

		Little 1	2	Moderate 3	4	Much 5
33. *Popularity.* Others seem to enjoy and want to be with this child; frequently seen interacting with others in a social friendly manner.	With same sex					
	With opp. sex					
34. *Acceptance of Others.* Relates to others with genuine interest and concern; enjoys others; seeks them out; shows warmth.						
35. *Status.* Assumes public roles and leadership positions or enjoys considerable status in peer group.						
36. *Social Maturity.* Able and willing to work with others, can "give and take," is sensitive to the needs and feelings of others, shows consideration, observes rules of social conduct.						
37. *Sense of Humor.* Ability to laugh at himself or herself; gets enjoyment of pleasure from lighter moments in school day, laughs easily and comfortably.						
38. *Sense of Well-being.* Seems self-confident, happy, and comfortable in most situations.						
39. *Rapport with Teacher.* Two-way communication which seems to bring enjoyment to both child and teacher; relatively open, relaxed, and personal relationship.						

Measuring Intelligence in Other Countries

Although intelligent life may or may not exist on other planets, it is a fact that intelligent life—as well as tests to measure same—exist outside of the United States. Here's a brief, country by country, "world tour" of intelligence tests as compiled by Aiken (1987):

Emotional Development

Check the column that best describes this child's emotional development. Please note that a high score may not be desirable on all of the items that follow.

	Little 1	2	Moderate 3	4	Much 5
42. *Emotional Stability.* Is able to cope with normal frustrations of living; adjusts to change with minimum of difficulty.					
43. *Emotional Control.* Expresses and displays emotions appropriately; emotional outbursts rarely occur.					
44. *Openness to Experience.* Appears to be receptive to new tasks or experiences; seems able to take reasonable risks; can respond naturally to unusual or unexpected stimuli.					
45. *Enthusiasm.* Enters into most activities with eagerness and wholehearted participation; maintains enthusiasm for duration of activity.					
46. *Self-Acceptance.* Seems to understand and accept self; able to view self in terms of both limitations and abilities.					
47. *Independence.* Behavior usually is dictated by his or her own set of values; is concerned with the freedom to express ideas and feelings.					

Australia

ACER Advanced Test B40 (Revised) © 1983; grade 11–adult (15+ years); Australian Council for Educational Research.

ACER Intermediate Tests F and G; © 1982; grades 5–9 (10–15 years); Australian Council for Educational Research.

ACER Tests of Learning Ability (TOLA); © 1976; TOLA 4—year 4 or ages 8 years 6 months to 11 years 5 months; TOLA 6—year 6 or ages 10 years 3 months to 13 years 2 months; Australian Council for Educational Research.

Naylor-Harwood Adult Intelligence Scale, by G. F. K. Naylor & E. Harwood; © 1972; adults; Australian Council for Educational Research.

Non-Verbal Ability Tests, by H. Rowe; © 1985; 8 years–adult; Australian Council for Educational Research.

Pacific Design Construction Test, by I. G. Ord; © 1968; 5 years and over; Australian Council for Educational Research.

Canada

Canadian Intelligence Examination, by H. Amoss, C. G. Stogdill, & C. E. Stothers; © 1940–1947; ages 3–16; Ryerson Press.

Canadian Intelligence Test, by C. E. Stothers, B. R. Collier, T. W. Covert, & J. C. Williams; © 1940–1947, 1966; ages 3 years and over; Ryerson Press.

Non-Language Multimental Test, by E. L. Terman, W. A. McCall, & J. Lorge; grades 2 and above; Institute of Psychological Research.

Safran Culture Reduced Intelligence Test, by C. Safran; 1960–1969; grades 1–6; published by C. Safran.

England

British Ability Scales, by C. D. Elliott, D. J. Murray, & L. S. Pearson; © 1977–1979; 2 years 5 months to 8 years; 5–17 years; NFER-Nelson Publishing Co.

Children's Abilities Scales, by R. Childs & C. Whetton; 11 years–12 years 6 months; NFER-Nelson.

Deeside Picture Test, by W. G. Emmet; 5–11 years; Harrap Ltd.

Educational Abilities Scales, by A. Stillman & C. Whetton; 1970; 13+–14+ years; NFER-Nelson Publishing Co.

General Ability Tests: Numerical, Perceptual, Verbal, by J. R. Morrisby; 1970; all ages; Educational and Industrial Test Service Ltd.

Group Test of General Ability, by A. W. Heim, K. P. Watts, & V. Simmons; parallel tests AH2 and AH3; 1970; 10 years–adulthood; NFER-Nelson.

Group Test of General Intelligence, by A. W. Heim; 1970; 10 years–adults; form AH4; NFER-Nelson.

Group Test of High Grade Intelligence, by A. W. Heim; 1970; 13 years–university level; form AH5; NFER-Nelson.

Group Test of High Level of Intelligence, by A. W. Heim, K. P. Watts, & V. Simmons; 1970; 16-year-olds–college and university level; form AH6; NFER-Nelson.

Moray House Tests (Verbal Reasoning Test 82, Junior Reasoning Test 6, Verbal Reasoning Test (Adv.) 10), by G. Thomson; 8½–13½ and over; © 1968–1970; Hodder & Stoughton.

Non-Readers Intelligence Test (3d ed.), by D. Young; 1964–1978; 6 years 7 months to 8 years 11 months, and less able children to 13 years 11 months; Hodder & Stoughton.

Oral Verbal Intelligence Test, by D. Young; 1973; 7 years 6 months to 10 years 11 months and to 14 years 11 months for children of less than average ability; Hodder & Stoughton.

Ravens Progressive Matrices and Vocabulary Scales, by J. C. Raven; Coloured Progressive Matrices and the Crichton Vocabulary Scales (ages 6 years up, elderly or mentally retarded people); Standard Progressive Matrices and the Mill Hill Vocabulary Scale (6 years and over); Advanced Progressive Matrices (11 years and over); NFER-Nelson.

Reynell-Zinkin Scales for Young Visually Handicapped Children, by J. Reynell & P. Zinkin; birth–5 years; untimed; NFER-Nelson.

Verbal Reasoning Test Series; Verbal Test BC, by D. A. Pidgeon (age range 8 years–10 years 6 months); Verbal Test CD, by V. Land (age range 9–11 years); Verbal Test D, by T. N. Postlethwaite (age range 10–12 years); Verbal Test EF, by O. Wood & V. Land (age range 11–13 years 6 months); Verbal Test GHJ, by V. Land (age range 13–15 years).

Williams Intelligence Test for Children with Defective Vision, by M. Williams, © 1956; blind and partially sighted ages 5–15 years; NFER-Nelson.

India

Non-Language Test of Verbal Intelligence, by S. Chatterji & M. Mukerjee; © 1968; ages 11–13; Statistical Publishing Society.

Netherlands

Snijders-Oomen Non-Verbal Intelligence Scale, by J. T. Snijders & N. Snijders-Oomen; © 1958; 30 months–17 years; SWETS Test Services.

Starren-Snijders-Oomen Non-Verbal Intelligence Scale, by J. Starren; 1976; 7–17 years; SWETS Test Services.

New Guinea

New Guinea Performance Scale, by I. G. Ord; © 1961–1971; 17 years and over; Society for New Guinea Psychological Research and Publications.

New Zealand

Test of Scholastic Abilities, by N. Reid et al.; © 1981; 9 years to 12 years 5 months; 10 years 6 months to 14 years 5 months; 12 years 6 months to 14 years 11 months; New Zealand Council for Educational Research.

Scotland

Cotswold Tests, by C. M. Fleming; © 1949–1961; mental ability series 9, 10, 11, 12 for ages 10–10½; mental ability series C, D, E, F for ages 8½–9½, Robert Gibson, Publisher.

Essential Intelligence Test, by F. J. Schonell & R. H. Adams; 1940–52; ages 8–12; Oliver & Boyd.

Kelvin Tests, by C. M. Fleming; 1935; infants; Robert Gibson, Publisher.

Orton Intelligence Test, by C. M. Fleming; 1931; ages 9–14 years; Robert Gibson, Publisher.

Republic of South Africa

Figure Classification Test, by T. R. Taylor; © 1976; grades 7–9; National Institute for Personnel Research.

Group Test for Indian South Africans, by F. W. O. Heinichen et al.; © 1967–1971; Junior (grades 4–6), Intermediate (grades 7–8), and Senior (grades 9–10); Human Science Research Council.

Individual Scale for Indian South Africans, by R. J. Prinsloo & F. W. O. Heinichen; © 1971; 8–17 years; Human Sciences Research Council.

Mental Alertness: Test B/1 and B/2; © 1945–1968; Test B/2, job applicants with 9–11 years of education; Test B/1, job applicants with 12 or more years of education; National Institute for Personnel Research.

New South African Group Test, © 1931–1965; Junior (8–11 years), Intermediate (10–14 years), Senior (13–17 years); Human Sciences Research Council.

New South African Individual Scale; © 1964; 6–17 years; Human Sciences Research Council.

The South African Individual Scale for the Blind; © 1979; children and adolescents; Human Sciences Research Council.

THE HERITABILITY ISSUE

Do you believe that intellectual ability is innate and that it simply "unfolds" from birth onward? How stable are IQ scores over time? What factors influence measured intelligence? These are some of the many questions and issues that have been raised with respect to intelligence and its measurement. Before reading on, make a note of your own answers to these questions—and then see if (and if so, how) your answers have changed when you reach the end of the chapter.

Preformationists and Predeterminists

Although most behavioral scientists today believe that measured intellectual ability represents an interaction between (1) innate ability and (2) environmental influences, such a belief was not always popular.

The doctrines of preformationism and predeterminism hold that intelligence is genetically encoded and will "unfold" with maturation. The roots of these doctrines go at least as far back as 1672, when one scientist reported that butterflies were preformed inside their cocoons and that their maturation was a result of an "unfolding." In that same year, another scientist, this one studying chick embryos, generalized from his studies to draw a similar conclusion about humans (Malphigi, *De Formatione Pulli in Ovo,* 1672; cited in Needham, 1959, p. 167).

The invention of the compound microscope in the late seventeenth century provided a new tool with which preformationists could attempt to gather supportive evidence. Scientists confirmed their expectations by observing semen under the microscope. Various investigators "claimed to have seen a microscopic horse in the semen of a horse, an animalcule with very large ears in the semen of a donkey, and minute roosters in the semen of a rooster" (Hunt, 1961, p. 38). Figure 8–7 illustrates one scientist's rendition of a human sperm cell as seen through the microscope—dramatic testimony to the way in which one's beliefs can affect perception.

Figure 8–7 *A Human Sperm Cell According to a Preformationist.* This is how one scientist drew a human sperm cell as he saw it through a microscope. (From Hartsoeker, 1694, cited in Needham, 1959, p. 20)

For approximately a hundred years after the invention of the compound microscope, the preformationist theory prevailed. However, the influence of this theory waned as evidence inconsistent with it was brought forth. For example, the theory could not explain the regeneration of limbs by crayfish and other organisms. With the progression of work in the area of genetics, preformationism, as the dominant theory of development, was slowly replaced by predeterminism—the belief that behavior "unfolds" as a result of genetic inheritance. Experimental work with animals was often cited in support of the predeterminist position. For example, a study by Carmichael (1927) showed that newly born salamanders and frogs that were anesthetized and deprived of an opportunity to swim, swam at about the same time as unanesthetized controls. Carmichael's work did not take into consideration the influence of the environment in the swimming behavior of salamanders and frogs. In parallel studies with humans, Dennis and Dennis (1940) observed the development of walking behavior in Hopi Indian children. Comparisons were made between children who spent much of their first year of life bound to a cradle board and children who had spent no such time constricted. Their conclusion was that there was no significant difference between the two groups of children at time of onset of walking and that walking was not a skill that could be enhanced by practice. Walking had been "proved" to be a human activity that unfolded with maturation.

Another proponent of the determinist view was Arnold Gesell. Generalizing from early twin studies that showed that practice had little effect on tasks such as climbing stairs, cutting with scissors, building with cubes, and buttoning buttons, Gesell (with Helen Thompson, 1929) concluded that "training does not transcend maturation." For Gesell, it was primarily the maturation of neural mechanisms and not learning or experience that was most important in the development of what might be referred to as intelligence. Gesell described mental development as a "progressive morphogenesis of patterns of behavior" (Gesell et al., 1940, p. 7) and argued that behavior patterns are determined by "innate processes of growth" that he viewed as synonymous with maturation (Gesell, 1945). Gesell (1954, p. 335) described infancy as "the period in which the individual realizes his racial inheritance" and has argued that this inheritance "is the end product of evolutionary processes which trace back to an extremely remote antiquity."

How valid is the predeterminist viewpoint? Let us ask the question a bit more directly.

Is Intelligence Genetically Encoded?

Is intelligence genetically encoded and something that unfolds with maturation? Or does the learning environment account for our intelligence? Nature/nurture questions like these have been raised for as long as there have been concepts of intelligence and tests to measure these concepts—sometimes amidst great publicity and controversy (figure 8–8). Galton firmly believed that genius was hereditary, a belief that was expressed in works such as *Hereditary Genius* (1869) and *English Men of Science* (1874). Richard Dugdale, another predeterminist, argued that degeneracy, like genius, was also inherited. Dugdale (1877) traced the immoral, lecherous lineage of the infamous Jukes family and hypothesized that the

Figure 8–8 *Dr. Jensen and Mr. Hyde?*

Arthur R. Jensen is perhaps best known for his 1969 article in the prestigious *Harvard Educational Review* entitled "How Much Can We Boost IQ and Scholastic Achievement?" In that article, Jensen presented evidence that blacks score lower on average than whites on standardized intelligence tests. Jensen argued that this difference was due primarily to genetic (nature) rather than environmental influences (nurture). More specifically, after analyzing the research on the black-white IQ score discrepancy, he concluded that the frequency of genes carrying higher intelligence is lower in the black population as a whole than in the white population. He estimated that the variability in measured intelligence was about 20% due to environmental influences and about 80% due to heredity. While the *Harvard Educational Review* article catapulted Jensen to the national spotlight with some members of the professional and public communities praising him and others damning him, an article published by Jensen two years prior to the widely read 1969 article (Jensen, 1967) had employed the same data—though Jensen had not come to the same conclusion. This little-known disparity in views was brought to light by Dworkin (1974), who analogized Jensen to the fictional multiple personality, Dr. Jekyll and Mr. Hyde. Dworkin speculated that the two different interpretations of the data and conclusions might have been due to different social conditions prevailing at the time (in 1969 there existed a social climate more disposed to cutting social welfare programs).

Jensen's rebuttal to Dworkin was entitled "Dr. Jensen and Mr. Hyde," and in it Jensen (1974) acknowledged the change in position

Arthur R. Jensen

but also noted that it was not unusual for investigators to change their view of research data and their interpretations and areas of emphases with respect to it over a period of years. Jensen defended his controversial position on the nature of intelligence.

In subsequent work, Jensen (1980) has attempted to document through logical and statistical analyses of the scholarly literature that genetic differences between the races in measured intelligence do exist. He has conceded, however, that such a position is hotly disputed and that most geneticists would find the idea of a genetic component in racial IQ differences to be "a scientifically legitimate but unproved hypothesis" (Jensen, 1980, p. 58). Perhaps indicative of his sensitivity to those who would label him a racist, Jensen has advocated equal education opportunities for minorities who have been denied this right in the past,

and he has argued that differences in measured intelligence between the races "should not be permitted to influence the treatment accorded to *individuals* of any race—in education, employment, legal justice, and political and civil rights. The well-established finding of a wide range of individual differences in IQ and other abilities within all major-racial populations and the great amount of overlap of their frequency distributions, absolutely contradicts the racist philosophy that persons of different races should be treated differently, one and all, only by reasons of their racial origins. Those who would accord any treatment to individuals solely by virtue of their race will find no rational support in any of the scientific findings from psychological testing or present day theories of differential psychology" (Jensen, 1980, pp. 737–738).

observed trail of poverty, harlotry, and laziness was a matter of heredity. Complementing the work of Dugdale was Henry Goddard's book, *The Kallikak Family* (1912). Goddard traced the family lineage resulting from the legitimate and illegitimate unions of a man given the pseudonym "Martin Kallikak" (the last name was a combination of the Greek words for "good" and "bad"). Kallikak had fathered children with a mentally defective waitress and with the reportedly normal woman he married. Goddard documented how Kallikak's illegitimate descendents were far less socially desirable than the legitimate ones.

Using intelligence tests on newly arrived immigrants to this country, Goddard (1913, 1917) found more than 80 percent of most groups of immigrants to be feeble-minded—a finding we can attribute to the English-language administration of the tests. Based on his testing of a sample of Mexican and Native American children, the father of the American version of Binet's test, Lewis M. Terman, drew similar conclusions about the genetic inferiority of persons from other cultures. The noted English statistician, Karl Pearson, wrote that as compared to the native Britishers, immigrating Jews were "somewhat inferior physiologically and mentally" (Pearson & Moul, 1925, p. 126). Although such observations seem flawed, even prejudiced—if not racist—by current standards, we should remember that they tended to reflect the prevailing truisms of the day.

While a scholarly consideration of the role of environmental and cultural factors (not to mention language barriers) is not evident in the writings of behavioral scientists such as Dugdale, Goddard, Terman, and Pearson, a research literature that shed light on the environment side of the heredity/environment issue subsequently began to mount. It was found, for example, that when identical twins are reared apart, they still show remarkably similar intelligence test scores, though not so similar as if they had been reared together (Newman, Freeman, & Holzinger, 1937; Johnson, 1963). Children born to poverty-stricken parents, but adopted at an early age by better-educated, middle-class families, tend to have higher intelligence test scores than do their counterparts who are not adopted by families of higher socioeconomic status—though the natural mothers with the higher IQs tend to have the children with the higher IQs irrespective of the family in which the adopted child is raised (Leahy, 1932, 1935).

In general, proponents of the "nurture" side of the nature/nurture controversy emphasize the crucial importance of factors such as prenatal and postnatal environment, socioeconomic status, educational opportunities, and parental modeling with respect to intellectual development. Proponents of this view characteristically suspect that opposing arguments which champion the role of nature in the controversy are based more on factors such as political leanings, than on sound and impartial scientific inquiry and analysis.

Somewhere between the rhetoric arguing that heredity plays *no* part in intelligence (Kamin, 1974) and assertions like "Nature has color coded groups of individuals so that statistically reliable predictions of their adaptability to intellectually rewarding and effective lives can easily be made and profitably be used by the pragmatic man-in-the-street." (Shockley, 1971, p. 375) lies the middle ground of the interactionist position: the position that intelligence, as measured by intelligence tests, is the result of the interaction between heredity and environment.

Inheritance and interactionism People differ in intelligence levels just as they differ in blood pressure levels, cerebrospinal fluid levels, and many other ways.

Once this is understood, it is natural to wonder *why* people differ in intellectual abilities; to wonder what accounts for the variability. According to the interactionist view, people inherit a certain intellectual potential and exactly how much of that genetic potential is realized depends partially on the nature of the environment in which it is nurtured. No one to date has inherited the ability to fly or to have "X-ray vision." You might spend your entire life in libraries or on mountaintops visiting gurus, but all of your studies cannot result in your acquiring the ability to fly or to see through things, since these abilities have not been encoded in your genetic makeup; all the learning in the world cannot provide you with the ability to do something that you do not have the genetic potential to do. As a psychologist, you may one day administer an intelligence test to a mentally deficient adult who does not have the ability required to reiterate five digits or to tell you how a ball and an apple are similar. You may wonder to yourself, as you administer that test, whether the deficiency was inherited, whether it was the result of some environmental insult (anything from improper prenatal nutrition on the part of the mother to inferior educational opportunities), or whether it was the result of a combination of the two. Remember that the intelligence test data you obtain will indicate predefined strengths or weaknesses in various subject areas, but it will not necessarily tell you why that deficiency exists.

The interactionist perspective on intellectual development tends to be a very optimistic one; according to it, we are free to become all that we can be. The notion that we can use the environment to push our genetic potential to the limit can be illustrated most graphically by reference to the honing of physical abilities by dedicated sports people. In the 1980 Olympic winter games in Lake Placid, New York, Eric Heiden won five gold medals for the United States in speed skating events ranging from the 500-meter sprint to the grueling 10,000-meter. He broke Olympic marks in each. It can be presumed that Heiden had fulfilled (or had come very close to fulfilling) the full extent of his genetic ability with respect to his ice-skating ability.

How many of us come that close to fulfilling our genetic potential with respect to our physical abilities? our mental abilities? Probably not that many of us. Environmental conditions have to be conducive to allow us to pursue such a course. We also have to have other needs satisfied first, such as the need for financial or other security. Also entering into the equation are personality factors such as the degree to which we are motivated to achieve. Finally, we have to be fortunate enough to be born in the right place at the right time. Would Eric Heiden have been a world-renowned Olympic ice-skater had he been born in the Bronx? Appalachia? Cairo? had he been born in 1945? had he been born to royalty? Born at some other time or in some other place, might he have achieved greatness via some other route or, alternatively, would he have faded into obscurity? Although such rhetorical questions defy any simple answer, they provide a useful point of departure in considering the nature/nurture controversy.

HOW STABLE IS INTELLIGENCE OVER TIME?

Assume for the sake of illustration that you and the other members of your measurement class were administered an individual adult intelligence test today.

Assume further that your measured IQ on the test used was 126 and that this placed you at the 99th percentile. How likely would it be that you and your classmates would achieve similar estimates of your intellectual abilities if retested with a parallel form of the same intelligence test next week? next year? ten years from today? twenty years from today? Longitudinal research studies have in general suggested that above the age of 7, IQs tend to remain relatively stable over time. Below the age of 7 and particularly below the age of 5, measured IQs have not generally been shown to be very stable, although evidence to the contrary may also be found (see Lamp & Krohn, 1990; and Smith, Bolin, & Stovall, 1988). A lack of stability in measured intelligence in very young children is understandable in light of the fact that there is typically a great amount of intellectual growth during the early childhood years. There is little reason to have great confidence that the measured intelligence of infants and preschool children would correlate highly with measures of intelligence obtained in later years (Wesman, 1968). This is so because the types of measures used in infant and preschool tests differ so markedly from those used to measure intelligence in school-age, adolescent, and adult individuals.

The correlation coefficient referred to as a *stability coefficient* is used to express the degree of the relationship that exists between scores on the same test (or parallel forms of the same test) observed at two points in time. The stability coefficient does not necessarily represent the degree of consistency between the measurements, but rather the degree of consistency in the person's relative standing among others on the same test. If all the subjects in the longitudinal research study improved or lowered their scores by approximately the same magnitude and a particular individual's relative standing in the group remained the same, the stability coefficient would be high.

We mention in passing that the responsible test user would, if possible, look to more than a test's stability coefficient in determining the degree of confidence with which projections could be made about a particular examinee's future intellectual ability; generalizations about data obtained in the course of longitudinal research with a group of subjects may not hold true for any one individual in the group. Especially when working with young children, any predictions about future intellectual ability must be considered tenuous and should ideally be made not only on the basis of measured IQ with a valid test, but also on the basis of an assessment of the child's personality and the environmental resources available at home, school, and elsewhere to foster intellectual growth.

The Rise and Fall of IQ

Since the early 1900s, it has been widely held that intellectual growth begins to decline at about age 20 or so. If this were true and you are at about that age, this would mean that you're at the height of your intellectual powers right now— you've "peaked" and it's all downhill from here.

The conclusion that an intellectual decline occurs at about age 20 or so was based on cross-sectional research studies in which people of different ages were examined and compared at the same time. Results of these studies did in fact suggest that mean IQ scores declined after around age 20. However, several factors were overlooked by the interpreters of the data; most importantly, decrements in measured intelligence as a result of age appeared to be confounded with decrements in measured intelligence as a function of cultural changes between the younger and older subjects. In a cross-sectional research study that compares a group of, say, 20-year-olds to a group of, say, 70-year-olds, it cannot be overlooked that the experimental background of members of these two groups is quite different; perhaps it was the experiential background and exposure to society at two different points in time that was primarily responsible for the differences in measured intelligence. Additionally, it should be noted that educational opportunities for the younger group may have been much greater than those available to the older subjects. Further, the younger group may have also had a wider range of potential learning experiences because of the widespread accessibility of radio and television. Indirect benefits were also accorded the younger group in terms of variables related to improvements in nutrition, medical care, and general quality of life.

Contrary to what turn-of-the-century behavioral scientists believed, it may well be that intellectual ability continues to increase as one gets older. In one longitudinal study, a mean increase of 11.3 IQ points from age 13 to age 29, and a mean increase of 6 IQ points between the ages of 29 and 42 were reported (Bradway & Thompson, 1962). On average, significant intellectual decrements do not begin to appear until people get into their sixties; and even at that point, it appears that a decline in general intellectual functioning may be related to overall level of health as opposed to age per se (Birren, 1968; Palmore, 1970). When intellectual decrements do occur, they are more likely to occur in fluid rather than crystallized abilities (see page 240). Exactly how, and if, such intellectual decline affects an individual may be based on numerous factors, such as whether or not education is continued in later life (Kaufman, 1990).

WHAT FACTORS INFLUENCE MEASURED INTELLIGENCE?

Measured intelligence may be influenced by numerous factors such as the measuring procedure used, heredity, and environment (as well as numerous related factors such as personality, gender, family constellation, and culture). These factors are not discrete in their influence on measured intelligence but rather interactive.

The Process of Measurement as a Factor

Measured intelligence may vary as a result of factors related to the measurement process, such as the instrument used to measure intelligence (including the test author's definition of intelligence, the standardization sample employed, and so forth), the competency of the test administrator, and the accuracy of the scoring. Other factors related to the measurement process itself include the amount of test-taking experience and/or prior coaching on the part of the examinee and numerous personality and situational factors (such as the examinee's level of anxiety or fatigue and the extent to which the conditions of the test's administration conform to the requirements of the test manual).

Genetic and Environmental Factors

Stated broadly, genetic and environmental factors clearly contribute to measured intelligence scores and also play no small part in recorded changes in measured intelligence over time. Overall growth patterns in people differ widely; some develop rather uniformly at a uniform pace while others grow in nonuniform ways in spurts. Such growth patterns may affect factors such as the ability and receptivity to new learning that would enhance intellectual ability. In addition, most professionals and nonprofessionals alike believe that people are born with a certain intellectual potential. Interacting with genetic factors are environmental influences that are also potent factors with respect to measured intelligence. The category "environmental factors" is quite broad, including variables as diverse as general learning and cultural opportunities, physical health and illness, socioeconomic status, family constellation, and cultural membership. Some subcategories of genetic and environmental factors, such as personality, are themselves factors that represent an interaction of heredity and environment.

Personality factors   Alfred Binet and David Wechsler, among others, considered personality to be an integral part of measured intelligence. Binet had conceived of the study of intelligence as being synonymous with the study of personality; he was sensitive to the manifestations of intelligence in *all* human behavior. Wechsler (1958) also believed that all tests of intelligence measure traits of temperament and personality, such as drive, energy level, impulsiveness, persistence, and goal awareness.

Longitudinal and cross-sectional studies of children have explored the relationship between various personality characteristics and measured intelligence. Aggressiveness with peers, initiative, high need for achievement, competitive striving, curiosity, self-confidence, and emotional stability are some personality factors that are associated with gains in measured intelligence over time. Passivity, dependence, and maladjustment are some of the factors present in children whose measured intellectual ability has not increased over time.

In discussions of the role of personality in the measured intelligence of infants, the term "temperament" (rather than "personality") is typically employed. There is evidence to suggest that infants differ quite markedly in temperament with respect to a number of dimensions, including vigor of responding, general activity rate, restlessness during sleep, irritability, and "cuddliness" (Chess & Thomas, 1973). An infant's temperament can affect his or her measured intellectual ability in that irritable, restless children who do not enjoy being held have a negative reciprocal influence on their parents—perhaps even test administrators as well. Parents are less likely to want to pick such children up and spend more time with them engaging in activities that are known to stimulate intellectual development, such as talking to them (White, 1971).

Gender and measured intelligence   It is generally believed that the sexes do not differ significantly in general intelligence as measured by the most widely used standardized intelligence tests (Matarazzo, 1972). While differences in some specific abilities have been observed, these differences tend to be insignificant statistically (Maccoby & Jacklin, 1974). Thus, for example, it has been found that females as a group tend to score slightly higher than males as a group in tasks involving verbal ability, while males tend to outscore females in tasks involving quantitative or mathematical ability (Maccoby & Jacklin, 1974; Silverstein & Fisher, 1960; Terman & Tyler, 1954).

Family environment and measured intelligence Environmental factors such as parental ability and parental concern regarding the child's achievement have been shown to correlate positively with the child's measured intelligence (Honzik, 1967). High measured intelligence in children has also been associated with warm democratic homes in which there are explanations for discipline policies (Baldwin, Kalhorn, & Breese, 1945; Kent & Davis, 1957; Sontag, Baker, & Nelson, 1958).

The relationship of maternal age to measured IQ has also been studied. Generally, children of older mothers have higher mean IQ scores (Davis, Butler, & Goldstein, 1972; Record, McKeown, & Edwards, 1969). The effect of maternal age on measured intelligence is often attributed to social class, because younger mothers often tend to be of lower socioeconomic status. However, this positive relationship between maternal age and measured intelligence has also been reported after social class, birth order, and family size were controlled (Davis, Butler, & Goldstein, 1972; Zybert, Stein, & Belmont, 1978).

Culture as a factor in measured intelligence As a group, members of some minority groups, including blacks (Baughman & Dahlstrom, 1968; Dreger & Miller, 1960; Lesser, Fifer, & Clark, 1965; Shuey, 1966), Hispanics (Gerry, 1973; Holland, 1960; Lesser, Fifer, & Clark, 1965; Mercer, 1976; Simpson, 1970), and Native American Indians (Cundick, 1976), score lower on average on intelligence tests than do those who are not members of a minority group. In one sense, such findings are not surprising. A culture provides specific models for ways of thinking, acting, and feeling; it enables people to survive both physically and socially and to master and control the world around them (Chinoy, 1967). Items on tests of intelligence tend to reflect the culture of the society where such tests are employed; to the extent that a score on such a test reflects the degree to which test takers have been integrated into the society and the culture, it would be expected that members of subcultures (as well as others who for whatever reason choose not to perceive themselves as identified with mainstream society) would score lower. Zuckerman (1990), however, cautions that there is much more variation within racial groups than between racial groups on such variables as temperament and basic personality traits. It is therefore possible that studies purporting to show differences between various minority groups may reflect sampling differences and not "true" group differences.

At one time in the history of intelligence testing, developers of intelligence tests sought to develop "pure" measures of intelligence that would be "culture-free." The assumption was that if cultural factors could be controlled, scores of average measured intelligence for minority and majority group members should not significantly differ. One way that the effect of culture could be controlled was through the elimination of verbal items and exclusive reliance on nonverbal, performance items. Researchers thought that the nonverbal items represented the best available means for determining the cognitive ability of minority-group children and adults. On the face of it, such an assumption seemed reasonable. However, the presumption that the use of nonverbal test items would eliminate the differences between minority and majority groups in measured intelligence was not found to be true for native-born, English-speaking minority groups. For example, on the average, blacks tended to score as low on performance as on verbal tests (Cole & Hunter, 1971; McGurk, 1975). Superior performance on these non-language tests as compared to more conventional IQ tests administered in English has been observed with non-English-speaking or bilingual groups such as Mexican-Americans, Puerto Ricans, Chinese, Japanese, and Native American Indians (Jensen, 1980). This difference in performance on the two types of tests (verbal and performance) is attributed more to language effects than to intellectual abilities. It may be speculated that blacks tend to score low on nonverbal tests for the same reasons that account for lower performance on verbal tests (for example, cultural deprivation). Another problem with exclusive reliance on nonverbal or nonlanguage tests was that they did not have the same high level of predictive validity as did the more verbally loaded tests, primarily because these items do not sample the same psychological processes as do the more verbally loaded, conventional tests of intelligence. Further, most academic courses and business and industrial jobs require at least some verbal facility. It should therefore come as no surprise to find that the nonverbal (performance) items have a low relation to success in the setting the tests were intended to predict for. Finally, although the idea of developing a truly culture-free test had great intuitive appeal, it was a practical impossibility; all tests of intelligence, to a greater or lesser degree, reflect the culture in which (1) they were devised and (2) will be used.

The concept of *cultural loading* is used in discussions regarding the magnitude with which cultural influence is reflected in the measured intelligence. For example, a test item such as "Name three words for snow" is a highly cultural-loaded item—one that draws heavily from the Eskimo culture where many words exist for snow. By contrast, people from Brooklyn would be hard put to come up with more than one word for snow (well, maybe two, if you count *slush*). Soon after it became evident that no test could legitimately be called "culture-free," a number of tests referred to as "culture-fair" began to be published. Some of the ways in which items for such tests were developed appear in Table 8–5.

In general, the rationale behind "culture-fair" test items was to include only those tasks that seemed to reflect experiences, knowledge, and skills common to all different cultures. In addition, all the tasks were designed to be motivating to all groups (Samuda, 1982). An attempt was made to minimize the importance of factors such as verbal skills thought to be responsible for the lower mean scores of various minority groups. Therefore, the culture-fair tests tended to be nonverbal in nature, with directions that were simple, clear, and administered orally by the examiner. The nonverbal tasks typically consisted of assembling, classifying, selecting, or manipulating objects, and drawing or identifying geometric designs. Some sample items from the Cattell Culture Fair Test are illustrated in Figure 8–10. Another test designed to be culture-fair, the System of Multicultural Pluralistic Assessment (SOMPA) will be discussed in Chapter 10.

While the cultural loading of these tests may indeed have been reduced, so was their value as tests of intelligence. These tests provided insufficient informa-

Table 8–5

Ways of Reducing the Culture Loading of Tests

Culture loaded	Culture loading reduced
Paper-and-pencil tasks	Performance tests
Printed instructions	Oral instructions
Oral instructions	Pantomime instructions
No preliminary practice	Preliminary practice items
Reading required	Purely pictorial
Pictorial (objects)	Abstract figural
Written response	Oral response
Separate answer sheet	Answers written on test itself
Language	Nonlanguage
Speed tests	Power tests
Verbal content	Nonverbal content
Specific factual knowledge	Abstract reasoning
Scholastic skills	Nonscholastic skills
Recall of past-learned information	Solving novel problems
Content graded from familiar to rote	All item content highly familiar
Difficulty based on rarity of content	Difficulty based on complexity of relation education

Source: Jensen (1980)

tion and lacked what has been the hallmark of traditional tests of intelligence: predictive validity. And still, minority group members tended to score lower on these tests than did majority group members.

Frustrated by their seeming inability to develop culture-fair equivalents of traditional intelligence tests, some test developers attempted to develop equivalents of traditional intelligence tests that were "culture specific"; the assumption here being that a test expressly developed for members of the subculture might yield a more valid measure of the mental development of minority group members. Some have argued, for example, that Americans living in urban ghettos share common beliefs and values that are quite different from those of mainstream America. Included among these common beliefs and values, for example, is an inability to delay gratification, a "live for today" orientation, and a reliance on slang in verbal communication. It has been argued, for example, that blacks living in poverty tend to share common modes of thinking, feeling, and acting that may affect their measured intelligence. Native American Indians also share a common subculture with core values that may negatively influence their measured intelligence. Central to these values is the belief that individuals should be judged with respect to their relative contribution to the group rather than individual accomplishments. Native Americans also value their relatively unhurried and present-time-oriented lifestyle (Foerster & Little Soldier, 1974).

Subcultural characteristics such as those cited have been presumed to penalize unfairly minority group members who take intelligence tests that are culturally loaded with American white, middle-class values. One culture-specific intelligence test developed expressly for use with blacks was the Black Intelligence Test of Cultural Homogeneity (Williams, 1975), a 100-item multiple-choice test containing items such as the following:[3]

1. *Mother's Day* means
   a. Black independence day
   b. a day when mothers are honored
   c. a day the welfare checks come in
   d. every first Sunday in church
2. *Blood* means
   a. a vampire
   b. a dependent individual
   c. an injured person
   d. a brother of color
3. The following are popular brand names. Which one does not belong?
   a. Murray's
   b. Dixie Peach
   c. Royal Crown
   d. Preparation H

As you read the items above you may be smiling and asking yourself questions like "Is this really an intelligence test?" or "Should I be taking this seriously?" If you were thinking such questions, you are in good company; many psychologists probably asked themselves the same questions. In fact a kind of parody of the BITCH (the acronym for the test) was published in the May 1974 issue of *Psychology Today* (p. 101) and it was called the "S.O.B. (Son of the Original BITCH) Test." However, the Williams (1975) test was purported to be a genuine culture-specific test of intelligence, a test that was standardized on 100 black high school students in the St. Louis area and a test that Williams was awarded $153,000 by the National Institute of Mental Health to develop.

In what was probably one of the few published studies designed to explore the test's validity, the Wechsler Adult Intelligence Scale (WAIS) and the BITCH were both administered to black ($n = 17$) and white ($n = 116$) applicants for a job with the Portland, Oregon, police department. The black subjects performed much better on the BITCH than did the white subjects with a mean score that exceeded the white mean score by 2.83 standard deviations. The white mean IQ as measured by the WAIS exceeded the black mean IQ by about 1.5 standard deviations. None of the correlations between the BITCH score and any of the following variables for either the black or white test takers differed significantly from zero: WAIS Verbal IQ, WAIS Performance IQ, WAIS Full Scale IQ, and years of education. It was also noteworthy that despite the fact that the black sample in this study had an average of more than 2½ years of college education, and despite the fact that their overall mean on the WAIS was about 20 points higher than blacks in general, their scores on the BITCH fell below the average of the standardization sample (high school pupils ranging in age from 16 to 18). What then is the BITCH measuring? The study authors, Matarazzo and Wiens

---

3. The answers keyed correct are as follows: 1(c), 2(d), and 3(d).

(1977) concluded that the test was measuring "street wiseness" though Jensen (1980, p. 681) has commented that "Whether it is even a psychometrically good test of black slang and 'street wiseness' is not known." At the other end of the spectrum from the culturally disadvantaged is the culturally privileged; and a culture-specific test has even been devised for that population (see Figure 8–9).[4]

Although many of the culture-specific tests did yield higher mean scores for the minority group they were specifically designed for use with, they lacked predictive validity and provided little useful and practical information.[5] The knowledge that is required to score high on all of the culture-specific and culture-reduced tests has not been seen as relevant for educational purposes within our pluralistic society. Such tests have low predictive validity for the criterion of success in academic as well as vocational settings.

At various phases in the "life history" of an intelligence test—including its development, administration, and interpretation—a number of approaches to reduce cultural bias may be employed. Panels of experts may evaluate the potential bias inherent in a newly developed test and those items judged to be biased are eliminated. The test may be devised so that relatively few verbal instructions are needed to administer it, and/or provide for demonstrations of how to respond to what is required—all in an effort to minimize any possible language bias. A tryout or pilot testing with ethnically mixed samples of test takers may be undertaken. If differences in scores emerge solely as a function of ethnic group membership, the individual items can be studied further for possible bias.

Major tests of intelligence have undergone a great deal of scrutiny for bias in many investigations—ranging from study of individual items to study of the validity of the predictions that can be made from their administration—and it has generally been concluded that these tests are relatively free of any systematic bias. However, even if an individual test is free of bias, it is important to remember that there are other potential sources of bias ranging from the criterion for referral for assessment, to the conduct of the assessment, to the scoring of items (particularly those items that are somewhat subjective), and, finally, to the interpretation of the findings.

A PERSPECTIVE ON INTELLIGENCE AND TESTS OF INTELLIGENCE

Variously referred to by a dozen or so other designations such as "mental ability," "learning potential," and "cognitive ability," *intelligence* is an abstract, multifaceted construct that defies simple definition; subsumed in this global and broad term are numerous special abilities and talents such as the ability to reason, judge, remember, understand, calculate, hypothesize, think abstractly, visualize spa-

---

4. According to Herlihy (1977), the answers keyed correct are 1(c), 2(b), 3(d), 4(a), 5(b), 6(b), 7(a), 8(c), 9(c), 10(d).
5. Perhaps the most psychometrically sound of the instruments designed especially for use with black subjects was the Listening Comprehension Test (Orr & Graham, 1968; Carver, 1968–1969, 1969). On this test, however, blacks tended to score lower than whites even when the groups were matched with respect to socioeconomic status.

Mazes

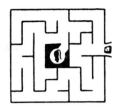

Classification

Pick out the two odd items in each row of figures.

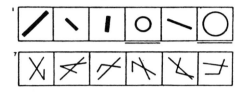

Figure Matrices

Choose from among the six alternatives, the one that most logically completes the matrix pattern above it.

Series

Choose one figure from the six on the right that logically continues the series of three figures at the left.

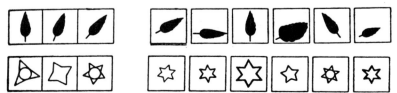

Figure 8–9 *Sample Items from the Culture Fair Test of Intelligence (Cattell, 1940).* 273

tially, and learn quickly. Intelligence sometimes overlaps (and sometimes does not overlap) with other abilities such as creativity and with various personality traits such as curiosity, persistence, and goal awareness. People who have high measured intelligence typically earn high grades in school and then go on to succeed in many varied vocational settings.

The construct of intelligence has value to psychologists in their efforts to understand and predict human behavior. Intelligence tests have proved to be of great value not only in basic research but also in applied settings where they may be used as an aid in selection, classification, placement, and diagnostic decisions.

Questions concerning the role of nature versus nurture in measured intelligence have not gone away (Reschly, 1981). Some (such as Burt, 1958; Herrnstein, 1971) have argued that the preponderance of the evidence points to the conclusion that differences in measured intelligence are due primarily to heredity. Others have argued that this position has been used to foster racist ideology and amounts, in essence, to a political tool to oppress many of society's religious, ethnic, and racial minorities.

It is likely that the nature/nurture dichotomy is too simplistic; it is impossible to separate out the confounding influences of personal, family, socioeconomic, and cultural variables associated with racial and ethnic group memberships. Although human beings do certainly differ in size, shape, and color—and it is therefore reasonable to consider that there is also a physical base for differences in intellectual ability—researchers have found it impossible to develop a pure measure of innate genetic potential. And though few would deny that genetic factors influence measured intelligence, a problem that defies solution is the determination of the amount of the variance in intellectual ability that can reasonably be attributed to genetics (not to mention the difficulty in determining which abilities are indeed hereditary). It is quite likely that nature as opposed to nurture is responsible for at least some of the variance for some abilities. But notwithstanding genetic technology, we have control only over the environmental factors that play a part in intellectual development; and it is those (environmental) factors that will play a great role in determining whether or not the genetic potential—or more likely, a portion of that potential—will ever indeed be realized. It would therefore seem incumbent on future researchers in this area to identify and develop a taxonomy of the essential environmental factors responsible in intellectual development. Some of these factors may be found to be "direct" in that once they are introduced to a group of subjects, the measured intelligence of that group rises. Other factors may be found to be "indirect" in that they do not directly affect measured intelligence but act as a catalyst to some preexisting genetic potential that had been dormant.

As our overview of intelligence and its measurement draws to a close, let's return for a moment to the hypothetical situation posed at the beginning of this chapter—the one about the letter from the school board requesting your assistance in identifying "slow" children who might require, and profit from, a special education program. Any new thoughts on the question of how you would proceed?

Because you are taking a course in measurement, your reflexive reaction might be, "develop a test!" Fine. But how will you define intelligence, and how will your measuring instrument reflect that definition? Will your test be derived from a one-factor model of intelligence, much like Spearman's (1927) notion of general intelligence, or *g*? Or will your definition reflect a two-factor model—verbal and performance abilities—much like Wechsler's conception. How about a three-factor model, complete with factors such as (1) analytic skills, (2) insightful-thinking skills, and (3) practical or adaptive skills—much like Sternberg's (1985) triarchic theory. Perhaps you lean more toward Guilford (1967), and prefer to conceptualize—and measure—"intelligence" in terms of over a hundred distinct abilities. In the following chapters, we will see how various theories of intelligence have been put into practice.

Figure 8–10 *Items from the CRUST (Cultural/Regional Uppercrust Savvy Test).* This tongue-in-cheek test of intelligence was designed by Herlihy (1977) to be a snap for test takers with "uppercrust savvy."

1. When you are "posted" at the country club, (a) you ride horses with skill, (b) you are elected to the governance board, (c) you are publicly announced as not having paid your dues, (d) a table is reserved for you in the dining room, whether you use it or not.
2. An arabesque in ballet is (a) an intricate leap, (b) a posture in which the dancer stands on one leg, the other extended backward, (c) a series of steps performed by a male and a female dancer, (d) a bow similar to a curtsy.
3. The Blue Book is (a) the income tax guidelines, (b) a guide to pricing used cars, (c) a booklet used for writing essay exams, (d) a social register listing 400 prominent families.
4. Brookline is located (a) in suburban Boston, (b) on Cape Cod, (c) between Miami Beach and Fort Lauderdale, (d) on the north shore of Chicago.
5. Beef Wellington is (a) the king's cut of roast beef, (b) tenderloin in a pastry crust lined with pâté, (c) an hors d'oeuvre flavored with sherry, (d) roast beef with béarnaise sauce.

6. Choate is (a) a gelded colt used in fox hunts, (b) a prep school, (c) an imported brandy, (d) the curator of the Metropolitan Museum of Art.
7. The most formal dress for men is (a) white tie, (b) black tie, (c) tuxedo, (d) décolletage.
8. *The Stranger* is (a) the . . . family who moved into the neighborhood, (b) Howard Hughes, (c) a book by Camus, (d) an elegant restaurant in San Francisco.
9. Waterford is (a) a health spa for the hep set, (b) a "fat farm," (c) hand-cut crystal from Ireland, (d) the Rockefeller family estate in upper New York.
10. Dining "alfresco" means (a) by candlelight, (b) a buffet supper, (c) at a sidewalk cafe, (d) outdoors.

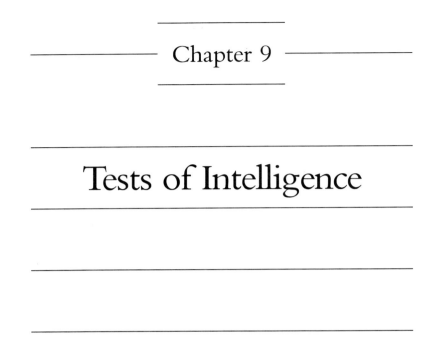

Chapter 9

Tests of Intelligence

EMERSON ONCE WROTE: "If a man write a better book, preach a better sermon, or make a better mousetrap than his neighbor, though he build his house in the woods, the world will make a beaten path to his door." Indeed the world "made a beaten path" to Binet's door at the turn of the century after he introduced a test that was helpful in identifying exceptional schoolchildren. Another "beaten path" was made to David Wechsler's door with the publication of a series of tests that offered unique advantages over existing tests. To whose door will the next such "beaten path" be made? Although the Binet and Wechsler tests have traditionally been widely used individually administered intelligence tests, they already have dozens of competitors. Further, there exist other tests more specialized than tests of general intelligence (such as tests of creativity) and a whole class of intelligence tests designed primarily for administration to groups and to infants. In this chapter we review a sampling of the many existing individual and group intelligence tests as well as some tests designed to assess related abilities. As you read about these tests, contemplate how the types of tasks on them fit into your own conception of what intelligence is and how you believe "intelligence" as you conceive it can best be measured.

Binet's Test in France

Charged with the task of developing a test to screen for mentally retarded children in the Paris schools, Alfred Binet collaborated with Théodore Simon in the preparation of a 30-item scale designed for individual administration. Items on this test were arranged in ascending order of difficulty. For example, item 1 of the 1905 Binet-Simon Scale called for the examiner to pass a lighted match in front of the child while noting the degree of eye-head coordination on the part of the subject. Item 15 required the subject to repeat sentences of 15 words each immediately after hearing them. Item 30 required the subject to verbally distinguish between abstractions such as "liking" and "respecting."

The 1905 test sampled a wide range of abilities and could be administered quite quickly. A major problem, however, was that there was no definitive scoring method; the examiner obtained a rough estimate of the child's level of intellectual development by comparing the subject's performance with—by current standards—crude normative data. The norm group consisted of 50 children presumed to be of average ability, ten of whom were 3 years old, 5 years old, 7 years old, 9 years old, and 11 years old. A revised edition of the Binet-Simon Scale was published three years later. The 1908 revision contained nearly twice as many items as its predecessor. One of the new items appears in Figure 9-1. Items from the 1905 scale deemed to be more appropriate for use with infants than with children of at least 3 years of age were eliminated.

A historically significant innovation was the grouping of items by the age when the majority of the children of a given age in the standardization sample could pass the item. The standardization sample consisted of 203 "average" schoolchildren, aged 3 to 12, from working-class Parisian homes. A child of 7, for example, who performed on the test like the average child of 11, was said to have a "mental age" of 11. The concept of "mental age" had great intuitive appeal and served to attract widespread attention to the 1908 Binet-Simon Scale.

Another revision of the Binet-Simon Scale was published in 1911. New in this test was the appearance of "adult" scales. Also embodied in the 1911 scale were items expressly designed to be as free from cultural bias as possible. Binet was sensitive to the fact that children of upper socioeconomic status tended to outperform working-class children on the test, and he eliminated some items and added new ones in an effort to make the test more culturally fair. Binet died on October 18, 1911, at the age of 54, shortly after the publication of the 1911 scale.

Binet's Test in America

Adaptations and translations of Binet's work appeared in many countries throughout the world. The original Binet-Simon Scale had been in use in this country at a training school in New Jersey as early as 1908 (Goddard, 1908, 1910), and by 1912 a modified version of the scale that extended the range of the test downward to 3 months had been published (Kuhlmann, 1912). However, it was the work of Lewis Madison Terman at Stanford University that ultimately culmi-

Figure 9–1 *Item from the 1908 Binet-Simon Scale.* The subject's task in these unfinished picture test items from year VIII of the 1908 scale was to complete the unfinished pictures. For example, in the female full-body item, the arms had to be drawn in by the subject in order to receive credit.

nated in what would become the most-used and most-researched offspring of the Binet-Simon Scale, the Stanford-Binet Intelligence Scale.

Terman's interest in intelligence testing was a matter of published record quite early in his career (Terman, 1911; Terman & Childs, 1912); he had had exposure to Binet's test as a graduate student at Clark University where his doctoral dissertation was on the subject of gifted children. As a faculty member of the School of Education at Stanford, Terman was concerned about high failure rates in American elementary schools—as high as 30 to 50 percent prior to 1915—and the economic drain that resulted from attempting to reteach children things it was felt they should and could learn. Sorely needed was a test to identify children who would require a special classroom in order to learn. Responding to that need, Terman, inviting the collaboration of his graduate students, first published an adaptation of the 1911 Binet Scale in 1916; the test was christened the Stanford-Binet (after the university where he had done his research and the man who was the primary impetus for and senior author of the original test).

Figure 9–2 *Lewis M. Terman (1877–1956).* Terman's name has become virtually synonymous with the Binet test of intelligence—and perhaps that's how it should be,
because he spent many more years working on it than Binet! But Terman's academic
interests and explorations extended beyond intelligence testing. His three-volume study,
Genetic Studies in Genius (1926 through 1948), was novel for the time, because in it he
speculated about the IQs of famous men and women, using letters, speeches, products,
and other case study–type materials. Terman explored the meaning of masculinity and
femininity with Catherine Cox Miles in *Sex and Personality* (1936), and he offered insights for marital bliss in *Psychological Factors in Marital Happiness* (1938). Terman was a
lifelong advocate of the gifted, and he felt that they should be encouraged to develop
their full potential not only in special classes but in special schools.

Although the Stanford-Binet published in 1916 was certainly not without
major flaws (such as the lack of representativeness of the standardization sample),
it also contained some major innovations. It was the first published intelligence
test to provide organized and detailed administration and scoring instructions.
Another milestone was that it was the first American test to employ the concept
of "IQ." And it was also the first test to introduce the concept of an "alternate
item": an item to be used only under certain conditions, for instance, if the regular item had not been administered properly by the examiner.

In 1926 Terman began a collaboration with a Stanford colleague, Maude Merrill, in a project to revise the test—a project that would take 11 years to complete. Innovations in the 1937 scale included the development of two equivalent forms labeled "L" and "M" and new types of tasks for use with preschool-level and adult-level test takers.[1] In addition, the manual for this test contained many scoring examples to aid the examiner. Although the test authors went to then-unprecedented lengths in attempting to achieve an adequate standardization sample (Flanagan, 1938) and the test was praised for its technical achievement in the areas of validity and especially reliability, a serious criticism of the test was, again, the lack of representativeness of the sample.

Another revision of the Stanford-Binet was well under way at the time of Terman's death at age 79 in 1956. The 1960 Stanford-Binet consisted of only a single form (labeled L-M) composed of the items considered to be the best from the two forms of the 1937 test with no new items added to the test. A major innovation, however, in the 1960 test manual was the use of the deviation IQ tables in place of the ratio IQ tables. The test was revised again in 1972 and, as with previous revisions, was criticized with respect to the standardization sample employed. A test user would be unable to determine from the manual how representative of the United States school-age population the sample actually was. For example, it said in the manual that a "substantial portion" of black and Spanish-surnamed individuals were included in the sample. But obviously a "substantial portion" could be either an overrepresentation or underrepresentation of people from these groups. It has also been suggested that another problem with the 1972 norms was the overrepresentation of the West and of large, urban communities (Waddell, 1980).

The Stanford-Binet Today

The most recent (fourth) edition of the Stanford-Binet (SB:FE) was published in 1986; its authors were Robert Thorndike, Elizabeth Hagen, and Jerome Sattler. The test represents a significant departure from previous versions of the Stanford-Binet in terms of theoretical organization, test organization, test administration, test scoring, and test interpretation. The test is no longer an age scale but a point scale, with 15 separate subtests yielding scores in the following four areas of cognitive ability: "Verbal Reasoning," "Abstract/Visual Reasoning," "Quantitative Reasoning," and "Short Term Memory" (see Table 9–1). The rationale for the change was that clinically useful diagnostic information could more easily be obtained from such a format than from the former one—one in which heterogeneous tests were grouped by age. Nine of the subtests were based on the types of items that appeared in previous versions of the test, while six of the subtests are new. In addition to scores in the four general areas listed, a *test composite*—formerly referred to as a deviation IQ score—may also be obtained.

Also new is an explicit exposition by the test's authors of the theoretical model of intelligence that guided the revision. The interested reader is referred to

---

1. Why the letters *L* and *M* for the two forms of the Stanford-Binet? What do these letters stand for? They are the first letters in the first names of the test's authors, Lewis and Maude. L. M. Terman left no clue as to what initials would have been used if his co-author's name had not begun with the letter *M*.

Table 9-1

281

TESTS OF
INTELLIGENCE

The Subtests of the Stanford-Binet Intelligence Scale: Fourth Edition (SB:FE)

Subtest	Description
Verbal Reasoning	
Vocabulary	Consists of 14 picture vocabulary items (in which the subject's task is to identify the pictured object) and 32 items that are words the subject defines—words that may be presented visually as well as orally.
Comprehension	Items range in difficulty from identifying parts of the body to questions regarding social judgment, reasoning, and evaluation (such as "Why should people be quiet in a hospital?"). Again, items may be both read to the examinee and presented visually.
Absurdities	The examinee's task on these items is to identify what is wrong or silly about a picture. This type of item taps the subject's visual-analysis skills.
Verbal Relations	Each of these items presents the examinee with four words and it is the examinee's task to state what it is that is similar about the first three things but different about the fourth. An example: "Newspaper. Magazine. Book. But not television." A correct response here would indicate that newspapers, magazines, and books are all read but television is not.
Abstract/Visual Reasoning	
Pattern Analysis	Exactly which items will be administered from this subtest will vary with the entry level of the examinee; the timed tasks range from placing cut-out forms into a form-board to reproducing complex designs with blocks.
Copying	The examinee's task here is to copy a design. At the earliest level, the design is made from blocks. Subsequently, the designs are copied directly into a record booklet.
Matrices	Here the examinee's task is to solve increasingly difficult matrices that use geometric symbols, letters, and common objects as stimuli. Items on this nonverbal test are presented in a multiple-choice format, and the items are deemed to be especially useful in gauging the general mental ability of non-English-speaking people.
Paper Folding and Cutting	These multiple-choice-type items present the examinee with the task of identifying how a folded and cut piece of paper will look when unfolded.
Quantitative Reasoning	
Quantitative Subtest	Items on this subtest range from simple counting to knowledge of various arithmetic concepts and operations.
Number Series	The examinee's task is to complete a number sentence with the next logical number in the sequence. For example, consider the following sequence of numbers and determine which two numbers should come next: 1 2 4 ___ ___. The answer is 8 and 16 and the reasoning is that each number in the sequence has been added to itself to yield the next number (1 + 1 = 2; 2 + 2 = 4; 4 + 4 = 8; 8 + 8 = 16; and so on).

Table 9–1 *(continued)*

The Subtests of the Stanford-Binet Intelligence Scale: Fourth Edition (SB:FE)

Subtest	Description
Quantitative Reasoning Equation Building	The examinee's task here is to rearrange a scrambled arithmetic equation so that it makes sense. As an example, rearrange the numbers and/or signs in the following equation in order to make a true number sentence: $5 + 12 = 7$. An acceptable rearrangement would be: $5 + 7 = 12$.
Short-Term Memory Bead Memory	Examinees study a picture of a bead sequence for five seconds and then must replicate the sequence using actual beads. The beads come in three different colors and four different shapes.
Memory for Sentences	The examiner orally presents a sentence and the examinee's task is to repeat it. The length of the sentence may vary from 2 to 22 words depending on the level of the examinee.
Memory for Digits	The examiner orally presents sequences of digits, forward and backward, and it is the examinee's task to repeat the digits presented in the same order.
Memory for Objects	Familiar objects are presented at one-second intervals and the examinee's task is to recall the presentation in the correct order.

the test manual (Thorndike, Hagen, & Sattler, 1986b) for a more in-depth discussion, but briefly the model is a hierarchical one with general intelligence or *g* at the top of the hierarchy. The term *general mental ability* is wide-ranging but encompasses, among other things (1) information-processing abilities, (2) planning and organizing abilities, and (3) reasoning and adaptation skills. Included in the second level of the theoretical hierarchy are (1) "crystallized abilities" (also referred to as scholastic or academic abilities), (2) "fluid-analytic abilities" (that is, nonlanguage abilities that relate to variables such as spatial skills and originality in problem solving), and (3) short-term memory. At the third level are included the following areas: verbal reasoning, abstract/visual reasoning, and quantitative reasoning. These three areas, along with short-term memory at the second level of the hierarchy, make up what are called the "area scores" of the test.

Items from the previous edition of the test that were deemed to be outdated or biased or weakly correlated with a particular area of ability the item was supposed to tap were dropped. Items were balanced for gender, ethnic, racial, and disabled representation. Pictures of children representing various ethnic appearances, a child in a wheelchair, and related modifications were made in the test materials. The test's authors were assisted in the editorial process by a panel of minority-member psychologists who reviewed the materials; expressed concerns led to the revision or discarding of items. Thus, for example, the word *brunette* was eliminated from the vocabulary test because of its lack of saliency to black children.

The standardization sample   The standardization sample consisted of 5,013 subjects ranging in age from 2 years through 23 years, 11 months. The sample was stratified with respect to the following variables based on the 1980 U.S. census data: geographical region, community size, race/ethnic group, gender, parental occupation, and parental education. In approximating the population of the United States in the sample, blacks were somewhat overrepresented and whites were somewhat underrepresented. More significant, however, was the overrepresentation of families from higher socioeconomic-status homes (43.1% of the sample versus 19.0% of the United States population). To correct this situation the norms had to be weighted. This meant, for example, that a subject from a more advantaged background was counted as a fraction of a case in the construction of the norms but a subject from a less advantaged background was counted as more than one case. An assumption inherent in such a weighting process is that the examinees in the sample are indeed representative of the entire population (Glutting, 1989).

Psychometric properties   Thorndike, Hagen, & Sattler (1986b) reported Kuder-Richardson (KR-20) internal consistency measures of reliability, and test-retest measures of stability. The median reliabilities for all of the tests with the exception of the Memory for Objects subtests were in the .80s to .90s range, which is acceptable. No inter-scorer reliability estimates were reported by the test authors.

Because the SB:FE consists of subtests that are not continuous throughout the scale and because different subtests are administered at different ages, the factor structure of the test has been examined by age. The test manual reports the presence of two factors at the preschool level, three factors at the school-age level, and four factors at the adolescent/adult level. One of the co-authors of the test, Sattler (1988), conducted his own factor analysis, and his findings indicated a somewhat different factor structure, with the group of subtests for the factors varying by age level: two factors at the preschool level and three factors at ages 7 through 23. Another study (Kline, 1989) supported Sattler's findings and urged that the scoring method in the manual be changed accordingly. Although these different factor analyses may yield different groupings of factors, they all suggest that the SB:FE is tapping *g*. Table 9–2 contains a summary of some factor-analytic studies.

Evidence in support of the construct validity of the test is presented in the test's technical manual. Included are studies that were conducted with "normal" subjects, correlating their scores on the Stanford-Binet with other tests. A summary of these correlational studies appears in Table 9–3. The fact that composite scores on the Binet were highly correlated with scores on each of the five criterion tests (with correlations ranging from .80 to .91) may be taken as evidence in support of the construct validity of the Binet. Eight additional correlation studies using four of the five same tests (with the exception of the WPPSI) were also reported in the test's technical manual. These eight studies used subjects identified as "exceptional" (that is, there were three samples of mentally retarded subjects, three samples of learning-disabled subjects, and two samples of gifted subjects). Thorndike, Hagen, and Sattler argued that these results too were supportive of the construct validity of the test.

Table 9–2

Factor-Analytic Research with the SB:FE

Researcher(s)	Age level	Factors identified
Thorndike, Hagen, & Sattler (1986b)	Preschool	Verbal Abstract/Visual
	School age	Verbal Memory Abstract/Visual
	Adolescent/ Adult	Verbal Memory Abstract/Visual Quantitative
Sattler (1988) Kline (1989)	Preschool	Verbal Comprehension Nonverbal Reasoning/Visualization
	Ages 7–23 years	Verbal Comprehension Nonverbal Reasoning/Visualization Memory
Keith, Cool, Novak, White, & Pottebaum (1988)	Preschool	Verbal Reasoning Abstract/Visual Reasoning
	Ages 7–23 years	Verbal Reasoning Quantitative Reasoning Abstract/Visual Reasoning Short-Term Memory

A number of additional studies employing a variety of criterion measures have been conducted with the SB:FE (Good & Thornton, 1988; Green, Sapp, & Chissom, 1990; Knight, Baker, & Minder, 1990; Krohn & Lamp, 1989; Lukens, 1988; McCall et al., 1989; McCallum & Karnes, 1987; Rothlisberg, 1987, 1990; Smith & Bauer, 1989; Smith & Knudtson, 1990; Smith, St. Martin, & Lyon, 1989; Swerdlik, 1988; Swerdlik & Ryburn, 1989). In general, a strong relationship has been found to exist between the SB:FE Composite score and (1) WISC-R Full Scale score, (2) Kaufman Assessment Battery for Children "mental processing composite" score, and (3) IQ as measured by the test's predecessor, the Stanford-Binet, Form LM. Correlations were not as high as would have been expected when samples of gifted students were tested.

Administering the test Developers of intelligence tests, and particularly developers of intelligence tests designed for use with children, have traditionally been sensitive to the need for beginning the test at a level that represents an optimal level of difficulty for the test taker; the items should not be so difficult as to leave the test taker frustrated nor so easy as to lull examinees into a false sense of security—and lead them into not taking the task seriously enough. There are three other advantages of beginning any ability test at an optimal level of difficulty: (1) it allows the test user to collect the maximum amount of information in the minimum amount of time, (2) it maintains examinee interest in the test and facilitates rapport, and (3) it minimizes the potential for examinee fatigue as a result of being administered an overabundance of items.

After the examiner has established a rapport with the test taker, the examination formally begins with an item from the Vocabulary subtest. The level of the item employed at the outset is determined by the examinee's chronological age, though the level of subsequent items will be based on the test taker's performance; the highest level of the Vocabulary subtest wherein the examinee passes two consecutive items is the level at which further testing will begin. In this context, the Vocabulary subtest is referred to as the *routing test* since it is used to direct or route the examinee to a particular level of questions (and in so doing directs or routes the examiner as well). Vocabulary was selected as the routing test primarily because general word knowledge is highly correlated with overall intellectual ability.

Once the examinee has passed four items at two consecutive levels, a *basal* (base) level is said to have been established. After the examinee has failed three out of four or four out of four items at two consecutive levels, a *ceiling* level is said to have been reached and testing is discontinued. *The Examiner's Handbook: An Ex-*

Table 9–3

Correlations Between the SB:FE and Other Tests

| Test | Subjects | Stanford-Binet Fourth Edition | | | | |
		Verbal reasoning	Abstract/ visual reasoning	Quantitative reasoning	Short-term memory	Composite
Stanford-Binet	139 children; mean age 7 years 11 months					
Form L-M		.76	.56	.70	.67	.81
WISC-R	205 children; mean age 9 years 5 months					
Verbal		.72	.68	.64	.64	.78
Performance		.60	.67	.63	.63	.73
Full Scale		.73	.73	.69	.70	.83
WPPSI	75 children; mean age 5 years 6 months					
Verbal		.80	.46	.70	.71	.78
Performance		.63	.56	.66	.59	.71
Full Scale		.78	.54	.73	.71	.80
WAIS-R	47 adults; mean age 19 years 5 months					
Verbal		.86	.68	.85	.82	.90
Performance		.79	.81	.80	.65	.85
Full Scale		.86	.76	.86	.78	.91
K-ABC	175 children; mean age 7 years 0 months					
Sequential		.77	.68	.73	.82	.84
Simultaneous		.71	.77	.72	.73	.82
MPC		.80	.78	.78	.83	.89
Achievement		.87	.75	.75	.83	.89

Source: Thorndike and Scott (1986)

panded Guide for Fourth Edition Users (Delaney & Hopkins, 1987) elaborates on the administration and scoring procedures for each subtest and provides suggestions for administering the subtests to special populations.

Scoring and interpreting the test   A *Guide for Administering and Scoring the Fourth Edition* (Thorndike, Hagen, & Sattler, 1986a) contains explicit directions for administering, scoring, and interpreting the test, as well as numerous examples of correct and incorrect responses useful in the scoring of individual items. Each item is scored either correct (1 point) or incorrect (0 points). Scores on the individual items of the various subtests are tallied to yield raw scores on each of the various subtests. The scorer then employs tables found in the manual to convert each of the subtest scores into a standard score. From these standard scores a composite score as well as scores in each of the four general areas tested may be derived.

In addition to formal scoring, the occasion of an individually administered test affords the examiner an opportunity for behavioral observation; the way the examinee copes with frustration, how the examinee reacts to items considered very easy, the amount of support the examinee seems to require, the general approach to the task, how anxious, fatigued, cooperative, distractable, or compulsive the examinee appears to be—these are the types of behavioral observations that will supplement formal scores.

In the tradition of the 1905 scale, the test data may be used to make decisions about the proper class placement of children. Alternatively, data from an intelligence test may have a bearing on the clinical or neurological diagnosis or treatment of a child. The test manual provides guidelines for interpreting the test scores. Other interpretation guides (such as Delaney & Hopkins, 1987; Swerdlik & Dornback, 1988) may be more focused and detailed with respect to the guidelines offered. Focusing on how Stanford–Binet data may be used in a school setting, for example, Swerdlik & Dornback (1988) advise that further testing may be advisable in the case of a student who does poorly on the quantitative subtest. The data from the Stanford–Binet as well as the additional tests would then be analyzed with the objective being the generation of effective instructional strategies.

Sattler (1988) has suggested that his alternative factor model for the SB:FE be used for interpretation. According to this model, there are two factors (Verbal Comprehension and Nonverbal Reasoning/Visualization) at the preschool level, and three factors (Verbal Comprehension, Nonverbal Reasoning/Visualization, and Memory) at the other age levels. Sattler recommends use of these factor scores as an alternate to area scores for interpretation because "area scores are not supported by factor analysis" (Sattler, 1988, p. 261). The subtests comprising the factors by age levels are presented in Table 9–4.

Delaney and Hopkins (1987) recommend emphasis in interpretation on the Test Composite and the inferred abilities measured by clusters of subtests, with less attention to the factor scores and area scores. Inferred abilities are the abilities, skills, or strategies that are assumed to underlie performance on subtests. Delaney and Hopkins analyzed each subtest and determined the most important skills necessary for solving the items presented in the subtest. Next, they developed a table that summarizes the skills involved for each subtest. The *Inferred Abilities and In-*

Table 9–4

Interpretive Factors Suggested by Sattler (1988)

Age level	Factors	Subtests
Preschool	Verbal Comprehension	Vocabulary
		Comprehension
		Absurdities
		Memory for Sentences
	Nonverbal Reasoning/Visualization	Pattern Analysis
		Copying
		Quantitative
		Bead Memory
School age	Verbal Comprehension	Vocabulary
		Comprehension
		Absurdities
	Nonverbal Reasoning/Visualization	Pattern Analysis
		Copying
		Quantitative
		Bead Memory
	Memory	Memory for Sentences
		Memory for Digits
		Memory for Objects
Upper age levels	Verbal Comprehension	Vocabulary
		Comprehension
		Verbal Relations
	Nonverbal Reasoning/Visualizations	Pattern Analysis
		Matrices
		Quantitative
		Bead Memory
	Memory	Memory for Sentences
		Memory for Digits
		Memory for Objects

fluences Chart for the Stanford-Binet: Fourth Edition (see Figure 9–3) indicates the specific skills measured by the subtests of the SB:FE as well as the subtest or subtests that measure them. For example, verbal expression is a skill that is involved in the Vocabulary, Comprehension, Absurdities and Verbal Relations subtests. If an individual does well on these four subtests, it is likely that the person has well-developed verbal expression skills. The inferred abilities approach systematically examines patterns of subtest performance to identify assets and deficits.

An evaluation   Even at this relatively early stage in the life history of the SB:FE, a number of observations, both pro and con, can reasonably be made.

In its various revisions, the Stanford-Binet Intelligence Scale has been a mainstay of assessors for decades and has traditionally been not only a good predictor of academic success at early age levels (Kaufman, 1973b), but a reliable and valid gauge of general reasoning and social judgment (Janzen, 1981). The SB:FE appears to provide a valid and reliable measure of overall general ability, including general reasoning and social judgment skills.

Inferred Abilities and Influences Chart for the Stanford-Binet: Fourth Edition

Name _____

Age _____

Personal SAS Mean _____

The Riverside Publishing Company
Copyright © 1987 by The Riverside Publishing Company.
All rights reserved.

	Verbal Reasoning Area				Abstract/Visual Reasoning Area				Quantitative Reasoning Area			Short-Term Memory Area				Strength (S) or Weakness (W)
	Vocabulary	Comprehension	Absurdities	Verbal Relations	Pattern Analysis	Copying	Matrices	Paper Folding & Cutting	Quantitative	Number Series	Equation Building	Bead Memory	Memory for Sentences	Memory for Digits	Memory for Objects	
1. Record the Standard Age Score.																
2. Record the personal SAS mean.																
3. Record the score difference.																
4. Record an S or W or + or −.*																
Vocabulary development																
Verbal expression																
Concept formation																
Verbal comprehension																
Knowledge of English syntax																
Part-to-whole synthesis																
Visual analysis																
Visual imagery																
Visual memory																
Spatial visualization																
Visual perception																
Numerical fluency																
Mathematical concepts/computation																
Ability to impose structure on randomly presented material																
Ability to analyze word problems																
Discrimination of essential details from nonessential details																
Planning ability																
Inductive reasoning																
Range of factual information																
Meaningful long-term memory																
Sequencing, chunking, or clustering strategies																
Short-term auditory memory																
Reorganized recalled material																
Verbal labeling/memory strategy																
Ability to use and relate general life experiences																
Visual-motor coordination																
Social knowledge																
Attention																
Flexibility																
Manual dexterity																
Time pressure																

*S: + 7 or more points   W: −7 or more points   +: 0 to +6 points   −: −1 to −6 points

ABCDEFG-BAW-93210/898

Figure 9–3 *Using the Inferred Abilities and Influences Chart.* Individual tests are identified across the top of the chart in the order in which they appear on the front cover of the record booklet. Space to record the examinee's name, age, and personal Standard Age Score (SAS) mean is provided in the upper left-hand corner. Abilities and influences are listed down the left side of the chart. The blank boxes on the chart indicate which tests measure a specific ability or influence. There is a summary column on the right side of the chart to record an *S* for strength or a *W* for weakness for each ability or influence listed. Note that the shaded boxes on the chart indicate shared abilities and influences that are not applicable to some tests. The following steps outline how to use the Inferred Abilities and Influences Chart:

1. Record the examinee's name and age in the upper left-hand corner.
2. Enter the Standard Age Score for each test in the box directly below the test title (line 1).
3. Compute the personal SAS mean by adding the test SASs and dividing the total by the number of tests taken that have SAS values. Round to a whole number. Record this score in the upper left-hand corner and for each applicable test on line 2.
4. Subtract the personal SAS mean from each test SAS. On line 3, labeled "Record the score difference," record a score difference for each test. Be sure to indicate a plus sign (+) or a minus sign (−) if appropriate.
5. On line 4, record an S (for a strength) for each test in which the score difference is +7 or more points.
6. For each test judged to be a strength (S), go down that test column and mark an S in each blank box, which corresponds to an ability or influence.
7. On line 4, record a plus sign (+) for all remaining tests in which the score difference is 0 to +6 points.
8. For each test identified in step 7 (0 to +6 points), record a plus sign (+) in each appropriate blank box.
9. On line 4, record a W (for a weakness) for each test in which the score difference is −7 or more points.
10. For each test judged to be a weakness (W), go down that test column and mark a W in each appropriate blank box.
11. On line 4, record a minus sign (−) for all remaining tests in which the score difference is −1 to −6 points.
12. For each test identified in step 11 (−1 to −6 points), record a minus sign (−) in each appropriate blank box.
13. An ability or influence that is followed by an S, several Ss, or a combination of Ss and plus signs is judged to be a strength. Record an S for that ability or influence in the summary column at the extreme right of the chart. An S must be obtained in a row to be summarized as a strength. All plus signs do not constitute a strength.
14. An ability or influence that is followed by a W, several Ws, or a combination of Ws and minus signs is judged to be a weakness. Record a W for that ability or influence in the summary column at the extreme right of the chart. A W must be obtained in a row to be summarized as a weakness. All minus signs do not constitute a weakness.
15. When a mixed pattern for an ability or influence is obtained involving Ss and Ws or Ss and minus signs, or Ws and plus signs, no clear indication is provided by the quantitative data in the pattern of test results. Examiners need to confirm or disprove mixed patterns based on the qualitative information gained during the evaluation.

The confirmatory model may be integrated or supplemented by a more specific analysis for special populations.

A major strength of the test is the size of the standardization sample and the nonbiased, nondiscriminatory nature of the test materials. The adaptive testing format of the test provides the examiner with flexibility in assessing children; the number of test items administered is minimized with no parallel loss of test data. The examiner may also select the subtests to be administered based on the objectives of the testing. Whether the entire test or only selected subtests are administered, the examiners can calculate a reliable composite score of general ability.

Although the SB:FE appears to hold great promise, some areas of concern also exist. The test kit for previous editions of this test came packed with actual objects (such as a spoon or a thimble) that were considered to be especially useful in assessing the intellectual ability of examinees of limited intellectual ability. However, the SB:FE contains only pictures of such objects on cards—a fact that may well make the test less useful with some examinees, such as those lacking satisfactory visual representation skills.

Factor-analytic studies do not support the hypothesized factor structure of the test across all age levels. Certain subtests (Bead Memory and Matrices) do not load on the factors they were designed to load on. Although the test composite clearly measures g, it is not entirely clear what each of the individual subtests is measuring. Thorndike, Hagen, and Sattler (1986b) recommend use of area scores, whereas Sattler (1988) recommends use of factor scores rather than area scores. To date, definitive research to resolve this apparent conflict regarding test interpretation strategies is lacking.

Another problem from a psychometric perspective is the fact that no inter-scorer reliability estimates are provided in the manual, and only KR-20 estimates of inter-item consistency are provided. Based only on the assumption that all items above the ceiling item would be failed,[2] the latter estimates may be inflated.

Although the standardization sample for the SB:FE is impressive for its size and the extent to which it is generally representative of the United States population, there are aspects of the sample that may be cause for concern. For example, according to the 1980 census, about 22% of the households in the United States may be classified as professional/managerial. Yet subjects from professional/managerial households represented about 43% of the Stanford-Binet sample. There was also overrepresentation of children from homes where the parents were college-educated. Perhaps such overrepresentation was unavoidable given that the schoolchildren who participated in the study were required to have permission notes signed by their parents; the better-educated and socioeconomically better-off parents may have been more willing than their less-educated counterparts to grant permission to have their children participate in the study. Although the norms were weighted to correct for the overrepresentations, the full effect of the imbalance in scoring and interpretation of data remains to be seen.

As practitioners come to familiarize themselves and use the SB:FE and as independent researchers investigate this test's effectiveness, a more complete picture of its value will emerge.

THE WECHSLER TESTS

David Wechsler (Figure 9–4) developed a series of individually administered tests designed to assess the intelligence of adults, school-age children, and preschool

---

2. Experienced examiners who have had occasion to "test the limits" of an examinee will tell you that this assumption is not always correct. *Testing the limits* is a procedure that entails the administration of test items beyond the level at which the test manual dictates discontinuance. The procedure may be employed when an examiner has reason to believe that an examinee can respond correctly to items at the higher level.

children. The wide acceptance enjoyed by the Wechsler tests stems not only from their psychometric soundness but also from their relative ease of administration. And because there is great overlap in the kinds of tasks required of the test takers, once the examiner has been trained to administer one Wechsler test, mastery of another will be much easier. After a brief look at the evolution of this series of tests and at some of the items that appear in each, we discuss the following four tests: the Wechsler Adult Intelligence Scale—Revised (WAIS-R), the Wechsler Intelligence Scale for Children—Revised (WISC-R) and its most recent revision, the WISC-III, and the Wechsler Preschool and Primary Scale of Intelligence—Revised (WPPSI-R).

The Wechsler Tests in General

The three Wechsler tests represent a continuum designed to asess the intellectual ability of people from preschool through adulthood. The original Wechsler Intelligence Scale for Children (WISC) was published in 1949, and it represented a

---

Figure 9–4 *David Wechsler (1896–1981).*

Born in Romania in 1896, David Wechsler came to New York City six years later with his parents and six older siblings. He completed his bachelor's degree in 1916 at City College (New York) and obtained a Master's degree at Columbia University the following year. While awaiting induction into the Army at a base in Long Island, Wechsler came in contact with the renowned historian of psychology, E. G. Boring.

Wechsler assisted Boring by evaluating the data from one of the first large-scale administrations of a group intelligence test (the Army Alpha test) as the nation geared up for World War I. Wechsler was subsequently assigned to an Army base in Fort Logan, Texas, where his primary duty was administering individual intelligence tests such as the newly published Stanford-Binet Intelligence Scale. Discharged from the Army in 1919, Wechsler spent two years studying in Europe where he had the opportunity to study with Charles Spearman and Karl Pearson, two brilliant English statisticians known primarily for their work in the area of correlation. Upon his return to New York City he took a position as a staff psychologist with the Bureau of Child Guidance. In 1935 Wechsler earned a Ph.D. from Columbia University. His dissertation was entitled "The Measurement of Emotional Reactions." By 1932 Wechsler was appointed Chief Psychologist at Bellevue Psychi-

atric Hospital. Seven years later, the individually administered test Wechsler had designed to measure an adult's intelligence in adult terms, the Wechsler-Bellevue Intelligence Scale, was a reality. Three years later in 1942 came a revision of that test referred to variously as the Wechsler-Bellevue II and as the Army Wechsler. In 1949 Wechsler published the Wechsler Intelligence Scale for Children (WISC). This was followed in 1955 by a revision of the Wechsler-Bellevue II that was named the Wechsler Adult Intelligence Scale (WAIS). The Wechsler Preschool and Primary Scale of Intelligence (WPPSI) was published in 1967 and in 1974 a revision of the WISC, the Wechsler Intelligence Scale for Children—Revised (WISC-R) was published. Wechsler's revision of the WAIS, the Wechsler Adult Intelligence Scale—Revised (WAIS-R) was published in 1981, the same year that this prolific and internationally respected psychologist died.

downward extension of another Wechsler test—a predecessor of the WAIS called the Wechsler-Bellevue Scale. In fact, most of the original WISC items were originally developed for a second form of the Wechsler-Bellevue Scale. The WISC-R, published in 1974, shares a number of specific items with the WAIS-R published in 1981. The WPPSI was first published in 1967 and revised in 1989. The WISC-R was revised to become the WISC-III in 1991.

Each of the Wechsler tests was designed to assess an individual's "overall capacity to understand and cope with the world around him" (Wechsler, 1974, p. 5). Because the tests share this common theoretical foundation, they are also similar in structure. As you can see from Table 9–5, each of the tests is made up of subtests that are part of either a Verbal Scale or a Performance Scale within the test. Note, for example, that the subtests called "Animal Pegs" and "Geometric Design" appear only on the WPPSI-R, the test designed for use with the youngest test takers. For the most part, similar types of items can be found in the various subtests of all three Wechsler tests. A brief description of these subtests appears in Table 9–6.

In general, the Wechsler tests have been evaluated favorably from a psychometric standpoint. While the coefficients of reliability vary as a function of the specific type of reliability assessed, it is fair to say that the Wechsler tests are generally satisfactory with respect to internal consistency and test-retest reliability. Thus, for example, average test-retest reliability estimates for people in the 25 to

Table 9–5

The Composition of the Wechsler Tests

	WPPSI-R	WISC-R	WISC-III	WAIS-R
Verbal Scales				
Information	X	X	X	X
Comprehension	X	X	X	X
Similarities	X	X	X	X
Arithmetic	X	X	X	X
Vocabulary	X	X	X	X
Digit Span		X[1]	X[1]	X
Sentences	X[2]	—	—	—
Performance Scales				
Picture Completion	X	X	X	X[1]
Picture Arrangement		X	X	X
Block Design	X	X	X	X
Object Assembly	X	X	X	X
Coding[3]	X	X	X	X
Mazes	X	X[1]	X[1]	—
Geometric Design	X	—	—	—
Animal Pegs	X	—	—	—
Symbol Search[4]	—	—	X[1]	—

[1]Optional supplementary subtest that is not included to determine IQ Score.
[2]Similar to Digit Span on WISC-R and WAIS-R but sentences rather than digits are orally presented.
[3]This subtest is labeled Digit Symbol on the WAIS-R and Animal Pegs on the WPPSI-R.
[4]This subtest only appears on the WISC-III.

Table 9–6

A Brief Description of the Wechsler Subtests

Subtest	Description
Information	"In what continent is Brazil?" This is the general type of question on the Wechsler Information subtests. In general the questions tap general knowledge and in part assess learning and memory. Interests, education, cultural background, and reading skills are some influencing factors in the Information subtest score.
Comprehension	In general, these questions tap social comprehension, the ability to organize and apply knowledge, and what is colloquially referred to as "common sense." An illustrative question is, "Why should children be cautious in speaking to strangers?"
Similarities	"How are a pen and a pencil alike?" This is illustrative of the general type of question that appears in this subtest; pairs of words are presented to the examinee and the task is to determine how they are alike. The ability to analyze relationships and engage in logical, abstract thinking are two of the intellectual functions tapped by this type of test.
Arithmetic	Arithmetic problems, presented and solved entirely verbally for older test takers are presented (at the lowest levels this subtest may involve simple counting). Learning of arithmetic, alertness and concentration, and short-term auditory memory are some of the intellectual functions tapped by this test.
Vocabulary	The test taker is called on to define words in this subtest that is generally viewed as the best single measure of general intelligence. Matarazzo (1972, p. 218) put it this way: "The number of words a man knows is at once a measure of his learning ability, his fund of verbal information, and the general range of his ideas." Needless to say, education and cultural opportunity are two factors that greatly influence scores on vocabulary tests.
Digit Span	Here the examiner verbally presents a series of numbers, and the examinee's task is to repeat the numbers in the same sequence. This subtest taps attention and concentration ability as well as short-term auditory memory. Performance on this subtest could be influenced by factors such as impulsivity, fatigue, and anxiety.
Sentences	This subtest appears only in the WPPSI-R and is similar to Digit Span though stimuli more meaningful to the younger test taker are employed. Sentences composed of vocabulary within preschoolers' range (such as "Jane goes to school") are presented, and the child's task is to repeat the sentence verbatim. This subtest appears to be more dependent on verbal facility than Digit Span, though it still taps factors such as attention, concentration ability, and short-term auditory memory.
Picture Completion	The subject's task here is to identify what important part is missing from a picture. For example, the test taker might be shown a picture of a chair with one leg missing. This subtest draws on visual perception abilities, alertness, memory, concentration, attention to detail, and ability to differentiate essential from nonessential detail. Because respondents may point to the missing part, this test provides a good nonverbal estimate of intelligence. However, successful performance on a test such as this still tends to be highly influenced by cultural factors.
Picture Arrangement	In the genre of a comic strip panel, this subtest requires the test taker to resort a scrambled set of cards with pictures on them into a story that makes sense. Because the test taker must understand the whole story before a successful resorting will occur, this subtest is thought to tap the ability to comprehend or "size-up" a whole situation. Additionally, attention, concentration, and ability to see temporal and cause-and-effect relationships are tapped.
Block Design	A design with colored blocks is illustrated either with blocks themselves or a picture of the finished design, and the examinee's task is to reproduce the design. This test draws on perceptual-motor skills, psychomotor speed, and the ability to analyze and synthesize. Factors that may influence performance on this test include the examinee's color vision, frustration tolerance, and flexibility or rigidity in problem solving.

293

34-year-old range on the WAIS-R were .94 on the Verbal Scale, .89 on the Performance Scale, and .95 on the Full Scale.

Evidence for the content validity of each Wechsler test can be found in the individual test manuals along with a detailed presentation of the rationale for inclusion of the specific subtests. Factor-analytic studies by a number of independent investigators have tended to provide support for the construct validity of the Wechsler tests as have studies of (1) correlations between a Wechsler test and other tests purporting to measure intelligence and (2) the intercorrelations of the individual subtests.

Table 9–6 (continued)

A Brief Description of the Wechsler Subtests

Subtest	Description
Object Assembly	The task here is to assemble, as quickly as possible, a cut-up picture of a familiar object. Some of the abilities called on here include pattern recognition, assembly skills, and psychomotor speed. Useful qualitative information pertinent to the examinee's work habits may also be obtained here by careful observation of the approach to the task (for example, does the examinee give up easily or persist in the face of difficulty?).
Coding/Digit Symbol	Labeled "Digit Symbol" on the WAIS-R and "Coding" on the WISC-R, the examinee's task is to follow a printed code. If you were given the dots and dash equivalents for several letters in Morse code and then had to write out letters in Morse code as quickly as you could, this would be an example of a coding task. This subtest taps learning ability, rote recall ability, psychomotor speed, and concentration and attention. The equivalent subtest on the WPPSI-R is called Animal Pegs.
Mazes	This subtest does not appear on the WAIS-R and is a supplementary test (not included for purposes of calculating IQ) on the WISC-R. On the WPPSI-R, this subtest is composed of paper-and-pencil mazes, some of which are identical to those that appear on the WISC-R. Perceptual-motor skills, psychomotor speed, and visual planning abilities are tapped by this subtest.
Geometric Design	In no other Wechsler test but the WPPSI-R, this subtest consists of geometric designs which the child is required to copy with a pencil. In general, this subtest provides an index of the child's perceptual-motor skills. Sattler (1974, p. 223) cautioned that, "High scores may be difficult to obtain even by bright young children because the motor ability needed for successful performance is associated in part with maturational processes that may be independent of the development of cognitive processes."
Animal Pegs	Also only in the WPPSI-R, the task here is to place different-colored cylinders in the holes under a picture of the appropriate animal. The dog, the chicken, the fish, and the cat each have a specific color cylinder, and it is the child's task to follow the code illustrated at the top of the board. Success on this task is dependent on factors such as concentration and visual memory, manual dexterity, and attention span.
Symbol Search	This is a new, optional performance subtest found only on the WISC-III. The child's task is to visually scan two groups of symbols, one search group and one target group, and determine whether the target symbol appears in the search group. Two levels, each containing 45 items, are contained in a booklet separate from the record form. There is a time limit of 120 seconds, and the score is equal to the number of correct responses less the number of incorrect responses. The test is presumed to tap cognitive processing speed.

Though they are similar in many ways, an important difference between the three Wechsler tests—as you might guess—has to do with the samples used in each of the test's standardization. Each test was independently standardized on a stratified representative sample of people from across the United States. Other similarities and differences between the Weschler adult, children's, and pre-school child's test will become evident as our discussion of these tests continues.

Administering the Tests

Each subtest has its own beginning point, usually determined by the test taker's age. In testing a younger individual in the designated age range, the examiner might begin, for example, with the first item in the Information subtest, whereas in testing an older person the examiner might begin with the fourth. The stopping point in a subtest occurs where the test taker has failed a certain prescribed number of items in a row or has passed every item for that subtest. Many of the items, especially for the younger test takers, call for demonstrations of what is required before the actual testing. The manual contains explicit directions for administering the subtests as well as a number of standard prompts for dealing with virtually any contingency, question, or comment that might arise during the test session. The administration of Verbal and Performance subtests are alternated; first a Verbal subtest might be given, followed by a Performance subtest, followed by a Verbal subtest, and so forth.

Figure 9–5 *Learning to Administer the WAIS-R.*

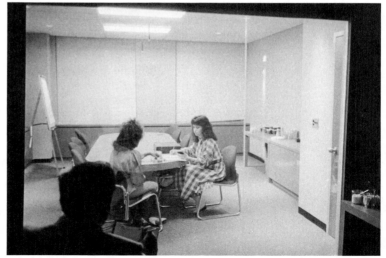

It takes a trained examiner to administer an intelligence test such as the Stanford-Binet or any of the Wechsler tests. Fantuzzo and Moon (1984) described a competency-based training model for teaching graduate students how to administer the WAIS-R. The program evaluates competence in test administration in terms of very discrete examiner behaviors and assesses performance of the examiner under conditions that approximate clinical situations. The trainee's administration of the test is observed through a one-way mirror, and the trainee is given detailed feedback based on a criteria checklist. Also involved in the program is observation by the trainee—and subsequent discussion of—a videotape of a model administering the test. The trainee then administers the WAIS-R, again being observed and obtaining feedback. Fantuzzo and Moon (1984) reported that such a procedure resulted in competent test administration at posttraining.

Scoring and Interpretation

Manuals for the Wechsler intelligence tests tend to be very clear about the scoring of responses, and many supplementary books and other publications are available. On some items, extra points may be earned depending on the quality of the response. On some Performance subtest items, extra points may be earned as a function of the speed with which the task is completed. Scores on the individual items are tallied to yield raw scores on each of the subtests. Using tables in the manual, the raw scores for each subtest are converted into scaled scores, and all of the scaled scores on each subtest have a mean of 10 and a standard deviation of 3. From these scaled scores, a Verbal Scale IQ, a Performance Scale IQ, and a Full Scale IQ (composite) can be derived. On any one of the Wechsler tests, a Full Scale IQ calculated to be 100 will be considered "average." And because the Wechsler tests are all point scales that yield deviation IQs with a mean of 100 (interpreted as "average") and a standard deviation of 15, any Full Scale IQ in the range of 85 to 115 will also be considered "average." On each of the Wechsler tests, a test taker's performance is compared with scores earned by individuals in his or her own age group.

The manuals for the Wechsler tests tend to contain barebones guidelines for the interpretation of the test data. More detailed interpretive information can be obtained from any of a number of publications devoted to the subject. Kaufman (1979) described what he termed a "successive levels" approach to Wechsler test interpretation, which entails successive evaluation of scale scores for the Verbal Scale, the Performance Scale, and the Full Scale, followed by an analysis and comparison of other data, such as clusters of selected subtests. In practice, a great deal of the data obtained during the testing, including and beyond scores and score clusters (such as the examiner's notes regarding the test taker's extra-test behavior), may hold great interpretive significance for the capable examiner. Ultimately, test interpretation skills for a Wechsler—like many other tests—are honed through a combination of activities, such as administering the test and observing firsthand a variety of test takers as they take it, reading about test interpretation in various sources, and scoring and interpreting a number of test protocols under the tutelage of a skilled, experienced, and knowledgeable supervisor.

The Wechsler Adult Intelligence Scale—Revised (WAIS-R)

The WAIS-R is the latest in a series of instruments, each designed to measure the intelligence of adults. Predecessors of the WAIS-R were the Wechsler-Bellevue I, the Wechsler-Bellevue II, and the Wechsler Adult Intelligence Scale. In the early 1930s Wechsler's employer, Bellevue Hospital in Manhattan, needed an instrument suitable for evaluating the intellectual capacity of multilingual, multinational, and multicultural clients being referred there. Wechsler was dissatisfied with existing intelligence tests when used with such a population, and he began to experiment with various tests to find one more appropriate for measuring adult intelligence. The eventual result, the Wechsler-Bellevue I (W-B I), was a new test that borrowed in format (not content) from existing tests.

Unlike the most popular individually administered intelligence test of the time, the Stanford-Binet, the W-B I was a *point scale* rather than an age scale; the items were classified by subtests rather than by age. The test was organized into six verbal subtests and five performance subtests, and all of the items in each test were arranged in order of increasing difficulty. Another form of the test designed to be an equivalent alternate, the Wechsler-Bellevue II (W-B II), was also published, though it was never thoroughly standardized (Rapaport, Gill, & Schafer, 1968). Unless a specific reference is made to the W-B II, reference here (and in the literature in general) to "the Wechsler-Bellevue" is to Wechsler-Bellevue I.

Problems identified with the Wechsler-Bellevue eventually led to the development of a new test. Although the research had suggested that the W-B was indeed measuring something comparable to what other intelligence tests were measuring (Matarazzo, 1972), the test had the following problems: (1) the standardization sample was rather restricted, (2) some subtests lacked sufficient inter-item reliability, (3) some of the subtests were made up of items that were too easy, (4) the scoring criteria for certain items were too ambiguous. Sixteen years after publication of Form I of the W-B, a revised form with a new name, the Wechsler Adult Intelligence Scale (Wechsler, 1955) was published.

The WAIS contained 257 items, 147 of which had been retained from the Wechsler-Bellevue. Like its predecessor, the WAIS was organized into six subtests designated as "Verbal" and six subtests designated as "Performance." Again, scoring yielded a Verbal IQ, a Performance IQ, and a Full Scale IQ. Modifications were made to improve the directions for administering and scoring the subtests. The WAIS was a widely researched test thought by many to be the best available measure of adult intelligence. As one reviewer observed, the WAIS "was carefully constructed and carefully standardized. The norms were intelligently conceived and meticulously developed . . . this test has become the standard against which other adult tests can be compared" (Lyman, 1972, p. 429). Primarily because of the need for a more contemporary norm group, the WAIS was revised and published as the Wechsler Adult Intelligence Scale—Revised (Wechsler, 1981).

Although the WAIS-R was ultimately published after his death, Wechsler assumed a very active role in its development. Approximately 80 pecent of the WAIS-R items remained essentially unchanged from the WAIS. The WAIS-R directions for scoring and the record form were changed as were the administration instructions for the tests (in the older version, verbal subtests were administered before the performance subtests, whereas in the WAIS-R the examiner alternates between administering a verbal and a performance subtest; see Figure 9–2).

The standardization sample   The WAIS-R sample of 1,880 white and non-white Americans was stratified along the variables of age, sex, race, geographic region, occupation, education, and urban-rural residence in a manner representative of the 1970 U.S. census. People whose primary language was not English were included only if they were able to both speak and understand English. Excluded from the sample were institutionalized mental retardates, brain-damaged or severely behaviorally or emotionally disturbed individuals, or subjects physically disabled in some way who would be restricted in their ability to respond to test items. No more than one member of any family was tested.

Psychometric properties   Correlations reported between total score and individual subtest scores ranged from .52 to .82 for the 25–34 years age range and are

Table 9-7

The WAIS-R: Some Factor-Analytic Studies

Researcher(s)	Factors identified
Silverstein (1982)	Verbal (Information, Digit Span, Vocabulary, Arithmetic, Comprehension, Similarities)
	Performance (Picture Completion, Picture Arrangement, Block Design, Object Assembly, Digit Symbol)
Gutkin, Reynolds, & Galvin (1984)	Verbal Comprehension (Information, Vocabulary, Comprehension, Similarities)
	Perceptual Organization (Block Design, Object Assembly)
Parker (1983) Ryan & Sattler (1988)	Verbal Comprehension (Information, Vocabulary, Comprehension, Similarities)
	Perceptual Organization (Picture Completion, Block Design, Object Assembly)
	Freedom from Distractibility (Digit Span, Arithmetic)
Waller & Waldman (1990)	Verbal Comprehension (Information, Vocabulary, Comprehension, Similarities)
	Perceptual Organization (Picture Completion, Block Design, Object Assembly)
	Freedom from Distractibility (Digit Span, Arithmetic, Digit Symbol)

good estimates of the internal consistency of the test (Kaufman, 1990). Subtest split-half reliability coefficients range from .70 to .92.

One type of validity study employs the technique of factor analysis to explore whether a test is measuring the factors it purports to measure. Such factor-analytic procedures have been employed for the standardization sample and a variety of clinical populations, and the number of factors that the test has been deemed to tap has varied by study from one to three. A summary of a sampling of the studies in which the WAIS-R standardization data were used is presented in Table 9-7.

An evaluation   The WAIS-R is the standard by which other tests of adult intelligence are compared and judged. The WAIS-R standardization is sound, and a multitude of research has shown it to be a valid measure of adult intelligence. As Matarazzo (1985) put it, "No other test . . . is as reliable, valid, or clinically useful for assessing the measurable aspects of adult intelligence."

The Wechsler Intelligence Scale for Children—Revised (WISC-R)

The Wechsler Intelligence Scale for Children (WISC) was first published in 1949; and, as one observer put it, this test was "probably more directly instrumental in influencing life decisions of school age children than any other intelligence test" (Freides, 1972, p. 800). Burstein (1972, p. 844) referred to the WISC as "a well standardized, stable instrument correlating well with other tests of intelligence." Although generally well-received in the professional community, the WISC was not without its flaws. One major deficiency was that the standardization sample contained no nonwhites. Another problem had to do with the lack of clarity in the test's manual, which led to ambiguities with respect to the administration of the test and the scoring of responses. As time passed, the test, standardized in the 1940s, became subject to criticism regarding gender/cultural stereotypes in some of the items. As a result of such considerations and the need for updated normative data, a revision of the WISC was undertaken. The revision, referred to as the WISC-R, was published in 1974.

The WISC-R contained a number of important advantages over its predecessor. For example, the WISC-R included nonwhites in the standardization sample. The test contained innovations with respect to the administration and scoring of the test. For example, in the WISC-R manual, the test administrator was directed to administer subtests from the Verbal Scale and Performance Scale in alternating fashion. The test language and format were also modernized and "child-ized." The word "cigars" was replaced with "candy bars" in the Arithmetic subtest. The picture of the car in the Object Assembly subtest was redrawn to reflect more contemporary styling. Materials were changed to make them more racially and culturally balanced with more nonwhites pictured in the various subtests.

The standardization sample   The WISC-R standardization sample consisted of 2,200 children representative of the 1970 U.S. population according to census data. The sample was stratified on the basis of age, sex, race, geographic region, occupation of head of household, and urban-rural residence. There were 200 children in each of 11 age groups (6 years 6 months to 16 years 6 months).

Psychometric properties   Average split-half reliability coefficients for the subtests range from .70 to .86, while average consistency reliability coefficients for the global scales range from .90 (Performance Scale) to .96 (Full Scale). Test–retest reliability coefficients for the subtests range from .63 to .95.

Although relatively few validity studies are reported in the WISC-R manual, the test has been the subject of hundreds of research studies. In fact, at this writing, the WISC-R is the most frequently used children's intelligence test and is also the most researched instrument. One computer search of published articles on the WISC-R between 1974 and 1987 turned up over twelve hundred publications (Puleo, 1989). Some of the studies designed to identify the factors tapped by the WISC-R have concluded that the test is indeed measuring two factors, one that could be labeled "verbal," and one that could be labeled "performance" (see Table 9–8). Other studies have identified three factors, typically referred to as verbal comprehension, perceptual organization (tapped primarily by Performance Scale subtests), and a factor called "freedom from distractibility." Although the latter three factors have been identified in WISC-R research with males and females, with normal and exceptional subjects, and in Spanish-speaking as well as English-speaking children (Reynolds & Kaufman, 1990), the meaning and interpretation of the "freedom from distractibility" factor has been a matter of some debate (Wielkiewicz, 1990; see also Bannatyne, 1974). It has been variously argued, for example, that this factor is more related to academic achievement (Piersel, Bush, Zabel, & Lee, 1988) and memory (Jensen, 1984) than the behavioral attribute of distractibility.

A number of correlational studies have examined the relationship between WISC-R scores and scores on other well-established individual tests of mental ability that employ a wide variety of subtests (Bloom, Raskin, & Reese, 1976; Brooks, 1977; Covin & Lubimiv, 1976; Dean, 1979; Hale, 1978; Hartlage & Steele, 1977; Kaufman & Van Hagen, 1977; Nagle & Lazarus, 1979; Raskin, Bloom, Klee, & Reese, 1978; Sattler & Ryan, 1981; Schwarting & Schwarting, 1977; Supp & Sutherland, 1980; Wechsler, 1974, 1981; Weiner & Kaufman, 1979; White, 1979; Wikoff, 1979). In general, the findings suggest that these tests tend to yield similar information regarding a child's overall intellectual functioning. The test has been viewed as "useful in predicting achievement or in helping to explain that general intelligence is a factor that would limit the teacher's success in teaching children within a regular classroom" (Brooks, 1977, p. 33). Kaufman (1979) and others (such as Covin & Lubimiv, 1976; Dean, 1979; Kaufman & Weiner, 1976; Raskin, Bloom, Klee, & Reese, 1978; Reschly & Reschly, 1979; Wikoff, 1979) have concluded that the WISC-R is a useful tool in predicting academic success.

The publisher of the Wechsler tests has made available to users software for computer-assisted interpretation of findings. The user enters a test taker's raw scores and subsequently obtains a printout including (1) the raw score, scaled score, and percentile rank for each subtest, (2) scaled scores, IQ, and percentile

Table 9–8

The WISC-R: Some Factor-Analytic Studies

Researcher(s)	Sample	Factors identified
Kaufman (1975) Silverstein (1977)	WISC-R standardization sample	Verbal Comprehension (Vocabulary, Information, Comprehension, Similarities, and, to a lesser extent, Arithmetic) Perceptual organization (Block Design, Object Assembly, Picture Completion, Picture Arrangement, and Mazes) Freedom from Distractibility (Arithmetic, Digit Span, and Coding B)
Gutkin & Reynolds (1981) Vance & Wallbrown (1978) Reschly (1978)	Anglo, Chicano, black, and Native American children	Verbal and Performance
Van Hagen & Kaufman (1975)	Mentally retarded children	Verbal Comprehension (Information, Similarities, Arithmetic, Vocabulary, Comprehension, and Digit Span) Perceptual Organization (Picture Completion, Picture Arrangement, Object Assembly, Coding, and Mazes) Freedom from Distractibility (Arithmetic, Digit Span, Coding, Picture Arrangement)
Schooler, Beebe, & Koepke (1978)	Learning disabled, educably mentally retarded, emotionally disturbed	Verbal and Performance

rank for Verbal, Performance, and Full Scale, (3) a reporting of scaled scores in profile format, (4) statistical information such as confidence intervals for Full Scale IQ, Verbal IQ, and Performance IQ, (5) a narrative report including discussion of any observed discrepancy between Verbal and Performance IQ and of the scatter among subtest scores—the meaning of the deviation of various subtest scores from the mean of the profile. Similar programs are also available from other commercial scoring and interpretation services.

An evaluation   The WISC-R is technically sound, well-constructed and standardized, relatively easy to learn to administer, and very useful in clinical, educational, and other settings.

The Wechsler Intelligence Scale for Children—Third Edition (WISC-III)   Published in 1991, the WISC-III is a revision of the WISC-R. In addition to updated normative information, what is new about the test is not so much the types of subtests used (only one new subtest has been added), but rather the form of the subtests. The artwork in the Picture Arrangement, Picture Completion, and Object Assembly has been dramatically modernized and rendered in color. The Mazes subtest contains enlarged mazes, and the Coding subtest contains enlarged printing for greater clarity. Additionally, the Coding subtest was lengthened in an effort to extend the range of possible scoring, and the "key" in that subtest was moved to the top of the paper to ensure that it would not be blocked by the left-hand of left-handed test takers. Some items were added, particularly at the low and high ends of the scale. For example, using the WPPSI-R as a guide, items tapping concepts of number and the test taker's ability to count were added at the bottom of the Arithmetic scale. Relatively difficult, multi-step word problems were added at the high end of this scale. The new subtest, "Symbol Search," is a second supplementary performance subtest (Mazes being the first), which, like Coding, was designed to tap cognitive processing speed.

The procedures used to revise the WISC-R and create the WISC-III illustrate many sound principles of test construction and revision. The publisher began the process with an in-house review of the test, including suggestions received from WISC-R users, recommendations solicited by experts, and ongoing correspondence with test users before and during the revision. New items and subtests were piloted, and a "tryout version" of the new test was administered to 500 children nationally. On the basis of the resulting data and in consultation with experts and high-volume users of the WISC-R, the WISC-III was then constructed. As has become standard practice in the development of new tests designed for wide commercial distribution, great pains were taken by the test developer to minimize any potential source of bias in any of the test's items. Using data from the WISC-R normative sample, each item was statistically analyzed in terms of performance as a function of gender, ethnicity, and age. Proposed replacement items underwent the same statistical review for item bias. WISC-R items and draft WISC-III items were reviewed by a panel of experts in an effort to balance them in terms of references to ethnicity and gender. Items deemed to be outdated were deleted. Color vision experts were consulted to ensure that color-blind test takers would not be adversely affected by the new color artwork in the test materials.

The norm sample for the WISC-III consisted of 2,200 children between the ages of 6 and 16. There were 200 children in each of 11 age groups, divided equally by gender. Variables in the stratification were closely matched to 1988 U.S. Census data for race/ethnicity, region of the country, and parental education level. Parental education level instead of parental occupation was used because prior research had indicated that parental education level accounts for more variance in test scores than parental occupation. Additional testing was conducted with black and Hispanic children to ensure accuracy of item bias statistics. Additional testing was also conducted for the purpose of comparing same-subject performance on the WPPSI-R and the WISC-III (the subjects were 200 6-year-olds), the WAIS-R and the WISC-III (the subjects were 200 16-year-olds), and the WISC-R and the WISC-III (the subjects were 200 children across the age range). About 300 children who had taken the WISC-III were re-tested for research purposes within 4 to 8 weeks between test administrations. In all, upwards of 4,500 test administrations at various sites around the country were conducted.

Who administered all of these tests and how was quality control ensured? Most test publishers do not maintain an in-house staff of trained examiners who can arrange for the administration of, and actually administer, 4,500 tests throughout the country within a reasonable amount of time. Rather, the publisher contracts with experienced examiners throughout the country who may be screened by means of a background questionnaire that solicits information on educational and background experience. This was the case with respect to the standardization of the WISC-III. Additionally, graduate students under the supervision of a qualified professional were employed. The test publisher used several tools of examiner "quality control" throughout the standardization, including

1. the completion and submission of practice protocols prior to testing,
2. feedback to the examiner on the practice protocol on both administration and scoring via telephone and letter,
3. frequent communication with examiners during the standardization process such as through a "standardization newsletter," and
4. rigorous checking procedures to evaluate each protocol for completeness and accuracy of administration and scoring.

The reliability of persons responsible for checking the accuracy of the other examiners' scoring of test protocols was ensured by means such as the use of *anchor protocols;* that is, protocols generated by the test publisher and given to an examiner for scoring for the purpose of checking the accuracy of the examiner's scoring.

An attempt was made to make the WISC-III more "user friendly" to both examiners and examinees than prior versions of this test. In addition to changes in the test itself, improvements were made in the test materials. For example, the cardboard "shield" used by the examiner in administering the Object Assembly subtest was constructed so that it could stand on its own. Previously, this shield had to be held with one hand while the examiner awkwardly tried to arrange pieces of the object to be assembled with the other hand. A computer-based interpretive program called WISC-III Writer was designed to generate numerous interpretive options and statistical indices applicable to a variety of evaluation settings and purposes.

Reliability and validity data presented in the test manual suggest that the WISC-III is a psychometrically sound instrument. Clinical validity studies with groups of children whose diagnoses included learning disabilities, mental retardation, general neurological impairment, hearing impairment, emotional dysfunction, conduct and attention disorders, and giftedness are also reported. If the history of the forerunners to the WISC-III can serve as a predictor, expect intense independent exploration of the reliability, validity, diagnostic value, and various other aspects of this test in relevant professional journals and books.

The Wechsler Preschool and Primary Scale of Intelligence—Revised (WPPSI-R)

Project Head Start as well as other 1960s programs for preschool children who were culturally different, or exceptional (defined in this context as atypical in terms of ability—gifted or retarded) fostered interest in the development of new tests (Zimmerman & Woo-Sam, 1978). The Stanford-Binet had traditionally been the test of choice for use with preschoolers, though test users were open to experimenting with alternative methods. While some advocated a restandardization of the WISC for children under 6, Wechsler (1967) had decided that a new scale, especially developed for and standardized on children under age 6, would be developed. The new test was the WPPSI (usually pronounced like "whipsy"), and with its publication the Wechsler series of intelligence tests was extended downward in age range to age 4. The WPPSI was the first major intelligence test that "adequately sampled the total population of the United States, including racial minorities" (Zimmerman & Woo-Sam, 1978, p. 10)—a fact that contributed to the success of the WPPSI, especially in an era when standardized tests were under attack for not having adequate minority representation in the standardization sample.

The WPPSI-R was published in 1989 and is designed to assess the intelligence of children from ages 3 years through 7 years 3 months. Major changes from the WPPSI included extension of the age range, addition of the Object Assembly subtest, and the renaming of the Animal Pegs subtest, (formerly Animal House). Approximately 48% of the WPPSI items (excluding Animal Pegs) were retained intact or with only slight modifications from the WPPSI. New items were developed for the younger age range and for the older age range. There is a one-year overlap with the WISC-R at ages 6 years, 0 months (6-0) through 7 years 3 months (7-3).

The standardization sample   The WPPSI-R was standardized on 1,700 children, including 100 boys and 100 girls in each of eight age groups, ranging in half-year intervals from age 3 years to 7 years, and one age group of 50 boys and 50 girls in the 7 years to 7 years 3 months interval. The sample closely reflects 1986 census estimates on stratification variables such as geographic region, ethnicity, parental education and occupation, and urban-rural residence.

Psychometric properties   Average subtest split-half reliability estimates for internal consistency range from .80 to .86 on the Verbal Scale, and from .63 to .85 on the Performance Scale. Test-retest reliability coefficients for the subtests range from .70 to .81 for the Verbal Scale and from .52 to .82 for the Performance Scale. For the global scales the split-half reliability coefficients range from .92 (Performance Scale) to .96 (Full Scale) and test-retest reliability coefficients range from .88 (Performance Scale) to .91 (Full Scale). Inter-scorer reliability coefficients for the Comprehension, Vocabulary, Similarities, Mazes, and Geometric Design subtests range from .88 to .96 (Gyurke, 1991).

Factor analyses of the data from the standardization sample yielded findings consistent with two previous studies of the WPPSI; a verbal factor and a performance factor were the two primary factors tapped by the test (Gyurke, Stone, & Beyer, 1990). Several validity studies, all of which support the validity of the test, are reported in the WPPSI-R manual, and a summary of these, as well as other studies, can be found in Table 9–9.

An evaluation   Standardization procedures for the WPPSI-R can perhaps best be described as, or as nearly, "state-of-the-art," and the psychometric properties

Table 9–9

WPPSI-R Validity Studies

Researcher(s)	Sample	Criterion	WPPSI-R Correlations		
			Verbal IQ	Performance IQ	Full Scale IQ
Not provided in WPPSI-R manual	144 children from the standardization sample	WPPSI-R	.85	.82	.87
Urbina & Clayton (in press)	50 children ages 72–86 months	WISC-R	.76	.75	.85
Terrell, Convy, & Kirby	115 children ages 48–86 months	SB:FE			
		VR	.63	.30	.55
		AVR	.50	.54	.59
		QR	.52	.47	.55
		STM	.57	.32	.52
		TC	.73	.56	.74
Jacob & Faust (cited in WPPSI-R manual)	93 children ages 4–6 years	MSCA			
		Verbal	.75	.37	.64
		PP	.53	.71	.72
		Q	.63	.59	.69
		GCI	.77	.66	.81
		Memory	.64	.46	.64
		Motor	.19	.25	.25
Thomas & Romero (cited in WPPSI-R manual)	59 children ages 37–76 months primarily Hispanic and black	K-ABC			
		SEQ	.41	.31	.43
		SIM	.31	.37	.41
		MPC	.42	.41	.49
		ACH		not reported	
Faust & Oakes (1990)	33 children ages 48–60 months in a private, preschool program	MSCA			
		GCI	.67	.50	.67
		PPVT-R	.31	.30	.34

of the test are strong. Scoring criteria for the subtests are clear, and as a result, inter-rater reliability in scoring overall tends to be impressive. More discussion of this test can be found in Chapter 11.

The Wechsler Tests in Perspective

The standardization of all of the Wechsler tests closely approximates the highest level of standards advocated by professional groups such as the American Psychological Association. In addition, each test has been thoroughly researched with respect to all facets of reliability and validity and in general has been found to be psychometrically sound.

The organization of the Wechsler Scales into a Verbal and Performance Scale with individual subtests constituting each scale facilitates the interpretation of the test data and the generation of diagnostic hypotheses. Additionally, the identification of areas of the test taker's strengths and weaknesses can be delineated from analysis of performance on Wechsler subtests.

The clarity of the instructions for administering the Wechsler tests is exemplary when it comes to test-manual writing. For example, if an examiner poses a question that requires the respondent to provide not one, but two reasons for something (in order for the examinee to earn full and not partial credit for the item), the administration manual provides not only the "permission" to probe for a second reason if only one is initially given, but the precise language in which to probe. And while the trained examiner may find the Wechsler tests fairly easy to administer, test takers generally find the materials "easy to take"—that is, engaging. After an item or two on a particular subtest are failed, it's on to a new subtest and another intellectually challenging task. Preschool children, older children, and adults tend to respond favorably to the Wechsler test materials designed for use with their respective age groups.

One problem an examiner might have with the Wechsler materials may come not while administering the test but while attempting to score it. Wechsler (1955) himself noted that the evaluation of a test taker's responses to some of the items— perhaps most noticeably on subtests such as Comprehension, Similarities, and Vocabulary—may require subjective judgment on the part of the examiner. For example, the manual can offer only a sampling of the many different definitions a child can give for a word on the Vocabulary subtest—and then it is up to the examiner to determine whether the response should be credited or not. This element of subjectivity in some of the scoring has been thought to depress correlations observed in some studies of inter-scorer reliability (Sattler, Winget, & Roth, 1969; Sattler, Andres, Squire, Wisely, & Maloy, 1978; Woo-Sam & Zimmerman, 1973), and level of inter-scorer agreement may not be related to amount of examiner experience (Miller, Chansky, & Gredler, 1972). In addition to differences in scoring as a function of subjectivity, differences in scoring resulting from clerical-type errors (for example, errors in addition or in transforming scores) may also arise (Sherrets, Gard, & Langner, 1979).

Although the Wechsler Scales are generally considered to be well standardized, some have raised questions about the standardization process for specific tests. For example, Tittle (1975) noted that the account of the standardization process in the manual for the WISC-R leaves unanswered questions concerning a comprehensive assessment of the proportional representation of people from various socioeconomic levels in the standardization sample. The applicability of the WISC-R normative data for children younger than 6 years 4 months of age and older than 16 years 8 months is questioned. Only children whose date of birth was at mid-year (plus or minus 1½ months) were included in the WISC-R standardization sample and, therefore, no children included were between 6 years 0 months and 6 years 3 months of age. Neither were there children between the ages of 16 years 8 months and 16 years 11 months of age.

Scaled scores for the various age ranges and Wechsler Scale subtests are not uniform; the same number of scaled-score points cannot be earned on all subtests. For example, the highest number of scaled-score points possible on the WISC-R Arithmetic subtest is 19 points at years 6 through 10. At age 11 years the highest number of scaled-score points is 18. At age 16 years 8 months the highest number of scaled-score points that can be earned is only 16. For the WAIS-R, in the reference group (ages 20–34) that is used to transform raw scores into scaled scores and then into deviation IQs, scaled scores of 19 can be earned on five subtests, a score of 18 on three subtests, and 17 on another three subtests. This lack of conformity among scaled scores may complicate the analysis and interpretation of the test data.

What do you do when you, as an examiner, want to administer a Wechsler (or other) intelligence test but don't have time to administer the whole test? The solution for which some examiners have opted is to administer what is called a "short form" of the test, that is, administer one or more selected subtests and then estimate from the data in hand what the examinee might have scored had he or she taken the entire test. Short forms of intelligence tests are nothing new; in fact, they have been around almost as long as the "long forms." Shortly after the Binet-Simon scale reached our shores a "short form" of it was proposed (Doll, 1917). Wechsler (1958) found nothing wrong with using short forms of as little as only two subtests, provided it was done only for screening purposes. But years later, perhaps in reaction to possible abuses of short forms, Wechsler (1967) advised that "reduction in the number of [subtests] as a time-saving device is unjustifiable and not to be encouraged" (p. 37). He further advised those who might claim that they did not have enough time to administer the test in its entirety to "find the time" (p. 37). Subsequent reviews of the literature on short forms have borne out the wisdom of Wechsler's later advice. Reviewers such as Watkins (1986) have concluded that short forms may be used for screening purposes only, and they should not be used to make placement or educational decisions. Silverstein (1990) provided an incisive review of the history of short forms focusing on four choices related to creating one: (1) how to abbreviate the original test, (2) how to select subjects; (3) how to estimate scores on the original test, and (4) the criteria to apply when comparing the short form to the original.

The Wechsler tests of intelligence are among the most-used tests of intelligence. Should you elect to pursue a career in psychology, you will no doubt obtain more detailed training in these tests and you will observe firsthand how they can provide an index of not only the examinee's intelligence but other factors as well, such as personality and neurological intactness.

Psychologists who have occasion to administer intelligence tests are familiar not only with names such as "Binet" and "Wechsler" but also with names such as "Slosson," "Kaufman," and "Peabody"—to name but a few. "Slosson" is the name associated with one of a variety of intelligence tests—the variety that is speedily administered and scored. After our rather speedy discussion of the Slosson—"the Slosson" is how psychologists typically refer to the Slosson Intelligence Test—we proceed to another variety of intelligence test, group-administered tests of intelligence.

The Slosson Intelligence Test (SIT)

Also referred to by some practitioners as the "Short Intelligence Test," the Slosson was designed to be a quick, easily administered, yet valid measure of intelligence. The test was originally conceived of as an abbreviated version of the Stanford–Binet (Slosson, 1963), and like Form L-M, the SIT is an age scale. The test also has many of the types of items found in infant intelligence scales and does extend downward in range to the infant level (as well as upward to age 27). Above age 7, the test becomes increasingly weighted with verbal items, though items assessing motor, perceptual-motor, and related abilities are also included. The test "kit" contains only two items: the test manual and score sheets. In contrast to the administration of a Binet or a Wechsler test, which may take as much as an hour (or more), the administration of the Slosson seldom takes more than 15 to 20 minutes. Further, the items can be scored quickly, with little room for subjectivity.

In the past, studies comparing scores achieved on the 1981 Slosson with scores achieved on other established intelligence tests such as the Stanford–Binet Form L-M tended to yield relatively high correlations in part because the two tests shared many of the same items. We hasten to add, however, that this does not mean that scores from one test can routinely be substituted for scores on the other; intellectual functioning tended to be overestimated with the SIT and, in at least in one study, misclassifications with the SIT occurred in 40 percent of the cases (Stewart & Jones, 1976).

Unlike previous editions of the test, which were based on the Stanford–Binet, the 1991 revision of the Slosson (SIT-R) contains, in addition, items similar to those found on the Wechsler scales. Intended for use as "a screening test of intelligence specifically measuring the verbal intelligence factor" (Slosson, 1991, p. 2), the SIT-R taps skills in the following domains: vocabulary, general information, similarities and differences, comprehension, auditory memory, and quantitative ability. It was standardized on 1,854 individuals loosely matched to the U.S. population with respect to educational and social characteristics; "loosely" since, for example, 83% of the standardization sample, as compared to 74% of the U.S. population, was white. The members of the standardization sample also tended to be better educated than the general U.S. population.

As reported in the test manual, the test-retest reliability coefficient for 41 examinees retested after one week was .96. Validity studies with 234 children divided into four groups ranging in age from 6 to 16 compared the Verbal scale scores of the SIT-R with those of the WISC-R and yielded validity coefficients ranging from .83 to .91. When full scale scores of the two tests were compared, correlations ranged from .61 to .92. In another study with adults, correlations between the SIT-R and WAIS-R verbal scales were found to be .88, and the SIT-R/WAIS-R full scale correlation was found to be .82.

In contrast to the Stanford-Binet and the Wechsler scales, a highly trained examiner is not required to administer the Slosson. The test has been promoted as one that can be used for screening purposes by personnel who may have had only minimal exposure to principles of psychological testing (such as counselors, special education teachers, reading specialists, and speech therapists). A potential problem, however, is that although such users may appreciate the convenience of the test, they may not appreciate the great limitations of the data derived from it. The Slosson must be viewed as a good test for what it is: a quick screening device that can be used to generate hypotheses about specific problem areas that could then be more fully explored using in-depth and specialized measures.

Group Intelligence Tests

If you are like many students, reading about intelligence tests may have piqued your curiosity about what your own IQ is. And if you are like many students, if you ever have taken an intelligence test, the chances are good it was a group test, not an individual test. That is probably the case, since out of the many millions of psychological tests administered annually in a variety of settings (Brim, Glass,

---

Close-up

Mensa

You may belong to a social, professional, or religious fraternity or sorority in which you engage in a wide variety of activities such as athletics, discussion groups, museum trips, speaker presentations, and parties. There is one social organization that is like these groups in all respects except that the requirement for membership is proof of high intelligence. That organization is called Mensa and it has more than seventy thousand members worldwide, with chapters not only throughout the United States but also in Europe, South America, Australia, India, Israel, and Japan. Members include cab drivers, physicians, homemakers—in short, a wide variety of people in a wide variety of occupations.

Mensa was founded in England by two attorneys as a kind of roundtable discussion club for a group of intellectual equals; in fact, the word *Mensa* is derived from the Latin word for "table." The group was founded shortly after World War II, its primary agenda then to discuss and arrive at ways of preserving world peace. Today, the objectives of the organization would not appear quite so ambitious; the group is a social club that also fosters scientific pursuits through an educational and research foundation and through a research journal. The group also awards scholarships to postsecondary students to encourage them to fulfill their intellectual potential; some chapters have a group to aid in the rehabilita-

Nevlinger, Firestone, & Lerner, 1969; Holmen & Docter, 1972), a relatively small fraction of those tests are individually administered intelligence tests; most people who have taken an intelligence test have taken a group test of intelligence (Hopkins & Bracht, 1975).

Perhaps the most obvious advantage of group tests over individual tests is that they can be administered to large numbers of people at the same time and so are more efficient. Most group tests can be reliably machine- or computer-scored. They are also more economical than individual tests because, in most cases, only a one-page computer answer sheet is used, thus avoiding the necessity for expensive, nonreusable test booklets. Inherent in this efficiency is a lowered "turn-around time" in scoring and thus a larger—and, in some instances, more representative— sample of respondents can be tested, an important consideration in research settings. The test administrator need not be highly trained, thus further bringing down the cost and ease with which such a test may be administered; the test administrator usually needs do no more than read the directions to the test taker and keep time. Another advantage of the lessened role of the test administrator is the fact that the test administrator may have less effect on the examinee's score than a test administrator in a one-on-one situation. Because of the general ease of administering and scoring group tests, they often are normed on larger and more representative standardization samples than are many individual tests.

A primary use of group tests of inelligence tests is screening. Tests results can suggest which subjects require more extensive assessment with individually administered intelligence tests. In the schools, group intelligence tests may also be helpful in identifying children who require extensive preparation and/or enrich-

tion of high-IQ prison inmates. Special-interest groups existing within Mensa cover different kinds of activities ranging from astronomy to motorcycles to Zen.

According to Mensa, each year about thirty thousand people attempt to qualify for membership; but since only people whose measured IQs fall within the top 2 percent in intelligence qualify, only about 2 of every 50 people who apply are admitted. Are you interested in joining Mensa? If so, contact the local chapter and request a membership application. They will send you a list of intelligence tests that you may have taken at one time or another in your life; and if you can document that your score on any of the tests meets the club's cutoff point, you pay your dues and you're in. If you are unable to document your IQ to the club's satisfaction, it's going to take a bit more effort on your part. For a nominal fee, the club will send you a take-home IQ test with questions similar to those in Table 1. If you pass the take-home test, you then will be invited to take, for a nominal fee, a proctored test. If you then score high enough to pass Mensa muster on the proctored test, you're invited to join. Needless to say, there are some people—many of whom might qualify for membership—who do not view such an organization in positive terms but who instead see it as elitist and snobbish. (*continued*)

Mensa (continued)

Table 1

———

Try these typical IQ-test questions.

1. What word means the same as (p-a-y) in one sense and the same as (b-o-t-t-o-m) in another sense?
2. Which of the following sentences best describes the meaning of the old bromide "The used key is always bright"?
   a. Keep on the scene in order to stay with it.
   b. If you use a test key, you will appear bright.
   c. New devices often don't work well.
   d. Old ideas are the best.
3. Which one of the following games does not belong in the group?
   a. Chess
   b. Bridge
   c. Go
   d. Mah-jongg
   e. Backgammon
4. The word procure is the opposite of which of the following words?
   a. Retain
   b. Abscond
   c. Forfeit
   d. Appropriate
   e. Purchase
5. Complete the following analogy: Green is to yellow as orange is to _____?
   a. Blue
   b. Purple
   c. Brown
   d. Yellow
   e. White
6. The word aggravate means the same as which of the following words?
   a. Burden
   b. Enrage
   c. Infect
   d. Intensify
   e. Complain
7. Which of the following words are most opposite in meaning?
   a. Intense
   b. Extensive
   c. Majority
   d. Extreme
   e. Diffuse
8. Which one of the following words does not belong in the group?
   a. Stone
   b. Brick
   c. Canoe
   d. Pontoon
   e. Oar
9. Which two of the following words have the most similar meanings?
   a. Divulge
   b. Divert
   c. Reveal
   d. Revert
10. Complete the following analogy: Mountain is to land as whirlpool is to _____?
    a. Fluid
    b. Wet
    c. Sea
    d. Sky
    e. Shower
11. The old saying "Don't trade horses when crossing a stream" most nearly means which of the following?
    a. You might fall off and get wet.
    b. Don't attempt something until you are fully prepared.
    c. Decide what you are going to do before you do it.
    d. Don't change plans when something is half completed.
12. If a house is 36 feet long and 27 feet wide, how wide would a house of the same proportions be if it were 72 feet long?

13. Which number, when multiplied by 4, is equal to $\frac{3}{4}$ of 112?
14. What word means the same as (h-i-r-e) in one sense and the same as (b-e-t-r-o-t-h) in another sense?
15. Which word does not belong in the following group?
    a. Car   d. Happy
    b. Moon   e. Belief
    c. Fish
16. If seven belly dancers can lose 20 pounds altogether in eight hours of dancing, how many additional belly dancers would be needed to lose that same 20 pounds in only four hours of dancing, providing the new dancers shed weight only half as fast as the original seven dancers?
    a. 7   d. 14
    b. 21   e. 12
    c. 27
17. Which two of the following words are the most similar in meaning?
    a. Autonomy   c. Oligarchy
    b. Autocracy   d. Dictatorship
18. What number comes next in the following series? 2, 3, 5, 9, 17 _____
19. Some Mensa members are geniuses. All geniuses have some human virtue as re-deeming qualities. Using these two facts, which of the following conclusions is most correct?
    a. Mensa members all have some virtues.
    b. All geniuses are quality Mensa members.
    c. Some Mensa members have redeeming qualities.
20. The old saying "The good is the enemy of the best" most nearly means which of the following?
    a. If you are good, you will best your enemy.
    b. Be good to your best enemy.
    c. Don't accept less than your best.
    d. The good struggle against the best.

Mensa Quiz Answers

1. (Foot). 2. (a). 3. (b). 4. (c). 5. (d).
6. (d). 7. (a & e). 8. (a). 9. (a & c).
10. (c). 11. (d). 12. (54 feet). 13. (21).
14. (engage). 15. (d). 16. (d). 17. (b & d).
18. (33). 19. (c). 20. (c).

Scoring Scale

Give yourself one point for each correct answer. You receive an additional four points if you completed the test in less than 10 minutes; three points if you completed it in less than 15 minutes; two points if you completed it in less than 20 minutes; and one point if you completed it in less than 25 minutes.

The authors of this text note that the original article contained a score interpretation guide indicating that a score of 20–24 qualified you as a "perfect candidate" for Mensa; 15–19 and you were still a candidate; 10–14 and "you might want to try the Mensa test"; and fewer than 10—"forget about joining." Of course, how much faith you place in a test interpretation guide should at least in part be a function of your evaluation of the psychometric soundness of the test. With no evidence as to reliability or validity of this test, we would advise that regardless of your test score, should you desire to join—go for it!

Source: Grosswirth (1980)

ment experience prior to beginning first grade. In research settings, group intelligence tests may be used, for example, to provide valuable feedback to an agency or institution (such as a school or the military) for program-planning purposes.

Lest we paint too rosy a picture in our overview of group tests, let us also point out that these tests also carry with them distinct disadvantages. Two assumptions inherent in the use of group tests are that people taking the test understand what is expected of them and that they are motivated to perform on the test. If these assumptions are violated, the results obtained will be invalid. During an individually administered test, the examiner is able to observe the subject's "individual learning style," such as a tendency to solve problems by a trial-and-error approach or in an impulsive rather than reflective manner. The examiner is also able to observe confusion, anxiety, lack of interest, or other factors that would hinder the examinee's performance; during the group test, the examiner has no such opportunity and not only is the opportunity for extra-test behavior lost, but so might be important information bearing on the test score. Group tests are, as their name implies, designed for the masses, and they therefore place the atypical person (for example, the individual with some disability not identified prior to testing or the individual who "walks to the beat of a different drummer") at a greater risk of obtaining a score on the test that does not accurately approximate that individual's hypothetical "true score."

With specific reference to group intelligence tests, the relative stability of scores obtained on such tests by test takers age 7 and above has been empirically demonstrated (Bloom, 1963), but few or no data exist to support the consistency of general intelligence measures obtained from group intelligence tests administered before age 7 in grades 1 and 2 (Hopkins & Bracht, 1975).

All examinees taking a group test, regardless of ability, typically start on the same item and frequently end on the last item as well. This state of affairs stands in marked contrast to the more custom-designed individually administered test situation in which all examinees need not start with or end on the same item and need not be exposed to all of the items on the test. Most individually administered intelligence tests contain specific rules for beginning the test (such as "begin at the level of the examinee's chronological age provided he or she answers the first two consecutive items correctly; if not, work backward until the first two consecutive items of a level are answered correctly") and for discontinuing the test ("discontinue after four consecutive failures"). Such procedures serve to prevent boredom or a failure to take the test seriously (because of the administration of too many easy items) and feelings of discouragement resulting from a sequence of too-difficult items.

Most group intelligence tests require the test taker to be able to read. And while the reading level required may be simpler than the cognitive demands of the item, the fact that the item does require reading may confound the value of the score achieved on the test by certain test takers (Cassell, 1971). In addition to reading ability, another skill expected of the test taker is the ability to manipulate a pencil and to mark an answer sheet—a task with which some normal first- and second-graders may have difficulty even if given prior practice sessions (Ramseyer & Cashen, 1971). Children who have eye-hand coordination or concentration difficulties will be especially vulnerable to difficulties with a test administered in such a format.

Although the standardization samples for group intelligence tests are often large, they are rarely as representative as they may appear. Group intelligence tests designed for use in the schools, for example, tend to be standardized on school districts rather than on individuals. While a particular district may be viewed as representative of a state, the particular individuals who make up that district and who participate in the testing are not necessarily representative of the population of individuals the test publisher would like to sample from. This is so because (1) the particular district may have volunteered to take part in the standardization process and (2) test takers within the district may be required to obtain parental permission to participate. The latter situation will almost certainly bias the composition of the sample as there is a tendency on the part of better-educated, higher-socioeconomic-status parents to consent to testing, as opposed to parents of lower socioeconomic status with little education. The fact that such subtle biasing factors exist may not be noted in a description of the sample in the test's manual.

The data from group intelligence tests—like the data from any test administration—can be misused. In the schools, for example, it is not unknown for such data to be used to track students into various types of special educational programs—a misuse of the test, since such tracking should ideally be done only on the basis of a comprehensive evaluation that includes an individually administered intelligence test. Data from the administration of a group intelligence test—administered in a school, employment, military, or any other setting—may also be misused when they become the basis for unrealistic academic expectations from children.

Despite our list of limitations and caveats, it cannot be denied that group intelligence tests can be of great value when used as screening instruments. We now briefly discuss the application of such tests in various settings.

Group intelligence tests in the schools   At one time, perhaps no more than a decade or two ago, approximately two-thirds of all school districts in the United States used group intelligence tests on a routine basis to screen 90% of their students; the other 10% were administered individual intelligence tests (Macmillan & Myers, 1980). Litigation and legislation surrounding the routine use of group intelligence tests have altered this picture somewhat (see Chapter 1), though the group intelligence test, now also referred to as a "school ability test," is by no means extinct. In many states, legal mandates exist prohibiting the use of group intelligence test data alone for tracking purposes. However, group intelligence test data, combined with other data, can be extremely useful in developing a profile of a child's intellectual assets.

Group intelligence test results provide school personnel with information of value for instruction-related activities and increased understanding of the individual pupil. One primary function of data from a group intelligence test is to alert educators to students who require more extensive assessment with individually administered IQ tests—and possible placement in a special class or program. Group intelligence test data can also help a school district plan educational goals for all children.

Group intelligence tests in the schools are used in special forms as early as the kindergarten level. The tests are administered to groups of 10–15 children, each of whom receives a test booklet that includes printed pictures and diagrams. For the most part, simple motor responses are required to answer items; oversized alternatives in the form of pictures in a multiple-choice test might appear on the pages, and it is the child's job to circle or to place an "X" on the picture that represents the correct answer to the item presented orally by the examiner. In some tests, machine-scorable booklets are used as early as first grade, though reading or writing is not required. During such testing in small groups the test takers will be carefully monitored to make certain they are following the directions.

The California Test of Mental Maturity, the Kuhlmann-Anderson Intelligence Tests, the Henmon-Nelson Tests of Mental Ability, and the Cognitive Abilities Test are some of the many group intelligence tests available for use in school settings. The first group intelligence test to be used in American schools—the one we have chosen to acquaint you with in the remainder of this section—is the Otis-Lennon School Ability Test.

After being convinced of the effectiveness and economy of the group-testing method through his experience in the mass testing of army recruits in World War I, Arthur Otis attempted to adapt his objective group-testing procedure for use in the school setting. Otis was a graduate student of Lewis Terman at Stanford University before World War I. He recognized the increased utility of a test that could be constructed specifically for testing groups of persons, and he set out to construct such a scale.

Otis became one of a group of 100 distinguished American psychologists who developed the Army Alpha Test, the first group intelligence test. The Army Alpha was used to assess the intelligence of an estimated 1,700,000 army draftees during World War I; and of that total, Otis estimated that he had personally examined some 50,000. As an outgrowth of his work with the Army Alpha, Otis developed several different item types that, due to his association with Terman, were adaptations of Binet tasks. He was also the person responsible for the use of an objective (multiple-choice) format in the construction of the Army Alpha.

Between 1922 and 1929 Otis developed a paper-and-pencil group intelligence test that sampled a broad range of cognitive abilities. This test was published as the Otis Group Intelligence Scale, and it was the first group test used in American schools. This test was actually a paper-and-pencil equivalent of the individually administered Stanford-Binet. The Otis Self-Administered Tests of Mental Ability were also developed between 1922 and 1929, and the Otis Quick Scoring Mental Ability Tests were developed in later years. The Otis Mental Ability Test was renamed a "School Ability Test" by the authors of its fifth edition, Arthur Otis and Roger Lennon (1979), with their stated objective being to "discharge overinterpretation of the nature of the ability assessed."

Designed for use in grades kindergarten through 13, the major purpose of the sixth edition of the Otis-Lennon School Ability Test (OLSAT), is to assess examinees' "ability to cope with school learning tasks, to suggest their possible placement for school learning functions, and to evaluate their achievement in relation to the talents they bring to school learning situations." From a pool of over 4,000 items submitted by fifty free-lance item writers, new items were considered for use in the sixth edition. In 1987, approximately 354,000 students from 65 schools participated in a national tryout of new items. Stratification variables included geographic region, socioeconomic status, and average school district enrollment per grade as per 1980 census data. Both qualitative analysis in the form of editorial examination of items by experts, as well as quantitative methods were used in an effort to eliminate possible item biases. The items presented in Figure 9–6 are representative of the types of tasks the test taker encounters on the OLSAT. Different levels of items designated as Levels "A" thru "G" (replacing confusing terms such as "primary" and "intermediate" in the prior edition of the test) are included in the sixth edition and there are an equal number of verbal and nonverbal items at each level. In a break with a tradition of this instrument that dates as far back as 1918—that of yielding only a Total Score—the sixth edition of the OLSAT yields both Verbal and Nonverbal part scores. These scores may be expressed in the form of School Ability Indexes or SAIs, which are normalized standard scores with a mean of 100 and a standard deviation of 16. Looking at the Verbal SAI, the Performance SAI, and the Total SAI, the seasoned examiner might experience a sense of deja vu with respect to the concept of IQ—and exactly how SAI differs from IQ is never quite made clear.

In his *Tenth Mental Measurements Yearbook* review of the OLSAT, Swerdlik (1992) concluded that although the test was technically adequate, it could be improved if the following problems were addressed:

1. more specific details regarding the procedures used in the standardization process could be provided in the test manual
2. the brief (one paragraph) account of the theory underlying this test is insufficient and needs to be expanded
3. the manual requires more detail in helping the test user to make meaningful and actionable interpretations from the test data, and
4. some caveat in the test manual regarding the need for caution in interpreting and acting on group test data would seem desirable.

Group Intelligence Tests in the Military

Group intelligence measures such as the Army Alpha (primarily verbal in nature) and the Army Beta (primarily nonverbal in nature) were first developed in response to manpower problems of the military during World War I. At that time there was the need to select potential officer candidates and to eliminate draftees who were mentally unfit for military service.

Today, group intelligence tests—as well as more specialized group tests—are still administered to prospective recruits not only for routine screening purposes but also as an aid in assigning soldiers to training programs and jobs. Data from group intelligence testing have indicated that there is a downward trend in the mean intelligence level of recruits since the ending of the draft and the inception of an all-volunteer army. In response to such findings, the military has developed new weapons training programs incorporating, for example, lower-level vocabulary in programmed instruction, a strategy designed to provide a better match between the learning ability of the trainee (recruit) and the material to be learned.

Included among many group tests used by the armed forces are the Officer Qualifying Test (a 115-item multiple-choice test used by the Navy as an admissions test to Officer Candidate School), the Airman Qualifying Exam (a 200-item multiple-choice test given to all Air Force volunteers), and the Armed Services

• Verbal Analogy items assess the ability to infer the relationship between a pair of words and to select a word that bears the same relationship to a given stimulus word.

Bird is to **nest** as **bee** is to —

    f hive   **g** flower   **h** buzz   **j** sting   **k** wasp

• Verbal Classification items assess the ability to determine which word in a set does not belong, according to some principle operative within the set.

Which word does *not* go with the other four?

    a tall   **b** big   **c** small   **d** short   **e** loud

• Sentence Completion items assess the ability to determine logical relationships among words in a sentence in order to supply a missing word.

Choose the word that *best* completes this sentence:

We will not begin the meeting _____ everybody is here.

    a because   **b** until   **c** if   **d** when   **e** after

• Sentence Arrangement items assess the ability to integrate a group of words into a meaningful sentence.

If the words below were arranged to make the *best* sentence, with which letter would the <u>last</u> word of the sentence <u>begin</u>?

streets	the	caused	to	rain	heavy	flood

  a s   **b** f   **c** h   **d** r   **e** c

• Numeric Inference items assess the ability to evaluate the relationship among pairs or trios of numbers and to select a number that is related to a stimulus number in the same way.

The numbers in each box go together by following the *same* rule. Decide what the rule is, and then find the number that goes where you see the question mark (?) in the last box.

  | 10, 5 | | 6, 3 | | 16, ? | **a** 2   **b** 4   **c** 8   **d** 11   **e** 13

• Quantitative Reasoning is dependent on the ability to evaluate groups of numbers in order to infer relationships among them and to infer and apply computational rules.

• Figural Analogy items assess the ability to infer the relationship between a pair of geometric shapes and to apply that relationship in selecting a shape that is related to a stimulus shape in the same way.

• Series Completion items assess the ability to predict the next step in a geometric series in which each element changes according to a given rule.

The drawings in the first part of the row go together to form a series. In the next part of the row, find the drawing that goes where you see the question mark (?) in the series.

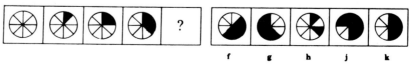

Figure 9–6 *Sample OLSAT Items.*

Vocational Aptitude Battery (ASVAB). The ASVAB is administered to prospective new recruits in all of the armed services. Let's look at it in more detail.

The ASVAB consists of 334 multiple-choice items organized into ten different subtests. A description of the subtests and some sample items are presented in Figure 9–7.

A set of 100 selected items included in the subtests of arithmetic reasoning, numerical operations, word knowledge, and paragraph comprehension make up a measure within the ASVAB called the Armed Forces Qualification Test (AFQT). The AFQT is a measure of general ability used in the selection of recruits into the military. The different armed services employ different cutoff scores in making accept/reject determinations for service based on considerations such as their pre-set quotas for people from a particular demographic group. In addition to the AFQT score, ten aptitude areas are also tapped on the ASVAB, including general technical, general mechanics, electrical, motor-mechanics, science, combat operations, and skill-technical. These are combined to assess aptitude in five separate career areas, including clerical, electronics, mechanics, skill-technical (medical, computers), and combat operations. A form of the test is also available for administration to high school students for counseling purposes.

A large-scale study bearing on the validity of the test compared the performance of high- and low-scoring men who were all accepted into the Air Force. It was found that the lower-scoring men were less likely to complete basic training, had more unsuitable discharges, and were less likely to attain the required level of success (Grunzke, Gunn, & Stauffer, 1970). In general, the test has been deemed to be quite useful in making selection and placement decisions in the armed forces.

MEASURES OF SPECIFIC INTELLECTUAL ABILITIES

There are certain intellectual abilities and talents that are not—or are only indirectly—assessed by the more widely used measures of intelligence. One such ability is creativity. And while it is true that most tests of intelligence do not measure creativity, the reverse of that statement cannot be stated with equal certainty. To the extent that the components of creativity include numerous variables related to general intellectual ability (such as originality in problem solving, originality in perception, originality in abstraction, ideational fluency, and inductive reasoning abilities), measures of creativity may also be thought of as tools for assessing aspects of intellectual functioning.

Measures of Creativity

A criticism frequently leveled at group standardized intelligence tests (as well as other ability and achievement tests) is that evaluation of test performance is too heavily focused on whether the answer is correct—as opposed to giving more weight to the examinee's thought process in arriving at the answer. On most achievement tests, for example, the skill that is required is called *convergent thinking;* after a consideration of the facts and after making a logical series of logical judgments, a solution to a problem is arrived at. Convergent thinking is a deduc-

Figure 9-7   The Armed Services Vocational Aptitude Battery (ASVAB).

The ASVAB is used by the armed services to determine qualifications for enlistment as well as most suitable job assignment. Test takers are advised to do their best since ASVAB scores "will determine which job areas you are qualified to enter. The better your scores are, the more opportunities you will have available to you."

The test is administered in a group setting with a two-hour, 24-minute time limit. All of the items on the ASVAB are multiple-choice with four or five possible answers. Score is based on the number right and test takers are encouraged to guess if they are unsure of the correct response; there is no penalty for guessing. Test takers are further advised to "get a good night's rest before taking the test." Sample items from each of the ten subtests follow with the answer key printed at the end. To get a feel for the type of questions asked, why not sample these items yourself—even if you perchance didn't get a good night's rest last night.

I. General Science
   Included here are general science questions, including questions from the areas of biology and physics.

   1. An eclipse of the sun throws the shadow of the
      A moon on the sun
      B moon on the earth
      C earth on the sun
      D earth on the moon

II. Arithmetic Reasoning
   The task here is to solve arithmetic problems. Test takers are permitted to use (government supplied) scratch paper.

   2. It cost $0.50 per square yard to waterproof canvas. What will it cost to waterproof a canvas truck that is 15' × 24'?
      A $ 6.67
      B $ 18.00
      C $ 20.00
      D $180.00

III. World Knowledge
   Which of four possible definitions best defines the underlined word?

   3. Rudiments most nearly means
      A politics
      B minute details
      C promotion opportunities
      D basic methods and procedures

IV. Paragraph Comprehension
   A test of reading comprehension and reasoning.

   4. Twenty-five percent of all household burglaries can be attributed to unlocked windows or doors. Crime is the result of opportunity plus desire. To prevent crime, it is each individual's responsiblity to
      A provide the desire
      B provide the opportunity
      C prevent the desire
      D prevent the opportunity

V. Numerical Operations
This speeded test contains simple arithmetic problems that the test taker must do quickly; it is one of two speeded tests on the ASVAB.

5. $6 - 5 =$
   A 1
   B 4
   C 2
   D 3

VI. Coding Speed
This subtest contains coding items which measure perceptual/motor speed among other factors.

KEY

green . . . 2715	man . . . 3451	salt . . . 4586
hat . . . 1413	room . . . 2864	tree . . . 5972

	A	B	C	D	E
6. room	1413	2715	2864	3451	4586

VII. Auto and Shop Information
This test assesses knowledge of automobiles, shop practices, and the use of tools.

7. What tool is shown above?
   A Hole saw
   B Keyhole saw
   C Counter saw
   D Grinding saw

VIII. Mathematics Knowledge
This is a test of ability to solve problems using high school level mathematics. Use of scratch paper is permitted.

8. If $3X = -5$, then $X =$
   A -2
   B $-\frac{5}{3}$
   C $-\frac{3}{5}$
   D $\frac{3}{5}$

IX. Mechanical Comprehension
Knowledge and understanding of general mechanical and physical principles are probed by this test.

319

Figure 9–7 *(continued)*

9. Liquid is being transferred from the barrel to the bucket by
A capillary action
B gravitational forces
C fluid pressure in the hose
D water pressure in the barrel

X. Electronics Information
Here, knowledge of electrical, radio, and electronics information is assessed.

10. Which of the above is the symbol for a transformer?
A A
B B
C C
D D

Answer Key
1. B
2. C
3. D
4. D
5. Why are you looking this one up?
6. C
7. A
8. B
9. B
10. A

tive reasoning process that emphasizes one solution to a problem. In his structure of intellect model discussed in Chapter 8, Guilford (1967) drew a distinction between the intellectual processes of convergent and *divergent* types of thinking. Divergent thinking involves a reasoning process in which thought is permitted the freedom to move in many different directions; as a result, several possible solutions to a problem are arrived at. This type of thinking requires flexibility of thought, originality, and imagination; and though facts are considered, there is much less emphasis on them than in convergent thinking. Guilford's model has served as a stimulus to focus research attention on not only the products of creative thought but the process as well.

A number of tests and test batteries designed to measure creativity in children and adults are available. Guilford (1954) described tasks such as Consequences ("Imagine what would happen if . . .") and Unusual Uses (for example, "Name as many uses as you can think of for a rubber band") as ways of assessing

320

creativity. Included in Guilford et al.'s (1974) test battery, the Structure-of-Intellect Abilities, are Consequences and Unusual Uses subtests, four Christensen-Guilford Fluency tests (Word Fluency, Ideational Fluency, Expressional Fluency, and Associational Fluency), and other verbally oriented subtests (such as Simile Interpretation) as well as relatively nonverbal subtests (such as Sketches, Making Objects, and Decorations).

Based on the work of Mednick (1962), the Remote Associates Test (RAT) presents the test taker with three words and the task is to find a fourth word that is associated with the other three. The Torrance (1966) Tests of Creative Thinking consist of word-based, as well as picture-based and sound-based test materials. In a subtest of different sounds administered with the aid of a phonograph record, for example, the examinee's task is to respond with what thoughts each sound conjures. Each subtest is designed to measure some or all of four characteristics deemed to be important in the process of creative thought: flexibility, originality, fluency, and elaboration—and responses are scored in three or more of these four areas. Flexibility refers to the variety of ideas presented and the ability to shift from one approach to another. Fluency involves the number of ideas or total responses actually produced. Elaboration alludes to the richness of detail in a verbal explanation or pictorial display. Originality refers to the ability to produce nonobvious ideas or figures. Test-retest reliability on this battery has not been encouraging though such findings may be similar with respect to other measures of creativity—an ability that may be highly susceptible to the effect of emotional or physical health, motivation, and related factors. And while a number of studies have explored aspects of the construct validity of this test (see, for example, Lieberman, 1965), many test reviewers (such as Wallach & Kogan, 1965) have remained skeptical, wondering aloud whether the test might more properly be thought of as one of intelligence. One large-scale factor-analytic study did not support the distinction of the fluency, flexibility, originality, and elaboration factors (Yamamoto & Frengel, 1966).

What interests and personality characteristics do creative people share? Using this question as a point of departure, tests such as The Group Inventory for Finding Creative Talent (Rimm, 1976), otherwise known as "the GIFT," the Group Inventory for Finding Interests (Davis & Rimm, 1979; 1982), and the Preschool and Kindergarten Interest Descriptor (Rimm, 1981) each approach the study of creativity by examining factors known to be related to creativity. The GIFT is a self-report instrument containing items related to independence, imagination, and interests. The Group Inventory for Finding Interests, and the Preschool and Kindergarten Interest Descriptor similarly survey interests as well as personality and biographical variables known to be related to creativity, such as self-confidence, adventurousness, risk taking, curiosity, and humor. Interested students are advised that a library of over two hundred creativity tests exists at the University of Georgia and at the State University College at Buffalo (Haensly & Torrance, 1990).

Other Measures

A number of tests exist to measure specific intellectual abilities ranging in diversity from critical thinking (such as the Watson-Glaser Critical Thinking Appraisal) to music listening skills (such as the Seashore Measures of Musical Tal-

Figure 9–8 *A Sample Item from the Meier Art Judgment Test.* The difference between the two pictures has to do with the positioning of the objects on the shelf.

ents). The Meier Art Tests (including the Meier Art Judgment Test and the Meier Aesthetic Perception Test) were based on the research of Norman Charles Meier in the area of aesthetic sensitivity. The task in the Aesthetic Perception Test is to rank four versions of the same work of art in order of perceived aesthetic merit. The Art Judgment Test consists of 100 pairs of paintings or drawings reproduced in black and white, one rendering of the original altered in some way. Examinees are informed of the difference between the two pictures (in order to control for potential problems in perception) and then asked which of the two versions of the artwork they like best. While some validation studies have examined the preferences of people with varying degrees of training or expertise in the area of art, the University of Iowa, the publisher of the Art Judgment Test, sells it with the following position statement appended to the test booklet:

> The application of the Meier Art Judgment Test for the purpose of disclosing artistic ability is no longer considered applicable and valid. Nonetheless, the test remains a significant document in the history of testing and measuring artistic ability. The researcher concerned with historical development in the area of testing and measuring ability will find Norman C. Meier's Art Judgment Test one of the most directed and extensive pursuits in the field. Therefore, the Meier Art Judgment Test is sold for historical and research purposes only.

Creativity. Critical thinking. Music listening ability. Art judgment. As you read about each of these skills and how they all might be related to that intangible construct "intelligence," you may have said to yourself, "Why doesn't anyone create a test that measures all of these diverse aspects of intelligence?" Although no one has undertaken that ambitious project, in recent years, test packages have been developed to test not only intelligence but related abilities in the context of an educational setting. These test packages, called "psychoeducational batteries," are discussed in the following chapter, along with other tests used in the schools.

-------- Chapter 10 --------

-------- Educational Assessment --------

WHAT ARE SOME of the things you associate with the word "school"? If the word *test* comes to mind, you probably have lots of company. This is so because many different tests are administered in public and private schools: intelligence tests, personality tests, tests of physical and sensory abilities—all kinds of tests. Educators are interested in answers to questions ranging from "How good is your reading ability?" to "How far can you broad jump?" In this chapter, we focus attention on those tests designed to facilitate the process of education. Included here are tests designed to measure achievement, identify aptitude, and point to areas of deficiency that require remediation. Our overview of educational assessment begins with a consideration of the type of test with which you have probably had the most firsthand experience.

ACHIEVEMENT TESTS

Achievement tests are designed to measure accomplishment. An achievement test for a first-grader might have as its subject matter the English language alphabet, whereas an achievement test for someone such as yourself might contain questions relating to principles of psychological assessment. In short, achievement tests are designed to measure the degree of learning that has taken place as a result of exposure to a relatively defined learning experience. The "relatively defined learning experience" may be something as broad as a sampling of "what you learned from four years of college" to something as narrow as "administering first aid for snake bites." A test of achievement may be standardized nationally, regionally, or locally, or it may not be standardized at all; the "pop quiz" on the anatomy of a frog given by your high school biology teacher qualifies every bit as much for the title "achievement test" as does the statewide examination you may have been given in biology at the completion of the school year. Like other tests, achievement tests vary widely with respect to their psychometric soundness. A sound achievement test is one that adequately samples the targeted subject matter and reliably gauges the extent to which all of the examinees learned it.

Achievement tests assist school personnel in making decisions concerning a student's advancement to higher levels and the grouping of students for instructional purposes. Achievement tests are sometimes used to screen for difficulties, and in such instances they may be preludes to the administration of diagnostic tests (discussed later) employed to identify areas where remediation will be necessary. Achievement test data can be used to gauge the quality of instruction vis à vis one particular teacher, an entire school district, or a state, though such a use of test data presumes that students' abilities and related factors are relatively constant across situations—a tenuous assumption in some situations.

Measures of General Achievement

Measures of general achievement may survey learning in one or more academic areas. Tests that cover a number of academic areas are typically divided into several subtests and are referred to as *achievement batteries*. Such batteries may be individually administered (such as the Peabody Individual Achievement Test) or group-administered (such as the Metropolitan Achievement Test). They may consist of a few subtests, as does the Wide Range Achievement Test—Revised (Jastak & Jastak, 1984) with its measures of reading, spelling, and arithmetic, or be as comprehensive as the STEP Series that includes subtests in reading, vocabulary, mathematics, writing skills, study skills, science, social studies, a behavior inventory, an educational environment questionnaire, and an activities inventory. Some batteries, such as the SRA California Achievement Tests, span kindergarten through grade 12, whereas others are grade- or course-specific. Some batteries are constructed to provide both norm-referenced and criterion-referenced analyses. Others are concurrently normed with scholastic aptitude tests to enable a comparison between achievement and aptitude. Some batteries are constructed with practice tests that may be administered several days prior to actual testing. Such practice tests serve to help students familiarize themselves with test-taking procedures. Other batteries contain "locator" or "routing" tests: pretests administered for purposes of determining the level of the actual test most appropriate for administration.

Of the many available achievement batteries (see Table 10–1), the test that is most appropriate for use is the one most consistent with the educational objectives of the individual teacher or school system. It may be that for a particular purpose a battery that focuses on achievement in a few select areas is preferable to one that attempts to sample achievement in several areas. On the other hand, a

Table 10–1

Some Achievement Test Batteries

Test	Subtests	Grade level	Forms	Normative data
California Achievement Test	Prereading Reading Spelling Language Mathematics Use of References	K–12 10 overlapping levels	2	X
Iowa Tests of Basic Skills	Vocabulary Reading Language Work Study Mathematics	K–9* 10 levels	2	X
Metropolitan Achievement Test	Reading Comprehension Mathematics Language Social Studies Science	K–12 8 levels	1 (for pre-primer) 2 at remaining levels	X
Peabody Individual Achievement Test—Revised	Mathematics Reading Recognition Reading Comprehension Spelling Written Expression General Information	K–12	1	X
SRA Achievement Series	Reading Mathematics Language Arts	K–12 8 levels	2	X
Stanford Achievement Test**	Vocabulary Spelling Reading Comprehension Word Study and Skills Language Arts Mathematics Science Social Studies Listening Comprehension	1.5–9.5 6 levels	3	X
Wide Range Achievement Test—Revised	Reading Spelling Arithmetic	K–adult 2 levels (1) for those under 12 (2) for those over 12	1	X

*The Tests of Achievement and Proficiency (TAP) expand the Iowa through high school levels. Additional subtests included in TAP are Use of Information Sources, Science, and Social Studies.

**The Stanford Early School Achievement Test (SESAT) and the Stanford Test of Academic Skills (TASK) extend the Stanford Series from kindergarten through grade 13.

Criterion-referenced data	Concurrent norming	Locator test	Practice test	Diagnostic information	Group/ individual
X	ShortForm Test of Academic Aptitude	X	—	—	Group
X	Cognitive Abilities Test	—	—	—	Group
X	Otis-Lennon School Ability Test	—	X	Reading Mathematics Language	Group
—	—	—	—	—	Individual
X	Educational Ability Series	—	—	—	Group
X	Otis-Lennon Mental Ability Test	—	X	—	Group
—	—	—	—	—	Individual

test that samples many areas may be advantageous when an individual comparison of performance across subject areas is desirable. If a school or local school district undertakes to follow the progress of a group of students as measured by a particular achievement battery, the battery of choice will be one that spans the targeted subject areas in all of the grades to be tested. If ability to distinguish individual areas of difficulty is of primary concern, achievement tests with strong diagnostic features will be chosen. Although achievement batteries sampling a wide range of areas, across grades, and standardized on large, national samples of students have much to recommend them, they also have certain drawbacks. For example, such tests usually take years to develop; in the interim the items, especially in fields such as social studies and science, may become outdated. Further, any nationally standardized instrument is only as good as the extent to which it meets the (local) test user's objectives.

Measures of Achievement in Specific Subject Areas

Whereas achievement batteries tend to be standardized instruments, most measures of achievement in specific subject areas are teacher-made tests; every time a teacher gives a quiz, a test, or a final examination in a course, a test in a specific subject area has been created. In the following discussion, we survey some of the types of tests administered at various stages of the educational process.

At the elementary school level, emphasis is placed on the acquisition of basic skills such as reading, writing, and arithmetic, and many of the standardized instruments available for this age level tap these skills. From the sampling of tests listed in Table 10–2, you can see that the test user has a great deal of choice with respect to variables such as individual or group administration, silent or oral reading, and type of subtest data provided. In general, the tests present the examinee with words, sentences, or paragraphs to be read silently or aloud, and reading ability is assessed by variables such as comprehension and vocabulary. When the material is read aloud, accuracy and speed will be measured. Tests of reading comprehension also vary with respect to the intellectual demands placed on the examinee over and above mere comprehension of the words read. Thus, for example, some tests might require the examinee to simply recall facts from a passage whereas other tests might require interpretation and the formation of inferences.

One battery designed for use in secondary schools is the Cooperative Achievement Test; it contains a series of separate achievement tests in areas as diverse as English, mathematics, literature, social studies, science, and foreign language. Each test was standardized on different populations appropriate to the grade level, and in general the tests tend to be technically sound instruments. For example, the American History component of the Social Studies series was standardized on seventh- and eighth-graders who represented 44 junior and 73 senior high schools. The sample was randomly selected and stratified in terms of public, parochial, and private schools. Alternate-form reliability for the test was found to be .87 for the junior high school sample and .79 for the senior high school sample. Kuder-Richardson reliability estimates of internal consistency at the junior high school level resulted in reliability coefficients of .88 and .90 for Forms A and B, respectively, and .90 for both forms at the high school level.

Table 10-2

Some Reading Achievement Tests

Test	Group/individual	Grade	Scores	Forms	Time required	Description of subtests
Gray Oral Reading Test	Ind.	1–12	Grade equivalents by sex	4	3–10 min. (untimed)	13 reading passages of varying difficulty: Accuracy, Speed, Comprehension, Error Analysis
Gilmore Oral Reading Test	Ind.	1–8	Stanines, percentiles, grade equivalents	2	15–20 min. (untimed)	10 reading passages: Accuracy, Speed, Comprehension, Error Analysis
Durrel Listening Reading Series	Group	1–9 (3 levels)	Grade and age equivalents, stanines, percentiles, and a score reflecting difference between Listening and Reading achievement	2	140–170 min.	Combination oral/silent reading test. Reading Test assesses Vocabulary Knowledge and Comprehension. Listening Test assesses comprehension of the spoken word.
Iowa Silent Reading Test	Group	Level 1 (6–9) Level 2 (9–14) Level 3 (accelerated high school & college)	Stanines, standard scores, percentiles, Reading Efficiency Index (relating speed with accuracy)	1	60–90 min.	Vocabulary Comprehension Speed Skimming material Use of reference material
Gates-MacGinitie Reading Test	Group	K–12 (7 levels)	Raw scores for 1.0 and 1.9 Other levels: percentiles, stanines, grade equivalent, extended scale scores	2 3 at grades 4–9	55 min.	Vocabulary Comprehension
Nelson Reading Skills Test	Group	3–9 (3 levels)	Stanines, percentile rank, percentile rank band, grade equivalent, normal curve equivalent	2	33 min.	Word Meaning Reading Comprehension Speed Test (optional) Word Parts (optional)

At the college level, recent years have witnessed growing interest on the part of state legislatures to mandate end-of-major outcomes assessment in state colleges and universities; apparently, taxpayers are increasingly desirous of some concrete affirmation that their education tax dollars are being well spent. Thus, for example, undergraduate psychology students attending a state-run institution where such legislation is in effect would be required in their senior year to sit for a final—in the literal sense—examination encompassing a range of subject matter that could be described as "everything that an undergraduate psychology major should know." And if that sounds formidable to you, trust us when we advise you that the task of developing such examinations will be all the more formidable.

Another use for achievement tests at the college as well as the adult level is for the purpose of placement. The Advanced Placement Program developed by the College Entrance Examination Board offers high school students the opportunity to achieve college credit for work completed while in high school. Successful completion of the advanced placement test may result in advanced standing and/or advanced course credit depending on the college policy. Since its inception, the advanced placement program has resulted in advanced credit or standing for over a hundred thousand high school students in approximately two thousand colleges. Another type of test that has application for placement purposes, particularly in areas of the country where English may be spoken as a second language by a relatively large segment of the population (such as areas of California, Florida, and Texas) is a test of English proficiency. A listing of some of the instruments currently available to assess English proficiency appears in Table 10-3. One way in which data from an English proficiency test are currently used is in the placement of applicants to college programs in an appropriate level of an English-as-a-second-language program. However, other uses of data from measures of English proficiency can be foreseen. In an era in which there appear to be growing numbers of native as well as immigrant Americans with limited English proficiency, and in a social climate that has legislators writing bills proclaiming English to be the official language of the state, one can foresee the increasing importance of issues related to the testing of English proficiency.

Achievement tests at the college or adult level may also be of the variety that assess whether college credit should be awarded for learning acquired outside of a college classroom. Numerous programs exist that are designed to systematically assess whether or not sufficient knowledge has been acquired to qualify for course credit. The College Level Examination Program (CLEP) is based on the premise that knowledge may be obtained through independent study and sources other than formal schooling. The program includes exams in subjects ranging from Afro-American History to Tests and Measurement. Participants in programs such as CLEP tend to think very favorably of them (Losak, 1978). The Proficiency Examination Program (PEP) offered by the American College Testing Program is another service designed to assess achievement and skills learned outside of the classroom.

The special needs of adults with a wide variety of educational backgrounds are addressed in tests such as the Adult Basic Learning Examination (ABLE), a test intended for use with examinees age 17 and older who did not complete eight years of formalized schooling. The test is designed to assess achievement in the

Table 10–3

Tests of English Proficiency

A brief description of some of the instruments available for measuring proficiency in the English language follows. Critical reviews as well as articles dealing with these or other English language proficiency tests may be found in specialized publications such as *Foreign Language Annals; Journal of Reading; Language Learning; Language, Speech, and Hearing Services in the Schools; Language Testing; Modern Language Journal; NABE Journal; TESOL Quarterly;* and *TESOL Canada Journal* or other compendiums of reviews (such as Alderson, Krahnke, & Stansfield, 1987, or Mitchell, 1985).

Test	Description
Basic English Skills Test (BEST) The Psychological Corporation San Antonio, Texas	Although this test of basic language skills was initially intended for use with Southeast Asian refugees in adult education programs, it can be used with any adult with limited proficiency in English. The test contains an individually administered section of items (that employs oral as well as pictorial stimuli which demand oral or written responses) and a section that may be individually or group administered (requiring only writing or marking responses). The test is designed to be useful as a diagnostic as well as a vocational counseling tool.
Basic Inventory of Natural Language (BINL) CHECpoint Systems, Inc. San Bernardino, California	The BINL (usually pronounced like "vinyl" with a *b*) is a test designed for use with children in grades K through 12. Pictures are used to elicit the examinee's natural speech, and the verbal productions are then analyzed with respect to variables such as fluency and syntactic complexity. The test is available in 32 languages, including Chinese, Japanese, Portuguese, and Vietnamese.
Bilingual Vocational Oral Proficiency Test (BVOPT) Resource Development Institute, Inc. Austin, Texas	According to its manual, this test was designed in part to "screen people for enrollment in a bilingual vocational training program" and to "determine the gain in English proficiency achieved during the training period." The test must be administered in the examinee's native tongue (either by an examiner proficient in the language or by a prerecorded tape), and it contains subtests tapping the ability to (1) respond appropriately in an interview, (2) repeat sentences, (3) respond correctly when orally instructed to manipulate an object. The test comes in two forms, one typically administered as a pretest and the other administered subsequent to training.
Comprehensive English Language (CELT) McGraw-Hill Book Company New York, New York	The CELT (pronounced like "felt" with a *k*) was designed for use with high school, college, and adult education students for whom English is either a second language or a foreign language. The 1986 revision of this test comes in two forms which may be used as a pre- and postinstruction outcome measure. The three subtests of the CELT are Listening (administered via a prerecorded tape), Structure (in which it is the examinee's task to supply a missing word by choosing from four alternatives), and Vocabulary (containing two parts: one in which a missing word in a sentence must be supplied from four alternatives, and another where the task is to select from four alternatives of the word that is being defined).
Diagnostic Assessment of Basic Skills—Spanish Curriculum Associates North Billerica, Massachusetts	Authored by A. H. Brigance and typically referred to as "the Brigance," this test is designed to assess English- and Spanish-language proficiency among other skills (such as math and reading skills). Testing in ten areas (Readiness, Speech, Functional Word Recognition, Oral Reading, Reading Comprehension, Word Analysis, Listening, Writing and Alphabetizing, Numbers and Computation, and Measurement) in levels from prekindergarten through sixth grade is designed to yield diagnostic information, including an assessment of language dominance. Directions to the student are mostly administered in Spanish, though some, for the language dominance assessment, are administered in English. See Swerdlik (1985) for a review of the English-language version of this test.

Table 10-3 (*continued*)

Tests of English Proficiency

Test	Description
Dos Amigos Verbal Language Scales Academic Therapy Publications Novato, California	This test is designed to provide a measure of English- or Spanish-language dominance as well as information as to the comparative development of the test taker's English- or Spanish-language proficiency. Appropriate for use in kindergarten through sixth grade, this individually administered test consists of lists of English and Spanish words that are read to the examinee. The child's task is to supply the antonym to the stimulus word. After five consecutive failures in one language, the test continues with words being read in the alternate language. The test was standardized on 1,224 Mexican-American children in Texas whose first language was Spanish.
Ilyin Oral Interview (IOI) Newbury House/HarperCollins Scranton, Pennsylvania	Pictures depicting everyday activities provide the stimuli for this individually administered oral interview. Examinees are instructed to respond with whole sentences and these responses are scored with respect to variables such as appropriateness, intelligibility, and grammatical accuracy. Information on the relationship between IOI test scores and course levels in the San Francisco Community College District is contained in the test manual though its author cautions that this information "should be used only as tentative until test users can see their own norms and guidelines for their particular programs" (Ilyin, 1976, p. M2).
Michigan Test of English Language Proficiency The University of Michigan Ann Arbor, Michigan	Usually referred to as simply as "the Michigan," this test is designed for use as a part of a battery to determine if the examinee, typically a foreign-born applicant to an American university, is proficient enough in the English language to undertake university-level coursework. First published in 1968, this multiple-choice test contains vocabulary, structure, and reading comprehension items that may be administered to groups or individuals.
Secondary Level English Proficiency Test (SLEP) Educational Testing Service Princeton, New Jersey	The SLEP (usually pronounced like "slept" without the *t*) is a group-administered test appropriate for use in grades 7 through 12. The test is designed to be helpful in making various kinds of language-related placement decisions such as whether or not a bilingual education program is indicated. The test contains a Listening Comprehension and a Reading Comprehension section, with each of these sections containing four subtests. A criterion-related validity study conducted by the test publisher with 1,239 students in 20 states indicated that statistically significant correlations existed between SLEP test scores, number of years of English study, and number of years the examinee has lived in the United States.
Test of English as a Foreign Language (TOEFL) Jointly sponsored by: The College Board, New York, New York The Graduate Record Examinations Board, Princeton, New Jersey Educational Testing Service, Princeton, New Jersey	Referred to as the TOEFL (pronounced like "toe" and "full" combined), this test is the most widely used instrument for determining if a nonnative English speaker has proficiency in English sufficient to do university-level coursework. The TOEFL is a secure test that is only administered at authorized test centers—approximately a thousand such centers exist in 135 countries. Administered to groups or individuals, the TOEFL consists of multiple-choice items grouped into three separately timed sections: Listening Comprehension (administered via audiotape), Structure and Written Expression (including items which tap knowledge of grammar), and Reading Comprehension and Vocabulary. A new equated form of the test is published monthly as are statistical reports for each test form. Included among the many supplementary materials made available by the test publisher are publications and a videotape for use in training personnel involved in test administration and bulletins covering various aspects of test administration, scoring, and interpretation.

area of vocabulary, reading, spelling, and arithmetic; it was developed in consultation with experts in the field of adult education.

Before leaving the topic of achievement tests, we will briefly point out that there are at least two distinctly different types of achievement test items. One such type of item demands only rote memory. An example of such an item on an examination designed to measure mastery of the material in this chapter might be question 1 below:

1. One type of item that could be used in an achievement test is an item that requires
   a. remote memory
   b. rote memory
   c. memory loss
   d. none of the above

Alternatively, items in achievement tests could require the test taker to not only know and understand the material but to be able to apply it. In a test of English proficiency, for example, it might be important for the examinee to know more than vocabulary or rules of grammar; items that gauge the ability of the examinee to understand or speak conversational English might be of far greater importance.

TESTS OF APTITUDE

True or false: "Achievement tests measure learned knowledge whereas aptitude tests measure innate potential." The correct answer to this question is "False." To

---

Figure 10–1 *The World (of test items) According to Students.*

Would you study longer for a test composed of fill-in-the-blank items than you would for a test of true/false items? According to Thomas Rocklin, the answer is "Yes." In a study designed to examine the different ways students perceive different types of items, Rocklin (1987) asked college student subjects ($n = 31$) to make judgments concerning the dissimilarity between each possible pair created from eight item types (true/false, multiple-choice, essay, fill-in-the-blank, matching, short-answer, analogy, and arrangement). Suggestive evidence was found to support the idea that college students discriminate among test items on three dimensions; included here is the degree to which items are perceived as (1) difficult, (2) objective (presumably with respect to scoring), and (3) drawing on reasoning or analytic skills. An interesting finding was that objectivity was negatively correlated with fairness—presumably, Rocklin hypothesizes, "because objective tests either 'don't let you demonstrate what you know' or because they can be 'tricky'" (p. 7). Rocklin writes that "Students make important decisions about their study strategies based on expectations about testing" (p. 2) and that "students report that they spend considerably more time reviewing for supply items than for selection items" (p. 8).

understand why this is so, consider for a moment how we acquire knowledge. Each of us is born with a mental and physical apparatus that does have certain limitations—not everyone is born with the same mental and physical gifts as everyone else. Working with the biological equipment we have in conjunction with psychological factors (such as motivation) and environmental factors (such as educational opportunities), we are constantly acquiring information through everyday life experiences and through formal learning experiences such as coursework in school. The primary difference between tests that are referred to as "achievement tests" and those that are referred to as "aptitude tests" is that aptitude tests tend to focus more on informal learning or life experiences as their subject matter, whereas achievement tests tend to focus on the learning that has occurred as a result of relatively structured input. Keeping this distinction in mind, consider the two items below, the first from a hypothetical achievement test and the second from a hypothetical aptitude test:

1. A correlation of .7 between variables X and Y in a predictive validity study accounts for what percentage of the variance?
   a. 7%
   b. 70%
   c. .7%
   d. 49%
   e. 25%
2. o is to O as x is to
   a. /
   b. %
   c. X
   d. Y

At least on the face of it, item 1 appears to be more dependent on formal learning experiences than does item 2. The successful completion of item 1 hinges on familiarity with the concept of correlation and the knowledge that the variance accounted for by a correlation coefficient is equal to the square of the coefficient (in this case, $.7^2$, or .49—choice "d"). The successful completion of item 2 requires experience with the concept of size, as well as the ability to grasp the concept of analogies, two abilities that tend to be gleaned from life experiences (witness how quickly you determined that the correct answer was choice "c"). It must also be kept in mind that the label "achievement" or "aptitude" for a test is very much dependent on the intended use of the test, not just on the type of items contained in it. It is possible for two tests to contain some of the same items and for one of these tests to be called an "aptitude" test whereas the other is referred to as an "achievement" test. Item 2 in our example was presented as representing an item that might appear on some aptitude test, though it might well appear on an achievement test if the area of learning covered by the latter test encompassed the concept of size and/or analogous thinking. Similarly, item 1, presented as an illustrative achievement test item, might well be used to assess aptitude (in statistics, or psychology, for example) were it to be included in a test that was not expressly designed to measure achievement in this area.

Aptitude tests, frequently referred to as "prognostic tests," are tests typically used to make predictions. Some of the tests we discuss illustrate how aptitude tests have been used to measure readiness for school, aptitude for college level work or graduate school, and aptitude for work in a particular profession (such as medicine, law, art, or music). Achievement tests may also be used for predictive purposes. Thus, for example, an individual who performs well on a first-semester foreign-language achievement test might be considered to be a good candidate for the second term's work. The assumption is made that, since the individual was able to master certain basic skills, the individual will be able to master more advanced skills—hence the achievement test has been used as if it were a test of aptitude. Few situations exist where the reverse is true—where a test expressly designed to test for aptitude is used as an achievement test. Note that when achievement tests are used to make predictions, they tend to draw on narrower (more formal) learning experiences and are therefore typically used to make predictions with respect to some equally narrow variable (for example, success in Basic French predicts success in Advanced French). Aptitude tests draw on a broader fund of information and abilities and are typically used to predict to broader variables (just as "general fund of information" might be used to predict to success in higher education). Another hallmark of the aptitude in contrast to the achievement test is the utilization of tasks that are not formally taught in the schools (such as figural analogies and number series)—chosen to reduce the likelihood that they had been specifically taught to the examinee.

To summarize the sometimes blurry distinction between achievement and aptitude tests: while both types of tests measure learning to some degree, achievement tests are typically more limited in scope in the learning they assess. Achievement tests reflect learning that has occurred under controlled and definable conditions, usually where there has been specific training. Aptitude tests tap a combination of learning experiences and inborn potential that was obtained under uncontrolled and nondefined conditions. Predictions about future learning and behavior can be made from both kinds of tests, though predictions made on the basis of achievement tests are usually limited to the subject matter of the test.

In the following sections, we survey some aptitude tests used in schools from entry level through graduate and professional institutions. Note that at the entry level an aptitude test is often referred to as a "readiness" test since its primary purpose is to assess the child's readiness for learning. As the level of education climbs, however, the term "readiness" is dropped in favor of the term "aptitude," although readiness is very much implied at all levels. The Scholastic Aptitude Test (SAT), given late in high school and widely used as a predictor of ability to do college-level work, might well have been called the "College Readiness Test." Similarly, the Graduate Record Examination (GRE) given in college and used as a predictor of ability to do graduate-level work, might have been christened the "Graduate School Readiness Examination." Both tests are presumed to be predictive of aptitude or readiness for advanced-level work. Such tests provide more than a mere indicator of "readiness." Especially at the upper levels, educational standards vary not only from community to community, but from school to school—even from class to class. Additionally, teacher prejudices as well as a host of other factors may enter into grading procedures. Aptitude tests represent a kind of "equalizer," for they provide a sample of academic performance on a standardized test that can be compared to the performance of all other students taking the test. When used in conjunction with grades and various other criteria, aptitude test data can be a good predictor of future academic success.

The Elementary School Level

The law mandates that children enter school at a particular chronological age (the age varies from state to state), though individual children of the same chronological age may vary in how ready they are to (1) separate from their parents, and (2) begin academic learning. Children come from a wide range of backgrounds and experiences, and their rates of physiological, psychological, and social development also vary widely. School readiness tests provide educators with a yardstick by which to assess pupils' abilities in areas as diverse as general information and sensory-motor skills.

The Metropolitan Readiness Tests (MRT)   The MRT is one of the many instruments designed to assess children's readiness and aptitude for formal education (see Table 10–4).

It is a group-administered battery that assesses the development of reading and mathematics skills important in the early stages of formal, school learning. The test is divided into two levels: Level I, to be used with beginning and middle kindergarteners, and Level II, which spans the end of kindergarten through first grade. There are two forms of the test at each level. The tests are orally administered in several sessions and are untimed though they typically require about 90 minutes or so to administer. A practice test (especially useful with young children who have had minimal or no prior test-taking experience) may be administered several days prior to the actual testing to help familiarize students with procedures and the format involved in taking such a test.

Normative data for the 1986 edition of the MRT are based on a national sample of approximately thirty thousand children. The standardization sample was stratified in terms of geographic regions, socioeconomic factors, prior school experience, and ethnic background. Data were obtained from both public and parochial schools and from both large and small schools. Split-half reliability coefficients for both forms of both levels of the MRT as well as Kuder-Richardson measures of internal consistency were in the acceptably high range. Content validity was developed through an extensive review of the literature, analysis of the skills involved in the reading process, and the development of test items that reflected these skills. Items were reviewed by minority consultants in an attempt to reduce (if not eliminate) any potential ethnic bias. The predictive validity of MRT scores has been examined with reference to later school achievement indices and the obtained validity coefficients have been acceptably high.

Another test battery, developed at least in part to provide a measure of aptitude that would be culturally fair, is the System of Multicultural Pluralistic Assessment or "SOMPA" as it is commonly known. We review this battery next, though as the reader will appreciate shortly, this multifaceted battery would also have qualified for placement elsewhere in this chapter. A closer look at one of the

Table 10–4

The Subtests of the Metropolitan Readiness Tests

Level I

Auditory Memory: four pictures containing familiar objects are presented. The examiner reads aloud several words. The child must select the picture that corresponds to the same sequence of words that were presented orally.

Rhyming: the examiner supplies the names of each of the pictures presented and then gives a fifth word that rhymes with one of them. The child must select the picture that rhymes with the examiner's word.

Letter Recognition: the examiner names different letters and the child must identify each from the series presented in the test booklet.

Visual Matching: a sample is presented and the child must select the choice that matches the sample.

School Language and Listening: the examiner reads a sentence and the child is instructed to select the picture that describes what was read. The task involves some inference-making and awareness of relevancy of detail.

Quantitative Language: comprehension of quantitative terms and knowledge of ordinal numbers and simple mathematical operations are assessed.

Level II

Beginning Consonants: four pictures representing familiar objects are presented in the test booklet and are named by the examiner. The examiner then supplies a fifth word (not presented), and the child must select the picture that begins with the same sound.

Sound-Letter Correspondence: a picture is presented followed by a series of letters. The examiner names the pictures and the child selects the choice that corresponds to the beginning sound of the pictured item.

Visual Matching: similar to the corresponding subtest at Level I, a model is presented and the child must select the choice that matches the model.

Finding Patterns: a stimulus consisting of several symbols is presented followed by a series of representative options. The child must select the option that contains the same sequence of symbols, even though presented in a larger grouping with more distractions.

School Language: similar to the School Language and Listening Test at Level I, the child must select the picture that corresponds to an orally presented sentence.

Listening: material is orally presented and the child must select the picture represented that reflects comprehension of, and the drawing of conclusions from, that material.

Quantitative Concepts ⎱ Both are optional tests that like the Quantitative Language
Quantitative Operations ⎰ of Level I assess comprehension of basic mathematical concepts and operations.

tests from the SOMPA, the Adaptive Behavior Inventory for Children, appears in the section on adaptive behavior in Chapter 17.

The SOMPA The SOMPA is an assessment system for measuring the cognitive abilities, perceptual-motor skills, and adaptive behavior of children from ages 5 through 11. The test is "pluralistic," as it is designed in part to compare test takers' scores to those of other children from similar sociocultural backgrounds. The tests used in the SOMPA include six instruments administered to the child and three instruments administered to the child's parent or primary caregiver. The instruments used with the child are (1) Physical Dexterity Tasks, (2) Bender

Visual Motor Gestalt Test, (3) Weight by Height, (4) Visual Acuity, (5) Auditory Acuity, and (6) the Wechsler intelligence scale appropriate for the age of the child. The three instruments administered to the parent are (1) Sociocultural Scales, (2) Adaptive Behavior Inventory for Children, and (3) Health History Inventory. Among the indices the user of the test can derive is an "Estimated Learning Potential" (ELP)—in essence, a Wechsler IQ score transformed with respect to "eth-class" (sociocultural) norms so that the examinee is being compared to members of his or her own sociocultural group.

In the light of PL 94-142, which mandated that social or cultural background be one of the factors considered in placement of children into special classes, there has been widespread interest in developing formal ways of identifying cognitive deficits as differentiated from physical or sociocultural deficits. Enter the SOMPA (Mercer & Lewis, 1979), which purports to be a comprehensive and culturally fair system of assessment from three perspectives—medical, social systems, and pluralistic—and one can readily appreciate why this test battery was greeted with a great deal of anticipation in the early 1980s.

Unfortunately, as numerous reviewers (such as Humphreys, 1985; Reynolds, 1985; Sandoval, 1985) of the system have now concluded, the SOMPA has failed to live up to its promise. Some of the many criticisms that have been leveled at this instrument are as follows:

- *The basic assumption on which the test rests is more a matter of opinion than fact and is very much open to question.* Test author Jane Mercer (1979), a sociologist, argues in the 164-page test manual that intelligence and learning potential are equally distributed among all ethnic and racial groups. According to this view, all prior mental testing has been from a perspective of "Anglo conformity" and all data derived from such tests are therefore artifacts of the tests used; real differences between the races do not exist.
- *Claims are made without substantiation.* It is asserted, for example, that an ELP "enables one to make inferences concerning the child's probable potential for future learning." While Mercer presents no data to support this claim, others (such as Reschly, 1982) have noted that ELP, unlike more traditional measures of intelligence, has not been meaningfully correlated to anything. Further, data from one study conducted over a four-year period suggested that ELP could be quite unstable; it could change rather dramatically over a four-year period (Wilkinson & Oakland, 1983a).
- *Aspects of the test do not appear to be technically sound.* In addition to questions raised concerning the stability of the ELP index, differences within scales as a function of demographic group have been noted; Wilkinson and Oakland (1983b) calculated a stability coefficient of .74 for females and only .23 for males on the SOMPA Trauma scale. With respect to that same scale, Sandoval (1985) observed that "a child who has been operated upon for removal of an appendix and had a long hospital stay and who later had an abssessed [sic] tooth removed might receive the same score as one who had to be operated upon for the removal of a brain tumor and who had a tooth removed" (p. 1523). Test-retest reliability coefficients for the SOMPA Health History Inventory have been recorded to be as low as −.08. Further, as Sandoval (1985) has noted, the SOMPA technical manual contains

"a number of inconsistencies from table to table with respect to numbers of subjects" (p. 1522).

- *Emphasis on classification supersedes emphasis on intervention with the result that the test data provide comparatively little help with the development of individual educational programs.* Reynolds (1985, p. 1521) could not justify committing so much time to administer this battery: "The emphasis on classification seems misplaced; an emphasis on prevention-intervention-habilitation is more in keeping with the needs of the field." Humphreys (1985) came to a similar conclusion and stated bluntly that what black and Hispanic children needed were "higher scores on measures of reading, listening, writing, computing, mathematics, and science, not ethclass IQs" (p. 1519).

One relatively favorable reviewer of the SOMPA summed up whatever contribution the test has made in the following way:

> The SOMPA represents an important, pragmatic, ideological, and theoretical challenge to traditional psychometric practice. Pragmatically, it reminds us that comprehensive child assessment demands the services of a multidimensional professional team; ideologically, it questions the fundamental value systems that permeate our standard techniques and argues for a dramatic shift in philosophical perspective; and, theoretically it raises several issues with respect to prevailing views about the constructs of intelligence, learning and achievement. (Rosenbach, 1984, p. 651)

The Secondary School Level

Perhaps the most obvious example of an aptitude test widely used in the schools at the secondary level is the Scholastic Aptitude Test (SAT). The test has been of value not only in the college selection process but also as an aid to high school guidance and job placement counselors in advising students about what course of action might be best for them. In addition to the SAT, the American College Testing (ACT) programs provide another well-known aptitude test.

How much do colleges really rely on criteria such as SAT scores in making college entrance decisions? Probably less than most people believe. Institutions of higher learning in this country differ widely with respect to their admission criteria. In one large-scale national survey of college admissions officers, it was found that only 48 percent of the responding institutions required SAT or ACT scores of all applicants (Undergraduate Admissions, 1980). Even among the schools that required these test scores, varying weights were accorded to the scores with respect to admission decisions. Highly selective institutions may admit large numbers of students with lower test scores and reject large numbers of students with high test scores (Harnett & Feldmesser, 1980). It has been argued that higher education is available to any American citizen who wants it and that "In no major system of higher education in the world is access to higher education less dependent on the results of a single examination or set of examinations than in the United States" (Hargadon, 1981, p. 1112). With that preface, we now go on to briefly describe the SAT—a test with which many of our readers have had some firsthand experience.

The Scholastic Aptitude Test (SAT)   The SAT was first introduced as an objective exam in 1926. In its present form the SAT is a three-hour test divided into two parts: Verbal and Mathematics. The Verbal part consists of sections that include Analogies, Reading Comprehension, Antonyms, and Sentence Completion. The Reading Comprehension section consists of reading passages containing subject material from a variety of academic areas such as science, social studies, and the humanities. The Sentence Completion section consists of single sentences or paragraphs in which one or two words have been omitted, and the examinee's task is to select the choice that best completes the written thought. Vocabulary knowledge is measured by performance on the Antonyms and Analogies items. In 1974, a Test of Standard Written English was introduced for the first time to assess the student's ability to comprehend the type of language utilized in most college textbooks. It consists of 50 multiple-choice questions and requires 30 minutes to complete. A Reading Comprehension score based on the Sentence Completion and Reading Comprehension sections is also computed. The Mathematics part of the SAT assesses the understanding and application of mathematical principles, as well as numerical reasoning ability. The subject matter of the test questions on this section assumes knowledge of the basic arithmetic operations such as addition, subtraction, multiplication, division, averages, percentages, odd-even integers, and geometric and algebraic concepts, including linear and quadratic equations, exponents, and factoring (Braswell, 1978).

Test items for the SAT are constructed by experts in the field and pretested on national samples during the actual examination. The experimental items are placed in separately timed sections of the examination. Such a pretesting procedure on a sample of examinees who are representative of the group that will be taking future forms of the test provides the test constructors with useful information regarding the value of proposed new items. The responses of students are statistically analyzed to determine the percent answering each question correctly, the percent choosing each of the distractor items, and the percent who omit the item; and an index of the response to each item with the total score on the test (that is, a difficulty rating for each item) is computed (Jones, Rowan, & Taylor, 1977). The test is under continual revision and the total time to develop an item may be upwards of 18 months.

The technical quality of the SAT is excellent. Reliability of recent forms of the test as measured by internal-consistency estimates have resulted in reliability coefficients in the .90s for both the Verbal and Mathematics scales. Research concerning the validity of the SAT has focused mostly on correlations between SAT scores and college grades, or on a combination of SAT scores and high school grades with college grades. In general, high school grades have been found to correlate higher with college grades than do SAT scores. When SAT scores and high school grade point average are combined, the correlation with college performance increases. In one study involving 4,283 students, it was found that high school percentile rank was the best single predictor of first-semester grade-point average in college. Combining high school percentile rank with SAT scores increased the correlation (Aleamoni & Oboler, 1978). Correlations between the Verbal and Mathematics parts of the SAT have been in the high .60s, a finding that suggests that overlapping skills, probably verbal in nature, are tapped on both parts of the exam.

The SAT is administered several times a year under carefully controlled conditions in cities throughout the United States and in foreign countries. Foreign language editions of the test have been made available, as have special editions for handicapped students. A special form (the Preliminary Scholastic Aptitude Test, or PSAT) is available for administration as a practice exam and as a tool for counselors. An authoritative source for more information, particularly technical information on this test, is *The College Board Technical Handbook for the Scholastic Aptitude Test and Achievement Tests* (Donlon, 1984).

In the fall of 1990, the College Board announced major changes in the SAT that began in 1991 and will be completed in 1994. The SAT will have two components: SAT-I: Reasoning Tests, and SAT-II: Subject Tests. SAT-I is set for introduction in 1994 and is to be composed of revised and expanded versions of the current SAT verbal and mathematical tests. An increased emphasis on critical reading will be incorporated into the verbal sections along with longer reading passages. Some math questions will require the student to produce a response and for the first time in the history of the examinations, students will be allowed to use calculators. SAT-II, as the achievement tests will be known, represents an expansion and revision of the current achievement tests. Tests will be in areas such as writing, literature, history, foreign languages, mathematics, and sciences (College Board Review, 1990–91). These changes in the SAT, field-tested over a three-year period with 100,000 students, are designed to make the test more "educationally relevant" with respect to its objectives of predicting college performance (Moses, 1991).

Detroit Tests of Learning Aptitude   Let us note at the outset that our discussion of this test under the subheading of secondary schools is somewhat arbitrary, for the test is designed for use with examinees ranging in age from 6 years to 17 years 11 months. We might also point out that our discussion of this test under the major heading of aptitudes is also somewhat arbitrary given the fact that its author (Hammill, 1985) sees little if any meaningful distinction between the terms *aptitude* and *intelligence*. At times Hammill (1985) uses these two terms interchangeably (see p. 2), and at other times he uses the terms as if they had different meanings (as on p. 8 of the manual, in the description of possible uses of the test: "to serve as a measurement device in research studies investigating aptitude, intelligence, and cognitive behavior"). But while Hammill treats *aptitude* and *intelligence* as synonyms, he does draw a distinction between the terms *tests of aptitude* and *tests of achievement*. After Gronlund (1985), Hammill (1985) views *achievement tests* as "built to sample specific knowledge and skills that are usually acquired through special formal or informal instruction (e.g., typing, algebra, phonics)" and *aptitude tests* as "built to sample behaviors that are common to all people in a society and that are generally acquired incidentally (e.g., discrimination, reasoning, concentration, vocabulary, recall ability, etc.)" (p. 2).[1]

---

1. As we saw in Chapter 8, scholars may—and often do—disagree as to the definition of intelligence. Although the present authors understand the logic of Hammill's (1985) conceptualization of *intelligence* as synonymous with *aptitude,* we have difficulty accepting it. We view intelligence as a broader concept than aptitude, and one that subsumes aptitude (as well as *achievement*). The sentence "Bill is an intelligent person" implies achievement as well as capability, whereas sentences such as "Bill has aptitude" or "Bill is a person with aptitude" would appear to speak more to Bill's capability than to his achievement or learning.

Table 10–5

The Subtests of the Detroit Tests of Learning Aptitude

Subtest	Description
Word Opposites	Knowledge of antonyms and, more generally, vocabulary, is tapped by this test. Given a word, it is the examinee's task to provide its opposite.
Sentence Imitation	The examinee's task here is to repeat a sentence read by the examiner. The test taps concentration ability as well as rote sequential memory.
Oral Directions	This test assesses the examinee's ability to follow directions administered orally with respect to paper-and-pencil tasks. A number of skills such as attention, short-term memory, manual dexterity, and spatial relations may be assessed in this manner.
Word Sequence	The examiner reads a series of unrelated words and it is the examinee's task to repeat them in the same order. Concentration, attention, and short-term memory are some of the skills tapped by this subtest.
Story Construction	The ability to create a logical story is assessed in this task; the examinee is presented with pictures and asked to make up a story about them.
Design Reproduction	Various designs are shown to the examinee for a brief period of time and it is the examinee's task to reproduce the designs. A number of skills such as attention to detail, short-term visual memory, spatial relations, and manual dexterity are assessed.
Object Sequences	Attention and visual short-term memory are assessed in this test, which requires the examinee to recall a numbered row of pictures after exposure to the same pictures in a different order.
Symbolic Relations	Problem-solving and visual short-term memory are two of the abilities tapped by this test, which requires the examinee to look at a design that has a part missing and then select from a series of designs the part that was missing from the first design.
Conceptual Matching	Below a stimulus picture are ten other pictures; the examinee's task is to select the pictures most closely related to the stimulus pictures. The test taps the examinee's ability to abstract and to see theoretical as well as practical relationships.
Word Fragments	Words with varying amounts of print missing are presented for the examinee to read aloud; the ability to form closure and to recognize partially printed words is necessary for the examinee to be successful on these items.
Letter Sequence	Short-term visual memory and attention are two of the skills tapped by this test, which requires the examinee to recreate a series of letters that is presented visually.

First published in 1935, revised in the mid-1960s (Baker & Leland, 1967), and revised and restandardized more recently (Hammill, 1985), the Detroit Tests of Learning Aptitude—or the DTLA-2 as it is now referred to—is an individually administered test composed of the 11 subtests listed in Table 10–5. Raw scores on the subtests are converted to standard scores, and the sum of the standard scores on various combinations of the 11 subtests is used to compute 9 composite scores (or "quotients"—a misnomer since there is no division involved in obtaining them), including a composite score indicative of general intelligence/overall aptitude (Figure 10–2). The individual subtest scores as well as the 9 composite scores were designed to be useful for diagnostic purposes. Decisions regarding retaining or dropping particular subtests of the original DTLA were made on the basis of a survey of 100 professionals who were known users of the test. Each user was asked to list the five subtests found to be most useful, and the five subtests found to be least useful.

According to the test manual, the DTLA-2 was standardized on 1,532 people in 30 states selected with respect to various demographic characteristics, including gender, age, race, ethnicity, level of education of parents, geographic area (Northeast, North Central, South, and West), and residence (rural/urban). Each DTLA user (contacted by means of the publisher's customer files) who consented to participate in the standardization process was "asked to test approximately 20 children who would represent their area" (Hammill, 1985, p. 55), though no details are provided concerning how the children were actually selected. Some studies attesting to the psychometric soundness of this instrument are reported in the test manual. One independently undertaken factor analysis of the intercorrelation among subtest scaled scores yielded "three interpretable factors that provide little support for combining the subtest scores into the nine aptitude areas described in the manual" (Aiken, 1987, p. 233).

The College Level and Beyond

If you are a college student planning to pursue further education after graduation, you are probably familiar with acronyms such as GRE, MAT, MCAT, and LSAT. Respectively, these acronyms stand for the Graduate Record Examination, the Miller Analogies Test, the Medical College Admission Test, and the Law School Admission Test. The GRE is widely used as one criterion for admission to many graduate school programs. The MAT is a 100-item multiple-choice analogy test that draws not only on the examinee's ability to perceive relationships, but also on general intelligence, vocabulary, and academic learning. As an example, complete the following analogy:

Classical conditioning is to *Pavlov,* as *operant conditioning* is to
  (a) Freud
  (b) Rogers
  (c) Skinner
  (d) Jung
  (e) Westheimer

Successful completion of this item demands not only the ability to understand the relationship between classical conditioning and Pavlov, but also knowing that it was B. F. Skinner (choice "c") whose name—of the names listed—is best associated with operant conditioning.

Applicants for training in certain professions are required to take specialized examinations. Students applying to medical school are required to take the Medical College Admission Test (MCAT). Offered twice a year, the MCAT is a mul-

Summary and Profile Sheet

D T L A-2

Detroit Tests of Learning Aptitude

Donald D. Hammill

Name _Jane Sanford_ Male ☐ Female ☑

	Year	Month	Day
Date tested	79	9	25
Date of birth	65	3	4
Age	14	6	21

School _Jefferson Elem._ Grade _9_

Examiner's Name _Mr. Bryant_

Examiner's Title _diagnostician_

SECTION I   RECORD OF SUBTEST SCORES

Subtests	Raw Scores	%iles	Std. Scores
I Word Opposites	34	16	7
II Sentence Imitation	18	50	10
III Oral Directions	25	5	5
IV Word Sequences	22	91	14
V Story Construction	31	98	16
VI Design Reproduction	40	63	11
VII Object Sequences	37	37	9
VIII Symbolic Relations	25	75	12
IX Conceptual Matching	19	5	5
X Word Fragments	38	75	12
XI Letter Sequences	65	95	15

SECTION II   OTHER TEST SCORES

Name	Date	Std. Score	DTLA-2 Equiv.
SIT	79-6	104	104
DAB - Total	79-4	90	90
CTBS - Reading	79-2	4	93
CTBS - Language	79-2	4	93
CTBS - Math	79-2	3	85

SECTION III   PROFILE OF SUBTEST SCORES

Figure 10–2 *A Sample Profile Sheet from the Detroit Tests of Learning Aptitude (DTLA-2).*

tiple-choice test divided into four separately timed sections. These include Verbal Ability (comprising 75 items to be completed in 20 minutes), Quantitative Ability (50 items to be completed in 45 minutes), General Information (75 items to be completed in 25 minutes), and Science (86 items to be completed in 60 minutes). Items in the Verbal Ability section consist of analogy items, synonyms, and antonyms. The Quantitative section assesses knowledge and application of algebraic, geometric, and arithmetic principles. The General Information section includes items pertaining to a variety of subject areas such as music and sports; and the Science section, probably the most closely related to the field of medicine, includes test items pertaining to biology, chemistry, and physics. While the test

SECTION IV WORKSPACE FOR COMPUTING COMPOSITE QUOTIENTS

DTLA-2 COMPOSITES	WO	SI	OD	WS	SC	DR	OS	SR	CM	WF	LS	SUM OF STD. SCORES	QUOTS.
GEN. INTELLIGENCE OR APTITUDE (GIQ)	7	10	5	14	16	11	9	12	5	12	15	= 116	(104)
VERBAL (VBQ)	7	10	5	14	16					12		= 64	(105)
NONVERBAL (NVQ)						11	9	12	5		15	= 52	(103)
CONCEPTUAL (COQ)	7	10	5		16			12	5	12		= 67	(97)
STRUCTURAL (STQ)				14		11	9				15	= 49	(115)
ATTENTION-ENHANCED (AEQ)		10	5	14		11	9				15	= 64	(105)
ATTENTION-REDUCED (ARQ)	7				16			12	5	12		= 52	(103)
MOTOR-ENHANCED (MEQ)			5			11	9				15	= 40	(100)
MOTOR-REDUCED (MRQ)	7	10		14	16			12	5	12		= 76	(106)

SECTION V PROFILE OF COMPOSITE QUOTIENTS

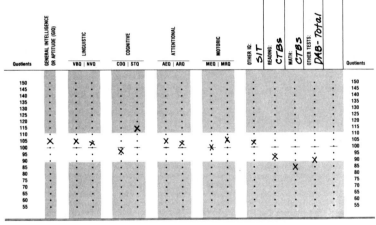

Figure 10–2 *(continued)*

continues to be used as one criterion in medical school admission, scores on it have not been found to be predictive of class rank in medical school.

Applicants to law school are required to take the Law School Admissions Test (LSAT). The test is presented in two testing sessions, one in the morning and one in the afternoon, and a separate score is obtained for each session. The morning session consists of five separately timed sections: Logical Reasoning, Practical Judgment, Data Interpretation, Quantitative Comparisons, and Principles and Cases. Based on the premise that the legal profession itself relies heavily on verbal skills (both in comprehension and communication), the LSAT is purposely developed to primarily reflect verbal abilities. The test items themselves are designed to assess comprehension, interpretation, critical analysis, evaluation, and application of information. To this end, each test item presents a body of information followed by multiple-choice items. The Logical Reasoning and Practical Judgment sections present information in the form of reading passages while the Data Interpretation section employs graphs and tables. Subject matter representative of many different fields of study is included in the test. The only section that contains legally oriented subject material is the Principles and Cases section, which presents hypothetical situations involving legal principles. It is assumed, however, that the test taker has had no previous legal training and that the answers may be obtained through general reasoning skills. The afternoon session is divided into three sections (Error Recognition, Sentence Correction, and Usage) that together form the Writing Ability Score. Taken together, these sections provide an indication of ability to express oneself in writing. Predictive validity studies examining the relationship between score obtained on the LSAT and grade-point average of first-year law students have yielded relatively low correlations.

Numerous other aptitude tests have been developed to assess specific kinds of academic and/or occupational aptitudes. For example, the Seashore Measures of Musical Talents (Seashore, 1938) is a musical aptitude test administered with the aid of a prerecorded record or tape. The six subtests measure specific aspects of musical talent (for example, comparing different notes and rhythms on variables such as loudness, pitch, time, and timbre). The Horn Art Aptitude Inventory is a measure of art aptitude that is divided into two sections. The Scribbles and Doodles section contains items thought to measure variables such as clarity of thought and originality. Items in the Imagery section contain key lines or "springboards" from art masterpieces to be incorporated in the examinee's artistic production. Scoring categories for the Imagery section include Design, Imagination, and Scope of Interests.

DIAGNOSTIC TESTS

In medical jargon, the noun *diagnosis* may be defined as "the act or process of identifying or determining the nature of a disease through examination." In the language of educational assessment, a diagnostic test is designed to pinpoint where a student is having difficulty with a particular academic skill. Typically included in such a test will be a number of subtests, each analyzing a specific knowledge or skill required to successfully perform a specific task. Thus, for example, a diagnostic reading test is designed to segment the various components of reading so that the specific problem areas with respect to the skill of reading will be brought into full relief. It is important to emphasize that diagnostic tests do not necessarily provide information that will answer questions concerning *why* the learning difficulty exists; it will remain for other educational, psychological, and perhaps medical examinations to answer the "why" question. In general, diagnostic tests are administered to students who have already demonstrated their problem with a particular subject area either through their poor performance in the classroom or their poor performance on some achievement test. It is therefore understandable that diagnostic tests tend to contain simpler items than do achievement tests designed for use with members of the same grade.

Reading Tests

The ability to read is integral to virtually all classroom learning, and so it is not surprising that many diagnostic tests are available to help pinpoint difficulties in acquiring this skill (for example, the Stanford Diagnostic Reading Test, the Metropolitan Reading Instructional Tests, the Diagnostic Reading Scales, the Durrell Analysis of Reading Test). For illustrative purposes we briefly describe one such diagnostic battery, the Woodcock Reading Mastery Tests.

The Woodcock Reading Mastery Tests—Revised (WRMT-R)   Developed by Richard W. Woodcock and typically referred to as "the Woodcock," the tests were revised in 1987, and are suitable for children age 5 and older, and adults up to age 75—and beyond according to the promotional literature. The subtests include:

- *Letter Identification:* This subtest consists of items that measure the ability to name letters presented in different forms. Both cursive/manuscript and uppercase/lowercase letters are presented.
- *Word Identification:* This subtest consists of words in isolation arranged in order of increasing difficulty. The student is asked to read each word aloud.
- *Word Attack:* This subtest consists of nonsense syllables that incorporate phonetic as well as structural analysis skills. The student is asked to pronounce each nonsense syllable.
- *Word Comprehension:* This subtest consists of items that assess word meaning by using a four-part analogy format.
- *Passage Comprehension:* This subtest consists of phrases, sentences, or short paragraphs read silently in which a word is missing. The student must supply the missing word.

The tests are individually administered and are designed to measure skills inherent in reading. The tests come in two forms labeled G and H and each form contains the five subtests listed above (Form G also contains a test labeled "Visual Auditory Learning"). A cassette tape is packaged with the tests, and serves as a guide to the proper pronunciation of the Word Attack items and the Word Identification items. Test scores may be combined to form what are referred to as "clusters" such as a Readiness cluster (the Visual-Auditory Learning and Letter Identification tests), a Basic Skills cluster (the Word Identification and Word Attack tests), a Reading Comprehension cluster (the Word Comprehension and Passage Comprehension tests), a Total Reading—Full Scale cluster (the Word Identification, Word Attack, Word Comprehension, and Passage Comprehension tests), and a Total Reading—Short Scale (the Word Identification and Passage Comprehension tests). The latter scale may be used for quick-screening (about 15 minutes) purposes, although each cluster of tests typically takes between 10 and 30 minutes to administer. An optional microcomputer software program is also available for score conversion and storage of pre- and posttest scores.

Math Tests

The Stanford Diagnostic Mathematics Test, the Metropolitan Mathematics Instructional Tests, the Diagnostic Mathematics Inventory, and the KeyMath Revised: A Diagnostic Inventory of Essential Mathematics exemplify some of the many tests that have been developed to help diagnose difficulties with arithmetic and mathematical concepts. Items on such tests typically analyze the skills and knowledge necessary for segregating mathematical operations into component parts. The KeyMath Revised test, for example, contains 13 subtests designed to assess areas such as basic concepts (including knowledge of symbols, numbers, and fractions), operations (including skill in addition, subtraction, multiplication, division, and mental computation), and applications (numerical problems employing variables such as money and time). Diagnostic information is obtained from an evaluation of the examinee's performance in the various areas, subtests, and items. Total test scores are translated into grade equivalents, area performance may be translated into a general pattern of mathematical functioning, and subtest performance may be translated into a profile illustrating strengths and weaknesses. For each item on the test, the manual lists a description of the skill involved and a corresponding behavior objective—information useful in determinations concerning skills to be included in a remedial program. A computerized scoring program converts raw scores into derived scores, summarizes the examinee's performance, and offers suggestions for remedial instruction.

Other Diagnostic Tests

In addition to individually administered diagnostic tests such as the KeyMath Revised, a number of diagnostic tests designed for group administration have also been developed. Two examples of group diagnostic tests are the Stanford Diagnostic Reading Test (SDRT) and the Stanford Diagnostic Mathematics Test (SDMT). Although developed independently and standardized on separate populations, the two instruments share certain characteristics related to test design and format. Both instruments are available in two forms, and both are divided into four overlapping levels that assess performance from grade 1 through high school. The SDRT consists of ten subtests that reflect skills required in three major areas of reading: decoding, vocabulary, and comprehension. The SDMT consists of three subtests administered at all levels. Norm-referenced as well as criterion-referenced information is provided in the test manual for each of these tests. Normative data are presented in terms of percentile ranks, stanines, grade equivalents, and scaled scores. Criterion-referenced information is provided for each skill through the use of a "progress indicator," a cutoff score that shows if the student is sufficiently competent in that skill to progress to the next stage of the instructional program. The manuals for both instruments include an index of behavioral objectives useful in prescriptive teaching strategies.

Learning Disabilities Assessment

Some children do poorly in school despite the fact that they are at least in the average range of intellectual ability. When the source of the learning problem is not a physical handicap or the result of emotional disturbance, economic deprivation, or mental retardation, the diagnosis "specific learning disability" is applicable. Samuel A. Kirk is credited with coining the term *learning disability* at a conference in support of the Fund for Perceptually Handicapped Children. Kirk suggested that this term be used to describe children with learning problems in the area of language, communication, and reading. As a result of Kirk's efforts, the Association for Children with Learning Disabilities—since renamed the Association for Children and Adults with Learning Disabilities—was formed. But what exactly is a "learning disability"? An answer to this question can be found in the definition published in the *Education for All Handicapped Children Act of 1975* (Public Law 94-142), at Section 5(b)(4):

> Specific learning disability means a disorder in one or more of the basic psychological processes involved in understanding or in using language, spoken or written, which may manifest itself in an imperfect ability to listen, think, speak, read, write, spell, or to do mathematical calculations. The term includes such conditions as perceptual handicaps, brain injury, minimal brain dysfunction, dyslexia, and developmental aphasia. The term does not include children who have learning problems which are primarily the result of visual, hearing, or motor handicaps, or mental retardation, or of environmental, cultural, or economic disadvantages.

Other characteristics often associated with learning disabilities (LD) include hyperactivity, perceptual-motor impairments, emotional disability, general coordination deficits, disorders of attention (such as distractibility or perseveration), impulsivity, disorders of memory and thinking, equivocal neurological signs, language problems, and disorders of speech and hearing. The *Federal Register* dated December 29, 1977, mandated that the diagnosis of specific learning disability be multidisciplinary in nature and be made by three people, including (1) a teacher or other specialist knowledgeable in the field of the suspected handicap, (2) the child's regular teacher, and (3) at least one person qualified to conduct individual diagnostic examinations of children (such as a school psychologist, speech language pathologist, or remedial reading teacher). The diagnosis of specific learning disability could be made only if the child demonstrated a discrepancy between ability and achievement in one or more of the following areas: oral expression, listening comprehension, written expression, basic reading skill, reading comprehension, mathematics calculation, or mathematics reasoning. The existence of a discrepancy between the child's achievement and expected level of achievement (the latter criterion based on the child's ability as measured by an intelligence test and the child's age) is emphasized in the federal guidelines partly to emphasize the view that a learning disability is not a minor or temporary condition.

In the years following the federal mandate to identify children with a "severe discrepancy between achievement and intellectual ability" (Procedures for Evaluating Specific Learning Disabilities, 1977, p. 65083), individual states employed a wide array of methods in an attempt to comply (Shepard, 1983). In its general form, the most common solution to the problem has entailed three steps: (1) quantifying achievement, (2) quantifying intellectual ability, and (3) developing some formula for determining when a "severe discrepancy" exists between the two. Existing formulas in the states have employed a number of variables such as grade-level deviation scores or standard scores on ability and achievement tests. Telzrow (1985) presents a highly readable account of some problems inherent in the use of some common discrepancy methods. Her review of the area also covers nonmeasurement variables affecting LD identification such as pressure on teachers to "find and fill" (that is, *find* LD children and *fill* the classes funded for that purpose) or "keep and teach" (that is, *keep* as many children as possible in the regular classroom when funding for special classes dries up).

A wealth of clinical leads contained in the intelligence test protocol can provide the clinician with clues regarding a suspected learning disability. More specialized tests might then be employed to bring into relief the areas of impaired functioning as well as areas of strength in the examinee's receptive, expressive, and information-processing abilities. Tests and observational procedures designed to evaluate sensory functioning, motor functioning, sensory-motor integration, cognitive processes, and language may all be employed in the examination. Current thought on linking such assessments can be found in Brown and Campione (1986), Embretson (1987, 1988), and Feuerstein et al. (1987).

PSYCHOEDUCATIONAL TEST BATTERIES

Psychoeducational test batteries are test kits that generally contain two types of tests: those that measure abilities related to academic success and those that measure educational achievement in areas such as reading and arithmetic. Data derived from these batteries allow for normative comparisons (how the student compares with other students within the same age group), as well as an evaluation of the test taker's own strengths and weaknesses—all the better to plan educational interventions.

Typical of the psychoeducational battery is the inclusion of a measure of cognitive ability. However, as we will see in our brief survey of three batteries below (the Kaufman Assessment Battery for Children, the Differential Ability Scales, and the Woodcock-Johnson Psycho-Educational Battery—Revised), the terminology used to label cognitive ability, as well as its definition and measurement, is varied. More uniformity exists with respect to the definition and measurement of areas related to educational achievement.

The Kaufman Assessment Battery for Children (K-ABC)

Alan and Nadine Kaufman, a husband/wife team of psychologists (Figure 10–3) approached the task of test development with some experience; both had previously worked closely with Dorothea McCarthy in the development of the McCarthy Scales of Children's Abilities, and Alan Kaufman had worked with David Wechsler on the development of the WISC-R.

The K-ABC is an individually administered test of both intelligence and achievement that was designed for use with normal and exceptional children from age 2½ through age 12½. According to the Kaufmans, a child's intelligence may be defined in terms of the effectiveness of his or her information-processing skills and problem-solving ability. This conception of intelligence is based at least in

Figure 10–3 *The Kaufmans—Nadine and Alan.*

part on the work of Luria (1966a, 1966b) and others (such as Das, Kirby, & Jarman, 1975), who identified two basic types of human information processing, sequential and simultaneous—which, you may recall, were discussed in detail in Chapter 8. Some characteristics of "sequential learners" and "simultaneous learners" along with corresponding teaching strategies are summarized in Table 10–6.[2] A rationale of the K-ABC is that an understanding of the abilities and problem-solving strategies of the test taker better equips the test user to diagnose and ultimately remediate educational deficits (Gunnison, 1984).

The K-ABC contains 16 subtests that yield scores in areas referred to as Mental Processing (conceptualized as "fluid" abilities) and Achievement (conceptualized as "crystallized" abilities and referring to school-related skills and knowledge). The Mental Processing Composite (MPC) score is derived from scores in its two component areas (referred to as Sequential Processing and Simultaneous Processing). The "fluid" versus "crystallized" dichotomy stems from Cattell's (1971) work, wherein knowledge of facts corresponds to crystallized ability and information-processing skills correspond to fluid ability. The test authors argued that an assessment strategy including assessment of achievement (crystallized ability) as well as intelligence (fluid ability) is optimal in the assessment of preschool and school-aged children. Table 10–7 contains a description of the 16 subtests of the K-ABC. Note that a maximum of 13 of these subtests will be administered to any one child.

---

2. Although the Kaufmans have made a convincing case for the utility of the distinction between sequential versus simultaneous learning, factor-analytic evidence supports the contention that these two types of learning are not entirely independent (Bracken, 1985; Keith, 1985).

Table 10–6

Characteristics and Teaching Guidelines for Sequential and Simultaneous Learners

Learner characteristics

The sequential learner:	*The simultaneous learner:*
The sequential learner solves problems best by mentally arranging small amounts of information in consecutive, linear, step-by-step order. He/she is most at home with verbal instructions and cues, because the ability to interpret spoken language depends to a great extent on the sequence of words.	The simultaneous learner solves problems best by mentally integrating and synthesizing many parallel pieces of information at the same time. He/she is most at home with visual instructions and cues, because the ability to interpret the environment visually depends on perceiving and integrating many details at once.

Sequential processing is especially important in:

- learning and retaining basic arithmetic facts
- memorizing lists of spelling words
- making associations between letters and their sounds
- learning the rules of grammar, the chronology of historical events
- remembering details
- following a set of rules, directions, steps
- solving problems by breaking them down into their component parts or steps

Sequential learners who are weak in simultaneous processing may have difficulty with:

- sight word recognition
- reading comprehension
- understanding mathematical or scientific principles
- using concrete, hands-on materials
- using diagrams, charts, maps
- summarizing, comparing, evaluating

Simultaneous processing is especially important in:

- recognizing the shape and physical appearance of letters and numbers
- interpreting the overall effect or meaning of pictures and other visual stimuli, such as maps and charts
- understanding the overall meaning of a story or poem
- summarizing, comparing, evaluating
- comprehending mathematical or scientific principles
- solving problems by visualizing them in their entirety

Simultaneous learners who are weak in sequential processing may have difficulty with:

- word attack, decoding, phonics
- breaking down science or arithmetic problems into their component parts
- interpreting the parts and features of a design or drawing
- understanding the rules of games
- understanding and following oral instructions
- remembering specific details and sequence of a story

The standardization sample Two thousand children between the ages of 2½ and 12½ years served as subjects in the standardization sample. The sample was designed to be representative of the population of the United States based on 1980 census data and it appears to be satisfactory in this regard (Coffman, 1985; Kamphaus & Reynolds, 1984; Mertz, 1984). The sample was stratified at each age group by the variables of sex, race, socioeconomic status, geographic region, and community size. Exceptional children, including children with learning disabilities and children with behavior problems, were included in the standardization sample.

Table 10–6 *(continued)*

Teaching guidelines	
For the sequential learner:	*For the simultaneous learner:*
1. Present material step by step, gradually approaching the overall concept or skill. Lead up to the big question with a series of smaller ones. Break the task into parts.	1. Present the overall concept or question before asking the child to solve the problem. Continue to refer back to the task, question, or desired outcome.
2. Get the child to verbalize what is to be learned. When you teach a new word, have the child say it, aloud or silently. Emphasize verbal cues, directions, and memory strategies.	2. Get the child to visualize what is to be learned. When you teach a new word, have the child write it and picture it mentally, see it on the page in the mind's eye. Emphasize visual cues, directions, and memory strategies.
3. Teach and rehearse the steps required to do a problem or complete a task. Continue to refer back to the details or steps already mentioned or mastered. Offer a logical structure or procedure by appealing to the child's verbal/temporal orientation.	3. Make tasks concrete wherever possible by providing manipulative materials, pictures, models, diagrams, graphs. Offer a sense of the whole by appealing to the child's visual/spatial orientation.
For example, the sequential learner may look at one or two details of a picture but miss the visual image as a whole. To help such a student toward an overall appreciation of the picture, start with the parts and work up to the whole. Rather than beginning with, "What does the picture show?" or "How does the picture make you feel?" first ask about details: "What is the little boy in the corner doing?" "Where is the dog?" "What expression do you see on the woman's face?" "What colors are used in the sky?" Lead up to questions about the overall interpretation or appreciation: "How do all these details give you clues about what is happening in this picture?" "How does this picture make you feel?" The sequential learner prefers a step-by-step teaching approach, one that may emphasize the gradual accumulation of details.	The simultaneous learner may react to a picture as a whole but may miss details. To help such a student notice the parts that contribute to the total visual image, begin by establishing an overall interpretation or reaction: "What does the picture show?" "How does the picture make you feel?" Then consider the details: "What is the expression on the woman's face?" "What is the little boy in the corner doing?" "What colors are used in the sky?" Relate the details to the student's initial interpretation: "How do these details explain why the picture made you feel the way it did?" The simultaneous learner responds best to a holistic teaching approach that focuses on groups of details or images and stresses the overall meaning or configuration of the task.

Source: Kaufman, Kaufman, and Goldsmith (1984)

Psychometric properties In general, satisfactory estimates of test-retest and split-half reliability for the test have been reported by the test's authors. Test-retest reliability coefficients ranged from .77 to .97 for 246 children who spanned the age range of the battery and were tested twice at intervals of two to four weeks.

The manual for the K-ABC presents the results of 43 validity studies conducted before publication of the test. Comparisons were made with other tests of ability and achievement using varied samples of subjects. In these, as well as other studies conducted subsequent to the test's publication, reported correlations have

Table 10–7

A Description of the K-ABC Subtests

Sequential Processing Scale

Hand Movements (ages 2-0 through 12-9)—Performing a series of hand movements in the same sequence performed by the examiner.

Number Recall (ages 2-6 through 12-5)—Repeating a series of digits in the same sequence spoken by the examiner.

Word Order (ages 4-0 through 12-5)—Touching a series of silhouettes of common objects in the same sequence as these objects were named orally by the examiner.

Simultaneous Processing Scale

Magic Window (ages 2-6 through 4-11)—Identifying a picture that the examiner exposes by slowly moving it behind a narrow window; hence, the picture is only partially visible at any one time.

Face Recognition (ages 2-6 through 4-11)—Selecting from a group photograph the one or two faces that were exposed briefly.

Gestalt Closure (ages 2-6 through 4-11)—Naming an object or scene pictured in a partially completed "inkblot" drawing.

Triangles (ages 4-0 through 12-5)—Assembling several identical triangles into an abstract pattern that matches a model.

Matrix Analogies (ages 5-0 through 12-5)—Selecting the meaningful picture or abstract design that best completes a visual analogy.

Spatial Memory (ages 5-0 through 12-5)—Recalling the placement of pictures on a page that was exposed briefly.

Photo Series (ages 6-0 through 12-5)—Placing photographs of an event in chronological order.

Achievement Scale

Expressive Vocabulary (ages 2-0 through 4-11)—Naming the object pictured in a photograph.

Faces and Places (ages 2-0 through 12-5)—Naming the well-known person, fictional character, or place pictured in a photograph.

Arithmetic (ages 3-0 through 12-5)—Demonstrating knowledge of numbers and mathematical concepts, counting and computational skills, and other school-related arithmetic abilities.

Riddles (ages 3-0 through 12-5)—Inferring the name of a concrete or abstract concept when given a list of its characteristics.

Reading/Decoding (ages 5-0 through 12-5)—Identifying letters and reading words.

Reading/Understanding (ages 7-0 through 12-5)—Demonstrating reading comprehension by following commands given in sentences.

tended to be high between measures such as the K-ABC Mental Processing Composite and (1) the SB:FE Test Composite, and (2) the WISC-R Full Scale IQ, as well as comparable measures on other tests (Bloom et al., 1988; Hayden, Furlong, & Linnemayer, 1988; Klanderman, Perney, & Kroeschell, 1985; Krohn & Lamp, 1989; Krohn, Lamp, & Phelps, 1988; Naglieri, 1985a, 1985b; Naglieri & Anderson, 1985; Smith & Lyon, 1987; Smith, St. Martin, & Lyon, 1989; Zucker, 1985; Zucker & Copeland, 1987).

A number of studies have examined the factor structure of the K-ABC—the factors measured by this test battery (Kamphaus, Kaufman, & Kaufman, 1982; Kaufman & Kamphaus, 1984; Kaufman & McLean, 1987; Keith, 1985; Keith & Dunbar, 1984; Keith, Hood, Eberhart, & Pottebaum, 1985; Naglieri & Jensen,

1987; Willson, Reynolds, Chatman, & Kaufman, 1985). These studies employed the standardization sample data as well as data contained from the study of other populations such as exceptional individuals. Many of the factor analyses suggested to the researchers that the test was, indeed, tapping three factors. But which three factors? Although most researchers agree on two of the factors, sequential and simultaneous processing, there is some disagreement regarding the third—the one the test manual for the K-ABC refers to as "achievement." This third factor has been variously identified as verbal comprehension and reading achievement (Good & Lane, 1988), achievement and reading ability in some cases (Kaufman & McLean, 1986), and reading achievement and verbal reasoning (Keith & Novak, 1987).

Administering the test   Starting and stopping points are based on the child's chronological age. The number of subtests administered varies from 7 at age 2-1/2 years, to 13 at ages 7 years and above. Test items are presented on an easel facing the child, while examiner instructions are printed on the side of the easel facing the examiner (Figure 10–4).

Oral instructions from the examiner and verbal responses from the examinee are minimal compared to other tests of intelligence, and the manual contains special instructions for test administration to bilingual, hearing-, speech-, or language-disabled test takers. Some of the mental processing subtests require the examiner to teach or demonstrate what is required although there are no sample or teaching items on the achievement portion of the test.

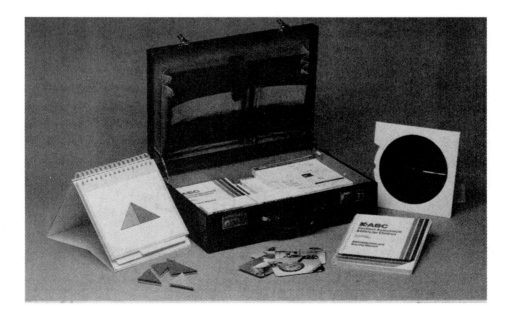

Figure 10–4   *The K-ABC Test Materials.*

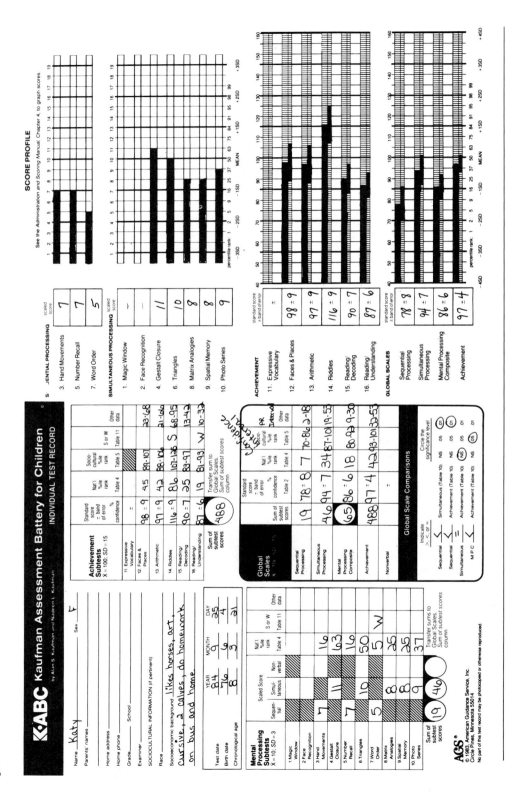

Figure 10–5 *A Sample K-ABC Test Record.*

356

Scoring and interpreting the test   Subtest items are scored correct (1 point) or incorrect (0 points) and the manual provides explicit directions and criteria for administering and scoring the test. Scores on the individual items are tallied to yield raw scores on each of the subtests. Tables in the manual are then used to convert each of the subtest scores into a standard score. From these standard scores Sequential Processing, Simultaneous Processing, Mental Processing Composite, and Achievement standard scores are derived. Sociocultural percentile ranks, based on the child's ethnic group and parents' educational level, can also be obtained. A sample K-ABC Test Record is presented in Figure 10–5.

One method of interpreting the K-ABC is the successive levels approach. As applied to the K-ABC, the test user evaluates processing style (simultaneous versus sequential), as well as the relationship between ability and achievement as reflected respectively by the Mental Processing Composite and Achievement scores. A subtest-by-subtest evaluation of assets and deficits follows. An alternative to the interpretation of the Achievement score suggested in the manual has been proposed by Kamphaus & Reynolds (1987).

Recommendations for teaching based on Kaufman and Kaufman's (1983) idea of "processing strength" can be derived from the K-ABC test findings. It may be recommended, for example, that a student whose strength is processing sequentially should be taught using the teaching guidelines for sequential learners. Students who do not have any particular processing strength may be taught using methods that employ a combination of methods. This model of test interpretation and consequential intervention has great intuitive appeal. However, research findings related to this approach have been mixed (Ayres & Cooley, 1986; Good et al., 1989; McCloskey, 1989; Salvia & Hritcko, 1984). Until this intervention model is employed in actual classrooms within the context of a regular curriculum over a reasonable period of time (one year or so), it will be impossible to know with any certainty of its effectiveness.

An evaluation   The K-ABC was introduced with extensive reliability and validity data supportive of its psychometric soundness. Factor-analytic studies were used to confirm the fact that the test taps three primary factors, although, as noted earlier, controversy remains regarding the nature and naming of one of them. The well-defined theoretical basis of the test facilitates continuing research into the validity of the instrument from a theoretical perspective. The K-ABC was designed to be as culture-fair as possible, and researchers have found this to be the case (Bracken, 1985; Chattin & Bracken, 1989). The use of sample items, teaching items, and the minimal verbal emphasis on the mental processing subtests all contribute to making the test culture-fair.

An unresolved issue for future research concerns the factor structure of the test; exactly what that third factor is measuring remains a nagging question that begs for an answer. The test authors' as yet unvalidated recommendations for teaching based on sequential or simultaneous processing skills is another source of controversy related to the K-ABC.

Differential Abilities Scales (DAS)

DAS is an American adaptation of BAS (the British Ability Scales) which, in turn, was a descendant of a test called the BIT (the British Intelligence Test). The BAS was first published in Great Britain in 1979, and a revision was published in 1983. Development of the American version of the DAS began in 1984, and the test was published about six years later (Elliott 1990a, 1990b). Appropriate for use with individuals from 2 years 6 months of age through 17 years 11 months, the DAS is not only a measure of ability (as one might expect from its name) but of achievement. As summarized in Table 10–8, the total battery consists of 17 cognitive subtests and 3 achievement subtests (tapping achievement in basic number skills, spelling, and word reading), though no more than 12 subtests are ever administered to any one test taker. In the words of the test's developer, school psychologist Colin Elliott (1990b), the DAS was developed

> to obtain and evaluate profiles of strengths and weaknesses. The achievement tests were co-normed with the cognitive battery to make direct ability-achievement discrepancy analyses possible. (p. 1)

Table 10–8

The Subtests of the DAS

Subtest	Description	Abilities Measured
Core Subtests		
Block Building (ages 2-6 through 3-5)	Copying a two- or three-dimensional design with blocks	Perceptual-motor ability
Verbal Comprehension (ages 2-6 through 5-11)	Pointing to pictures and manipulating toys or objects in response to examiner instructions	Receptive verbal knowledge
Picture Similarities (ages 2-6 through 5-11)	The child is shown a row of four pictures (such as geometric designs, or everyday objects) and is given a card with a fifth picture, which is to be placed under the picture sharing an element or concept	Nonverbal reasoning
Naming Vocabulary (ages 2-6 through 5-11)	Naming objects and pictures	Expressive verbal knowledge
Pattern Construction (ages 3-6 through 17-11)	Constructing a design with foam rubber squares or plastic blocks to match patterns depicted on cards	Nonverbal, spatial reasoning
Early Number Concepts (ages 3-6 through 5-11)	Responding to questions about number, size, and other numerical concepts using colored chips or pictures	Nonverbal and verbal knowledge
Copying (ages 3-6 through 5-11)	Copying drawings made by the examiner or displayed in a picture	Perceptual-motor ability
Recall of Designs (ages 6-0 through 17-11)	Reproducing an abstract geometric design after being exposed to it	Short-term visual spatial memory
Word Definitions (ages 6-0 through 17-11)	Defining words presented orally or visually	Expressive verbal knowledge
Matrices (ages 6-0 through 17-11)	The test taker is shown an incomplete matrix of abstract figures and selects the figure (from four or six choices) that completes the matrix	Nonverbal reasoning

Table 10–8 (*continued*)

Subtest	Description	Abilities Measured
Similarities (ages 6-0 through 17-11)	Stating how things are similar or go together	Verbal reasoning
Sequential and Quantitative Reasoning (ages 6-0 through 17-11)	The subtest is presented in two parts. The test taker is first shown a series of abstract figures and must complete it. In the second part, the test taker identifies a relationship within each pair of two pairs of numbers and then provides the missing number in an incomplete pair.	Detection of sequential patterns in figures or numbers
Diagnostic Subtests		
Recall of Objects— Immediate (ages 4-0 through 17-11)	Three immediate recall trials in which the test taker views a card with pictures of 20 objects for 20 to 60 seconds and then tries to recall as many objects as possible.	Short-term verbal memory
Recall of Objects— Delayed (ages 4-0 through 17-11)	The test taker recalls as many objects as possible from Recall of Objects— Immediate subtest. Administration occurs 10 to 30 minutes after initial presentation of the objects.	Intermediate verbal memory
Matching Letterlike Forms (ages 4-6 through 5-11)	Choosing a figure (from six choices) that matches an abstract figure.	Visual perceptual matching
Recall of Digits (ages 3-0 through 17-11)	Repeating a sequence of digits presented orally at the rate of two digits per second.	Short-term auditory memory
Recognition of Pictures (ages 3-0 through 7-11)	After being shown black-and-white pictures of common objects for 5 or 10 seconds, a second picture with the same objects as well as distractors (objects not in the first picture) is shown, the task being to point to the object(s) that were in the first picture.	Short-term visual memory
Speed of Information Processing (ages 6-0 through 17-11)	The test taker is presented with items consisting of rows of figures (circles containing small boxes or numbers). In each row the task is to mark the circle with the most boxes or highest number.	Quickness in performing mental operations
Achievement Subtests		
Basic Number Skills (ages 6-0 through 17-11)	Basic arithmetic skills, ranging from identifying numbers to problems requiring addition, subtracting, multiplication, or division. At upper age levels, word problems.	Numerical computation
Spelling (ages 6-0 through 17-11)	Writing words dictated by the examiner.	Spelling
Word Reading (ages 6-0 through 17-11)	Reading aloud words presented on a card.	Reading decoding skills

The conception of intelligence underlying the DAS is one that can best be described as a developmental, hierarchical, model of cognitive abilities with three levels: general conceptual ability (GCA, also known as *g*) at the top of this hierarchy, followed by general verbal and nonverbal abilities (as measured by cluster scores for clusters of subtests), followed by individual, specific verbal and non-verbal abilities as measured by individual subtests (see Figure 10–6). GCA is a composite measure of intelligence, that is, a composite measure of "conceptual and reasoning abilities" derived from the scores on "core subtests" forming the foundation of the battery. Additionally, "diagnostic subtests" measure specific cognitive skills such as short-term auditory memory and visual discrimination. Developmentally, it is presumed that only certain abilities are present at certain ages, and the actual structure of the battery varies by age.

The standardization sample   The standardization sample consisted of 3,475 subjects, with 175 subjects for each six-month age group from 2 years 6 months through 4 years 11 months and 200 subjects per age-group year in age-group years 5 through 17. The sample was stratified at each level on the basis of sex, race/ethnicity, parent education, geographic region, and preschool enrollment using 1988 census data as a criterion. Children enrolled in special education classes were included in the standardization sample. Children from smaller metropolitan and nonmetropolitan areas were underrepresented.

Psychometric properties   The DAS test author reports generally satisfactory estimates of internal reliability and test-retest reliability. Test-retest reliability co-efficients for the GCA range from .85 to .94. Test-retest reliability coefficients for

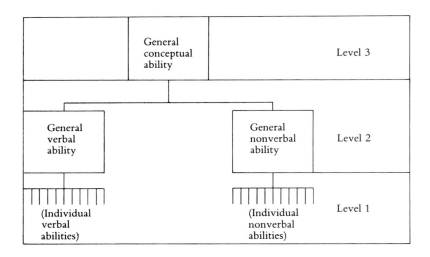

Figure 10–6   *A Three-Level Hierarchical Model of Cognitive Abilities.* The theory on which the DAS is based posits that individual abilities are at the first level and clusters of individual abilities are at the second level. At the third and highest level in this model is "general conceptual ability" (GCA).

Table 10–9

Internal Reliability Estimates by Age Level for the DAS

| | Internal reliability estimates | |
	Range	Mean
Preschool level		
Cognitive Subtests	.66 to .90	.81
Cluster Scores		
Verbal Ability	.86 to .90	.88
Nonverbal Ability	.88 to .90	.89
GCA (lower level)	.89 to .91	.90
GCA	.94 to .95	.94
School-Age Level		
Cognitive Subtests	.66 to .94	.83
Achievement Subtests	.82 to .95	.90
Cluster Scores		
Verbal Ability	.87 to .90	.88
Nonverbal Reasoning Ability	.88 to .92	.90
Spatial Ability	.89 to .94	.92
GCA	.95 to .96	.95

the clusters range from .79 to .90 for 393 children randomly selected from three age levels and tested twice at intervals of two to seven weeks. Internal reliability (Table 10–9) was established through a procedure which, in the words of the test author, "is based purely on the items expected to be taken by an individual and makes no assumptions about the person's performance on unadministered items" (Elliott, 1990b, p. 175). For subtests that entail subjective scoring (Copying, Recall of Designs, Similarities, and Word Definitions), mean inter-rater reliability estimates for each subtest were quite high, ranging from .90 to .96.

On the basis of factor-analytic research reported in the test's manual, the test taps one factor (GCA) at ages 2 years 6 months through 3 years 5 months; two factors (a verbal and a nonverbal factor) at ages 3 years 6 months through 5 years 11 months; and three factors (a verbal, a nonverbal reasoning, and a spatial ability factor) at ages 6 years 0 months through 17 years 11 months. Subsequent research with exceptional test takers as well as test takers from other populations will be necessary to further validate the factor structure of the DAS.

Several validity studies comparing the DAS to other measures of ability and achievement using nonhandicapped as well as exceptional children are reported in the test manual. Although the studies are limited in terms of sample size and region of the country, they tend to support the validity of the DAS as a measure of ability and achievement.

Administering the test Administration instructions are clearly presented in the manual, with starting and stopping points based on the test taker's chronological age and number of successes and failures. The core subtests are administered in a prescribed order, while the examiner has some discretion with regard to the sequence of administration of diagnostic and achievement subtests. Some subtests

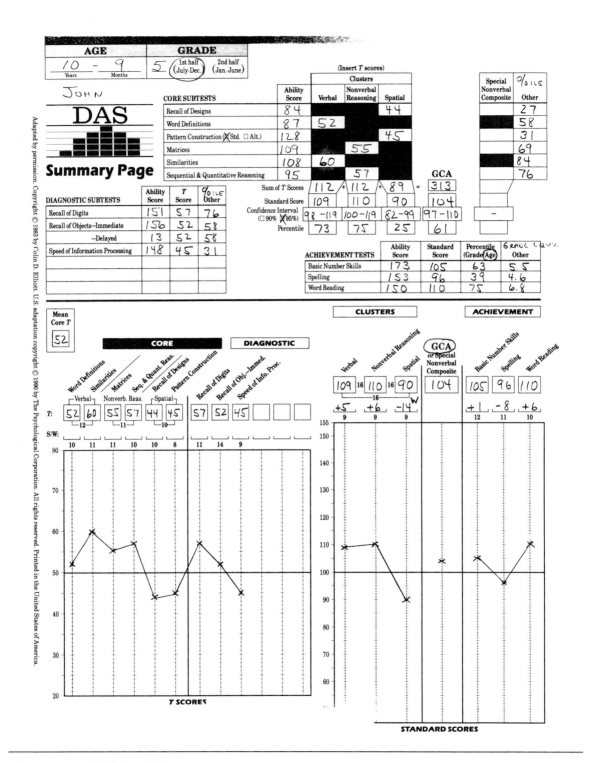

Figure 10-7 *DAS Record Form.*

DIFFERENTIAL ABILITY SCALES

Examiner _____

	YEAR	MONTH	DAY
Date Tested	___	___	___
Birth Date	___	___	___
Age	___	___	■

(Disregard the days)

Name _____ ID_____ Sex ☐ Male ☐ Female

Address _____
STREET   CITY   STATE   ZIP

Grade _____ School _____ Teacher _____

Does the examinee have glasses or corrective lenses? ☐ Yes ☐ No   If yes, were they worn during testing? ☐ Yes ☐ No

     Is there a known uncorrected vision problem? ☐ Yes ☐ No

Does the examinee have a hearing aid? ☐ Yes ☐ No   If yes, was it used during testing? ☐ Yes ☐ No

     Is there a known uncorrected hearing problem? ☐ Yes ☐ No   Handedness ☐ Left ☐ Right ☐ Mixed

Are there any other personal or physical characteristics or medications that might affect test results? _____

_____

Dominant language _____ Language spoken at home _____

Referred by _____ Reason for referral _____

_____

Comments _____

INFORMAL BEHAVIOR SCALE
Characteristics of the Examinee

Calm, relaxed	☐☐☐☐☐	Anxious, nervous
Mature	☐☐☐☐☐	Immature
Neat, well groomed	☐☐☐☐☐	Unkempt
Independent	☐☐☐☐☐	Fearful of leaving parent/classroom
Physically coordinated	☐☐☐☐☐	Physically uncoordinated
Speaks clearly	☐☐☐☐☐	Difficult to understand
Proficient in English	☐☐☐☐☐	Limited English proficiency
Overactive, fidgety	☐☐☐☐☐	Lethargic

Coping Skills (Attitude Toward Performance)

Optimistic, positive	☐☐☐☐☐	Pessimistic, complaining
Persistent in face of difficulty	☐☐☐☐☐	Gives up easily
Handles failure well	☐☐☐☐☐	Becomes upset by failure
Overconfident	☐☐☐☐☐	Lacking in confidence
Unconcerned with details	☐☐☐☐☐	Obsessive about minor details
Overcritical of own performance	☐☐☐☐☐	Uncritically accepts own performance

Approach to Testing

Attentive, on task	☐☐☐☐☐	Distractible, off task
Deliberate	☐☐☐☐☐	Impulsive
Highly interested in testing	☐☐☐☐☐	Uninterested in testing
Methodical	☐☐☐☐☐	Haphazard, random
Eager to speak	☐☐☐☐☐	Reluctant to speak
Does not require encouragement	☐☐☐☐☐	Requires constant encouragement

Social Interaction with the Examiner

Cooperative, friendly	☐☐☐☐☐	Uncooperative
Talkative, outgoing	☐☐☐☐☐	Withdrawn, shy
Behaves appropriately	☐☐☐☐☐	Behaves inappropriately
Easily establishes rapport	☐☐☐☐☐	Has difficulty establishing rapport

Figure 10–7 *(continued)*

(1) make provision for sample items, teaching items, and examiner demonstration of items, (2) may be administered through gestures rather than verbal instructions to produce a Nonverbal Composite score, and/or (3) have an "out of level range" permitting their administration to high-ability or low-ability children—the net effect being an extension of the age and ability range of these subtests. Administration time for the complete battery ranges from about 35 minutes at age 2 years 6 months to about 90 minutes for the school-age test taker.

Scoring and interpreting the test   Two record forms are provided, one for the preschool level, and one for the school-age level. The record forms are "user-friendly," with clearly marked starting/stopping points and instructions for scoring. Most test items are scored correct (1 point) or incorrect (0) points, though some provide for 0, 1, or 2 scoring; bonus points are awarded for rapid, successful completion of timed items. Raw scores are tallied and converted to subtest scores, which, in turn, are converted into standard scores (having a mean of 50 and a standard deviation of 10 for the cognitive subtests, and a mean of 100 and a standard deviation of 15 for the achievement subtests). From these standard scores, the GCA and cluster scores, both of which have a mean of 100 and a standard deviation of 15, are derived. A sample summary page from the School-Age Record Form is presented in Figure 10–7.

Interpreting the DAS is similar in many ways to interpreting other ability-achievement batteries. Composite and cluster scores are compared and evaluated as are individual subtest scores—all in an effort to profile the test taker's strengths and weaknesses. Additionally, extra-test behavior and other test-related findings may find their way into the experienced examiner's interpretation of the testing.

Evaluation   For preschool and school-age children alike, the DAS materials tend to be engaging; a variety of colorful, manipulable objects (as opposed to two-dimensional pictures) aid in maintaining interest and keeping test takers task-oriented. Because testing is tailored or adapted to the profile of responses—a style of testing known as "adaptive testing,"—overall testing time is reduced. Because out-of-level norms were developed for the test, children within a broad ability range can be evaluated appropriately. The psychometric properties of the battery appear to be strong; reliability and validity data are in the acceptable range and the battery's factor structure has been confirmed in studies reported in the test manual. We would caution, however, that the samples with which the validity research was conducted tended to be relatively small and not geographically diverse. During the test's development, procedures were employed to reduce or eliminate any possible race or gender bias, though the manual does not report any comparative data for white, black, and Hispanic test takers.

How comparable are scores on the DAS as compared to scores on other ability-achievement batteries? It will be interesting to see how the answer to this question emerges in independent studies in the coming years, especially since the operative definition of intelligence, general conceptual ability, differs from many existing tests. How useful will the DAS be in developing educational interventions? This, too, is a question that awaits careful research in the years to come.

The Woodcock-Johnson Psycho-Educational Battery—Revised (WJ-R)

The WJ-R (Woodcock & Johnson, 1989) was designed to measure cognitive abilities, academic achievement, and scholastic aptitude. How much of a discrepancy is there between the test taker's ability, as reflected by the test, and his or her achievement or aptitude? What are the test taker's strengths and weaknesses with respect to her or his achievement and abilities? These are the types of questions that may be addressed using, at least in part, data derived from an administration of the WJ-R.

Developed for use with individuals ranging in age from 2 to 95, the WJ-R has two parts: the Woodcock-Johnson Tests of Cognitive Ability and the Woodcock-Johnson Tests of Achievement. As listed in Table 10–10, a total of 21 tests compose the Cognitive Ability battery (7 standard and 14 supplemental), and a total of 18 tests make up the Achievement battery (9 standard and 9 supplemental). Subtests are organized into clusters, which yield measures such as one of "broad cognitive ability" (similar to a WISC-R Full Scale score), as well as measures of aptitude in various areas. For example, the cluster score for reading aptitude is based on performance on the Memory for Sentences, Visual Matching, Sound Blending, and Oral Vocabulary subtests. Cognitive abilities measured by the cognitive subtests are summarized in Table 10–11. Curriculum areas tapped by the WJ-R achievement tests are summarized in Table 10–12.

Table 10–10

Subtests of the WJ-R

Subtest	Description
Cognitive Ability Subtests	
Memory for Names	Measures the ability to learn associations between unfamiliar auditory and visual stimuli
Memory for Sentences	Measures the ability to remember and repeat phrases and sentences
Visual Matching	Measures the ability to locate and circle the two identical numbers in a row of six numbers
Incomplete Words	Measures auditory closure
Visual Closure	Measures the ability to identify a drawing or picture that is altered in one of several ways
Picture Vocabulary	Measures the ability to name familiar and unfamiliar pictured objects
Analysis-Synthesis	Measures the ability to analyze the presented components of an incomplete logic puzzle and to determine the missing components
Visual-Auditory Learning	Measures the ability to associate new visual symbols with familiar words and to translate a series of symbols into verbal sentences
Memory for Words	Measures the ability to repeat lists of unrelated words in the correct sequence
Cross Out	Measures the ability to scan and compare visual information quickly

Table 10–10 (*continued*)

Subtests of the WJ-R

Subtest	Description
Sound Blending	Measures the ability to integrate and then say whole words after hearing parts of the words
Picture Recognition	Measures the ability to recognize a subset of previously presented picture within a field of distracting pictures
Oral Vocabulary	Measures knowledge of word meanings
Concept Formation	Measures the ability to identify the rules for concepts when shown illustrations of both instances and noninstances of the concepts
Delayed Recall— Memory for Names	Measures the ability to recall (after 1 to 8 days) the space creatures presented in Memory for Names
Delayed Recall— Visual-Auditory Learning	Measures the ability to recall (after 1 to 8 days) the symbols presented in Visual-Auditory Learning
Numbers Reversed	Measures the ability to say a series of random numbers backward
Sound Patterns	Measures the ability to indicate whether pairs of complex sound patterns are the same or different
Spatial Relations	Measures the ability to match shapes visually
Listening Comprehension	Measures the ability to listen to a short tape-recorded passage and supply the single word missing at the end of the passage
Verbal Analogies	Measures the ability to complete phrases with words that indicate appropriate analogies
Achievement Subtests	
Letter-Word Identification	Measures reading identification skills by identifying isolated letters and words
Passage Comprehension	Measures skill in reading a short passage and identifying a missing key word
Calculation	Measures skill in performing mathematical calculation
Applied Problems	Measures skill in analyzing and solving practical mathematical problems
Dictation	Measures prewriting skills and skill in providing written responses to a variety of questions requiring knowledge of letter forms, spelling, punctuation, capitalization, and word usage
Writing Samples	Measures skill in writing responses to a variety of demands
Science	Measures knowledge in the various areas of biological and physical sciences
Social Studies	Measures knowledge of history, geography, government, economics, and other aspects of social studies
Humanities	Measures knowledge in various areas of art, music, and literature
Word Attack	Measures skills in applying phonic and structural analysis skills to the pronunciation of unfamiliar printed words
Reading Vocabulary	Measures skill in reading words and supplying appropriate meanings
Quantitative Concepts	Measures knowledge of mathematical concepts and vocabulary
Proofing	Measures skill in identifying a mistake in a typed passage and indicating how to correct the mistake
Writing Fluency	Measures skill in formulating and writing simple sentences quickly

Source: Adapted from Examiner's Manuals for the WJ-R

Table 10–11

Cognitive Factors Measured by the WJ-R Subtests

Cognitive Factors	Standard Battery	Supplemental Battery
Long-Term Retrieval	Memory for Names	Visual-Auditory Learning Delayed Recall—Memory for Names Delayed Recall—Visual-Auditory Learning
Short-Term Memory	Memory for Sentences*	Memory for Words* Numbers Reversed*
Processing Speed	Visual Matching	Cross Out
Auditory Processing	Incomplete Words*	Sound Blending* Sound Patterns*
Visual Processing	Visual Closure	Picture Recognition Spatial Relations
Comprehension-Knowledge	Picture Vocabulary	Oral Vocabulary Listening Comprehension* Verbal Analogies*
Fluid Reasoning	Analysis-Synthesis	Concept Formation Spatial Relations Verbal Analogies

*Audio-taped subtest

Table 10–12

Curriculum Areas Measured by the WJ-R Subtests

Curriculum Areas	Standard Battery	Supplemental Battery
Reading	Letter-Word Identification Passage Comprehension	Word Attack Reading Vocabulary
Mathematics	Calculation Applied Problems	Quantitative Concepts
Written Language	Dictation Writing Samples	Proofing Writing Fluency *Punctuation and Capitalization *Spelling *Usage **Handwriting
Knowledge	Science Social Studies Humanities	

*Composed of selected items from the Dictation and Proofing subtests
**Utilizes the examinee's response on Writing Samples subtest

The standardization sample The WJ-R was standardized on 6,359 subjects selected from communities across the country, including 705 preschool children, 3,245 individuals from the kindergarten through twelfth-grade level, 916 college/university students, and 1,493 adults not in school. A stratified sampling based on the 1980 census that controlled for variables such as geographic region, community size, race, educational level, and occupation was used. The norms were weighted to approximate the distribution of the United States population (Woodcock & Mather, 1989).

Psychometric properties   As reported in the test manual, internal consistency reliability estimates for the cognitive ability subtests ranged from .62 to .98, with median reliability coefficients of .69 to .93 for the nine age groups (ages 2, 4, 6, 9, 13, 30–39, 50–59, and 70–79 years). Cluster reliabilities range from .73 to .98 with median reliability coefficients of .81 to .97 (Woodcock & Mather, 1989). For the achievement subtests, internal reliability coefficients range from .75 to .98 with median reliability coefficients of .76 to .93 for the nine age groups. Cluster reliabilities range from .85 to .99 with median reliability coefficients of .91 to .96 (Woodcock & Mather, 1989, 1990). Test-retest reliability except for the Writing Fluency subtest was not reported.

Three concurrent validity studies are reported in the test manuals (Woodcock & Mather, 1989; Woodcock & Mather, 1989, 1990). These studies related the WJ-R performance of individuals with a mean age of 3 years, 9 years, and 17 years to performance on a number of other ability and achievement measures. The age 3 sample was administered the WJ-R, Boehm Tests of Basic Concepts, Bracken Basic Concept Scale, K-ABC, McCarthy Scales of Children's Abilities, Peabody Picture Vocabulary Test—Revised, and SB:FE. The age 9 sample completed the WJ-R, K-ABC, SB:FE, WISC-R, Basic Achievement Skills Individual Screener (BASIS), Kaufman Test of Educational Achievement (KTEA), Peabody Individual Achievement Test (PIAT), and the Wide Range Achievement Test—Revised (WRAT-R). The age 17 sample was given the WJ-R, SB:FE, WAIS-R, BASIS, KTEA, PIAT, and WRAT-R. Correlation coefficients between the WJ-R cognitive battery and the other ability measures were in the .60 to .70 range, except for the preschool level, at which the correlation coefficients were lower (ranging from .48 to .69). Correlations between the WJ-R achievement battery and other achievement measures yielded coefficients in the .60 to .70 range at the school-age level. Interpretation of these findings is hampered, however, by the fact that little detail was provided regarding sample selection, test administration procedures, and sample attrition over the course of the studies. Factor-analytic studies as described by Woodcock (1990) were construed as supportive of the theory underlying the cognitive battery.

Administering the test   Starting points based on the examinee's estimated ability level are provided on several subtests. Other subtests begin with the first item regardless of the examinee's age or estimated ability. Three of the subtests are timed (Visual Memory, Cross Out, and Writing Fluency). Several subtests are administered by means of audiocassette to minimize the possibility of examiner error or deviation from the standardization protocol. The estimated administration time is 40 minutes for the standard cognitive battery and 40 minutes for the supplemental cognitive battery. The estimated administration time for the standard achievement battery is 50–60 minutes.

Scoring and interpreting the test   Items are scored correct or incorrect though there are exceptions to this general rule. Raw scores for each subtest are converted to age-equivalent scores, grade-equivalent scores, and "*W*" scores—the latter being a "special transformation of the Rasch ability scale" (Woodcock & Mather, 1989, p. 66). *W* scores are converted to standard scores with a mean of 100 and a standard deviation of 15. Cluster scores are calculated from various combinations of subtests, and discrepancies between individual subtests and clusters are analyzed. A computer scoring system is available for calculating cluster and discrepancy scores.

Interpretation of WJ-R data, like that of data from many other tests, may take many different forms. Individual subtest scores, aptitude scores, and cluster scores may be compared to scores of examinees of similar age to determine whether the examinee is at, above, or below average as compared to peers. Alternatively, the data may be used not to compare the examinee to others but to analyze the examinee's performance with respect to her or his own performance; what discrepancy, if any, exists between measured ability and measured achievement? How do aptitude clusters in areas such as reading, mathematics, written language, and oral language compare? What are the examinee's unique strengths and weaknesses? A guide to facilitate WJ-R interpretation is available (Mather, 1991).

Evaluation The WJ-R is relatively easy to administer; scoring and interpretation are another matter. The conversion of raw scores to standard scores and the calculation of cluster scores can be difficult and time-consuming. And even after scores on the WJ-R are calculated, exactly what these scores mean is open to question. At this writing, reliability and validity data for the WJ-R are lacking and although an examiner's manual is available, a technical manual is not. Initial factor-analytic studies are supportive of the factor structure of the WJ-R, though Woodcock himself has observed that most of the reading and written language subtests "have not been studied thoroughly" (Woodcock, 1990, p. 235) within the theoretical framework (that of fluid versus crystallized abilities) in which the test is couched (see also Reschly, 1990; and Ysseldyke, 1990). Additionally, there is a dearth of validity studies to satisfactorily relate WJ-R data to those obtained with more proven instruments.

OTHER TESTS USED IN EDUCATIONAL SETTINGS

The Peabody Picture Vocabulary Test—Revised (PPVT-R)

Working in the special education department at the George Peabody College for Teachers, Lloyd Dunn (1959) developed the Peabody Picture Vocabulary Test, which was subsequently revised (Dunn & Dunn, 1981) and is now simply referred to as the PPVT-R. The test consists of pictures that are exposed to the test taker four at a time. The examiner reads a word and the test taker points to (or otherwise indicates via head-nodding, blinking—whatever) the picture that best describes that word.[3] The two parallel forms of the test employ the identical sets

---

3. The 300 stimulus pictures included in the older version were criticized as being sex-role- and racially stereotyped. Women were depicted only in domestic activities and only one minority member, a black train porter, was included. Dunn and Dunn (1981) attempted to remedy this problem in the revision of the test.

of pictures but different stimulus words. The test is most frequently administered individually though it can be adapted for group administration.

The entire test typically takes less than 15 minutes to administer and can be scored quickly (Figure 10–8). Raw scores are converted to age equivalents and/or standard scores that have a mean of 100 and a standard deviation of 15. In the older version of the test, raw scores were converted into "mental age" or "IQ" scores, though this practice has been recognized as misleading; the PPVT-R is not an intelligence test but rather one that measures one facet of cognitive ability— receptive (hearing) vocabulary for standard American English. It is also useful as a language assessment tool for people who have expressive language disorders (Maxwell & Wise, 1984) and as a rough measure of scholastic aptitude for multiply-handicapped individuals (Umberger, 1985). The test enjoys rather wide usage, particularly by school psychologists who employ it for screening purposes (Levy, 1982).

The PPVT-R was standardized on a sample of 4,200 children between the ages of 2-1/2 and 18 years of age. The sample was designed to be nationally representative in terms of geographic location, community size, age, sex, race, and occupation of the primary wage earner according to 1970 U.S. Census data. A second sample of 828 adults (defined here as age 19 or over) was also tested; however, this sample was only representative of the U.S. population with respect to

Figure 10–8 *An Examiner Administering the PPVT-R.*

the variables of geographic location, age, sex, and occupation—not race or community size. The standardization sample for the original PPVT had been limited to whites residing in the Nashville, Tennessee, area.

Satisfactory reliability evidence has been reported for the PPVT-R (Bracken, Prasse, & McCallum, 1984; McCallum & Bracken, 1984). A number of studies examining the relationship between the PPVT-R and traditional measures of intelligence such as the Stanford-Binet (Form L-M) and the WISC-R have yielded low to moderate correlation coefficients (Bracken & McCallum, 1981; Bracken & Prasse, 1982; Breen, 1981; Naglieri, 1981; Naglieri & Naglieri, 1981; Prasse & Bracken, 1981; Pound & McChesney, 1982). These types of correlations should be expected once it is acknowledged that, unlike some of the tests to which it has been compared, the PPVT-R is not a test of general intelligence.

Peer Appraisal Techniques

One method of obtaining information about an individual is by asking that individual's peer group to make the evaluation. Techniques employed to obtain such information are referred to as *peer appraisal* methods. A teacher, supervisor, or other group leader may be interested in peer appraisals for a variety of reasons. Peer appraisals can help call needed attention to an individual who is experiencing academic, personal, social, or work-related difficulties—difficulties that for whatever reason have not come to the attention of the person in charge. Peer appraisals allow the individual in charge to view individuals in a group from a different perspective, the perspective of people who work, play, socialize, eat lunch, and walk home with the individual being evaluated. In addition to providing information about behavior that is rarely observable, peer appraisals supply information about the group's dynamics: who takes which roles under what conditions. Knowledge of an individual's place within the group is an important aid in guiding the group to optimal efficiency.

Peer appraisal techniques may be used in university settings (Klockars, 1978) as well as in grade school, industrial, and military settings. Such techniques tend to be most useful in settings where the individuals doing the rating have functioned as a group long enough to be able to evaluate each other on specific variables. The nature of peer appraisals may change as a function of changes in the assessment situation and the membership of the group (Veldman & Sheffield, 1979); thus, for example, an individual who is rated as the "shiest" in the classroom can theoretically be quite gregarious—and perhaps even be rated "the rowdiest"—in a peer appraisal undertaken at an after-school center.

One method of peer appraisal that can be employed in elementary school (as well as other) settings is called the "Guess Who?" technique. Brief descriptive sentences (such as "This person is the most friendly") are read or handed out in the form of questionnaires to the class and the children are instructed to "guess who?" Decisions concerning whether or not negative attributes should be included in the peer appraisal (for example, "This person is the least friendly") must be made on an individual basis in consideration of the potential negative consequences such an appraisal could have on one member of the group.

The *nominating technique* is a method of peer appraisal in which individuals are asked to select or "nominate" other individuals for various types of activities.

Tests of Minimum Competency

Soon after the founding of the United States as an independent nation, one citizen commented in a book entitled *Letters from an American Farmer* that a "pleasing uniformity of decent competence appears throughout our habitations" (Crevecoeur, 1782, cited in Lerner, 1981). Over two hundred years later, widespread dissatisfaction with the *lack* of competence in this country has become evident. At about the time of the nation's bicentennial celebration, a grassroots movement aimed at eradicating illiteracy and anumeracy began taking shape. By 1980, 38 states had legislated regulations requiring that the schools administer a test to determine whether its secondary school graduates had developed "minimum competence." Exactly what constituted minimum competence would vary from one jurisdiction to the next but it generally referred to some basic knowledge of reading, writing, and arithmetic. The movement has gained momentum with the realization that the illiterate and anumerate often wind up not only unemployed, but unemployable as well. The unfortunate consequence is that too many of these individuals require public assistance or, alternatively, turn to crime—some finding their way to jail.

A minimum competency testing program is designed to ensure that the student given the high school diploma has at least acquired the minimal skills to become a productive member of society. Representative of such minimal skills necessary in everyday living are the ability to fill out an employment application and the ability to write checks, balance a checkbook, and interpret a bank statement.

As an example of one test for minimal competency, we focus attention on the Alabama High School Graduation Exam (AHSGE). A publication of the Alabama State Department of Education (Teague, 1983) sets forth very detailed specifications for items to be used in the AHSGE. The skills that are tested are based on ninth grade minimal competencies in the areas of Reading, Language, and Mathematics. Some of the skills listed in the area of Language are as follows:

- *Observe pronoun-antecedent agreement*
  Items for this competency require the student to choose the pronoun that agrees with its antecedent.
- *Use correct forms of nouns and verbs*
  Items for this competency require the student to choose the correct form of the nouns (singular and/or plural) and of verbs (regular and/or irregular) and to select verbs that agree with the subjects.
- *Include in a message or request all necessary information (who, what, when, where, how, or why)*
  Items for this competency require the student to demonstrate knowledge about what information is necessary in a message or request.
- *Determine what information is missing from a message, an announcement, or a process explanation; or what information is irrelevant*
- *Identify the comma to separate words in a series*
- *Identify question marks, periods, and exclamation points to punctuate sentences*
- *Identify words frequently used in daily activities*
  Items for this competency require the student to recognize frequently used words which are spelled incorrectly.
- *Complete a common form such as a driver's license application or change of address form*
- *Identify the proper format of a friendly letter*
- *Identify the proper format of a business letter*
  Items for this competency require the student to demonstrate knowledge of the proper format of a business letter, which includes punctuation and capitalization. Test questions refer to business letters reproduced in the test booklet. Figure 1 is an example.

Although the idea of "minimum competency" may on the face of it seem like a good idea, it has not gone unchallenged in the courts. Who should determine the skills necessary for "minimum competence" and the lack of "minimum competence"? What should the consequence be if an individual is not found to be "minimally competent"? Will a minimum competence requirement for a high school diploma act to motivate the academically unmotivated? In 1979, a federal judge in Florida held the scheduled application of that state's minimum competency law to be unconstitutional. Condemning the judge's decision, Lerner (1981) wrote that "disputes over empirical questions cannot be resolved by judicial fiat," and she went on to document that (1) substantial numbers of Americans are failing to master basic skills like reading, (2) the consequences of such deficits warrant action, and (3) the actions recommended by minimum competence advocates offer reasonable hope of bringing about the desired change (see also Lerner, 1980). Critics of such programs (such as Airasian, Madaus, & Pedulla, 1979; Haney & Madaus, 1978; Tyler, 1978) object primarily on grounds pertaining to the potential for abuse inherent in such programs, though some criticisms regarding the psychometric soundness of the instruments have also been voiced.

---

120 Drewry Road
Monroeville Alabama   36460

Miss Ann Andrews, Director
Parks and Recreation
Monroeville, Alabama   36460

Dear Miss Andrews:

    Our class would like to use the Community House for our senior prom. The tentative date for the prom is April 30, 1982. Please let me know if the ballroom is available on this date and the charges for the use of this facility.

                yours truly,

                Jan Austin

---

1. What part of the letter is the salutation?

   a. Jan Austin
*b. Dear Miss Andrews:
   c. Yours truly,
   d. Miss Ann Andrews

2. Which part of the letter has an error in punctuation?

   a. The salutation
   b. The closing
   c. The signature
*d. The heading

3. Which part of the letter has an error in capitalization?

*a. The closing
   b. The body
   c. The inside address
   d. The heading

4. Which part of this business letter has been omitted?

*a. The date of the letter
   b. The salutation
   c. The closing
   d. The inside address

Figure 1 *Sample Items Designed to Evaluate the Test Taker's Knowledge of the Format for a Business Letter.*

A child being interviewed in a psychiatric clinic may be asked, "Who would you most like to go to the Moon with?" as a means of determining which parent or other individual is most important to the child. Members of a police department might be asked, "Who would you most like as your partner for your next tour of duty and why?" as a means of finding out which police officers are seen by their peers as being especially competent or incompetent.

The results of a peer appraisal can be graphically illustrated. One graphic method of organizing such data is called the *sociogram*. Here figures such as circles or squares are drawn to represent different individuals, and lines and arrows are drawn to indicate various types of interaction. At a glance the sociogram can provide information such as who is popular in the group, who tends to be rejected by the group, and who is relatively "neutral" in the opinion of the group. Nominating techniques have been the most widely researched of the peer appraisal techniques and they have generally been found to be highly reliable and valid (Kane & Lawler, 1978, 1980). Still, the careful users of such techniques must be aware that an individual's perceptions within a group are constantly changing. As some members leave the group and others join it, the positions and roles the members hold within the group change; new alliances form and members may be looked at in a new light. It is therefore important to update periodically information obtained from peer appraisal methods so that accurate, up-to-date information is maintained.

Study Habits, Interests, and Attitudes

Academic performance is the result of a complex interplay of a number of factors. Ability and motivation are inseparable partners in the pursuit of academic success. A number of instruments designed to look beyond ability and toward factors such as study habits, interests, and attitudes have been published. For example, the Study Habits Checklist, designed for use with students in grades 9 through 14, consists of 37 items that assess study habits with respect to note taking, reading material, and general study practices. In developing the test, potential items were presented for screening to 136 Phi Beta Kappa members at three colleges. This procedure was based on the premise that good students are the best judges of important and effective study techniques (Preston, 1961). The judges were asked to evaluate the items in terms of their usefulness to students having difficulty with college course material. Although the judges conceded that they did not always engage in these practices themselves, they identified the techniques they deemed to be the most useful in study activities. Standardization for the Checklist took place in 1966, and percentile norms were based on a sample of several thousand high school and college students residing in Pennsylvania. In one validity study, 302 college freshmen who had demonstrated learning difficulties and had been referred to a learning skills center were evaluated with the Checklist. As predicted, it was found that these students demonstrated poor study practices, particularly in the areas of note taking and proper use of study time (Bucofsky, 1971).

If a teacher knows what a child's areas of interest are, instructional activities engaging those interests can be employed. The What I Like to Do Interest Inventory (Meyers, 1975) consists of 150 forced-choice items that assess four areas of interests: academic interests, artistic interests, occupational interests, and interests in leisure time (play) activities. Included in the test materials are suggestions for designing instructional activities that are consonant with the designated areas of interest.

Attitude inventories used in educational settings assess student attitudes toward a variety of school-related factors. Interest in student attitudes is based on the premise that "positive reactions to school may increase the likelihood that students will stay in school, develop a lasting commitment to learning, and use the school setting to advantage" (Epstein & McPartland, 1978, p. 2). Instruments have been developed that assess attitudes in one specific subject area such as reading (Engin, Wallbrown, & Brown, 1976; Wallbrown, Brown, & Engin, 1978; Heathington & Alexander, 1978), as well as in several other areas (for example, the Survey of School Attitudes, the Quality of School Life Scales). Other instruments, such as the Survey of Study Habits and Attitudes (SSHA) and the Study Attitudes and Methods Survey combine an attitude assessment with the assessment of study methods. The SSHA, intended for use in grades 7 through college, consists of 100 items tapping poor study skills and attitudes that could affect academic performance. Two forms, Form H for grades 7–12 and Form C for college, are available, each requiring 20–25 minutes to complete. Students respond to items on the following five-point scale: "Rarely," "Sometimes," "Frequently," "Generally," or "Almost Always." Test items are divided into six areas, which include Delay Avoidance, Work Methods, Study Habits, Teacher Approval, Education Acceptance, and Study Attitudes. The test yields a study skills score, an attitude score, and a total orientation score.

While on the subject of study habits, skills, and attitudes, perhaps a self-assessment as we end this chapter will prove useful. How have your own study habits, skills, and attitudes been? Might they be improved in any way? Experiment with your answer to the latter question by employing what you believe to be a more effective approach as you read the next chapter.

Chapter 11

Preschool Intelligence and

Ability Assessment

BEYOND AN ever-present concern with making the school experience as rewarding as possible for school-age children, public and governmental attention has expanded in recent years to focus on the nature of the preschool experience. The evolution of this increasing focus can be seen in federal legislation regarding the evaluation and education of gifted, culturally disadvantaged, and disabled children. In the 1950s' cold war climate, Congress allocated funds to help identify and educate gifted children—this in an effort to ensure that America would have the "brains" needed to stay ahead of the Soviets in the years to come. In the 1960s, Project Head Start was designed to enhance the academic readiness of educationally disadvantaged preschool children. In the mid-1970s, Congress enacted Public Law (PL) 94-142, which mandated that children age 3 and up suspected of having physical or mental disabilities be evaluated professionally to determine what their special educational needs might be. The law also provided federal funds to help the states meet these educational needs. In 1986, a set of amendments to PL 94-142, known as PL 99-457, extended downward to birth the obligation of states toward disabled children. It further mandated that beginning with the school year 1990–1991, all disabled children, from ages 3 to 5, be provided with a free, appropriate education.

Amidst the social reality of a burgeoning number of parents who are employed full-time (so-called two paycheck households, or single-parent, one paycheck households) and in need of day care for their children, Congress is currently wrestling with various child care bills. Although the current legislative focus is on payment for services and on facility and personnel qualifications, it is likely in the not-too-distant future that these concerns will be displaced by issues of assessment and early intervention (when, and if, necessary) for the growing number of preschoolers (nondisabled as well as disabled) in public and private child care facilities.

What tools are used in the assessment of preschoolers, and what do they really tell us about them? This as well as related questions will be addressed in this chapter. We begin with some background about the preschool years.

THE PRESCHOOL PERIOD: BIRTH TO AGE 5

The first five years of life—the span of time referred to by the term *preschool period*—is a time of profound change. Basic reflexes develop, affording many proud moments for the parents as the child passes through a number of sensory-motor milestones—crawling, sitting, standing, walking, running, grasping an object, and so forth. Usually between 18 and 24 months, the child becomes capable of symbolic thought and develops language skills. By age 2, the average child has a vocabulary of over two hundred words. Of course, all such observations about the development of children are of more than mere academic interest to professionals charged with the responsibility of assessing children.

An Overview of Preschool Measures

At the earliest levels, "intelligence" is gauged by infant intelligence scales that, in essence, note the presence or absence of various developmental achievements through means such as observation and parental (or caretaker) interviews. By age 2, the child enters into a challenging period for psychological assessors. Language and conceptual skills are beginning to emerge, yet the kinds of verbal and performance tests traditionally used with older children and adults are inappropriate; different types of measures have had to be developed. We will acquaint you with a sampling of these measures in the pages to come.

The attention span of the preschooler—much like an undergraduate stricken with "spring fever"—is short. Ideally, test materials are colorful, engaging, and attention-maintaining. Approximately one hour is a good rule-of-thumb limit for an entire test session with a preschooler, and less time is preferable; as testing time increases, so does the possibility of fatigue and distraction—with a resultant underestimation of the examinee's ability. An examiner should be well schooled in dealing with the many potential demands standardized testing of a preschooler entails (such as special problems in establishing and maintaining rapport, scoring and interpreting responses that "test the limits" of sample responses in the published manual, and so forth). The examiner must be well acquainted with the test materials and administer the tests with efficiency. Most welcomed by examiners who regularly work with preschoolers are tests that are relatively easy to administer, have simple start/discontinue rules, and allow the examiner ample opportunity to make behavioral observations of the examinee. Dual-easel test

Figure 11–1 *A "Dual-Easel" Format in Test Administration.* An "easel format" in the context of test administration refers to test materials, usually some sort of book that contains test-stimulus materials and that can be folded and placed on a desk; pages are turned by the examiner to reveal to the examinee, for example, objects to identify or designs to copy. When corresponding test-administration instructions or notes are printed on the reverse side of the test-stimulus pages for the examiner's convenience during test administration, the format is sometimes referred to as "dual easel."

administration format (see Figure 11–1), sample and teaching items for each subtest, and dichotomous scoring (for example, right/wrong) all serve to facilitate test administration.

Stability and predictive validity   How stable over time are measures obtained on preschool intelligence and ability tests? How predictive are such measures of future intelligence test results and school achievement?

Early studies addressed to such questions suggested that test stability tends to increase with the age of the child tested (Bayley, 1949, 1955; Honzik, 1976; Honzik, McFarlane, & Allen, 1948). Such findings are understandable because preschool measures—especially in the youngest ages—tap abilities that are quite different from the verbal/performance, and sequential/simultaneous-type tasks typically administered to school-age children.

Preliminary findings from two currently-in-progress, longitudinal studies examining stability in measured intelligence are beginning to appear in the literature. One study (Lamp & Krohn, 1990) began with 89 randomly selected Head Start children who were administered the K-ABC, SB:FE, and SB:LM at age 4.

Table 11–1

A Comparison of Two Longitudinal Studies

	Correlation between Test 1 and Test 2 scores		Gain scores (Differences in mean scores from Test 1 to Test 2)	
	Krohn & Lamp	Smith et al.	Krohn & Lamp	Smith et al.
K-ABC				
MPC	.82	.77	4.2*	1.1*
SEQ	.78	.73	6.0*	−5.0*
SIM	.74	.76	2.6*	5.2*
ACH	.84	.80	5.5*	−5.8*
SB:FE				
TC	.84	—	0.2	—
VR	.85	—	−4.5*	—
AVR	.61	—	−2.6	—
QR	.55	—	4.6*	—
STM	.70	—	2.4	—

Test abbreviations:
K-ABC: Kaufman Assessment Battery for Children
  MPC: Mental Processing Composite
  SEQ: Sequential Processing
  SIM: Simultaneous Processing
  ACH: Achievement
SB:FE: Stanford-Binet Intelligence Scale: Fourth Edition
  TC: Test Composite
  VR: Verbal Reasoning
  AVR: Abstract/Visual Reasoning
  QR: Quantitative Reasoning
  STM: Short-Term Memory

*Statistically significant, $p < .05$

Two years later 71 children (42 girls, 29 boys) of the original sample were re-tested. At the time of this second testing, the children ranged in age from 6 years 3 months to 7 years 5 months, and most were in the first grade. Stability coefficients and mean gain/loss scores are presented in Table 11–1. Lamp and Krohn found the scores on the two instruments to be highly stable from age 4 to age 6. Annual retesting is planned until the children are in sixth grade.

Another study (Smith, Bolin, & Stovall, 1988) began with 49 randomly selected, nonhandicapped children from a middle class, midwestern community. The children, ranging in age from 3 years 8 months to 4 years 10 months at initial testing, were administered the K-ABC. Two years later the K-ABC was read-ministered to 25 of these children (13 boys and 12 girls). At this time the children ranged in age from 5 years 11 months to 6 years 11 months. Stability coefficients and mean gain/loss scores are presented in Table 11–1. Smith et al. (1988) also found the scores on the K-ABC to be stable over the two-year period. Although the stability coefficients were similar for both studies, there were differences in the gain scores. On the K-ABC, for example, Krohn and Lamp reported that the mean gain scores on the global scales were all positive and statistically significant, whereas Smith et al. (1988) found positive gain scores on two scales and negative gain scores on two others. These results may reflect differences in the samples, as the Krohn and Lamp study used Head Start children of lower socioeconomic status, and the Smith study used middle-class children who presumably had not received analogous preparatory schooling. Subsequent testings of both samples should provide additional data on this unexpected finding. Taken together, the studies provide evidence that the preschool measures studied evidence stability in the 4–6 age range.

What of the predictive validity of preschool measures? As we will see in the following section on infant assessment, it appears that, in general, the younger the child at the time of intelligence testing, the less the findings will correlate with adolescent or adult measures. One review of a wide range of studies examining the nature of the relationship between preschool measures and later school achievement noted that in about a third of these studies, a preschool measure of intelligence was among the best predictors of later academic achievement. They reported that testing near the end of kindergarten—just before the preschooler becomes school age—appeared to be the optimal time of testing. Why did such predictive relationships exist? The authors of the study left to future research the problem of determining how and why various aspects of cognitive functioning are related to future academic achievement. When such important information is finally gained, optimally effective early-childhood intervention programs can be designed.

ASSESSING THE INTELLECTUAL ABILITY OF INFANTS

Assessment of the intelligence—very broadly defined—of infants tends to be synonymous with the assessment of various sensory-motor capabilities and non-verbal responses (such as gestural imitation, following a moving object with the eyes, and reaching for an object). In essence then, intelligence tests for infants tend to be standardized observational techniques designed to gauge the presence of various landmarks and stages in human growth. Most of the tests have in common items providing for the assessment of alertness and motor coordination. Involuntary and goal-directed movements are also assessed by observing the infant. Provisions for assessing interpersonal communication in the form of gestures and vocalizations are also provided. Emotional attitudes may be assessed by observing the infant interact with the examiner and other adults. For example, is the infant slow to "warm up" to the examiner? In the later stages of infancy, both receptive and expressive language is assessed.

Data from infant intelligence tests, especially when combined with other information (such as birth history, emotional and social history, health history, data on the quality of the physical and emotional environment, and measures of adaptive behavior) have proved useful to health professionals when suspicions about mental retardation and related developmental deficits have been raised. The tests have also proved useful in helping to define the abilities, as well as the extent of disability, in older, psychotic children. Furthermore, the tests have been in use for a number of years by many adoption agencies that will disclose and interpret such information to prospective adoptive parents. Infant tests also have wide application in the area of research and can play a part in selecting infants for specialized early educational experiences or measuring the outcome of educational, therapeutic, or prenatal care interventions.

What is the meaning of a score on an infant intelligence test? Whereas some of the developers of infant tests (such as Cattell, 1940; Gesell, 1940) claimed that such tests were predictive of future intellectual ability because they measured the developmental precursors to such ability, others have insisted that performance on such tests is at best reflective of the infant's physical and neuropsychological intactness. It would seem that a middle ground between these extreme positions is best supported by the research literature. In general, the tests have not been found to be predictive of performance on child or adult intelligence tests—tests that tap vastly different types of abilities and thought processes (Bayley, 1955, 1959; Bradway, 1945; Honzik, McFarlane, & Allen, 1948; Welcher et al., 1971). The predictive efficacy of the tests does tend to increase with the extremes of the infant's performance; the test interpreter can say with authority more about the future performance of an infant whose performance was either profoundly below age expectancy or significantly precocious (Sattler, 1982). Still, infancy is a developmental period of many spurts and lags and infants who are slow or precocious at this age might catch up or fall back in later years.

Bayley Scales of Infant Development

The first editions of Nancy Bayley's test were originally designed for use in a study called the Berkeley Growth Study and were published in 1933 and 1935 under the name of the California Scales of Infant Mental and Motor Development. The Bayley Scales of Infant Development (frequently referred to by psychologists as simply "the Bayley") is an expanded, restandardized edition of that test. The test is appropriate for the assessment of infants and children 2 months through 2-1/2 years. The test is administered while the mother holds the infant. The 163 Mental Scale and 81 Motor Scale items are arranged in ascending order of difficulty. The score on the Mental Scale yields a Mental Developmental Index (MDI) obtained from the assessment of factors such as perception, memory, learning, problem solving, vocalization, verbal communication, and rudimentary abstract thinking. A Psychomotor Developmental Index (PDI) is obtained from the motor scale, which taps gross motor body control and fine motor coordination, including balance, creeping, standing, and reaching for and manipulating objects. A third scale is referred to as the Infant Behavior Record. It contains 30 items tapping 25 areas of infant behavior that are observed by the examiner during the testing and rated after the testing has ended. Ratings are made of behaviors such as attention span, reactivity, and cooperation (see Figure 11–2).

The 1969 standardization sample consisted of 1,262 normal infants and children organized into 14 age groups ranging from 2 months to 30 months of age with from 83 to 94 children included in each age group. The sample was stratified in accordance with 1960 U.S. census data with respect to variables such as race, socioeconomic background, highest level education of the head-of-household, geographical area, urban-rural residence, and sex. The children included in the standardization sample were located through hospitals, well-baby clinics, pediatricians, city birth records, and social agencies. Only one child per family was included in the standardization sample. Children over 12 months of age from bilingual homes, or children who had observable difficulty in English, those born more than one month prematurely, and institutionalized children with severe behavioral or emotional problems were excluded from the sample (Bayley, 1969, pp. 7–8).

Evidence of satisfactory internal (split-half) reliability has been presented (Werner & Bayley, 1966), though there is evidence to suggest that inter-scorer reliability may be a problem especially with respect to the scoring of items that require the parent's assistance (such as an item on the Motor subtest where the child's task is to pull to a standing position). The test has been judged to be reliable relative to existing infant tests (Alessi & Lesiak, 1981; Collard, 1972), though it has limited predictive value. Bayley scores should be used to determine an infant's current level of functioning in comparison to other same-age babies and not to predict future developmental trends. Additionally, the test has value as a neuropsychological screening instrument and as a tool in the assessment of the intelligence of young psychotic children (Sattler, 1982). The test has been extensively used in research and in the evaluation of various programs ranging from prenatal care to child abuse programs (Koski & Ingram, 1977).

Figure 11–2 *Testing the "Alerting" Response.*

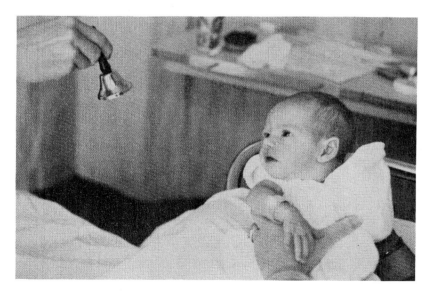

One assessment technique common to infant development tests is a test of the "alerting" response. An *alerting response* is indicative of an infant's capacity for responsiveness and it is deemed to be present when the infant's eyes brighten and widen—this in contrast to the term *orientation*, which is used to define the response of turning in the direction of a stimulus (Erickson, 1976). Here the child is exhibiting an alerting response to the sound of the bell.

Gesell Developmental Schedules

Physician Arnold Gesell and his colleagues at the Yale University Clinic of Child Development conducted pioneering work in the area of infant testing. As a result of intensive observation of numerous infants, they developed what they called "schedules," standardized normative instruments used to observe and evaluate behavioral development in children aged 4 weeks to 6 years. Each of these schedules assesses development in a number of different developmental areas. Ten such schedules were developed to be used in assessing infants during various age ranges beginning at 4 to 8 weeks of age.

Each of the schedules provides for assessment in the four areas of motor behavior, language behavior, adaptive behavior, and personal-social behavior. Motor behavior is assessed, for example, by observing gross bodily control (such as balance of neck and head, sitting, creeping, walking) and fine motor coordination (such as grasping and manipulation of objects). The language area is assessed by observation of communicative behaviors such as babbling. Adaptive behavior is assessed in various ways such as by observing reaction to a dangling ring, drawing, and simple form boards. Personal-social behavior is assessed by observing feeding, play behavior, and responses to people. Ratings—most are pass/fail—are assigned either as a result of examiner observation or in some cases as a result of parental report. After the child has progressed up the schedules to his or her maximal performance level, the scores in each of the four areas are tallied and an all-inclusive "developmental quotient" (DQ) is derived.

Norms for the Gesell are based on a longitudinal study of 107 children and, according to the test authors, "upon hundreds of preschool children both normal and atypical" (Gesell et al., 1940, p. 319). These 107 children represented a restricted sample of white, full-term babies from lower-middle-class families of northern European extraction. The children were observed at 4, 6, and 8 weeks after birth and at 4-week intervals until age 56 weeks. Follow-up observations were conducted at 2, 3, 4, 5, and 6 years of age. The placement of particular items in each of the schedules was determined by the percentage of subjects in the standardization sample passing the items. The sample used to develop norms has been criticized as being too small and restricted, and the meaning of the reference to the "hundreds of preschool children" lacks the specificity to make such a reference meaningful. Because of the inadequate and poorly specified standardization sample, critics of the test such as Thomas (1970) have charged that the Gesell is a crudely constructed test because many items were arbitrarily placed.

While acceptably high test-retest reliability and inter-scorer reliability coefficients have been reported for the Gesell Schedules (Knobloch & Pasamanick, 1960; McTurk & Neisworth, 1978), the evidence for the validity of this test is mixed at best. Some factor-analytic research suggested that the test appeared to primarily be measuring alertness and fine and gross motor skills (Stott & Ball, 1965). No relationship was found to exist between scores on the test by normal infants ranging in age from 3 to 33 weeks and retests administered years later (Escalona & Moriarty, 1961). Using a sample of 16 infants with Down's Syndrome, Share, Webb, and Koch (1961) noted that the DQ obtained during the first 13 months of life was a poor predictor of later DQs. However, these same investigators noted that DQs obtained between 15 and 24 months were much better predictors of future DQs. Others (such as McTurk & Neisworth, 1978) have suggested that performance on the Gesell may in some instances be predictive of classroom performance. Wittenborn et al. (1956) reported a nonsignificant (.28) correlation coefficient between the Gesell administered at 40 weeks and subsequent performance on the Stanford-Binet at age 3. Like the Bayley, the Gesell can perhaps best be thought of as a useful screening instrument.

ASSESSMENT: INFANCY THROUGH SCHOOL AGE

Beyond infancy, the number of available instruments to gauge children's developmental level, intelligence, and related abilities begins to mushroom. Some, such as tests based on Piaget's conceptualization of intelligence (which we survey below) have a strong theoretical foundation. In other tests, the link to an overall theory of cognitive development is far less obvious, if existent at all. Our sam-

---

Close-up

"At Risk"

Gamblers and investors place a sum of money "at risk" every time they wager or invest. People with a long history of heart disease in the family may be "at risk" for themselves developing circulatory disorders. Many species are "at risk" for extinction. Get a failing grade in your psych measurement class, and you may be "at risk" for having the checks from home terminated.

The term "at risk" may be used in many different contexts, and, for the most part, we don't have to think twice about the meaning of it when we hear it. But what does the term "at risk" mean in the context of a preschool child who has been evaluated psychologically?

One definition has it that *at risk* means in danger of not being ready for first grade (Martin, 1981). Another has it that the term refers to a level of functioning that is not within normal limits (Paget, 1985). In truth, a multitude of definitions have arisen. States—even individual school districts within many—have developed their own definitions of the term. From its origins as an alternative to a diagnostic classification that might have detrimental effects on young children (Knudtson, 1990), the term itself is at

high risk for being misinterpreted when it is used.

Some preschool children do very poorly on some or all of the many areas in which they are asessed, including sensory functioning, motor functioning, cognitive skills, communication skills, and behavior (see NJCLD, 1985 for an elaboration on these areas of assessment). When a child's poor performance in any or all of these areas is significant—say, for the purpose of this example, one standard deviation or more below the mean—"at risk" becomes a euphemism in describing a child with a documented problem, developmental lag, or disability that requires remediation. In contrast, many school districts prefer, more appropriately, to apply this term to children who have difficulties but who nonetheless might "fall through the cracks" were it not for routine screening and individualized follow-up assessment. In essence, these are children who are at risk for not being identified as having a problem and who therefore would not receive the tailored educational interventions that could make their school years fulfilling.

pling of instruments available for use with preschoolers continues with a consideration of screening tests.

Screening Tests

To better appreciate the concept of a *screening test* in the context of preschool testing, it may be useful to begin by thinking of a somewhat analogous but more familiar type of screening test, a blood test. Human blood is composed of many substances, and after many analyses of what an average blood sample should contain, various levels of these substances have come to be regarded as "within normal limits," or "wnl." Levels of these substances above or below the "wnl" mark, or the presence of some foreign substance, signals the need for further medical testing. In like fashion, psychological testing with a sample of youngsters serves to establish a kind of "wnl" mark for performance on a test. Performance that falls on the low side of the "wnl" range signals the need for further psychological

"At risk" can have many meanings. In the film *Home Alone,* the child "at risk" was at risk of becoming a crime statistic.

evaluation; the child may be "at risk" (see the Close-up for this chapter). Following is a brief look at two screening tests used with preschoolers.

Battelle Developmental Inventory (BDI)   The Battelle Developmental Inventory (BDI) (Newbourg, Stock, Wnek, Guidubaldi, & Svinicki, 1984) yields measures of cognitive, motor, adaptive, communication, and personal/social development in children from birth to age 8, and a composite Development Quotient (with a mean of 100 and a standard deviation of 15). The full battery requires 1 to 1½ hours to administer, though a special screening version can be administered in as little as ten minutes. The test was normed in late 1982 through March 1983 on 800 children matched to the 1981 census estimates on the variables of sex and race. The manual presents adequate reliability data but limited validity data. Subsequent studies with it have reported mixed findings (Boyd, 1989; Harrington, 1985a, 1985b; Molitor & Kramer, 1987; Smith, Bauer, & Lyon, 1987).

Early Screening Profiles (ESP)   The Early Screening Profiles (ESP) (Harrison, in press) was developed for the purpose of screening the developmental areas specified in Public Law 99-457. It measures cognitive/language, motor, and self-help/social development using measures to which the test taker responds as well as questionnaires completed by parents, teachers, and screening examiners. The battery yields a Cognitive/Language profile incorporating data from four subtests (Verbal Concepts, Visual Discrimination, Logical Relations, and Basic School Skills), a Motor Profile that incorporates data from two subtests (Gross Motor and Fine Motor), and a Self-Help Social Profile that draws on the communication, daily living, socialization, and motor scales. Separate scores for Expressive Language and Receptive Language are determined from performance on selected items of the Verbal Concepts and Basic School Skills subtests. The battery can be administered in 15 to 30 minutes, and the parent and teacher questionnaires can be completed in about 10 minutes each. The standardization sample was stratified on the basis of 1990 census estimates according to sex, race or ethnic membership, community size, region of the country, and parents' level of education. The sample consisted of 1,149 children, with 76 to 172 children in each of ten half-year groups between 2 years 0 months, and 6 years 11 months. Some of the types of tasks the child is presented with on this test include: pointing to pictures that match stimulus pictures or that are described aloud by the examiner; pointing to pictures to solve visual analogies; and answering questions having to do with conceptual knowledge of numbers, quantity, letters, and words.

Test-retest reliability for 74 children retested at an interval of 21 days or less ranged from .70 on the Motor Profile to .90 on the Cognitive/Language Profile. Stability coefficients for 23 children retested in 5 to 15 months ranged from .51 on the Motor Profile to .54 on the Cognitive Profile (Smith, Lasee, & McCloskey, 1990; Smith, Lasee, Steenson, & Ouradnik, 1990). ESP scores were compared to K-ABC scores in one concurrent validity study with 29 subjects (Lasee & Smith, 1990), and a correlation of .58 was calculated between the ESP Cognitive/Language Profile and the K-ABC Mental Processing Composite. The correlation between the ESP Cognitive/Language Profile and the K-ABC Achievement Scale was .71.

Piagetian Scales

Jean Piaget (1896–1980) is the French developmental psychologist whose work you probably became acquainted with in your introductory psychology course. Piaget's theory (reviewed very briefly in Chapter 8) stresses the uniform progression of cognitive development through successive, invariant stages. Test developers who subscribe to Piaget's theory have constructed tests to gauge exactly how far along a child is within a Piagetian framework. For example, from about age 7 to about age 12 a child is presumed to be in the Piagetian stage known as concrete operations; such a child should be able to perform certain mental operations identified with that stage of cognitive development. The Ordinal Scales of Psychological Development and the Concept Assessment Kit—Conservation are two tests based on Piaget's developmental theory.

The Ordinal Scales of Psychological Development (OSPD)   Uzgiris and Hunt (1975) initially designed the OSPD as a research instrument to measure the effects of environment on child development. It is appropriate for use with normal children aged 2 weeks to 2 years and can be of value in assessing older retarded children (Wachs, 1970; Kahn, 1976). All of the items are scored on a pass/fail basis, and then scores on six ordinal "scales" are computed. An ordinal scale is one designed to reveal the important aspects of each major cognitive developmental period. The attainment of one stage is contingent on the completion of the earlier stage. Emphasis is on qualitative description of the child's characteristic behavior. A description of these scales appears in Table 11–2.

No large-scale standardization of the OSPD has ever been undertaken. The test is criterion- as opposed to norm-referenced, and it is designed to assess the individual examinee's progress with respect to a sequence of cognitive skills. Evidence for the validity of this instrument comes from studies comparing findings from it with comparable findings from more traditional intelligence tests. For example, in one study, scores on the OSPD obtained at three-month intervals between the ages of 12 and 24 months were found to be positively and significantly correlated with scores achieved on the Stanford-Binet (Form L-M) at age 31 months (Wachs, 1975). Less correlation was found between the two instruments in a study that employed children who were at the lower end of the spectrum in intellectual functioning; with a sample of children who had a Stanford-Binet measured IQ of 50 or less, the coefficient of correlation between the Binet and the OSPD was found to be .62 (Wachs, 1975). While not a widely used test, the test is useful in illustrating the application of one theory of intelligence to the measurement of intelligence.

Concept Assessment Kit—Conservation (CAK-C)   The Piagetian principle of conservation is that "certain properties of objects—their quantity, number, weight—stay the same, even when the shape or spatial arrangement is changed" (Bee, 1978, p. 214). For example, while the number of pennies in a row is not increased by spreading them apart, the preoperational child, influenced by the irrelevant perceptual cues of the stimulus, might think there are more pennies if they are more spread out. According to Piaget, conservation of quantity and con-

Table 11–2

The Ordinal Scales of Psychological Development

Scale I. The Development of Visual Pursuit and the Permanence of Objects
   This scale examines the child's emerging representational thought by focusing on understanding of the permanence of objects. Tasks include visually following an object and then searching for it when it is hidden.
Scale II. The Development of Means for Obtaining Desired Environmental Events
   The child's understanding of causality and means-end relationships as well as aspects of the child's ability to exercise control over his or her environment is tapped by this scale. For example, does the child use his own hands to reach for a toy or instead pull a towel on which the toy has been placed to reach it?
Scale III. The Development of Imitation
   Imitative behavior is critical in the learning of a wide variety of skills including language. The items on this scale all probe the child's ability to imitate verbal (vocal) as well as nonverbal (gestural) behavior.
Scale IV. The Development of Operational Causality
   This scale is designed to assess the child's emerging understanding of the way she or he can affect the environment. The examiner observes the extent to which a child will engage in certain behavior to obtain a desired outcome (such as ringing and then ringing again a bell or activating and then reactivating a toy).
Scale V. The Construction of Object Relations in Space
   How well does the child understand spatial relationships? This is the primary question of interest here. Tasks include the localizing of sounds, using the concept of gravity in play, and alternately observing two objects.
Scale VI. The Development of Schemes for Relating to Objects
   How does a child relate to—manipulate, explore, symbolically use—objects? In the scoring of this scale, the child's spontaneous play is observed and aspects of the way the child holds, drops, waves, names, or otherwise relates to objects are examined.

servation of number are reached at approximately age 5 or 6. Conservation of weight is gained at about the age of 8. Lastly, conservation of volume is gained anywhere between ages 11 and 13 or later.

The CAK-C was designed for use with children aged 4 through 7, and it comprises items designed to assess the child's ability to exhibit conservation of numbers, substance, weight, space, and quantity. For example, an item designed to assess conservation of weight involves the examiner showing the subject two equal balls of Play-Doh. The examiner then flattens one ball into a pancake and asks the child whether the ball is as heavy as the pancake.

The standardization sample for the CAK-C consisted of 560 children aged 4 to 7. Included in the sample were both black and white children, all from the Los Angeles area. Children from a variety of socioeconomic levels were included, though lower-middle-class families were overrepresented (Goldschmid & Bentler, 1968a). Satisfactory reliability coefficients for the test's internal consistency, its alternate forms, and its test-retest reliability have been reported (Silverstein, Brownlee, & Legutki, 1980). In support of the validity of the tests, its authors have presented factor-analytic evidence that, they argue, demonstrates conservation as the factor being measured by the test (Goldschmid & Bentler, 1968b). The test authors have also noted that CAK-C scores correlated significantly with first-grade achievement. It is noted parenthetically that training in conservation can improve scores (Zimmerman & Rosenthal, 1974a, 1974b).

Piagetian tests in perspective   Some of the differences between Piagetian tests and more traditional instruments used to assess intelligence are summarized in Table 11–3. Note that, despite such differences, positive and significant correlations may be observed when scores from Piagetian-based tests are compared to scores on more traditional tests (see Gottfried & Brody, 1975; Jensen, 1980; Kohlberg, 1968). Piagetian tests do not enjoy widespread use in applied settings, in part because they tend to be more difficult and cumbersome to administer, more time-consuming, and not so readily interpretable with respect to the types of decisions test users must make on a daily basis. Still, Piaget's theory does have appeal to many test users and it is for this reason that psychologists and educators

Table 11–3

Some Differences Between Piagetian Scales and More Conventional IQ Tests

Piagetian scales	*Conventional IQ tests*
Based on Piaget's unitary theory of cognitive development.	Usually not based on any explicit theory.
Primary use for research on developmental psychology.	Used for clinical or diagnostic evaluation in applied settings such as hospitals, schools, and vocational institutions.
Flexible procedural approach but more time-consuming and difficult to administer.	Strict standardized administration and scoring procedures.
Emphasis on qualitative interpretation and descriptions of what the subject is able to do and how he or she does it.	Emphasis on quantitative interpretation and what the subject cannot do.
Scoring and interpretation focuses on the process of problem solving and quality of response.	Focus is on product and quantity.
Major object of test is to elicit the subject's explanation of an observed event and reasons that underlie that explanation.	Focus is on correct answers.
Typically small number of items or problems included.	Large number of items included.
Subject's incorrect responses are often of primary interest because of their value in revealing the subject's misconceptions.	Typically ignore incorrect responses except in determining total scores.
Ordinal scales consistent with Piaget's theory that the attainment of one stage is contingent on the completion of the earlier stages. Less susceptible to influence by specific instruction.	Interval scales that do not have an absolute zero point but have equal intervals. Items are selected on the bases of differentiating between successive ages. More susceptible to influence of specific instruction.
Emphasis less on tapping acquired knowledge than on cognitive structures or schemas; therefore less culture-loaded.	More emphasis on tapping acquired knowledge; therefore more culture-loaded.

have explored the applicability of these tests in various settings (Herron, 1973; Karplus & Karplus, 1970; Kaufman, 1971; Pinard & Laurendeau, 1964).

The McCarthy Scales of Children's Abilities (MSCA)

Dorothea McCarthy (1972) developed an individually administered ability test designed for use with children from ages 2½ through 8½. The objective was to develop a clinically useful tool that would help identify the learning strengths and weaknesses of both normal and exceptional children. Development of such a scale was given impetus by a climate stressing the need for early childhood education and by the void in tests other than the Stanford-Binet for measuring the intellectual ability of children between the ages of 30 and 48 months.

As you can see from Table 11–4, the McCarthy Scales of Children's Abilities (MSCA) consist of six scales with subtests composed of gamelike and colorful

Table 11–4

The McCarthy Scales of Children's Abilities[1]

Scales	Subtests
Verbal: Assesses the ability to understand and process verbal stimuli and to express thoughts vocally. Included are verbal abilities that the Wechsler scales test with an emphasis on verbal fluency and memory.	Pictorial Memory Word Knowledge Verbal Memory Verbal Fluency Opposite Analogies
Perceptual-Performance: Assesses visual-motor coordination and nonverbal reasoning through the manipulation of concrete materials. More visual-motor coordination is tapped than on the Wechsler scales but the MSCA does not include as many nonverbal reasoning items. The subject need not verbalize responses on this scale.	Block Building Puzzle Solving Tapping Sequence Right-Left Orientation (for ages 5 and above)[2] Draw-A-Child Conceptual Grouping
Quantitative: Assesses the facility in dealing with numbers and understanding of quantitative concepts.	Number Questions Numerical Memory Counting and Sorting
Memory: Assesses short-term memory across a wide range of visual and auditory stimuli. Includes more items than the Wechsler scales.	Pictorial Memory Tapping Sequence Verbal Memory Numerical Memory
Motor: Assesses gross and fine motor coordination. It is useful in diagnosing possible neurological impairment and includes more imitation than the Wechsler scales.	Leg Coordination Arm Coordination Imitative Action Draw-A-Design Draw-A-Child
General Cognitive: Assesses reasoning, concept formation, and memory when solving verbal and nonverbal problems and when manipulating concrete materials.	Verbal, Perceptual-Performance, and Quantitative Scales

[1]See McCarthy (1972) or Kaufman and Kaufman (1977) for a detailed description of individual subtests.
[2]Only Perceptual-Performance subtest that does not include visual stimuli. It tends to measure verbal concepts.

Table 11–5

Subtests of the McCarthy Scales of Children's Abilities

Subtest	Description[1]
Pictorial Memory	Names of objects pictured on a card are recalled
Word Knowledge	Common objects are identified and words are defined
Verbal Memory	Word series and sentences are repeated (Part I), and a story read by the examiner is retold (Part II)
Verbal Fluency	As many articles as possible in a given category are named in 20 seconds
Opposite Analogies	Sentences are completed by providing opposites
Block Building	Block structures built by the examiner are copied
Puzzle Solving	Cut-up pictures of common animals and foods are assembled
Tapping Sequence	Sequences of notes tapped by the examiner on a xylophone are copied
Right-Left Orientation	Knowledge of right and left is demonstrated (ages 5 and above)
Draw-A-Design	Geometrical designs are copied
Draw-A-Child	A picture of a child of the same sex is drawn
Conceptual Grouping	Blocks are classified on the basis of size, color, and shape
Number Questions	Questions involving number information or basic arithmetical computation are answered
Numerical Memory	Series of digits are repeated in the order presented by the examiner (Part I) and in reverse order (Part II)
Counting and Sorting	Blocks are counted and sorted into equal groups
Leg Coordination	Motor tasks involving the legs, such as walking backwards or standing on one foot, are performed
Arm Coordination	A rubber ball is bounced; a beanbag is caught and thrown through a hole in a target
Imitative Action	Simple movements, such as folding one's hands or looking through a tube, are copied

[1]Adapted from McCarthy (1972)

items arranged in order of increasing difficulty with specified cutoff points. A brief description of each subtest is provided in Table 11–5.

A General Cognitive Index (GCI), which can be calculated on the basis of performance on six of the subtests, is similar conceptually to the IQ yielded by conventional intelligence tests. However, McCarthy deliberately wished to avoid the use of the term *IQ*, since the test was being introduced at the height of the controversy about the relevancy of the concept of IQ to the testing of children from minority groups.

The sample consisted of 1,032 children with at least 100 subjects in each of ten half-year age levels ranging from 2½ to 8½ years old. The sample was representative of the 1970 census data and was stratified on the variables of sex, race, head-of-household's occupation, age, urban-rural residence, and geographical region. Potential subjects with obvious handicaps, who spoke a language other than English or who had poor comprehension of English, were eliminated from the sample. There was a large minority representation in the MSCA standardization sample and no strong evidence of cultural bias in the items exists. In general, the standardization of the test has been viewed as satisfactory (Davis & Rowland, 1974).

The test appears to be relatively sound from a psychometric perspective with short-term test-retest reliability coefficients acceptably high (McCarthy, 1972). Some of the scales at some of the age levels have been shown to have unsatisfactorily low internal-consistency reliability coefficients. The manual provides clear directions for administration and scoring, and inter-scorer agreement tends to be high. Numerous studies on this test have suggested that it is both content valid and construct valid; it does appear to be measuring abilities related to intelligence and the lack of such abilities do tend to be related to learning problems. High correlations have been noted between performance on the MSCA and the WPPSI (Phillips, Pasework, & Tindall, 1978), the Stanford-Binet (Naglieri & Harrison, 1978), and the WISC-R (Goh & Youngquist, 1979). Factor-analytic research on the test has generally supported the grouping of items into the six scales (Kaufman & Hollenbeck, 1973), though in one study, the quantitative factor was not observed in subjects under the age of 5 (Kaufman, 1975) or in children whose overall intellectual ability was low (Harrison, Kaufman, & Naglieri, 1980).

In general this test has proved itself to be useful in fulfilling its objective of aiding the diagnosis of specific learning strengths and weaknesses. An advantage of this test for use in school applications is the ease with which findings from the test can be translated into specific educational objectives. One problem that has been cited with the test is the great amount of clerical work that is required in transforming scores on the 18 subtests into scores on the six scales; the work leaves open the possibility of clerical errors. Some have viewed as a deficiency in the test the fact that it contains few items tapping abstract problem-solving ability and "social intelligence"—the ability tapped by the Comprehension items on the SB:FE and on the Comprehension subtests of the Wechsler tests. Also there are no alternate items or alternate tests if an item or test is for any reason invalidated.

Other Tests and Measures

If you have read the material in the two chapters prior to this one, you already have some familiarity with some of the other tests and measures available for use with preschool children. The Wechsler Pre-School and Primary Scale of Intelligence—Revised (WPPSI-R) has an age range of 3 to 7. A test that has been proved to be psychometrically sound, it is not necessarily the test of choice for physically challenged youngsters. Because some subtests require the use of a pencil or manipulation of blocks or other test materials, children with various disabling conditions will be unable to execute such tasks.

The Stanford-Binet: Fourth Edition (SB:FE) is designed for use with children as young as 2 years of age, and it contains eight subtests at the preschool level. One potential problem with the use of the SB:FE with preschool (as well as other) children has to do with the use of the Vocabulary subtest as the routing test. Many referrals for testing of preschoolers are language- or speech-related, and such children may begin the test experience on a frustrating note of failure—a situation that to some subtle or not-so-subtle degree may influence the rest of the testing, including perhaps the examiner's expectations regarding the child's ability. Additionally, many of the subtests call for lengthy verbal instructions, which in themselves may penalize test takers of limited verbal ability.

Containing at the preschool level 8–11 subtests, the Kaufman Assessment Battery for Children (K-ABC) tests an age range extending downward to age 2½. Many aspects of this test make it particularly appealing for use with preschoolers, including the provision of many sample and teaching items, concise subtest directions phrased in simple language, and "out of level" test administration procedures, complete with norms, for higher-ability 4-year-olds and lower-ability 5-year-olds.

The Differential Ability Scales (DAS) is appropriate for use with children as young as 2½ and at the preschool level. Six to 11 subtests are administered. The DAS contains colorful materials and numerous manipulables—all a great plus for use with preschoolers. Many subtests have an out-of-level range, indicating the ages at which they can be administered to children of atypically high or low ability.

Aspects of a preschooler's knowledge of basic concepts—for example, the concepts of "top/bottom" and "left/right"—may be assessed using tests such as the Boehm Test of Basic Concepts—Preschool Version and the Bracken Basic Concept Scale (BBCS). In the BBCS, for example, pictures are the primary instruments of evaluation; the child's task is to point to the picture (or other stimulus such as a color) that best depicts a particular concept. The BBCS contains norm-referenced screening and diagnostic components, with diagnostic subtests such as Numbers/Counting, Time/Sequence, and Social/Emotional. Designed for use with children ranging in age from 2 years 6 months to 7 years 11 months, one application of this test is described in the manual as follows:

> The results of the BBCS Screening Tests may be used to determine whether the child is "at risk" for future educational learning problems. By determining the "at risk" cut off point most suitable for a given school system, the individuals conducting the screening can recommend or perform a more intensive psychoeducational assessment for children who perform below the predetermined "at risk" cut off on the BBCS. (Bracken, 1984, p. 5)

In general, reviewers have found the BBCS to be technically adequate. Its strengths include its clearly written manual, its ease of administration, and its comprehensiveness in measuring basic concepts. The test has been criticized on technical grounds for its scoring system (Turco, 1989) and for the fact that the screening tests require conceptual prerequisites such as top/bottom and on/off. No predictive validity studies are reported in the manual, though seven concurrent validity studies (with satisfactory correlations with related tests such as the Boehm Test of Basic Concepts) are reported. Ysseldyke (1989) cautioned that some of the reported internal consistency reliability coefficients were too low for screening purposes at specific ages. Turco (1989) cautioned that the spiral-bound easel format used to present stimulus materials could be unruly at times: "The easel was somewhat temperamental to use because occasionally the spiral wiring twisted, which prevented the pages from flipping easily and lying flat" (p. 103).

An encapsulated comparison of some of the preschool measures we have discussed is presented in Table 11–6. Table 11–7 contains a summary of the factor structure for these tests, and Table 11–8 contains a comparison of these tests' subtests.

A number of correlational studies with varied populations have analyzed scores obtained on two or more of the instruments discussed above. For a sam-

Table 11–6

A Comparison of Selected Preschool Tests

	MSCA	WPPSI-R	SB:FE	K-ABC	DAS
Administration time (minutes)	45–60	60–75	60	30–45	35–65
Number of subtests	18	12	8	7–11	6–11
Age range (years)	2-6–8-7	3-0–7-3	2-6–adult	2-6–12-6	2-6–17-11
Census data for norms	1970	1986	1980	1980	1988
Standardization dates	10/70–9/71	Spring 1987–Spring 1989	1/85–7/85	4/81–9/81	2/87–3/89
Number tested for each one-year age level	200	400	200–400	200	350
Sociocultural norms	No	No	No	Yes	No
Sample items on ability subtests	No	No	No	Yes	Some not all
Teaching items on ability subtests	No	All except Arithmetic	No	Yes	Some not all
Nonverbal Scale	*	**	No	Yes	Yes

*Motor scale is present
**Performance scale is present

Table 11–7

Factor Structure of Selected Preschool Tests

Test	Measure of g	Factors
MSCA	General Cognitive Index (GCI)	Verbal Perceptual-Performance Quantitative Memory Motor
WPPSI-R	Full Scale IQ	Verbal Performance
SB:FE	Test Composite	Verbal Reasoning Abstract/Visual Reasoning Quantitative Reasoning Short-Term Memory
K-ABC	Mental Processing Composite (MPC)	Sequential Processing Simultaneous Processing Achievement
DAS	General Conceptual Ability (GCA)	Verbal Ability* Nonverbal Ability*

*Ages 3 years 6 months through 5 years 11 months

Table 11-8

Subtest Comparisons for Selected Preschool Tests

MSCA	WPPSI-R	SB:FE	K-ABC	DAS
Analogous Subtests				
Puzzle Solving	Object Assembly			
Draw a Design	Geometric Design	Copying		Copying
	Block Design	Pattern Analysis	Triangles	Pattern Construction
	Information		Faces & Places	
	Comprehension	Comprehension		Verbal Comprehension
Number Questions/ Counting and Sorting	Arithmetic	Quantitative	Arithmetic	Early Number Concepts
Word Knowledge	Vocabulary	Vocabulary	Expressive Vocabulary	Naming Vocabulary
	Similarities			Picture Similarities
Verbal Memory	Sentences	Memory for Sentences		
		Bead Memory	Spatial Memory	
Numerical Memory			Number Recall	Recall of Digits
Block Building				Block Building
Pictorial Memory				Recall of Objects

Nonanalogous Subtests

  MSCA: Tapping Sequence, Right-Left Orientation, Leg Coordination, Arm Coordination, Imitative Action, Draw-A-Child, Verbal Fluency, Opposite Analogies, Conceptual Grouping

  WPPSI-R: Mazes, Picture Completion, Animal Pegs

  SB:FE: Absurdities

  K-ABC: Magic Window, Face Recognition, Hand Movements, Gestalt Closure, Word Order, Matrix Analogies, Riddles, Reading Decoding

  DAS: Matching Letterlike Forms, Recognition of Pictures

pling of such studies, the interested reader is referred to Bloom et al. (1989), Faust and Oakes (1990), Krohn and Lamp (1989), Krohn, Lamp, and Phelps (1988), Smith and Bauer (1989), Smith and Knudtson (1990), Zucker (1985), and Zucker and Copeland (1987).

Despite which tests are employed with the preschool child, at least one objective of the testing and assessment seems universal—that of early identification of unique strengths and weaknesses, the better to enrich the individual's life in the many years to come. The enterprise of preschool evaluation has evolved from one that was, in essence, testing designed to screen for disability, to one that entails assessment for program planning.[1]

---

1. For more on this multipurpose conceptualization of preschool evaluation, see Kelley and Surbeck (1983).

Part

4

Personality

Assessment

Chapter 12

An Overview of

Personality Assessment:

Objective Methods

IN A 1950s' vintage oldie-but-goodie rock 'n' roll tune called "Personality," singer Lloyd Price described the subject of his song in terms of walk, talk, smile, and charm. In so doing, Price's use of the term *personality* was quite consistent with the way that most people tend to use it. For lay people, "personality" refers to components of an individual's makeup that can elicit positive or negative reactions from others. The individual who consistently tends to elicit positive reactions from others is thought to have a "good" personality. The individual who consistently tends to elicit not-so-good reactions from others is thought to have a "bad" personality or, perhaps worse yet, "no personality." Other descriptive epithets such as "aggressive personality," "cold personality," and "warm personality" also enjoy widespread usage.

   When behavioral scientists seek to define and describe personality, the terms they use are more rigorous than those describing simple social skills and are more precise than all-encompassing adjectives. The search has led to the serious study of constructs such as personality traits, personality types, and personality states. In this chapter we survey various approaches to assessing personality and constructing personality tests. Our survey continues in Chapter 13, where we focus exclusively on projective tests. In Chapter 14 we look at other tools that have been used in the process of personality assessment. We begin by defining some of the terms that we use throughout Part 4. As you will see, defining some of these terms is not at all easy. However, logically speaking, it is important to arrive at working definitions of these terms before proceeding to a discussion of how to measure them.

DEFINING AND MEASURING "PERSONALITY"

Dozens of distinctly different definitions of "personality" exist in the psychology literature (Allport, 1937). Some definitions appear to be all-inclusive in nature. For example, McClelland (1951, p. 69) defined personality as "the most adequate conceptualization of a person's behavior in all its detail." Menninger (1953, p. 23) defined it as "the individual as a whole, his height and weight and love and hates and blood pressure and reflexes; his smiles and hopes and bowed legs and enlarged tonsils. It means all that anyone is and that he is trying to become." Some definitions rely heavily on a particular aspect of the person such as the individual's phenomenal field (Goldstein, 1963) or the individual as a social being (Sullivan, 1953). At an extreme end of the spectrum of definitions are those proposed by theorists who have scrupulously avoided definition. For example, Byrne (1974, p. 26) characterized the entire area of personality psychology as "psychology's garbage bin in that any research which doesn't fit other existing categories can be labeled 'personality.'" Deploring personality theorists who avoid defining their subject matter, Dahlstrom (1970) observed that

> Some sidestep the issue, apparently to satisfy a demand for ostensive definitions. Thus, Sarason states, "We shall consider personality as an area of investigation rather than as an entity, real or hypothetical" (1966, p. 15). While such a definition makes it easy to point to the definienda ("I am studying what the personologist over there is doing"), it obviously leaves the central definition itself unformulated. (p. 2)

In their widely read and authoritative textbook *Theories of Personality,* Hall and Lindzey (1970, p. 9) wrote that "it is our conviction that *no substantive definition of personality can be applied with any generality*" and that "*personality is defined by the particular empirical concepts which are a part of the theory of personality employed by the observer*" [emphasis in the original]. They went on, "If this seems an unsatisfactory definition to the reader, let him take consolation in the thought that in the pages to follow he will encounter a number of specific definitions any one of which will become his if he chooses to adopt that particular theory" (p. 9).[1]

Traits, Types, and States

At this point you might well ask, "If venerable authorities like Hall and Lindzey aren't going to define personality, who are Cohen, Swerdlik, and Smith to think that they can do it?" Our response is to formulate a middle-of-the-road defini-

---

1. Hall and Lindzey (1970) did point out that important theoretical differences underlie the various different types of definitions of "personality" that exist. After Allport (1937), Hall and Lindzey (1970, p. 8) point out, for example, that a distinction can be made between *biosocial* types of definitions (that is, definitions that equate personality with the social stimulus value of the individual), and *biophysical* types of definitions (that is, definitions that do not take account of the social stimulus value of the individual but are solely rooted within the individual).

401

AN OVERVIEW
OF
PERSONALITY
ASSESSMENT:
OBJECTIVE
METHODS

tion: one that represents a middle ground between the all-inclusive "whole person" types of definitions and the nondefinition types of definitions. We find the following definition useful for our purposes (that is, the teaching of psychological testing): "*Personality* may be defined as *an individual's unique constellation of psychological traits and states.* Accordingly, *personality assessment* entails the measurement of traits and states." Before proceeding to a discussion of strategies used to accomplish such measurement, we should define *traits* and *states*. We also define another widely used personality-related term, *types.*

Personality traits The vocabulary of personality assessment relies heavily on trait terms (such as "warm," "reserved," "trusting," and "imaginative"). If you have taken a course in personality theory you are probably aware that just as there is no consensus about the definition of personality, no consensus exists regarding the word *trait.* Theorists such as Gordon Allport (1937) have tended to view personality *traits* as real physical entities that are "bona fide mental structures in each personality" (p. 289). For Allport, a trait is a "generalized and focalized neuropsychic system (peculiar to the individual) with the capacity to render many stimuli functionally equivalent, and to initiate and guide consistent (equivalent) forms of adaptive and expressive behavior" (p. 295). Robert Holt (1971) noted that there "*are* real structures inside people that determine their behavior in lawful ways" (p. 6), and he went on to conceptualize these structures in terms of changes in brain chemistry that might occur as a result of learning: "learning causes submicroscopic structural changes in the brain, probably in the organization of its biochemical substance" (p. 7). Raymond Cattell (1950) also conceptualized traits as "mental structures," but for him "structure" did not necessarily imply actual physical status.

Our own preference is to shy away from definitions that elevate *trait* to the status of physical existence; rather than physical entities, we tend to view psychological traits as attributions made in an effort to identify threads of consistency in behavioral patterns. A definition of *trait* offered by Guilford (1959, p. 6) has great appeal to us. He defined *trait* as, "any distinguishable, relatively enduring way in which one individual varies from another."

Inherent in this relatively simple definition are commonalities with the writings of other personality theorists such as Allport (1937), Cattell (1950, 1965), and Eysenck (1961). The word "distinguishable" conveys the idea that behavior labeled with one trait term can be differentiated from behavior that is labeled with another trait term. Thus, for example, behavior within a certain context that might be viewed as "religious" should ideally be distinguishable from behavior within the same or another context that might be viewed as "deviant." Note here that it is important to be aware of the *context* or situation in which a particular behavior is displayed when distinguishing between trait terms that may be applicable: a person who is kneeling and talking to God inside of a church may be described as "religious," while another person engaged in the exact same behavior in a public restroom might more readily be viewed as "deviant." The trait term that an observer applies, as well as the strength or magnitude of the trait presumed to be present, is based on an observation of a sample of behavior. The observed sample of behavior may be obtained in a number of ways, ranging from direct observation of the assessee (such as by actually watching the individual going to church regularly and praying) to the analysis of the assessee's statements on a self-report, pencil-and-paper personality test (on which, for example, the individual may have provided an indication of great frequency in church attendance).

In his definition of *trait,* Guilford did not assert that traits represent enduring ways in which individuals vary from one another; rather, the term *relatively enduring way* was used. The modifier "relatively" serves to emphasize that exactly how a particular trait manifests itself is, at least to some extent, situation-dependent. For example, a "violent" parolee may generally be prone to behave in a rather subdued way with her parole officer and much more violently in the presence of her family and friends. John may be viewed as "dull" and "cheap" by his wife but as "charming" and "extravagant" by his secretary, business associates, and others he is keenly interested in impressing. Allport (1937) addressed the issue of cross-situational consistency—or lack of it—as follows:

> Perfect consistency will never be found and must not be expected. . . . People may be ascendant and submissive, perhaps submissive only towards those individuals bearing traditional symbols of authority and prestige; and towards everyone else aggressive and domineering. . . . The ever changing environment raises now one trait and now another to a state of active tension. (p. 330)

Returning to our elaboration of Guilford's definition, note that *trait* is described as a *way in which one individual varies from another.* Here it is important to emphasize that the attribution of a trait term is always a *relative* phenomena. For instance, some behavior described as "patriotic" may differ greatly from other behavior also described as "patriotic." No absolute standards prevail here; in saying that one person is "patriotic," we are in essence making an unstated comparison to the degree of patriotic behavior that could reasonably be expected to be emitted by the average person.

Research demonstrating a lack of cross-situational consistency in traits such as honesty (Hartshorne & May, 1928), punctuality (Dudycha, 1936), conformity (Hollander & Willis, 1967), attitude toward authority (Burwen & Campbell, 1957), and introversion/extraversion (Newcomb, 1929) are the types of studies typically cited by Mischel (1968, 1973, 1977, 1979) and others who have been critical of the predominant role of the concept of traits in personality theory. Such critics may also allude to the fact that some undetermined portion of behavior exhibited in public may be governed more by societal expectations and cultural role restrictions than by an individual's personality traits (see Goffman, 1963; Barker, 1963). Research designed to shed light on the primacy of individual differences versus situational factors in behavior is methodologically complex (see Golding, 1975), and the verdict as to the primacy of the trait or the situation is far from being in (see Moskowitz & Schwartz, 1982).

Personality types Having defined personality as a unique constellation of traits and states we might define a personality *type* as a constellation of traits and states that is similar in pattern to one identified category of personality within a taxonomy of personalities. For assistance in elaborating on this definition of type, we can look to the work of Isabel Briggs Myers and Katherine C. Briggs, authors of the Myers-Briggs Type Indicator (Myers & Briggs, 1943/1962), a test inspired by the theoretical typology of Carl Jung (1923). An assumption guiding the develop-

Table 12–1

403

Two Typologies: Adler and Hippocrates

Adlerian type	*Corresponding type of Hippocrates*
Ruling type: High activity but in an asocial way; typical of "bossy" people and, in the extreme, homicidal people.	Choleric type
Getting type: This type of person has low social interest and a moderate activity level; typical of people who are constantly depending on others for support.	Phlegmatic or sluggish type
Avoiding type: This type of person has very low social interest combined with a very low activity level; method of coping is primarily avoidance.	Melancholic type
Good Man type: This type of person has high social interest combined with a high activity level; she or he lives life to the fullest and is very much concerned with the well-being of her or his fellow human beings.	Sanguine type

Source: Adler (1927/1965)

ment of this test was that people exhibit definite preferences in the way that they perceive or become aware of, and judge or arrive at conclusions about, people, events, situations, and ideas. According to Myers (1962, p. 1), these differences in perception and judging result in "corresponding differences in their reactions, in their interests, values, needs, and motivations, in what they do best, and in what they like to do."[2] While traits are frequently discussed as if they were something individuals possess, types are more clearly only descriptions of people—not something presumed to be inherent in them.

Hypotheses and notions about various *types* of people have appeared in the literature through the ages. Perhaps the most primitive personality typology was the humoral theory of Hippocrates (see Chapter 2). Centuries later, the personality theorist Alfred Adler would differentiate personality types in a way that was somewhat reminiscent of Hippocrates (Table 12–1). Adler's personality types represented different combinations of social interests and varying degrees of vigor with which they attacked life's problems. Adler (1933/1964, p. 127) never developed a formal system to measure these types since he realized that they were generalizations, useful primarily for teaching persons. By contrast, another personality theorist, physician William Sheldon, developed an elaborate typology based on measurements of body mass (see Figure 12–1).

Personality states The word *state* has been used in at least two distinctly different ways in the personality assessment literature. In one usage of this term, a personality state is an inferred psychodynamic disposition designed to convey the

2. In an interesting exploratory study designed to better understand the personality of chess players, the Myers-Briggs Type Indicator was administered to 2,165 chess players (including masters and senior masters). The chess players were found to be significantly more introverted, intuitive, and thinking (as opposed to feeling) than members of the general population. The investigator also found masters to be more judging than would be expected in the general population (Kelly, 1985).

Figure 12–1 *Sheldon's Typology.*

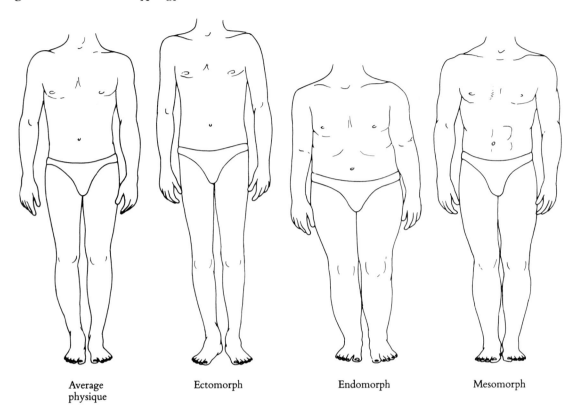

Average physique   Ectomorph   Endomorph   Mesomorph

William Sheldon and his associates (Sheldon & Stevens, 1942; Sheldon, Dupertuis, & McDermott, 1954) proposed a personality typology based on body build. This complicated typology involved measurements of body mass and ratio that culminated in classification with respect to three body types: the endomorph, the mesomorph, and the ectomorph. Associated with each of these body types are specific predispositions and temperaments. The endomorph, for example, was said to have a "viscerotonic" disposition, which implied, among other

things, a love of good food and good company and general even-temperedness. The mesomorph is "somatotonic": action-oriented, adventuresome, and dominating, among other things. The ectomorph is "cerebrotonic": physically and emotionally restrained, future-oriented, and introverted.

For Sheldon, the task of assessment was one of classifying persons with respect to three dimensions of physique. Each individual was rated on a scale from 1 to 7 according to the amount of endomorphy, mesomorphy, and

ectomorphy that was deemed to be present. An individual who was the epitome of an endomorph would thus be rated as a "7-1-1"; 7 for endomorphy (the highest possible rating), 1 for mesomorphy, and 1 for ectomorphy (the lowest possible rating). An individual who was high on mesomorphy, medium on endomorphy, and low on ectomorphy would be rated 3-7-1; presumably such an individual would also have a temperament that corresponded to this particular "somatotype" (or "body type").

dynamic quality of id, ego, and superego in perpetual conflict. Assessment of these psychodynamic dispositions may be made through the use of various psychoanalytic techniques such as free association, word association, symbolic analysis of interview material, dream analysis, and analysis of slips of the tongue, accidents, jokes, and forgetting.

405

AN OVERVIEW
OF
PERSONALITY
ASSESSMENT:
OBJECTIVE
METHODS

Presently, a more popular usage of the word *state*—and the one that we make reference to in the discussion that follows—refers to the transitory exhibition of some personality trait. Put another way, the use of the word "trait" presupposes a relatively enduring behavioral predisposition, whereas the term "state" is indicative of a relatively temporary predisposition. Thus, for example, Sally may be described as being "in an anxious state" before her midterms, though no one who knows Sally well would describe her as "an anxious person."

Measuring personality states amounts, in essence, to a search for and assessment of the strength of traits that are relatively transitory in nature and/or fairly situation-specific. Relatively few existing personality tests seek to distinguish traits from states. Seminal work in this area was done by Charles D. Speilberger and his associates. These researchers developed a number of personality inventories designed to distinguish various states from traits. Included here are the State-Trait Anxiety Inventory (Spielberger, Gorsuch, & Lushene, 1970), the State–Trait Anxiety Inventory for Children (Spielberger, Edwards, Montuori, & Lushene, 1973), the State-Trait Anger Scale (Spielberger et al., 1980a), and the Test Anxiety Inventory, Research Edition (Spielberger et al., 1980b).

In the manual for the State-Trait Anxiety Inventory (STAI), for example, we find that *state anxiety* refers to a transitory experience of tension because of a particular situation. By contrast, *trait anxiety* or "anxiety proneness" refers to a relatively stable or enduring personality characteristic. The STAI test items consist of short descriptive statements, and subjects are instructed to indicate either (1) how they feel "right now" or "at this moment" (and to indicate the intensity of the feeling), or (2) how they "generally feel" (and to record the frequency of the feeling). The test-retest reliability coefficients reported in the manual are consistent with the theoretical premise that trait anxiety is the more enduring characteristic, whereas state anxiety is transitory; test-retest reliability coefficients for the *state* anxiety measure over a one-hour interval were .33 and .16 for males and females, respectively, and the test-retest reliability coefficients for the *trait* anxiety measure for males and females were .84 and .76, respectively. Similar trends were observed in the test-retest reliability coefficients over longer intervals.

Three Basic Questions

Having considered some of the many ways personality can be conceived, let's proceed to consider various aspects of personality assessment and personality test construction. At the outset, some very basic questions need to be addressed: Why measure personality? What makes a "good" personality test? How does one construct a personality test?

Why measure personality? It will surely come as no surprise to you to hear that personality tests are designed to provide users with more information than they might otherwise have about the person being assessed; as the author of one widely used personality measure modestly implied with reference to his own creation, they yield something superior to "folk notions about personality" (Gough, 1989, p. 69). Clinicians and counselors seeking to identify their clients' problem areas and/or to confirm their own clinical hunches may use a test of personality to supplement interviews and other assessment tools. The test results may not only prove insightful as stand-alone data but may also be useful as a stimulus to further investigation of previously unexplored or underexplored areas. The test data may also prove useful in identifying strengths that can be drawn on and weaknesses that may be remediable within the context of a planned psychotherapeutic or behavioral intervention. In school situations, personality test data can point the way to nonacademic factors that may be acting to impede academic performance. In a private practice situation, personality test data may prove useful with respect to decisions regarding specific modes of intervention. For example, if there are strong indications that the assessee is a social isolate, these as well as other data should factor into a decision regarding the timing and appropriateness of group treatment.

Beyond the clinical arena, personality tests are widely used in occupational contexts. Vocational counselors administer such tests and on the basis of the resulting profile, advise examinees as to the lines of work in which they might best find their "niche." Depending on the entire record as well as other factors, a vocational counselor might advise a client with a decided preference for social isolation against going into a career that entails daily interpersonal contact (such as sales or bar tending) and urge the individual instead to consider occupations more along the lines of computer programming or copy editing.

Psychological research is another major area in which tests of personality are used. Here there are many possible subcategorizations, but for our purposes, we will dichotomize all such applications into (1) studies of individual psychological variables, and (2) studies of psychological theories. The researcher intent on learning about every possible facet and correlate of social isolationism through the use of personality tests exemplifies how personality tests might be used to study individual psychological variables. A researcher who has developed an "interpersonal theory of personality" might also use personality tests to test hypotheses derived from that theory. Hypotheses might concern the number of postulated primary, secondary, and tertiary personality dimensions there are, whether these personality dimensions are hierarchical in nature, and so forth. Personality test data may be used to research individual variables and to develop theory in many different ways. For example, suppose you subscribed to a theory that predicted that social isolates—let's refer to them as "introverts"—learned certain types of tasks more quickly than more socially oriented, gregarious people—let's refer to the latter group as "extraverts." Your classmate subscribes to another theory, which has it that the key to learning is not social isolationism or introversion-extraversion but, rather, drive level; according to the latter view, people with higher drive level learn more quickly. One way you might go about settling your dispute is to administer a test of drive level, a test of introversion/extraversion, and a learning task. Analysis of the learning curves for the subjects should provide insight into the question—provided, as Burisch (1984a) reminds us, the instruments used to gauge introversion/extraversion and drive level are satisfactory:

I recall trying to make sense out of the controversy between Hans Eysenck and Kenneth Spence during much of the 1960s on the question of whether "drive level" or "introversion-extraversion" governs speed of conditioning in human subjects. Drive level was almost always operationalized by Taylor's Manifest Anxiety Scale, introversion-extraversion by one scale of the Maudsley Personality Inventory. Even to a neophyte such as myself, it seemed that the two instruments were much too fragile a basis for carrying much weight in the argument. (p. 216)

407

AN OVERVIEW
OF
PERSONALITY
ASSESSMENT:
OBJECTIVE
METHODS

This brings us to our next question. . . .

What makes a "good" personality test?   You know from your reading of previous chapters that at least a partial answer to this question is going to have to do with the psychometric concepts of reliability and validity. But let's take the answer "validity" one step further and ask in this context, "Validity with respect to what?" To state this more concretely: "What sort of correlation with what kind of data should we be looking for?" (Burisch, 1984a, p. 217). What do we need to know, for example, about a "social isolation" personality scale to tell us that it is valid; against what criterion or criteria should we judge scores on this test? How about another hypothetical personality test, one we'll call the "Unresolved Oedipal Conflict Scale" (UnOCS); against what criterion or criteria should we judge scores on the UnOCS? And since the notion of an "unresolved oedipal conflict" is unique to psychoanalytic theory and not a universally accepted reality, must we also require evidence of its existence prior to entertaining notions about the validity of the UnOCS? These are the types of issues that must be satisfactorily resolved before judging the merits of a particular test.

According to Burisch (1984a), the use to which the test will be put must also figure into the evaluation of the instrument, as must the test's economy of administration time:

> Short scales not only save testing time but also avoid subject boredom and fatigue. . . . There are subjects (e.g., depressives) from whom you will not get any response if the test looks too long. There is, by the way, the likelihood that a long scale will actually be less valid than a short one. This is so because the assumptions of the Spearman-Brown formula may be unrealistic for most personality questionnaires. (p. 219)[3]

How does one construct a personality test?   Take a moment at this juncture to think about how you might go about developing and validating a paper-and-pencil test of personality. Jot down those ideas before continuing to read.

- What is the purpose of the personality test you've developed? What is it designed to do?
- Is it to be used to measure traits, types, states, or some combination thereof?

---

3. This "little known possibility" (Burisch, 1984a, p. 219) is discussed in greater detail by Burisch (1984b). Let's emphasize, however, that less validity as a function of test length would indeed be an unexpected finding.

- Is it to be used to gauge the relative strength of various traits? If so, which traits are to be measured?
- Is it to be used to distinguish people on the basis of the healthiness of their personality? Is it to be used to distinguish people on the basis of the suitability of their personalities for a particular kind of work? Is it to be used in general research on personality?
- What kinds of items would your test contain? How would you decide on the content and wording of these items? Would you, for example, rely on a particular theory of personality in devising these items? Or would you rely on no particular theory, but rather on your own life experiences?
- In writing your test items, did you use a true/false format or some other format? Will the items of your test be grouped in any particular order?
- How might you convincingly demonstrate that your test measures what it purports to measure?

Like yourself, would-be authors of personality tests have had to struggle with answering questions like these. Some test authors have relied on theories of personality in constructing their test items, whereas others have steered clear of personality theory and have used more empirical methods. Some test authors have devised forms designed to take a general "inventory" of personality, and others have devised forms to measure specific aspects of it such as the strength of a particular trait. Paper-and-pencil measures of personality differ with respect to the rationale of the measurement model that underlies the test construction. The different models or strategies of test construction have been classified in a number of different ways, and there is even disagreement as to the number of distinctly different models or strategies that exist (Gynther & Gynther, 1976). In the following discussion, we have distinguished four approaches to personality-test construction and have supplemented the discussion with an illustration of at least one test that was developed using each approach.[4] The four approaches are (1) logical or content test construction, (2) factor-analytic test construction, (3) test construction by empirical criterion keying, and (4) the theoretical approach to test construction.

LOGICAL OR CONTENT TEST CONSTRUCTION

One strategy of personality-test construction has been variously referred to as the "logical," "content," "intuitive," or "rational" approach. Here the personality inventory comprises items that logically, intuitively, or rationally seem to belong in the test. Inherent in the logical approach to personality-test construction is the assumption that the test constructor has indeed been logical in the selection of test items. As an adjunct to his or her own logic or intuition, the test developer frequently employs aids such as textbooks, clinical records, experimental data, and

---

4. It is important to note that these approaches to test development are not necessarily mutually exclusive; different aspects of a test's development may contain features of each. For example, prospective items for a test could be selected on a rational/logical basis and/or on a theoretical basis. The selected items could then be arranged into scales on the basis of factor analysis. The utility of each item might then be empirically demonstrated.

conversations with colleagues and others. Suppose you were going to follow the logical or content approach in the construction of a test designed to measure "attitudes toward school." Intuition might tell you that items such as the following should be included:

> (*Answer TRUE or FALSE*)
> I enjoy getting up in the morning for school.
> I like my teacher(s).
> I enjoy seeing my friends at school.
> I enjoy the subjects I learn about at school.

Logically, items like those listed would appear to belong in any test that purported to measure attitudes toward school. The first formal efforts to measure personality employed the logical approach to test construction. The Personal Data Sheet (Woodworth, 1917), later known as the Woodworth Psychoneurotic Inventory, was an early test of personality designed to screen World War I recruits for personality and adjustment problems. The test items tapped self-report of fears, sleep disorders, and other problems deemed to be symptomatic of a trait called psychoneuroticism; the greater the number of such problems, the more psychoneurotic the respondent was presumed to be.

In general the logically constructed test has a certain appeal to test takers since the content is so straightforward and so directly related to the objective of the test. The respondent typically feels more in control of the information he or she is revealing in a content-constructed device than, for example, on an indirect measure of personality such as the Rorschach Inkblots Test. A drawback inherent in the logically constructed test is the ease with which the respondent may withhold or distort important information by failing to respond to items honestly. For this reason, a test developer may initially approach a test's development by selecting logically appealing items, but then depart from logic in order to structurally modify the test to detect deceptive responses (see the discussion of "deviant" responses in the last section of this chapter). Another drawback of the logical approach to test construction pertains to the fact that test takers might not necessarily have the insight and perspective on their problems and the assets to accurately assess themselves. A classic example of a content-constructed instrument—one that is still in use over forty years since its development—is the Mooney Problem Checklist (Mooney & Gordon, 1950).

The Mooney Problem Checklist

Items on this checklist were developed after evaluating statements of problems obtained from approximately four thousand high school students, as well as on the basis of counseling interviews and a review of clinical records. The Checklist items relate to emotional functioning in areas such as home and family; boy/girl relations; courtship and marriage; morals and religion; school/occupation; economic security; social skills and recreation; and health and physical development. Respondents are instructed to underline all problems that are of concern to them and to circle those items that "are of most concern."

There are four forms of the instrument, each appropriate for administration to a different age group from junior high school through adult. The test may be administered individually or in groups. Test-retest reliability coefficients for the various forms of the Mooney Checklist have been found to be relatively high, suggesting consistency in the way that test takers perceive their problems over time. The test results have been found to be especially useful in counseling situations where they may be used as a kind of catalyst to treatment and as a pre- and post-measure of the effectiveness of treatment.

FACTOR-ANALYTIC TEST CONSTRUCTION

Recall from our previous discussion (see Chapter 6) that factor analysis is a data-reduction method. Here, we focus on the use of this statistical technique to identify the minimum number of variables or "factors" that account for the intercorrelations in a number of observed phenomena. To illustrate, let's use an example in which the "number of observed phenomena" are a multitude of colors. Let's suppose that you want to paint your apartment but have no idea as to the color that would go best with your "early undergraduate" decor. You go to the local paint stores in your area and obtain free card samples of every shade of color paint known to humanity—thousands of color samples. Let's further suppose you undertook a "factor analysis" of these thousands of color samples—that is, you attempted to identify the minimum number of variables or factors that account for the intercorrelations between all of these colors. You would discover that, accounting for the intercorrelations, there existed three factors (which might be labeled "primary factors") and four more factors (which might be labeled "secondary" or "second-order" factors), the latter set of factors being combinations of the first set of factors. Since all colors can be reduced to three primary colors and their combinations, the three primary factors would correspond to the three primary colors, red, yellow, and blue (which you might christen factor R, factor Y and factor B), and the four secondary or second-order factors would correspond to all of the possible combinations that could be made from the primary factors (factors RY, RB, YB, and RYB).

The color illustration may be helpful to keep in mind as we review how factor analysis can be used in the construction of personality tests. Popular tests such as the Eysenck Personality Inventory, the Guilford-Zimmerman Temperament Survey, and the Sixteen Personality Factor (16 PF) Questionnaire all were derived through the use of factor-analytic strategies. We have chosen the 16 PF to describe in greater detail.

The 16 PF

Just as you might have an idea that you wish to analyze all colors into their primary factors, so the notion Raymond Bernard Cattell had when he set out to construct a personality test was the analysis of all personality traits into what might be called primary or "source" traits. Construction of the test items began with a look at the previous research by Allport and Odbert (1936), which suggested that there were more than 18,000 personality trait names and terms in the English language. Of these, however, only about a quarter were "real traits of personality" or words and terms that designated "generalized and personalized

411

AN OVERVIEW
OF
PERSONALITY
ASSESSMENT:
OBJECTIVE
METHODS

determining tendencies—consistent and stable modes of an individual's adjustment to his environment . . . not . . . merely temporary and specific behavior" (Allport, 1937, p. 306). Cattell added to this list some trait names and terms employed in the professional psychology and psychiatric literature and then had judges rate "just distinguishable" differences between all of the words (Cattell, 1957). The result was a reduction in the size of the list to 171 trait names and terms. College students were asked to rate their friends with respect to these trait names and terms, and the factor-analyzed results of that rating further reduced the number of names and terms to 36, which were referred to by Cattell as "surface traits." Still more research indicated that 16 basic dimensions or "source traits" could be distilled. The Sixteen Personality Factor Questionnaire is a test that contains items tapping each of the 16 source traits listed in Table 12–2. (See also Figure 12–2.)

The 16 PF was designed for use with junior and senior high school students as well as college and general adult populations. The test was normed on more than fifteen thousand people. Short-term test-retest reliability estimates have been relatively high, though estimates of long-term test-retest reliability have been considerably lower. The poor long-term test-retest reliability coefficients raise questions concerning the stability of the traits the test purports to measure. Indeed, academicians are by no means in unanimous agreement that Cattell has discovered *the* "source traits" of personality or that the data from the test yield 16 factors (see Cattell & Krug, 1986). Still the test is among the most widely used objective personality tests (Karson & O'Dell, 1989).

Numerous other forms of this test have subsequently been developed, including an abbreviated version of the test, a "low literate" form for people with third- to sixth-grade reading levels, a taped version for the visually handicapped,

Table 12–2

Factors of the Sixteen Personality Factor Questionnaire (16 PF)

	Low score	*High score*
Sociable	Reserved	Warm, cooperative
Intelligent	Dull	Bright
Mature	Affected by feelings, undemonstrative	Emotionally stable, calm
Dominant	Obedient, submissive	Assertive
Cheerful	Sober, serious	Enthusiastic
Persistent	Disregards rules, undependable	Conscientious
Adventurous	Shy	Venturesome
Effeminate	Toughminded, realistic, vigorous	Tenderminded, sensitive
Suspicious	Trusting	Suspicious
Imaginative	Practical, conventional	Imaginative
Shrewd	Forthright, naive	Sophisticated, shrewd
Insecure	Self-assured	Guilt prone, timid
Radical	Conservative, traditional	Experimenting
Self-sufficient	Group-dependent	Self-sufficient, resourceful
Controlled	Uncontrolled	Controlled
Tense	Relaxed	Tense

Figure 12–2 *George Washington's 16 PF.* A computerized, narrative report is available for the scoring and interpretation of the 16 PF. The examinee in this case is George Washington (as in "father of our country") at age 44. No, the publishers of the 16 PF were not distributing the test as early as 1776. Rather, several psychologists familiar with the test were asked to study biographical information on Washington and then derive a profile showing how they think he would have scored.

"Now where am I supposed to get a number 2 pencil?"

```
            N A R R A T I V E    S C O R I N G    R E P O R T
          for The Sixteen Personality Factor Questionnaire- 16 PF


     This report is intended to be used in conjunction with professional
     judgment. The statements it contains should be viewed as hypotheses
     to be validated against other sources of data.   All information in
     this report should be treated confidentially and responsibly.

     NAME-George Washington
                                                      July 4, 1776
                                                      AGE-44; SEX-M

     * * * * * * * * * * * *  VALIDITY SCALES  * * * * * * * * * * * * * *
     *                                                                   *
     *   Validity indicators are within acceptable ranges.              *
     *      Faking good/MD (sten) score is very low (2).                *
     *      Faking bad (sten) score is extremely low (i).               *
     * * * * * * * * * * * * * * * * * * * * * * * * * * * * * * * * * * *
```

Figure 12–2 *(continued)*

```
       SCORES                          16 PF     PROFILE
      Raw   Sten      LEFT MEANING   1 2 3 4 5 6 7 8 9 10  RIGHT MEANING       %
            U   C                           average
                                      ------------------------
       7    4   4   A  Cool, Reserved      !<---    !       Warm, Easygoing    23
      12   10  10   B  Concrete Thinking   !   --------->   Abstract Thinking  99
      23    9   9   C  Easily Upset        !   ------->     Calm, Stable       96
      15    7   7   E  Not Assertive       !   --->!        Dominant           77
      10    4   4   F  Sober, Serious      !<---   !        Enthusiastic       23
      17    8   8   G  Expedient           !   ----->       Conscientious      89
      23    9   9   H  Shy, Timid          !   ------->     Venturesome        96
       4    3   3   I  Tough-Minded     <-----    !         Sensitive          11
       6    5   5   L  Trusting            !  <-   !         Suspicious         40
      10    4   4   M  Practical           !<---   !         Imaginative        23
       9    6   6   N  Forthright          !  ->   !         Shrewd             60
       6    4   4   O  Self-Assured        !<----  !         Self-Doubting      23
       8    5   5   Q1 Conservative        !  <-   !         Experimenting      40
      16    9   9   Q2 Group-Oriented      !   ------ -->    Self-Sufficient    96
      19    9   9   Q3 Undisciplined       !   ------->      Self-Disciplined   96
       9    5   5   Q4 Relaxed             !  <-   !         Tense, Driven      40
                                      ------------------------
```

Note: "U" indicates uncorrected sten scores. "C" indicates sten scores corrected for distortion (if appropriate). The interpretation will proceed on the basis of corrected scores. This report was processed using male adult (GP) norms for Form A.

SECOND-ORDER FACTORS   COMPOSITE SCORES

Extraversion..average (4.5)   Neuroticism...below average (3.6)
Anxiety........low (2.9)   Leadership....very high (9.4)
Tough Poise...high (7.8)   Creativity....very high (8.7)
Independence..high (7.5)
Control.......very high (8.9)   Profile Pattern Code = 2133

PERSONAL COUNSELING OBSERVATIONS

Adequacy of adjustment is above average (7.4).
Rigidity of behavior controls is very high (8.9).

PRIMARY PERSONALITY CHARACTERISTICS OF SPECIAL INTEREST

Capacity for abstract skills is extremely high.
Problems are approached with calm emotional stability and realism.
Regard for strict moral standards, duty, and conscientious perseverance is high.
He is venturesome, socially bold and spontaneous, and not easily inhibited. This tendency is very high.
As a person, he is realistic, tough-minded, and unsentimental.
Being self-sufficient, he prefers tackling things resourcefully, alone.
He has a definite self-concept and sets out to control himself to fit what he feels his social reputation requires.

413

Figure 12–2 *(continued)*

BROAD INFLUENCE PATTERNS

His attention is directed about equally toward the outer environment and toward inner thoughts and feelings. Extraversion is average (4.5).

At the present time, he sees himself as less anxious than most people. His anxiety score is low (2.9).

Tasks and problems are approached with emphasis upon rationality and getting things done. Less attention is paid to emotional relationships. This tendency is high (7.8).

His life style is independent and self-directed leading to active attempts to achieve control of the environment. In this respect, he is high (7.5).

He tends to conform to generally accepted standards of conduct and has probably internalized societal standards as his own. He feels strongly obligated to meet his responsibilities. This tendency is very high (8.9).

VOCATIONAL OBSERVATIONS

At client's own level of abilities, potential for creative functioning is very high (8.7).

Potential for benefit from formal academic training, at client's own level of abilities, is very high (9.4).

In a group of peers, potential for leadership is very high (9.4).

Potential for success in jobs that reward interpersonal, sales, and persuasive skills is very high (8.5).

Potential for success in job areas that reward precision and dependability is high (7.8).

Potential for growth to meet increasing job demands is extremely high (10.0).

The extent to which the client is accident prone is very low (2.1).

OCCUPATIONAL FITNESS PROJECTIONS

In this segment of the report his 16 PF results are compared with various occupational profiles. All projections should be considered with respect to other information about him, particularly his interests and abilities.

1. ARTISTIC PROFESSIONS

    Artist.........................extremely high (10.0)
    Musician.......................high (8.1)
    Writer.........................extremely high (10.0)

2. COMMUNITY AND SOCIAL SERVICE

    Employment Counselor...........high (8.2)
    Firefighter....................extremely high (10.0)
    Nurse..........................very high (8.6)
    Physician......................average (6.2)
    Police Officer.................high (8.0)
    Priest (R.C.)..................average (5.3)
    Service Station Dealer.........average (5.9)
    Social Worker..................below average (4.4)

Figure 12-2 *(continued)*

3. SCIENTIFIC PROFESSIONS

```
        Biologist.....................extremely high (10.0)
        Chemist.......................extremely high (10.0)
        Engineer......................very high (9.4)
        Geologist.....................very high (9.4)
        Physicist.....................extremely high (10.0)
        Psychologist..................extremely high (9.7)
```

4. TECHNICAL PERSONNEL

```
        Accountant....................extremely high (10.0)
        Airline Flight Attendant......average (6.1)
        Airline Pilot.................very high (9.1)
        Computer Programmer...........extremely high (10.0)
        Editorial Worker..............extremely high (10.0)
        Electrician...................extremely high (10.0)
        Mechanic......................extremely high (10.0)
        Psychiatric Technician........extremely high (10.0)
        Time/Motion Study Analyst.....high (8.0)
```

5. INDUSTRIAL/CLERICAL PERSONNEL

```
        Janitor.......................very high (8.5)
        Kitchen Worker................average (5.7)
        Machine Operator..............high (8.1)
        Secretary-Clerk...............high (7.8)
        Truck Driver..................above average (7.4)
```

6. SALES PERSONNEL

```
        Real Estate Agent.............high (7.9)
        Retail Counter Clerk..........above average (6.9)
```

7. ADMINISTRATIVE AND SUPERVISORY PERSONNEL

```
        Bank Manager..................very high (8.5)
        Business Executive............extremely high (9.8)
        Credit Union Manager..........high (8.4)
        Middle Level Manager..........very high (9.3)
        Personnel Manager.............high (7.6)
        Production Manager............very high (8.8)
        Plant Foreman.................high (8.2)
        Sales Supervisor..............very high (8.5)
        Store Manager.................below average (4.4)
```

8. ACADEMIC PROFESSIONS

```
        Teacher-Elementary Level......above average (6.5)
        Teacher-Junior High Level.....below average (3.5)
        Teacher-Senior High Level.....below average (3.7)
        University Professor..........high (7.5)
        School Counselor..............above average (7.3)
        School Superintendent.........very high (9.3)
        University Administrator......extremely high (10.0)
```

Item Summary

Item responses have not been provided.

and translations into various languages. The philosophy of the 16 PF was extended downward in the construction of various other personality tests, including the Early School Personality Questionnaire (for ages 6 to 8), the Children's Personality Questionnaire (for ages 8 to 12), and the High School Personality Questionnaire (for ages 12 to 18). The use of this series of tests from childhood through adulthood could provide a relatively consistent yardstick by which to gauge personality functioning at various developmental stages.

One of the limitations inherent in the factor-analytic technique is the problem of naming factors that have been identified through the statistical analysis. Suppose, for example, you obtained high intercorrelations between the following traits on a test of personality:

Depression
Anger
Fatigue
Conservative
Bright

How would you name the factor that all of these traits seemed to "load on"? Of course there is no rule to naming factors, and the name that you choose might be meaningful for you but not necessarily a name that others would readily accept. Another limitation inherent in factor-analytic approaches to test construction concerns the controversy that may arise concerning the selection of a particular factor-analytic technique. As has been pointed out by Comrey, Backer, and Glaser (1973, p. 11), "There are many different methods of carrying out a factor analysis. Several different factor analysts can take the same data and come up with as many different solutions . . . all of these different solutions for the same data by different analysts represent interpretations of the original correlation matrix that may be equally correct from the mathematical point of view."

TEST CONSTRUCTION BY EMPIRICAL CRITERION KEYING

Personality-test construction by the strategy of empirical criterion keying may be summed up in the following simplified way:

1. Create a number of test items that presume to measure one or more traits.
2. Administer the test items to at least two groups of people:
   a. a "criterion group" composed of people you know to possess the trait being measured, and
   b. a control group of people who are presumed not to possess the trait in question
3. Items that discriminate in a statistically significant way with respect to the criterion and control groups are retained, whereas those items that do not discriminate between the two groups are discarded.

This method of test construction is referred to as "empirical" because only those items that demonstrate an actual (empirical) relationship between the test item and the trait in question are retained. It is called "criterion keying" because each item of the test is keyed to a criterion, the criterion being related to the particular trait in question. Burisch (1984a) characterized the essence of this approach by saying, "If shoe size as a predictor improves your ability to predict performance as an airplane pilot, use it" (p. 218). He offered this tongue-in-cheek description of how a test developer might develop an "M-F" test—a test to differentiate males from females—by means of empirical criterion keying:

> Allegedly not knowing where the differences were, he or she would never dream of using an item such as "I can grow a beard if I want to" or "In a restaurant I tend to prefer the ladies' room to the men's room." Rather, a heterogeneous pool of items would be assembled and administered to a sample of men and women. Next, samples would be compared item by item. Any item discriminating sufficiently well would qualify for inclusion in the M-F test. (p. 214)

Since test construction by means of empirical criterion keying always involves the comparison of at least two groups of people (one group possessing the trait, the other not), this approach to test construction has also been referred to as the method of "contrasted groups." Two well-known personality tests developed by this method are the Minnesota Multiphasic Personality Inventory (MMPI) as well as its revision, the MMPI-2, and the California Psychological Inventory (CPI).

The MMPI

Conceived in the 1930s by psychologist Starke R. Hathaway and psychiatrist/neurologist John C. McKinley as an aid in assessing the mental health of patients seen in medical practice, a test first called the "Medical & Psychiatric Inventory" was renamed when published by the University of Minnesota Press in 1941 as the "Minnesota Multiphasic Personality Inventory" (MMPI). Hathaway (Figure 12–3) reminisced that "It was difficult to persuade a publisher to accept the MMPI" (Dahlstrom & Welsh, 1960, p. vii), though the test quickly gained popularity among psychologists and has become the single most widely used objective personality test (Lubin, Larsen, & Mattarazzo, 1984).

The MMPI consists of 550 statements to which the examinee responds "true" or "false." In one form of the test, statements are printed on cards, and a third category, "cannot say," is included (Dahlstrom, Welsh, & Dahlstrom, 1972). For the group-administered version of the test, all unanswered items in the test booklet are scored in the "cannot say" category. The MMPI may be used with persons 16 or older who have at least a sixth-grade education (or an IQ of 80). Tape-recorded and foreign-language versions of the inventory have also been constructed.

As reported by the test authors (Hathaway & McKinley, 1940, 1951), research preceding the final selection of items involved the study of psychiatric textbooks, psychiatric reports, and previously published personality-test items. The test items that were ultimately selected reflected 26 content categories, including general health, family issues, religious attitudes, sexual identification, and psychiatric symptomatology (Hathaway & McKinley, 1951). These items were then presented to both criterion groups and a control group. Lanyon and Goodstein (1971, p. 76) described the normal control group as follows: "1500 control sub-

Figure 12–3 *Starke Rosecrans Hathaway (1903–1984).*

"With his consistent emphasis on objectivity and eclecticism, his insistence on data in preference to inference, his commitment to collegiality and scientific openness, and his scholarly respect for both the biological and psychological dimensions of human personality, Starke Hathaway has an assured place as one of the founders of modern clinical psychology"—so read the obituary for the co-developer of the MMPI, a test that in "its many versions and in nearly 50 languages . . . has been employed in hundreds of different research uses and practical applications for nearly five decades" (Dahlstrom, Meehl, & Schofield, 1986).

Born in Michigan, Hathaway spent much of his youth in Marysville, Ohio. He earned his bachelor's and master's degree at Ohio University in Athens and his Ph.D. at the University of Minnesota. Through the efforts of a psychiatrist at the University Medical School, J. Charnley McKinley, Hathaway was granted a position in the neuropsychiatry division. The two men would subsequently collaborate in the development of the Minnesota Multiphasic Personality Inventory MMPI (Hathaway & McKinley, 1940).

Dahlstrom, Meehl, & Schofield (1986, p. 835) remind us that:

Hathaway's identification with the MMPI overshadowed his equally important contributions as a teacher and therapist. He was a master clinician to whom medical colleagues frequently referred puzzling or difficult patients for diagnosis or treatment. The more difficult and challenging the case was, the more intense, persistent, and innovative were Hathaway's efforts. He rarely failed to achieve a significant result. . . . Many of Hathaway's treatment methods anticipated the behavioral interventions of today,

including such methods as mild aversive shock, suggestion and hypnosis, modeling, and habit retraining.

Hathaway's long list of lifetime achievements includes being recipient of the American Psychological Association's award for Distinguished Contributions for Applications in Psychology. Hathaway retired from the University of Minnesota in 1971 and he died in his home in Minneapolis on July 4, 1984.

"When I came to the University hospitals in about 1937 and began to work with patients, I started to change from a physiological psychologist toward becoming a clinical psychologist. As we went on grand rounds, I, with my white coat and newly developing sense of role, expected that the medical staff would want the data and insights of a psychologist. I still remember one day when I was thinking this and suddenly asked myself, suppose they *did* turn to me for aid in understanding the patients' psychology; what substantive information did I have that wasn't obvious on the face of the case or that represented psy-

chology rather than what the psychiatrist had already said. I could, perhaps, say that the patient was neurotic or an introvert or other such items suggested from my available tests. I had intelligence tests, . . . and a few other inventories. I didn't have any objective personality data that would go deeper or be more analytically complex than what would suggest general statements, such as that the patient was maladjusted. . . . [As] I then perceived [personality inventories, the] variables and interpretation were not in current jargon nor did they develop suggestions that would be of value to a staff required to make routine diagnostic, prognostic, and treatment decisions.

The real impetus for the MMPI came from reports of results with insulin shock treatment of schizophrenia. The early statistics on treatment outcomes, as is characteristic of new treatment ideas, promised everything from 100% cure to no effect and no value. It occurred to me that the enormous variance in effectiveness as reported from hospital to hospital depended partly upon the unreliability of the validity criterion—the diagnostic statements. If there were some way in which we could pick experimental groups of patients using objective methods, then outcome tests for treatment efficacy should be more uniform and meaningful. I did not have any objective personality instrument that was adaptable to such a design; and, thinking about the needs, I got the idea of an empirically developed inventory that could be extended indefinitely by development of new scales." (S. R. Hathaway, quoted in Mednick, Higgins, & Kirschenbaum, 1975, pp. 350–351).

jects were drawn from hospital visitors, normal clients at the University of Minnesota Testing Bureau, local WPA workers, and general medical patients." The criterion group was eight clinical groups of psychiatric inpatients from the University of Minnesota hospital. Those items reflecting statistically significant differences between the responses of the clinical criterion group and the control subjects were retained. Analysis of the clinical groups' responses in contrast to the control group made it possible to develop "scales" that corresponded to each disorder. The MMPI consists of eight clinical scales that were developed in this fashion (as well as two additional scales, Masculinity-Femininity and Social Introversion-Extraversion, that employed nonpsychiatric criterion groups in their development). A brief description of each criterion group used in the development of the ten clinical scales appears in Table 12–3. More detailed information concerning the construction and validation of the MMPI can be found in Welsh and Dahlstrom (1956).

419

AN OVERVIEW
OF
PERSONALITY
ASSESSMENT:
OBJECTIVE
METHODS

Table 12–3

The Clinical Criterion Groups for MMPI Scales

Scale	Criterion group
1. Hypochondriasis (Hs)	The criterion group for this scale was patients who showed exaggerated concerns about their physical health.
2. Depression (D)	The criterion group for this scale was clinically depressed patients; unhappy and pessimistic about their future.
3. Hysteria (Hy)	The criterion group for this scale included patients with conversion reactions.
4. Psychopathic deviate (Pd)	The criterion group for this scale was patients who had had histories of delinquency and other antisocial behavior.
5. Masculinity-femininity (Mf)	The criterion group for this scale was Minnesota draftees, airline stewardesses, and male homosexual college students from the University of Minnesota campus community.
6. Paranoia (Pa)	The criterion group for this scale was patients who exhibited paranoid symptomatology such as ideas of reference suspiciousness, delusions of persecution, and delusions of grandeur.
7. Psychasthenia (Pt)	The criterion group for this scale was anxious, obsessive-compulsive, guilt-ridden, and self-doubting patients.
8. Schizophrenia (Sc)	The criterion group for this scale was patients who were diagnosed as schizophrenic (various subtypes)
9. Hypomania (Ma)	The criterion group for this scale was patients, most diagnosed as manic-depressive, who exhibited manic symptomatology such as elevated mood, excessive activity, and easy distractibility.
10. Social introversion (Si)	The criterion group for this scale was college students who had scored at the extremes on a test of introversion-extraversion.

In addition to ten clinical scales, the MMPI contains three "validity scales" that were designed to serve as indicators of factors such as the operation of response sets, attitudinal factors, or misunderstandings of directions that may influence test results. These include the L scale (sometimes referred to as the "Lie" scale), the F scale (sometimes referred to as the "Infrequency" scale), and the K (correction) scale. The L scale contains 15 items that are somewhat negative but that apply to most people, such as "I do not always tell the truth," or "I gossip a little at times" (Dahlstrom et al., 1972, p. 109). The preparedness of the examinee to reveal *anything* negative about himself or herself will be called into question if the score on the L scale does not fall within certain limits. The 64 items on the F scale (1) are infrequently endorsed by members of nonpsychiatric populations (that is, normal people), and (2) do not fit into any known pattern of deviance. A response of "True" to an item such as the following would be scored on the F scale: "It would be better if almost all laws were thrown away" (Dahlstrom et al., 1972, p. 115). An elevated F score may mean that the respondent did not take the test seriously and was just responding to items randomly. Alternatively, the individual with a high F score may be a very eccentric individual or someone who was attempting to "fake bad." Malingerers in the armed services, people intent on committing fraud with respect to health insurance, and criminals attempting to "cop a psychiatric plea" are some of the groups of people who might be expected to have elevated F scores on their profiles.

Like the L score and the F score, the K score is a reflection of the frankness of the test taker's self-report. An elevated K score is associated with defensiveness and the desire to present a favorable impression. A low K score is associated with excessive self-criticism, desire to detail deviance, and/or desire to fake bad. A "True" response to the item "I certainly feel useless at times" and a "False" response to "At times I am all full of energy" (Dahlstrom et al., 1972, p. 125) would be scored on the K scale. The K scale is sometimes used to "correct" scores on five of the clinical scales; the scores are statistically corrected for an individual's overwillingness or unwillingness to admit deviancy.

The MMPI may be computer-scored, even computer-interpreted; computerized reports range in detail from simply a numerical score for each scale to long and detailed narrative reports. Whether computer-scored or hand-scored, the raw test scores are converted to standard scores that have a mean of 50 and a standard deviation of 10. Standard scores of 70 or greater on the clinical scales are considered to indicate a problem that must be investigated. For example, a score of 88 on the Depression scale would suggest an extremely depressed and pessimistic individual, while an 85 on the Hypochondriasis scale would be reflective of an individual who has frequent physical complaints and excessive concern with bodily functioning. Interpretations on the MMPI are generally made, however, on the basis of the entire test pattern or profile, not on the basis of a score on any one scale.

In contemporary usage, MMPI scales are referred to by number rather than their original name. This is so because literal interpretation of the names of the scales would be inaccurate. A high score on the Schizophrenia (Sc) scale does not necessarily mean that the test taker would be diagnosed as schizophrenic; the test taker might well be diagnosed as suffering from some other form of psychosis. It might even be possible for an individual with an elevated Sc scale to be diagnosed

421

AN OVERVIEW
OF
PERSONALITY
ASSESSMENT:
OBJECTIVE
METHODS

as normal. In practical usage, the scales are viewed as continuums with respect to particular personality traits associated with the criterion group the scale was based on. For example, a person scoring high on the Paranoia scale would be regarded as high in suspiciousness, feelings of persecution, and distrust. Note that this use is inconsistent with the purpose of the test as conceived by the test authors (to be an instrument used for classification and differential diagnosis).

Since its inception in the early 1940s, the MMPI has been used in clinical and research settings with a variety of individuals. The consequence of decades of use and research is a proliferation of new MMPI scales based on the test patterns of various populations. Over 400 new MMPI scales have been devised since the test's publication and new scales, made up of various constellations of MMPI data, are created and reported on regularly. Recently, for example, MMPI scales for possible use or research were reported on for identifying adolescents with over-controlled hostility (Truscott, 1990), as well as people with panic disorders (Lewis, Turtletaub, Pohl, Rainey, & Rosenbaum, 1990), drug misuse habits (Lavelle, Hammersley, & Forsyth, 1991), and memory and concentration difficulties due to closed-head trauma (Gass, Russell, & Hamilton, 1990). In addition to creating new scales, researchers frequently reevaluate, and suggest new uses for, existing scales. For example, in their reevaluation of the MMPI Masculinity-Femininity scale, Ward and Dillon (1990) reported that male and female patients who scored high on femininity were rated higher on anxiety, depressed mood, guilt feelings, and tension than were low-scorers. Researchers have examined and compared not only the MMPI responses of normals and persons with various psychiatric diagnoses, but also the test protocols of members of more "offbeat" populations as well. Included in the latter category is research with members of groups as diverse as a serpent-handling religious cult (Tellegen et al., 1969), castrated males (Yamamoto & Seeman, 1960), submarine school dropouts (King, 1959), and civilians selected for isolated northern stations (Wright, Sister, & Chylinski, 1963). Several encyclopedias of MMPI profiles—referred to in the profession as "cookbooks"—are available for use by clinicians (for example, Hathaway & Meehl, 1951; Dahlstrom, Welsh, & Dahlstrom, 1972; see also, Swenson, Pearson, & Osborne, 1973; Butcher, 1979; Dahlstrom, Lachar, & Dahlstrom, 1986).

Critics of the MMPI have cited limitations relating to its construction and use. In light of the widespread use of this instrument, the original normative sample has been criticized as being deficient in terms of size and the representativeness of the general population. Other criticism has been leveled at the sheer age of the norms; as Dahlstrom et al. pointed out (1972, p. 8): "Each subject taking the MMPI, therefore, is being compared to the way a typical man or woman endorsed those items. In 1940, such a Minnesota normal adult was about thirty-five years old, was married, lived in a small town or rural area, had had eight years of general schooling, and worked at a skilled or semiskilled trade (or was married to a man with such an occupational level)."

In October 1983 a new set of MMPI norms for normal adults was published. The norms were developed by a group of researchers from the Mayo Clinic of Rochester, Minnesota (Colligan, Osborne, Swenson, & Offord, 1983), and included MMPI responses from 1,408 normal subjects (people who were not under the care of any health-care professional), ranging in age from 18 through 99 years and living in the same general geographic area as the sample used by Hathaway and McKinley (1940). The results indicated that people living in the 1980s tended to have elevated MMPI profiles in contrast to a comparable sample of people living in the 1940s (and the increases tended to be greater for men than for women). Colligan, Osborne, Swenson, and Offord (1984) offered two alternative (though not mutually exclusive) explanations for this finding: (1) people in the 1980s may be under more psychological and physical stress than were people in the 1940s, and (2) changes in response patterns may be due to changes in societal mores and perceptions. Colligan et al. (1984) interpreted their findings as being of practical as well as statistical significance, and they cautioned that "clinicians take a somewhat more conservative approach to profile interpretation with more careful consideration of the impact of age and sex on profile configuration."

At this writing, published experience with the updated norms has been scarce and the byword with respect to their use seems to be "caution." Miller and Streiner (1986) examined MMPI data for 2,083 people using the original norms and those from Colligan et al. (1983). These researchers noted sufficient lack of comparability between the two sets of norms to caution that the newer norms not be used independently—but rather in conjunction with the original norms—until the clinical relevance of the differences are determined. In reviewing the work of Colligan et al., Greene (1985) reached a similar conclusion:

> The real issue is whether the use of contemporary MMPI norms results in more accurate predictions. . . . In the empirical spirit with which the MMPI was developed, it seems that we must wait to see the data. Until then, all we can say is that contemporary adults earn somewhat different scores on the various MMPI scales than the adults of the 1930s. Hopefully, such research will be forthcoming so we can begin to evaluate the issue of interpretive accuracy. (p. 109)

Whether the new or original norms are employed, it has always been important for the test user to temper interpretations made from the test data with reference to the limitations of the population used as a normative sample. Thus, for example, Colligan et al. (1983) pointed out that their norms would not be appropriate for use with ethnic minority groups, and they encouraged the development of norms expressly designed for such use. In this vein, it would also be important to learn more about the applicability of the new norms to other geographic areas and groups (Miller & Streiner, 1986).

From the standpoint of test construction, the MMPI has been criticized for having some of the same items used in the different scales. The result of this structural redundancy is that some of the scales are highly correlated with one another. If the instrument is to be used as a tool of differential diagnosis, it would be preferable for the scales not to correlate with one another. There also exists some confusion as to the meaning of a low score on the clinical scales; while the meaning of an elevated score on a clinical scale may be clear, Wiggins (1973) has pointed out that given the way the MMPI was constructed, the meaning of a significantly low score is unclear. Other frequently cited limitations of the MMPI have to do with the ready availability of its computerized scoring and the possible misuses inherent in any computer-generated test reports (more on that subject in Chapter 20); the offensiveness of some of the questions to some test takers (Butcher & Tellegen, 1966; Gallucci, 1986), particularly questions related to sex, religion, bladder and bowel functions; and the length of the test (which has been viewed by some as excessive). One attempted remedy for the latter criticism has been the development of short forms of the test—forms that contain only a sampling of items from each of the scales and a fraction of the original total of items (Stevens & Reilley, 1980). In general, however, the short form of the MMPI seems not to have lived up to its promise in terms of psychometric soundness or clinical utility (Helmes & McLaughlin, 1983; Hart, Lutz, McNeill, & Adkins, 1986).

In spite of its limitations, the MMPI remains the most used and researched of all the existing personality inventories. Its use as a tool to describe aspects of one's personality has found application in a variety of clinical, counseling, educational, worksite, and research settings. The large and ever-expanding literature on this test provides a library of reference material to MMPI users. Although the test is seldom used in the way it was designed to be used—as a measure of differential diagnosis—it is no doubt of value to clinicians in their everyday work with psychiatric patients; MMPI results provide insight into the extent and magnitude of patients' problems. The test results are frequently viewed as tentative hypotheses about the examinee's psychopathology that await clarification and validation from other sources of data (see Graham, 1977).

The MMPI-2

Though the MMPI has gained widespread acceptance, and is, in fact, the most frequently administered clinical test in the United States (Butcher, 1990), the test, as we have seen, was in need of revision. The sample on which the MMPI was standardized was limited and unrepresentative of the United States population. The language and content of some of the items were not contemporary and in some instances could be construed as being sexist. There was also concern that "the original MMPI item pool was not broad enough to permit assessment of many characteristics judged important by many test users" (Graham, 1990a, p. 9). James Butcher, W. Grant Dahlstrom, John R. Graham, and Auke Tellegen (1989) were charged with the task of revising the test, and in August of 1989 the MMPI-2 became a reality.

Several changes are apparent in the revision. Approximately 14% of the original items were rewritten to correct grammatical errors and to make the language more contemporary, nonsexist, and readable. Items from the original scale judged to have been objectionable because they contained references to religion, sex, or bodily functions were eliminated. Added were items addressing topics such as drug abuse, suicide potential, "Type A" behavior patterns, marital adjustment, and attitudes toward work.[5]

The MMPI-2 still contains its original clinical scales as well as its original validity scales, although three new validity scales—Back-Page Infrequency (Fb), True Response Inconsistency (TRIN), and Variable Response Inconsistency

5. First described by cardiologists Meyer Friedman and Ray Rosenman (1974; Rosenman, Brand, Jenkins, Friedman, Straus, & Wurm, 1975), the "Type A" personality is characterized by competitiveness, haste, restlessness, impatience, feelings of being time-pressured, and strong needs for achievement and dominance. In contrast, "Type B" behavior is more mellow and "laid-back." A 52-item, self-report inventory called the Jenkins Activity Survey (Jenkins, Zyzanski, & Rosenman, 1979) has been widely used to measure the degree to which a respondent is Type A or Type B.

(VRIN)—each considered experimental as of this writing (Graham, 1990) have been added. Some test takers' diligence in test taking wanes as the test wears on so that by the "back pages," a random and/or inconsistent pattern of responses is in evidence. The Fb scale contains seldom-endorsed items and is designed to detect such a pattern. The TRIN scale consists of 23 pairs of items worded as opposites; that is, consistency would dictate a "True" response to one form of the item, and a "False" response to its opposite wording. Similar to the TRIN scale, the VRIN scale also yields a measure of consistency; it contains item pairs worded as either opposites or as similar statements.

A new set of content scales designed to assess personality factors such as anxiety, fears, obsessiveness, depression, health concerns, anger, cynicism, anti-social practices, self-esteem, social discomfort, family problems, and work inter-ference was developed for the MMPI-2 by Butcher, Graham, Williams, and Ben-Porath (1989). These scales were developed using "both rational and statistical procedures to assure rational content relevance and strong statistical properties" (Butcher & Pope, 1990, p. 37). Studies are currently in progress to determine how reliable and valid these new scales are. A summary comparison of the MMPI-2 with its predecessor along selected dimensions is presented in Table 12–4.

The 2,600 individuals (1,462 females, 1,138 males) from seven states who made up the MMPI-2 standardization sample had been matched to 1980 United States census data on the variables of age, gender, minority status, social class, and education (Butcher, 1990). Whereas the original MMPI did not contain any nonwhites in the standardization sample, the MMPI-2 sample was 81% white and 19% nonwhite. Age of subjects in the sample ranged from 18 years to 85 years. Formal education ranged from 3 years to 20+ years, with higher educated people overrepresented in the sample (Graham, 1990). Median annual family income for females in the sample was $25,000 to $30,000. Median annual family income for males in the sample was $30,000 to $35,000. For research purposes, MMPI-2 test

Table 12–4

A Comparison of the MMPI and MMPI-2

MMPI	*MMPI-2*
566 items, including 16 repeated items	567 items with no repeated items
Includes nonworking, nonscored items	No nonworking, nonscored items
4 validity scales (?, L, F, K)	7 validity scales (?, L, F, K, Fb, VRIN, TRIN)
10 clinical scales (Hs, D, Hy, Pd, Mf, Pa, Pt, Sc, Ma, Si)	10 clinical scales (Hs, D, Hy, Pd, Mf, Pa, Pt, Sc, Ma, Si) with objectionable content eliminated from F, Hs, D, Mf, and Si scales
Standardized on 724 individuals with mean educational level of eighth grade from rural, white Minnesota	Standardized on 2,600 individuals with mean educational level of 13 years and representative of 1980 U.S. census on gender, ethnicity, and socioeconomic level
Can be hand-scored or computer-scored	Can be hand-scored or computer-scored

Adapted from Butcher and Graham (1989)

data were also collected from samples of various populations such as airline pilot applicants, people in chronic pain, college students, psychiatric inpatients, and couples in marital counseling. Research with this instrument in its finished or pilot form has been reported regarding its utility in areas as diverse as chemical dependency evaluation (McKenna & Butcher, 1987), marital counseling and assessment (Hjemboe & Butcher, 1990), psychiatric evaluation in inpatient settings (Graham & Butcher, 1988), and evaluation of patients with chronic pain (Keller & Butcher, 1989).

425

AN OVERVIEW
OF
PERSONALITY
ASSESSMENT:
OBJECTIVE
METHODS

The new test is not without its critics. Adler (1990), for example, has questioned the comparability of MMPI and MMPI-2 scores, the validity of the new content scales, and the utility of treatment recommendations made on the basis of MMPI-2 scores. However, preliminary research with the new instrument has been encouraging (Ben-Porath & Butcher, 1989; Graham, 1990a, 1990b) and there is every reason to believe that the MMPI-2 will continue in the tradition of its predecessor as one of the world's most widely used—and widely researched—psychological tests.

California Psychological Inventory

Another test constructed by the method of empirical criterion keying is the California Psychological Inventory (CPI). This test is a "kissing cousin" of the MMPI in that many of its items were drawn directly or revised from the MMPI. In contrast to the MMPI, which was developed to assess maladjustment, the CPI was designed for use with normal populations aged 13 and older, and its scales emphasize more positive and socially desirable aspects of personality than do the scales of the MMPI.

The CPI is available from its publisher in its original form (Gough, 1956) or in a revised edition (Gough, 1987). The original edition of the test contains 18 scales, which may be grouped into four categories depending on whether they primarily measure interpersonal effectiveness (including measures of poise, self-assurance, and self-acceptance), intrapersonal controls (including measures of self-control and tolerance), academic orientation (including measures of achievement potential), or general attitudes toward life (including measures of conformity and interests). Eleven of the personality scales were empirically developed based on the responses of subjects known to display certain kinds of behaviors. Factors such as course grades, participation in extracurricular activities, and peer ratings were used in selecting the criterion groups (see Gough, 1957, 1975). Four scales, Social Presence, Self-Acceptance, Self-Control, and Flexibility were developed through internal-consistency item-analysis procedures. Also built into the inventory were scales designed to detect response sets for faking favorable and bad impressions.

The 1987 revision of the test retained the 18 original scales with only minor changes in content and some rewriting or deletion of items to reduce sexist and/or other bias. Two new scales were added, Independence and Empathy, bringing the total number of scales contained in the 1987 revision of the test to 20. The 20 scales can be organized with reference to three independent themes derived from factor-analytic studies: (1) interpersonal orientation, (2) normative orientation, and (3) realization. Like its predecessor, this edition of the CPI may be hand- or computer-scored. Unlike its predecessor, the 1987 CPI manual provided a theoretical model of personality structure—one subsequently elaborated on in terms of its implications by Gough (1989, 1990) as well as by others (see, for example, Helson & Picano, 1990; Helson & Wink, 1987; Sundberg, Latkin, Littman, & Hagan, 1990).

Normative data for the original version of the CPI were obtained from the testing of 6,000 males and 7,000 females of varying age, socioeconomic status, and place of residence. Test-retest reliability coefficients reported in the CPI manual range from .55 to .75. Included in the manual is research concerning the feasibility of making various kinds of predictions with the test scores, predictions ranging from the probability of delinquency or dropping out of school to the probability of success among those in training for various occupations (such as dentists, optometrists, accountants, and so on). An abbreviated form of the original edition of the CPI has been found to correlate in the range of .74 to .91 with the original (Armentrout, 1977).

Like the MMPI, the CPI is a widely used instrument, with published versions of it available in more than two-dozen languages ranging from Arabic to Maylasian to Urdu (Pakistanese) and guides to assist in interpretation (see, for example, McAllister, 1988). Numerous studies reporting on new scales can be found in the professional literature. For example, Gough (1985) reported on the development of a "Work Orientation" (WO) scale for the CPI. The WO scale is composed of 40 items that were found to be correlated with criterion measures such as job performance rating. It was reported that high scorers on WO were dependable, moderate, optimistic, and persevering.

Professionals tend toward extremes when reviewing the CPI—either enthusiastically recommending its use, or not recommending it at all. These extremes were both represented in two reviews published in the *Ninth Mental Measurements Yearbook*. Acknowledging that the then existing edition of the test could be faulted for its lack of an underlying personality theory, the lack of research on profile interpretation, and the fact that the scales correlated with each other, Baucom (1985) went on to commend Gough for "the fruits yielded thus far from the CPI" (p. 252). Eysenck (1985) criticized Gough for his rationale for the test, which he found to be at best, vague, and at worst, the product of convoluted logic. Eysenck struggled with Gough's assertion that terms used in the CPI such as "dominance" and "sociability" were not traits. Eysenck (1985) also had trouble accepting Gough's rationale for rejecting factor analysis, and ultimately did not recommend use of the test:

> Factor analysis is one important way of imposing some degree of order on this field, and attempting to reach agreed conclusions along methodologies. Gough's refusal to accept this discipline, which he does not attempt even to justify in terms of any kind of acceptable statistical or philosophical argument, leads us straight into a situation where personality models, different inventories, and choice of scales are subject to a kind of Dutch auction, rather than a scientific debate which might result in a universally acceptable conclusion. . . . On the principle that all possible information should be given the test user, the absence in the manual of item intercorrelations and factorial analyses is to be deplored, particularly as no rational argument is advanced to justify it. In the absence of such supporting evidence of internal validity, it is difficult to recommend the test to prospective users. (p. 253)

THE THEORETICAL APPROACH
TO TEST CONSTRUCTION

427

AN OVERVIEW
OF
PERSONALITY
ASSESSMENT:
OBJECTIVE
METHODS

Perhaps in reaction to the widespread popularity of computerized personality testing, complete with neatly printed narrative interpretations, at least a few voices have begun to call for more clinical and more theoretically based approaches to personality assessment. In the latter camp, we can include Sugarman (1991), who has argued that personality theory as applied in personality assessment serves an organizing function, an integrative function, clarifies gaps in test data, and better allows for prediction. Using an article entitled "Psychiatric Diagnosis: Are Clinicians Still Necessary?" (Spitzer, 1983) as their point of departure, Pilkonis, Heape, Ruddy, and Serrao (1991) explored how multifaceted assessments employing multiple sources of data could be brought to bear to enhance the validity of diagnoses of personality disorder.

Instruments used in personality testing range from what we might term "theory-saturated," to relatively atheoretical—allowing for the test users, should they so desire, to impose their own theoretical preferences with respect to the interpretation of the findings. An example of a theory-saturated instrument is "The Blacky Pictures Test" (Blum, 1950). This test, now seldom if ever used, consists of pictures of Blacky, a dog, in various situations, each image designed to elicit fantasies associated with various psychoanalytic themes. For example, one card depicts Blacky with a knife hovering over his tail, a scene, according to the test's author, designed to elicit material related to the psychoanalytic concept of castration anxiety. The respondent's task is to make up stories in response to such cards, and the stories are then analyzed according to the parameters set forth by Blum (1950).[6] More contemporary psychoanalytically based assessment efforts can be found in other sources such as the writings of Robert Plutchik, Hope Conte, and their associates (Conte et al., 1991; Plutchik & Conte, 1989; Conte & Plutchik, 1981).

One widely used, theoretically based personality test is the Myers-Briggs Type Indicator. This test is based on the personality typology of Carl Jung (see Myers & Briggs, 1943/1962; Myers & McCaulley, 1985; and Briggs, Myers, & Saunders, 1987). Other personality tests, such as the Personality Research Form (Jackson, 1984; see the Close-up in Chapter 7), and the Edwards Personal Preference Schedule (described below), are based on the theory of personality developed by Henry Murray.

The Edwards Personal Preference Schedule (EPPS)

The EPPS (Edwards, 1953) is a personality inventory based on the theory of personality presented by Henry Murray in *Explorations in Personality* (1938). *Explorations* presented a complex but academically elegant theory of personality that not only introduced new concepts (such as "press," "regnancy," and "serial programs"), but also provided the impetus for renewed study of more traditional

---

6. This brief description of a test that employs pictures used as a stimulus for story telling will serve as a preview of things to come in the following chapter on projective instruments.

Table 12–5

List of Needs Presented in Murray (1938)*

Need	Definition (the need to . . .)
Abasement	submit passively
	accept blame, injury, criticism, or punishment
	admit inferiority, error, wrongdoing, or defeat
Achievement	accomplish and excel
	rival and surpass others
Affiliation	please, win affection of, and remain loyal to a friend
	draw near others
Autonomy	be independent, unattached, and defy convention
	resist restrictions
Counteraction	make up for failure with renewed efforts
	overcome a weakness or a fear
Defendance	protect or shield from blame, criticism, assault, and humiliation
Dominance	influence or direct others by authority or force
Exhibition	influence others by entertaining, shocking, exciting, or enticing them
Harmavoidance	avoid physical injury, pain, illness, and death
Infavoidance	avoid embarrassment and humiliation
Nurturance	help, support, protect, comfort, nurse, heal, and give sympathy
Order	achieve balance, precision, and organization
Play	participate in games, sports, other pleasurable activities
	act sheerly for "fun"
Rejection	separate or snub a person deemed to be inferior in some way
Sentience	seek and enjoy sensuous activities
Sex	have erotic relationships and sexual outlets
Succorance	be nursed, supported, sustained, protected, advised, forgiven, consoled
	have a steadfast, sympathetic supporter
Understanding	question, theorize, analyze, speculate, generalize

* We have abbreviated the definitions of these needs for the purposes of this tabular presentation. Consult Murray (1938, pp. 152–226) for complete definitions.

concepts.[7] In the latter context, for example, Murray explored the parameters of the word *need*, defining it, writing about its consequences, and detailing how various needs could be inferred. According to Murray, needs could be either primary or secondary, overt or covert, focal or diffuse, proactive (determined from within) or reactive (occurring in response to or as a result of some environmental event), and modal (done for the sheer pleasure of doing) or effect (done to effect some result). The list of needs originally published in *Explorations* appears in Table 12–5.

Edwards selected 15 of the needs listed by Murray and constructed items designed to assess each of those needs. He next conducted research designed to assess the social desirability of each of the items he wrote. Items assessing different

---

7. "Press" is a construct Murray used to refer to significant determinants of behavior that lie outside of the person. It is a term used in contrast to the construct "need," which refers to the significant determinants of behavior from *within*. "Regnancy" is a concept Murray used to link physiological (brain) processes to psychological processes (see Murray, 1938, p. 45). "Serial program" is used to refer to a set of subgoals that must be reached before some final goal can be attained.

429

AN OVERVIEW
OF
PERSONALITY
ASSESSMENT:
OBJECTIVE
METHODS

needs that were found to be generally equivalent with respect to social desirability were then placed into pairs (Edwards, 1957a, 1957b, 1966). For example, a pair of statements deemed to be approximately equivalent with respect to social desirability might be

I feel depressed when I fail at something.

I feel nervous when giving a talk before a group.

Edwards constructed his test of 210 pairs of statements in a way such that respondents were "forced" to answer "True" or "False" or "Yes" or "No" to one of two statements that were equivalent in terms of social desirability. This "forced-choice" technique represented an attempt to control for respondents' attempts to fake good or fake bad. Note also that each of the two statements above, like each of the statements in every pair of EPPS statements, is keyed to a different need in Murray's system. Endorsement of an item keyed to one scale in essence serves to reject an item keyed to an alternative scale. The score that is computed for each of the EPPS needs or scales thus represents the intensity of a particular need *in relation* to the intensity of the individual respondent's other needs. EPPS scores are, in psychometric jargon, *ipsative* in nature; the scores do not represent the strength of the need in absolute terms but rather the strength of the need in relation to the individual respondent's other needs. To elaborate, ipsative scoring allows for comparison of personality characteristics exhibited by an individual examinee with respect only to that examinee and does not allow for comparison between examinees. Stated another way, such scoring is useful in *intra*-individual comparison and not in *inter*-individual comparison. For example, on the basis of personality inventory data derived by means of ipsative scoring, it might be ap-

---

Close-up

Clinical Versus Actuarial Prediction

There are two different general approaches to interpreting data derived from personality (as well as more clinically oriented) tests and related sources. Referred to as the *clinical* and the *actuarial* approaches, these approaches represent two distinctly different ways in which data are combined to yield forecasts of future performance. Underlying the clinical approach is a reliance on clinical experience and judgment. Underlying the actuarial approach is a reliance on normative data and statistical formulas.

Data derived from tests, interviews, case-history material, and other sources will ultimately be used to formulate a description of, predict something about, or make a decision pertinent to an assessee. Questions concerning the optimal method for integrating all of the data and formulating such descriptions, predictions, and/or decisions have been a matter of long-standing controversy within the profession of psychology. One method, referred to as the *actuarial* approach (Meehl, 1954), is distinguished by its exclusive reliance on statistical procedures, empirical methods, and formal rules as opposed to reliance on the interpreter's own judgment in evaluating the data. By contrast, the *clinical* approach is characterized by less formal rules and reliance on the clinician's own intuition, judgment, and experience.

To illustrate some of the differences inherent

Clinical Versus Actuarial Prediction (continued)

in these two approaches, suppose that two psychologists, one who subscribes to the actuarial approach, "Dr. Actu," and one who subscribes to the clinical approach, "Dr. Clin," were called on to make a recommendation concerning whether a "Mr. T. Taker" should be hired as an executive with a large corporation. Both clinicians are given identical files on Mr. Taker, containing scores on various standardized tests, case-history data, projective-test data, and interview material. Both clinicians are aware that the corporation wants to hire executives with superior abilities in the areas of leadership, decision making, organizing and planning, interpersonal skills, and creativity.

Dr. Actu might approach his task by going through all of the available data on Mr. Taker and then applying certain preset rules (for example, some equation to combine the data for each variable) to come up with a score on each of the five variables to be judged. If the scores on, say, three out of five of these variables exceed a certain preset cutoff score, Dr. Actu would recommend that Mr. Taker be hired. Dr. Clin may or may not arrive at the same recommendation on the basis of his analysis of the same data. The process employed by Dr. Clin is more free-wheeling and less replicable than that employed by Dr. Actu. Something—virtually anything—in the data on Mr. Taker is capable of influencing Dr. Clin's judgment as to whether this applicant has executive potential. For example, Dr. Clin may have noticed that the written physical description of Taker included the fact that he wore one gold earring to the interview. On the basis of this fact alone, Dr. Clin might recommend that Taker not be hired; having interviewed hundreds of executives and prospective executives for this firm, Dr. Clin has mentally formulated an image of what the successful male executive looks like—and there is no provision for one gold earring in that picture.

The sample situation we describe is exaggerated for the purposes of illustration, for the clinical approach is characterized by careful scrutiny of all available data; and conclusions are typically drawn on the basis of a constellation of factors,

not just one (such as preference for wearing earrings). Still, our summary is useful in highlighting the nature of clinical as opposed to actuarial judgments. Dr. Clin may have rejected Taker solely on the basis of an element of his attire. Taker might also have "lost points" with Dr. Actu for this manner of dress as well, but only if "manner of dress" were one of the preset criteria to be rated in the assessment equation; exactly what importance, weight, or relevance the earring would be given in the hiring equation would have to have been placed into the selection equation before the selection procedure had begun. The actuarial approach, in contrast to the clinical one, is strictly empirical in nature. If a large body of existing data indicates that males who wear one earring to employment interviews (or, stated more broadly, persons who dress in a manner inconsistent with the "image" of a particular corporation) turn out to be poor executives, such persons will lose points in their evaluation. With respect to the clinical approach, the body of data being used as a reference is the information, knowledge, and experience of the clinician making the judgment.

A difference between the two approaches that must be emphasized concerns the *meaning* assigned to certain data. Because the actuarial approach is so empirical in nature, meaning of responses and behaviors is deemphasized in favor of how such responses and behaviors correlate with a certain criterion. If successful male executives for the company in question do not tend to sport earrings, that will be sufficient for Dr. Actu to reject the applicant. Alternatively, Dr. Clin might overlook and "see beyond" the earring, noting that other data suggest Taker to be a highly creative, artistic, and independent individual who would do well in a particular executive slot that the corporation needs to fill. Clin's report to the corporation might recommend Taker be offered the executive position, conditional on his removal of the earring. If Taker was hired, consented to removing the earring, and did very well in the position, the corporation might then seek to recruit other applicants who fit a similar profile.

Since there is a finite set of data available to the clinician, it would be nice if there was one best way to interpret that data. An architect of the actuarial approach, Meehl (1984) likened the clinical approach to leaving a supermarket and saying, "Well, it looks like I spent about 17 bucks worth" instead of consulting the cash register receipt to know what was actually spent. Citing reasons why the actuarial approach has failed to achieve widespread adoption, Meehl's list included the following factors: (1) the ubiquity of irrationality in the conduct of human affairs, (2) sheer ignorance, (3) the threat of technological unemployment, (4) strong theoretical identifications on the part of some clinicians, (5) claims that actuarial techniques are "dehumanizing," (6) mistaken concepts of ethics, and (7) computer phobia.

Einhorn (1984) has asked how we can presume to make predictions about the course of human life if we can't even do it for interest or mortgage rates. Einhorn argued that clinicians must accept the reality that there will always be error in prediction. Since clinicians have more limited information-processing than computers, there would appear to be more room for error in the clinical approach.

Others have added that the process of making predictions clinically may be tedious whereas computers may make the same or better decisions within seconds. And others have argued that computers compute and can at best show low levels of relations; in essence, they yield regression equations with neither understanding, compassion, nor the ability to anticipate unforeseen and unanticipated (that is, nonprogrammed) events. With respect to the latter point, no computer ever predicted that there would be a national oil shortage in this country in the early 1970s. The shortage arose as a result of an Arab fuel boycott, which arose in part as a consequence of the support of the United States for Israel in the *Yom Kippur* war. Thus while there was no shortage of computer printouts indicating rates of fossil fuel consumption and production in this country and throughout the world,

no computer could have forecasted the unlikely chain of events that resulted in not only the oil shortage but also a number of related consequences (such as gas-station lines, federal energy usage restrictions and incentives, and the imposition of a national speed limit of 55 miles per hour).

Clearly, both the clinical and the actuarial approach have much to be said for them. The actuarial approach tends to be much more efficient than the clinical one in terms of making predictions in a variety of situations, especially those in which many predictions must be made and a large data base for making those predictions exists (Meehl, 1954, 1959, 1965). Owing to its rigor, the actuarial approach lends itself well to research; volumes have been written, for example, concerning descriptions of persons with particular MMPI patterns. Being less subject to empiricism and to rules, the clinical approach has as its chief advantage flexibility and the potential for using the novel combination of data ("programmed" as well as "unprogrammed") to arrive at decisions, descriptions, predictions, and hypotheses.

In summary, the difference between the clinical and the actuarial approach to assessment is in some ways similar to the difference between a courtroom trial that will result in a ruling by either a judge or a computer. Both the computer and the judge will take in all of the evidence and weigh it. Each will arrive at a verdict on the basis of the weight of the evidence and the applicable standard ("guilty beyond a reasonable doubt" in a criminal proceeding and "preponderance of the evidence" in a civil proceeding). The computer will weigh the evidence according to preprogrammed rules and arrive at a verdict. The judge will also weigh it according to ("preprogrammed") rules but with more openness to nuances of information that might not be in the "rulebook." Whereas the computer's decision can be expected to conform to the letter of the law, the judge's decision can be expected to conform with not only the letter of the law but its spirit as well.

propriate to make a statement like "John's need for achievement is higher than his need for succorance." However, it would be inappropriate on the basis of such data to compare any of John's needs to those of another person's as in a statement like, "John's need for achievement is higher than Jane's need for achievement."

In addition to the use of the forced-choice format, Edwards built other precautionary measures into the EPPS in an effort to detect and/or minimize the effects of faking, response sets, and other factors that would threaten the validity of the obtained scores. A Consistency scale is designed to check on the consistency of the examinee's responses. This scale consists of 15 identical items that are repeated in various places throughout the inventory.

As a further measure of consistency, a "stability" score may be obtained; this score is equal to the correlation coefficient that describes the relationship between two halves of the test (odd and even scores in the 15 scales).

Normative data for the EPPS were initially gathered on a sample of 760 male and 749 female college students from 29 campuses throughout the country and approximately 9,000 men and women from the general adult population. Subsequently, data based on the test results for 559 male and 986 female high school students were added. Test-retest reliability coefficients for the 15 scales based on one-week intervals were found to range between .74 and .87. Internal-consistency measures resulted in split-half reliability coefficients ranging from .60 to .87 with a median of .78. Interpretation of these findings is complicated because the test contains repeated items. In general, the test is viewed as being within acceptable standards of test-retest and inter-item reliability; the objection many reviewers have raised concerns the lack of compelling validity data (Heilbrun, 1972). Additionally, questions have been raised concerning the extent to which the forced-choice format of the test does indeed eliminate the social desirability response set from affecting scores (Heilbrun & Goodstein, 1961a, 1961b; Rorer, 1965; Wiggins, 1966). Reviewers have also questioned the appropriateness of converting ipsative scores into normative percentiles and the representativeness of the normative sample. The test was originally designed for use with college students and adults and is often used for research, teaching, and counseling purposes (Drummond, 1984).

SOME PROBLEMS AND ISSUES IN ASSESSING PERSONALITY

Many personality assessment instruments of the paper-and-pencil variety rely heavily either on the self-report of the assessee or on a rating made by the assessor(s). We conclude this chapter by considering some limitations inherent in the use of such techniques.

Potential Limitations of Self-Report Techniques

Were employers to faithfully rely on job applicants' representations concerning their personality and their suitability for a particular job, they might well receive universally glowing references—and still not hire the most suitable personnel. This is so because many job applicants, as well as other people in a wide variety of other contexts—contexts as diverse as singles bars, custody hearings, and high

433

AN OVERVIEW
OF
PERSONALITY
ASSESSMENT:
OBJECTIVE
METHODS

school reunions—attempt to "fake good" in their presentation of themselves to other people. The other side of the "faking good" coin is, as you might expect, "faking bad." Litigants in civil actions who claim injury may seek high awards to compensate them for their alleged pain, suffering, and emotional distress—all of which may be exaggerated and dramatized for the benefit of a judge and jury. The accused in a criminal action may view time in a mental institution as preferable to time in prison (or capital punishment) and strategically opt for an insanity defense—with accompanying behavior and claims to make such a defense as believable as possible. A homeless person who prefers the environs of mental hospital to that of the street may attempt to "fake bad" on tests and in interviews if failure to do so will result in discharge. In the days when a military draft existed, it was not uncommon for draft resistors to attempt to be deferred from their obligation to serve on psychiatric grounds—and many such people went to great lengths to "fake bad" when assessed.

Consideration of situations such as those described above can help you to appreciate that a problem inherent in personality testing and assessment—one that is particularly acute with respect to self-report methods—is the problem of "seeing through" assessees' attempts to present themselves in a favorable or unfavorable light. *Impression management* is a term social psychologists use to describe the behavior of attempting to manipulate others' impressions, and below we discuss this phenomenon as well as related behaviors.

Impression management   After Goffman (1959), Braginsky, Braginsky, and Ring (1969) used the term *impression management* to refer to the fact that:

> we can and generally do manage our expressive behavior so as to control the impressions that others form of us. Through selective exposure of some information (it may be false information) consistent with the character we mean to sustain for the purpose of an interaction, coupled with suppression of information incompatible with that projection of self, we establish a certain definition of ourselves that we attempt to maintain throughout the interaction episode. (p. 51)

In essence, we all try (to varying degrees) to "manage impressions" of ourselves to others. According to Goffman (1959), an individual may want the audience "to think highly of him, or to think that he thinks highly of them, or to perceive how in fact he feels toward them, or to obtain no clear-cut impression; he may wish to ensure sufficient harmony so that the interaction can be sustained, or to defraud, get rid of, confuse, mislead, antagonize, or insult them" (p. 3). Another variation of impression management concerns not the desire to fake good or bad, but simply to manage the impression—good, bad, or indifferent— that the actor believes the audience is expecting. This point has been elaborated on by Goffman (1959):

> Doctors who are led into giving placebos, filling station attendants who resignedly check and recheck tire pressures for anxious women motorists, shoe clerks who sell a shoe that fits but tell the customer it is the size she wants to hear—these are cynical performers whose audiences will not allow them to be sincere. (p. 18)

> If a baseball umpire is to give the impression that he is sure of his judgment he must forego the moment of thought which might make him sure of his

judgment: he must give an instantaneous decision so that the audience will be sure that he is sure of his judgment. (p. 30)

In the process of personality assessment, it is possible for examinees to employ any number of impression management strategies for any number of reasons. Del Paulhus (1984, 1986, 1990; Paulhus & Levitt, 1987) and his colleagues have explored impression management in test taking as well as the related phenomena of *enhancement* (the claiming of positive attributes), *denial* (the repudiation of negative attributes), and *self-deception*—"the tendency to give favorably biased but honestly held self-descriptions" (Paulhus & Reid, 1991, p. 307).[8] Test takers who consistently engage in impression management or other such identifiable ways of responding are said to be exhibiting what has been referred to as a "response style" (Jackson & Messick, 1962).[9]

Response styles   Also referred to as "response set," *response style* refers to the tendency to respond to a question in some characteristic manner regardless of the content of the question. For example, some individuals are more apt to answer "Yes" or "True" than "No" or "False" on short-answer tests. Although there are those who consider the notion of a response style to be a myth (Rorer, 1965), the vast amount of research done in this area suggests it is a reality. Table 12–6 contains a sampling of some of the different response styles psychologists have distinguished. Nunnally (1978) made the point that response styles may themselves be important personality measures:

> Some of the response styles that have been catalogued sound like important personality traits, e.g., cautiousness, acquiescence, and extremeness. To the extent that such stylistic variables can be measured independently of content relating to nonstylistic variables or to the extent that they can somehow be separated from the variance of other traits, they might prove useful as measures of personality traits. (p. 660)

As we have seen, some personality tests contain items that are part of the test for the express purpose of identifying the respondent who has a tendency to give unusual or uncommon responses. Thus, for example, a "True" response to an item like "I recently vacationed in downtown Baghdad" might lead the test scorer/interpreter to raise some questions about the findings: Did the test taker understand the instructions? Did the test taker take the test seriously? Did the test taker respond "True" to all of the items on the test? Did the test taker respond randomly to items on the test? Analysis of the entire protocol might help to provide additional answers.

Feedback to the test taker   A potential drawback of self-report instruments that is not often mentioned is the lack of insights such tests, when administered alone, can offer to the test taker. Burisch (1984a) put it this way:

---

8. Others view self-deception differently; for example, Gur and Sackheim (1979) saw it as a concept in search of a phenomenon. See also Flett, Blankstein, Pliner, and Bator (1988).
9. Nunnally (1978, pp. 658–677) provides a more technical explanation and discussion of response style. For him, it is "(1) a reliable source of variance in individual differences which (2) is an artifactual product of measurement methods and (3) is at least partially independent of the trait which the measurement methods are intended to measure" (p. 658).

435

AN OVERVIEW
OF
PERSONALITY
ASSESSMENT:
OBJECTIVE
METHODS

Table 12–6

A Sampling of Response Styles

Response style name	Explanation: A tendency to respond on a test . . .
Socially desirable responding	to present oneself in a favorable (read "socially acceptable" or "socially desirable") light
Acquiescence	to agree with whatever is presented
Nonacquiescence	to disagree with whatever is presented
Deviance	to make unusual or uncommon responses
Extreme	to make extreme, as opposed to middle, ratings on a rating scale
Gambling/cautiousness	to guess—or not guess—when in doubt

> On the basis of self-ratings alone, clinicians cannot tell patients anything they do not already know. But this is precisely what the patients came for! The mystery of a projective device or the glamour of a computer-scored inventory profile is painfully missing. (p. 225)

It is probably overstating the case to say that on the basis of self-ratings alone, "clinicians cannot tell patients anything they do not know." Clinicians may well be able to accomplish that feat on the basis of looking at various patterns or clusters of response. The more compelling question for us is, "How much can the clinician tell about the patient on the basis of self-ratings alone?" And in the context of our discussion of impression management strategies, we might rephrase that question: "How much can the clinician *really* tell about the patient on the basis of self-rating alone?"

Potential Limitations of Rating Scales

Some measures involve procedures where one individual observes and evaluates someone else. The considerations that need to be kept in mind in such a situation have already been touched on in Chapter 6, in the section on bias. Here we review and expand on that discussion with reference to rating scales and raters.

The rater Mrs. Jones, a third-grade teacher, had Alvin Farkas's brother Fred in her class five years ago. She remembers Fred to be an excellent, all-around student, and he was every bit the "teacher's pet." Will this fact enter into Mrs. Jones's judgment when she evaluates Alvin? Maybe it shouldn't, but few people would be surprised if it did. Teachers are human, too, and experience, attitudes, hopes, and fears are some of the factors that might enter into—and bias—their ratings. In the situation of two brothers, a "halo effect" may be operative with respect to Mrs. Jones's ratings of Alvin; the Farkas name has generated so much goodwill in the mind of Mrs. Jones that Alvin may be perceived as "capable of doing no wrong." More broadly, a *halo effect* is a type of error in rating wherein some single attribute or combination of attributes biases judgments or ratings regarding other attributes.

Many raters have an investment in the people they rate. Thus the school, industrial, or organizational instructor who has spent six months teaching a particular course has a personal investment in the ratings of the students; it doesn't look good for the instructor if too many of the students fail on some final measure of outcome. Thus, situations might exist where the rater's own self-interests are at odds with—and may interfere with—a fair and unbiased rating (Figure 12–4).

Numerous other factors may contribute to bias in a rater's ratings. The rater may feel competitive with, physically attracted to, or physically repulsed by, the subject of the ratings. The rater may not have the proper background, experience, and "trained eye" needed for the particular task. The rater's judgments may be limited by his or her general level of conscientiousness and willingness to devote the time and effort required to do the job properly. The rater may harbor biases concerning various stereotypes. The rater may have a tendency to rate highly (a *leniency* or *generosity error*), a tendency to rate harshly (a *severity error*), or a tendency to rate everyone at some point around the midpoint of the rating scale (an *error of central tendency*). Subjectivity based on the rater's own subjective prefer-

Figure 12–4 *A Halo Effect.*

"Monsters and screaming women have always worked for me; I give it 'thumbs up,' Roger."

ences and taste may also enter into judgments. Bo Derek was a perfect "10" for Dudley Moore in the film by the same name, though others may find this woman less than perfect to greater or lesser degrees.

437

AN OVERVIEW
OF
PERSONALITY
ASSESSMENT:
OBJECTIVE
METHODS

One attempt at controlling for raters' biases involves educating raters as to the types of biases that exist and the ways in which they may interfere with the accuracy of ratings. Another attempt at controlling for raters' biases has been to provide training sessions for raters. Such training sessions afford the opportunity for raters to (1) clarify terminology to increase the reliability of their ratings (for example, terms such as "satisfactory" and "unsatisfactory" may be construed differently by different people), (2) to obtain practice in observing and rating others, and (3) to compare their ratings with those of experienced raters. Research has demonstrated the effectiveness of rater-training programs (see Bernardin, 1978).

The instrument   By now you have already acquired much firsthand experience with a small sample of the various rating systems that have an impact on everyone's academic, business, and social life. Some of these familiar rating systems are as follows:

"NC17" is a rating of a motion picture in which there is rather graphic presentation of sexual and/or violent material. When you were younger, such a rating prohibited you from entering the theater.

"****" is a rating used in many travel guidebooks to denote the highest quality accommodations and dining.

"√√√" is something your friend Jane uses in her little black book next to the names of men she has dated to distinguish those who have conformed to her highest specifications in terms of mental, physical, and related attributes.

"D" is the rating your instructor gave you as a final grade in your economics course. This is why you decided to shun the business world and become a psychology major.

Rating scales are used to classify, to determine eligibility, and to predict effectiveness. Ratings are also useful in the process of validating a particular test because they provide a convenient criterion against which test scores can be compared. Thus, for example, scores on a paper-and-pencil "Work Effectiveness Test" taken by a worker might be compared against a supervisor-filled-out "Work Effectiveness Rating Scale." Given that rating scales may play a large part in terms of individuals' academic and business futures, a word about the construction of these types of instruments is in order. Rating scales (like tests) with the same name may be focusing on vastly different things. For example, one "Worker Effectiveness Rating Scale" might contain items on it that relate mostly to a worker's creativity and initiative, whereas another "Worker Effectiveness Rating Scale" might contain items that focus more on the worker's ability to cooperate with fellow workers. Thus, a rating scale, like a test, must be judged by its validity for use in a specific context and for a specific purpose, not by its name.

Rating scales come in many varieties. There are rating scales to rate the self and there are rating scales to rate others. Some rating scales require the rater to make careful observations (such as "Does the patient make his bed?"), whereas others require the rater to make evaluations and express opinions (such as "How well does the patient get along with the other patients on the ward?"). Rating scales vary in format; in general, they are either alphabetical, numerical, graphic, or of the forced-choice variety. The alphabetical rating scale uses letters keyed to some type of description as the rating system. The letter-grade rating system of A to F (excluding the letter "E") is an example of an alphabetical rating system as is the movie industry's "G," "PG," "PG13," "R," and "NC17" rating system. A numerical format, as its name implies, employs numbers keyed to descriptions (for example, 0 = the least, 100 = the most). With graphic rating scales, the rater's task is to check off or mark some line, number, letter, or point on a figure. One widely used rating scale of the graphic variety is called the "semantic differential." Developed by Osgood, Suci, & Tannenbaum (1957), the *semantic differential* is a technique that employs bipolar adjectives and a seven-point rating scale (Figure 12–5). The examinee is instructed to respond to the presentation of some idea, concept, or issue by checking off one of the seven spaces between the bipolar adjectives. Forced-choice rating scales contain two or more descriptions from which the rater must select the most appropriate. Forced-choice ratings are useful in self-rating instruments and in other situations where there might exist a special need to minimize errors in ratings as a function of bias or response sets.

One special form of rating is ranking. In essence, ranking entails an ordering of ratings with reference to some bipolar variable (such as highest-lowest, most-least, or strongest-weakest). Like forced-choice procedures, ranking procedures may force the rater to make fine distinctions and to identify positive as well as negative choices. The *paired-comparison method* of ranking entails individually comparing every item to be ranked with every other item to be ranked. Another ranking method entails comparing each item or individual to be ranked according to some preestablished standard or criterion. Rankings generally provide little information in and of themselves. For example, what does it mean to be ranked fifth in a class of gifted children? To make such a ranking meaningful, we would

Myself

Warm	____:____:____:____:____:____:____	Cold
Tense	____:____:____:____:____:____:____	Relaxed
Optimistic	____:____:____:____:____:____:____	Pessimistic
Frugal	____:____:____:____:____:____:____	Extravagant
Weak	____:____:____:____:____:____:____	Strong
Brooks Brothers suit	____:____:____:____:____:____:____	Hawaiian shirt

Figure 12–5 ***The Semantic Differential.*** This is a technique that can be applied to the rating of people, products—most anything. Here the rater is being asked to place checkmarks at the point in the continuum that best describes himself or herself.

have to know more (such as measures of central tendency and variability, the method by which the ranking was derived, and so forth).

Inter-rater reliability tends to increase as a function of the clarity and specificity with which terms on a particular rating scale are defined. Thus, all other things being equal, a random group of raters will probably exhibit less agreement on a rating scale that merely has categories such as "Excellent," "Good," "Fair," and "Poor" than on one where clear behavioral referents to these terms are specified.

439

AN OVERVIEW
OF
PERSONALITY
ASSESSMENT:
OBJECTIVE
METHODS

Chapter 13

Projective Methods

SUPPOSE THE LIGHTS in your classroom were dimmed and everyone was told to stare at the clean chalkboard for about a minute or so. And suppose everyone was then asked to take out some paper and write down what he or she thought he or she could "see" on the chalkboard—other than the chalkboard itself. If you examined what each of your fellow students wrote, you would probably find as many different things "seen" on that blank chalkboard as there are students responding. You might even assume that the students "saw" on the chalkboard—or, more accurately, *projected* onto the chalkboard—something that was not really on the chalkboard, but rather something that was in (or on) their own minds. You might further assume that each student's response to the blank chalkboard reflected something very telling about the student's personality structure.

The *projective hypothesis* holds that an individual supplies structure to unstructured stimuli in a manner consistent with the individual's own unique pattern of conscious and unconscious needs, fears, desires, impulses, conflicts, and ways of perceiving and responding. In the chalkboard exercise described, a blank chalkboard served as the unstructured stimulus upon which respondents projected. However, any relatively unstructured stimulus will do. In a scene in Shakespeare's play *Hamlet,* Polonius and Hamlet discuss what can be seen in clouds. Indeed, clouds could be used as a projective stimulus.[1] But psychologists, slaves to practicality (and scientific methods) as they are, have developed projective measures of personality that are more reliable than clouds and more portable than chalkboards. In the sampling of tests to be discussed in this chapter, ink-blots, pictures, words, drawings, cartoons, and other things have been used as projective stimuli.

Unlike self-report methods, projective tests are *indirect* methods of personality; the examinee's task is to talk about something or someone other than herself or himself, and inferences about the examinee's personality will be made from the response. On such a task, the ability—and presumably the inclination—of examinees to fake is greatly minimized. Also somewhat minimized is the test taker's need for great proficiency in the English language; minimal language skills are required in order to respond to—or create—a drawing. For this reason as well as the fact that some projective methods may be less culture-linked than other measures of personality, proponents of projective testing believe that there is a promise of crosscultural utility with these tests that has yet to be fulfilled. Proponents of projective measures also argue that a major advantage of such measures is that they tap unconscious as well as conscious material. And in the words of the man who first coined the term *projective techniques,* "the most important things about an individual are what he cannot or will not say" (Frank, 1939, p. 395).[2]

Projective tests were born in the spirit of rebellion against normative data and through attempts by personality researchers to break down the study of personality into the study of specific traits of varying strengths. This orientation is exemplified in the following excerpts from Frank (1939):

> It is interesting to see how the students of personality have attempted to meet the problem of individuality with methods and procedures designed for study of uniformities and norms that ignore or subordinate individuality, treating it as a troublesome deviation which derogates from the real, the superior, and only important central tendency, mode, average, etc. (pp. 392–393).
>
> . . . physicists are using such devices as the Wilson Cloud Chamber and the Geiger Counter to obtain data on the *individual* electrical particle, which reveals its presence and energy by the path traced in water vapor, or by activation of the Counter, although never itself observable or directly measurable.
>
> These methodological procedures are being refined and extended because they offer possibilities for ascertaining what is either unknowable by other means or is undeterminable because the older analytic methods destroyed part or all of that which was to be studied (pp. 398–399) [Emphasis in the original].

---

1. In fact, clouds *have* been used as projective stimuli. Wilhelm Stern's Cloud Picture Test, in which subjects were asked to tell what they saw in pictures of clouds, was one of the earliest projective measures.
2. The first published use of the term *projective methods* that we are aware of was in an article entitled "Projective Methods in the Psychological Study of Children," by Ruth Horowitz and Lois Barclay Murphy (1938). However, these authors had read Lawrence K. Frank's (1939) as-yet-unpublished manuscript and had credited him for having "applied the term 'projective methods.'"

Thus, in contrast to methods of personality assessment that focused on the individual from a statistics-based, normative perspective, projective techniques were at one time viewed as the technique of choice for focusing on the individual from a purely clinical perspective—a perspective that examined the unique way an individual projects onto an ambiguous stimulus "his way of seeing life, his meanings, significances, patterns, and especially his feelings" (Frank, 1939, p. 403). As we will see, however, years of clinical experience with these tests and a growing volume of research data have led interpretation of responses to projective stimuli to become increasingly norm-referenced in nature.

INKBLOTS AS PROJECTIVE STIMULI

In the film *Take the Money and Run,* Woody Allen, as Virgil Starkwell, a confirmed sociopath, responds to an inkblot similar to that presented in Figure 13–1 with: "It looks like two elephants making love to a men's glee club."

The public has become familiar with inkblot measures of personality through many such media gags. However, as is the case with a lot of mass media psychology, many misconceptions attend the publicity. For example, one misconception concerning inkblot tests pertains to the importance of *what* an individual sees. In actuality, what an individual sees in the inkblots is important, but it is only one facet of a multifaceted task; factors related to *how* the individual sees the blot (that is, does he or she respond to large or small parts of it? to primarily the white or black area?) are all important in the interpretation process. Here we review the two major tests of this type, the Rorschach Inkblot Test and the Holtzman Inkblot Technique.

The Rorschach

Developed by the Swiss psychiatrist Hermann Rorschach (1921/1942), the Rorschach Inkblot Test consists of ten bilaterally symmetrical—mirror-imaged if

Figure 13–1 *A Rorschach-like Inkblot.*

folded in half—inkblots that are printed on separate cards (Figure 13–2). Five inkblots are achromatic (meaning "without color" or black and white); two are black, white, and red; and three are multicolored. The test comes with the cards only: no test manual, nor any administration, scoring, or interpretation instructions, nor any rationale for why some of the inkblots are achromatic and others

Figure 13–2 *Hermann Rorschach (1884–1922).*

Over a hundred years ago on November 8, Hermann Rorschach was born in Zurich, Switzerland. Hermann studied medicine in Zurich, Nuremberg, Bern, and Berlin and by 1909 had earned his license to practice medicine in Switzerland. Specializing in psychiatry, Rorschach came into contact with members of the psychoanalytic community in Zurich and himself employed psychoanalytic procedures with some of his patients. During his studies he met a Russian female colleague, whom he married. At the end of 1913, Rorschach left his position in a Swiss mental asylum and moved with his wife to Russia, where he worked in a private clinic. But by July 1914, Rorschach had returned to Switzerland, where he served as an assistant director at a regional asylum. Rorschach's wife was detained from leaving the country due to a declaration of war and did not rejoin him in Switzerland until the spring of 1915. Mrs. Rorschach's explanation for her husband's return to Switzerland was that "In spite of his interest in Russia and the Russians, he remained a true Swiss, attached to his native land. . . . He was European and intended to remain so at any price" (cited in Pichot, 1984, p. 591).

Complementing Rorschach's interest in psychoanalysis was an interest in art and drawing—an interest that perhaps stemmed from the fact that his father had been a teacher of art and drawing. By 1913 Rorschach had published papers on analyzing mental patients' artwork as a means of learning more about the personality. Among the more specific influences that may have contributed to Rorschach's development of his now-famous test were his familiarity with the work of his contemporary, Carl Jung. Jung was a pioneer in the area of word association testing—an assessment technique that employed a stimulus (a word) as an aid in bringing unconscious material to light. The published use of inkblots as a stimulus for association had appeared as early as 1857:

The utilization of forms obtained "through chance" by folding over a piece of paper into the center of which some ink had been dropped had a

long history. In 1857 Justinus Kerner had published a collection of poems entitled "Kleksographien." Kerner, who belonged to the so-called romantic school of German psychiatry, had been at one and the same time both a physician and a painter of repute. . . . In "Kleksographien" he had published a series of "chance inkblots" for each of which he had composed a poem. . . . In the collection of the "Kleksographien," each page showed, in justaposition [sic], an inkblot form and the poem it had evoked. It was a very successful book in German-speaking countries. Later it was republished and was thus known to Rorschach. (Pichot, 1984, pp. 594–595)

In turn-of-the-century France, Alfred Binet had experimented with inkblots as a test of imaginative ability. As Pichot (1984) says, the contribution of Hermann Rorschach lies not only in his development of the test but also in his "viewing the responses as determined by the *peculiarities of perception* which, in turn, were dependent upon the underlying structure of the personality." (p. 595, emphasis added). Rorschach's test was published in 1921 and was not an immediate success. He died the following year from appendicular peritonitis at the age of 38, unaware of the great legacy he was to leave.

are chromatic (with color). Filling the need for a test manual and administration, scoring, and interpretation instructions have been a number of manuals and handbooks that set forth a variety of methods (such as Beck, 1944, 1945, 1952, 1960; Klopfer & Davidson, 1962; Exner, 1974, 1978, 1986; Exner & Weiner, 1982; Piotrowski, 1957). Although there are differences between the systems in terms of administration, scoring, and interpretation instructions, what follows is a description of the process in very general terms.

The cards are presented to the subject one at a time in a prescribed sequence. The subject is instructed to tell what is on each of the cards with a question such as "What might this be?" from the examiner. The examiner records the subject's responses verbatim as well as the length of time required before the first response to each card. Other factors such as the position of the card, spontaneous statements that the subject makes, and noteworthy nonverbal gestures or body movements are also recorded. The examiner does not engage in any discussion concerning the subject's responses during the initial administration of the cards. Every effort is made to provide the subject with the opportunity to "project," free from any outside distractions.

After the entire set of cards has been adminstered once, a second administration, referred to as the "inquiry," is conducted. During the inquiry, the examiner attempts to determine what features of the inkblot played a role in formulating the subject's perceptions. Questions such as "What made it look like _____ ?" and "How do you see _____ ?" are asked in an attempt to clarify what was seen and which aspects of the inkblot were most influential in forming these percepts. The inquiry provides information that is useful in scoring and interpreting the responses. Also learned in the inquiry is whether the examinee remembers earlier responses, whether the original percept is still seen, and whether any new responses are now perceived.

A third component of the administration, referred to as "testing the limits," may also be included. This procedure enables the examiner to restructure the situation for the subject by asking specific questions that provide additional information concerning personality functioning.

If, for example, the subject has utilized the entire inkblot when forming percepts throughout the test, the examiner might want to determine if the subject would be able to respond to particular details within the inkblot. Under these conditions the examiner might say, "Sometimes people use a part of the blot to see something." Alternatively, the examiner might point to a specific area of the card and ask the subject, "What does this look like?" A limit-testing procedure may also be undertaken with the objective being (1) to identify any confusion or misunderstanding concerning the task, (2) to aid the examiner in determining if the subject is able to refocus his or her percepts given a new frame of reference, and (3) to see if a subject made anxious by the ambiguous nature of the task is better able to perform given this added structure. At least one Rorschach researcher has advocated the technique of trying to elicit "one last response" from test takers who think they have already given as many responses as they are going to give; the rationale is that "endings have many meanings," and the one last response may provide a source of questions and inferences applicable to treatment considerations (Cerney, 1984).

Hypotheses concerning personality functioning will be formed on the basis of all the variables we have outlined (such as the content of the response, the location of the response, the length of time to respond) plus many additional ones. In general, Rorschach protocols are scored according to several categories, including location, determinants, content, popularity, and form. *Location* refers to the part of the inkblot that was utilized in forming the percept. Individuals may use the entire inkblot, a large section, a small section, a minute detail, or white spaces. *Determinants* refer to the qualities of the inkblot that determine what the individual perceives: the form, color, shading, and/or movement that the individual attributes to the inkblot. *Content* refers to the content category of the response; although different scoring categories vary in terms of some of the categories scored, certain general content areas such as human figures, animal figures, anatomical parts, blood, clouds, X-rays, and sexual responses are usually included. *Popularity* refers to the frequency with which a certain response has been found to correspond with a particular inkblot or section of an inkblot. A popular response is one that has frequently been obtained from the general population. A rare response is one that has been perceived infrequently by the general population. The *form* of a response refers to how accurately the individual's perception matches or fits the corresponding part of the inkblot. Form level may be evaluated as being adequate or inadequate, or good or poor.

The scoring categories are considered to correspond to various aspects of personality functioning, and hypotheses concerning aspects of personality are based both on the number of responses that fall within each category and the interrelationships among the categories. For example, the number of Whole responses (using the entire inkblot) in a Rorschach record is thought to be associated with conceptual thought processes. Form level is associated with reality testing; human movement with imagination; and color responses with emotional reactivity. Patterns of response, recurrent themes, and the interrelationships among the different scoring categories are all considered in arriving at a final description of the individual from a Rorschach protocol. Data concerning the responses of various clinical and nonclinical groups of adults, adolescents, and children have been compiled and are available for comparisons (see Goldfried, Stricker, & Weiner, 1971; Ames, Metraux, Rodell, & Walker, 1974; Ames, Metraux, & Walker, 1971; Exner, 1978, 1986; Exner & Weiner, 1982).

Psychometric properties   Assessing the reliability of the Rorschach test—regardless of the particular scoring system employed—presents difficulties, because traditional methods for assessing reliability have not proved feasible for this test (or other projective tests; see McClelland, 1980). It would be inappropriate, for example, to assess reliability by means of the split-half method, as each inkblot is considered to have a unique stimulus quality and is not comparable to any other inkblot on the test. In a study involving 67 emotionally disturbed children who were in residential treatment, Hayden (1981) found certain cards to be associated with parental figures. When asked to select the card "which in some way makes you think of your mother/father" (p. 227), two cards (IV and VII) were selected significantly more often than chance would allow. We should note that a subsequent analysis of the literature on those Rorschach cards that have come to be known as the "Mother" (Card VII) and "Father" (Card IV) cards has called into question the practice of evaluating parental relationships based on responses to these cards (Liaboe & Guy, 1985). However, if we concede that each card does have a unique stimulus quality, then we must also accept that a procedure such as the split-half method for evaluating the reliability of the test would be inappropriate.

The test-retest procedure for determining reliability has similarly been found to be lacking as a measure of reliability because responses to the stimulus cards are the result of many factors (needs, conflicts, concerns) occurring within the individual at the time of administration. While certain themes may persist, the extent to which these factors are operative varies from administration to administration and with any changes that occur in the subject. Even the fact that the subject is familiar with the test may influence the responses obtained. The difficulties inherent in devising an alternate form equivalent to the Rorschach were exemplified in the work of Behn, who, under Sigmund Freud's direction, was able to develop a similar but not alternate form of the test called the Behn-Rorschach (Eichler, 1951; Buckle & Holt, 1951; Swift, 1944).

With respect to inter-scorer reliability, a distinction must be made between (1) inter-scorer agreement on the basic scoring categories for a given system of scoring the Rorschach, and (2) inter-scorer agreement on interpretations made from Rorschach protocols. In general, studies have shown acceptable levels of inter-scorer reliability with respect to basic scoring categories among trained scorers for a given scoring system. In an early study of the degree of inter-scorer agreement, 90% agreement was found for the location category; 83% agreement was found for the determinants of form and movement; and 75% agreement was found for the color and shade determinants (Remzy & Pickard, 1949). The highest degree of agreement was found to exist for the category of content (99%). These findings are similar to those obtained by Ames and her associates, who reported product-moment correlation coefficients of .92 (location), .90 (form and movement), .80 (color and shading), and .97 (content) among different scorers (Ames, Learned, Metraux, & Walker, 1952). Exner (1986) reported inter-rater agreement ranging from 87% to 99% for form, movement, color, and shading determinants. As illustrated in Figure 13–3, one journal that publishes a number of Rorschach studies, the *Journal of Personality Assessment,* began in 1991 to require evidence of at least 80% inter-scorer agreement with respect to "variables central to the particular study" (Weiner, 1991, p. 1).

Studies of inter-scorer reliability with respect to interpretations made from Rorschach protocols have not been nearly so encouraging. A study done as a doctoral dissertation at Yale University by Lisansky (1956) is noteworthy on two counts. First, the six Rorschach experts who participated in the study were polled in advance of the experiment to list the kinds of items they would feel confident in predicting from the Rorschach. The evolved list contained nine items (such as intellectual capacity, rigidity, and ambition) to be checked off on as many as five adjectives ranging from "very superior" to "dull" and a tenth item that asked for outstanding symptoms or diagnostic features. Second, the study represented an early sensitivity to the problems inherent in attempts to simulate clinical conditions. Thus, the study was responsive to the most frequently cited criticism of experimental work on personality tests:

Figure 13–3 *The Agreement Requirement.* Satisfied that adequately trained examiners can agree on the scoring of the variables of interest in a Rorschach study, the *Journal of Personality Assessment* published this notice in its first issue of 1991. Note that agreement with respect to how specific responses should be scored according to a particular scoring system does not necessarily imply agreement with respect to the interpretation of the scoring; interpretation is another matter entirely.

Editor's Note:
Inter-Scorer Agreement in
Rorschach Research

Ample evidence indicates that adequately trained examiners can agree reasonably well in their scoring of Rorschach variables for which clearly defined scoring criteria have been explicated. Although these data demonstrate the potential reliability of Rorschach scoring, they do not assure that Rorschach protocols will be reliably scored in each instance. The potential for reliable scoring is sometimes taken by researchers as sufficient basis for assuming scorer reliability of the protocols used in their studies. Such assumptions are unwarranted.

Accordingly, in keeping with sound psychometric practice, the *Journal of Personality Assessment* will now routinely require evidence of interscorer agreement in articles reporting Rorschach research. Investigators unfamiliar with methodology for examining scoring reliability on the Rorschach should follow the following procedures.

At least 20 protocols in a study should be scored by two or more examiners to monitor scoring reliability. For the purposes of this reliability check, the scores should be partitioned into such categories as location, determinants, form level, contents, and so on. For each category, a percentage tally should be made of the agreement between examiners on that category. For example, 20 protocols with a mean of 20 responses will yield 400 location scores. Of these 400 location scores, on what percentage were the scorers in agreement? Likewise, on what percentage of the 400 responses were the examiners in agreement concerning what the determinants should be, the form level, the content categories, and so on? Instances in which a researcher's examiners are unable to reach at least 80% agreement on a category indicate a need for revised scoring prior to any attempts to relate the Rorschach variables to other test or behavioral variables.

Reports of Rorschach research that do not include information on scoring reliability or indicate less than 80% agreement on variables central to the particular study will be returned for further work before being accepted for publication.

Irving B. Weiner

Blind interpretations are considered to be parlor tricks by most competent Rorschach interpreters. On the other hand, a history including description of the patient's symptoms and a psychiatric evaluation undoubtedly influences interpretation so that we are no longer dealing with the reliability of the Rorschach test alone as a clinical instrument. The aim of the study was to simulate clinic conditions but to minimize cues other than the Rorschach test. Each Rorschach protocol was therefore accompanied by an abstract of the patient's life history containing some facts of his life but no information about the patient's personality traits, emotional reactions or the opinions of others about him. The life history abstract included the patient's age and sex and the most important facts of his family, educational, occupational, marital, religious, military and medical history. (Lisansky, 1956, pp. 311–312)

A total of 40 Rorschach protocols chosen so that there were at least 15 and not more than 60 responses were given to two groups of three Rorschach experts to score on the prearranged checklist. The experts had an average of 10.5 years of experience in clinical psychology and at least 8 years' experience with the Rorschach. All had published on the Rorschach and all had taught the Rorschach. As a control group, 6 other clinicians who averaged 7½ years of experience were given only the abstracts and asked to complete the same checklist. The degree of agreement among the clinicians in the control group was only .32 as measured by the phi coefficient. The degree of agreement among the expert Rorschach users—who not only had the case history and Rorschach to judge with but were also using an outcome measure that they had devised—was only .33 (virtually the same low degree of reliability as that of the controls). The finding is particularly compelling because the questionnaire had been specifically designed to tap question areas that the Rorschach (and not the life history abstract) was supposed to be able to answer.

In another inter-scorer reliability study (Korner & Westwood, 1955) degree of agreement among three trained Rorschach users was only .31. Even two researchers who were clearly sympathetic to the use of this test were compelled to conclude from their data that "a substantial majority of Rorschach reports have very little communication value" (Datel & Gengerelli, 1955, p. 380).

Answers to questions concerning the validity of the Rorschach test, regardless of the scoring system employed, have been matters of heated controversy; academicians have traditionally claimed that experimental data, primarily from the large number of studies executed in the 1950s, provide no evidence or justification for the widespread use of this test, whereas clinicians have retorted that the Rorschach is a rich source of valuable clinical data. Studies such as those indicating that the Rorschach test is ineffective in differentiating between clinical groups (for example, Guilford, 1948; Wittenborn & Holzberg, 1951) or is not predictive of psychotherapy outcome (Rogers, Knauss, & Hammond, 1951) have been cited frequently. Further, clinical experience with the test was *not* shown to enhance accuracy of interpretation. In one study (Turner, 1966) four groups of 25 judges ($n = 100$) were asked to score Rorschach protocols and then to predict statements pertaining to the patient that had previously been made by the hospital staff. The members of the four groups were varied in their familiarity with the Rorschach and in their knowledge of the Rorschach scoring system. In one group were 25 Fellows of the Society for Projective Techniques who were considered experts in the use of the Rorschach. The other three groups consisted of recently graduated clinical psychologists, graduate students in clinical psychology, and undergraduates who had little or no familiarity with the Rorschach. The results were that all of the four groups were right in about 65 percent of their predictions.

Goldfried, Stricker, and Reiner (1971) suggested that interpretation based on the Rorschach is most justified in those situations where the test is viewed as a structured interview, the results of which are analyzed by skilled clinicians. In a similar vein, Korchin and Schuldberg (1981) took note of a trend to regard the Rorschach as "less of a test" and more as "an open and flexible arena for studying interpersonal transactions" (p. 1151). Commenting on that trend, Berg (1984) wrote that "This shift in perspective opens the door to a range of useful interventions and ways of understanding test data not otherwise available to the examiner" (p. 11). One such new way of understanding Rorschach data—indeed, a relatively new way of administering, scoring, and interpreting the test—is the "consensus method of administration," described and illustrated with case material on two couples (Klopfer, 1984).

It has been argued that even if the validity of the Rorschach has not been satisfactorily demonstrated for clinical use, it is still useful as a research instrument. In fact, the Rorschach has been utilized extensively for research purposes (see Figure 13–4). A perusal of any relatively recent edition in the *Mental Measurements Yearbook* series will list not dozens of references, not hundreds of references, but thousands of references to this test. And regardless of the question of its validity, the Rorschach remains a widely used clinical tool (Howes, 1981). In a survey of 194 members of the Society for Personality Assessment that included a checklist for reporting frequency of usage of 18 popular psychological tests, it was found that "The Rorschach was by far the most frequently utilized projective technique" (Piotrowski, Sherry, & Keller, 1985, p. 117). A survey of universities in the United States offering graduate-level training in clinical psychology indicated that "the greatest proportion of required diagnostic training is allocated to projective testing" (Kolbe, Shemberg, & Leventhal, 1985, p. 60) followed by training in intelligence testing. When members of the Division of Clinical Psychology of the American Psychological Association were asked which tests they would advise graduate students to learn, the Rorschach was at the top of the list. The survey authors hypothesized that clinicians were probably unaffected by negative research in part because they accord greater weight to personal clinical experience than to experimental evidence (Wade & Baker, 1977). The Rorschach is the most frequently taught projective technique in counseling psychology programs (Watkins, Campbell, & Manus, 1990) and is widely used at practicum sites (Craig, 1990).

Exner's Comprehensive System   By the mid-1950s, no less than five different systems for administering and scoring the Rorschach test were in use—systems developed by Samuel J. Beck, Marguerite R. Hertz, Bruno Klopfer, Zygmunt Piotrowski, and David Rapaport with Roy Schafer. Despite differences between the systems and even though many clinicians might "pick and choose" elements from each of the different systems to employ in their own administra-

Figure 13–4 *The Computerized Rorschach.*

Computer-assisted scoring and interpretation of the Rorschach can be accomplished in the clinician's office with specially developed software, or through centralized scoring services where protocol data are processed. In both cases, the trained clinician administers the test and then prepares the raw data for computer scoring and interpretation. The computer may be programmed with any one of a variety of existing Rorschach scoring systems—each with its own rules for scoring and interpreting individual responses and combinations of responses. All of the findings may be integrated in narrative summaries that deal with cognitive, emotional, and other aspects of the test taker's functioning.

To illustrate the type of information obtained from such an administration of the Rorschach, consider the case of Hermann Goering (1893–1946), a high-ranking official in Germany during Hitler's reign. Born to a distinguished family in Bavaria, Goering distinguished himself as a member of Germany's Air Force during World War I and received the Iron Cross, First Class. After meeting Hitler, he became active

in the Nazi party in Germany. He helped organize the secret police as well as the concentration camps and held more than 20 offices in Nazi Germany, among them the title of "Chief Liquidator." Goering is also credited—or discredited—with having signed the most drastic of the anti-Semitic decrees issued by the German state. Described as one of the world's most powerful industrialists of the time and as the economic dictator of Germany, Goering had been designated as Hitler's successor.

However, Goering was convicted of war crimes at the Nuremberg trials and sentenced to death. Goering committed suicide by taking poison the night before he was to be executed.

Shortly after the German surrender in 1945, while the captured Nazis were awaiting trial, Rorschach tests were adminstered to them by the prison psychologist, Gustave Gilbert. The Rorschach responses were published in a book entitled *The Nuremberg Mind* (Miale & Selzer, 1975), and these published data served as the raw data by which two Rorschach experts independently scored the test and then fed their findings into a computerized program based on the Klopfer et al. (1954; Klopfer & Davidson, 1962) scoring system (the Century Diagnostics Computer Interpreted Rorschach). What the computer had to say about Hermann Goering on the basis of his Rorschach data follows. Compare these findings with the profile of a typical healthy adult as published in Klopfer & Davidson (1962, pp. 147–148) or as shown here in the second profile.

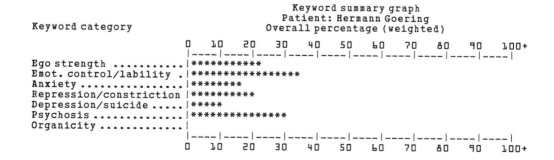

```
                              Keyword summary graph
                             Patient: Hermann Goering
        Keyword category      Overall percentage (weighted)

                             0   10   20   30   40   50   60   70   80   90  100+
                             |----|----|----|----|----|----|----|----|----|----|
Ego strength ..........      |**********
Emot. control/lability .     |******************
Anxiety ...............      |*******
Repression/constriction      |*********
Depression/suicide .....      |*****
Psychosis .............      |***************
Organicity ............      |
                             |----|----|----|----|----|----|----|----|----|----|
                             0   10   20   30   40   50   60   70   80   90  100+
```

Patient ID: Goering   Sex: M
Cognitive function
    This individual's ego strength score which represents his overall adaptive capacity for
cognitive processing, reality function and ability to handle stress effectively is POOR.

Figure 13–4 *(continued)*

There will likely be difficulties in coping with stress cognitively. In addition, this individual may be uncomfortable in new social situations and experience difficulties in his outward adjustment with others. Because of his limited cognitive resources, his level of sexual and/or aggressive impulses, although not excessive, may result in disruption of judgment and intermittent acting out. However, he shows an ability to react to situations in a calm, dispassionate, and impartial manner when such a response is appropriate. A tendency toward distorted perceptual/thought processes is present, but may or may not be indicative of psychosis.

Emotional function

This individual's emotional control/lability score is ELEVATED. The possibility of emotional lability and subsequent loss of control when placed under stress should be carefully considered. This individual exhibits a definite lack in the ability to meet emotional needs in an adaptive, socially appropriate manner. There are high levels of emotional lability and impulsivity. There is a strong likelihood of breakdown of emotional control when placed under stress. This individual is likely to be unable to delay gratification of his immediate emotional needs. Impulsive or explosive behavior and egocentric personality features are prominent. A MODERATE level of anxiety is indicated.

Interpersonal function

The ability to meet dependency and security needs through socially appropriate interactions with others is very poor. Success in meeting these needs through secondary channels of gratification, such as recognition, achievement, or adaptive conformity is unlikely. Overall reduced awareness, repression and/or denial of dependency and security needs may result in unsuccessful and frustrating interpersonal relationships.

THIS NARRATIVE SUMMARY IS BASED UPON THE PRECEDING RORSCHACH REPORT. IT IS NOT INTENDED AS A SUBSTITUTE FOR THAT REPORT, WHICH SHOULD BE READ IN ITS ENTIRETY. THIS REPORT IS INTENDED FOR PROFESSIONAL USE ONLY.

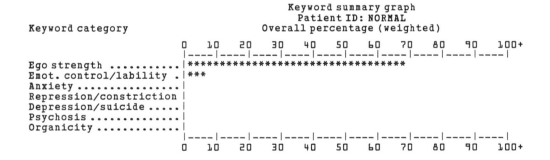

```
                               Keyword summary graph
                                 Patient ID: NORMAL
       Keyword category          Overall percentage (weighted)

                       0   10   20   30   40   50   60   70   80   90  100+
                       |----|----|----|----|----|----|----|----|----|----|
Ego strength ..........|*********************************
Emot. control/lability .|***
Anxiety ...............|
Repression/constriction |
Depression/suicide .....|
Psychosis ..............|
Organicity ............|
                       |----|----|----|----|----|----|----|----|----|----|
                       0   10   20   30   40   50   60   70   80   90  100+
```

Patient ID: Normal   Sex: F   Age: 38
Cognitive function

This individual's ego strength score which represents her overall adaptive capacity for cognitive processing, reality function and ability to handle stress effectively is EXCELLENT. This individual appears capable of taking a balanced intellectual and perceptual approach to problem solving situations. She has the ability to develop an overview of situations while simultaneously dealing with the common sense aspects of a problem. This person is fully able to utilize her adaptive resources in her interaction with others. She has a reasonable acceptance regarding the presence of a sexual and aggressive impulse life. No maladaptive cognitive defensive strategies are noted. She shows an ability to react to situations in a calm, dispassionate, and impartial manner when such a response is appropriate.

Emotional function

This individual's emotional control/lability score is LOW and suggests the possibility of emotional overcontrol. However, this individual is capable of considering others in the expression of her emotions. She has the capacity to delay gratification of her emotional

Figure 13-4 *(continued)*

needs in the face of environmental stress. There is a healthy control over emotional impact
without loss of flexibility. Responsiveness is appropriately modulated. Overall, this individual shows potential for appropriate emotional spontaneity which is likely to be an
asset to her adjustment.

Interpersonal function

This individual appears to have adequate potential for meeting dependency and security
needs through socially appropriate interactions with others. She is capable of meeting her
needs through derived secondary channels of gratification, such as, recognition, achievement, or adaptive conformity. In addition, there is adequate potential for deeper, more
primary affectional responsivity, such as physical contact and closeness. Overall, this
person appears to have achieved an appropriate level of socialization, wherein she should
be able to meet her needs through socially satisfying interaction with others.

THIS NARRATIVE SUMMARY IS BASED UPON THE PRECEDING RORSCHACH REPORT. IT IS NOT INTENDED AS A
SUBSTITUTE FOR THAT REPORT, WHICH SHOULD BE READ IN ITS ENTIRETY. THIS REPORT IS INTENDED FOR
PROFESSIONAL USE ONLY.

---

tions of the test, general usage of the test by clinicians flourished and it tended to
be referred to as *the* Rorschach—as if it were a standardized test.[3]

Which of the five existing Rorschach systems had the greatest clinical utility?
This was the question John E. Exner, Jr., tackled in a study designed to compare
the empirical strengths of each existing system. Exner's (1969) work highlighted
the differences between the existing systems and served as a stimulus to the establishment of a Rorschach Research Foundation, with an objective of surveying
practitioners and reviewing and cross-referencing the scholarly literature on the
test. Using the findings and experimentally exploring the efficacy of a sixth system that integrated into it the best features of the five existing systems, Exner
(1974) published what he called a "Comprehensive System" for administering,
scoring, and interpreting the Rorschach test. Subsequent volumes (Exner, 1978,
1986; Exner & Weiner, 1982) have elaborated on—and made yet more comprehensive—the comprehensive system. After administration of the ten cards and an
inquiry, responses to each card are scored or, to use Exner's preferred term,
"coded." The coding process is too complicated to detail in its entirety here. In
general, each response is coded with reference to the following seven categories:
Location, Determinant(s), Form Quality, Content(s), Popularity, Organizational
Activity, and Special Scores. Using the category scores, interpretive scores and
indices such as an obsessive style index, a depression index, a coping deficit
index, and a schizophrenia index may be derived. Exner and associates (for example, Exner, Armbruster, & Viglione, 1978) have reported impressive test-
retest reliability coefficients for the system. However, as Exner (1983) has pointed

---

3. An example of "picking and choosing" in the context of interpretative criteria can be found in a
recent article having to do with Rorschach indicators of child abuse. Describing the measures she used
in her study, Saunders (1991, p. 55) writes: "Rorschach protocols were scored using Rapaport et al.'s
(1945–46) system as the basic framework, but special scores of four different types were added. I borrowed two of these additional measures from other researchers (Holt, 1977; Wilson, 1985) and developed the other two specifically for this study."

out, some scoring categories are, of necessity, unreliable since they are sensitive to the present state of the test taker:

> The psychological state of the subject at the time of testing is one variable that potentially affects a test's psychometric properties. Using the Comprehensive System, this variable does not effect [sic] the entire Rorschach test or many of the scoring variables. There are, however, some variables that are *state* related. For example, the scores for inanimate movement (m) and diffuse shading (Y) are very unstable over short periods and longer intervals of time. Yet, their interpretive significance seems unquestionable; both are clearly correlated with external variables which indicate the presence of situational stress (Exner, 1978; Exner & Weiner, 1982). Thus, some Comprehensive System scores defy the axiom that something cannot be valid unless it is also reliable. (pp. 410–411)

Normative findings that employed a sample of more than 2,500 subjects were reported by Exner (1978, 1986), and findings with respect to 1,970 nonpatient children were reported by Exner and Weiner (1982). Interpretation of a properly coded test protocol with reference to this normative base of data can lead, according to Exner (1990; in press) and others, to interpretive statements that are sound from a psychometric viewpoint. As the use of the system grows in popularity, we can look forward to the publication of more studies by independent investigators with respect to the psychometric soundness of the system. As we saw previously, however, studies of the psychometric soundness of the Rorschach test that employed a variety of systems other than the Comprehensive System have tended to reinforce the image of the test as a tool that may be clinically useful but unable to pass muster under rigorous scrutiny from a psychometric perspective.

The Holtzman Inkblot Technique (HIT)

Based on the same underlying premise as the Rorschach, the HIT was constructed to be a psychometrically sound projective instrument. The test consists of two parallel forms (A and B), each composed of 45 inkblots with two additional trial blots identical in both test forms. Included are inkblots that are achromatic and chromatic. Unlike the Rorschach, which consists of symmetrical blots (similar on both sides), asymmetrical blots were also included in the HIT. *Inkblot Perception and Personality* (Holtzman, Thorpe, Swartz, & Herron, 1961) serves as a manual and a scoring guide for the test. The inkblots are presented one at a time to the subject, and (unlike the Rorschach) subjects are instructed to produce only one response per blot. A brief inquiry follows immediately, wherein the examiner seeks to determine where the percept was seen and the qualities of the blot that contributed to the forming of the percept.

Responses on the HIT are scored according to 22 variables, some (such as "reaction time") quite familiar to Rorschach users, with others (such as "penetration") less familiar. For the record, "penetration" refers to that which "might be symbolic of an individual's feeling that his body exterior is of little protective value and can be easily penetrated" (Holtzman, 1975, p. 247). Factor analysis of the different scoring categories has resulted in the establishment of six clusters or dimensions that reflect interrelationships among the variables. Some of these in-

Table 13–1

Key Variables on the Holtzman Inkblot Test (HIT)

Factor number	Variables
I	Movement
	Integration
	Human
	Barrier
	Popular
II	Color
	Shading
	Form definiteness (reversed)
III	Pathognomic verbalization
	Anxiety
	Hostility
	Movement
IV	Form appropriateness
	Location
V	Reaction time
	Rejection
	Animal (reversed)
VI	Penetration
	Anatomy
	Sex

terrelationships are listed in Table 13–1. A computer-based interpretive scoring system has been developed for the HIT.

Psychometric properties   The HIT was standardized on over 1,400 normal, schizophrenic, depressed, and retarded individuals who ranged in age from 5 years through adulthood. Percentile norms based on these groups were developed. Several differences in test construction between the HIT and the Rorschach result in the HIT being more adaptable to psychometric analyses. The limitation of only one response per inkblot eliminates the problem of variability in productivity that may sometimes complicate statistical analyses of the Rorschach (that is, since there is no restriction on the number of responses a subject may give to each Rorschach card, responses may theoretically range from 0 to however many the examiner will sit for before stopping the respondent—a situation that makes for difficulty when trying to compare protocols from different people). The availability of two forms of the instrument constructed concurrently during test development and "carefully paired on both stimulus and response characteristics to enhance the equivalence" (Holtzman, 1975, p. 244) enables test-retest and alternate form-reliability procedures to be conducted. Additionally, the order of presentation of "achromatic and chromatic blots is sufficiently random to minimize undesirable sequential effects" (Holtzman, 1975, p. 245), enabling split-half reliability procedures to be conducted.

Internal consistency measures based on 50 samples and employing split-half (odd-even blots) procedures resulted in median reliability coefficients mostly in the .70s and .80s, with some being above .90. Inter-scorer reliability with respect to the HIT system was found to be exceptionally high, with reliability coefficients above .95 on all but two scoring categories. Test-retest reliability estimates using alternate forms of the test and extending over intervals from one week to one year were found to range from .36 to .81 for the standardization sample. In one cross-cultural longitudinal study of test-retest reliability, Holtzman (1975) used alternate forms of the test with a population of American and Mexican children. Over a six-year period, children were tested at 6 years 8 months, 9 years 8 months, and 12 years 8 months. Retesting intervals varied from one to five years. Test-retest reliability was found to be highest at the older age levels. In addition, as the length of time of the testing interval increased, the reliability decreased. Test-retest reliability estimates were found to be the highest for the Location scoring category (reliability coefficients falling mostly in the .80s), followed by estimates for the Movement, Human, and Form Definiteness categories.

Validity investigations have compared HIT findings with data obtained from other assessment instruments. For example, a study comparing HIT scores with scales on the Personality Research Form (PRF) resulted in significant correlations between high color scores on the HIT and high scores on the PRF scales of Impulsiveness, Exhibitionism, and Nurturance. These findings appear to be consistent with Rorschach theory, which holds that "the ways . . . color is handled in responding to the blots are believed to cast light upon the overt emotional reactions of the subject to the impact of his social environment" (Klopfer, Ainsworth, Klopfer, & Holt, 1954, p. 278). Also found to be positively correlated was the HIT score of Integration and the PRF scale of Understanding, both of which reflect intellectual abilities.

Information concerning intergroup differences in performance on the HIT was illustrated in data obtained from the standardization sample, where the performance of "normals" was compared with such groups as depressives, chronic schizophrenics, and retardates. Mosely's (1963) reanalysis of Holtzman's standardization sample data resulted in differentiation of normals from schizophrenics, depressives from schizophrenics, and depressives from normals. Computer analysis of over five thousand cases of individuals, including depressives, neurotics, schizophrenics, the brain-damaged, and alcoholic groups, from the United States and 16 other countries have led to the development of additional normative data (Gorham, Mosely, & Holtzman, 1968). Mittenberg and Petersen (1984) explored the validity of the HIT measure of anxiety in a study that employed biofeedback measures and concluded that their findings supported the validity of the HIT as a measure of anxiety (though they weren't sure whether the anxiety was state or trait in nature).

A standardized edition of the HIT designed for group administration by means of projection of slides has also been developed. The reliability of the group technique using split-half and test-retest procedures has been found to approximate that of individual administrations. However, certain scoring categories, such as Location, Color, or Space, were found to receive higher scores during group administration, suggesting that when viewed from a distance, these qualities of the inkblots become more prominent. In addition, higher variance on the variable of anxiety was found to occur in group administration of the HIT, possibly substantiating the premise that the interpersonal relationship between examiner/examinee is of consequence in test taking.

Table 13–2

The Rorschach and the HIT Compared

Rorschach	HIT
Intended for individual administration	May be administered individually or in groups
One form of the test	Two forms of the test
Comprises 10 inkblots	45 inkblots in each form
No trial blots	Two trial blots
Inkblots are bilaterally symmetrical	Both symmetrical and asymmetrical inkblots are included
Both achromatic and chromatic cards are included	Both achromatic and chromatic cards are included
No limit on the number of responses a subject may give	Only one response per card is allowed
Inquiry follows presentation of *all* the cards and allows for additional responses	Inquiry follows immediately after each response
Traditional methods for assessing reliability have not proved easily adaptable	Test construction results in its being conducive to assessment of reliability
Computer scoring and interpretation available	Computer scoring and interpretation available

In spite of what many view as the superior qualities of the HIT from a purely psychometric standpoint, the Rorschach has prevailed as the dominant projective inkblot method (see Table 13–2). We may speculate as to the possible reasons: (1) for many years the Rorschach was the only technique available, and clinicians interested in projective techniques would be routinely trained in its use—familiarity with the Rorschach, lack of familiarity with the HIT, and sheer inertia may therefore be factors; (2) the Rorschach is viewed as supplying more clinical content since there is no limit on the number of responses obtainable and the procedure allows for extensive inquiry; and (3) some users of projective techniques may place their clinical intuition above any touted benefits of superiority with respect to psychometric qualities. At the very least, the HIT does seem to have been of value in stimulating thought and investigation with respect to the use of inkblots as a projective technique.

PICTURES AS PROJECTIVE STIMULI

Look at Figure 13–5. Having looked at it, make up a story about it. Your story should have a beginning, a middle, and an end. Write it down using as much paper as you need. Bring the story to class with you and compare it to some other student's story.[4] What does the story reveal about your needs, fears, desires, im-

---

4. Do it! At the very least, it's a good way of introducing yourself to someone in the class whom you haven't yet met.

pulse control, ways of viewing the world—your personality? What does the story written by your classmate reveal about her or him?

This exercise introduces you to the use of pictures as projective stimuli. Pictures used as projective stimuli may be photos of real persons, of animals, of objects, or anything; they may be paintings, drawings, etchings, or any other variety of picture. One of the earliest uses of pictures as projective stimuli came at the turn of the century. An article by Brittain (1907) in a journal called *The Pedagogical Seminary* reported sex differences in stories that children gave in response to nine pictures. The author reported that the girls were more interested in religious and moral themes than were the boys. The next year another experimenter used pictures and a story-telling technique to investigate the imagination of children, and differences in themes as a function of age were observed (Libby, 1908). In 1932 a psychiatrist working at the Clinic for Juvenile Research in Detroit developed the Social Situation Picture Test (Schwartz, 1932), a projective instrument that contained pictures relevant to juvenile delinquents. Working at the Harvard Psychological Clinic in 1935, Christiana D. Morgan and Henry Murray published the Thematic Apperception Test (TAT)—pronounced by saying the letters and not by rhyming with "cat"—the instrument that has come to be the most widely used of all of the picture/story-telling projective tests. We discuss the TAT as well as some related instruments.

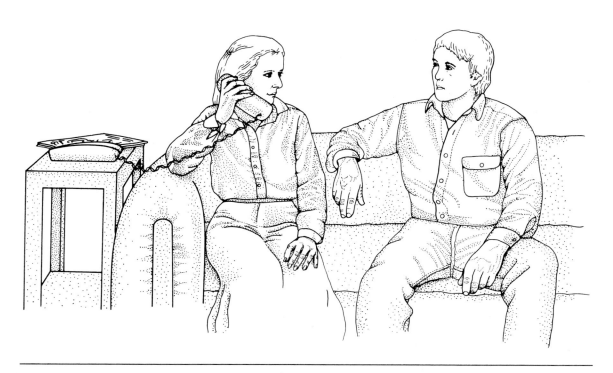

Figure 13–5 *A TAT-like Picture.*

The Thematic Apperception Test (TAT)

The TAT was originally designed as an aid to eliciting fantasy material from patients in psychoanalysis (Morgan & Murray, 1935). The stimulus materials consist of 31 cards, of which one is blank. The 30 picture cards, all black-and-white, contain a variety of scenes that were designed to present the test taker with "certain classical human situations" (Murray, 1943). Some of the pictures contain a lone individual, some contain a group of people, and some contain no people. Some of the pictures appear to be as real as a photo and others are surrealistic drawings. Examinees are introduced to the examination with the "cover story" that it is a "test of imagination" in which it is their task to tell what events led up to the scene in the picture, what is happening at that moment, and what the outcome will be. Examinees are also asked to tell what the people depicted in the cards are thinking and feeling. In the TAT *Manual*, Murray (1943) also advised that the examiners attempt to find out what the source of the story was; in this context it is noteworthy that the noun "apperception" is derived from the verb *apperceive,* which is defined as "to perceive in terms of past perceptions." The source of a story could be anything—a personal experience, a dream, an imagined event, a book, an episode of *Roseanne,* and so on. When and if the blank card is administered, examinees are instructed to imagine that there is a picture on the card and then proceed to tell a story about it.

In clinical practice, examiners tend to take liberties with various elements pertaining to the administration, scoring, and interpretation of the TAT. For example, while 20 cards is the recommended number for presentation, in practice an examiner might administer as few as one or two cards or as many as all 31. If a clinician is assessing a patient who has a penchant for telling stories that fill reams of the clinician's notepad, it's a good bet that fewer cards will be administered. If, on the other hand, a patient tells brief, one- or two-sentence stories, more cards may be administered in an attempt to collect more raw data with which to work. Some of the cards are suggested for use with adult males, females, or both, and some are suggested for use with children. This is so because certain pictorial representations lend themselves more than others to identification and projection with respect to members of these groups. In one study involving 75 males (25 each of 11-, 14-, and 17-year-olds), Cooper (1981) identified the ten most productive cards for use with adolescent males. *In practice,* however, any card—be it one recommended for use with males, with females, or children—may be administered to any subject; the clinician administering selects the cards that he or she believes will elicit responses pertinent to the objective of the testing.

The raw material used in drawing conclusions about the individual examined with the TAT are (1) the stories as they were told by the examinee, (2) the clinician's notes about the way or the manner in which the examinee responded to the cards, and (3) the clinician's notes about extra-test behavior and verbalizations. The latter two categories of raw data (test and extra-test behavior) are sources of clinical interpretations for almost any individually administered test. Analysis of the story content requires special training. One illustration of how a test taker's behavior during testing may influence the examiner's interpretations of the findings was provided by Sugarman (1991, p. 140), who told of a "highly narcissistic patient [who] demonstrated contempt and devaluation of the examiner (and presumably others) by dictating TAT stories complete with spelling and punctuation as though the examiner was a stenographer."

A number of systems for interpreting TAT data exist, though all are based to a greater or lesser degree in Henry Murray's influential theory of personality, excellent summaries of which are available (in, for example, Hall & Lindzey, 1970; Murray, 1959; Murray & Kluckhohn, 1953). In particular, interpretive systems for the TAT tend to incorporate the Murrayan concepts of *need* (determinants of behavior arising from within the individual), *press* (determinants of behavior arising from within the environment), and *thema* (a unit of interaction between needs and press). In general, the guiding principle in interpreting TAT stories is that the test taker is identifying with someone (the protagonist) in the story and that the needs, environmental demands, and conflicts of the protagonist in the story are in some way related to the concerns, hopes, fears, or desires of the examinee. In his discussion of the TAT from the perspective of a clinician, William Henry (1956) examined each of the cards in the test in terms of such variables as "manifest stimulus demand," "form demand," "latent stimulus demand," frequent plots, and significant variations. To get an idea of how some of these terms are used, look again at Figure 13–4—a picture which is *not* a TAT card—and then read Tables 13–3 and 13–4, which are descriptions of the card and some responses to the card from college-age respondents. Although a clinician may obtain bits of information from the stories told about every individual card, the clinician's final impressions will usually derive from a consideration of the overall patterns of themes that emerge.

TAT scoring and interpretation systems based on the work of personality theorists other than Henry Murray may also be found. For example, an "Affect Maturity Scale" that has its basis in Anna Freud's notion of affect development and maturation has been described by Thompson (1986). Westen and his colleagues (Westen, Silk, Lohr, & Kerber, 1985; Westen, Barends, Leigh, Mendel, & Silbert, 1988) have reported on the development of the Object Relations and Social Cognition Scale (ORSCS), a measure used in conjunction with the TAT and based in object relations theory as well as social-cognitive psychology.

Reliability   Inter-scorer reliability for trained examiners using the same scoring methods can be acceptably high. However, although scorers can be trained to agree with respect to specific scoring criteria, the reliability of interpretations made from TAT data is not readily amenable to assessment by the usual means of determining reliability (such as split-half, test-retest, alternate-form) because of the nature of the task (see McClelland, 1980) and the susceptibility of responses on the test to various factors, including those discussed in the following paragraphs.

Situational factors can affect TAT responses. Variables such as the examiner, experiences just prior to test administration, and even the manner in which instructions and/or comments are given during the test administration all have an effect on TAT responses. In a study that examined the effect of the age of the examiner on TAT performance (Mussen & Scodel, 1955), two groups of male college students were shown slides of nude females and were instructed to rate their attractiveness. One group had the slides presented by a "stern man" in his sixties; the other by a "young, informal" graduate student. TATs were then administered

Table 13–3

A Description of the Sample TAT-like Picture

Author's description

A male and a female are seated in close proximity on a sofa. The female is talking on the phone. There is an end table with a magazine on it next to the sofa.

Manifest stimulus demand

Some explanation of the nature of the relationship between these two persons and some reason the woman is on the phone are required. Less frequently noted is the magazine on the table and its role in this scene.

Form demand

Two large details, the woman and the man, must be integrated. Small details include the magazine and the telephone.

Latent stimulus demand

This picture is likely to elicit attitudes toward heterosexuality and, within that context, material relevant to the examinee's "place" on optimism-pessimism, security-insecurity, dependence-independence, passivity-assertiveness, and related continuums. Alternatively, attitudes toward family and friends may be elicited with the two primary figures being viewed as brother and sister, the female talking on the phone to a family member, etc.

Frequent plots

We haven't administered this card to enough people to make judgments about what constitutes "frequent plots." We have, however, provided a sampling of plots (Table 13–4).

Significant variations

Just as we cannot provide information on frequent plots, we cannot report data on significant variations. We would guess, however, that most college students viewing this picture would perceive the two individuals in it as being involved in a heterosexual relationship. Were that to be the case, a significant variation would be a story in which the characters are not involved in a heterosexual relationship (for example, they are employer/employee). Close clinical attention will also be paid to the nature of the relationship of the characters to any "introduced figures" (persons not pictured in the card but introduced into the story by the examinee). The "pull" of this card is to introduce the figure to whom the woman is speaking. What is the phone call about? How will the story be resolved?

and scored for expressed sexual themes. The scores from the group with the "informal" presenter were higher than those of the other group, suggesting that the aroused need was inhibited to a greater degree in the presence of a presenter viewed as an authority figure. Significant differences in TAT scores as a function of the examiner's presence or absence have also been found to occur (Bernstein, 1956). In examining the way experiences just prior to TAT administration may affect performance, Lindzey (1950) found that exposing subjects to socially frustrating situations just prior to TAT administration resulted in a greater incidence

Table 13–4

Some Responses to the Sample Picture

Respondent	Story
1. (Male)	This guy has been involved with this girl for a few months. Things haven't been going all that well. He's suspected that she's been seeing a lot of guys. This is just one scene in a whole evening where the phone hasn't stopped ringing. Pretty soon he is just going to get up and leave.
2. (Female)	This couple is dating. They haven't made any plans for the evening and they are wondering what they should do. She is calling up another couple to ask if they want to get together. They will go out with the other couple and have a good time.
3. (Male)	This girl thinks she is pregnant and is calling the doctor for the results of her test. This guy is pretty worried because he has plans to finish college and go to graduate school. He is afraid she will want to get married, and he doesn't want to get trapped into anything. The doctor will tell her she isn't pregnant, and he'll be really relieved.
4. (Female)	This couple has been dating for about two years and they're very much in love. She's on the phone firming up plans for a down-payment on a hall that's going to cater the wedding. That's a bridal magazine on the table over there. They look like they're really in love. I think things will work out for them even though the odds are against it—the divorce rates and all.
5. (Male)	These are two very close friends. The guy has a real problem and needs to talk to someone. He is feeling really depressed and that he is all alone in the world. Every time he starts to tell her how he feels, the phone rings. Pretty soon he will leave feeling like no one has time for him and even more alone. I don't know what will happen to him, but it doesn't look good.

of aggressive acts carried out by the hero of the stories, while Feshback (1961) found subjects insulted prior to TAT administration exhibited more aggression in their stories than did a noninsulted group. Bellak (1944) was able to demonstrate that subjects criticized *during* TAT administration increased their use of aggressive words on the remaining cards. While the variables in these studies cited were carefully manipulated and controlled, in most cases the extent to which situational factors are operative and affect performance is unknown, making measurement of the test's reliability difficult.

Transient internal-need states can affect TAT responses. Need states such as hunger, thirst, fatigue, and higher-than-ordinary levels of sexual tension experienced by the subject during a particular administration of a picture story task can affect the subject's responses on that occasion. For example, the effect of food deprivation on TAT protocols has been investigated (Sanford, 1936; McClelland & Atkinson, 1948), with the findings indicating that food responses were found to vary as a function of the degree of food deprivation experienced (that is, the greater the deprivation, the higher the number of food responses). Investigations of the effect of sleep deprivation and other variables on TAT protocols have also been conducted (see Atkinson, 1958). To the extent that responses on the TAT are subject to temporary states, determination of the more enduring personality characteristics becomes difficult, and the accuracy of reliability estimates becomes questionable.

The TAT cards themselves have different stimulus "pulls." Some of the TAT pictures are more likely than others to elicit stories with themes of depression or despair, for example, than are other cards (see Goldfried & Zax, 1965). Some cards are more apt to elicit stories that deal with such needs as the need for achievement, for example, than are other cards. Given the fact that the cards themselves have different stimulus "pulls" or, more technically stated, different "latent stimulus demands," it would become difficult for a psychometrist to determine the inter-item reliability of the test; card 1 might reliably elicit need achievement themes while card 16, for example, might not usually elicit any such themes.

The open-ended nature of the task contributes to methodological difficulties in determining psychometric soundness. One can readily appreciate the methodological difficulties in determining the inter-item reliability inherent in a test where one item may have only one or two sentences written in response to it and another item might have one or two pages. While on the one hand the open-ended nature of the TAT enables highly individualistic responses, it also creates numerous possibilities for response patterns. Variations occur not only in length of response but also in content, story themes, and levels of abstraction as well. While it may be established that certain factors affect these variables, such as intelligence contributing to number of story themes (Rubin, 1964) and length of response (Webb & Hilden, 1953), developing a psychometrically rigorous procedure to account for all these variables would be an unenviably complex task.

Intentional desire to fake good or to fake bad can affect TAT response. One of the assumptions inherent in the TAT and in projective measures in general is that the examinee is unaware of the significance of his or her responses. This point has been made by the author of the TAT: "Whatever peculiar virtue the TAT may have, if any, it will be found to reside not as some have assumed in its power to mirror overt behavior or to communicate what the patient knows and is willing to tell, but rather in its capacity to reveal things that the patient is unwilling to tell because he is unconscious of them" (Murray, 1951, p. 577). But research designed to explore this assumption has questioned its validity. Weisskopf and Dieppa (1951) instructed a group of subjects to produce stories that would create the best impression of themselves possible while another group was instructed to produce stories that would create the worst impression possible. Not only were the subjects successful in conveying the desired impresssion, but judges were only able to correctly identify 58 percent of those who had faked good impressions. The ability of subjects to fake a need for achievement was demonstrated in a study by Holmes (1974). In another study (Hamsher & Farina, 1967), subjects who were playing the roles of people attending a psychological clinic were able to successfully present the impression of being "open" or "guarded," depending on what they had been instructed to convey. The extent to which the TAT may be sensitive to faking must be considered by test users in assessing reliability.

Validity   In general, validity research on the TAT has focused on questions like "What is the relationship between expressions of fantasy stories and real-life behavior?" A sampling of some of the research that has been conducted with respect to one variable, aggressive behavior, follows. One study addressing this question focused on the relationship between aggression expressed in fantasy and overt aggression (Mussen & Naylor, 1954). These researchers observed that need for aggression expressed on the TAT was predictive of overt aggressive behavior and that a low expectation of punishment for aggression led to an even stronger likelihood that aggression would be expressed. The subjects in this study were 29 adolescent delinquent males (between the ages of 9 and 16) from lower-class environments. Kagan (1956) examined the relationship between TAT-expressed aggression in 118 middle-class boys in grades 1 through 3 (mean age of 7.9) and teacher ratings of the subjects with respect to their tendency to express or inhibit feelings of anger. Although Kagan noted a positive relationship between fantasy aggression and ratings of overt aggression, the relationship was not significant. In a study on hostility involving 51 neuropsychiatric patients in an army hospital, Gluck (1955) hypothesized that the greater the hostility expressed on the TAT, the greater the hostile behavior that would be exhibited when presented with a frustrating situation. The results did not, however, support this hypothesis. Barends, Westen, Leigh, Silbert, & Byers (1990) found a significant correlation between TAT and interview measures with respect to the psychoanalytic concept of "affect tone"—the extent to which people and relationships tend to be seen as enriching versus hostile and malevolent.

Conflicting opinions and questioning appear in the literature not only with respect to validity of the assumptions of the test, but also with respect to the validity of diagnostic inferences. Some have concluded that the validity of the interpretation of the data derived from a TAT administration is based more on the clinician's skills than the psychometric properties of the test (Worchel & Dupree, 1990). With so many questions about the psychometric soundness of the TAT, the student might well ask why this test remains one of the most popular in terms of clinical assessment.[5] Among the possible reasons that could be cited is the test's longevity; like the Rorschach test, the TAT is a test that many practicing clinicians were taught when they were in graduate school and it is a projective test with which they are very familiar. Another reason is the great intuitive appeal of the projective hypothesis as applied to this test; it makes sense that people would project their own motivation when asked to construct a story with respect to ambiguous scenes. Because many of the pictures with figures in them contain more than one figure, the instrument is particularly well suited to uncovering information related to those needs, desires, and conflicts that are related to social, interpersonal, and familial relationships. Unlike personality inventories with items that are set and administration procedures that are rigorously standardized, the TAT examiner not only selects the particular cards to be used for a given testing, but also has a fair amount of leeway with respect to the type of probing during the test. Such "hands-on" involvement in preparing for the testing and administering the test—not to mention scoring and interpreting the test—may have great appeal to a clinician; the opportunity to take an active and vital role in the assessment is becoming harder and harder to come by in an age when "testing" is almost always tantamount to handing the test taker an answer sheet, an answer book, a

---

5. But while the TAT remains a popular clinical tool, it has not, in recent years, served as a great stimulus for research. Polyson, Norris, and Ott (1985) counted TAT references in *Psychological Abstracts* and in the Buros series of yearbooks for the years 1970 to 1983 and found that research with the TAT had declined substantially.

number 2 pencil—and then waiting for the narrative summary and profile to come back from the computer.

Other Picture-Story Tests

Since the publication of the TAT in the mid-1930s, many adaptations of it have appeared. For example, the Thompson (1949) modification of the TAT was expressly designed for administration to black subjects, and pictures contained both black and white protagonists. The Children's Apperception Test (CAT), authored by Leopold Bellak and first published in 1949, was designed specifically for use with children aged 3 to 10 and featured animals instead of humans in the pictures. However, in response to research indicating that children might produce more clinically valuable material when cards featured humans in the pictures (see Murstein, 1963, for example), an alternative version of the CAT called the CAT-H ("H" standing for the use of human figures in the pictures) was published (Bellak & Bellak, 1965). The clinician's choice of either the CAT or CAT-H was to be influenced by his or her judgment concerning the mental age and personality of the child subject (Bellak & Hurvich, 1966). Subsequently, Bellak developed a TAT-like test for the elderly and christened it the Senior Apperception Technique (Bellak & Bellak, 1973). Some of the other published modifications of the original TAT include tests designed for American Indians, South Africans, and South Micronesians (Bellak, 1971). The Blacky Pictures Test (Blum, 1950) was a psychoanalytically based TAT-like projective test for children that employed "Blacky" the dog as well as his family and friends. Phillipson (1955) devised a measure containing more diffuse, less differentiated pictures than the TAT. The test, described as "a cross between the TAT and the Rorschach," is reportedly "more widely used in Great Britain, but gaining in popularity here" (Stricker & Healey, 1990, p. 226).

Numerous other picture-story instruments have been published, and we will briefly describe a sampling of them. In general, the tests are designed to elicit information from respondents in a particular age group and/or in a particular situation (such as school) or diagnostic category. Like the TAT, the picture-story tests tend not to offer strong evidence for their psychometric soundness; to a greater degree than most objective personality tests, the validity of such instruments is often limited by the skill, ability, and clinical acumen of the test user.

The Picture Story Test (Symonds, 1949) was designed expressly for use with adolescents, and the 20 pictures contained in it were designed to elicit stories pertinent to those years (for example, coming home late, leaving home, and planning for the future). The Education Apperception Test (Thompson & Sones, 1973) and the School Apperception Method (Solomon & Starr, 1968) are two picture-story instruments designed to tap children's attitudes toward school and learning. The Michigan Picture Test was developed for use with children between the ages of 8 and 14, and it contains 16 pictures designed to elicit various responses, ranging from conflicts with authority figures to feelings of personal inadequacy (Andrew, 1953). A thematic apperception technique designed for use with urban Hispanic children called TEMAS depicts Hispanic characters in urban settings (Malgady, Costantino, & Rogler, 1984; Costantino, Malgady, & Rogler, 1988). The Roberts Apperception Test for Children (RATC; McArthur & Roberts, 1972) contains cards depicting a variety of situations, including family confrontation, parental conflict, parental affection, attitudes toward school, and peer action. Developed with one objective being a standardized scoring system, reviews of this instrument to date can at best be described as mixed (Sines, 1985; Obrzut & Boliek, 1986). The Children's Apperceptive Story-Telling Test (CAST; Schneider, 1989; Schneider & Perney, 1990) has its basis in Adlerian theory, contains color cards, and was designed to reflect "contemporary figures in contexts of modern problems while retaining stimulus ambiguity" (Schneider, 1989, p. 9).

In one projective test, test takers construct their own pictures and then tell a story. The Make A Picture Story Method (Shneidman, 1952) consists of 67 cut-up figures of people and animals that may be presented on any of 22 pictorial backgrounds. The figures (which vary in posture and position) represent males, females, children, nudes, minority groups (such as blacks, Mexicans, and Orientals), legendary characters, and well-known fictitious characters (such as Superman). A number of figures with blank faces are also included. The backgrounds represent diverse settings (for example, a living room, street, nursery, stage, schoolroom, bathroom, bridge, dream, camp, cave, raft, cemetery, cellar), and there is also one blank background onto which the test taker may assign any background. Designed for use with individuals 6 years of age or older, examinees are instructed to arrange the figures on the backgrounds "as they might be in real life" (Shneidman, 1952, p. 7). The subject is then instructed to construct a story pertinent to their creation and indicate who the characters are, what they are doing, what they are thinking, how they are feeling, and what the outcome of the story will be.

One projective personality test that employed pictures as stimuli is now more a matter of historical interest than anything else. Still, the theory on which the test was based remains a source of fascination to students of projective techniques. It is a test that was designed in part to explore "the German characterologic assumption that within the frame of the total personality there is a nucleus of innate, permanent psychological features that cannot be modified by environmental factors" (Webb, 1987, p. 600). And so we refer you to our chapter Close-up and a brief look at an instrument unique among picture projective techniques for its grounding in both genetics and personality theory: the Szondi Test.

Close-up

Of Historical Interest . . .

The Szondi Test was published in Europe along with accompanying books (Szondi, 1947, 1948) and popularized in the United States by Susan K. Deri (Figure 1). Deri had been psychiatrist Lipot Szondi's student in Hungary, had worked with him in the development of the test, and wrote *Introduction to the Szondi Test* (1949a), a test manual. In the foreword to that book, Szondi praised Deri for her effort to bridge the gap between then existing European and American approaches in the mental health field:

> We Europeans still pursue an "epic" form of psychology of a kind that we learned from Dostoevski and Freud. The story of the *soul* of man to us is still a heroic novel that we like to tell unhurriedly in long sentences. (pp. vii–viii)

Of Historical Interest (continued)

Figure 1 *From left to right: Susan K. Deri and Dr. and Mrs. Szondi in a photo taken in September 1982, a year before Mrs. Deri died. Lipot Szondi died at the age of 93 in 1986, leaving behind 25 books and tracts and 350 journal articles.*

Indeed, the Szondi Test could be conceived as one attempt to uncover, if not the test taker's soul, drives and conflicts presumed to be, at least in part, inborn. The test was developed by Szondi to be a therapeutic aid and it was only within the context of *Schicksalanalysis* (a confrontational therapy) that the test findings would have diagnostic meaning (Webb, 1987). The test materials consist of 6 sets of 2-inch by 3-inch photographs, with each set containing 8 photographs, a total of 48 in all. Each of the photographs of a set is of a different person who had been diagnosed into one of the following then-existing psychodiagnostic categories: (1) homosexual, (2) sadistic, (3) epileptic, (4) hysteric, (5) catatonic, (6) paranoid, (7) depressive, and (8) manic (see Figure 2). According to Deri (1949b):

> The eight types of mental disorders in the test are those which Szondi believes follow Mendelian laws of inheritance. That is why these

pictures were used and not others. Szondi's basic hypothesis is that we respond to these pictures in the basis of inner promptings originating in our own genetic structure. (p. 448)

Set I of 8 photographs is laid out before the test taker in a manner prescribed in the test manual and the examiner asks, "Now look at all these faces and pick out first the two you like most and then the two you dislike most. Don't think long, just do it spontaneously (or quickly); you don't have to give any reason for your choice." After the two liked and disliked pictures have been selected and put aside, all of the remaining photographs in Set I are put back into the test kit and the procedure is repeated, one set at a time with the remaining five sets of photographs. At the conclusion of the sorting of Set VI, the examiner now places the accumulated total of 12 "liked" cards before the test taker and asks which 4 were liked the most. The administration of the test is completed with the selection of the 4 most disliked cards from the pile of 12 disliked cards previously chosen, though an optional addition to the test administration could be a story-telling component where the respondent would use the Szondi pictures much like TAT cards. Deri (1949a, p. 14) advised that "The administration of the test has to be repeated at least six, preferably ten, times, with at least one day intervals between administrations, to be able to give a valid clinical interpretation of the personality." When repeated, it would be important to make the test taker understand that the purpose of the readministration was not to check on consistency, but rather to see "how he feels today in regard to these pictures" (Deri, 1949a, p. 15).

The test taker's responses are scored and interpreted according to an elaborate scoring system that has some theoretical basis in the work of Kurt Lewin (1935), particularly with respect to Lewinian concepts pertaining to organismic needs and drives. The eight types of Szondi pictures were designed to correspond to eight types of psychological needs "which to some degree

Figure 2 *Some Sample Photographs from the Szondi Test.* The diagnostic categories for the patients pictured in the top row, from left to right are: homosexual, sadist, epileptic, and hysteric. For the bottom row, left to right: catatonic, paranoid, depressive, and manic.

exist in everybody. . . . Depending on the degree of (or intensity of) the state of tension in each of the eight need-systems, the pictures representing the corresponding needs will assume valence character in various proportions . . . the subject *chooses* pictures from the factor corresponding to his own need in tension. . . . Relatively great numbers of choices (four or more) from one category means that the corresponding need is in a state of strong tension . . . lack of choices in a certain category means that the corresponding need is *not* in state of tension" (Deri, 1949a, pp. 26–27). Deri (1949a) discussed at length the psychological needs associated with each of the eight psychodiagnostic categories included in the test. Thus, for example, the focus in her discussion of the diagnostic category of

homosexuality was not sexual preference, but rather the feminine, "tender, more yielding part of sexuality" (p. 67) and the desire "to be loved by somebody the way they were loved by their mother" (p. 68).

Research has not supported the assumptions on which the Szondi Test is based (Guertin, 1951; Gordon, 1953; Lubin & Malby, 1951; Prelinger, 1950, 1952; Mussen & Krauss, 1952; Wiegersma, 1950); and, except as the subject of a dissertation once every great while, one seldom reads of any research being conducted with it. Still, this test holds a place of fascination in the annals of psychological testing, perhaps because of the age-old fascination and intuitive appeal of being able to tell something about people from their face.

WORDS AS PROJECTIVE STIMULI

Although all projective techniques involve the use of verbalizations either in providing directions or in obtaining responses, there are those instruments that use words as the projective stimulus material. Projective techniques that employ open-ended words, phrases, and sentences are referred to as semistructured techniques because, while they are open-ended and allow for a variety of responses, they still provide a framework within which the subject must operate. The two best-known examples of verbal projective techniques are word association and sentence completion tests.

Word Association Tests

The first attempt at investigating word association was made by Galton (1879). Galton's method consisted of presenting a series of unrelated stimulus words and instructing the subject to respond with the first word that came to mind. Continued interest in the phenomenon of word association resulted in additional studies being conducted. Precise methods for recording the responses given and the length of time elapsed before obtaining a response were developed (Cattell, 1887; Trautscholdt, 1883). Cattell and Bryant (1889) were the first to use cards with stimulus words printed on them, and Kraepelin's (1896) investigations studied the effect of physical states such as hunger and fatigue as well as the effect of practice on word association. Mounting experimental evidence led psychologists to believe that the associations individuals made to words were not chance happenings, but rather were the resultant interplay of the individual's life experiences, attitudes, and unique personality characteristics.

Jung (1910) maintained that by selecting certain key words that represented possible areas of conflict, word association techniques could be employed for psychodiagnostic purposes. Jung's experiments served as an inspiration to developers of such tests as the Word Association Test developed by Rapaport, Gill, & Schafer (1946) at the Menninger Clinic. This test consisted of three parts. In the first part, each stimulus word is administered to the examinee, who has been instructed to respond quickly with the first word that comes to mind. The examiner records the length of time it takes the subject to respond to each item. In the second part of the test, each stimulus word is again presented to the examinee. Here the examinee is instructed to reproduce the original responses. Any deviation between the original and this second response is recorded, as is the length of time before reacting. The third part of the test is the inquiry. Here the examiner asks questions to try to clarify the relationship that exists between the stimulus word and the response (for example, "What were you thinking about?" or "What was going through your mind?"). In some cases, the relationship may be obvious but in others the relationship between the two words may be idiosyncratic or even bizarre.

The test consists of sixty words, some considered neutral by the test authors (for example, *chair, book, water, dance, taxi*) and some termed "traumatic." In the latter category are "words that are likely to touch upon sensitive personal material according to clinical experience, and also words that attract associative disturbances" (Rapaport, Gill, & Schafer, 1968, p. 257). Examples of words designated as "traumatic" are *love, girlfriend, boyfriend, mother, father, suicide, fire, breast,* and *masturbation.*

Responses on the Word Association Test are evaluated with respect to variables such as popularity, reaction time, content, and test-retest responses. Normative data are provided on the percentage of occurrence of certain responses for college students and schizophrenic groups. For example, to the word *stomach,* 21% of the college group responded with "ache"; 13% with "ulcer." Ten percent of the schizophrenic group responded with "ulcer." To the word *mouth,* 20% of the college sample responded with "kiss"; 13% with "nose"; 11% with "tongue"; 11% with "lips"; and 11% with "eat." In the schizophrenic group, 19% responded with "teeth," while 10% responded with "eat."

The Kent-Rosanoff Free Association Test.[6]   The Kent-Rosanoff Free Association Test (1910) represents an attempt at standardizing the responses of individuals to specific words. The test consists of 100 stimulus words, all commonly used and believed to be neutral with respect to emotional impact. The standardization sample consisted of 1,000 normal adults who varied in terms of geographic location, educational level, occupation, age, and intellectual capacity. Frequency tables based on the responses of these 1,000 cases were developed. These tables were used to evaluate examinees' responses in terms of the clinical judgment of psychopathology. Psychiatric patients were found to have a lower frequency of popular responses than did the normals in the standardization group. However, as it became apparent that individuality of response may be influenced by many variables other than psychopathology (such as creativity, age, education, and socioeconomic factors), the popularity of the Kent-Rosanoff as a differential diagnostic instrument diminished. Still, the test endures as a standardized instrument of word association responses, and over 80 years since its publication, it continues to be used in experimental research and clinical practice.

Sentence Completion Tests

Other projective techniques that use verbal material as projective stimuli are sentence completion tests. How might *you* complete the following sentences?

I like to _____.

Someday, I will _____.

I will always remember the time _____.

I worry about _____.

I am most frightened when _____.

My feelings are hurt _____.

---

6. The term *free association* refers to the technique of having subjects relate all their thoughts as they are occurring and is most frequently used in psychoanalysis; the only structure imposed is provided by the subjects themselves. The technique employed in the Kent-Rosanoff is that of *word association* (not free association) in which the examinee relates the first word that comes to mind in response to a stimulus word. The term "free association" in the test's title is, therefore, a misnomer.

My mother _____.

I wish my parents _____.

Sentence completion tests may contain items that, like the items listed, tend to be quite general in nature and appropriate for administration in a wide variety of settings. Alternatively, sentence completion *stems* (the first part of the item) may be developed for use in very specific types of settings (such as school or business) or for highly specific purposes. Sentence completion tests may be relatively atheoretical in nature or linked very closely to some theory. As an example of the latter, the Washington University Sentence Completion Test (Loevinger, Wessler, & Redmore, 1970) was based on the writings of Loevinger and her colleagues in the area of ego development. Loevinger (1966; Loevinger & Ossorio, 1958) has argued that with maturity, knowledge, and awareness comes a transformation from a self-image that is essentially stereotypic and socially acceptable to one that is more personalized and realistic. The Washington University Sentence Completion Test was constructed in an attempt to assess self-concept according to Loevinger's theory.

A number of standardized sentence completion tests are available to the clinician. One such test, the Rotter (pronounced like "rote," not "rot," with an "r" added on) Incomplete Sentences Blank (Rotter & Rafferty, 1950) is the most popular of all (Lah, 1989a). Consisting of 40 incomplete sentences, the test was developed for use with populations from grade 9 through adulthood and is available in three levels: high school (grades 9 through 12), college (grades 13 through 16), and adult. Test takers are instructed to respond to each item in a way that expresses their "real feelings." The manual suggests that responses on the test be interpreted according to several categories: family attitudes, social and sexual attitudes, general attitudes, and character traits. Each response is evaluated in terms of a seven-point scale that ranges from "need for therapy" to "extremely good adjustment." The responses of several subjects on the Rotter, as well as some background information about the subjects, are presented in the test manual to provide illustrations of the different categories. The manual also contains normative data for a sample of 85 female and 214 male college freshmen, but no norms for high school and adult populations. Reliability estimates for male and female college students were found to be .84 and .83, respectively. Estimates of inter-scorer reliability with respect to scoring categories were in the .90s. The majority of the validity studies with the Rotter were conducted in the 1950s and 1960s, and they employed "expert judge" and/or "known group" experimental designs. More recently, sociometric techniques have been used to demonstrate the validity of the Rotter as a measure of adjustment (Lah, 1989b).

In general, a sentence completion test may be a useful method for obtaining diverse information relating to an individual's interests, educational aspirations, future goals, fears, conflicts, needs, and so forth. The tests have a high degree of "face validity"; a child having difficulty in school, for example, would consider it appropriate to answer a list of questions or statements concerning feelings toward school. However, with this high degree of face validity comes a certain degree of transparency with respect to the objective of this type of test; for this reason, sentence completion tests are perhaps the most vulnerable of all the projective methods to faking on the part of the examinee intent on making a good—or bad—impression.

One relatively quick and easy-to-administer projective technique is the analysis of drawings. Drawings can provide the psychodiagnostician with a wealth of clinical hypotheses to be confirmed or discarded as the result of other findings. The use of drawings in clinical and research settings has extended beyond the area of personality assessment, and attempts have been made to use artistic productions as a source of information about intelligence, cognitive development, visual-motor coordination, and neurological intactness (see Figure 13–6). Figure drawings are an appealing source of diagnostic data since the instructions for them can be administered individually or in a group by nonclinicians such as teachers and no materials other than a pencil and paper are required.

Machover's Draw-A-Person Test

The classic work on the use of figure drawings as a projective stimulus is a book entitled *Personality Projection in the Drawing of the Human Figure: A Method of Personality Investigation,* by Karen Machover (1949). Machover wrote that "The human figure drawn by an individual who is directed to 'draw a person' related intimately to the impulses, anxieties, conflicts, and compensations characteristic of that individual. In some sense, the figure drawn is the person, and the paper corresponds to the environment" (p. 35).

The instructions for administering the Draw-A-Person (DAP) test are quite simple; the examinee is given a pencil and an 8½-by-11-inch blank sheet of white paper and is told to "Draw a person." Inquiries on the part of the examinee concerning how the picture is to be drawn are met with statements such as "Make it the way you think it should be" or "Do the best you can." Immediately after the first drawing is completed, the examinee is handed a second sheet of paper and instructed to draw a picture of a person of the opposite sex from the person just drawn.[7] Subsequently, many clinicians will ask questions concerning the drawings such as "Tell me a story about that figure," "Tell me about that boy/girl, man/lady," "What is the person doing?" "How is the person feeling?" "What is nice or not nice about the person?" Responses to these questions are used in forming various hypotheses and interpretations concerning personality functioning.

Performance on a figure-drawing test is formally evaluated through analysis of various characteristics of the drawing. Attention is given to such factors as the length of time required for completing the picture, placement of the figures, the size of the figure, pencil pressure used, symmetry, line quality, shading, the presence of erasures, facial expressions, posture, clothing, and overall appearance. Various hypotheses have been generated based on these factors. For example, the placement of the figure on the paper is seen as representing how the individual functions within the environment; the person who draws a tiny figure at the bottom of the paper might have a poor self-concept or be insecure and/or depressed.

---

7. Most people will draw a person of the same sex when instructed to simply "draw a person." It is deemed to be clinically significant if the person draws a person of the opposite sex when given these instructions. Reirdan and Koff (1981) found that in some cases, children are uncertain as to the sex of the figure drawn and hypothesize that in such cases "the child has an indefinite or ill-defined notion of sexual identity" (p. 257).

Figure 13–6 *Some Sample Interpretations Made from Figure Drawings. (Source: Hammer, 1981)*

Drawing by a 25-year-old schoolteacher after becoming engaged. Previously, she had entered psychotherapy because of problems relating to men and a block against getting married. The positioning of the hands is indicative of a fear of sexual intercourse that remains.

Drawing by a male with a "Don Juan" complex—a man who pursued one affair after another. The collar pulled up to guard the neck and the excessive shading of the buttocks is suggestive of a fear of being attacked from the rear. It is possible that this man's Don Juanism is an outward defense against the lack of masculinity—even feelings of effeminacy—he may be struggling with within.

Drawing by an authoritarian and sadistic male who had been head disciplinarian of a reformatory for boys before he was suspended for child abuse. His description of this picture was that it "looked like a Prussian or a Nazi General."

The manacled hands, tied feet, exposed buttocks, and large foot drawn to the side of the drawing taken together are reflective, according to Hammer, of masochistic, homosexual, and exhibitionistic needs.

This drawing by an acutely paranoid, psychotic man was described by Hammer (1981, p. 170) as follows: "The savage mouth expresses the rage-filled projections loose within him. The emphasized eyes and ears with the eyes almost emanating magical rays reflect the visual and auditory hallucinations the patient actually experiences. The snake in the stomach points up his delusion of a reptile within, eating away and generating venom and evil."

The individual who draws a picture that cannot be contained on one sheet of paper and goes off the page is considered to be impulsive. A sampling of some other hypotheses related to various aspects of figure drawings are as follows:

- Unusually light pressure suggests character disturbance (Exner, 1962).
- Placement of drawing on the right of the page suggests orientation to the future; to the left, orientation to the past; upper right suggests desire to suppress an unpleasant past plus excessive optimism about the future; lower left suggests depression with desire to flee into the past (Buck, 1948, 1950).
- Large eyes and/or large ears suggest suspiciousness, ideas of reference, or other paranoid characteristics (Machover, 1949; Shneidman, 1958).
- Unusually large breasts drawn by male suggest unresolved oedipal problems with maternal dependence (Jolles, 1952).
- Long and conspicuous ties suggest sexual aggressiveness, perhaps overcompensating for fear of impotence (Machover, 1949).
- Button emphasis suggests dependent, infantile, inadequate personality (Halpern, 1958).

For a comprehensive and readable summary of various interpretations of projective drawings, the interested reader is referred to Knoff (1990a).

Other Figure-Drawing Tests

Another projective test employing figure drawings is the House-Tree-Person test (HTP) developed and popularized by Buck (1948). In this procedure, as its name implies, the subject is instructed to draw a picture of a house, a tree, and a person. In much the same way that different aspects of the human figure are presumed to be reflective of psychological functioning, so too the way in which an individual represents a house and a tree are considered to have symbolic significance. In this context, one might find, for example, an account of how the House-Tree-Person test has been used to identify physically abused children (Blain, Bergner, Lewis, & Goldstein, 1981). A Draw-An-Animal procedure was developed based on the assumption that more projective material may be obtained through representations of animals as opposed to human figures (see Campo & Vilar, 1977, for an example of a study comparing the clinical utility of animal and human figure drawings).

Another projective drawing technique, this one of particular value in learning about the examinee in relation to her or his family, is the Kinetic Family Drawing (KFD). Derived from Hulse's (1951, 1952) Family Drawing Test, an administration of the KFD (Burns & Kaufman, 1970, 1972) begins with the examinee being given an 8½-by-11-inch piece of paper (which can be positioned any way) and a pencil with an eraser. The examinee, usually though not necessarily a child, is instructed as follows:

> Draw a picture of everyone in your family, including you, DOING something. Try to draw whole people, not cartoons or stick people. Remember, make everyone DOING something—some kind of actions. (Burns & Kaufman, 1972, p. 5)

In addition to yielding graphic representations of each family member for analysis, this procedure may yield a wealth of information in the form of examinee verbalizations while the drawing is being executed. After the examinee has completed the drawing, a rather detailed inquiry follows. The examinee is asked to identify each of the figures, talk about their relationship, and detail what they are doing in the picture and why (see Knoff & Prout, 1985). A number of formal scoring systems for the KFD are available (such as McPhee & Wegner, 1976; Meyers, 1978; Mostkoff & Lazarus, 1983). Related techniques include a school adaptation called the Kinetic School Drawing (KSD; Prout & Phillips, 1974), a test that combines aspects of the KFD and KSD called the Kinetic Drawing System (KDS; Knoff & Prout, 1985), and the Collaborative Drawing Technique (Smith, 1985), a test that provides an occasion for family members to collaborate on the creation of a drawing—the better to "draw together."

Like other projective techniques, figure-drawing tests, while thought to be clinically useful, have had a rather embattled history when the literature on psychometric soundness is reviewed. Questions have been raised concerning the reliability and validity of the KFD (see, for example, Harris, 1978; Cummings, 1981) as well as other such tests. No compelling evidence has been adduced to date to support the claim that human figure drawings approximate self-representations. Quite the contrary, the literature tends to support the view that there is no relationship between figure drawings and self-representations. In one study, DAP test data from 25 obese and 20 ideal-weight women were matched for age, education, I.Q., marital status, and the career versus housewife dichotomy. Out of 129 chi-squares run on 43 criteria, only seven of the tests achieved significance and this result could have occurred by chance. In short, contrary to the body-image hypothesis, there were no differences between the drawings of obese and ideal-weight women (Kotkov & Goodman, 1953). Another study compared the DAP protocols of 49 hemiplegic and 43 normals and found no differences (Prater, 1957). However, body image *concerns* have been found to be reflected in human figure drawings by psoriasis (an unattractive skin ailment) patients (Leichtman, Burnett, & Robinson, 1981). In a study that employed DAP and KFD drawings from children ages 9 to 14 (some with diagnosed mood or anxiety disorders and the rest normal controls), quantitative scoring of emotional indicators failed to differentiate the groups (Tharinger & Stark, 1990).

It is somewhat paradoxical that the common lay argument against the DAP ("but, I'm not a good artist!") is well-founded. Contrary to Hammer's (1958) summary dismissal of this argument, drawing ability *is* a source of variance affecting the quality of drawings (Swensen, 1968; Sherman, 1958). As early as 1953, at least one experimenter concluded that "as judged by the 'average' clinical psychologist today, human figure drawings executed by persons of average or above average intelligence seem to indicate art achievment but do not seem to show any consistent relationship to level of personal adjustment" (Whitmyre, 1953, p. 424).

In the heyday of the use of the DAP, numerous objective scales detailing constellations of DAP indices for the purpose of differential diagnosis were available. For example, Hozier's (1959) schizophrenic scale was said to differentiate normal from schizophrenic women on the basis of a 15 item-DAP checklist that included items related to presence or absence of various features, proportion, flexibility of joint, and clothing transparencies. The Reznikoff-Tomblen (1956) scale differentiated the neurologically impaired from neurotics on the basis of such variables as synthesis, misplacement of parts, emptiness of figures, and various distortions at the extremities. The Baugh-Carpenter (1962) scale differentiated delinquents from nondelinquents on the basis of such factors as presence or absence of parts, nudity, nonstick drawings, and other factors (such as "gangster identification"). A review of such scales did not support their validity (Watson, Felling, & Maceacherr, 1967). A study on differential diagnosis (Covetkovic, 1979) involving 70 hospitalized schizophrenic adults and 71 normal subjects sought to determine if differences existed between the two groups' conception and representation of space in human figure drawings. The results revealed similar tendencies for both groups, and any differences that did exist were related to sex rather than diagnostic category.

One tacit assumption is that all other things being equal, the more experience the clinician has with the DAP, the better—the more valid—the clinical interpretations. Yet experimental work with the DAP has yielded the rather unexpected finding that experience and expertise do not necessarily correlate with greater judgmental accuracy as measured by an external criterion. In one study, 25 DAP experts assigned rank-ordered probabilities of diagnosis to pairs of drawings made by patients from five criterion groups. It was found that the experts were able to identify only the drawings of the mental defectives beyond chance—even after being given a second try to make the correct diagnosis (Wanderer, 1967). In another study (Watson, 1967), psychologists of three different levels of familiarity and expertise with the DAP were asked to categorize 48 DAP protocols as either organic, paranoid schizophrenic, nonparanoid schizophrenic, or normals. The psychologists in the study included ten psychologists who said they frequently used the DAP, ten who said they did not use it, and four "experts" (defined as such by their extensive writing on projective tests; the author noted that 21 experts had been petitioned to participate but 17 refused). Diagnostic acuity was not found to vary as a function of familiarity or sophistication with the DAP. The author concluded that "the results suggest that reliance on the DAP as a diagnostic indicator is actually detrimental to overall diagnostic acuity, except in those rare settings where the base-rate frequencies of the various nosological categories are essentially equal" (p. 145). Indeed, a psychologist whose name has become virtually synonymous with figure drawings as a means of assessment, Karen Machover, expressed "grave misgivings" about the misuse of the DAP in diagnosis (Machover, cited in Watson, 1967, p. 145).

OTHER PROJECTIVE AND SEMIPROJECTIVE TECHNIQUES

As you no doubt realize by now, almost any object that lends itself to varied interpretations may be used as a projective stimulus by a creative clinician. For example, children's use of toys—especially dolls, puppets, and household furniture—has been found to be a rich source of otherwise unobtainable clinical data impacting on the nature of the child's family and peer relationships. Kits such as the Driscoll Play Kit, which consists of a family of 5, a 5-room apartment, and 27 pieces of furniture, have been packaged for the convenience of therapists who prefer to obtain clinical data by observing children's projections during play. In the following sections, we briefly describe two other of the many projective methods available to clinicians.

The Hand Test

This test consists of nine cards with pictures of hands on them and one blank card. When presented with each picture card, the examinee's task is to tell what the hands might be doing. When presented with the blank card, the examinee is instructed to imagine hands on the card and then proceed to tell what they might be doing. The test's author advises that the test may be administered to anyone over six years of age. The examinee may make several responses to each card, and the examiner records all the responses as well as the time period that elapsed before the first response was produced. Responses are interpreted according to 24 categories, including categories such as affection, dependence, and aggression.

Normative data based on 1,020 cases that included normal adults, children, college students, mental retardates, neurotics, psychotics, and antisocial personalities are provided in the test manual. Inter-scorer reliability with respect to scoring criteria based on a sample of 100 protocols was found to range from .86 to .96. In a study involving 71 college students, the test-retest reliability coefficient on 21 of the variables of the Hand Test were found to range from .30 to .89, with approximately half the coefficients clustering in the .60s and .70s (Panek & Stoner, 1979). Research investigating differences in children's responses as a function of gender has yielded significant differences in the length of time, number of responses, and the content of the responses of a sample of second-grade boys ($n = 69$) and girls ($n = 65$). Girls were found to produce more exhibition and failure responses, whereas boys were found to produce more active, acting out, environmental, description, withdrawal, and pathology responses. The boys in the sample were also found to respond more quickly to the cards and to produce a greater number of responses (Stoner, 1978).

The Rosenzweig Picture Frustration Study

An example of a projective instrument using a story-completion approach is the Rosenzweig Picture Frustration Study (Rosenzweig, 1945, 1950, 1978, 1981a, 1981b; Rosenzweig, Fleming, & Clarke, 1947; Rosenzweig, Fleming, & Rosenzweig, 1948). Available in three levels, one for children aged 4 through 13, one for adolescents aged 12 to 18, and one for adults aged 18 and over, this test was developed to investigate reactions to frustrating situations. The Rosenzweig consists of cartoonlike pictures in which two characters are represented. Each picture is considered to represent a commonly experienced frustrating situation. One of the characters in the picture is placed in the position of being frustrated, while the other character is presented as either frustrating the first character or as describing

Figure 13-7 *Sample Item from the Rosenzweig Picture-Frustration Study.*

the frustrating situation. "Balloons" for dialogue are presented above the figures (see Figure 13-7). An empty balloon is placed above the figure that is being frustrated. The subject is instructed to supply the missing dialogue in the empty balloon by giving the first reply that comes to mind. It is assumed that subjects will identify with the frustrated character and that their responses are indicative of their own reactions to frustrating situations.

Young children respond orally to these pictures, while older children and adults may either present their responses orally or write them down. The test author (Figure 13-8) suggests that an inquiry period be conducted after administration of the cards to clarify the subject's responses.

Responses on the Rosenzweig are evaluated in terms of the type of reaction and the direction of the aggression expressed. The direction of the aggression may be "intropunitive" (aggression turned inward) or it may be "extrapunitive" (outwardly expressed); alternatively, it may be "inpunitive" in nature in which case aggression is evaded so as to avoid or gloss over the situation. The types of reactions are grouped into categories: "obstacle-dominance," in which the response concentrates or centers on the frustrating barrier; "ego-defense," in which attention is focused on protecting the frustrated person; and "need-persistence," in which attention is focused on solving the frustrating problem.

The children's version of the Rosenzweig was standardized on 131 boys and 125 girls between the ages of 4 and 13. Those children aged 7 and under attended private schools, whereas the rest of the sample was drawn from public schools.

Figure 13–8 *Saul Rosenzweig.*

These data have been augmented with an additional 143 white middle-class children from the public schools in the St. Louis, Missouri, area and have resulted in revised norms for the children's version of the Rosenzweig (Rosenzweig, 1988). The version of the test developed for use at older age levels was standardized on 236 males and 224 females between the ages of 20 and 30. The sample was drawn mostly from the middle class, and although a small number of skilled and unskilled workers were included, the mean educational level for the group was high (13.5 years of schooling).

For each scoring category on the Rosenzweig, the percentage of responses is computed and compared with those of the normative group. A group conformity rating (GCR), representing the degree to which the subject's responses conform or are typical of those of the standardization group, is obtained. Examples of responses representing the different scoring categories are presented in the manual. Test-retest reliability coefficients at the adult level reported by the author were found to range from .60 to .80. Bernard (1949) obtained test-retest reliability coefficients ranging from .50 to .75 based on a four-month interval. Inter-scorer reliability was found to be adequate (Clarke, Rosenzweig, & Fleming, 1947). In one validity study, teacher judgments of the social functioning of the 4-to-7-year-olds in the standardization group were compared with this group's performance on the Rosenzweig. Although some trends were noted between teacher classifications and Rosenzweig results for those identified as socially inadequate, none of the findings was statistically significant (Rosenzweig & Mirmow, 1950). Others (e.g., French, Graves, & Levitt, 1983) have also questioned the validity of the children's form. Graybill (1990) and his colleagues (Graybill, Heuvelman, & Reeder, 1991; Graybill, Peterson, & Williams, 1989; Graybill, Williams, Bodmer, & Peterson, 1991) have suggested that a simpler scoring system may yield more valid findings. In general, questions remain concerning how reactions to cards depicting frustrating situations on the Rosenzweig are related to real-life situations.

PROJECTIVE TECHNIQUES IN PERSPECTIVE

Although projective tests remain in wide use by clinicians, the psychometric soundness of many of them in terms of the usual standards remains to be documented. Perhaps some specially devised standards sensitive to the unique nature of these tests will be required; the lingering coexistence of widespread clinical use of these instruments with widespread criticism makes such action seem reasonable. In general, critics have attacked projective methods on grounds related to the assumptions inherent in their use, the situational variables that attend their use, and the paucity of sound reliability and validity data. A brief review of these arguments follows.

Assumptions

Murstein (1961) examined ten assumptions of projective techniques and argued that none of them was scientifically compelling. Several assumptions concern the stimulus material. For example, it is assumed that the more ambiguous the stimuli, the more subjects reveal about their personality. However, Murstein describes the stimulus material as only one aspect of the "total stimulus situation." Environmental variables, response sets, reactions to the examiner, and related factors all contribute to response patterns. In addition, in situations where the stimulus properties of the projective material were designed to be unclear, hazy, or are presented with uncompleted lines—thereby increasing ambiguity—projection on the part of the subject was not found to increase. Another assumption concerns the supposedly idiosyncratic nature of the responses evoked by projective stimuli. In fact, similarities in the response themes of different subjects to the same stimulus cards suggest that the stimulus material may not be as ambiguous and as amenable to projection as had been previously assumed. Some consideration of the stimulus properties and the ways in which they affect the subject's responses is therefore indicated. The assumption that projection is greater to stimulus material that is similar to the subject (in physical appearance, gender, occupation, and so on) has also been found to be questionable.

Other assumptions questioned by Murstein concern how responses on projective tests are interpreted. These include the assumption that every response provides meaning for personality analysis; that a relationship exists between the strength of a need and its manifestation on projective instruments; that subjects are unaware of what they are disclosing about themselves; that a projective protocol reflects sufficient data concerning personality functioning to formulate judgments; and finally, that there is a parallel between behavior obtained on a projective instrument and behavior displayed in social situations. It is Murstein's contention that these "cherished beliefs have been accepted by some clinical psychologists without the support of sufficient research validation" (p. 343).

Another assumption basic to projective testing is that there is such a thing as an "unconscious." Though the term *unconscious* is used by many psychologists and lay people as well, some academicians have questioned whether in fact the "unconscious" exists in the same way that the "liver" exists. The scientific studies typically cited to support the existence of the unconscious (or perhaps more accurately, the efficacy of the construct "unconscious") have used a very wide array of methodologies—see, for example, Diven (1937), Erdelyi (1974, 1978, 1979), Greenspoon (1955), McGinnies (1949), and Razran (1961). The conclusions from each of these types of studies are subject to alternative explanations. Additionally, conclusions about the existence of the unconscious based on experimental testing of predictions derived from hypnotic phenomena, from signal detection theory, and from specific personality theories have been, at least, inconclusive (Brody, 1972).

Situational Variables

Proponents of projective techniques have claimed that such tests are capable of illuminating the recesses of the mind in a manner similar to the way that X-rays illuminate the body. Frank (1939) conceptualized projective tests as tapping personality patterns without disturbing the pattern being tapped. If this were true, then variables related to the test situation should have no effect on the data obtained. However, as we have seen, the variable of the examiner being present or absent can significantly affect the responses of experimental subjects. TAT stories written in private are likely to be less guarded, less optimistic, and more affectively involved than those written in the presence of the examiner (Bernstein, 1956). The age of the examiner is likely to affect projective protocols (Mussen & Scodel, 1955) as are the specific instructions (Henry & Rotter, 1956) and the subtle reinforcement cues provided by the examiner (Wickes, 1956).

Masling (1960) reviewed the literature on the influence of situational and interpersonal variables in projective testing and concluded that there was strong evidence for the role of situational and interpersonal influences in projection. Moreover, Masling argued that it was not only the subjects who utilized every available cue in the testing situation (for example, the room or the actions and appearance of the examiner) but also the examiners, who capitalized on cues over and above their training and orientation. Examiners appeared to interpret projective data with regard to their own needs and expectations, their own subjective feelings about the subject being tested, and their own constructions regarding the total test situation. In a later study, Masling (1965) experimentally demonstrated that Rorschach examiners are capable of unwittingly eliciting the responses they expect through postural, gestural, and facial cues.

Even in "nonprojective" situations like taking a psychiatric history or taking an objective test, the effect of the clinician's training (Fitzgibbons & Shearn, 1972; Chapman & Chapman, 1967) and role perspective (Snyder, Shenkel, & Schmidt, 1976), the patient's social class (Hollingshead & Redlich, 1958; Lee, 1968; Routh & King, 1972) and motivation to manage a desired impression (Edwards & Walsh, 1964; Wilcox & Krasnoff, 1967) may influence ratings of pathology (Langer & Abelson, 1974) as well as attribution of the locus of the problem (Batson, 1975). These and other variables are given wider latitude in the projective test situation in which the examiner may be at liberty to choose not only the test and extra-test data on which interpretation will be focused, but also the scoring system that will be used to arrive at that interpretation; as we have noted, for many of the projective methods, a number of different alternative scoring systems are available.

Psychometric Considerations

The psychometric soundness of many widely used projective instruments has yet to be demonstrated. Kinslinger (1966) has cited the failure of researchers to cross-validate findings as a source of spurious validity estimates for projective techniques. Others (such as Cronbach, 1949; Vernon, 1964; Zubin, Eron, & Schumer, 1965) have called attention to variables such as uncontrolled variations in protocol length, inappropriate subject samples, inadequate control groups, and poor external criteria as factors contributing to spuriously increased ratings of validity. Recall that there are very real methodological difficulties in demonstrating the psychometric soundness of *any* instrument, let alone projective instruments. If it is difficult to scientifically document the reliability of more traditional tests by the usual techniques (test-retest method or the split-half method), imagine trying to obtain reliability of the DAP, the TAT, or the Rorschach. Mention must also be made of the difficulty of designing reliability and validity studies that effectively rule out, limit, or statistically take into account the situational variables and extra-test cues that attend the administration of such tests.

The debate between academicians who argue that projective tests are not technically sound instruments and clinicians who find such tests useful has been raging ever since projectives came into widespread use. This chapter contained some quoted material from Frank (1939) in its beginning and it is appropriate that we end this chapter with some words from him as well—here responding to those who would reject projective methods because of their lack of technical rigor:

> These leads to the study of personality have been rejected by many psychologists because they do not meet psychometric requirements for validity and reliability, but they are being employed in association with clinical and other studies of personality where they are finding increasing validation in the consistency of results for the same subject when independently assayed by each of these procedures. . . .
> If we face the problem of personality, in its full complexity, as an active

dynamic process to be studied as a *process* rather than as entity or aggregate of traits, factors, or as static organization, then these projective methods offer many advantages for obtaining data on the process of organizing experience which is peculiar to each personality and has a life career. (Frank, 1939, p. 408) [emphasis in the original]

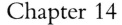

Chapter 14

Other Methods

of Assessing Personality

and Behavior

SOME PEOPLE SEE the world as filled with love and good, where others see hate and evil. Some people equate "living" with behavioral excess, whereas others strive for moderation in all things. Some people have relatively realistic perceptions of themselves and other people, while others labor under grossly distorted self-images and inaccurate perceptions of family, friends, and acquaintances. Many tests and assessment techniques that do not necessarily fall into the category of "personality inventory" or "projective technique" can be used to shed light on these and other aspects of individuals—their behavior, their thought processes, their attitudes, beliefs, fears, hopes, perceptions, social skills, internal physiological states—all that constitutes the multifaceted construct "personality."

In this chapter we cover measures of cognitive style and situational performance, as well as behavioral assessment. We begin with a consideration of self-concept measures.

MEASURES OF SELF-CONCEPT

Measures of self-concept are self-report measures whose object is to obtain a picture or description of the assessee from the perspective of the assessee. Among other potential uses of such data, self-concept data are thought to be of value in assessing risk for, or severity of, psychological disorders (Ingham, Kreitman, Miller, Sashidharan, & Surtees, 1986). Additionally, self-concept data may also hold possible application in the assessment of a variety of other life difficulties, including marriage and family problems and academic and workplace problems. In addition to methods such as personality inventories and projective tests that are capable of yielding information pertinent to self-concept, other, more specialized techniques have been found to be effective. We present a sampling of such techniques, cautioning, however, that it has not been established that each of the many available tests purporting to measure self-concept is indeed measuring the same thing (Demo, 1985; Robson, 1988; Wylie, 1974, 1979).

Q-Sort Techniques

The term *Q-sort* refers to a method of personality assessment in which the assessee's task is to sort a group of index cards with certain statements printed on them into some kind of rank order, usually ranging from "least descriptive" to "most descriptive." Some sample statements printed on the cards might be "I try hard to please others," "I am sensitive to criticism," "I'm often uncomfortable in social situations," and "If I put my mind to it, I can do anything." The technique was originally developed by Stephenson (1953), though a number of variations on this method—in terms of variables such as the content of the statements on the card and the administration instructions—designed for use in various settings have since appeared in the assessment literature (Stephenson, 1980).

One of the most well-known applications of Q-methodology in clinical and counseling settings was the use of the Q-sort as advocated by the personality theorist and psychotherapist Carl Rogers. Rogers (1959) used the Q-sort as a method of determining how much discrepancy there was between clients as they saw themselves and how they would like to be: the discrepancy between the present and "idealized" self. At the beginning of a course of psychotherapy, clients might be asked to sort cards twice, once in terms of how they perceived themselves to be and once again in terms of how they would ultimately like to be. The larger the discrepancy between the sortings, the more work that would be needed in therapy. Presumably the retesting of the client who successfully completed a course of psychotherapy would reveal much less discrepancy between the present and idealized self. Beyond the application of the Q-sort technique in initial assessment and re-evaluation of a therapy client, the technique has also been used extensively in basic research in the area of personality as well as in other areas. Some of the highly specialized kinds of Q-sorts that have been published include the Leadership Q-Test (Cassel, 1958) and the Tyler Vocational Classification System (Tyler, 1961). The former test was designed for use in military settings and contains cards with statements the subject is instructed to sort with respect to their perceived importance to effective leadership. The Tyler Q-sort contains cards on which occupations are printed, the subject's task being to sort them into piles representing occupations that he or she might choose, would not choose, or have no opinion about. Further sortings help to yield a listing of occupations that are perceived to be most and least desirable. Modifications of these and other Q-sorts may be made as the situation warrants. For example, Williams (1978) expanded the list of occupations represented in the original Tyler cards to include a wider range of occupations.

Q-methodology is a very flexible measurement technique and one that can be adapted to virtually any assessment situation. Insights into self-concept may be obtained by asking test takers to sort cards not only with respect to how they see themselves in general, but also with respect to how they see themselves in specific situations (such as alone at home, in school, in the office, in social/sexual situations), how they see others (such as family members, friends, instructors, employers, spouse, dates), how they would like to see others—the opportunities are limitless. The California Q-Sort (Block, 1961) was originally designed for sorting by professionally trained observers, though a modified version of it designed for lay people has since been developed.

485

OTHER
METHODS OF
ASSESSING
PERSONALITY
AND BEHAVIOR

The primary advantage in using a Q-sort lies in its versatility and relative ease of application. It is of great utility when the assessor requires relatively precise comparative responses from a large number of stimuli, though, as Nunnally (1978, p. 625) cautioned, "before the Q-sort is employed, it is important to ensure that sensible comparative responses can be made among the stimuli employed in the particular study." Nunnally cited other advantages of the Q-sort in terms of the versatility with which such data could be analyzed:

> if one elects to use the Q-sort as a rating method, one is not necessarily tied to the use of particular techniques of mathematical analysis rather than others . . . choices among approaches to mathematical analysis . . . are mainly matters of taste and hunch. In the long run we shall learn which approaches are generally more fruitful, but at this early stage in the growth of science, it is good that all of the research eggs are not being placed in the same methodological basket. (p. 625)

The Q-sort is of course subject to all of the limitations of any self-report measure in terms of the willingness and ability of sorters to make accurate and insightful revelations about themselves. It must be noted, however, that there is a wealth of evidence to support the view that respondents can generally supply meaningful and predictive information about themselves (see Bem & Funder, 1978; Bem & Allen, 1974).

Other Measures of Self-Concept

Another general approach to measuring self-concept is referred to as the adjective checklist method. The popularity of such techniques derives in no small part from their great intuitive appeal; present examinees with a list of adjectives and then have them check off the ones they deem to be most descriptive of themselves. One such test, the Adjective Check List (ACL), consists of 300 adjectives arranged in alphabetical order. Gough (1960; Gough & Heilbrun, 1980) devised an elaborate scoring system for this test with 37 scales based in part on the personality theory of Henry Murray. The ACL is a popular research instrument and has been used in many different ways such as in the study of parents' perceptions of their children (Brown, 1972) and clients' perceptions of their therapists (Reinehr, 1969) and therapeutic environment (Sutker, Allain, Smith, & Cohen, 1978). In a study employing middle-level managers as subjects, Hills (1985) found that subjects who had described themselves on the ACL as assertive, competitive, self-confident, and willing to function autonomously were subsequently rated by others as more effective in problem-solving exercises than were subjects who had given relatively higher emphasis to characteristics such as cooperativeness, self-discipline, and tact.

The great popularity of the ACL spurred the development of other adjective checklists that focus on specific affective conditions. The Depression Adjective Checklist (Lubin, 1967, 1981; Lubin & Levitt, 1979) instructs test takers to indicate which adjectives best describe how they are feeling at that moment. The Multiple Affect Adjective Checklist (Zuckerman & Lubin, 1965) is another affective adjective checklist, this one consisting of 132 adjectives arranged in alphabetical order. The test may be administered under two test sets, both of which have been standardized. One set, the "Today" form, instructs the examinee to select those adjectives that describe how he or she feels at the time of the testing. The other, called the "In General" form, instructs the examinee to select those adjectives that describe how the individual usually feels. On both forms respondents are instructed to place a double check next to the adjective if it definitely describes them, a single check if it is only slightly applicable, a question mark if the subject is undecided, and a "no" if the adjective is not applicable. A score is obtained for each of the affective states. Factorial analyses suggest the identification of 6 to 12 mood factors that may be helpful in interpreting data (see Zuckerman & Lubin, 1965). Anecdotal support of the validity of this instrument can be found in the test manual as well as in investigations reported in the literature. For example, in one study, students were found to obtain higher scores on the affective scales of this test when threatened with examinations (Zuckerman, Lubin, Vogel, & Valerius, 1964).

Scales employing a variety of methods have been developed to assess the self-concept of adults (such as the Beck Self-Concept Test) and children (such as the Piers-Harris Children's Self Concept Scale).

The Beck Self-Concept Test (BST)

The Beck Self-Concept Test (BST; Beck & Stein, 1961) was initially designed as a method of evaluating the negative view of the self held by depressed patients, as has been observed and described by Aaron T. Beck (1963, 1967, 1976). For Beck, the self-concept construct consists of various characteristics that people can ascribe to themselves (such as interpersonal attractiveness), each of which may be operationally defined by descriptors (such as "attractive"). According to Beck, Steer, Epstein, and Brown (1990):

> The descriptors, in turn, are weighed by an individual with respect to how much they are valued by himself or herself. The overall self-concept thus reflects the summation of an individual's self-evaluations of the set of descriptors and represents how good the person feels about himself or herself. The self-concept is the product of input of self-relevant data and relatively stable structures (self-schemata) that serve as information processors. The stronger a self-schema, the greater its influence on the input of self-relevant information (i.e., data supporting the self-concept will be processed, whereas data not supporting the self-concept will be ignored). For example, in depression, individuals direct their cognitive processing toward critical self-evaluations, and self-schemata assume a crucial role. Data supporting a depressed person's negative self-concept are more readily acceptable to the individual than data fostering positive self-evaluations. (p. 191)

487

OTHER
METHODS OF
ASSESSING
PERSONALITY
AND BEHAVIOR

The BST was developed on the basis of personality- and ability-related characteristics that psychiatric patients considered to be important aspects of themselves (for example, looks, knowledge, memory, and telling jokes). Test takers describe themselves with these 25 traits by selecting the phrase next to the trait that best describes them in comparison with people they know. For example, for the trait "telling jokes," test takers will indicate whether they are better than nearly anyone they know, better than most people they know, about the same as most people, worse than most people they know, or worse than nearly anyone they know. Scores are calculated by summing the ratings for the 25 traits; the higher the score, the higher the self-concept.

The BST is self-administered and takes only about ten minutes to complete. Beck, Steer, Epstein, and Brown (1990) reviewed research on the psychometric soundness of this instrument and found it to be satisfactory, though they acknowledged the need for more research on it. They suggested that in addition to other possible applications, the test may have value as an indicator of suicidal risk in psychiatric outpatients.

An awareness of the importance of self-concept in childhood with respect to subsequent adjustment has compelled test developers to turn their attention toward the measurement of children's self-concept (see, for example, Fitts, 1965; Coopersmith, 1967). One scale designed to assess children's perceptions of themselves is the Piers–Harris Children's Self Concept Scale (Piers, 1969).

Piers–Harris Children's Self Concept Scale (CSCS)   Appropriate for use with subjects in grades 3 through 12, the CSCS consists of 80 statements about oneself (such as "I like the way I look"; "I don't have any friends"). The subject responds either "yes" or "no" to each item. A factor analysis of the CSCS indicated that the items covered six general areas of self-concept: (1) behavior, (2) intellectual and school status, (3) physical appearance and attributes, (4) anxiety, (5) popularity, and (6) happiness and satisfaction.

The CSCS was standardized on 1,183 children who were enrolled in grades 4 through 12 in one school district in Pennsylvania. Estimates of internal consistency were found to range from .78 to .93, and test-retest reliability coefficients were in the .70's range. The test manual reports moderate correlations of the CSCS with similar instruments. In a study exploring the validity of the test, the CSCS was administered along with another self-concept scale, the Self Esteem Inventory, to 248 fourth-graders from five elementary schools and to 321 seventh-graders from one junior high school. A correlation coefficient of .78 was obtained between scores on the two instruments (Franklin, Duley, Rousseau, & Sabers, 1981). Saylor (1984) noted a significant relationship between the Piers-Harris and the Children's Depression Inventory. In another study that bears on the validity of this test, the CSCS was administered to 39 mentally retarded and emotionally disturbed children between the ages of 11 and 16. In this study, the test items in many instances had to be read aloud to the test takers, given their reading difficulties. The responses on the CSCS were compared with the observations of teachers and teachers' aides on two rating scales: the Behavior Problem Checklist (which assesses, among other things, deviant behavior) and the Conners Teacher Rating Scale (which assesses, among other things, activity level). The results indicated that although behavior and activity level were positively correlated (children high in deviant behavior were also high in activity level), self-concept was negatively correlated with activity level and deviant behavior; children with high activity levels who exhibited deviant behaviors expressed negative self-concepts, while those with low activity levels and nondeviant behaviors expressed positive self-concepts (Wolf, 1981).[1]

MEASURES OF COGNITIVE STYLE

Are you reflective or impulsive? Dependent or independent? Flexible or rigid? A "sharpener" or a "leveler"? These are some of the terms used by psychologists to denote *cognitive styles,* the particular thought patterns characteristically used by an individual in problem-solving (in the broadest sense) situations. Although quite similar to the way the term "trait" is used, "cognitive style" implies something more than "trait" about thought processes. The distinction is admittedly fine but one that we hope you will understand after a brief review of some of the instruments that were designed to measure it.

Field Dependence and Independence

Herman Witkin and his associates (Witkin, Lewis, Hertzman, Machover, Meissner, & Wapner, 1954; Witkin, Dyk, Fatterson, Goodenough, & Karp, 1962; Berry, 1976; Witkin & Berry, 1975; Witkin & Goodenough, 1981) have devoted considerable research energy to investigating a cognitive style related to how much an individual relies on environmental cues in perception. In perceiving an object, people who are highly "field-dependent" rely heavily on the visual field that surrounds that object. On the other hand, people who are highly "field-independent" rely less on the surrounding visual field and are able to focus more on the object itself. As illustrated and described in Figure 14–1, the tools used by Witkin in his experimental investigations of this cognitive style have been the rod-and-frame-test, the tilting-room/tilting-chair test, and the Embedded Figures Test (Oltman, Raskin, & Witkin, 1971). In general, the person labeled "field dependent" rather than "field independent" would be one who was unable to adjust the rod or the chair to a true upright position when a background of confusing environmental cues was present. The field-dependent person may also be identified as such on the basis of a paper-and-pencil measure, the Embedded Figures Test. Low scores on this test reflect difficulty or slowness in separating the targeted figure from the complex background.

What started out as a program of basic research has led to an impressive array of findings with applied value. Primarily through correlational studies, a profile of the personality of people with respect to this cognitive style has emerged. In contrast to the field-independent person, a field-dependent person tends to have less self-esteem and tends to be more conforming, more socially oriented, more passive, less creative, less analytic, and less self-aware. The field-independent in-

---

1. For a sampling of various research applications of the CSCS, see Chiu (1989), Gill and Hayes-Butler (1988), and McWatters (1989).

dividual is more independent in social relations and tends to have more initiative than does the field-dependent person (Heesacker, 1981; Witkin et al., 1954; Witkin et al., 1962; Witkin & Goodenough, 1977, 1981). In a study involving 102 suburban Philadelphia students enrolled in grades 2 through 4, the cognitive style of field independence was found to be related to high achievement in mathematics (Vaidya & Chansky, 1980). The field-dependence measure has more recently found application in the study of the reading comprehension processes. Meng and Patty (1991) observed differences in the reading patterns of their elementary school subjects as a function of cognitive style.

Paper-and-pencil measures of field dependence and independence include the Embedded Figures Test (Oltman, Raskin, & Witkin, 1971), the Children's Embedded Figures Test (Karp & Konstadt, 1963/1971), the Preschool Embedded Figures Test (Coates, 1972), and the Group Embedded Figures Test, this last test now described in greater detail.

The Group Embedded Figures Test   The Group Embedded Figures Test, or GEFT (Oltman, Raskin, & Witkin, 1971), was designed for use with subjects 10 and older. It consists of 25 embedded-figure problems printed in a booklet, the subject's task being to identify a simple design from within a more complex one

489

OTHER
METHODS OF
ASSESSING
PERSONALITY
AND BEHAVIOR

Figure 14–1   *Measuring Field Dependence and Independence.*

If someone asked you, "Which way is up?" you would probably have no difficulty in pointing the right way. But think of the visual cues you rely on to make that judgment: the floor, the ceiling, other objects in your line of vision, and so forth. What if those cues were taken away? Worse yet, what if those cues were purposely distorted? Do you think you would still be able to readily answer the question, "Which way is up?"

Measurement techniques designed to explore questions such as these were devised by Witkin and his associates (1962). In the tilting-room/tilting-chair device (see **a**), the subject sits in a chair that may be tilted and is in a room that may be tilted as well—this can get you dizzy just thinking about it! The subject's task is to identify which way is up after the chair and the room have been set

at different angles. On the rod-and-frame test (see **b**), the frame and the rod may be rotated, and—

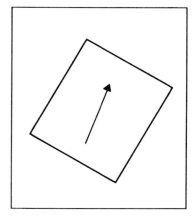

here again—the subject's task is to indicate which direction is true upright with reference to the rod. Both of these techniques are designed to measure the cognitive style of field dependence/independence.

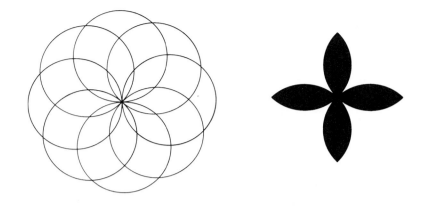

Figure 14–2 *An Illustration of a Sample Embedded-Figure Type Item.* The examinee's task on one type of embedded-figure item would be to locate the target figure (at the right) within a stimulus figure (at the left).

(see Figure 14–2). Normative data for the GEFT are based on a college sample of 155 men and 242 women. Correlations between the GEFT and the Embedded Figures Test were found to be .82 for males and .63 for females, a difference that is unexplained in the test manual. In a study involving 22 sixth-grade students, internal-consistency coefficients were found to range from .83 to .98, and long-term-stability coefficients were found to be .80 for boys and .71 for girls (Lis & Powers, 1979).

A study with 88 sixth-grade boys explored the relationships between cognitive style, self-concept, and leadership ability (Hoffman, 1978). Subjects were administered the Group Embedded Figures Test to determine field dependence/independence. The Piers-Harris Children's Self Concept Scales (discussed earlier in this chapter) provided a measure of self-concept. Leadership ability was assessed by assigning the subjects to groups for the purpose of completing an unstructured task and recording the amount of participation and verbalization of each subject. In addition, each member in the group rated the other members on a leadership rating scale. Boys identified as field independent were more likely to have been evaluated by their peers as demonstrating leadership ability and were more likely to have exhibited a positive self-image as measured by the Piers-Harris.

Other research has raised questions concerning the meaning of performance on the GEFT. Lusk and Wright (1981) have suggested that higher scores obtained on the second half of the GEFT are the result of learning that occurs during the test administration—learning that may influence subsequent performance on the test. In another study the researchers concluded that when the GEFT is used with an adult alcoholic population, cognitive impairment rather than cognitive style is the dimension assessed (O'Leary, Calsyn, & Fauria, 1980). It has also been suggested that the skills involved in tests of field dependence and independence may be confounded with general intelligence (Brody, 1972) or general spatial ability.

Reflective versus Impulsive Cognitive Styles

491

OTHER
METHODS OF
ASSESSING
PERSONALITY
AND BEHAVIOR

The *reflective-versus-impulsive* cognitive-style dimension has been described as the "consistent tendency to display slow or fast response times in problem situations with high response uncertainty" (Kagan, 1965, p. 134). Persons exhibiting a reflective style will spend more time examining the problem, considering alternative solutions, and will check for the accuracy and completeness of each hypothesis. The impulsive style is characterized by a tendency to make quick decisions and to respond with what comes to mind rather than with critical examination. Reflective versus impulsive style has been shown to be stable over time, though there is a tendency for reflection to increase as the subject gets older (Kagan, 1965).

The theoretical formulation of reflective-versus-impulsive style was an outgrowth of the work of Kagan and his associates (Kagan, Rossman, Day, Albert, & Phillips, 1964) at the Fels Institute. Kagan et al. observed that there were differences in the way children approach those "problem situations where many solution hypotheses are available simultaneously, (and where) the child has to evaluate the differential adequacy of each possibility" (p. 13). The Matching Familiar Figures Test (MFFT) was developed as an instrument to research the reflective-impulsive dimension in children. The construct of impulsivity has also been studied by means of situational tests that involve delay of gratification (see Mischel, 1966) and by the use of a combination of procedures such as the MFFT and situational tests (Block, Block, & Harrington, 1974).

The MFFT consists of 12 items that represent familiar objects (such as telephone, airplane, and cowboy) and two sample items. The subject is presented with a standard picture and six "strikingly similar" pictures of which only one is identical to the standard. The subject is instructed to select that picture which is identical to the standard. Scores are based on the length of time required before responding and on the number of errors produced. Respondents with short response times and a high number of errors will earn scores indicative of impulsivity, while respondents with longer response times and a low number of errors will earn scores indicative of being "reflective." It has been demonstrated that high negative correlations exist between response time on the MFFT and the number of errors produced; that is, test takers who respond quickly tend to make more errors than those who respond more slowly (Kagan, 1965).

In research comparing the performance of 58 11-year-olds on the MFFT with performance on the Wechsler Intelligence Scale for Children—Revised (WISC-R), children designated as reflective based on MFFT performance were found to perform significantly higher on visual organization and attention-concentration subtests of the WISC-R than did children designated as impulsive (Brannigan, Ash, & Margolis, 1980).

The MFFT has been criticized for a lack of normative data and the lack of an alternate form to reduce practice effects in retesting (Arizmendi, Paulsen, & Domino, 1981). Still, the test has been used in a number of research projects, including studies exploring how impulsivity in children might be modified. Kagan, Pearson, & Welch (1966) were able to lengthen MFFT response times of impulsive first-graders by providing training experiences in visual matching, inductive reasoning, and enforced periods of delay before giving a response. In a study involving 48 impulsive second- and third-graders, Nelson and Birkimer (1978) demonstrated that training in self-reinforcement could lengthen response time on the MFFT and significantly reduce errors. In another study it was shown that training in verbal self-instruction could result in an increase in MFFT response time, a decrease in MFFT errors for impulsive subjects as well as improved teacher ratings of classroom behavior (Kendall & Finch, 1978). Although primarily used in research with children, investigations of Kagan's formulations with adult populations have been conducted (for example, Brodzinsky & Dein, 1976; O'Keefe & Argulewicz, 1979).

Other Cognitive Styles

A number of other cognitive styles have been identified by psychologists, and clearly a volume or two could be devoted just to this subject. Much has been written about the construct *locus of control,* and indeed you may already have become acquainted with this term in another psychology course. *Locus*—meaning "place" or "site"—*of control* refers to the perception people have about the source of things that happen to them; do they see themselves as largely responsible for what happens to them in their lives, or do they attribute what happens to them to other factors (such as fate, luck, other forces, or other people)? Rotter first introduced this construct in a 1966 monograph and with it provided an Internal/External (I/E) scale. Other scales designed to measure internal/external orientations or styles (in the broadest sense) have since been published. The following item is representative of the items typically found on such tests; answer it "True" or "False" and, before reading further, "score" your response as to whether you think it places you more on the internal or external end of the locus-of-control continuum:

Sample Item: I believe in the value of seat belts and use them willingly.

True or False

If you answered "True" to this statement, it would indicate an internal rather than an external orientation. People who believe in the value of seat belts perceive themselves as being able to do something to help prevent serious injury in the event of an automobile accident. At the other end of the spectrum are people who do not believe in the value of seat belts and who—sometimes in violation of state safety-belt laws—refuse to buckle them. Among the familiar rationales offered for not using seat belts are some (such as "if it's meant to be, it's meant to be") that exemplify an orientation representative of an external (as opposed to an internal) locus of control.

From a psychometric standpoint, Rotter's (1966) measure of locus of control is reliable and numerous studies have attested to the validity of the construct. A survey of the recent scholarly literature will reveal hundreds of experimental investigations that relate scores on a measure of internal/external locus of control to numerous variables such as academic achievement, occupational success, psychiatric diagnosis, marital adjustment, and so forth.

Moving from Rotter and the highly researched internal-versus-external dichotomy to the far less researched—but noteworthy—dichotomy of rigidity versus flexibility, we come to the classic work of Abraham Luchins on the *einstellung* (rigidity in problem solving) phenomenon. Luchins (1946; Luchins & Luchins,

1959; Luchins & Luchins, 1970) provided a methodology for measuring *einstellung* by means of a series of "water jar problems" (paper-and-pencil problems in which the subject's task was to solve a sequence of problems involving the transfer of water between jars of different sizes) as well as a delightful account of how his mentor, Max Wertheimer, first inspired this line of research.

493

OTHER
METHODS OF
ASSESSING
PERSONALITY
AND BEHAVIOR

Finally, a cognitive dimension of "leveling/sharpening" refers to differences in the way people perceive and recall stimuli. *Levelers* tend to minimize differences in a stimulus field and to organize and recall stimuli in a simple and diffuse manner. *Sharpeners,* on the other hand, tend to maximize differences in stimuli and to prefer complex and detailed organization (Holzman, 1954). The process of leveling and sharpening has been illustrated in experimentation with the Schematizing Test (Gardner, Holzman, Klein, Linton, & Spence, 1959). Described briefly, this procedure has subjects judge the size of 150 squares. The squares vary in size from 1 to 14 inches and are projected onto a screen in groups of five, according to a prescribed order. The five smallest squares were presented three times in ascending order, then randomly. Following random presentation, the smallest square was removed and replaced with one slightly larger than any previously shown. In like manner, the new group of squares was presented first in ascending order, then randomly; finally, the substitution of the smallest square with a larger one was made. This procedure continued until all the squares were shown. Continuous substitution of a larger for a smaller square created a gradual shift in the relative position each square held within the group. The way in which the subjects incorporated these changes in their judgments of size was analyzed. Some subjects were alert to differences, able to adapt to changes as new stimuli were introduced, and to adjust their estimations accordingly (sharpeners). Others (levelers) were less attuned to differences, more influenced by the stimuli they had previously observed, and less likely to modify their judgments as new stimuli were introduced (Holzman & Klein, 1954; Klein & Holzman, 1950).

In a separate investigation, the effect leveling and sharpening had on the recall of early experiences was explored (Holzman & Gardner, 1960). The Schematizing Test was administered to 41 undergraduate female students of similar socioeconomic background between the ages of 18 and 22. In a separate testing session, the subjects were asked to recount the childhood story of the Pied Piper, which was scored for the presence of eleven thematic elements. The Pied Piper was selected as a tale that most people have been exposed to but are not overly familiar with. In general, sharpeners recalled more of the key elements of the story in a more organized fashion than did levelers. Levelers tended to be vague in their accounts and often supplied only "an indistinct general impression" (Holzman & Gardner, 1960, p. 178). These findings led the authors to conclude that the phenomenon of leveling and sharpening not only operates in the laboratory setting, but also may be an "enduring aspect of cognitive organization" (p. 179) that may be generalized to a variety of situations.

SITUATIONAL PERFORMANCE MEASURES

If you have ever applied for a part-time secretarial job and been required to take a typing test, you have had firsthand experience with what we are calling "situational performance measures." Broadly stated, a *situational performance measure* is a procedure that allows for observation and evaluation of an individual under a standard set of circumstances. A situational performance measure typically involves performance of some specific task under actual or simulated conditions. The road test you took to obtain your driver's license was a situational performance measure that entailed an evaluation of your driving skills in a real car, on a real road, in real traffic. On the other hand, situational performance measures used to assess the skills of prospective astronauts are done in rocket simulators in scientific laboratories that are firmly planted on Mother Earth.

The range of variables that may be focused on in situational performance measures is virtually limitless. In addition to evaluating skills such as typing and driving, situational performance measures have been used to assess a wide variety of variables related to personality. For example, the responses of prospective astronauts placed in simulated space conditions are closely observed with respect to such variables as tolerance for weightlessness; irritability; ability to eat, sleep, and exercise routine duties; and ability to get along with others under such conditions for a prolonged time. In the next sections, we discuss a sampling of the situational performance measures that have been used by researchers in academic and applied psychology. We begin with a consideration of the oft-cited work of Hartshorne and May (1928).

The Character Education Inquiry

The Character Education Inquiry was the name of a project designed to explore the nature of children's "character," and it represented one of the earliest psychological assessment research projects that employed situational performance measurements. The behaviors to be observed took place in the context of tasks and activities that regularly occurred during the pupils' day, and none of the research subjects knew that they were being observed and evaluated. The component of "character" that was focused on in most of the tests was honesty, though measures of self-control and altruism were also included. In one measure of honesty, for example, children were presented with the opportunity to cheat on the grading of a test. This measure involved the administration of a test, the collection of the test papers, and, unbeknownst to the students, the scoring of the papers. No marks were actually made on the test papers. The following day the test papers were returned to the students with instructions to grade their own papers. The grades made by the students were compared with the grades the examiners had obtained prior to returning the test papers to the students.

Another index of honesty was stealing. A test that provided the opportunity for stealing involved having each child receive a box containing coins that were to be used in playing a game. Upon completion of the game, the children were instructed to place the coins back into the box and return the box to the person in charge. A record of the number of coins in each box was made before the boxes were distributed. The number of coins returned in the different boxes was compared with the original number; thus, it was possible to ascertain if the children did in fact return all the coins, or if they decided to keep some for themselves.

The results obtained on the different tests of the Character Education Inquiry indicated that the children's responses varied depending on the situation they were in. Stated another way, the children could not be absolutely classified as "honest" or "dishonest"; their behavior was a function of the circumstances they were in, not of an absolute "character." Low correlations were observed for different measures purporting to measure the same trait (here, honesty). The findings of Hartshorne and May (1928) have been cited as evidence for Mischel's (1968) position that a cross-situational trait "honesty" does not exist but rather that people are honest in some situations but not in others. To this day, one still occasionally reads of research being conducted with measures very much like those pioneered by Hartshorne and May (for example, Leming, 1978).

495

OTHER
METHODS OF
ASSESSING
PERSONALITY
AND BEHAVIOR

Leaderless-Group Situations

The leaderless group is another situational assessment procedure, one in which the subjects being evaluated are usually aware that their behavior is being observed and/or recorded. The procedure typically involves organizing several people into a group for the purpose of carrying out a specific task. Although the group knows the objectives of the exercises, no one is placed in the position of leadership or authority. In addition, purposely vague instructions are typically provided for the group. The group determines how it will accomplish the task and who will be responsible for what duties. An observer monitors the group's progress and evaluates both the group's functioning as a whole and the way in which each individual member functions within the group. The leaderless-group situation provides an opportunity to observe the degree of cooperation exhibited by each individual group member and the extent to which each individual is able to function as part of a team.

The leaderless-group technique has been employed in military and industrial settings. Its use in the military developed out of the U.S. Office of Strategic Service's (OSS, 1948) attempts to assess such characteristics as cooperation, leadership, and initiative. The procedure was designed to aid in the establishment of cohesive military units—cockpit crews, tank crews, and so forth—in which members would work together well and each could make a significant contribution. Assessees might, for example, be assigned the task of transporting equipment over some obstacle-ridden terrain. The way in which the group as a group proceeded through the assignment, as well as how each individual member of the group contributed—or failed to contribute—to the group's process would be carefully noted. From such a sample of behavior, information about an individual's leadership ability, initiative, organization and planning abilities, communication skills, social skills, and related skills and abilities could be obtained.

The use of the leaderless-group procedure in industrial settings has similarly been useful in identifying leaders—persons with managerial or executive potential. Less commonly, the technique has also been employed to identify those combinations of personnel that would have a high probability of functioning well together. Manz and Sims (1984) have called attention to a puzzling paradox that exists in an era when more and more organizations are adopting the self-managed work-group approach: How does one lead those who are supposed to lead themselves? On the basis of their research with 320 employees in a production plant that used a self-managed work system, Manz and Sims identified a unique type of leader required in such a work system—"the unleader." These authors described the effective "unleader" as primarily a facilitator who is able to balance both a "hands-off" and directive management style in a variety of situations.

Situational Stress Tests

Situational stress tests are measures designed to assess how an individual will react to a specific type of anxiety, frustration, or stress. Most situational stress tests are designed to present a task that must be completed, an activity that must be carried out, or a problem that must be solved. Frustrating obstacles, such as a "helper" who hinders more than helps, are typically an integral part of the exercise. The way in which the examinee responds to this situation provides some indication of the way the examinee tends to respond to frustration in stressful situations.

Situational stress tests were frequently employed by the U.S. Office of Strategic Services (OSS, 1948) during the Second World War in efforts to select candidates for military intelligence and other positions. This technique is still widely used by military organizations for selection as well as research purposes. Tziner and Eden (1985) described the use of such techniques by the Israeli military to determine what the ideal composition of a crew is.

Today some of the larger corporations have personnel departments that administer measures quite reminiscent of the OSS's situational stress tests. Of

---

Figure 14–3 *A Hypothetical "Stockbroker Stress Test."*

It is not inconceivable that some major brokerage houses use performance work samples as one method by which candidates for positions are selected. What might such a stockbroker stress test be like? Using imagination as well as knowledge of the typical compo-

nents of such procedures, we could envision the following.

Initially, candidates for the position of stockbroker might be told that they will be observed by trained raters in a performance work test that will be one of the criteria used in deciding whether they are given further consideration for the position. They might then be led to the room where the experiment will be conducted, a room designed to look very much like the typical work environment of a broker. And now the "stress test" begins. . . .

Candidates are told that they have just been hired by a hypothetical brokerage house—let's call the firm "Merry Lynch." Next, candidates are given time sufficient to familiarize themselves with a number of written materials, including (1) a listing of various personnel in the firm, (2) information on various (hypothetical) stocks, (3) a listing and description of the personality and holdings of seven of their best clients, and (4) a listing of a hundred or so prospects (potential customers).

After studying these materials, each candidate is placed in an office situation (along with three or four other candidates) where each person has a desktop computer (from which current quotes on the hypothetical stocks may be obtained) and (1) an office assistant (who seldom assists and is more apt to hinder), (2) a phone that seems to keep ringing with clients wishing to place orders or ask advice on certain stocks, (3) a number of pieces of correspondence and interoffice memos that must be answered, and (4) the delivery of company advisories on various stocks and newly issued stocks. Within a certain time limit, the candidates must deal with all of these tasks; how competently and professionally candidates establish priorities and policies, communicate information to clients and fellow employees, and generally deal with the duties and stresses of the "Merry Lynch" situation will in part determine whether they are given further consideration for a position at the firm.

497

OTHER
METHODS OF
ASSESSING
PERSONALITY
AND BEHAVIOR

course, we are not privy to published descriptions of such tests, which are typically kept confidential. However, it would not be too difficult to conceive, for example, of a "Stockbroker Stress Test" that might proceed as outlined in Figure 14–3.

OTHER MEASURES OF PERSONALITY

Various other techniques have been devised for assessing personality and/or specific aspects of personality. The IPAT Humor Test of Personality (Cattell & Luborsky, 1952; Luborsky & Cattell, 1947) represents an attempt at formalizing measurement of reactions to humorous situations. Form A of the test consists of 104 pairs of jokes to which the examinee indicates which of the two jokes is funnier. Form B consists of 130 jokes or cartoons. The examinee responds to each item by indicating whether the item is "funny" or "not funny." Both forms are scored according to personality dimensions derived from factor analysis. Test-retest reliability coefficients between the two forms of the test were found to range from .10 to .60 (Cattell & Luborsky, 1952).

Proverb interpretation tasks have also been regarded by many as a useful clinical and research tool in assessment of personality (Bass, 1956, 1957, 1958; Benjamin, 1964; Cancro, 1969; Gorham, 1956; Kim, Siomopoulos, & Cohen, 1977; Walsh, 1966). In the Famous Sayings Test (Bass, 1958), the task is to evaluate 130 proverbs and aphorisms by indicating "Agree," "Disagree," or "Uncertain" with respect to each item. Scores are obtained on three factor-analytically derived scales—Conventional Mores, Fear of Failure, and Hostility—as well as a fourth scale, Social Acquiescence (a measure of the subject's general tendency to agree or disagree with the statements).

Some people seem to see the world through "rose-colored glasses" whereas others seem to see the world through much darker lenses. In order to better understand and assess how an individual tends to see the world, a clinician or counselor may wish to administer a test called the Role Construct Repertory Test (Kelly, 1955)—the "Rep Test" as it is referred to by psychologists. The purpose of this test is to investigate those personal constructs—templates or patterns—through which individuals perceive their world; templates that influence not only perception but behavior as well. This test may be administered in different ways. In one variation, the subject is presented with a Role Title List with a number of roles listed such as "liked teacher," "boss," "liked acquaintance," "disliked co-worker," "mother," "sibling," "neighbor"—24 in all (in the individually administered version of this instrument, the group version lists only 15 roles). The respondent is presented with the task of relating the important ways in which two of the people listed are similar, but different from a third person. In presenting the respondent with varying three-person combinations, much qualitative data about the respondent's interpersonal relations evolve.

Among the lesser known and "off-the-beaten-path" personality measures is a technique developed by Blatt, Wein, Chevron, and Quinlan (1979) that calls for the assessee to create a written description of his or her parents. The written material is then scored with respect to the strength of various traits on a 7-point scale. The Comprehensive Early Memories Scoring System (CEMSS; Last, 1983; see also, Last & Bruhn, 1983, 1985) is a measurement technique that has its basis in psychoanalytic theory. Although conceptually intriguing, this test does not enjoy widespread usage, perhaps because early memories are difficult to reliably obtain and validate. Also difficult to reliably obtain—and impossible to validate—are dreams, the basis for a psychoanalytically linked scale called the Object Representation Scale for Dreams (ORSD; Mayman & Faris, 1960; see also Mayman, 1968; Krohn & Mayman, 1974; Ryan & Bell, 1984; and Ryan & Cicchetti, 1985). This scale was designed, in part, to assess the way the assessee characteristically views other people.

Throughout Part 4, we have seen how some personality tests originally designed for use with adults have been adapted for use with children (for example, the Children's Personality Questionnaire and the Children's Apperception Test). In recent years, a number of personality tests and measurement techniques designed expressly for use with children have appeared. We have already reviewed one self-report measure designed for use with children (the Piers-Harris Children's Self-Concept Scale) in this chapter. Now we look at a measure where someone other than the child is the respondent: the Personality Inventory for Children.

The Personality Inventory for Children (PIC)

One of the best ways a person has of learning about a child's personality with an economy of time is to talk to the child's parent. Child psychologists and others who work with children know this well, and an interview with a child's parent or guardian has always been standard operating procedure in mental health facilities where children are treated. The Personality Inventory for Children is a kind of standardized interview of a child's parent; though the child is the subject of the test, the respondent is the child's parent. In a research program that began at the University of Minnesota, investigators (Wirt, Lachar, Klinedinst, & Seat, 1977/1984) developed the empirical scales of the PIC in the "mold" of the MMPI; the method of contrasting groups that is characteristic of the MMPI was used along with an additional item-analytic procedure described by Darlington and Bishop (1966). The other scales were constructed using a content-oriented strategy or an internal-consistency strategy, or both (Lachar & Gdowski, 1979a).

The PIC consists of 600 true/false items answered by the parent (usually the mother) or other appropriate adult (such as the child's guardian). The standardization sample for the PIC included 2,400 normal males and females within the 6- to 16-year-old age range and 200 males and females within the 3- to 5-year-old age range. There are 13 clinical scales, 1 screening scale (labeled "Adjustment"), and 3 validity scales (labeled "Lie," "Frequency," and "Defensive"; see Table 14–1). Additionally, there are 4 broad-band factor-derived scales and a critical-item list that may be useful in the diagnostic process. Respondents complete the first 131, 280, or 420 items to allow the scoring of various screening, short-form, or full-length scale measures. Empirically derived interpretations have been developed for individual scales (Lachar, 1982; Lachar & Gdowski, 1979b) and for profile types (Lachar, Kline, & Boersma, 1986).

The PIC has been the subject of numerous studies by many different researchers since its publication in 1977. The application of the PIC to pre-school screening issues (Keenan & Lachar, 1988) and to problems such as hyperactivity (Forbes, 1985) and cognitive dysfunction (Kline, Lachar, & Sprague, 1985) only

499

OTHER
METHODS OF
ASSESSING
PERSONALITY
AND BEHAVIOR

Table 14–1

The Scales of the Personality Inventory for Children

Validity scales

Lie Scale (L)—designed to detect lying as evidenced by a tendency to ascribe the most virtuous kinds of behaviors to the child while denying minor but fairly common behavior problems.

Frequency Scale (F)—composed of infrequently endorsed items and designed, in part, to identify a deviant or random response set or difficulty in following directions. An elevated F scale may also be indicative of the child's presentation of extreme or delinquent behavior.

Defensiveness Scale (DEF)—designed to detect defensiveness on the part of the respondent.

Screening scale

Adjustment Scale (ADJ)—designed to identify children with problems in need of professional intervention.

Clinical scales

Achievement Scale (ACH)—designed to detect the presence of poor academic achievement independent of cognitive and neurological status.

Intellectual Screening Scale (IS)—designed to detect the need for an intellectual evaluation.

Development Scale (DVL)—detects not only cognitive and neurological impairment but impairment in areas of social functioning as well.

Somatic Concern Scale (SOM)—taps the child's expression and exhibition of physical symptoms such as headache and fatigue.

Depression Scale (D)—related to various behavioral indices of depression, including sleep disturbances and social withdrawal.

Family Relations Scale (FAM)—designed to assess family effectiveness and cohesion.

Delinquency Scale (DLQ)—taps dimensions such as compliance, hostility, impulsivity, and antisocial behaviors.

Withdrawal Scale (WDL)—designed to detect withdrawal from social contact.

Anxiety Scale (ANX)—designed to detect anxiety as manifested in behavioral correlates such as sleep disturbances.

Hyperactivity Scale (HPR)—reflects distractibility, overactivity, impulsivity, and the absence of perfectionistic behavior.

Social Skills Scale (SSK)—designed to measure the various characteristics that reflect effective social relations.

begin to sample the number of published studies with this instrument. According to the test's publisher, over one million children have been assessed with it.

In general the PIC appears to be psychometrically sound; measures of test-retest reliability for the various profile scales as well as measures of internal consistency are acceptably high. Evidence of the validity of the test lies in studies such as those which have demonstrated the ability of the test to predict observations of teachers, clinicians, and peers (see Wirt et al., 1977/1984). Some (such as Achenbach, 1981; Cornell, 1985) have expressed concern about the reliance on parental report for the derivation of PIC scores; these concerns have been persuasively rebutted with reference to research on the validity of the test (Lachar & Wirt, 1981; Lachar, Gdowski, & Snyder, 1985).

An Overview

Traits, states, motives, needs, drives, defenses, and related psychological constructs have no tangible existence; they are constructs whose existence must be inferred from behavior. In the traditional approach to clinical assessment, tests as well as other tools are employed to gather data; from these data diagnoses and inferences are made concerning the existence and strength of psychological constructs. The traditional approach to assessment might therefore be termed a "sign" approach, since test responses are deemed to be signs or clues to underlying personality or ability. In contrast to this traditional approach is an alternative philosophy of assessment that may be termed the "sample" approach. This approach focuses on the behavior itself; emitted behavior is not viewed as a sign of something but rather as a sample to be interpreted in its own right. The emphasis in behavioral assessment is on "what a person *does* in situations rather than on inferences about what attributes he *has* more globally" (Mischel, 1968, p. 10). Predicting what a person will do is thought to entail an understanding of the assessee in terms of antecedent conditions and consequences for the particular situation in question. Upon close scrutiny, however, the trait concept is still present in many behavioral measures though more narrowly defined and more closely linked to specific situations (Zuckerman, 1979).

To illustrate behavioral observation as an assessment strategy, consider the plight of the single female client who presents herself at the university counseling center complaining that even though all her friends tell her how attractive she is, she is experiencing great difficulty in meeting men—so much so that she doesn't even want to try anymore. A counselor confronted with such a client might, among other things, (1) interview the client with respect to this problem, (2) administer an appropriate test to the client, (3) ask the client to keep detailed diaries of her thoughts and behaviors with respect to her efforts to meet men, and/or (4) accompany the client to a singles bar and observe her behavior. The latter two strategies come under the heading of behavioral observation; in one situation the counselor is doing the actual observing, in another it is the client herself.

The administration of a psychological test or test battery to a client such as this single woman might yield signs that then could be inferred to relate to the problem. For example, if a number of the client's TAT stories involved themes of demeaning, hostile, or otherwise unsatisfactory heterosexual encounters as a result of venturing out into the street, the counselor might make an interpretation at a "deeper" or "second" level of inference: the client's expressed fear of going outdoors (and ultimately her fear of meeting men) might in some way be related to an unconscious fear of promiscuity—a fear of becoming a "street-walker."

In contrast to the sign approach, the clinician employing the sample or behavioral approach to assessment might examine the behavioral diary that the client kept with respect to her problem and design an appropriate therapy program on the basis of these records. Thus, for example, the antecedent conditions under which the client would feel most distraught and unmotivated to do anything about the problem might be delineated and worked on in counseling sessions.

501

OTHER
METHODS OF
ASSESSING
PERSONALITY
AND BEHAVIOR

An advantage of the sign as opposed to the sample approach is that in the hands of a skillful, perceptive clinician, the client might be put in touch with feel-ins that even she was not really aware of before the assessment. The client may have been consciously (or unconsciously) avoiding certain thoughts and images (say those attendant on the expression of her sexuality, for example) and this in-ability to deal with those thoughts and images may indeed have been a factor con-tributing to her ambivalence with respect to meeting men.

Behavioral assessors seldom make such "deeper level" inferences; and if the area of sexuality is not raised as an area of difficulty by the client (either in an interview, a checklist, or by some other behavioral assessment technique), this problem area may well be ignored or given short shrift. The behavioral assessor does, however, tend to be more comprehensive and systematic in his or her ap-proach to assessing the breadth and magnitude of the client's problem. Instead of searching for signs in Rorschach or other test protocols, the behaviorally oriented counselor or clinician might simply ask such a client a question like, "What are some of the reasons you think you are unable to meet men?" and then take it from there. By obtaining a complete self-report either verbally or through a pencil-and-paper behavioral checklist and by obtaining behavioral observation data, the behaviorally oriented assessor will discover specific areas that need to be focused on in therapy. You can see that the behavioral approach does not require as much "clinical creativity" as the sign approach; perhaps for this reason, it is generally considered to be the more scientific of the two approaches to psychological assessment.

Unlike traditional psychological assessors, behaviorally oriented clinicians have characteristically found little use for traditional psychological tests and pro-cedures in their work. This division in the field of clinical psychology was taken note of as early as 1967 by Greenspoon and Gersten, who observed that "Psychol-ogists in the practicum agencies contend that tests are the 'bread and butter' of the clincial psychologist and the university personnel contend that if such is the case the clinical psychologist is on an ersatz diet" (p. 849). In their article entitled "A New Look at Psychological Testing: Psychological Testing from the Standpoint of a Behaviorist," they argued that "psychological tests should be able to provide the behavior therapist with information that should be of value in doing behavior therapy. This contention is based on the assumption that the behavior on any psy-chological test should be lawful" (Greenspoon & Gersten, 1967, p. 849). Accord-ingly, psychological tests could be useful, for example, in helping the behavior therapist to identify the kinds of contingent stimuli that would be most effective with a given patient. For example, patients with high percentages of Color or Color/Form responses on the Rorschach and with IQs in excess of 90 might be most responsive to positive verbal contingencies (such as "good," "excellent") whereas patients with high percentages of movement or vista (three-dimensional) responses and IQs in excess of 90 might be most responsive to negative verbal contingencies ("no," "wrong"). Although the ideas expressed by Greenspoon and Gersten seem not to have been greeted with a rush of experimental enthusi-asm—perhaps because there exist more direct ways to assess responsiveness to various contingencies—their article did represent a truly innovative attempt to narrow a widening schism in the field of clinical assessment.

Differences between traditional and behavioral approaches to assessment have to do with varying assumptions about the nature of personality and the causes of behavior. The data from traditional assessment are used primarily to describe, classify, or diagnose, whereas the data from a behavioral assessment are typically more directly related to the formulation of a specific treatment program. Some of the other differences between the two approaches are summarized in Table 14–2.

The Who, What, When, Where, and How of It

The name says it all; *behavior* is the focus of assessment in behavioral assessment—not traits, states, or other constructs presumed to be present in various strengths,

Table 14–2

Differences Between Behavioral and Traditional Approaches to Psychological Assessment

	Behavioral	Traditional
Assumptions		
Conception of personality	Personality constructs mainly employed to summarize specific behavior patterns, if at all	Personality as a reflection of enduring, underlying states or traits
Causes of behavior	Maintaining conditions sought in current environment	Intrapsychic or within the individual
Implications		
Role of behavior	Important as a sample of person's repertoire in specific situation	Behavior assumes importance only insofar as it indexes underlying causes
Role of history	Relatively unimportant, except, for example, to provide a retrospective baseline	Crucial in that present conditions seen as a product of the past
Consistency of behavior	Behavior thought to be specific to the situation	Behavior expected to be consistent across time and settings
Uses of data	To describe target behaviors and maintaining conditions	To describe personality functioning and etiology
	To select the appropriate treatment	To diagnose or classify
	To evaluate and revise treatment	To make prognosis; to predict
Other characteristics		
Level of inferences	Low	Medium to high
Comparisons	More emphasis on intraindividual or idiographic	More emphasis on interindividual or nomothetic
Methods of assessment	More emphasis on direct methods (e.g., observations of behavior in natural environment)	More emphasis on indirect methods (e.g., interviews and self-report)
Timing of assessment	More ongoing; prior, during, and after treatment	Pre- and perhaps posttreatment, or strictly to diagnose
Scope of assessment	Specific measures and of more variables (e.g., of target behaviors in various situations, of side effects, context, strengths as well as deficiencies)	More global measures (e.g., of cure, or improvement) but only of the individual

Source: Hartmann, Roper, and Bradford (1979).

just behavior. This will become clear as we continue our overview with a look at what we could call the "who, what, where, when, and how" of behavioral assessment.

503

OTHER
METHODS OF
ASSESSING
PERSONALITY
AND BEHAVIOR

Who is assessed? Most typically, only one person at a time. Regardless of whether the assessment is for research, clinical, or other purposes, the hallmark of behavioral assessment is intensive study of individuals—this is in contrast to mass testing of groups of people to obtain normative data with respect to some hypothesized trait or state. *Who* is the assessor? Depending on the particular assessment, the assessor may be a highly qualified professional, or a technician/assistant trained to conduct a particular assessment (such as recording the number of times young Johnny leaves his seat during hygiene class).

What is measured in behavioral assessment? Not surprisingly, the behavior or behaviors targeted for assessment will vary as a function of the objectives of the assessment. Whatever behavior or behaviors are being measured, a careful definition of what constitutes a targeted behavior must be drawn. And for the purposes of assessment, the targeted behavior must be measurable—quantifiable in some way. Examples of such measurable behaviors can range from "the number of seconds Johnny spends out of his seat during hygiene class" to "the number of degrees Centigrade body temperature is altered"—the latter being an observable event that may be considered "behavior" in its broadest sense. Note that descriptions of targeted behaviors in behavioral assessment typically begin with the phrase "the number of. . . ."

When is an assessment of behavior made? Beyond fairly general types of answers to this question (such as "during the school day except at lunch"), behavioral assessors may employ any of various schedules or formats of assessment. For example, one schedule of assessment is referred to as *frequency,* or *event recording.* Here, each time the targeted behavior occurs, it is recorded. Another schedule of assessment is referred to as *interval recording.* Assessment according to this schedule only occurs during predefined intervals of time (for example, every other minute, every 48 hours, every third week, and so forth). Beyond merely tallying the number of times a particular behavior is emitted, the assessor may also maintain a record of the intensity of the behavior as gauged by observable and quantifiable events such as the *duration* of the behavior, stated in terms such as number of seconds, minutes, hours, days, weeks, months, or years, or some ratio or percentage of time that the behavior occurs during a specified interval of time.

Where does the assessment take place? Unlike the administration of psychological tests, which are most likely to be administered in a psychologist's office or in some institutional setting such as a hospital or school, behavioral assessment may take place virtually anywhere—usually preferably in the environment where the targeted behavior is most likely to occur naturally. For example, a behavioral assessor studying the obsessive-compulsive habits of a patient might wish to visit the patient at home to see firsthand the variety and intensity of the compulsive behavior the patient exhibits (for example, whether the patient checks the oven for having left the gas on and, if so, how many times per hour).

How is behavioral assessment conducted? Again, the answer to this question will vary of course according to the purpose of the assessment. In some situations, the only special equipment required will be a trained observer with pad and pencil. In other types of situations, highly sophisticated recording equipment may be necessary. As an example of the latter situation, imagine that you were a NASA psychologist studying the psychological and behavioral effects of space travel on astronauts; what types of behavioral measures might you employ, and what special equipment would you need—or design—to obtain those measures?

As you consider this question, our brief overview of behavioral assessment continues with a look at some of the tools used in this discipline.

Behavioral Observation and Behavior Rating Scales

A child psychologist observes a patient in a playroom through a one-way mirror; a family therapist views a videotape of a troubled family attempting to resolve a conflict; a psychologist's assistant accompanies a patient lacking in interpersonal skills to a disco for the purpose of observing her; these are all examples of the use of an assessment technique called *behavioral observation*. As its name implies, this technique entails watching the activities of targeted clients or research subjects and, typically, maintaining some kind of record of those activities. Researchers, clinicians, or counselors may themselves serve as observers, or they may designate trained assistants or other people (such as parents, siblings, teachers, supervisors, and so forth) to be the observers. Even the observed person herself or himself can be the behavior observer, as is the case of the dieter maintaining a diary of food intake and emotional feelings—although in that instance the term *self-observation* would be more appropriate than *behavioral observation*. In some instances, behavioral observation entails mechanical means, such as a videorecording of an event; this relieves the clinician, researcher, or other observer of the necessity to be physically present at the time the behavior occurs and to view its occurrence when it is convenient to do so. Regardless of who actually does the observing, and whether the observation is accomplished through a "live" or recorded viewing, factors noted in behavioral observation will typically include a notation of the presence or absence of specific, targeted behaviors, behavioral excesses, behavioral deficits, behavioral assets, and the situational antecedents and consequences of the emitted behaviors.

The "nuts-and-bolts" of behavioral observation may take many forms, though underlying watchwords in such endeavors are standardization and reliability; every observer using the technique should be trained to systematically look for and record the same well-defined behavior. In one form of behavioral observation, the observer may, in the tradition of the naturalist, record a running narrative of events, using tools such as pencil and paper, a video, film, or still camera, and/or a cassette recorder. Another form of behavioral observation employs what is called a *behavior rating scale*—a preprinted sheet on which the observer notes the presence and/or intensity of targeted behaviors, usually by checking boxes, or by filling in coded terms. For example, if the focus of interest was whether or not an institutionalized patient took out the garbage on a daily basis, an "Emptying Garbage" behavioral scale or checklist like the one to which we were first introduced on page 18 might be employed. Sometimes the user of a behavior rating form writes in coded descriptions of various behaviors; the code is preferable to a running narrative, as it takes far less time to enter the data and frees the observer familiar with the code to enter data relating to any of hundreds of possible behaviors, not just the ones printed on the sheets. For example, a number of coding systems for observing the behavior of couples and families are available. Two such systems are the Marital Interaction Coding System (Weiss & Summers, 1983) and the Couples Interaction Scoring System (Notarius & Markman, 1981). In an attempt to facilitate the work of the observer, Filsinger (1983) describes the use of a handheld data-entry device for the observer to use while entering coded observations made from a combination of the Marital Interaction Coding System, the Couples Interaction Scoring System, and two other systems.

Behavior rating scales and systems, as approaches to behavioral assessment in general, may be categorized in different ways. A categorization of "direct" to "indirect" has to do with the setting in which the observed behavior occurs, and how closely that setting approximates the setting in which the behavior naturally occurs. The more natural the setting, the more "direct" the measure; the more removed from the natural setting, the less direct the measure (Shapiro & Skinner, 1990). According to this categorization, assessing a client's reactions in a real disco would provide a direct measure, whereas assessment of behavior in a simulated or videotaped evening at a disco would provide an indirect behavioral measure. Shapiro and Skinner (1990) also draw a distinction between "broad band" instruments that seek to measure a wide variety of behaviors, and "narrow band" instruments that may focus on behaviors related to single, specific constructs such as hyperactivity, shyness, or depression.

A number of behavior rating scales designed to assess various aspects of children's behavior are available, among them the Child Behavior Checklist (Achenbach & Edelbrock, 1983; see also Achenbach & Edelbrock, 1986, 1987; Edelbrock, 1988; McConaughty & Achenbach, 1988; Christenson, 1990; Martin, 1988; Martin, Hooper, & Snow, 1986; Mooney, 1984), the Behavior Rating Profile (Brown & Hammill, 1978), the Eyberg Child Behavior Inventory (Eyberg & Robinson, 1983; Eyberg & Ross, 1978; Burns & Patterson, 1990); the Revised Behavior Problem Checklist (Quay & Peterson, 1983), the Play Performance Scale for Children (Lansky et al., 1985, 1987), and the Walker Problem Behavior Identification Checklist (Walker, 1983). Below we examine one such checklist, which focuses on social skills assessment. Then we look at an innovative newcomer to the field of behavioral assessment instruments—one designed to gauge tissue damage as a result of self-injurious behavior.

The Social Skills Rating System (SSRS) The SSRS (Gresham & Elliott, 1990) is designed to measure social skills in individuals from preschool through high school (ages 3 to 18 years) using Teacher and Parent forms and a Student self-report form (grades 3 through 12). The Social Skills Scale assesses positive social behaviors in five areas (cooperation, assertion, responsibility, empathy, and self-control) and the Problem Behavior Scales measure behavior in three areas referred to as "externalizing" problems (including behaviors with observable impact and consequences, such as delinquent-type behaviors), "internalizing" problems (including problems such as fearfulness and inhibitions), and hyperactivity. Items on the Social Skills Scales are rated on the basis of frequency (never, sometimes, or very often) and their importance (not important, important, critical), whereas the Problem Behavior Scales are rated on frequency (never, sometimes, or very often). Sample items from the Social Skills Scales and Problem Behavior Scales are presented in Table 14–3.

The SSRS was standardized on a national sample of 4,170 children during the spring of 1988. An attempt was made to approximate the 1990 United States census estimates for the variables of race or ethnicity, geographic region, and community size. Overall, the standardization was 73% white and 27% minority. Southern and North Central states as well as central city, suburban, and small-town communities were somewhat overrepresented in the standardization sample, whereas Western and Northeastern areas along with rural communities were underrepresented. The number of handicapped students in the standardization sample was greater than in the United States population (17.3% versus 11.0%). Median coefficient alpha reliabilities were .90 for the Social Skills Scale and .84 for the Problem Behavior Scale, respectively, across all forms and levels. Test-retest reliability was assessed, with samples of teachers, parents, and students rating the same students four weeks after the original ratings. Test-retest correlations for Social Skills ranged from .68 (students) to .85 (teachers) to .87 (parents) and for Problem Behaviors from .65 (parents) to .84 (teachers). Initial validity studies compared the SSRS with similar instruments, including the Child Behavior Checklist, and produced moderate to high correlations.

Table 14–3

Sample Items from the Social Skills Rating System—Elementary Level

Social Skills Subscales	*Teacher Form*	*Parent Form*	*Student (Self-Rating) Form*
Cooperation	Finishes class assignments within time limits.	Completes household tasks within a reasonable time.	I finish classwork on time.
Assertion	Initiates conversations with peers.	Starts conversations rather than waiting for others to talk first.	I start talks with class members.
Responsibility	(Not in this form)	Reports accidents to appropriate persons.	(Not in this form)
Empathy	(Not in this form)	(Not in this form)	I feel sorry for others when bad things happen to them.
Self-Control	Controls temper in conflict situations with peers.	Controls temper when arguing with other children.	I control my temper when people are angry at me.

Problem Behaviors Subscales	*Teacher Form*	*Parent Form*	*Student (Self-Rating) Form*
Externalizing Problems	Gets angry easily.	Gets angry easily.	Not rated by students
Internalizing Problems	Appears lonely.	Appears lonely.	Not rated by students
Hyperactivity	Is easily distracted.	Is easily distracted.	Not rated by students

Adapted from Gresham and Elliott (1990).

The Self-Injury Trauma (SIT) Scale   The Self-Injury Trauma (SIT) Scale provides a method for quantifying surface tissue damage caused by self-injurious behavior. Injuries are categorized in terms of their location, type, and number, as well as an estimate as to severity (see Figure 14–4). Fifty pairs of independently scored SIT Scale records were subjected to inter-rater reliability analyses and the percentage of agreement for all of the variables measured ranged from a low of 92% agreement for the test's "Severity Index," to a high of 100% agreement for the test's "Estimate of Current Risk" measure (Iwata, Pace, Kissel, Nau, & Farber, 1990). Such a scale may have many potential applications, including (1) measuring pre- and posttreatment changes in injuries, (2) assessing the level of risk a patient may be at for evidencing self-injurious behavior, and (3) designing or instituting effective treatments for self-injurious behavior, and monitoring their effectiveness.[2]

Analogue studies   The behavioral approach to clinical assessment and treatment has been likened to the researcher's approach to experimentation; the behavioral assessor proceeds in many ways like a researcher, with the patient's problem being the dependent variable and the factor(s) responsible for causing and/or maintaining the problem behavior being the independent variable(s). Behavioral assessors will typically use the phrase *functional analysis* of behavior to convey the process of identifying the dependent and independent variables with respect to the presenting problem. However, just as it is true that experimenters must frequently employ independent and dependent variables that imitate how those variables occur in the "real world," so behavioral assessors must too. This type of study, where a variable or two are similar or analogous to the "real" variable the investigator wishes to examine, is referred to as an *analogue study*. The subjects for most of the analogue research in experimental psychology have been white rats and introductory psychology students. However, as we shall see, real patients with real problems can also be assessed in an analogue study.

Suppose Mr. Johnson, a weekend hunter, presents himself at the office of a behavior therapist to be treated for a fear of snakes (harmless and otherwise)—a fear that is seriously interfering with his weekend activities. The therapist, desirous of learning more specific behavioral information about this fear, might arrange to accompany Johnson on one of his forays into the woods. More likely, however, Johnson and his therapist would simply discuss the problem—what types of snakes bother him, to what degree, what effect they have on him, and so forth. Alternatively, the therapist might arrange to perform an analogue study in the office. When Johnson shows up for his appointment the following week, the therapist may present him with a harmless snake, caged or free, at some distance from him. The assessment would then be made in terms of the number of feet Johnson could approach the snake without self-reported debilitating anxiety. Incidentally, the goal of the therapy would have been reached when Johnson was able to comfortably walk right up to the animal and pet it. This is *analogue research*

507

OTHER
METHODS OF
ASSESSING
PERSONALITY
AND BEHAVIOR

---

2. Somewhat related in potential application to the SIT scale are methods of quantifying various effects of medical treatment, such as nausea and vomiting (Morrow, 1984) and pain (Jay, Elliott, Ozolines, Olson, & Pruitt, 1987).

THE SELF-INJURY TRAUMA (SIT) SCALE

Patient:_____ Examiner:_____ Date:_____

PART I. GENERAL DESCRIPTION AND SUMMARY OF HEALED INJURIES

Check each type of self-injurious behavior exhibited by the patient. Next, note any physical evidence of healed injuries (scars, permanent disfigurement, missing body parts), along with the specific site.

Self-Injurious Behaviors:

___ Forceful contact with head or face
___ Forceful contact with other body part
___ Scratching, picking, rubbing skin
___ Biting
___ Eye gouging

___ Ingestion of inedible materials (pica)
___ Vomiting or rumination
___ Air swallowing (aerophagia)
___ Hair pulling (trichotillomania)
___ Other:_____

Healed Injuries:

1 _____
2 _____
3 _____
4 _____
5 _____

PART II. MEASUREMENT OF SURFACE TRAUMA

For each area of the body containing a current (unhealed) injury, identify the location and number of wounds, and note the type and the severity of the worst wound at that particular location.

Number:	Score:	1)--One wound 2)--Two-four wounds 3)--Five or more wounds
Type:		Abrasion or Laceration (AL): A break in the skin, either superficial or deep, caused by tearing, biting, excessive rubbing, or contact with a sharp object.
		Contusion (CT): A distinct area marked by abnormal discoloration or swelling, with or without tissue rupture, caused by forceful contact.
Severity:	Score AL as:	1)--Area is red or irritated, with only spotted breaks in the skin. 2)--Break in the skin is distinct but superficial; no avulsion. 3)--Break in the skin is deep or extensive, or avulsion is present.
	Score CT as:	1)--Local swelling only or discoloration without swelling. 2)--Extensive swelling. 3)--Disfigurement or tissue rupture.

(scoring chart on next page)

Figure 14–4 *A Page from the SIT Scale.* The complete scale, as well as a detailed description of its development, use, and potential applications, is provided by its authors, Iwata, Pace, Kissel, Nau, and Farber (1990).

because an attempt has been made to replicate in the consulting room the conditions that exist in the wild; Johnson's reaction to the snake in the laboratory is analogous—though not identical to—his reaction to a snake in the wild.

A problem with such an assessment procedure is the problem inherent in all analogue research; that problem may be stated succinctly in the question, "How analogous are the findings to the real world?" In the present example, Johnson might feel secure enough to warmly embrace a boa constrictor if the assessment was being executed in the environs of a university psychology laboratory. However, it would remain for a "real world" test to see if Johnson's fear had truly been ameliorated as a result of the laboratory experience.

Self-monitoring   If you have ever attempted to stop smoking or lose weight you are probably familiar with the assessment technique of self-monitoring. As its name implies, self-monitoring converts the assessee into an assessor: the assessee carefully records the emission of target behaviors (such as the number of cigarettes smoked per hour or the number of calories consumed in different situations). Self-monitoring-type tasks have also been attempted with other, less overt "behavior" (in the broadest sense of that word), such as thoughts and feelings (Lee & Piersel, 1989). The utility of this assessment technique obviously depends almost entirely on factors related to the competence, diligence, and motivation of the assessee. Additionally, there is a problem of reactivity; if you're on a diet and recording everything you eat—as you should be if you're watching your weight (Cohen, 1979a)—perhaps you will forego the blueberry cheesecake if you know you have to write it down and then have your behavioral diary read aloud by the therapist. As we will see, the problem of reactivity in behavioral assessment and research can be circumvented when so-called unobtrusive measures are employed. Self-monitoring has proved its utility as a cost-effective method of ongoing assessment in many different types of behavioral intervention programs (Kratochwill & Sheridan, 1990).

Psychophysiological Methods

In the broadest sense, certain activity within the body that is observable through the use of special devices—the rise and fall of blood pressure, heart rate, temperature, and the like—may be considered "behavior." The search for clues to understanding and predicting human behavior has led researchers to the study of variables such as heart rate, respiration rate, blood pressure, electrical resistance of the skin, brain waves, voice waves, and pupillary response.

Biofeedback   Biofeedback instrumentation provides a vehicle by which individuals can monitor—or obtain feedback from—some of their own biological processes. This monitoring usually takes the form of visual displays such as lights or scales or auditory stimuli such as bells and buzzers. The stage was set for biofeedback technology in the early 1960s when it was reported that animals given rewards (and hence feedback) for the emission of certain involuntary responses (such as heart rate, urine production, and intestinal contraction) could successfully modify such responses in a predictable direction (Miller, 1969). In some of the early studies with humans, Kamiya (1962, 1968) showed that people with attached electrodes from an *electroencephalograph* (a machine that produces a continuous written record of brain wave activity) could learn to produce alpha-type brain waves on command; the subjects were given previous training in identifying alpha waves by the experimenter, who sounded a bell when their brain was emitting such waves. Since that time, two dozen or so American companies have become manufacturers of biofeedback equipment (Schwitzgebel & Rugh, 1975) offering machines that provide feedback not only to alpha waves, but to other physiological responses as well—muscle tension, galvanic skin response, and changes in skin temperature, for example.

Biofeedback has been used as a psychotherapeutic technique in alleviating unpleasant or unhealthy physiological conditions (such as high blood pressure) or psychological problems. In the latter context, for instance, it has been used as an aid to relaxation in therapeutic interventions where the patient must be in a relaxed state while mentally creating prescribed imagery. Biofeedback techniques may be employed in conjunction with the monitoring of physiological processes to help the patient learn to control body functioning. Although biofeedback as a psychotherapeutic technique is not without its critics (see Blanchard & Young, 1974), encouraging results have been observed with respect to problems ranging from hyperactivity (Omizo & Williams, 1981) to headaches (Satinsky & Frerotti, 1981). As an adjunct to assessment, biofeedback may be used in various ways—for example, as a tool to reduce initial anxiety (via relaxation) or as an aid in identifying the way that psychological conflicts may be related to physical conditions (Sarnoff, 1982).

The polygraph   Commonly referred to as a "lie detector," the *polygraph* (literally, "more than one graph") is an apparatus used to provide a written record of selected physiological responses during a specially devised interview by a polygrapher (also referred to as a polygraphist). Proceeding on the theory that certain measurable physiological changes take place when a person lies, polygraphers claim that they can determine whether the subject is lying or telling the truth in response to a question (or, alternatively, declare the testing to be inconclusive). Is this claim true? Is the polygraph really a lie detector? This is an important question given that an estimated two hundred thousand to a half-million polygraph examinations are administered annually in the private sector alone (Youth, 1986) and given that the consequences of a polygraph examination can be more momentous than the consequences of the administration of a Rorschach, an MMPI, or any other psychological test. In his book *A Tremor in the Blood,* Lykken (1981) refers to the lie-detector industry as "one of the most important branches of applied psychology both in dollar volume and, especially, in its social consequences" (p. 4). He argues that psychologists must learn more about it:

> There is a great body of knowledge and theory concerning psychological testing in that branch of psychology known as psychometrics or psychological assessment, a data base with which only a handful of polygraphers are able to make contact. . . . Psychologists specializing in psychometrics or in clinical psychology know something about the perils and pitfalls of psychological assessment, the factors that diminish accuracy, and they understand how to measure the reliability and validity of a test in an objective and credible fashion (p. 43). . . . Fewer than 0.03% of the accredited psychologists

511

OTHER
METHODS OF
ASSESSING
PERSONALITY
AND BEHAVIOR

in the United States have contributed to the polygraphy literature; it is doubtful that 46 of the 46,000 members of the American Psychological Association know enough about the topic to offer an informed opinion. Yet polygraphic interrogation is unquestionably one of the most important areas of applied psychology in the United States, whether measured as a multimillion dollar industry or in terms of its wide social impact. . . . Perhaps . . . the lie detector now carries a taint of sensationalism which threatens to embarrass the respectable scientist. Psychologists rather should be embarrassed about their ignorance of this important and burgeoning development. (pp. 44–45)

In the Close-up below, we take a detailed look at the concept of lie detection and at the polygraph as a lie detector. As you will see, it seems reasonable to conclude, as others have (Alpher & Blanton, 1985, for example) that the promise of a machine that can detect dishonesty has gone unfulfilled. The American Psychological Association has supported legislation that would outlaw polygraph employee testing, a practice that the Congressional Office of Technology Assessment found to be "undergoing a revival that may surpass the heyday of psychological testing in the 1950s" (Bales, 1987a, 1987b).

Plethysmography   The *plethysmograph* is an instrument that records changes in the volume of a part of the body due to variations in blood supply. Investigators have been interested in determining any changes that occur in flow of blood as a result of personality factors. Kelly (1966) found significant differences in the blood supply of normal, anxiety-ridden, and psychoneurotic groups (the anxiety group having the highest mean) by using a plethysmograph to measure blood supply in the forearm. In another investigation, changes in finger volume by use of a plethysmograph were compared with results on the "emotional-stability" factor of the Bell Adjustment Inventory (Van der Merwe & Theron, 1947; Theron, 1948); those identified as emotionally labile were found to exhibit greater rates of change in finger volume.

A *penile plethysmograph* is designed to measure changes in penis volume during periods of sexual arousal. Freund (1963) developed one such instrument for use in his research concerning differences in penile volume of homosexual and heterosexual males when shown slides of male nudes. On the basis of summed reactions, Freund was able to correctly identify 48 of the 58 homosexuals who participated in the study, and all of the 65 heterosexual subjects. This type of device in variously modified forms, and the subsequent collection of what is referred to as "phallometric" data, has unique value in the assessment and treatment of male sexual offenders (Abel, Blanchard, Murphy, Becker, & Djenderedjian, 1981; Barbaree & Marshall, 1989; Blader & Marshall, 1984; Earls & Marshall, 1983; Earls, Quinsey, & Castonguay, 1987; Farrall & Card, 1988; Freund, Sadlaceck, & Knob, 1965; Laws & Osborne, 1983; Marshall, Barbaree, & Butt, 1988; Quinsey, Steinman, Bergersen, & Holmes, 1975). In one such type of application, the offender—a rapist, child molester, exhibitionist, or other sexual offender—is exposed to visual and/or auditory stimuli depicting scenes of normal and deviant behavior while penile tumescence is simultaneously gauged (see, for example, Malcolm, Davidson, & Marshall, 1985). In one study with rapists, the subjects demonstrated more sexual arousal to descriptions of rape, and less arousal to con-

Truth or Falsehood?

Deception is part of life. Deception has always existed in Nature; in their efforts to survive, living organisms may change form or appearance or behavior in order to deceive would-be predators or prey. And perhaps as far back as the day humans began meaningfully communicating with other humans, a need to determine the veracity of such communications has existed. In different times and in different places throughout the world, society's need to determine the truthfulness of communications has been met through various methods. In most primitive cultures, the methods of lie detection used were not civilized; torture of one sort or another was used to extract confessions. The general rule of thumb when torture was used as a means of lie detection was that the truth teller would not be harmed by the procedure given that he or she was a virtuous person. In Arab cultures, for example, truth was discerned by means of the application of a hot iron to the tongue; the investigators believed that the person telling the truth would not be harmed by the heat.

By current standards, more civilized methods of determining fact or fiction relied on supposed indices of deception such as an inability to look the questioner directly in the eye, trembling, blushing, or a quickened pulse rate. Perhaps one of the oldest of the "physiological methods" of lie detection, one employed by the ancient Chinese and ancient Hindus among others, involved salivary responses. Truth was discerned by means of a test that required only a bowl of rice in the way of "equipment." After having answered a critical question, the person under investigation had to chew some rice and then spit it out; presumably, only the innocent would be able to discharge the rice.

In the light of current physiological knowledge, some basis for the use of lie-detection methods such as the ancient Chinese "rice test" can be discerned. If we grant that the person who was lying was extremely fearful of being discovered, then we can say that this strong emotional state prompted a number of physiological changes to take place. Some of the physiological changes that usually accompany a state of arousal—the state the body is in when a strong emotion such as intense fear or anger is being displayed—include an increase in heart rate, bronchial dilation in the lungs, pupillary dilation, increased sweat-gland activity, and decreased digestive activity. With respect to the latter condition, salivation would be inhibited and the saliva already in the mouth would become more viscid; the person physiologically aroused by having told a lie would therefore be unable to discharge the rice.

In modern times, some of the techniques employed in an effort to discern truth from falsehoods have included word association tests, hypnosis, drugs (so-called truth serums), the polygraph, and voice analyzers.

WORD ASSOCIATION TESTS

The task in a word association test is to respond to a (usually orally administered) word with an immediate association to that word. Sir Francis Galton may have been the first person to experiment with the use of word association tests as a means of lie detection, the rationale being that an individual who intends to deceive the examiner will attempt to mentally censor his or her associations to certain critical words; the individual will therefore take longer, on average, to respond to words seen as "critical" as opposed to words seen as "neutral." Upon retesting, the liar would be expected to change associations to critical words more frequently than associations to neutral words. If, for example, a suspect was under investigation for the strangulation murder of a man named Smith, longer latencies would be expected in response to critical words such as "rope" and "Smith" as opposed to neutral words such as "lamp" or "horse." The point was made by a pioneer in the field of applied psychology, Harvard psychologist Hugo Munsterberg (1918):

> Those words which by their connection with the crime stir up deep emotional complexes of ideas will throw ever new associations into consciousness, while the indifferent ones will link themselves in a superficial way without change. To a certain degree, this variation of the dangerous associations is reinforced by the intentional effort of the suspected. He does not feel satisfied with his first words, and hopes that other words may better hide his real thoughts, not knowing that just this change is to betray him.

Although some preliminary reports using this technique showed it to have promise, it soon became evident that the method was of limited utility. For the test to be of any use at all, the test taker must faithfully follow the direction to "immediately say the first thing that comes into your mind." Since responses could easily be faked and latencies in responding increased to *all* stimulus words (critical as well as neutral), word association tests have not been judged to be a useful method of lie detection.

HYPNOSIS AND "TRUTH SERUMS"

The state of hypnosis is an altered state of consciousness in which mental imagery and thoughts are focused on something suggested by the hypnotist. Although there exist some anecdotal reports of confessions, hypnosis cannot be considered to be a reliable way of discerning truth; not all people are able or willing to enter into the deep hypnotic state that would probably be required for the dramatic confession to materialize, and the individual with something to hide could be expected to resist. Further, rather than entering into a bona fide hypnotic state, an individual intent on deception could feign hypnosis

and perpetuate lies while presumed to be in a state of hypnosis. There also exists the danger that some innocent and highly hypnotizable people might confess to something they actually did not do while in this altered state of consciousness.

So-called truth serums such as sodium amytal, sodium pentothal, and scapolomine have not fared much better than hypnosis as a means of lie detection. These drugs render the subject semiconscious, and what results are soft-spoken (sometimes to the point of being garbled and unintelligible) verbalizations that are presumed by advocates of the technique to be uncensored truths—even unconscious material brought to consciousness. But even groggy people are capable of making up stories. Further, people placed into such a state may be even more apt than the fully conscious person to let their fantasies run rampant. The search for the perfect lie-detection method has therefore had to move forward beyond the level of a syringe.

THE POLYGRAPH

As early as the late 1800s Cesare Lombroso, an Italian criminologist, experimented with the use of a plethysmograph (an apparatus designed to provide a continuous record of pulse rate and blood volume—similar to one channel of a polygraph) as a means of lie detection. The approach would subsequently be refined by William Moulton Marston, a student of Munsterberg's at Harvard who acted on his teacher's call for the application of the techniques of experimental psychology to the forensic field (see Figure 1). Marston's work inspired others, and what has evolved is the modern polygraph and various techniques for its use.

Specific instrumentation on polygraphic equipment may vary, but typically these instruments contain three sensors: one for monitoring respiration, one for monitoring galvanic skin response, and one for monitoring blood volume

Truth or Falsehood? (continued)

Figure 1 *Dr. and Mrs. William Marston Demonstrate a Lie Detector Test in 1938.* Marston, a psychologist/attorney, claimed to have the ability to discern truth from falsehoods with his machine, and it was he who coined the term "lie detector" (Marston, 1938). In reading about Marston, one gets a picture of a colorful, imaginative, commercial-minded individual. Lykken (1981) informs us that Marston appeared with his machine in print advertising for razor blades, and he was featured in a 1938 article in *Look Magazine* where readers were informed how the polygraph might be employed in comparing a husband's response to two kisses—one from his wife and one from an attractive stranger. In addition to all of his other accomplishments, under the pen name of "Charles Moulton," William Moulton Marston was the creator of the "Wonder Woman" character.

and pulse rate. As the subject responds with "yes" or "no" answers to a series of questions posed by the polygrapher, the machine produces a continuous written record of physiological changes that occurred during questioning. This written record (variously referred to as "tracing," "graphs," "charts," or the "polygram") provides a basis for the polygrapher's judgment concerning the subject's honesty in responding. The judgment might be made by informally "eyeballing" the graphs or, more formally, by means of a numerical scoring system.

Prior to the actual examination, the polygrapher may collect and review data pertinent to the subject matter at hand and interview the person to be tested. The interview serves as a means of establishing a rapport with the test taker and it also provides the polygrapher the opportunity to obtain more background information. Additionally, this pretest exposure to the test taker provides the examiner with an opportunity to informally assess the vocabulary and communication skills of the test taker so that the questions used in testing can be devised accordingly.

Different methods of conducting polygraph tests exist. In one common method, the polygrapher will ask a number of different types of questions, including those referred to as "neutral," "relevant," "outside issue," and "control" questions. The *neutral* question typically concerns demographic data such as "Is your date of birth June 2nd?" An *outside issues* question may be asked if the examiner suspects that something, such as the fear that some information not relevant to the present investigation will be discovered, may be influencing the subject's response. The outside issues question may be phrased, "Are you concerned that I am also going to ask you about the strangulation murder of Jones?" or, if the questions to be covered have been reviewed by both parties to the test, "Are you afraid that I will ask you a question that hasn't been reviewed?" A *control* question serves to shed light on how motivated the subject is to make a favorable impression on the examiner, and it typically includes reference to some human foible that is (1) unrelated to the testing, and (2) something to which most people would admit.

The use of the polygraph as an instrument of detecting lies in employment screening, judicial proceedings, and other settings has been criticized on a number of grounds. In his book *A Tremor in the Blood,* psychologist David Lykken (1981) critically scrutinizes and ultimately rejects as untenable the very premise that the business of lie detecting (by means of the polygraph, by voice analysis, or other such devices) is based on: the notion that there exists a specific lie response—"a distinctive, involuntary, bodily reaction that everyone produces when lying but never when telling the truth" (p. 55). Lykken also rejected as inappropriate the statistical analyses of another psychologist (and attorney), Stanley Abrams (1977), who argued for the validity of polygraphy. Lykken (1981) expressed a great deal of skepticism about claims made by polygraph proponents in general, most of which are in nonrefereed publications and based on unscientific studies:

> For someone attempting, as I am here, a fair and reasonably comprehensive critical survey of this literature, the vast bulk of which has not had such preliminary screening, this situation is a kind of nightmare. I would expect that anyone with a scientific background who attempted to read critically all 1700 references cited in Ansley and Horvath's bibliography of polygraphy, *Truth and Science,* might risk serious psychiatric consequences. (p. 44)

Claims being made for the efficacy of polygraphy are particularly frustrating for the psychologist when one notes the relatively uncritical acceptance and receptivity such claims enjoy in the eyes of the general public:

> If we administer the MMPI to 100 schizophrenic patients and to 100 random citizens off the street, then ask an expert psychologist to tell us which MMPI profiles had been produced by the patients and which by the healthy people, he will be correct about 80% of the time. If I now announce to my scientific colleagues that I have invented a new test that can identify schizophrenia with 90% or 95% accuracy, my colleagues will be interested—but skeptical. I would be expected to support my assertions with experimental evidence and that evidence would be very critically examined. Even if my proofs withstood such scrutiny, many would reserve judgment until an independent investigator had confirmed my findings. All this skepticism about a claim that my new test can distinguish "crazy people" from normal ones! The tools of the psychologist are not precision instruments; really high accuracy is seldom achieved. Skepticism is appropriate.
>
> Nevertheless, when the polygrapher announces that his psychological test can separate liars from the truthful with a validity of 90%, or 95%, or even 99%, the typical reaction is a kind of marveling acceptance. The critic who questions these claims is greeted with surprise and skepticism. Nearly every American has heard of the lie detector; without really knowing what is involved, many assume that it is nearly infallible. So deeply ingrained is that mystique that, gradually over the past 50 years, the burden of proof has somehow shifted to the critic. (Lykken, 1981, pp. 80–81)

Instrumentation used in polygraphy is not standardized (Skolnick, 1961). Even Abrams (1977), a proponent of the polygraph, has noted that while machines equipped with three sensors (described earlier) are used by most polygraphers, "there are several others that are available and used by a relatively small number of examiners" (p. 54).

Focusing on the role of the examiner in the process of polygraphy, it would appear that

Truth or Falsehood? (continued)

these individuals have a great deal of input—perhaps more input than many polygraphers realize—as to the outcome of a test. Abrams (1977) repeatedly asserts how essential it is for the polygrapher to be well trained, experienced, ethical, and competent; for even slight nuances of the examiner's behavior may influence the resulting charts. The examiner must be able to "direct the fears of the innocent to the control items and the concerns of the guilty toward the critical questions" (p. 109). The examiner must be able to remain impartial to nontest accounts of the investigation, such as sometimes impassioned accounts of what happened in a crime by witnesses or police. Impartiality is important because the polygrapher "can unconsciously make his opinion known to the examinee and affect him accordingly. Any added emphasis upon the relevant questions in the form of inflection or loudness could result in a greater reaction to those items because of those factors rather than deception." (p. 45). Elsewhere Abrams (1977) continues, "it would be a simple matter to produce charts so that they would appear deceptive or nondeceptive. The inflection used when presenting a question would be sufficient to cause a reaction that resembles a deceptive response. Even questioning a subject between tests on only the relevant questions will give him the feeling that he is doing poorly on these items and increase his concerns and therefore his reactions to them. The opposite effect would occur if the emphasis were placed on the controls" (p. 152).

Use of the polygraph is deemed inappropriate with subjects who are mentally retarded or psychotic. Further, transient internal states such as pain, fatigue, or intoxication may seriously bias polygraph data. Thus, in addition to being an ethical, honest person, a trained observer, a skillful interviewer, and a competent interpreter of polygrams, the polygrapher must also be prepared to recognize and exclude from testing subjects for whom the testing would be invalid on medical, psychological, or other grounds. It would seem that much is expected, required, and demanded from individuals who may have had no other formal training in such matters other than six weeks or so of classroom instruction at polygraph school.

A problem with polygraphy discussed by Kleinmuntz and Szucko (1984) is the problem of false positives; test results that indicate that a person is lying when in reality the person is telling the truth. These researchers estimated that false-positive judgments "may label more than 50% of the innocent subjects as guilty" (p. 774). Others (such as Lykken, 1981; Alpher & Blanton, 1985) have also criticized the use of the polygraph with respect to related psychometric considerations.

Polygraph data have been ruled inadmissible in many jurisdictions on a variety of grounds, including those having to do with the reliability and standardization of the instrument itself, the validity of the theories on which the procedure rests, and the competence of polygraphers. In some jurisdictions, testimony based on a polygraph test can be admitted into evidence only under certain conditions, such as if both sides agree that they would like the results entered into evidence. Polygraph tests have been used frequently in employment selection, especially by large retailers as part of loss prevention programs. They have also been used as part of pre-employment selection procedures. The Employee Polygraphy Protection Act of 1988, however, prohibited the use of the polygraph in employment selection. In many cases, paper-and-pencil tests designed to measure traits associated with desirable employee characteristics have been developed. These so-called honesty tests, discussed in Chapter 18, are in many respects as controversial as the instruments they would replace.

senting sex stories than did control subjects (Quinsey, Chaplin, & Upfold, 1984). Offenders who continue to deny deviant sexual object choices may be confronted with the findings from such studies as a means of compelling them to speak more openly about their thoughts and behavior (Abel, Rouleau, & Cunningham-Rathner, 1986).

Researchers in this area have cautioned that it may be misleading to rely exclusively on phallometric data for the purposes of understanding sexual preferences; such data must ideally be complemented by other data such as interviews (Haywood, Grossman, & Cavanaugh, 1990). Legal and ethical issues that attend the use of plethysmography have been discussed by Travin, Cullen, & Melella (1988).

Pupillary responses Another involuntary physiological response upon which some researchers have sought to make inferences about psychological functioning is the response of the eye's pupil (the part of the eyeball through which light enters). Referred to as "pupillometrics," the research conducted pertains to changes that occur in the pupil in response to a variety of personality aspects (Hess, 1972; Janisse, 1973; Goldwater, 1972). Among the dimensions found to affect the functioning of the pupil are interests, attitudes, and preferences (Hess, 1965; Hess & Polt, 1960, 1964, 1966). Some investigators have attempted to identify differences in the pupillary responses of different diagnostic groups (Rubin, 1974). Other investigators have applied pupillometrics to psychotherapeutic research. For example, in his work with alcoholics, Kennedy (1971) found that those patients nearing completion of treatment whose pupils dilated in response to their favored alcoholic beverage had a higher rate of recidivism than did those patients who exhibited decreased pupil dilation. Pupillometrics have also been employed to assess consumer preferences—with dubious results (see Chapter 19).

Other Behavioral Measures

Self-report Verbal self-report, a commonly used technique in traditional approaches to assessment, is also very much a part of the behavioral assessor's tools. Verbal behavior is, after all, behavior, and is therefore amenable to behavioral assessment. Moreover, as Tasto (1977) put it:

> in the realm of clinical practice, *the operational criteria for the existence of problems are self-report verbalizations.* . . . Therapeutic intervention is considered to be progressing to the extent that the patient (and others who may be involved) report that things are better. (p. 154)

Unobtrusive measures Another class of measures referred to by Webb, Campbell, Schwartz, and Sechrest (1966) as *unobtrusive measures* are nonreactive and do not require a willing patient or research subject. In the words of Webb et al., these are measures that "do not require the cooperation of a respondent and that do not themselves contaminate a response" (p. 2). The length of a nailbiter's nails might be used by a clinician as an unobtrusive or nonreactive measure of anxiety; the client's verbalizations may express a bright picture and may verbalize that all is well, but the nails may speak to the contrary (allowance must be made

517

OTHER
METHODS OF
ASSESSING
PERSONALITY
AND BEHAVIOR

for manicures and other possible confounding variables here). In a book that was almost entitled *The Bullfighter's Beard*,[3] Webb et al. (1966, p. 2) listed numerous examples of unobtrusive measures, including the following:

- The degree of fear induced by a ghost-story-telling session can be measured by noting the shrinking diameter of a circle of seated children.
- Popularity of a museum exhibit can be measured by examination of the erosion of the floor around it relative to the erosion of other exhibits.
- Amount of whiskey consumption in a town can be measured by counting the number of empty bottles in ashcans.
- The effect of the introduction of television into a community can, among other ways, be assessed by examining library book withdrawal records.

In general, the case was made that unobtrusive measures such as physical traces and records were underutilized measurement techniques that could usefully complement other research techniques such as interviews and questionnaires. In at least one research study, referred to by its authors as a "garbology analysis" (Cote, McCullough, & Reilly, 1985), one of the unobtrusive (?!) dependent measures employed was subjects' garbage.

Role play—acting a particular role in a simulated situation—can be a technique used in teaching and therapy. Police departments, for example, routinely prepare rookies for emergency situations by having them play roles—such as that of an officer confronted by a criminal holding a hostage at gunpoint. A therapist might use role play to help a feuding couple avoid hurtful shouting matches and to learn more effective methods of conflict resolution. Role play may also be used as an assessment technique. For example, part of the prospective police officer's final exam may be successful performance of role-playing tasks. And a couple's successful resolution of role-played issues may be one of a therapist's criteria for terminating therapy.

A large and growing literature exists on role play as a method of assessment (see, for example, Becker & Heimberg, 1988; Bellack, 1983; Bellack, Hersen, & Lamparski, 1979; Helzel & Rice, 1985; Higgins, Alonso, & Pendleton, 1979; Wessberg, Mariotto, Conger, Conger, & Farrell, 1979). In general, role play can provide a relatively inexpensive and highly adaptable means for assessing various behavior potentials; we say "potentials" because of the uncertainty that role-played behavior will be elicited in a naturalistic situation (Kern, Miller, & Eggers, 1983; Kolotkin & Wielkiewicz, 1984).

To explore the social skills of psychiatric patients as compared to those of nonpatient controls, for example, Bellack, Morrison, Mueser, Wade, and Sayers

---

3. Webb et al. (1966) explained that the provocative, if uncommunicative, title *The Bullfighter's Beard* was a "title drawn from the observation that toreadors' beards are longer on the day of the fight than on any other day. No one seems to know if the toreadors' beard really grows faster that day because of anxiety or if he simply stands further away from the blade, shaking razor in hand. Either way, there were not enough American afficionados to get the point." (p. v). The title they finally settled on was *Unobtrusive Measures: Nonreactive Research in the Social Sciences*.

(1990) employed a role-play test, videotaped on a living room–type "set." After enacting two practice scenes, the subjects were presented with 12 social encounter–type scenes to which they had to react. The investigators described one such sample scene involving the subject and a "confederate" (in research, someone working with the experimenter):

> in one scene the subject is home watching television and someone walks in and changes the channel, saying "let's watch this instead." If the subject demurred [objected], the confederate said, "You always get to watch your show. Now let's watch mine instead." If the subject complied with the original prompt, the confederate said, "Movies are really much better." (pp. 249–250)

The videotaped interactions were subsequently rated on a number of variables and the data were analyzed. It was found that role play not only discriminated between patient and nonpatient groups but also between diagnostic groups of patients. The authors acknowledged that, "The ultimate validity criterion for any laboratory- or clinic-based assessment is unobtrusive observation of the target behavior in the community" (p. 253). However, the inability, inconvenience, or expense of such observations may lead investigators to role-play techniques in the first place. Bellack et al. (1990) suggest that role play as an assessment technique has diagnostic applications and can be used to identify specific strengths and weaknesses. It may even have application one day as a technique to assess psychiatric patients' readiness for return to the community. What do you think?

Issues in Behavioral Assessment

One issue, not unique to behavior assessment methods, is what we might term the issue of definition—how to define the targeted behavior well enough so that it is both meaningful and measurable. Suppose, for example, that you wished to behaviorally assess newly released inmates of a juvenile house of detention for aggressive behavior. How would you define *aggression?* Would your definition and/or criteria of "aggressive behavior" be the same—and if not, how would it differ—from the way that you would define "aggressive behavior" on the part of the officers and detectives of your municipal police department? the current members of the National Hockey League? the top 1% in the country life insurance salespeople? the winner and runner-ups in the last running of the Indianapolis 500? the pilot with the most "kills" in the Persian Gulf War? United States senators on the Judiciary Committee who interviewed Judge Clarence Thomas, Anita Hill, and other witnesses in the Thomas confirmation hearings? One may speak of aggressive behavior in many contexts, including, for example, criminal, noncriminal, managerial, political, and familial contexts. And as you can begin to see, "aggressive behavior" may have vastly different meanings depending on the context in which it is considered; an important first step in behavioral assessment, then, is to specify clearly the context, meaning, and method of measurement for whatever behavior is being assessed.

Having developed what you believe to be is a solid foundation for behavioral assessment—that is, a sound definition of what it is you will be measuring—the next step is to demonstrate that what you wish to measure can in fact be reliably measured. To do that, you may employ one or more of the techniques described in Chapter 5, such as the split-half method if you have developed a paper-and-pencil behavioral scale, or estimates of inter-rater reliability if you have developed a measure that requires behavioral observation. In the latter situation, many potential pitfalls await. Training behavioral observers so that they can agree some agreed on percentage of the time on what has been observed and how to record it may seem easier to accomplish than it typically is in practice. For example, teaching professionals how to use the behavior observation and coding system of The Marital Interaction Coding System "takes two to three months of weekly instruction and practice to learn how to use its 32 codes" (Fredman & Sherman, 1987, p. 28). Borman and Hallam (1991) studied human observation accuracy using jet engine mechanics watching a videotape of mechanics installing a jet engine; these investigators concluded, in part, that "even relatively simple human-evaluation tasks have a substantial subjective component" (p. 17). Various strategies for dealing with this "substantial subjective component," that is, for reducing measurement error, have been proposed. For example, Tsujimoto, Hamilton, and Berger (1990) propose that such error could be reduced by the computation of a "composite judge," an averaging of multiple judgments.

The reliability and validity of behavioral observation hinge directly on the accuracy of the report by the behavioral observer and the extent to which observer bias enters into the reporting. There may be one or more observers, each with his or her own biases concerning variables such as the assessee, the purpose of the assessment, and the judgments to be made. Some types of observer bias may be prevented by careful training of observers to the point that they agree on what they are to observe and how they are to go about it. However, other types of bias do not practically or readily lend themselves to remedy. For example, in behavioral observation involving the use of videotape equipment, it would on many occasions be advantageous if multiple cameras and recorders could be used to cover various angles of the ongoing action, to get close-ups, and so forth. The practicality of the situation in terms of economics (let alone other factors such as the limited engineering skills on the part of the clinician using such equipment) is that more than one camera in a fixed position recording the action is seldom feasible. The camera in a sense is "biased" in that one fixed position, because in many instances it is recording information that may be quite different from the information that would have been obtained had it been placed in another position—or if multiple recordings were being made. The practicality of most such situations, however, mandates the use of one recording of the action.

Another factor that must be recognized and dealt with in behavioral measurement has to do with a particular type of rating error behavioral raters can make, one referred to as a "contrast effect." To understand what this is, think of yourself as a behavioral rater of professorial performance; during the course of one day of classes, you are going to rate each of the class lectures you are exposed to on a number of variables such as how informative and how thought-provoking you thought it was. At one point in the day, perhaps it is just after lunch, you sit through what you rate as the world's worst lecture—it took a great deal of effort to stay awake and mark the rating scale! Your next class features a lecture which, under other circumstances, you probably would have rated only "average"; however, in contrast to the previous lecture, this one seems so much better that you rate it "excellent." Here, a contrast effect has occurred.

Stated informally, a contrast effect might be termed an error of "unfair comparison" or "shifting standards." Stated formally, a *contrast effect* occurs when "the magnitude of a rating assigned to behavioral stimuli is contrasted away from the level observed in the same context or a preceding context" (Maurer & Alexander, 1991, p. 3). How important are contrast effects? They can be very important and have a great impact on the findings. They have been observed in interview situations (Kopelman, 1975; Schuh, 1978; Wexley, Sanders, & Yukl, 1973), in performance evaluations in laboratory settings (Murphy, Balzer, Lockhart, & Eisenman, 1985; Smither, Reilly, & Buda, 1988), and in field performance evaluations (Grey & Kipnis, 1976; Ivancevich, 1976). In one study, 80% of the total variance could be explained by contrast effects (Wexley, Yukl, Kovacs, & Sanders, 1972).[4]

Reactivity is another possible limitation inherent in behavioral observation techniques. This term refers to the fact that people react differently in experimental as opposed to natural situations; microphones, cameras, and one-way mirrors may themselves alter the observed behavior. Some patients may attempt, for example, to minimize the amount of psychopathology they are willing to record for posterity whereas others may exaggerate it. Illustrations of reactivity are probably quite familiar to you; even the most unruly child in the classroom can manage to appear angelic when the school principal is seated in the back with a pad and pencil. One possible solution to the problem of reactivity is the use of hidden observers and/or clandestine recording techniques, though such methods raise serious ethical issues. Many a time all that is required to solve the problem is an adaptation period in which the people being observed are given some time to adjust to the idea of observation. They soon pay little attention to the observer and/or the recording device. Most clinicians are aware from personal experience that a tape recorder in the therapy room might put off some patients at first but in only a matter of minutes, the chances are good that it will be ignored.

One final issue that we will consider with respect to behavioral measures is one that may be referred to as the issue of *generalizability:* how generalizable are the findings? When we find on the basis of laboratory or field observation of behavior, for example, that a child meets specified criteria for being considered "hyperactive," or that an adolescent's behavior meets our criteria for being termed "aggressive," or that a couple meets our criteria for being termed "argumentative"—how generalizable are such findings to other contexts? This issue is a complicated one and one that mirrors some of the same types of questions raised when we considered the cross-situational application of traits and states. Perhaps it is, as Funder and Colvin (1991) among others have noted, that behavior elicited or triggered by specific situational stimuli are not likely to occur across a broad range of situations. For example, a sales executive eager to impress a prospective account may welcome the opportunity to engage in the behavior of "picking up

4. Detailed discussion of contrast and related effects, as well as ways to avoid them, may be found in a number of sources (for example, Bernardin & Buckley, 1981; Latham, Wexley, & Pursell, 1975; Maurer & Alexander, 1991; Pulakos, 1986; and Wexley, Sanders, & Yukl, 1973).

the check and paying for the dinner" at a posh restaurant. Yet the executive might dread the thought of engaging in that same behavior when the fellow diners at the table are, not prospective accounts, but the in-laws along with their nine children.[5]

Having gained at least an acquaintance with the theory of psychological testing and assessment and with some of the major instruments and techniques used, we are ready to proceed to Part 5 and to take a more detailed look at how theory is put into practice in various areas.

---

5. More detailed discussion of the generalizability as well as related issues in behavioral assessment can be found in numerous sources, such as Bellack and Hersen (1988), Cone and Hawkins (1977), Goldberg (1978), Hersen and Bellack (1988), Jackson (1982), Kuncel and Fiske (1974), Mash and Terdal (1988), Shapiro and Kratochwill (1988), and Wicklund and Koller (1991).

TESTING AND
ASSESSMENT
IN ACTION

Chapter 15

Clinical and Counseling

Assessment

CLINICAL PSYCHOLOGY IS that branch of psychology that has as its primary focus the prevention, diagnosis, and treatment of abnormal behavior. Clinical psychologists receive training in psychological assessment and in psychotherapy and are employed in hospitals, public and private mental health centers, independent practice, and academia. Like clinical psychology, counseling psychology is a branch of psychology that is also concerned with the prevention, diagnosis, and treatment of abnormal behavior; but its province tends to be the less severe behavior disorders and the "everyday problems in living" (such as marital and family communication problems, career decisions, and difficulties with school study habits). Although counseling psychologists work in a variety of settings, most are employed by schools, colleges, and universities, where they teach and/or work in the school counseling center. The distinction between clinical and counseling psychology is sometimes blurred by the overlap of the domains, but it is fair to say that clinical psychologists are more apt to focus their research and treatment efforts on the more severe forms of behavior pathology; members of both fields have in common the objective of fostering personal growth. Toward that end, both clinical and counseling psychologists may use many of the same tools in the process of assessment—the interview, psychological tests, the case history, and behavioral measures. Counseling psychologists are most apt to employ psychological tests when the presenting problem involves a career choice decision

(Fee, Elkins, & Boyd, 1982; Watkins & Campbell, 1989; Watkins, Campbell, & McGregor, 1988).

Tests have many uses in clinical settings, though they are perhaps most typically used as diagnostic aids and in researching pre- and posttreatment measures of psychopathology to assess outcome as a result of treatment. You may well appreciate that virtually any of the tests we have covered in this book to this point—ranging from tests of intelligence, to general measures of personality, to measures of self-concept, to measures of cognitive style—would be appropriate for coverage in this chapter, for all have potential application in clinical and counseling contexts. Further, other specialized instruments might be appropriate for coverage here as well (such as tests and assessment procedures designed to measure various personal and social problems related to school, family, and employment). In an introductory text such as this, however, choices must be made as to coverage and organization, and it is important to remind you of that where appropriate.

In the previous chapter, a variety of behavioral measures were introduced, along with discussion of a sampling of applications in clinical and counseling contexts. In this chapter we will look at the interview, the case history, and psychological tests in the context of clinical and counseling applications. The chapter concludes with a look at the end product of an assessment undertaken for clinical or counseling purposes—the psychological report.

AN OVERVIEW

Clinical and counseling practitioners are typically trained in the administration, scoring, and interpretation of individual intelligence tests, personality tests, and other specialized testing and assessment methods. For example, because many counseling psychologists may have occasion to evaluate and counsel individuals regarding potential career choices, one type of specialized test widely used by counseling psychologists is an inventory of interests called the Strong Campbell Interest Inventory, discussed in Chapter 18 of this text. In this section, however, our focus will be more on the nature of assessment in clinical contexts.

Clinical assessment may be undertaken for various reasons, depending on the referral question to be answered. It may, for example, be initiated to provide the clinician (or other parties responsible for treatment) with a clearer picture of the patient's intellectual, emotional, and neurological resources and deficits. Such an understanding is sometimes critical for making the proper diagnosis and/or recommending the best possible course of treatment. Clinical assessment can shed light on the etiology of behavior disorders and can therefore be useful in prevention. In instances where there are questions concerning the suicidal or homicidal potentiality of an individual, clinical assessment data provide a vital supplement to related information (such as court and police records) that will be taken into consideration when momentous decisions regarding involuntary hospitalization—decisions that may ultimately be made by a judge—are made. Clinical assessment data gathered at one point in time can become a standard by which to gauge the cognitive, emotional, and behavioral consequences of some intervening event (such as a course of psychotherapy, a psychiatric medication, or a traumatic event) when clinical assessment data are obtained on the same person at some later date. From the standpoint of basic research, clinical assessment data can be useful in helping to enhance knowledge about various behavior disorders, including knowledge of the evaluation and course of the disorder under various kinds of treatment and no-treatment conditions.

The practicing clinician—whether in private practice, a hospital, or some other setting—may be called on to render a professional opinion on questions such as the following: What is the proper psychiatric diagnosis for this patient? Will this person be able to function in this type of setting? Who should get custody? Is this person competent to stand trial? Why isn't this child doing well in school? Is the insured malingering? What is the extent of emotional damage resulting from this event? Is this individual suicidal? Is this individual homicidal? Can this convict be rehabilitated? Why has this person been unable to hold a job? What is needed for this person to kick a drug habit? Why isn't this person acting "right"? The clinician's tools—the interview, psychological tests, case history data, and behavioral observation—will be indispensable in answering such questions.

From surveys in the professional literature we know that while psychologists tend to express confidence in the value of psychological assessment (Lubin, Larsen, & Matarazzo, 1983; Levy & Fox, 1975), actual usage of psychological tests by clinicians has been declining over the years. According to one survey of clinicians employed in mental health facilities, the amount of professional time devoted to psychological assessment dropped from about 44% in the late 1950s to about 28% in the late 1960s (Lubin & Lubin, 1972). Subsequently, others (such as Glaser, 1981; Korchin & Schuldberg, 1981; Cleveland, 1976) have taken note of what appears to be declining interest in traditional psychodiagnostic testing. Some of the reasons typically cited for this decline include (1) disappointing reliability and validity estimates of many instruments, (2) the amount of time necessary in the administration, scoring, interpretation, and reporting for many traditional tests—time that is not cost-effective—and (3) the rise in prominence of behavioral observation and other behaviorally oriented assessment techniques (Elbert, 1984). Still, the tests used by the psychologists in applied settings who use tests tend, for the most part, to be "traditional" tests. From their literature review of 1980 through 1990 publications regarding psychological testing practices in applied settings, Piotrowski and Keller (1991) concluded that the MMPI appears to be the most frequently used objective personality instrument, the Wechsler scales are the most popular measures of intelligence, and the Bender-Gestalt (covered in the following chapter) is perhaps the most popular measure of neuropsychological impairment. Two of the more popular measures of depression, the Beck Depression Inventory and the Children's Depression Inventory, will be covered in this chapter, as will the Millon Clinical Multiaxial Inventory and the Millon Adolescent Personality Inventory—the latter two tests being among what Piotrowski and Keller (1991) referred to as "noteworthy newcomers" evidencing increasing use in recent years. We begin with another look at the assessment tool you were first introduced to in Chapter 1, the interview—in its many possible forms, the most popular tool of assessment in psychology.

An interview is a technique for gathering information by means of discussion. Except for rare circumstances (such as an individual known to be totally noncommunicative), an interview will be part of every clinician's or counselor's typical individual assessment. In a clinical situation, for example, an interview may be conducted to arrive at a diagnosis, to pinpoint areas that must be addressed in psychotherapy, or to determine whether an individual will be harmful to himself or others. In a typical counseling application, an interview is conducted to assist the interviewee in learning more about himself or herself—the better to make a career or other life choice. Usually face to face in clinical and counseling applications, interviewers learn about interviewees not only from what the interviewees say, but also from how they say it and how, in general, they present themselves during the interview.

The training of most clinicians and counselors has sensitized them to issues concerning the role of the interviewer in an interview situation. Having been interviewed yourself on any number of occasions, you are probably aware that not only does the content of the interview vary from one situation to the next, but the tone of the interview as set by the interviewer may vary widely as well. Some interviewers, by virtue of their manner and their verbal and nonverbal responses to you and what you say, may make you feel relaxed and responsive, whereas others do not. Some interviewers may convey to you that they are "with you" and understand you, whereas others prompt you to feel that they have no comprehension of you or "where you're at." Some interviewers are warm and accepting; others are cold and aloof. Some interviewers prefer to ask open-ended questions (such as "Could you tell me something about yourself?"), and others prefer to pose closed questions—some posed so sharply as to be reminiscent of the Inquisition (such as "Are you now, or have you ever been, a member of the Communist Party?"). In general, the clinician or counselor strives to create an atmosphere throughout the interview that will put the interviewees at ease and will motivate them to answer questions to the best of their ability.

An interview may be wide-ranging in subject matter covered or narrowly focused on a particular area—depending on variables such as the nature of the referral question, the nature and quantity of available background information, the demands (with respect to time, the willingness or ability of the interviewee to respond, and so forth) of the particular situation, and the judgment of the clinician or counselor.

Interviews may also vary with respect to *structure*. A highly structured interview is one in which all of the questions that will be asked have been prepared in advance. An interview with little structure has few or no questions prepared in advance, and the interviewer is free to enter (or not to enter) into subject areas as his or her judgment dictates. The structured interview represents a cost-efficient, quick, uniform method of interviewing when the objective is to screen large numbers of people. In clinical or counseling research, for example, a structured interview provides a uniform method of gauging subjects' psychopathology at both the pre- or postintervention stage; thus the effect on interview behavior of counseling, a new psychiatric drug, or some other therapeutic intervention can be assessed.

One of the many standardized interviews is the Structured Clinical Interview (SCI). Like other such published instruments in the hands of a trained interviewer, the SCI provides a carefully controlled stimulus situation. This interview focuses primarily on the interviewee's observable behavior and responses (in contrast to other interviews where there are many questions concerning the interviewee's history). It consists of 179 items administered orally by the interviewer from an eight-page booklet; the interviewer checks off 1 ("Yes") or 2 ("No") to the questions. According to the authors of the SCI:

> The tone of the inquiry is relatively mild, with stimulus questions which focus on specific content areas relevant for evaluation of psychopathology but that do not insist on detailed disclosures, thus avoiding the effect of pressure. The inquiry is open-ended and somewhat ambiguous, making it necessary for the subject to work out his responses, which thus tend to reflect his own rather than the examiner's idea. . . . The procedure strikes an effective compromise between detail and brevity. . . . The comparatively neutral stimuli used in the SCI are intended to minimize any tendency of the subject toward acquiescence or disavowal. It is, therefore, desirable that the SCI be administered before any more probing inquiries, so as to avoid possible after-effects of reinforcement of such response tendencies. (Burdock & Hardesty, 1969, p. 7)

The completed protocol is interpreted with reference to 10 "subtests" with labels such as "incongruous ideation," "incongruous behavior," and "sexual problems." As illustrated in Figure 15–1, the examiner is, in effect, taking a behavioral inventory while carrying out the verbal interview. Thus, for example, item 53 has little to do with the last question above it ("How is your hearing?"), but it would be checked "1" if at that point (or at any other point in the interview) the patient had admitted to feeling sensations of creeping or crawling over the body. The SCI manual contains detailed administration instructions and scoring criteria as well as information about the instrument's standardization and psychometric soundness. In general, the test has been shown to be sensitive to postintervention changes, with the majority of the test variance attributable to individual differences. Like other self-report measures, the test is vulnerable to examiner effects and patient response sets. The effective use of the SCI requires, as the authors rightly caution, "an examiner who can combine the experimental with the clinical attitude" (Burdock & Hardesty, 1969, p. 5).

Areas that may be covered in an initial, exploratory clinical interview include:

- *Demographic data.* Name, age, sex, religion, number of persons in family, race, occupation, marital status, socioeconomic status, address, telephone numbers.
- *Reason for referral.* Why is this individual requesting or being sent for psychological assessment? Who is the referral source?
- *Past medical history.* What significant events are there in this individual's medical history?
- *Present medical condition.* What current medical complaints does this individual have? What medications are currently being used?

	Yes	No	C 1
33. Says that he cannot make up his mind or that he has difficulty making decisions.	1	0	(68)
34. Indicates that he thinks about committing or feels he might commit some horrible act (e.g., that he might attack or kill someone.)	1	0	(69)
35. Indicates that he enjoys thinking about tragic or horrible events.	1	0	(70)
"How is your mood today?" *("What's your state of mind?")*	/////	/////	/////
36. Indicates that he feels elated or high.	1	0	(71)
37. Mentions that he feels depressed or despondent.	1	0	(72)
38. Mentions that he feels he is getting nowhere.	1	0	(73)
"What is your health like?"			
39. Indicates that he has trouble sleeping or that he requires drugs to sleep.	1	0	(74)
"How do you feel today?"	/////	/////	/////
40. Indicates that he feels tired, sleepy or without energy	1	0	(75)
41. Mentions that he has various aches and pains or physical dysfunctions.	1	0	(76)
42. Reports a motor or sensory dysfunction not confirmed by medical evidence.	1	0	(77)

	Yes	No	C 1
43. Insists that an organ or organ system is diseased in spite of negative medical findings.	1	0	(78)
44. Expresses dissatisfaction with his size or strength.	1	0	(79)
45. Says that a part of his body is inexplicably changing in size or shape.	1	0	(80)
46. Says that his body is decaying or rotting.	1	0	C 2 (36)
47. Imagines that he has a fatal illness or that he is about to die.	1	0	(37)
48. Expresses dissatisfaction with the appearance of his body or part of his body.	1	0	(38)
How is your eyesight?" *"What happens when you close your eyes?"*	/////	/////	/////
49. Indicates that he experiences visual perceptions in the absence of an adequate or appropriate stimulus.	1	0	(39)
50. Indicates that objects or people look unusually large or small.	1	0	(40)
51. Indicates that people or things look weird or distorted.	1	0	(41)
"How is your hearing?"	/////	/////	/////
52. Indicates that he experiences auditory perceptions in the absence of an adequate or appropriate s.imulus.	1	0	(42)
53. Says that he gets creeping or crawling sensation on his body.	1	0	(43)

Figure 15–1 *A Sample Page from the Structured Clinical Interview. (Burdock & Hardesty, 1969)*

- *Familial medical history.* What chronic or familial types of disease are present in the family history?
- *Past psychological history.* What traumatic events has this individual suffered? What psychological problems (such as disorders of mood or disorders of thought content) have troubled this individual?
- *Current psychological conditions.* What psychological problems are currently troubling this person? How long have these problems persisted? What is causing these problems? What are the "psychological strengths" of this individual?

Throughout the interview, the interviewer may be jotting down subjective impressions about the interviewee's general appearance (appropriate?), personality (sociable? suspicious? shy?), mood (elated? depressed?), emotional reactivity (appropriate? blunted?), thought content (hallucinations? delusions? obsessions?), speech (normal conversational? slow and rambling? rhyming? singing? shouting?), and judgment (regarding such matters as prior behavior and plans for the future). During the interview any chance actions by the patient that may be relevant to the purpose of the assessment are noted.[1]

Seasoned interviewers endeavor to create a positive, accepting climate in which to conduct the interview. They may use open-ended questions initially and then closed questions to obtain specific information. The effective interviewer conveys understanding to the interviewee by verbal or nonverbal means; a statement summarizing what the interviewee is trying to convey and an attentive posture and understanding facial expression are some of the ways by which understanding can be conveyed. Responses conveying that the interviewer is indeed listening attentively include head-nodding behavior and vocalizations such as "um-hmm." However, here the interviewer must exercise caution: such vocalizations and head-nodding have been observed to act as reinforcers that increase the emission of certain interviewee verbalizations (Greenspoon, 1955). For example, if a therapist vocalized an "um-humm" every time John Smith brought up material related to the subject of "mother," then—other things being equal—it is conceivable that John Smith would spend more time talking about the subject of mother than would other patients not "reinforced" for bringing up that topic. An interview conducted to determine whether a student has the social skills and maturity to function effectively in a particular classroom setting will vary greatly in content from an interview designed to determine if an accused sex offender is competent to stand trial. Clearly, many types of interviews exist. One type commonly used in clinical settings is the "mental status examination."

The mental status examination   A parallel to the general physical examination conducted by a physician is a *mental status examination* conducted by a clinician. This examination, used to screen for intellectual, emotional, and neuro-

---

1. Tangentially we note the experience of the senior author (RIC) while conducting a clinical interview in the Bellevue Hospital Emergency Psychiatric Service. Throughout the intake interview, the patient sporadically blinked his left eye. At one point in the interview, the interviewer said, "I notice that you keep blinking your left eye"—in response to which the interviewee said, "Oh, this . . ." as he proceeded to remove his (glass) eye. Once he regained his breath, the interviewer noted this vignette on the intake sheet.

logical deficits, will typically include provision for questioning or observation with respect to each area discussed in the following list.

- *Appearance.* Are the patient's dress and general appearance appropriate?
- *Behavior.* Is anything remarkably strange about the patient's speech or general behavior during the interview? Does the patient exhibit facial tics, involuntary movements, difficulties in coordination or gait?
- *Orientation.* Is the patient oriented to person; that is, does he know who he is? Is the patient oriented to place; that is, does she know where she is? Is the patient oriented to time; does he or she know the year, the month, and the day?
- *Memory.* How is the patient's memory for recent and long-past events?
- *Sensorium.* Are there any problems related to the five senses?
- *Psychomotor activity.* Does there appear to be any abnormal retardation or quickening of motor activity?
- *State of consciousness.* Does consciousness appear to be clear, or is the patient bewildered, confused, or stuporous?
- *Affect.* Is the patient's emotional expression appropriate? For example, does the patient (inappropriately) laugh while discussing the death of an immediate family member?
- *Mood.* Throughout the interview, has the patient generally been angry? depressed? anxious? apprehensive? What?
- *Personality.* In what terms can the patient best be described? Sensitive? Stubborn? Apprehensive? What?
- *Thought content.* Is the patient hallucinating—seeing, hearing, or otherwise experiencing things that aren't really there? Is the patient delusional—expressing untrue, unfounded beliefs (such as the delusion that someone follows him or her everywhere)? Does the patient appear to be obsessive—does the patient appear to think the same thoughts over and over again?
- *Thought processes.* Is there under- or overproductivity of ideas? Do ideas seem to come to the patient abnormally slow or fast? Is there evidence of loosening of associations? Are the patient's verbal productions rambling or disconnected?
- *Intellectual resources.* What is the estimated intelligence of the interviewee?
- *Insight.* Does the patient realistically appreciate his or her situation and the necessity for professional assistance if such assistance is necessary?
- *Judgment.* How appropriate has the patient's decision making been with regard to past events and future plans?

A mental status examination begins from the first moment the interviewee enters the room. The examiner takes note of the examinee's appearance, gait, and so forth. Orientation is assessed by straightforward questions such as "What is your name?" "Where are you now?" and "What is today's date?" If the patient is indeed oriented to person, place, and time, the assessor may note in the record of the assessment "Oriented × 3" (read "oriented times 3"). Different kinds of questions based on the individual examiner's own preferences will typically be employed to assess the other areas in the examination. For example, to assess intellectual resources, a variety of questions may be asked, ranging from those of the general information (such as "What is the capital of this state?"), to arithmetic calculations (such as "What is 81 divided by 9?"), to proverb interpretations (such as "What does this saying mean: People who live in glass houses shouldn't throw stones?"). Insight may be assessed, for example, simply by asking the interviewee why he or she is being interviewed; having little or no appreciation of the reason for the interview will indicate little insight (if not malingering). As a result of a mental status examination, a clinician might be better able to diagnose the interviewee, if in fact the purpose of the interview was diagnostic (see Figure 15–2). The outcome of such an examination might be, for example, a decision to hospitalize, a decision not to hospitalize, or a request for a more in-depth psychological or neurological examination.

A number of published mental status examinations are available, including one called the Mini-Mental State Exam (MMS; Folstein, Folstein, & McHugh, 1975)—so called because of its relative ease of administration. Although widely used, especially in the assessment of cognitive impairment in the elderly, the instrument does have its limitations (Anthony et al., 1982). For example, the MMS may lack structure for administration and scoring sufficient for obtaining acceptable inter-rater reliabilities (Molloy, Alemayehu, & Roberts, 1991). There is also evidence that people tested with it who have an eighth-grade education or less are more apt to be diagnosed as suffering from dementia than people with education beyond eighth grade (Murden, McRae, Kaner, & Bucknam, 1991). A number of researchers have cited the need for revision of the MMS.

Other specialized interviews   Numerous other specialized types of interviews have appeared in the literature, and only a sampling of them can be reviewed here. The Diagnostic Interview for Borderlines is designed to distinguish people with the *DSM III* diagnosis of borderline personality disorder from people who fall into other diagnostic categories. Hurt (1986) found this instrument to be useful in distinguishing patients diagnosed as borderline from inpatients diagnosed as psychotic and outpatients diagnosed as personality-disordered, though he questioned the psychometric rationale of the construction of some of the scales. The Schedule for Affective Disorders and Schizophrenia (SADS; Endicott & Spitzer, 1978) is a standardized interview designed to detect schizophrenia and disorders of affect. A recent study with one form of the SADS suggested that this interview may be of particular value in detecting schizophrenia in mentally retarded adults (Meadows et al., 1991). A number of different approaches have been attempted in long-standing efforts to detect psychologically related malingering— the feigning or deliberate exaggeration of symptoms related to mental disorder (see, for example, Davidson, 1949; Greene, 1988; Lachar & Wrobel, 1979; Ritson & Forrest, 1970; Wachspress, Berenberg, & Jacobson, 1953; and Resnick, 1988). One relatively new instrument in this ongoing field of study is the Structured Interview of Reported Symptoms (SIRS; Rogers, 1986; Rogers, Gillis, Dickens, & Bagby, 1991). The authors reported that this interview may be useful as an adjunct to tests such as the MMPI or in situations where a suspected malingerer refuses to take the MMPI.

A *stress interview* is the general name applied to any interview where one objective is to place the interviewee in a pressured state for some particular reason. The stress may be induced in order to test for some aspect of personality (such as aggressiveness or hostility) that might only be elicited under such conditions.

Screening for work in the security or intelligence fields might well entail stress interviews if one of the criteria for the job is the ability to remain "cool" under pressure. Exactly what the source of the stress will be varies as a function of the specific purpose of the evaluation, though disapproving facial expressions, critical remarks, condescending reassurances, and relentless probing are among the interviewer behaviors that have been employed. In order to induce a stressed condition in a neurological examination, the examiner might say something like "You have only 5 seconds in which to complete this task." Then, the interviewer emphasizes the stressful condition by counting the numbers 1 through 5 while the examinee attempts to respond.

In Chapter 14 we referred to another type of specialized interview: the interview conducted after an altered state of consciousness has been induced in the interviewee (by means of hypnosis or a drug). In addition to the use of such techniques in clinical assessment, proponents of the amytal interview have claimed that this method has therapeutic value in treating conditions such as amnesia (loss

---

Figure 15–2 *The DSM-III-R.*

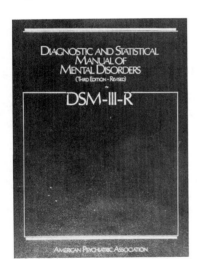

Now in its third edition and revised in 1987, the *Diagnostic and Statistical Manual of Mental Disorders* (DSM-III-R) names and describes all known mental disorders and even includes a category called "conditions not attributable to a mental disorder that are a focus of attention or treatment." A DSM-III-R diagnosis immediately conveys a great deal of descriptive information about the nature of the behavioral deviance, deficits, or excesses in the diagnosed person. Whether for treatment or related purposes (such as general record keeping, insurance reimbursement, or research) mental health professionals frequently have occasion to diagnose patients. Psychological tests and measures may be a useful adjunct to other tools of assessment (such as the interview, the case study, or behavioral observation) in arriving at a diagnosis.

Some clinical psychologists, most vocally the behaviorally-oriented clinicians, have expressed dissatisfaction with DSM-III-R on many grounds, including the fact that it is firmly rooted in the medical model; patterns of behavior are described in DSM-III-R in a way akin to diseases as opposed to a scientific description of behavior. This diagnostic system has also been criticized for being relatively unreliable; different clinicians interviewing the same patient may well come up with different diagnoses. An additional criticism is that even if the "right" diagnosis is made, this system of assessment provides no guidance as to what method of treatment will be optimally effective.

Proponents of DSM-III-R argue that this diagnostic system is useful because of the wealth of information that is conveyed by a psychiatric diagnosis. They argue that perfect inter-diagnostician reliability cannot be achieved due to the nature of the subject matter. In response to the medical model criticism, DSM-III-R supporters maintain that the diagnostic system is useful regardless whether any particular diagnostic category is or is not actually a disease; each of the disorders listed is associated with pain, suffering, and disability. The classification system, it is argued, provides useful subject headings under which practitioners can search for (or add) to the research literature with respect to the different diagnostic categories.

of memory) and posttraumatic stress disorder (Perry & Jacobs, 1982). Claims for the therapeutic value of such interventions continue despite longstanding reservations regarding the efficacy of such procedures (see Dysken, Chang, Cooper, et al., 1979; Dysken, Kooser, Haraszti et al., 1979). Note that because such a procedure entails injection of a drug, it may be performed only by a physician, most typically a psychiatrist, competent and legally entitled to engage in such procedures.

The Case History

As we noted in Chapter 1, a case history is composed of biographical data about the subject. The data may be obtained by interviewing the patient and/or "significant others" in the patient's life. Additionally, hospital records, school records, employment records, and related documents may be useful in piecing together a picture of subjects and at least some of the foundations on which their current life

Figure 15–2 *(continued)*

In DSM-III-R, diagnoses are coded according to five dimensions or axes. The types of disorders subsumed under each axis are as follows:

Axis 1: Disorders of infancy, childhood, and adolescence; dementias such as those caused by Alzheimer's disease; disorders arising out of drug use; mood and anxiety disorders; and schizophrenia. Also included here are conditions that may be the focus of treatment (such as academic or social problems) but not attributable to mental disorder.

Axis 2: Mental retardation; autism; specific developmental disorders, including impairments in academic skills, language and speech, and motor coordination and development; and personality disorders.

Axis 3: Physical conditions that may affect mental functioning—ranging from migraine headaches to allergies—are included here.

Axis 4: Different sources of stress, or "stressors," may be operative in an individual's life at any given time. Financial, legal, marital, occupational, or other sources of stress may precipitate behavior ranging from starting to smoke after having quit to attempting suicide. The presence, severity, and duration of stressors are noted on this axis.

Axis 5: This axis calls for a global rating of overall functioning. At the high end of this scale are ratings indicative of no symptoms and just everyday kinds of concerns. At the low end of this scale are ratings indicative of people who are a clear and present danger to themselves or others and must therefore be confined in a secure facility.

DSM-III-R diagnoses are descriptive and atheoretical; that is,

they merely describe behavior but make no theoretical assumptions regarding its origin. The first two axes contain all of the diagnostic categories for mental disorders while the remaining three axes provide additional information regarding an individual's level of functioning and current life situation. Multiple diagnoses are possible; an individual may be diagnosed, for example, as exhibiting behavior indicative of the disorders listed on both Axis 1 and Axis 2.

Research with DSM-III-R has shown it to be generally reliable, though clinicians are less apt to agree with respect to the Axis 2 personality disorders (Drake & Vaillant, 1985). Perhaps that problem will be remedied in DSM-IV—in preparation at the time of this writing (see Stoudemire and Hales, 1991).

Hopefully, with the refinement of descriptions of the nature and course of various disorders, increasingly productive treatment strategies will evolve.

circumstances might be based. In the rather unique circumstance where there exist factual, published accounts of a biographical or autobiographical nature, this material too might be incorporated into the case history.[2]

Case history data may be invaluable in helping a counselor or clinician gain understanding of an individual, yet as others have noted, "Sources and textbooks on psychological assessment have paid little attention to the importance and value of case history data" (Maloney & Ward, 1976, p. 85). The usefulness, meaningfulness, and interpretability of data derived from other sources such as interviews and tests depend to no small degree on the context in which such data are viewed.

Psychological Tests

Virtually any of the tests we have described so far could be used in clinical or counseling assessment; tests such as the MMPI and the Rorschach would certainly be near the top of the list with respect to use by clinicians. However, clinicians and counselors employ a wide range of tests in their work, and each year brings with it the publication of new tests designed to assist in the identification and/or assessment of various conditions. It is also true that more than one test is frequently used in assessing an individual. The term psychologists use to describe a group of tests used in an assessment is *test battery*. Some of our students have asked what a "battery" is in this context. You are probably aware that the term *batter* refers to a beaten liquid mixture that typically contains a number of ingredients. Somewhat similar in meaning to this definition of *batter* is one definition of the word *battery*: an array or grouping of like things to be used together. When psychological assessors speak of a battery, they are referring to a group of tests administered together for the purpose of gathering information about an individual from a variety of instruments.

The psychological test battery A *personality test battery* refers to a group of personality tests. A *projective test battery* also refers to a group of personality tests, though this term is more specific because it additionally tells us that the battery is confined only to projective techniques (such as the Rorschach, the TAT, figure drawings, sentence completion, and word association tests). In "shop talk" among clinicians, if the specific type of battery referred to is left unspecified or if the clinician refers to a battery of tests as a "standard" battery, what is usually being referred to is a group of tests, including one intelligence test, at least one personality test, and a test designed to screen for neurological deficit (discussed in Chapter 16).

Each test in the standard battery provides the clinician with information that goes beyond the specific area that the test is designed to tap. Thus, for example, a

2. For an example of a case study from the psychology literature, the interested reader is referred to "Socially Reinforced Obsessing: Etiology of a Disorder in a Christian Scientist" (Cohen & Smith, 1976) wherein the authors suggest that a woman's exposure to Christian Science predisposed her to an obsessive disorder. The article stirred some controversy and elicited a number of comments (for example, London, 1976; Halleck, 1976; Coyne, 1976; McLemore & Court, 1977), including one from a representative of the Christian Science church (Stokes, 1977)—all rebutted by Cohen (1977, 1979, pp. 76–83).

test of intelligence may yield not only information about intelligence, but also information about personality and neurological functioning. Conversely, information about intelligence and neurological functioning can be gleaned from personality test data (and here we refer specifically to projective tests rather than personality inventories). The insistence on using a battery of tests and not a single test in evaluating patients was one of the many contributions of David Rapaport (see Figure 15–3). At a time when using a battery of tests might mean using more

Figure 15–3 *David Rapaport (1911–1960).*

Born in Budapest, Hungary, Rapaport specialized in mathematics and physics in college. However, after entering into psychoanalysis, his interest shifted to psychology and philosophy, and he earned a Ph.D. in psychology from the University of Budapest in 1938, the same year he emigrated to the United States. After working for a brief period as a psychologist at Mount Sinai Hospital in New York City, Rapaport moved to Kansas to accept a position as a staff psychologist at the Osawatamie State Hospital. He worked there until 1940, when Karl Menninger offered him a position at the Menninger Clinic in Topeka, Kansas; Rapaport was to be the clinic's first full-time psychologist.

The years 1940 through 1948

witnessed Rapaport's rise to prominence through a number of publications, including his now-classic work *Diagnostic Psychological Testing* (1945–1946), co-authored by Roy Schafer, B.S. [now, Ph.D.] and Merton Gill, M.D. While hailed by many clinicians as a milestone in the assessment literature, the work was criticized on many counts, such as its lack of statistical rigor. By 1960, all of the remaining stock from the numerous re-printings of the book had been exhausted, and the plates used for reprinting were no longer usable. Two publishers were prepared to republish the two volumes of *Diagnostic Psychological Testing* in their original form. However, as Holt (1968) tells us:

David Rapaport had been hurt by the criticisms of the book and had taken them to heart; he realized that many were justified, and he did not feel that he could allow so many undeniable errors to stand in a reissued book; yet he did not have time or inclination to undertake a revision. His own interests and practice had turned toward theory, experimental research, and therapy, and those of Roy Schafer had similarly grown away from testing into psychoanalysis. As for the third member of the original team, though he remained interested in and informed about testing

beyond most of his psychiatric and psychoanalytic colleagues, Merton Gill was clearly not the man for the job. (p. 1)

The person who turned out to be "the man for the job" was Robert R. Holt; Rapaport had spent a sabbatical year at New York University between 1959 and 1960 and had met Holt, who had discussed his ideas for revision. Some time later, shortly before Rapaport's death, Rapaport wrote Holt and asked if he would undertake the revision (which he did).

While at Menninger, Rapaport had been head of the psychology department and chairman of research. In 1948 Rapaport left Topeka for Stockbridge, Massachusetts, and a position at the Austen Riggs Foundation there. Unburdened of administrative duties, he immersed himself in the study of psychoanalysis and produced, among other publications, *Organization and Pathology of Thought* and *Structure of Psychoanalytic Theory: A Systematizing Attempt*. At the age of 49 and very much involved in his work, David Rapaport died in Stockbridge, Massachusetts, while dining with friends. He was survived by his two daughters and by his wife, Elvira, whom he had met on a kibbutz in Israel prior to his emigration to the United States.

than one projective test, Rapaport (1946/1967) argued that a testing would be incomplete if there weren't "right or wrong answers" to at least one of the tests administered; here he referred to a test of intellectual ability. This orientation is reflected in Rapaport's now-classic work in the area of clinical assessment, *Diagnostic Psychological Testing* (Rapaport, Gill, & Schafer, 1945–1946). Ogdon (1982) provides a useful sourcebook of studies from the research literature that sample the various interpretations that can be made from some of the tests typically used in a standard battery.

Beyond the small circle of widely used intelligence, personality, and neuropsychological measures lie thousands of other tests, which vary not only with respect to their frequency of use but also with respect to their breadth of applicability to assessment situations. Following is a brief look at one thin slice of the universe of clinical tests and measures.

Diagnostic Tests

Some tests are designed primarily to be of diagnostic assistance to clinicians and counselors. One such group of tests was developed by Theodore Millon.

The Millon tests   The Millon Clinical Multiaxial Inventory (MCMI; Millon, 1983) consists of 175 true/false items which yield scores related to enduring personality features as well as acute clinical symptoms. Such information may be useful in assisting clinicians to make diagnoses with respect to the "multiaxial" DSM-III and to assess outcome in psychotherapy. A revision of this test, the MCMI-II (Millon, 1987), yields scores for 22 clinical scales (including personality styles and clinical syndromes), and three validity scales. The Millon Adolescent Personality Inventory (MAPI; Millon, Green, & Meager, 1982) consists of 150 true/false items written at a sixth-grade level, and it yields scores on eight personality scales and three "behavior correlate" scales (referred to as impulse control, societal conformity, and scholastic achievement). All of these tests must be computer-scored and cannot be hand-scored. At the foundation of each of these tests is Millon's (1969, 1981, 1986a, 1986b) notion of two primary dimensions of personality. One dimension refers to ways of gaining satisfaction and avoiding stress; the other refers to an overall pattern of coping, which may be described as active or passive. Scores on the Millon tests may be interpreted with respect to these two dimensions of personality, which, in turn, may be interpreted according to DSM-III categories. For example, an individual who exhibits, according to Millon's system, a passive-dependent personality style, may be diagnosed as "dependent personality" according to DSM-III-R.

The Millon tests were constructed and meant to be interpreted from actuarial base-rate data. In practice, this means that raw scores on the scales are transformed into base-rate scores corresponding to known diagnostic prevalence data. A transformed score on any clinical scale of 75 or higher is considered significant and said to "correspond to the clinically judged prevalence rate for presence of a personality disorder or clinical syndrome's symptom features" (Millon & Green, 1989, p. 10). Suppose, for example, you administered the MCMI to the person who sits next to you in class and that person was found to have scored 75 on the Drug Abuse scale. What would this mean?

The by-the-book (or in this case, the by-the-manual) answer to the question raised above might be something like, "I think the person who sits next to me in class is a drug abuser." Such a response would be quite reasonable, especially in light of the fact that Millon (1983) reported that his Drug Abuse scale correctly classified 94% of his sample, with a false-positive rate—that is, a rate of misidentifying non–drug abusers as abusers—of only 4%. Similarly, Millon reported that the MCMI Alcohol Abuse scale correctly classified 88% of his sample with a false positive rate of 9%.

Researchers who have investigated the validity of the MCMI might answer the same question posed above somewhat differently—perhaps by saying something like, "I'm not really sure what that means." In one study that employed known alcohol and drug abusers, only 49% of the alcoholics and only 43% of drug abusers scored 75 or higher on the corresponding MCMI scales (Bryer, Martines, & Dignan, 1990; see also Marsh, Stile, Stoughton, & Trout-Landen, 1988, whose study yielded similar findings). Rates of false positives—that is, scores of 75 or higher in non–alcohol- or non–drug abusers on the corresponding MCMI scales—were 50% for each scale. Moreover, Millon's (1983) claims that the two scales measure independent constructs and correlate insignificantly ($r = -.08$), are at odds with the data from at least two studies, which indicate that a significant positive correlation exists between the MCMI Alcohol Abuse and Drug Abuse scales (Jaffe & Archer, 1987; Bryer et al., 1990). Bryer et al. (1990) noted that the MCMI-II retained most of the items from the MCMI Alcohol Abuse and Drug Abuse scales, and they advised readers that more direct and face-valid measures, such as the Michigan Alcohol Screening Test (Selzer, 1971), might prove a useful alternative to the comparable MCMI scale.

Other independent inquiries into the psychometric soundness and related aspects of the MCMI (Choca, Bresolin, Okonek, & Ostrow, 1988; Choca, Shanley, Peterson, & Van Denburg, 1990; Dana & Cantrell, 1988; McCormack, Barnett, & Wallbrown, 1989; Libb et al., 1990; Overholser, 1990; Wetzler, 1990), the MCMI-II (McCann, 1990, in press; Retzlaff, Sheehan, & Lorr, 1990; Streiner & Miller, 1989), and the MAPI (Pantle, Evert, & Trenerry, 1990; Reidy & Carstens, 1990; Witt, Heffer, & Pfeiffer, 1990) have yielded findings that, taken as a whole, can best be described as equivocal. Suffice to say that additional research into the use of these instruments for specific applications will be necessary before the tests may be used with confidence.

Measures of Depression

Depression is the most common mental health problem and reason for psychiatric hospitalization (Dean, 1985). From 4.5% to 9.3% of adult women, from 2.3% to 3.2% of adult men (American Psychiatric Association, 1987), and from 18% to 35% of adolescents (Clarizio, 1989) may experience depression at any given time. The DSM-III-R criteria for diagnosing depression are presented in Table 15–1. Depression may be diagnosed through an interview alone or through the use of varied other clinical tools (Ponterotto, Pace, & Kavan, 1989). Here we will briefly survey some of the many instruments that exist to screen for depression and explore the nature of an individual's experience of the disorder.

Beck Depression Inventory (BDI) Originally published in 1961 (Beck, Ward, Mendelson, Mock, & Erbaugh, 1961), and twice revised since (Beck &

Table 15–1

DSM-III-R Criteria for Depression

A. At least five of the following symptoms have been present during the same two-week period and represent a change from previous functioning; at least one of the symptoms is either (1) depressed mood, or (2) loss of interest or pleasure. (Do not include symptoms that are clearly due to a physical condition, mood-incongruent delusions or hallucinations, incoherence, or marked loosening of associations.)
  (1) depressed mood (or can be irritable mood in children and adolescents) most of the day, nearly every day, as indicated either by subjective account or observation by others
  (2) markedly diminished interest or pleasure in all, or almost all, activities most of the day, nearly every day (as indicated either by subjective account or observation by others of apathy most of the time)
  (3) significant weight loss or weight gain when not dieting (e.g., more than 5% of body weight in a month), or decrease or increase in appetite nearly every day (in children, consider failure to make expected weight gains)
  (4) insomnia or hypersomnia nearly every day
  (5) psychomotor agitation or retardation nearly every day (observable by others, not merely subjective feelings of restlessness or being slowed down)
  (6) fatigue or loss of energy nearly every day
  (7) feelings of worthlessness or excessive or inappropriate guilt (which may be delusional) nearly every day (not merely self-reproach or guilt about being sick)
  (8) diminished ability to think or concentrate, or indecisiveness, nearly every day (either by subjective account or as observed by others)
  (9) recurrent thoughts of death (not just fear of dying), recurrent suicidal ideation without a specific plan, or a suicide attempt or a specific plan for committing suicide
B. (1) It cannot be established that an organic factor initiated and maintained the disturbance.
  (2) The disturbance is not a normal reaction to the death of a loved one (Uncomplicated Bereavement). Note: Morbid preoccupation with worthlessness, suicidal ideation, marked functional impairment or psychomotor retardation, or prolonged duration suggest bereavement complicated by Major Depression.
C. At no time during the disturbance have there been delusions or hallucinations for as long as two weeks in the absence of prominent mood symptoms (i.e., before the mood symptoms developed or after they have remitted).
D. Not superimposed on Schizophrenia, Schizophreniform Disorder, Delusional Disorder, or Psychotic Disorder NOS.

Source: American Psychiatric Association (1987). Diagnostic and Statistical Manual of Mental Disorders (3rd ed., revised, p. 232). Washington, DC: Author.

Beamesderfer, 1974; Beck, 1978), the BDI is among the most frequently used measures of depression (Ponterotto, Pace, & Kavan, 1989). The test consists of 21 items, each tapping a specific symptom or associated attitude. For each item, test takers circle one of four statements—each reflecting increasing intensity—that best describes how they have been feeling the past week, "including today." Scoring for each item, done by computer or by hand, is on a 0–3 basis, and a total score of 16 or higher suggests the presence of depression.

Studies of this test's psychometric soundness have been generally favorable. Perhaps its greatest drawback is its face validity (Stehouwer, 1985); test takers can handily fake depression, or its absence, if they so desire. Another problem is that a response set may emerge; that is, a test taker might simply choose a particular type of response on each item, such as the extreme response indicative of the most or least depression. Researchers who randomly ordered the alternative statements for each item reported obtaining what they believed to be more accurate scores than when they presented the BDI in its original form (Dahlstrom, Brooks, & Peterson, 1990).

Hamilton Depression Rating Scale (HDRS)   The HDRS (Hamilton, 1960) is used primarily in research settings (Whisman et al., 1989) as a gauge of the severity of depression with persons who are already diagnosed as depressed. The HDRS consists of 21 items, each item rated by a clinician as to the severity of the symptom presentation. A client-completed, computer-administered version of this instrument is being developed (Kobak, Reynolds, Rosenfeld, & Greist, 1990).

Children's Depression Inventory (CDI)   Similar to the BDI, the CDI (Kovacs & Beck, 1977) is a self-report questionnaire containing 27 items, each item consisting of three statements from which one is selected as reflective of how the respondent has felt over the course of the last two weeks. Appropriate for use with children and adolescents, the CDI has been studied extensively (see, for example, Carey, Faulstich, Gresham, Ruggerio, & Enyart, 1987; Kavan, 1990; Knoff, 1990b; Mattison, Handford, Kales, Goodman, & McLaughlin, 1990; Saylor, Finch, Spirito, & Bennett, 1984; Semrud-Clikeman, 1990; Siegel, 1986; Smucker, Craighead, Craighead, & Green, 1986). In general, the test has been shown to be reliable and valid, capable of distinguishing depressed children and adolescents from normal controls. The CDI is less robust in its ability to distinguish children and adolescents diagnosed as depressed from children and adolescents with other psychiatric diagnoses. The factor structure of the test appears to vary as a function of the age of the children and adolescents tested. The CDI appears particularly useful in identifying children and adolescents as depressed when used as part of a multiinstrument battery (Kazdin, Colbus, & Rodgers, 1986).

Other measures of depression   Numerous other measures of depression are available to clinicians and counselors. The Center for Epidemiological Studies (CES) at the National Institute of Mental Health developed its own measure of depressive symptoms in adults, a measure commonly referred to as the CES-D (Radloff, 1977). As explained by Roberts, Lewinsohn, and Seeley (1991), in the context of a study that compared the CES-D with the BDI in terms of utility for use with adolescents:

> The CES-D and BDI were intended to measure syndromal depression (i.e., the symptoms of depression) and not nosological depression, the presence or absence of an episode of depression as variously defined by the RDC, *DSM-III, DSM-III-R,* and eventually *DSM-IV* (Kendall et al., 1987). Since syndromal depression accompanies so many other psychiatric and medical conditions, it may be inevitable that to the extent that a screener measures only depression symptoms there will be *many* false positives. Perhaps this problem can be alleviated by designing a second screening instrument for those who screen with positive results on the first screen. The purpose of the second screen would be to discriminate between true and false positives. (p. 65)

Among the relatively new self-report instruments designed to be of value in diagnosing depression according to DSM-III-R criteria and assessing its severity is the Inventory to Diagnose Depression (IDD; Zimmerman, Coryell, Corenthal, & Wilson, 1986). The IDD has shown promise in research use with psychiatric inpatients (Zimmerman et al., 1986), community samples (Zimmerman & Coryell, 1987, 1988), and college subjects (Goldston, O'Hara, & Schartz, 1990). A self-report instrument not keyed to the DSM-III-R but designed only to screen for depression in adolescents is the Reynolds Adolescent Depression Scale (RADS; Reynolds, 1987). Test takers respond to items such as "I feel happy" or "I feel sad," using the following four-point scale: Almost never, Hardly ever, Sometimes, and Most of the time. Published opinion regarding this test has been mixed. For example, Kaplan (1990) opined that the test adds little to existing measures, while others (for example, Evans, 1988; Kundert, 1990) intimate that the test shows promise as a screening measure.

The primary function of other measures of depression is neither diagnosis nor screening. Rather, these tests focus on one aspect of depression. One such test, called the Automatic Thoughts Questionnaire (ATQ-N; Hollon & Kendall, 1980) focuses only on negative cognitions that may accompany depression. The other side of the coin—that is, positive cognitions that may accompany depression—has been explored via a test called the Positive Automatic Thoughts Questionnaire (ATQ-P; Ingram & Wisnicki, 1988). Both instruments may be of value in exploring changes over time in positive and negative thought in depressed individuals (Ingram, Slater, Atkinson, & Scott, 1990).

Measures of Values

A synonym for the word *value* is *worth,* and when we speak of an individual's "values," we are talking about whatever the individual prizes or believes in. Knowledge of an individual's priorities with respect to values can be helpful in counseling that individual about career choice; if, for example, the individual prizes independence above all, he or she is probably not very happy—and probably not optimally productive—punching a time clock on a 9-to-5 job. Knowledge of priorities with respect to values can also be helpful in making myriad other life choices, among them decisions to get married (or get divorced). How well do the values of the two individuals mesh? This is an important question with regard to the choice of a lifetime mate. And although common folklore—mythology—has it that "opposites attract," any psychologist who has done marital or premarital counseling will tell you that when it comes to values of a husband and a wife, the more similar the better.

Clinicians may find information on a patient's values useful in understanding factors that contribute to or serve to maintain maladaptive behavior. The management of a company—a multinational corporation or a small business—may have certain values to which they would like their employees to subscribe. Educators, especially educators in the private and parochial sectors, may seek to obtain knowledge of an individual's values as one admission criterion. There are many potential applications—within and beyond counseling settings—of data from a test of values. The classic measurement instrument in this area is the Study of Values, and that is where we begin our review of some of the available tests.

The Study of Values   A book published in 1928 with the title *Types of Men* contained the following six categories of people and what they value:

Theoretical—values discovery of truth through empirical and rational approaches; values attempt at order and systematizing knowledge

Esthetic—values form and harmony

Economic—values the practical and useful

Political—values personal power and influence

Social—values love of people

Religious—values unity of the cosmos as a whole

The categorization of values in *Types of Men* (Spranger, 1928) was a source of inspiration to psychologists Gordon Allport and Phillip Vernon, who used it in constructing a questionnaire they called the Allport-Vernon Study of Values. Since its revision in 1951—a revision Gardner Lindzey collaborated on—this questionnaire has been known as the Allport-Vernon-Lindzey Study of Values (A-V-L).

Designed for use with people at or above the second year of high school, the A-V-L contains 45 items distributed in two parts of the test. Part 1 contains items such as the following, to which examinees indicate their agreement or disagreement: "The main object of scientific research should be the discovery of pure truth rather than its practical applications."

Such an item is designed to tap a theoretical-values orientation, and if the examinee agrees with the statement, he or she would earn points in the theoretical-values category. The second part of the test contains 15 four-choice items. Examinees must rank-order the four alternatives into an order consistent with their values. A sample item follows:

Do you think good government should aim chiefly at:
(a) More aid for the poor, sick, and old.
(b) Development of manufacturing and trade.
(c) Introducing more ethical principles into its policy and diplomacy.
(d) Establishing a position of prestige and respect among nations.

If an examinee's rank-ordering of these alternatives matched the order in which they appear, the examinee would earn four points on the social-values scale, three points on the economics-values scale, two points on the religious (also referred to as the "ethical") scale, and one point on the political-values scale.

Revised again in 1960, the A-V-L test manual contains normative data on more than six thousand high school students and 8,360 college students, as well as normative data on persons from a wide variety of occupational groups. In 1968, additional normative data based on a national sample of 5,320 male and 7,296 female high school students in grades 10 through 12 were obtained and published in a revised test manual. Both split-half and test-retest reliability estimates have been computed for the Study of Values. The median split-half reliability coefficient for the different scales was found to be .82; and the median test-retest reliability coefficients based on one- or two-month intervals were found to be .88 and .89 for the different subscales. The validity data presented in the manual are based on the profiles that were obtained from various educational and occupational groups. These profiles were found to exhibit significant differences in ways that would be predicted by the descriptions of the various value types. For example, theological students were found to obtain their highest score on the religious-value type. Scores on the test are plotted on a profile and indicate the examinee's own position relative to each of the values; the scoring is ipsative.

The Rokeach Value Survey   Suppose you were given two lists of gummed labels with a word or term imprinted on each label. Your task: to detach the labels and readhere them in creating a rank-ordering for two new lists that reflects their importance to you as guiding principles. How would you reorder the following lists?

List 1	*List 2*
ambitious	a comfortable life
broad-minded	an exciting life
capable	a sense of accomplishment
cheerful	a world at peace
clean	a world of beauty
courageous	equality
forgiving	family security
helpful	freedom
honest	happiness
imaginative	inner harmony
independent	mature love
intellectual	national security
logical	pleasure
loving	salvation
obedient	self-respect
polite	social recognition
responsible	true friendship
self-controlled	wisdom

If you'd like to know more about what Rokeach says your lists reveal about you, consult his (1973) book, *The Nature of Human Values,* the book that is also the manual for the Rokeach Value Survey (RVS). Reprinted from the RVS, list 1 contains values that are modes of conduct designed to help people get to where they would like to be in life. List 2 contains places or end points where one would like to be at some time in the future. In the terminology of the test's developer, Milton Rokeach (1973), list 1 comprises "instrumental" values and list 2 comprises "terminal" values.

Test-retest reliability coefficients with samples of college students over intervals of from three to seven weeks ranged from .70 to .72 for instrumental values and from .78 to .80 for terminal values. Median test-retest reliability coefficients (with a three-week interval) for a younger sample of seventh- and ninth-graders were mostly in the .60's range. No normative data are included in the test's manual; users of this test develop their own (local) norms.

The Work Values Inventory (WVI)   Would you prefer to work at a job that offers economic rewards, security, or prestige? What would you need in order to be motivated to work hard and to feel satisfied in a job? The Work Values Inventory (Super, 1970) was designed to assess the degree to which individuals value different work-related factors, the rationale being that job satisfaction contributes to job success. The test is designed for vocational guidance use with junior and senior high school students and college and adult populations. The test consists of 45 items arranged to represent 15 areas of values important in determining job satisfaction (such as surroundings, associates, and independence). The items are presented in a Likert-scale format, and test takers indicate the extent to which the statement presented is important to them. The entire test takes only 15 minutes or so to administer. The test manual contains normative data based on a national sample of close to ten thousand students in grades 7 through 12. Test-retest reliability estimates obtained for the WVI based on a two-week interval were found to range from .74 to .88 with a median reliability coefficient of .83. Also presented in the manual are some suggestive findings with respect to the test's concurrence and construct validity. In a study designed to examine differences in WVI scores as a function of gender and job level, the test was administered to a sample of approximately 200 males and females between the ages of 18 and 25 (Drummond, McIntire, & Skaggs, 1978). These investigators reported that, in contrast to the females, males were more apt to value intellectual stimulation, independence, and creativity. Females were found to value the personal work environment (that is, surroundings and supervisory relations) as more important than did the male group. Differences in values were not found to be related to job level.

Other Tests

Literally thousands of other tests are available for use in clinical and counseling contexts. Moreover, as different types of problems in living and psychopathology require greater attention, so different tests and measures can be expected to be created to meet the changing need. Consider in this context, for example, the history of the assessment of posttraumatic stress disorder (PTSD). Although it had long been recognized that war can produce its own brand of emotional distress and behavioral aberrance in prisoners (Bing & Vischer, 1919) as well as veterans and others (Freud, Ferenczi, Abraham, Simmel, & Jones, 1921; Grinker & Spiegel, 1945), the study of PTSD—one possible consequence of war or other catastrophic stress—did not receive a great deal of attention until the Vietnam era. It has been estimated that the war in Vietnam left in its wake nearly half a million veterans suffering from PTSD and an additional 350,000 veterans with partial PTSD (Kulka, Schlenger, Fairbank, Hough, Jordan, Marmar, & Weiss, 1988). Comparable data addressing PTSD among veterans of World War II and the Korean conflict are hard to come by although estimates range from 46% (Zeiss & Dickman, 1986) to 90% (Sutker, Winstead, Galina, & Allain, 1990; see also, Sutker, Bugg, & Allain, 1991). As one group of researchers put it with specific reference to the large number of Vietnam veterans: "Development of reliable and valid diagnostic instruments is essential for identifying these troubled veterans, the majority of whom have not yet received formal psychiatric assistance" (McFall, Smith, Mackay, & Tarver, 1990, p. 114).

Techniques developed to assess PTSD in recent years have ranged from elaborate interviews to psychophysiological methods (Blanchard, Kolb, & Prins,

Marital and Family Assessment

"Are you happily married?" "How does the family get along?" Beyond such general, straightforward questions, how else might you obtain information on the functioning of a married couple or a family? What other questions would you pose? What other methods might you employ?

Stated succinctly, that's the challenge of the would-be constructor of a scale designed to assess aspects of the functioning of a married couple or a family. Through the years, hundreds of researchers have attempted to answer the call to that challenge with sundry different approaches to couple—also referred to in this

context as marital—assessment and family assessment.

MARITAL AND FAMILY ASSESSMENT USING "TRADITIONAL" TESTS

With few exceptions, most of the tests discussed in this book to this point have at least some applicability to marital and family assessment and can yield insights into family relationships, insights that other techniques, including interviews, behavioral observation, and other test data, may ultimately corroborate. For example, verbal responses to various subtests of many in-

Figure 1 Question: Who says the American family is on the decline? Answer: Popular culture as reflected in the form of television sitcoms. Contrast the contemporary Bundy family (that's Bud, Al, Peg, and Kelly seated on the couch) as depicted in the popular series *Married with Children* with the Andersons (that's Kathy, Jim, and Margaret seated, and Betty and Bud standing) of *Father Knows Best* (which was aired nationally from 1954 through 1963). Jim Anderson was a content-enough agent for General Insurance Company, who would typically come home from work, put on his sweater, have dinner with the family, and then proceed to sort-out the day's problems. Al Bundy is a horribly frustrated shoe salesman in a mall, who doesn't know from day to day what he will come home to, though no dinner, no respect, and a heavy dose of life's frustrations are a given.

From what you know of the Bundys, or some other family—even your own—think about the types of responses you would expect to find on the marital and family assessment tools discussed in this Close-up. The next step would be to think about how such data could be used therapeutically to make each of the family members' lives, as well as the family's life as a whole, more fulfilling.

telligence tests (even some nonverbal responses on subtests such as a Wechsler Picture Arrangement task) may yield provocative clues with respect to family relationships. Similarly, personality inventories and other measures of personality may be revealing in this context. One of the scales of the MMPI deals with family conflicts, and the responses to many of the individual items may be further explored for their implications with respect to family issues. Family assessment by means of some situational performance measure is also a possibility. What types of alliances form in the course of solving the problem? How is communication directed? Who is most and least dominant? These are important questions that could be answered in the context of a group exercise and later used as a stimulus to more general discussion and assessment.

Projective measures may provide a wealth of leads to pursue regarding marriage and family assessment. On the TAT, for example, a test administrator interested in focusing on couple or family issues would select cards with a relevant stimulus. For other cards, what would be noteworthy would be the extent to which people designated as family members are introduced into stories, their roles in the stories, and their relationships to the protagonist. The Rorschach, while not typically thought of as the instrument of choice for couple or family assessment, may be adapted for just such purposes (Dudek, 1954; Dudek & Gottlieb, 1954; Loveland, Wynne, & Singer, 1963; Levy & Epstein, 1964). Projective drawing tests such as the Draw-A-Person and the House-Tree-Person are "naturals" for assessment in a couple or family context, as are kinetic family drawing techniques. Other projective measures, such as word association tests, sentence completion tests, and the Rosenzweig Picture Frustration Study, are also capable of yielding valuable insights with respect to marital and family functioning.

Other measures of personality and behavior, such as those discussed in Chapter 14 and elsewhere in this text, may also prove useful in marital or family assessment. For example, a measure of values may yield important clues regarding each family member's worldview. Such an assessment may be particularly important for married couples that do not share the same religion; issues ostensibly related to religion may mask values orientations that typically accompany a particular religious persuasion. A measure of values administered to each member of the couple can help to bring differences to the fore for discussion.

MARITAL AND FAMILY ASSESSMENT USING SPECIALIZED TESTS AND MEASURES

Alongside the more customary measures, increasingly specialized instruments and procedures have been developed to assess marital and family functioning. In the period from 1934 to 1975, over eight hundred marital and/or family measures were in fact produced (Strauss & Brown, 1978). In general, the bulk of such measures can be categorized as being paper-and-pencil inventories, structured interviews, behavior observation systems, projective measures, or other techniques—the latter category including assessment procedures such as family sociograms and genograms. There are inventories and adjustment methods focused on various aspects of married and family life, including adjustment (Epstein, Baldwin, & Bishop, 1983; Spanier, 1976; Spanier & Filsinger, 1983), assets (Olson, Larsen, & McCubbin, 1985), communication (Bienvenu, 1978), feelings (Lowman, 1980), satisfaction (Roach, Frazier, & Bowden; Snyder, 1981), stability (Booth & Edwards, 1983), trust (Larzelere & Huston, 1980), expectancies (Notarius & Vanzetti, 1983), coping strategies (McCubbin, Larsen, & Olson, 1985), strength of

Marital and Family Assessment (continued)

family ties (Bardis, 1975), intimacy (Waring & Reddon, 1983), and overall satisfaction with quality of life with respect to financial well-being, neighborhood and community, and other variables (Olson & Barnes, 1985). What follows is a nonevaluative listing and brief description of some of the available instruments and assessment techniques.

Adult-Adolescent Parenting Inventory (Bavolek, 1984)

Using a five-point scale (Strongly agree, Agree, Uncertain, Disagree, Strongly disagree) with reference to 32 items stating opinions about parenting (for example, "Parents will spoil their children by picking them up and comforting them when they cry"), this test is designed to yield insights about parents' beliefs about child rearing, as well as their expectations and empathy for their children.

Beavers-Timberlawn Family Evaluation Scale (Beavers, 1985)

The test is designed as a structured interview in which a family as a group discuss what they would like to change about the family. The session is videotaped and the last ten minutes of the discussion is rated on dimensions such as "structure of the family" (encompasses questions of power, coalitions, and closeness) and "family affect" (which includes expression of feelings, mood and tone of communications, and presence or absence of empathy).

Beier-Sternberg Discord Questionnaire (Beier & Sternberg, 1977)

How much agreement exists between marital partners on topics such as money, children, sex, and politics? How much of a problem is the amount of agreement (or disagreement) that

exists for each marital partner? These are the types of questions posed directly on this seven-point Agree/Disagree scale and corresponding seven-point Happy/Unhappy scale.

Child's Attitude Toward Mother Scale (Hudson, 1982)
Child's Attitude Toward Father Scale (Hudson, 1982)

Each of these two 25-item tests contains statements about the examinee's mother or father. The wording is virtually identical except for the word *mother* or *father*—for example, "My mother [father] doesn't understand me." For each item, respondents indicate whether what is stated is true on the following five-point scale:

Rarely or none of the time
A little of the time
Some of the time
Good part of the time
Most or all of the time

Each of the tests is designed to yield clinical data about the nature and extent of problems the test taker expresses having with a parent.

Conflict Tactics Scales (Straus, 1979)

Marital and/or family conflict is inevitable. Given that premise, what tactics or techniques do the parties involved characteristically use to resolve conflict? Are the issues calmly discussed? Is someone else brought in to mediate? Is crying, sulking, or the "silent treatment" used? Is a threat or physical contact made? In this paper-and-pencil inventory, both the husband and wife respond to items questioning the number of times in the last year various types of conflict-resolution tactics have been used. Different forms of the test are available to assess conflict tactics as seen through the eyes of husbands, wives, parents, and children.

Family Enviroment Scale
(Moos & Moos, 1981)
The "environment" referred to in the name of this scale means social climate—a gauge of various dimensions of relationship and personal growth within the family. How well do family members get along? How expressive can family members be about telling each other problems? How important to family members are recreational pursuits? religion? How much control is exercised over family members? These are the types of issues addressed. The authors have also developed similar scales for measuring social climate in other systems such as school, work, military, and treatment environments.

Family Inventory of Life Events and Changes (McCubbin, Patterson, & Wilson, 1985)
Changes such as a move, loss of employment, a death, having an unanticipated pregnancy, or starting a new business may prove disruptive in many ways to a family. This 71-item test in yes/no format surveys such changes over the previous 12-month period and yields a measure of how stressed the family is. The data may be of diagnostic value for use with distressed families.

Family Task Interview (Kinston, Loader, & Miller, 1985)
As its name implies, this measurement technique entails observing how a family handles various tasks (such as planning something together, building a tower out of blocks, and discussing likes and dislikes), after which family members' observations are discussed. Ratings are made on a "Family Health Scale," which covers topics such as "Alliances," "Family Competence" (encompassing observations on areas such as conflict resolution and parental management of children), and "Communication" (encompassing observations on expression and reception of messages).

Marital Adjustment Test
(Locke & Wallace, 1959)
This 15-item paper-and-pencil inventory test may take only five minutes, give or take a few, to administer. Respondents are asked to indicate, "everything considered," their degree of happiness with their marriage. They are also asked to indicate how often they agree with their mate on various matters such as financial, sexual, and recreational issues. Some of the other areas tapped by this brief self-report instrument concern leisure-time pursuits, ways of handling disagreements, and willingness to confide in one's spouse. The test was originally published with a scoring system based on weighted responses, though a simplified scoring system was subsequently proposed by Hunt (1978).

Marital Alternatives Scale (Udry, 1981)
This is a multiple-choice, paper-and-pencil test designed to probe the respondent's feelings regarding alternatives to being married—remaining single, getting divorced, and marrying someone else. Data from it may be used to shed light on the question of how better- or worse-off individuals would be were they not married.

Marital Comparison Level Index
(Sabatelli, 1984)
How do spouses feel about their marital experience relative to their expectations? Using a scale

Marital and Family Assessment (continued)

ranging in degree from "Worse than I expect," to "About what I expect" to "Better than I expect," the test taker responds to 32 items, which all begin with "The amount" (such as "The amount your partner is willing to listen to you"). Marital dissatisfaction is presumed to be in evidence where a negative discrepancy exists between expectations and experience.

Parent-Adolescent Relationship Questionnaire (Robin, Koepke, & Moye, 1990).

Based on the behavioral family-systems model of Robin and Foster (1989) that regards "parent-adolescent conflict as a developmental phenomenon of families whose functioning has been disrupted by the biologically driven, culturally mediated striving for independence of the young adolescent" (Robin et al., 1990, p. 451), this self-report inventory assesses problem-solving communication skills, belief systems, and family structure.

Productivity Environmental Preference Survey (Price, Dunn, & Dunn, 1982)

Individual preferences may play a very important role in a couple's compatibility. To better appreciate that, simply take note of some of the many preferences expressed by people seeking to meet other people via personal ads in a newspaper: for example, "non-smoker preferred," "enjoys dining out, discos, and long walks on the beach," and "loves quiet evenings at home." This 100-item test surveys preferences with respect to areas such as the physical environment (addressing factors such as temperature, lighting, and noise level) and the social environment (self- versus other-oriented). The test has potential application not only with respect to home environments but workplace environments as well.

Self-Report Jealousy Scale— Revised (Bringle, Roach, Andler, & Evenbeck, 1979)

On a five-point scale of "Pleased," "Mildly upset," "Upset," "Very upset," and "Extremely upset," how would you indicate you felt if your partner went to a bar several evenings without you? Or commented to you about how attractive another person is? How would you feel if someone flirted with your partner? Or your best friend suddenly shows interest in doing things with someone else? These are some of the types of items contained in this 25-item test designed to measure romantic as well as nonromantic aspects of jealousy. The test has been used as an aid in the counseling of heterosexual as well as homosexual couples.

1991; Lyons, Gerardi, Wolfe, & Keane, 1988; Wolfe, Keane, Lyons, & Gerardi, 1987). The PTSD scale of the MMPI (Keane, Malloy, & Fairbank, 1984) has also been used, although it fails to measure the full domain of symptoms as specified in DSM-III-R. Watson (1990) has reviewed the comparative merits of a sampling of what he referred to as the "large, rather bewildering assortment of post-traumatic stress disorder (PTSD) measuring instruments" (p. 460).

As you may readily appreciate, there are certain areas of specialization within the general fields of clinical and counseling psychology, in which unique types of assessment tools and approaches may be employed or more traditional techniques used in some not-so-traditional way. We now turn our attention to clinical assessment in special contexts.

Forensic Psychological Assessment

The word *forensic* means "pertaining to or employed in legal proceedings," and the term *forensic psychological assessment* can be defined broadly as the theory and application of psychological evaluation and measurement for legal ends. Psychologists, psychiatrists, and other health professionals may be called on by courts, corrections and parole personnel, attorneys, and others involved in the criminal justice system to offer expert opinion on some matter. With respect to criminal proceedings, the opinion may, for example, concern an individual's competency to stand trial or his or her criminal responsibility (that is, "sanity") at the time a crime is committed. With respect to a civil proceeding, the opinion might have to do with issues as diverse as the extent of emotional distress suffered in a personal injury suit, the suitability of one or the other parents in a custody proceeding, or the testamentary capacity (capacity to make a last will and testament) of a deceased person.

Before discussing some of the assessment-related aspects in a sampling of the many areas of forensic psychology, it is important to note that there are important differences between forensic and general clinical practice. As noted by Rappeport (1982), the major difference is that in the forensic situation, the clinician is not serving the patient but a third party such as a court or an attorney, and this fact (as well as its implications with respect to issues such as confidentiality) must be made clear to the assessee. Another difference stems from the fact that the patient is consulting the professional not for therapy but for help in dealing with the third party. There is therefore "a great likelihood that the patient will not be as truthful as he or she would be in other circumstances" (Rappeport, 1982, p. 333). Consequently, it is imperative that the assessor rely not only on the assessee's representations but on all available documentation, such as police reports and interviews with persons who may have pertinent knowledge. The mental health professional who performs forensic work would do well to be educated with respect to the language of the law. As Rappeport put it:

> To go into court and render the opinion that a person is not responsible for a crime because he is psychotic is to say nothing of value to the judge or jury. However, to go into the same court and state that a man is not responsible because as a result of a mental disorder, namely, paranoid schizophrenia, "he lacked substantial capacity to conform his behavior to the requirements of the law"—because he was hearing voices that told him he must commit the crime to protect his family from future harm—would be of great value to the judge or jury. It is not because the man had a psychosis that he is not responsible; it is how his illness affected his behavior and his ability to form the necessary criminal intent or to have the *mens rea,* or guilty mind, that is important. (p. 333)

The forensic assessor may sometimes be placed in the role of psycho-historian, as in the case in which an individual's testamentary capacity has been called into question. Here the assessor may offer an opinion about an individual he or she may have never personally seen—a situation that seldom if ever arises in nonforensic assessments.

The very appropriateness of mental health professionals as expert witnesses in many situations has been vigorously challenged in recent years. Faust and Ziskin (1988a, 1988b) point to the unreliability of psychiatric diagnoses, the unreliability and invalidity of certain tests for specific purposes, and questionable conclusions reached by mental health professionals on the basis of interviewing, testing, and other methods of assessment. The interested reader is referred to the writings of Faust and Ziskin as well as the response of Matarazzo (1990) for a firsthand look at this spirited debate.

Competency to stand trial   "Competency" in the legal sense has many different meanings. One may speak, for example, of competence to make a will, enter into a contract, commit a crime, waive constitutional rights, consent to medical treatment . . . the list goes on. Before convicted murderer Gary Gilmore was executed in Utah, he underwent an examination designed to determine whether or not he was competent to be executed. That is so because the law mandates that a certain propriety exists with respect to state-ordered executions, and it would not be morally proper to execute insane persons. *Competency to stand trial* has largely to do with a defendant's ability to understand the charges against him or her and assist in his or her own defense. As stated in the Supreme Court's ruling in *Dusky v. United States,* a defendant must have "sufficient present ability to consult with his lawyer with a reasonable degree of rational . . . (and) factual understanding of the proceedings against him." This "understand and assist" requirement, as it has come to be called, is in effect an extension of the constitutional prohibition against trials *in absentia;* a defendant must be not only physically present during the trial, but mentally present as well.

The competency requirement serves to protect an individual's right to choose and assist counsel, the right to act as a witness on one's own behalf, and the right to confront opposing witnesses. The requirement also increases the probability that the true facts of the case will be developed, since the competent defendant is able to monitor continuously the testimony of witnesses and help bring discrepancies in testimony to the attention of the court. In general, persons who are mentally retarded, psychotic, or suffering from a debilitating neurological disorder are persons held to be incompetent to stand trial. However, it cannot be overemphasized that any one of these three diagnoses is not sufficient in itself for a person found to be incompetent. Stated another way: it is possible for a person to be mentally retarded, psychotic, or suffering from a debilitating neurological disorder—or all three—and still be found competent to stand trial. The person will be found to be incompetent if and only if he or she is unable to understand the charges against him or her and is unable to assist in his or her own defense.

To help psychologists and other mental health professionals determine whether a defendant meets the "understand and assist" requirement, a number of test instruments have been developed. For example, researchers at Georgetown University Law School (Bukatman, Foy, & DeGrazia, 1971) enumerated thirteen criteria of competency to stand trial and specific questions for a competency screening interview (see Tables 15–2 and 15–3).

According to Bukatman et al., a thorough competency evaluation would entail answers to each of the interview questions listed "with sufficient information on each point to indicate whether there is, or might be in the future, a problem in that area" (p. 1226). Lipsitt, Lelos, and McGarry (1971) developed a sentence

Table 15–2

Georgetown Criteria for Competency to Stand Trial

Factual items

Defendant's ability to:
1. understand his [or her] current legal situation
2. understand the charges made against him [or her]
3. understand the legal issues and procedures in the case
4. understand the possible dispositions, pleas, and penalties
5. understand the facts relevant to the case
6. identify and locate witnesses

Inferential items

Defendant's ability to communicate with counsel and to:
7. comprehend instructions and advice
8. make decisions after advice
9. follow testimony for contradictions or errors
10. maintain a collaborative relationship with his [or her] attorney
11. testify if necessary and be cross-examined
12. tolerate stress at the trial or while awaiting trial
13. refrain from irrational behavior during the trial

Source: Bukatman, Foy, and DeGrazia (1971)

Table 15–3

Georgetown Screening Interview for Competency to Stand Trial

Understanding of current situation
Who is your lawyer at this time?
Have you had other lawyers in this case?
How did you get them?
What is your lawyer's job?
What is the purpose of the judge?
What does the jury do?
What will the prosecutor do?
Since your arrest, have you spent time in jail?
If so, how long?
Have you been questioned by the police?
When? Where?
Did they tell you what rights you have in this case?

What are the charges against you?
What do they mean to you?
Why were they made against you?

When is your trial going to take place?
In which court is your trial going to take place?
Can the judge or prosecutor make you take the witness stand in court and make you
    answer questions?

Since your arrest have you gone before any court or court official?
When? Where? What was the reason?
What kind of official was it?
What was decided?
Did you have a lawyer?
If so, how did you get him [or her]?

Table 15–3 (*continued*)

Georgetown Screening Interview for Competency to Stand Trial

Understanding of current situation (continued)

What is the difference between guilty and not guilty?

If the court should find you guilty, what are the possible sentences in your case?

What do you think will happen? Why?

What does a suspended sentence mean?

What does probation mean?

Cooperation and participation in own defense

What is your plea at this time?

What alibi or defense do you think you have now?

Does your lawyer agree with this?

Why are you going to use this alibi? Defense?

Have you and your lawyer discussed any other alibi or defense that you could use, but don't plan to use? What are they?

Why are you not using them?

What does incompetent to stand trial mean to you?

Do you think there is any reason why you should be found incompetent?

Would you like to be found incompetent to stand trial? If so, why?

Will there be any witnesses against you?

Do you think you know what they might say?

If one of them tells a lie, or makes a mistake, what would you do?

Will there be any witnesses for you?

What have you done to contact them and make sure they will be at your trial?

What have you done to be certain that what they say will help your case?

Has your lawyer been helpful in letting you know about your rights . . . ?

Has there been anything you thought your lawyer could do to help your case which you have been reluctant to ask him or her to do? If so, what?

Is there something about your lawyer that makes it difficult for you to work with him [or her]?

Is your lawyer charging you for his [or her] service in this case?

Have you ever testified before? When?

Describe what happened.

Do you think you have to testify at your trial?

If so, how do you feel about doing so?

What will you do if you are asked a question you don't want to answer?

Source: Bukatman, Foy, and DeGrazia (1971)

completion test (see Table 15–4) that contains 22 items, each of which relates to a legal criterion of competency to stand trial. The test is scored on a three-point scale, ranging from 0 to 2 with appropriate responses being scored 2, marginally appropriate responses being scored 1, and clearly inappropriate responses being scored 0. For example, a 2-point response to the item, "When I go to court, the lawyer will _____," would be "defend me." Such a response indicates that the assessee has a clear understanding of the lawyer's role. By contrast, a 0-point response might be "have me guillotined," which would be indicative of an inappropriate perception of the lawyer's role. Lipsett et al. reported an inter-rater reliability among trained scorers of this test to be $r = .93$ ($p < .001$). They also reported that their test was successful in discriminating seriously disturbed, state-hospitalized men from control groups consisting of students, community adults,

Table 15–4

Competency Screening Test

1. The lawyer told Bill that _____.
2. When I go to court, the lawyer will _____.
3. Jack felt that the judge _____.
4. When Phil was accused of the crime, he _____.
5. When I prepare to go to court with my lawyer _____.
6. If the jury finds me guilty, I _____.
7. The way a court trial is decided _____.
8. When the evidence in George's case was presented to the jury _____.
9. When the lawyer questioned his client in court, the client said _____.
10. If Jack had to try his own case, he _____.
11. Each time the D.A. asked me a question, I _____.
12. While listening to the witnesses testify against me, I _____.
13. When the witness testifying against Harry gave incorrect evidence, he _____.
14. When Bob disagreed with his lawyer on his defense, he _____.
15. When I was formally accused of the crime, I thought to myself _____.
16. If Ed's lawyer suggests that he plead guilty, he _____.
17. What concerns Fred most about his lawyer _____.
18. When they say a man is innocent until proven guilty _____.
19. When I think of being sent to prison, I _____.
20. When Phil thinks of what he is accused of, he _____.
21. When the [members of the jury hear] my case, they will _____.
22. If I had a chance to speak to the judge, I _____.

Source: Lipsitt, Lelos, and McGarry (1971)

club members, and civilly committed hospitalized patients. Subsequent research by independent investigators (Nottingham & Mattson, 1982) further supports the clinical utility of the Competency Screening Test.

Criminal responsibility   "Not guilty by reason of insanity" is a plea to a criminal charge that we have all heard about at one time or another. But stop and think about the meaning the legal term *insanity* has to mental health professionals and the evaluation procedures by which psychological assessors could identify the "insane." The insanity defense has its roots in the idea that only blameworthy persons (that is, those with a "criminal mind") should be punished. Possibly exempt from blame, therefore, are children, mental incompetents, and others who may be irresponsible, lack control of their actions, or have no conception that what they are doing may be criminal. As early as the sixteenth century, it was argued in an English court that an offending act should not be considered a felony if the offender had no conception of good and evil. By the eighteenth century, the focus had shifted from good and evil as a criterion for evaluating criminal responsibility to the issue of whether the defendant "doth not know what he is doing no more than . . . a wild beast." Judicial history was made in nineteenth century England, when in 1843 Daniel M'Naghten was found not guilty by reason of insanity after attempting to assassinate the British Prime Minister (and mistakenly shooting and killing the Prime Minister's secretary). In the words of the court that acquitted M'Naghten, exculpation would be made if "at the time of the committing of the act, the party accused was laboring under such a defect of reason from disease of the mind as not to know the nature and quality of the act he was doing, or if he did know it, that he did not know he was doing what was wrong."

The decision in the M'Naghten case has come to be referred to as the "right or wrong test." To the present day this test of sanity is adhered to in England as well as a number of jurisdictions in the United States as well. However, a deficiency in the "right or wrong test" is that it does not allow for the exculpation of persons who might know right from wrong but are unable to control impulses to commit criminal acts. In 1954, an opinion written by the United States Court of Appeal for the District of Columbia in the case of *Durham v. United States* held a defendant not to be culpable for criminal action "if his unlawful act was the product of a mental disease or defect." Still another standard of legal insanity was set forth by the American Law Institute (ALI) in 1956, and this standard has become one of the most widely used throughout the United States (Weiner, 1980). With slight alterations from one jurisdiction to another, this legal test of sanity provides as follows:

> A person is not responsible for criminal conduct i.e., insane if, at the time of such conduct, as a result of a mental disease or defect, he lacks substantial capacity either to appreciate the criminality (wrongfulness) of his conduct, or to conform his conduct to the requirements of the law.
>
> As used in this article, the terms "mental disease or defect" do not include an abnormality manifested only by repeated criminal or otherwise antisocial conduct.

In clinical practice, defendants who are either mentally retarded, psychotic, or neurologically impaired are persons who are likely to be the ones found to be not guilty by reason of insanity. However, as was the case with considerations of competency to stand trial, the mere fact that a person is judged to be mentally retarded, psychotic, or neurologically impaired is in itself no guarantee that the individual will be found not guilty; other criteria, such as the ALI standards cited, must be met. To help psychological assessors determine if those standards are met, a number of instruments such as the Rogers Criminal Responsibility Assessment Scale (RCRAS) have been developed. Psychologist Richard Rogers and his colleagues (Rogers & Cavanaugh, 1980, 1981; Rogers, Dolmetsch, & Cavanaugh, 1981) designed the RCRAS to be a systematic and empirical approach to insanity evaluations. This instrument consists of 25 items tapping both psychological and situational variables. The items are scored with respect to five scales: reliability (including malingering), organic factors, psychopathology, cognitive control, and behavioral control. After scoring, the examiner employs a hierarchical decision model for the purpose of arriving at a decision concerning the assessee's sanity. Tables 15–5 and 15–6 contain a listing of the scales as well as sample items from the RCRAS. Validity studies done with this scale (for example, Rogers, Seman, & Wasyliw, 1983; Rogers, Wasyliw, & Cavanaugh, 1984) have shown it to be useful in discriminating between sane and insane patients/defendants.

Debate about the reasonableness of insanity as a defense has been a fact of life perhaps as long as there has been an insanity defense (Fingarette & Hasse, 1979; Finkel, Shaw, Bercaw, et al., 1985; Goldstein, 1967; Keilitz, 1987; Lanyon, 1986; Morse, 1985; Reynolds, 1984; Simon, 1967; Simon & Aaronson, 1988; Slobogin, 1985). In recent years, the rhetoric has become even more heated, however, as

Table 15–5

Scales and Items of the RCRAS

Item name		Range	Score
Scale 1. Patient's Reliability			
1 Reliability of patient's self report (voluntary)		1–5	
2 Involuntary interference with patient's self report		1–5	
	Summation	(2–10)	_____
Scale 2. Organicity			
3 Intoxication		1–6	
4 Brain damage or disease		1–5	
5 Brain damage and crime		1–5	
6 Mental retardation		1–6	
7 Retardation and the crime		1–5	
	Summation	(5–27)	_____
Scale 3. Psychopathology			
8 Bizarre behavior		1–5	
9 Anxiety		1–6	
10 Amnesia		1–6	
11 Delusions		1–5	
12 Hallucinations		1–5	
13 Depressed mood		1–6	
14 Elevated or expansive mood		1–6	
15 Verbal coherence		1–5	
16 Affect		1–5	
17 Thought disorder (list)			_____
	Summation	(9–49)	
Scale 4. Cognitive Control			
18 Planning and preparation		1–6	
19 Awareness of criminality		1–4	
15 Verbal coherence		1–5	
17 Thought disorder (list)			_____
	Summation	(3–15)	
Scale 5. Behavioral Control			
20 Focus of the crime		1–5	
21 Level of activity		1–6	
22 Responsible social behavior		1–5	
23 Reported self-control		1–6	
24 Estimated self-control		1–6	
25 Control and psychosis		1–4	
8 Bizarre behavior		1–6	
	Summation	(7–38)	_____

10. Amnesia about the alleged crime.
     (This refers to the examiner's assessment of amnesia, not necessarily the patient's reported amnesia).
     (0) No information
     (1) None. Remembers the entire event in considerable detail.
     (2) Slight; of doubtful significance. The patient forgets a few minor details.
     (3) Mild. Patient remembers the substance of what happened but is forgetful of many minor details.
     (4) Moderate. The patient has forgotten a major portion of the alleged crime but remembers enough details to believe it happened.
     (5) Severe. The patient is amnesic to most of the alleged crime but remembers enough details to believe it happened.
     (6) Extreme. Patient is completely amnesic to the whole alleged crime.

Table 15–6

Sample Items of the RCRAS

11. Delusions at the time of the alleged crime
    (0) No information
    (1) Absent
    (2) Suspected delusions (e.g., supported only by questionable self-report)
    (3) Definite delusions but not actually associated with the commission of the alleged crime
    (4) Definite delusions which contributed to, but were not the predominant force in the commission of the alleged crime
    (5) Definite controlling delusions on the basis of which the alleged crime was committed

attempts have been made at the federal and state level to modify or even abolish existing statutes affecting a defense of insanity. Different insanity defense standards will have differential effects on court findings. Empirical research on how changed standards might affect court findings is currently in an exploratory stage (see, for example, Wettstein, Mulvey, & Rogers, 1991).

Readiness for Parole or Probation

Some people convicted of a crime will "pay their dues" to society and go on to lead fulfilling, productive lives after their incarceration. At the other extreme are career criminals who will violate laws at the first opportunity upon their release— or escape—from prison. Predicting who is ready for parole or probation and what the outcome of such a release might be has proved no easy task, yet this has not deterred psychologists from trying to develop effective measures.

A classic work by Cleckley (1976) provided a detailed profile of *psychopaths*—people with few inhibitions who may pursue pleasure or money with callous disregard for the welfare of others. Based on a factor-analytic study of Cleckley's description, Robert D. Hare (1980) developed a 22-item Psychopathy Checklist (PCL) that reflects both personality characteristics as rated by the assessor (such as callousness, impulsiveness, and empathy) as well as prior history, as gleaned from the assessee's records (such as "criminal versatility"). In the revised version of the test, the Revised Psychopathy Checklist (PCL-R; Hare, 1985), two items from the original PCL were omitted because of their relatively low correlation with the rest of the scale, and the scoring criteria for some of the remaining items were modified. Hare et al. (1990) report that the two forms are equivalent.

Preliminary findings with the PCL have been impressive. Harris, Rice, and Cormier (1989) report that in a maximum-security psychiatric sample, the PCL correctly identified 80% of the violent recidivists. A study by Hart, Kropp, and Hare (1988) indicates that psychopaths are four times more likely than non-psychopaths to fail on release. A version of the PCL specially modified for use with young male offenders produced scores that correlated significantly with variables such as number of conduct disorder symptoms, previous violent offenses, violent recidivism, and violent behavior within the maximum security institution in which the study was conducted (Forth, Hart, & Hare, 1990). In another study, psychopathy ratings were found to predict outcome for both temporary absence and parole release; psychopaths were recommitted four times more frequently than nonpsychopaths (Serin, Peters, & Barbaree, 1990).

Another line of research in this area has been undertaken by Glenn Walters (in press) at the federal penitentiary in Leavenworth, Kansas. Walters and White (1989) have characterized the criminal lifestyle as one marked by self-indulgence, interpersonal intrusiveness, social rule breaking, and irresponsibility. The 14-item Lifestyle Criminality Screening Form (LCSF; Walters, White, & Denne, in press) yields scores on such characteristics based on information from an offender's presentence investigation report. In a study in which the subjects' probation officers served as the raters, offenders obtaining high scores on the LCSF exhibited a higher rate of parole and probation failure than offenders obtaining lower scores (Walters, Revella, & Baltrusaitis, 1990). Walters et al. (1990) caution, however, that additional research is required to explore the generalizability and implications of their findings.

CUSTODY EVALUATIONS

As the number of divorces in this country continues to climb, so does the number of custody proceedings. Prior to the 1920s, it was fairly commonplace for the father to be granted custody of the children (Lamb, 1981). The pendulum swung, however, with the widespread adoption of what was referred to as the "tender years" doctrine, and the belief that the child's interest would be best served if the mother was granted custody. In recent years, and with the coming of age of the dual-career household, the courts have begun to be more egalitarian in their custody decisions; it is recognized that the best interest of the child may be served by father custody, mother custody, or joint custody (McClure-Butterfield, 1990). Psychological assessors can assist the court in making awards of custody with reports that detail the parental capacity of the parents, and/or the parental preferences of the children (Weithorn, 1987). Ideally, one impartial expert in the mental health field should be responsible for assessing *all* family members and submitting a report to the court (Gardner, 1982). More often than not, however, the husband has his doctor, the wife has hers, and the battle is on.

Evaluation of the parent   The evaluation of the parental capacity typically entails a detailed interview that focuses primarily on various aspects of child rearing, though tests of intelligence, personality, and adjustment may be employed if questions remain after the interview. The assessor might begin with open-ended questions designed to let the parent ventilate some of his or her feelings and then proceed to more specific questions tapping a wide variety of areas, including:

- the parent's own childhood: how happy? abused?
- the parent's own relationship with parents, siblings, peers
- the circumstances that led up to the marriage and the degree of forethought that went into the decision to have (or adopt) children
- the adequacy of prenatal care and attitudes toward the pregnancy
- the parent's description of the child

- the parent's own evaluation of himself or herself as a parent, including strengths and weaknesses
- the parent's evaluation of his or her spouse regarding strengths and weaknesses as a parent
- the quantity and quality of time spent caring for and playing with children
- the parent's approach to discipline
- the parent's receptivity to the child's peer relationships

During the course of the interview the assessor may find evidence that the interviewee really does not want custody of the children but is undertaking the custody battle for some other reason. For example, the issue of custody may be nothing more than another issue to bargain over with respect to the divorce settlement. Alternatively, a mother might, for example, be embarrassed to admit to herself and to all observers of the proceedings that she really doesn't want custody of the children. Sometimes a parent, emotionally scathed by all that has gone on prior to the divorce, may be employing the custody battle as a technique of vengeance—to threaten to take away that which is most prized and adored by the spouse. The clinician performing the evaluation must appreciate that such ill-motivated intentions do underlie some custody battles; and, in the best interest of the children, it is the obligation of the clinician to report such findings.

Evaluation of the child   The court will be interested in knowing if the child in a custody proceeding has a preference with respect to future living and visitation arrangements. Toward that end, the psychological assessor can be of assistance with a wide variety of tests and techniques. Most authorities agree that the preferences of children under the age of 5 are too unreliable and too influenced by recent experiences to be accorded much weight. However, if intelligence test data indicate that the child who is chronologically 5 is functioning at a higher level, then his or her preferences may be accorded greater weight. This is particularly true if the Comprehension subtest score on a Wechsler test (such as the Wechsler Preschool and Primary Scale of Intelligence—Revised) is elevated; for, you will recall, the Comprehension subtest requires the child to draw on the knowledge of social situations. Some methods that can be useful in assessing a child's parental preference include structured play exercises with dolls that represent the child and other family members, figure drawings of family members followed by story telling to the drawings, and the use of projective techniques such as the TAT and related tests (see Figure 15–4).

Sometimes impromptu innovation on the part of the examiner is required. In performing a custody evaluation on a 5-year-old child, the senior author of this text (RJC) noted that the child seemed to identify very strongly with the main character in a then-popular film, *E. T., The Extraterrestrial*. The child had seen the film three times, came into the test session carrying two *E. T.* bubblegum cards, and identified as "E. T." the picture he drew when instructed to draw a person. As a means of obtaining a measure of parental preference, the examiner took four figures and represented them as "E. T.," "E. T.'s mother," "E. T.'s father," and "E. T.'s sister." An empty cardboard box was then labeled a "spaceship," and the child was told that E. T. (stranded on Earth and longing to return to his home planet) had the opportunity to go home but that the spaceship had room for only

Figure 15–4 *Projective Techniques Used in Custody Evaluation.* The picture on the left is from the Children's Apperception Test—H (Bellak & Bellak, 1965), and the one on the right is from the *The Boys and Girls Book About Divorce* (Gardner, 1971). These as well as TAT and other pictures used as projective stimuli may be useful in evaluating children's parental preferences.

two other passengers. The child boarded his mother and his sister in addition to "E. T." and told the examiner that E. T.'s father would "wave goodbye."

Specially constructed sentence completion items can also be of value in the assessment of parental preferences. For example, the following items might prove to be useful in examining the differing perceptions of each parent:

Mothers _____ .

If I do something wrong my father _____ .

It is best for children to live with _____ .

Fathers _____ .

Mommies are bad when _____ .

I like to hug _____ .

I don't like to hug _____ .

Daddies are bad when _____ .

The last time I cried _____ .

My friends think that my mother _____ .

My friends think that my father _____ .

The data-gathering process for the evaluation begins at the moment the child and the parent(s) come into the office. The assessor takes careful note of the quality of the interaction between the parent(s) and the child. The child will then be interviewed alone, and questions about the nature and quality of the relationship will be posed. If the child expresses a strong preference for one parent or the other, it is the burden of the assessor to evaluate how meaningful that preference is. For example, a child who sees his rancher father only every other weekend might have a "good ol' time" on the brief occasions that they are together and express a preference for living there—unaware that life in the country would soon become just as routine as life in the city with Mom. For those children with no expressed preference, insight into their feelings can be obtained by using the tests described earlier, combined with skillful interviewing. Included among the topics for discussion will be the child's physical description of his or her parents as well as his or her living quarters. Questions about the routine aspects of life (such as, "Who makes breakfast for you?") as well as questions about recreation, parental visitation, parental involvement with their education, their general well-being, and their siblings and friends will be asked.

Child Abuse and Neglect

A legal mandate exists in most states for many licensed professionals to report child abuse and child neglect when they have knowledge of it. The legal definition of the terms "child abuse" and "child neglect" vary from state to state. Typically, definitions of *abuse* refer to the creation of conditions that may give rise to abuse of a child (a person under the state-defined age of majority) by an adult responsible for the care of that person. The abuse may be in the form of (1) the infliction or allowing of infliction of physical injury or emotional impairment that is nonaccidental, (2) the creation or allowing the creation of substantial risk of physical injury or emotional impairment that is nonaccidental, or (3) the committing or allowing of a sexual offense to be committed against a child. Typical definitions of *neglect* refer to a failure on the part of an adult responsible for the care of a child to exercise a minimum degree of care in providing the child with food, clothing, shelter, education, medical care, and supervision.

A number of excellent general sources for the study of child abuse and child neglect are currently available (see, for example, Helfer & Kempe, 1988; Fontana, Donovan, & Wong, 1963; Cicchetti & Carlson, 1989; Kelley, 1988; Reece & Groden, 1985; Ellerstein, 1981). More specifically, literature is available to assist professionals in recognizing child abuse in the form of head injury (Billmire & Myers, 1985), eye injury (Gammon, 1981), mouth injury (Becker, Needleman, & Kotelchuck, 1978), central nervous system injury (Klein, 1981), emotional trauma (Brassard et al., 1986), burns (Lung, Miller, Davis, & Graham, 1977; Alexander, Surrell, & Cohle, 1987), bites (American Board of Forensic Odontology, 1986), fractures (Worlock et al., 1986), poisoning (Kresel & Lovejoy, 1981), sexual abuse (Adams-Tucker, 1982; Faller, 1988; Friedrich, Urquiza, & Beike, 1986; Sanfillipo et al., 1986; Sebold, 1987), and shaken infant syndrome (Dykes, 1986). What follows are some brief, very general guidelines to the assessment of physical and emotional signs of child abuse.

Physical signs of abuse and neglect   Although psychologists and other mental health professionals without medical credentials do not typically have occasion to physically examine children, a knowledge of physical signs of abuse and neglect is important. Obvious physical injuries may be described by abused children or abusing adults as the result of an accident, and it is incumbent on the knowl-

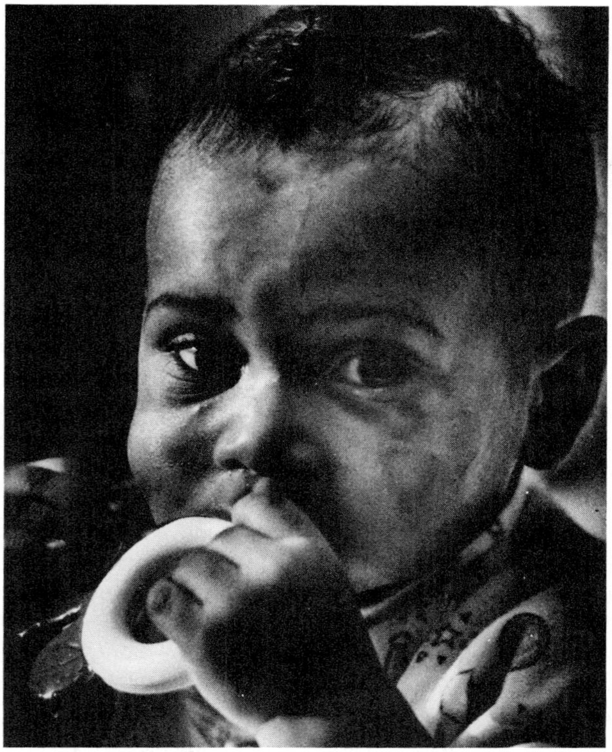

Figure 15–5 *Abused and neglected.* This physically abused child (note facial bruises) was abandoned by his parent and left in a shopping cart outside of a supermarket on a cold winter night.

edgeable professional to have a working familiarity with the various kinds of injuries that may signal more ominous causes. For example, in the case of injury to the face, in most veritable accidents, only one side of the face is injured. It may therefore be significant if a child evidences injury on both sides of the face—both eyes and both cheeks. Marks on the skin may be telling—"grab" marks made by an adult-size hand, marks that form a recognizable pattern, such as the tines of a fork, a belt buckle, a cord or rope, or human teeth. Burns from a cigarette or lighter may be in evidence as marks on the soles of the feet, the palms of the hands, the back, or the buttocks, while burns from scalding water may be in evidence as a "glovelike" redness on the hands or feet. Any bone fracture or dislocation should be investigated, as should head injuries, particularly when a patch of hair appears to be missing—as would be the case if the child's hair was pulled.

Physical signs that may or may not be indicative of neglect include dress that is inappropriate for the season, poor hygiene, and lagging physical development. Physical signs indicative of sexual abuse are not present in the majority of cases. In many instances, there is no penetration or only partial penetration by the abusing adult and no physical scars. In young children, physical signs that may or may not be indicative of sexual abuse include difficulty in sitting or walking, itching or reported pain or discomfort of genital areas, stained, bloody, or torn under-clothing, and foreign bodies in orifices. In older children, the presence of sexually transmitted diseases or a pregnancy may or may not signal child sexual abuse.

Emotional and behavioral signs of abuse and neglect   Emotional and be-havioral indicators may reflect something other than child abuse and neglect; child abuse or neglect is only one of several possible explanations underlying the ap-pearance of such signs. Fear of going home or fear of adults in general, as well as reluctance to remove outer garments may be signs of abuse. Other emotional and behavioral signs that may be abuse-related include unusual reactions or apprehen-sion in response to other children crying, low self-esteem, extreme or inappropri-ate moods, aggressiveness, social withdrawal, and nail biting, thumb sucking, or other habit disorders. Frequent lateness or absence at school, chronic fatigue, chronic hunger, and age-inappropriate behavior (such as that of a child who has taken on the role of an adult because of the absence of a caregiver at home) may be signs of neglect.

In children under 8 years of age, problems such as fear of sleeping alone, eat-ing disorders, enuresis, encopresis, sexual acting out, change in school behavior, tantrums, crying spells, sadness, and suicidal thoughts may or may not be indica-tive of sexual abuse. In older children, a professional might additionally observe memory problems, emotional numbness, violent fantasies, hyperalertness, self-mutilation, and sexual concerns or preoccupations, which may be accompanied by guilt or shame.

Interviews, behavioral observation, and psychological tests may all be brought to bear in the process of identifying child abuse. Of particular value in this endeavor has been the use of children's figure drawings (Burgess, Mc-Causland, & Wolbert, 1981; Kelley, 1985).

Issues in reporting child abuse and neglect   Child abuse, when it occurs, is a tragedy. Claims of child abuse when in fact there has been no such abuse is also a tragedy—one that can irrevocably scar an accused but innocent individual for life. It is incumbent on professionals who undertake the weighty obligation of as-sessing a child for potential abuse not to approach their task with any precon-ceived notions, as such notions can be conveyed to the child and be perceived as the "right answer" to questions that are posed (King & Yuille, 1987; White, San-tilli, & Quinn, 1988). Children from the ages of about 2 to 7 are highly suggest-ible and their memory is not as well-developed as that of older children; for this reason, it is possible that events that occur after the alleged incident—including events only referred to in conversations—may be confused with the actual inci-dent (Ceci, Ross, & Toglia, 1987; Goodman & Reed, 1986; Loftus & Davies, 1984). Other such considerations in the psychological examination of a child for abuse have been discussed in detail by Weissman (1991). Sensitivity to the rights of the accused in a child abuse proceeding are critical to making certain that justice is served (Ackerman, 1987; Besharov, 1985; Coleman, 1989; Corwin, Berlinger, Goodman, Goodwin, & White, 1987; Green, 1986; Jones & McGraw, 1987; Raskin & Yuille, 1987; Wong, 1987).

A critical component of any testing or assessment procedure is the reporting of the findings. The high reliability or validity of a test or assessment procedure may be "cast to the wind" if the assessment report is not written in an organized and readable fashion. Of course, what constitutes an "organized" and "readable" report will vary as a function of the goal of the assessment and the audience for whom the report is aimed; a psychoanalyst's report exploring a patient's unresolved oedipal conflict designed for presentation to the New York Psychoanalytic Society will look and sound a lot different from a school psychologist's report to a teacher concerning a child's learning disability. Reports differ not only in the extent to which they rely on one or another assessment procedure. Of course, reports also are written and used in widely different settings; although we will be focusing our attention on the writing of clinical reports, it should be clear that report writing is a skill necessary for educational, industrial/organizational, and any other setting where psychological assessment takes place.

Writing the Clinical Report

Because there is no one universally accepted style or form for psychological report writing, most assessors develop a style and form that they believe best suits the goal of the assessment. In their comprehensive review of clinical report-writing styles and forms, Hammond and Allen (1953) noted that reports differ widely in the extent to which they focus on specific referral questions and on the data derived from tests; they also differ on the extent to which they rely on particular theories of personality. Generally, however, most clinical reports of psychological evaluation contain, at a minimum, the following elements: demographic data, reason for referral, findings, recommendations, and summary (see Table 15–7).

Now that we've specified some of the types of material that belong in the clinical report, we proceed to outline some of the types of material that have no place in it. Here we are referring to what psychologists call "the Barnum effect."

The Barnum Effect

The showman P. T. Barnum is credited with the quote "There's a sucker born every minute." Psychologists, among others, have taken P. T. Barnum's words about the widespread gullibility of people quite seriously. In fact, *Barnum effect* is a term that should be familiar to any psychologist called on to write a psychological report. Before reading on to find out exactly what the Barnum effect is, imagine that you have just completed a computerized personality test and that the printout describing the results reads as follows:

> You have a strong need for other people to like you and for them to admire you. You have a tendency to be critical of yourself. You have a great deal of unused capacity which you have not turned to your advantage. While you have some personality weaknesses, you are generally able to compensate for them. Your sexual adjustment has presented some problems for you. Disciplined and controlled on the outside, you tend to be worrisome and insecure

Table 15-7

Elements of a Typical Report of Psychological Assessment

Demographic data

Included here are all or some of the following: the patient's name, address, telephone number, education, occupation, religion, marital status, date of birth, place of birth, ethnic membership, citizenship, date of testing. The examiner's name must also be considered part of the identifying material in the report.

Reason for referral

Why was this patient referred for psychological assessment? This section of the report may sometimes be as short as one sentence (for example, "Johnny was referred for evaluation to shed light on the question of whether his inattention in class is due to personality, neurological, or other difficulties"). Alternatively, this section of the report may be extended with all relevant background information (for example, "Johnny complained of hearing difficulties in his fourth-grade class according to a note in his records"). If all relevant background information is not covered in the "Reason for Referral" section of the report, it may be covered in a separate section labeled "Background" or in a section labeled "Findings."

Tests administered

Here the examiner simply lists the names of the tests that were administered. Thus, for example, this section of the report may be as brief as the following:

Wechsler Intelligence Scale for Children—Revised (1/8/90; 1/12/90)
Bender Visual-Motor Gestalt Test (1/8/90)
Rorschach Test (1/12/90)
Thematic Apperception Test (1/12/90)
Sentence Completion Test (1/8/90)
Figure drawings (1/8/90)

Note that the date of the test administration has been inserted next to the name of each test administered. This is a good idea under any circumstances and particularly important if testing was executed over the course of a number of days, weeks, or longer. In the sample section above, it will be noted that the WISC-R was administered over the course of two testing sessions on two days (1/8/90 and 1/12/90) and that the Bender, the Sentence Completion Test, and figure drawings were administered on 1/8/90, while the Rorschach and the Thematic Apperception Test were administered on 1/12/90.

Also in this section, the examiner might place the names and the dates of tests known to have been previously administered to the examinee. If the examiner has a record of the findings (or better yet, the original test protocols) from this prior testing, this information may be integrated into the next section of the report, "Findings."

Findings

Here the examiner reports not only findings (for example, "On the WISC-R Johnny achieved a Verbal IQ of 100, a Performance IQ of 110, yielding a full-scale IQ of 106") but also all extra-test considerations, such as observations concerning the examinee's motivation (for instance, "the examinee did/did not appear to be motivated to do well on the tests"), the examinee's level of fatigue, the nature of the relationship and rapport with the examiner, indices of anxiety, and method of approach to the task. The section labeled "Findings" may begin with a description of the examinee that is adequate enough for the reader of the report to almost visualize him or her. For example:

John is a 20-year-old college student with brown, shoulder-length, stringy hair and a full beard. He came to the testing wearing a "psychedelic" shirt, cut-off and ragged shorts, and sandals. He sat slouched in his chair for most of the test session, tended to speak only when spoken to, and spoke in a slow, lethargic manner.

Also included in this section is mention of any extraneous variables that might in some way have affected the test results. Was testing in a school interrupted by any event such as a fire drill, earth tremor, or other disturbance? Did loud or atypical noise in or out of the test site affect the test takers' concentration? Did the hospitalized patient receive any visitors just prior to an evaluation and could such a visit have affected

Table 15–7 (*continued*)

567

CLINICAL AND
COUNSELING
ASSESSMENT

Elements of a Typical Report of Psychological Assessment

Findings (continued)

the findings? Answers to these types of questions may prove invaluable in interpreting assessment data. Some unusual but dramatic real-life examples of the importance of considering the context of assessment can be found in figure 15-6.

The "Findings" section of the report is where all of the background material, behavioral observations, and test data are integrated to provide an answer to the referral question. Whether or not the examiner makes reference to the actual test data is a matter of personal preference. Thus, for example, one examiner might simply state, "There is evidence of neurological deficit in this record" and stop there. Another examiner would document exactly why this was being asserted: "There is evidence of neurological deficit as indicated by the rotation and preservation errors in the Bender-Gestalt record. Further, on the TAT, this examinee failed to grasp the situation as a whole and simply enumerated single details. Additionally, this examinee had difficulty abstracting—still another index of neurological deficit—as evidenced by the unusually low score on the WAIS Similarities subtest." The findings section should logically lead into the "Recommendations" section.

Recommendations

On the basis of the psychological assessment, with particular attention to factors such as the personal assets and deficiencies of the examinee, recommendations addressed to ameliorating the presenting problem are given. The recommendation may be for psychotherapy, a consultation with a neurologist, placement in a special class, short-term family therapy addressed to a specific problem—whatever the examiner believes is required to ameliorate the situation is spelled out here.

Summary

The summary section includes in "short form" a statement concerning the reason for referral, the findings, and the recommendation. This section is usually only a paragraph or two, and it should provide a concise and succinct statement of who the examinee is, why the examinee was referred for testing, what was found, and what needs to be done.

---

inside. At times you have serious doubts as to whether you have made the right decision or done the right thing. You prefer a certain amount of change and variety and become dissatisfied when hemmed in by restrictions and limitations. You pride yourself as being an independent thinker and do not accept others' opinions without satisfactory proof. You have found it unwise to be too frank in revealing yourself to others. At times you are extraverted, affable, and sociable while at other times you are introverted, wary, and reserved. Some of your aspirations tend to be pretty unrealistic.

Still imagining that the preceding test results had been formulated specifically for you, please rate the accuracy of the description as it does or does not apply to you personally:

I feel that the interpretation was:

_____ Excellent

_____ Good

_____ Average

_____ Poor

_____ Very Poor

Figure 15–6 *The Context of Assessment*

The setting in which people are assessed, including their immediate past experiences, may be of critical importance in arriving at an accurate evaluation. In clinical settings, for example, behavior that may appear to be the product of paranoid or severely confused thinking may actually only represent a temporary and situation-specific reaction to an environmental event. Dramatic examples of this point were provided by Thompson and Smith (1991) who chronicled how the mere exposure to people in costume precipitated in certain individuals behavior that mimicked severe psychiatric symptoms. One case involved a 67-year old man who had undergone an operation to remove his gallbladder. Day 1 after the operation, the patient suffered from post-operative agitation, insomnia, and a condition called delirium. *Delirium* is a medical term used to describe a state of confusion and clouded consciousness that could be brought on by any of a number of different factors such as surgery, a high fever, shock, or intoxication. Thompson and Smith (1991) describe post-operative Day 2:

In many cities, a number of services exist where for a fee, a costumed individual will be dispatched to perform at sites such as a party to help commemorate some occasion. For some people, exposure to costumed individuals may result in psychiatric symptoms such as confusion or paranoia.

> On the second postoperative day, his well-meaning family arranged to have him visited in the hospital for his 68th birthday by a costumed singer from a business that will send singers to deliver birthday or other messages. A lively young woman dressed in a bumble bee costume burst into his hospital room, then in an operatic-style voice sang "Happy Birthday" to him while pretending to "buzz" around his bed.
> He had been alone in his room, was intially frightened, and then summoned a nurse, who on arrival looked on, enjoyed the show, and thanked him for calling her so that she could see it. He later reported

that, "It took me a couple of minutes to get my thinking straight" and "laughingly said, "I thought for a second that thing was real and would sting or hurt me. When the nurse didn't look scared, I still wasn't sure what was happening but I figured it was safe." (pp. 2–3).

Now consider the case of another hospital patient on a medical ward, "Mr. P." He is recovering from pneumonia and also suffering from delirium, though this condition was thought to be improving as the pneumonia improved. It is late October

On Halloween afternoon, several ward nurses, medical students, and house staff held a

costume party and walked through the ward to "cheer up the patients." Mr. P was awakened from a nap by this "parade" and became terrified at seeing "a band of dead and deformed people singing all around me." He initially believed that the costume figures were real and wondered if he had "died and gone to hell." (Thompson & Smith, 1991, p. 2)

A psychiatrist consult was called in to see Mr. P for what was described as a "brief reactive psychosis." In reality, it was another cae of a phenomenon whereby a patient in a delirim state is exposed to a costumed person and develops what appears to be severe psychiatric symptoms.

Now that you have completed the exercise we can say, "Welcome to the ranks of those who have been subject to the Barnum effect." This psychological profile is, as you no doubt have noticed, vague and general. The same paragraph (sometimes with slight modifications) has been used in a number of psychological studies (Forer, 1949; Merrens & Richards, 1970; Sundberg, 1955; Ulrich, Stachnick, & Stainton, 1963; Jackson, O'Dell, & Olson, 1982) with similar findings: *People tend to accept vague and general personality descriptions as uniquely applicable to themselves without realizing that the same description could be applied to just about anyone.*

The finding that people tend to accept vague personality descriptions as accurate descriptions of themselves came to be known as "The Barnum Effect" after psychologist Paul Meehl's (1956) condemnation of "personality description after the manner of P. T. Barnum."[3] Meehl suggested that the term *Barnum effect* be used "to stigmatize those pseudo-successful clinical procedures in which personality descriptions from tests are made to fit the patient largely or wholly by virtue of their triviality." Tallent (1958) made a related observation. Deploring the generality and vagueness that seemed to plague too many psychological reports, Tallent wrote:

> Quite similar to the Barnum phenomenon is what might be called the *Aunt Fanny description* in clinical reports. Superfluous statements, such as, "This client has difficulty in performing at optimal capacity when under stress," or "The client has unconscious hostile urges" might readily prompt the report reader to think "so has my Aunt Fanny!"

The "Barnum" or "Aunt Fanny" effect has been the subject of numerous research studies. In one study conducted by Ulrich, Stachnick, and Stainton (1963), 57 college students were given two personality tests by their psychology instructor, who promised to score the tests and have the results back to each individual student at a later date. One week later, all students were given the identical personality description—the one that appears earlier in this section—though the descriptions were arranged in different orders. The students were asked to rate the interpretations as either excellent, good, average, poor, or very poor and to make any additional comments. The ratings were as follows:

Excellent	27
Good	26
Average	3
Poor	1
Very Poor	0

Some of the comments made by the students were as follows:

> I feel that you have done a fine job with the material which you had to work with. I agree with almost all of your statements and think they answer the problems I may have.

---

3. Meehl credited D. G. Patterson with having first used the term *Barnum effect.*

On the nose! Very good. I wish you had said more, all you did mention was all true without a doubt. I wish you could go further into this personality sometime.

The results have brought out several points which have worried me because I was not sure if I had imagined these to be personality traits of mine. Tests like this could be valuable to an individual in helping him to solve some of his own problems.

In a follow-up study executed by these same researchers, 79 other college students were shown how to administer two personality tests (the same tests that had been administered by the instructor in the first experiment). The students were then asked to play the role of test examiner and to use as an examinee any one available person such as a roommate or neighbor. At the completion of the test administration, the student examiner would tell the examinee that the test would be scored and returned with an interpretation. The "interpretation" was the same as in the prior study and once again the ratings of its applicability were quite high:

Excellent	29
Good	30
Average	15
Poor	5
Very Poor	0

Some of the comments made by the examinees on the accuracy of the student examiners' "results" were as follows:

I believe this interpretation applied to me individually, as there are too many facets which fit me too well to be a generalization.

The interpretation is surprisingly accurate and specific in description. I shall take note of many of the things said.

I feel that the interpretation does apply to me individually. For the first time things I have been vaguely aware of have been put into concise and constructive statements which I would like to use as a plan for improving myself.

It appears to me that the results of this test are unbelievably close to the truth. For a short test of this type, I was expecting large generalizations for results, but this was not the case; and I give all the credit to the examiner whose conclusions were well calculated.

It can be seen that even in a situation in which nonexperienced, student examiners were involved, 59 of the 79 examinees rated the generalized interpretation as excellent or good. In reviewing the surprising results of their experiments, Ulrich and his collaborators concluded that the persons given the phony test interpretations were not only "taken in" by the interpretations, but they were also "very likely to praise highly the examiner on his conclusions."

Other research serves to underscore just how powerful the Barnum effect can be. In one study, students were unable to select their actual personal description when it was paired with a generalized description (Sundberg, 1955). In another, students actually preferred a generalized interpretation to an interpretation written on the basis of their actual psychological test scores (Merrens & Richards, 1970). The effect has since been explored with reference to situational variables (Snyder, Shenkel, & Lowery, 1977; Snyder & Shenkel, 1976; Hinrichsen & Bradley, 1974) such as the prestige of the diagnostician (Dmitruk, Collins, & Clinger, 1973; Snyder & Larson, 1972; Bradley & Bradley, 1977; Halperin, Snyder, Shenkel, & Houston, 1976), the sex of the diagnostician (Zeren & Bradley, 1982), the number of assessees (Snyder & Newburg, 1981), and the type of assessment instrument used (Snyder, 1974; Weinberger & Bradley, 1980). Cognizance of this effect and the factors that may heighten or diminish it is necessary if psychological assessors are to avoid making interpretations "in the manner of P. T. Barnum." In Appendix A we present what we consider to be a typical psychological report.

Chapter 16

Neuropsychological

Assessment

WHAT IS THE nature of the link between the brain and the body? The philosopher René Descartes (1596–1650) postulated that a gaseous distillate from the blood flowed through hollow nerves to or from the brain in order to receive or send information. In accordance with prevailing church dogma, Descartes divorced the brain and the body from the soul (mind) and argued that in some activities only the body was operating, in others just the soul was operating, and in still others there was an interaction. The French physiologist and humanitarian Pierre Cabanis (1757–1808) explored the mind/body question from a slightly more graphic perspective with "field research"; he personally observed the state of consciousness of guillotined victims of the French Revolution. Cabanis concluded that the mind and the body were so intimately related that the swift guillotine was probably a painless mode of execution. Franz Joseph Gall (1758–1828) saw fit to explore the relationship between the brain and behavior through the study of curvatures of the head. The rationale behind this approach, called *phrenology*, was that functions and special talents were localized in concentrations of brain fiber and these clusters pressed outward (manifesting themselves as bumps on the head). By 1911, phrenology and the *Journal of Phrenology* (which had been founded in 1823) were laid to rest by an onslaught of rigorous behaviorial and neuroanatomical experimentation.

Modern-day investigators exploring the link between the brain and the body use a number of varied tools and procedures in their work, including laboratory testing and field observation of head-trauma victims, experimentation involving the electrical or chemical stimulation of various human and animal brain sites, experimental lesioning of the brain of animal subjects, and autopsies of normal and abnormal human and animal subjects.

The branch of medicine that focuses on the nervous system and its disorders is *neurology.* The branch of psychology that focuses on the relationship between brain functioning and behavior is *neuropsychology.* Formerly a specialty area within clinical psychology, neuropsychology has evolved into a specialty in its own right in recent years. Psychologists doing routine clinical evaluations are trained to screen for signs and symptoms of neurological deficit. Such signs or symptoms may present themselves during history taking (for example, the examinee reports a fall in which consciousness was lost for a few minutes), interviewing (the examinee complains of severe, long-lasting headaches), or test taking (involuntary movements are observed); signs may also be evident in data derived from an intelligence test (such as a large discrepancy between measured verbal and performance IQ) or other tests. If, on the basis of such signs, neurological deficit is suspected, the examinee will be referred to a neurologist or neuropsychologist for further evaluation. In this chapter some of the tools used by clinicians and neuropsychologists to screen for and diagnose the existence of neurological disorders will be surveyed. We begin with a brief introduction to neuroanatomy and brain-behavior relationships. This material is presented to help lay a foundation for appreciating how test-taking (as well as other) behavior can be evaluated to form hypotheses about the level of intactness or functioning in various parts of the brain.

THE NERVOUS SYSTEM AND BEHAVIOR

The nervous system is composed of various kinds of *neurons* (nerve cells) and can be divided into the *central* nervous system (consisting of the brain and the spinal cord) and the *peripheral* nervous system (consisting of the neurons that convey messages to and from the rest of the body). Viewed from the top, the large, rounded portion of the brain called the cerebrum can be divided into two sections or hemispheres (see Figure 16–1). This mass appears gray in color since mixtures of capillary blood vessels and cell bodies of neurons have a gray-brown color. Connecting the left and right hemispheres is a band of nerve fibers called the *corpus callosum.* Much of the surface of the cerebral hemispheres constitutes what is called the cerebral *cortex* (from the Latin meaning "bark, shell, rind," or outer layer). The cortex appears wrinkled due to the many clefts or indentations in its surface. A cleft is technically referred to as a *fissure* or a *sulcus* depending on its depth (fissures are deeper than sulci), and the ridge between the depression is called a *gyrus* (the plural is *gyri*). Fissures divide each cerebral hemisphere into four areas referred to as *lobes:* the frontal, temporal, occipital, and parietal lobes. Just beneath the corpus callosum, at the approximate center of the brain, lies a group of nuclei called the *thalamus,* and below that lies another group of nuclei called the *hypothalamus* ("hypo" meaning "below"). The thalamus and the hypothalamus are actually part of the structure called the brainstem that connects the

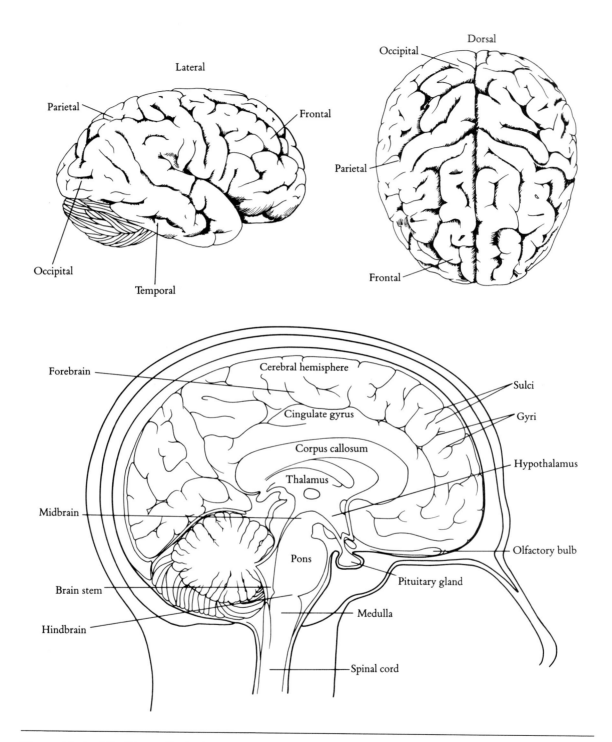

Figure 16–1 *The Human Brain from Three Perspectives.*

574

brain to the spinal cord. Also part of the brainstem, just above the spinal cord, is a mass of nuclei and fibers called the *reticular formation.*

Some brain-behavior correlates are summarized in Table 16–1. In Figure 16–2, we see the projection of sensory information onto the somatosensory area of the brain and the corresponding motor areas. Note that the two cerebral hemispheres each receive sensory information from the opposite side of the body and also control motor responses on the opposite side of the body—a phenomenon called *contralateral control.* It is due to the brain's contralateral control of the body

Table 16–1

Some Brain-Behavior Characteristics for Selected Nervous System Sites

Site	Characteristic
Temporal lobes	These lobes contain auditory reception areas as well as certain areas for the processing of visual information. Damage to the temporal lobe may affect sound discrimination, recognition, and comprehension; music appreciation; voice recognition; and auditory or visual memory storage.
Occipital lobes	These lobes contain visual reception areas. Damage to this area could result in blindness to all or part of the visual field or deficits in object recognition, visual scanning, visual integration of symbols into wholes, and recall of visual imagery.
Parietal lobes	These lobes contain reception areas for the sense of touch and for the sense of bodily position. Damage to this area may result in deficits in the sense of touch, disorganization, and distorted self-perception.
Frontal lobes	These lobes are integrally involved in ordering information and sorting out stimuli. Concentration and attention, abstract-thinking ability, concept-formation ability, foresight, problem-solving ability, speech, as well as gross and fine motor ability may be affected by damage to the frontal lobes.
Thalamus	The thalamus is a kind of communications relay station for all sensory information being transmitted to the cerebral cortex. Damage to the thalamus may result in altered states of arousal, memory defects, speech deficits, apathy, and disorientation.
Hypothalamus	The hypothalamus is involved in the regulation of bodily functions such as eating, drinking, body temperature, sexual behavior, and emotion. It is sensitive to changes in environment that call for a "fight or flight" response from the organism. Damage to it may elicit a variety of symptoms ranging from uncontrolled eating or drinking to mild alterations of mood states.
Cerebellum	Together with the pons (another brain site in the area of the brain referred to as the hindbrain), the cerebellum is involved in the regulation of balance, breathing, and posture—among other functions. Damage to the cerebellum may manifest itself as problems in fine motor control and coordination.
Reticular formation	In the core of the brain stem, the reticular formation contains fibers en route to and from the cortex. Because stimulation to this area can cause a sleeping organism to awaken and cause an awake organism to become even more alert, it is sometimes referred to as the *reticular activating system.* Damage to this area can cause the organism to sleep for long periods of time.
Limbic system	Composed of the amygdala, the cingulate cortex, the hippocampus, and the septal areas of the brain, the limbic system plays an integral part in the expression of emotions. Damage to this area may profoundly affect emotional behavior.
Spinal cord	Many reflexes necessary for survival (such as withdrawing from a hot surface) are carried out at the level of the spinal cord. In addition to its role in reflex activity, the spinal cord plays an integral part in the coordination of motor movements. Spinal cord injuries may result in various degrees of paralysis or other motor difficulties.

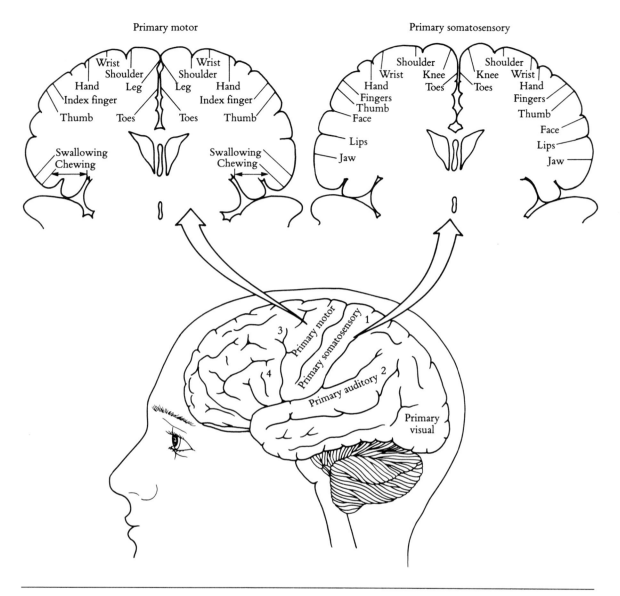

Figure 16–2 *Cross-Sections of Two Areas of the Brain.* Cross-sections of the primary motor and somatosensory areas of the brain are pictured. Although it is not clear from the illustration, the amount of space that a body area has represented in the cortex is determined by the degree of fine motor control associated with that body area, not by its size. Thus, for example, the fingers have far greater representation on the motor cortex than does the trunk. The lips are given a great amount of representation on the somatosensory cortex.

576

that an injury to the right side of the brain may result in sensory and/or motor defects with respect to the left side of the body. The "meeting ground" of the two hemispheres is the corpus callosum, though one hemisphere, most frequently the left one, is dominant. It is because the left hemisphere is most frequently dominant that most people are right-handed. The dominant hemisphere dominates in activities such as reading, writing, arithmetic, and speech while the nondominant hemisphere has as its forte tasks involving spatial and textural recognition as well as art and music appreciation. In the normal, neurologically intact individual, one hemisphere works to complement the other.

Neurological Damage and the Concept of "Organicity"

Neurological damage may take the form of a *lesion* in the brain or any other site within the central or peripheral nervous system. A lesion is a pathological alteration of tissue such as that which could result from injury or infection. Neurological lesions may be physical or chemical in nature, and they may be focal (relatively circumscribed at one site) or diffuse (scattered at various sites). Since different sites of the brain control various functions, focal and diffuse lesions at different sites will manifest themselves in terms of varying behavioral deficits. A partial listing of the technical names for the many varieties of sensory and motor deficits appears in Table 16–2.

Note that a focal lesion may have what could be referred to as diffuse ramifications in terms of behavioral deficits (that is, a circumscribed lesion in one area of the brain may affect many different kinds of behaviors). Conversely, it is possible that a diffuse lesion may affect one or more areas of functioning so severely that it masquerades as a focal lesion. In a sense, the neuropsychologist works backwards—examining behavior by means of a variety of tests and proce-

Table 16–2

Technical Names for Various Kinds of Sensory and Motor Deficits

Name	*Description of deficit*
Acalcula	Inability to perform arithmetic calculations
Acopia	Inability to copy geometric designs
Agnosia	Deficit in recognizing sensory stimuli (for example, *auditory agnosia* is a difficulty in recognizing auditory stimuli)
Agraphia	Deficit in writing ability
Akinesia	Deficit in motor movements
Alexia	Inability to read
Amnesia	Loss of memory
Amusia	Deficit in ability to produce or appreciate music
Anomia	Deficit associated with finding words to name things
Anopia	Deficit in sight
Anosmia	Deficit in the sense of smell
Aphasia	Deficit in communication due to impaired speech or writing ability
Apraxia	Voluntary movement disorder in the absence of paralysis
Ataxia	Deficit in motor ability and muscular coordination

dures and trying to determine from the pattern of findings where a neurological lesion, if any, exists. Neuropsychological assessment also plays a critical role in determining the extent of behavioral impairment that has occurred or can be expected to occur due to a neurological disorder. Such information is useful not only in designing remediation programs but also in assessing the consequences of drug treatments, physical training, and other therapy.

The terms "brain damage," "neurological damage," and "organicity" have, unfortunately, been used interchangeably in much of the psychological literature. The term *neurological damage* is most all-inclusive, since it covers not only damage to the brain but also damage to the spinal cord and to all the components of the peripheral nervous system. The term *organicity,* still very popular in usage with clinicians, derives from the post–World War I research of the German neurologist Kurt Goldstein. Studies of brain-injured soldiers led Goldstein to the conclusion that the factors differentiating organically impaired individuals ("organics" for short) from normals included the loss of abstraction ability, deficits in reasoning ability, and inflexibility in problem-solving tasks. Accordingly, Goldstein (1927, 1939, 1963a) and his colleagues developed psychological tests that tapped these factors and were designed to help in the diagnosis of organic brain syndrome or "organicity" for short. Some of these tests are illustrated in Figure 16–3.

In the tradition of Goldstein and his associates, two German psychologists named Heinz Werner and Alfred Strauss examined brain/behavior correlates in brain-injured, mentally retarded children (Werner & Strauss, 1941; see also Strauss & Lehtinen, 1947). Like their predecessors who had worked with brain-injured adults, these investigators attempted to delineate characteristics common to *all* brain-injured people, including children. Although such work led to a better understanding of the behavioral consequences of brain injury in children, one unfortunate consequence was that a unitary picture of brain injury emerged; all "organic" children were presumed to share a similar pattern of cognitive, behavioral, sensory, and motor deficits—regardless of the specific nature or site of their impairment. The unitary concept of "organicity" prevailed through the 1950s at which time researchers like Birch and Diller (1959) began to complain about what they termed the "naivete of the concept of 'organicity'":

> It is abundantly clear that "brain damage" and "organicity" are terms which though overlapping are not identities and serve to designate interdependent events. "Brain-damage" refers to the fact of an anatomical destruction, whereas "organicity" represents one of the varieties of functional consequences which may attend such destruction. (p. 195)

Through the 1960s, a number of researchers echoed the view that "organicity" and "brain damage" should not be viewed as unitary in nature and that no one set of behavioral characteristics can be applied to all brain-injured persons. Thus, for example, Haynes and Sells (1963) observed that "both native practice and the overwhelming bulk of published research appear to accept the term brain damage as a unitary diagnostic entity, although the predominant evidence indicates that it represents a complex and multifaceted category" (p. 316). The conceptualization of "organicity" and "brain damage" as nonunitary in nature was supported by a number of observations, which are summarized in Table 16–3.

Figure 16–3 *The Goldstein-Scheerer Tests of Abstract and Concrete Thinking.*

The Stick Test is a measure of recent memory. The subject's task is to reproduce designs from memory using sticks. **(a)**

The Cube Test challenges the subject to replicate with blocks a design printed in a booklet. This subtest was the predecessor to the Block Design task on Wechsler intelligence tests. It is used as a measure of nonverbal abstraction ability. **(b)**

The Color-Form Sorting Test contains 12 objects, including 4 triangles, 4 circles, and 4 squares (each piece in one of four colors). The objects are presented in a random order, and the subject is instructed to sort according to which belong together. Once sorted, the subject is next asked to sort the objects a different way. The subject's flexibility in shifting from one sorting principle to another is noted. **(c)**

The Object Sorting Test consists of 89 objects, which the subject is required to group. Concrete thinking and organic impairment may be inferred if the subject sorts, for example, by color instead of function. **(d)**

The Color Sorting Test employs several woolen skeins of varying colors. The task here is to sort the skeins according to a sample sketch displayed by the examiner. **(e)**

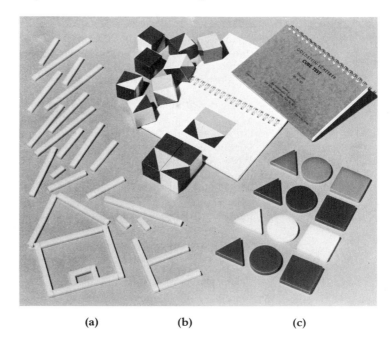

(a)   **(b)**   **(c)**

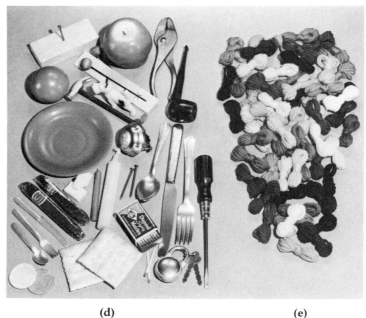

(d)   **(e)**

Table 16-3

The Nonunitary Nature of "Organicity." Evidence for the nonunitary nature of organicity derives from observations and research such as the following.

* Persons who have identical lesions in the brain may exhibit markedly different symptoms. Reed, Reitan, and Klove (1965) have observed that "behavior deficits associated with cerebral lesions in children may be quite different from the ability losses typically demonstrated by brain-damaged adults" (p. 250). In a similar vein, Pincus and Tucker (1974) noted that "large unilateral injuries in infants . . . tend to produce a more widespread deficit in intellectual abilities than similar injuries in adults" (pp. 123–124).

* Many interacting factors such as the patient's premorbid functioning, the site and diffuseness of the lesion, the cause of the lesion and its rate of spread may make one "organic" appear quite dissimilar clinically from another (Goldfried, Stricker, & Weiner, 1971; Reitan & Davison, 1974; Smith, 1962).

* Considerable similarity may exist in the symptoms exhibited by persons who have entirely different types of lesions. Further, these different types of lesions may arise from a variety of causes, such as trauma with or without loss of consciousness, infection, nutritional deficiencies, tumor, stroke, neuronal degeneration, toxins, insufficient cardiac output, and a variety of metabolic disturbances.

  * Many conditions that are not due to brain damage produce symptoms that mimic those produced by brain damage. For example, an individual who is psychotic, depressed, or simply fatigued may produce data on an examination for organic brain damage that is characteristically diagnostic of neuropsychological impairment.

* Factors other than brain damage (such as psychosis, depression, fatigue) influence the responses of brain-damaged persons. Some types of responses are consequences (rather than correlates) of the brain damage. For example, if brain-injured children as a group tend to be described as more "aggressive" than normals, this may reflect more on the way such children have been treated by parents, teachers, and peers than on the effect of any lesions per se. Conversely, persons who are in fact brain-damaged are sometimes able to compensate for their deficits to such an extent that some functions are actually taken over by other, more intact parts of the brain.

THE NEUROPSYCHOLOGICAL EXAMINATION

The tests and other procedures employed in a neuropsychological examination will vary as a function of several factors—such as the purpose of the examination, the neurological intactness of the examinee, and the thoroughness of the examination. In a sense, any routine administration of a battery of psychological tests within a clinical setting can also serve the purpose of neuropsychological screening; in the course of intelligence testing, personality testing, or other psychological testing, the clinician may be alerted to suspicious findings signaling that a more in-depth neuropsychological examination should be conducted. Sometimes a patient is referred to a psychologist for screening for neurological problems; in such a case, a battery of tests will be administered—consisting, at a minimum, of an intelligence test, a personality test, and a perceptual-motor/memory test.[1] In

1. We have listed here what we believe to be the minimum amount of testing to suffice for an adequate neuropsychological screening. It is, however, not uncommon for some clinicians to administer only a perceptual-motor/memory test such as the Bender Visual Motor Gestalt test as a screening device. In the light of strong cautions against such practices (see, for example, Bigler & Ehrenfurth, 1981), some have stated flatly that the singular use of such a test "could certainly be considered negligent" (Kahn & Taft, 1983, p. 79).

the course of the evaluation, if neurological signs are discovered, the examinee will be referred for further and more detailed evaluation.

In addition to general screening purposes, an individual might be referred for an in-depth neuropsychological evaluation because of the nature of the presenting problem (such as memory impairment). A neuropsychological examination might be ordered by a neurologist who seeks to find out more about the site of a suspected or known lesion. A neurologist's referral note to a neuropsychologist in such an instance might read:

> My examination was negative but I feel I might be missing something. This patient did have a head injury about six months ago and he still complains of headaches and slight memory problems for recent events. I found no hard signs, some soft signs such as a right hand tremor (possibly due to anxiety), and a pattern of findings on laboratory tests ranging from negative to equivocal. Please evaluate this patient and let me know whether you find the headaches and other vague complaints to be organic or functional in origin.[2]

In addition to asking whether any observed deficits are organic (physically based) or functional (psychologically based), the referral note might also ask the neuropsychologist other kinds of questions such as: Is this condition acute or chronic? Is the damage focal (local in one area) or diffuse (present in a number of areas)? Will there be progressive deterioration? Is this individual ready to go back to school or work? What skills require remediation?

The neuropsychological examination will vary widely as a function of the nature of the referral question. In contrast to referral questions concerning the location and nature of suspected lesions, for example, questions concerning the functional or organic origin of observed behavior will require more in-depth examination of personality and psychiatric history.

The content and nature of the examination will also vary as a function of the neurological intactness of the assessee. Neuropsychologists have occasion to assess persons exhibiting a wide range of physical and psychological disabilities. Some, for example, have known visual or auditory deficits, concentration and attention problems, speech and language difficulties, and so forth. Allowance must be made for such deficits and a way must be found to administer the appropriate tests in such a way that meaningful results can be obtained. Frequently, neuropsychologists will administer preliminary visual, auditory, and other such examinations to ascertain the gross intactness of sensory and motor functioning before proceeding with more specialized tests. An olfactory (sense of smell) deficit, for example, may be symptomatic of a great variety of neurological and non-neurological problems as diverse as Alzheimer's disease (Serby, Larson, & Kalkstein, 1991), Parkinson's disease (Serby, Corwin, Conrad et al., 1985), and AIDS (Brody, Serby, Etienne, & Kalkstein, 1991). The discovery of such a deficit by means of a test such as the University of Pennsylvania Smell Identification Test

---

2. In the jargon of neuropsychological assessment, a *hard sign* may be defined as an indicator of definite neurological deficit (for example, abnormal reflex performance). Hard signs may be contrasted to *soft signs,* which are suggestive of neurological deficit but not necessarily indicative of such deficit (for example, a 15-point discrepancy between the verbal and performance scales on a Wechsler intelligence test).

(Doty, Shaman, & Dann, 1984) would be a stimulus for continued diagnostic assessment.

Common to all thorough neuropsychological examinations is a history taking, a mental status examination, and the administration of tests and procedures designed to uncover any problems with respect to neuropsychological functioning. Throughout the examination, the neuropsychologist's knowledge of neuroanatomy, neurochemistry, and neurophysiology will be essential for optimal interpretation of the data gathered. In addition to guiding decisions concerning what to test for and how to test for it, such knowledge will also come into play with respect to the decisions concerning *when* to test. Thus, for example, it would be atypical for a neuropsychologist to psychologically test a stroke victim immediately after the stroke occurred. Because some recovery of function could be expected to spontaneously occur in the weeks and months following the stroke, testing the patient immediately after the stroke would therefore yield an erroneous picture of the extent of the damage.

The History

The typical neuropsychological examination begins with a careful history taking. Areas that will be of interest to the examiner include the following:

- the medical history of the patient
- the medical history of the patient's immediate family and other relatives. A sample question here might be, "Have you or any of your relatives experienced dizziness, fainting, blackouts, or spasms?"
- the presence or absence of certain developmental milestones; a particularly critical part of the history-taking process when examining young children. A listing of some of these milestones appears in Table 16–4.
- psychosocial history, including level of academic achievement and estimated level of intelligence; an estimated level of adjustment at home and at work or school; observations regarding personality (for example, is this individual hypochondriacal?), thought processes, and motivation (is this person willing and able to respond accurately to these questions?).
- the character, severity, and progress of any history of complaints involving disturbances in sight, hearing, smell, touch, taste, or balance; disturbances in muscle tone, muscle strength, and muscle movement; disturbances in autonomic functions such as breathing, eliminating, and body temperature control; disturbances in speech; disturbances in thought and memory; pain (particularly headache and facial pain); and various types of thought disturbances.

A careful history is critical to the accuracy of the assessment. Consider, for example, a patient who exhibits flat affect, is listless, and seems not even to know what day it is or what time of day it is. Such an individual might be suffering from something neurological in origin (such as a dementia); however, a functional disorder (such as severe depression) might instead be causing the problem. A good history taking will shed light on the answer to the referral question of whether the observed behavior is the result of a genuine dementia or a product of what is referred to as a pseudodementia. History-taking questions might include

Table 16–4

Some Developmental Milestones

Age	Development
16 weeks	Gets excited, laughs aloud
	Spontaneous smile in response to people
	Anticipates eating at sight of food
	Sits propped for 10 to 15 minutes
28 weeks	Smiles and vocalizes to a mirror and pats at mirror image
	Many vowel sounds
	Sits unsupported for brief period and then leans on hands
	Takes solids well
	When lying on back, places feet to mouth
	Grasps objects and transfers objects from hand to hand
	When held standing, supports most of weight
12 months	Walks with only one hand held
	Says "mamma" and "dada" and perhaps two other "words"
	Gives a toy in response to a request or gesture
	When being dressed, will cooperate
	Plays "peek-a-boo" games
18 months	Has a vocabulary of some ten words
	Walks well, seldom falls, can run stiffly
	Looks at pictures in a book
	Feeds self, although spills
	Can pull a toy or hug a doll
	Can seat self in a small or adult chair
	Scribbles spontaneously with a crayon or pencil
24 months	Walks up and down stairs alone
	Runs well, no falling
	Can build a tower of six or seven blocks
	Uses personal pronouns ("I" and "you") and speaks a three-word sentence
	Identifies simple pictures by name and calls self by name
	Verbalizes needs fairly consistently
	May be dry at night
	Can pull on simple garment
36 months	Alternates feet when climbing stairs and jumps from bottom stair
	Rides a tricycle
	Can copy a circle and imitate a cross with a crayon or pencil
	Comprehends and answers questions
	Feeds self with little spilling
	May know and repeat a few simple rhymes
48 months	Can dry and wash hands, brushes teeth
	Laces shoes, dresses and undresses with supervision
	Can play cooperatively with other children
	Can draw figure of a person with at least two clear body parts
60 months	Knows and names colors, counts to 10
	Skips on both feet
	Can print a few letters, can draw identifiable pictures

Source: Gesell and Amatruda (1947)

the following: How long has the patient been in this condition and what emotional or neurological trauma may have precipitated it? Does this patient have a personal or family history of depression or other psychiatric disturbance? What factors appear to be operating to maintain the patient in this state? Regardless of whether the disorder is organic or functional in origin, the history will also shed light on questions relative to its progressive or nonprogressive nature.

The Neuropsychological Mental Status Examination

An outline for a general mental status examination was presented in Chapter 15. The neuropsychological mental status examination overlaps greatly with respect to questions concerning the assessee's consciousness, emotional state, thought content and clarity, memory, sensory perception, performance of action, language, speech, handwriting, and handedness. The mental status examination administered for the express purpose of evaluating neuropsychological functioning may delve more extensively into specific areas of interest. For example, during a routine mental status examination, the examiner might require the examinee to interpret the meaning of only one or two proverbs; on the neurological mental status examination, many proverbs may be presented in order to obtain a more comprehensive picture of the patient's capacity for abstract thought. Throughout the history taking and the mental status examination, the clinician will take note of gross and subtle observations pertinent to the evaluation. For example, the examiner will note the presence of involuntary movements (such as facial tics), locomotion difficulties, and other sensory and motor problems that may become apparent during the interview. The examiner may note, for example, that one corner of the mouth is slower to curl than the other when the patient smiles—a finding suggestive of damage to the seventh (facial) cranial nerve.

The Physical Examination

Most neuropsychologists do perform some kind of physical examination on patients, but the extent of this examination varies widely as a function of the expertise, competence, and confidence of the examiner. Some neuropsychologists have had, as part of their education, extensive training in performing physical examinations under the tutelage of neurologists in teaching hospitals. Such psychologists feel confident and competent in performing many of the same *noninvasive* procedures (procedures that do not involve any intrusion into the examinee's body) that neurologists perform as part of their neuropsychological examination. In the course of the following discussion, we list some of these noninvasive procedures. We precede this discussion with the caveat that it is the physician and not the neuropsychologist who is always the final arbiter of medical questions.

In addition to making observations about the examinee's appearance, the examiner may also physically examine the scalp and skull for any unusual enlargements or depressions. Muscles may be inspected for their tone (soft? rigid?), strength (weakness or tiredness?), and size relative to other muscles. With respect to the latter point, the examiner might find, for example, that Ralph's right biceps are much larger than his left biceps. Such a finding could indicate muscular dystrophy in the left arm, but it also could be reflective of the fact that the patient has been working as a shoemaker for the last forty years—a job in which he is constantly hammering with and building up the muscle in his right arm. This patient's case serves to underscore the importance of careful history taking when evaluating physical findings. In addition to physical examination of the skull and the musculature, simple reflexes may be tested. *Reflexes* are involuntary motor responses to stimuli. Many reflexes have survival value for infants but then disappear as the child grows older. One such reflex is the mastication (chewing) reflex. Stroking the tongue or lips will elicit chewing behavior in the normal infant; however, if chewing is elicited in the older child or adult, it is indicative of neurological deficit. In addition to testing for the presence or absence of various reflexes, the examiner might examine muscle coordination by using tests such as those listed in Table 16–5.

Table 16–5

Tests Used to Evaluate Muscle Coordination

Walking-running-skipping

If the examiner has not had a chance to watch the patient walk for any distance, he may ask the patient to do so as part of the examination. We tend to take walking for granted; but, neurologically speaking, it is a highly complex activity that involves proper integration of many varied components of the nervous system. Sometimes abnormalities in gait may be due to nonneurological causes; if, for example, a severe case of bunions is suspected as the cause of the difficulty, the examiner may ask the patient to remove his or her shoes and socks so that the feet may be physically inspected. Highly trained examiners are additionally sensitive to subtle abnormalities in, for example, arm movements while the patient walks, runs, or skips.

Standing-still (technically, the Romberg test)

The patient is asked to stand still with feet together, head erect, and eyes open. Whether patients have their arms extended straight out or at their sides and whether or not they are wearing shoes or other clothing will be a matter of the examiner's preference. Patients are next instructed to close their eyes. The critical variable is the amount of sway exhibited by the patient once the eyes are closed. Since normal persons may sway somewhat with their eyes closed, experience and training is required to determine when the amount of sway is indicative of pathology.

Nose-finger-nose

The patient's task here is to touch her nose with the tip of her index finger, then touch the examiner's finger, and then touch her own nose again. The sequence is repeated many times with each hand. This test, as well as many similar ones (such as the toe-finger test, the finger-nose test, the heel-knee test), are designed to assess, among other things, cerebellar functioning.

Finger wiggle

The examiner models finger wiggling (that is, playing an imaginary piano or typing), and then the patient is asked to wiggle his own fingers. Typically, the nondominant hand cannot be wiggled as quickly as the dominant hand, but it takes a trained eye to pick up a significant decrease in rate. The experienced examiner will also be looking for abnormalities in the precision of the movements and the rhythm of the movements, "mirror movements" (uncontrolled similar movements in the other hand when instructed to only wiggle one), and other abnormal involuntary movements. Like the nose-finger test, finger wiggling supplies information concerning the quality of involuntary movement and muscular coordination. A related task involves tongue wiggling.

Medical Diagnostic Aids in Neuropsychological Examinations

Data from neuropsychological testing combined with data derived from various medical procedures can in some cases yield a thorough understanding of a neurological problem. For example, certain behavioral indices evident in neuropsychological testing may lead the neuropsychologist to recommend that a particular site in the brain be further explored for the presence of lesions—a suspicion that may be confirmed by a diagnostic procedure that yields cross-sectional pictures of the site.

The trained neuropsychologist has a working familiarity with the armamentarium of nonpsychological—medical—tests that may be brought to bear on neuropsychological problems. In this discussion we describe a sampling of such tests and measurement procedures. We begin with a brief description of the medical procedure and apparatus that is perhaps most familiar to us all—whether from experience in a dentist's chair or elsewhere—the X-ray.

To the radiologist, the X-ray photograph's varying shades convey information about the corresponding density of the tissue through which the X-rays have been passed. With front, side, back, and other X-ray views of the brain and the spinal column, the diagnosis of tumors, lesions, infections, and other abnormalities can frequently be made. There are many different types of neuroradiologic procedures that can be employed. These range from the simple X-ray of the skull to more complicated procedures involving the injection of some tracer element into the bloodstream (as is required for a cerebral angiogram).

Perhaps you have also heard or read about another X-ray-type of procedure, the "CAT (computerized axial tomography) scan" or "CT" scan (Figure 1). The *CT scan* is superior to traditional X-rays because the structures in the brain may be represented in a systematic series of three-dimensional views, a feature that is extremely important in assessing conditions such as spinal anomalies. *PET* (positron emission tomography) scans are a tool of nuclear medicine particularly useful in diagnosing biochemical lesions

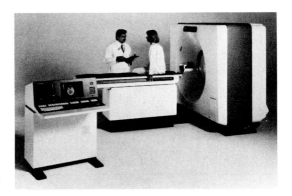

Figure 1 The CT scan is useful in pinpointing the precise location of tumors, cysts, degenerated tissue or other abnormalities and its use may eliminate the need for exploratory surgery or painful diagnostic procedures used in brain or spinal studies.

in the brain. PET has also been used as a tool in evaluation research with schizophrenics and other psychiatric patients (Trimble, 1986). Conceptually related to the PET scan is *SPECT* (single photon emission computed tomography), a technology that records the course of a radioactive tracer fluid (iodine) producing exceptionally clear photographs of organs and tissues (Figure 2).

Also referred to as a "radioisotope scan," the *brain scan* procedure involves the introduction of radioactive materials into the brain via an injection. The cranial surface is then scanned with a special camera to track the flow of material. Alterations in blood supply to the brain are noted, including alterations that may be associated with disease such as tumors.

The *electroencephalograph* (EEG) is a machine that measures the electrical activity of the brain by means of electrodes pasted to the scalp. It is a relatively safe, painless procedure that can be of significant value in diagnosing and treating seizure and other disorders. The electroencephalographer is trained to distinguish normal from abnormal brain wave activity. EEG activity will

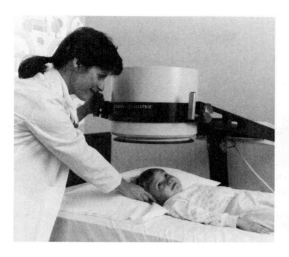

Figure 2 SPECT technology has been found to be of promising value in evaluating conditions such as cerebral vascular disease, Alzheimer's disease, and seizure disorders.

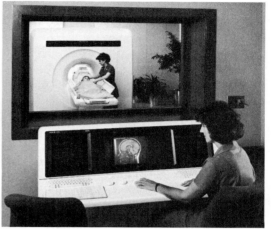

Figure 3 This magnetic resonance system utilizes a magnetic field and radio waves to create detailed images of the body. These and related imaging techniques may be employed not only in the study of neuropsychological functioning but in the study of abnormal behavior as well; see, for example, Kellner et al.'s (1991) study of obsessive-compulsive disorder.

vary as a function of age, level of arousal (awake, drowsy, asleep), and other variables in addition to brain abnormalities. EEG technology has been used to study a wide variety of neuropsychological phenomena such as electrical activity of the brain in Alzheimer's disease (see, for example, Martin-Loeches et al., 1991).

The *electromyograph* (EMG) is a machine that records electrical activity of muscles by means of an electrode that is inserted directly into the muscle. Abnormalities found in the EMG can be used with other clinical and historical data as an aid in making a final diagnosis. The *echoencephalograph* is a machine that transforms electric energy into sound (sonic) energy. The sonic energy ("echoes") transversing the tissue area under study is then converted back into electric energy and displayed as a printout. This printout is used as an adjunct to other procedures in helping the neurologist to determine the nature and location of certain types of lesions in the brain. Radio waves in combination with a magnetic field can also be used to create detailed anatomical images—as illustrated in Figure 3.

Information about nerve damage and related abnormalities may be obtained by direct electrical stimulation of nerves and notation of

movement or lack of movement in corresponding muscle tissue. Examination of the cerebrospinal fluid for blood and other abnormalities is an important diagnostic aid to the neurologist. A sample of the fluid is obtained by means of a medical procedure called a *lumbar puncture*—in everyday terminology, a spinal tap. This procedure entails the insertion of a special needle into the widest spinal interspace, after a local anesthetic has been applied. In addition to providing information concerning the chemical normality of the fluid, the test also provides the neurologist with the opportunity to gauge the normality of the intracranial pressure.

Laboratory analysis of blood, urine, and other cells will provide the physician with a wealth of leads concerning possible bases for suspected neurological difficulties. For example, a presenting problem of decreased sensation may be due to a number of different causes such as diabetes mellitus (which could be diagnosed by a procedure called a glucose tolerance test).

A complete examination is designed to assess not only the functioning of the brain but aspects of the functioning of the nerves, muscles, and other organs and systems as well. Some procedures used to shed light on the adequacy and functioning of some of the 12 cranial nerves are summarized in Table 16–6. Needless to say, other more specific tests and procedures may be employed as the examiner sees fit. Additionally, medical practitioners have at their disposal a variety of so-

Table 16–6

*Sample Tests Used by Neurologists to Assess
the Intactness of Some of the 12 Cranial Nerves*

Cranial nerve	Test
I (olfactory nerve)	Closing one nostril with a finger, the examiner places some odiferous substance under the nostril being tested and asks whether the smell is perceived. Subjects who perceive it are next asked to identify it. Failure to perceive an odor when one is presented may be indicative of lesions of the olfactory nerve, a brain tumor, or other medical conditions. Of course, failure may be due to ther factors, such as oppositional tendencies on the part of the patient or intranasal disease, and such factors must be ruled out as causal.
II (optic nerve)	Assessment of the intactness of the second cranial nerve is a highly complicated procedure, for this is a sensory nerve with functions related to visual acuity and peripheral vision. A Snellen eye chart will therefore be one of the tools used by the physician in assessing optic nerve function. If the subject at a distance of 20 feet from the chart is able to read the small numbers or letters in the line labeled line "20," then the subject is said to have 20/20 vision in the eye being tested. 20/20 vision is only a standard; and while many persons can read only the larger print at higher numbers on the chart (that is, a person who reads the letters on line "40" of the chart would be said to have a distant vision of 20/40), some persons have better than 20/20 vision. An individual who could read the line labeled "15" on the Snellen eye chart would be said to have 20/15 vision.
V (trigeminal nerve)	The trigeminal nerve supplies sensory information from the face, and it supplies motor information to and from the muscles involved in chewing. Information regarding the functioning of this nerve will be examined by the use of tests for facial pain (pinpricks will be made by the physician), facial sensitivity to different temperatures, and other sensations. Another part of the examination will entail having the subject clamp his jaw shut. The physician will then feel and inspect the facial muscles for weakness and other abnormalities.
VIII (acoustic nerve)	The acoustic nerve has functions related to the sense of hearing and the sense of balance. Hearing may be formally assessed by the use of an apparatus called the audiometer. More frequently, the routine assessment of hearing will involve the use of a so-called "dollar watch." Provided the examination room is quiet, an individual with normal hearing should be able to hear a dollar watch ticking at a distance of about 40 inches from each ear (30 inches if the room is not very quiet). Other quick tests of hearing involve the placement of a vibrating tuning fork on various portions of the skull. Individuals who complain of dizziness, vertigo, disturbances in balance, and so forth may have their vestibular system examined by means of specific tests.

phisticated apparatuses and procedures to assist in the answering of diagnostic questions. Some of these diagnostic aids are illustrated in the Close-up for this chapter.

Neuropsychologists have at their disposal a wealth of psychological tests that may be valuable in assessing deficits, particularly deficits in the mild to moderate range. We now turn our attention to some of these instruments.

NEUROPSYCHOLOGICAL TESTS

Tests and assessment procedures have been created to assess virtually all conceivable aspects of neuropsychological functioning, including sundry aspects of perceptual, motor, verbal, memory, cognitive, and related functioning. Neuropsychological tests are used in screening for deficit and are also used as an adjunct to medical examinations, especially when the suspected deficit is mild or questionable in nature. Further, data derived from psychological testing are capable of providing information as to the site, progression, or regression of a neurological disease and can therefore be essential to accurate diagnosis and treatment (Pincus & Tucker, 1974). Additionally, neuropsychological tests can also be helpful in the assessment of:

- change in mental status or other variables as a result of medication, surgery, or some disease process
- abnormalities in function before abnormalities in structure can be detected
- strengths and weaknesses of the neurologically impaired patient, thus facilitating the rehabilitation process
- the ability of an individual to stand trial (that is, the ability to understand the charges against him)
- changes in a disease process over the course of a longitudinal neurological study

A detailed review of the hundreds of available neuropsychological tests is beyond the scope of this brief overview. In the following sections, we review a sampling of techniques used by neuropsychologists in their in-depth evaluations and by clinicians and school psychologists in their neuropsychological screenings. Note that while we discuss these tests under certain headings, most of the tests yield information that overlaps into other areas; a test that is primarily designed to test for memory, for example, might well be capable of yielding a wealth of information about perceptual functioning.

Specialized Interviews and Rating Scales

A number of structured interviews and rating forms are available as aids in the neuropsychological screening and evaluation process. Neuropsychological screening devices point the way to further areas of inquiry with more extensive evaluation methods. Such devices can be used economically with members of varied populations who may be at risk for neuropsychological impairment, such as psychiatric patients, the elderly, and alcoholics (Berg, Franzen, & Wedding, 1987; Errico, Nixon, Parsons, & Tassey, 1990; Goldstein, 1986; Yozawitz, 1986). Some of these measures, such as the Short Portable Mental Status Questionnaire (Pfeiffer, 1975) are completed by an assessor, while others, such as the Neuropsychological Impairment Scale (NIS; O'Donnell & Reynolds, 1983) are self-report instruments completed by the assessee. The NIS contains 50 items that survey complaints indicative of neuropsychological difficulties and requires the assessee to rate the intensity with which they experience symptoms. Past research with another self-report-type neuropsychological instrument, the Patient's Assessment of Own Functioning (PAF), has not been encouraging; studies suggest that when used with populations of general neuropsychological referrals and alcoholics, the PAF may yield a measure more reflective of affective state than actual neuropsychological impairment (Chelune, Heaton, & Lehman, 1986; Shelton & Parsons, 1987).

Intellectual Ability Tests in Neuropsychology

Tests of intellectual ability, particularly the Wechsler scales, occupy a prominent position among the diagnostic tools available to the neuropsychologist. In fact, a survey of members of the APA Division of Clinical Neuropsychology and members of the National Academy of Neuropsychologists indicated that of all psychological tests and test batteries, the Wechsler scales were far and away the single most frequently used in practice by neuropsychologists; while many neuropsychologists use a variety of different techniques in their daily practice, one test virtually all of them use is a Wechsler intelligence test (Seretny, Dean, Gray, & Hartlage, 1986).

The varied nature of the tasks on the Wechsler scales and the wide variety of responses required of the subject make it a good bet that if a neuropsychological deficit exists, some clue to the existence of the deficit will be brought to light. Thus, for example, difficulties in attention, concentration, or conceptualization might be noted during the administration of the Arithmetic items—a possible clue to a neurological deficit as opposed to a lack of arithmetic ability. Because certain patterns of test response are indicative of particular deficits, the examiner will look beyond performance on individual tests to a study of the pattern of test scores, a process referred to as *pattern analysis*. Thus, for example, extremely poor performance on the Block Design and other performance subtests in a record that contains relatively high scores on all of the verbal subtests might, in combination with other data, lead the examiner to suspect damage in the right hemisphere. A number of researchers intent on developing a definitive sign of brain damage have devised various ratios and quotients based on patterns of subtest scores. David Wechsler himself referred to one such pattern called a "deterioration quotient" or "DQ" (also referred to by some as a "deterioration index"). However, neither the DQ nor any formula subsequently developed has performed satisfactorily enough in investigations to be a stand-alone definitive measure of neurological impairment.

We have already noted the need to administer standardized tests in a manner that rigidly conforms to the instructions in the test manual. Yet due to the limited ability of the test taker, such "by the book" test administrations are not always possible or desirable when testing members of the neurologically impaired population. Because of various problems or potential problems (such as the shortened attention span of some neurologically impaired individuals), the experienced examiner may find it necessary to modify the test administration in ways that will accommodate the test taker yet yield clinically useful information. The examiner administering a Wechsler scale may deviate from the prescribed order of test administration when administering the test to an individual who becomes fatigued quickly; in such cases, the more taxing subtests will be administered early in the exam. In the interest of shortening the total test administration time, the trained examiner might judge it necessary to omit certain subtests that he or she suspects will not provide any information over and above that already obtained. Let us reiterate that such deviations in the administration of standardized tests such as the Wechsler scales can be made—and meaningfully interpreted—by trained and experienced neuropsychologists. For the rest of us, it's *by the book!*

Memory Tests

Memory is an important, multifaceted, cognitive function. The thorough neuropsychological evaluation of memory will include assessments of immediate memory, remote memory, and addition of new information to immediate memory. A clinician may informally test for the latter form of memory by mentioning something (for example, three states—Mississippi, Rhode Island, and Idaho) at the beginning of an examination; then, ten minutes or so later, the clinician asks the examinee to recall the states mentioned. Formal testing for memory may involve the use of instruments such as the Wechsler Memory Scale—Revised (WMS-R), a psychometrically sound instrument (Holden, 1988) appropriate for use with people from age 16 to 74 (D'Elia, Satz, & Schretlen, 1989), that has many potential applications (see, for example, O'Leary, Brouwers, Gardner, & Cowdry, 1991). In general, the task of the test taker is to recall stories and other verbal stimuli, and the test yields composite scores for Verbal Memory, Visual Memory, General Memory (Verbal and Visual Memory), Attention/Concentration, and Delayed Recall (see Table 16–7 for a description of the subtests). Verbal memory can also be assessed by any number of existing tests that involve the presentation of words, digits, nonsense syllables, sentences, or other such stimuli which must subsequently be recalled. Such tests include the Randt Memory Test (Randt & Brown, 1983), the Rey Auditory Verbal Learning Test, and the Selective Reminding Test.

Nonverbal memory may be assessed by means of tests such as the Benton Test of Visual Retention—Revised and the Memory for Designs Test, two tests that provide a measure of the test taker's ability to perceive and retain images of visually presented geometric figures.[3] Milner (1971) devised another nonverbal memory measure, this one employing twisted pieces of wire that are in essence "tactile nonsense figures." The examinee's task is to match the figures using the

---

3. A comparison of the effectiveness of these two instruments indicated that the Benton was preferable to the Memory for Designs Test in evaluating patients with mild to moderate brain damage (Marsh & Hirsch, 1982). Another study (Tamkin & Kunce, 1985) indicated that the Benton was a valid predictor of neuropsychological problems by itself, but that its predictive validity increased when used in combination with two other neuropsychological tests (the Hooper Visual Organization Test and the Weigl Color-Form Sorting Test).

right or left hand (Figure 16–4). Another tactile memory test involves an adaptation in the administration of the Seguin-Goddard Formboard. Although the formboard was initially designed to assess visuopractic ability, Halstead (1947a) suggested that it could be used to assess tactile memory if subjects were blindfolded during the test and a recall trial was added.

One effort to make memory tests more "real world" in nature is to substitute memory tasks that people must perform each day (for example, those related to driving, meeting new people, remembering lists) for memory tasks that involve memorizing strings of numbers or words. In one 15-test computerized battery developed by Thomas Crook and described by Hostetler (1987), such "real world" tasks are incorporated in measures such as telephone dialing and name-face association. Crook's memory test battery is currently being used not for diagnostic purposes, but for evaluating the effects of various drugs in the treatment of Alzheimer's disease.

Tests of Cognitive Functioning

Difficulty in thinking abstractly is a relatively common consequence of brain injury regardless of the site of the injury. One popular measure of verbal-abstraction ability is the Wechsler Similarities subtest, isolated from the age-appropriate version of the Wechsler intelligence scale. The task is to identify how

Table 16–7

Subtests of the WMS-R

Index	Subtest	Description
Verbal Memory	Logical Memory I	Two stories are read to the examinee, who then retells them from memory
	Verbal Paired Associates II	Eight word pairs are read to the examinee. Then the first word is read and the examinee supplies the second word from memory
Visual Memory	Figural Memory	A set of abstract designs is shown to the examinee, who must identify them from a larger set
	Visual Paired Associates I	The examinee identifies the color associated with each of six abstract designs
	Visual Reproduction I	The examinee draws from memory geometric designs that are presented
	Delayed Recall (administered 30 minutes after original presentation)	
	Logical Memory II	Examinee retells the stories originally presented
	Verbal Paired Associates II	Examinee recalls the second word from the eight word pairs originally presented
	Visual Paired Associates II	Examinee identifies the colors associated with the previously presented designs
	Visual Reproduction II	Examinee reproduces from memory the previously presented geometric designs
Attention/ Concentration	Digit Span	Examinee repeats sequences of numbers in forward order (Part I) and in reverse order (Part II)
	Visual Memory Span	Examinee taps sequences of squares in forward order (Part I) and in reverse order (Part II)

two objects (for instance, a ball and an orange) are alike. Proverb interpretation is another method used to assess ability to think abstractly. As an example, interpret the following proverb before reading on:

A stitch in time saves nine.

If your interpretation got across the idea that "haste makes waste," then you evidenced an ability to think abstractly. By contrast, some people with neurological deficits might have interpreted that proverb more concretely—with less abstraction. An interpretation such as "When sewing, take one stitch at a time—it'll save you from having to do it over nine times" might—or might not depending on other factors—betray a deficit in abstraction ability. The Proverbs Test (Gorham, 1956) contains a number of proverbs along with standardized administration instructions and normative data. In one form of this test the subject is instructed to write an explanation of the proverb. In another form of the test, this

---

Figure 16–4 *Two Tools Used in the Measurement of Tactile Memory.*

Illustrated at right is one form of the Seguin-Goddard Formboard. Blindfolded examinees are instructed to fit each of the 10 wooden blocks into the appropriate space in the formboard with each hand separately and then with both hands. Afterward the examinee may be asked to draw the formboard from memory. All responses are timed and scored for accuracy.

Four pieces of wire bent into what are in essence "tactile nonsense figures" can be used in a tactile test of immediate memory. Examinees may be instructed to feel one of the figures with their right or left hand (or both hands) and then locate a matching figure.

one multiple-choice, each proverb is followed by four choices, three of which
may be either common misinterpretations or representative of a concrete-type
response.

Nonverbal tests of abstraction include any of the various sorting tests—tests
that require the respondent to sort objects in some logical way. Common to most
of the sorting tests are instructions like "Group together all the ones that belong
together" followed by questions such as, "Why did you group those objects together?" Representative of such tests is the Object Sorting Test (see Figure 16–3),
a test that contains familiar objects which the subject is required to sort according
to various categories (such as color or use). Alternatively, the examiner may
group a few of the objects together and ask the subject to determine why those
objects go together or to select the object that does not belong with the rest. Another such sorting test is the Color Form Sorting Test (also referred to as Weigl's
Test) wherein the subject's task is to sort objects of different shapes and colors
according to the directions of the examiner. The Wisconsin Card Sorting Test requires the subject to sort a pack of 64 cards with different geometric figures of
different colors according to rules that (1) must be inferred and (2) shift as the test
progresses.

Brain damage may result in deficits with respect to organizing and planning
abilities as well as ability to reason. One tool used in assessing ability to organize
and plan is the Porteus Maze Test (see Figure 16–5). Here the subject's task is to

Figure 16–5 *Make the "right choice," Charly.* A Porteus-mazelike task is being illustrated by the woman in the white coat to actor Cliff Robertson as "Charly" in the now-
classic film of the same name.

trace a path through mazes, from start to finish without entering a blind alley. Insight into a subject's reasoning abilities may be assessed by means of the Comprehension subtest on Wechsler subtests or by Binet-type Verbal Absurdities or Picture Absurdities items (see item *a* in Figure 16–6). Wechsler subtests such as Digit Span, as well as numerous other tests, including the MMPI (Gass, Russell, & Hamilton, 1990), may be useful in the assessment of other indices of cognitive functioning, such as concentration.

Common to many types of neurological impairment are disorders of orientation—a lack of awareness of one's relationship to one's surroundings. Orientation difficulties usually become apparent during the mental status interview. One formal, now-classic measure of personal orientation is Head's (1925) Eye, Hand and Ear Test. The examiner sits in front of the examinee and alternately points to his right and left eye, and right and left ear, while the patient's task is to imitate this movement on his or her own body. Noting that the examiner giving this test might model the desired movements to the examinee, Maloney, Ball, and Edgar (1970) modified and standardized the procedure by using large pictures of a person pointing to the right or left ear or eye with the right or left hand. Another aspect of spatial orientation can be assessed by the Standardized Road-map Test of Direction Sense (Money, 1976). On that test, the task of the assessee is to describe turns in a path the examiner traces on a grid.

Tests of Verbal Functioning

Aphasia, not to be confused with *aphagia,* refers to a loss of ability to express oneself and/or to understand spoken or written language due to some neurological deficit.[4] A number of batteries such as the Neurosensory Center Comprehensive Examination of Aphasia (NCCEA) have been designed to help identify the extent and nature of the communication deficit. The NCCEA (Spreen & Benton, 1969), for example, is composed of 24 subtests, 20 of which are designed to assess various aspects of auditory and visual comprehension and oral/written expression. The remaining 4 subtests address visual and tactile functioning, and these subtests are administered only when the examiner suspects a visual or tactile sensory deficit.

Verbal fluency and fluency in writing are sometimes affected by injury to the brain, and there are tests to assess the extent of the deficit in such skills. In the Controlled Word Association Test (formerly called the Verbal Associative Fluency Test), the examiner says a letter of the alphabet and it is the subject's task to say as many words as he or she can think of that begin with that letter. Each of three trials employing three different letters as a stimulus lasts one minute, and the test taker's final score on the test reflects the total number of correct words produced weighted by other factors (that is, the sex, age, and education of the test taker). A counterpart of this test applicable to the assessment of written fluency can be found in the Primary Mental Abilities tests (Thurstone & Thurstone, 1962). Here the examiner provides the test taker with letters of the alphabet, and the test taker writes down as many four-letter words as he or she can that begin with each letter within stated time limits.

---

4. *Aphagia* refers to an inability to eat.

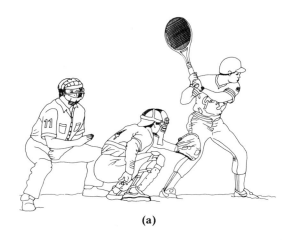

(a)

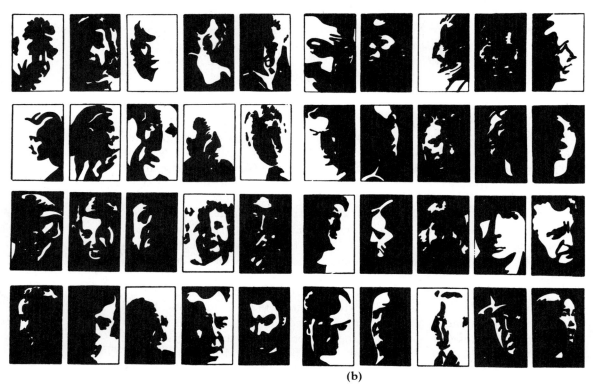

(b)

Figure 16–6 *Sample Items from Some Tests That May Be Used in a Neuropsychological Examination.*
(a) "What's wrong or silly about this picture?" This is the type of question asked in conjunction with picture absurdity–type items; (b) the Mooney Closure Faces Test requires subjects to sort the faces—shaded to varying degrees of ambiguity—into piles labeled boy, girl, grown man, grown woman, old man, and old woman. (c) The task in a Field of Search item is to locate a match to a sample figure as quickly as possible; (d) the Trail Making Test is a connect-the-circles task that provides information about visual-conceptual and visual-motor tracking ability.

For use in assessing the development of receptive and expressive communication in children aged 4 months to 4 years, the Sequenced Inventory of Communication Development contains a number of observation and test procedures designed to assess various aspects of the young child's awareness and understanding. Two neuropsychological measures of language deficit designed expressly for use with Hispanic children are the Del Rio Language Screening Test (Toronto, 1973; Toronto, Leverman, Hanna et al., 1975) and the Developmental Assessment of Spanish Grammar (Toronto, 1976); both tests can be used as aids in evaluating various aspects of receptive and expressive communication in Spanish-speaking children.

Perceptual, Motor, and Perceptual-Motor Tests

Brain injury can have a disruptive effect on perceptual, motor, and perceptual-motor functioning, and a number of tests designed to assess functioning in these areas exist (see Figure 16–6). Neurologically impaired individuals may exhibit difficulty in making sense out of fragmented or jumbled stimuli, and tests such as Mooney's Closure Faces Test are designed to assess the existence and extent of this deficit. People with right hemisphere lesions may exhibit deficits in visual scanning ability, and a test such as the Field of Search can be of value in discovering such deficits. Color blindness may be screened for using the Ishihara (1964) test, though more specialized instruments are available if rare forms of color perception deficit are suspected. Among the tests available for measuring deficit in auditory functioning is the Wepman Auditory Discrimination Test. This brief, easy-to-administer test requires that the examiner read a list of 40 pairs of monosyllabic meaningful words (such as "muss"/"much") pronounced with lips covered. The examinee's task is simply to determine if the two words just presented

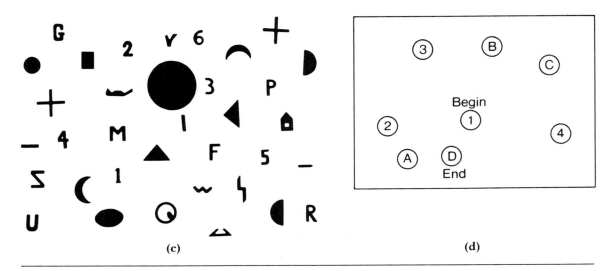

(c)   (d)

Figure 16–6 *(continued)*

are the same or different. It's quite a straightforward test—provided that the examiner (1) isn't suffering from a speech defect, (2) has no heavy foreign accent, and (3) exhibits no proclivities toward muttering.

An example of a test designed to assess gross and fine motor skills is the Bruininks-Oseretsky Test of Motor Proficiency. Designed for use with children aged 4½ to 14½, this instrument includes subtests that assess running speed and agility, balance, strength, response speed, and dexterity. A sphere referred to by its manufacturer as a "Neuro Developmental Training Ball" (see Figure 16–7) may be used to assess balance and the vestibular sense. A measure of manual dexterity that was originally developed in the late 1940s as an aid in employee selection is the Purdue Pegboard Test (Figure 16–8). The object here is to insert pegs into holes using one hand, then the other hand, and then both hands. Each segment of these three segments of the test has a time limit of 30 seconds, and the score is equal to the number of pegs correctly placed. Normative data are available and it is noteworthy that in a non-brain-injured population, women generally perform slightly better on this task than men. With brain-injured subjects, this test may be employed to help answer questions regarding the lateralization of a lesion.

A number of tests are designed to assess visual-motor integration. The Beery-Buktenica Development Test of Visual-Motor Integration is a test in which the examinee's task is to copy geometric forms arranged in increasing order of difficulty. The Frostig Developmental Test of Visual Perception measures some

Figure 16–7 *Neuro Developmental Training Balls.*

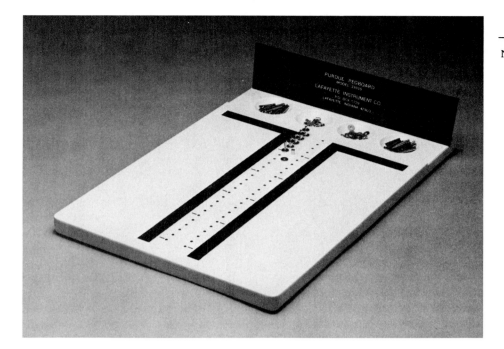

Figure 16–8 *The Purdue Pegboard Test.*

aspects of visual perception and eye-hand coordination by means of subtests that entail drawing lines between boundaries, finding embedded figures, distinguishing target shapes from other shapes, locating a rotated figure, and copying simple forms and patterns by joining dots. The Motor-Free Visual Perception Test is designed for use with children aged 4 to 9, and it contains items that involve tasks such as matching of geometric forms, locating stimulus drawings on various backgrounds, drawing a stimulus from memory, and determining which of a selection of drawings is different in terms of spatial orientation.

One of the most widely used psychological tests among the general population of users is the Bender-Gestalt test (Lubin, Wallis, & Paine, 1971). Because of its widespread use by clinicians, school psychologists, and others who have occasion to administer psychological tests, we provide an in-depth look at this test in the following section. It is noteworthy that while this test enjoys widespread usage among clinicians in general, one survey of test usage of neuropsychologists indicated that fewer than 50 percent of these specialists reported that they use this test in their practice—perhaps because they have more specialized instruments at their disposal (Seretny, Dean, Gray, & Hartlage, 1986).

The Bender Visual-Motor Gestalt Test

Frequently referred to simply as the "Bender-Gestalt" or even just "the Bender," this is the most popular, though not necessarily the best, of all the quick, neuropsychological screening instruments used by clinical, school, counseling, and other psychologists. In their survey of the American Psychological Association's approved clinical and counseling psychology graduate programs, Golden and Kupperman (1980) found that the Bender was the only assessment technique for evaluating cerebral function taught in a substantial number of them. The test materials are nine index-sized cards on each of which is printed one design. These designs, as well as others, had been used by the psychologist Max Wertheimer (1923) in his study of the perception of *gestalten* (a German word which loosely translates to "configurational wholes"). Physician Lauretta Bender (Figure 16–9) recognized the potential clinical application such designs might have in assessing perceptual maturation and neurological impairment in her 1938 monograph entitled "A Visual-Motor Gestalt Test and Its Clinical Use." We describe the administration, scoring, and psychometric properties of Bender's test.

Administration A desk with a smooth writing surface, two sharp, number 2 pencils with good erasers, and one 8½-inch-by-11-inch sheet of paper (placed on the desk so that the 11-inch edge is vertical) are required in preparation for the administration of the Bender-Gestalt. The examiner instructs the examinee as follows: "I have here nine cards with designs on them. I will show them to you one at a time and I want you to copy them as exactly as you can. Here is the first card. Copy it as best you can." The first card is then placed directly above the white paper with its length horizontal to the paper. After the first drawing is complete, the rest of the cards are administered in consecutive order. No time limit is imposed, but the total administration time for this component of the test seldom runs more than five minutes. Regardless, the clinician times the test session because an unusually long or short time with the test will be of diagnostic significance. If an examinee begins to rotate either the card or the paper he or she is instructed by the examiner that this is not permissible and the materials are returned to the proper angle. Erasing and starting a design over is permissible, while use of rulers or other aids and tracing is not.

After the ninth design has been copied, a procedure employed by many clinicians is to remove the cards and the completed sheets and place in their stead another blank sheet of paper in front of the examinee. The following instructions are then given: "Now please draw all of the designs you can remember." This phase of the test, referred to as the *recall* phase, had not appeared in the original test instructions published by Bender but was rather a modification proposed by Gobetz (1953). Although the recall data provide the clinician with an index of the examinee's concentration abilities and short-term visual-memory capacity, this procedure had initially been proposed by Gobetz as a means of testing a notion about how neurotic adults would perform as compared to normals on the task.[5] At the conclusion of the recall, the test is over. Examinees may then be asked to sign and date each sheet of paper. The examiner may draw an arrow on the back

---

5. Gobetz (1953) had hypothesized that owing to the pressure of the unexpected second test, subjects diagnosed as neurotic would be able to recall fewer figures on the recall portion of the test than would normal subjects. The recall procedure is routinely used with the Bender today, not to provide personality data, but rather to provide additional neuropsychological data.

Figure 16–9 *Lauretta Bender (1897–1987).*

Born on August 9, 1897, to John Oscar Bender, an attorney, and Katherine Irvine Bender, Lauretta was the youngest of four children. Lauretta repeated first grade three times and was thought to be mentally retarded in large part because of her tendency to reverse letters in reading and writing. However, by the time she completed grammar school any concerns about mental retardation were quelled as she had proved herself as an able student.

The family moved often. Lauretta attended high school in Los Angeles, where she cultivated an interest in biological research. She earned her B.S. and M.A. degrees at the University of Chicago and while there pursued research that led to her first scientific publications—hematological studies on experimental tuberculosis of the Guinea pig. Accepted at the State University of Iowa Medical School, she was granted a research and teaching assistantship and assigned to Dr. Samuel Orton in the department of neuropathology. In 1926 she earned her M.D. degree. This was followed by some study overseas, an internship at the University of Chicago, a residency at Boston Psychopathic Hospital, and a research appointment at the Henry Phipps Psychiatric Clinic of Johns Hopkins Hospital. While at Hopkins she met and co-authored a publication with the Viennese psychoanalyst and contemporary of Freud's, Paul Schilder, M.D., Ph.D. Despite the fact that Schilder was married and eleven years her senior, Bender is said to have fallen in love with Schilder and moved to New York with him in 1930 to work at Bellevue Hospital once Schilder had been offered and accepted a position there. After Schilder's divorce, the two were married in November of 1936 and within the following four years the couple had three children. Tragedy struck shortly after the birth of their third child in 1940; leaving the hospital after visiting Lauretta and his newborn daughter, Paul was struck down and killed by a car. Lauretta did not marry again until she was 70 years old, this time to Henry B. Parkes, Ph.D., and was widowed again after only five years of marriage.

Lauretta Bender is perhaps best remembered for her "Visual-Motor Gestalt Test" first published in 1938, though this prolific psychiatrist's writings have made contributions in a very wide range of areas. Bender served on the psychiatric staff at Bellevue Hospital from 1930 through 1956 and was appointed head of the Children's Psychiatric Division in 1934. Bender also held numerous other positions ranging from a professorship at New York University to an editorial advisor to Action Comics—the latter position stemming in part from an article she wrote that focused on the role of comics in developing children's reading skills. Lauretta Bender's accomplishments have been acknowledged by numerous professional organizations, who have bestowed on her a variety of honors and awards. Even in retirement in Maryland, Bender served as a consultant to various organizations, including the Anne Arundel County Board of Education.

of the sheets to indicate the direction or slant in which the paper was tilted as the
subject wrote. Also noted on the reverse side of the paper will be other extra-test
data (such as handedness of the examinee, any possible distractions, and so forth).

Scoring and interpretation In her original monograph Bender proposed that
the test not be scored according to a scoring system, but rather by the clinician's
own qualitative judgment. In subsequent writings (such as Bender, 1970) this
view has been reaffirmed. But necessity is the mother of invention and the need
for guidelines in scoring this appealingly simple test soon outweighed the recommendation of the test's author to the contrary. A number of different scoring systems were soon available, including some for use with adults (Hutt, 1985; Pascal
& Suttell, 1951; Watkins, 1976) and with children (Koppitz, 1963, 1975). Some
terms common to each scoring system are defined and illustrated in Figure
16–10.

Bender stimulus	Reproduction	Type of error
5.		Rotation
8.		Angulation
A.		Integration
1.		Perseveration
3.		Distortion of shape
A.		Disproportion

Figure 16–10 *Terms Used in Bender-Gestalt Scoring Systems.* Some sample types of
errors on the Bender that may be suggestive of organic impairment. Not all of the illustrated errors are signs of organic impairment at all ages.

The Pascal and Suttell (1951) scoring procedure assigns each response a numerical value with a total of 106 different scorable characteristics. Each card (excluding card A) has from 10 to 13 scorable items and 7 layout organization variables applied to the drawings as a whole. Examples of scorable characteristics include tremor (4 points), workover (2 points), and rotation (8 points). The higher the subject's score, the poorer his or her Bender performance. The mean score for seven age groups composed of both men and women with a high school education was found to be 18.0 (with a standard deviation of 9.4) and 12.7 (with a standard deviation of 8.8) for persons with a college education.

While working in a New York child guidance clinic, psychologist Elizabeth Koppitz was struck by the large number of children referred for learning or emotional problems who had concomitant perceptual problems. The Bender scoring system she developed for use with children from age 5 to age 11 is the most popular scoring system used by psychologists in the schools. As is true for the Pascal and Suttell (1951) system, points are awarded for incorrect reproductions of the stimulus figure, and the larger scores reflect poorer performance. In contrast with the adult system, however, the Koppitz system does not include differential weighting of scorable errors. The 1963 Koppitz standardization sample consisted of 637 male and 467 female schoolchildren (98% of whom were white) enrolled in 46 classes in 12 public schools. The schools were located in rural, urban, and suburban areas; however, the exact percentage from each area was not specified.

The 1975 restandardization included 975 children between the ages of 5 and 11. Geographically, the sample was unevenly distributed, with 15% from the West, 2% from the South, and 83% from the Northeast. Members of the 1975 norm group resided in rural areas (7%), small towns (31%), suburban areas (36%), and large metropolitan areas (25%). By comparison with the 1963 standardization sample, a better racial balance was obtained with 86% of the sample being white, 8.5% black, 4.5% Mexican and Puerto Rican, and 1% Oriental. Koppitz (1975) provides no information relating to the socioeconomic level of the sample, maintaining that this factor is not significantly related to Bender performance, though others (such as Buckley, 1978; Marmorale & Brown, 1977) have not agreed with this view.

Psychometric properties Koppitz (1975, pp. 27–31) reviewed test-retest reliability research reported for her scoring system. Eight studies were reviewed using samples of normal children from kindergarten through sixth grade with test-retest time intervals ranging from two testings on the same day to eight months between tests. Koppitz concluded: "Research findings showed conclusively that Bender test scores of normal elementary school pupils (end of kindergarten to sixth grade) are reliable" (p. 30). The total Koppitz score was more reliable than total time spent working or subscores of any of the four error categories (distortion, rotation, integration, perseveration). Other research supports this conclusion (Engin & Wallbrown, 1976; Wallbrown, Wallbrown, & Engin, 1976; Wallbrown & Fremont, 1980) though reported reliability coefficients have ranged from as little as .50 to .90. With respect to inter-scorer reliability using the Koppitz system, Koppitz (1975) summarized 23 studies and found the range of coefficients to be from .79 to .86 with most coefficients exceeding .85. Satisfactory inter-scorer reliability coefficients have also been reported by Buckley (1978).

Reviews of the research bearing on the validity of the Bender suggest that the test is a valid neuropsychological screening tool (Heaton, Baade, & John, 1978; Spreen & Benton, 1965) though many of the studies reviewed contained methodological deficiencies such as inappropriate subject selection procedures. Performance on the Bender, as Pascal and Suttell (1951) noted, "can indicate damage to the cortex *only when the damage shows its effect by pronounced disturbance of the ability to execute the test . . .* actual lesions may exist which cannot, on the basis of deviations noted by us, be detected in performance on this test" (pp. 62–66, emphasis added). Hain (1964) noted that "the test is not picking up impairment associated with small localized lesions in many parts of the brain" (p. 40).

A danger in using the Bender as a single test for neurological deficit is a high rate of false negatives (that is, no indication of organic damage on the Bender protocol while in actuality organic damage does exist). Bigler and Ehrenfurth (1980, 1981) provided numerous examples of satisfactory performance on the Bender in individuals with documented organic damage, and they estimated that the rate of false negatives for the Bender is "in the neighborhood of 40% or worse" (p. 567). These researchers emphasized that any single test for organic impairment tapping only selected dimensions of brain functioning can similarly be expected to produce an unacceptably high rate of false negatives. Lezak (1976, p. 320) is among those neuropsychologists who has marvelled that "the Bender is as effective as it is since many kinds of brain pathology simply do not affect the specific functions involved in this visuographic exercise."

The cost of false negatives is high (Satz, 1966) and the consequences of not diagnosing neurological deficit when it in fact exists may be grave (Krug, 1971). Such considerations must be kept in mind when conducting neuropsychological screenings.

Modifications of the traditional Bender   Numerous modifications of Lauretta Bender's test have been proposed since the test procedure was first published. For example, Canter (1963, 1966) developed a background interference procedure (the "BIP Bender") in an effort to reduce the number of false negatives obtained with it. Canter's procedure entails a standard administration of the Bender followed by one in which the examinee must copy the designs on paper that has randomly interwoven curved lines. Canter (1966; Adams, Kenney, & Canter, 1973) has argued that the BIP Bender is more sensitive to organic impairment than the traditional administration, although exactly how much more sensitive it is remains a matter of controversy (Tolor & Brannigan, 1980). In an effort to distinguish perceptual from motor deficits, Labrentz, Linkenhoker, and Aaron (1976) developed a multiple-choice Bender that measures visual perception without measuring motor responses. Other modifications of the Bender procedure have included the manufacturing of oversized Bender cards suitable for group administration and the manufacturing of Bender booklets for the same purpose. It is noted, however, that when the designs are individually drawn in booklets, information on how the examinee would have organized the drawings is lost. In general, group administration of this test is inadvisable due to the loss of important information concerning the individual examinee's mode of responding.

Clinicians have attempted to make the Bender serve "double duty" and yield information about not only neuropsychological intactness, but personality func-

Table 16–8

Emotional Indicators on the Bender

1. *Confused order:* Associated with poor planning and inability to organize material.
2. *Wavy line on Figures 1 and 2:* Associated with poor motion coordination and/or emotional instability
3. *Dashes substituted for circles on Figure 2:* Associated with impulsivity and lack of interest in young children.
4. *Increasing size on Figures 1, 2, or 3:* Associated with low frustration tolerance and explosiveness.
5. *Large size:* Associated with acting-out behavior in children.
6. *Small size:* Associated with anxiety, withdrawal, and timidity in children.
7. *Fine line:* Associated with timidity, shyness, and withdrawal in young children.
8. *Careless overwork or heavily reinforced lines:* Associated with impulsivity, aggressiveness, and acting-out behavior in children, although some researchers have found it to be related to high intelligence and good achievement.
9. *Second attempt:* Associated with impulsivity and anxiety.
10. *Expansion:* Associated with impulsivity and acting-out behavior in children.
11. *Box around design:* Associated with children who have weak inner control; they need and want limits and controls in order to function in school and at home.
12. *Spontaneous elaboration or additions to design:* Associated with children who are overwhelmed by fears and anxieties and are totally preoccupied with their own thoughts; they often have a tenuous hold on reality and may confuse fact and fantasy.

Adapted from Koppitz (1975)

tioning as well. Some have made inferences about the symbolic significance of errors in producing specific designs. For example, Halpern (1951) believed that a disturbance in reproducing Bender Figure 8 was indicative of homosexuality. Koppitz (1963, 1975) listed twelve "emotional indicators" or "EIs" (see Table 16–8) and cautioned that the "presence of three or more EIs on a Bender test protocol tends to reflect emotional difficulties that warrant further investigation" (Koppitz, 1975, p. 92). Suczek and Klopfer (1952) proposed that the Bender could be used as a kind of projective test if examinees were asked to discuss their associations to the stimuli. The Hutt (1977) Adaptation of the Bender Gestalt entails a copying task (in which examinees are not told how many designs they will be given nor how much paper they will need), an elaboration task (in which examinees are instructed to copy the stimulus cards with any modification or elaborations they see fit to make), and an association task (in which examinees are instructed to verbalize their associations to the Bender stimuli). Research on such adaptations has served to remind clinicians that even neuropsychological screening instruments can tangentially provide insight into personality. It must be kept in mind, however, that the test user's goal in general is to make optimal use of both the professional and the patient's time and that requires the administration of tests that are directly—not tangentially—designed for use with respect to the subject matter of the assessment. Evidence in support of the use of the Bender-Gestalt as an instrument to assess personality is tenuous (Holmes, Dungan, & Medlin, 1984).

The "Flexible" Battery

The tests we've listed only begin to illustrate the diversity that exists with respect to the numerous techniques and methods available to the clinician doing neuro-psychological assessment. On the basis of the mental status examination, the physical examination, and the case history data, the neuropsychologist will typically administer a *flexible battery* of neuropsychological tests; specific tests will be chosen for some purpose relevant to the unique aspects of the patient and the presenting problem. This so-called flexible battery of tests hand-picked by the neuropsychologist stands in contrast to a standard or prepackaged battery of neuropsychological tests wherein all examinees are administered the same subtests in the context of a standardized procedure.

The clinician who administers a flexible battery has not only the responsibility of selecting the tests to be used, but also the burden of integrating all of the findings from each of the individual tests—no simple task since each test may have been normed on different populations. Another problem inherent in the use of a flexible battery is that the tests administered frequently overlap with respect to some of the functions tested, and the result is some waste in testing and scoring time. Regardless of these and other drawbacks attendant on the administration of a flexible battery, it is the preference of most highly trained neuropsychologists to tailor a battery of tests to the unique and specific demands of a particular testing situation.

The Prepackaged Battery

Prepackaged neuropsychological test batteries are designed to comprehensively sample the patient's neuropsychological functioning. The prepackaged battery is appealing to clinicians, especially clinicians who are relatively new to the area of neuropsychological assessment, because it tends to be less demanding in many ways. While a great deal of expertise and skill is required to fashion a flexible battery that will adequately answer the referral question, a prepackaged battery represents a non-tailor-made but comprehensive alternative. Various tests sampling various areas are included in the battery, and each is supplied with clear scoring methods. One major drawback of the prepackaged variety of tests, however, is that the specific handicap of the patient may greatly—and adversely—influence performance on the test; thus, an individual with a visual impairment, for example, may perform poorly on many of the other subtests of a battery that require certain visual skills.

Keeping in mind that trained neuropsychologists may administer a prepackaged battery, may modify a prepackaged battery for the purposes of a particular case at hand, or administer their own hand-picked assortment of tests, we now look at some representative test batteries.

The Halstead-Reitan Neuropsychological Battery Ward C. Halstead (1908–1969) was an experimental psychologist whose interest in the study of brain/behavior correlates led him to the establishment of a laboratory for that

purpose at the University of Chicago in 1935—the first such laboratory of its kind in the world. During the course of 35 years of research, Halstead studied over 1,100 brain-damaged persons. From his observations, Halstead (1947a, 1947b) derived a series of 27 tests designed to assess the presence or absence of organic brain damage—the Halstead Neurological Test Battery. A student of Halstead's, Ralph M. Reitan, would subsequently elaborate on his mentor's findings. In 1955, Reitan published two papers that dealt with the differential intellectual effects of various brain lesion sites (Reitan, 1955a, 1955b). Fourteen years and much research later, Reitan (1969) would privately publish a book entitled *Manual for Administration of Neuropsychological Test Batteries for Adults and Children*—the forerunner of the Halstead-Reitan Neuropsychological Test Battery (H-R).

Administration of the H-R requires a highly trained examiner conversant with the procedures necessary to administer the various subtests (see Table 16–9). Even with such an examiner, the test generally requires a full workday to complete. Subtest scores are interpreted not only with respect to what they mean by themselves, but by their relation to scores on other subtests. Appropriate interpretation of the findings requires the eye of a trained neuropsychologist, though H-R computer interpretation software—no substitute for clinical judgment but an aid to it—is available. Scoring yields a number referred to as the "Halstead Impairment Index," and an index of .5 or above the cutoff point is indicative of a neurologic problem; data on over 10,000 patients in the standardization sample were used to establish that cutoff point. Normative information has also been published with respect to other populations such as epileptics (Klove & Matthews, 1974), the retarded (Matthews, 1974), and neurologically intact, nonpsychiatric adults (Fromm-Auch & Yeudall, 1983). Leckliter and Matarazzo (1989) have cautioned that H-R performance may be affected by factors such as age, education, IQ, and gender, and that there is a "critical need to use clinical judgment in the selection of appropriate reference norms" (p. 509).

Conducting test-retest reliability studies on the H-R is a prohibitive endeavor in light of the amount of time it may take to complete one administration of the battery as well as other factors (such as practice effects and effects of memory). Still, as Matarazzo, Matarazzo, Wiens, Gallo, and Klonoff (1976) observed after their review of a number of reliability studies, "Despite the lack of comparability across the four samples on many dimensions, including age and test-retest intervals, the results again reveal a high degree of clinical as well as purely psychometric reliability for most of the tests in the neuropsychological battery" (pp. 348–349). A growing body of literature attests to the validity of the instrument in differentiating brain-damaged from normal subjects. One study with a children's version of the battery yielded findings supportive of the test's construct validity. The battery has also been used to identify neuropsychological impairment associated with learning disabilities (Batchelor, Gray, & Dean, 1990), and to aid in the localization of neurological lesions, as well as their associated cognitive, perceptual, motor, and behavioral deficits. This battery has achieved widespread acceptance as a standardized means of assessing neuropsychological capabilities (Dean, 1983; Guilmette & Faust, 1991; Guilmette, Faust, Hart, & Arkes, 1990; Whitworth, 1984).

A distinction has been made between tests that are theoretical versus relatively atheoretical in approach (Kelly & Dean, 1990). The Halstead-Reitan battery

Table 16-9

Subtests of the Halstead-Reitan Battery

Category

This is a measure of abstracting ability in which stimulus figures of varying size, shape, number, intensity, color, and location are flashed on an opaque screen. Subjects must determine what principle ties the stimulus figures together (such as color) and indicate their answer among four choices by pressing the appropriate key on a simple keyboard. If the response is correct a bell rings; if incorrect, a buzzer sounds. The test primarily taps frontal lobe functioning of the brain.

Tactual performance

Blindfolded examinees complete the Seguin Formboard (see Figure 16-5) with their dominant and nondominant hands and then with both hands. Time taken to complete each of the tasks is recorded. The formboard is then removed, the blindfold is taken off, and the examinee is given a pencil and paper and asked to draw the formboard from memory. Two scores are computed from the drawing: the *memory* score, which includes the number of shapes reproduced with a fair amount of accuracy, and the *localization* score, which is the total number of blocks drawn in the proper relationship to the other blocks and the board. Interpretation of the data includes consideration of the total time to complete this task, the number of figures drawn from memory, and the number of blocks drawn in proper relationship to the other blocks.

Rhythm

First published as a subtest of the Seashore Test of Musical Talent and subsequently included as a subtest in Halstead's (1947a) original battery, the subject's task here is to discriminate between like and unlike pairs of musical beats. Difficulty with this task has been associated with right temporal brain damage (Milner, 1971).

Speech sounds perception

This test consists of 60 nonsense words administered via an audiotape adjusted to the examinee's preferred volume. The task is to discriminate a spoken syllable, selecting from four alternatives presented on a printed form. Performance on this subtest is related to left hemisphere functioning.

Finger-tapping

Originally called the "finger oscillation test," this test of manual dexterity measures the tapping speed of the index finger of each hand on a tapping key. The number of taps from each hand is counted by an automatic counter. The number of taps from each hand is counted over five consecutive, 10-second trials with a brief rest period between trials. The total score on this subtest represents the average of the five trials for each hand. A typical, normal score is approximately 50 taps per 10-second period for the dominant hand and 45 taps for the non-dominant hand (a 10 percent faster rate is expected for the dominant hand). Cortical lesions may differentially affect finger-tapping rate of the two hands.

Time sense

The examinee watches the hand of a clock sweep across the clock and then has the task of reproducing that movement from sight. This test taps visual motor skills as well as ability to estimate time span.

Other tests

Also included in the battery is the Trail Making Test (see Figure 16-7) in which the examinee's task is to correctly connect numbered and lettered circles. A strength-of-grip test is also included; strength of grip may be measured informally by a hand-shake grasp and more scientifically by an instrument called a dynamometer (see Figure 16-12).

To determine which eye is the preferred or dominant eye, the Miles ABC Test of Ocular Dominance is administered. Also recommended is the administration of a Wechsler intelligence test, the MMPI (useful in this context for shedding light on questions concerning the possible functional origin of abnormal behavior), and an aphasia screening test adapted from the work of Halstead and Wepman (1959).

Various other sensory-motor tests may also be included. A test called the "critical flicker fusion test" was also at one time part of this battery but has since been discontinued by most examiners. If you have ever been in a disco and watched the action of the "strobe" light, you can appreciate what is meant by a light that flickers. To administer the flicker fusion test, an apparatus that emits a flickering light at varying speeds is required, and the examinee is instructed to adjust the rate of the flicker until the light appears to be steady or fused.

lies at the atheoretical end of the spectrum. We now look at a battery that lies at the other end.

The Luria Nebraska Neuropsychological Battery   Based on the theoretical postulations of the eminent Russian neuropsychologist, Aleksandr Luria, and first published in English as a test battery as recently as 1975 by Christensen, the Luria-Nebraska Neuropsychological Battery (Golden, Hammeke, & Purisch, 1980) is available in two equivalent forms. Form I consists of 269 items that individually and collectively are designed to explore the following areas: cerebral dominance, motor functions, perception and reproduction of pitch and rhythm, visual functions, receptive and expressive speech, reading, writing, arithmetic, memory, concept formation, and other intellectual processes. A "pathognomonic score" (reminiscent in intent to the Halstead Impairment Index) based on 31 of the items on the test most sensitive to brain damage is computed as a right and left hemisphere score. Form II consists of 279 items and includes an additional scale, Intermediate Memory. Form I can be computer-scored or hand-scored, but Form II is computer-scored only.

In terms of convenience, The Luria-Nebraska is an appealing test because it typically takes about one-third the time taken to administer the H–R, is more portable than the H–R, and can be administered at bedside (whereas the H–R cannot due to the need for special equipment).[6] However, the psychometric soundness of this test has been called into question. While it has been claimed that the test is relatively reliable and valid for its stated purposes (Golden et al., 1981), independent researchers have not been in agreement on this point (see Adams, 1984; Stambrook, 1983). The test has also been criticized for being overdependent on language skills (Franzen, 1985) and for yielding a high rate of false negative findings, especially with respect to aphasia (Crosson & Warren, 1982; Delis & Kaplan, 1982).

Other neuropsychological batteries   Among the other available neuropsychological batteries is the Montreal Neurological Institute Battery (Taylor, 1979), a test devised in large part as a result of intensive observation of neurosurgical patients. This battery contains many published tests, including the Wechsler intelligence tests, Mooney Faces, and Wisconsin Card Sorting tests. The battery is particularly useful to trained neuropsychologists in locating specific kinds of lesions. The battery was administered preoperatively and postoperatively to hundreds of patients who underwent a surgical excision of a defined area of brain tissue as the method of treatment for a brain tumor or epilepsy. Since the research on the battery was executed primarily with individuals who had surgically induced focal lesions, it is understandable that the battery has more utility in cases involving focal as opposed to diffuse lesions.

Many published and unpublished neuropsychological test batteries are designed to probe deeply into one area of neuropsychological functioning instead of

---

6. A portable and inexpensive version of the Halstead-Reitan Category Test that eliminates the need for a cumbersome projection box apparatus has been described by Slay (1984); a parts list for the "do-it-yourself" neuropsychological assessor is included in the article.

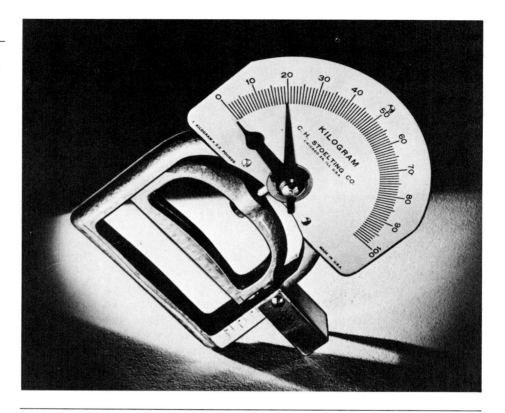

Figure 16–11   *A Dynamometer of the Kind Used as Part of the Halstead-Reitan Battery to Measure Strength of Grip.* The examinee is instructed to squeeze the grips as hard as possible, two trials with each hand. The score is recorded in terms of number of pounds of pressure exerted.

surveying for possible behavioral deficit in a variety of areas. Thus test batteries exist that focus on visual, sensory, memory, and communication problems; indeed batteries can focus on virtually any specific area of brain-behavior functioning. One such specialized battery is the Southern California Sensory Integration Tests. Designed to assess sensory–integrative and motor functioning in children 4 to 9 years of age, this battery consists of 18 standardized subtests. The Southern California is helpful not only in identifying children who are having sensory-motor problems but also in identifying the nature of those problems. A well-trained examiner is required to administer the tests and interpret the findings. The manual (Ayres, 1972) for this battery contains research bearing on the psychometric data of the individual tests and the battery as a whole as well as appropriate cautions regarding interpretations of test performance. Normative data provided in the test manual are sketchy, and some critics suspect that many of the functions assessed in this battery may be related more to intelligence than to the targeted functions.

Relatively new on the scene of neuropsychological batteries is one called the Severe Impairment Battery (SIB; Saxton, McGonigle-Gibson, Swihart, Miller, &

Boller, 1990). As its name implies, this series of tests is designed for use with severely impaired assessees who might otherwise perform at or near the floor of existing tests. The battery is divided into six subscales: Attention, Orientation, Language, Memory, Visuoperception, and Construction. Additionally, there are brief measures of responding to name, praxis, and social skills—the latter abstracted from Holland's (1980) test of Communicative Abilities in Daily Living. Many of the tasks included in this battery—as well as the kinds of abilities measured by each of the tasks—will (or should) sound familiar to the reader completing this chapter. For example, some of the tasks include counting and repeating digits, naming photographs of everyday objects, and drawing and copying shapes. Experimenting with a relatively small sample of subjects (41), Saxton et al. (1990, p. 301) tentatively concluded that the SIB "successfully elicits a range of performance in a variety of cognitive domains in severely demented patients." Based on what you now know about assessing neurological deficit, what other kind of test(s) would you advise the authors of the SIB to add to their new test?

Chapter 17

The Assessment of

People with

Disabling Conditions

WE ARE LIVING in an era in which the special needs of our physically challenged citizens are being acknowledged more than they ever before have been. The effects of this ever-increasing acknowledgment are visibly evident in things like special access ramps alongside flights of stairs; specially equipped buses designed to accommodate passengers in wheelchairs; large-print newspapers, books, and magazines for the visually impaired; captioned television programming for the hearing impaired; and signing and pantomiming of important speeches for the hearing impaired.[1] As medical technology continues to increase the chances that society's disabled citizenry will survive, so society has reponded with environmental aids and legal protection for the exceptional individual.[2] In 1973 Congress passed the Rehabilitation Act, a law that has been referred to as "The Bill of Rights for Handicapped Citizens," since it addressed many of the special needs of

---

1. Like the noun "mime," the verb *pantomime* has to do with communication by gesturing. As used in the context of psychological testing, pantomime is something that a test administrator might do with a deaf or hearing-impaired examinee in order to help convey the meaning of some instruction, question, or response.
2. In accordance with general usage of the word in educational contexts, the word "exceptional" is used here in its broadest sense; an *exceptional* individual is someone who differs from most other people with respect to some physical and/or mental ability. People with disabling conditions—as well as the gifted—may in this context be referred to as "exceptional."

the handicapped and outlawed job discrimination on the basis of handicap. In 1975 Congress passed Public Law 94-142, The Education for All Handicapped Children Act, mandating appropriate educational assessment and programs to meet the needs of the handicapped aged 3 to 18. The psychologist charged with assessing the exceptional child was now legally obliged to "use tests and other assessment materials which have been validated for the purposes for which they are being used" (Department of Health, Education, and Welfare, 1977a, 1977b). In 1986, Public Law 99-457, The Education for All Handicapped Children Act Amendments, extended the reach of the law downward to birth.

613

THE ASSESS-
MENT OF
PEOPLE WITH
DISABLING
CONDITIONS

In this chapter we survey some of the special considerations that must be taken into account in testing people who have sensory, motor, and/or cognitive deficits. We begin with a consideration of the factors that must be taken into account when testing blind or visually impaired people.

THE VISUALLY IMPAIRED AND THE BLIND

A three-category taxonomy of visual impairment useful in considerations related to testing and assessment was proposed by Bauman (1974). Included in the first category are people for whom vision is of no practical use in a testing or working assignment. The totally blind fall into this classification. Also included in this category are individuals who can differentiate between light and dark or even some who can distinguish shapes but can do so only when those shapes are held between the eyes and the source of light. The next category includes people for whom vision is of some assistance in handling large objects, locating test pieces in a work space, or following the hand movements of the examiner during a demonstration, but who cannot read even enlarged ink print effectively enough to be tested using such materials. Such individuals may be tested with materials that do not rely heavily on vision but rather require a combination of vision and touch. The third category includes people who read ink print efficiently although they may need large type, may hold the page very close to their eyes, or may use a magnifier or other special visual aid.

Issues in Test Administration and Interpretation

A valid assessment of a visually impaired or blind examinee requires an examiner who is attuned not only to the examinee's visual deficit but also to related deficits that may or may not be present in areas such as language development, socialization skills, and personality in general.[3] Sensitivity to these factors may be developed through experience with such a population and from reading about the experiences of various assessment specialists such as Bauman and Kropf (1979),

---

3. The phenomenon whereby one problem (such as a physical disability) may cause other kinds of difficulties for a particular individual (for example, personality-related problems) is referred to informally by clinicians as a "ripple effect." Needless to say, our caveat here concerning test-user sensitivity with respect to how one problem in an examinee's life could have affected other areas of the examinee's life is applicable to the assessment of all people and not just the blind or visually impaired.

Bradley-Johnson (1986); Bradley-Johnson and Harris (1990), Drinkwater (1976), Evans (1978), Tillman (1973), and Vander Kolk (1977).

While the nature of the specific assessment procedures employed will of course vary with the particular objective of the assessment, in general, the examiner will proceed in much the same way as with a fully sighted person, except that special attention will be paid to the developmental nature of the deficit and its consequences. Background information collected in the course of a comprehensive assessment may include information about the circumstances of the mother's pregnancy; health in infancy; health in early childhood; adjustment; socialization history; full health history, including age of onset of visual deficit; complete diagnosis, including related deficits such as color recognition skills, prognosis (including the findings of all specialists who have treated the patient), treatments administered (including lens prescription if available); records of previous testing and school attendance, as well as related records. The choice of the test instrument will of course depend on the specific purpose of the assessment, but the instrument should contain pictures, diagrams, and the like only to the extent that the examinee will be capable of seeing such visual materials. Some other commonsense guidelines in testing a visually impaired or blind person are:

- Modify the amount of light in the room so that it is optimal for the person being tested. Some examinees may require more light, and all that may be required is an extra lamp on an adjacent desk. Other examinees may be disturbed by excessive light and glare.
- It is important under any testing conditions to have a quiet testing room that is free of distractions. However, this requirement takes on added importance in the testing of blind or visually impaired people since these individuals may be more distracted by extraneous sounds than are the fully sighted.
- The work space should be relatively compact so that all equipment is within grasp of the examinee.
- If the test stimulus materials to be administered require some reading and the test is being administered to a partially seeing person, then it is advisable to retype the materials in large type if they are not already in large type. For the totally blind, an administration in braille may be appropriate; however, it is a fact that relatively few totally blind individuals read braille and relatively few of these people read it well.
- For the partially seeing examinee, writing instruments and written materials should be appropriate for the task. Thus, for example, a black felt-tip pen or crayon in most instances will be more appropriate than a fine-point ballpoint pen. Similarly, special wide-lined paper may be in order.
- In general, persons with impaired vision require more time than do non-impaired individuals. It may take longer to dictate materials than for the examinees to read the material themselves. When the partially sighted person is asked to use residual vision, test fatigue may set in, evidenced by behavior such as eye rubbing or other extraneous movements. Adequate time must be allowed for when testing the visually impaired.
- The use of multiple-choice questions, even when such questions are presented in braille, is frowned on by experts in this area, because this type of

615

THE ASSESS-
MENT OF
PEOPLE WITH
DISABLING
CONDITIONS

question places an extra burden of concentration on the visually impaired examinee.

- Introduction to the testing situation should include time for the examinee with a severe visual impairment to touch all the materials he or she will be working with during the test. During testing, more verbal feedback regarding what is going on may be required than with a sighted individual.

It is difficult, time-consuming, and expensive to develop norms applicable for use with the blind and the visually impaired; the group is relatively small in terms of number of cases and quite varied in terms of sightedness and related factors, including time of life in which vision became impaired or was lost, experience with respect to rehabilitative efforts, and other deficits compounding the effect of the visual impairment. Interpretation of standardized tests that have been modified for administration to blind or visually impaired people—like the interpretation of standardized tests that have been modified for administration to people with any other disabling conditions—is a matter of professional judgment; in many instances no relevant normative data will be available.

Available Instruments

In assessing the intellectual functioning of the blind and the visually impaired, the Verbal Scale of the Wechsler test of intelligence that is appropriate to the age of the examinee has been used frequently. The scale is orally administered and does not include any visual stimuli except for some portions of the Arithmetic subtest that can easily be modified. The latest (fourth) edition of the Stanford-Binet contains two subtests (Memory for Sentences, Memory for Digits) that can be administered without modification to visually impaired individuals. The use of braille versions for other subtests has been recommended (Delaney & Hopkins, 1987), although interpretation of findings must be cautious because of the absence of relevant norms. An intelligence test specifically designed for use with the blind and the visually impaired is the Haptic Intelligence Scale (HIS). The word *haptic* refers to the sense of touch, and the HIS exclusively employs the sense of touch in its administration; partially sighted examinees must wear a blindfold when taking this test, for viewing the test materials would invalidate the findings. Some of the subtests are described in Figure 17–1.

A number of other tests of intellectual ability have been developed for use with the visually impaired. Some have been modeled after existing intelligence tests (such as the Interim Hayes-Binet and the Perkins Binet) whereas others are independent in rationale from existing tests (for example, the Vocational Intelligence Scale for the Adult Blind, the Tactile Progressive Matrices, the Tactile Reproduction Pegboard, and the Blind Learning Aptitude Test).

In the area of personality assessment, most existing methods available for use with the sighted (see Part 4 of this book) can be readily adapted for use with the visually impaired and the blind. Test materials that must be read can be reprinted in large type, read to the examinee, or prerecorded on tape. Even a test such as the Thematic Apperception Test can be administered to a blind person if the blind person hears a description of the card and then proceeds to tell a story about it. A specially developed TAT-like test for the blind is the Sound Test, which contains prerecorded sounds such as footsteps, running water, and music, combined in some instances with verbal interchanges; the examinee's task is to construct a story about such aural stimuli. Other specially devised personality tests include The Emotional Factors Inventory and the Adolescent Emotional Factors Inventory, two tests that include scales measuring the examinee's adjustment to blindness. The Maxfield-Bucholz Social Competency Scale for Blind Preschool

---

Figure 17–1 *The Haptic Intelligence Scale.*

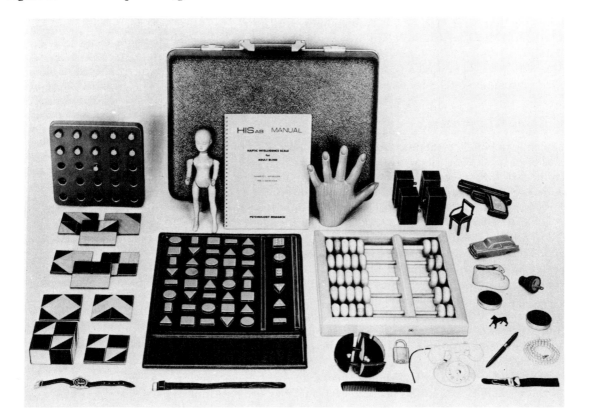

The Haptic Intelligence Scale (Shurrager & Shurrager, 1964) is an individually administered intelligence test designed for use with the adult blind. The test is composed of the following subtests:

Digit Symbol—Different patterns of raised dots (not braille) on sample geometric forms provide the code that the examinee uses to identify and "decode" like objects.

Block Design—Blocks with two rough sides and two sides diagonally bisected into half rough/half smooth sides are arranged in designs that reproduce a model design.

Object Assembly—As in the Wechsler tests, jigsawlike pieces are assembled into objects (such as a hand, a ball, a human figure).

Object Completion—Modeled after the Wechsler Picture Com-

pletion subtests, the subject's task here is to identify the missing part of a familiar object through touching it.

Pattern Board—The test taker's task on this subtest is to reproduce the pattern felt on a board that has rows of holes with pegs in them.

Bead Arithmetic—An abacus is used to solve arithmetic problems of varying difficulty.

Children is a measure of social competence and adaptive behavior designed for use with blind children from birth to age 6. The scale is administered to a third party such as the parent, guardian, or primary caregiver, and it is designed to explore areas such as the subject's physical development, ability with respect to self-care, and social competency.

Tests have also been developed to help the blind and the visually impaired with vocational guidance. Many of the available tests of finger and hand dexterity are used with this population. Available vocational interest inventories are administered to this population in large-print editions, braille, or other adaptations. One such test, the PRG Interest Inventory, was based entirely on the content of the types of jobs held by and the types of hobbies indulged in by blind respondents. In the test's instructions, examinees are advised to respond as if they have the visual capabilities to handle the description of the various jobs. The instructions were worded this way so that the test would yield a veritable measure of interest as opposed to perceived capability.

617

THE ASSESS-
MENT OF
PEOPLE WITH
DISABLING
CONDITIONS

THE HEARING-IMPAIRED AND THE DEAF

Hearing-impaired individuals differ with respect to variables such as magnitude of hearing loss, age of onset of loss, and consequential effects of the loss on language skills and social adjustment. Examiners who work with this population typically have access to a wealth of background information on each examinee (such as developmental, family, and school history; medical history, including audiological and speech evaluation; and so forth). Such background information will be useful not only in answering the particular assessment question asked, but also in formulating meaningful recommendations for treatment or remediation. For example, the examinee whose history shows the onset of severe hearing loss prior to the development of speech and language will require a remedial program that will be quite different from an examinee who suffered the hearing loss after the development of speech, although the two examinees might have had the exact same test scores on some psychological tests.

Issues in Test Administration and Interpretation

Most psychologists do not have technical expertise in American Sign Language (ASL) or other languages that have been devised for communication with the deaf. It is also true that many of the deaf or hearing-impaired people to be examined with psychological tests are not proficient enough in lipreading for the examiner to be certain that all test-related communications have been received. If the hearing impairment is mild, amplification of the examiner's voice through the use of an electronic amplification apparatus (or a hearing aid worn by the examinee) may be all that is required to be able to administer the test. However, if the hearing problem is more severe, the communication problem may be solved by one or more of the following solutions: (1) presenting written instructions at a reading level appropriate to the examinee, (2) pantomiming instructions and questions, and (3) conducting the examination through the use of an "interpreter" who will sign and/or pantomime all communication to the examinee and translate the examinee's responses when need be.

Necessary as one or more of the solutions outlined are, there are drawbacks associated with each. For example, using written communication instead of spoken communication introduces another variable (reading proficiency) into the task where no such variable had existed before. Pantomiming instructions and cues in the absence of explicit directions for doing so in the test manual results in a

---

Close-up

Attitudes toward the Disabled

Besides assessment of the disabled, psychological tests may serve related purposes, such as increasing our understanding of attitudes existing toward the disabled. With this latter goal in mind, you may wish to try the following exercise. Make up a story with a beginning, a middle, and an end in response to the TAT-like picture that appeared on page 457. Now do the same thing in response to Figure 1. Finally, analyze the content of your two stories with re-spect to any differences that emerge solely as a function of the prosthetic device the man is wearing in Figure 1. What do these differences tell you, if anything, about your own attitudes toward the disabled? You and your classmates may wish to try this exercise with a few people willing to serve as your research subjects—perhaps some who are disabled and some who are not—to get a sense of the nature of narrative specifics pertaining to the prosthetic device.

situation where different pantomimists (that is, different test administrators) may well have different ideas about how to get a point across by gestures; hence, the standardization of the instructions to the examinee will suffer. The introduction of an interpreter into the situation may have the effect of diminishing the rapport between the examiner and the examinee. Further, a certain amount of error in expressive and receptive translations can also be expected. The interpreter's signing skills must be compatible with the assessee's receptive skills. It would be inappropriate, for example, for the interpreter to sign in Coded Sign English (a method of communication more closely linked to the written/verbal expression of people with no hearing handicap), if the assessee is more fluent in ASL. Verbal information, especially idioms and proverbs, is not readily amenable to translation into sign, and the assessor must carefully examine test materials in advance with this fact in mind—and appropriately modify the administration materials if need be.

In the interpretation of test findings, an important distinction arises between performance that is due to substandard English-language skills and performance that is due to lack of intelligence or psychopathology. Relatively few psychologists have a great deal of experience assessing the deaf (Gibbins, 1989) and to the inexperienced assessor, the communication style of a deaf person may seem fragmented or concrete, much like the communication style of schizophrenics or people with other disorders (Misaszek et al., 1985). An inexperienced assessor might readily see intellectual and/or personality deficits, whereas a more experienced assessor might see only speech and language difficulties along with a certain amount of immaturity that is typically associated with such difficulties (Chess & Fernandez, 1981; Sullivan & Vernon, 1979). Prevention of such problems can be fostered by supervised work in assessment settings for the deaf and hearing impaired under the aegis of an experienced assessor, and by familiarity with the relevant literature (see, for example, Cates & Lapham, 1991; Elliot, Glass, & Evans, 1987; and Zieziula, 1982). Where appropriate, test findings should be supplemented with case history data, as well as information derived from behavioral observation and reports from caregivers such as parents or teachers.

Available Instruments

The Wechsler tests for test takers in the appropriate age group are in popular usage with the hearing-impaired and the deaf to assess intellectual functioning. WISC-R norms have been developed for hearing-impaired children (Anderson & Sisco, 1977), thus allowing comparison of an individual's performance to that of similarly disabled and/or hearing peers. Ray (1979) developed an adapted WISC-R Performance Scale designed to minimize examiner-examinee communication through the use of supplemental and alternate instructions that make great use of examples. These sample items are unscored and are repeated until the task is understood by the examinee. The Kaufman Assessment Battery for Children contains a nonverbal scale for children from age 4 through 12½. The subtests are administered in pantomime or gesture and require a nonverbal or motoric response. Nonverbal norms allow for comparison with similarly challenged and/or hearing peers. Validity studies with this scale have generally supported its use (Gibbins, 1988; Kennedy & Hiltonsmith, 1988; Phelps & Branyan, 1988).

619

THE ASSESS-
MENT OF
PEOPLE WITH
DISABLING
CONDITIONS

Measures of academic achievement using tests such as the Metropolitan Achievement Test and the Stanford Achievement Tests can be useful, since both of these tests have been standardized with members of this population. In general, hearing-impaired and deaf children do not perform as well on such tests as do their hearing peers. This is due not only to their language impairment but also to the lack of curriculum methods developed specifically to meet the educational needs of the deaf. Only 5% of graduates from educational programs for the deaf attain a tenth-grade education; 41% achieve a seventh- or eighth-grade-level education, and 30% are functionally illiterate.

Experts in the area of the personality assessment of the deaf, especially children who have never had hearing, do not encourage such assessment by means of paper-and-pencil inventories. A reading level above sixth grade is rare among the prelingual deaf because of the great obstacles to language acquisition they face (Trybus, 1973). A modification of the 16-PF (Form E), expressly designed to be at a reading level between third and fifth grade, was once thought to have great promise for use with the prelingual deaf, but poor intratest reliability has plagued it (Jensema, 1975).

The Rorschach has been recommended for use with only those deaf people known to be above average in intelligence and able to sign fluently (Vernon & Brown, 1964), although clinicians experienced with this special population may be able to use it more routinely (Sachs, 1976). Other projective measures, such as those involving drawings (Johnson, 1989; Ouellette, 1988), the Bender Visual-Motor Gestalt Test used projectively (Gibbins, 1989), and the TAT (Vernon & Brown, 1964), may prove insightful. Cates and Lapham (1991) caution that although the TAT may be useful, deaf children and adolescents may concretely label the cards, then perseverate on themes in an effort to supply the "right" answer:

> A potential difficulty in administering apperception techniques to deaf children and adolescents is a tendency toward response perseveration. For example, if unfamiliar with the task, the deaf student may initially attempt to label the picture. If this response is corrected, the deaf student may then perceive the first story told as the correct response. If the first correct response is a story containing a violent theme, then the deaf client may assume that violence is desired or appropriate in the stories and perseverate on violent themes. The clinician must decide whether to allow the perseveration or restructure the response set of the child or adolescent. The authors generally noted the perseverative phenomenon, then restructured the response set, indicating that each picture may elicit differing themes. (p. 125)

Cates and Lapham (1991) also reported on concrete types of response that may be given on another projective measure, the Hand Test. They found that

> deaf children and adolescents give a higher frequency of concrete responses to the Hand Test than do their hearing counterparts. For example, in response to the first card—a hand held up, palm outward—the deaf child may initially provide a description of the hand (e.g., "It's a hand, held up. Five fingers.") rather than describe the hand in some form of activity, as requested in the instructions. In the Hand Test scoring system, this type of descriptive response is considered indicative of severe disturbance. The clinician using the Hand Test, then, may wish to administer the test according to standardized procedure, followed by a testing-the-limits procedure, in which the deaf

child is urged to provide more appropriate responses. Alternatively, follow-ing the first descriptive response, the clinician may wish to reemphasize the instructions, elicit a more appropriate response, and consider the initial re-sponse as training. The deaf subject may also benefit from an inclusion to the standard directions that the hands are not signing. (p. 122)

Behavior checklists and rating scales can prove to be valuable tools of assess-ment with the deaf (McCoy, 1972). The single most extensively used checklist with deaf children and adolescents is the Meadow-Kendall Social-Emotional As-sessment Inventory (Meadow, Karchmer, Petersen, & Rudner, 1980), appropriate for use with individuals age 7 to 21 years old. Other such instruments, not neces-sarily designed especially for the deaf, include the Behavior Problem Checklist (Quay & Peterson, 1967, 1983), the Devereaux Adolescent Behavior Rating Scale (Spivack, Spotts, & Haimes, 1967), the Devereaux Child Behavior Rating Scale (Spivack & Spotts, 1966), the Child Behavior Checklist (Achenbach, 1978), and the Walker Problem Behavior Identification Checklist (Walker, 1976).

A measure of general aptitude in common usage with the deaf and the hear-ing-impaired is the Nebraska Test of Learning Aptitude developed by Marshall S. Hiskey (1966) and frequently referred to as "the Hiskey Nebraska." Another widely used measure of aptitude is the Arthur Adaptation of the Leiter Inter-national Performance Scale (Arthur, 1950). Vocational aptitude testing with this population may include tests of manual dexterity, mechanical aptitude, and spatial relations ability. Vocational interests tests designed for use with the hearing-impaired rely heavily on pictures as opposed to words (for example, The Geist Picture Interest Inventory).

THE DEAF-BLIND

In response to the rubella epidemic that spread across the United States from 1963 to 1965 and the resulting increase in multiply handicapped babies, Congress cre-ated 10 Regional Centers for Deaf-Blind Youths and Adults in 1967. These centers were charged with the responsibility of identifying and assessing such children.

Although relatively few in number, the deaf-blind as a group are legally en-titled by federal law to a free and appropriate public school education. Unfortu-nately, few school psychologists or other professional personnel in the schools have much training or experience in working with such multiply handicapped youngsters. The assessment of members of this population represents the "most difficult diagnosis task a psychologist can be asked to do" (Vernon, Blair, & Lotz, 1979, p. 291). The psychologist must be particularly wary of diagnostic errors that might lead to the placement of such children into programs for the mentally or emotionally impaired when in fact such programs would be inappropriate for the particular child.

Few standardized tests are appropriate for use with the deaf-blind. Standard-ized tests developed for and standardized on individuals with other disabling con-ditions do not adequately take into account the multiplicity and the pervasiveness of impairments of the deaf-blind. Psychological assessment of the deaf-blind most typically involves assessment of adaptive behavior (to be discussed later ir greater detail) as well as interviews with caregivers and analysis of case-history material. One of the few tests designed for use with, and standardized on, this population is the Callier-Azusa Scale (CAS).

The CAS is a behavior checklist that enables the examiner to compare the subject's development in a number of areas (motor, perceptual, language, daily living skills, and socialization) with typical development for deaf-blind children, ages birth to 9 years, who have received appropriate interventions. The test is useful in both educational program planning and as a posttest to assess behavior change after a specific intervention.

Stillman (1974) recommends that more than one rater assess the child's behavior both at home and school for at least two weeks. Information is usually provided by the mother, teacher, and/or other person having extensive contact with the child. Adequate reliability has been reported with respect to the test's 16 subscales. The test authors also reported that the scale's reliability was not significantly influenced by the child's educational setting nor the number of people rating the child (Bennett, Hughes, & Hughes, 1979). Related to validity evidence, Diebold, Curtis, and Dubose (1978) have demonstrated the strong relationship for a sample of 6- to 13-year-old deaf-blind children between systematic observation of daily behavior measures and performance on a set of developmental scales. The 16 subscales of the CAS yield an age-equivalent score rather than an IQ, but the conversion table is psychometrically unsound and therefore few professionals use it. Credit for particular items is awarded only if the behavior is "present fully and regularly." Behaviors that are just emerging are not credited. If the deaf-blind child has additional disabilities such as a motor deficit, specific CAS items can be omitted.

MOTOR DISABILITIES

Motor deficits come in many forms, from many varied causes, and may involve any muscle or muscle group in the body. Paralysis, tremors, involuntary movement, gait difficulties, and problems with volitional movement and speech are some of the many types of motor problems that may exist. The cause of the motor problem may be an inherited muscular or neurological difficulty or one acquired as a result of a trauma to the muscle, the brain, or spinal cord. Other causal factors include the wide range of neuromuscular diseases. Cases of cerebral palsy, for example, are believed to occur at the rate of 1.6 to 5 per 1,000 in the under 21 population. The palsy may be caused by an endocrine imbalance, low blood sugar, anoxia, a high forceps delivery, or any of a variety of other factors before, during, or after birth.

Issues in Test Administration and Interpretation

Most of the tests used to assess intellectual functioning rely at least in part on the respondent's ability to manipulate some materials—be they cards, blocks, beads, or whatever; the test that does not contain such tasks would be criticized by experts as being too loaded on verbal as opposed to performance measures of intelligence. Examiners wishing to assess the intelligence of motor-handicapped people will attempt to select an existing test that does not need to be modified in any way for administration to the particular individual being assessed. If all available tests would require modification, the test requiring the least modification would be selected. An example of a modification that might be employed when administering a block design task, for example, would involve the examiner physically turning the blocks until the examinee indicates that the rotation of the block is his or her response. The examinee might indicate this with a verbal response or, if there is a speech deficit, with another response such as a wink of the eye. On paper-and-pencil tasks that require fine motor coordination, such as tests that involve blackening tiny grids with number 2 pencils, the motor-handicapped individual might require a writer to enter the responses. The alternative (not to administer any motor tasks to the motor-handicapped examinee) is the approach taken by some examiners; the rationale here is that a verbal test such as the vocabulary subtest of a Wechsler examination correlates highly with the rest of the examination and may therefore be used as a rough estimate of both verbal and nonverbal intelligence. However, such a procedure provides only a *rough estimate* and is never in good practice if used for placement decisions in the absence of other assessment data.

Available Instruments

Many existing instruments used to assess intelligence, personality, educational achievement, and the like are amenable to adaptation for use with motor-handicapped examinees. Sattler (1972) investigated the adaptation of selected Stanford-Binet (Form L-M) and WISC items for use with members of this population. Using "normal" and mentally retarded children and children with cerebral palsy, Sattler modified all subtests (between levels I and V) that involved a verbal or motor response. These modifications included changes in test stimuli and changes in the method of response (similar to the yes–no response discussed earlier). The tests that couldn't be modified were omitted and alternate tests were used. Overall, this modified form appeared to have an acceptable level of concurrent validity (Sattler, 1972). Perhaps the primary finding was that mentally retarded and cerebral-palsied children scored higher mean IQs on the modified form than on the original standard form. Sattler also continued with modifications at the upper levels (ages 9 to 12), particularly in memory subtests. The results at this age level were not as encouraging. Sattler believed that modification of the memory tests made them easier. Sattler also modified some of the WISC subtests (Digit Span, Block Design, and Coding) and concluded that there was a significant correlation between the modified and the standardized form and the modification would therefore be appropriate for use with handicapped children.

Katz (1955) also conducted studies with cerebral palsied and nonhandicapped children with the Stanford-Binet (Form L). Again, response modifications such as pointing were used on certain subtests. His results suggested that at least for the levels of the questions he had employed in his study (levels II through VI), the Stanford-Binet was an appropriate tool for use in evaluating the intelligence of cerebral-palsied children. Other possible ways to modify existing instruments for use with members of this population include the "eye-pointing" method proposed by Reynell (1970) and the "halfstep" method introduced by Theye (1970). Theye administered the WISC Block Design and Picture Arrangement subtests using cues he called halfsteps in order to help the examinees complete the items.

623

THE ASSESS-
MENT OF
PEOPLE WITH
DISABLING
CONDITIONS

Conceivably, the notion of "halfsteps"—graduated cues to facilitate item completion—could be applied to various kinds of motor tasks administered to persons with motor deficits.

Psychologists and special educators who have occasion to assess variables such as the severity of a motor deficit have a number of tests at their disposal for use. Four test batteries in current usage are the Purdue Perceptual-Motor Survey, the Bruininks-Oseretsky Test of Motor Proficiency, the Frostig Movement Skills Test Battery, and the Southern California Sensory Integration Tests. The Purdue is a screening device that provides guidelines for assessing various gross and fine motor functions in children aged 6 to 10 years. The Bruininks-Oseretsky also tests gross and fine motor skills as well as general motor proficiency. It is a technically sound test but one that requires (1) a very well trained examiner to administer and interpret, and (2) extensive space to administer (such as a playground or a specially equipped room). The Frostig is designed to assess sensory-motor development, gross and fine motor coordination, balance, strength, and flexibility in children aged 6 to 12 years. It is popular among many examiners because it is relatively simple to administer, contains a relatively wide range of motor skills sampled, and is easy to score. The Southern California is also a measure of sensory integrative functioning designed for use with children aged 4 to 9 years of age. It is, however, time-consuming to administer and a test that requires a highly trained examiner to administer and interpret.

COGNITIVE DISABILITIES

Throughout this text we have discussed assessment considerations that are applicable in assessing people who are cognitively exceptional in some way. Particularly relevant, of course, are the chapters on the assessment of intelligence and personality. In Chapter 10 (Educational Assessment) we focused on the definition and assessment of learning disabilities, which also may be thought of as a cognitive exceptionality. In Chapter 15 (Clinical and Counseling Assessment) there was some discussion of people with thought disorders and psychoses, and these categories too might qualify for discussion as "cognitive disabilities." Here we focus our discussion on the mentally retarded. Keep in mind that many of the assessment techniques we present are applicable in the assessment of a variety of people. Thus, for example, although we discuss assessment of adaptive behavior with reference to the mentally retarded, it might also be appropriate to assess adaptive behavior of the psychotic, the neurologically impaired, the gifted, or other different kinds of individuals.

The Mentally Retarded

The most widely accepted definition of mental retardation is the one set forth in 1983 by the American Association of Mental Deficiency (AAMD): "Mental retardation refers to significantly subaverage general intellectual functioning existing concurrently with deficits in adaptive behavior, and manifested during the developmental period."

The deficits in adaptive behavior refer to deficits in adjusting to the demands of the environment, and the diagnosis of mental retardation is made not only on the basis of an individual intelligence test but also on the basis of an assessment of adaptive behavior. Table 17–1 describes levels of mental retardation. Most mentally retarded people can be classified according to the AAMD classification system as mildly retarded. The remaining 15 percent or so may be classified as either moderate, severe, or profound in retardation.

625

THE ASSESS-
MENT OF
PEOPLE WITH
DISABLING
CONDITIONS

Assessing Adaptive Behavior

The concept of "adaptive behavior" has a long history rooted not only in psychology but in anthropology and sociology as well. Lambert (1978) notes that references to concepts like adaptive behavior were being made by authorities in the field of mental retardation prior to 1850. In 1905 Alfred Binet made reference to a concept we would now recognize as "adaptive behavior" when he said "an individual is normal if he is able to conduct his affairs of life without having need of supervision of others, if he is able to work sufficiently remunerative to supply his own personal needs . . ." (Binet, quoted in Goddard, 1916). The concepts of intelligence and adaptive behavior are indeed very closely related—so closely related that at least in one introductory psychology textbook, intelligence tests were defined as "measures of an individual's adaptive behavior in meeting a particular set of environmental challenges" (Zimbardo & Ruch, 1975, p. 206). Although there is clearly overlap between the two concepts, adaptive behavior has been more traditionally viewed as synonymous with terms such as adjustment, social maturity (Doll, 1953), adaptive capacity (Fullan & Loubser, 1972), and personal and social competence (Cain, Levine, & Elzey, 1963). Matarazzo (1972, pp. 147–148) defined adaptive behavior as follows:

> Adaptive behavior refers primarily to the effectiveness with which the individual copes with, and adjusts to, the natural and social demands of his environment. It has two principal facets: (a) the degree to which the individual is able to function and maintain himself independently, and (b) the degree to which he meets satisfactorily the culturally imposed demands of personal and social responsibility. It is a composite of many aspects of behavior . . . [subsumed] under the designation intellectual, affective, motivational, social, motor, and other non-cognitive elements [that] all contribute to and are a part of total adaptation to the environment.

Tests of adaptive behavior are in structure more like interviews than they are "tests" per se. Typically, a third party familiar with the assessee is asked a series of questions about the assessee's behavior in a variety of situations. Exactly what situations are asked about will depend in part on the chronological age of the individual being assessed. For infants, the assessment of adaptive behavior might take the form of questioning whether the infant is able to stand up without assistance. For the preschooler, questions concerning personal hygiene and self-care will be asked. Through the school years and into adulthood, additional questions concerning self-care and personal hygiene will be asked as well as questions concerning interpersonal relations, finances, social awareness, and other areas. We now briefly describe some of the available measures of adaptive behavior.

The Vineland   The Vineland Social Maturity Scale was developed by Edgar A. Doll (1953), then the Director of Research at the Vineland Training School in Vineland, New Jersey. Doll believed that in addition to measures assessing intelligence, personality, and academic achievement, a measure of social competence was needed for a thorough assessment of a mentally retarded person. Doll (1953, p. 2) defined *social competence* as "a functional composite of human traits which subserves social usefulness as reflected in self-sufficiency and service to others."

A structured interview, the Vineland was designed for use in assessing people from birth to age 30. In its original form, the interview was conducted with an informant who was typically the primary caregiver to the subject (the subject's parent or legal guardian). The interview began with questions concerning the informant's degree of acquaintance with the subject. This information was recorded on the record form and the interview proceeded with questions concerning whether or not the examinee habitually performed or engaged in various types of behavior. Responses were numerically scored, and the net result was a raw score that was then converted into what Doll called a "social age." Doll also provided for the conversion of the social age into a "social quotient" by use of the following formula:

Table 17–1

Levels of Mental Retardation

Level	Preschool age: birth to 5 yrs.	School age: 6 to 21 yrs.
Mild retardation	Can develop social and communication skills; minimal retardation in sensory-motor areas; rarely distinguished from normal until later age.	Can learn academic skills to approximately sixth-grade level by late teens. Cannot learn general high school subjects. Needs special education, particularly at secondary school age levels.
Moderate retardation	Can talk or learn to communicate; poor social awareness; fair motor development; may profit from self-help; can be managed with moderate supervision.	Can learn functional academic skills to approximately fourth-grade level by late teens if given special education.
Severe retardation	Poor motor development; speech is minimal; generally unable to profit from training in self-help; little or no communication skills.	Can talk or learn to communicate; can be trained in elemental health habits; cannot learn functional academic skills; profits from systematic habit training.
Profound retardation	Gross retardation; minimal capacity for functioning in sensory-motor areas; needs nursing care.	Some motor development present; cannot profit from training in self-help; needs total care.

$$\text{Social Quotient} = \frac{\text{Social Age}}{\text{Chronological Age}} \times 100$$

627

THE ASSESS-
MENT OF
PEOPLE WITH
DISABLING
CONDITIONS

The social quotient can be compared to the intelligence quotient for diagnostic purposes. Such a comparison was deemed to be helpful, for example, in discriminating intellectually handicapped people who are relatively competent in handling their own affairs from those who are incompetent in doing so.

In the Vineland Adaptive Behavior Scales (Sparrow, Balla, & Cicchetti, 1984), the format of an individually administered scale given to a parent or caregiver very familiar with the subject is retained. However, a number of major changes have been made in the revision. The concepts of "social age" and "social quotient" have been abandoned in favor of a point scale, and a complete restandardization was undertaken. Appropriate for use with individuals under the age of 19, the new test is available in three forms—referred to as the Survey Form of the Interview Edition (requiring about 20 to 60 minutes to administer), the Expanded Form of the Interview Edition (which is more comprehensive and will require one hour or more to administer), and the Classroom Edition (which takes about 20 minutes to administer to the subject's teacher). Each of the tests contains

Table 17–1 (*continued*)

Adult: over 21 yrs.	Range in standard deviation value	Approximate mental age at adulthood	Percent in population	Stanford-Binet Form L-M IQ range	Wechsler Scale IQ range
Capable of social and vocational adequacy with proper education and training. Frequently needs guidance when under serious social or economic stress.	−2.01 to −3.00	8.3 to 10.9	2.7	67–52	69–55
Capable of self-maintenance in unskilled or semiskilled occupations; needs supervision and guidance when under mild social or economic stress.	−3.01 to −4.00	5.7 to 8.2	.2	51–36	54–40
Can contribute partially to self-support under complete supervision; can develop self-protection skills to a minimal useful level in controlled environment.	−4.01 to −5.00	3.2 to 5.6	.1	35–20	39–25
Some motor and speech development; totally incapable of self-maintenance; needs complete care and supervision.	>−5.00	<3.2	.05	<20	<25

items tapping areas such as daily living skills, socialization skills, and motor functioning. Additionally, the two interview editions also have items designed to assess maladaptive behavior.

A sample of respondents that was generally representative of the U.S. population according to the 1980 census was employed in the norming of the test (though there were some deviations in terms of geographic region, parental education, and community size). Approximately three thousand individuals were tested with the Classroom Edition, and another three thousand were tested with the interview editions. There are also supplementary norms available for the institutionalized and noninstitutionalized mentally retarded adults and for institutionalized children who were either visually impaired, hearing impaired, or emotionally disturbed.

Reliability estimates reported in the test's manual generally suggested that the Expanded form was the most reliable of the three forms available, the Classroom form the least reliable. Also reported in the manual are concurrent validity studies which indicate that this test, like other tests designed to measure the same construct, is indeed measuring adaptive behavior.

Adaptive Behavior Inventory for Children (ABIC)   The ABIC is one of the tests included in the System of Multicultural Pluralistic Assessment (SOMPA)—discussed in Chapter 10—though it can be and is used by itself as a measure of adaptive behavior. Like the SOMPA, the ABIC is designed for use with children from 5 to 11 years old and, also like the SOMPA, the test was developed from a social systems perspective; in part, how adaptive the subject's behavior is can be determined from examination of that behavior with respect to the role expectations of the family, the community, the peer group, and the school. Self-maintenance and earner/consumer roles are also examined. The test is a structured individual interview, available in English or Spanish, consisting of 242 questions administered to the child's parent or primary caregiver. Each item, like the following sample item from the Earner/Consumer domain of questions, has three alternative answers that can be scored either 0, 1, or 2:

> Does (insert child's name) make correct change for a dollar
> (2) without help
> (1) only with help
> (0) not at all?

Standard scores having a mean of 50 and a standard deviation of 15 are provided for each of the domains assessed by the test, and the average of all these standard scores provides a single composite measure of adaptive behavior. Special validity scales include a Veracity Scale designed to aid in discovering whether the respondent is trying to "fake good" and "Don't Know" and "No Opportunity/ Not Allowed" scales, scores on which may signal excessive informant ignorance or restrictiveness. The usual administration time is about 45 minutes—though this doesn't include transportation time to the respondent's home (the place where it is recommended that the interview take place).

Norms for the ABIC are based on a random sample of 2,085 children in California schools, stratified with respect to ethnic group membership (Anglo, Black, Hispanic), size of community, gender, and age. Because only children from California were used in the normative study, the development of local norms for use of this test outside of California is strongly encouraged. Also, although the test surveys a number of role areas for children, one area that it conspicuously neglects is academic role performance, a critically important area for school-age children. This important limitation must be kept in mind when using this test. Another limitation inherent in the test is its reliance on one informant, rendering it highly vulnerable to the informant's biases and areas of ignorance. Parent informants tent to paint a more adaptive picture of their child than do other informants such as teachers (Wall & Paradise, 1981; see also Kazimour & Reschly, 1981). No test-retest data are presented in the manual, and no studies to date have attested to the stability of ABIC scores. One practical limitation is that the test's manual provides little guidance for interpreting the profile of a child found to be "at risk" for being diagnosed as mentally retarded.

On a more positive note, the test represents one of the few designed expressly from a social systems perspective, and that fact alone gives it great appeal for a wide variety of test users. Care was taken in empirically deriving the items; they appear to have high face validity and have been shown to have good internal-consistency reliability. The utility in the school setting of this somewhat controversial instrument will better be understood as more data regarding its validity as a measure of adaptive behavior become available.

Other measures of adaptive behavior Other tests of adaptive behavior include the Adaptive Behavior Scale (ABS) and the Adaptive Behavior Scale, School Edition (ABSSE), both published by the American Association of Mental Deficiency. The ABS is appropriate for ages 3 to 69 and the ABSSE is appropriate for ages 3 to 16. The ABS was developed as a result of detailed studies of deficient behaviors in the retarded. The instrument is designed to identify behaviors that need remediation. A description of the domains assessed in these scales (such as independent functioning, physical development, and so forth) appears in Table 17–2. The test yields raw scores that can then be converted to decile scores (though the manual labels them percentile scores). Graphic representations of scores can be made so that visual comparison of scores across behavioral domains can be made.

The ABS was standardized on approximately 4,000 persons aged 3 to 59 residing in 68 residential facilities for the mentally retarded throughout the United States. The ABSSE was standardized on approximately 6,500 people ranging in age from 3 to 16 in classes for the retarded and in normal classes in the states of California and Florida. The scales can be criticized for having unrepresentative standardization samples and for the lack of compelling reliability and validity data presented in the test manuals. In one study using parents and teachers as informants with respect to a child, it was found that parents tended to rate the child's level of adaptive behavior more favorably than did the teacher (Mealor & Richmond, 1980). In another study addressed to the validity of the ABS, performance on the scale was found to be related to productivity in a sheltered workshop setting (Cunningham & Presnall, 1978). Factor-analytic studies of the items on the scales have consistently yielded factors labeled "Personal Independence," "Social Maladaption," and "Personal Maladaption" across ages (Nihira, 1969a; 1969b). Still, the content of the individual items is probably too vague in most instances

629

THE ASSESS-
MENT OF
PEOPLE WITH
DISABLING
CONDITIONS

Table 17–2

Domains Assessed by the ABS and ABSSE

Part 1 66 items on ABS; 56 on ABSSE
  I. Independent functioning
     A. Eating (use of utensils, table manners)
     B. Toilet use
     C. Cleanliness (bathing, menstruation)
     D. Appearance (posture)
     E. Care of clothing
     F. Dressing and undressing
     G. Travel (sense of direction and use of public transportation)
     H. Other independent functioning (telephone use)
  II. Physical development
     A. Sensory development (vision and hearing)
     B. Motor development (balance, ambulation, motor control)
  III. Economic activity
     A. Money handling (knowledge of money) and budgeting
     B. Shopping skills
  IV. Language development
     A. Expression (articulation, writing, word usage)
     B. Comprehension (understanding complex sentences and reading)
     C. Social language development (conversational language skills)
  V. Numbers and time
  VI. Vocational activity (performance of complex jobs safely and reliably)
  VII. Self-direction
     A. Initiative (initiation of activities and passivity)
     B. Perseverance (attention and persistence)
     C. Leisure time (free-time activities)
  VIII. Responsibility (care of personal belongings and general responsibility)
  IX. Socialization (appropriate and inappropriate behaviors)
  X. Domestic activity (ABS only; cleaning, food, and serving)

Part 2 44 items on ABS; 39 on ABSSE. For each of these ratings the subject responds
        either "occasionally" or "frequently"
  I. Rebelliousness (disobedience and insubordination)
  II. Antisocial vs. social behavior (teasing, bossing, disruptive behavior, inconsiderate
      behavior)
  III. Aggressiveness (personal property damage and temper tantrums)
  IV. Trustworthiness (lying, stealing)
  V. Withdrawal vs. involvment (inactivity, withdrawal, and stress)
  VI. Stereotyped behavior and odd mannerisms
  VII. Appropriateness or interpersonal manners
  VIII. Acceptability of vocal habits
  IX. Acceptability of habits (unacceptable or eccentric habits)
  X. Activity level (hyperactive tendencies)
  XI. Symptomatic behavior (possible emotional disturbance)
  XII. Use of psychoactive medications (for control of hyperactivity, seizures, etc.)
  XIII. Self-abusive behavior (ABS only)
  XIV. Sexually aberrant behavior (ABS only; masturbation, homosexuality, rape)

for use in developing detailed intervention programs, and the ABS and ABSEE
are probably best thought of as screening instruments, not to be used in important diagnostic or program placement decisions.

One instrument specifically designed for use in assessing the sexual knowledge and attitudes of the developmentally disabled is the Socio-Sexual Knowl-

631

THE ASSESS-
MENT OF
PEOPLE WITH
DISABLING
CONDITIONS

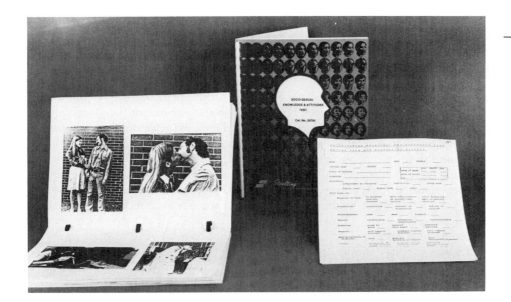

Figure 17-2 *The Socio-Sexual Knowledge & Attitudes Test.*

edge & Attitudes Test (Wish, McCombs, & Edmonson, 1980). Topic areas covered by the instrument include anatomy terminology, menstruation, mastur-bation, dating, marriage, intimacy, intercourse, pregnancy, childbirth, alcohol and drugs, homosexuality, and venereal disease (Figure 17-2). Since expressive language required by the examinee is minimal—most responses are made by pointing or indicating "yes" or "no"—the test is suitable for administration to those with limited language skills or ability. Though the test manual includes nor-mative data on developmentally disabled individuals aged 18 to 42, the intent of the test authors is that the test be used in a criterion-referenced as opposed to norm-referenced fashion; as a measure of what the individual test taker knows, believes, or doesn't know. Using a testing-the-limits procedure, it is possible for the examiner to employ some of the pictorial stimuli to explore the examinee's understanding of diseases such as AIDS, and concepts such as sexual abuse and sexual harassment.

A PERSPECTIVE

The disabled individual must be able to take the test the examiner wishes to ad-minister; the examiner who wishes to administer, for example, the Wepman Auditory Discrimination Test to a totally deaf individual is engaging in an exer-cise in futility, as the examinee will be unable to hear the stimulus words. When working with the disabled individual, then, the examiner must either devise a new test designed for administration to people with the identified disability or modify an existing test so that it can be administered to the disabled person. If, for example, an existing test such as the WISC-III is administered with modifications to an individual with sensory deficits, the question arises, "How relevant are these norms—based solely on the performance of nondisabled people—to the performance of people with disabling conditions who have the test administered to them in ways that deviate from the standardized guidelines?"

The problem of normative comparisons of the performance of disabled and nondisabled individuals is a thorny one to be sure. It is incumbent on the examiner to keep in mind the question being asked in the assessment before relying on a particular set of norms. If the question asked in the assessment concerns how a disabled individual would perform in a mainstream classroom, a regular job situation, or any situation in which the disabled individual will be competing or working with nondisabled individuals, it is generally appropriate to judge the disabled individual with reference to norms gathered on nondisabled persons. If, however, the question being asked in the assessment concerns how the disabled individual compares to others with the same disability—for diagnostic purposes, placement in a sheltered workshop, or any other purpose that would necessitate evaluation of the disability per se—then norms developed on a population of people with that specific disability would be an appropriate reference source. When a standardized test in use with nondisabled people is modified for use with people with one or another deficit, there are in many instances no published norms that are directly applicable. The assessor in such an instance will then rely on the published norms applicable to nondisabled individuals but use caution in making interpretations with respect to the performance of a nonmember of someone characteristic of the normative population who was administered a modified version of the test. All of this may sound unscientific and nonstandardized to the reader. It is. In practice, however, appropriate norms are not readily available for every type of modification that may be made in an existing standardized test so that it is amenable for administration to a person who is disabled in some way. In practice, the assessor of members of a disabled population may be compelled to improvise not only with respect to administration procedures but in making interpretations as well.

Chapter 18

Industrial/Organizational

Assessment

INDUSTRIAL PSYCHOLOGY IS defined as "the application of the methods, facts, and principles of psychology to people at work" (Schultz, 1982, p. 6). The subspeciality areas of organizational psychology, personnel psychology, and engineering psychology are all included within this definition. *Organizational psychology* focuses on the nature and quality of the structure of the organization (corporation, business, military, or other), including such variables as formal and informal lines of communication, management–staff relations, public relations, research and development, and related areas. Underscoring how closely related the areas of industrial and organizational psychology are is the fact that, in 1970, the division of the American Psychological Association then known as the Division of Industrial Psychology officially changed its name to the Division of Industrial and Organizational Psychology. *Personnel psychology* is that area of industrial/organizational (I/O) psychology that deals with matters related to the hiring, firing, promotion, and transfer of workers as well as issues of worker productivity, motivation, and job satisfaction. *Engineering psychology* involves the study of human factors involved in the operation of mechanical things ranging from household gadgets to spacecraft. In this chapter, we provide a brief overview of the assessment instruments and methods used in each of these two I/O subspecialties. We begin with a look at some of the *preemployment* tools of assessment that might be used not only by personnel psychologists but also by psychologists and counselors in a school counseling center or other agency.

As a starship captain, James T. Kirk had a five-year mission to seek new worlds and explore new civilizations. As a company clerk in a mobile army surgical hospital (MASH), Radar O'Reilly prepared daily reports, filled out supply depositions, and telephoned all over Korea. As a superhero in need of a disguise, reporter Clark Kent (alias "Superman") sought out and wrote news stories for his employer, *The Daily Planet*. Kent was well suited to his job because of a more-than-passing curiosity in world events, superior written communication skills, and his willingness—not to mention his superior ability—to travel. Similarly, Kirk and O'Reilly proved themselves well suited to their jobs because of their respective abilities.

Whether a starship captain, a clerk, a reporter, or something else, individuals will enjoy their work most—and probably be optimally productive at it—if the demands of the job reasonably match their own unique needs, abilities, interests, and aptitudes. Researchers in the I/O subspecialty area of personnel psychology have developed a number of tests and methods to help match individuals to jobs. High school guidance counselors, college counseling centers, and private agencies with similar goals employ many different instruments to assist their clientele in making career choices. Our overview of some of these tests and techniques begins with a look at some of the tests used to provide information about the interest patterns of prospective employees.

Measures of Interest

On the presumption that interest in one's work promotes better performance, greater productivity, and greater job satisfaction, both employers and prospective employees have much to gain from methods that can help individuals identify their interests and a job tailored to those interests. Using such methods, individuals can discover, for example, if their interests lie in "seeking new worlds and exploring new civilizations" or in something more along the lines of veterinary dermatology. Employers can use information about their employees' interest patterns in formulating job descriptions and attracting new personnel. For example, a company could design an employment campaign emphasizing that the position offers security if security was found to be the chief interest of the workers currently holding the same job. Although many instruments designed to measure interests have been published, our discussion will focus on the one with the longest history of continuous use, the Strong-Campbell Interest Inventory of the Strong Vocational Interest Blank, now abbreviated SVIB-SCII.

Strong Vocational Interest Blank (SVIB-SCII)   As early as 1907, psychologist G. Stanley Hall had developed a questionnaire to assess children's recreational interests. However, it was not until the early 1920s that Edward K. Strong, Jr., after attending a seminar on the measurement of interest, began a program of systematic investigation into the measurement of human interests—an investigation that would lead to (1) a 420-item measure of interests for men published by Stanford University Press with a test manual in 1928 (subsequently revised in 1938), (2) a 410-item measure of interests for women published with a manual in 1935 (subsequently revised in 1946), (3) major revisions of the men's form and women's form in the mid-1960s, (4) the publication of the first Merged Form of 325 items under the direction of David P. Campbell in 1974, and (5) a revised and expanded edition of the test published in 1985 (Strong, Hansen, & Campbell, 1985).

Strong's approach to test construction was empirical and straightforward: (1) select hundreds of items that might conceivably distinguish the interests of a person by that person's occupation, (2) administer this "rough cut" of the test to several hundred people selected so as to be representative of certain occupations or professions, (3) sort out which items seemed of interest to persons by occupational group and discard items with no discriminative ability, and (4) construct a final version of the test that would yield scores describing how an examinee's pattern of interest corresponded to people actually employed in various occupations and professions. With the availability of such a test, college students majoring in psychology could, for example, see how closely their pattern of interests paralleled that of working psychologists. Presumably, if your interests closely match those of psychologists (in contrast to the interests of, say, tow truck operators), you would probably enjoy the work of a psychologist.

Figure 18–1 *It's Not Just a Job, It's an Adventure!* Had Orin Scrivello, D.D.S. (Steve Martin) in the film *Little Shop of Horrors* taken an interest survey, the results might have been quite bizarre. As a child, young Orin's interests leaned toward bashing the heads of pussy cats, shooting puppies with a BB gun, and poisoning guppies. He was able to put what his mother described as his "natural tendencies" to use in gainful employment: he became a dentist.

The test as it exists today consists of a total of 325 items to which the examinee responds by blackening boxes on an answer sheet grid to indicate preference of some sort. Items 1 through 281 require respondents to indicate whether they "Like," "Dislike," or are "Indifferent" to various occupations, school subjects, activities, amusements, and types of people. For example, do you like, dislike, or are you indifferent to the work of a bookkeeper? to algebra? sewing? golf? people who live dangerously? For items 282 through 311, respondents indicate their preference between two activities (such as, "taking a chance" or "playing it safe") or indicate that they cannot make up their mind. For items 312 through 325, respondents describe themselves by indicating "yes," "no," or uncertainty ("?") to statements like "win friends easily."

Men and women in the standardization sample for the test were all between the ages of 25 and 55. The sample was divided into members of a general reference group and an occupational reference group; members of the latter all had to like their work and have at least three years of experience at it to be included. The general reference group served as a kind of control group; its members were selected to represent men or women "in general."

The test protocols can be scored only by computer; not only would scoring by hand be inordinately difficult and time-consuming, but also the item weights and scoring algorithms are registered trade secrets of the copyright owner. Along with scoring (a Profile Report), a computer-prepared narrative description of the test taker's pattern of scores (an Interpretive Report) is available to the test user. Also available with the 1985 Revised Edition of the test is an individualized, interactive video interpretation of the findings along with career counseling and exploration. Three types of general scales—General Occupational Themes, Basic Interest Scales, and Occupational Scales—are scored and interpreted with reference to six personality types distinguished by Holland (1973). The personality characteristics associated with each of these types are included in each SVIB-SCII report. The General Occupational Theme score is a kind of summary statement of how similar the respondent is to some theoretically ideal occupational type—be it the enterprising, the conventional, realistic, the social, the investigative, or the artistic occupational type. Scores on the Basic Interest Scales and Occupational Scales allow the interpreter of the test to see at a glance how similar or dissimilar the respondent's interests are to people holding a variety of jobs. In addition to these primary scales, scores on two "special scales" are reported. One of these is called the "Academic Comfort" scale, and it is designed to discriminate between students who might and might not feel comfortable in an academic setting. The other special scale is the IE (introversion-extraversion) scale; the higher the score on this scale, the more introverted the test taker is presumed to be. Also on the answer sheet are two administrative indices ("Total Responses" and "Infrequent Responses"), there for the purpose of detecting carelessness, random responding to items, misunderstanding of directions, the presence of response sets, and possible errors in the computer scoring. Since there are 325 items, a Total Responses "score" of anything less than 325 may prompt further investigation. The "Infrequent Responses" index provides a measure of the number of rare or unusual responses to items made by the test taker.

SVIB-SCII data may be used by counselors to assist in the counseling of students as well as others (such as job applicants, current employees, and prisoners) in making employment and career decisions. It is also true that a scored report with a narrative interpretation returned to a test taker may require little or no interpretation by a counselor since it comes with a very clear test guide for interpreting the findings. SVIB-SCII data can assist individuals in a particular line of work to better understand why they might not be happy with that line of work. The possible research applications of the test are many. A partial listing of the ways this test could potentially be used in research is as follows: studying characteristics of particular occupations, individuals, and groups; studying general societal trends and crosscultural influences; and studying interpersonal relationships such as the interest patterns of friends, lovers, and happily married versus divorced couples.

The SVIB-SCII is a psychometrically sound instrument with median test-retest reliability coefficients reported to be in the high .80s and low .90s for intervals ranging from two weeks to three years. Concurrent validity, defined as the ability of the scale to "discriminate between people of different occupations" (Campbell & Hansen, 1981, p. 67) is acceptably high. The test is one that has proved itself able to "keep up with the times" and the latest (1985) edition contains 34 new Vocational/Technical Occupational Scales (ranging from Emergency Medical Technician to Travel Agent) and 12 new Professional Occupational Scales including, for example, Athletic Trainer, Broadcaster, and Medical Illustrator. A companion book which provides a job description of each of the occupations in the professional, nonprofessional, vocational, and technical jobs listed in the Occupational Scales is also available (Hansen, 1986).

The Kuder Preference and Interest Scales G. Frederick Kuder is the author of a number of interest and preference tests that bear his name, including the Kuder Vocational Preference Record, the Kuder Personal Preference Record, the Kuder Occupational Interest Survey, and the Kuder General Interest Survey.

In contrast to the empirically derived SVIB-SCII, the initial versions of the Kuder were *theoretically* derived by using sophisticated statistical procedures to identify items that clustered into general themes. However, an instrument developed subsequently, the Kuder Occupational Interest Survey, Revised (Kuder, 1979), is an empirically keyed instrument; unlike the SVIB-SCII, no general reference group was employed in its standardization sample. A feature of this Kuder test is its normative data on patterns of interest of college students enrolled in different courses of study. With such information it is possible to compare an examinee's pattern of interests with those characteristics of other college students who are enrolled in the same or different courses of study. Another feature of one of the Kuder tests, the General Interest Survey, is its appropriateness for use in grades 6 through 12. This test is used to aid in decisions concerning course of study as well as in general guidance counseling.

One general difference between the Kuder tests and the SVIB-SCII concerns the format of the tests; the Kuder tests require the examinee to indicate most- and least-liked alternatives from three statements. This forced-choice format is particularly useful in identifying attempts on the part of the test taker to fake good or fake bad. In general, the Kuder tests have been found to be at acceptable levels of psychometric soundness.

Other interest inventories A number of interest inventories are more specialized in some way than the SVIB-SCII and the Kuder, and we briefly mention some of them. Holland (1979, 1985) developed two such measures that stemmed from his research on the relationship between personality and occupational choice. The Occupational Preference Inventory is an examiner-administered and examiner-interpreted instrument, whereas the Self-Directed Search, an outgrowth and expansion of the former test, is self-administered and self-interpreted. The Minnesota Vocational Interest Inventory is an empirically keyed instrument designed to compare the respondents' interest patterns with those of persons employed in a variety of nonprofessional occupations (such as stock clerks, painters, printers, truck drivers). An instrument called the Career Decision Scale has been used to examine cognitive processes associated with general career indecision (see Osipow & Reed, 1985) as well as specialty indecision among people who have decided on a career (Savickas, Alexander, Osipow, & Wolf, 1985).

In the area of preemployment counseling, the delineation of a client's interests is only part of the story; a client may, for example, exhibit a great deal of interest in becoming a diamond cutter. However, if the client has a severe perceptual motor deficit or a persistent tremor in the hands, it would be judicious on the part of the I/O psychologist to steer such a client toward a profession other than diamond cutting—perhaps something else within the field of gemology, like appraising. This brings us to the subject of aptitude.

Measures of Aptitude

More than interest is needed to succeed in a career; aptitude is essential. A number of tests have been designed to assess potential for learning the knowledge and skills required in various occupations. Some of these instruments, such as the widely used Differential Aptitude Test, are designed to survey a number of aptitudes so that the examinee can discover the field for which she or he appears to have the greatest aptitude. Other aptitude tests, such as the O'Connor Finger Dexterity Test, focus on one particular ability.

The Differential Aptitude Test First introduced in 1947 and revised several times since then, the Differential Aptitude Test (DAT) is a vocational aptitude battery developed for use with students in grades 7 through 12. The rationale for this test is that people have not one but a variety of vocational aptitudes and these aptitudes are measurable. Useful as a tool in vocational counseling, the test consists of eight subtests, which yield separate scores on eight aptitudes (see Table 18–1). A ninth score, Scholastic Aptitude (derived from a combination of the scores on Verbal Reasoning and Numerical Reasoning), is designed to yield information about academic ability. With the 1990 revision of this test came the Career Interest Inventory, which combines DAT data with data from a supplementary questionnaire tapping interests, educational goals, and preferences. The computerized test report analyzes and discusses the resulting pattern of aptitudes and interests in terms of the appropriateness of various occupational choices.

Approximately 100,000 students from 520 school districts and an additional 22,000 students from research programs participated in the 1990 standardization, with stratification according to grade, sex, region of the country, socioeconomic status, ethnicity, and urban/rural/suburban residence. Normative data for males and females are presented separately in the manual. Intercorrelations among the

Table 18–1

The Subtests of the Differential Aptitude Test

Test	Type of items
Verbal Reasoning	Double-ended analogies designed in part to test ability to abstract. This type of item requires the test taker to select the pair of words that best completes the beginning and end of a sentence. An example: _____ is to end, as appetizer is to _____ 1. beginning _____ dessert 2. ending _____ appetizing 3. sunset _____ dusk 4. final _____ midterm 5. fruit cup _____ open bar
Numerical Reasoning	Items on this subtest measure computational skills and understanding of numerical relationships.
Abstract Reasoning	The test taker's task here is to determine which of several alternative figures would logically be next in a series of figures.
Perceptual Speed and Accuracy	Includes tasks resembling those required for clerical jobs (such as filing and coding).
Mechanical Reasoning	Items on this subtest are pictures designed to assess the test taker's understanding and knowledge of various physical laws and forces affecting activities such as lifting, turning, and pulling.
Space Relations	A two-dimensional picture or pattern is presented, and it is the examinee's task to select which of several alternative pictures or patterns could be produced from the original; this subtest taps the process of visualization—and the ability to mentally rotate objects in space.
Spelling	A word is presented and the test taker indicates whether the word is or is not spelled correctly.
Language Usage	Basic language skills such as grammar, punctuation, and capitalization are tapped by this subtest.

subtests are low enough to suggest that they are, in fact, measuring relatively independent areas.

The General Aptitude Test Battery   The United States Employment Service (USES) developed the General Aptitude Test Battery (GATB) and first put it into use in 1947 after extensive research and development. The GATB (pronounced like the name "Gatsby" would be without the *s*) is available for use by state employment services as well as other agencies and organizations (such as certain school districts and nonprofit organizations that have obtained official permission from the government to administer the test). The GATB is a tool used to identify aptitudes for occupations, and it is a test just about anyone of working age can take. The test is administered regularly at local state offices (referred to by names such as the "Job Service," "Employment Security Commission," or "Labor Security Commission") to people who want the agency to help find them a job, to people who are unemployed and have been referred by a state office of unemployment, or to employees who work at a company that has requested such aptitude

Validity Generalization and the GATB

Can a test validated for use in personnel selection for one occupation also be valid for use in personnel selection for another occupation? Must the validation of a test used in personnel selection be situation-specific? Stated more generally, can validity evidence for a test be meaningfully applied to situations other than those in which the evidence was obtained? These are the types of questions that are raised when the topic of *validity generalization* is discussed.

As applied to employment-related decision making on the basis of test scores achieved on the General Aptitude Test Battery (GATB), *validity generalization* refers to the fact that the same test score data may be predictive of aptitude for all jobs; the implication is that if a test is validated for a few jobs selected from a much larger cluster of jobs—each requiring similar skills at approximately the same level of complexity—the test is valid for all jobs in that cluster. For example, if a validation study conclusively indicated tht GATB scores are predictive of aptitude for (and ultimately proficiency in) the occupation of assembler in an aircraft assembly plant, an entirely new validation study may not necessarily be needed to apply such data to the occupation of assembler in a shipbuilding plant; if the type and level of skill required in the two occupations can be shown to be sufficiently similar, it may be that the same or similar procedures used to select aircraft assemblers can profitably be used to select assemblers of ships.

Validity generalization (VG) as applied to personnel selection using the GATB makes unnecessary the burden of conducting a separate validation study with the test for each and every one of the over 12,000 jobs that exist in the American economy. The application of VG to GATB scores also enables GATB users to supply employers with more precise information about test takers. To understand why this is so, let's begin by consulting the "pie chart" (Figure 1).

Note that the inner circle of the chart lists the 12 tests in the General Aptitude Test Battery and that the next ring of the circle lists eight aptitudes derived from the 12 tests. Not illustrated here is a ninth aptitude, General Learning

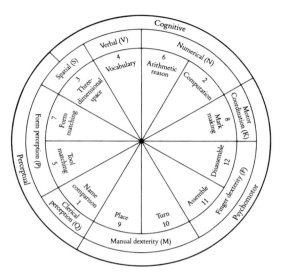

Figure 1 *Aptitudes Measured by the General Aptitude Test Battery.*

Ability, which is derived from scores on the Vocabulary, Arithmetic Reasoning, and Three-Dimensional Space tests. A brief description of each of the nine aptitudes measured by the GATB follows:

General Learning Ability (also referred to as *intelligence*), (G)—"Catching on" and understanding instructions and principles as well as reasoning and judgment are tapped here. G is measured by Tests 3, 4, and 6 in the diagram.

Verbal Aptitude (V)—Understanding the meaning of words and relationships between them as well as using words effectively are some of the abilities tapped here. V is measured by Test 4.

Numerical Aptitude (N)—N is measured by tasks requiring the quick performance of arithmetic operations. It is measured by Tests 2 and 6.

Spatial Aptitude (S)—The ability to visualize and mentally manipulate geometric forms is tapped here. S is measured by Test 3.

Form Perception (P)—Attention to detail, including the ability to discriminate slight differences in shapes, shading, lengths, and widths, as well as ability to perceive pertinent detail is measured. P is measured by Tests 5 and 7.

Clerical Perception (Q)—Attention to detail in written or tabular material as well as the ability to proofread words and numbers and to avoid perceptual errors in arithmetic computation is tapped here. Q is measured by Test 1.

Motor Coordination (K)—This test taps the ability to quickly make precise movements that require eye-hand coordination. K is measured by Test 8.

Finger Dexterity (F)—This test taps the ability to quickly manipulate small objects with the fingers. F is measured by Tests 11 and 12.

Manual Dexterity (M)—The ability to work with one's hands in placing and turning motions is measured here. M is measured by Tests 9 and 10.

Referring back to the diagram and more specifically to the outermost ring, note that the three composite aptitudes can be derived from the nine specific aptitudes: a Cognitive composite, a Perceptual composite, and a Psychomotor composite. The nine aptitudes that compose the three composite aptitudes may be summarized as follows:

	The nine GATB aptitudes	The three composite scores
G	General Learning Ability (also referred to as *intelligence*)	
V	Verbal Aptitude	Cognitive
N	Numerical Aptitude	
S	Spatial Aptitude	
P	Form Perception	Perceptual
Q	Clerical Perception	
K	Motor Coordination	
F	Finger Dexterity	Psychomotor
M	Manual Dexterity	

Traditionally—prior to the advent of VG—test takers who sat for the GATB might subsequently receive counseling as to how they did in each of the nine aptitude areas. Further they might have been informed (1) how their own pattern of GATB scores compared to patterns of aptitude (referred to as Occupational Aptitude Patterns or OAPs) deemed necessary for proficiency in various occupations, and/or (2) how they performed with respect to any of the 467 constellations of a Special Aptitude Test Battery (SATB) that could potentially be extracted from a GATB protocol. Using VG makes possible additional information useful in advising prospective employers and counseling prospective employees. Such information includes more precise data concerning a test taker's performance with respect to OAPs, as well as scores (usually expressed in percentiles) with respect to the five job families. Research (Hunter, 1982) has indicated that the three composite aptitudes can be used to validly predict to job proficiency for all jobs in the United States economy. All jobs may be categorized according to five job families and the aptitude required for each of these families can be described with respect to various contributions of the three composite GATB scores. For example, Job Family 1 is 59% Cognitive, 30% Perceptual, and 11% Psychomotor in nature. GATB scoring is done by computer as is weighting of scores to determine suitablity for employment in jobs in each of the five job families.

In addition to weighting of composite aptitude scores for the purpose of deriving percentile scores for each of the five job families, VG as applied to the GATB has also brought with it an attempt to avoid adverse impact on any racial group. For this reason, an individual's score on the GATB represents a comparison only to members of his or her own racial group—well, not quite. The following four categories were established:

1. Black
2. Hispanic
3. Native American (Indian)
4. Other (including whites—Jewish Americans, Italian Americans, French Canadians, and so forth—Orientals, and anyone else who is not described in the aforementioned three categories)

Validity Generalization and the GATB (continued)

Proponents of VG as applied to use with the GATB list the following advantages:

1. *The decreased emphasis on multiple cutoffs as a selection strategy has advantages for both prospective employers and employees.* In a multiple cutoff selection model, a prospective employee would have to achieve certain minimum GATB scores in each of the aptitudes deemed critical for proficiency in a given occupation; failure to meet the minimal cutting score in these aptitudes would mean elimination from the candidate pool for that occupation. Using VG, a potential benefit for the prospective employee is that the requirement of a minimum cutting score on any specific aptitude is eliminated. For employers, VG encourages the use of a "top-down" hiring policy: one in which the best qualified people (as measured by the GATB) are offered jobs first.

2. *Research has suggested that the relationship between aptitude tests scores and job performance is linear, a relationship that is statistically better suited to VG as opposed to the multiple cutoff selection model.* The nature of the relationship between scores on a valid test of aptitude and ratings of job performance is illustrated in Figure 2. Given that such a relationship exists, Hunter (1980, 1982) notes that from a technical standpoint, linear data are better suited to analysis via a VG model than via one that employs multiple cutoffs.

3. *More precise information can be reported to employers regarding a test taker's relative standing in the continuum of aptitude test scores.* Consider in this context Figure 3 and let's suppose that an established and validated cutoff score for selection in a particular occupation using this hypothetical test of aptitude is 155. Examinee X and Examinee Y both meet the cutoff requirement but Examinee Y is probably better qualified for the job—we say "probably" because there may be exceptions to this general rule depending on variables such as the actual demands of the specific job. While the score

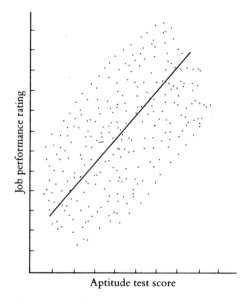

Figure 2   *The Linear Relationship Between Aptitude Test Scores and Job Performance Ratings.*

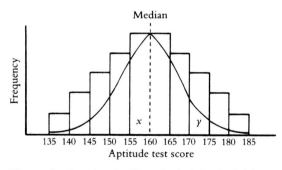

Figure 3   *Results of a Hypothetical Aptitude Test.*

for Examinee X falls below the median score for all test takers, the score for Examinee Y lies at the high end of the distribution of scores. All other factors being equal, which individual would you prefer to hire if you owned the company? Using a simple cutoff procedure, no distinction with respect to aptitude score would have been made between Examinee X and Examinee Y provided both scores met the cutoff criterion.

4. *The potential for adverse impact is minimized or at least made no worse than previously with test performance comparisons limited to members of one's own racial group.* However, as was intimated earlier, it is not entirely true that all test taker data are analyzed with respect to the race of individual test takers. The fourth category in the racial taxonomy used by the government (the "Other" category) clumps together whites, Orientals, and everyone else who is not described by the other three categories.

5. *G better assists employers in their efforts to hire qualified employees.* Studies such as one conducted at the Philip Morris Company suggest that a significant increase in the rate of training success can be expected for employees hired using a selection procedure that uses VG as compared to employees hired by other means (Warmke, 1984).

Is VG "The Answer" to all personnel selection problems? Not at all. VG is, to put it simply and straightforwardly, one rationale for justifiably avoiding the time and expense of conducting a separate validation study for every single test with every possible group of test takers under every possible set of circumstances—too often with too few subjects to achieve meaningful findings. It should be noted, however, that with the convenience of VG come many concerns about the efficacy of the procedures employed. And while we have devoted a fair amount of time to acquainting you with this important concept in the personnel selection literature, it is equally important for you to be aware that a number of technical issues with respect to VG are currently being debated in the professional literature.

You will recall that in the development of VG as applied to personnel selection, Hunter and his colleagues used a process called meta-analysis to cumulate findings across a number of studies. One important aspect of this work involved sta-

tistically correcting for the small sample sizes that occurred in the studies analyzed. The types of procedures used in such a process and the types of interpretations that can legitimately be made as a result have been the subject of a number of critical analyses of VG. The amount of unexplained variance that remains even after statistical corrections for differences in sample size have been made (Cascio, 1987), the unknown influence of a potential restriction-of-range problem with respect to subject self-selection (Cronbach, 1984), objections with respect to using employer ratings as a criterion (Burke, 1984), and the fact that alternative models may explain variation in validity coefficients as well as the cross-situational consistency model (James, Demaree, & Mulaik, 1986) are some of the technical issues that have been raised with respect to the use of VG (see also Zedeck & Cascio, 1984). With specific reference to VG as applied to use with the GATB, one might inquire further: What problems arise when over twelve thousand occupations are grouped into five job families? Is it really meaningful to group an occupation such as "truck driver" in the same job family as "secretary"? Is adverse impact really minimized by the procedure previously described?

Clearly, much remains to be learned about how VG can most effectively be brought to bear on problems related to personnel testing. Difficult questions—some psychometric in nature, others that relate more to societal values—will have to be addressed. Compounding the task of addressing such questions is a litany of variables that are neither psychometric in nature nor directly related to values; included here are variables such as the strength of the economy, the size of the available labor pool, the experience of the available labor pool, the general desirablity of specific jobs, and the salaries being offered for various kinds of work. Regardless of whether one looks favorably or not at the government's experimentation with VG in personnel selection, it seems reasonable to assume that there is much to be learned in the process, and the field of personnel selection may ultimately profit from the experience.

assessment. If you're curious about your own aptitude for work in fields as diverse as psychology, education, and plumbing, you may just want to visit your local state employment office. Be prepared to sit for an examination that will take about three hours or so if you take the entire test; the GATB consists of twelve timed tests that measure nine aptitudes that in turn can be divided into three composite aptitudes (see the Close-up). About one-half the time will be spent involved in psychomotor tasks and the other half of the time will be spent on paper-and-pencil tasks. In some instances, depending on factors such as the reason assessment is undertaken, only selected tests of the battery will be administered—this (referred to as a Special Aptitude Test Battery or SATB) as a means of measuring aptitude for a specific line of work. And even if you take the full GATB, various SATBs—aptitudes deemed necessary for specific occupations—can be isolated for study from the other test data.

In recent years the GATB has evolved from a test with multiple cutoffs to one that employs regression and validity generalization for making recommendations based on test results. The rationale and process by which the GATB has made this evolution has been described by John E. Hunter (1980, 1986), Frank Schmidt, and their associates (Hunter & Schmidt, 1983; Hunter, Schmidt, & Jackson, 1982; Hunter & Hunter, 1984—the latter Hunter is more than an associate; she's John's wife), and validity generalization is the subject of our chapter Close-up. Briefly, recommendations with respect to aptitude for a particular job had in the past been made with respect to GATB validity studies bearing on specific jobs; if, for example, there existed 500 job descriptions covering 500 jobs for which scores on the GATB were to be applied, there would be 500 individual validation studies with the GATB—one validation study for each individual job, typically with a relatively small sample size (many of these single studies containing an average of only 76 subjects). Further, there were no validation studies for the other 12,000-plus jobs that exist in the American economy according to the *Dictionary of Occupational Titles* published by the United States Department of Labor (1977). Using various techniques to cumulate results across a number of validation studies and statistically correct for error such as sampling error—a process called *meta-analysis* (see Glass, McGaw, & Smith, 1981; Hunter et al., 1982)—Hunter demonstrated that all of the jobs could be categorized within five families of jobs, these families based on what are called "worker function codes" of the *Dictionary of Occupational Titles*. The five families of jobs are: (1) Setting Up, (2) Feeding and Off-Bearing, (3) Synthesizing and Coordinating, (4) Analyzing, Compiling, and Computing, and (5) Copying and Comparing. Regression equations for each of the families were then developed, and using these equations it was found that recommendations for individual test takers could be generalized to various jobs.

In recent years and with the realization that minority test takers fare less well on the GATB than their nonminority counterparts, the GATB has become a race-normed test. *Race norming* refers to the process of adjusting scores to show an individual test taker's standing within her or his own racial group. With the GATB, high scorers from all racial groups are recommended to employers for employment; employers are not given access to raw scores. In response to a Labor Department request to assess race norming and other aspects of the test, the National Academy of Science (NAS) issued a report in 1989 that was supportive of such adjustment of minority members' scores. Additionally, the NAS found the GATB to be an adequate predictor of job performance for many jobs, although it did not recommend its use for all jobs. In July of 1990, the Labor Department proposed a two-year suspension in the use of the GATB, during which time the efficacy of the test and the scoring procedures used would be further researched. Should the suspension take effect, users of the GATB will be forced to rely on private sources of aptitude testing or be left to their own resources. At this writing, no decision has been made on the suspension. However, even if there is none, the future of the GATB is unclear because of congressional opposition to score adjusting and racial quotas. One government industrial psychologist stated flatly, "My sense is the GATB is as good as dead" (cited by Adler, 1991, p. 14). Psychologist Frank Schmidt's response to these events can perhaps best be summed up by his observation that "The problem isn't in the test. . . . the problem is a social problem—it is a failure to develop the job skills equally well in all groups" (cited in Adler, 1991, p. 14).

Another aptitude test developed by USES is the Nonreading Aptitude Test Battery, a test designed for use with culturally and educationally disadvantaged individuals. There is also a Spanish-language version of the GATB—no small feat since differences between East Coast and West Coast spoken and written Spanish had to be taken account of in its development. A version of the GATB for the deaf and hearing-impaired is also available. In addition to measures of aptitude, USES also administers interest measures, tests of clerical skills, and an achievement test called the Basic Occupational Literacy Test (BOLT). Measures of general aptitude are sometimes administered along with tests of general intelligence; there is overlap in the constructs measured (Anderson, Mohenshil, Buckland-Meer, & Levison, 1990), but taken together such measures can yield a more complete profile of skills and abilities.

Other measures of general aptitude   Other measures of general aptitude, or more precisely, vocational aptitude, include the previously discussed Armed Services Vocational Aptitude Battery and one general aptitude test battery that may take as long as 11 hours to administer in its entirety: the Flanagan Aptitude Classification Tests. Needless to say, the Flanagan is one battery that will require at least two appointments for administration. Intended for use with high school students and a general adult population, it consists of 19 subtests, including some labeled Precision, Ingenuity, and Alertness. The subtests were developed on the basis of research that suggested which behaviors were critical to successful job performance in specific occupations. When time is at a premium, an examiner might opt for an aptitude test like the Career Ability Placement Survey, which requires only about 50 minutes to administer. This test yields scores on the following eight scales: Mechanical Reasoning, Spatial Relations, Verbal Reasoning, Numerical Ability, Language Usage, Word Knowledge, Perceptual Speed and Accuracy, and Manual Speed and Dexterity. Studies examining the test-retest and alternate-forms reliability of this test have yielded correlation coefficients ranging from the .70s to the .90s. This test's correlation with relevant portions of other vocational aptitude tests—tests that take much longer to administer—such as the DAT and the GATB has been found to vary widely as a function of the particular subtest compared (Knapp, Knapp, & Michael, 1977).

Measures of specific aptitudes   If an employee's job consists mainly of securing tiny transistors into the inner workings of some electronic appliance or game,

Figure 18–2 *The O'Connor Tweezer Dexterity Test.*

the chances are good that the employer is not particularly interested in a prospective employee's verbal aptitude, numerical aptitude, or general intelligence; there will, however, be great interest focused on perceptual-motor abilities, finger dexterity, and related variables. In such an instance the test user might find a test like the O'Connor Tweezer Dexterity Test to be the instrument of choice (see Figure 18–2). This test requires the examinee to insert brass pins into a metal plate using a pair of tweezers. Other tests designed to measure specific aptitudes exist for a wide variety of occupational fields ranging from art appreciation (Meier, 1942) to mechanical reasoning (Bennett, Seashore, & Wesman, 1947). As we saw in Chapter 10, testing programs designed for use with admission to professional schools, such as the Dental Admission Testing Program, the Medical College Admissions Test, the Law School Admission Test, and specialized tests that are part of the Graduate Record Examination (for example, the Psychology Test), are all designed to shed light on the test taker's aptitude.

Personality Measures

Is a likeable, dominant, persuasive person better suited for work in sales or work on an assembly line? Clearly such an individual, at least with respect to the personality traits described, seems better suited for work in sales. In addition to examining interests and aptitudes, preemployment counseling may also entail the administration of personality tests. Such tests "round out" the vocational assessment by providing additional input. Suppose an individual with an interest in a television news career and a high aptitude for writing is weighing the merits of becoming a television news personality or a television news writer. And suppose further that one of the findings in a personality test was that this individual has a very high need for exhibitionism. The personality test findings, combined with other findings, might lead the consulting psychologist to steer the client toward pursuit of an on-air career. Contrariwise, if the findings from personality tests indicated that this client was low in exhibitionism, had a strong need for independence and autonomy combined with little tolerance for relating to authority figures, the client might be asked to consider the merits of freelance work within the field of television news.

Any personality test like those described in Chapters 12 through 14 could conceivably be used within the context of vocational counseling. We now look at two of the many personality tests that have found specific application in the field of employment and preemployment decision making.

The Guilford-Zimmerman Temperament Survey The Guilford-Zimmerman Temperament Survey (GZTS) is a self-report test that yields scores on the ten personality dimensions listed in Table 18–2. The scores on each of these dimensions or factors are derived from responses to 30 statements that may take

Table 18–2

Guilford-Zimmerman Temperament Survey (GZTS) Personality Dimensions

Dimension name	Description
General Activity (G)	A measure of energy level and the rate at which the individual operates. A high scorer would be a person who moves quickly, works at a rapid rate, and is full of vitality.
Restraint (R)	A measure of self-control, persistence, and deliberate action; to some extent this score provides a measure of responsibility. A person scoring low on this scale would be impulsive, spontaneous, and seemingly carefree.
Ascendance (A)	A measure of the degree to which the individual exhibits leadership, initiative, and assertiveness. A low score on this scale reflects submissiveness.
Sociability (S)	The extent to which the individual seeks and develops social contacts.
Emotional Stability (E)	An indication of evenness or fluctuation of moods, optimism, or pessimism, and whether there are feelings of or freedom from feelings of worry, guilt, or loneliness.
Objectivity (O)	A measure of the degree to which the individual is thick-skinned or sensitive.
Friendliness (F)	A measure of congeniality, respect for others, acceptance, and tolerance.
Thoughtfulness (T)	An indication of observation and reflectiveness of self and others.
Personal Reactions (P)	Acceptance and tolerance of others and faith in social institutions.
Masculinity (M)	A measure of the degree to which the individual is interested in masculine activities and exhibits behavior traditionally associated with masculine roles.

the form of "yes," "no," or "?" (uncertain).[1] Interpretation is typically not made with respect to any one score but rather on the basis of all the scores—a profile. Thus, for example, consideration of a high score in General Activity alone might lead the interpreter to suspect that the assessee is one who works quickly. However, if such a score is coupled with a low score on the Restraint dimension, the interpretation might change from "highly energetic" to "highly impulsive," the latter description being more accurate for someone who acts quickly but with little restraint. In addition to the dimension scales, the GZTS has built into it three verification scales designed to detect response sets, intentional faking, and carelessness.

Normative data for the GZTS are based on a college sample of 523 men and 389 women; profiles of patterns of scores for various high school, college, and adult occupational groups are reported in the test manual (Guilford, Zimmerman, & Guilford, 1976). Reliability estimates obtained on each of the different factors were found to range from .75 to .85. Test-retest reliability based on varying intervals of from one to three years tend to lie in the .50s and .60s range. An overview of the extensive amount of research conducted on this test in the years since its publication is presented in the manual. Included are studies exploring scores on the test as a function of variables such as age, education, gender, occupational group, psychiatric diagnosis, socioeconomic status, ethnic group, and political affiliation.

The Edwards Personal Preference Schedule   The Edwards Personal Preference Schedule (EPPS) is a personality inventory based in part on the work of Murray (1938) in the area of motivation. Murray distinguished between primary needs (that is, food, water, sex) and secondary (psychological) needs. The EPPS was designed to measure the strength of the following 15 psychological needs: achievement, deference, order, exhibition, autonomy, affiliation, intraception, succorance, dominance, abasement, nurturance, change, endurance, heterosexuality, and aggression.

The EPPS consists of 210 pairs of statements arranged in a forced-choice format; the examinee is instructed to select the statement from the pair that is most descriptive of himself or herself. The statements are arranged so that they reflect equal social desirability, each statement representing a different need scale. A score representing the intensity of each need is derived. Note that as each of the test statements in any pair of statements corresponds to one of the test scales, the choice of one statement serves to reject the item representative of the alternative. As a result, the scores are *ipsative* in nature: that is, the score obtained does not represent the strength of a need in absolute terms, but rather in *relation* to the strength of the other needs. Because the items on the EPPS are ipsative in nature, caution is in order when comparing scores between individuals. In addition to the scale scores, a Consistency Score and a Profile Stability Score are also computed. The Consistency Score reflects how consistent the respondent has been in selecting choices by comparing responses on a selected number of items that are identi-

---

1. The GZTS in its present form is actually the distillation of three personality inventories previously developed by its authors. The establishment of these "personality dimensions" was done by means of factor analysis, so they are sometimes referred to as "factors."

cally repeated in different parts of the inventory. The Stability Score represents the correlation between scores obtained on two halves of the inventory.

Normative data for the EPPS were obtained from a sample of approximately 1,500 college students (760 males and 749 females) from 29 campuses throughout the country and from close to 9,000 men and women from the general adult population. Additional normative data for 559 male and 986 female high school students have been compiled, and a comparison between the mean scores of the high school sample and the mean scores of the original college sample is available (Pasewark & Sawyer, 1979). Test-retest reliability for the 15 scales based on one-week intervals was found to range from .74 to .87. Internal-consistency measures resulted in split-half reliability coefficients ranging from .60 to .87 with a median of .78. Interpretation of these findings is complicated because certain items are repeated. Data concerning the validity of this test are meager, and this remains a major criticism of the EPPS.

Job Previews

Once the vocational search has been narrowed to a specific field, the question sometimes arises as to what area or specialty within that field would be best. At this point, a valuable preemployment assessment technique—one employed by clients themselves and not counselors—is the job preview: the opportunity for the prospective employee to see and assess firsthand exactly what the job entails and the working conditions that can be expected. Reading about a job in a classified ad or being told about the job by an employment agent or company representative doesn't compare to actually visiting the worksite and obtaining an account of the advantages and disadvantages of a particular line of work from the employer as well as current employees. When an on-site visit to the place of employment is impractical, an organization might make a job preview available through printed or audiovisual materials and/or in-person visits by organizational representatives.

The prospective employee who undertakes a job preview might be instructed by a vocational counselor to return to that office to report on impressions. Like measures of interests, aptitudes, and personality, a report of a job preview can be useful for counseling purposes.

PERSONNEL PSYCHOLOGY

Screening, Selection, Classification, and Placement

Screening refers to a relatively superficial selection process based on an evaluation with respect to certain minimal criteria. For example, the military might screen prospective soldiers with respect to intelligence, height, weight, and physical health. Perhaps the most widely used tools for employment screening include application blanks, letters of recommendation, and the interview.

A distinction may be made between the terms *selection, classification,* and *placement*. It is appropriate to use the term *selection* only when each person (or "object" with respect to some applications) considered will either be selected or rejected; the decision to hire or not and the decision to admit or deny admission are examples of situations that involve selection. By contrast, *classification* does not imply acceptance or rejection, but rather a rating (or "pigeon-holing") with respect to two or more criteria. A military draft board, for example, might *classify* registrants on the basis of criteria such as physical suitability for military service, marital status, age, and related variables. Like classification, *placement* also carries no implication of acceptance or rejection. It is appropriate to use the term placement when a rating is being made on the basis of one criterion. If, for example, you took a college-level course when still in high school, the score you earned on the advanced placement test in that subject area may have been the sole criterion used to place you in an appropriate section of that college course upon your acceptance to college.

Businesses, schools, the military, and other organizations regularly select, classify, and/or place individuals according to their needs. To help in decision making, tools such as those discussed in the section on preemployment counseling may be used (for example, measures of aptitude, interest, and personality). Other measures and techniques, such as those discussed next, may also be used.

Application blanks Application blanks may be thought of as biographical sketches that supply employers with information pertinent to the acceptability of job candidates. In addition to demographic information (such as name, address, and telephone number), pertinent details about other areas such as educational background, military service, and previous work experience may be requested. As noted in Table 18–3, each item in an application blank should ideally be relevant to the issue of whether the employer should continue to consider the application for employment. The application blank is a highly useful tool for quick screening in numerous settings.

Table 18–3

Checklist for an Application Blank Item

---

1. Is the item necessary for identifying the applicant?
2. Is it necessary for screening out those who are ineligible under the company's basic hiring policies?
3. Does it help to decide whether the candidate is qualified?
4. Is it based on analysis of the job or jobs for which applicants will be selected?
5. Has it been pretested on the company's employees and found to correlate with success?
6. Will the information be used? How?
7. Is the application form the proper place to ask for it?
8. To what extent will answers duplicate information to be obtained at another step in the selection procedure—for example, through interviews, tests, or medical examinations?
9. Is the information needed for selection at all, or should it be obtained at induction or even later?
10. Is it probable that the applicants' replies will be reliable?
11. Does the question violate any applicable federal or state legislation?

Source: Ahern (1949)

Letters of recommendation Another useful tool in terms of preliminary screening of applicants is the letter of recommendation (Arvey, 1979; Glueck, 1978). Such letters may be a unique source of detailed information pertaining to areas such as how the applicant has performed in the past, the quality of the applicant's relationships with peers, and so forth. Of course, such letters are not without their drawbacks. It is no secret that applicants solicit letters from those individuals who they believe will say only positive things about them. Another possible drawback with respect to letters of recommendation is the variance due to the observational and writing skills of the letter writers. In research that employed application files for admission to graduate school in psychology, it was found that an applicant might variously be described as "analytically oriented, reserved, and highly motivated" or "free-spirited, imaginative, and outgoing" depending on the letter writer's perspective. As the authors of that study pointed out, "Although favorable recommendations may be intended in both cases, the details of and bases for such recommendations are varied" (Baxter et al., 1981, p. 300). Efforts to minimize the drawbacks inherent in the open-ended letter of recommendation have in some instances taken the form of "questionnaires of recommendation" wherein former employers, professors, and other letter writers respond to structured questions concerning the applicant's prior performance. Some such questionnaires employ a forced-choice format designed to force respondents to make negative as well as positive statements about the applicant.

Interviews Interviews, be they individual or group in nature, provide an occasion for the face-to-face exchange of information between interviewers and interviewees. Like other interviews, the employment interview may fall anywhere on a continuum from highly structured, with uniform questions being asked to all, to highly unstructured, with the questions to be asked left largely to the interviewer's discretion. Like other interviews, too, the interviewer's biases and prejudices may creep into the evaluation and ultimately influence the outcome. Other factors such as the order of interviewing might also affect outcomes by reason of contrast effects. For example, an average applicant may appear better or less qualified depending on whether the preceding candidate was particularly poor or outstanding. A summary of some of the interacting factors that contribute to the outcome of an employment interview is presented in Figure 18–3.

Performance samples If you have ever taken a word-processing or typing test as a prerequisite for employment you have had firsthand experience with a performance sample. Sometimes the work sample required for employment takes the form of the administration of a standardized test. For example, the Seashore-Bennett Stenographic Proficiency Test is a standardized measure of stenographic competence. The test materials include a recording in which a voice dictates a series of letters and manuscripts that the assessee is to transcribe in shorthand and then type. The recorded directions provide a uniform clarity of voice and rate of dictation. Sometimes the work sample required for the job cannot reasonably be completed within the relatively brief period of time allotted for the personnel evaluation. For example, an individual applying for a position as an art director might be expected to have a portfolio of paintings and/or drawings attesting to artistic abilities. A performance sample might use elaborately constructed en-

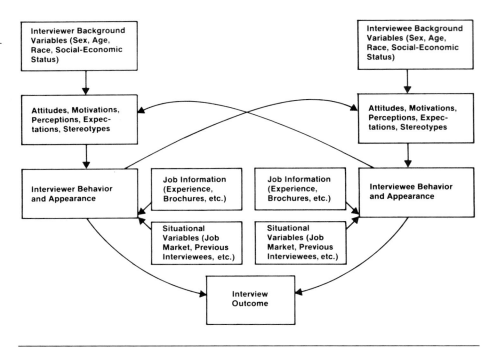

Figure 18-3 *Interacting Factors Influencing Interview Outcome (Source: Schmitt, 1976).*

vironments and special equipment to mimic the conditions under which the successful applicant might have to function (see Figure 18–4). For example, during World War II, the assessment staff of the Office of Strategic Services (OSS) selected American secret agents, saboteurs, propaganda experts, and other personnel for overseas assignments. In addition to interviews, personality tests, and other paper-and-pencil tests, OSS administered situational performance tests. One such test was the "brook exercise," wherein a group of candidates, given only boards, rope, a pulley, and a barrel, had to transport a log and a rock across a stream. Today, the Israelis, among other military powers, use similar methods; Tziner and Eden (1985) described experiments with three-person military crews performing military tasks in a military field setting. Individuals were assigned to the crews on the basis of levels of ability and motivation, and assignment by all possible combinations of these levels were varied in an effort to determine the optimal composition of a crew.

A commonly used performance test in the assessment of business leadership ability is a leaderless group situation. Communication skills, problem-solving ability, the ability to cope with stress, and other skills can also economically be assessed by a group exercise in which the participants' task is to work together in the solution of some problem or the achievement of some goal. As group members interact, the assessors make judgments with respect to questions such as "Who is the leader?" and "What role do other members play in this group?" The answers to such questions will no doubt figure into decisions concerning the indi-

Figure 18–4 *Games Psychologists Play.* Psychologists have long recognized the value of gamelike situations in the process of evaluating prospective personnel. These photos illustrate some of the "games" that have been utilized by psychologists in this regard.

(a)

(a) During World War II the Office of Strategic Services (OSS) assessed leadership ability and emotional stability by means of in-the-field performance tests. Here, subjects were called on to rebuild a blown bridge though they were not supplied with sufficient materials to do so. In some of the OSS exercises, "assistants"—actually confederates of the experimenters—acted in ways to further frustrate the efforts of the assessees (for example, by being sluggish or by being eager but incorrect).

(b) A task referred to as the "Manufacturing Problem" was used as part of the AT&T Management Progress Study conducted in 1957. The assessee's task here is to collaborate with others in the buying of parts and the manufacture of a "product." The people pictured here from left to right are Drs. Warren D. Bachelis, John Paul McKinney, Douglas W.

(b)

(c)

Bray, and H. Weston Clarke, Jr.

(c) Video games have been employed by many researchers such as those at the Naval Biodynamics laboratory who explored the viability of using such materials in the selection and training of military personnel. According to Kennedy et al. (1982, p. 51), "With respect to stability and task definition, commercially available

video games compare favorably with more than 40 conventional tests of psychomotor skills and cognition." They also found video games to be economical relative to other apparatuses, reliable, safe, adaptable for use in varied environments, readily available in departments stores throughout the country, and capable of being group-administered.

vidual assessee's future position in the organization. Another performance test frequently used to assess leadership or managerial ability is the in-basket technique. This technique is an exercise that simulates the way a manager or executive deals with his or her "in-basket" filled with mail, memos, announcements, and various other notices and directives. Assessees are instructed that they have only a limited amount of time, usually two or three hours, to deal with all of the items in the "basket" (more commonly, a manila envelope). Through post-test interviews and an examination of the way that the assessee handled the materials, assessors can make judgments concerning variables such as organizing and planning, problem solving, decision making, creativity, leadership, and written communication skills. The in-basket was first developed by Educational Testing Service as a means of assessing the effectiveness of the curriculum at the Air College of the United States Air Force (Frederiksen, Saunders, & Wand, 1957).

Test batteries and assessment centers Major corporations may employ full-time I/O psychologists whose duties include administering psychological test batteries to prospective employees. Recounting a major U.S. airline's experience in this regard, Holt, Taylor, and Carter (1985) reported that during the period from 1975 to 1982, 368 applicants for pilot positions underwent preemployment screening that included tests of intelligence and personality. A total of 73 of these prospective employees were rejected for various reasons—the majority deemed unsuitable as a result of the personality assessment or a finding of low intelligence. The United States Air Force (USAF) Human Resources Laboratory frequently develops programs designed to improve the selection of pilot trainees and the classification of student pilots for either fighter or heavy aircraft training. In one such program, a battery of experimental tests, including tests of psychomotor skills, personality, and cognitive abilities are administered by computer prior to flight training. These results are then analyzed with respect to subjects' performance in both training and operational flying (Kantor & Bordelon, 1985).

A widely used tool in selection, classification, and placement is the *assessment center*. Although it sounds as if it might be a place, the term actually denotes an organizationally standardized *procedure* involving multiple assessment techniques such as paper-and-pencil tests and situational performance tests. The assessment-center concept had its origins in the writings of Henry Murray and his associates (1938). Assessment-center-like activities were first pioneered by military organizations both in this country and abroad (Thornton & Byham, 1982). In 1956, the first application of the idea in an industrial setting occurred with the initiation of the Management Progress Study (MPS) at American Telephone and Telegraph (Bray, 1964). MPS was to be a longitudinal study that would follow the lives of over 400 telephone company management and nonmanagement personnel. Each participant would attend a 3½-day assessment center in which he or she would be interviewed for two hours, would take a number of paper-and-pencil tests designed to shed light on their cognitive abilities and personality (for example, the School and College Ability Test and the Edwards Personal Preference Schedule), and would participate in individual and group situational exercises (such as the in-basket test and a leaderless group). Additionally, projective tests such as the Thematic Apperception Test and the Sentence Completion Test were administered. All of the data on each of the assessees were integrated at a meeting of the assessors, and judgments concerning the variables are listed in Table 18–4.

Table 18–4

655

Original Management Progress Study Dimensions

Area	Dimension
Administrative skills	Organizing and planning—How effectively can this person organize work, and how well does he or she plan ahead?
	Decision making—How ready is this person to make decisions, and how good are the decisions made?
	Creativity—How likely is this person to solve a management problem in a novel way?
Interpersonal skills	Leadership skills—How effectively can this person lead a group to accomplish a task without arousing hostility?
	Oral communication skills—How well would this person present an oral report to a small conference group on a subject he or she knew well?
	Behavior flexibility—How readily can this person, when motivated, modify his or her behavior to reach a goal? How able is this person to change roles or style of behavior to accomplish objectives?
	Personal impact—How forceful and likeable an early impression does this person make?
	Social objectivity—How free is this person from prejudices against racial, ethnic, socioeconomic, educational, and other social groups?
	Perceptions of threshold social cues—How readily does this person perceive minimal cues in the behavior of others?
Cognitive skills	General mental ability—How able is this person in terms of the functions measured by tests of intelligence, scholastic aptitude, and learning ability?
	Range of interests—To what extent is this person interested in a variety of fields of activity such as science, politics, sports, music, art?
	Written communication skill—How well would this person compose a communicative and formally correct memorandum on a subject he or she knew well? How well-written are memos and reports likely to be?
Stability of performance	Tolerance of uncertainty—To what extent will this person's work performance stand up under uncertain or unstructured conditions?
	Resistance to stress—To what extent will this person's work performance stand up in the face of personal stress?
Work motivation	Primacy of work—To what extent does this person find satisfactions from work more important than satisfactions from other areas of life?
	Inner work standards—To what extent will this person want to do a good job, even if a less good one is acceptable to the boss and others?
	Energy—How continuously can this person sustain a high level of work activity?
	Self-objectivity—How realistic a view does this person have of his or her own assets and liabilities, and how much insight into his or her own motives?
Career orientation	Need for advancement—To what extent does this person need to be promoted significantly earlier than his or her peers? To what extent are further promotions needed for career satisfaction?

Table 18–4 (*continued*)

Original Management Progress Study Dimensions

Area	Dimension
	Need for security—How strongly does this person want a secure job?
	Ability to delay gratification—To what extent will this person be willing to wait patiently for advancement if confident advancement will come?
	Realism of expectations—To what extent do this person's expectations about his or her work life with the company conform to what is likely to be true? (Convention: If *under-*estimates, rate 5.)
	Bell System value orientation—To what extent has this person incorporated Bell System values such as service, friendliness, justice of company position on earnings, rates, wages?
Dependency	Need for superior approval—To what extent does this person need warmth and nurturant support from immediate supervisors?
	Need for peer approval—To what extent does this person need warmth and acceptance from peers and subordinates?
	Goal flexibility—To what extent is this person likely to reorient his or her life toward a different goal?

Source: Hogan and Quigley (1986)

Is the assessment-center approach a valid approach to a personnel assessment? According to Olshfski and Cunningham (1986), this question is premature because certain methodological and theoretical questions need to be clarified. For example, issues regarding (1) the concept of manager competence, (2) the assessment exercises, and (3) the role of the assessors need to be addressed. Olshfski and Cunningham cautioned that, lacking such conceptual clarification, an important management evaluation tool might be rejected on the basis of quantitative studies.

Physical tests   A lifeguard who is visually impaired is seriously compromised in his or her ability to perform the job. A wine taster with damaged tastebuds is of little value to a vintner. An aircraft pilot who has lost the use of his arms . . . the point is clear: physical requirements of a job must be taken into consideration when screening, selecting, classifying, and placing applicants. Depending on the specific requirements of the job, a number of physical subtests may be used. Thus, for example, for a job in which a number of components of vision are critical, a test of visual acuity might be administered along with tests of visual efficiency, stereopsis (distance/depth perception), and color blindness. General physical fitness is required in many jobs, such as in police work where successful candidates might one day have to chase a fleeing suspect on foot or defend themselves against a suspect resisting arrest. The tests used in assessing such fitness might include a complete physical examination, tests of physical strength, and a performance test that meets some determined criterion with respect to running speed and running agility. Tasks like vaulting some object, stepping through tires, and going through a window frame would be included to simulate running on difficult terrain.

In some instances, an employer's setting certain physical requirements for employment are so reasonable and so necessary that they would readily be upheld by any court if challenged. Other physical requirements for employment, however, may fall into a gray area. How reasonable is it, for example, for a municipal police or fire department to maintain height and weight standards or weight-lifting requirements? In an extensive review of court rulings pertaining to physical standards for employment, Hogan and Quigley (1986) suggested that for a physical standard to be upheld the standard, in general, must be proved to be (1) nondiscriminatory, and (2) job-related. A summary of some of the litigation in this area is presented in Tables 18–5 and 18–6.

Table 18–5

Cases Litigated Involving Height and Weight Standards for Employment Selection

Case	Claim/job	Requirement/ impact	Defense	Decision/ judicial comments
Callery v. New York City Parks and Recreation Department	Sex discrimination Exec. Law §298 Lifeguard	5 ft 7 in. height Excluded 90% of female and 20% of male applicants 135 lb weight Excluded 60% of female and 30% of male applicants	Judge concluded that the real basis for the standard was that there had to be a "line of demarcation" (4 Empl. Prac. Dec. [CCH] ¶5252)	No job analysis or reference to job duties presented as evidence Judge cited that "testimony showed that persons both shorter and lighter might be able to perform duties" (4 Empl. Prac. Dec. [CCH] ¶7593) Department ordered to discontinue use of requirements
Castro v. Beecher	Race discrimination Fourteenth Amendment Police officer	5 ft 7 in. height No impact demonstrated	Police commissioner and Civil Service Commission denied that requirement was enforced	No prima facie case established Court declared that "in the absence of a showing of a prima facie case, the standard of review is a relaxed one . . . which a minimum height requirement for policeman clearly meets" (459 F.2d 734) Requirement upheld
Pond v. Braniff Airways, Inc.	Sex discrimination Title VII Airline worker	5 ft 8 in. height No impact demonstrated 4 ft 5 in. woman and 6 ft 4 in. man applied for a job unloading cargo (200 lb to 600 lb loads)	Airline claimed that height requirement was not applied and that the better qualified applicant was hired	Braniff did not discriminate by hiring better qualified applicant; that is, the man

Table 18–5 (*continued*)

Cases Litigated Involving Height and Weight Standards for Employment Selection

Case	Claim/job	Requirement/impact	Defense	Decision/judicial comments
Meadows v. Ford Motor Co.	Sex discrimination Title VII Automobile worker	150 lb weight Excluded 80% of female and 30% of male applicants	No defense discussed	No evidence given of strength of persons less than or greater than 150 lb Ford enjoined and prohibited from further use of the tests
Hail v. White	Sex discrimination Title VII Police officer	5 ft 7 in. height 135 lb weight No impact demonstrated	Police department witnesses testified that the requirements were selected on the basis of "generally prevailing standards among police departments (8 Empl. Prac. Dec. [CCH] ¶9637)	Plaintiff's expert testified that 90% of police work is "service and non-violent" Requirements upheld and found "not unreasonable" and "job related" (8 Empl. Prac. Dec. [CCH] ¶9637)
Hardy v. Stumpf	Sex discrimination Fourteenth Amendment Police officer	5 ft 7 in. height 135 lb weight Excluded over 80% of female applicants	Police department claimed that size is a measure of strength and that persons under the size requirement could not perform efficiently (7 Fair Empl. Prac. Cas. [BNA] 1084)	No direct evidence presented other than claim about size and strength Lower court dismissal of plaintiff's claim reversed
Guardians Association v. Civil Service Commission	Race and national origin discrimination Title VII Fourteenth Amendment Police officer	5 ft 7 in. height Excluded 54.1% of Spanish-American, 19.1% of black, and 22.1% of white men	Defendants claimed that a height requirement is a "well established practice," supported by survey showing that 97% of police departments had height requirements in 1973, with an average requirement of 68 in. (18 Fair Empl. Prac. Cas. [BNA] 82)	No job-relatedness established The court declared that "the fact that the use of height requirements is a time honored or widely established practice does not automatically save it from a claim of discrimination" (18 Fair Empl. Prac. Cas. [BNA] 18) No intent established; Fourteenth Amendment claim not supported Title VII violated; defendant enjoined from further use of height requirement

Table 18–5 (*continued*)

Cases Litigated Involving Height and Weight Standards for Employment Selection

Case	Claim/job	Requirement/ impact	Defense	Decision/judicial comments
Boyd v. Ozark Air Lines, Inc.	Sex discrimination Title VII Airline attendant	5 ft 5 in. height Excluded 25.8% of male and 93% of female applicants age 18–34 years and 11% of male and 74% of female applicants without regard to age	Defendants claimed business necessity based on claim that persons less than 5 ft 5 in. cannot adequately see to operate cockpit instruments	Quoting *Spurlock v. United Airlines* (1972): "When the job clearly requires a high degree of skill and the economic and human risks involved in hiring an unqualified applicant are great, the employer bears a correspondingly lighter burden [than with jobs requiring low degree of skill] to show that his employment criteria are job-related. The job of airline flight officer is clearly such a job." (17 Fair Empl. Prac. Cas. [BNA] 630) Requirement upheld
United States v. New York	Race discrimination Title VII State trooper	Physical agility test included "disguised" height requirement— shotgun aiming over a patrol vehicle	Defendant personnel claimed that officers need to be able to shoot over a patrol car	Shotgun test is disguised height requirement Defendants enjoined from further use of requirement
Costa v. Markey	Title VII Sex discrimination Police officer	5 ft 6 in. height Excluded 80% of female and 20% of male applicants	Requirement applied to all female applicant pool, therefore no discrimination	Prima facie case established All female applicant pool "is no defense to a prima facie case" (30 Empl. Prac. Dec. [CCH] ¶33137) Court declared: "*Teal* requires us, however, to look behind the result and evaluate the disparate impact of the height requirement itself, not the end result of its application in a particular case" (30 Empl. Prac. Dec. [CCH] ¶33137)

Table 18–5 (*continued*)

Cases Litigated Involving Height and Weight Standards for Employment Selection

Case	Claim/job	Requirement/impact	Defense	Decision/judicial comments
				In a dissenting opinion: "When only women are competing for a job as police officer, a height requirement may be unfair but it is not a violation of Title VII" (30 Empl. Prac. Dec. [CCH] ¶33173)
				Requirement in violation of Title VII (28 Empl. Prac. Dec. [CCH] ¶33173), reversed and remanded

Source: Hogan and Quigley (1986)

Table 18–6

Cases Litigated Involving Physical Tests for Employee Selection

Case	Claim/job	Selection battery	Defense	Decision
Hail v. White	Sex discrimination Title VII Police officer	Physical agility tests: Squat thrusts (25 in 1 min) Sit-ups (25 required) Push-ups (22 required) Squat jumps (27 required) Pull-ups (6 required)	"Synthetic validation" claimed No empirical evidence given	Tests upheld as "not unreasonable" and not non-job related" (8 Empl. Prac. Dec. [CCH] ¶9637)
Officers for Justice v. Civil Service Commission	Sex discrimination and national origin discrimination Title VII Fourteenth Amendment Police officer	Physical agility tests: Primarily upper-body strength Sandbag lift Wall test Dynamometer strength test 63% of men passed 1.2% of women passed	Concurrent study attempted	Job performance not predicted Tests in violation of Title VII Job analysis "not careful" and not done in accordance with guidelines No search for alternatives with less adverse impact Defendants enjoined from further use of tests
Hardy v. Stumpf	Sex discrimination Title VII	Physical agility tests: Run 300 ft, scale 6 ft wall	Content validity claimed based on job	Tests found reasonable and supported by job analysis

Case	Claim/job	Selection battery	Defense	Decision
	Fourteenth Amendment Police officer	Run 300 ft, register 75 lb on grip dynamometer, drag 140 lb dummy 50 ft, and raise it to a 2 ft high platform Complete above in 2.5 min. 15% of women passed 85% of men passed	analysis and concurrent study	Tests therefore upheld and not in violation of Title VII or Fourteenth Amendment
United States v. City of Buffalo	Sex discrimination Title VII Police officer	MPTC* standards score based on weighted sum of (a) numerical score for height/ weight and (b) agility, strength, speed, and endurance test scores	MPTC* standards adopted after abandoning height requirement	Undue advantage given to taller persons Defendants enjoined from further use of tests
Hull v. Cason	Race discrimination Title VII Fourteenth Amendment Fire fighter	Physical agility tests: Dummy carry (up a ladder) Pull-ups (2 required)	No defense presented in text decision	Use of tests upheld: "That an occupational function consumes a *de minimis* proportion of one's workday . . . does not necessarily diminish the need for selecting one who can best perform that function" (18 Fair Empl. Prac. Dec. [BNA] 1930)
Blake v. City of Los Angeles	Sex discrimination Title VII Fourteenth Amendment Police officer	Physical abilities tests: Run 50 yd, scale 6 ft wall Run 50 yd, 1 min overhand hang from chinning bar Run 50 ft, drag 140 lb dead weight 50 ft "Tremor" test—holding a stylus steady for 17 sec. Endurance run—12 min run on 1/8 mi track—scored on number of laps	Concurrent and content validation attempted	Job-relatedness not established Validation studies flawed Prediction of training success insufficient Defendants enjoined from further use of tests
United States v. City of Philadelphia	Sex discrimination Police officer	Physical performance test: 1/2 mi shuttle run Obstacle course Jump reaction time Hand grip 30.9% of women passed 97.2% of men passed	Concurrent validity claimed	Defendants enjoined from further use of tests No showing of job-relatedness

Table 18–6 (*continued*)

Cases Litigated Involving Physical Tests for Employee Selection

Case	Claim/job	Selection battery	Defense	Decision
United States v. New York	Race discrimination Sex discrimination Title VII Fourteenth Amendment State trooper	Physical performance test Phase I P/F test: Shotgun aiming Tire change Portable scale life Pull deer off roadway Physical coordination course Phase II: Competitive combative v. noncombative Attic opening Mile run Police pursuit course Nonweapon physical contact Drag person from vehicle 40.3% of men scored higher than highest scoring woman	Content validity claimed	Defendants enjoined from further use of tests Job analysis inappropriate for content validation Different scoring could have reduced adverse impact
Harless v. Duck	Sex discrimination Title VII Fourteenth Amendment Police officer	Physical agility test: 15 push-ups 25 sit-ups 6 ft standing broad jump 25 ft obstacle course (complete 3 or 4 to pass)	Developed through an "intuitive process"	Tests in violation of Title VII Tests not proved valid or job-related Job did not specify amount of strength or exertion required Test used elsewhere but never validated No justification for tests chosen or scoring used Tests deleted in 1975 with apparently no detrimental effect on police department
Berkman v. City of New York	Sex discrimination Title VII Fourteenth Amendment Fire fighter	Physical agility test: Dummy carry Hand grip Free-style broad jump Flexed arm hang Agility test Ledge walk Mile run 0% of women passed 46% of men passed	Content validity claimed Criterion-related by validity generalization	Defendants enjoined from further test use Validation strategy inappropriate—should have conducted construct or criterion-related validation Job analysis results contradictory "Ex post facto" rationalization of test selection Tests used from other study declared "irrelevant"

*MPTC = Municipal Police Training Council.

Widespread concern over drug abuse has prompted some to call for other types of physical screening and testing in the workplace: urinalysis for the purpose of detecting drugs in the body. The legal and ethical issues attendant to such testing are complex and beyond the scope of this book.

Integrity Tests

Whereas most tests used by corporate personnel offices are derived on the basis of a job analysis (that is, identification of the specific behavioral elements of a job performance), not all of the tests and measures used fall into this category. Integrity tests may serve to screen new employees as well as to "keep honest" those already hired. Paper-and-pencil screening instruments purporting to predict who will and will not be an honest employee—so-called *integrity tests*—have been around for many years. However, the use of such tests has increased dramatically with the passage of legislation prohibiting the use of lie detectors in most employment settings. In fact, it has been estimated that integrity testing has mushroomed into a thirty-million-dollar-a-year industry (Lawlor, 1990), with an estimated 15 million people taking such tests annually (Gavzer, 1990).

Sackett, Burris, and Callahan (1989) dichotomize existing instruments into what they term "overt integrity tests" (which may straightforwardly ask the examinee questions like "Do you always tell the truth?"), and "personality-based measures," which resemble in many ways objective personality inventories like the MMPI. Items on the latter type of tests may be far more subtle than on the former. Also, responses to items on the personality-based measures are less likely to be interpreted on the basis of the face validity of the item and more likely to be interpreted with reference to the responses of groups of people known to have, or lack, "integrity" as defined by the particular test.

Integrity tests have been criticized on many grounds, chief among them their questionable—and for the most part untested—validity (Sackett & Harris, 1984; Sackett, Burris, & Callahan, 1989). The American Psychological Association's Task Force on the Prediction of Dishonesty and Theft in Employment Settings issued a report (APA, 1991) noting the high variability in the ways that publishers of such tests describe them as well as "in the evidence that they assemble to substantiate claims of their validity and utility" (p. 25). The report did allow, however, that "for those few tests for which validity information is available, the preponderance of the evidence is supportive of their predictive validity" (APA, 1991, p. 26).

Beyond issues concerning the validity of many of the available tests are broader questions relating to the use of such tests. For example, is privacy being invaded when a prospective employee is asked to sit for such a test? Can such tests be used in support of discrimination practices? Should such tests be used alone or in combination with other measurement procedures as a basis for granting or denying employment? Interestingly, White (1984) suggests that preemployment honesty testing may induce negative work-related attitudes. Further, having to undergo such a test may be interpreted by prospective employees as evidence of high levels of employee theft—with the (paradoxical) result being a new and higher norm of stealing by employees.

Model Guidelines for Preemployment Integrity Testing Programs is a document developed by the Association of Personnel Test Publishers (APTP, 1990) that addresses many of the issues surrounding integrity tests, including issues relating to test development, administration, scoring, interpretation, confidentiality, public statements regarding the tests, and test-marketing practices. Specific guidelines in these areas are provided and the responsibilities of test users and publishers are discussed (see Jones, Arnold, & Harris, 1990, for an overview).

Other procedures   Many organizations employ various other tests and measures to aid in their decision making about personnel. For example, an autobiographical statement that includes the applicant's goals and objectives may be part of the application process. The United States Office of Personnel Management has developed special applications of the biographical approach that focus on prior experiences relevant to a particular job rather than on diplomas and other educational credentials (see Primoff, 1980). In managerial selection as in employee selection, a number of different methods are used, including tests, interviews, work samples, and peer or supervisor ratings. More subtle factors, including such job-irrelevant factors as race, may enter into judgments (Hitt & Barr, 1989). Focusing on the role of attention in managerial ability, Stankov, Fogarty, and Watt (1989) concluded that factors such as selective attention (ability to concentrate on a particular task), attention-switching ability (ability to shift attention as needed), and breadth of attention (ability to handle a variety of competing stimuli simultaneously) were generally desirable traits in managers. These researchers developed a test battery to assess these attentional abilities.

Issues in Personnel Selection

Who should be hired? Who should be fired? Who should be promoted? Who should be laid off? What criteria should be employed in making decisions such as these? Psychometric, ethical, and legal considerations enter into the process of answering such questions.

Psychometric considerations   Stated succinctly, the ideal, psychometrically sound personnel test is one that would reliably provide answers to questions concerning test takers' ability to do a job competently. The employer who uses a psychometrically sound selection procedure can reap great financial rewards for doing so. As we pointed out in Chapter 6, Schmidt, Hunter, and their associates have impressively documented the dollars-and-cents savings that are possible through the use of valid personnel tests and assessment programs (see Schmidt, Hunter, Outerbridge, & Trattner, 1986; Schmidt, Hunter, & Pearlman, 1981; Hunter & Schmidt, 1981; Pearlman, Schmidt, & Hunter, 1980; Schmidt, Gast-Rosenberg, & Hunter, 1980; Schmidt, Hunter, Pearlman, & Shane, 1979; Schmidt, Hunter, McKenzie, & Muldrow, 1979; Schmidt & Hunter, 1977, 1984; Schmidt, Hunter, & Urry, 1976).

But a psychometrically sound test is not enough; considerations other than ability frequently enter into hiring decisions. In one study of federal entry-level jobs, Hunter and Hunter (1984) concluded that while hiring by ability alone might save the government $15.61 billion per year, this practice would adversely impact on minority groups. What price, if any, can society afford to place on selection procedures that adversely impact on a segment of society? This is a very thorny issue—and one that is only marginally related to psychometrics.

An issue that clearly has a great deal to do with psychometrics concerns the very framework within which judgments concerning the validity of tests are evaluated. In a provocative article entitled "Stamp Collecting Versus Science: Validation as Hypothesis Testing," Landy (1986) challenged the use of the traditional three-model taxonomy of validity—especially in the light of litigation resulting from Title VII of the Civil Rights Act of 1964 (the portion of the Act that precludes employment discrimination on the basis of race, color, religion, national origin, or sex):

> Either directly or indirectly, many Title VII decisions are influenced by a judge's decision with respect to whether the correct model has been chosen. The jeopardy inherent in this labeling process is eloquently expressed in *Guardians Association v. Civil Service Commission of the City of New York* (1980). One aspect of the litigation involved the plaintiffs' assertion that a particular test measured "constructs" and, as a result, the only appropriate validation strategy would be a construct-validation approach. The validity strategy chosen by the defendants was a content-oriented approach. In writing the decision for the Second Circuit Court of Appeals, Judge Newman clearly identified the pivotal issue: "This content-construct distinction has a significance beyond just selecting the proper technique for validating the exam; it frequently determines who wins the lawsuit" (p. 92).
>
> As a result of this tendency to label validity approaches as correct or incorrect in a given situation, Title VII cases often take on the appearance of a primitive form of stamp collecting. There are only three spaces to be filled—the content space, the construct space, and the criterion-related space. The test in question is the metaphorical stamp. If it is a test of constructs, then it is pasted in the construct space, and the litigants set out to determine if all of the requirements for construct validation efforts have been met. If it is a test of knowledges, then either the content or criterion-related space is filled and the litigants consider a different checklist of requirements. These list checkers take on the appearance of the modern-day equivalent of the biblical Pharisees, checking scripture to determine if law or tradition has been violated. (p. 1184)

Landy argued that the traditional three-category taxonomy of validity may have outlived its usefulness and that the process of validating a test should be considered as "nothing more and nothing less than traditional hypothesis testing" (p. 1183). In partial support of this view is the thinking of Lawshe (1985) who had previously argued that "kinds of validity" really do not exist but that "kinds of validity analysis strategies" do exist. A corollary to this view is that it is inappropriate to refer to the validity of a test; instead one would refer to the validity of inferences from test scores. We noted that the position expressed by Lawshe (1985) could only be deemed to be partially supportive of Landy (1986). This is so because Lawshe suggested that the different kinds of analyses would yield three types of evidence: content-related, criterion-related, and construct-related evidence.

Whether the traditional "trinitarian" (Guion, 1980) view of validity will ultimately prevail over what has been referred to as the unitarian view (Landy, 1986) remains to be seen. Interestingly, some support for both positions can be found in the *Standards* (1985). On the first page of Chapter 1 (Validity), we find the following:

Traditionally, the various means of accumulating validity evidence have been grouped into categories called *content-related, criterion-related,* and *construct-related evidence of validity.* These categories are convenient, as are other more refined categorizations (e.g., the division of the criterion-related category into predictive and concurrent evidence of validity), but the use of the category labels does not imply that there are distinct types of validity or that a specific validation strategy is best for each specific inference or test use. Rigorous distinctions between the categories are not possible. (*Standards,* 1985, p. 9)

However, the notion that the three categories are simply convenient labels does not come through elsewhere in the *Standards.* As Landy (1986) points out, "Standards 1.6, 1.10, 1.11, 1.16, 1.19, and 1.20 clearly invoke the traditional models, and the 'convenient label' concept is not substantially advanced by these references. In a later section on employment testing (pp. 59–62), the extent of the recidivism is apparent. Standards 10.1, 10.4, 10.5, 10.6, 10.7, and 10.8 clearly rest on the content-criterion-construct distinction. The addition of the suffix *related* to each of these concepts does not address the problem. This suffix is intended to emphasize the fact that tests do not 'possess' validity. It does nothing to dispel the notion of three "acceptable models of validation." (p. 1184)

Ethical considerations   Decisions such as hiring one person over another, promoting one person over another, firing one person instead of another, and so forth, are typically (we hope) made on the basis of more considerations than an individual's score on a test. Other criteria that may be entered into personnel decision equations include the gender, race, and national origin of the applicant, as well as the applicant's physical condition. As a means of compensating for prior inequities, some companies have developed strong affirmative action programs designed to attract members of minority populations who may have been rejected for employment or discriminated against in the past. Companies with such commitments to affirmative action may give disproportionate weight to gender, race, or national origin in their hiring formulas.

Legal considerations   Employment practices are also affected by—indeed to a large extent regulated by—law. For example, the Americans with Disabilities Act of 1990 (PL 101-336) prohibits an employer from refusing to hire or promote someone on the basis of disability if the individual is qualified to perform the job. In effect as of July 26, 1992, for employers with 25 or more employees, and July 26, 1994, for employers with 15 to 24 employees, PL 101-336 covers most individuals with mental disabilities and all individuals with physical disabilities, including those in treatment for drug and alcohol abuse and those with AIDS or H.I.V. infection. Employers will be prohibited from asking a prospective employee whether he or she has been treated for mental health problems. The skills measured by any preemployment tests must be directly related to the skills necessary for successful performance of the job. Individuals who do not possess fine motor coordination skills sufficient enough to take a paper-and-pencil test might not be required to take such a test if the job does not require such skills. Visually impaired or blind individuals will be provided with a recorded version of job applications. The hearing-impaired and the deaf will have to be interviewed in such a way that they are not penalized for their disability. The law further requires employers to make reasonable accommodation for individuals with a disability if such accommodation will enable the individual to perform the job.

Productivity, Motivation, and Job Satisfaction

Up to this point, our overview of personnel psychology has focused on testing and assessment considerations with respect to preemployment counseling and personnel selection. Next, we focus on other concerns of employers and personnel psychologists: productivity, motivation, and job satisfaction.

Productivity "Productivity" is used here in the broadest sense to be meaningful with reference to workers in all occupations, including those who do not necessarily "produce" (such as service workers). If a business endeavor is to succeed, monitoring output with the ultimate goal of maximizing output is essential. Measures of productivity not only help to define where a business is, but also what it needs to do to get where it wants to be. A manufacturer of television sets, for example, might find that the people who are manufacturing the wood casing for the sets are working at optimal efficiency but that the people responsible for installing the picture tubes in the cabinets are working at one-half the expected efficiency. A productivity evaluation can help identify the factors responsible for the sagging performance of the picture tube people.

Using techniques such as supervisor ratings, interviews with employees, and the planting of undercover employees in the picture tube workshop, management might determine what—or who in particular—is responsible for the unsatisfactory performance. Perhaps the most common method of evaluating worker productivity or performance is through the use of rating and ranking procedures by superiors in the organization. One type of ranking procedure used when large numbers of employees are being assessed is called the *forced distribution technique*. This procedure involves the distribution of a predetermined number or percentage of assessees into various categories that describe performance (such as Unsatisfactory, Poor, Fair, Average, Good, Superior). Another index of on-the-job performance is number of absences within a given period. It typically reflects more poorly on an employee if he or she is absent on, say, twenty separate occasions than on twenty consecutive dates as the result of a bout with illness. The *critical incidents* technique (Flanagan & Burns, 1955) involves the recording of positive and negative employee behaviors by the supervisor. The notations are catalogued according to various categories (for example, "dependability; initiative") for ready reference when an evaluation needs to be made. There is some evidence to suggest that a "honeymoon" period of about three months or so occurs when a new worker starts a job and that supervisory ratings will be more truly reflective of the worker at the conclusion of that period (see Helmreich, Sawin, & Carsrud, 1986).

Peer ratings or evaluations made by other workers of the same level have proved to be a valuable method of identifying talent among employees. Although peers have a tendency to rate their counterparts higher than these people would be rated by superiors, the information obtained from the ratings and rankings of peers can be highly predictive of future performance. For example, one study in-

Table 18–7

Peer Ratings and Performance of Life Insurance Salespeople*

	Job tenure		Production	
	6 months	1 year	6 months	1 year
Peer rating	.18*	.29**	.29**	.30**
Age	.18*	.24**	.06	.09
Starting salary	.01	.03	.13	.26**
Final course grade	.02	.06	−.02	.02

*$p = .05$ (one-tailed test)
**$p = .01$ (one-tailed test)
Source: Mayfield (1972)

volved 117 inexperienced life insurance agents who attended a three-week training class. At the conclusion of the course, the budding insurance agents were asked to list the three best people in their class with respect to each of 12 situations. From these data, a composite score for each of the 117 agents was obtained. After one year, these peer ratings and three other variables were correlated with job tenure (number of weeks on the job) and with production (number of dollars of insurance sold). As can be seen from Table 18–7, peer ratings had the highest validity in all of the categories. By contrast, a near zero correlation was obtained between final course grade and all categories.

As we have already noted, error in ratings may result from different types of bias on the part of the raters (for example, a leniency effect or a halo effect).

Motivation Why do some people skip lunch, work overtime, and take home work nightly while others strive to do as little as possible and live a life of leisure at work? At a practical level, light may be shed on such questions using assessment instruments such as *The Study of Values* (see Chapter 15), which tap the values of the assessee. When dealing with a population of unskilled personnel, specially devised techniques may be required. Champagne (1969) responded to the challenge of knowing little about what might appeal to rural, unskilled people in attempts to attract them to work, so he devised a motivational questionnaire. As illustrated by the three items in Figure 18–5, the questionnaire used a paired comparison (forced-choice) format that required the subject to make choices relative to 12 factors used by companies to entice employment applications: fair pay, steady job, vacations and holidays with pay, job extras such as pensions and sick benefits, a fair boss, interesting work, good working conditions, chance for promotion, a job close to home, working with friends and neighbors, nice people to work with, and praise for good work. The job-seeking factor found to be most important in Champagne's sample of 349 male and female, rural unskilled subjects was "steady job." The least important factor was found to be "working with friends and neighbors." "Praise for good work" was a close runner-up for being least in importance. In interpreting the findings, Champagne cautioned that "the factors reported here relate to the job seeking behavior of the unskilled and are not measures of how to retain and motivate the unskilled once employed. . . . what

Vacations and holidays with pay . . .   OR   . . . Job extras such as pensions, sick benefits, etc.

A job close to home . . .   OR   . . . A fair boss

Working with friends and neighbors . . .   OR   . . . chance for a promotion

Figure 18–5 *Studying Values with the Unskilled.* Champagne (1969) used test items such as those pictured in a recruitment study with a rural, unskilled population.

prompts a person to accept a job is not necessarily the same as what prompts a person to retain a job or do well in it" (p. 268).

On a theoretical level, there exists an abundance of theories that seek to delineate the specific needs, attitudes, social influences, and other factors that might account for differences in motivation. For example, Vroom (1964) proposed an expectancy theory of motivation, which essentially holds that employees expend energy in ways designed to achieve the outcome they want; the greater the expectancy that an action will achieve a certain outcome, the more energy that will be expended to achieve that outcome. Maslow (1943, 1970) constructed a theoretical hierarchy of human needs (see Figure 18–6) and proposed that as one category of need is met, people move on to satisfy the next category of need. Employers who subscribe to Maslow's theory would seek to identify (1) the need "level" the job requires of the employee, and (2) the need level the prospective employee is at. Alderfer (1972) proposed an alternative need theory of motivation, one that was not hierarchical in nature. Whereas Maslow saw the satisfaction of one need leading to the satisfaction of the next need in the hierarchy, Alderfer proposed that once a need was satisfied it was possible that the organism strove to satisfy it to an even greater degree. The Alderfer theory also provides that the frustration of one need might lead to the channeling of energy into the achievement of a need at another level.

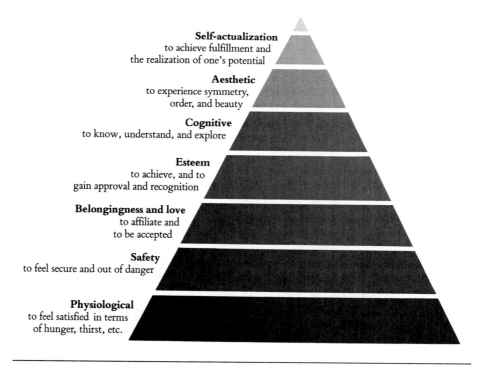

Self-actualization
to achieve fulfillment and
the realization of one's potential

Aesthetic
to experience symmetry,
order, and beauty

Cognitive
to know, understand, and explore

Esteem
to achieve, and to
gain approval and recognition

Belongingness and love
to affiliate and
to be accepted

Safety
to feel secure and out of danger

Physiological
to feel satisfied in terms
of hunger, thirst, etc.

Figure 18–6 *Maslow's Hierarchy of Needs (Adapted from Maslow, 1970).*

In a widely cited program that undertook to define the parameters of achievement motivation, McClelland (1961) used as his measure of that motivation stories written under special instructions about TAT and TAT-like pictures. McClelland described the individual with a high need for achievement as one who prefers a task that is not too simple or extremely difficult; something with moderate as opposed to extreme risks. A situation with little or no risk will not lead to feelings of accomplishment if the individual succeeds. On the other hand, an extremely high-risk situation may not lead to feelings of accomplishment because of the high probability of failure. Persons with high need for achievement enjoy taking responsibility for their actions because they desire the credit and recognition for their accomplishments. Such individuals also desire feedback concerning their performance in order to constantly improve their output. Other researchers also used TAT-like pictures and their own specially devised scoring systems to study related areas of human motivation such as the fear of failure (Birney, Burdick, & Teevan, 1969; Cohen & Teevan, 1974, 1975; Cohen & Houston, 1975; Cohen, Becker, & Teevan, 1975; Cohen & Parker, 1974) and the fear of success (Horner, 1973).

Job satisfaction   If you enjoy what you do (that is, if you derive satisfaction from your life's work), you are going to try to minimize your absences from that work and probably do a better job at it than if you do not enjoy what you do. Conversely, if you do not enjoy what you do, you may find more and more occasions to be absent from work, not care very much about the quality of work that you are doing, and so forth. Absenteeism is costly to organizations, as it may result in the underutilization of some personnel, the overloading of other personnel, and/or the generally inefficient operation of the organization. Organizations would also prefer to have their members working at optimal efficiency rather than simply going through the motions with a yawn. Researchers in this area have examined "job satisfaction" and developed various instruments to measure what are believed to be components of it. For example, the Job Discrimination Index (Smith, Kendall, & Hulin, 1969) contains five subscales labeled Work, Pay, Co-Workers, Supervision, and Promotions. Another instrument developed by Kavanaugh, MacKinney, and Wolins (1970) focuses on the dimensions of group morale versus individual satisfaction. Numerous other instruments have been published, and many researchers have developed their own questionnaires, interviews, critical incident techniques, or other techniques for assessing job satisfaction.

The effects of job satisfaction have been explored from the perspective of both the employer and the employee. Studies examining this variable from the employer's perspective might focus on its relationship to, for example, corporate earnings. Studies examining the variable of job satisfaction from the perspective of the employee might, for example, focus on the relationship between job satisfaction and the employee's health. As an example of the latter, it was reported in one study of 40 female workers in a cigar factory that the mean heart rate of satisfied workers was lower than the mean heart rate of dissatisfied workers (Khaleque, 1981). The index of job satisfaction in that study was a measure developed by Brayfield and Rothe (1951). As the literature in this area burgeons, the relationship between the various components of job satisfaction and other variables such as satisfaction with life in general, productivity, and physical and mental health will be better understood.

ENGINEERING PSYCHOLOGY

The relationship between equipment and the workers and/or consumers who use that equipment is the province of the engineering psychologist. The engineering psychologist is also concerned with the design of work and play environments that are (1) safe, and (2) maximally conducive to whatever purpose they are being used for. The tools of engineering psychologists involve specialized application of the testing and assessment methods used by their counterparts in other areas of psychology.

Also referred to as "human engineering" and as "human factors psychology," engineering psychology had its orgins at about the turn of this century. It was not, however, until the time of World War II that developments in this field accelerated faster than ever before. The war brought with it an urgent need for machinery (such as weapons) and equipment (such as aircraft cockpits) to be designed in a manner that would facilitate ready operation by military personnel. What is the best height for the placement of the altimeter on the aircraft's instrument panel? Should that gauge be to the left or the right of the pilot? These are the types of questions that engineering psychologists of the day, in collaboration with other engineers and scientists, were assigned to answer. The scope of engineering psychology has since expanded to include the design of a wide array of instrumentation and equipment in all areas of industry, the professions (medical and dental equipment), and consumer goods. Additionally, engineering psychologists have been active in the design of safe and effective work environments as well as play environments that are indeed conducive to play. Some examples follow.

Designing Instrumentation and Equipment

Do the symbols in Figure 18–7 look familiar to you? They should, for they might well be on the dashboard of your car or that of your friend's car. The pictured symbol, or pictogram, has become a popular mode of communication as international travel and commerce increase. Pictures are an international language, and if manufacturers of equipment can convey instructions, labeling of parts, and related information in pictures instead of their native tongues, they can greatly widen the potential market for their product. More importantly, since "one picture is worth a thousand words," as the saying goes, a good pictogram can be recognized with greater speed and accuracy than can words. But what constitutes a good pictogram? Research such as that conducted by Green and Pew (1978) is designed to find out. These investigators tested 50 University of Michigan students with a variety of tasks, each designed to shed light on the effectiveness of certain automotive pictograms. For example, the subjects might be asked to imagine that they were sitting in a car with the pictograms in Figure 18–7 before them. The experimenter would then say, "You have just tried to start your car, and you forgot to fasten your seat belt. The seat belt light goes on. Please point to

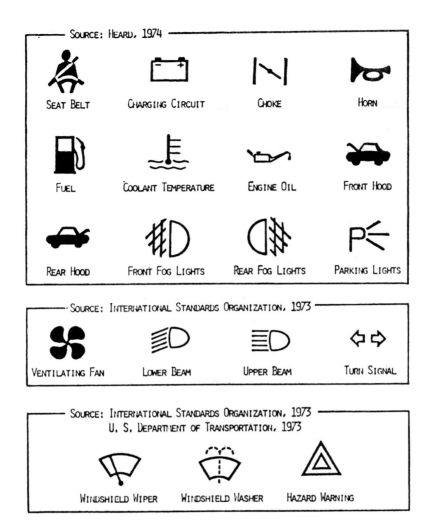

SOURCE: HEARD, 1974

SEAT BELT	CHARGING CIRCUIT	CHOKE	HORN
FUEL	COOLANT TEMPERATURE	ENGINE OIL	FRONT HOOD
REAR HOOD	FRONT FOG LIGHTS	REAR FOG LIGHTS	PARKING LIGHTS

SOURCE: INTERNATIONAL STANDARDS ORGANIZATION, 1973

VENTILATING FAN	LOWER BEAM	UPPER BEAM	TURN SIGNAL

SOURCE: INTERNATIONAL STANDARDS ORGANIZATION, 1973
U. S. DEPARTMENT OF TRANSPORTATION, 1973

WINDSHIELD WIPER	WINDSHIELD WASHER	HAZARD WARNING

Figure 18–7 *Dashboard Pictograms Used by Green & Pew (1978).*

the seat belt symbol." Another task required the students to rate how communicative each symbol was. These investigators found that only 6 of the 19 symbols
tested met their minimum criteria for recognition.

Pictograms are used not only in the manufacturing of products but also in
the design of signs. In addition to the greater speed and accuracy with which they
may be perceived, it is also true that they may be perceived from farther away
than words. Collins and Lerner (1982) undertook to assess the understandability
of 25 proposed fire-safety symbols such as those in Figure 18–8. How well
did the symbols convey the message they were intended to convey? To answer
this question, the investigators had their subjects engage in tasks like taking a
multiple-choice test on the symbols, writing their own definitions for symbols,
and drawing their own symbols to depict fire-safety referents.

Imagine for a moment that it was you who came up with the idea for a push-button phone to replace the rotary-dial phone. The next question might concern how the buttons should be arranged. Should they be arranged in circular fashion? A triangular pattern? You can be sure that the engineering psychologists working for Bell Laboratories did extensive experimentation to determine the most efficient arrangement of the buttons on a pushbutton phone before that phone was introduced. Engineering psychologists have applied their skills to a wide variety of other kinds of design questions, including some with respect to household items, surgical instruments, spacecraft—and beyond.

Designing Environments

Have you given much thought to the suitability of the environment in which you do *your* work? Is the space where you do your studying quiet and properly lit? Are the chairs and tables you use the proper height? Work-related environments as varied as tractor seats, subway cars, and deep-sea diving bells may be the work sites studied by industrial/organizational psychologists. In one study that focused on the design of school furniture, Mandal (1982) observed that as the average height of children is increasing, the average height of school furniture has been decreasing. According to this investigator, furniture that is too low imposes tension on the muscles and tendons of the back and could, especially in taller pupils,

Fire Exit (black on white, red flame)

Emergency Exit

Not an Exit

Do Not Use Water To Extinguish (black on white, red circle & slash)

Do Not Lock (black on white, red circle & slash)

No Smoking (black on white, red circle & slash)

No Open Flame (black on white, red circle & slash)

Figure 18–8 *Samples of the Fire-Safety Alerting Symbols Used by Collins and Lerner (1982).*

result in a back deformity. School authorities show an unfortunate tendency to set their priorities on furniture that is easily stored and stacked. Manufacturers of furniture have not paid enough attention to the anatomy of the seated person. According to Mandal, the optimal height of a table or desk is at least one-half the person's height, and the chair must be at least one-third the person's height. As illustrated in Figure 18–9, furniture that is not high enough can promote poor posture (and attendant health problems such as backaches). Where the furniture is the proper height, the model's back is relatively straight (the way it should be) even though she or he is in a backless chair.

An area that has been receiving increasing attention in the design of environments is the use of color. Because evidence indicates that bubblegum pink tends to have a calming effect, the walls in some rooms of institutions as diverse as penal institutions and locker rooms (for the visiting team) have been painted this hue (Gruson, 1982). Wohlfarth (1984) reported that a change in one schoolroom's color scheme produced concomitant changes in blood pressure and behavior. The walls of the room were changed from orange and white to royal and light blue. An orange rug was replaced by a gray carpet, and the fluorescent lighting was replaced with full-spectrum lighting. The result was a mean systolic blood pressure drop of 17%, less fidgeting in seats, less aggressive behavior, and more attentive behavior. Returning the room to its previous state restored rowdy behavior. Exactly why the change in color scheme worked as it did is unknown,

Figure 18–9 *Assessing Environments: Furniture.* Low furniture evokes a maximum flexion of the back (as in **A,** where the seat and table are respectively only 18 inches and 28 inches off the ground), whereas high furniture is more comfortable and produces a straight back (as in **B,** where the seat and table are respectively 25 inches and 36 inches off the ground).

although Wohlfarth postulated that the minute amounts of electromagnetic energy that light is made up of may affect one or more of the brain's neurotransmitters in some as yet undefined way.

We now turn from discussion of the use of psychological testing and assessment in the workplace to a look at the use of such tools in the marketplace; how psychological tests and assessment procedures are used in the creation, design, and promotion of consumer products.

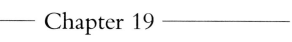

Chapter 19

Consumer Assessment*

CONSUMER PSYCHOLOGY IS that branch of social and industrial/organizational (I/O) psychology that deals primarily with the development, advertising, and marketing of products and services. Working closely with professionals in fields such as marketing and advertising, consumer psychologists bring behavioral research methods to bear on questions such as the following:

- Does a market exist for this new product?
- Does a market exist for this new use of an existing product?
- Exactly who, in terms of age, sex, race, social class, and other demographic variables, constitutes the market for this product?
- How can the targeted consumer population cost-effectively be made aware of this product?
- How can the targeted consumer population most cost-effectively be persuaded to purchase this product?
- What is the best way to package this product?[1]

---

* This chapter was written by Ronald Jay Cohen and David W. Stewart.
1. Questions concerning packaging and how to make a product stand out on the shelf have been referred to as questions of "shelf-esteem" by consumer psychologists with a sense of humor.

AN OVERVIEW

One area of interest shared by the consumer psychologist and psychologists in other specialty areas is the measurement of attitudes; for the consumer psychologist, however, the attitude of interest might be one toward a particular product or concept. We begin our survey of tests and measurement in consumer psychology with a brief look at the process of measuring attitudes.

The Measurement of Attitudes

An *attitude* may be defined as a presumably learned predisposition to react in some characteristic manner with respect to a particular stimulus. The stimulus might be virtually anything, though we most typically think of it as an object, a group, or an institution. The "characteristic manner" of reaction might run the gamut from love to hate to fear to anger. Attitudes can semantically be distinguished from beliefs or opinions. In contrast to attitudes, beliefs and opinions tend to be more specific, less "ingrained," and more subject to change as a result of factual input than are attitudes. Although it is commonly presumed that attitudes—as gauged by tests, questionnaires, and the like—are predictive of behavior, this is not necessarily the case (Tittle & Hill, 1967; Wicker, 1969). People differ not only in their ability to introspect but also in the extent to which they allow themselves to be totally honest. Further, people differ in terms of level of self-awareness; many people are genuinely unable to accurately predict how they would act or even feel in a given situation. Most psychologists infer the existence of specific attitudes on the basis of tests that rely heavily on the assessee's self-report—and the limitations of such an approach are kept firmly in mind when the data are interpreted. Further, there is evidence that under limited-time and low-involvement conditions, attitude formation may occur only reactively in response to the measure of attitude used (see Sandelands & Larson, 1985).

A classic treatment of the assessment of attitude can be found in *The Measurement of Attitude* (Thurstone & Chave, 1929), wherein the authors described how they employed the scientific method in their construction of a test to measure attitudes toward the church (as well as other things). The first step involved getting "several groups of people and many individuals" (p. 22) to write out statements concerning their opinons about the church. The authors conducted a search of the literature for material that could be made into statements with which examinees could agree or disagree. In general, brief statements were preferred and "double-barreled" statements (that is, statements representing more than one thought or idea) were avoided. A total of 130 statements were selected that were considered to express relatively favorable, unfavorable, or neutral attitudes toward the church.

Thurstone and Chave's next step in constructing the attitude scale was to present these statements to a sample of 300 judges (no description of who the judges were or how they were selected is presented), who were asked to provide an indication of where on the favorable to neutral to unfavorable part of the continuum each of the statements fell. The judges were instructed to arrange the statements into eleven piles designated as piles "A" through "K" with "A" being composed of statements most favorable toward the church, "F" being neutral, and "K" being composed of statements that were strongly negative.

The responses of the judges to the different statements were investigated by the construction of graphs, and the percentages of the judges who placed the statements in the different categories (piles) were determined. Numerical designations replaced the alphabetical designations of the piles with "A" being equivalent to "1" and "K" being equivalent to "11." By reviewing the graph, the authors determined the 50th percentile or median position assigned to the statement by the judges. This value, representing the median of the judgments, was referred to as the *scale value* of the statement. Figure 19–1 is the graphic representation of the judges' responses to the item: "I believe the church is absolutely needed to overcome the tendency to individualism and selfishness. It practices the golden rule fairly well" (Thurstone & Chave, 1929, p. 25). As you can see from the graph, the scale value for this statement was 1.8, indicating that 50% of the judges viewed this statement as representing a rather positive attitude toward the church. The graph also enabled determination of the ambiguity of the statement by indicating how variable the judges were in their placement of statements into different categories. Statistically, ambiguity was computed by determining the distance between the 25th and 75th percentiles. The ambiguity value (or Q-value) for this statement above was low (1.3), indicating that the statement was not ambiguous and generally conveyed a similar meaning to the judges. Each item for the final version of the scale was selected primarily on the basis of (1) low ambiguity, and (2) how appropriately the item represented one component of the possible range of attitudes.

A final list of 45 statements reflecting a wide range of possible attitudes toward the church was compiled. Subjects were instructed to check each statement

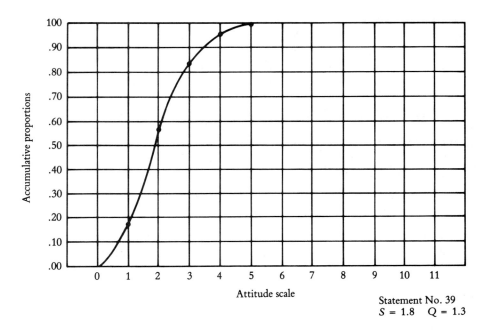

Statement No. 39
$S = 1.8$ $Q = 1.3$

Figure 19–1 *A Graphic Representation of Judges' Ratings.* Illustrated is a graphic representation of judges' responses to Statement 39 in Thurstone & Chave (1929): "I believe the church is absolutely needed to overcome the tendency to individualism and selfishness. It practices the golden rule fairly well."

that expressed their own sentiments. The subject's score on the scale was the mean of the scale values obtained from all the items checked. Scores on the test were deemed to be neither "good" nor "bad," but merely descriptive of the attitudes expressed. Thurstone and Chave administered their scale to samples of students in different years of study at the University of Chicago and to divinity students. No distinct trend in attitude toward the church was found to be related to year of study in college. However, as might be expected, divinity students expressed more favorable attitudes toward the church than did other groups.

The construction of a measure of attitude need not necessarily entail the rather elaborate methodology used by Thurstone and his colleagues. A monograph entitled "A Technique for the Measurement of Attitudes" (Likert, 1932) provided researchers in this area with a much simpler procedure for constructing an instrument for measuring attitudes. Essentially, this procedure consists of listing statements (either favorable or unfavorable) that are reflective of a particular attitude. These statements are then administered to a group of respondents whose responses are analyzed in order to identify the most discriminating statements— items that best discriminate people at different points on the hypothetical continuum—which are then included in the final scale. Each statement included in the final scale is accompanied by a five-point continuum of alternative responses that may range, for example, from "Strongly Agree" to "Strongly Disagree." Scoring is accomplished by assigning numerical weights of 1 through 5 to each category such that "5" represents the strongest favorable response and "1" reflects the least favorable response.

Measures of attitude found in the psychological literature run the gamut from instruments devised solely for research and testing of academic, theoretical formulations, to scales with wide-ranging, "real world" applications. In the latter context, we might find sophisticated industrial/organizational measures designed to gauge workers' attitudes toward their work, or scales designed to measure the general public's attitudes toward some politician or issue. Attitude scales with applied utility may also be found in the educational psychology literature—consider, for example, measures such as the Study Attitudes and Methods Survey (a scale designed to assess study habits), and the Minnesota Teacher Attitude Survey (a scale designed to assess student-teacher relations). And given the title of this chapter, you may have already correctly assumed that attitude measurement is very much a part of consumer psychology.

The Tools of the Consumer Psychologist

To answer questions such as those posed at the beginning of this chapter (as well as others such as those concerned with the *positioning* of products—see Figure 19–2), consumer psychologists rely on a variety of methods, used individually or

---

Figure 19–2 *Positioning a Product.* Positioning of a product in the marketplace generally refers to highlighting a particular benefit of a product. Thus, for example, one dishwashing detergent might be positioned as the "best cleaning," another as "gentlest to your hands," and another as "most economical." Sometimes products undergo radical changes in their positioning. For example, although Listerine is currently positioned in the marketplace as a plaque-killer and conqueror of gingivitis, it was at one time positioned not as a mouthwash, but as a scalp rinse.

Scalp troubles?
Loose DANDRUFF?

Read letters below—

they tell much better than we could
the amazing results accomplished by
Listerine in treating scalp disorders.

MEN and women are constantly writing us of the beneficial effects of using full strength Listerine on the scalp and hair, either as a part of the usual shampoo or independent of it. In many cases they report that Listerine brought relief from scalp troubles after other methods of treatment had failed.

The letters below, selected from many hundreds, show a number of uses to which Listerine has successfully been put. The value of this safe antiseptic lies primarily in its ability to destroy germs almost instantly, and therefore combat infection. At the same time it is soothing and healing to tissue. Lambert Pharmacal Co., St. Louis, Mo.

Relieved Itching Scalp

My husband and I can't find praise enough for Listerine. It sure is wonderful. For months he was troubled with dandruff and his scalp itched him terribly. He'd come home from work so grouchy, that you could hardly speak to him and he'd always say "How can I help it? My scalp itches so badly, that it nearly drives me crazy, and I have so much dandruff that I'm ashamed to be seen anywhere."

One of our friends advised him to try Listerine. At first he laughed, but I finally persuaded him to try it. He did and with such wonderful results the first time that he went right to the druggist's and purchased a large bottle. He has been using it regularly once a week and I can truthfully say that he hasn't a bit of dandruff, or noticed any itching of the scalp since he's been using it.

Yours truly,
MRS. VIRGIL HELBIG
Newport, Kentucky

Ended Baby's "Milk Crust"

When my infant daughter reached the age of four months, a fine film of "milk crust" commonly known as "cradle cap" formed on her scalp. I attempted to soften this film with olive oil, hoping thereby, to release it from the scalp but soon discovered that this treatment was ineffective as the "cap" had thoroughly imbedded itself in the scalp. Combing with a fine tooth comb helped somewhat but was not recommended as it tended to irritate the sensitive scalp and one had to be extremely careful of the soft opening at the top of the head. The scalp not only was unsightly but refused to respond to treatment.

Finally my husband suggested Listerine, two parts of Listerine to one part of warm water, and rinsing the baby's head with this solution.

Skeptical, I gave it a trial for a week, soaking baby's head thoroughly once daily with the diluted Listerine. At the end of the week I noticed that the "crust" had almost disappeared and that the remaining flakes were quite loose and could be combed out with gentle movements. I continued using the diluted Listerine for the two successive weeks and at the end of that time baby's scalp was clean. I noticed no irritation or discomfiture on her part, therefore was certain that Listerine was as harmless to infants' sensitive scalps as to adults' more hardened ones.

Sincerely yours,
MRS. MILDRED S. MACLEOD
Jamaica, L. I., N. Y.

Relieves Itching of Diabetic Patient

Early in our education as student nurses we are taught, among other important duties, the Nurse should not prescribe, and also, she should be seen and not heard.

But, as regards Listerine, and its valuable properties, I feel it is necessary that I be heard. If I may so express myself, I find Listerine to be the last word in securing a cooling, refreshing and permanent relief or cure from the annoyance of, not alone dandruff, but skin conditions, especially those of the scalp so often prevalent in diabetes.

A small piece of cotton dipped in Listerine and applied to the scalp, after parting the hair, not only relieves the itching, but refreshes the patient confined to bed (which automatically reacts on the general physical health and soothes them to sleep many times) and it entirely removes the large itching spots that occur on the scalp in the diabetic patient.

These spots often appear on the forehead, on the sides of the face and around back of the neck, bordering the hair and are visible, about the size of a quarter. They not only itch but are embarrassing; as skin desquamates and falls on the eyebrows finally rests on the chest and shoulders. These irritated spots, thanks to Listerine which I always apply to the infected area, are controlled, at the same time soothed, and ultimately obliterated.

Cordially yours,
MARY WILSON PATTON, R. N.
San Antonio, Texas

Got Rid of Dandruff

I would like to state just two of my reasons for recommending Listerine to our patients who have scalp diseases or irritations. One is that it is a permanent remover, and the other is that it is so pleasant to use, as it does not leave that unpleasant odor as do so many of the others, but leaves the hair with a soft, luxurious texture, and with a sweet fragrance. And as the scalp is, in most cases, very sensitive, we must use something that not only removes the dandruff, but that will also cool and soothe the irritations. After recommending Listerine, I find that innumerable people return to thank me for my suggestion. Personally I believe that Listerine is the only treatment for dandruff.

Sincerely yours,
ETHELWYNE D. AKER
Registered Certified Nurse
San Diego, California

Too Much Oil in Hair

I use Listerine exclusively to correct oily and dull hair. My method is simple. Every morning I set a water-wave in my hair with a mixture of Listerine and water, using a quarter cupful of each. I dip a small, clean hairbrush in this solution, and brush the hair with it until thoroughly wet. Then I set the wave and let it dry.

By washing the brush in soapy water after using, this process serves to clean the hair and remove the oil; thus doing away with the necessity of frequent shampoos, which only aggravate the oily condition.

As the hair comes back into condition, clear water may be substituted for the Listerine solution on alternate days, or oftener.

The improvement in my hair is remarkable; it is now soft, fluffy and a bright brown, with those much-desired "highlights"; instead of the forlorn, hair-colored mass of an earlier time. And I am always free of scalp troubles and dandruff.

Cordially,
MRS. CLAIRE B. BURCHETT
Derby, Colorado

LISTERINE *cleans, cools, soothes the scalp*

KILLS 200,000,000 GERMS IN 15 SECONDS

in combination with each other. Included here are surveys and polls, motivation research, behavioral observation, as well as a variety of other methods.

Surveys and polls   When the attitudes, opinions, or beliefs of large numbers of people need to be known, the measurement method of choice is a survey or a poll. Politicians frequently engage pollsters to obtain a sense of how their constituency is feeling with respect to controversial issues (such as abortion, gun control, and surrogate motherhood). The consumer psychologist might use this tool to gauge the receptivity of consumers to a new product or a new use for an existing product. As we will see, survey or poll questions may be put to the consumer in a face-to-face interview, over the phone, through the mail, or, at least hypothetically, through other means as well (for example, through a computer terminal).

Occasions arise when research questions cannot be answered through a survey or a poll; consumers may be unable or unwilling to cooperate. As an example of an inability to cooperate, consider the hypothetical case of "Ralph," who smokes a hypothetical brand of cigarettes we will call "Cowboy." When asked why he chooses to smoke "Cowboy" brand cigarettes, Ralph might reply "taste." It may in fact be the case, however, that Ralph began smoking "Cowboy" because the advertising for this brand appealed to Ralph's image of himself as an independent, macho type—this despite the fact that Ralph is employed as a clerk for a dry cleaner. Consumers may also be unwilling or reluctant to respond to some survey or poll questions. Suppose, for example, that the manufacturers of Cowboy cigarettes wished to know where on the product's packaging the Surgeon General's warning could be placed so that it would be least likely to be read. How many consumers would be willing to entertain such a question? Indeed, what would even posing such a question do for the public image of the product? It can be seen that if this hypothetical company was interested in obtaining an answer to such a question, it would have to do so through means other than a survey or a poll.

Motivation research methods   Motivation research is so named because it typically involves the analysis of motives with respect to consumer behavior and attitudes. Motivation research methods include individual interviews and focus groups, and these methods are used to examine in depth a representative group of consumers' reactions to whatever the focus of the study is—be it a concept for a new product, the packaging of a new product, a particular television or radio commercial, or an entire advertising campaign. Such research may be useful in determining what is appealing about a product that is in wide use and what is unappealing about a product that the public has rejected. For example, in the late 1940s it became evident that instant coffee, a revolutionary convenience item at that time, did not enjoy wide acceptance by the public. Polling indicated that people didn't buy instant coffee because they didn't like the flavor. However, innovative, in-depth market research suggested that the real reason people weren't buying it was that they might be perceived, either by themselves or others, as lazy, extravagant, and shirking their household duties (Haire, 1950).

One variety of motivation research involves a technique called a *focus group,* so named because it involves a group of people whose members, with the aid of a group moderator, focus on some issues presented in the group. Another technique used in motivation research is the in-depth interview. Each of these techniques is discussed in greater detail later in this chapter.

Behavioral observation   In October 1982, the sales of pain relievers such as aspirin, Bufferin, Anacin, and Excedrin rose sharply. Was this rise in sales due to the effectiveness of the advertising campaigns for these products? No. The sales rose sharply in 1982 when it was learned that seven people had died from Tylenol capsules that had been laced with cyanide. As Tylenol, the pain reliever with the largest share of the market, was withdrawn from the shelves of stores nationwide, there was a corresponding rise in the sale of alternative preparations. A similar phenomenon occurred in 1986. The point here is that if market researchers were to base their judgments concerning the effectiveness of an ad campaign on sales figures alone, the interpretation of the data would, no doubt, be spurious. Thus, it is not unusual for market researchers to sometimes station behavioral observers in stores as a technique for monitoring what really prompts a consumer to buy this or that product at the point of choice. Such an observer at a store selling pain relievers in October of 1982 might have observed, for example, a conversation with the clerk concerning what the best alternative for Tylenol would be. Behavioral observers in a supermarket who studied the purchasing habits of people buying breakfast cereal concluded that children accompanying the purchaser requested or demanded a specific brand of cereal (Atkin, 1978). Hence, it would be wise for breakfast cereal manufacturers to gear their advertising to children and not the adult consumer.

Other methods   A number of other methods and tools may be brought to bear on marketing and advertising questions. Consumer psychologists at times have occasion to employ projective tests—existing as well as custom-designed—as an aid in answering the questions raised by their clients. As we will see, special instrumentation ranging from tachistoscopes to electroencephalographs have also been used in efforts to uncover consumer motivation. Consumer input through interviews and focus groups combined with special computer programs—as well as some creativity—may be used to derive brand names for new products. Thus, for example, when Honda wished to position a new line of its cars as "advanced precision automobiles," a company specializing in the naming of new products conducted a computer search of over 6,900 English language morphemes to locate word roots that mean or imply "advanced precision." The applicable morphemes were then computer-combined in ways the phonetic rules of English would allow. From the resulting list the best word (that is, one that has visibility among other printed words, one that will be recognizable as a brand name, and so forth) was then selected; in this case that word was *Acura* (Brewer, 1987).

Finally, literature reviews represent another method available to consumer psychologists in their armamentarium of tools that can be brought to bear on clients' questions. A literature review might suggest, for example, that certain sounds or imagery in a particular brand tend to be more popular with consumers than other sounds or imagery (see Figure 19–3). Schloss (1981) observed that the sound of the letter *K* was represented better than six times more than would be expected by chance in the initial letters of 200 top brand name products (such as

REACHES ALL
—Cleans All

PRO-PHY-LAC-TIC protects
every tooth in
your mouth

When you have found a tooth brush that reaches *all* your teeth, you have taken the most important step in keeping your teeth permanently sound and beautiful.

Study the picture of the Pro-phy-lac-tic Tooth Brush, shown here. Notice how the bristles are arranged. See how they form a curve ending in a large pyramidal tuft. You can see that this curve is sensibly shaped to fit snugly against the outside and inside profiles of *all* your teeth. The molars in the rear, so hard to get at with an ordinary tooth brush, are easily reached by this convenient end tuft.

The bent handle is the third feature which makes it easy to reach *all* thirty-two of your teeth. Nature aligned most of your teeth on a curve. It naturally follows that a curved handle accommodates itself to this formation more easily and more comfortably than a handle that is straight.

Sold in three sizes by all dealers in the United States, Canada, and all over the world. Prices in the United States and Canada are: Pro-phy-lac-tic Adult, 50c; Pro-phy-lac-tic Small, 40c; Pro-phy-lac-tic Baby, 25c. Made in three different bristle textures—hard, medium, and soft—and with white handles or colored transparent handles—red, green, or orange. *Always sold in the yellow box.* (A larger Pro-phy-lac-tic with four rows of bristles is priced 60 cents.) Pro-phy-lac-tic Brush Company, Florence, Massachusetts.

© 1927, P. B. Co.

Are you sure you don't need a new tooth brush?

A Pro-phy-lac-tic Tooth Brush is made so well that it doesn't look worn out even when it should be replaced with a new one. The handle and even the bristles appear as good as ever. But the best bristle will after continued use lose its springiness and elasticity. Pro-phy-lac-tic bristles are the best that Nature provides, but three or four months of steady twice-daily use will take away their liveliness.

Don't try to wear out your Pro-phy-lac-tic Tooth Brush. Get a new one every three months. Keep several on hand. To present a Pro-phy-lac-tic in a yellow box to an overnight guest is a thoughtful courtesy.

FREE . . . an interesting booklet containing valuable information on the care of the teeth.

Pro-phy-lac-tic Brush Company,
Dept. 210, Florence, Mass.

Please send me your instructive booklet on the care and preservation of the teeth.

Name ....

Address ....

City .... State ....

684

Sanka, Quaker, Nabisco—and, we might also add, Acura). Schloss went on to speculate about the ability of this as well as other sounds of words to elicit emotional as opposed to rational reactions.

MEASUREMENT WITH SURVEYS AND POLLS

Survey Techniques

Survey research attempts to obtain answers to relatively structured questions from a reasonably representative set of individuals. Most often the sample is large (several hundred at a minimum) so that statistical inferences may be drawn about the larger population that the survey respondents represent. Because survey research seeks to reach relatively large numbers of people, it is not possible to obtain the depth and richness of information from any one individual that would be possible with individual interviews or focus groups. This loss of information is compensated for by the types of analyses and inferences that may be made from survey data. Survey research may be carried out by face-to-face personal interviews, telephone interviews, mail questionnaires, or some combination of these methods.

Face-to-face survey research   Personal interviews involve a face-to-face encounter with the respondent. The interviewer asks questions and records responses as they are given. This personal interaction helps assure that questions are clearly understood and can provide such clarifications as the parties desire. This face-to-face encounter may, however, introduce some bias into the responses of individuals. Respondents may seek to give answers they think the interviewer wants or they may be reluctant to provide information on sensitive or potentially embarrassing topics.

Personal interviewing is a very common method of survey research and it can be conducted almost anywhere—on a commuter bus or ferry, at a ball game, or in the vicinity of an election polling station. A common site for face-to-face survey research on consumer products is a shopping mall; "mall intercept studies" (as they are called) can be conducted by interviewers with clipboards who ap-

---

Figure 19–3 *What's in a Name?* "What's in a name? A rose by any other name would smell as sweet." Sentiments such as this may be touching to read and beautiful to behold when spoken by talented actors on Broadway. However, they wouldn't have taken William Shakespeare very far on Madison Avenue. The name given to a product is an important part of what is referred to as the "marketing mix": the way a product is positioned, marketed, and promoted in the marketplace. In the ad shown, reproduced from a 1927 magazine, the benefits of a toothbrush with the brand name Pro-phy-lac-tic are touted. The creator of this brand name no doubt wished to position this toothbrush as being particularly useful in preventing disease. However, the word *prophylactic* (defined as "protective") became more identified in the public's mind with condoms, a fact that could not have helped the longevity of this brand of toothbrush in the marketplace. Today, researchers use a variety of methods, including word association, to create brand names.

proach shoppers. The shopper may be asked to participate in a survey by answering some questions right then and there or may be led to a booth or room where a more extended interview takes place. Another face-to-face survey method, this one more popular with political pollsters, is the door-to-door approach; here an entire neighborhood may be polled by knocking on the door at individual households and soliciting responses to the questionnaire.

A unique advantage in face-to-face survey research is the ability to present respondents with stimuli (such as a product or a list of items from which to select) to which they may be asked to respond. The advantage of having an interviewer who can interact with the respondent creates a need for careful selection and training of the interviewer. Thus, since personal interviewing is labor-intensive, it is the most expensive and time-consuming method of survey research. The least expensive method of survey research, and the fastest method for obtaining information, is the telephone survey.

Telephone surveys   Perhaps the most widely used form of survey research is the telephone survey. Since telephone interviews require less social interaction between the interviewer and respondent, the biases inherent in such interaction and the intensive training required for personal interviewing are reduced. In addition, it is easy to coordinate and monitor the performance of telephone interviewers since telephoning can take place in a centralized location. And with new technology currently available to telephone survey researchers, subjects are called by a computer, called back if the subject isn't home, and interviewed by a pretaped voice—all without the necessity of a human interviewer.

One type of telephone poll in common use in consumer research is designed to obtain a measure of the memorability of advertising, most typically, a television commercial. Thus, for example, the day after the airing of the Academy Awards on television, randomly selected households in selected communities might be telephoned and the interviewer might ask questions such as, "Did you watch the Academy Awards last evening? . . . What commercials do you recall seeing on that show? . . . Do you recall seeing a commercial for Mermaid Brand Sardines?"

While the telephone survey offers a number of advantages, it does, however, suffer from some limitations. Generally, the amount of information that can be obtained by telephone is less than that which can be obtained by personal interview or mail. It is not possible to show respondents visual stimuli via telephone. Also, bias may be introduced if telephone directories are used for identifying respondents. As many as 40 percent of all telephones in some cities are not listed. A partial solution to this latter problem is random-digit dialing (see Glaser & Metzger, 1972), a procedure that randomly changes the last one or two digits of a telephone number taken from a directory. Use of this process generally yields contacts with households that have unlisted telephone numbers, as well as those with listed numbers. However, even with this procedure, it is necessary to exercise caution by calling at different times of the day and on different days of the week. Otherwise, households that have no one home at particular times will be missed (Bureau of the Census, 1973). One study indicated, for example, that the greater the number of attempts to reach a household, the greater the likelihood that the household reached would be in the higher income brackets (Lansing & Morgan, 1971).

Lest we stray too far from the subject of psychology in measurement, let us hasten to point out that although telephone surveys may be viewed with favor on the part of members of the marketing community, they may be viewed in less glowing terms by interviewees; they may be viewed at best as an unwelcome annoyance and at worst as an unwarranted invasion of privacy.

Mail surveys   A mail survey may be the most appropriate survey method when the survey questionnaire is particularly long and will require some time to complete. In general, mail surveys tend to be relatively low in cost, as they do not require the services of a trained interviewer and can provide large amounts of information. They are also well suited for obtaining information about which respondents may be sensitive or shy in a face-to-face or even a telephone situation. They are also well suited to posing questions that require the use of records or consultation with others (such as family members) for an answer. Note also that much of what we say about mail surveys also applies to "electronic mail surveys" or surveys conducted via fax machines.

The major disadvantages of mail questionnaires are (1) the possibility of no response at all from the intended recipient of the survey (for whatever reason ranging from a situation in which it was never delivered to one in which it was thrown out as "junk mail" as soon as it arrived), (2) the possibility of response from someone (perhaps a family member) who was not the intended recipient of the survey, and (3) the possibility of a late—and hence useless for tabulation purposes—response. If, for whatever reason, large numbers of people fail to respond to a mail questionnaire, it is impossible to determine whether those individuals who did respond are representative of those who did not. People may not respond to a mail questionnaire for many different reasons; and various techinques, ranging from incentives to follow-up mailings, have been suggested for dealing with various types of nonresponse (Furse & Stewart, 1984).

It is possible to combine the various survey methods to obtain the advantages of each. For example, the survey researcher might mail a lengthy questionnaire to potential respondents, then obtain responses by telephone. Alternatively, those individuals not returning their responses by mail might be contacted by telephone or in person.

A number of commercial research firms maintain a list of a large number of people or families who have agreed to respond to questionnaires that are sent to them; the people who make up this list are referred to as a *consumer panel*. In return for their participation, panel members may receive incentives ranging from cash to free samples of all of the products about which they are asked to respond in surveys. One special type of panel is called a *diary panel,* and here the respondents must keep detailed records of their behavior (for example, keeping a record of products they purchased, use of coupons, radio stations they listened to while driving to and from work, or what newspapers and magazines were read). Specialized panels exist that monitor general product or advertising awareness, attitudes, and opinions regarding social issues as well as a variety of other variables.

As with any research, care must be exercised when interpreting the results of a survey. Both the quantity and quality of the data may vary from survey to survey. Response rates may differ, questions may be asked in different forms, and data collection procedures may vary from one survey to another. Ultimately, the utility of any conclusions rests on the integrity of the data on which the conclusions are based.[2] More guidelines may be needed in survey research because of the differences that exist in the methodologies of various polling firms (Henry, 1984).

Designing Survey Research Questionnaires

Whether the survey will be conducted face-to-face or over the telephone, the questionnaire must be designed so that it will not take a substantial amount of a respondent's time. With a mail survey, the length of the questionnaire may be longer; respondents can complete the questionnaire at their convenience and can pace themselves in completing it. However, because the mail survey will be completed at home without the presence of an interviewer to clarify questions, the mail survey must be written very clearly lest the frustration of not understanding the intention of an item prompt the respondent to "forget the whole thing."

Some of the standard items on a survey (such as demographic information) will not require very much talent in preparing while it may require considerable effort to word other questions to best reflect the objective of the question. Two broad approaches to the assessment of attitudes in surveys are referred to as *aggregate scaling* and *multidimensional scaling*. We review these approaches in the pages to follow. In addition, we look at the application of the semantic differential technique—discussed earlier in Part 4—in the field of consumer psychology.

Aggregate scaling methods   Aggregate methods represent the average of some group of people on some measure. The measure may range from an opinion item (such as "Should the death penalty be abolished?") to a self-report of behavior (such as "How often do you eat in a fast food restaurant each month?"). The federal government and large corporations are among the largest users of aggregate measures; they can be used to "take the pulse" of a given population on a given issue, determine who buys certain products or services, or assess what customers think of products and services. The user of an aggregate measure is typically keenly interested not only in a measure of central tendency, but also in dispersion or variance about the mean; such dispersion will tell whether or not people tend to be heavily divided with respect to the issue assessed. Attitudes may be based on many factors. For example, consumers may judge an automobile on the basis of its styling, its power, its comfort, its fuel economy, its price, or any number of other attributes. When using aggregate scaling methods, the assumption is made that attitudes toward all of these attributes can be combined into a single or composite score.

The simplest aggregative method is the *one-dimensional preference* scale in which respondents are asked to provide an overall rating for an object, person, or institution rather than rating individual attributes. For example, respondents might be asked to use the scale below to rate, say, various brands of canned sardines:

Like	*Like Somewhat*	*Neutral*	*Dislike Somewhat*	*Dislike*
1	*2*	*3*	*4*	*5*

---

2. Further discussion of the evaluation of survey research may be found in Wheeler (1977) and in marketing research textbooks (such as Kinnear & Taylor, 1983; Lehmann, 1985).

The numbers 1 through 5 are assigned to scale values, and ratings can be expressed in quantitative form.

A five-point preference scale, such as that used in this example, is an example of a *Likert* scale. Note that an assumption inherent in the use of such a technique is that respondents can sort out their opinions about the various attributes of the product in question and come up with a valid, overall reaction ranging from "like" to "neutral" to "dislike."

One shortcoming of this form of scaling is that the different ratings are not necessarily interval in nature and therefore the number of statistical manipulations that can legitimately be performed with such data is limited. A rating of 3 on the scale may not be viewed by respondents as three times greater than a rating of 1. The scale is an *ordinal* one, and a rating of 3 may legitimately be viewed only as greater than 1. Another limitation inherent in such aggregative data is the fact that there is no assurance that respondents have considered all relevant attributes in arriving at their conclusion. Additionally, the use of an overall rating obscures the possibility that respondents may, indeed, have quite different attitudes toward different attributes of the object being rated.

An alternative approach would be to rate each attribute separately and then sum the individual ratings to obtain an overall score. For example, let us assume that respondents are asked to rate a particular brand of sardines on four attributes—flavor, freshness, aroma, and appearance—using a Likert scale. And let's further assume that one respondent has rated a particular brand as follows:

Flavor	4
Freshness	2
Aroma	3
Appearance	5

The total rating for these sardines would be 14—obtained by summing the ratings of the individual attributes. This total rating can then be treated in a variety of statistical ways in making comparisons between brands.

Aside from questions about the level of measurement represented in the scaling device, this approach has one major limitation: namely, each attribute is treated as though it were equally important in arriving at an overall attitude toward the sardines. And while this may be true in some cases, it certainly cannot be presumed to be true all of the time. One way of avoiding this potential pitfall is by employing a variation of the Fishbein-Rosenberg method of scaling. In this approach, respondents are asked two sets of questions. First, they are asked to rate relevant attributes in terms of their importance. Then, individual objects are rated in terms of the extent to which they possess each of the attributes in question. Applying this approach to our example, we might find that the attribute of flavor is rated 5 in terms of importance, freshness is also rated 5, and aroma and appearance are rated 4 and 2, respectively. We can now combine the rating of the individual attribute with the rating of attribute importance as shown in the matrix in Table 19–1. Through the procedure, each attribute rating is multiplied by the importance of the attribute in order to weight it properly. The weighted results can then be submitted to various statistical treatments for making comparisons between brands.

Figure 19–4 *Literature in the Area of Consumer Assessment Is Growing.* Specialized journals such as one officially sponsored by the Consumer Psychology Division of the American Psychological Association, *Psychology & Marketing,* regularly contain articles dealing with aspects of consumer assessment, as well as articles in related areas (see, for example, Alpert & Alpert, 1990; Batra & Holbrook, 1990; Butter et al., 1991; Kuykendall & Keating, 1990; LaTour, 1990; Merikle, 1988; Pratkanis & Greenwald, 1988; Synodinos, 1988; and Stith, 1989). Articles pertaining to consumer assessment and related areas may also be found in many other journals, including *Journal of Advertising Research, Journal of Applied Communication Research, Journal of Consumer Research, Journal of Marketing, Journal of Marketing Research,* and in selected publications of the Marketing Science Institute (such as Dickson & Sawyer, 1986; Hunt, 1977; Olson & Ray, 1983; May, 1971; and Wilkie & Dickson, 1985).

Table 19–1

Individual Ratings
Combined with Attribute Importance

Attributes	Brand rating		Attribute importance		Total
Flavor	4	×	5	=	20
Freshness	2	×	5	=	10
Aroma	3	×	4	=	12
Appearance	5	×	2	=	10
Total				=	52

Another method of aggregate scaling designed to give greater weight to some attributes than to others is an adaptation of Guttman scaling (Guttman, 1944). The Guttman method employs an ordered set of statements about a stimulus object such as a hypothetical brand of sardines called "Mermaid":

Mermaid Sardines taste good	Yes	No
Mermaid Sardines stay fresh	Yes	No
Mermaid Sardines have a nice aroma	Yes	No
Mermaid Sardines look appetizing	Yes	No

The statements are ordered according to their relative importance, with the first statement being most important and the last statement being the least important. The specific statements used and their order are usually determined by interviews with persons familiar with the stimulus object. Often, several orderings are investigated to find the most appropriate one. The global rating is computed by counting the "yes" responses to the ordered questions. A "yes" is counted as 1 and a "no" as 0. The preference score is determined by asking the questions in order and adding 1 to the total score for each "yes" answer obtained. Whan a "no" is encountered, the process stops. The overall rating is a summation of the number of "yes" responses.

A number of other aggregate scaling techniques may be used. Those shown have been introduced to clarify the nature of aggregate scaling and to point up one of the problems of summing attribute ratings—namely, that certain attributes are more important than others and must be weighted in some way in order to provide a valid rating.

Multidimensional scaling (MDS)   Multidimensional scaling is a relatively recent development in psychometric research. Unlike aggregate scaling methods, MDS methods reject the notion that attitudes about a stimulus object can be combined into a single score. MDS attempts to locate objects within the framework of an "attribute space" based on perceptions of similarities and differences among the objects.

Figure 19–5 is an example of multidimensional scaling. Several points should be noted about this figure. First, consumer perceptions and preferences for pain relievers can be ordered in terms of a two-dimensional space made up of the two attributes of gentleness and effectiveness. Second, each pain reliever can be

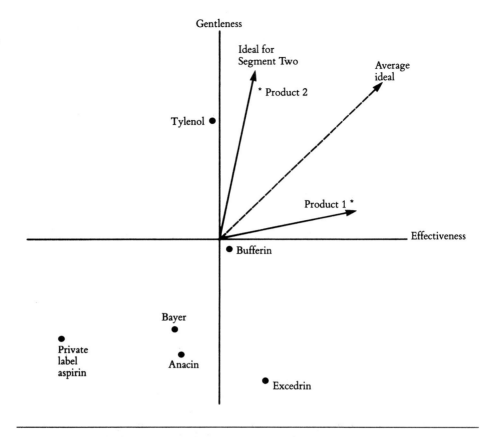

Figure 19–5 *An Illustration of Similarities (Adapted from Urban & Hauser, 1980).*

located in this space in a position that represents a specific combination of these two attributes. Thus, Tylenol is perceived as very gentle relative to other pain relievers, but not so effective as Excedrin. Excedrin, on the other hand, is perceived as highly effective, but not at all gentle. Third, different pain relievers may cluster in terms of their perceived similarity. Bayer, Anacin, and private label aspirin are perceived as similar on both gentleness and effectiveness. Bufferin, Excedrin, and Tylenol tend to occupy unique positions within the space. The optimal combination of gentleness and effectiveness is represented at point 3. Note that different groups of consumers may, in fact, have different ideals. Tylenol is the product most similar to the ideal product for segment one. It is apparent that multidimensional scaling is a useful technique for identifying the position of products in a relevant product space and for relating existing products to the ideal product of consumers.

The construction of a product space through the use of multidimensional scaling is beyond the scope of this text. Essentially, however, it is a computer-based technique that locates products in a space of minimum dimensionality based on perceived similarities and differences. Since MDS is wholly a numerical procedure, it ignores the problem of axis labeling. It is not necessary, therefore, when employing the MDS technique, to specify the attributes on which objects are to be judged. One simply obtains judgments of similarity about the objects being studied in the hope that the most salient attributes will be identifiable by the ultimate structure obtained in the analysis. By examining the location of objects within the space that is generated, and by being familiar with the characteristics of the objects, the analyst is often able to identify the most salient features on which the data have been mathematically ordered. It is also possible to map attributes on to the derived space in order to facilitate interpretation of the axes.

Multidimensional scaling, using as input data the naive perceptions of consumers, appears to have promise as a systematic approach for ordering and analyzing perceptions and preferences and is widely used by researchers in the area of consumer behavior (see Schiffman, Reynolds, & Young, 1981).

The semantic differential technique   The semantic differential is one of the most widely used and versatile scaling techniques employed in marketing research. Originally developed as a clinical tool for defining the meaning of concepts and relating concepts to one another in a "semantic space," the basic technique has undergone modification in its adaptation to a wide range of purposes.

As initially conceived by Osgood, Suci, and Tannenbaum (1957), the semantic differential involved repeated judgments of a concept using a series of descriptive bipolar adjectives (such as good/bad or strong/weak) on a seven-point scale such as this one:

GOOD_____/_____/_____/_____/_____/_____/_____/ BAD

In the fields of consumer and social psychology, the semantic differential has been used to measure opinions of brands, products, companies, social programs, stores, product users, political candidates, and so forth. A number of modifications in the semantic differential as originally described by Osgood, Suci, and Tannenbaum (1957) are made when this technique is used in consumer-related studies (Mindak, 1961). For example, the bipolar adjective might be replaced by descriptive phrases (such as "something very special" versus "just another drink" with reference to a particular brand of beer).

The semantic differential is a very popular tool in consumer-related research because it provides a relatively simple, efficient way of collecting quantifiable data from large samples and can be used effectively as a "before" and "after" test (for example, before and after exposure to a commercial or informational film). It is useful in obtaining an index of attitude that might be difficult to obtain through other approaches, and it can provide a quantifiable "benchmark" to which competing brands can be compared. Since it requires very little verbal skill, it is quite useful in measuring the attitudes of children and adult respondents who have limited language abilities. Data from the use of this technique also tend to be quite reliable.

QUALITATIVE ASSESSMENT

A distinction can be made between *quantitative* research, which typically involves large numbers of subjects and elaborate statistical analyses, and *qualitative* research, which typically involves few respondents and little or no statistical analysis; the emphasis in the latter type of research is not on quantity (of subjects or of data) but on the qualities of whatever it is that is under study. Included under the heading of "qualitative assessment" are the motivation research techniques of one-on-one interviews, focus groups, and specially designed projective techniques.

There are many occasions when it is important to study in detail a small number of individuals. This may occur when one desires a great deal of information from each individual and when relatively little is known about the phenomenon of interest. Qualitative research often provides the opportunity to develop hypotheses about why consumers behave as they do. These hypotheses may then be tested with a larger number of consumers. Qualitative research also has diagnostic value. The best way to obtain highly detailed information about what a consumer likes and dislikes about a product, a store, or an advertisement is to use qualitative research. Qualitative research may help a government service agency determine how individuals will respond to new intervention programs or how to better deliver their services. Such research might also assist a compensation manager to assess reaction to compensation programs, benefits packages, or commission structures for sales personnel. It may also help detect problems that might otherwise be unidentified.

One-on-One Interviews

Individual interviews with consumers have the advantage of providing very rich information and avoiding the influence of others on the opinion of any one individual. However, individual interviews tend to be expensive and time-consuming. As a result, it is unlikely that large numbers of people will be interviewed for any one research project.

One type of individual interview is sometimes referred to as a "depth interview." A depth interview is a relatively unstructured interview that involves considerable probing of an individual consumer's beliefs and attitudes. The purpose of this type of interview is to get beyond surface or superficial reactions of a consumer to more fundamental processes underlying responses to some stimulus. Sometimes a depth interview may contain some structured questions relating to how the consumer chooses a particular product; what information is sought (for example, price? quality? name-brand?) and how the information is evaluated and processed. And when it comes to the question, "to buy or not to buy," what factors are primarily responsible for the choice?

The same factors that make for a good interview in other settings make for a good interview to assess social or economic phenomena. In fact, such interviews are often carried out by psychologists with clinical training or other experience in interviewing. As an exercise in depth-interviewing, approach some (approachable) person you know who wears Coca-Cola clothing that prominently displays the company's symbol. Tell the person you are conducting a survey for one of your classes, and your assignment is to determine what motivates people to buy such clothing. Next, conduct a depth interview. At some point in the interview you may discover that your interviewee is—though it may not be fashionable to admit—quite patriotic; the Coca-Cola symbol may be seen as synonymous with "American," and sporting such clothing may be quite analogous to the blue-collar workers' wearing of American flag patches and lapel pins (Cohen, 1986).

Focus Groups

A *focus group* is a group interview led by a trained, independent moderator who ideally has a knowledge of group discussion facilitation techniques and group dynamics.[3] As their name implies, "focus groups" are designed to focus group discussion on something—such as a particular commercial, a concept for a new product, or packaging for a new product. Focus groups usually consist of from 6 to 12 participants who may have been recruited off the floor of a shopping mall or may have been selected in advance in order to meet some preset qualifications for participation in the group; the usual objective here is to have the members of the group be in some way representative of the population of targeted consumers for the product or service being focused on. Thus, for example, only beer drinkers (defined, for example, as males who drink at least two six-packs per week and females who drink at least one six-pack per week) might be solicited for participation in a focus group designed to explore one or various attributes of a new brand of beer—including such variables as its taste, its packaging, its advertising, and its "bar call," this last phrase being an industry term that refers to the ease with which one could order the brew in a bar. Due to the high costs associated with introducing a new product and advertising a new or established product, professionally executed focus groups complete with a representative sampling of the targeted consumer population are a valuable tool in market research.

Depending on the requirements of the moderator's client (usually an advertiser or an advertising agency), the group discussion can be relatively structured (with a number of points to be covered) or relatively unstructured (with few points to be covered exhaustively). After establishing a rapport with the group, the moderator may, for example, show some advertising or a product to the group and then pose a general question to the group (such as "What did you think of the beer commercial?") to be followed up by more specific kinds of questions (such as "Were the people in that commercial the kind of people *you* would like to have a beer with?"). The responses of the group members may build on those of other group members, and the result of the free-flowing discussion may be new information, new perspectives, or some previously overlooked problems with the advertising or product.

Focus groups typically last from one to two hours and are usually conducted in rooms (either conference rooms or living rooms) equipped with one-way mirrors (from which the client's staff may observe the proceedings) and audio or video equipment so that a record of the group session will be preserved. Aside from being an "active listener" and an individual who is careful not to suggest answers to questions or draw conclusions for the respondents, the focus group moderator's duties include (1) following a discussion guide and keeping the discussion on the topic, (2) drawing out "silent" group members so that everyone is heard from, (3) limiting the response time of group members who might domi-

---

3. Ideally, a focus group moderator should be independent so that he or she can dispassionately discuss the topics at hand with some distance and perspective. It is true, however, that some advertising agencies maintain an in-house focus group moderator staff to test the advertising produced by the agency. Critics of the practice of using advertising agency employees to test advertising developed by the agency have likened the process of using in-house, non-independent moderators to assigning wolves to guard the hen-house.

nate the group discussion, and (4) writing a report that provides not only a summary of the group discussion but also psychological and/or marketing insights to the client. Recent years have witnessed experimentation with computer equipment in focus groups so that second-by-second reaction to stimulus materials such as commercials can be monitored. Cohen described the advantages (1985) and limitations (1987) of a technique whereby respondents watching television commercials pressed a calculatorlike keypad to indicate how positive or negative they were feeling on a moment-to-moment basis while watching television. The response could then be visually displayed as a graph and played back for the respondent who could be probed for the reasons concerning the spontaneous response.

The focus group was a tool used by the publisher of the Strong Vocational Interest Blank (SVIB-SCII) when, in 1984, the profile was undergoing redesign in preparation for its 1985 revision. A group of counseling psychologists from a variety of work settings served as the respondents; an objective was to make the profile optimally responsive to the needs of users of the test. As a result, the new SVIB-SCII (1) is color-coded for easy reference to different scales, (2) reads from left to right by type of scale, (3) has a large, easily read type size, and (4) has a white background in which test users, counselors, or others can make notations.

Focus groups are widely employed in consumer research, and there is a growing literature on various aspects related to their potential (for example, Greenbaum, 1988; Langmaid & Ross, 1984; Schlackman, 1984; Skibbe, 1986). Among the uses of these groups are the following:

1. To generate hypotheses that can be further tested quantitatively
2. To generate information for designing or modifying consumer questionnaires
3. To provide general background information about a product category
4. To get impressions on new product concepts for which little information is available
5. To obtain new ideas about older products
6. To generate ideas for product development
7. To interpret the results of previously obtained quantitative results

In general, the focus group tends to be thought of as a highly useful technique for exploratory research, a technique that can provide a valuable springboard to more comprehensive quantitative studies. Because so few respondents are typically involved in such groups, the findings from them cannot automatically be thought of as representative of the larger population. Still, many a client (including advertising agency creative staff) has received inspiration from the words spoken by ordinary consumers on the other side of a one-way mirror.

Projective Techniques

Various projective techniques have been applied in consumer research. Word association techniques may be used to screen brand names for negative connotations or to help uncover consumers' feelings about new products. A study by the Governor's Advisory Committee on the Tourist Industry in Hawaii used word associations to obtain emotional reactions to words associated with the islands. Among the results was the finding that, while the word *Hawaii* had no negative associations, *Waikiki* gave rise to responses such as "cheap and gaudy," "crowded," "flashy," and "overpublicized" (Grossack, 1964).

A number of variations of the word association approach have been devised. Controlled word association is a variation in which respondents are asked to respond with a class of words. For example, a list of products may be read, one at a time, and the subjects are asked to respond with brand names. Chain or successive word association requires that the subject respond with a series of words rather than just a single word in response to the stimulus. There is some evidence that deeper levels of feeling may be reached through chain associations, since concealed resentments often do not appear until the third or fourth word in the chain (Grossack, 1964).

Another frequently used projective technique in consumer research is the sentence completion test. Like word association techniques, sentence completion techniques may be used in an effort to obtain information that for whatever reason may otherwise be inaccessible. Kassarjian and Cohen (1965) asked 179 smokers who thought cigarettes were a health hazard why they continued to smoke. The majority of the answers gave the impression that smokers were relatively happy with their lot and smoked because they enjoyed it or felt that moderate smoking was all right. When these same respondents were given the opportunity to finish the sentence "People who never smoke are _____," they responded with comments such as "happier," "smarter," "wiser," and so forth. For the sentence "Teenagers who smoke are _____," respondents completed the thought with comments such as "foolish," "crazy," "uninformed," "stupid," "showing off," and "immature." Clearly, the sentence completion test shows cigarette smokers to be more anxious, concerned, and dissatisfied with their habit than was revealed by the direct question.

Other projective techniques employed in consumer research include TAT-like pictures about which respondents are asked to construct stories, and cartoon-like characters with "empty balloons" to be filled in by respondents (similar in structure to the stimuli of the Rosenzweig Picture-Frustration Study), though depicting situations relevant to the research question; see Figure 19–6.

Other Techniques

Before leaving the realm of the perceptual to proceed to the realm of the psychophysiological, we should also mention the use of an instrument called a *tachistoscope* in consumer (as well as other) research. The tachistoscope is an apparatus used to present visual stimuli for extremely minute instants of time. The machine may be set for the desired length of presentation of a stimulus, usually in milliseconds (thousandths of a second). Traditionally used in perceptual and psychophysiological research, the tachistoscope has found application in consumer psychology where researchers use it primarily to assess the effectiveness of trademarks, brand names, and corporate logograms. Often abbreviated to simply *logo,* a *logogram* is a symbol that represents an abbreviation, such as $ for "dollars(s)." Some examples of corporate logos are the specially designed letter *N* symbolizing the National Broadcasting Company, the McDonalds' *M,* and the distinctive *31* in a circle, symbolic of the 31 ice cream flavors offered each month by Baskin-Robbins. Consumer psychologists use the tachistoscope in research designed to

Figure 19–6 *Projective Stimuli in Consumer Research.*

In his overview of the use of projectives in consumer research, Levy (1985) described the use of the picture of "two boys buying hot dogs" (above). After being told that one of the boys purchased the brand his mother told him to get and the other bought the brand that he wanted, respondents were asked to make up stories about the pictures. The obedient boy tended to be seen as middle class and the purchaser of a national brand whereas the other child was seen as purchasing a more frivolous-seeming brand and pocketing the change.

More ambiguous, TAT-like pictures have also been employed in research with consumers. Stories in response to the picture below served to differentiate two groups of consumers as a function of the brand of a particular product they used. For users of one brand, the stories tended to be relatively calm, peaceful, and accepting of the figure as relaxed, contemplative, idle—suggestive to Levy (1985) that this market seg-ment was conventional, able to relax, and accepting of the moment. Stories in response to this picture from users of a competitive brand tended to be more "troubled," with more negative emotions and adverse events being described. Levy found this latter group to be "people who saw more complexity in life"—an outlook that was "compatible with a brand that represented a stronger sense of striving and achievement" (p. 76).

Cohen (1983b) used a projective-like task to study corporate images as reflected in corporate logos. Respondents were told that they were participating in a "test of symbolism" and were asked to verbalize their immediate association to symbols such as the Post Office eagle, the Merrill-Lynch bull, and the Bell telephone. One of the more interesting findings was that the Bell logo conjured associations to reliability and security but not high technology.

test the ease of recognition and recall of corporate brand names and logos. Is the logo recalled amidst other logos? Is the logo recognized when flashed for an instant? What does the subject recall about the logo after seeing it for a period of time so brief that it is just recognizable? These types of questions may be asked in assessing consumer response to various logos with a tachistoscope.

Other types of consumer assessment may entail situational testing; consumers are placed in hypothetical situations where the object is to determine what factors prevail in motivating them to buy one product rather than another. A number of situational as well as paper-and-pencil measures purport to measure constructs referred to as *purchase intent, brand loyalty,* and *involvement* in products (see Jacoby & Chestnut, 1978; Lilien & Kotler, 1983; Traylor & Joseph, 1984; Zaichowsky, 1985). A common situational approach in new-product research places the consumer in a simulated shopping situation where he or she has the opportunity to actually purchase the new product—even though the product may not be available in the "real world."

PSYCHOPHYSIOLOGICAL MEASURES

In search of an uncontaminated and "pure" measure of consumer response to products and their promotion of same, some researchers in the fields of marketing and advertising have looked to psychophysiological measures for answers to their questions. Here we briefly describe and review a number of these measurement techniques, all of which have been employed in experimental situations where the subject watches a commercial or discusses a product while psychophysiological measurements are simultaneously taken.

Pupillary Response

Pupillary response first gained attention as a potential psychophysiological measure of consumer response in the early 1960s when research suggested that pupil size seemed to vary directly with the pleasurableness of observed stimuli (Hess & Polt, 1960). Subsequent study of the phenomenon has suggested that the interpretation of those initial findings were probably an oversimplification (Stewart & Furse, 1982). While pupillary response may be related to affect, exactly how it is related and the nature of the physiological mechanism that is operating remains unclear. The best data available to date suggest that pupillary response appears to be related to the amount of information processing evoked by a stimulus and therefore may be viewed as a measure of attention and cognitive effort—not affect.

Electrodermal Response

The term *electrodermal response* refers to a measure of the degree to which a small electric current is conducted or resisted by the surface of the skin (a measure that is usually, but not always, gauged by taping an electrode to the palm or putting a ringlike monitor around a finger). There is evidence that electrodermal responses may be related to arousal, affect, and amount of information processing. However, these responses tend to be very unstable over time, and attempts to establish the reliability of this measurement technique have not proved to be successful. Further, some important methodological issues are as yet unresolved with respect to this method. For example, different results may be obtained depending on whether resistance (sometimes referred to as Galvanic Skin Response, or GSR) or conductance is the measured response; conductance and resistance are reciprocally related. Perhaps the primary complaint on the part of those who have experimented with electrodermal response as a criterion measure is that while it may indicate an affective response, there is no way of discerning by means of the technique whether the response is favorable or unfavorable to the stimulus. Moreover, the specific mechanisms that give rise to electrodermal responses are not well understood.

Brain Wave Measurement

Attempts have been made to gauge consumer response to stimuli such as commercials by having the consumer watch the commercials while an electroencephalograph (EEG) simultaneously monitors brain wave activity (Price, Rust, & Kumar, 1986). While it has been noted that brain wave patterns do change in response to stimuli, the reasons for such change and even the meaning of such changes remain a matter of controversy (Stewart & Furse, 1982; Stewart, 1984; Nevid, 1984; Cacioppo & Petty, 1985).

Other Measures

Numerous other psychophysiological measures have been experimented with in the search for the "pure" measure of consumer reaction. The electromyograph (EMG) measures minute movement in muscles, and it has been applied to facial muscles as subjects are exposed to various stimuli (Ekman, Friesen, & Ellsworth, 1982). Voice-pitch analysis is another method that has been experimented with, the rationale here being that voice pitch is an involuntary consequence of muscular contractions of the larynx (Nighswonger & Martin, 1981; Brickman, 1980). However, it is not always clear what the factors responsible for a change in voice pitch may be. Factors such as time of day of the recordings, the method of recording, characteristics of the interviewer, and the general health of the respondent are all capable of influencing voice pitch. Perhaps most importantly, a discrepancy exists in the literature on voice-pitch analysis between reports of accuracy of vocal-auditory recognition and the lack of evidence for the acoustic differentiation of vocal expression (Scherer, 1986).

One measure shown to be of value in assessing consumer response to print advertising is eye-movement tracking equipment. In some of the older versions of this equipment, the subject is strapped into a harness and looks through lenses at slides of print ads while eye-movement recorders simultaneously record exactly where in the ad the gaze of the subject's eye is going. A newer version of the eye-tracking device features a tiny fiberoptic material embedded in a specially prepared pair of glasses that acts as a camera; virtually everywhere the subjects look

Figure 19–7 *But Is Anybody Watching?*

A videocamera/recorder mounted directly on a television set in the home of subjects enabled the experimenters to observe and subsequently analyze subjects' behavior during the viewing of television commercials.

A television commercial may cost $100,000 or more to develop and produce. The budget for airing the commercial may be ten times that amount. Add to that sum of money the cost of pre- and post-research of the commercial's effectiveness and there you have a very rough estimate of what it can cost to advertise on television . . . But is anybody watching the commercials?

This question was addressed in a study by Nevid and Cohen (1987) that employed an at-home behavioral observation technique. An encased television camera and videorecorder was installed on the living room television for the purpose of recording subjects' behavior as they watched television. All subjects were given a video tape that ran for approximately two hours. On the tape was (1) a movie that ran approximately 90 minutes, and (2) a pilot situation comedy that ran for 30 minutes, with order of presentation of program material randomly assigned to households. Different commer-

cials varying in length (120 seconds, 60 seconds, 30 seconds, and 15 seconds) were interspersed in pods throughout the tape in a manner similar to the way they would usually be interspersed in a commercial television presentation. Subjects were given instructions to "watch television as you normally do." The video record of subjects' commercial-watching behavior was analyzed with respect to a number of variables such as "fixed attention" and "absent from room." Additionally, about one hour after their viewing of the program, all subjects were called and asked a number of questions designed to determine which commercials they remembered viewing. These questions were classified as being of the "product category prompt" variety (such as "Do you remember seeing a commercial for a long distance telephone company?") and as the "specific brand prompt" variety (such as "Do you remember seeing a commercial for MCI?").

The mounds of resulting behav-

ioral data were analyzed for each commercial length by each response category. Suffice to say that the results from this one study cannot be taken as very encouraging for television advertisers or their agencies. In general, a rather low level of attending to television commercials was observed. Focusing on the data for the seven 30-second commercials on the tape, it was found that about half the subjects watched them an average of less than one second; the median viewing time for these seven commercials ranged from a low of 0.4 second to a high of 7 seconds. Recall of commercials was also quite low; generally, only 2 or 3 of the 20 subjects in this study were able to recall 30-second commercials on the reel—and that was true even after a category or brand prompt.

Generalization from this research must be made with extreme caution due to factors such as the limited sample size (ten married couples) and geographical location (all from Brooklyn, New York). Additionally, although subjects were instructed to watch television as they normally would, common sense dictates that the presence of a television camera recording behavior would alter it (to varying and unknown degrees). Further, it was deemed judicious to place the television camera recording subjects' behavior on top of televisions located in the living room of the home only. Although subjects typically had televisions in other rooms of their homes and presumably watched television in those rooms as well, placement of a television camera in rooms other than the living room could potentially have resulted in unique dilemmas regarding the analysis of the recorded behaviors.

as they go through specially constructed magazines or other test stimuli is recorded on videotape by this pinhead-size recording device.

Psychophysiological Measures in Perspective

In general, psychophysiological measures as applied to consumer research offer promise—but a promise that has yet to be fulfilled. Rather than the "pure" measures of attitude and/or affect their proponents had hoped they would be, psycho-

---

Close-up

Psychographics

Demography is the study of characteristics of human populations in terms of variables such as size, growth, density, height, weight, age, and so forth—all referred to by the plural noun *demographics. Psychographics* is a term in marketing, advertising, and consumer psychology (though it may not yet have made it to an English-language dictionary) that refers to the study of psychological characteristics of populations—more specifically, the psychological characteristics of populations of consumers. Why describe groups of consumers in terms of psychological traits? The notion underlying the use of psychographics is that people who share the same or similar personality traits, attitudes, interests, beliefs, and activities will be attracted by the same or similar products and services—and be influenced by the same kinds of advertising and promotion.

Psychographic studies are quantitative studies that tend to employ large numbers of subjects responding to a relatively large number of items. The responses are usually obtained via a format that readily lends itself to quantification (such as Likert scales or semantic differential items), and the data are carefully analyzed in different ways to determine what relationships exist. The object of a typical psychographic study is to identify common psychological and related characteristics of a particular population of people (for example, all people who sent in $400 for a home-study course in "How to Get Rich Quick in Real Estate," after exposure to a television commercial). Alternatively, a psychographic study might

employ as subjects a large, random group of people on whom many psychological measures have been taken and from whom much consumer information has been obtained; from such information psychographic profiles of different "types" of consumers might emerge.

Perhaps the best-known and most widely used typology of consumers, one that is based on psychographic research, is the typology developed by the Stanford Research Institute (SRI). The SRI typology is referred to as VALS (an acronym for an ongoing program of Values and Lifestyles), and in the VALS taxonomy, nine basic types of consumers have been identified: two types of "need-driven" consumers, three types of "outer-directed" consumers, and four types of "inner-directed" consumers (see Table 1). As you read the description of each, try to decide which of these categories best describes yourself, your siblings, and your parents.

The "Outer-Directed" general category of consumer consists of three distinctive groups that combined represent two-thirds of the U.S. population—and account for almost 78 percent of all purchases. These groups are concerned with appearance and conformity to established social norms. The *Achievers* within this broad category are the leaders of business, professions, and government. They value efficiency, status, materialism, and creature comforts. They have a high median income and a median age of 42. The *Emulators* are ambitious, upwardly mobile, and status conscious. They are younger than the

physiological measures can at best be thought of as indicating such factors as type and stage of information processing (Stewart & Furse, 1982).

Numerous, as yet unresolved, methodological issues regarding such measures exist. For example, the fact that some changes in psychophysiological measures are not independent of the baseline measures (a phenomenon referred to as the *law of initial values*) suggests that such dependence must be controlled by statistical means. Second, while there is a generalized response to similar stimuli that is common to all individuals (stimulus-response specificity), each individual has a

Achievers, have a lower median income than the Achievers, and aspire to attain the success of the Achievers (some will, but others will fail due to a lack of skills, education, or resources). The *Belongers* are the largest VALS category. They tend to be conservative and traditional, and their lives are focused on the home. They seek to fit in with society rather than stand out.

People who are "Inner-Directed" according to the VALS taxonomy can be characterized by a desire for self-expression and a need to fulfill individual needs. The four groups that make up this category represent about one-fifth of the U.S. population, and they make about 15 percent of the total purchases made in this country. The largest group of Inner-Directeds is the *Socially Conscious* group, a group that places emphasis on simple living, conservation, and environmentalism. The *Experientials* want experience and involvement. They participate in a wide range of activities for the experiences these activities provide. They tend to be hedonistic but often engage in activities such as crafts, building, and do-it-yourself projects because these projects provide opportunities for new experiences. The youngest VALS group is the *I-Am-Me's*. Members of this group are individualistic, impulsive, experimental, and highly energetic. They enjoy faddish items and tend to be innovators, particularly with respect to fashion. Many young adults and students fall into this latter category.

The *Integrated* make up about 2 percent of the population of the United States and spend about $28 billion annually. They are the most highly educated of the groups and have a median age of 40 and a median income of $40,000. This group combines the outward orientation of the outer-directed lifestyle and the sensitivity of the inner-directed. The buying habits of this group revolve around quality, uniqueness, high standards, and ecology. They embrace the values of individualism, tolerance, and a global view.

People who fall into the VALS general category of "Need-Driven" tend to be concerned primarily with security and simply "getting by." Although they represent about 11 percent of the U.S. population they account for only about 4 percent of total annual purchases in the United States. The *Sustainers* include a large number of females, single heads of household, as well as others who are struggling on the verge of poverty. The *Survivors* are typically older and poor. They tend to be cautious, conservative, authoritarian, and removed from mainstream society.

Members of the different VALS groups do exhibit differences in behavior in the marketplace, and a number of firms have found this taxonomy to be useful in defining their markets. Achievers tend to buy luxury cars, belongers tend to buy family-size cars, the socially conscious buy gas-efficient cars, and the need-driven tend to buy used cars (Capeli, 1984). Timex Medical Products Group focuses its marketing activities for digital thermometers, digital blood pressure monitors, and digital scales on the achievers and

Psychographics (continued)

socially conscious because consumers in these groups tend to be more concerned with staying healthy, are more highly educated, and are more receptive to innovation than are members of the other groups. Belongers are not considered a viable market for these products because their traditional orientation makes them less receptive to high-tech items ("Timex," 1984).

Critics of the psychographic approach have argued that psychographic categories overlap so much as to be virtually meaningless. It has been further argued that when all is said and done, psychographic studies reveal nothing that savvy researchers or practitioners do not already know or could not figure out for themselves. Proponents of psychographics concede that there is overlap in defined lifestyle groups but argue that real differences do exist—marginal as they may be in some instances—and may still be quite useful. Proponents of the psychographic approach would further argue that such studies provide insights that cannot be obtained in any other way. Readers interested in more detailed discussions of various aspects of psychographics are referred to the following sources: Wells (1975); Demby (1974); Veltri & Schiffman (1984); Mitchell (1978); Bearden, Teel, & Durand (1978); and Runyon & Stewart (1987).

Table 1

VALS Lifestyle Segmentation

Percentage of population	Consumer type	Values and lifestyles	Demographics	Buying patterns	Spending power
Need-Driven consumers					
6	Survivors	Struggle for survival Distrustful Socially misfitted Ruled by appetites	Poverty-level income Little education Many minority members	Price dominant Focus on basics Buy for immediate needs	$3 billion
10	Sustainers	Concern with safety, security Insecure, compulsive Dependent, following Want law and order	Low income Low education Much unemployment Live in country as well as cities	Price important Want warranty Cautious buyers	$32 billion
Outer-Directed consumers					
32	Belongers	Conforming, conventional Unexperimental, traditional, formal Nostalgic	Low to middle income Low to average education Blue-collar jobs Trend toward non-city living	Family Home Fads Middle and lower market makers	$230 billion

Table 1 (*continued*)

VALS Lifestyle Segmentation

Percentage of population	Consumer type	Values and lifestyles	Demographics	Buying patterns	Spending power
Outer-Directed consumers (continued)					
10	Emulators	Ambitious, show-off Status conscious Upwardly mobile Macho, competitive	Good to excellent income Youngish Highly urban Traditionally male, but changing	Conspicuous consumption "In" items Imitative Popular fashion	$120 billion
28	Achievers	Achievement, success, fame Materialism Leadership, efficiency Comfort	Excellent incomes Leaders in business, politics, etc. Good education Suburban and city living	Give evidence of success Top of the line Luxury and gift markets "New and improved" products	$500 billion
Inner-Directed consumers					
3	I-Am-Me	Fiercely individualistic Dramatic, impulsive Experimental Volatile	Young Many single Study or starting job Affluent backgrounds	Display one's taste Experimental fads Source of far-out fads Clique buying	$25 billion
5	Experimental	Drive to direct experience Active, participative Person-centered Artistic	Bimodal incomes Mostly under 40 Many young families Good education	Process over product Vigorous, outdoor "sports" "Making" home pursuits Crafts and introspection	$56 billion
4	Societally Conscious	Societal responsibility Simple living Smallness of scale Inner growth	Bimodal low and high incomes Excellent education Diverse ages and places of residence Largely white	Conservation emphasis Simplicity Frugality Environmental concerns	$50 billion
2	Integrated	Psychological maturity Sense of fittingness Tolerant, self-actualizing World perspective	Good to excellent incomes Bimodal in age Excellent education Diverse jobs and residential patterns	Varied self-expression Ethically oriented Ecologically aware One-of-a-kind items	$28 billion

unique response set (individual response stereotype) that must be controlled. Third, the use of a single physiological measure, which has been typical of many applications of these measures, fails to provide information concerning individual response sets and provides an incomplete picture of response. Current psycho-physiological texts suggest the use of multiple measures; and the use of measurement from a number of different psychophysiological assessment devices requires that all of the measures be converted to comparable scaling units. Fourth, numerous experimental controls are required to assure that an individual is responding only to the intended stimulus rather than to the experimental situation and/or extraneous events in the environment. Finally, there are a variety of issues related to instrumentation that must be considered when using psychophysiological measures; such charcteristics as sensitivity, precision, and accuracy must be carefully examined when selecting instrumentation for use in psychophysiological studies.

Chapter 20

Computer-Assisted

Psychological

Assessment*

COMPUTERS AS ADMINISTRATORS, scorers, and interpreters of test and other assessment-related data, have the potential of being a boon to the field of psychological testing. Computers don't come in to work irritable because they stayed out too late the night before. Nothing is dull, monotonous, boring, routine, or too mundane for a computer. They wouldn't rather be out jogging, they don't wonder whether they're getting enough fiber or where their kids are, and they couldn't care less about the price of oil; in short, *nothing* distracts them. Minute after minute, hour after hour, day after day, week after week they rigorously pay close attention to detail, adhering to the finest points of a standardized testing procedure—all of this with a cordial if not pleasing "voice," a letter-perfect "penmanship," and an enviable capacity for creating, modifying, and reproducing artwork. Computers are exemplary in their "understanding" of the term *service*. They can be loyal, friendly, and understanding. They thrive on processing data from multitudes of test takers, on multiple dates—ever ready to remember and compare findings within or between test takers. Computers have nothing, after all, if they don't have great memory. They don't see the world through rose-colored glasses or prejudicial blinders. They are as patient and as nonbiased as they are pro-

*This chapter was written by Ronald Jay Cohen and Kevin L. Moreland.

grammed to be and have outrageous organizational and planning abilities. They are capable of recording to the millisecond test takers' response time to an item. They can be programmed to interact with test takers in any language—even sign language for the deaf or hearing-impaired. They can dispense praise or rewards if so programmed. And they'll even turn themselves off on cue.

In the context of the umbrella term "computer-assisted psychological assessment" (CAPA), *assistance* refers to the use of computers in the administration, scoring, and/or interpretation of psychological tests, interviews, and other assessment techniques. Economy of assessors' time in administering, scoring, and interpreting assessments is perhaps the most oft-cited advantage of CAPA. Another major advantage, albeit more controversial, is that computers can do a more efficient and accurate job of test interpretation—analyzing voluminous amounts of assessment data while simultaneously comparing such data to other data and known facts in memory.

Much has been, and will be, written on the intricacies and issues associated with psychological assessment by, or with, computers. *Psychological Abstracts* lists over five hundred references to articles on computerized assessment—articles running the gamut from the practical to the theoretical—and that list is growing steadily. In this chapter, our modest objective is to acquaint you with selected aspects of the CAPA process, some of the advantages and disadvantages of using CAPA procedures, as well as the issues associated with its use.

AN OVERVIEW

In his article "Landmarks in Computer-Assisted Psychological Assessment," Fowler (1985) reminds us that the use of machines to process psychological assessment data is not a recent innovation. As early as 1930, electromechanical scoring for at least one psychological test, the Strong Vocational Interest Blank (SVIB), was available (Campbell, 1971). In 1946, thanks to the efforts of a Minneapolis engineer named Elmer Hankes, SVIB scoring and profiling had become mechanized. One year later, Hankes adopted the same technology to score and profile the MMPI (Dahlstrom, Welsh, & Dahlstrom, 1972). By the late 1950s, computers were being used not to merely score or develop profiles, but to interpret test data (Rome, Mataya, Pearson, Swenson, & Brannick, 1965). And by 1965, the Roche Psychiatric Service Institute had initiated the first national, mail-in MMPI service: clinicians could administer the MMPI, mail in the protocol, and get back a computer-scored and computer-interpreted report.

Perhaps the greatest stimulus to the growth of the field of computer-assisted psychological assessment, was the development of the desktop microcomputer. Affordably priced IBM-PCs, Apples, and other such hardware held out the promise of in-office, computerized test administration, combined with quick and accurate test data interpretation. Recent years have witnessed the development of a burgeoning number of psychological and educational testing software packages, as well as the establishment of a number of new companies marketing various computer-related assessment services. Computerized tests to assess intelligence, personality (projectively as well as other ways), neuropsychological functioning, adjustment, vocational aptitudes and interests, scholastic achievement, as well as sundry other variables are all either currently on the market or soon will be.

The Process

Use of the term "computer-assisted assessment" in its broadest sense always implies that the assessor is somehow being assisted by a computer; it does *not* necessarily imply that the assessee is directly being assisted by a computer or even using a computer to enter data. The SAT and the GRE are examples of instruments of assessment that can be considered "computer-assisted," as they are designed for computer scoring. Yet these instruments are not administered on a computer terminal; you may recall that the only "word processor" you used in taking such tests was a number 2 pencil applied to sheets of paper with printed grids.

Increasingly, computer-assisted assessment entails computerized test administration: the individual test taker sits before a computer video display and responds to prompts that appear on the screen (or prompts "spoken" by a speech simulator). The examinee's responses may be made by pressing keys on a keypad, by using a "light pen" and indicating a response by pointing to some area of the display, or by some other means. The nature of the interaction between the computer and the examinee will depend on how interactive the computer has been programmed to be. *Computerized adaptive testing* is the term used to denote an interactive process of test taking; the directions and/or test items administered to individual test takers will vary as a function of the test taker's response. As in traditional testing, the test might begin with some sample, practice items. However, the computer may not permit the test taker to continue with the test until the practice items have been responded to in a satisfactory manner and the test taker has provided evidence that he or she understands the test procedure. Computerized adaptive testing gets much more complicated than that. A test may be different for each test taker depending on individual performance on the items presented. Each item on an achievement test, for example, may have a known difficulty level and discrimination index. These data as well as other data (such as a statistical allowance for blind guessing) will be factored in when it comes time to derive a final score on the items administered—we deliberately don't say "final score on the test" because "the test" is ultimately different for different test takers. Computer-adaptive testing has been found to reduce the number of test items that need to be administered by as much as 50% while simultaneously reducing measurement error by 50% (Weiss & Vale, 1987). The items statistics used in such tests must be very precise, so very large samples of respondents are needed to establish those statistics.

The Advantages

Butcher (1987) described the advantages of CAPA in terms of the objectivity, accuracy, reliability, and efficiency such techniques can offer. According to Jackson (1986, p. 5), the advantages, or at least what he called the "perceived advantages" of computer-assisted assessment, can be summarized as follows:

1. economy of professional time
2. the possibility of employing trained assistants to monitor test administration at times when no psychologist is available
3. the negligible time lag between the administration of a test and its scoring and interpretation

4. the virtual elimination of scoring errors resulting from human lapses of attention or judgment
5. the capacity of a computer to combine data according to a rule more accurately than the capacities of humans
6. the standardization of interpretations by eliminating unreliability traceable to differing points of view in professional judgment
7. the potential for systematically gathering and accessing extensive normative data bases that transcend the capacities of human test interpreters
8. the possibility of employing complex scoring and data combination strategies that are not otherwise practical
9. the application of computer-based assessment to special populations

As an example of the latter advantage, Jackson cites the work of Wilson, Thompson, & Wylie (1982), who developed a dental plate activated by the tongue as the mechanism for test response to be used by test takers who lacked the capacity for speech or control of their hands or limbs. The device permitted five distinct responses, depending on the area of the plate depressed by the tongue. As demonstrated by such apparatuses, CAPA would appear to offer a seemingly limitless number of potential applications.

On conventional, paper-and-pencil tests, test takers are usually able to see all of the test's items; they can preview items coming up or review items they have completed. For some test takers, seeing the entire test at one time heightens test anxiety, leading to hurried responses, which may not have been adequately thought out. By contrast, items presented on a computer monitor are presented a few at a time, at most; the respondent typically has no way of knowing the total number of items on the test. Thus, in some cases, administration by computer might lead to more careful attention to items.

Computer programs designed to facilitate the construction of administration, scoring, and interpretation of assessor-made tests, such as teacher-made achievement tests, are proliferating in record numbers. These programs, some with names such as *Make-A-Test* (see Figure 20–1), *Create-A-Test, The Grand Inquisitor,* and *The First National Item Bank and Criterion-Referenced Scoring System,* typically make use of two advantages of computerized testing: the ability to store items in an "item bank" and the ability to individualize testing through a technique called "item branching."

Item banking An *item bank* is a relatively large, easily accessible collection of test questions. Instructors who regularly teach a particular course sometimes create their own item bank of questions they have in the past found to be useful on examinations. One of the many potential advantages of an item bank is accessibility to a large number of test items conveniently classified by subject area, item statistics, or other variables. And just as funds may be added to or withdrawn from a more traditional bank, so may items be added to, withdrawn from, and even modified in an item bank.

Developing a bank of items for an item bank is typically no easy chore; many questions and issues relating to the development of such a bank and to the maintenance of a satisfactory pool of items will need to be resolved (Hiscox, 1983; Hiscox & Brzezinski, 1980). As an introduction to the many potential problems inherent in developing an item bank, consider the following: You are a testing

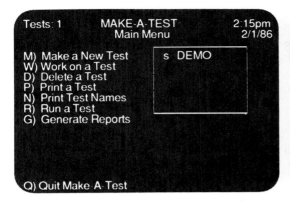

Manager Main Menu Screen: All program options are accessed through simple menu structures. Submenus and prompts help users know available options.

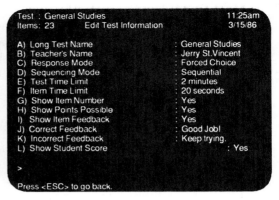

Edit Test Information Screen: Tests of up to 500 items may be given with one of several presentation options.

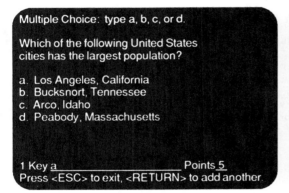

Test Item Creation Screen: Test items are created with a simple text editor. Editing is performed using the same word processing-style editor.

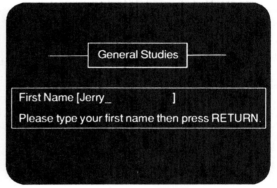

Run a Test Screen: The Run a Test option allows instructor preview of the test in student mode with timing and scoring.

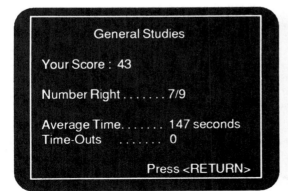

On-Line Test Completion Screen: At the end of a computer-administered test, immediate scoring results can be displayed to the student.

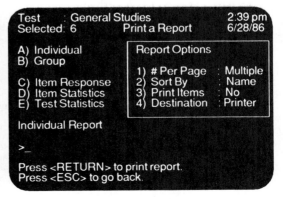

Individual Report Screen: A wide range of report types and styles can be ordered by the user. Reports can also be viewed on-line before printing.

Figure 20–1 *Sample Display Screens from the WICAT Make-A-Test Program.*

consultant who has been asked by a national association of people who go to people's homes and exercise with them—we'll call this group "The Association of Personal Physical Trainers Who Make House Calls (APPTHC)"—to develop an item bank of questions. This item bank will be made up of questions that any physical trainer who makes house calls should reasonably be able to answer. APPTHC officials inform you that their ultimate objective will be to use this item bank to develop an APPTHC certification examination. How would you go about developing such an item bank? What questions would need to be asked?

Struggle with the APPTHC exercise (above) before looking at Table 20–1 (below); as an APPTHC member in good standing might say, "No pain, no gain!"

Table 20–1

Questions to Be Answered in Designing Item Banking Systems

I. Items
    A. *Acquisition and development*
        1. Develop/use your own item collection or use collections of others?
            a. If develop your own item collection, what development procedures will be followed?
            b. If use collections of others, will the items be leased or purchased, and is the classification scheme sufficiently documented and the item format specifications sufficiently compatible for easy transfer and use?
        2. What types of "items" will be permitted?
            a. Will open-ended (constructed response) items, opinion questions, instructional objectives, or descriptions of performance tasks be included in the bank?
            b. Will all the items be made to fit a common format (e.g., all multiple-choice with options a, b, c, and d)?
            c. Must the items be calibrated, validated, or otherwise carry additional information?
        3. What will be the size of the item collection?
            a. How many items per objective/subtopic (collection depth)?
            b. How many different topics (collection breadth)?
        4. What review, tryout, and editing procedures will be used?
            a. Who will perform the review/editing?
            b. Will there be a field tryout, and if so, what statistics will be gathered, and what criteria will be used for inclusion in the bank?
    B. *Classification*
        1. How will the subject matter classifications be performed?
            a. Will the classification by subject matter use fixed categories, keywords, or some combination of the two?
            b. Who will be responsible for preparing, expanding, and refining the taxonomy?
            c. How detailed will the taxonomy be? Will it be hierarchically or non-hierarchically arranged?
            d. Who will assign classification indices to each item, and how will this assignment be verified?
        2. What other assigned information about the items will be stored in the item bank?
        3. What measured information about the items will be stored in the bank? How will the item measures be calculated?*

Table 20–1 (continued)
Questions to Be Answered in Designing Item Banking Systems

713

COMPUTER-
ASSISTED PSY-
CHOLOGICAL
ASSESSMENT

C. *Management*
1. Will provision be made for updating the classification scheme and items? If so:
   a. Who will be permitted to make additions, deletions, and revisions?
   b. What review procedures will be followed?
   c. How will the changes be disseminated?
   d. How will duplicate (or near duplicate) items be detected and eliminated?
   e. When will a revision of an item be trivial enough that item statistics from a previous version can be aggregated with revisions from the current version?
   f. Will item statistics be stored from each use, last use, or aggregated across uses?
2. How will items that require pictures, graphs, special characters, or other types of enhanced printing be handled?
3. How will items that must accompany other items, such as a series of questions about the same reading passage, be handled?

II. Tests
A. *Assembly*
1. Must the test constructor specify the specific items to appear on the test or will the items be selected by computer?
2. If the items are selected by computer:
   a. How will one item out of several that matches the search specification be selected (randomly, time since last usage, frequency of previous use)?
   b. What happens if no item meets the search specifications?
   c. Will a test constructor have the option to reject a selected item, and if so, what will be the mechanism for doing so?
   d. What precautions will be taken to ensure that examinees who are tested more than once do not receive the same items?
3. What item or test parameters can be specified for test assembly (item format restrictions, limits on difficulty levels, expected score distribution, expected test reliability, etc.)?
4. What assembly procedures will be available (options to multiple-choice items placed in random order, the test items placed in random order, different items on each test)?
5. Will the system print tests or just specify which items to use? If the former, how will the tests be printed or duplicated and where will the answers be displayed?

B. *Administration, scoring, and reporting*
1. Will the system be capable of on-line test administration? If so:
   a. How will access be managed?
   b. Will test administration be adaptive, and if so, using what procedures?
2. Will the system provide for test scoring? If so:
   a. What scoring formula will be used (rights only, correction for guessing, partial credit for some answers, weighting by discrimination values)?
   b. How will constructed responses be evaluated (off-line by the instructor, on-line/off-line by examiners comparing their answers to a key, on-line by computer with/without employing a spelling algorithm)?
3. Will the system provide for test reporting? If so:
   a. What records will be kept (the tests themselves, individual student item responses, individual student test scores, school or other group scores) and for how long? Will new scores for individuals and groups supplement or replace old scores?
   b. What reporting options (content/format) will be available?
   c. To whom will the reports be sent?

Table 20–1 (*continued*)

Questions to Be Answered in Designing Item Banking Systems

    C. *Evaluation*
       1. Will reliability and validity data be collected? If so, what data will be collected by whom, and how will they be used?
       2. Will norms be made available and, if so, based on what norm-referenced measures?
 III. System
    A. *Acquisition and development*
       1. Who will be responsible for acquisition/development, given what resources, and operating under what constraints?
       2. Will the system be made transportable to others? What levels and what degree of documentation will be available?
    B. *Software/hardware features*
       1. What aspects of the system will be computer assisted?
         a. Where will the items be stored (computer, paper, card file)?
         b. Will requests be filled using a batch, on-line, or manual mode?
       2. Will a microcomputer be used and, if so, what special limits does such a choice place on item text, item bank size, and test development options?
       3. Will items be stored as one large collection or will separate files be maintained for each user?
       4. How will the item banking system be constructed (from scratch; by piecing together word processing, data-base management, and other general purpose programs; by adopting existing item banking systems)?
       5. What specific equipment will be needed (for storage, retrieval, interactions with the system, etc.)?
       6. How user and maintenance friendly will the equipment and support programs be?
       7. Who will be responsible for equipment maintenance?
    C. *Monitoring and training*
       1. What system features will be monitored (number of items per classification category, usage by user group, number of revisions until a user is satisfied, distribution of test lengths or other test characteristics, etc.)?
       2. Who will monitor the system, train users, and give support (initially, ongoing)?
       3. How will information about changes in system procedures be disseminated?
    D. *Access and security*
       1. Who will have access to the items and other information in the bank (authors/owners, teachers, students)? Who can request tests?
       2. Will users have direct access to the system or must they go through an intermediary?
       3. What procedures will be followed to secure the contents of the item bank (if they are to be secure)?
       4. Where will the contents of the item bank be housed (centrally or will each user also have a copy)?
       5. Who will have access to score reports?
 IV. Use and Acceptance
    A. *General*
       1. Who decides to what uses the item bank will be put? And will these uses be the ones that the test users need and want?
       2. Who will develop the tests and who will be allowed to use the system? Will these people be acceptable to the examinees and recipients of the test information?
       3. Will the system be able to handle the expected demand for use?
       4. Is the output of the system likely to be used and used as intended?
       5. How will user acceptance and item bank credibility be enhanced?

Table 20–1 (*continued*)

Questions to Be Answered in Designing Item Banking Systems

715

COMPUTER-
ASSISTED PSY-
CHOLOGICAL
ASSESSMENT

B. *Instructional improvement.* If this is an intended use:
  1. Will the item bank be part of a larger instructional/decision-making system?
  2. Which textbooks, curriculum guidelines, and other materials, if any, will be keyed to the bank's items? Who will make that decision and how will the assignments be validated?
  3. Will items be available for drill and practice as well as for testing?
  4. Will information be available to users that will assist in the diagnosis of educational needs?

C. *Adaptive testing.* If this is an option:
  1. How will the scheduling of the test administrations take place?
  2. How will the items be selected to ensure testing efficiency yet maintain content representation and avoid duplication between successive test administrations?
  3. What criteria will be used to terminate testing?
  4. What scoring procedures will be followed?

D. *Certification of competence.* If this is an intended use:
  1. Will the item bank contain measures that cover all the important component skills of the competence being assessed?
  2. How many attempts at passing the test will be allowed; when? How will these attempts be monitored?

E. *Program/curriculum evaluation.* If this is an intended use:
  1. Will it be possible to implement the system so as to provide reliable measures of student achievement in a large number of specific performance areas?
  2. Will the item bank contain measures that cover all the important stated objectives of the curriculum? That go beyond the stated objectives of the curriculum?
  3. Will the item bank yield commensurable data that permit valid comparisons over time?

F. *Testing and reporting requirements imposed by external agencies.* If meeting these requirements is an intended use:
  1. Will the system be able to handle requirements for program evaluation, student selection for specially funded programs, assessing educational needs, and reporting?
  2. Will the system be able to accommodate minor modifications in the testing and reporting requirements?

V. Costs
  A. *Cost feasibility*
    1. What are the (fixed, variable) costs (financial, time, space, equipment, and supplies) to create and support the system?
    2. Are these costs affordable?
  B. *Cost comparisons*
    1. How do the item banking system costs compare to the present or other testing systems that achieve the same goals?
    2. Do any expanded capabilities justify the extra cost? Are any restricted capabilities balanced by cost savings?

---

*This question is the subject of considerable controversy and discussion in the technical measurement literature. For example, to obtain a latent trait difficulty parameter, concern has been expressed about sample size, calibration procedure (Rasch, 3-parameter), linking models (major axis, least squares, maximum likelihood), and number of items common to the equating forms.
Source: Millman and Arter (1984).

Item branching   One of the major advantages of computer-based test admin-istration is the capability of *item branching*—the ability of the computer to tailor the content and order of presentation of test items on the basis of responses to previous items. A computer may have a bank, for example, of achievement test items of different difficulty levels. The computer may be programmed (1) not to present an item of the next difficulty level until two consecutive items of the pre-vious difficulty level are answered correctly, and (2) to terminate the test when five consecutive items of a given level of difficulty have been answered incor-rectly. Alternatively, the pattern of items to which the test taker is exposed may be based not on the test taker's response to preceding items but on a random drawing from the total pool of test items. Green (1984) commented on the advan-tage of such a procedure:

> Conventional tests can be compromised by theft of test forms, or by each of several applicants memorizing a few items for later mutual benefit. Future applicants can then be coached on specific item content, or even furnished with test answer keys. But when the computer selects items at random from its pool, each applicant gets a different test form, and such specific coaching is much less effective. In fact, if the item pool is sufficiently large and exten-sive, it can be published for all to see, on the grounds that anyone who can answer all these items, knows the material being tested.

Green went on to cite the case of a computer-administered driving-license test—the written portion—as an instance that might be particularly amenable to the administration of randomly drawn items. And given a large enough bank of items, it would even be possible to keep a record of the items administered to an applicant on a first administration of the test—an administration on which the applicant did not receive a passing score—and randomly draw from the remaining (unused) items in the bank for succeeding administrations to the same applicant.

Jackson (1986) mused about how item branching might be employed in a computer-administered personality test, the better to get a more accurate picture of the test taker:

> If a respondent has already responded to four items in such a way as to deny visual hallucinations, it would be reasonable to conclude that this [is] a less fruitful avenue of investigation than that of depression, where three or four items have been endorsed. By selecting items to present to the respondent from the depression area, one might obtain a more complete and accurate picture of psychopathology in terms of such sub-dimensions as suicidal ten-dencies, despair over the future, fatigue and eating disorders. (p. 11)

Another potential application of item-branching technology in personality tests has to do with the monitoring of the purposefulness of examinees' re-sponses. Should a profile of responses appear indicative of a situation wherein the examinee is responding in nonpurposive or inconsistent fashion or in a manner indicative of faking, the computer may be programmed to respond in a prescribed way such as by admonishing the respondent to be more careful and/or refusing to proceed until a purposive response is given. For example, on a computer-based true/false test, if the examinee responds "True" to an item such as "I spent Christmas in Beirut last year," there would be reason to suspect that the examinee is responding nonpurposively, randomly, or in some way other than genuinely.

You might conclude at this point in our overview that automation has done for psychological assessment exactly what it has done in many other spheres of daily living—greatly enhanced the quality of life. Is this, in fact, the case?

As our overview continues, you will become acquainted with some of the problems and issues that the rush to computer technology has left in its wake. Subsequently, we'll examine some of the more technical pros, cons, and issues associated with CAPA.

The Disadvantages

The test-taker's perspective   From the perspective of a test taker, particularly a test taker who is not "computer savvy" or experienced, a computer-administered test may be in itself an intimidating experience. Test takers may find themselves prevented from engaging in various test-taking strategies that have worked for them in the past, such as previewing or reviewing test materials and skipping around to answer only questions they are certain of first. Examinees whose practice it is to skim through and survey all of the items on a test at the outset may not be able to do so during a computerized test administration. Typically, an answer is required to an item before the computer's cursor proceeds to the next. Having completed the test or any portion of it, test takers may be electronically prohibited from reviewing previously entered answers. During the test, because an answer may be required before the next item is presented for response, the examinee is deprived of the option of purposefully omitting items. And because every item must be answered (and in many instances verified with a prompt from the computer, such as "You answered TRUE; if that is correct press RETURN"), the computer administration of a test may actually take longer than the administration of the same test via paper and pencil. Note, however, that computer administrations of tests typically take less time than conventional administrations (White, Clements, & Fowler, 1985).

The test user's perspective   A great paradox of the computer era is that although such technology is designed to be time-saving, many long hours must frequently be invested reading tomes of documentation—perhaps even a number of ancillary books written as easy guides to the primary books—before the technology can be used. Once the obstacle of learning to use computer software and/or specially designed hardware is overcome, and the inevitable "bugs" have been worked out, other problems may arise.

In contrast to psychological tests administered by clinicians themselves, automated test administrations are typically designed for administration by a nonprofessional member of the clinician's staff, or for self-administration by the assessee. Thus, in contrast to the clinician-administered test, an automated testing situation may provide diminished, if any, opportunity for the assessor to (1) establish a rapport with the assessee, (2) observe the assessee's test-taking behavior, and (3) note any unusual extra-test conditions that may have affected responses.

When computers are used to administer tests, they can be "tied up" for relatively long periods of time and clinicians, as a result, deprived of their use. For example, although some test takers can complete a computer-administered version of the MMPI-2 in as little as 45 minutes, others may take as long as two hours. Given that a clerk can key in all 567 MMPI-2 responses from an answer sheet in about five minutes or so, and given that an optical mark reader could process an answer sheet in less than five seconds, why should the computer be tied up for as long as two hours?

The age of computers has brought with it new kinds of crime: computer theft and computer mischief, the latter exemplified by computer "viruses" capable of altering or erasing a computer's memory. Just as clinicians have for decades protected the security of tests and test data with tools such as locked, steel filing cabinets, so clinicians who use CAPA technology have the obligation of protecting these tests and test data. A significant obstacle modern clinicians face, however, is the time and expense entailed in keeping up with the latest and most effective means of electronic security.

Perhaps the most vexing concern of clinicians who use computerized assessment software, particularly software that provides automated interpretations of findings, concerns the paucity of studies documenting the validity of computer-generated interpretations of findings (Spielberger & Piotrowski, 1990). A related question has to do with the equivalence of data obtained from a computerized version of a test with data derived from the more traditional paper-and-pencil administration.

One way to conceptualize CAPA-related products and services is in terms of computer inputs and outputs; that is, what goes into and what comes out of the computer. Below we delve in detail into the intricacies of CAPA in terms of input and output.

COMPUTER INPUT

For purposes of discussion, let's dichotomize "computer input" into two categories: (1) the test taker's input of responses directly into a computer—a process referred to as *on-line test administration*—and (2) the test user's input of assessees' responses into a computer for the purpose of scoring and/or interpretation.

On-line Test Administration

Most tests that are currently available for on-line administration were originally developed for conventional (that is, paper-and-pencil) administration. A primary concern of test users is how factors related to on-line test administration—factors that are irrelevant to the original design of the test—might influence test-taker performance. For example, in a computer-assisted administration of a test, test takers typically must enter their responses through a keyboard. But what if the test taker is woefully unfamiliar with it? In some tests, such as one in which the test taker's task is to quickly list words (as in some tests of divergent thinking or creativity), the test takers unfamiliar with computer keyboards are penalized. Concerns have also been expressed regarding the applicability of published norms and of reliability and validity data; typically such data are obtained using conventional test administrations, and generalizing these data to a computer-assisted test administration is risky, at best, and inappropriate, at worst.

"Can scores on a conventionally administered test be considered equivalent to scores on a computer-assisted administration of the same test?" Ultimately, this question will have to be answered on an individual, test-by-test basis. In general, research into the equivalency of test scores as a function of method of administration has focused on, among other variables, the effect of item type, item content, and the test taker's attitude. A brief sampling of representative research in each of these areas follows.

Effects of item type   There is evidence that certain types of items may yield significantly different scores as a function of the mode of test administration. Significant differences in scores on speeded arithmetic tests as a function of whether the tests were conventionally administered or computer-administered have been found (Greaud & Green, 1986). By contrast, on tests involving mostly multiple-choice and true-false items, the two modes of test administration were deemed equivalent (Hoffman & Lundberg, 1976). A clear exception to the latter finding was matching-type items: the computer presentation of matching items resulted in significantly lower scores, different numbers of changed responses, and different patterns of changed responses, as compared to conventionally presented matching items.

On paper-and-pencil tests, a test taker can, by design or omission, fail to respond to a particular item by not placing pencil to paper to respond to it. But in a mode of test administration whereby the computer will not proceed unless an item is responded to in some way, the test taker who wishes not to respond is compelled, in some way, to enter this "nonresponse." This fact of life of computerized test adminsitration has implications for the data obtained in many types of tests, including personality tests (Honaker, 1988). For example, when the Adjective Checklist is administered by computer, respondents must actively reject an adjective, rather than passively fail to endorse it—a fact that may lead to differences in scores (Allred & Harris, 1984).

Effects of item content   The content of items—whether, for example, they call for the respondent to reveal something very personal—may also be affected by mode of administration of the item. Writing decades ago, Smith (1963) mused that test takers might prefer an impersonal computer to face-to-face contact when "confession-type" questions were being asked. This hypothesis has been explored in a number of studies, some of which have yielded conflicting findings. In one study (Skinner & Allen, 1983), no differences were found in respondents' willingness to describe their alcohol and illegal drug use when using a paper-and-pencil questionnaire or a computer, though such differences have been observed by others (Evan & Miller, 1969; Hart & Goldstein, 1985; Koson, Kitchen, Kochen, & Stodolsky, 1970). Koson et al. (1970) found that females tended to be more honest than males on computerized tests. More pathological MMPI scores were found as a function of computerized versus conventional test administration (Bresolin, 1984). Rezmovic (1977) found mode-of-administration effects most pronounced at the extreme ends of a distribution of test scores; computer administration caused extreme scorers to become even more extreme.

Although studies both support and fail to support the "honest confession to an impersonal computer" hypothesis, perhaps the most reasonable conclusion on the basis of the available literature is that nonequivalence as a function of mode of test administration is typically small enough to be of no practical consequence (Beaumont & French, 1987; Harrell & Lombardo, 1984; Holden & Hickman, 1987; Honaker, Harrell, & Buffaloe, 1988; Lukin, Dowd, Plake, & Kraft, 1985).

The test taker's attitude and emotional reaction   Most people have favorable attitudes regarding computerized test administration (Burke, Normand, & Raju, 1987; French & Beaumont, 1987; Honaker, 1988; Llabre, Clements, Fitzhugh, & Lancelotta, 1987), even if a computer is initially more anxiety-provoking than paper-and-pencil questionnaires (Lushene, O'Neil, & Dunn, 1974). Indeed, many people even seem to prefer computer to conventional testing (Bresolin, 1984; Honaker, 1988; Rozensky, Honor, Rasinski, Tovian, & Herz, 1986).

There is, however, a minority of test takers who are uncomfortable with computerized testing. The elderly compose one demographic group who tend to be uncomfortable with keyboards, monitors, and other even more exotic instruments of assessment (Carr, Wilson, Ghosh, Ancil, & Woods, 1982; Volans & Levy, 1982). Whether or not such discomfort with automated tools significantly affects test scores has yet to be explored.

Inputting Data from Tests

Placing yourself in the shoes of a test user, consider some of your options with regard to having the tests you administer scored and/or interpreted: central processing, teleprocessing, and local processing.

Central processing   Central processing entails sending test protocols completed (usually using the traditional paper-and-pencil method) at one location to some other central location for processing; that is, for scoring and/or interpretation. The results may then be returned to the test user via an oral report by telephone or by a written report via mail, fax, or other delivery system. An example of central processing is the Roche Psychiatric Service Institute service for computerized scoring of MMPI protocols.

Because ownership of any expensive equipment is not required, the chief advantage of central processing is its low cost. Particularly when test results do not have to be "turned around" very quickly, and when there are large numbers of protocols to be processed, central processing offers the most economical test-scoring and interpretation alternative. Clincians who test clients only on occasion, or companies, such as personnel selection firms testing large numbers of people, may find central processing to be best suited to their needs.

As the prices of technology such as microcomputers and optical mark readers continue to go down, and as mailing, shipping, and related costs rise, the cost-efficiency edge of central processing will dwindle. Another factor militating against widespread future use of central processing is the increasingly interactive nature of many tests. More and more computer-administered tests are designed to be individually tailored to the responses of the test taker; that is, the sequence, even the total number of items administered to a test taker, may depend on responses to previous questions. Users of central processing can only administer tests with a fixed item sequence.

Teleprocessing   The processing of test data at a remote location via telephone lines is referred to as *teleprocessing*. An interface between a personal computer and the central computer, called a *modem,* may be used to send the raw data in and receive the processed scores and/or interpretive data back. Test users pay a fee to the company offering teleprocessing services. The user must also pay for the telephone time charges, which can be substantial if large numbers of tests are being processed. In general, teleprocessing represents an attractive alternative to central processing because test results are available in minutes.

Teleprocessing is also an attractive alternative to local processing (see below) because start-up costs are much lower. The only equipment needed for teleprocessing is a data communications terminal. Such a terminal, which does nothing but transmit, receive, and print data, can be purchased for a few hundred dollars. Alternatively, many relatively inexpensive microcomputers can be adapted for use as a data communications terminal. Further, such relatively inexpensive microcomputers purchased for the purpose of teleprocessing, can "double" in some other capacity (such as a word processor, a computer bulletin board, or some other non-assessment-related application) during down time.

Perhaps the chief disadvantage of teleprocessing is its inavailability for processing many different types of tests.

Local processing   Local processing refers to on-site computer processing, whether by home microcomputer, optical mark reader, or some other automated technology. A microcomputer used for local test processing can also be used for teleprocessing, though the reverse isn't necessarily true; software used for local test processing is typically available only for the most popular microcomputers.

The two primary advantages of local processing for the test user are control and flexibility. By having the system entirely "in-house," the test user has total control over every facet of the processing of the tests, including factors such as hours of operation and down time, when servicing of the system will take place, and quality control of the operation. And because the user of local processing typically has at least one powerful computer on the premises, the flexibility to use that computer for test administration purposes—or some other non-assessment-related purpose—is another advantage.

Software for local test processing is plentiful; such software is not necessarily published by the test publisher and may be produced by any number of competing manufacturers. Most software for local test processing yields an interpretive report but seldom contains a program for administering the test or a scoring program. This is because of legal issues surrounding ownership of the items in the test and the system used to score the test. Test items and scoring information are owned by the test developer or publisher and cannot legally be copied into a computer without the owner's permission—permission that is seldom forthcoming. Central processing and teleprocessing services that involve scoring are only available legally from the test publisher or licensees. By contrast, local processing involves the generation of interpretive findings (in various forms, such as a narrative report), based on scoring that was done either by hand or by owner-licensed computer software. Most test publishers offer only one "official" interpretive system for a given application of a particular test, though independent companies may offer a variety of test-interpretation software.

The costs of launching local-processing services, including the cost of purchasing computer hardware and software, and the time that must be invested to
get the system running properly are the major potential disadvantages of such
testing services.

Computer Output

Perhaps the most fundamental "output question" is, "What does the computer
put out when I use this product or service, and does whatever it puts out meet my
needs and objectives?" To state this another way, the questions a prospective user
might ask about a test-interpretation service or test-interpretation software product include: "What is the output? Will I get a simple scoring report such as a tally
of scores? item analysis data? graphically drawn profiles? an interpretive report
complete with a narrative summary? Is this computer output service appropriate
and feasible for use with this client? Is it feasible for me as a user in terms of cost
and time considerations?"

Generally, two broad categories of computer output options exist, each with
at least one subcategory: scoring reports and interpretive reports.

Scoring Reports

Simple scoring reports   With simple scoring reports, the name says it all—
what you get are test scores. Some tests, such as vocational interest inventories
that contain over a hundred scales (for example, the Strong), are much too cumbersome—if not impossible—to score by hand. The scores may be listed or
drawn on a profile. Some tests, such as the 13 scales of the MMPI in use since the
test was first published, can readily be scored by hand; it takes approximately a
minute to hand-score and plot each scale. But what if you had dozens of protocols
to score? Or what if you wished to make use of any of the hundreds of MMPI
special scales that have been developed in the years since the test was first published? In such instances, time considerations dictate that the most prudent approach would be automated scoring. The scoring of tests with as few as 20 scales,
with each protocol costing approximately five dollars for a computer-generated
simple scoring report, is typically less expensive and more accurate than having
a trained clerk manually do the same job. And given the dollar value of a clinician's time, automated scoring represents a great advantage over hand scoring;
few clinicians would consider scoring large numbers of tests or large numbers of
scales by hand.

Extended scoring reports   A scoring report that also contains detailed statistical output but little or no case-specific narrative is referred to as an *extended scoring report* (Zachary, 1984). Extended scoring reports are particularly useful when
it is important for the test user to know at a glance whether certain differences
between subtest or scale scores are statistically significant, or merely the result of
measurement error. Extended scoring reports that provide key statistical information about the results, as well as the relationships between the various subtests
or scales for intelligence tests, ability tests, neuropsychological test batteries, and
vocational interest tests, can provide a great deal of information in a glance to the

trained eye. Figure 20–2 illustrates an extended scoring report from the Jackson Vocational Interest Survey.

Interpretive Reports

When raw assessment data are fed into a computer, in many cases it is possible to get back output that goes much further than a mere reporting of scores, profiles, or statistics; it is possible to obtain a written interpretation of the findings, referred to as an *interpretive report*. The process of computer-assisted test interpretation (CATI) may yield one or another, or some combination, of the following types of interpretive reports: a descriptive report, a screening report, and/or a consultative report.

Descriptive reports "Description" in the term *descriptive report* refers to a comment—typically a most succinct and to-the-point comment—on each of the scales on the test (see Figure 20–3). Such reports are especially helpful when a particular test contains scales reported in terms of different types of standard scores or different normative samples; such reports allow the test user to quickly identify the most important scores.

Screening reports Screening reports typically supply more information than descriptive reports; comments are not necessarily limited to one scale at a time, and interpretation of the relationship between different scales may be provided.

A computerized screening report may present the results of a dedicated screening instrument—that is, a self-contained test used solely for screening or screening data regarding particular variables from some other test. In the latter context, various computerized screening reports based on an MMPI administration have been developed. One such "screener" (as it may be referred to in the vernacular of industry professionals) is The Minnesota Report: Personnel Screening System for the MMPI (University of Minnesota, 1984; see Figure 20–4). Although this screening device is based on the MMPI, there is no direct correspondence between any scale on it and any one MMPI scale. Rather, a complex set of decision rules govern the scale values that will emerge on The Minnesota Report—and ultimately the interpretations that will be made. For example, in order for this screening report to spew out an interpretive comment (such as "The client may keep problems to himself too much"), the following conditions must be met:

- Lie and Correction scales are greater than the Infrequency scale, *and*
- the Infrequency scale is less than a T-score of 55, *and*
- the Depression, Paranoia, Psychasthenia, and Schizophrenia scales are less than a T-score of 65, *and*
- the Conversion Hysteria scale is greater than 69T, *or*
- the Need for Affection subscale is greater than 63T, *or*
- the Conversion Hysteria scale is greater than 64T, and the Denial of Social Anxiety subscale or Inhibition of Aggression subscale is greater than 59T, *or*
- the Repression scale is greater than 59T, *or*
- the Brooding subscale is greater than 59T.

Figure 20–2 *An Extended Scoring Report.* In the Jackson Vocational Interest Survey
(JVIS), Jackson (1984b) provides statistical indices of similarity between JVIS profiles and
the average profiles of large groups of people holding similar jobs or having the same
college majors. Note that the "scores" in this excerpt from the computer-generated (extended scoring) report don't look like any test scores you've seen recently; in fact, they
may look like something else—such as correlations. That's exactly what they are! For
example, the score of -0.57 on Agriculture indicates that this test taker's profile of scores
on the various JVIS scales correlates poorly with the average JVIS profile of college students studying agriculture; the report indicates that the similarity to such students is
"very low."

Note that this application of a coefficient of correlation is different from the more
typical types of applications that appear elsewhere in this book. Instead of correlating
two scores, each produced by a large group of people, a large number of scores produced
by one person is correlated with the average of those same scores for various groups—
such as agriculture students, student counselors, and so forth. Because so many correlations must be calculated, the JVIS must be computer-scored.

```
Respondent-CASE, M .          1234567890    Male    16-JUL-91    Page   5


       **************************************************
       *****     UNIVERSITY MAJOR FIELD CLUSTERS     *****
       **************************************************


   JVIS   profiles   from  over  10,000  university  students  who  were   enrolled   in
   more  than  150  different  major  fields,  ranging  from  accounting  to  zoology,
   have  been  collected  and  analyzed.     That  analysis  indicated  that  the  major
   fields  could  be  classed  into  17  broad  academic  clusters.     Each  cluster   is
   based   on   data   from   both   males   and   females   and   represents   a   set   of
   educational  majors  that  shared  a  similar  pattern  of  JVIS  scores.

   The   profile   below   describes   the   similarity  of  your  JVIS   Basic   Interest
   Profile  to  each  of  the  student  clusters.     A  high  score  indicates  that  your
   pattern   of  interests  is  similar  to  students  in  the  fields  of  concentration
   defining   the   cluster,   while   a   low   score   indicates   dissimilarity.      These
   scores  indicate  your  probable  interest  and  satisfaction  with  these  academic
   major   fields.     These   scores   do   not   tell   you   whether   or   not   you   will   be
   succesful  in  any  particular  field.

   Following   the   profile   is   a   brief   analysis   of   the   three   academic   clusters
   most   similar   to   your   pattern   of   interest,   together   with   sample   areas   of
   specialization.

                                      DISSIMILAR                         SIMILAR
                                      -1.0      -.5      0.0      +.5        1.0
                                R  .       .        .        .        .
   Agribusiness & Economics      -0.16 XXXXXXXXXXXXXXXXX
   Environmental Resource Mgt.   -0.43 XXXXXXXXXXX
   Education                     +0.49 XXXXXXXXXXXXXXXXXXXXXXXXXXXXXXXXX
   Health,Physical Educ. & Rec   +0.08 XXXXXXXXXXXXXXXXXXXXXXX
   Mathematical Sciences         -0.42 XXXXXXXXXXXX

   Engineering                   -0.60 XXXXXXXXX
   Food Science                  -0.34 XXXXXXXXXXXXX
   Art & Architecture            -0.60 XXXXXXXXX
   Communication Arts            +0.26 XXXXXXXXXXXXXXXXXXXXXXXXXX
   Science                       -0.51 XXXXXXXXXXX

   Health Services & Science     -0.17 XXXXXXXXXXXXXXXXX
   Business                      +0.51 XXXXXXXXXXXXXXXXXXXXXXXXXXXXXXXXXX
   Behavioral Science            +0.45 XXXXXXXXXXXXXXXXXXXXXXXXXXXXXXX
   Social Science,Law & Politi   +0.35 XXXXXXXXXXXXXXXXXXXXXXXXXXXX
   Performing Arts               +0.18 XXXXXXXXXXXXXXXXXXXXXXX

   Computer Science              -0.10 XXXXXXXXXXXXXXXXXXX
   Social Service                +0.49 XXXXXXXXXXXXXXXXXXXXXXXXXXXXXXXX

   Your   JVIS   profile   is   most   similar   to   university   students   whose   academic
   areas  of  specialization  are  in  the  following  three  field  clusters:

   Business
   Social Service
   Education

   Sample  majors  for  each  of  these  three  areas  are  listed  below.


         MAJOR FIELD CLUSTER                    SAMPLE MAJORS
   --------------------------    --------------------------------------------
   Business                      Finance, Industrial Engineering, Accounting,
                                 Business, Administration and Management,
                                 Agricultural Business Management, Marketing.

   Social Service                Social Welfare, Education and Exceptional
                                 Children, Psychology, Speech Pathology and
                                 Audiology, Individual and Family Studies,
                                 Rehabilitation Education.

   Education                     Secondary Education, Music Education,
                                 Special Education, Elementary and
                                 Kindergarten, Counselor Education.
```

Figure 20-2   *(continued)*

725

COMPUTER-
ASSISTED PSY-
CHOLOGICAL
ASSESSMENT

```
Respondent-CASE, M .          1234567890    Male    16-JUL-91   Page  6

         ********************************************************
         *****   SIMILARITY TO OCCUPATIONAL CLASSIFICATIONS   *****
         ********************************************************

Below  are  ranked the occupational classifications found to be similar  to
your interest profile.  A positive score indicates that your profile  shows
some  degree  of  similarity  to those already working  in  the  occupational
cluster, while a negative score indicates dissimilarity.

SCORE     SIMILARITY               OCCUPATIONAL CLASSIFICATION
------    ----------------         --------------------------------------------
+0.66  VERY SIMILAR        Teaching and Related Occupations
+0.64  VERY SIMILAR        Counselors / Student Personnel Workers
+0.59  SIMILAR             Occupations in Pre-school and Elementary Teaching
+0.56  SIMILAR             Administrative and Related Occupations
+0.49  SIMILAR             Clerical Services
+0.48  SIMILAR             Assembly Occupations-Instruments & Small Products
+0.46  SIMILAR             Occupations in Religion
+0.43  SIMILAR             Occupations in Social Welfare
+0.42  SIMILAR             Occupations in Accounting, Banking and Finance
+0.40  SIMILAR             Personnel / Human Management
+0.38  MODERATELY SIMILAR  Sales Occupations
+0.36  MODERATELY SIMILAR  Occupations in Law and Politics
+0.36  MODERATELY SIMILAR  Service Occupations
+0.26  MODERATELY SIMILAR  Occupations in Merchandising
+0.17  NEUTRAL             Occupations in Social Science
+0.01  NEUTRAL             Occupations in Writing
+0.01  NEUTRAL             Occupations in Music
-0.12  NEUTRAL             Protective Services Occupations
-0.13  NEUTRAL             Sport and Recreation Occupations
-0.16  NEUTRAL             Health Service Workers
-0.20  NEUTRAL             Military Officers
-0.23  NEUTRAL             Agriculturalists
-0.29  DISSIMILAR          Occupations in Entertainment
-0.45  DISSIMILAR          Mathematical and Related Occupations
-0.45  DISSIMILAR          Medical Diagnosis and Treatment Occupations
-0.48  DISSIMILAR          Occupations in Fine Art
-0.49  DISSIMILAR          Construction / Skilled Trades
-0.49  DISSIMILAR          Occupations in The Physical Sciences
-0.51  DISSIMILAR          Life Sciences
-0.53  DISSIMILAR          Engineering and Technical Support Workers
-0.56  DISSIMILAR          Machining / Mechanical and Related Occupations
-0.57  DISSIMILAR          Occupations in Commercial Art
```

Figure 20-3   *A Descriptive Computer-Assisted Test Interpretation.* The MMPI report developed at the Mayo Clinic in Rochester, Minnesota (Rome et al., 1965), was one of the earliest examples of a descriptive, computer-assisted test-interpretation report. Note the characteristically brief but descriptive comment after each of the scale codes ("D," "Pt," etc.). Note that the scales are interpreted in descending order of elevation and that, in this case, no interpretation is provided for the Hy scale.

NCS (MAYO) MMPI ANALYSIS

Sex: Male. Education: 20. Age: 34. Marital Status: Married. Outpatient.
MMPI Code: 27"5'8064–391/–KLF/

D   2 Severely depressed, worrying, indecisive, and pessimistic
Pt   7 Rigid and meticulous. Worrisome and apprehensive. Dissatisfied
       with social relationships. Probably very religious and moralistic
MfM 5 Probably sensitive and idealistic with high esthetic, cultural, and
       artistic interests
Sc   8 Tends toward abstract interests such as science, philosophy, and
       religion
Si   0 Probably retiring and shy in social situations
Pa   6 Sensitive. Alive to opinions of others
Pd   4 Independent or mildly nonconformist
Hy   3
Ma   9 Normal energy and activity level
Hs   1 Number of physical symptoms and concern about bodily
       functions fairly typical for clinic patients
Consider psychiatric evaluation

THE MINNESOTA PERSONNEL SCREENING REPORT TM*   Page 1
                                                   TM
        for the Minnesota Multiphasic Personality Inventory

                  By James N. Butcher, Ph.D.

    Client No.   : 000067890   Gender: Male
    Report Date : 7-JAN-86   Age: 23
    PAS Code Number: 531 0002
    Occupation: Flight Crew

                ****
                *   OPENNESS TO EVALUATION   *
                ****

    OVERLY   QUITE   OVERLY
    FRANK   OPEN   ADEQUATE   CAUTIOUS   GUARDED   INDETERMINATE

    -------------------------------------x----------------------------

                ****
                *   SOCIAL FACILITY   *
                ****

                                      PROBLEMS
    EXCELLENT GOOD   ADEQUATE   POSSIBLE   POOR   INDETERMINATE

    --x---------------------

    NOTE: This MMPI report can serve as a useful guide for employment
    descisions in which personality adjustment is considered important for
    success on the job. The decision rules on which these classifications
    are based were developed through a review of the empirical literature
    on the use of the MMPI with "normal-range" individuals (including job
    applicants) and the author's practical experience using the test in
    employment selection. The report can assist psychologists and physicans
    involved in personnel selection by providing an "outside opinion" about
    the applicant's adjustment. The MMPI should NOT be used as the SOLE
    means of determining the applicant's suitability for employment. The
    information in this report should be used by qualified test
    interpretation specialists ONLY.

                MINNESOTA MULTIPHASIC PERSONALITY INVENTORY
                 Copyright THE UNIVERSITY OF MINNESOTA
         1943, renewed 1970. This report 1983. All rights reserved.
        Scored and Distributed Exclusively by NCS PROFESSIONAL ASSESSMENT
           SERVICES Under Licence from the University of Minnesota

    *   "The Minnesota Personnel Screening Report," "MMPI," and
    "Minnesota Multiphasic Personality Inventory" are trademarks owned by
    the University Press of the University of Minnesota.

Figure 20–4 *A Computer-Assisted Test Interpretation Screening Report.* This excerpt from the interpretive output of the Minnesota Report: Personnel Screening System for the MMPI and MMPI-2 developed by Butcher (1989; University of Minnesota, 1984) is deceptively simple; complex decision rules underlie each of the possible ratings.

Screening reports may prove useful in alerting test users to patterns of test findings that may require further investigation. Suppose you were a psychologist responsible for screening the mental health of applicants for state police positions in your state. And let's further suppose that you were using The Minnesota Report for that purpose. This instrument might interpret as "suspect" the mental health of a candidate whose test responses indicated that the applicant (1) is a thrill-seeker who, among other things, enjoys fast cars and shooting guns, (2) is obsessive to the extent that the ability to act effectively in an emergency is impaired, and/or (3) may have a substance abuse problem.

Before denying employment with the state police to an applicant with such a pattern of test findings, further investigation would be required. For example, it may well be that in your state, just about every current employee on the force in your state scored high in thrill seeking on this instrument. Further, it may be the case that officers who have had long, satisfying, and successful careers in administrative and clerical state police positions scored high in obsessiveness. As for the finding of substance abuse, further investigation here might take the form of a blood test, a urinalysis, and/or research into other medical records. It would not be enough to merely suspect substance abuse on the basis of a screening report; before a momentous decision such as the denial of employment is made, you would have to *know* that such abuse was indeed taking place.

Consultative reports   A consultative report is one that provides a detailed analysis of test data in language appropriate for communication between testing professionals (Dahlstrom, Welsh, & Dahlstrom, 1972). Of the various types of computerized reports that are available, a consultative report is perhaps the one most readily associated with "computer-assisted test interpretation" in the minds of most psychologists. In a manner analogous to a professional consultation, a consultative report provides a test user with the expert opinion of an individual, or group of individuals, who may have devoted years of study to the interpretation of a particular instrument. The Roche Psychiatric Service Institute system for interpreting the MMPI was the first such system to produce consultative reports. Ideally, a consultative report generated by a computer is in many ways indistinguishable from a report written by a highly trained and knowledgeable testing professional. An example, this one a Personality Inventory for Children Report, can be found within the chapter Close-up.

ISSUES IN CAPA

Various issues associated with mechanizing aspects of psychological assessment have always existed, though the recent explosion of technology has brought with it a greater urgency to resolve satisfactorily these issues. In general, many of these issues can be categorized as relating to aspects of (1) computer-assisted test administration, (2) computer-assisted test interpretation, (3) access to CAPA products, and (4) standards for CAPA products.

Computer-Assisted Test Administration: Equivalency

The key issue regarding the computerized administration of tests that were originally developed for more conventional, paper-and-pencil administration is one of equivalence: are the results of these two different methods of test administration equivalent? Addressing this issue in what could certainly be described as a pessimistic presentation—one subtitled, "Everything You Should Know About Com-

Actuarial Test Interpretation: The Personality Inventory for Children

As we saw in Chapter 14, The Personality Inventory for Children (PIC) differs from other personality inventories in that the primary respondent is not the child but the parent. Another distinguishing feature of the PIC in the context of CAPA is that unlike most other psychological tests, the PIC was expressly designed for computerized interpretation. Long before this test was published, David Lachar (1987) and his associates were gathering data that would provide an actuarial basis for test interpretation.

Initially, the "raw materials" in this endeavor were a clinic application form to be filled out by the parent or guardian, a form to be completed by the clinician who evaluated the child and his or her parent, and a number of "real-world" events or observations (such as teacher observations and juvenile delinquent records) that could be correlated with PIC test scores. The nature of the correlation, if any, between such real-world events and PIC test scores was studied. Next, rules for correlate assignment were developed (see Table 1). An analysis of how various patterns of scores occurred with respect to real-world correlates yielded the basis for the development of a computer program for narrative test interpretation (see Table 1).

The numbers in the column labeled "Correla-

Table 1

Actuarial Correlates of the Personality Inventory for Children Delinquency Scale

					T-score ranges			
Descriptor[a]	Correlations[b]	Base rate	30– 59	60– 69	70– 79	80– 89	90– 99	100– 109
Impulsive behavior	.25, .39	68[c]	40	57	61	72	76	72
Temper tantrums	.27, .25	43	18	42	40	38	44	63
Involved w/police	.44, .49	17	0	4	6	10	21	19
Dislikes school	.18, .38	39	28	28	28	30	48	55
Mother inconsistent in setting limits	.26, .30	59	27	45	61	59	64	82

Source: Lachar and Gdowski (1979).
[a] Clinician ratings.
[b] n's = 215 and 216, respectively.
[c] Percentage of children rated as displaying the characteristic.

tions" indicate the strength of the relationship between the presence or absence of the descriptors in the left-most column ("Impulsive behavior," "Temper tantrums," etc.) and scores on the PIC Delinquency Scale. The column labeled "Base rate" provides information concerning the percentage of children in the entire study for whom the descriptors applied. For example, 68% of the children in the study were described as "impulsive." The next eight columns also list percentages of children for whom each of the descriptors applied. However, these percentages are based on children with certain T-scores on the Delinquency Scale. Recall that T-scores are standard scores whereby the mean of the normative sample is set at 50, and the standard deviation is set at 10. According to this table, only 40% of the children with Delinquency scores between 30T and 59T were rated "impulsive," whereas 84% of the children with scores of 110T to 119T were described as impulsive. The test developers analyzed such data to derive what are called "decision rules." As a result of one such decision rule, children with Delinquency scores greater than 99T are described in computer-generated PIC interpretations as likely to have temper tantrums, while children with scores less than 60T are described as unlikely to have them. The last, "True positive rate," column provides an indication of how well the decision rule works. We can see, for example, that 66% of the children with Delinquency scores greater than 99T had temper tantrums, and 47% of those with scores less than 60T did not have temper tantrums.

Also included in the test report is a section labeled "Critical Items." Selected items that suggest areas for further inquiry are reprinted here along with a notation regarding the relative frequency of item endorsement in normative and clinical samples. Various graphic representations of scale profiles are also included in the report as are narrative interpretations of profiles. In a section of the report labeled "Classroom Placement Analysis," the child's profile is compared to average profiles of groups of elementary school children placed in regular or different categories of special education settings.

110–119	>120	Decision rule	True positive rate
84	100	>79 T	79%
64	69	>99 T	66%
		<60 T	47%
58	63	>109 T	15%
63	70	>89 T	57%
89	67	>99 T	79%
		<60 T	63%

Actuarial Test Interpretation: The Personality Inventory for Children (continued)

PERSONALITY INVENTORY FOR CHILDREN (PIC)
by David Lachar, Ph.D. and Charles L. Gdowski, Ph.D.
A WPS TEST REPORT by Western Psychological Services
12031 Wilshire Boulevard
Los Angeles, California 90025
Version: S800-001
Copyright (c) 1985, 1989 by Western Psychological Services

CLIENT: 000000000
SEX: Male
AGE: 11 Years
SCHOOL GRADE: 5 th

ANSWER SHEET NUMBER: 00000000
PROCESSING DATE: 01/21/91
INFORMANT: Mother
ETHNICITY: White

Form: II (Factor and Shortened Clinical Scales)

* * * * * PIC INTERPRETATION * * * * *

This PIC interpretation is based on the systematic analysis of data obtained in the evaluation of behaviorally disturbed children and adolescents. This report consists of a series of hypotheses that may serve to guide further investigation.

GENERAL ADJUSTMENT AND INFORMANT RESPONSE STYLE:

Inventory responses do not suggest that this informant attempted to minimize or deny any problems that this child may have.

The description of this child's behavior suggests that a psychological/ psychiatric evaluation may assist in the remediation of current problems.

PERSONALITY AND FAMILY EVALUATION:

A history of poor peer relations may lead this child to expect criticism and rejection from others. Parents and teachers frequently observe that similar children have few, if any, friends. Poor social skills may be demonstrated by a failure to initiate relationships, with resulting isolation, or by conflict with peers that reflects poor sportsmanship and limited frustration tolerance.

This child's behavior is likely to be characterized by social

isolation and emotional lability. Similar children are frequently described by their parents as "often confused or in a daze." Additional strange or peculiar behaviors may be noted. Excessive daydreaming or delayed motor and language developmental milestones may also be reported. Other problems may include self-destructive behavior (such as head-banging), destruction of objects, poor judgment, rapid mood shifts, difficulty getting to sleep, or early morning awakening. A psychological/psychiatric evaluation may determine whether these behaviors reflect a serious or progressive disability in empathic skills or thought processes.

Child behavior is likely to reflect the presence of depression, anxiety, and fearfulness. Presenting complaints frequently include eating disturbances, trouble falling asleep, nightmares, distrust of others, isolation, emotional lability, fear of school, or excessive worry, self-blame, or self-criticism. Among adolescents, these symptoms may be associated with suicidal thought and behavior. The mothers of these children may be seen as overly permissive and often have difficulty setting limits on the demands of children.

Health-related complaints are

Western Psychological Services • 12031 Wilshire Boulevard • Los Angeles, California 90025

TEST REPORT

likely to require professional
attention. Sustained fatigue, aches
and pains, or headaches may be
present. A careful evaluation will
be necessary to determine whether
physical symptoms are employed to
avoid responsibilities, are used to
withdraw from uncomfortable
situations, are in response to
stress, accompany depression or other
emotional states, and/or require
medical intervention.

A disregard for rules and
societal expectations is likely to be
evidenced by behavior displayed at
both home and school. Similar
children may express a dislike for
school and demonstrate a hostile,
defiant response to school personnel.
Current behavior is likely to
reflect impulsivity, poor judgment,
or unmodulated hostility. An
antisocial adjustment may be
suggested by symptoms such as lying,
theft, or association with similarly
troubled children, or by an
established tendency to blame others
for current problems.

A history of problematic peer
relations is suggested that may be
characterized by poorly controlled
expression of hostility, fighting,
provocation and teasing, or poor
sportsmanship. Current and/or past
behavior may also suggest
hyperactivity, distractibility,
restlessness, or impulsivity. Similar
children are often inattentive in
class, do not complete homework
assignments, and may require adult
intervention to conform to stated
limits. A limited frustration
tolerance may be associated with
temper tantrums, destruction of
objects, projection of blame, direct

expression or displacement of anger,
or a lack of trust in others. Other
problems may include excessive
seeking of attention and approval,
clumsiness, frequent accidents or
fire setting.

A history of marital discord,
as well as subsequent separation or
divorce, is suggested. One or both
parents may be judged to require
professional assistance to deal with
their emotional instability,
alcoholism, or substance abuse.
Parental inconsistency in setting
limits may contribute to the
development of child behavior
problems.

Also included in the test report is a section labeled "Critical Items." Selected items that suggest areas for further inquiry are reprinted here along with a notation regarding the relative frequency of item endorsement in normative and clinical samples. Various graphic representations of scale profiles are also included in the report as are narrative interpretations of profiles. In a section of the report labeled "Classroom Placement Analysis," the child's profile is compared to average profiles of groups of elementary school children placed in regular or different categories of special education settings.

NOTE: The studies that form
the foundation for this PIC REPORT
are presented in three publications
published by Western Psychological
Services: "Multidimensional
Description of Child Personality: A
Manual for the Personality Inventory
for Children" (WPS Catalog No.
W-152G), "Actuarial Assessment of
Child and Adolescent Personality: An
Interpretive Guide for the
Personality Inventory for Children
Profile" (W-305), and "Personality
Inventory for Children Revised Format
Manual Supplement" (W-152GS).

Western Psychological Services • 12031 Wilshire Boulevard • Los Angeles, California 90025

TEST REPORT

Actuarial Test Interpretation: The Personality Inventory for Children (continued)

Personality Inventory for Children (PIC)

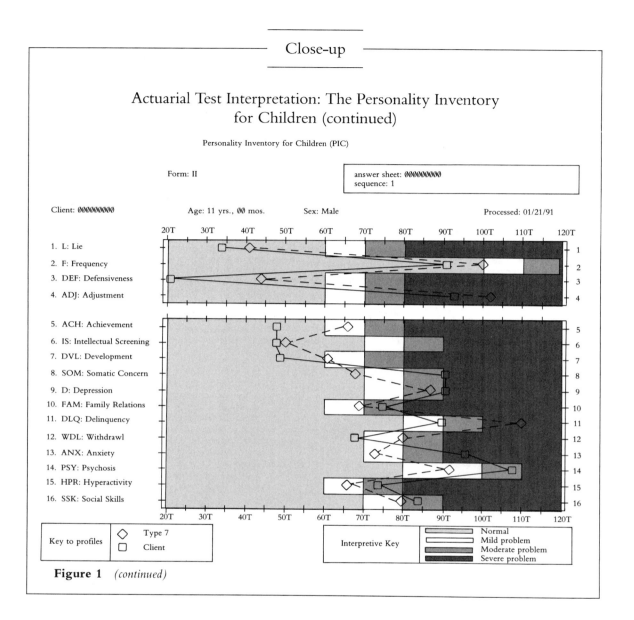

Figure 1 *(continued)*

puter Administration But Will Be Disappointed If You Ask"—Honaker (1990) noted that

> in light of the large number of psychologists who use [computer-administered] tests . . . it is disheartening to know that there is not one . . . program available for which we know all the answers [to the questions listed in Table 20–2]. For most programs there is little or no research data which addresses whether or not the computer version is psychometrically equivalent to its traditional counterpart. When research is available, it is either incomplete or inconclusive. . . . software developers should consider them-

Table 20–2

*Questions to Raise When Considering the Use
of a Computer-Administered Version of a Conventional Test*

1. Is the computer administration psychometrically equivalent to its traditional counterpart?
   a. Are there differences in the rank order of the scores? If so, data from the conventional version of the test cannot be used with the computerized version.
   b. Are there differences in the mean scores or in the shape of the distribution of scores? If so, data from the conventional version of the test can be used with the computerized version only if an equating formula has been used to adjust the computerized scores for these differences.
2. Has this particular program of a computerized version of the test been shown to be equivalent?
3. Will this computerized version be equivalent on my particular computer? Is my computer different, in some critical way, from the computers used to do the equivalency research?
4. For which of my clients will this computerized version be equivalent? Stated another way: for what types of clients has the program been demonstrated to be equivalent?
5. How will my clients react to the computerized test?

Source: Adapted from Hofer & Green (1985) and Honaker (1990)

selves lucky that the current *Guidelines for Computer-Based Tests Interpretations . . .* are guidelines rather than standards. (pp. 3–4)

Honaker went on to caution that if a psychologist doubts the equivalency of a particular mode of test administration, the questionable test-administration method should not be used. Of course, as Honaker readily acknowledged, strict adherence to such a caution would render unusable most of the CAPA products currently on the market! Hofer and Green (1985, p. 832) took a somewhat more liberal position when they advised that "Interpretation of computer-obtained scores with conventionally obtained data should be rejected if there are plausible reasons for expecting nonequivalence." Moreland (1987, p. 36) directed attention to the unique skills demanded by each of the many different ways a test can be administered when he wrote that "if a computerized administration procedure is comparable to a conventional one, comparable results will be obtained."

In summary, state-of-the-art computer-assisted test administration has not yet progressed to the point where there are more answers than questions regarding the equivalency of various modes of test administration. But research on the many variables involved (such as the work described previously in the On-line Test Administration section of this chapter) shows promise in helping us to understand better exactly why and how data derived from various modes of test administration may differ.

Computer-Assisted Test Interpretation: Validity

Perhaps the single most thorny issue regarding computer-assisted test interpretation has to do with the validity of the burgeoning number of such interpretation programs becoming available on the market. "Is this system valid for administration to the people I test?" is the key question of interest for users of CAPA products. For tests users in many settings, especially settings that differ markedly from the setting where the CAPA instrument was developed, the answer to this question is probably "No."[1] Some of the reasons why that might be the case are touched on below. And as you will see, some of the problems are not confined to CAPA instruments.

A CAPA may be invalid for widespread use because the standardization sample on which the program was based was not representative of the general population with which the test might be used. Thus, for example, Goldstein and Shelly (1982) questioned the advisability of using an actuarial interpretation system for the Halstead-Reitan Neuropsychological Battery (Russell, Neuringer, & Goldstein, 1970) developed in a United States armed forces veteran hospital, outside of veteran hospitals.

Neuropsychological test data may be validated against "hard" evidence such as brain tumors (Adams, Kvale, & Keegan, 1984). However, other instruments, such as personality inventories, are frequently validated against things like other tests or expert opinions (see, for example, Vale & Keller, 1987, and Labeck, Johnson, & Harris, 1983). Unfortunately, the standard of accuracy in such studies hinges on the reliability and the validity of the specific test(s) and/or clinician(s) used as a standard; it is possible for the CAPA instrument in question to be at variance with such standards, yet still be a useful tool (Graham, 1967).

Another potential problem in the validation of many CAPA personality inventories—as well as non-CAPA inventories—is the Barnum effect (see pp. 566–571 for a complete description of this phenomenon). The concern here is that raters charged with the task of assessing the accuracy of computer-derived personality descriptions may rate such descriptions as accurate not because they are in fact individualized descriptions of the test takers but because they contain generalities true of most people; such generalities cannot be dismissed as inaccurate, but they are probably not very useful.[2]

In his survey of available test-interpretation programs, Lanyon (1984, p. 690) opined that "lack of demonstrated program validity has now become the norm." Joseph Matarazzo (1983, 1986a), a former APA president, characterized the majority of the available programs as unvalidated and pulled no punches in his critique of the burgeoning CAPA industry:

> for-profit companies and individual psychologist-entrepreneurs . . . are vigorously touting and overselling the products of a new computer technology to some ill-prepared and professionally undereducated users who erroneously equate the products of this technology with a full and responsible psychological assessment . . . safeguards for the client and society [are] being replaced by undisguised hucksterism of the crassest kind. (1986a, pp. 14–15)

---

1. For somewhat more technical material on why generalization from CAPA products may be difficult, see Mitchell (1986) and Payne and Wiggins (1968).
2. In recent years, several studies using various instruments have attempted to control for the Barnum effect. See, for example, Eyde, Kowal, and Fishburne (1990), Guastello and Rieke (1990), Jackson and Murray (1986), Moreland and Onstad (1985), Prince and Guastello (1990), Snyder and Hoover (1989), and Snyder, Lachar, and Wills (1988).

Table 20-3

735

Evaluating "Customer Satisfaction" Studies

1. Did raters have prior experience with the interpretive systems under study?
2. Were raters given experience with the rating system prior to the beginning of the study?
3. Was the sample of raters representative of those using the interpretation in applied contexts?
4. Was the sample of test respondents unbiased?
5. Was the content of the criterion instruments representative of the content covered by the interpretative system?
6. Were ratings completed with the appropriate time frame in mind? For example, the adequacy of inferences about transient affective states should not be rated on the basis of observations conducted weeks after the test was administered.
7. Was discriminant validity of the interpretations assessed? This can be accomplished by obtaining ratings of both genuine and bogus reports (Moreland & Onstad, 1985) or genuine reports generated by different interpretive systems (Eyde et al., 1991).
8. Was inter-rater reliability assessed?
9. Was intra-rater reliability assessed?
10. Was reliability of the interpretations themselves, across time, assessed?
11. Could raters indicate contradictory elements of interpretations?
12. Could raters indicate useless elements of interpretations?
13. Could raters indicate when interpretations omitted significant information?
14. Were interpretive statements produced by different rules assessed independently? Ideally, if different rules produce different paragraphs, accuracy ratings should be obtained for each paragraph.

Simply put, "customer satisfaction" studies of computer-assisted test interpretations (CATIs) involve asking someone well acquainted with the person described whether the interpretation is any good. This table describes the real-world complexities that must be attended to when judging the adequacy of such research—such as the careful selection of judges, not just convenience samples of judges who may be unfamiliar with CATIs. The table also addresses the way in which researchers can structure the ratings for maximum utility. For example, the rating system should permit separate assessment of independent statements in CATIs and allow raters to describe exactly what is wrong with errant statements.

Writing in 1978, Butcher observed what he called "misstatements of staggering proportions" in some test-interpretation programs—a situation that had only gotten worse as time went on and such programs proliferated (Butcher, 1987). Yet Butcher's ire was clearly tempered by his belief that as invalid as many actuarial interpretation programs might or might not be, they were still generally preferable to strictly clinical interpretations. This point was made in an article co-authored by Raymond Fowler, another former APA president:

> Studies of clinician-generated "interpretations" have yielded unimpressive results. . . . Although the studies of the validity of computerized interpretations thus far reported in the literature leave much to be desired, they are more extensive by far than the studies of individually prepared clinical reports. . . . in the two studies that have made a direct comparison, human test interpreters did not do much better than the computer. (Fowler & Butcher, 1986, pp. 94-95)

Moreover, Fowler and Butcher (1986) suggested that hucksterism in CAPA was nonexistent and that "crassness may be in the eye of the beholder." Matarazzo's (1986b) rejoinder to Fowler and Butcher stressed that all of the parties to the debate over the validity of CAPA test interpretation products were actually on the same side of the issues raised.

In recent years, organizations of professionals concerned with testing have published special guidelines for CAPA interpretation systems. Typically, such guidelines encourage the gathering and publication of information to ensure that the computerized interpretation does indeed mimic expert interpretation (see Moreland, 1987; and Bartram, Beaumont, Cornford, & Dann, 1987). For example, what follows are two of the American Psychological Association's *Guidelines for Computer-Based Tests and Interpretations* (1986) dealing respectively with reliability and validity:

23. Information should be provided to users of computerized interpretations concerning the [reliability of interpretive] classifications, including, for example, the number of classifications and the interpretive significance of changes from one classification to adjacent ones. (p. 21)
24. When predictions of particular outcomes or specific recommendations are based on quantitative research, information should be provided showing the . . . relationship between the classification and the probability of [the prediction or recommendation being accurate] in the validation group. (p. 22)

However, since the field of computer-assisted psychological assessment has preceded the development of these guidelines by at least 35 years, it can reasonably be expected that it will be some time before years of professional practice catch up with recent guidelines.

Standards for CAPA Products

Professional groups like the American Psychological Association develop guidelines and standards with regard to the use of CAPA products. Unfortunately, it is only APA members who can be held to adherence to such guidelines and standards. Many people who use tests do not belong to professional organizations and indeed may not even be members of a licensed profession.

Traditionally, quality control in test-related materials has been maintained by a combination of factors, including (1) efforts made by commercial publishers to publish only materials that pass muster with their professional reviewers, and (2) a professional marketplace sufficiently knowledgeable about such products as to embrace or reject them. But the computer era in testing is, in at least some respects, changing all of that. Mom-and-Pop-type operations offering CAPA-related products are getting into the publishing game in record numbers; and just about anyone with a computer, something the person feels he or she has to offer professionals in the field, and an entrepreneurial bent can play. The phenomenon is due at least in part to the small amount of capital needed to start such a business, in comparison to the large investment that would be needed to found a more traditional publishing company. With a computer, many aspects of such a business—from accounting on spreadsheet programs to the design of advertising on desktop publishing programs—can be done rather cheaply in-house. The major cash out-lay for the would-be publisher may be not in the development or research of the product but rather its advertising and marketing. The CAPA-related product it-self, usually a piece of software, may be available in the form of a blank floppy disk that the publisher purchases for small change. Once the publisher's program has been copied onto this disk, that same disk might be sold for hundreds of dollars. Of course, the validity of the test interpretation (or other) program that the publisher has copied onto the disk is an entirely different matter; it may well be worth hundreds of dollars, or it may not be worth the small change spent on the blank floppy disk.

Currently, no governmental regulation exists for CAPA-related publishing or traditional psychological test publishing. Opinion is divided as to whether such regulation should be introduced. Some have called for governmental regulation of psychological tests, in a manner akin to the way that the Food and Drug Administration oversees the pharmaceutical and cosmetics industries. Others believe that the hodgepodge of checks and balances currently in place for years with respect to traditional tests will also be sufficient for CAPA-related products; according to this view, the marketplace has sufficient sophistication to reject products lacking professional merit. It is probably reasonable to expect no governmental regulation of published psychological testing–related products, until "solid" evidence of public harm comes as the result of some unscrupulous publisher.

Access to CAPA Products

The issue of access to CAPA-related products is perhaps the least controversial of the many issues facing test users; professionals tend to agree that only qualified professionals should have access to CAPA-related products. The problem, of course, is much the same as the one that has existed, and continues to exist, with regard to more traditional testing products; and that is the definition of a "qualified professional." Licensing laws help solve that problem in some, but not all, states, and even where licensing laws exist, there is often sufficient vagueness to allow just about anyone access to and the use of psychological assessment–related products.

A fear on the part of many testing professionals is that the widespread availability of testing software increases the danger that test security will be breached. Further, as such software falls into the "wrong hands," the stage will be set for abuse of such tests, and public disenchantment with, if not total rejection of, psychological tests altogether. As a result, special committees of concerned professional organizations have been formed to study the potential problems (see, for example, Eyde, Moreland, Robertson, Primoff, & Most, 1988). To date, there is no research to confirm or disconfirm the gnawing suspicion of many testing professionals that CAPA products are being abused any more than more conventional test–related products.

And while we are on the subject of the qualified user of psychological tests, we conclude by extending our best wishes to you, the reader, should *you* continue to pursue a career path that will make you a "qualified user." As you have seen in our survey of psychological testing and assessment, many challenging opportunities await individuals with psychometric expertise in a wide range of applied and academic areas in clinical counseling, or other specialties within psychology, business and industry, education and special education, . . . the list goes on. And should you decide to pursue such a career, we hope you will think about some of the issues we have raised here as well as elsewhere throughout this book; perhaps it will be *your* contribution and insights we will be citing in some future edition of *Psychological Testing and Assessment: An Introduction to Tests and Measurement.*

─── Appendix A ───

A Sample Report of

Psychological Assessment

IN OUR DISCUSSION of the psychological assessment report (see Chapter 15, Clinical and Counseling Assessment), we noted that the elements of a typical report were as follows:

- Demographic data
- A statement of the reason for referral for testing
- A listing of the tests administered
- Findings
- Recommendations
- Summary

What follows is a sample psychological report that exemplifies the type of report that a staff psychologist at an in-patient hospital or other facility might write.

REPORT OF PSYCHOLOGICAL ASSESSMENT

NOTE: *This material is privileged and confidential.*

Name: William Freddy

Address: 1313 Elm Street
               Bronx, New York

Telephone: (212) 666-1234

	Year	Month	Day
Date of testing	1987	12	15
Date of birth	1973	6	6
Age at testing	14	6	9

Name/address
of parent
or guardian: Mrs. Wilhimena Freddy (same address and telephone number
as above).

Reason for Referral

On December 6, 1987, William and seven companions were standing in front of a
liquor store they were planning to rob when a 17-year-old female high school
student passing by overheard the conversation and went into the store to warn the
store owner. When she came out of the store, a verbal altercation ensued, a knife
was drawn, and the high school student was left dead. Later that day William confessed to police that he was responsible for the murder. However, William has
since claimed that this confession was motivated by a desire to "cover" for a companion who actually committed the murder.

William was taken into custody by the police and brought before a juvenile
court judge for a preliminary hearing. At the hearing, William told the judge that
he would kill himself if the judge sent him to Medford (an adolescent detention
center). William had previously spent time at Medford for his involvement in a
"boom box" radio theft—involvement in which he has also claimed to have had
only a bystander role. While he was at Medford some of the bigger boys tried
(unsuccessfully) to force him to indulge in homosexual activities. Psychological
assessment was initiated at the request of the court to assess the boy's general level
of cognitive and emotional functioning as well as his current suicidal as well as
homicidal potential.

Tests Administered

Wechsler Intelligence Scale for Children—Revised (12/15/87)
Bender Visual-Motor Gestalt Test (12/15/87)
Rorschach Test (12/15/87)
Thematic Apperception Test (12/15/87)
Sentence Completion Test (12/15/87)
Figure Drawings (12/15/87)

There was no record of any prior psychological test administration.

Findings

William is currently an inpatient of the Adolescent Psychiatry Service of Mc-
Donald Memorial. He is an average-looking, 5-feet-4-inch 14½-year-old whose
pockmarked and wrinkled face, combined with his rather serious disposition,

tends to make him appear four or five years older than his actual chronological age. He was well groomed and came to the test session wearing jeans, sneakers, and a purple tank top. He was cooperative and well behaved in all interactions with this examiner, readily acclimating to the cognitive demands of the various psychometric instruments. His responses to the projective materials, especially the TAT, Sentence Completion Test, and Rorschach, impressed me as being most spontaneous and candid. This spontaneity was also manifest on the WISC-R as exemplified by his response to the question, "What is the thing to do if a fellow much smaller than yourself starts to fight with you?" William answered, "What I'd do, right? I'd smack him in the head." While candor and spontaneity are desirable and admirable qualities in a testing situation, as well as other life situations, marked impulsivity is not. A tendency toward impulsivity was suggested by some of William's test responses as well as by some of his extra-test behavior. For example, when presented with the WISC-R Object Assembly task (in which pieces of a puzzle are first arranged in mixed order behind a screen and then exposed to the test taker), William pulled the exposed puzzle toward him with such force that pieces fell to the floor. Other indicators of the boy's impulsivity permeated the test record. When asked to make up a story about a picture of a rowboat drawn up on the bank of a woodland stream, William said, "Maybe the boat belongs to a little kid . . . somebody could take it. If I see a boat there I'd take it and go fishing." When asked to reproduce Figure "A" of the Bender series he responded, "I don't have to put them that close like you have them." It is appropriate to note here that accurate reproduction of this figure does require a disciplined hand. When reminded of the instruction to "draw exactly what you see," William was able to satisfactorily capture the gestalt of the figure. On the WISC-R coding subtest William inappropriately dotted many of the figures, a behavior seldom if ever noted in most test records; further, he seemed to do so with all of the deliberation of a graffiti artist embellishing some public place even though he knows he's not supposed to do it. Whatever the meaning of these marks, their presence on an otherwise uncontaminated WISC-R protocol must be noted.

Perhaps the most dramatic testimony to William's tendency to act on impulse is his admitted participation in the planned robbery of the liquor store, a robbery that was conceived only about half an hour before it was attempted. Although the full extent of William's involvement in the subsequent murder is unclear at this time, it seems not critically important to this examiner whether William, as he has variously claimed, did all of the stabbing, did only some of the stabbing, or went to stab the victim but missed. What must be given due consideration is that, by William's own admission, he was so angered by the bystander's benevolent actions that he produced a knife and—at the very least—attempted to stab the bystander with the intent of killing her.

On the WISC-R, William achieved a Verbal IQ of 70 and a Performance IQ of 84, yielding a full-scale IQ of 75. According to Wechsler norms this places him in the borderline range of intellectual functioning. There was little variability in the scaled scores and this consistency of performance, in and of itself, might lead one to conclude that the full-scale IQ of 75 is a valid estimate of this child's intelligence. However, there was evidence from some of the projective material (such as the high number of whole and vista-type responses on the Rorschach) to suggest that the borderline description may, to some degree, underestimate William's intellectual potential. Before leaving discussion of the results of the intelligence testing, it will be noted that the Performance IQ being significantly higher than the Verbal IQ is a frequent occurrence in the records of diagnosed psychopaths, sociopaths, and adolescent delinquents.

On the Rorschach, William produced a greater than average number of CF responses, a phenomenon that has been associated with impulsivity, emotional immaturity, and a tendency to "act out." William's response to card 6GF of the TAT could be construed as anything from a deviant conception of heterosexual relations to a non sequitur with psychotic flavor. As described by Murray, this card depicts a young woman sitting on the edge of a sofa looking back over her shoulder at an older man with a pipe in his mouth who seems to be addressing her. William's response to this card was: "Love scene I think. She's surprised . . . he said something to her. He's gonna kill her or ask her to marry him." The matter-of-fact delivery of the statement, especially in the context of his present predicament (awaiting trial for murder charges) provided further evidence regarding this child's volatility, impulsivity, and violent proclivities.

When asked to draw a person, William drew a female first. Because subjects of all ages are expected to draw their own sex first, the possibility of conflict or ambivalence regarding sexual identification exists. In his figure drawings, the female head was larger than the male, teeth were showing on the female, and the female tended to look more menacing than the male—all indices, perhaps, of William's perception of being threatened either by females or by any of his own identification with females. On the Sentence Completion Test, William completed the stem "One of the troubles with women is" with "they act bad, real tough." Other items on the Sentence Completion Test were equally revealing and perhaps more relevant to immediate treatment concerns:

Sometimes I think that I will kill myself.

What I could do is escape.

Throughout the protocol there was no clear cluster of indicators of psychosis (other than the non sequitur in his story to Card 6GF on the TAT) or neurological deficit. The Bender required only about five minutes to administer in its entirety, and William captured the gestalt of all of the figures, even producing six of the nine figures on the recall.

Recommendations

Although William has not presented any problem to the staff while on our service, it seems clear from the test record that a strong tendency for this child to act on impulse exists in combination with relatively high homicidal, suicidal, and elopement potential. Accordingly, it is recommended that:

1. All staff be apprised of these findings so that they might take proper precautions in all of their dealings with William.
2. The court be notified of these findings immediately so that this information may be used in its disposition of this case.
3. William be placed on a regular schedule of psychotherapy while at this facility, such therapy to have included among its specific goals (a) the lessening of his impulsivity and acting out potential, (b) the improvement of

his social judgment, and (c) exploration of his attitudes toward women and cognitive restructuring where necessary.

Summary

William is a 14½-year-old boy, looking older than his chronological age, who has been implicated in the murder of a female high school student. William has previously spent time at an adolescent correctional facility and has threatened to kill himself if sent back there. Psychological assessment was ordered by the court to provide the court with more information as to the reality of William's threat. The findings indicated that William is a very impulsive and volatile youngster with poor social judgment whose measured intelligence falls in the borderline range. In this examiner's opinion, William is quite capable of exhibiting suicidal (as well as homicidal) behavior and must be treated accordingly. It is recommended that he undergo psychotherapeutic treatment while at this institution.

———————
Factor Analysis: What It
———————
Is, How It's Done, and
———————
What to Do with It*
———————

ALL SCIENTISTS ATTEMPT to identify the basic underlying dimensions which can be used to account for the phenomena they study. For example, physicists refer to inferred dimensions or constructs such as "force" or "energy" in their attempt to identify and account for a large number of physical phenomena that occur in the universe. Behavioral scientists speak of other dimensions, constructs, or factors in their own attempt to identify, label, and understand behavioral phenomena.

Consider the case of a psychologist involved in personality research who has accumulated data on hundreds of test takers who each sat for a dozen personality tests—personality tests that are supposed to measure about six dozen personality dimensions (also called "traits"). After analyzing the data, the psychologist may come to the conclusion that only three or four dimensions of personality are being measured by all those tests. Or, how about a hypothetical instrument we'll call the "Test of Executive Potential" (TEP)—a test which claims to provide scores on 21 dimensions or factors related to managerial success. After extensive research and experience with the TEP, an industrial/organizational psychologist might conclude that the TEP actually measures only 10 dimensions or factors related to managerial success. In each of these cases, the behavioral scientist began with

———————
*Prepared by Louis H. Primavera and Bernard S. Gorman.

measurements on several variables, analyzed the data, and concluded as a result of data analyses that some basic dimensions or factors could more efficiently account for the observed data. Several different, related procedures may be used to analyze data for the purpose of identifying basic dimensions or factors. Collectively, these techniques are known as _factor analysis_.[1]

WHAT IS FACTOR ANALYSIS?

We will define _factor analysis_ as "a set of mathematical techniques used to identify dimensions underlying a set of empirical measurements." In order to examine the process, let's do an informal kind of factor analysis. Imagine that you are a clinical psychologist and a new patient, a 45-year-old woman whom you refer to as "Annette O." has just entered your office for her first consultation. Days before, when she had made the appointment, this woman would not explain over the phone why she sought therapy. In fact, she wouldn't even tell you her last name! After a brief exchange of pleasantries you say, "How may I be of help to you?" And then it all comes out.

Annette tells you how unhappy and miserable she is; a long-term relationship ended abruptly three months before this consultation when the man she was seeing suddenly decided that he wanted to go to school full-time to become a court-reporter. Since that day she's been experiencing headaches, stomach pains, poor appetite, an inability to get a good night's sleep (or even feel very calm anytime during the day), a reluctance to get out of bed in the morning, a general and overwhelming feeling of dread, and an outbreak of acne—the likes of which she hadn't seen since adolescence.

During the course of this initial session with Annette you are not only an "active listener" but an "active watcher." You pay close attention not only to her verbal behavior but her nonverbal behavior as well. You note the generally sad expression on her face, the nonstop hand-wringing behavior, the plaintive cry in her voice, and the fact that you're almost completely out of tissues.

As your clock signals the end of the session, two words—neither one of them uttered among the hundreds of words spoken during the course of the session—seem to summarize much of the information you obtained in this first session with Annette: "depression" and "anxiety."

Turning the pages in your calendar with one hand while you try gracefully to fumble for your pen (which during the course of the session fell between the cracks of your leather chair) with the other, your mind races to thoughts of alternative therapy plans. You are too preoccupied to reflect on the elements of the process that has just transpired. One way of looking at that process is to think of it as data reduction. You have mentally reduced mounds of data to a more manageable and workable amount. More specifically, there were five steps in that process. Step 1 involved your observation of the person's behavior during the therapy session. In Step 2, you tried to understand how the themes that you observed

_____

1. Keep in mind, however, that while for our purposes we speak of "factor analysis" in the singular sense—as if it were one technique, like "simple addition"—there are many different ways of factor-analyzing data, and some may yield results that differ from others.

went together; that is, what observations were similar to one another. Step 3 involved decisions regarding what everything you saw and heard had in common; that is, what the processes or underlying dimensions were. Step 4 involved a decision on your part regarding the relative weights or importance of each of the dimensions; depression and anxiety were the dimensions that struck you as most prominent. Step 5 involved your formulation of a plan of therapeutic intervention—a plan for using the data in a way that you deem will best help Annette.

As we shall soon see, the five-step process described above in many ways parallels the five-step description of factor analysis that follows. A major difference, of course, is that factor analysis, as it is typically used in psychology, is based on the administration of a number of measures to a scientifically selected sample of people—not one person's subjective observations and judgments about another person. Also, before moving on from the question, "What is factor analysis?" we might make note of what factor analysis is *not*. The process of factor analysis is sometimes confused with the process of *cluster analysis*—a set of methods for grouping similar measures without necessarily searching for underlying, quantifiable dimensions.

HOW IS FACTOR ANALYSIS DONE?

Our goal here is to convey a general understanding of the process of factor analysis, as used in psychological measurement, not a "nuts-and-bolts" primer on how to do it. The mathematical procedures used in factor analysis are very complex. The reader who is interested in a more mathematically detailed, how-to-do-it presentation is referred to other sources, such as Gorsuch (1983).

Step 1

The first step in doing a factor analysis involves choosing a set of tests or measures. These measures or variables could be items on one test or two or more complete tests. For the purpose of this discussion, we will refer to these variables—either test items or whole tests—simply as "measures." Once you choose the measures that you wish to use, you administer them to a sample of test takers. This sample is selected—as in all good empirical research—to represent the population to which you wish to generalize your results. This first step is similar to the initial step in the therapy session described above: careful observation of the patient's behavior.

Step 2

The second step in factor analysis is to compute all correlations among the set of measures that you have chosen to represent the construct or constructs. Recall that in Step 2 in Annette's initial therapy session, you decided, through some subjective process, which of the patient's behaviors were similar to each other. The second step in a factor analysis may also be thought of as a process of distilling relationships, though here, the method is not so subjective. Instead, mathematically computed coefficients of correlation are used.

Correlation coefficients provide a gauge of the degree of similarity that exists between measures. Correlations quantify the degree to which two variables share something in common. The squared value of the correlation coefficient, called the *coefficient of determination,* is interpreted as the proportion of variance shared by two variables. It provides a quantitative index of how much two measures have in common. For example, if we found that a test of anxiety correlated .60 with a test of neuroticism then we could conclude that they had .36 or 36 percent shared variance; that is, 36 percent of what was being measured by the anxiety test was also measured by the neuroticism test. The correlations are arranged into a matrix of intercorrelations and this matrix is used in the next step of the process.

Step 3

The third step in a factor analysis is to factor the matrix of intercorrelations among a set of measures. This step is similar to the third step in the therapy session; there decisions were made regarding what the major underlying dimensions of the patient's behaviors were. The matrix of intercorrelation is factored using one or more mathematical procedures.

Factoring is a term that you may already have some familiarity with. You probably remember hearing a grade-school teacher use the term to describe a method in algebra by which a large, unwieldy expression was made more manageable by division of common factors. In modern factor-analysis methods, computer programs analyze the matrix of intercorrelations into a smaller matrix of a few common factors.

Most of the factoring procedures used in factor analysis produce a set of independent, uncorrelated factors. Most of them also can produce as many factors as there are variables. Some of these factors are thought to be *common factors* and others are thought to be *specific factors* and *error factors*. Common factors represent the dimensions which all the measures have in common. They are the underlying, basic dimensions which scientists seek to identify—the basic taxonomies of fields of scientific endeavor. Specific factors are simply those factors which are related to some specific aspect of the measuring procedure but are not common to any of the other measures in the analysis. Error factors refer to error of measurement or unreliability, which is always a part of any measuring process.

It is up to the researcher to decide which of the factors produced by the factor analysis are the common factors, since that is usually the purpose for doing factor analysis. The problem of identifying which of the factors are the common factors has occupied a great deal of the factor analysis literature and will not be covered here. Most factor analysts agree that this identification process is complex and difficult. A great deal of converging evidence is needed to make the decision as to which factors are the common factors. However, as we shall see shortly, common factors usually "stand out" in an understandable pattern.

Now, let's see how the first three steps of a factor analysis might work.

An Example of Steps 1 through 3 in Practice

Suppose that an educational psychologist wants to study both mathematics and verbal ability. She researches the literature and comes up with a test plan from

Table 1

The Matrix of Intercorrelations Among the Five Items

	Item				
	1	2	3	4	5
1 Vocabulary	1.00	.22	.77	.20	.50
2 Algebra	.22	1.00	.21	.65	.48
3 Analogy	.77	.21	1.00	.19	.52
4 Geometry	.20	.65	.19	1.00	.47
5 Algebra-Word	.50	.48	.52	.47	1.00

which she constructs the five items that she believes will measure both these abilities. It's a good bet that, in practice, many more than five items would be needed to adequately represent the two factors of interest, but for now, five items provide a manageable example. Item 1 is a vocabulary item and item 3 is a word analogy problem. Item 2 tests a basic algebra concept and item 4 tests a basic geometry concept. Item 5 is an algebra word problem.

The researcher uses a standard factor-analysis computer program which first computes the matrix of intercorrelations among the measures. The matrix of intercorrelations for the five items is presented in Table 1. Each entry in the matrix is a correlation coefficient between two of the items. Note in Table 1 that the correlation between the vocabulary item and the algebra concept item is .22 and that the correlation between the geometry item and the algebra word problem is .47. Now, examine the rest of this matrix of intercorrelations. Is any particular pattern present?

The vocabulary and the word analogy items have a high correlation but each has low correlations with the algebra concept and geometry concept items. The algebra concept and geometry items have a high correlation but each has a low correlation with the vocabulary and word analogy items. The algebra word problem has a moderate correlation with the other four items. These results suggest that there are two factors underlying these five items, with the vocabulary and word analogy items being most associated with one factor and the algebra and geometry concept items being associated with the second factor. It also seems that the algebra word problem may be associated with both factors.

In the present example, it's relatively easy to see that the patterns of correlations suggest what the two underlying factors might be for this set of five items. However, finding common factors would be an overwhelming task if you had a large number of items (for example, 100 or more). For this reason, you would probably need a method which would find these underlying dimensions in an objective way. Mathematical factoring is just such a method.

After the computer program computes the matrix of intercorrelations among all the measures, it next factors that matrix. Using the results from the computer program and several converging criteria which include some mathe-

Table 2

The Results of the Factor Analysis of the Five Items

	Factors		
	I	II	Communality
Vocabulary	.917	.101	.851
Algebra	.113	.885	.796
Analogy	.925	.094	.864
Geometry	.086	.891	.801
Algebra-Word	.594	.573	.681
Eigenvalue	2.700	1.30	
Percent of Total Variance	54.000	26.000	

matical indices as well as interpretability, the educational researcher decides that there are two common factors underlying these five items.[2]

The entries in Table 2 are called "factor loadings" and can be treated like correlations between the measure and the underlying factors. Item 1, a vocabulary item, "loads" or correlates very highly with Factor I and very low with Factor II. Item 2, an algebra problem, correlates very low with Factor I and very highly with Factor II. In interpreting this factor matrix, it is necessary to decide what size or magnitude a factor loading should have before we can consider it to have a meaningful or important contribution to a factor. There is no agreed-upon significance test for factor loadings and, therefore, it is necessary to specify some value which indicates that a factor loading is meaningful or important. Cattell (1978) proposed a concept he called *salience*—a concept which is analogous to another concept which is no doubt more familiar to you, that of *significance*. Cattell proposed that, as a rule, a factor loading might be considered salient if it is greater than either .30 or .40. The choice of the value for salience is dependent on the size of the sample of subjects. If the sample is small (say, less than 100), factor loadings of .40 or greater may be thought to be salient. If the sample is large, a value of .30 or greater may be used as the cutoff for salience. For the present example, we chose a value of .30 as the cutoff because we know—since we made up the example—that the educational psychologist used a very large sample of subjects for her study.

The salient factor loadings have been underlined in Table 2. Using this criterion for salience or meaningfulness, you can see that the vocabulary and word analogy items load saliently on Factor I and that the algebra concept and geometry concept items load saliently on Factor II. These items are called *factorially simple* items because they load saliently on only one factor. It can be seen that

2. In order to make the factors most interpretable, it is often necessary to use another mathematical procedure called "rotation." *Rotation* is a mathematical procedure which adjusts the results of factor analysis so that it will be more interpretable without distorting the relationship of the factors to the original data. The interested reader is again directed to Gorsuch (1983) for a more detailed explanation.

these factorially simple items reflect only one dimension or factor. The algebra word problem loads saliently on both Factors I and II. A variable which loads saliently on more than one factor is called *factorially complex* because it reflects more than one dimension.

Nowhere in the statistical procedure of factor analysis is it written, or even suggested, how the names for common factors should be derived. That is a task left to the factor analyst and, sometimes, there is a lot of subjectivity when naming them. Common factors may be named anything from "Factor I" to "Introversion" to "Belief in an Afterlife" to . . . whatever seems reasonable on the basis of the data at hand. With respect to factorially simple measures, the investigator typically makes some decision on the name of the factor based on the dimension the factors seem to have in common. The factorially complex items are, hopefully, interpretable and understandable in terms of the names given the factors. Before reading on, what names would *you* give the factors in Table 2?

We named Factor I "Verbal Ability" because we judged verbal ability to be a primary dimension or ability for completing vocabulary and analogy problems. We named Factor II "Mathematical Ability" because we judged this ability to be the primary dimension or ability used for solving algebra and geometry problems. Using the names that we gave to the two factors, the algebra word problem can be interpreted as a measure of *both* mathematical and verbal abilities.

You may have chosen different names for the factors from the names we chose. Similar problems—those related to different names for observations—often arise in factor analytic research and may even be responsible for theoretical debates about what the underlying dimensions for a given set of behaviors really are. As one example, the interested reader is referred to the debate over how many factors there *really* are in the factor analytically derived 16PF (Personality Factors) test (see Comrey & Duffy, 1968; Eysenck, 1972; Guilford, 1975; Howarth & Browne, 1971; and Cattell & Krug, 1986).

Step 4

Getting back to Annette O.'s therapy session and more specifically, the fourth step in the model presented above, recall that the psychologist decided that Annette's behavior was symptomatic of depression and, secondarily, of anxiety. In making this judgment, the psychologist assigned relative importance to each of the factors or dimensions. Similarly, the results of a factor analysis provide a numerical index called an *eigenvalue,* or characteristic root. An eigenvalue is a number which indicates the relative strength or importance of each of the factors. Eigenvalues from most factor analyses will vary from a value of 0.0 to that equal to the number of measures that are being factored. Divide the eigenvalue by the number of variables in the analysis and multiply the result by 100, and you will obtain the percent of total variance accounted for by a given factor. The eigenvalues and the total percent of variance associated with each of the two factors for the five items are given at the bottom of Table 2. Note that for these five items, the Verbal Ability Factor (54%) is more than twice as strong as the Mathematical Ability Factor (26%). The results of a factor analysis will allow us to estimate not only how many factors or dimensions there are for a set of measures, but also the relative importance or strength of each of these factors.

Step 5

The final step in the therapy session scenario described above entailed your planning of a therapeutic intervention, perhaps with regard to your judgment concerning the relative importance of the observed symptomatology. Analogously, once factor analysts decide on the number of factors in a factor analysis, they can compute an index called *communality*. Communality assesses how well each measure is explained by the common factors. You will recall that the square of a correlation can be interpreted as the proportion of variance that two measures have in common. The square of a factor loading provides an indication of how much a factor and measure have in common. Square each factor loading for a measure and then add the sum of the squares; the sum will be equal to the total proportion of variance of all of the common factors that is accounted for by that measure. The communality for the algebra concept item was computed by squaring its factor loadings, .113 and .885, and adding them together. Since communalities can vary between 0.0 and 1.0 we can see that all the measures in this analysis have a moderate to strong communality. Try computing the communalities for the other four items yourself.

WHAT DOES ONE DO WITH A FACTOR ANALYSIS?

Over the last 20 years, a great increase in the use of factor analysis in many areas of psychological research has occurred. This increase is partially due to the availability of high-speed computers and relatively easy-to-use computer programs. Factor analysis is used in numerous ways such as:

- Finding underlying factors of ability tests;
- Identifying personality dimensions;
- Identifying clinical syndromes;
- Finding dimensions of worker satisfaction, and
- Finding the dimensions that people use when judging social behaviors.

One way that factor analysis should *never* be used is as a haphazard method to attempt to make order from chaos; *it is totally inappropriate to factor-analyze just any set of measures with the hope of finding meaningful common factors.* A factor analysis should be planned as a tool that will be used at some appropriate point in a study. Do I understand the problem thoroughly? Do I understand the phenomena for which I am attempting to identify common factors? Are the measures I've chosen the best available ones with respect to the phenomena I'm investigating? These are only some of the questions that must be raised (and satisfactorily answered) prior to the execution of a factor analysis.

Suppose you were interested in identifying the dimensions of the construct "anxiety." Ideally, you would need to choose the test(s) or test items that most clearly represented what is known about anxiety. To accomplish this, you would read as much of the psychological literature about anxiety as possible and choose the measure(s) which you thought best represented the domain of anxiety. Again, the measuring tool you ultimately select must ideally be one about which a good deal is known; one with demonstrated reliability and validity. To do otherwise would be to impair your ability to—and jeopardize the likelihood of—identifying meaningful factors. Further, poor "up front" homework will lessen the likelihood that your work will be replicable; the factors you identify will probably not be found in subsequent studies by other researchers. In this context, a modern saying springs to mind: "Garbage in, Garbage out."

There are many technical issues in conducting a factor analysis that are beyond the scope of this introductory presentation. Our main goal was to introduce you to some of the basics. More in-depth approaches to this very important technique of data analysis are as far away as your campus library!

Appendix C

Selected Suppliers of Psychological and Educational Tests and Measurement-Related Services*

---

*This list contains only a sampling of the hundreds of suppliers of measurement-related materials and is not meant to be comprehensive. Contact these or other suppliers for a complete list of their product offerings.

755

Academic Therapy Publications
20 Commercial Boulevard
Novato, CA 94947-6191
(415) 883-3314
List includes: The Larsen-Hammill Test of Written Spelling and the Motor-Free Visual Perception Test.

Alemany Press
2501 Industrial Parkway West
Hayward, CA 94545
1-800-227-2375
(415) 887-7070
List includes: The Henderson-Moriarity ESL Placement Test, the Maculaitis Assessment Program, and the Test of English Proficiency Level.

Ambulatory Monitoring, Inc.
731 Saw Mill River Road
Ardsley, NY 10502
(914) 693-9240
Products include: Wrist Actigraph and Respitrace biofeedback systems.

American Association of State Psychology Boards
P.O. Box 4389
Montgomery, AL 60611
(205) 832-4580
Publisher of the Examination for Professional Practice in Psychology

American College Testing Program (ACT)
P.O. Box 168
Highway 1 and 180
Iowa City, IA 52240
(319) 337-1000
List includes: ACT Career Planning and ACT Proficiency Examination programs.

American Guidance Service, Inc.
Publishers' Building
Circle Pines, MN 55014-1796
1-800-328-2560
(203) 322-6135
List includes: The Bruininks-Oseretsky Test of Motor Proficiency, the Goldman-Fristoe Test of Articulation, the Kaufman Assessment Battery for Children, the Kaufman Adolescent and Adult Intelligence Test, the Kaufman Brief Intelligence Test, the KeyMath Diagnostic Arithmetic Test, the Vineland Adaptive Behavior Scales–Revised, and the Woodcock Reading Mastery Tests.

American Orthopsychiatric Association, Inc.
19 West 44th Street
New York, NY 10036
(212) 354-5770
Publisher of the Bender Visual-Motor Gestalt Test.

Autogenics-Cyborg
1350 S. Kostner Avenue
Chicago, IL 60623
(312) 522-7777
Products include: BioLab computerized feedback.

Ball Foundation
800 Roosevelt Road
Glen Ellyn, IL 60137
(312) 469-6270
List includes: Computerized Ball Aptitude Battery.

Century Diagnostics, Inc.
2101 E. Broadway
Tempe, AZ 85282
(602) 966-6006
Services include the Century Diagnostics Computer Interpreted Rorschach Report.

CHECpoint Systems, Inc.
1520 W. Waterman Avenue
San Bernadino, CA 92404
(714) 888-3296
List includes: The Basic Inventory of Natural Language.

Clinical Psychology Publishing Co.
4 Conant Square
Brandon, VT 05733
(802) 247-6871
List includes: The Questionnaire on Resources and Stress.

Consulting Psychologists Press, Inc.
577 College Avenue
Palo Alto, CA 94306
(415) 857-1444
List includes: Adjective Check List, the California Psychological Inventory, the California Q-Sort Deck, the Myers-Briggs Type Indicator, and the SVIB-SCII.

C.P.S., Inc.
P.O. Box 83
Larchmont, NY 10538
List includes: The Children's Apperception Test and the Senior Apperception Technique.

Curriculum Associates
5 Esquire Road
No. Billerica, MA 01862-2589
1-800-225-0248
List includes: The Brigance Diagnostic Inventory of Basic Skills and the Brigance Diagnostic Inventory of Early Development.

DLM Teaching Resources
P.O. Box 4000
One DLM Park
Allen, TX 75002
1-800-527-4747
1-800-442-4711
List includes: Battelle Developmental Inventory, Birth to Three Assessment and Intervention System, Peabody Developmental Motor Scales, Test of Word Finding, and the Woodcock-Johnson Psychoeducational Battery.

The College Board
45 Columbus Avenue
New York, NY 10023-6917
(212) 713-8000
List includes: The College Board Achievement tests, the Graduate Record Examinations, and the Test of English as a Foreign Language (note that some tests are sponsored jointly with Educational Testing Service).

Educational Testing Service (ETS)
Rosedale Road
Princeton, NJ 08541-6736
(609) 921-9000
List includes: Advanced Placement Examinations, College-Level Examination Program, Interagency Language Roundtable Oral Proficiency Interview, the Scholastic Aptitude Test, the Secondary Level English Proficiency Test, the Test of Spoken English, the Test of Written English (note that some tests are sponsored by arrangement with The College Board).

Futurehealth, Inc.
975-A Bristol Pike
Bensalem, PA 19020
1-800-338-8873
Products include BioPro, a computerized biofeedback system.

Harvard University Press
79 Garden Street
Cambridge, MA 02138
(617) 495-2600
Publisher of the Thematic Apperception Test.

Institute of Personality and Ability Testing (IPAT)
P.O. Box 188
Champaign, IL 61820
(217) 352-4739
List includes: Children's Personality Questionnaire, Early School Personality Questionnaire, High School Personality Questionnaire, IPAT Anxiety Scale, IPAT Depression Scale, IPAT Humor Test of Personality, and the 16PF.

Jastak Associates, Inc.
1526 Gilpin Avenue
Wilmington, DE 19806
1-800-221-WRAT
List includes: The Wide Range Achievement Test-Revised, the Wide Range Interest and Opinion Test, and the Wide Range Employability Sample Test.

Lafayette Instrument Company
P.O. Box 5729
Lafayette, IN 47903
1-800-428-7545
Products include: various kinds of instruments for assessment, including The Purdue Pegboard and the O'Connor Tweezer Dexterity Test.

Multi-Health Systems, Inc.
10 Parfield Drive
Willowdale, Ontario
Canada M2J 1B9
Products include: various software packages ranging from intake history to corporate culture.

National Computer Systems, Inc. (NCS)
5605 Green Circle Drive
Minnetonka, MI 55343
1-800-523-8805
List includes: Career Assessment Inventory, Millon Clinical Multiaxial Personality Inventory, Inventory of College Activities, and various computer scoring services. NCS is also the distributor of the Minnesota Multiphasic Personality Inventory (MMPI), and the MMPI-2.

Newbury House/Harper & Row
Keystone Industrial Park
Scranton, PA 18512
1-800-242-7737
List includes: Ilyin Oral Interview, Listening Comprehension Picture Test, and the Listening Comprehension Written Test

New York City Board of Education
49 Flatbush Avenue Extension
Brooklyn, NY 11201
(718) 596-5226
Publisher of the Language Assessment Battery.

Northwestern University Press
1735 Benson Avenue
Evanston, IL 60201
(312) 491-5313
List includes: Developmental Sentence Scoring, Northwestern Syntax Screening Test, Screening Test of Spanish Grammar.

Oblique Solutions, Inc.
P.O. Box 16595
Tampa, FL 33687-6595
1-800-553-1433
Products include software for administering and scoring psychological tests on a personal computer.

Personnel Decisions, Inc.
821 Marquette Avenue
2300 Forshay Tower
Minneapolis, MN 55402
(612) 339-0927
List includes: Retail Employment Inventory and the Management Success Profile.

PRO-ED
5341 Industrial Oaks Boulevard
Austin, TX 78735
(512) 892-3142
List includes: The Detroit Tests of Learning Aptitude—2.

Psychological Assessment Resources, Inc.
P.O. Box 98
Odessa, FL 33556
1-800-331-TEST
List includes: the Eating Disorder Inventory, Reynolds Adolescent Depression Scale, Rogers Criminal Responsibility Assessment Scales, Self-Directed Search, the Suicidal Ideation Questionnaire, and the Wisconsin Card Sorting Test.

Psychological Corporation/Harcourt Brace Jovanovich, Inc.
555 Academic Court
San Antonio, TX 78204
1-800-228-0752
(516) 543-6914
(202) 342-2205
List includes: Boehm Test of Basic Concepts—Revised, McCarthy Scales of Children's Abilities, Nonverbal Test of Cognitive Skills, Wechsler Adult Intelligence Scale—Revised, Rorschach Test (one U.S. distributor), Wechsler Intelligence Scale for Children—III, Wechsler Preschool & Primary Scale of Intelligence—Revised, and Wechsler Memory Scale—Revised.

Research Psychologists Press, Inc.
1110 Military Street
P.O. Box 984
Port Huron, MI 48061-0984
List includes: Personality Research Form, Psychological Screening Inventory, Jackson Personality Inventory, and report generation software.

Riverside Publishing Co.
8420 Bryn Mawr Avenue
Chicago, IL 60631
1-800-323-9540
(201) 729-6031
List includes: Cognitive Abilities Test, Gates-MacGinitie Reading Test, and the Stanford-Binet Intelligence Scale: Fourth Edition.

Saul Rosenzweig
8029 Washington Avenue
St. Louis, MO 63114
Publisher of the Rosenzweig Picture Frustration Study.

Slosson Educational Publishing, Inc.
P.O. Box 280
East Aurora, NY 14502
1-800-828-4800
(716) 652-0930
List includes: Slosson Intelligence Test, Slosson Oral Reading Test, and the Slosson Articulation, Language Test with Phonology.

Stoelting Company
1350 S. Kostner Avenue
Chicago, IL 60623
(312) 522-4500
List includes: Creativity Checklist, Dole Vocational Sentence Completion Blank, Gross Geometric Forms Creativity Test, Inventory of Perceptual Skills, Joseph Pre-School & Primary Self Concept Screening Test, and the Khatena-Torrance Creative Perception Inventory.

Thought Technology Ltd.
2180 Belgrave Avenue
Montreal, Quebec
Canada H4A 2L8
Products include: biofeedback equipment.

United States Military Entrance Processing Command
Department of Defense
2500 Green Bay Road
North Chicago, IL 60064-3094
Contact concerning the Armed Services Vocational Aptitude Battery.

University of Michigan
English Language Institute
Ann Arbor, MI 48109
(313) 747-0456
List includes: Michigan Test of English Language Proficiency, Michigan Test of Aural Comprehension.

University of Minnesota Press
2037 University Avenue, S.E.
Minneapolis, MN 55455
(612) 624-2516
List includes: The Minnesota Multiphasic Personality Inventory—2 (MMPI-2) and the Minnesota Test for Differential Diagnosis of Aphasia. The MMPI-A (a version of the MMPI-2 for adolescents) is under development at this writing.

University of Iowa
Publications Order Department
Iowa City, IA 52240
(319) 335-8777
List includes: The Meier Art Judgment Test, and the Templin-Darley Tests of Articulation.

Western Psychological Services
12031 Wilshire Boulevard
Los Angeles, CA 90025
1-800-222-2670
(213) 478-2061
List includes: The Auditory Discrimination Test, The Hand Test, The Luria-Nebraska Neuropsychological Battery, and the Southern California Sensory Integration Tests.

WICAT Systems, Inc.
1875 South State Street
Orem, UT 84058
(800) 453-1145
(801) 224-6400
Products include computer programs such as WICAT Early Childhood Profile, WICAT Occupational Profile, Make-A-Test, and Test Creation Package.

Wonderlic & Associates, Inc.
P.O. Box 8007
820 Frontage Road
Northfield, IL 60093-9990
(312) 446-8900
List includes the Wonderlic Personnel Test.

760

Appendix D

Selected Suppliers of

Computer-Assisted

Psychological Assessment

Resources

INDIVIDUAL AND GROUP INTELLIGENCE/APTITUDE TESTS

Service	Publisher or Service Provider*
Kuhlmann-Anderson Tests: Mail-in scoring	Scholastic Testing Service
Otis-Lennon School Ability Test (OLSAT): Local or mail-in scoring services	Psychological Corporation
Cognitive Abilities Test: Mail-in scoring and interpretation services	Riverside Publishing

---

*Included in this non-comprehensive listing are service providers that may not be licensed or authorized by the test publisher to offer scoring and interpretation services. If in doubt, check with the test publisher regarding the availability of authorized scoring and interpretation services.

Watson Glaser Critical Thinking Tests: Local machine scoring services	Psychological Corporation
Differential Aptitude Tests: Mail-in scoring and interpretation services	Psychological Corporation
Slosson Intelligence Test: Software program to score and provide narrative report	Slosson Publishing
Wechsler Adult Intelligence Scale: Software for scoring, interpretation, and narrative report	Slosson Publishing
Wechsler Intelligence Scale for Children—Revised (WISC-R): Software for scoring, interpretation, and narrative report	Slosson Publishing
WISC-R Scoring and Interpretation	Happ Electronics
WISC-III Scoring and Interpretation	Psychological Corporation
WISC-R Recompilation: Prints out age appropriate goals and objectives for each deficiency	Slosson Publishing
Wechsler Preschool and Primary Scale of Intelligence—Revised (WPPSI-R) Report Writer	Psychological Assessment Resources
Stanford-Binet Intelligence Scale, Fourth Edition: Software for scoring and interpretation	Riverside Publishing Happ Electronics
Kaufman Assessment Battery for Children (K-ABC): Software for scoring and interpretation	American Guidance Service
Report Writer for the K-ABC: Generates narrative report	Psychological Assessment Resources
ASSET: A Student Advising/Placement and Retention Service: Local microcomputer administration, scoring, and interpretation. Includes basic skill measures (writing, numerical, reading, and study skills), advanced math measures (elementary algebra, intermediate algebra, college algebra, and geometry), additional skills (such as English essay, chemistry, ACT, or SAT), and career awareness measures (such as mechanical reasoning, clerical speed/accuracy, and space relations)	ACT

INDIVIDUAL/GROUP ACHIEVEMENT

Stanford Achievement Test: Mail-in scoring and interpretation	Psychological Corporation
Metropolitan Achievement Tests: Mail-in scoring and interpretation	Psychological Corporation

SELECTED
SUPPLIERS OF
COMPUTER-
ASSISTED PSY-
CHOLOGICAL
ASSESSMENT
RESOURCES

Metropolitan Readiness Test: Local and mail-in scoring available	Psychological Corporation
Academic Instructional Measurement System: Software systems offers technology for constructing, editing, storing, and retrieving tests and test items	Psychological Corporation
Basic Achievement Skills Individual Screener (BASIS): Scoring	Psychological Corporation
Stanford Diagnostic Reading Tests: Mail-in scoring and interpretation	Psychological Corporation
Metropolitan Achievement Test Reading Diagnostic Tests: Machine-scorable	Psychological Corporation
Gates-MacGinitie Reading Tests: Scanning, scoring, and reporting	Riverside Publishing
Stanford Writing Assessment Program, The Language Arts Performance Assessment, Metropolitan Achievement Test, Writing Test: Mail-in scoring available through Writing Assessment Center	Psychological Corporation
Stanford Diagnostic Math Test: Mail-in scoring or local, machine-scorable	Psychological Corporation
Metropolitan Achievement Test Math Diagnostic Tests: Mail-in scoring	Psychological Corporation
Iowa Tests of Basic Skills: Scoring and interpretation service. Follow-through service also available that offers individualized instruction in specific skills targeted for remediation by the Iowa Tests of Basic Skills	Riverside Publishing
Stanford Adaptive Mathematics Screening Test: Computer-administered math achievement screening test	Harcourt Brace Jovanovich, Inc.
Detroit Tests of Learning Aptitude: Software scoring available	Slosson Publishing
Detroit Tests of Learning Aptitude—Adult: Software scoring available	Slosson Publishing
Test of Language Development: Software scoring available	Slosson Publishing
Test of Adolescent Language: Software scoring available	Slosson Publishing
Test of Early Reading Ability: Software scoring available	Slosson Publishing
Test of Written Language—2: Software scoring available	Slosson Publishing

Woodcock Reading Mastery Test—Revised: Software for scoring and interpretation	American Guidance Service
Kaufman Test of Educational Achievement: Software for scoring and interpretation	American Guidance Service
Wide Range Achievement Test—Revised: Scoring and interpretive reports	Jastak Associates
Vineland Adaptive Behavior Scale: Software for scoring and interpretation	American Guidance Service
Academic Instructional Measurement System: Enables construction, editing, storing, and retrieving of tests and test items	Harcourt Brace Jovanovich, Inc.
Reportwriter—Children's Intellectual and Achievement Tests: Produces a comprehensive interpretive report for the most commonly used intelligence and achievement tests.	Psychological Assessment Resources

PERSONALITY

Microtest Assessment System: Enables administration, scoring, and interpretation of a variety of leading clinical instruments such as Alcohol Use Inventory (Profile and Report), Guilford-Zimmerman Temperament Survey (narrative report), Inventory for Counseling and Development (Profile Report), Millon Adolescent Personality Inventory (clinical narrative report), Millon Behavioral Health Inventory (narrative report), Millon Multiaxial Inventory I & II (profiles and narrative reports), Automated Child/Adolescent Social History (computerized interview, scoring, and interpretation), MMPI (narrative report), MMPI-2 (narrative report), 16 PF (narrative report)	National Computer Services
MMPI Adult and Adolescent Interpretive Systems: Software for interpretation and to integrate MMPI data with information from other sources	Psychological Assessment Resources
MMPI: Narrative reports available	National Computer Systems
16 PF: Scoring, interpretation, and narrative reports	Institute for Personality and Ability Testing (IPAT)
High School Personality Questionnaire, Karson Clinical Report, Marriage Counseling Report, Children's Personality Questionnaire: Teletest links examiner's	Institute for Personality and Ability Testing (IPAT)

computer to IPAT's test-scoring and interpretation service through telephone modem connection. Reports are sent back over the telephone

765

SELECTED
SUPPLIERS OF
COMPUTER-
ASSISTED PSY-
CHOLOGICAL
ASSESSMENT
RESOURCES

Survey of School Attitudes: Machine-scorable	Psychological Corporation
The Mooney Problem Checklist: Machine-scorable	Psychological Corporation
Dimensions of Self-Concept: Mail-in scoring services	EDITS
Eating Disorders Inventory (EDI-2): Test administration, scoring, and interpretation	Psychological Assessment Resources
Reynolds Adolescent Depression Scale: Mail-in scoring	Psychological Assessment Resources
Rorschach: Exner's scoring and interpretation	Psychological Assessment Resources
Parenting Stress Index: Software for scoring and interpretation. Provides narrative report	Psychological Assessment Resources
Connors Rating Scales: Software for administration and scoring of Parent and Teacher Rating Scales. Graphs and interpretative statements are also provided	Psychological Assessment Resources
ADD-H Comprehensive Teachers Rating Scale: Software for scoring and interpretation	Meritech
Student Adjustment Inventory: Software for administration and scoring	Meritech
Mental Status Checklist: Software for narrative report	Psychological Assessment Resources
Myers-Briggs Type Indicator California Personality Inventory: Scoring and reporting of results	Consulting Psychologists Press
Barclay Classroom Assessment System Interpersonal Style Inventory, Learning Styles Inventory, Marital Satisfaction Inventory, MMPI 1 & 2, Multiscore Depression Inventory, Personality Inventory for Children, Piers Harris Self-Concept Scale, Suicide Probability Scale, Tennessee Self-Concept Scale, Western Personality Inventory: Software available to administer, score, and/or interpret these and other tests	Western Psychological Services

Projective Drawing Tests—House-Tree-Person, Draw-A-Person, Kinetic Family Drawing Test, and Rorschach: Software to score and provide narrative report

Reason House

VOCATIONAL INTEREST/APTITUDE

Wonderlic Personnel Test: Software for scoring and interpretation

Scholastic Testing Service

Strong Vocational Interest Test: Machine-scorable and mail-in scoring

Psychological Corporation

College Admissions Practice Test: Machine-scorable

Psychological Corporation

Wide Range Interest Opinion Test: Mail-in scoring

Jastak Associates

Self-Directed Search (SDS): Computer administration, scoring, and interpretation; provides written report

Psychological Assessment Resources

Dictionary of Holland Occupational Titles: Computer search program

Psychological Assessment Resources

Ohio Vocational Interest Survey: Software available for administration and scoring

Harcourt Brace Jovanovich

Career Directions Inventory: Mail-in scoring, interpretation, and narrative report

Research Press

NEUROPSYCHOLOGICAL ASSESSMENT

Halstead-Reitan Neuropsychological Test Battery for Adults: Software for scoring, interpretation, and generating a narrative report

Psychological Assessment Resources

Luria-Nebraska Neuropsychological Battery: Mail-in scoring and interpretation

Western Psychological Services

Report Writer: Adult intellectual achievement and neuropsychological screening tests

Psychological Assessment Resources

References

Abel, G. G., Blanchard, E. B., Murphy, W. D., Becker, J. V., & Djenderedjian, A. (1981). Two methods of measuring penile response. *Behavior Therapy, 12,* 320–328.

Abel, G. G., Rouleau, J., & Cunningham-Rathner, J. (1986). Sexually aggressive behavior. In W. J. Curran, A. L. McGarry, & S. Shah (Eds.), *Forensic psychiatry and psychology: Perspectives and standards for interdisciplinary practice* (pp. 289–314). Philadelphia: Davis.

Abrams, S. (1977). *A polygraph handbook for attorneys.* Lexington, MA: Heath.

Achenbach, T. M. (1978). *Child Behavior Profile.* Bethesda, MD: Laboratory of Developmental Psychology, National Institute of Mental Health.

Achenbach, T. M. (1981). A junior MMPI? *Journal of Personality Assessment, 45,* 332–333.

Achenbach, T. M., & Edelbrock, C. (1983). *Manual for the Child Behavior Checklist and Revised Child Behavior Profile.* Burlington, VT: University of Vermont, Department of Psychiatry.

Achenbach, T. M., & Edelbrock, C. (1986). *Manual for the Teacher's Report Form and Teacher Version of the Child Behavior Profile.* Burlington, VT: University of Vermont, Department of Psychiatry.

Achenbach, T. M., & Edelbrock, C. (1987). *Manual for the Youth Self-Report and Profile.* Burlington, VT: University of Vermont, Department of Psychiatry.

Ackerman, M. (1987). Child sexual abuse: Bona fide or fabricated? *American Journal of Family Law, 2,* 181–185.

Adams, J., Kenny, T. J., & Canter, A. (1973). The efficacy of the Canter Background Interference Procedure in identifying children with cerebral dysfunction. *Journal of Consulting and Clinical Psychology, 40,* 489.

Adams, K. M. (1984). Luria left in the lurch: Unfulfilled promises are not valid tests. *Journal of Clinical Neuropsychology, 6,* 455–458.

Adams, K. M., Kvale, V. I., & Keegan, J. R. (1984). Relative accuracy of three automated systems for neuropsychological interpretation based on two representative tasks. *Journal of Clinical Neuropsychology, 6,* 413–431.

Adams-Tucker, C. (1982). Proximate effects of sexual abuse in childhood: A report on 28 children. *American Journal of Psychiatry, 139,* 1252–1256.

Adler, A. (1927/1965). *Understanding human nature.* Greenwich, CT: Fawcett.

Adler, A. (1933/1964). *Social interest: A challenge to mankind.* New York: Capricorn.

Adler, T. (1990). Does the 'new' MMPI beat the 'classic'? *APA Monitor, 20* (4), 18–19.

Adler, T. (1991, May). Tug-of-war develops over use of GATB. *APA Monitor, 22* (5), 14.

Ahern, E. (1949). *Handbook of personnel forms and records.* New York: American Management Association.

Aiken, L. R. (1987). *Assessment of intellectual functioning.* Newton, MA: Allyn and Bacon.

Airasian, P. W., Madaus, G. F., & Pedulla, J. J. (1979). *Minimal competency testing.* Englewood Cliffs, NJ: Educational Technology Publications.

Alderfer, C. (1972). *Existence, relatedness and growth: Human needs in organizational settings.* New York: Free Press.

Alderson, J. C., Krahnke, K. J., & Stansfield, C. W. (1987). *Reviews of English language proficiency tests.* Washington, DC: TESOL.

Aleamoni, L., & Oboler, L. (1978). ACT versus SAT in predicting first semester GPA. *Educational and Psychological Measurement, 38,* 393–399.

Alessi, G. L., & Lesiak, W. J. (1981). *Non-biased assess-*

ment of high incidence special education students: Tests used in evaluating educable mentally impaired. Lansing: Michigan Department of Education.

Alexander, R. C., Surrell, J. A., & Cohle, S. D. (1987). Microwave oven burns in children: An unusual manifestation of child abuse. *Pediatrics, 79,* 255–260.

Algera, J. A., Jansen, P. G., Roe, R. A., & Vijn, P. (1984). *Journal of Occupational Psychology, 57,* 197–210. Validity generalization: Some critical remarks on the Schmidt-Hunter procedure.

Allen, M. J., & Yen, W. M. (1979). *Introduction to measurement theory.* Monterey, CA: Brooks/Cole.

Allport, G. W. (1937). *Personality: A psychological interpretation.* New York: Holt.

Allport, G. W., & Odbert, H. S. (1936). Trait-names: A psycholexical study. *Psychological Monographs, 47* (Whole No. 211).

Allport, G. W., Vernon, P. E., & Lindzey, G. (1951). *Study of values* (Rev. ed.). Boston: Houghton Mifflin.

Allred, L. J., & Harris, W. G. (1984). *The nonequivalence of computerized and conventional administrations of the Adjective Checklist.* Unpublished manuscript, Johns Hopkins University.

Alpert, J. I., & Alpert, M. I. (1990). Music influences on mood and purchase intentions. *Psychology & Marketing, 7,* 109–133.

Alpher, V. S., & Blanton, R. L. (1985). The accuracy of lie detection: Why lie tests based on the polygraph should not be admitted into evidence today. *Law & Psychology Review, 9,* 67–75.

Ambrosini, P. J., Metz, C., Bianchi, M. D., Rabinovich, H., & Undie, A. (1991). Concurrent validity and psychometric properties of the Beck Depression Inventory in outpatient adolescents. *Journal of the American Academy of Child and Adolescent Psychiatry, 30,* 51–57.

American Board of Forensic Odontology, Inc. (1986). Guidelines for analysis of bite marks in forensic investigation. *Journal of the American Dental Association, 12,* 383–386.

American College Testing Program (1973). *Highlights of the ACT technical report.* Iowa City: American College Testing Program.

American College Testing Program. (1978). *The ACT assessment counselor's handbook.* Iowa City: American College Testing Program.

American Law Institute. (1956). *Model penal code.* Tentative Draft Number 4.

American Psychiatric Association. (1987). *Diagnostic and statistical manual of mental disorders* (3rd ed., rev.). Washington, DC: Author.

American Psychological Association. (1953). *Ethical standards of psychologists.* Washington, DC: Author.

American Psychological Association (1954). *Technical recommendations for psychological tests and diagnostic techniques.* Washington, DC: Author.

American Psychological Association. (1966). Automated test scoring and interpretation practices. In Proceedings of the American Psychological Association. *American Psychologist, 21,* 1141.

American Psychological Association. (1967). *Casebook on ethical standards of psychologists.* Washington, DC: Author.

American Psychological Association. (1977). Standards for providers of psychological services. *American Psychologist, 32,* 495–505.

American Psychological Association, Division of Industrial and Organizational Psychology. (1980). *Principles for the validation and use of personnel selection procedures* (2nd ed.). Washington, DC: American Psychological Association.

American Psychological Association. (1981a). *Ethical principles of psychologists.* Washington, DC: Author.

American Psychological Association, Committee on Professional Standards. (1981b). Specialty guidelines for the delivery of services by clinical psychologists. *American Psychologist, 36,* 640–651.

American Psychological Association, Committee on Professional Standards. (1981c). Specialty guidelines for the delivery of services by counseling psychologists. *American Psychologist, 36,* 652–663.

American Psychological Association, Committee on Professional Standards. (1981d). Specialty guidelines for the delivery of services by industrial/organizational psychologists. *American Psychologist, 36,* 664–669.

American Psychological Association, Committee on Professional Standards. (1981e). Specialty guidelines for the delivery of services by school psychologists. *American Psychologist, 36,* 670–681.

American Psychological Association. (1981f). Ethical principles of psychologists. *American Psychologist, 36,* 633–638.

American Psychological Association, Committee on Professional Standards and Committee on Psychological Tests and Assessment. (1986). *Guidelines for computer-based tests and interpretations.* Washington, DC: Author.

American Psychological Association. (1987). *Casebook on ethical principles of psychologists*. Washington, DC: Author.

American Psychological Association, (1991a). *Questionnaires used in the prediction of trustworthiness in pre-employment selection decisions: An APA Task Force Report*. Washington, DC: Author.

American Psychological Association, (1991b). Ethical principles revised. *APA Monitor, 21*(6), 28–32.

Ames, L. B., Learned, J., Metraux, R. W., & Walker, R. N. (1952). *Child Rorschach responses*. New York: Paul B. Hoeber.

Ames, L. B., Metraux, R. W., Rodell, J. L., & Walker, R. N. (1974). *Child Rorschach responses: Developmental trends from two to ten years* (Rev. ed.). New York: Bruner/Mazel.

Ames, L. B., Metraux, R. W., & Walker, R. N. (1971). *Adolescent Rorschach responses: Developmental trends from ten to sixteen years*. New York: Bruner/Mazel.

Amidon, E., Kumar, V. K., & Treadwell, T. (1983). Measurement of intimacy attitudes: The Intimacy Attitude Scale—Revised. *Journal of Personality Assessment, 47*, 635–639.

Amrine, M. (Ed.). (1965). Special issue. *American Psychologist, 20*(11), 857–991.

Anastasi, A. (1968). *Psychological testing* (3rd ed.). New York: Macmillan.

Anderson, R. J., & Sisco, F. H. (1977). *Standardization of the WISC-R Performance Scale for deaf children*. Washington, DC: Office of Demographic Studies, Gallaudet College.

Anderson, B., Broffitt, B., Karlsson, J., & Turnquist, D. (1989). A psychometric analysis of the Sexual Arousability Index. *Journal of Consulting and Clinical Psychology, 57*, 123–130.

Anderson, W. T., Hohenshil, T. H., Buckland-Heer, K., & Levison, E. M. (1990). Best practices in vocational assessment of students with disabilities. In A. Thomas & J. Grimes (Eds.), *Best practices in school psychology II* (pp. 787–797). Washington, DC: National Association of School Psychologists.

Andrew, G. (1953). The selection and appraisal of test pictures. In G. Andrew, S. W. Hartwell, M. L. Hutt, & R. E. Walton (Eds.), *The Michigan Picture Test* (No. 7-2144). Chicago: Science Research Associates.

Angoff, W. H. (1962). Scales with nonmeaningful origins and units of measurement. *Educational and Psychological Measurement, 22*, 27–34.

Angoff, W. H. (1964). Technical problems of obtaining equivalent scores on tests. *Educational and Psychological Measurement, 1*, 11–13.

Angoff, W. H. (1966). Can useful general-purpose equivalency tables be prepared for different college admissions tests? In A. Anastasi (Ed.), *Testing problems in perspective* (pp. 251–264). Washington, DC: American Council on Education.

Angoff, W. H. (1971). Scales, norms, and equivalent scores. In R. L. Thorndike (Ed.), *Educational measurement* (2nd ed.). Washington, DC: American Council on Education.

Anthony, L., LeResche, L., Niaz, U., et al. (1982). Limits of the "Mini-Mental State" as a screening test for dementia and delirium among hospital patients. *Psychological Medicine, 12*, 397–408.

Arizmendi, T., Paulsen, K., & Domino, G. (1981). The Matching Familiar Figures Test: A primary, secondary, and tertiary evaluation. *Journal of Clinical Psychology, 37*, 812–818.

Armentrout, J. A. (1977). Comparison of the standard and short form score of Canadian adults on the California Psychological Inventory. *Perceptual & Motor Skills, 45*(3, Pt. 2), 1088.

Arthur, G. (1950). The Arthur adaptation of the Leiter International Performance Scale. *Journal of Clinical Psychology, 5*, 345–349.

Arvey, R. D. (1979). *Fairness in selecting employees*. Reading, MA: Addison-Wesley.

Association for Personnel Test Publishers (APTP). (1990). Model guidelines for preemployment integrity testing programs. Washington, DC: APTP.

Atkin, C. K. (1978). Observation of parent-child interaction in supermarket decision-making. *Journal of Marketing, 42*, 41–45.

Atkinson, J. W. (Ed.). (1958). *Motives in fantasy, action, and society*. Princeton, NJ: Van Nostrand.

Atkinson, J. W. (1981). Studying personality in the context of an advanced motivational psychology. *American Psychologist, 36*, 117–128.

Austin, J. J. (1970). *Educational and Developmental Profile*. Muskegon, MI: Research Concepts.

Ayres, A. J. (1972). *Southern California Sensory Integration Test*. Los Angeles: Western Psychological Services.

Back, R., & Dana, R. H. (1977). Examiner sex bias and Wechsler Intelligence Scale for Children scores. *Journal of Consulting and Clinical Psychology, 45,* 500.

Baker, H., & Leland B. (1967). *Detroit Tests of Learning Aptitude, revised edition.* Indianapolis: Bobbs-Merrill.

Baker, F. B. (1988). Computer technology in test construction and processing. In R. L. Linn (Ed.), *Educational measurement* (3rd ed.). New York: American Council on Education/Macmillan.

Baldwin, A. L., Kalhorn, J., & Breese, F. H. (1945). Patterns of parent behavior. *Psychological Monographs, 58* (Whole No. 268).

Bales, J. (1987a, December). Agency sounds alarm on work test technology. *APA Monitor, 18,* 16.

Bales, J. (1987b, December). House bill outlaws worker polygraphs. *APA Monitor, 18,* 17.

Bales, J. (1987c, December). Agency sounds alarm on work test technology. *APA Monitor, 18,* 16.

Bales, J. (1987d, December). House bill outlaws worker polygraphs. *APA Monitor, 18,* 17.

Bales, J. (1987e, December). Judge upholds university, NCS copyright on MMPI. *APA Monitor, 18,* 26.

Bannatyne, A. (1974). Diagnosis: A note on recategorization of the WISC scaled scores. *Journal of Learning Disabilities, 7,* 272–274.

Barbaree, H. E., & Marshall, W. L. (1989). Erectile responses among heterosexual child molesters, father-daughter incest offenders, and matched non-offenders: Five distinct age preference profiles. *Canadian Journal of Behavioral Science, 21,* 70–82.

Barclay, A., & Yater, A. (1969). A comparative study of the Wechsler Preschool and Primary Scale of Intelligence and the Stanford-Binet Intelligence Scale, Form L-M among culturally deprived childen. *Journal of Consulting and Clinical Psychology, 33,* 257.

Bardis, P. D. (1975). The Borromean family. *Social Science, 50,* 144–158.

Barends, A., Westen, D., Leigh, J., Silbert, D., & Byers, S. (1990). Assessing affect-tone of relationship paradigms from TAT and interview data. *Psychological Assessment: A Journal of Consulting & Clinical Psychology, 2,* 329–332.

Barker, R. (1963). On the nature of the environment. *Journal of Social Issues, 19,* 17–38.

Bartell, T. P., & Fremer, J. (1986). *Procedures for developing a code of fair testing in education.* Paper presented at the annual meeting of the American Psychological Association, Washington, DC.

Bartlett, F. C. (1916). An experimental study of some problems of perceiving and imaging. *British Journal of Psychology, 8,* 222–266.

Bartram, D., Beaumont, J. G., Cornford, T., & Dann, P. L. (1987). Recommendations for the design of software for computer based assessment: Summary statement. *Bulletin of the British Psychological Society, 40,* 86–87.

Bass, B. M. (1956). Development of a structured disguised personality test. *Journal of Applied Psychology, 40,* 393–397.

Bass, B. M. (1957). Validity studies of proverbs personality test. *Journal of Applied Psychology, 41,* 158–160.

Bass, B. M. (1958). Famous Sayings Test: General manual. *Psychological Reports, 4,* Monograph Number 6.

Batchelor, E. S., Gray, J. W., & Dean, R. S. (1990). Empirical testing of a cognitive model to account for neuropsychological functioning underlying arithmetic problem solving. *Journal of Learning Disabilities, 23*(1), 38–42.

Batchelor, E. S., Sowles, G., Dean, R. S., & Fischer, W. (1991). Construct validity of the Halstead-Reitan Neuropsychological Battery for Children with learning disorders. *Journal of Psychoeducational Assessment, 9*(1), 16–31.

Batra, R., & Holbrook, M. B. (1990). Developing a typology of affective responses to advertising. *Psychology & Marketing, 7,* 11–25.

Batson, D. C. (1975). Attribution as a mediator of bias in helping. *Journal of Personality and Social Psychology, 32,* 455–466.

Baughman, E. E., & Dahlstrom, W. B. (1968). *Negro and white children: A psychological study in the rural south.* New York: Academic Press.

Bauman, M. K. (1974). Blind and partially sighted. In M. V. Wisland, (Ed.). *Psychoeducational diagnosis of exceptional children* (pp. 159–189). Springfield, IL: Charles C Thomas.

Bauman, M. K., & Kopf, C. A. (1979). Psychological tests used with blind and visually handicapped persons. *School Psychology Digest, 8,* 257–270.

Baugh, V. S., & Carpenter, B. L. (1962). Comparison of delinquents and non-delinquents. *Journal of Social Psychology, 56,* 73–78.

Bavolek, S. J. (1984). *Handbook for the adult-adolescent parenting inventory.* Eau Claire, WI: Family Development Associates.

Baxter, J. C., Brock, B., Hill, P. C., & Rozelle, R. M.

(1981). Letters of recommendation: A question of value. *Journal of Applied Psychology, 66,* 296–301.

Bayley, N. (1949). Consistency and variability in the growth of intelligence from birth to eighteen years. *Journal of Genetic Psychology, 75,* 165–169.

Bayley, N. (1955). On the growth of intelligence. *American Psychologist, 10,* 805–818.

Bayley, N. (1959). Value and limitations of infant testing. *Children, 5,* 129–133.

Bayley, N. (1969). *Bayley Scales of Infant Development: Birth to two years.* New York: Psychological Corporation.

Bear, D. M., & Fedio, P. (1977). Quantitative analysis of interictal behavior in temporal lobe epilepsy. *Archives of Neurology, 34,* 454–467.

Bearden, W. O., Teel, J. E., Jr., & Durand, R. M. (1978). Media usage, psychographic, and demographic dimensions of retail shoppers. *Journal of Retailing,* Spring, 65–77.

Beaumont, J. G., & French, C. F. (1987). A clinical field study of eight automated psychometric procedures: The Leicester/DHSS Project. *International Journal of Man-Machine Studies, 26,* 311–320.

Beavers, R. (1985). *Manual of Beavers-Timberlawn Family Evaluation Scale and Family Style Evaluation.* Dallas, TX: Southwest Family Institute.

Beck, S. J. (1944). *Rorschach's test: Vol. 1. Basic processes.* New York: Grune & Stratton.

Beck, S. J. (1945). *Rorschach's test: Vol. 2. A variety of personality pictures.* New York: Grune & Stratton.

Beck, S. J. (1952). *Rorschach's test: Vol. 3. Advances in interpretation.* New York: Grune & Stratton.

Beck, S. J. (1960). *The Rorschach experiment.* New York: Grune & Stratton.

Beck, A., Steer, R., & Ranieri, W. (1988). Scale for suicide ideation: Psychometric properties of a self-report version. *Journal of Clinical Psychology, 44,* 499–505.

Beck, A. T. (1978). Depression Inventory. Philadelphia, PA: Center for Cognitive Therapy.

Beck, A. T., & Beamesderfer, A. (1974). Assessment of depression: The Depression Inventory. In P. Picket (Ed.), *Psychological measurements in psychopharmacology: Modern problems in pharmacopsychiatry* (Vol. 7; pp. 151–169). Basel, Switzerland: Kargel.

Beck, A. T., Ward, C. H., Mendelson, M., Mock, J., & Erbaugh, J. (1961). An inventory for measuring depression. *Archives of General Psychiatry, 4,* 561–571.

Beck, A. T. (1963). Thinking and depression: 1. Idiosyncratic content and cognitive distortions. *Archives of General Psychiatry, 9,* 324–333.

Beck, A. T. (1967). *Depression: Causes and treatments.* Philadelphia: University of Pennsylvania Press.

Beck, A. T. (1976). *Cognitive theory and emotional disorders.* New York: International Universities Press.

Beck, A. T., Rush, A. J., Shaw, B. F., & Emery, G. (1979). *Cognitive therapy for depression.* New York: Guilford Press.

Beck, A. T., Steer, R. A., Epstein, N., & Brown, G. (1990). Beck Self-Concept Test. *Psychological Assessment: A Journal of Consulting & Clinical Psychology, 2,* 191–197.

Beck, A. T., & Stein, D. (1961). Development of a Self-Concept test. Unpublished manuscript, University of Pennsylvania School of Medicine, Center for Cognitive Therapy, Philadelphia.

Becker, H. A., Needleman, H. L., & Kotelchuck, M. (1978). Child abuse and dentistry: Orificial trauma and its recognition by dentists. *Journal of the American Dental Association, 97*(1), 24–28.

Becker, R. E., & Heimberg, R. G. (1988). Assessment of social skills. In A. S. Bellack & M. Hersen (Eds.), *Behavioral assessment: A practical handbook* (3rd ed.). New York: Pergamon Press.

Bee, H. (1978). *The developing child* (2nd ed.). New York: Harper & Row.

Beier, E. G., & Sternberg, D. P. (1977). Marital communication. *Journal of Communication, 27,* 92–100.

Bellack, A. S., & Hersen, M. (Eds.). (1988). *Behavioral assessment: A practical guide* (3rd ed.). Elmsford, NY: Pergamon Press.

Bellack, A. S. (1983). Recurrent problems in the behavioral assessment of social skill. *Behaviour Research and Therapy, 21,* 29–42.

Bellack, A. S., Hersen, M., & Lamparski, D. (1979). Role-play tests for assessing social skills: Are they valid? Are they useful? *Journal of Consulting and Clinical Psychology, 47,* 335–342.

Bellack, A. S., Morrison, R. L., Mueser, K. T., Wade, J. H., & Sayers, S. L. (1990). Role play for assessing the social competence of psychiatric patients. *Psychological Assessment: A Journal of Consulting & Clinical Psychology, 2,* 248–255.

Bellak, L. (1944). The concept of projection: An experimental investigation and study of the concept. *Psychiatry, 7,* 353–370.

Bellak, L. (1971). *The TAT and CAT in clinical use* (2nd ed.). New York: Grune & Stratton.

Bellak, L., & Bellak, S. (1965). *The CAT-H—A human modification*. Larchmont, NY: C.P.S.

Bellak, L., & Bellak, S. S. (1973). *Senior Apperception Technique*. New York: C.P.S.

Bellak, L., & Hurvich, M. (1966). A human modification of the Children's Apperception Test. *Journal of Projective Techniques, 30,* 228–242.

Bem, D. J., & Allen, A. (1974). On predicting some of the people some of the time: The search for cross-situational consistencies in behavior. *Psychological Review, 81,* 506–520.

Bem, D. J., & Funder, D. C. (1978). Predicting more of the people more of the time: Assessing the personality of situations. *Psychological Review, 85,* 485–501.

Bender, L. (1938). A visual–motor gestalt test and its clinical use. *American Orthopsychiatric Association Research Monographs,* No. 3.

Bender, L. (1970). The visual–motor gestalt test in the diagnosis of learning disabilities. *Journal of Special Education, 4,* 29–39.

Benjamin, J. (1964). A method for distinguishing and evaluating formal thinking disorders in schizophrenia. In L. Kasanin (Ed.), *Language and thought in schizophrenia* (pp. 65–88). New York: Norton.

Bennett, F., Hughes, A., & Hughes, H. (1979). Assessment techniques for deaf-blind children. *Exceptional Children, 45,* 287–288.

Bennett, G., Seashore, H., & Wesman, A. (1947). *Mechanical Reasoning Test*. New York: Psychological Corporation.

Bennett, G., Seashore, H., & Wesman, A. (1974). *The fifth edition manual for the Differential Aptitude Tests—Forms S and T*. New York: Psychological Corporation.

Ben-Porath, Y. S., & Butcher, J. N. (1989). The comparability of MMPI and MMPI-2 scales and profiles. *Psychological Assessment: A Journal of Consulting and Clinical Psychology, 1,* 345–347.

Berg, M. (1984). Expanding the parameters of psychological testing. *Bulletin of the Menninger Clinic, 48,* 10–24.

Berg, M. (1985). The feedback process in diagnostic psychological testing. *Bulletin of the Menninger Clinic, 49,* 52–68.

Berg, R., Franzen, M., & Wedding, D. (1987). *Screening for brain impairment: A manual for mental health practice*. New York: Springer.

Berk, R. A. (Ed.). (1982). *Handbook of methods for detecting test bias*. Baltimore: The Johns Hopkins University Press.

Berkeley, G. (1710). *A treatise concerning the principles of human knowledge*.

Bernard, J. (1949). The Rosenzweig Picture-Frustration Study: I, Norms, reliability, and statistical evaluation. *Journal of Psychology, 28,* 325–332.

Bernardin, H. J. (1978). Effects of rater training on leniency and halo errors in student ratings of instructors. *Journal of Applied Psychology, 63,* 301–308.

Bernardin, H. J., & Buckley, M. R. (1981). Strategies in rater training. *Academy of Management Review, 6,* 205–212.

Bernstein, L. (1956). The examiner as an inhibiting factor in clinical testing. *Journal of Consulting Psychology, 20,* 287–290.

Berry, J. W. (1976). *Human ecology and cognitive style: Comparative studies in cultural and psychological adaptation*. Beverly Hills: Sage.

Bersoff, D. N., & Hofer, P. (1988). Legal implications of computer-based test interpretation. In T. B. Gutkin & S. L. Wise (Eds.), *The computer as adjunct to the decision-making process*. Hillside, NJ: Erlbaum.

Besharov, D. J. (1985). "Doing something" about child abuse: The need to narrow the grounds for state intervention. *Harvard Journal of Law and Public Policy, 8,* 539–589.

Bienvenu, M. J., Sr. (1978). *A counselor's guide to accompany a Marital Communication Inventory*. Saluda, NC: Family Life.

Bigler, E. E., & Ehrenfurth, J. W. (1980). Critical limitations of the Bender-Gestalt test in clinical neuropsychology: Response to Lacks. *Clinical Neuropsychology, 2,* 88–90.

Bigler, E. D., & Ehrenfurth, J. W. (1981). The continued inappropriate singular use of the Bender Visual Motor Gestalt Test. *Professional Psychology, 12,* 562–569.

Billmire, M. G., & Myers, P. A. (1985). Serious head injury in infants: Accident or abuse? *Pediatrics, 75,* 34–342.

Binet, A., & Henri, V. (1895a). La psychologie individuelle. *L'Année Psychologique, 2,* 411–465.

Binet, A., & Henri, V. (1895b). La mémoire des mots. *L'Année Psychologique, 1,* 1–23.

Binet, A., & Henri, V. (1895c). La memoire des phrases. *L'Année Psychologique, 1,* 24–59.

Binet, A., & Simon, T. (1905). Méthodes nouvelles pour le diagnostic du niveau intellectuel des anormaux. *L'Année Psychologique, 11*, 191–244.

Bing, R., & Vischer, A. L. (1919, April 26). Some remarks on the psychology of internment, based on observations of prisoners of war in Switzerland. *Lancet*, 696–697.

Birch, H. G., & Diller, L. (1959). Rorschach signs of "organicity": A physiological basis for perceptual disturbances. *Journal of Projective Techniques, 23*, 184–197.

Birney, R. C., Burdick, H., & Teevan, R. C. (1969). *Fear of failure*. New York: Van Nostrand Reinhold.

Birren, J. E. (1968). Increments and decrements in the intellectual status of the aged. *Psychiatric Research Reports, 23*, 207–214.

Black, H. (1963). *They shall not pass*. New York: Morrow.

Black, H. C. (1979). *Black's law dictionary* (Rev. ed.). St. Paul: West Publishing.

Blader, J. C., & Marshall, W. L. (1989). The relationship between cognitive and erectile measures of sexual arousal in non-rapist males as a function of depicted aggression. *Behaviour Research and Therapy, 22*, 623–630.

Blain, G. H., Bergner, R. M., Lewis, M. L., & Goldstein, M. A. (1981). The use of objectively scorable House-Tree-Person indicators to establish child abuse. *Journal of Clinical Psychology, 37*, 667–673.

Blanchard, E. B., & Young, L. D. (1974). Clinical applications of biofeedback training: A review of evidence. *Archives of General Psychiatry, 30*, 573–589.

Blanchard, E. B., Kolb, L. C., & Prins, A. (1991). Psychophysiological responses in the diagnosis of posttraumatic stress disorder in Vietnam veterans. *The Journal of Nervous and Mental Disease, 179*, 97–101.

Blatt, S. J., Wein, S. J., Chevron, E., & Quinlan, D. M. (1979). Parental representations and depression in normal young adults. *Journal of Abnormal Psychology, 88*, 388–397.

Block, J. (1961). *The q-sort method in personality assessment and psychiatric research*. Springfield, IL: Charles C Thomas.

Block, J., Block, J. H., & Harrington, D. M. (1974). Some misgivings about the Matching Familiar Figures Test as a measure of reflection-impulsivity. *Developmental Psychology, 10*, 611–632.

Bloom, A. S., Raskin, L. M., & Reese, A. H. (1976). A comparison of the WISC-R and Stanford-Binet Intelligence Scale classifications of developmentally disabled children. *Psychology in the Schools, 13*, 288–290.

Bloom, A. S., Allard, A. M., Zelko, F. A. J., Brill, W. J., Topinka, C. W., & Pfohl, W. (1988). Differential validity of the K-ABC for lower functioning preschool children versus those of higher ability. *American Journal of Mental Retardation, 93*(3), 273–277.

Bloom, B. (1964). *Stability and change in human characteristics*. New York: Wiley.

Bloom, B. S. (1963). Testing cognitive abilities and achievement. In N. L. Gage (Ed.), *Handbook of research on teaching*. Chicago: Rand McNally.

Blum, G. S. (1950). *The Blacky pictures: A technique for the exploration of personality dynamics*. New York: Psychological Corporation.

Blum, M. L., & Naylor, J. C. (1968). *Industrial psychology: Its theoretical and social foundations*. (Rev. ed.). New York: Harper & Row.

Bock, R. D., & Jones, L. V. (1968). *The measurement and prediction of judgment and choice*. San Francisco: Holden-Day.

Bonnie, R. J. (1983). The moral basis of the insanity defense. *American Bar Association Journal, 69*, 194–197.

Booth, A., & Edwards, J. (1983). Measuring marital instability. *Journal of Marriage and the Family, 45*, 387–393.

Boring, E. G. (1923, June 6). Intelligence as the tests test it. *The New Republic*, pp. 35–37.

Boring, E. G. (1950). *A history of experimental psychology* (Rev. ed.). New York: Appleton-Century-Crofts.

Borman, W. C., & Hallam, G. L. (1991). Observation accuracy for assessors of work-sample performance: Consistency across task and individual-differences correlates. *Journal of Applied Psychology, 76*, 11–18.

Bowd, A. D. (1984). Development and validation of a scale of attitudes toward the treatment of animals. *Educational & Psychological Measurement, 44*, 513–515.

Boyd, R. D. (1989). What a difference a day makes: Age-related discontinuities and the Battelle Developmental Inventory. *Journal of Early Intervention, 13*, 114–119.

Bracken, B. A. (1984). *Examiner's manual for the Bracken*

Basic Concept Scale. San Antonio, TX: The Psychological Corporation.

Bracken, B. A. (1985). A critical review of the Kaufman Assessment Battery for Children (K-ABC). *School Psychology Review, 14,* 21–36.

Bracken, B. A., & McCallum, R. S. (1981). Comparison of the PPVT and PPVT-R for white and black preschool males and females. *Educational and Psychological Research, 1,* 79–85.

Bracken, B. A., & Prasse, D. P. (1982). Comparison of the PPVT, PPVT-R, and intelligence tests used for the placement of black, white, and Hispanic EMR students. *Journal of School Psychology, 19,* 304–311.

Bracken, B. A., Prasse, D. P., & McCallum, R. S. (1984). Peabody Picture Vocabulary Test—Revised. An appraisal and review. *School Psychology Review, 13,* 49–60.

Bradley, G. W., & Bradley, L. A. (1977). Experimenter prestige and feedback related to acceptance of genuine personality interpretations and self-attitude. *Journal of Personality Assessment, 41,* 178–185.

Bradley-Johnson, S. (1986). *Psychological assessment of visually impaired and blind students: Infancy through high school.* Austin, TX: Pro-Ed.

Bradley-Johnson, S., & Harris, S. (1990). Best practices in working with students with a visual loss. In A. Thomas & J. Grimes (Eds.), *Best practices in school psychology II* (pp. 871–885). Washington, DC: National Association of School Psychologists.

Bradway, K. P. (1945). Predictive values of Stanford-Binet preschool items. *Journal of Educational Psychology, 36,* 1–16.

Bradway, K. P., & Thompson, C. W. (1962). Intelligence at adulthood: A twenty-five year follow-up. *Journal of Educational Psychology, 53,* 1–14.

Braginsky, B. M., Braginsky, D. D., & Ring, K. (1969). *Methods of madness.* New York: Holt, Rinehart & Winston.

Brannigan, G. G., Ash, T., & Margolis, H. (1980). Impulsivity-reflectivity and children's intellectual performance. *Journal of Personality Assessment, 44,* 41–43.

Brantley, P., Dietz, L., McKnight, G., & Jones, G. (1988). Convergence between the Daily Stress Inventory and endocrine measures of stress. *Journal of Consulting and Clinical Psychology, 56,*(4), 549–551.

Brassard, M., et al. (Eds.). (1986). *The psychological maltreatment of children and youth.* Elmsford, NY: Pergamon Press.

Braswell, J. (1978). The College Board Scholastic Aptitude Test: An overview of the mathematical portion. *Mathematics Teacher, 71*(3), 168–180.

Bray, D. W. (1964). The management progress study. *American Psychologist, 19,* 419–429.

Bray, D. W. (1982). The assessment center and the study of lives. *American Psychologist, 37,* 180–189.

Brayfield, A. H., & Rothe, H. F. (1951). An index of job satisfaction. *Journal of Applied Psychology, 35,* 307–311.

Breen, M. J. (1981). Comparison of the Wechsler Intelligence Scale for Children—Revised and the Peabody Picture Vocabulary Test—Revised for a referred population. *Psychological Reports, 49,* 717–718.

Bresolin, M. J., Jr. (1984). A comparative study of computer administration of the Minnesota Multiphasic Personality Inventory in an inpatient psychiatric setting. *Dissertation Abstracts International, 46,* 295B. (University Microfilms No. 85-06, 377)

Brewer, S. (1987, January 11). A perfect package, yes, but how 'bout the name? *Journal-News* (Rockland County, NY), pp. H-1, H-18.

Breyer, J. B., Martines, K. A., & Dignan, M. A. (1990). Millon Clinical Multiaxial Inventory Alcohol Abuse and Drug Abuse scales and the identification of substance-abuse patients. *Psychological Assessment: A Journal of Consulting & Clinical Psychology, 2,* 438–441.

Brickman, G. A. (1980, April). Uses of voice-pitch analysis. *Journal of Advertising Research, 20,* 69–73.

Briggs, K. C., Myers, I. B., & Saunders, D. (1987). *Type Differentiation Indicator (Research Edition).* Palo Alto, CA: Consulting Psychologists Press.

Brim, D., Glass, D., Nevlinger, J., Firestone, I., & Lerner, S. (1969). *American beliefs and attitudes about intelligence.* New York: Russell Sage Foundation.

Bringle, R., Roach, S., Andler, C., & Evenbeck, S. (1979). Measuring the intensity of jealous reactions. *Catalogue of Selected Documents in Psychology, 9,* 23–24.

Brittain, H. L. (1907). A study in imagination. *The Pedagogical Seminary, 14,* 137–207.

Brody, D., Serby, M., Etienne, N., & Kalkstein, D. S. (1991). Olfactory identification deficits in HIV infection. *American Journal of Psychiatry, 148,* 248–250.

774

Brody, N. (1972). *Personality: Research and theory*. New York: Academic Press.

Brodzinsky, D. M., & Dein, P. (1976). Short-term stability of adult reflection-impulsivity. *Perceptual and Motor Skills, 43*, 1012–1014.

Brogden, H. E. (1946). On the interpretation of the correlation coefficient as a measure of predictive efficiency. *Journal of Educational Psychology, 37*, 65–76.

Brogden, H. E. (1949). When tests pay off. *Personnel Psychology, 2*, 171–183.

Brooks, C. R. (1977). WISC, WISC-R, S-B:LM, WRAT: Relationships and trends among children ages six to ten referred for psychological evaluation. *Psychology in the Schools, 14*, 30–33.

Brotemarkle, R. A. (1947). Clinical psychology, 1896–1946. *Journal of Consulting and Clinical Psychology, 11*, 1–4.

Brown, A. L., & Campione, J. C. (1986). Psychological theory and the study of learning disabilities. *American Psychologist, 41*, 1059–1068.

Brown, L. L., & Hammill, D. D. (1978). *The Behavior Rating Profile: An ecological approach to behavioral assessment*. Austin, TX: Pro-Ed.

Brown, R. D. (1972). The relationship of parental perceptions of university life and their characterizations of their college sons and daughters. *Educational and Psychological Measurement, 32*, 365–375.

Bruch, H. (1962). Perceptual and conceptual disturbances in anorexia nervosa. *Psychosomatic Medicine, 24*, 187–194.

Bruininks, R. H., Woodcock, R. W., Weatherman, R. F., & Hill, B. K. (1984). *Scales of Independent Behavior*. Allen, TX: DLM Teaching Resources.

Buck, J. N. (1948). The H-T-P technique: A qualitative and quantitative scoring manual. *Journal of Clinical Psychology, 4*, 317–396.

Buck, J. N. (1950). *Administration and interpretation of the H-T-P test: Proceedings of the H-T-P workshop at Veterans Administration Hospital, Richmond, Virginia*. Beverly Hills: Western Psychological Services.

Buckle, M. B., & Holt, N. F. (1951). Comparison of Rorschach and Behn Inkblots. (1951). *Journal of Projective Techniques, 15*, 486–493.

Buckley, P. D. (1978). The Bender-Gestalt test: A review of reported research with school-age subjects 1966–1977. *Psychology in the Schools, 15*, 327–338.

Bucofsky, D. (1971). Any learning skills taught in the high school? *Journal of Reading, 15*(3), 195–198.

Bukatman, B. A., Foy, J. L., & De Grazia, E. (1971). What is competency to stand trial? *American Journal of Psychiatry, 127*, 1225–1229.

Bureau of the Census. (1973). *Who's home when*. Washington, DC: U.S. Government Printing Office.

Burdock, E. I., & Hardesty, A. S. (1969). *Structured clinical interview manual*. New York: Springer.

Burgess, A. W., McCausland, M. P., & Wolbert, W. A. (1981, February). Children's drawings as indicators of sexual trauma. *Perspectives in Psychiatric Care, 19*, 50–58.

Burisch, M. (1984a). Approaches to personality inventory construction: A comparison of merits. *American Psychologist, 39*, 214–227.

Burisch, M. (1984b). You don't always get what you pay for: Measuring depression with short and simple versus long and sophisticated scales. *Journal of Research in Personality, 18*(1), 81–98.

Burke, M. J. (1984). Validity generalization: A review and critique of the correlation model. *Personnel Psychology, 37*, 93–115.

Burke, M. J., Normand, J., & Raju, N. S. (1987). Examinee attitudes toward computer-administered ability testing. *Computers in Human Behavior, 3*, 95–107.

Burks, N., & Martin, B. (1983). Everyday problems and life-change events: Ongoing versus acute sources of stress. *Journal of Human Stress, 11*, 27–35.

Burns, G. L., & Patterson, D. R. (1990). Conduct problem behaviors in a stratified random sample of children and adolescents: New standardization data on the Eyberg Child Behavior Inventory. *Psychological Assessment: A Journal of Consulting & Clinical Psychology, 2*, 391–397.

Burns, R. C., & Kaufman, S. H. (1970). *Kinetic Family Drawings (K-F-D): An introduction to understanding through kinetic drawings*. New York: Brunner/Mazel.

Burns, R. C., & Kaufman, S. H. (1972). *Actions, styles, and symbols in Kinetic Family Drawings* (K-F-D). New York: Brunner/Mazel.

Burnkrant, R. E., & Page, T. J. (1984). A modification of the Fenigstein, Scheier, and Buss Self-consciousness Scales. *Journal of Personality Assessment, 48*, 627–628.

Buros, O. K. (1938). *The 1938 mental measurements*

yearbook. New Brunswick, NJ: Rutgers University Press.

Buros, O. K. (1974). *Tests in print II*. Highland Park, NJ: Gryphon Press.

Burstein, A. G. (1972). Review of the Wechsler Adult Intelligence Scale. In O. K. Buros (Ed.), *The seventh mental measurements yearbook* (pp. 786–788). Highland Park, NJ: Gryphon Press.

Burt, C. (1958). The inheritance of mental ability. *American Psychologist, 13*, 1–15.

Burwen, L. S., & Campbell, D. T. (1957). The generality of attitudes toward authority and non-authority figures. *Journal of Abnormal and Social Psychology, 54*, 24–31.

Butcher, J. N. (Ed.). (1979). *New developments in the use of the MMPI*. Minneapolis: University of Minnesota Press.

Butcher, J. N. (1978). Computerized scoring and interpreting services [Re: Minnesota Multiphasic Personality Inventory]. In O. K. Buros (Ed.), *The eighth mental measurements yearbook* (Vol. 1, pp. 942–945, 947–956, 958, 960–962). Highland Park, NJ: Gryphon Press.

Butcher, J. N. (1987). The use of computers in psychological assessment: An overview of practices and issues. Available. In J. N. Butcher (Ed.), *Computerized psychological assessment: A practitioner's guide* (pp. 3–14). New York: Basic Books.

Butcher, J. N. (1990). *MMPI-2 in psychological treatment*. New York: Oxford University Press.

Butcher, J. N., Dahlstrom, W. G., Graham, J. R., Tellegen, A., & Kaemmer, B. (1989). *Manual for the restandardized Minnesota Multiphasic Personality Inventory: MMPI-2. An administrative and interpretive guide*. Minneapolis: University of Minnesota Press.

Butcher, J. N., & Graham, J. R. (1989). *Topics in MMPI-2 Interpretation*. Minneapolis, MN: MMPI-2 Workshops and Symposia.

Butcher, J. N., Graham, J. R., Williams, C. L., & Ben-Porath, Y. (1989). *Development and use of the MMPI-2 Content Scales*. Minneapolis: University of Minnesota Press.

Butcher, J. N., & Pope, K. S. (1990). MMPI-2: A practical guide to psychometric, clinical, and ethical issues. *The Independent Practitioner, 10*(1), 33–40.

Butcher, J. N., & Tellegen, A. (1966). Objections to MMPI items. *Journal of Consulting Psychology, 30*, 527–534.

Butter, E. J., Weikel, K. B., Otto, V., Wright, K. P., & Deinzer, G. (1991). TV advertising of OTC medicines and its effects on child viewers. *Psychology & Marketing, 8*, 117–128.

Byrne, D. (1974). *An introduction to personality* (2nd ed.). Englewood Cliffs, NJ: Prentice Hall.

Cacioppo, J. T., & Petty, R. E. (1985). Physiological responses and advertising effects: Is the cup half full or half empty? *Psychology & Marketing, 2*, 115–126.

Cain, L. F., Levine, S., & Elsey, F. F. (1963). *Cain-Levine Social Competency Scale*. Palo Alto, CA: Consulting Psychologists Press.

Camilli, G., & Shepard, L. A. (1985). A computer program to aid the detection of biased test items. *Educational & Psychological Measurement, 45*, 595–600.

Campbell, D. P. (1968). The Strong Vocational Interest Blank: 1927–1967. In P. McReynolds (Ed.), *Advances in psychological assessment* (Vol. 1, pp. 105–130). Palo Alto, CA: Science and Behavior Books.

Campbell, D. P. (1971). *Handbook for the Strong Vocational Interest Blank*. Palo Alto, CA: Stanford University Press.

Campbell, D. P., & Hansen, J. C. (1981). *Manual for the SVIB-SCII—Third Edition*. Stanford, CA: Stanford University Press.

Campbell, D. T., & Fiske, D. W. (1959). Convergent and discriminant validation by the multitrait-multimethod matrix. *Psychological Bulletin, 56*, 81–105.

Campo, V., & Vilar, N. P. (1977). Clinical usefulness of the Draw-An-Animal Test. *British Journal of Projective Psychology and Personality Study, 22*(1), 1–7.

Cancro, R. (1969). Abstraction on proverbs in process-reactive schizophrenia. *Journal of Consulting and Clinical Psychology, 33*, 267–270.

Canter, A. (1963). A background interference procedure for grapho-motor tests in the study of deficit. *Perceptual and Motor Skills, 16*, 914.

Canter, A. (1966). A background interference procedure to increase the sensitivity of the Bender Gestalt Test to organic brain disorders. *Journal of Consulting Psychology, 30*, 91–97.

Capeli, E. (1984, September). Detroit goes psycho! *Automotive Industries*, pp. 44–48.

Carey, M. P., Faulstich, M. E., Gresham, F. M., Ruggerio, L., & Enyart, P. (1987). Children's Depression Inventory: Construct and discriminant validity across clinical and nonreferred (control) populations. *Journal of Consulting and Clinical Psychology, 55,* 755–761.

Carlson, L., & Reynolds, C. R. (1981). Factor structure and specific variance of the WPPSI subtests at six age levels. *Psychology in the Schools, 18,* 48–54.

Carmichael, L. (1927). A further study of the development of behavior in vertebrates experimentally removed from the influence of external stimulation. *Psychological Review, 34,* 34–47.

Carr, A. C., Wilson, S. L., Ghosh, A., Ancil, R. J., & Woods, R. T. (1982). Automated testing of geriatric patients using a microcomputer-based system. *International Journal of Man-Machine Studies, 17,* 297–300.

Carr, M. A., Sweet, J. J., & Rossini, E. (1986). Diagnostic validity of the Luria-Nebraska Neuropsychological Battery—Children's Revision. *Journal of Consulting and Clinical Psychology, 54,* 354–358.

Carroll, J. B. (1985, May). Domains of cognitive ability. Symposium: Current theories and findings on cognitive abilities. Los Angeles: AAAS.

Carver, R. P. (1968–1969). Designing an aural aptitude test for Negroes: An experiment that failed. *College Board Review, 70,* 10–14.

Carver, R. P. (1969). Use of a recently developed listening comprehension test to investigate the effect of disadvantagement upon verbal proficiency. *American Educational Research Journal, 6,* 263–270.

Cascio, W. F. (1987). *Applied psychology in personnel management (3rd Edition).* Englewood Cliffs, NJ: Prentice-Hall.

Cash, T. F., & Brown, T. A. (1987). Body image in anorexia nervosa and bulimia nervosa: A review of the literature. *Behavior Modification, 11,* 487–521.

Cassel, R. N. (1958). *The leadership q-sort test: A test of leadership values.* Murfreesboro, TN: Psychometric Affiliates.

Cassel, R. N. (1971). The group intelligence test IQ paradox. *College Student Journal, 5,* 31–33.

Castiglioni, A. (1946). *Adventures of the mind.* New York: Knopf, 1946.

Cates, J. A., & Lapham, R. F. (1991). Personality assessment of the prelingual, profoundly deaf child or adolescent. *Journal of Personality Assessment, 56,* 118–129.

Cattell, R. B. (1978). *The scientific use of factor analysis in behavioral and life sciences.* New York: Plenum.

Cattell, J. M. (1887). Experiments on the association of ideas. *Mind, 12,* 68–74.

Cattell, J. M., & Bryant, S. (1889). Mental association investigated by experiment. *Mind, 14,* 230–250.

Cattell, P. (1940). *Cattell Infant Intelligence Scale.* New York: Psychological Corporation.

Cattell, R. B. (1940). A culture free intelligence test, Part I. *Journal of Educational Psychology, 31,* 161–179.

Cattell, R. B. (1950). *Personality: A systematic theoretical and factual study.* New York: McGraw-Hill.

Cattell, R. B. (1957). *Personality and motivation, structure and measurement.* Yonkers, NY: World Book.

Cattell, R. B. (1965). *The scientific analysis of personality.* Baltimore: Penguin Books.

Cattell, R. B. (1971). *Abilities: Their structure, growth, and action.* Boston: Houghton Mifflin.

Cattell, R. B., & Krug, S. E. (1986). The number of factors in the 16 PF: A review of the evidence with special emphasis on methodological problems. *Educational and Psychological Measurement, 46,* 509–522.

Cattell, R. B., & Luborsky, L. B. (1952). *IPAT humor test of personality: Manual.* Champaign, IL: Institute for Personality and Ability Testing.

Ceci, S. J., Ross, D. F., & Toglia, M. P. (1987). Suggestibility of children's memory: Psycholegal implications. *Journal of Experimental Psychology, 116,* 38–49.

Cerney, M. S. (1984). One last response to the Rorschach test: A second chance to reveal oneself. *Journal of Personality Assessment, 48,* 338–344.

Chambless, D. L., Caputo, G. C., Bright, P., & Gallagher, R. (1984). Assessment of fear in agoraphobics: The Body Sensations Questionnaire and the Agoraphobic Cognitions Questionnaire. *Journal of Consulting & Clinical Psychology, 52,* 1090–1097.

Champagne, J. E. (1969). Job recruitment of the unskilled. *Personnel Journal, 48,* 259–268.

Chandler, L. A., Shermis, M. D., & Lampert, M. E. (1989). The need-threat analysis: A scoring system for the Children's Apperception Test. *Psychology in the Schools, 26,* 47–53.

Chapman, L., & Chapman, J. (1967). Genesis of popular but erroneous psychodiagnostic observations. *Journal of Abnormal Psychology, 72,* 193–204.

Chattin, S. H., & Bracken, B. A. (1989). School psychologists' evaluation of the K-ABC, McCarthy

Scales, Stanford-Binet IV, and WISC-R. *Journal of Psychoeducational Assessment, 7*(2), 112–130.

Chelune, G., Heaton, R., & Lehman, R. (1986). Neuropsychological and personality correlates of patients' complaints of disability. In G. Goldstein (Ed.), *Advances in clinical neuropsychology* (Vol. 3, pp. 95–126). New York: Plenum Press.

Chess, S., & Fernandez, P. (1981). Do deaf children have a typical personality? *Annual Progress in Child Psychiatry and Child Development,* 295–305.

Chess, S., & Thomas, A. (1973). Temperament in the normal infant. In J. C. Westman (Ed.), *Individual differences in children.* New York: Wiley.

Chiu, C. (1989). A study of self-concept of Cambodian children in two Richmond Public schools. Paper presented at the Annual Meeting of the Eastern Educational Research Association, Savannah, GA. (ERIC Document Reproduction Service No. ED 303 559).

Chinoy, E. (1967). *Society: An introduction to sociology.* New York: Random House.

Choca, J., Bresolin, L., Okonek, A., & Ostrow, D. (1988). Validity of the Millon Clinical Multiaxial Inventory in the assessment of affective disorders. *Journal of Personality Assessment, 52,* 96–105.

Choca, J. P., Shanley, L. A., Peterson, C. A., & Van Denburg, E. (1990). Racial bias and the MCMI. *Journal of Personality Assessment, 54,* 479–490.

Christensen, A. L. (1975). *Luria's neuropsychological investigation.* New York: Spectrum.

Christenson, S. L. (1990). Review of Child Behavior Checklist. In J. J. Kramer & J. C. Conoley (Eds.), *The supplement to the tenth mental measurements yearbook* (pp. 40–41). Lincoln: The Buros Institute of Mental Measurements of the University of Nebraska-Lincoln.

Chun, K., Cobb, S., & French, J. R. P., Jr. (1975). *Measures for psychological assessment.* Ann Arbor, MI: Survey Research Center of the Institute for Social Research.

Cicchetti, D., & Carlson, V. (Eds.). (1989). *Child maltreatment: Theory and research on the causes and consequences of child abuse and neglect.* New York: Cambridge University Press.

Cieutat, V. J. (1965). Examiner differences with the Stanford-Binet IQ. *Perceptual and Motor Skills, 20,* 317–318.

Clarizio, H. F. (1989). *Assessment and treatment of depression in children and adolescents.* Brandon, VT: Clinical Psychology Publishing.

Clark, B. (1979). *Growing up gifted.* Columbus, OH: Merrill.

Clark, B. (1988). *Growing up gifted* (3rd ed.). Columbus, OH: Merrill.

Clarke, H. J., Rosenzweig, S., & Fleming, E. E. (1947). The reliability of the scoring of the Rosenzweig-Picture-Frustration Study. *Journal of Clinical Psychology, 3,* 364–370.

Cleckley, H. (1976). *The mask of sanity* (5th ed.). St. Louis, MO: Mosby.

Cleveland, S. E. (1976). Reflections on the rise and fall of psychodiagnosis. *Professional Psychology, 7,* 309–318.

Cliff, N. (1984). An improved internal consistency reliability estimate. *Journal of Educational Statistics, 9,* 151–161.

Coates, S. (1972). *Preschool Embedded Figures Test.* Palo Alto, CA: Consulting Psychologists Press.

Code of Fair Testing Practices in Education. (1988). Washington, DC: Joint Committee on Testing Practices.

Coffman, W. E. (1985). Review of the Kaufman Assessment Battery for Children. In J. V. Mitchell, Jr. (Ed.), *The ninth mental measurements yearbook* (Vol. 1). Lincoln: University of Nebraska Press.

Cohen, E. (1965). Examiner differences with individual intelligence tests. *Perceptual and Motor Skills, 20,* 1324.

Cohen, J. (1960). A coefficient of agreement for nominal scales. *Educational and Psychological Measurement, 20,* 37–46.

Cohen, R. J. (1977). Socially reinforced obsessing: A reply. *Journal of Consulting and Clinical Psychology, 45,* 1166–1171.

Cohen, R. J. (1979a). *Malpractice: A guide for mental health professionals.* New York: Free Press.

Cohen, R. J. (1979b). *Binge! It's not a state of hunger . . . It's a state of mind.* New York: Macmillan.

Cohen, R. J. (1983a). The professional liability of behavioral scientists: An overview. *Behavioral Sciences & the Law, 1*(1), 9–22.

Cohen, R. J. (1983b). *A study of the goodwill associated with the Bell Symbol.* Unpublished manuscript.

Cohen, R. J. (1985). Computer-enhanced qualitative research. *Journal of Advertising Research, 25*(3), 48–52.

Cohen, R. J. (1986). Patriotic chic (Editor's Note). *Psychology & Marketing, 3,* 239–241.

Cohen, R. J. (1987). Overview of emerging evaluative and diagnostic methods technologies. In *Proceed-*

ings of the fourth annual advertising research foundation workshop: Broadening the horizons of copy research. New York: Advertising Research Foundation.

Cohen, R. J. (1988). *A student's guide to psychological testing*. Mountain View, CA: Mayfield.

Cohen, R. J. (1992). *65 exercises in psychological testing and assessment*. (2nd ed.). Mountain View, CA: Mayfield.

Cohen, R. J., Becker, R. E., & Teevan, R. C. (1975). Perceived somatic reaction to stress and hostile press. *Psychological Reports, 37*, 676–678.

Cohen, R. J., & Houston, D. R. (1975). Fear of failure and rigidity in problem solving. *Perceptual and Motor Skills, 40*, 930.

Cohen, R. J., & Mariano, W. E. (1982). *Legal guidebook in mental health*. New York: Free Press.

Cohen, R. J., & Parker, C. (1974). Fear of failure and death. *Psychological Reports, 34*, 54.

Cohen, R. J., & Smith, F. J. (1976). Socially reinforced obsessing: Etiology of a disorder in a Christian Scientist. *Journal of Consulting and Clinical Psychology, 44*, 142–144.

Cohen, R. J., & Teevan, R. C. (1974). Fear of failure and impression management: An exploratory study. *Psychological Reports, 35*, 1332.

Cohen, R. J., & Teevan, R. C. (1975). Philosophies of human nature and hostile press. *Psychological Reports, 37*, 460–462.

Colarusso, R. P., & Hammill, D. D. (1972). *Motor-Free Visual Perception Test*. San Rafael, CA: Academic Therapy.

Cole, S. T., & Hunter, M. (1971). Pattern analysis of WISC scores achieved by culturally disadvantaged children. *Psychological Reports, 20*, 191–194.

Coleman, L. (1989). Medical examination for sexual abuse: Are we being told the truth? *Family Law News, 12*(2).

Collard, R. R. (1972). Review of the Bayley Scales of Infant Development. In O. K. Buros (Ed.), *The seventh mental measurements yearbook* (pp. 402–404). Highland Park, NJ: Gryphon Press.

Colligan, R. C., Osborne, D., Swenson, W. M., & Offord, K. P. (1983). *The MMPI: A contemporary normative study*. New York: Praeger.

Colligan, R. C., Osborne, D., Swenson, W. M., & Offord, K. P. (1984). Contemporary norms for the MMPI: Summarizing one year of clinical experience. Paper presented at the 93rd annual meeting of the American Psychological Association, Toronto, Ontario, Canada.

Collins, B. L., & Lerner, N. D. (1982). Assessment of fire-safety symbols. *Human Factors, 24*, 75–84.

Commons, M. (1985, April). How novelty produces continuity in cognitive development within a domain and accounts for unequal development across domains. Toronto: SRCD, Ontario, Canada.

Comrey, A. L., Backer, T. E., & Glaser, E. M. (1973). *A sourcebook for mental health measures*. Los Angeles: Human Interaction Research Institute.

Comrey, A. L., Michael, W. B., & Fruchter, B. (1988). J. P. Guilford (1897–1987). *American Psychologist, 43*, 1086–1087.

Comrey, A. L., & Duffy, K. E. (1968). Cattell and Eysenck factor scores related to Comrey personality factors. *Multivariate Behavioral Research, 4*, 379–392.

Cone, J. D., & Hawkins, R. P. (Eds.). (1977). *Behavioral assessment: New directions in clinical psychology*. New York: Brunner/Mazel.

Conger, A. J. (1985). Kappa reliabilities for continuous behaviors and events. *Educational and Psychological Measurement, 45*, 861–868.

Connolly, A. J., Nachtman, W., & Pritchett, E. W. (1976). *KeyMath Diagnostic Arithmetic Test Manual*. Circle Pines, MN: American Guidance Service.

Conoley, J. C., & Kramer, J. J. (Eds.). (1989). *The tenth mental measurements yearbook*. Lincoln: The Buros Institute of Mental Measurements of the University of Nebraska-Lincoln.

Conte, H. R., Plutchik, R., Buck, L., Picard, S., & Karasu, T. B. (1991). Interrelations between ego functions and personality traits: Their relation to psychotherapy outcome. *American Journal of Psychotherapy, 45*, 69–77.

Conte, H. R., & Plutchik, R. (1981). A circumplex model for interpersonal personality traits. *Journal of Personality and Social Psychology, 40*, 701–711.

Cooper, A. (1981). A basic TAT set for adolescent males. *Journal of Clinical Psychology, 37*(2), 411–414.

Cooper, Z., Cooper, P. J., & Fairburn, C. G. (1985). The specificity of the Eating Disorder Inventory. *British Journal of Clinical Psychology, 24*, 129–130.

Coopersmith, S. (1967). *The antecedents of self-esteem*. San Francisco: Freeman.

Corah, N. L., O'Shea, R. M., Pace, L. F., & Seyrek, S. K. (1984). Development of a patient measure of satisfaction with the dentist: The Dental Visit Satisfaction Scale. *Journal of Behavioral Medicine, 7*, 367–373.

Cornell, D. G. (1985). External validation of the Personality Inventory for Children—Comment on Lachar, Gdowski, and Snyder. *Journal of Consulting & Clinical Psychology, 53,* 273–274.

Corwin, D., Berlinger, L., Goodman, G., Goodwin, J., & White, S. (1987). Child sexual abuse and custody disputes: No easy answers. *Journal of Interpersonal Violence, 2,* 91–105.

Costantino, G., Malgady, R., & Rogler, L. H. (1988). *Tell-Me-A-Story—TEMAS—Manual.* Los Angeles: Western Psychological Services.

Cote, J. A., McCullough, J., & Reilly, M. (1985). Effects of unexpected situations on behavior-intention differences: A garbology analysis. *Journal of Consumer Research, 12,* 188–194.

Covetkovic, R. (1979). Conception and representation of space in human figure drawings by schizophrenic and normal subjects. *Journal of Personality Assessment, 43*(3), 247–256.

Covin, T. M., & Lubimiv, A. J. (1976). Concurrent validity of the WRAT. *Perceptual and Motor Skills, 43,* 573–574.

Coyne, J. C. (1976). The place of informed consent in ethical dilemmas. *Journal of Consulting and Clinical Psychology, 44,* 1015–1017.

Cozby, P. C., Worden, P. E., & Kee, D. W. 1989. *Research methods in human development.* Mountain View, CA: Mayfield Publishing Company.

Craig, R. J. (1990). Current utilization of psychological tests at diagnostic practicum sites. Paper presented at Annual Meeting of the Society for Personality Assessment, San Diego, CA.

Crevecoeur, M. G. St. J. de. (1951). What is an American letter? In H. S. Commager (Ed.), *Living ideas in America.* New York: Harper. (Originally published in *Letters from an American farmer,* 1762.)

Crino, M. D., White, M. C., & Looney, S. W. (1985). In the eye of the beholder: A reply to Ilgen and Moore. *Academy of Management Journal, 28,* 950–954.

Cronbach, L. J. (1949). Statistical methods applied to Rorschach scores: A review. *Psychological Bulletin, 46,* 393–429.

Cronbach, L. J. (1951). Coefficient alpha and the internal structure of tests. *Psychometrika, 16,* 297–334.

Cronbach, L. J. (1970). *Essentials of psychological testing* (3rd ed.). New York: Harper & Row.

Cronbach, L. J. (1975). Five decades of public controversy over mental testing. *American Psychologist, 30,* 1–13.

Cronbach, L. J. (1984). *Essentials of psychological testing.* New York: Harper & Row.

Cronbach, L. J., & Gleser, G. C. (1965). *Psychological tests and personnel decisions* (2nd ed.). Urbana: University of Illinois Press.

Cronbach, L. J., Gleser, G. C., Nanda, H., & Rajaratnam, N. (1972). *The dependability of behavioral measurements: Theory of generalizability for scores and profiles.* New York: Wiley.

Cronbach, L. J., & Meehl, P. E. (1955). Construct validity in psychological tests. *Psychological Bulletin, 52,* 281–302.

Crosson, B., & Warren, R. L. (1982). Use of the Luria-Nebraska Neuropsychological Battery in aphasia: A conceptual critique. *Journal of Consulting and Clinical Psychology, 50,* 22–31.

Crowne, D. P., & Marlowe, D. (1964). *The approval motive: Studies in evaluative dependence.* New York: Wiley.

Cummings, J. A. (1981). An evaluation of Kinetic Family Drawings. Paper presented at the annual meeting of the American Psychological Association. Los Angeles, California.

Cundick, B. P. (1976). Measures of intelligence on Southwest Indian students. *Journal of Social Psychology, 81,* 151–156.

Cunningham, T., & Presnall, D. (1978). Relationship between dimensions of adaptive behavior and sheltered workshop productivity. *American Journal of Mental Deficiency, 82,* 386–393.

Cureton, E. E. (1957). The upper and lower twenty-seven per cent rule. *Psychometrika, 22,* 293–296.

Dahlstrom, W. G. (1970). Personality. *Annual Review of Psychology, 21,* 1–48.

Dahlstrom, W. G., Brooks, J. D., & Peterson, C. D. (1990). The Beck Depression Inventory: Item order and the impact of response sets. *Journal of Personality Assessment, 55,* 224–233.

Dahlstrom, W. G., Lachar, D., & Dahlstrom, L. E. (Eds.). (1986). *MMPI patterns of American minorities.* Minneapolis: University of Minnesota Press.

Dahlstrom, W. G., Meehl, P. E., & Schofield, W. (1986). Obituary—Starke Rosecrans Hathaway (1903–1984). *American Psychologist, 41,* 834–835.

Dahlstrom, W. G., & Welsh, G. S. (1960). *An MMPI handbook: A guide to use in clinical practice and research.* Minneapolis: University of Minnesota Press.

Dahlstrom, W. G., Welsh, G. S., & Dahlstrom, L. E. (1972). *An MMPI handbook. Volume 1, Clinical in-*

terpretation. Minneapolis: University of Minnesota Press.

Dana, R. H., & Cantrell, J. D. (1988). An update on the Millon Clinical Multiaxial Inventory (MCMI). *Journal of Clinical Psychology, 44,* 760–763.

Darlington, R. B., & Bishop, C. H. (1966). Increasing test validity by considering interitem correlation. *Journal of Applied Psychology, 50,* 322–330.

Darlington, R. B., & Stauffer, G. F. (1966). Use and evaluation of discrete test information in decision making. *Journal of Applied Psychology, 50,* 125–129.

Darwin, C. (1859). *On the origin of species by means of natural selection.* London: Murray.

Das, J. P. (1972). Patterns of cognitive ability in nonretarded and retarded children. *American Journal of Mental Deficiency, 77,* 6–12.

Das, J. P., Kirby, J., & Jarman, R. F. (1975). Simultaneous and successive synthesis: An alternative model for cognitive abilities. *Psychological Bulletin, 82,* 87–103.

Das, J. P., Kirby, J. R., & Jarman, R. F. (1979). *Simultaneous and successive cognitive processes.* New York: Academic Press.

Datel, W. E., & Gengerelli, J. A. (1955). Reliability of Rorschach interpretations. *Journal of Projective Techniques, 19,* 322–338.

Davidson, H. A. (1949). Malingered psychosis. *Bulletin of the Menninger Clinic, 13,* 157–163.

Davis, A. (1951). Socioeconomic influences upon children's learning. *Understanding the Child, 20,* 10–16.

Davis, E. E., & Rowland, T. (1974). A replacement for the venerable Stanford-Binet. *Journal of Clinical Psychology, 30,* 517–521.

Davis, G. A. (1989). Testing for creative potential. *Contemporary Educational Psychology, 14,* 257–274.

Davis, G. A., & Rimm, S. B. (1979). *GIFFI I and II: Group inventories for finding interests.* Watertown, WI: Educational Assessment Service.

Davis, G. A., & Rimm, S. B. (1982). Group Inventory for Finding Interests (GIFFI) I and II: Instruments for identifying creative potential in the junior and senior high school. *Journal of Creative Behavior, 16,* 50–57.

Davis, R., Butler, N., & Goldstein, H. (1972). *From birth to seven: A report of the National Child Development Study.* London: Longman.

Davison, G. C., Feldman, P. M., & Osborn, C. E. (1984). Articulated thoughts, irrational beliefs, and fear of negative evaluation. *Cognitive Therapy & Research, 8,* 349–362.

Dean, A. (Ed.). (1985). *Depression in multidisciplinary perspective.* New York: Brunner/Mazel.

Dean, R. S. (1979). Predictive validity of the WISC-R with Mexican-American children. *Journal of School Psychology, 17,* 55–58.

Dean, R. S. (1983). Neuropsychological assessment. In Staff College (Ed.), *Handbook of diagnostic and epidemiological instruments.* Washington, DC: National Institute of Mental Health.

Dearborn, G. V. (1897). Blots of ink in experimental psychology. *Psychological Review, 4,* 390–391.

Dearborn, G. V. (1898). A study of imagination. *American Journal of Psychology, 9,* 390–391.

DeDombal, F. T. (1979). Computers and the surgeon: A matter of decision. *The Surgeon, 39,* 57.

Delaney, E. A., & Hopkins, T. F. (1987). *Examiner's handbook: An expanded guide for Fourth Edition users.* Chicago: Riverside Publishing Company.

D'Elia, L., Satz, P., & Schretlen, D. (1989). Wechsler Memory Scale: A critical appraisal of the normative studies. *Journal of Clinical and Experimental Neuropsychology, 11,* 551–568.

Delis, D. C., & Kaplan, E. (1982). The assessment of aphasia with the Luria Nebraska Neuropsychological Battery: A case critique. *Journal of Consulting and Clinical Psychology, 50,* 32–39.

De Longis, A., Coyne, J. C., Dakof, G., Folkman, S., & Lazarus, R. S. (1982). Relationship of daily hassles, uplifts and major life events to health status. *Health Psychology, 1,* 119–136.

Demby, E., (1974). Psychographics and from whence it came. In W. D. Wells (Ed.), *Lifestyles and psychographics.* Chicago: American Marketing Association.

Demo, D. H. (1985). The measurement of self-esteem: Refining our methods. *Journal of Personality and Social Psychology, 48,* 1490–1502.

Dennis, W., & Dennis, M. G. (1940). The effect of cradling practice upon the onset of walking in Hopi children. *Journal of Genetic Psychology, 56,* 77–86.

Dennis, W., & Najarian, P. (1957). Infant development under environmental handicap. *Psychological Monographs, 71,* No. 7 (Whole No. 436).

Department of Health, Education, and Welfare (1977a). Nondiscrimination on basis of handicap: Implementation of Section 504 of the Rehabilitation Act of 1973. *Federal Register, 42*(86), 22676–22702.

Department of Health, Education, and Welfare (1977b). Education of Handicapped Children: Implementation of Part B of the Education of the Handicapped Act. *Federal Register, 42*(163), 42474–42518.

Deri, S. (1949a). *Introduction to the Szondi Test.* New York: Grune & Stratton.

Deri, S. K. (1949b). The Szondi Test. *The American Journal of Orthopsychiatry, 19*, 447–454.

DeStefano, L. Y., & Thompson, D., S. (1990). Adaptive behavior: The construct and its measurement. In C. R. Reynolds & R. W. Kamphaus (Eds.), *Handbook of psychological and educational assessment of children: Personality, behavior & context* (pp. 445–469). New York: Guilford Press.

DeWitt, K. (1991). Looking overseas for school exams. *New York Times,* March 29, 1991, p. B6.

Dickson, P. R., & Sawyer, A. G. (1986). *Point-of-purchase behavior and price perceptions of supermarket shoppers.* Working paper, Cambridge, MA: Marketing Science Institute.

Diebold, M. H., Curtis, W. S., & DuBose, R. F. (1978). Developmental scales versus observational measures for deaf-blind children. *Exceptional Children, 44*, 275–278.

Diener, E., Emmons, R. A., Larsen, R. J., & Griffin, S. (1985). The Satisfaction With Life Scale. *Journal of Personality Assessment, 49*, 71–75.

Diven, K. (1937). Certain determinants in the conditioning of anxiety reactions. *Journal of Psychology, 3*, 291–308.

Dmitruk, V. M., Collins, R. W., & Clinger, D. I. (1973). The Barnum effect and acceptance of negative personal evaluation. *Journal of Consulting and Clinical Psychology, 41*, 192–194.

Dokecki, P. R., Frede, M. C., & Gautney, D. B. (1969). The criterion, construct, and predictive validities of the WPPSI. *Proceedings of the Annual Convention of the American Psychological Association, 4*, 505–506.

Doll, E. (1965). *Vineland Social Maturity Scale.* Minneapolis: American Guidance Service.

Doll, E. A. (1917). A brief Binet-Simon scale. *Psychological Clinic, 11*, 197–211, 254–261.

Doll, E. A. (1953). *Measurement of social competence: A manual for the Vineland Social Maturity Scale.* Circle Pines, MN: American Guidance Service.

Donion, T. (1984). *The College Board technical handbook for the Scholastic Aptitude and Achievement tests.* New York: College Board Publications.

Doty, R. L., Shaman, P., & Dann, M. (1984). Development of the University of Pennsylvania Smell Identification Test: A standard microencapsulated test of olfactory dysfunction. *Physiological Behavior, 32*, 489–502.

Down, J. L. (1887). *On some of the mental affections of childhood and youth.* London: J. & A. Churchill.

Drake, R. E., & Vaillant, G. E. (1985). A validity study of axis II of DSM-III. *American Journal of Psychiatry, 145*, 753–755.

Dreger, R. M., & Miller, K. S. (1960). Comparative studies of Negroes and Whites in the U.S. *Psychological Bulletin, 51*, 361–402.

Drinkwater, M. J. (1976). Psychological evaluation of visually handicapped children. *Massachusetts School Psychologists Association Newsletter, 6.*

Drummond, R. J. (1984). Review of Edwards Personal Preference Schedule. In D. J. Keyser & R. C. Sweetland (Eds.), *Test critiques* (Vol. 1; pp. 252–258). Kansas City, MO: Test Corporation of America.

Drummond, R. J., McIntire, W. G., & Skaggs, C. T. (1978). The relationship of work values to occupational level in young adult workers. *Journal of Employment Counseling, 15*, 117–121.

DuBois, P. H. (1966). A test-dominated society: China 1115 B.C.–1905 A.D. In A. Anastasi (Ed.), *Testing problems in perspective* (pp. 29–36). Washington, DC: American Council on Education.

DuBois, P. H. (1970). *A history of psychological testing.* Boston: Allyn and Bacon.

Dudek, S. (1954). An approach to fundamental compatibility in marital couples through the Rorschach. *Journal of Projective Techniques, 18*, 400.

Dudek, S., & Gottlieb, S. (1954). An approach to fundamental compatibility in marital couples through the Rorschach. *American Psychologist, 9*, 356.

Dudycha, G. J. (1936). An objective study of punctuality in relation to personality and achievement. *Archives of Psychology, 204*, 1–319.

Dugdale, R. (1877). *The Jukes: A study in crime, pauperism, disease, and heredity.* New York: Putnam.

Duncan, P. M., & Millard, W. (1866). *A manual for the classification, training, and education of the feeble-minded, imbecile, and idiotic.* London: Longmans, Green.

Dunn, L. M. (1959). *Peabody Picture Vocabulary Test.* Minneapolis: American Guidance Service.

Dunn, L. M., & Dunn, L. M. (1981). *Peabody Picture Vocabulary Test—Revised.* Circle Pines, MN: American Guidance Service.

Dunnette, M. D. (1963). A modified model for selection research. *Journal of Applied Psychology, 47,* 317–323.

Dunnette, M. D., & Borman, W. C. (1979). Personnel selection and classification systems. *Annual Review of Psychology, 30,* 477–525.

Dunphy, D. C. (1963) The social structure of urban adolescent peer groups. *Sociometry, 26,* 230–240.

Duran, R. P. (1986). *Purposes for a code of fair testing in education.* Paper presented at the annual meeting of the American Psychological Association, Washington, DC.

Duran, R. P. (1988). Testing of linguistic minorities. In R. L. Linn (Ed.), *Educational measurement* (3rd ed.). New York: American Council on Education/Macmillan.

Durrell, D. D., & Catterson, J. H. (1980). *Durrell Analysis of Reading Difficulty manual* (3rd ed.). New York: Psychological Corporation.

Dworkin, G. (1974). Two views on IQs. *American Psychologist, 29,* 465–467.

Dykes, L. (1986). The whiplash shaken infant syndrome: What has been learned? *Child Abuse and Neglect, 10,* 211.

Dysken, M. W., Chang, S. S., Cooper, R. C., et al. (1979). Barbiturate-facilitated interviewing. *Biological Psychiatry, 14,* 421–432.

Dysken, M. W., Kooser, J. A., Haraszti, J. S., et al. (1979). Clinical usefulness of sodium amytal interviewing. *Archives of General Psychiatry, 36,* 789–794.

Earls, C. M., & Marshall, W. L. (1983). The current state of technology in the laboratory assessment of sexual arousal patterns. In J. G. Greer & I. R. Stuart (Eds.), *The sexual aggressor: Current perspectives on treatment* (pp. 336–362). New York: Van Nostrand Reinhold.

Earls, C. M., Quinsey, V. L., & Castonguay, L. G. (1987). A comparison of three methods of scoring penile circumference changes. *Archives of Sexual Behavior, 6,* 493–500.

Ebel, R. L. (1973). Evaluation and educational objectives. *Journal of Educational Measurement, 10,* 273–279.

Eckenrode, J. (1984). Impact of chronic and acute stressors on daily reports of mood. *Journal of Personality and Social Psychology, 46,* 907–918.

Edelbrock, C. (1988). Informant reports. In E. S. Shapiro & T. R. Kratochwill (Eds.), *Behavioral assessment in schools* (pp. 351–383). New York: Guilford Press.

Educational Testing Service. (1977). *Graduate Record Examinations information bulletin: 1977–1978.* Princeton, NJ: Educational Testing Service.

Edwards, A. L. (1953). *Edwards Personal Preference Schedule.* New York: Psychological Corporation.

Edwards, A. L. (1957a). *Techniques of attitude scale construction.* New York: Appleton-Century-Crofts.

Edwards, A. L. (1957b). *The social desirability variable in personality assessment and research.* New York: Dryden.

Edwards, A. L. (1966). Relationship between probability of endorsement and social desirability scale value for a set of 2,824 personality statements. *Journal of Applied Psychology, 50,* 238–239.

Edwards, A. L., & Walsh, J. A. (1964). Response sets in standard and experimental personality scales. *American Educational Research Journal, 1,* 52–60.

Eichler, R. M. (1951). A comparison of the Rorschach and Behn-Rorschach inkblot tests. *Journal of Consulting Psychology, 15,* 185–189.

Einhorn, H. J. (1984). *Accepting error to make less error in prediction.* Paper presented at the 92nd annual meeting of the American Psychological Association, Toronto, Ontario, Canada.

Ekman, W., Friesen, V., & Ellsworth, P. (1982). *Emotions in the human face.* New York: Pergamon.

Elbert, J. C. (1984). Training in child diagnostic assessment: A survey of clinical psychology graduate programs. *Journal of Clinical Child Psychology, 13,* 122–123.

Ellerstein, N. S. (Ed.) (1981). *Child abuse and neglect: A medical reference.* New York: Wiley.

Elliot, H., Glass, L., & Evans, J. (Eds.). (1987). *Mental health assessment of deaf clients: A practical manual.* Boston: Little, Brown.

Elliott, C. D. (1990a). *The Differential Ability Scales.* San Antonio, TX: The Psychological Corporation.

Elliott, C. D. (1990b). *Technical Handbook: The Differential Ability Scales.* San Antonio, TX: The Psychological Corporation.

Embretson, S. E. (1987). Toward development of a psychometric approach. In C. S. Lidz (Ed.), *Dynamic assessment: An interactive approach to evaluating learning potential* (pp. 135–164). New York: Guilford Press.

Embretson, S. E. (1988). Diagnostic testing by measuring learning processes: Psychometric considerations for dynamic testing. In N. O. Frederiksen, R. Glaser, A. M. Lesgold, M. G. Shafto (Eds.). *Diagnostic monitoring of skill and knowledge acquisition*. Hillsdale, NJ: Erlbaum.

Endicott, J., & Spitzer, R. L. (1978). A diagnostic interview: The Schedule for Affective Disorders and Schizophrenia. *Archives of General Psychiatry, 35*, 837–844.

Engin, A., & Wallbrown, F. H. (1976). The stability of four kinds of perceptual errors on the Bender-Gestalt. *Journal of Psychology, 94*, 13–126.

Engin, A., Wallbrown, F., & Brown, D. (1976). The dimensions of reading attitude for children in the intermediate grades. *Psychology in the Schools, 13*(3), 309–316.

Epstein, J. L., & McPartland, J. M. (1978). *The Quality of School Life Scale administration and technical manual*. Boston: Houghton Mifflin.

Epstein, N., Baldwin, L., & Bishop, S. (1983). The McMaster Family Assessment Device, *Journal of Marital and Family Therapy, 9*, 171–180.

Epstein, Y. M., & Borduin, C. M. (1985). Could this happen? A game for children of divorce. *Psychotherapy, 22*, 770–773.

Erdelyi, M. H. (1974). A new look at the new look: Perceptual defense and vigilance. *Psychological Review, 81*, 1–25.

Erdelyi, M. H., & Goldberg, B. (1979). Let's not sweep repression under the rug: Toward a cognitive psychology of repression. In J. F. Kihlstrom & F. J. Evans (Ed.), *Functional disorders of memory*. Hillsdale, NJ: Erlbaum.

Erdelyi, M. H., & Kleinbard, J. (1978). Has Ebbinghaus decayed with time? The growth of recall (hypermnesia) over days. *Journal of Experimental Psychology: Human Learning and Memory, 4*, 275–289.

Erickson, M. L. (1976). *Assessment and management of developmental changes in children*. St. Louis, MO: Mosby.

Errico, A. L., Nixon, S. J., Parsons, O. A., & Tassey, J. (1990). Screening for neuropsychological impairment in alcoholics. *Psychological Assessment: A Journal of Consulting and Clininical Psychology, 2*, 45–50.

Ervin, S. J. (1965). Why Senate hearings on psychological tests in government. *American Psychologist, 20*, 879–880.

Escalona, S. K., & Moriarty, A. (1961). Prediction of school age intelligence from infant tests. *Child Development, 32*, 597–605.

Esquirol, J. E. D. (1838). *Des malades mentales considerées sous les rapports médical, hygiénique et médicolegal*. Paris: Balliere.

Evan, W. M., & Miller, J. R. (1969). Differential effects of response bias of computer vs. conventional administration of a social science questionnaire. *Behavioral Science, 14*, 216–227.

Evans, E. D. (1988). Review of Reynolds Adolescent Depression Scale. In D. J. Keyser & R. C. Sweetland (Eds.), *Test critiques* (Vol. 7; pp. 485–495). Kansas City, MO: Test Corporation of America.

Evans, M. (1978). Unbiased assessment of locally low incidence handicapped children. *IRRC practitioners talk to practitioners*. Springfield, IL: Illinois Regional Resource Center.

Exner, J. E. (1962). A comparison of human figure drawings of psychoneurotics, character disturbances, normals, and subjects experiencing experimentally induced fears. *Journal of Projective Techniques, 26*, 292–317.

Exner, J. E. (1966). Variations in WISC performance as influenced by differences in pretest rapport. *Journal of General Psychology, 74*, 299–306.

Exner, J. E. (1969). *The Rorschach systems*. New York: Grune & Stratton.

Exner, J. E. (1974). *The Rorschach: A comprehensive system*. New York: Wiley.

Exner, J. E. (1978). *The Rorschach: A comprehensive system: Vol. 2. Current research and advanced interpretations*. New York: Wiley-Interscience.

Exner, J. E. (1983). Rorschach assessment. In I. B. Weiner (Ed.), *Methods in clinical psychology* (2nd ed.). New York: Wiley.

Exner, J. E. (1986). *The Rorschach: A comprehensive system: Vol. 1. Basic foundations* (2nd ed.). New York: Wiley.

Exner, J. E. (1990). *Workbook for the comprehensive system* (3rd ed.). Asheville, NC: Rorschach Workshops.

Exner, J. E. (in press). *The Rorschach: A comprehensive system: Vol. 2. Current research and advanced interpretation* (2nd ed.). New York: Wiley.

Exner, J. E., Armbruster, G. L., & Viglione, D. (1978). The temporal stability of some Rorschach features. *Journal of Personality Assessment, 42*, 474–482.

Exner, J. E., & Weiner, I. B. (1982). *The Rorschach: A*

comprehensive system: Vol. 3, Assessment of children and adolescents. New York: Wiley.

Eyberg, S. M., & Robinson, E. A. (1983). Conduct problem behavior: Standardization of a behavioral rating scale with adolescents. *Journal of Clinical Child Psychology, 12,* 347–357.

Eyberg, S. M., & Ross, A. W. (1978). Assessment of child behavior problems: The validation of a new inventory. *Journal of Clinical Child Psychology, 7,* 113–116.

Eyde, L. D., Kowal, D. M., & Fishburne, F. J., Jr. (1990). The validity of computer-based test interpretations of the MMPI. In S. Wise & T. B. Gutkin (Eds.), *The computer as adjunct to the decision-making process.* Lincoln, NE: Buros Institute of Mental Measurements.

Eyde, L. D., Moreland, K. L., Robertson, G. J., Primoff, E. S., & Most, R. B. (1988). Test user qualifications: A data-based approach to promoting good test use. *Issues in Scientific Psychology.* Report of the Test User Qualifications Working Group of the Joint Committee on Testing Practices. Washington, DC: American Psychological Association.

Eyde, L. D., & Primoff, E. S. (1986). Test purchaser qualifications: A proposed voluntary system based on test ethics. In Scientific Affairs Office, American Psychological Association (Ed.), *Test purchaser qualifications: Present practice, professional needs, and a proposed system.* Washington, DC: American Psychological Association.

Eyde, L. D. (Ed.). (1987). Computerized psychological testing (Special issue). *Applied Psychology: An International Review, 36*(3–4).

Eysenck, H. J. (1961). The effects of psychotherapy. In H. J. Eysenck (Ed.), *Handbook of abnormal psychology: An experimental approach* (pp. 697–725). New York: Basic Books.

Eysenck, H. J. (1967). Intelligence assessment: A theoretical and experimental approach. *British Journal of Educational Psychology, 37,* 81–98.

Eysenck, H. J. (1972). Primaries or second-order factors: A critical consideration of Cattell's 16PF battery. *British Journal of Social and Clinical Psychology, 11,* 265–269.

Fagan, J., Broughton, E., Allen, M., Clark, B., and Emerson, P. (1969). Comparison of the Binet and WPPSI with lower class five year olds. *Journal of Consulting and Clinical Psychology, 33,* 607–609.

Falbo, T., & Belk, S. S. (1985). A short scale to measure self-righteousness. *Journal of Personality Assessment, 49,* 172–177.

Faller, K. C. (1988). *Child sexual abuse.* New York: Columbia University Press.

Fantuzzo, J. W., & Moon, G. W. (1984). Competency mandate: A model for teaching skills in the administration of the WAIS-R. *Journal of Clinical Psychology, 40,* 1053–1059.

Farrall, F. R., & Card, R. D. (1988). Advancements in physiological evaluation of assessment and treatment of the sexual transgressor. In R. A. Prentky & V. L. Quinsey (Eds.), *Human sexual aggression: Current perspectives* (pp. 261–273). New York: Annals of the New York Academy of Sciences.

Farrell, A. D. (1989). Impact of computers on professional practice. *Professional Psychology: Research and Practice, 20*(3), 172–178.

Farrell, A. D. (1989). Impact of standards for computer-based tests on practice: Consequences of the information gap. *Computers in Human Behavior, 5,* 1–11.

Faust, D. S., & Oakes, J. (1990). Concurrent validation of the WPPSI-R. Paper presented at the Annual Meeting of the American Psychological Association, Boston.

Faust, D. S., & Ziskin, J. (1988a). The expert witness in psychology and psychiatry. *Science, 241,* 31–35.

Faust, D. S., & Ziskin, J. (1988b). Response to Fowler and Matarrazo. *Science,* 1143–1144.

Fee, A. F., Elkins, G. R., & Boyd, L. (1982). Testing and counseling psychologists: Current practices and implications for training. *Journal of Personality Assessment, 46,* 116–118.

Ferguson, R. L., & Novick, M. R. (1973). Implementation of a Bayesian system for decision analysis in a program of individually prescribed instruction. *ACT Research Report,* Number 60.

Feshback, S. (1961). The influence of drive arousal and conflict. In J. Kagan & G. Lesser (Eds.), *Contemporary issues in thematic appercention methods.* Springfield, IL: Charles C Thomas.

Feuerstein, R., Rand, Y., Jensen, M. R., Kaniel, S., & Tzuriel, D. (1987). Prerequisites for assessment of learning potential: The LPAD model. In C. S. Lidz (Ed.), *Dynamic assessment: An interactive approach to evaluating learning potential* (pp. 35–51). New York: Guilford Press.

Filsinger, E. (1983). A machine-aided marital observation technique: The Dyadic Interaction Scoring

Code. *Journal of Marriage and the Family, 2,* 623–632.

Fingarette, H., & Hasse, A. F. (1979). *Mental disabilities and criminal responsibility.* Berkeley: University of California Press.

Finkel, N. J., Shaw, R., Bercaw, S., et al. (1985). Insanity defenses: From the jurors' perspective. *Law and Psychology Review, 9,* 77–92.

Fitts, W. H. (1965). *Manual for the Tennessee Self-Concept Scale.* Nashville: Counselor Recordings and Tests.

Fitzgibbons, D. J., & Shearn, C. R. (1972). Concepts of schizophrenia among mental health professionals: A factor-analytic study. *Journal of Consulting and Clinical Psychology, 38,* 288–295.

Flanagan, J. C. (1938). Review of Measuring Intelligence by Terman and Merrill. *Harvard Educational Review, 8,* 130–133.

Flanagan, J. C., & Burns, R. K. (1955). The employee business record: A new appraisal and development tool. *Harvard Business Review, 33*(5), 99–102.

Flett, G. L., Blankstein, K. R., Pliner, P., & Bator, C. (1988). Impression management and self-deception components of appraised emotional experience. *British Journal of Social Psychology, 27,* 67–77.

Fliess, J. L. (1971). Measuring nominal scale agreement among many raters. *Psychological Bulletin, 76,* 378–382.

Flugel, J. C., & West, D. J. (1964). *A hundred years of psychology: 1833–1933.* New York: Basic Books.

Foerster, L. M., & Little Soldier, D. (1974). Open education and native American values. *Educational Leadership, 32,* 41–45.

Folstein, M. F., Folstein, S. E., & McHugh, P. R. (1975). "Mini-Mental State": A practical method for grading the cognitive state of patients for the clinician. *Journal of Psychiatric Research, 12,* 189–198.

Fontana, V. J., Donovan, D., & Wong, R. J. (1963, December 8). The maltreatment syndrome in children. *New England Journal of Medicine, 269,* 1389–1394.

Forbes, G. B. (1985). The Personality Inventory for Children (PIC) and hyperactivity: Clinical utility and problems of generalizability. *Journal of Pediatric Psychology, 10,* 141–149.

Forer, B. R. (1949). The fallacy of personal validation: A classroom demonstration of gullibility. *Journal of Abnormal and Social Psychology, 44,* 118–123.

Forth, A. E., Hart, S. D., & Hare, R. D. (1990). Assessment of psychopathy in male young offenders. *Psychological Assessment: A Journal of Consulting and Clinical Psychology, 2,* 342–344.

Fourqurean, J. M. (1987). A K-ABC and WISC-R comparison for Latino learning-disabled children of limited English proficiency. *Journal of School Psychology, 25,* 15–21.

Forrest, D. W. (1974). *Francis Galton: The life and works of a Victorian genius.* New York: Taplinger.

Fowler, R. D. (1969). Automated interpretation of personality test data. In J. N. Butcher (Ed.), *MMPI: Research developments and clinical applications* (pp. 105–126). New York: McGraw-Hill.

Fowler, R. D. (1985). Landmarks in computer-assisted psychological assessment. *Journal of Consulting and Clinical Psychology, 53,* 748–759.

Fowler, R. D., & Butcher, J. N. (1986). Critique of Matarazzo's views on computerized testing: All sigma and no meaning. *American Psychologist, 41,* 94–96.

Fowler, R. D., & Matarazzo, J. D. (1988). Psychologists and psychiatrists as expert witnesses. *Science, 241,* 1143.

Frank, L. K. (1939). Projective methods for the study of personality. *Journal of Psychology, 8,* 389–413.

Franklin, M. R., Duley, S. M., Rousseau, E. W., & Sabers, D. L. (1981). Construct validation of the Piers-Harris Children's Self-Concept Scale. *Educational and Psychological Measurement, 41,* 439–443.

Franzen, M. D. (1985). Review of Luria-Nebraska Neuropsychological Battery. In D. J. Keyser & R. C. Sweetland (Eds.), *Test critiques* (Vol. 3; pp. 402–414). Kansas City, MO: Test Corporation of America.

Franzen, M. D. (1986). Review of Luria-Nebraska Neuropsychological Battery, Form II. In D. J. Keyser & R. C. Sweetland (Eds.), *Test critiques* (Vol. 4; pp. 382–386). Kansas City, MO: Test Corporation of America.

Frederiksen, N., Saunders, D. R., & Wand, B. (1957). The in-basket test. *Psychological Monographs, 71*(9), Whole No. 438.

Fredman, N., & Sherman, R. (1987). *Handbook of measurements for marriage & family therapy.* New York: Brunner/Mazel.

Freides, D. (1972). Review of the Wechsler Intelligence Scale for Children—Revised. In O. K. Buros (Ed.), *The seventh mental measurements yearbook* (pp. 349–351). Highland Park, NJ: Gryphon Press.

French, C. C., & Beaumont, J. G. (1987). The reaction of psychiatric patients to computerized assessment. *British Journal of Clinical Psychology, 26,* 267–278.

French, J. L. (Ed.) (1964). *Educating the gifted.* New York: Holt, Rinehart & Winston.

French, J., Graves, P.A., & Levitt, E.E. (1983). Objective and projective testing of children. In C. E. Walker & M. C. Roberts (Eds.), *Handbook of clinical child psychology* (pp. 209–248). New York: Wiley.

Freud, S., Ferenczi, S., Abraham, K., Simmel, E., & Jones, E. (1921). *Psychoanalysis and the war neuroses.* New York: International Psychoanalytic Press.

Freund, K. (1963). A laboratory method for diagnosing predominance of homosexual and heterosexual erotic interest in the male. *Behavior Research and Therapy, 1,* 85–93.

Freund, K., Sedlacek, E., & Knob, K. (1965). A simple transducer for mechanical plethysmography of the male genital. *Journal of Experimental Analysis of Behavior, 8,* 169–170.

Friedman, M., & Rosenman, R. H. (1974). *Type A behavior and your heart.* New York: Knopf.

Friedrich, W. N., Urquiza, A. J., & Beike, R. (1986). Behavioral problems in sexually abused young children. *Journal of Pediatric Psychiatry, 11,* 47–57.

Fromm-Auch, D., & Yeudall, L. T. (1983). Normative data for the Halstead-Reitan Neuropsychological Tests. *Journal of Clinical Neuropsychology, 5,* 221–238.

Frostig, M. (1966). *Frostig Developmental Test of Visual Perception.* Palo Alto, CA: Consulting Psychologists Press.

Fullan, M., & Loubser, J. (1972). Education and adaptive capacity. *Sociology of Education, 45,* 271–287.

Funder, D. C., & Colvin, C. R. (1991). Some behaviors are more predictable than others. *The Score, 13*(4), 3–4.

Furse, D. H., & Stewart, D. W. (1984). Manipulating dissonance to improve mail survey response. *Psychology & Marketing, 1,* 71–84.

Gallagher, J. J. (1966). *Research summary on gifted child education.* Springfield, IL: State Department of Public Instruction.

Gallucci, N. T. (1986). General and specific objections to the MMPI. *Educational and Psychological Measurement, 46,* 985–988.

Galton, F. (1869). *Hereditary genius.* London: Macmillan. (Macmillan edition published in 1892).

Galton, F. (1874). *English men of science.*

Galton, F. (1879). Psychometric experiments. *Brain, 2,* 149–162.

Galton, F. (1883). *Inquiries into human faculty and its development.* London: Macmillan.

Gammon, J. A. (1981). Ophthalmic manifestations of child abuse. In N. S. Ellerstein (Ed.), *Child abuse and neglect: A medical reference* (pp. 121–139). New York: Wiley.

Garbarino, J., et al. (1987). *The psychologically battered child.* San Francisco: Jossey-Bass.

Gardner, R. A. (1971). *The boys and girls book about divorce.* New York: Bantam.

Gardner, R. A. (1982). *Family evaluation in child custody litigation.* Cresskill, NJ: Creative Therapeutics.

Gardner, R. W., Holzman, P. S., Klein, G. S., Linton, H. B., & Spence, D. F. (1959). Cognitive control: A study of individual consistencies in cognitive behavior. *Psychological Issues, 1* (4).

Garfield, S., & Kurtz, R. M. (1973). Attitudes toward training in diagnostic testing. A survey of directors of internship training. *Journal of Consulting and Clinical Psychology, 40,* 350–355.

Garner, D. M., & Garfinkel, P. E. (1981). Body image in anorexia nervosa: Measurement, theory, and clinical implications. *International Journal of Psychiatry in Medicine, 11,* 263–284.

Garner, D. M., Garfinkel, P. E., Stancer, H. C., & Moldofsky, H. (1976). Body image disturbances in anorexia nervosa and obesity. *Psychosomatic Medicine, 38,* 327–336.

Garrett, H. E., & Schneck, M. R. (1933). *Psychological tests, methods and results.* New York: Harper.

Gass, C. S., Russell, E. W., & Hamilton, R. A. (1990). Accuracy of MMPI-based inferences regarding memory and concentration in closed-head-trauma patients. *Psychological Assessment: A Journal of Consulting & Clinical Psychology, 2,* 175–178.

Gaston, L. (1991). Reliability and criterion-related validity of the California Psychotherapy Alliance Scales—Patient version. *Psychological Assessment: A Journal of Consulting and Clinical Psychology, 3,* 68–74.

Gavzer, B. (1990, May 27). Should you tell all? *Parade Magazine,* pp. 4–7.

Gerken, K. C. (1991). Assessment of preschool children with severe handicaps. In B. A. Bracken (Ed.), *The psychoeducational assessment of preschool children* (2nd ed.; pp. 392–429). Needham, MA: Allyn and Bacon.

Gerry, M. H. (1973). Cultural myopia: The need for a corrective lens. *Journal of School Psychology, 11*, 307–315.

Gesell, A. (1945). *The embryology of behavior. The beginnings of the human mind.* New York: Harper.

Gesell, A. (1954). The ontogenesis of infant behavior. In L. Carmichael (Ed.), *Manual of child psychology.* New York: Wiley.

Gesell, A., & Amatruda, C. S. (1947). *Developmental diagnosis: Normal and abnormal child development* (2nd ed.). New York: Harper & Row.

Gesell, A., & Thompson, H. (1929). Learning and growth in identical twin infants. *Genetic Psychology Monographs, 6*, 1–124.

Gesell, A., et al. (1940). *The first five years of life.* New York: Harper.

Ghiselli, E. E., Campbell, J. P., & Zedeck, S. (1981). *Measurement theory for the behavioral sciences.* San Francisco: Freeman.

Gibbins, S. (1988, April). Use of the K-ABC and WISC-R with deaf children. Paper presented at the Annual Meeting of the National Association of School Psychologists, Chicago.

Gibbins, S. (1989). The provision of school psychological assessment services for the hearing impaired: A national survey. *The Volta Review, 91*, 95–103.

Gill, W., & Hayes-Butler, K. (1989). The effects of schoolwide discipline, role play, modeling and video utilization upon the self concept of elementary school children: A preliminary report. Paper presented at the Society of School Librarians International Conference, San Antonio, TX. (ERIC Document Reproduction Service No. ED 305 888).

Gillingham, W. H. (1970). An investigation of examiner influence on Wechsler Intelligence Scale for Children scores. (Doctoral dissertation, Michigan State University, 1970). *Dissertation Abstracts International, 31*, 2178-A. (University Microfilms No. Order 70-20, 458).

Glaser, G. J., & Metzger, G. D. (1972). Random digit dialing as a method of telephone sampling. *Journal of Marketing Research, 9*, 59–64.

Glaser, R. (1981). The future of testing: A research agenda for cognitive psychology and psychometrics. *American Psychologist, 36*, 923–936.

Glaser, R., & Nitko, A. J. (1971). Measurement in learning and instruction. In R. L. Thorndike (Ed.), *Educational measurement* (2nd ed.). Washington, DC: American Council on Education.

Glass, G. V., McGaw, B., & Smith, M. L. (1981). *Metaanalysis in social research.* Beverly Hills: Sage.

Gleghorn, A., Penner, L., Powers, P., & Schulman, R. (1987). The psychometric properties of several measures of body image. *Journal of Psychopathology and Behavioral Assessment, 9*, 203–218.

Gluck, M. R. (1955). The relationship between hostility in the TAT and behavioral hostility. *Journal of Projective Techniques, 19*, 21–26.

Glueck, W. F. (1978). *Personnel: A diagnostic approach.* Dallas, TX: Business Publications.

Glutting, J. J. (1989). Introduction to the structure and application of the Stanford-Binet Intelligence Scale—Fourth Edition. *Journal of School Psychology, 27*, 69–80.

Glutting, J. J., & McDermott, P. A. (1989). Using "teaching items" on ability tests: A nice idea, but does it work? *Educational and Psychological Measurement, 49*, 257–268.

Gobetz, W. A. (1953). Quantification, standardization, and validation of the Bender-Gestalt test on normal and neurotic adults. *Psychological Monographs, 67*, No. 6.

Goddard, H. H. (1908). The Binet and Simon tests of intellectual capacity. *Training School, 5*, 3–9.

Goddard, H. H. (1910). A measuring scale of intelligence. *Training School, 6*, 146–155.

Goddard, H. H. (1912). *The Kallikak family.* New York: Macmillan.

Goddard, H. H. (1913). The Binet tests in relation to immigration. *Journal of Psycho-Asthenics, 18*, 105–107.

Goddard, H. H. (1917). Mental tests and the immigrant. *Journal of Delinquency, 2*, 243–277.

Goddard, H. H. (1916). *Feeblemindedness.* New York: Macmillan.

Goffman, E. (1959). *The presentation of self in everyday life.* New York: Anchor.

Goffman, E. (1963). *Behavior in public places.* Glencoe, IL: Free Press.

Goh, D. S., & Cordonig, B. (1989). Comparison of the Stanford-Binet Fourth Edition with WAIS-R in college learning disabled students. Paper presented at the Annual Meeting of the National Association of School Psychologists, Boston.

Goh, D., & Youngquist, J. (1979). Comparing McCarthy Scales of Children's Abilities and the

WISC-R. *Journal of Learning Disabilities, 12,* 344–348.

Gokhale, D. V., & Kullback, S. (1978). *The information in contingency tables.* New York: Marcel Dekker.

Gold, Y. (1984). The factorial validity of the Maslach Burnout Inventory in a sample of California elementary and junior high school classroom teachers. *Educational & Psychological Measurement, 44,* 1009–1016.

Goldberg, L. R. (1970). Man vs. model of man: A rationale, plus some evidence, for a method of improving on clinical inferences. *Psychological Bulletin, 73,* 422–432.

Goldberg, L. R. (1978). The reliability of reliability: The generality and correlates of intra-individual consistency in response to structured personality inventories. *Applied Psychological Measurement, 2,* 269–291.

Golden, C. J., Hammeke, T. A., & Purisch, A. D. (1980). *The Luria-Nebraska Neuropsychological Battery: Manual.* Los Angeles: Western Psychological Services.

Golden, C. J., & Kupperman, S. K. (1980). Graduate training in clinical neuropsychology. *Professional Psychology, 11,* 55–63.

Golden, C. J., et al. (1981). Cross validation of the Luria-Nebraska Neuropsychological Battery for the presence, lateralization, and localization of brain damage. *Journal of Consulting and Clinical Psychology, 49,* 491–507.

Goldfarb, L. A., Dykens, E. M., & Gerrard, M. (1985). The Goldfarb Fear of Fat Scale. *Journal of Personality Assessment, 49,* 329–332.

Goldfried, M. R., & Davison, G. C. (1976). *Clinical behavior therapy.* New York: Holt, Rinehart, & Winston.

Goldfried, M. R., Stricker, G., & Weiner, I. B. (1971). *Rorschach handbook of clinical and research applications.* Englewood Cliffs, NJ: Prentice-Hall.

Goldfried, M., & Zax, M. (1965). The stimulus value of the TAT. *Journal of Projective Techniques, 29,* 46–57.

Golding, S. L. (1975). Flies in the ointment: Methodological problems in the analysis of the percentage of variance due to persons and situations. *Psychological Bulletin, 82,* 278–288.

Goldman, R., & Fristoe, M. (1972). *Goldman-Fristoe Test of Articulation.* Circle Pines, MN: American Guidance Service.

Goldman, R., Fristoe, M., & Woodcock, R. (1970). *Goldman-Fristoe-Woodcock Test of Auditory Discrimination.* Circle Pines, MN: American Guidance Service.

Goldschmid, M. L., & Bentler, P. M. (1968a). Dimensions and measurement of conservation. *Child Development, 39,* 787–802.

Goldschmid, M. L., & Bentler, P. M. (1968b). *Manual: Concept Assessment Kit—Conservation.* San Diego, CA: Educational and Industrial Testing Service.

Goldschmid, M. L., & Bentler, P. M. (1968). *Manual: Concept Assessment Kit—Conservation.* San Diego, CA: Educational and Individual Testing Service.

Goldstein, A. S. (1967). *The insanity defense.* New Haven, CN: Yale University Press.

Goldstein, G. (1986). The neuropsychology of schizophrenia. In I. Grant & K. M. Adams, (Eds.), *Neuropsychological assessment of neuropsychiatric disorders* (pp. 147–171). New York: Oxford University Press.

Goldstein, G., & Shelly, C. (1982). A further attempt to cross-validate the Russell, Neuringer, and Goldstein neuropsychological keys. *Journal of Consulting and Clinical Psychology, 50,* 721–726.

Goldstein, K. (1927). Die lokalisation in her grosshim rinde. *Handb. norm. pathol. psychiologie.* Berlin: J. Springer.

Goldstein, K. (1939). *The organism.* New York: American Book.

Goldstein, K. (1963a). *The organism.* Boston: Beacon.

Goldstein, K. (1963b). The modifications of behavior consequent to cerebral lesions. *Psychiatric Quarterly, 10,* 586–610.

Goldston, D. B., O'Hara, M. W., & Schartz, H. A. (1990). Reliability, validity, and preliminary normative data for the Inventory to Diagnose Depression in a college population. *Psychological Assessment: A Journal of Consulting & Clinical Psychology, 2,* 212–215.

Goldwater, B. C. (1972). Psychological significance of pupillary movements. *Psychological Bulletin, 77,* 340–355.

Good, R. H., Chowdhri, S., Katz, L., Vollman, M., & Creek, R. (1989, March). Effect of matching instruction and simultaneous/sequential processing strength. Paper presented at the Annual Meeting of the National Association of School Psychologists, Boston.

Good, R. H., & Lane, S. (1988). Confirmatory factor analysis of the K-ABC and WISC-R: Hierarchical models. Paper presented at the Annual Meeting of the American Psychological Association, Atlanta, GA.

Good, R. H., & Thornton, J. (1988). Stanford-Binet Intelligence Scale, Fourth Edition regional database: Preliminary results. Paper presented at the Annual Meeting of the National Association of School Psychologists, Chicago.

Goodman, G. S., & Reed, R. S. (1986). Age differences in eyewitness testimony. *Law and Human Behavior, 10,* 317–332.

Goodman, J. F. (1978). Wanted: Restoration of the mental age in the 1972 revised Stanford-Binet. *Journal of Special Education, 12,* 45–49.

Gordon, L. V. (1953). A factor analysis of the 48 Szondi pictures. *Journal of Psychology, 36,* 387–392.

Gorham, D. R. (1956). A Proverbs Test for clinical and experimental use. *Psychological Reports, Monograph Supplement, 2,* No. 1, 1–12.

Gorham, D. R., Mosely, E. C., & Holtzman, W. H. (1968). Norms for the computer scored Holtzman Inkblot Technique. *Perceptual & Motor Skills Monograph Supplement, 26,* 1279–1305.

Gorsuch, R. L. (1974). *Factor analysis.* Philadelphia: Saunders.

Gorsuch, R. L. (1983). *Factor analysis* (2nd ed.). Hillsdale, NJ: Erlbaum.

Gottfried, A. W., & Brody, N. (1975). Interrelationship between and correlates of psychometric and Piagetian scales of sensorimotor intelligence. *Developmental Psychology, 11,* 371–387.

Gough, H. G. (1956). *California Psychological Inventory.* Palo Alto, CA: Consulting Psychologists Press.

Gough, H. G. (1957). *California Psychological Inventory: Manual* (Revised 1964). Palo Alto, CA: Consulting Psychologists Press.

Gough, H. G. (1960). The Adjective Check List as a personality assessment research technique. *Psychological Reports, 6,* 107–122.

Gough, H. G. (1975). *California Psychological Inventory Manual (Revised).* Palo Alto, CA: Consulting Psychologists Press.

Gough, H. G. (1985). A Work Orientation scale for the California Psychological Inventory. *Journal of Applied Psychology, 70,* 505–513.

Gough, H. G. (1987). *California Psychological Inventory, 1987 Revised Edition.* Palo Alto, CA: Consulting Psychologists Press.

Gough, H. G. (1989). The California Psychological Inventory. In C. S. Newmark (Ed.), *Major psychological assessment instruments, Vol. II* (pp. 67–98). Needham Heights, MA: Allyn and Bacon.

Gough, H. G., & Heilbrun, A. B., Jr. (1980). *The Adjective Checklist manual (Revised).* Palo Alto, CA: Consulting Psychologists Press.

Graham, J. R. (1967). A Q-sort study of the accuracy of clinical descriptions based on the MMPI. *Journal of Psychiatric Research, 5,* 297–305.

Graham, J. R. (1977). *The MMPI: A practical guide.* New York: Oxford University Press.

Graham, J. R. (1990a). *MMPI-2: Assessing personality and psychopathology.* New York: Oxford University Press.

Graham, J. R. (1990b). Congruence between MMPI and MMPI-2 code types. *News and Profiles: A Newsletter of the MMPI-2 Workshops and Symposia, 1*(2), 1–2, 12.

Graham, J. R., & Butcher, J. N. (1988, March). Differentiating schizophrenic and major affective disorders with the revised form of the MMPI. Paper presented at the 23rd Annual Symposium on Recent Developments in the Use of the MMPI, St. Petersburg, FL.

Graybill, D. (1990). Developmental changes in the Response types versus Aggression Categories on the Rosenzweig Children's Form. *Journal of Personality Assessment, 55,* 603–609.

Graybill, D., Peterson, S. P., & Williams, P. G. (1989). Variability of responses within the Aggression Categories on the Rosenzweig Picture-Frustration Study, Children's Form. *Journal of Personality Assessment, 53,* 472–477.

Graybill, D., Heuvelman, L. R., & Reeder, G. D. (1991, March), *Validity of the Children's Picture-Frustration Study.* Paper presented at the meeting of the Society for Personality Assessment, New Orleans.

Graybill, D., Williams, P. G., Bodmer, B., & Peterson, S. P. (1991). Relationship of the Children's Form of the Rosenzweig Picture-Frustration Study to children's behavior, sex, and fantasies. *Psychological Reports, 68,* 747–753.

Grayson, H. M., & Backer, T. E. (1972). Scoring accuracy of four automated MMPI interpretation report agencies. *Journal of Clinical Psychology, 28,* 366–370.

Greaud, V. A., & Green, B. F. (1986). Equivalence of conventional and computer presentation of speed tests. *Applied Psychological Measurement, 10,* 23–34.

Green, A. (1986). True and false allegations of sexual abuse in child custody disputes. *Journal of the American Academy of Child Psychology, 25,* 449–456.

Green, B. F. (1984). *Computer-based ability testing.* Paper delivered at the 91st annual meeting of the American Psychological Association, Toronto, Ontario. Canada.

Green, P., & Pew, R. W. (1978). Evaluating pictographic symbols: An automotive application. *Human Factors, 20,* 103–114.

Greenbaum, T. L. (1988). *The practical handbook and guide to focus group research.* Lexington, MA: Heath.

Greene, A. C., Sapp, G. L., & Chissom, B. (1990). Validation of the Stanford–Binet Intelligence Scale: Fourth Edition with exceptional black male students. *Psychology in the Schools, 27,* 35–41.

Greene, R. L. (1985). New norms, old norms, what norms for the MMPI? *Journal of Personality Assessment, 49,* 108–110.

Greene, R. L. (1988). Assessment of malingering and defensiveness by objective personality measures. In R. Rogers (Ed.), *Clinical assessment of malingering and deception* (pp. 123–158). New York: Guilford Press.

Greenspoon, J. (1955). The reinforcing effect of two spoken sounds on the frequency of two responses. *American Journal of Psychology, 68,* 409–416.

Greenspoon, J., & Gersten, C. D. (1967). A new look at psychological testing: Psychological testing from the standpoint of a behaviorist. *American Psychologist, 22,* 848–853.

Gregg, N., & Hoy, C. (1985). A comparison of the WAIS-R and the Woodcock-Johnson Tests of Cognitive Ability with learning-disabled college students. *Journal of Psychoeducational Assessment, 3,* 267–274.

Gresham, F. M., & Elliott, S. N. (1990). Social Skills Rating System. Circle Pines, MN: American Guidance Service.

Grey, R. J., & Kipnis, D. (1976). Untangling the performance appraisal dilemma: The influence of perceived organizational context on evaluative processes. *Journal of Applied Psychology, 61,* 329–335.

Gridley, B. E. (1990). Best practices in working with gifted children. In A. Thomas & J. Grimes (Eds.), *Best practices in school psychology II* (pp. 811–821). Washington, DC: National Association of School Psychologists.

Grinker, R. R., & Spiegel, J. P. (1945). *Men under stress.* New York: Blakiston.

Gronlund, N. E. (1985). *Measurement and evaluation in teaching* (5th ed.). New York: Macmillan.

Gross, M. L. (1962). *The brain watchers.* New York: Random House.

Grossack, M. M. (1964). *Understanding consumer behavior.* Boston: Christopher.

Grosswirth, M. (1980). Mensa: It's a state of mind—but a mind finely tuned. *Science Digest, 87,* 74–79.

Grunzke, N., Gunn, N., & Staufer, G. (1970). *Comparative performance of low-ability airmen* (Technical Report 70-4). Lackland AFB, TX: Air Force Human Resources Laboratory.

Gruson, L. (1982, October 19). Color has powerful effect on behavior, researchers assert. *New York Times,* pp. C-1, C-6.

Guastello, S. J., & Rieke, M. L. (1990). The Barnum Effect and the validity of computer-based test interpretations: The Human Resource Development Report. *Psychological Assessment, 2,* 186–190.

Guertin, W. H. (1951). A factor analysis of some Szondi pictures. *Journal of Clinical Psychology, 7,* 232–235.

Guidelines for computer-based interpretation and assessment. (1985). Washington, DC: American Psychological Association.

Guidelines for computer-based tests and interpretations. (1986). Washington, DC: American Psychological Association.

Guilford, J. P. (1948). Some lessons from aviation psychology. *American Journal of Psychology, 3,* 3–11.

Guilford, J. P. (1954a). *Psychometric methods.* New York: McGraw-Hill.

Guilford, J. P. (1954b). A factor analytic study across the domains of reasoning, creativity, and evaluation. I. Hypothesis and description of tests. *Reports from the psychology laboratory.* Los Angeles: University of Southern California.

Guilford, J. P. (1959). *Personality.* New York: McGraw-Hill.

Guilford, J. P. (1967). *The nature of human intelligence.* New York: McGraw-Hill.

Guilford, J. P., et al. (1974). *Structure-of-Intellect Abilities.* Orange, CA: Sheridan Psychological Services.

Guilford, J. P. (1975). Factors and factors of personality. *Psychological Bulletin, 82,* 802–814.

Guilford, J. P. (1985). A sixty-year perspective on psychological measurement. *Applied Psychological Measurement, 9,* 341–349.

Guilford, J. S., Zimmerman, W. S., & Guilford, J. P. (1976). *The Guilford-Zimmerman Temperament Survey handbook: Twenty-five years of research and application.* San Diego, CA: Educational and Industrial Testing Service.

Guilmette, T. J., & Faust, D. (1991). Characteristics of neuropsychologists who prefer the Halstead-Reitan Battery or the Luria-Nebraska Neuropsychological Battery. *Professional Psychology: Research and Practice, 22*(1), 80–83.

Guilmette, T. J., Faust, D., Hart, K., & Arkes, H. R. (1990). A national survey of psychologists who offer neuropsychological services. *Archives of Clinical Neuropsychology, 5,* 373–392.

Guion, R. M. (1967). Personnel selection. *Annual Review of Psychology, 18,* 191–216.

Guion, R. M. (1980). On trinitarian doctrines of validity. *Professional Psychology, 11,* 385–398.

Gulliksen, H. (1950). *Theory of mental tests.* New York: Wiley.

Gulliksen, H., & Messick, S. (Eds.). (1960). *Psychological scaling: Theory and applications.* New York: Wiley, 1960.

Gunnison, J. (1984). Developing educational interventions from assessments involving the K-ABC. *Journal of Special Education, 18,* 325–344.

Gur, R., & Sackheim, H. A. (1979). Self-deception: A concept in search of a phenomenon. *Journal of Personality and Social Psychology, 37,* 147–169.

Gustafson, J. E. (1985). Measuring and interpreting *g. The Behavioral and Brain Sciences, 8,* 231–232.

Gutkin, T. B., & Reynolds, C. R. (1981). Factorial similarity of the WISC-R for white and black children from the standardization sample. *Journal of Educational Psychology, 73,* 227–231.

Gutkin, T. B., & Wise, S. L. (Eds.). (1988). *The computer as adjunct to the decision-making process.* Hillsdale, NJ: Erlbaum.

Gutkin, T. B., Reynolds, C. R., & Galvin, G. A. (1984). Factor analyses of the Wechsler Adult Intelligence Scale—Revised (WAIS-R): An examination of the standardization sample. *Journal of School Psychology, 22*(1), 83–93.

Guttman, L. (1944a). A basis for scaling qualitative data. *American Sociological Review, 9,* 139–150.

Guttman, L. A. (1944b). A basis for scaling qualitative data. *American Sociological Review, 9,* 179–190.

Guttman, L. (1947). The Cornell technique for scale and intensity analysis. *Educational and Psychological Measurement, 7,* 247–280.

Gwartney-Gibbs, P. A. (1986) The institutionalization of premarital cohabitation: Estimates from marriage license applications, 1970–1980. *Journal of Marriage and the Family, 48,* 423–434.

Gynther, M. D., & Gynther, R. A. (1976). Personality inventories. In I. B. Weiner (Ed.), *Clinical methods in psychology.* New York: Wiley.

Gyurke, J. S. (1991). The assessment of children with the Wechsler Preschool and Primary Scale of Intelligence—Revised. In B. A. Bracken (Ed.), *The psychoeducational assessment of preschool children* (2nd ed.; pp. 86–132). Needham Heights, MA: Allyn and Bacon.

Gyurke, J. S., Stone, B., & Beyer, M. (1990). A confirmatory factor analysis of the WPPSI-R. *Journal of Psychoeducational Assessment, 8*(1), 15–21.

Haensly, P. A., & Torrance, E. P. (1990). Assessment of creativity in children and adolescents. In C. R. Reynolds & R. W. Kamphaus (Eds.), *Handbook of psychological and educational assessment of children: Intelligence & achievement* (pp. 697–722). New York: Guilford Press.

Hagender, H. (1967). *Influence of creative writing experiences on general creative development.* Master's research paper, University of Minnesota, Minneapolis.

Hain, J. D. (1964). The Bender-Gestalt Test: A scoring method for identifying brain damage. *Journal of Consulting Psychology, 28,* 34–40.

Hainsworth, P. K., & Siqueland, M. L. (1969). *Meeting Street School Screening Test.* Providence, RI: Crippled Children and Adults of Rhode Island.

Haire, M. (1950). Projective techniques in marketing research. *Journal of Marketing, 14,* 649–652.

Hale, R. L. (1978). The WISC-R as a predictor of WRAT performance. *Psychology in the Schools, 15,* 172–175.

Hall, B. F. (1848). The trial of William Freeman. *American Journal of Insanity, 5*(2), 34–60.

Hall, C. S., & Lindzey, G. (1970). *Theories of personality.* New York: Wiley.

Halleck, S. L. (1976). Discussion of "Socially Reinforced Obsessing." *Journal of Consulting and Clinical Psychology, 44,* 146–147.

Halperin, K., Snyder, C. R., Shenkel, R. J., & Houston, B. K. (1976). Effects of source status and message favorability on acceptance of personality feedback. *Journal of Applied Psychology, 61*, 85–88.

Halpern, F. (1951). The Bender Visual Motor Test. In H. H. Anderson & G. Anderson (Eds.), *An introduction to projective techniques* (pp. 324–341). Englewood Cliffs, NJ: Prentice-Hall.

Halpern, F. (1958). Child case study. In E. F. Hammer (Ed.), *The clinical application of projective drawings* (pp. 113–129). Springfield, IL: Charles C Thomas.

Halstead, W. C. (1947a). *Brain and intelligence.* Chicago: University of Chicago Press.

Halstead, W. C. (1947b) *Brain and intelligence: A quantitative study of the frontal lobes.* Chicago: University of Chicago Press.

Halstead, W. C., & Wepman, J. M. (1959). The Halstead-Wepman Aphasia Screening Test. *Journal of Speech and Hearing Disorders, 14*, 9–15.

Hambleton, R. K. (1979). Latent trait models and their application. *New Directions in Testing and Measurement, 4*, 13–32.

Hambleton, R. K., & Cook, L. L. (1977). Latent trait models and their use in the analysis of educational test data. *Journal of Educational Measurement, 14*, 75–96.

Hambleton, R. K., & Jurgensen, C. (1990). Criterion-referenced assessment of school achievement. In C. R. Reynolds & R. W. Kamphaus (Eds.), *Handbook of psychological and educational assessment of children: Intelligence & achievement* (pp. 456–476). New York: Guilford Press.

Hambleton, R. K., & Novick, M. R. (1973). Toward an integration of theory and method for criterion-referenced tests. *Journal of Educational Measurement, 10*, 159–170.

Hambleton, R. K. (1988). Principles and applications of item response theory. In R. L. Linn (Ed.), *Educational measurement* (3rd ed.). New York: American Council on Education/Macmillan.

Hamilton, M. (1960). A rating scale for depression. *Journal of Neurology, Neurosurgery, and Psychiatry, 23*, 56–62.

Hammer, E. F. (1958). *The clinical application of projective drawings.* Springfield, IL: Charles C Thomas.

Hammer, E. F. (1981). Projective drawings. In A. I. Rabin (Ed.), *Assessment with projective techniques: A concise introduction* (pp. 151–185). New York: Springer.

Hammill, D. D. (1985). *Detroit Tests of Learning Aptitude (DTLA-2).* Austin, TX: PRO-ED.

Hammond, K. R., & Allen, J. M. (1953). *Writing clinical reports.* New York: Prentice-Hall.

Hamsher, J. H., & Farina, A. (1967). "Openness" as a dimension of projective test responses. *Journal of Consulting Psychology, 31*, 525–528.

Haney, W. (1981). Validity, vaudeville, and values: A short history of social concerns over standardized testing. *American Psychologist, 36*, 1021–1034.

Haney, W., & Madaus, G. F. (1978). Making sense of the competency testing movement. *Harvard Educational Review, 48*, 462–484.

Hansen, J. C. (1986). *Strong-Hansen occupational guide.* Palo Alto, CA: Consulting Psychologists Press.

Hare, R. D. (1980). A research scale for the assessment of psychopathy in criminal populations. *Personality and Individual Differences, 1*, 111–119.

Hare, R. D. (1985). *The Psychopathy Checklist.* Unpublished manuscript. University of British Columbia, Vancouver, Canada.

Hare, R. D., Harpur, A. R., Hakstian, A. R., Forth, A. E., Hart, S. D., & Newman, J. P. (1990). The Revised Psychopathy Checklist: Reliability and Factor Structure. *Psychological Assessment: A Journal of Consulting and Clinical Psychology, 2*, 338–341.

Hargadon, F. (1981). Tests and college admissions. *American Psychologist, 36*, 1112–1119.

Harnett, R., & Feldmesser, D. (1980). College admissions testing and the myth of selectivity: Unresolved questions and needed research. *AAHE Bulletin, 32*(7).

Harrell, T. H., & Lombardo, T. A. (1984). Validation of an automated 16PF administration procedure. *Journal of Personality Assessment, 48*, 638–642.

Harrington, R. G. (1985a). Review of Scales of Independent Behavior. In D. J. Keyser & R. C. Sweetland (Eds.), *Test critiques* (Vol. 3). Kansas City, MO: Test Corporation of America.

Harrington, R. G. (1985b). Review of Battelle Developmental Inventory. In D. J. Keyser & R. C. Sweetland (Eds.), *Test critiques* (Vol. 2; pp. 72–82). Kansas City, MO: Test Corporation of America.

Harris, D. B. (1978). A review of Kinetic Family Drawings. In O. K. Buros (Ed.), *The eighth mental measurements yearbook* (Vol. 1; pp. 884–885). Highland Park, NJ: Gryphon Press.

Harris, G. T., Rice, M. E., & Cormier, C. A. (1989).

Violent recidivism among psychopaths and non-psychopaths treated in a therapeutic community. *Penetanguishene Mental Health Centre Research Report VI* (No. 181). Penetanguishene, Ontario, Canada: Penetanguishene Mental Health Centre.

Harrison, P. L. (1990). *AGS Early Screening Profiles.* Circle Pines, MN: American Guidance Service.

Harrison, P. L., Kaufman, A. S., & Naglieri, J. A. (1980). Subtest patterns and recategorized groupings of the McCarthy Scales for EMR children. *American Journal of Mental Deficiency, 85*(2), 129.

Harrison, P. L., Kaufman, A. S., Hickman, J. A., & Kaufman, N. L. (1988). A survey of tests used for adult assessments. *Journal of Psychoeducational Assessment, 6*(3), 188–198.

Hart, R. R., & Goldstein, M. A. (1985). Computer-assisted psychological assessment. *Computers in Human Services, 1,* 69–75.

Hart, R. R., Lutz, D. J., McNeill, J. W., & Adkins, T. G. (1986). Clinical comparability of the standard MMPI and the MMPI-168. *Professional Psychology: Research and Practice, 17,* 269–272.

Hart, S. D., Kropp, P. R., & Hare, R. D. (1988). Performance of male psychopaths following conditional release from prison. *Journal of Consulting and Clinical Psychology, 56,* 227–232.

Hartlage, L. C., & Steele, C. (1977). WISC and WISC-R correlates of academic achievement. *Psychology in the Schools, 14,* 15–18.

Hartley, D. (1749). *Observations on man, his frame, his duty, and his expectations.*

Hartmann, D. P. (1977). Considerations in the choice of inter-observer reliability estimates. *Journal of Applied Behavior Analysis, 10,* 103–116.

Hartmann, D. P., Roper, B. L., & Bradford, D. C. (1979). Some relationships between behavioral and traditional assessment. *Journal of Behavioral Assessment, 1,* 3–21.

Hartshorne, H., & May, M. A. (1928). *Studies in the nature of character. Vol. 1: Studies in deceit.* New York: Macmillan.

Hathaway, S. R., & McKinley, J. C. (1940). A multiphasic personality schedule (Minnesota): 1. Construction of the schedule. *Journal of Psychology, 10,* 249–254.

Hathaway, S. R., & McKinley, J. C. (1951). *The MMPI manual.* New York: Psychological Corporation.

Hathaway, S. R., & Meehl, P. E. (1951). *An atlas for the clinical use of the MMPI.* Minneapolis: University of Minnesota Press.

Hayden, B. C. (1981). Rorschach cards IV and VII revisited. *Journal of Personality Assessment, 45,* 226–229.

Hayden, D. C., Frulong, M. J., & Linnemeyer, S. (1988). A comparison of the Kaufman Assessment Battery for Children and the Stanford-Binet IV for the assessment of gifted children. *Psychology in the Schools, 25,* 239–243.

Haynes, J. R., & Sells, S. G. (1963). Assessment of organic brain damage by psychological tests. *Psychological Bulletin, 60,* 316–325.

Haywood, T. W., Grossman, L. S., & Cavanaugh, J. L. (1990). Subjective versus objective measurements of deviant sexual arousal in clinical evaluations of alleged child molesters. *Psychological Assessment: A Journal of Consulting & Clinical Psychology, 2,* 269–275.

Head, H. (1925). *Aphasia and kindred disorders of speech.* New York: Cambridge University Press.

Heath, C. P., & Obrzut, J. E. (1988). An investigation of the K-ABC, WISC-R, and WJPB, Part Two, with Learning Disabled children. *Psychology in the Schools, 25,* 358–364.

Heathington, B. S., & Alexander, J. E. (1978). A child-based observation checklist to assess attitudes toward reading. *The Reading Teacher, 31,* 769–771.

Heaton, R. K., Baade, L. E., & John, K. L. (1978). Neuropsychological test results associated with psychiatric disorders in adults. *Psychological Bulletin, 85,* 141–162.

Heesacker, M. (1981). *A review of the history of field dependence.* Los Angeles, CA: Paper presented at the Annual Convention of the American Psychological Association. (ERIC Document Reproduction Service No. ED 211 888)

Heilbrun, A. B., & Goodstein, L. D. (1961a). Social desirability response set: Error or predictor variable. *Journal of Psychology, 51,* 321–329.

Heilbrun, A. B., & Goodstein, L. D. (1961b). The relationship between individually defined and group defined social desirability and performance on the Edwards Personal Preference Schedule. *Journal of Consulting Psychology, 25,* 200–204.

Heilbrun, H. B., Jr. (1972). Edwards Personal Preference Schedule. In O. K. Buros (Ed.), *The seventh mental measurements yearbook* (Vol. 1). Highland Park, NJ: Gryphon Press, 1972.

Helfer, R. E., & Kempe, R. S. (Eds.) (1988). *The bat-*

tered child (4th ed.). Chicago: University of Chicago Press.

Helmes, E., & McLaughlin, J. D. (1983). A comparison of three MMPI short forms: Limited clinical utility in classification. *Journal of Consulting and Clinical Psychology, 51,* 786–787.

Helmreich, R. L., Sawin, L. L., & Carsrud, A. L. (1986). The honeymoon effect in job performance: Temporal increases in the predictive power of achievement motivation. *Journal of Applied Psychology, 71,* 185–188.

Helsel, W. J., & Matson, J. L. (1984). The assessment of depression in children: The internal structure of the Child Depression Inventory (CDI). *Behaviour Research & Therapy, 22,* 289–298.

Helson, R., & Picano, J. (1990). Is the traditional role bad for women? *Journal of Personality and Social Psychology, 59,* 311–320.

Helson, R., & Wink, P. (1987). Two conceptions of maturity examined in the findings of a longitudinal study. *Journal of Personality and Social Psychology, 53,* 531–541.

Helzel, M. F., & Rice, M. E. (1985). On the validity of social skills assessments: An analysis of role-play and ward staff ratings of social behavior in a maximum security setting. *Canadian Journal of Behavioral Science, 17,* 400–411.

Henry, E. M., & Rotter, J. B. (1956). Situational influences on Rorschach responses. *Journal of Consulting Psychology, 20,* 457–462.

Henry, J. D. (1984). Syndicated public opinion polls: Some thoughts for consideration. *Journal of Advertising Research, 24,* I-5–I-8.

Henry, W. E. (1956). *The analysis of fantasy.* New York: Wiley

Herlihy, B. (1977). Watch out, IQ myth: Here comes another debunker. *Phi Delta Kappan, 59,* 298.

Hermann, B. P., & Whitman, S. (1984). Behavioral and personality correlates of epilepsy: A review, methodological critique, and conceptual model. *Psychological Bulletin, 95,* 451–497.

Herrnstein, R. J. (1971). IQ. *Atlantic Monthly, 228,* 43–64.

Herron, J. D. (1973). Piaget for chemists: Explaining what good students cannot understand. *Journal of Research in Science Teaching, 10,* 143–146.

Hersen, M., & Bellack, A. S. (1988). *Dictionary of behavioral assessment techniques.* Elmsford, NY: Pergamon Press.

Hess, E. H., & Polt, J. M. (1960). Pupil size as related to interest value of visual stimuli. *Science, 132,* 349–350.

Hess, E. H., & Polt, J. M. (1964). Pupil size in relation to mental activity during simple problem solving. *Science, 143,* 1190–1192.

Hess, E. H. (1965). Attitude and pupil size. *Scientific American, 212,* 46–54.

Hess, E. H., & Polt, J. M. (1966). Changes in pupil size as a measure of taste difference. *Perceptual and Motor Skills, 23,* 451–455.

Hess, E. H. (1972). Pupillometrics: A method of studying mental, emotional and sensory processes. In N. S. Greenfield & R. A. Sternbach (Eds.), *Handbook of psychophysiology* (pp. 491–531). New York: Holt, Rinehart & Winston.

Higgins, R. L., Alonso, R. R., & Pendleton, M. G. (1979). The validity of role-play assessments of assertiveness. *Behavior Therapy, 10,* 655–662.

Hills, D. A. (1985). Prediction of effectiveness in leaderless group discussions with the Adjective Check List. *Journal of Applied Social Psychology, 15,* 443–447.

Hinrichsen, J. J., & Bradley, L. A. (1974). Situational determinants of personal validation of general personality interpretations: A re-examination. *Journal of Personality Assessment, 38,* 530–534.

Hiscox, M. D. (1983). *A balance sheet for educational item banking.* Paper presented at the annual meeting of the National Council for Measurement in Education, Montreal, Canada.

Hiscox, M. D., & Brzezinski, E. (1980). *A guide to item banking in education.* Portland, OR: Northwest Regional Educational Laboratory, Assessment and Evaluation Division.

Hiskey, M. S. (1966). *Hiskey-Nebraska Test of Learning Aptitude.* Lincoln, NE: Union College Press.

Hitt, M. A., & Barr, S. H. (1989). Managerial selection decision models: Examination of configural cue processing. *Journal of Applied Psychology, 74*(1), 53–61.

Hjemboe, S., & Butcher, J. N. (1990, June). Analysis of MMPI-2 profiles of couples in marital counseling. Paper presented at the 25th Annual Symposium on Recent Developments in the Use of the MMPI (MMPI-2), Minneapolis, MN.

Hofer, P. J., & Green, B. F. (1985). The challenge of competence and creativity in computerized psychological testing. *Journal of Consulting and Clinical Psychology, 53,* 826–838.

Hoffman, B. (1962). *The tyranny of testing.* New York: Crowell-Collier.

Hoffman, D. A. (1978). Field independence and intelligence: Their relationship to leadership and self-concept in sixth grade boys. *Journal of Educational Psychology, 70,* 827–832.

Hoffman, K. I., Lundberg, G. D. (1976). A comparison of computer monitored group tests and paper-and-pencil tests. *Educational and Psychological Measurement, 36,* 791–809.

Hoffman, W. F. (1985). Hypnosis as a diagnostic tool. *American Journal of Psychiatry, 14,* 272–273.

Hogan, A. E., Quay, H. C., Vaughn, S., & Shapiro, S. K. (1989). Revised Behavior Problem Checklist: Stability, prevalence, and incidence of behavior problems in kindergarten and first-grade children. *Psychological Assessment: A Journal of Consulting and Clinical Psychology, 1,* 103–111.

Hogan, J., & Quigley, A. M. (1986). Physical standards for employment and the courts. *American Psychologist, 41,* 1193–1217.

Holden, R. H. (1988). Review of Wechsler Memory Scale—Revised. In D. J. Keyser & R. C. Sweetland (Eds.), *Test critiques Volume VII* (pp. 633–638). Kansas City, MO: Test Corporation of America.

Holden, R. R., & Hickman, D. (1987). Computerized versus standard administration of the Jenkins Activity Survey (Form T). *Journal of Human Stress, 13,* 175–179.

Holden, R., & Fekken, G. (1988). Test-retest reliability of the Hopelessness Scale and its items in a university population. *Journal of Clinical Psychology, 44,* 40–43.

Holland, A. (1980). *Communicative abilities in daily living: A test of functional communication for aphasic adults.* Baltimore, MD: University Park.

Holland, J. L. (1973). *Making vocational choices.* Englewood Cliffs, NJ: Prentice-Hall.

Holland, J. L. (1979)., *The Self-Directed Search: Professional manual, 1979 edition.* Palo Alto, CA: Consulting Psychologists Press.

Holland, J. L. (1985). *Self-Directed Search, 1985 Revision.* Odessa, FL: Psychological Assessment Resources.

Holland, W. R. (1960). Language barrier as an educational problem of Spanish speaking children. *Exceptional Children, 27,* 42–47.

Hollander, E. P., & Willis, R. H. (1967). Some current issues in the psychology of conformity and non-conformity. *Psychological Bulletin, 68,* 62–76.

Hollingshead, A. B., & Redlich, F. C. (1958). *Social class and mental illness: A community study.* New York: Wiley.

Hollon, S. D., & Kendall, P. C. (1980). Cognitive self-statements in depression: Development of an automatic thoughts questionnaire. *Cognitive Therapy and Research, 4,* 383–395.

Holmen, M., & Docter, R. (1972). *Educational and psychological testing.* New York: Russell Sage Foundation.

Holmes, C. B., Dungan, D. S., & Medlin, W. J. (1984). Reassessment of inferring personality traits from Bender-Gestalt drawing styles. *Journal of Clinical Psychology, 40,* 1241–1243.

Holmes, D. S. (1974). The conscious control of thematic projection. *Journal of Consulting and Clinical Psychology, 42,* 323–329.

Holt, G. W., Taylor, W. F., & Carter, E. T. (1985). Airline pilot disability: The continued experience of a major US airline. *Aviation, Space, & Environmental Medicine, 56,* 939–944.

Holt, R. R. (1968). Editor's foreword. In D. Rapaport, M. M. Gill, & R. Schafer, *Diagnostic psychological testing* (Rev. ed.). New York: International Universities Press.

Holt, R. R. (1971). *Assessing personality.* New York: Harcourt Brace Jovanovich.

Holzman, P. S. (1954). The relation of assimilation tendencies in visual, auditory, and kinesthetic time-error to cognitive attitudes of leveling and sharpening. *Journal of Personality, 22,* 375–394.

Holzman, P. S., & Gardner, R. W. (1960). Leveling-sharpening and memory organization. *Journal of Abnormal and Social Psychology, 61,* 176–180.

Holzman, P. S., & Klein, G. S. (1954). Cognitive system-principles of leveling and sharpening: Individual differences in assimilation effects in visual time-error. *Journal of Psychology, 37,* 105–122.

Holtzman, W. H. (1975). New developments in Holtzman Inkblot Technique. In P. McReynolds (Ed.), *Advances in psychological assessment.* (Vol. 3; pp. 243–274). San Francisco: Jossey-Bass.

Holtzman, W. H., Thorpe, J. S., Swartz, J. D., & Herron, E. W. (1961). *Inkblot perception and personality—Holtzman Inkblot Technique.* Austin, TX: University of Texas Press.

Honaker, L. M. (1988). The equivalency of computerized and conventional MMPI administration: A review. *Clinical Psychology Review, 8,* 561–577.

Honaker, L. M. (1990, August). Recommended guidelines for computer equivalency research (or everything you should know about computer administration but will be disappointed if you ask). In W. J. Camara (Chair), *The state of computer-based testing and interpretation: Consensus or chaos?* Symposium conducted at the Annual Convention of the American Psychological Association, Boston.

Honaker, L. M., Harrell, T. H., & Buffaloe, J. D. (1988). Equivalency of Microtest computer MMPI administration for standard and special scales. *Computers in Human Behavior, 4,* 323–337.

Honzik, M. P. (1967). Environmental correlates of mental growth: Prediction from the family setting at 21 months. *Child Development, 38,* 337–364.

Honzik, M. P. (1976). Value and limitations of infant tests: An overview. In M. Lewis (Ed.), *Origins of intelligence* (pp. 59–95). New York: Plenum Press.

Honzik, M. P., McFarlane, J. W., & Allen, L. (1948). The stability of mental test performance between 2 and 18 years. *Journal of Experimental Education, 17,* 309–324.

Hopkins, K. D., & Bracht, G. H. (1975). Ten years stability of verbal and nonverbal IQ scores. *American Educational Research Journal, 12,* 469–477.

Hopkins, K. D., & Glass, G. V. (1978). *Basic statistics for the behavioral sciences.* Englewood Cliffs, NJ: Prentice-Hall.

Horn, J. (1988). Thinking about human abilities. In J. R. Nesselroade & R. B. Cattell (Eds.), *Handbook of multivariate psychology.* New York: Plenum.

Horner, M. S. (1973). A psychological barrier to achievement in women: The motive to avoid success. In D. C. McClelland & R. S. Steele (Eds.), *Human motivation* (pp. 222–230). Morristown, NJ: General Learning Press.

Horowitz, R., & Murphy, L. B. (1938). Projective methods in the psychological study of children. *Journal of Experimental Education, 7,* 133–140.

Horst, P. (1953). Correcting the Kuder-Richardson reliability for dispersion of item difficulties. *Psychological Bulletin, 50,* 371–374.

Hoshmand, L., & Austin, G. (1987). Validation studies of a multifactor cognitive-behavioral Anger Control Inventory. *Journal of Personality Assessment, 51,* 417–432.

Hostetler, A. J. (1987). Try to remember. *APA Monitor 18*(5), 18.

Houston, B. K., Fox, J. E., & Forbes, L. (1984). Trait anxiety and children's state anxiety, cognitive behaviors, and performance under stress. *Cognitive Therapy & Research, 8,* 631–641.

Howarth, E., & Browne, J. A. (1971). An item factor analysis of the 16 P-F. *Personality, 2,* 117–139.

Howes, R. J. (1981). The Rorschach: Does it have a future? *Journal of Personality Assessment, 45,* 339–351.

Hozier, A. (1959). On the breakdown of the sense of reality: A study of spatial perception in schizophrenia. *Journal of Consulting Psychology, 23,* 185–194.

Hudson, W. W. (1982). *The clinical measurement package: A field manual.* Chicago: Dorsey Press.

Hughes, H. M., & Pugh, R. (1984). The Behavior Rating Form—Revised: A parent-report measure of children's self-esteem. *Journal of Clinical Psychology, 40,* 1001–1005.

Hulse, W. G. (1951). The emotionally disturbed child draws his family. *Quarterly Journal of Child Behavior, 3,* 151–174.

Hulse, W. G. (1952). Childhood conflict expressed through family drawings. *Quarterly Journal of Child Behavior, 16,* 152–174.

Hume, D. (1739). *A treatise on human nature.*

Humphreys, L. G. (1985). Review of the System of Multicultural Pluralistic Assessment. In J. V. Mitchell (Ed.), *The ninth mental measurements yearbook* (pp. 1517–1519). Lincoln: University of Nebraska Press.

Hunt, J. McV. (1961). *Intelligence and experience.* New York: Ronald Press.

Hunt, M. K. (Ed.) (1977). Conceptualization and measurement of consumer satisfaction and dissatisfaction. *Proceedings of Marketing Science Institute/National Science Foundation Conference.* Cambridge, MA: Marketing Science Institute.

Hunt, R. A. (1978). The effect of item weighting on the Locke-Wallace Marital Adjustment Scale. *Journal of Marriage and the Family, 40,* 249–256.

Hunter, J. E. (1980). *Validity generalization for 12,000 jobs: An application of synthetic validity and validity generalization to the General Aptitude Test Battery (GATB).* Washington, DC: U.S. Employment Service, U.S. Department of Labor.

Hunter, J. E. (1982). *The dimensionality of the General Aptitude Test Battery and the dominance of general factors over specific factors in the prediction of job perfor-*

mance. Washington, DC: U.S. Employment Service, U.S. Department of Labor.

Hunter, J. E. (1986). Cognitive ability, cognitive aptitudes, job knowledge, and job performance. *Journal of Vocational Behavior, 29,* 340–362.

Hunter, J. E., & Hunter, R. (1984). Validity and utility of alternate predictors of job performance. *Psychological Bulletin, 96,* 72–98.

Hunter, J. E., & Schmidt, F. L. (1976). A critical analysis of the statistical and ethical implications of various definitions of "test bias." *Psychological Bulletin, 83,* 1053–1071.

Hunter, J. E., & Schmidt, F. L. (1981). Fitting people into jobs: The impact of personal selection on normal productivity. In M. D. Dunnette & E. A. Fleishman (Eds.), *Human performance and productivity: Vol. 1. Human capability assessment.* Hillsdale, NJ: Erlbaum.

Hunter, J. E., & Schmidt, F. L. (1983). Quantifying the effects of psychological interventions on employee job performance and work-force productivity. *American Psychologist, 38,* 473–478.

Hunter, J. E., Schmidt, F. L., & Jackson, G. B. (1982). *Meta-analysis: Cumulating research findings across studies.* Beverly Hills, CA: Sage.

Hunter, N., & Kelley, C. K. (1986). Examination of the validity of the Adolescent Problems Inventory among incarcerated juvenile delinquents. *Journal of Consulting and Clinical Psychology, 54,* 301–302.

Hurt, S. W. (1986). Diagnostic Interview for Borderlines: Psychometric properties and validity. *Journal of Consulting and Clinical Psychology, 54,* 256–260.

Hutt, M. L. (1977). *The Hutt adaptation of the Bender-Gestalt* (3rd ed.). New York: Grune & Stratton.

Hutt, M. L. (1985). *The Hutt adaptation of the Bender-Gestalt Test* (4th ed.). Orlando, FL: Grune and Stratton.

Ingham, J. G., Kreitman, N. B., Miller, P. M., Sashidharan, S. P., & Surtees, P. G. (1986). Self-esteem, vulnerability, and psychiatric disorder in the community. *British Journal of Psychiatry, 148,* 375–385.

Ingram, R. E., Slater, M. A., Atkinson, J. H., & Scott, W. (1990). *Psychological Assessment: A Journal of Consulting & Clinical Psychology, 2,* 209–211.

Ingram, R. E., & Wisnicki, K. S. (1988). Assessment of positive automatic cognition. *Journal of Consulting and Clinical Psychology, 56,* 898–902.

Institute for Juvenile Research. (1937). *Child guidance procedures, methods and techniques employed at the Institute for Juvenile Research.* New York: Appleton-Century.

Ironson, G. H., & Subkoviak, M. J. (1979). A comparison of several methods of assessing item bias. *Journal of Educational Measurement, 16,* 209–225.

Ishihara, S. (1964). *Tests for color blindness* (11th ed.). Tokyo: Kanehara Shuppan.

Ilyin, D. (1976). *The Ilyin oral interview.* Rowley, MA: Newbury House.

Ivancevich, J. M. (1983). Contrast effects in performance evaluation and reward practices. *Academy of Management Journal, 26,* 46. 476.

Iwata, B. A., Pace, G. M., Kissel, P. C., Nau, P. A., & Farber, J. M. (1990). The Self-Injury Trauma (SIT) Scale: A method for quantifying surface tissue damage caused by self-injurious behavior. *Journal of Applied Behavior Analysis, 23,* 99–110.

Jackson, D. E., & Murray, B. S. (1986). Predicting accuracy and liking ratings for bogus and real personality feedback. *Journal of Psychology: Interdisciplinary and Applied, 119,* 495–503.

Jackson, D. E., O'Dell, J. W., & Olson, D. (1982). Acceptance of bogus personality interpretations: Face validity reconsidered. *Journal of Clinical Psychology, 38,* 588–592.

Jackson, D. N. (1964). Desirability judgments as a method of personality assessment. *Educational and Psychological Measurement, 24,* 223–238.

Jackson, D. N. (1970). A sequential system for personality scale development. In C. D. Spielberger (Ed.), *Current topics in clinical and community psychology.* New York: Academic Press.

Jackson, D. N. (1982). Some preconditions for valid person perception. In M. P. Zanna, E. T. Higgins, & C. P. Herman (Eds.), *Consistency in social behavior: The Ontario Symposium* (Vol. 2; pp. 251–279). Hillsdale, NJ: Erlbaum.

Jackson, D. N. (1984a). *Personality Research Form manual.* Port Huron, MI: Research Psychologists Press.

Jackson, D. N. (1984b). *Jackson Vocational Interest Survey manual* (2nd ed.). Port Huron, MI: Research Psychologists Press.

Jackson, D. N. (1986). *Computer-based personality testing.* Washington, DC: Scientific Affairs Office, American Psychological Association.

Jackson, D. N. (1988). Computer-based assessment

and interpretation: The dawn of discovery. In T. B. Gutkin & S. L. Wise (Eds.), *The computer as adjunct to the decision-making process*. Hillsdale, NJ: Erlbaum.

Jackson, D. N., & Messick, S. (1958). Content and style in personality assessment. *Psychological Bulletin, 55,* 243–252.

Jackson, D. N., & Messick, S. (1962). Response styles and the assessment of psychopathology. In S. Messick & J. Ross (Eds.), *Measurement in personality and cognition*. New York: Wiley.

Jacobs, J. (1970). Are we being misled by fifty years of research on our gifted children? *Gifted Child Quarterly, 14,* 120–123.

Jacoby, J., & Chestnut, R. (1978). *Brand loyalty: Measurement and management*. New York: Wiley.

Jaffe, L. T., & Archer, R. P. (1987). The prediction of drug use among college students from the MMPI, MCMI, and Sensation Seeking scales. *Journal of Personality Assessment, 51,* 243–253.

Jagim, R. D., Wittman, W. D., & Noll, J. O. (1978). Mental health professionals' attitudes towards confidentiality, privilege, and third-party disclosure. *Professional Psychology, 9,* 458–466.

Jahanshahi, M., & Philips, C. (1986). Validation of a new technique for the assessment of pain behavior. *Behavior Research and Therapy, 24,* 35–42.

James, L. R., Demaree, R. G., & Mulaik, S. A. (1986). A note on validity generalization procedures. *Journal of Applied Psychology, 71,* 440–450.

Janisse, M. P. (1973). Pupil size and affect: A critical review of the literature since 1960. *Canadian Psychologist, 14,* 311–329.

Janzen, H. L. (1981). Why use the Binet? *The Alberta School Psychologist, 2,* 25–38.

Jastak, J. F., & Jastak, S. (1984). *Wide Range Achievement Test—Revised*. Wilmington, DE: Jastak Associates.

Jay, S. M., Elliott, C. H., Ozolines, M., Olson, R., & Pruit, S. D. (1987). Behavioral management of children's distress during painful medical procedures. *Behavioral Research and Therapy, 23,* 513–520.

Jenkins, C. D., Zyzanski, S. J., & Rosenman, R. H. (1979). *Jenkins Activity Survey: Manual*. San Antonio, TX: Psychological Corporation.

Jensema, C. (1975). A statistical investigation of the 16PF Form E as applied to hearing impaired college students. *Journal of Rehabilitation of the Deaf, 9,* 21–29.

Jensen, A. R. (1962). The culturally disadvantaged: Psychological and educational aspects. *Educational Research, 10,* 4–20.

Jensen, A. R. (1967). The culturally disadvantaged: Psychological and educational aspects. *Educational Research, 10,* 4–20.

Jensen, A. R. (1969). How much can we boost IQ and scholastic achievement? *Harvard Educational Review, 39,* 1–123.

Jensen, A. R. (1974). The strange case of Dr. Jensen and Mr. Hyde. *American Psychologist, 29,* 467–468.

Jensen, A. R. (1980). *Bias in mental testing*. New York: Free Press.

Jensen, A. R. (1984). The black-white difference on the K-ABC: Implications for future tests. *Journal of Special Education, 18*(3), 377–408.

Johnson, G. S. (1989). Emotional indicators in the human figure drawings of hearing-impaired children: A small sample validation study. *American Annals of the Deaf, 134,* 205–208.

Johnson, O. G., & Bommarito, J. W. (1971). *Tests in child development: A handbook*. San Francisco: Jossey-Bass.

Johnson, R. C. (1963). Similarity in IQ of separated identical twins as related to length of time spent in same environment. *Child Development, 34,* 745–749.

Jolles, J. (1952). *A catalogue for the qualitative interpretation of the H-T-P*. Los Angeles: Western Psychological Services.

Jones, C., Rowan, M., & Taylor, H. (1977). An overview of the mathematics achievement tests offered in the admissions testing program of the College Entrance Examination Board. *Mathematics Teacher, 70*(3), 197–208.

Jones, D. P., & McGraw, J. M. (1987). Reliable and fictitious accounts of sexual abuse to children. *Journal of Interpersonal Violence, 2,* 27–45.

Jones, D. R. (1984). More on psychiatry and space flight. *American Journal of Psychiatry, 141,* 918.

Jones, J. W., Arnold, D., & Harris, W. G. (1990). Introduction to the Model Guidelines for Preemployment Integrity Testing. *Journal of Business and Psychology, 4,* 525–532.

Jung, C. G. (1910). The association method. *American Journal of Psychology, 21,* 219–269.

Jung, C. G. (1923). *Psychological types*. London: Rutledge & Kegan Paul.

Jupp, J. J. (1983). Change in unconscious concern with

body image following treatment for obesity. *Journal of Personality Assessment, 47*, 483–489.

Kagan, J. (1956). The measurement of overt aggression from fantasy. *Journal of Abnormal and Social Psychology, 52*, 390–393.

Kagan, J. (1965). Impulsive and reflective children: Significance of conceptual tempo. In J. D. Krumboltz (Ed.), *Learning and the educational process.* Chicago: Rand McNally.

Kagan, J., Pearson, L., & Welch, L. (1966). Modifiability of an impulsive tempo. *Journal of Educational Psychology, 57*, 359–365.

Kagan, J., Rossman, B. L., Day, D., Albert, J., & Phillips, W. (1964). Information processing in the child: Significance of analysis and reflective attitudes. *Psychological Monographs, 78*, 1–37.

Kahn, J. (1976). Utility of the Uzgiris-Hunt Scales of Sensorimotor Development with severely and profoundly retarded children. *American Journal of Mental Deficiency, 80*, 663–665.

Kahn, M., & Taft, G. (1983). The application of the standard of care doctrine to psychological testing. *Behavioral Sciences and the Law, 1*, 71–84.

Kaiser, H. F. (1958). A modified stanine scale. *Journal of Experimental Education, 26*, 261.

Kaiser, H. F., & Michael, W. B. (1975). Domain validity and generalizability. *Educational and Psychological Measurement, 35*, 31–35.

Kamin, L. J. (1974). *The science and politics of IQ.* New York: Wiley.

Kamiya, J. (1962). *Conditional discrimination of the EEG alpha rhythm in humans.* Paper presented at the annual meeting of the Western Psychological Association (April).

Kamiya, J. (1968). Conscious control of brain waves. *Psychology Today, 1*(11), 56–60.

Kamphaus, R. W., Kaufman, A. S., & Kaufman, N. L. (1982). A cross-validation study of sequential-simultaneous processing at ages 2½–12½ using the Kaufman Assessment Battery for Children (K-ABC). Paper presented at the Annual Meeting of the American Psychological Association, Washington, DC.

Kamphaus, R. W., & Reynolds, C. R. (1984). Development and structure of the Kaufman Assessment Battery for Children. *Journal of Special Education, 18*, 213–218.

Kamphaus, R. W., & Reynolds, C. R. (1987). *Clinical and research applications of the K-ABC.* Circle Pines, MN: American Guidance Service.

Kane, J. S., & Lawler, E. E., III. (1978). Methods of peer assessment. *Psychological Bulletin, 85*, 555–586.

Kane, J. S., & Lawler, E. E., III. (1980). In defense of peer assessment: A rebuttal to Brief's critique. *Psychological Bulletin, 85*, 555–586.

Kanner, A. D., Coyne, J. C., Schaefer, C., & Lazarus, R. S. (1981). Comparison of two modes of stress measurement: Daily hassles and uplifts versus major life events. *Journal of Behavioral Medicine, 4*, 1–39.

Kantor, J. E., & Bordelon, V. P. (1985). The USAF pilot selection and classification research program. *Aviation, Space, & Environmental Medicine, 56*, 258–261.

Kaplan, B. J. (1990). Review of Reynolds Adolescent Depression Scale. In J. J. Kramer & J. C. Conoley (Eds.), *The supplement to the tenth mental measurements yearbook* (pp. 217–218). Lincoln: The Buros Institute of Mental Measurements of the University of Nebraska-Lincoln.

Karp, S. A., & Konstadt, N. (1963/1971). *Children's Embedded Figures Test.* Palo Alto, CA: Consulting Psychologists Press.

Karplus, E., & Karplus, R. (1970). Intellectual development beyond elementary school deduction logic. *School Science and Mathematics, 70*, 398–406.

Karson, S., & O'Dell, J. W. (1989). The 16PF. In C. S. Newmark (Ed.), *Major psychological assessment instruments: Vol. II* (pp. 45–66). Needham Heights, MA: Allyn and Bacon.

Kassarjian, H. H., & Cohen, J. B. (1965). Cognitive dissonance and consumer behavior: Reaction to the Surgeon General's Report on Smoking and Health. *California Management Review, 8*, 55–64.

Katz, E. (1955). Success of Stanford-Binet Intelligence Scale test items of children with cerebral palsy as compared with nonhandicapped children. *Cerebral Palsy Review, 16*, 18–19.

Kaufman, A. S. (1971). Piaget and Gesell: A psychometric analysis of tests built from their tasks. *Child Development, 42*, 1341–1360.

Kaufman, A. S. (1973a). Comparison of the performance of matched groups of black children and white children on the Wechsler Preschool and Primary Scale of Intelligence. *Journal of Consulting and Clinical Psychology, 41*, 186–191.

Kaufman, A. S. (1973b). Comparison of the WPPSI, Stanford-Binet, and McCarthy Scales as predictors of first-grade achievement. *Perceptual and Motor Skills, 36,* 67–73.

Kaufman, A. S. (1975a). Factor analysis of the WISC-R at eleven age levels between 6½ and 16½ years. *Journal of Consulting and Clinical Psychology, 43,* 135–147.

Kaufman, A. S. (1975b). Factor structure of the McCarthy Scales at five age levels between 2½ and 8½. *Educational and Psychological Measurement, 35,* 641–656.

Kaufman, A. S. (1979). *Intelligent testing with the WISC-R.* New York: Wiley.

Kaufman, A. S. (1984). K-ABC and giftedness. *Roeper Review, 7*(2), 83–88.

Kaufman, A. S. (1990). *Assessing adolescent and adult intelligence.* Needham Heights, MA: Allyn and Bacon.

Kaufman, A. S., & Hollenbeck, G. P. (1973). Factor analysis of the standardization edition of the McCarthy Scales. *Journal of Clinical Psychology, 29,* 358–362.

Kaufman, A. S., & Kamphaus, R. W. (1984). Factor analysis of the Kaufman Assessment Battery for Children (K-ABC) for ages 2½ through 12½ years. *Journal of Educational Psychology, 76*(4), 623–637.

Kaufman, A. S., & Kaufman, N. L. (1977). *Clinical evaluation of young children with the McCarthy Scales.* New York: Grune & Stratton.

Kaufman, A. S., & Kaufman, N. L. (1983). *Kaufman Assessment Battery for Children (K-ABC) Interpretive Manual.* Circle Pines, MN: American Guidance Service.

Kaufman, A. S., Kaufman, N. L., & Goldsmith, B. (1984). *Kaufman Sequential or Simultaneous (K-SOS).* Circle Pines, MN: American Guidance Service.

Kaufman, A. S., & McLean, J. E. (1986). K-ABC/WISC-R factor analysis for a learning disabled population. *Journal of Learning Disabilities, 19,* 145–153.

Kaufman, A. S., & McLean, J. E. (1987). Joint factor analysis of the K-ABC and WISC-R with normal children. *Journal of School Psychology, 25,* 105–118.

Kaufman, A. S., & Van Hagen, J. (1977). Investigation of the WISC-R for use with retarded children: Correlation with the 1972 Stanford-Binet and comparison of WISC and WISC-R profiles. *Psychology in the Schools, 14,* 10–14.

Kaufman, A. S., & Weiner, S. (1976). *A comparison of the WISC-R and the WISC for black children aged 7 to 10 years.* Paper presented at the annual meeting of the Eastern Psychological Association, New York.

Kavan, M. G. (1990). Review of *Children's Depression Inventory.* In J. J. Kramer & J. C. Conoley (Eds.), *The supplement to the tenth mental measurements yearbook* (pp. 46–48). Lincoln: The Buros Institute of Mental Measurements, University of Nebraska-Lincoln.

Kavanaugh, M. J., MacKinney, A. C., & Wolins, L. (1970). Satisfaction and morale of foremen as a function of middle manager's performance. *Journal of Applied Psychology, 54,* 145–156.

Kazdin, A. E., Colbus, D., & Rodgers, A. (1986). Assessment of depression and diagnosis of depressive disorder among psychiatrically disturbed children. *Journal of Abnormal Child Psychology, 14,* 499–515.

Kazdin, A. E., Esveldt-Dawson, K., French, N. H., & Unis, A. S. (1987). Problem-solving skills training and relationship therapy in the treatment of antisocial child behavior. *Journal of Consulting and Clinical Psychology, 55,* 76–85.

Kazdin, A. E., Rodgers, A., & Colbus, D. (1986). The Hopelessness Scale for Children: Psychometric characteristics and concurrent validity. *Journal of Consulting & Clinical Psychology, 54,* 241–245.

Kazimour, K. K., & Reschly, D. J. (1981). Investigation of the norms and concurrent validity for the Adaptive Behavior Inventory for Children (ABIC). *American Journal of Mental Deficiency, 85,* 512–520.

Keane, T. M., Malloy, P. F., & Fairbank, J. A. (1984). Empirical development of an MMPI subscale for the assessment of combat-related posttraumatic stress disorder. *Journal of Consulting and Clinical Psychology, 52,* 881–891.

Keenan, P. A., & Lachar, D. (1988). Screening preschoolers with special problems: Use of the Personality Inventory for Children (PIC). *Journal of School Psychology, 26*(1), 1–11.

Keilitz, I. (1987). Researching and reforming the insanity defense. *Rutgers Law Review, 39,* 289–322.

Keith, T. Z. (1985). Questioning the K-ABC: What does it measure? *School Psychology Review, 14,* 21–36.

Keith, T. Z., Cool, V. A., Novak, C. G., White, L. J., & Pottebaum, S. M. (1988). Confirmatory factor analysis of the Stanford-Binet Fourth Edition: Testing the theory-test match. *Journal of School Psychology, 26*(3), 253–274.

Keith, T. Z., & Dunbar, S. B. (1984). Hierarchical factor analysis of the K-ABC: Testing alternate models. *Journal of Special Education, 18,* 367–375.

Keith, T. Z., Hood, C., Eberhart, S., & Pottebaum, S. M. (1985). Factor structure of the K-ABC for referred school children. Paper presented at the Annual Meeting of the National Association of School Psychologists, Las Vegas, NV.

Keith, T. Z., & Novak, C. G. (1987). Joint factor structure of the WISC-R and K-ABC for referred school children. *Journal of Psychoeducational Assessment, 5*(4), 370–386.

Keith, T. Z., & Reynolds, C. R. (1990). Measurement and design issues in child assessment research. In C. R. Reynolds & R. W. Kamphaus (Eds.), *Handbook of psychological and educational assessment of children: Intelligence & achievement* (pp. 29–61). New York: Guilford Press.

Keller, L. S., & Butcher, J. N. (1989, March). Use of the MMPI-2 with chronic pain patients. Paper presented at the 24th Annual Symposium on Recent Developments in the Use of the MMPI, Honolulu, HA.

Kelley, S. J. (1985). Drawings: Critical communications for the sexually abused child. *Pediatric Nursing, 11,* 421–426.

Kelley, S. J. (1988). Physical abuse of children: Recognition and reporting. *Journal of Emergency Nursing, 14*(2), 82–90.

Kelley, T. L. (1939). The selection of upper and lower groups for the validation of test items. *Journal of Educational Psychology, 30,* 17–24.

Kelley, M., & Surbeck, E. (1983). History of preschool assessment. In K. Paget, & B. Bracken (Eds.), *The psychoeducational assessment of preschool children* (pp. 1–16). New York: Grune & Stratton.

Kellner, C. H., Jolley, R. R., Holgate, R. C., Austin, L., Lydiard, R. B., Laraia, M., & Ballenger, J. C. (1991). Brain MRI in obsessive-compulsive disorder. *Psychiatry Research, 36,* 45–49.

Kelly, D. H. (1966). Measurement of anxiety by forearm blood flow. *British Journal of Psychiatry, 112,* 789–798.

Kelly, E. J. (1985). The personality of chessplayers. *Journal of Personality Assessment, 49,* 282–284.

Kelly, G. A. (1955). *The psychology of personal constructs.* New York: Norton.

Kelly, M. D., & Dean, R. S. (1990). Best practices in neuropsychology. In A. Thomas & J. Grimes (Eds.), *Best practices in school psychology-II.* Washington, DC: National Association of School Psychologists.

Kendall, M. G. (1948). *Rank correlation methods.* London: Griffin.

Kendall, P. C., & Finch, A. J., Jr. (1978). A cognitive-behavioral treatment for impulsivity. A group comparison study. *Journal of Consulting and Clinical Study, 46,* 110–115.

Kennedy, M. H., & Hiltonsmith, R. W. (1988). Relationships among the K-ABC Nonverbal Scale, the Pictorial Test of Intelligence and the Hiskey-Nebraska Test of Learning Aptitude for speech- and language-disabled preschool children. *Journal of Psychoeducational Assessment, 6*(1), 49–54.

Kennedy, O. A. (1971). Pupillometrics as an aid in the assessment of motivation, impact of treatment, and prognosis of chronic alcoholics. *Dissertation Abstracts International, 32,* 1214B–1215B.

Kennedy, R. S., Bittner, A. C., Harbeson, M., & Jones, M. B. (1982). Television computer games: A "new look" in performance testing. *Aviation, Space and Environmental Medicine, 53,* 49–53.

Kent, G. H., & Rosanoff, A. J. (1910). A study of association in insanity. *American Journal of Insanity, 67,* 37–96, 317–390.

Kent, N., & Davis, D. R. (1957). Discipline in the home and intellectual development. *British Journal of Medical Psychology, 30,* 27–33.

Kerlinger, F. N. (1973). *Foundations of behavioral research* (2nd ed.). New York: Holt.

Kern, J. M., Miller, C., & Eggers, J. (1983). Enhancing the validity of role-play tests: A comparison of three role-play methodologies. *Behavior Therapy, 14,* 482–492.

Kerr, M. M., & Nelson, C. M. (1989). *Strategies for managing behavior problems in the classroom* (2nd ed.). Columbus, OH: Merrill.

Keyser, D. J., & Sweetland, R. C. (Eds.). (1984–1988). *Test Critiques* (Vol. I–VII). Kansas City, MO: Test Corporation of America.

Khaleque, A. (1981). Job satisfaction, perceived effort and heart rate in light industrial work. *Ergonomics, 24,* 735–742.

Kim, S. P., Siomopoulos, G., & Cohen, R. J. (1977). Verbal abstraction and culture: An exploratory study with proverbs. *Psychological Reports, 41,* 967–972.

King, B. M. (1959). *Predicting submarine school attrition from the Minnesota Multiphasic Personality Inventory.* USN Medical Research Laboratory Report, New London, CT: *18* (Whole No. 313).

King, M. A., & Yuille, J. C. (1987). Suggestibility and the child witness. In S. J. Ceci, M. P. Toglia, & D. F. Ross (Eds.), *Children's eyewitness testimony.* New York: Springer-Verlag.

Kinnear, T. C., & Taylor, J. A. (1983). *Marketing research.* New York: McGraw-Hill.

Kinslinger, H. J. (1966). Application of projective techniques in personnel psychology since 1940. *Psychological Bulletin, 66,* 134–149.

Kinston, W., Loader, P., & Miller, L. (1985). *Clinical assessment of family health.* London: Hospital for Sick Children, Family Studies Group.

Kirchner, W. K. (1966). A note on the effect of privacy in taking typing tests. *Journal of Applied Psychology, 50,* 373–374.

Kirk, S. A., McCarthy, J. J., & Kirk, W. D. (1968). *Illinois Test of Psycholinguistic Abilities.* Urbana: University of Illinois Press.

Kirkpatrick, E. (1900). Individual tests of school children. *Psychological Review, 7,* 274–280.

Klanderman, J. W., Perney, J., & Kroeschell, Z. B. (1985). Comparison of the K-ABC and WISC-R for LD children. *Journal of Learning Disabilities, 18,* 524–527.

Klein, D. (1989). The Depressive Experiences Questionnaire: A further evaluation. *Journal of Psychological Assessment, 53,* 703–715.

Klein, G. S., & Holzman, P. S. (1950). The "schematizing process": Personality qualities and perceptual attitudes in sensitivity to change. *American Psychologist, 5,* 312.

Kleinke, C. (1988). The Depression Coping Questionnaire. *Journal of Clinical Psychology, 44,* 516–526.

Kleinmuntz, B., & Szucko, J. J. (1984). Lie detection in ancient and modern times: A call for contemporary scientific study. *American Psychologist, 39,* 766–776.

Kline, R. B. (1989). Is the Fourth Edition Stanford-Binet a four factor test? Confirmatory factor analyses of alternative models for ages 2 through 23. *Journal of Psychoeducational Assessment, 7(1),* 4–13.

Kline, R. B., Lachar, D., & Sprague, D. J. (1985). The Personality Inventory for Children (PIC): An unbiased predictor of cognitive and academic status. *Journal of Pediatric Psychology, 10,* 461–477.

Klockars, A. J. (1978). Personality variables related to peer selection. *Educational and Psychological Measurement, 32,* 513–517.

Klopfer, B., Ainsworth, M., Klopfer, W., & Holt, R. R. (1954). *Developments in the Rorschach technique: Vol. 1. Technique and theory.* Yonkers-on-Hudson, NY: World.

Klopfer, B., & Davidson, H. (1962). *The Rorschach technique: An introductory manual.* New York: Harcourt.

Klopfer, W. G. (1984). Application of the consensus Rorschach to couples. *Journal of Personality Assessment, 48,* 422–440.

Klove, H., & Matthews, C. G. (1974). Neuropsychological studies of patients with epilepsy. In R. M. Reitan & L. A. Davison (Eds.), *Clinical Neuropsychology: Current status and applications* (pp. 237–365). New York: Winston.

Knapp, R. R., Knapp, L., & Michael, W. (1977). Stability and concurrent validity of the Career Ability Placement Survey (CAPS) against the DAT and the GATB. *Educational and Psychological Measurement, 37,* 1081–1085.

Knight, B. C., Baker, E. H., & Minder, C. C. (1990). Concurrent validity of the Stanford-Binet: Fourth Edition and the Kaufman Assessment Battery for Children with Learning Disabled students. *Psychology in the Schools, 27(2),* 116–120.

Knight, R., Chisholm, B., Paulin, J., & Waal-Manning, H. (1988). The Spielberger Anger Expression Scale: Some psychometric data. *British Journal of Clinical Psychology, 27,* 279–281.

Knobloch, H., & Pasamanick, B. (1960). Environmental factors affecting human development before and after birth. *Pediatrics, 26,* 210–218.

Knobloch, H., & Pasamanick, B. (1966). Prediction from assessment of neuromotor and intellectual status in infancy. Paper presented at the American Psychopathological Association Meeting (February), Washington, DC.

Knoff, H. M. (1990a). Evaluation of projective drawings. In C. R. Reynolds and T. B. Gutkin (Eds.), *Handbook of school psychology* (2nd ed.; pp. 898–946). New York: Wiley.

Knoff, H. M. (1990b). Review of Children's Depression Inventory. In J. J. Kramer & J. C. Conoley (Eds.), *The supplement to the tenth mental measurements yearbook* (pp. 48–50). Lincoln: The Buros Institute of Mental Measurements, University of Nebraska-Lincoln.

Knoff, H. M., & Prout, H. T. (1985). *The Kinetic drawing system: Family and school.* Los Angeles: Western Psychological Services.

Kobak, K. A., Reynolds, W. M., Rosenfeld, R., & Greist, J. H. (1990). Development and validation of a computer-administered version on the Hamilton Depression Rating Scale. *Psychological Assessment: A Journal of Consulting and Clinical Psychology, 2,* 56–63.

Kohn, P. M., Lafreniere, K., & Gurevich, M. (1990). The Inventory of College Students' Recent Life Experiences: A decontaminated hassles scale for a special population. *Journal of Behavioral Medicine, 13,* 619–630.

Kohn, S. D. (1975, July–August). The numbers game: How the testing industry operates. *National Elementary Principal, 11*–23.

Kohlberg, L. (1968). Early education: A cognitive developmental view. *Child Development, 31,* 1013–1062.

Kolb, B., & Whishaw, I. Q. (1980). *Fundamentals of human neuropsychology.* San Francisco: Freeman.

Kolbe, K., Shemberg, K., & Leventhal, D. (1985). University training in psychodiagnostics and psychotherapy. *The Clinical Psychologist, 38*(3), 59–61.

Kolko, D. J., Kazdin, A. E., & Meyer, E. C. (1985). Aggression and psychopathology in childhood firesetters: Parent and child reports. *Journal of Consulting & Clinical Psychology, 53,* 377–385.

Kolotkin, R. A., & Wielkiewicz, R. M. (1984). Effects of situational demand in the role-play assessment of assertive behavior. *Journal of Behavioral Assessment, 6,* 59–70.

Kopelman, M. D. (1975). The contrast effect in the selection interview. *British Journal of Educational Psychology, 45,* 333–336.

Koppitz, E. M. (1963). *The Bender-Gestalt Test for young children.* New York: Grune & Stratton.

Koppitz, E. M. (1975). *The Bender-Gestalt Test for young children* (Vol. 2). New York: Grune & Stratton.

Korchin, S. J., & Schuldberg, D. (1981). The future of clinical assessment. *American Psychologist, 36,* 1147–1158.

Kordinak, S. T., Vingue, F. J., & Birney, S. D. (1968). Head Start: Who needs it? That is the question. *American Psychologist, 76,* 618.

Korner, I. N., & Westwood, D. (1955). Inter-rater agreement in judging student adjustment from projective tests. *Journal of Clinical Psychology, 11,* 167–170.

Koski, M. A., & Ingram, E. M. (1977). Child abuse and neglect. Effects on Bayley Scale scores. *Journal of Abnormal Child Psychology, 5,* 79–91.

Koson, D., Kitchen, C., Kochen, M., & Stodolsky, D. (1970). Psychological testing by computer: Effect on response bias. *Educational and Psychological Measurement, 30,* 803–810.

Kotkov, B., & Goodman, M. (1953). The Draw-A-Person tests of obese women. *Journal of Clinical Psychology, 9,* 362–364.

Kovacs, M. (1977). *Children's Depression Inventory.* Pittsburgh: Western Psychiatric Institute and Clinic.

Kraepelin, E. (1892). *Uber die Beeinflussung einfacher psychischer Vorgange durch einige Arzneimittel.* Jena: Fischer.

Kraepelin, E. (1895). Der psychologische versuch in der psychiatrie. *Psychologische Arbeiten, 1,* 1–91.

Kraepelin, E. (1896). Der psychologische versuch in der psychiatrie. *Psychologische Arbeiten, 1,* 1–91.

Kramer, J. J., & Conoley, J. C. (Eds.). (1990). *The supplement to the tenth mental measurements yearbook.* Lincoln: The Buros Institute of Mental Measurements, University of Nebraska-Lincoln.

Kratochwill, T. R., & Sheridan, S. M. (1990). Advances in behavioral assessment. In T. B. Gutkin & C. R. Reynolds (Eds.), *The handbook of school psychology* (2nd ed.; pp. 328–364). New York: Wiley.

Kresel, J. J., & Lovejoy, F. H. (1981). Poisonings and child abuse. In N. S. Ellerstein (Ed.), *Child abuse and neglect: A medical reference* (pp. 307–313). New York: Wiley.

Krohn, A., & Mayman, M. (1974). Object representations in dreams and projective tests. *Bulletin of the Menninger Clinic, 43,* 515–524.

Krohn, E. J., & Lamp, R. E. (1989). Concurrent validity of the K-ABC and Stanford-Binet—Fourth Edition for Head Start Children. *Journal of School Psychology, 27*(1), 59–67.

Krohn, E. J., Lamp, R. E., & Phelps, C. G. (1988). Validity of the K-ABC for a black preschool population. *Psychology in the Schools, 25,* 15–21.

Krug, R. S. (1971). Antecedent probabilities, cost efficiency, and differential prediction of patients with cerebral organic conditions or psychiatric disturbance by means of a short test for aphasia. *Journal of Clinical Psychology, 27,* 468–471.

Kuder, G. F. (1979). *Kuder Occupational Interest Survey, Revised: General manual*. Chicago: Science Research Associates.

Kuder, G. F., & Richardson, M. W. (1937). The theory of the estimation of reliability. *Psychometrika, 2*, 151–160.

Kuhlmann, F. (1912). A revision of the Binet-Simon system for measuring the intelligence of children. *Journal of Psycho-Asthenics Monograph Supplement, 1*(1), 1–41.

Kulka, R. A., Schlenger, W. E., Fairbank, J. A., Hough, R. L., Jordan, B. K., Marmar, C. R., & Weiss, D. S. (1988). *Contractual report of findings from the national Vietnam veterans readjustment study: Vol. 1. Executive summary, description of findings, and technical appendices*. Research Triangle Park, NC: Research Triangle Institute.

Kuncel, R. B., & Fiske, D. W. (1974). Stability of response process and response. *Educational and Psychological Measurement, 34*, 743–755.

Kundert, D. K. (1990). Review of Reynolds Adolescent Depression Scale. In J. J. Kramer & J. C. Conoley (Eds.), *The supplement to the tenth mental measurements yearbook* (pp. 218–219). Lincoln: The Buros Institute of Mental Measurements, University of Nebraska-Lincoln.

Kuykendall, D., & Keating, J. P. (1990). Mood and persuasion: Evidence for the differential influence of positive and negative states. *Psychology & Marketing, 7*, 1–9.

Labeck, L. J., Johnson, J. H., & Harris, W. G. (1983). Validity on an automated on-line MMPI interpretive system. *Journal of Clinical Psychology, 39*, 412–416.

Labrentz, E., Linkenhoker, F., & Aaron, P. G. (1976). Recognition and reproduction of Bender-Gestalt figures: A developmental study of the lag between perception and performance. *Psychology in the Schools, 13*, 128–133.

Lachar, D. (1987). Automated assessment of child and adolescent personality. In J. N. Butcher (Ed.), *Computerized psychological assessment: A practitioner's guide* (pp. 261–291). New York: Basic Books.

Lachar, D., & Gdowski, C. G. (1979). *Actuarial assessment of child and adolescent personality: An interpretive guide for the Personality Inventory for Children profile*. Los Angeles: Western Psychological Services.

Lachar, D. (1982). *Personality Inventory for Children (PIC): Revised format manual supplement*. Los Angeles: Western Psychological Services.

Lachar, D., & Gdowski, C. L. (1979a). Problem-behavior factor correlates of Personality Inventory for Children profiles scales. *Journal of Consulting and Clinical Psychology, 47*, 39–48.

Lachar, D., & Gdowski, C. L. (1979b). *Actuarial assessment of child and adolescent personality: An interpretive guide for the Personality Inventory for Children profile*. Los Angeles: Western Psychological Services.

Lachar, D., Gdowski, C. L., & Snyder, D. K. (1985). Consistency of maternal report and the Personality Inventory for Children: Always useful and sometimes sufficient—Reply to Cornell. *Journal of Consulting and Clinical Psychology, 53*, 275–276.

Lachar, D., Kline, R. B., & Boersma, D. C. (1986). The Personality Inventory for Children: Approaches to actuarial interpretation in clinic and school settings. In H. M. Knoff (Ed.), *The psychological assessment of child and adolescent personality* (pp. 273–308). New York: Guilford Press.

Lachar, D., & Wirt, R. D. (1981). A data-based analysis of the psychometric performance of the Personality Inventory for Children (PIC): An alternative to the Achenbach review. *Journal of Personality Assessment, 45*, 614–616.

Lachar, D., & Wrobel, T. A. (1979). Validating clinicians' hunches: Construction of a new MMPI critical item set. *Journal of Consulting and Clinical Psychology, 47*, 277–284.

Lah, M. I. (1989a). Sentence completion tests. In C. S. Newmark (Ed.), *Major psychological assessment instruments* (Vol. 2; pp. 133–163). Needham Heights, MA: Allyn and Bacon.

Lah, M. I. (1989b). New validity, normative, and scoring data for the Rotter Incomplete Sentences Blank. *Journal of Personality Assessment, 53*, 607–620.

Lake, D. G., Miles, M. B., & Earle, R. B., Jr. (1973). *Measuring human behavior*. New York: Teachers College Press.

Lamb, M. E. (Ed.). (1981). *The role of the father in child development* (2nd ed.). New York: Wiley.

Lambert, N. M. (1978). The Adaptive Behavior Scale—Public School Version: An overview. In W. A. Coulter & H. W. Morrow (Eds.). *Adaptive behavior: Concepts and measurements*. New York: Grune & Stratton.

Lamp, R. E., & Krohn, E. J. (1990). Stability of the Stanford-Binet Fourth Edition and K-ABC for young black and white children from low income families. *Journal of Psychoeducational Assessment, 8,* 139–149.

Landers, S. (1986, December). Judge reiterates I.Q. test ban. *APA Monitor,* p. 18.

Landy, F. J. (1986). Stamp collecting versus science. *American Psychologist, 41,* 1183–1192.

Landy, F. J., & Farr, J. H. (1980). Performance rating. *Psychological Bulletin, 87,* 72–107.

Langer, E. J., & Abelson, R. P. (1974). A patient by any other name: Clinician group difference in labeling bias. *Journal of Consulting and Clinical Psychology, 42,* 4–9.

Langmaid, R., & Ross, B. (1984). Games respondents play: A look at the importance of game analysis as a technique for enriching the understanding of group discussions. *Journal of the Market Research Society, 26,* 221–229.

Lansing, J. B., & Morgan, J. N. (1971). *Economic survey methods.* Ann Arbor: University of Michigan Press.

Lansky, L. L., List, M. A., Lansky, S. B., Cohen, M. E., & Sinks, L. B. (1985). Toward the development of a play performance scale for children (PPSC). *Cancer, 56,* 1837–1840.

Lansky, S. B., List, M. A., Lansky, L. L., Ritter-Sterr, C., & Miller, D. A. (1987). The measurement of performance in childhood cancer patients. *Cancer, 62,* 1651–1656.

Lanyon, R. I. (1984). Personality assessment. *Annual Review of Psychology, 35,* 667–701.

Lanyon, R. I. (1986). Psychological assessment procedures in court-related settings. *Professional Psychology: Research and Practice, 17,* 260–268.

Lanyon, R. I., & Goodstein, L. D. (1971). *Personality assessment.* New York: Wiley.

Lapoint, F. H. (1972). Who originated the term "psychology"? *Journal of the History of the Behavioral Sciences, 8,* 328–335.

Larzelere, R., & Huston, T. (1980). The Dyadic Trust Scale: Toward understanding interpersonal trust in close relationships. *Journal of Marriage and the Family, 43,* 595–604.

Lasee, M. J., & Smith, D. K. (1991). Relationships between the K-ABC and the Early Screening Profiles. Paper presented at the Annual Meeting of the National Association of School Psychologists, Dallas, TX.

Last, J. M. (1983). Comprehensive early memory scoring system manual. Unpublished manuscript.

Last, J. M., & Bruhn, A. R. (1983). The psychodiagnostic value of children's earliest memories. *Journal of Personality Assessment, 47,* 597–603.

Last, J. M., & Bruhn, A. R. (1985). Distinguishing child diagnostic types with early memories. *Journal of Personality Assessment, 49,* 187–192.

Latham, G. P., Wexley, K. N., & Pursell, E. D. (1975). Training managers to minimize rating errors in the observation of behavior. *Journal of Applied Psychology, 60,* 550–555.

LaTour, M. S. (1990). Female nudity in print advertising: An analysis of gender differences in arousal and response. *Psychology & Marketing, 7,* 65–81.

Lavelle, T., Hammersley, R., & Forsyth, A. (1991). A short scale for predicting drug misuse using selected items from the MMPI. *British Journal of Addiction, 86,* 49–55.

Lawlor, J. (1990, September 27). Loopholes found in truth tests. *USA Today,* p. D-1.

Laws, D. R., & Osborne, C. A. (1983). How to build and operate a behavioral laboratory to evaluate and treat sexual deviance. In J. G. Greer & I. R. Stuart (Eds.), *The sexual aggressor: Current perspectives on treatment* (pp. 293–335). New York: Van Nostrand Reinhold.

Lawshe, C. H. (1975). A quantitative approach to content validity. *Personnel Psychology, 28,* 563–575.

Lawshe, C. L. (1985). Inferences from personnel tests and their validities. *Journal of Applied Psychology, 70,* 237–238.

Leahy, A. (1932). A study of certain selective factors influencing prediction of the mental status of adopted children or adopted children in nature-nurture research. *Journal of Genetic Psychology, 41,* 294–329.

Leahy, A. M. (1935). Nature-nurture and intelligence. *Genetic Psychology Monographs, 17,* 241–306.

Leckliter, I. N., & Matarazzo, J. D. (1989). The influence of age, education, IQ, gender, and alcohol abuse on Halstead-Reitan Neuropsychological Test Battery performance. *Journal of Clinical Psychology, 45,* 484–512.

Lee, S. D. (1968). Social class bias in the diagnosis of mental illness. Unpublished doctoral dissertation, University of Oklahoma.

Lee, S. W., & Piersel, W. C. (1989). Reliability and reactivity of self-recording by preschool children. *Psychological Reports, 64,* 747–754.

806

Lehmann, D. R. (1985). *Market research and analysis.* Homewood, IL: Richard D. Irwin.

Leichtman, S. R., Burnett, J. W., & Robinson, H. M., Jr. (1981). Body image concerns of psoriasis patients as reflected in human figure drawings. *Journal of Personality Assessment, 45,* 478–483.

Leming, J. S. (1978). Cheating behavior, situational influence, and moral development. *Journal of Educational Research, 71,* 214–217.

Lennon, R. T. (1978). Perspective on intelligence testing. *Measurement in Education, 9,* 1–2.

Lerner, B. (1980). *Minimum competence, maximum choice: Second chance legislation.* New York: Irvington.

Lerner, B. (1981). The minimum competence testing movement: Social, scientific, and legal implications. *American Psychologist, 36,* 1056–1066.

Lesser, G. S., Fifer, G., & Clark, D. H. (1965). Mental abilities of children from different social-class and cultural groups. *Monographs of the Society for Research in Child Development, 30* (Serial No. 102).

Levitt, E. E., & Hutton, L. H. (1984). A psychometric assessment of the Mathematics Anxiety Rating Scale. *International Review of Applied Psychology, 33,* 233–242.

Levy, J., & Epstein, N. (1964). An application of the Rorschach test in family investigation. *Family Process, 3,* 344–376.

Levy, M. R., & Fox, H. M. (1975). Psychological testing is alive and well. *Professional Psychology, 6,* 420–424.

Levy, S. (1982). Use of the Peabody Picture Vocabulary Test with low functioning autistic children. *Psychology in the Schools, 19,* 24–27.

Levy, S. J. (1985). Dreams, fairy tales, animals and cars. *Psychology & Marketing, 2,* 67–81.

Lewin, K. (1935). *A dynamic theory of personality.* New York: McGraw-Hill.

Lewinsohn, P. M., Mermelstein, R. M., Alexander, C., & MacPhillamy, D. J. (1985). The Unpleasant Events Schedule: A scale for the measurement of aversive events. *Journal of Clinical Psychology, 41,* 483–498.

Lewis, C. (1986). Test theory and psychometrika: The past twenty-five years. *Psychometrika, 51,* 11–22.

Lewis, R., Turtletaub, J., Pohl, R., Rainey, J., & Rosenbaum, G. (1990). MMPI differentiation of panic disorder patients from other psychiatric outpatients. *Psychological Assessment: A Journal of Consulting & Clinical Psychology, 2,* 164–168.

Lezak, M. D. (1976). *Neuropsychological assessment.* New York: Oxford University Press.

Liaboe, G. P., & Guy, J. D. (1985). The Rorschach "Father" and "Mother" cards: An evaluation of the research. *Journal of Personality Assessment, 49,* 2–5.

Libb, J. W., Stankovic, S., Sokol, R., Freeman, A., Houck, C., & Switzer, P. (1990). Stability of the MCMI among depressed psychiatric outpatients. *Journal of Personality Assessment, 55,* 209–218.

Libby, W. (1908). The imagination of adolescents. *American Journal of Psychology, 19,* 249–252.

Lieberman, J. N. (1965). Playfulness and divergent thinking: An investigation of their relationship at the kindergarten level. *Journal of Genetic Psychology, 107,* 219–224.

Likert, R. (1932). A technique for the measurement of attitudes. *Archives of Psychology,* Number 140.

Lilien, G. L., & Kotler, P. (1983). *Marketing decision making: A model building approach.* New York: Harper & Row.

Lilly, R. S., Hoaglin, A., & Anderson-Kulman, R. (1989). The use of factor analysis in published psychological research. Paper presented at the Annual Meeting of the American Psychological Association, New Orleans, LA.

Lindgren, B. (1983, August). N or N-1? [Letter to the editor]. *American Statistician,* p. 52.

Lindholm, L., & Wilson, G. T. (1988). Body image assessment in patients with bulimia nervosa and normal controls. *International Journal of Eating Disorders, 7,* 527–539.

Lindzey, G. (1950). An experimental examination of the scapegoat theory of prejudice. *Journal of Abnormal and Social Psychology, 45,* 296–309.

Lippmann, W. (1922, October). The mental age of Americans. *New Republic.*

Lipsitt, P. D., Lelos, D., & McGarry, A. L. (1971). Competency for trial: A screening instrument. *American Journal of Psychiatry, 128,* 105–109.

Lis, D. J., & Powers, J. E. (1979). Reliability and validity of the Group Embedded Figures Test for a grade school sample. *Perceptual and Motors Skills, 48,* 660–662.

Lisansky, E. S. (1956). The inter-examiner reliability of the Rorschach test. *Journal of Projective Techniques, 20,* 310–317.

Llabre, M. M., Clements, N. E., Fitzhugh, K. B., & Lancelotta, G. (1987). The effect of computer-administered testing on test anxiety and perfor-

807

mance. *Journal of Educational Computing Research, 3,* 429–433.

Locke, H. J., & Wallace, K. M. (1959). Short marital adjustment and prediction tests: Their reliability and validity. *Marriage and Family Living, 21,* 251–255.

Locke, J. (1690). *An essay concerning human understanding.*

Loevinger, J. (1957). Objective tests as instruments of psychological theory. *Psychological Reports, 3,* 635–694.

Loevinger, J. (1966). The meaning and measurement of ego development. *American Psychologist, 21,* 195–206.

Loevinger, J., & Ossorio, A. G. (1958). Evaluation of therapy by self-report: A paradox. *American Psychologist, 13,* 366.

Loevinger, J., Wessler, R., & Redmore, C. (1970). *Measuring ego development: Vol. 1. Construction and use of a sentence completion test. Vol. 2. Scoring manual for women and girls.* San Francisco: Jossey-Bass.

Loftus, E. F. (1979). *Eyewitness testimony.* Cambridge, MA: Harvard University Press.

Lohman, D. F. (1989). Human intelligence: An introduction to advances in theory and research. *Review of Educational Research, 59,* 333–373.

London, P. (1976). Psychotherapy for religious neuroses? Comments on Cohen and Smith. *Journal of Consulting and Clinical Psychology, 44,* 145–147.

LoPiccolo, J., Heiman, J. R., Hogan, D. R., & Roberts, C. W. (1985). Effectiveness of single therapists versus cotherapy teams in sex therapy. *Journal of Consulting & Clinical Psychology, 53,* 287–294.

Lord, F. M. (1978). *A prediction interval for scores on a parallel test form* (Research Bulletin RB-78-5). Princeton, NJ: Educational Testing Service.

Lord, F. M. (1980). *Applications of item response theory to practical testing problems.* Hillsdale, NJ: Erlbaum.

Lord, F. M., & Novick, M. R. (1968). *Statistical theories of mental test scores.* Menlo Park, CA: Addison-Wesley.

Losak, J. (1978). What do the students say? *The College Board Review, 108,* 25–27.

Loveland, N., Wynne, L., & Singer, M. (1963). The Family Rorschach: A new method for studying family interaction. *Family Process, 2,* 187–215.

Lowman, J. C. (1980). Measurement of family affective structure. *Journal of Personality Assessment, 44,* 130–141.

Loyd, B. H., & Loyd, D. E. (1985). The reliability and validity of an instrument for the assessment of computer attitudes. *Educational & Psychological Measurement, 45,* 903–908.

Lung, R. J., Miller, S. H., David, T. S., & Graham, W. P. (1977). Recognizing burn injuries as abuse. *American Family Physician, 15,* 134–135.

Lubin, A., & Malby, M. (1951). An empirical test of some assumptions underlying the Szondi Test. *Journal of Abnormal and Social Psychology, 46,* 480–484.

Lubin, B. (1967). *Depression Adjective Check Lists: Manual.* San Diego, CA: Educational and Industrial Testing Service.

Lubin, B. (1981). Additional data on the reliability and validity of the brief lists of the Depression Adjective Check Lists. *Journal of Clinical Psychology, 37,* 809–811.

Lubin, B., Larsen, R. M., & Matarazzo, J. D. (1983). Patterns of psychological test usage in the United States: 1935–1982. Paper presented at the annual meeting of the American Psychological Association, Anaheim, CA.

Lubin, B., Larsen, R. M., & Matarazzo, J. D. (1984). Patterns of psychological test usage in the United States: 1935–1982. *American Psychologist, 39,* 451–454.

Lubin, B., Larsen, R. M., Matarazzo, J. D., & Seever, M. F. (1985). Psychological test usage patterns in five professional settings. *American Psychologist, 40,* 857–861.

Lubin, B., & Levitt, E. E. (1979). Norms for the Depression Adjective Check Lists: Age group and sex. *Journal of Consulting and Clinical Psychology, 47,* 192.

Lubin, B., & Lubin, A. W. (1972). Patterns of psychological services in the U.S.: 1959–1969. *Professional Psychology, 3,* 63–65.

Lubin, B., Wallis, R. R., & Paine, C. (1971). Patterns of psychological test usage in the United States: 1935–1969. *Professional Psychology, 2,* 70–74.

Luborsky, L. B., & Cattell, R. B. (1947). The validation of personality factors in humor. *Journal of Personality, 15,* 283–291.

Luchins, A. S. (1946). Classroom experiments on mental set. *American Journal of Psychology, 59,* 295–298.

Luchins, A. S., & Luchins, E. H. (1959). *Rigidity of behavior: A variational approach to the effect of Einstellung.* Eugene: University of Oregon Books.

Luchins, A. S., & Luchins, E. H. (1970). *Wertheimer's seminars revisited: Problem solving and thinking* (Vol. 3). Albany: Faculty Student Association of the State University of New York at Albany.

Lukens, J. (1988). Comparison of the Fourth Edition and the L-M Edition of the Stanford-Binet used with mentally retarded persons. *Journal of School Psychology, 26,* 87–89.

Lukin, M. E., Dowd, E. T., Plake, B. S., & Kraft, R. G. (1985). Comparing computerized versus traditional psychological assessment. *Computers in Human Behavior, 1,* 49–58.

Lund, M., Foy, D., Sipprelle, R., & Strachan, A. (1984). The Combat Exposure Scale: A systematic assessment of trauma in the Vietnam war. *Journal of Clinical Psychology, 40,* 1323–1328.

Lung, R. J., Miller, S. H., Davis, T. S., & Graham, W. P. (1977). Recognizing burn injuries as abuse. *American Family Physician, 15,* 134–135.

Luria, A. R. (1966a). *Human brain and psychological processes.* New York: Harper & Row.

Luria, A. R. (1966b). *Higher cortical functions in man.* New York: Basic Books.

Luria, A. R. (1970, March). The functional organization of the brain. *Scientific American, 222,* 66–78.

Luria, A. R. (1973). *The working brain: An introduction to neuropsychology.* New York: Basic Books.

Luria, A. R. (1980). *Higher cortical functions in man* (2nd ed.). New York: Basic Books.

Lushene, R. E., & Gilberstadt, H. (1972, March). *Validation of VA MMPI computer-generated reports.* Paper presented at the Veterans Administration Cooperative Studies Conference, St. Louis, MO.

Lusk, E. J., & Wright, H. (1981). Differences in sex and curricula on learning in the Group Embedded Figures Test. *Perceptual and Motor Skills, 53,* 8–10.

Lutey, C., & Copeland, E. P. (1982). Cognitive assessment of the school-age child. In C. R. Reynolds & T. B. Gutkin (Eds.), *The handbook of school psychology.* New York: Wiley.

Lykken, D. T. (1981). *A tremor in the blood: Uses and abuses of the lie detector.* New York: McGraw-Hill.

Lyman, H. B. (1972). Review of the Wechsler Adult Intelligence Scale. In O. K. Buros (Ed.), *The seventh mental measurements yearbook* (pp. 788–790). Highland Park, NJ: Gryphon Press.

Lyons, J. A., Gerardi, R. J., Wolfe, J., & Keane, T. M. (1988). Multidimensional assessment of combat-related PTSD: Phenomenological, psychometric, and psychophysiological considerations. *Journal of Traumatic Stress, 1,* 373–394.

Maccoby, E. E., & Jacklin, C. N. (1974). *The psychology of sex differences.* Stanford, CA: United Press.

MacFarlene, K., & Krebs, S. (1986). Techniques for interviewing and evidence gathering. In K. MacFarlene, et al. (Eds.), *Sexual abuse of young children.* New York: Guilford Press.

Machover, K. (1949). *Personality projection in the drawing of the human figure: A method of personality investigation.* Springfield, IL: Charles C Thomas.

MacMillan, D. L., & Meyers, C. E. (1980). Larry P.: An educational interpretation. *School Psychology Review, 9,* 136–148.

Magnello, M. E., & Spies, C. J. (1984). Francis Galton: Historical antecedents of the correlation calculus. In B. Laver (Chair), *History of mental measurement: Correlation, quantification, and institutionalization.* Paper session presented at the 92nd annual convention of the American Psychological Association, Toronto, Ontario, Canada.

Mahoney, T. A., & England, G. W. (1965). Efficiency and accuracy of employer decision rules. *Personnel Psychology, 18,* 361–377.

Malcolm, P. B., Davidson, P. R., & Marshall, W. L. (1985). Control of penile tumescence: The effects of arousal level and stimulus content. *Behaviour Research & Therapy, 23,* 273–280.

Malgady, R. G., Costantino, G., & Rogler, L. H. (1984). Development of a Thematic Apperception Test (TEMAS) for urban Hispanic children. *Journal of Consulting and Clinical Psychology, 52,* 986–996.

Malone, P. S., Brounstein, P. J., von Brock, A., & Shaywitz, S. S. (1991). Components of IQ scores across levels of measured ability. *Journal of Applied Social Psychology, 21,* 15–28.

Maloney, M. P., Ball, T. S., & Edgar, C. L. (1970). Analysis of the generalizability of sensory-motor training. *American Journal of Mental Deficiency, 74,* 458–469.

Maloney, M. P., & Ward, M. P. (1976). *Psychological assessment.* New York: Oxford University Press.

Mandal, A. D. (1982). The correct height of school furniture. *Human Factors, 24,* 257–269.

Mandell, C. J., & Fiscus, E. (1981). *Understanding exceptional people.* St. Paul, MN: West Publishing Company.

Manz, C. C., & Sims, H. P. (1984). Searching for the "unleader": Organizational member views on leading self-managed groups. *Human Relations, 37,* 409–424.

Maranell, G. M. (1974). *Scaling: A sourcebook for behavioral scientists.* Chicago: Aldine.

Mardell-Czudnowski, C. D., & Goldenberg, D. S. (1983, 1990). *Developmental Indicators for the Assessment of Learning—Revised.* Circle Pines, MN: American Guidance Service.

Marks, P. E., & Seeman, W. (1963). *The actuarial description of personality: An atlas for use with the MMPI.* Baltimore: Williams & Wilkins.

Marmorale, A. M., & Brown, F. (1977). Bender-Gestalt performance of Puerto Rican, White and Negro Children. *Journal of Clinical Psychology, 33,* 224–228.

Marquette, B. W. (1976). *Limitations on the generalizability of adult competence across all situations.* Paper presented at the annual meeting of the Western Psychological Association, Los Angeles, CA.

Marsh, D. T., Stile, S. A., Stoughton, N. L., & Trout-Landen, B. L. (1988). Psychopathology of opiate addiction: Comparative data from the MMPI and MCMI. *American Journal of Drug and Alcohol Abuse, 14,* 17–27.

Marsh, G. G., & Hirsch, S. H. (1982). Effectiveness of two tests of visual retention. *Journal of Clinical Psychology, 38,* 115–116.

Marshall, W. L., Barbaree, H. E., & Butt, J. (1988). Sexual offenders against male children: Sexual preferences. *Behavior Research and Therapy, 26,* 383–391.

Marston, W. M. (1938). *The lie detector test.* New York: Richard R. Smith.

Martin, R. P. (1986). Assessment of the social and emotional functioning of preschool children. *School Psychology Review, 15,* 216–232.

Martin, R. P. (1988). *Assessment of personality and behavior problems.* New York: Guilford Press.

Martin, R. P., Hooper, S., & Snow, J. (1986). Behavior rating scale approaches to personality assessment in children and adolescents. In H. M. Knoff (Ed.), *The assessment of child and adolescent personality* (pp. 309–351). New York: Guilford Press.

Martin, W. A. P. (1870). Competitive examinations in China. *North American Review, 111,* 62–77.

Martin-Loeches, M., Gil, P., Jimenez, F., Exposito, F. J., Miguel, F., Cacabelos, R., & Rubia, F. J. (1991). Topographic maps of brain electrical activity in primary degenerative dementia of the Alzheimer type and multiinfarct dementia. *Biological Psychiatry, 29,* 211–223.

Mash, E. J., & Terdal, L. G. (1988). *Behavioral assessment of childhood disorders* (2nd ed.). New York: Guilford Press.

Masling, J. (1959). The effects of warm and cold interaction on the administration and scoring of an intelligence test. *Journal of Consulting Psychology, 23,* 336–341.

Masling, J. (1960). The influence of situational and interpersonal variables in projective testing. *Psychological Bulletin, 57,* 65–85.

Masling, J. (1965). Differential indoctrination of examiners and Rorschach responses. *Journal of Consulting Psychology, 29,* 198–201.

Maslow, A. H. (1943). A theory of motivation. *Psychological Review, 50,* 370–396.

Maslow, A. H. (1970). *Motivation and personality* (2nd ed.). New York: Harper & Row.

Matarazzo, J. D. (1972). *Wechsler's measurement and appraisal of adult intelligence.* Baltimore: Williams & Wilkins.

Matarazzo, J. D. (1983, July 22). Computerized psychological testing. *Science, 221,* 323.

Matarazzo, J. D. (1985). Review of the Wechsler Adult Intelligence Scale—Revised. In J. V. Mitchell (Ed.), *The ninth mental measurements yearbook* (pp. 1703–1705). Lincoln: The Buros Institute of Mental Measurements, University of Nebraska.

Matarazzo, J. D. (1986a). Computerized clinical psychological test interpretations: Unvalidated plus all mean and no sigma. *American Psychologist, 41,* 14–24.

Matarazzo, J. D. (1986b). Response to Fowler and Butcher on Matarazzo. *American Psychologist, 41,* 96.

Matarazzo, J. D. (1990). Psychological assessment versus psychological testing: Validation from Binet to the school, clinic, and courtroom. *American Psychologist, 45,* 999–1017.

Matarazzo, J. D., Matarazzo, R. G., Wiens, A. N., Gallo, A. E., & Klonoff, H. (1976). Retest reliability of the Halstead Impairment Index in a normal, a schizophrenic and two samples of organic patients. *Journal of Clinical Psychology, 32,* 338–349.

Matarazzo, J. D., & Wiens, A. N. (1977). Black Intelligence Test of Cultural Homogeneity and Wechsler Adult Ingelligence Scale scores of black and white police applicants. *Journal of Applied Psychology, 62,* 57–63.

Mather, N. (1991). *An instructional guide to the Woodcock-Johnson Psycho-Educational Battery—Revised.* Allen, TX: DLM Teaching Resources.

Matthews, C. G. (1974). Applications of neuropsychological test methods in mentally retarded subjects. In R. M. Reitan & L. A. Davison (Eds.), *Clinical neuropsychology: Current status and applications* (pp. 267–287). New York: Winston.

Mattison, R. E., Handford, A., Kales, H. C., Goodman, A. L., & McLaughlin, R. E. (1990). *Psychological Assessment: A Journal of Consulting & Clinical Psychology, 2,* 169–174.

Maurer, T. J., & Alexander, R. A. (1991). Contrast effects in behavioral measurement: An investigation of alternative process explanations. *Journal of Applied Psychology, 76,* 3–10.

Maxwell, J. K., & Wise, F. (1984). PPVT IQ validity in adults: A measure of vocabulary, not of intelligence. *Journal of Clinical Psychology, 40,* 1044–1048.

May, E. G. (1971). *Image evaluation of a department store* (working paper). Cambridge, MA: Marketing Science Institute.

Mayfield, E. C. (1972). Value of peer nominations in predicting life insurance sales performance. *Journal of Applied Psychology, 56,* 319–323.

Mayman, M. (1968). Early memories and character structure. *Journal of Projective Techniques and Personality Assessment, 31,* 303–316.

Mayman, M., & Faris, M. (1960). Early memories as expressions of relationship paradigms. *American Journal of Orthopsychiatry, 30,* 507–520.

McAllister, L. W. (1988). *A practical guide to CPI interpretation* (2nd ed.). Palo Alto, CA: Consulting Psychologists Press.

McArthur, D. S., & Roberts, G. E. (1982). *Roberts Apperception Test for Children manual.* Los Angeles: Western Psychological Services.

McCall, V. W., Yates, B., Hendricks, S., Turner, K., & McNabb, B. (1989). Comparison between the Stanford-Binet: L-M and the Stanford-Binet: Fourth Edition with a group of gifted children. *Contemporary Educational Psychology, 14*(2), 93–96.

McCall, W. A. (1922). *How to measure in education.* New York: Macmillan.

McCall, W. A. (1939). *Measurement.* New York: Macmillan.

McCallum, M., & Piper, W. E. (1990). The psychological mindedness assessment procedure. *Psychological Assessment: A Journal of Consulting and Clinical Psychology, 2,* 412–418.

McCallum, R. S., & Bracken, B. A. (1981). Alternate form reliability of the PPVT-R for white and black preschool children. *Psychology in the Schools, 18,* 422–425.

McCallum, R. S., & Karnes, F. A. (1987). Comparison of intelligence tests. *School Psychology International, 8,* 133–139.

McCallum, R. S., Karnes, F. A., & Edwards, R. P. (1984). The test of choice for assessment of gifted children: A comparison of the K-ABC, WISC-R, and Stanford-Binet. *Journal of Psychoeducational Assessment, 2,* 57–64.

McCann, J. T. (1990). A multitrait-multimethod analysis of the MCMI-II clinical syndrome scales. *Journal of Personality Assessment, 55,* 465–476.

McCann, J. T. (1991). Convergent and discriminant validity of the MCMI-II and MMPI personality disorders scales. *Psychological Assessment: A Journal of Consulting and Clinical Psychology, 3*(1), 9–18.

McCarthy, D. (1972). *Manual for the McCarthy Scales of Children's Abilities.* New York: Psychological Corporation.

McClelland, D. C. (1951). *Personality.* New York: Holt-Dryden.

McClelland, C. D. (1961). *The achieving society.* Princeton, NJ: Van Nostrand.

McClelland, D. C. (1980). Motive dispositions: The merits of operant and respondent measures. In L. Wheeler (Ed.), *Review of personality and social psychology* (Vol. 1, pp. 10–41). Beverly Hills, CA: Sage.

McClelland, D. C., & Atkinson, J. W. (1948). The projective expression of needs: I. The effect of different intensities of the hunger drive on perception. *Journal of Psychology, 25,* 205–222.

McCloskey, G. W. (1989, March). The K-ABC sequential-simultaneous information processing model and classroom intervention: A report—the Dade County Classroom research study. Paper presented at the Annual Meeting of the National Association of School Psychologists, Boston.

McClure-Butterfield, P. (1990). Issues in child custody evaluation and testimony. In C. R. Reynolds & R. W. Kamphaus (Eds.), *Handbook of psychological* and educational assessment of children: Personality, behavior and context (pp. 576–588). New York: Guilford Press.

McConaughty, S. H., & Achenbach, T. M. (1988). *Practical guide for the Child Behavior Checklist and related materials.* Burlington: University of Vermont, Department of Psychiatry.

McCormack, J. K., Barnett, R. W., & Wallbrown, F. H. (1989). Factor structure of the Millon Clinical Multiaxial Inventory (MCMI) with an offender sample. *Journal of Personality Assessment, 53*(3), 442–448.

McCoy, G. F. (1972). *Diagnostic evaluation and educational programming for hearing impaired children.* Springfield, IL: Office of the Illinois Superintendent of Public Instruction.

McCubbin, H., Larsen, A., & Olson, D. (1985). F-COPES: Family Crisis Oriented Personal Evaluation Scales. In D. H. Olson, H. I. McCubbin, H. L. Barnes, A. S. Larsen, M. Muxen, & M. Wilson (Eds.), *Family inventories* (Rev. ed.). St. Paul: Family Social Science, University of Minnesota.

McCubbin, H. I., Patterson, J. M., & Wilson, L. R. (1985). FILE: Family Inventory of Life Events and Changes. In D. H. Olson, H. I. McCubbin, H. L. Barnes, A. S. Larsen, M. Muxen, & M. Wilson (Eds.), *Family inventories* (Rev. ed.). St. Paul: Family Social Science, University of Minnesota.

McCubbin, J. A., Wilson, J. F., Bruehl, S., Brady, M., Clark, K., & Kort, E. (1991). Gender effects on blood pressures obtained during an on-campus screening. *Psychosomatic Medicine, 53,* 90–100.

McCullough, C. S. (1990). Best practices for utilizing technology. In A. Thomas & J. Grimes (Eds.), *Best practices in school psychology II* (pp. 773–786). Washington, DC: National Association of School Psychologists.

McFall, M. E., Smith, D. E., Mackay, P. W., & Tarver, D. J. (1990). Reliability and validity of Mississippi Scale for Combat-Related Posttraumatic Stress Disorder. *Psychological Assessment: A Journal of Consulting and Clinical Psychology, 2,* 114–121.

McGinnies, E. (1949). Emotionality and perceptual defense. *Psychological Review, 56,* 244–251.

McGurk, F. J. (1975). Race differences—twenty years later. *Homo, 26,* 219–239.

McKenna, T., & Butcher, J. N. (1987, March). Use of the revised MMPI in the assessment of chemical dependency. Paper presented at the 22nd Annual Symposium on Recent Developments in the use of the MMPI, Seattle, WA.

McLemore, C. W., & Court, J. H. (1977). Religion and psychotherapy—ethics, civil liberties, and clinical savvy: A critique. *Journal of Consulting and Clinical Psychology, 45,* 1172–1175.

McNamara, J. R., Porterfield, C., Miller, L. G. (1969). The relationship of the WPPSI with the Coloured Progressive Matrices and the Bender Gestalt test. *Journal of Clinical Psychology, 25,* 65–68.

McNemar, Q. (1964). Lost: Our intelligence. Why? *American Psychologist, 19,* 871–882.

McPhee, J. P., & Wegner, K. W. (1976). Kinetic-Family-Drawing styles and emotionally disturbed childhood behavior. *Journal of Personality Assessment, 40,* 487–491.

McReynolds, P. (1987). Lightner Witmer: Little-known founder of clinical psychology. *American Psychologist, 42,* 849–858.

McTurk, R. H., & Neisworth, J. T. (1978). Norm referenced and criterion based measures with preschoolers. *Exceptional Children, 44,* 34–47.

McWatters, M. (1989). *The self-concept of the retarded reader and the achieving reader at the high school level.* Unpublished Master's thesis, Kean College, NJ. (ERIC Document Reproduction Service No. ED 313 681)

Meadow, K. P., Karchmer, M. A., Petersen, L. M., & Rudner, L. (1980). *Meadow-Kendall Social-Emotional Assessment Inventory.* Washington, DC: Gallaudet University.

Meadows, G., Turner, T., Campbell, L., Lewis, S. W., Reveley, M. A., & Murray, R. M. (1991). Assessing schizophrenia in adults with mental retardation: A comparative study. *British Journal of Psychiatry, 158,* 103–105.

Mealor, D. J., & Richmond, B. O. (1980). Adaptive behavior: Teachers and parents disagree. *Exceptional Children, 46,* 386–388.

Mednick, S. A. (1962). The associative basis of the creative process. *Psychological Review, 69,* 220–232.

Mednick, S. A., Higgins, J., & Kirschenbaum, J. (1975). *Psychology.* New York: Wiley.

Meehl, P. E. (1954). *Clinical versus statistical prediction: A theoretical analysis and a review of the evidence.* Minneapolis: University of Minnesota Press.

Meehl, P. E. (1956). Wanted: A good cookbook. *American Psychologist, 11,* 263–272.

Meehl, P. E. (1959). A comparison of clinicians with

five statistical methods of identifying psychotic MMPI profiles. *Journal of Consulting Psychology, 6,* 102–109.

Meehl, P. E. (1965). Seer over sign: The first good example. *Journal of Experimental Research in Personality, 1,* 27–32.

Meehl, P. E. (1984). Clinical and statistical prediction: A retrospective and would-be integrative view. In R. K. Blashfield (Chair), *Clinical versus statistical prediction.* Symposium presented at the 92nd annual meeting of the American Psychological Association, Toronto, Ontario, Canada.

Meeker, M., & Meeker, R. (1973). Strategies for assessing intellectual patterns in black, Anglo, and Mexican-American boys—or any other children—and implications for education. *Journal of School Psychology, 11,* 341–350.

Megargee, E. I. (1972). *The California Psychological Inventory handbook.* San Francisco: Jossey-Bass.

Meier, N. C. (1942). *Art in human affairs.* New York: McGraw-Hill.

Meier, S. T. (1984). The construct validity of burnout. *Journal of Occupational Psychology, 57,* 211–219.

Meier, S. T. (1991). Tests of the construct validity of occupational stress measures with college students: Failure to support discriminant validity. *Journal of Counseling Psychology, 38,* 91–97.

Meng, K., & Patty, D. (1991). Field dependence and contextual organizers. *The Journal of Educational Research 84,* 183–189.

Menninger, K. A. (1953). *The human mind* (3rd ed.). New York: Knopf.

Mentality tests: A symposium. (1916). *Journal of Educational Measurement, 7,* 229–240, 278–286, 358–360.

Mercer, J. R. (1976). A system of multicultural pluralistic assessment (SOMPA). In *Proceedings: With bias toward none.* Lexington: Coordinating Office for Regional Resource Centers, University of Kentucky.

Mercer, J. R. (1979). *System of Multicultural Pluralistic Assessment: Technical Manual.* Cleveland: Psychological Corporation.

Mercer, J. R., & Lewis, J. F. (1979). *System of Multicultural Pluralistic Assessment.* Cleveland: Psychological Corporation.

Merikle, P. M. (1988). Subliminal auditory messages: An evaluation. *Psychology & Marketing, 5,* 355–372.

Merrens, M. R., & Richards, W. S. (1970). Acceptance of generalized versus "bona fide" personality interpretation. *Psychological Reports, 27,* 691–694.

Merz, W. R. (1984). K-ABC critique. In D. J. Keyser & R. C. Sweetland (Eds.), *Test Critiques* (Vol. 1; pp. 393–405). Kansas City, MO: Test Corporation of America.

Meyers, C. E. (1975). *What I Like To Do—An inventory of students' interests.* Chicago: Science Research Associates.

Meyers, C. J. (1986). The legal perils of psychotherapeutic practice: The farther reaches of the duty to warn. In L. Everstine & D. S. Everstine (Eds.), *Psychotherapy and the law.* New York: Grune & Stratton.

Meyers, D. V. (1978). Toward an objective procedure evaluation of the Kinetic Family Drawings (KFD). *Journal of Personality Assessment, 42,* 358–365.

Miale, F. R., & Selzer, M. (1975). The *Nuremberg mind.* New York: Quadrangle Books.

Micceri, T. (1989). The unicorn, the normal curve and other improbable creatures. *Psychological Bulletin, 105,* 156–166.

Michael, W. B., Michael, J. J., & Zimmerman, W. S. (1980). *Study Attitudes and Methods Survey manual of instructions and interpretations.* San Diego, CA: Educational and Industrial Testing Service.

Michael, W., Young, L., Michael, J., Hooke, G., & Zimmerman, W. (1971). A partial redefinition of the factorial structure of the Study Attitudes and Methods Survey (SAMS) Test. *Educational and Psychological Measurement, 31,* 545–547.

Mill, J. (1829). *Analysis of the phenomena of the human mind.*

Miller, C. K., Chansky, N. M., & Gredler, G. R. (1972). Rater agreement on WISC protocols. *Psychology in the Schools, 7,* 190–193.

Miller, G. A. (1962). *Psychology.* New York: Harper & Row.

Miller, N. E. (1969). Learning of visceral and glandular responses. *Science, 163,* 434–445.

Miller, H. R., & Streiner, D. L. (1986). Differences in MMPI profiles with the norms of Colligan et al. *Journal of Consulting and Clinical Psychology, 54,* 843–845.

Miller, W. R., Heather, N., & Hall, W. (1991). Calculating standard drink units: International comparisons. *British Journal of Addiction, 86,* 43–47.

Millman, J. (1974). Criterion-related measurement. In W. J. Popham (Ed.), *Evaluation and education.* Berkeley, CA: McCutchan.

Millman, J. (1979). Reliability and validity of criterion-referenced test scores. *New Directions in Testing and Measurement, 1*(4), 75–92.

Millman, J., & Arter, J. A. (1984). Issues in item banking. *Journal of Educational Measurement, 21,* 315–330.

Millon, T. (1969). *Modern psychopathology.* Philadelphia, PA: Saunders.

Millon, T. (1981). *Disorders of personality: DSM-III, Axis II.* New York: Wiley.

Millon, T. (1983). *Millon Clinical Multiaxial Inventory manual.* Minneapolis, MN: National Computer Systems.

Millon, T. (1986a). Personality prototypes and their diagnostic criteria. In T. Millon & G. L. Klerman (Eds.), *Contemporary directions in psychopathology: Toward the DSM-IV.* New York: Guilford Press.

Millon, T. (1986b). A theoretical derivation of pathological personalities. In T. Millon & G. L. Klerman (Eds.), *Contemporary directions in psychopathology: Toward the DSM-IV.* New York: Guilford Press.

Millon, T. (1987). *Millon Clinical Multiaxial Inventory II manual.* Minneapolis, MN: National Computer Systems.

Millon, T., & Green, C. (1989). Interpretive guide to the Millon Clinical Multiaxial Inventory (MCMI-II). In C. S. Newmark (Ed.), *Major psychological assessment instruments* (Vol. 2; pp. 5–43). Needham Heights, MA: Allyn and Bacon.

Millon, T., Green, C. J., & Meagher, R. B. (1982). *Millon Adolescent Personality Inventory.* Minneapolis, MN: National Computer Systems.

Milner, B. (1971). Interhemispheric differences in the localization of psychological processes in man. *British Medical Bulletin, 27,* 272–277.

Milner, B., & Taylor, L. (1972). Right-hemisphere superiority in tactile pattern-recognition after cerebral commissurotomy: Evidence for nonverbal memory. *Neuropsychologia, 10,* 1–15.

Milner, J. (1989). Additional cross-validation of the Child Abuse Potential Inventory. *Psychological Assessment: A Journal of Consulting and Clinical Psychology, 1,* 219–223.

Mindak, W. A. (1961). Fitting the semantic differential to the marketing problem. *Journal of Marketing, 25,* 28–33.

Misaszek, J., Dooling, J., Gieseke, M., Melman, H., Misaszek, J. G., & Jorgensen, K. (1985). Diagnostic considerations in deaf patients. *Comprehensive Psychiatry, 26,* 513–521.

Mischel, W. (1966). Theory and research on the antecedents of self-imposed delay of reward. In B. A. Maher (Ed.), *Progress in experimental personality research* (Vol. 3; pp. 85–132). New York: Academic Press.

Mischel, W. (1968). *Personality and assessment.* New York: Wiley.

Mischel, W. (1973). Toward a cognitive social learning reconceptualization of personality. *Psychological Review, 80,* 252–283.

Mischel, W. (1977). On the future of personality measurement. *American Psychologist, 32,* 246–254.

Mischel, W. (1979). On the interface of cognition and personality: Beyond the person-situation debate. *American Psychologist, 34,* 740–754.

Mishlove, M., & Chapman, L. J. (1985). Social anhedonia in the prediction of psychosis proneness. *Journal of Abnormal Psychology, 94,* 384–396.

Mitchell, A. (1978). *Consumer values: A typology.* Menlo Park, CA: Stanford Research Institute.

Mitchell, J. V., Jr. (Ed.). (1983). *Tests in print III.* Lincoln: University of Nebraska Press.

Mitchell, J. V., Jr. (Ed.). (1985). *The ninth mental measurements yearbook.* Lincoln: University of Nebraska Press.

Mitchell, J. V., Jr. (1986). Measurement in the larger context: Critical current issues. *Professional Psychology: Research and Practice, 17,* 544–550.

Mittenberg, W., & Petersen, J. D. (1984). Validation of the Holtzman Anxiety Scale by vasomotor biofeedback. *Journal of Personality Assessment, 48,* 360–364.

Molitor, D. L., & Kramer, J. J. (1987). Battelle Developmental Inventory. *Journal of Psychoeducational Assessment, 5,* 114–119.

Molloy, D. W., Alemayehu, E., & Roberts, R. (1991). Reliability of a standardized Mini-Mental State Examination compared with the traditional Mini-Mental State Examination. *American Journal of Psychiatry, 148,* 102–105.

Money, J. (1976). *The Standardized Road-map Test of Direction Sense: Manual.* San Rafael, CA: Academic Therapy Publications.

Monroe, S. M. (1983). Major and minor life events as predictors of psychological distress: Further issues and findings. *Journal of Behavioral Medicine, 6,* 189–205.

Mooney, C. M. (1957). Age in the development of closure ability in children. *Canadian Journal of Psychology, 11,* 219–226.

814

Mooney, K. C. (1984). Review of Child Behavior Checklist. In D. J. Keyser & R. C. Sweetland (Eds.), *Test critiques* (Vol. 1, pp. 168–184). Kansas City, MO: Test Corporation of America.

Mooney, R. L., & Gordon, L. V. (1950). *Mooney Problem Check Lists*. New York: Psychological Corporation.

Moore, M. K., & Neimeyer, R. A. (1991). A confirmatory factor analysis of the Threat Index. *Journal of Personality and Social Psychology, 60*, 122–129.

Moos, R. H., & Moos, B. S. (1981). *Family Environment Scale manual*. Palo Alto, CA: Consulting Psychologists Press.

Moreland, K. L. (1983, April). *A comparison of the validity of the two MMPI interpretation systems: A preliminary report*. Paper presented at the 18th Annual Symposium on Recent Developments in the Use of the MMPI, Minneapolis, MN.

Moreland, K. L. (1985). Validation of computer-based test interpretations: Problems and prospects. *Journal of Consulting and Clinical Psychology, 53*, 816–825.

Moreland, K. L. (1986). An introduction to the problem of test user qualifications. In R. B. Most (Chair), *Test purchaser qualifications: Present practice, professional needs, and a proposed system*. Symposium presented at the 94th annual convention of the American Psychological Association, Washington, DC.

Moreland, K. L. (1987). Computerized psychological assessment: What's available. In J. N. Butcher (Ed.), *Computerized psychological assessment: A practitioner's guide* (pp. 26–49). New York: Basic Books.

Moreland, K. L. (1990). Some observations on computer-assisted psychological testing. *Journal of Personality Assessment, 55*, 820–823.

Moreland, K. L., & Onstad, J. A. (1985). *Validity of the Minnesota Report: 1. Mental health outpatients*. Paper presented at the 20th Annual Symposium on Recent Developments in the Use of the MMPI, Honolulu, HI.

Morgan, C. D., & Murray, H. A. (1935). A method for investigating fantasies: The Thematic Apperception Test. *Archives of Neurology and Psychiatry, 34*, 289–306.

Morrow, G. R. (1984). The assessment of nausea and vomiting: Past problems, current issues, and suggestions for future research. *Cancer, 53*, 2267–2278.

Morse, S. J. (1985). Excusing the crazy: The insanity defense reconsidered. *Southern California Law Review, 58*, 777–836.

Mosely, E. C. (1963). Psychodiagnosis on the basis of the Holtzman Inkblot Technique. *Journal of Projective Techniques and Personality Assessment, 27*, 86–91.

Moses, S. (1991). Major revision of SAT goes into effect in 1994. *APA Monitor, 22*(1), 35.

Mostkoff, D. L., & Lazarus, P. J. (1983). The Kinetic Family Drawing: The reliability of an objective scoring system. *Psychology in the Schools, 20*, 16–20.

Moskowitz, D. S., & Schwartz, J. C. (1982). Validity comparison of behavior counts and ratings by knowledgeable informants. *Journal of Personality and Social Psychology, 42*, 518–528.

Mueller, C. G. (1949). Numerical transformations in the analysis of experimental data. *Psychological Bulletin, 46*, 198–223.

Mulvey, E. P., & Lidz, C. W. (1984). Clinical considerations in the prediction of dangerousness in mental patients. *Clinical Psychology Review, 4*, 379–401.

Mungas, D., Blunden, D., Bennington, K., Stone, A., & Palma, G. (1990). Reliability and validity of scales for assessing behavior in epilepsy. *Psychological Assessment: A Journal of Consulting and Clinical Psychology, 2*, 423–431.

Murden, R. A., McRae, T. D., Kaner, S. T., & Bucknam, M. E. (1991). Mini-Mental State Exam scores vary with education in blacks and whites. *Journal of the American Geriatric Society, 39*, 149–155.

Murphy, G. (1949). *Historical introduction to modern psychology* (Rev. ed.) New York: Harcourt, Brace, & World.

Murphy, G. E. (1984). The prediction of suicide: Why is it so difficult? *American Journal of Psychotherapy, 38*, 341–349.

Murphy, K. R., Balzer, W. K., Lockhart, M. C., & Eisenman, E. J. (1985). Effects of previous performance on evaluations of present performance. *Journal of Applied Psychology, 70*, 72–84.

Murray, H. A. (1940). What should psychologists do about psychoanalysis? *Journal of Abnormal and Social Psychology, 35*, 150–175.

Murray, H. A. (1938). *Explorations in personality*. Cambridge, MA: Harvard University Press.

Murray, H. A. (1943). *Thematic Apperception Test manual*. Cambridge, MA: Harvard University Press.

Murray, H. A. (1951). Uses of the TAT. *American Journal of Psychiatry, 1071,* 577–581.

Murray, H. A. (1959). Preparations for the scaffold of a comprehensive system. In S. Koch (Ed.), *Psychology: A study of science* (Vol. 3). New York: McGraw-Hill.

Murray, H. A., & Kluckhohn, C. (1953). Outline of a conception of personality. In C. Kluckholn, H. A. Murray, & D. Schneider (Eds.), *Personality in nature, society, and culture* (2nd ed.; pp. 3–52). New York: Knopf.

Murray, H. A., & MacKinnon, D. W. (1946). Assessment of OSS personnel. *Journal of Consulting Psychology, 10,* 76–80.

Murstein, B. J. (1961). Assumptions, adaptation level, and projective techniques. *Perceptual and Motor Skills, 12,* 107–125.

Murstein, B. J. (1963). *Theory and research in projective techniques*. New York: Wiley.

Mussen, P. H., & Krauss, S. R. (1952). An investigation of the diagnostic validity of the Szondi test. *Journal of Abnormal and Social Psychology, 47,* 399–405.

Mussen, P. H., & Naylor, H. K. (1954). The relationship between overt and fantasy aggression. *Journal of Abnormal and Social Psychology, 49,* 235–240.

Mussen, P. H., & Scodel, A. (1955). The effects of sexual stimulation under varying conditions on TAT sexual responsiveness. *Journal of Consulting Psychology, 19,* 90.

Myers, I. B., & Briggs, K. C. (1943/1962). *The Myers-Briggs Type Indicator*. Palo Alto, CA: Consulting Psychologists Press.

Myers, I. B., & McCaulley, M. H. (1985). *Manual for the Myers-Briggs Type Indicator: A guide to the development and use of the MBTI*. Palo Alto, CA: Consulting Psychologists Press.

Nagle, R. J., & Lazarus, S. C. (1979). The comparability of the WISC-R and WAIS among 16-year old EMR children. *Journal of School Psychology, 17,* 362–367.

Naglieri, J. A. (1981). Concurrent validity of the Revised Peabody Picture Vocabulary Test. *Psychology in the Schools, 18,* 286–289.

Naglieri, J. A. (1985a). Use of the WISC-R and K-ABC with learning disabled, borderline mentally retarded, and normal children. *Psychology in the Schools, 22,* 133–141.

Naglieri, J. A. (1985b). Normal children's performance on the McCarthy Scales, Kaufman Assessment Battery and Peabody Individual Achievement Test. *Journal of Psychoeducational Assessment, 3,* 123–129.

Naglieri, J. A. (1989). A cognitive processing theory for the measurement of intelligence. *Educational Psychologist, 24,* 185–206.

Naglieri, J. A. (1990). Das-Naglieri Cognitive Assessment System. Paper presented at the conference "Intelligence: Theories and Practice," Memphis, TN.

Naglieri, J. A., & Anderson, D. F. (1985). Comparison of the WISC-R and K-ABC with gifted students. *Journal of Psychoeducational Assessment, 3,* 175–179.

Naglieri, J. A., & Das, J. P. (1988). Planning-arousal-simultaneous-successive (PASS): A model for assessment. *Journal of School Psychology, 26,* 35–48.

Naglieri, J. A., & Harrison, P. L. (1978). Comparison of the McCarthy and Cognitive Indexes and Stanford-Binet for educable mentally retarded children. *Perceptual and Motor Skills, 48,* 1252–1254.

Naglieri, J. A., & Jensen, A. R. (1987). Comparison of black-white differences on the WISC-R and the K-ABC: Spearman's hypothesis. *Intelligence, 11,* 21–43.

Naglieri, J. A., & Naglieri, D. A. (1981). Comparison of the PPVT and PPVT-R for preschool children: Implications for the practitioner. *Psychology in the Schools, 18,* 434–436.

Narens, L. & Luce, R. D. (1986). Measurement: The theory of numerical assignments. *Psychological Bulletin, 99,* 166–180.

National Association of School Psychologists. (1984). *Principles for professional ethics*. Washington, DC: Author.

National Joint Committee on Learning Disabilities. (1985). Learning disabilities and the preschool child: A position paper of the National Joint Committee on Learning Disabilities. Baltimore, MD: Author.

Naylor, J. C., & Shine, L. C. (1965). A table for determining the increase in mean criterion score obtained by using a selection device. *Journal of Industrial Psychology, 3,* 33–42.

Needham, J. (1959). *A history of embryology*. New York: Abelard-Schuman.

Neisser, U. (1979). The concept of intelligence. *Intelligence, 3,* 217–227.

Nelson, R. O., Sigmon, S., Amodei, N., & Jarrett, R. B. (1984). The Menstrual Symptom Questionnaire: The validity of the distinction between spasmodic and congestive dysmenorrhea. *Behavior Research & Therapy, 22,* 611–614.

Nelson, W. J., & Birkimer, J. C. (1978). Role of self-instruction and self-reinforcement in the modification of impulsivity. *Journal of Consulting and Clinical Psychology, 46,* 183.

Nevid, J. S. (1984). Methodological considerations in the use of electroencephalographic techniques in advertising research. *Psychology & Marketing, 1*(2), 5–19.

Nevid, J. S. & Cohen, R. J. (1987). Watching people watch: But is anybody watching? In R. J. Cohen (Chair), *Aspects of the consumer experience.* Symposium presented at the 95th annual convention of the American Psychological Association, August 31, 1987, New York.

Newborg, J., Stock, J. R., Wnek, L., Guidubaldi, U., & Svinicki, J. (1984). *Battelle Developmental Inventory.* Allen, TX: DLM Teaching Resources.

Newcomb, T. M. (1929). *Consistency of certain extravert-introvert behavior patterns in 51 problem boys.* New York: Columbia University Bureau of Publications.

Newman, H. H., Freeman, F. N., & Holzinger, K. J. (1937). *Twins.* Chicago: University of Chicago Press.

Nighswonger, N. J., & Martin, J. R. (1981). On using voice analysis in marketing research. *Journal of Marketing Research, 18,* 350–355.

Nihira, K. (1969a). Factorial dimensions of adaptive behavior in adult retardates. *American Journal of Mental Deficiency, 73,* 868–878.

Nihira, K. (1969b). Factorial dimensions of adaptive behavior in mentally retarded children and adolescents. *American Journal of Mental Deficiency, 74,* 130–141.

Nitko, A. J. (1988). Designing tests that are integrated with instructions. In R. L. Linn (Ed.), *Educational measurement* (3rd ed.). New York: American Council on Education/Macmillan.

Noles, S. W., Cash, T. F., & Winstead, B. A. (1985). Body image, physical attractiveness, and depression. *Journal of Consulting & Clinical Psychology, 53,* 88–94.

Notarius, C., & Markman, H. (1981). Couples Interaction Scoring System. In E. Filsinger & R. Lewis, (Eds.), *Assessing marriage: New behavioral approaches.* Beverly Hills, CA: Sage.

Notarius, C. I., & Vanzetti, N. A. (1983). The Marital Agendas Protocol. In E. Filsinger (Ed.), *Marriage and family assessment: A sourcebook for family therapy.* Beverly Hills, CA: Sage.

Nottingham, E. J., IV, & Mattson, R. E. (1981). A validation study of the Competency Screening Test. *Law and Human Behavior, 5,* 329–335.

Novick, M. R. (1981). Federal guidelines and professional standards. *American Psychologist, 36,* 1035–1046.

Novick, M. R., & Lewis, C. (1967). Coefficient alpha and the reliability of composite measurements. *Psychometrika, 32,* 1–13.

Nunnally, J. C. (1978). *Psychometric theory* (2nd ed.). New York: McGraw-Hill.

Oakland, T. (1985). Review of the Slosson Intelligence Test. In J. V. Mitchell (Ed.). *The ninth mental measurements yearbook* (pp. 1401–1403). Lincoln: University of Nebraska Press.

Obrzut, A., Nelson, R. B., & Obrzut, J. E. (1987). Construct validity of the Kaufman Assessment Battery for Children with mildly mentally retarded students. *American Journal of Mental Deficiency, 92*(1), 74–77.

Obrzut, J. E., & Bolick, C. A. (1986). Thematic approaches to personality assessment with children and adolescents. In H. M. Knoff (Ed.), *The assessment of child and adolescent personality* (pp. 173–198). New York: Guilford Press.

O'Donnell, W. E., & Reynolds, D. McQ. (1983). *Neuropsychological Impairment Scale (NIS) manual.* Annapolis, MD: Annapolis Neuropsychological Services.

O'Farrell, T. J., Cutter, H. S., & Floyd, F. J. (1985). Evaluating behavioral marital therapy for male alcoholics: Effects on marital adjustment and communication from before to after treatment. *Behavior Therapy, 16,* 147–167.

Ogdon, D. P. (1982). *Psychodiagnosis and personality assessment: A handbook.* Los Angeles: Western Psychological Services.

O'Keefe, T., & Argulewicz, E. N. (1979). Test-retest reliability of the Matching Familiar Figures Test scores of female undergraduates. *Perceptual and Motor Skills, 49,* 698.

O'Leary, K. M., Brouwers, P., Gardner, D. L., & Cowdry, R. W. (1991). Neuropsychological testing of patients with borderline personality disorder. *American Journal of Psychiatry, 148,* 106–111.

O'Leary, M. R., Calsyn, D. A., & Fauria, T. (1980). The Group Embedded Figures Test: A measure of cognitive style or cognitive impairment. *Journal of Personality Assessment, 44,* 532–537.

Oliver, J. M., & Baumgart, E. P. (1985). The dysfunctional attitude scale: Psychometric properties and relation to depression in an unselected adult population. *Cognitive Therapy & Research, 9,* 161–167.

Oliver, J., May, M., & Handel, P. (1988). The factor structure of the Family Environment Scale: Factors derived from subscales. *Journal of Clinical Psychology, 44,* 723–727.

Ollendick, T. H. (1983). Reliability and validity of the Revised Fear Survey Schedule for Children (FSSC-R). *Behavior Research & Therapy, 21,* 685–692.

Olshfski, D. F., & Cunningham, R. B. (1986). Establishing assessment center validity: An examination of the methodological and theoretical issues. *Public Personnel Management, 15,* 85–98.

Olson, D. H., & Barnes, H. L. (1985). Quality of Life. In D. H. Olson, H. I. McCubbin, H. L. Barnes, A. S. Larsen, M. Muxen, & M. Wilson (Eds.), *Family inventories (Rev. ed.).* St. Paul: Family Social Science, University of Minnesota.

Olson, D. H., Larsen, A. S., & McCubbin, H. I. (1985). Family Strengths. In D. H. Olson, H. I. McCubbin, H. L. Barnes, A. S. Larsen, M. Muxen, & M. Wilson (Eds.), *Family inventories* (Rev. ed.). St. Paul: Family Social Science, University of Minnesota.

Olson, J. C., & Ray, W. J. (1983). *Using brain-wave measures to assess advertising effects* (Working paper). Cambridge, MA: Marketing Science Institute.

Oltman, P. K., Raskin, E., & Witkin, H. A. (1971). *Group Embedded Figures Test.* Palo Alto, CA: Consulting Psychologists Press.

Omizo, M. M., & Williams, R. E. (1981). Biofeedback training can calm the hyperactive child. *Academic Therapy, 17,* 43–46.

Ornstein, R. (1988). *Psychology: The study of human experience* (2nd ed.). San Diego, CA: Harcourt Brace Jovanovich.

Orr, D. B., & Graham, W. R. (1968). Development of a listening comprehension test to identify educational potential among disadvantaged junior high school students. *American Educational Researcher Journal, 5,* 167–180.

Osgood, C. E., Suci, G. J., & Tannenbaum, P. H. (1957). *The measurement of meaning.* Urbana: University of Illinois Press.

Osipow, S. H., & Reed, R. (1985). Decision making style and career indecision in college students. *Journal of Vocational Behavior, 27,* 368–373.

OSS Assessment Staff. (1948). *Assessment of men: Selection of personnel for the Office of Strategic Service.* New York: Rinehart.

Otis, A., & Lennon, R. (1979). *Otis-Lennon School Ability Test.* New York: Psychological Corporation.

Ouellette, S. E. (1988). The use of projective drawing techniques in the personality assessment of prelingually deafened young adults: A pilot study. *American Annals of the Deaf, 133,* 212–217.

Overholser, J. C. (1990). Retest reliability of the Millon Clinical Multiaxial Inventory. *Journal of Personality Assessment, 55*(1 & 2), 202–208.

Ozer, D. J. (1985). Correlation and the coefficient of determination. *Psychological Bulletin, 97,* 307–315.

Paget, K. D. (1985). Assessment in early childhood education. *Diagnostique, 10,* 76–87.

Palmore, E. (Ed.). (1970). *Normal aging.* Durham, NC: Duke University Press.

Panek, P. E., & Stoner, S. (1979). Test-retest reliability of the Hand Test with normal subjects. *Journal of Personality Assessment, 43,* 135–137.

Panell, R. C., & Laabs, G. J. (1979). Construction of a criterion-referenced, diagnostic test for an individualized instruction program. *Journal of Applied Psychology, 64,* 255–261.

Pantle, M. L., Evert, J. M., & Trenerry, M. R. (1990). The utility of the MAPI in the assessment of depression. *Journal of Personality Assessment, 55,* 673–682.

Parker, K. C. (1983). Factor analysis of the WAIS-R at nine age levels between 16 and 74 years. *Journal of Consulting and Clinical Psychology, 51,* 302–308.

Parsons, C. J. (1917). Children's interpretations of inkblots. *British Journal of Psychology, 9,* 74–92.

Pascal, G. R., & Suttell, B. J. (1951). *The Bender-Gestalt Test: Quantification and validity for adults.* New York: Grune & Stratton.

Pasewark, R. A., Rardin, M. W., & Grice, J. E. (1971). Relationship of the WPPSI and the Stanford-Binet L-M in lower class children. *Journal of School Psychology, 9,* 45–50.

Pasewark, R. S., & Sawyer, R. N. (1979). Edwards Personal Preference Schedule scores of rural high school students. *Educational and Psychological Measurement, 39,* 81–84.

Paulhus, D. L. (1984). Two-component models of socially desirable responding. *Journal of Personality and Social Psychology, 46,* 598–609.

Paulhus, D. L. (1986). Self-deception and impression management in test responses. In A. Angleitner & J. S. Wiggins (Eds.), *Personality assessment via questionnaire* (pp. 142–165). New York: Springer.

Paulhus, D. L. (1990). Measurement and control of response bias. In J. P. Robinson, P. R. Shaver, & L. Wrightsman (Eds.), *Measures of personality and social-psychological attitudes* (pp. 17–59). San Diego, CA: Academic Press.

Paulhus, D. L., & Levitt, K. (1987). Desirable response triggered by affect: Automatic egotism? *Journal of Personality and Social Psychology, 52,* 245–259.

Paulhus, D. L., & Reid, D. B. (1991). Enhancement and denial in socially desirable responding. *Journal of Personality and Social Psychology, 60,* 307–317.

Payne, F. D., & Wiggins, J. S. (1968). Effects of rule relaxation and system combination on classification rates in two MMPI "cookbook" systems. *Journal of Consulting and Clinical Psychology, 32,* 734–736.

Pearlman, K., Schmidt, F. L., & Hunter, J. E. (1980). Validity generalization results for tests used to predict job proficiency and training success in clerical occupations. *Journal of Applied Psychology, 65,* 373–406.

Pearson, K., & Moul, M. (1925). The problem of alien immigration of Great Britain illustrated by an examination of Russian and Polish Jewish children. *Annals of Eugenics, 1,* 5–127.

Pedersen, D. M., Shinedling, M. M., & Johnson, D. L. (1968). Effects of sex of examiner and subject on children's quantitative test performance. *Journal of Personality and Social Psychology, 10,* 251–254.

Pellegrini, A., & Putman, P. (1984). The amytal interview in the diagnosis of late onset psychosis with cultural features presenting as catatonic stupor. *Journal of Nervous & Mental Disease, 172,* 502–504.

Penner, L. A., Thompson, J. K., & Coovert, D. L. (1991). Size estimation among anorexics: Much ado about very little? *Journal of Abnormal Psychology, 100,* 90–93.

Perry, J. C., & Jacobs, D. (1982). Overview: Clinical applications of the amytal interview in psychiatric emergency settings. *American Journal of Psychiatry, 139,* 552–559.

Peterson, C. A., & Knudson, R. M. (1983). Anhedonia: A construct validation approach. *Journal of Personality Assessment, 47,* 539–551.

Petrie, K., & Chamberlain, K. (1985). The predictive validity of the Zung Index of Potential Suicide. *Journal of Personality Assessment, 49,* 100–102.

Pfeiffer, E. (1975). A Short Portable Mental Status Questionnaire for the assessment of organic brain deficit in elderly patients. *Journal of the American Geriatric Society, 23,* 433–441.

Phelps, L., & Branyon, B. (1988). Correlations among the Hiskey, K-ABC Nonverbal Scale, Leiter, and WISC-R Performance Scale with public school deaf children. *Journal of Psychoeducational Assessment, 6,* 354–358.

Phillips, B. L., Pasework, R. A., & Tindall, R. C. (1978). Relationships among McCarthy Scales of Children's Abilities, WPPSI, and Columbia Mental Maturity Scale. *Psychology in the Schools, 15,* 352–356.

Phillipson, H. (1955). *The object relations technique.* Glencoe, IL: Free Press.

Piaget, J. (1954). *The construction of reality in the child.* New York: Basic Books.

Piaget, J. (1971). *Biology and knowledge.* Chicago: University of Chicago Press.

Pichot, P. (1984). Centenary of the birth of Hermann Rorschach. (S. Rosenzweig & E. Schreiber, Trans.). *Journal of Personality Assessment, 48,* 591–596.

Piers, E. V. (1969). *Manual for the Piers-Harris Children's Self-Concept Scale.* Nashville, TN: Counselor Recordings and Tests.

Piersel, W. C., Bush, B., Zabel, M., & Lee, S. W. (1988). The third factor on the WISC-R: Does it measure anything? Paper presented at the Annual Meeting of the American Psychological Association, Atlanta, GA.

Pilkonis, P. A., Heape, C. L., Ruddy, J., & Serrao, P. (1991). Validity in the diagnosis of personality disorders: The use of the LEAD standard. *Psychological Assessment: A Journal of Consulting and Clinical Psychology, 3,* 46–54.

Pinard, A., & Laurendeau, M. (1964). A scale of mental development based on the theory of Jean Piaget: Description of a project. *Journal of Research in Science Teaching, 2,* 253–260.

Pincus, J. H., & Tucker, G. J. (1974). *Behavioral neurology.* New York: Oxford.

Pintner, R. (1931). *Intelligence testing.* New York: Holt.

Piotrowski, C., & Keller, J. (1991, March). *Psychological testing practices in applied settings: A literature review from 1980–1990.* Paper presented at the annual meeting of the Southeastern Psychological Association, New Orleans, LA.

Piotrowski, C., & Keller, J. W. (1989). Psychological testing in outpatient mental health facilities: A national study. *Professional Psychology: Research and Practice, 20*(4), 423–425.

Piotrowski, C., & Lubin, B. (1990). Assessment practices of health psychologists: Survey of APA Division 38 clinicians. *Professional Psychology: Research and Practice, 21,* 99–106.

Piotrowski, C., Sherry, D., & Keller, J. W. (1985). Psychodiagnostic test usage: A survey of the Society for Personality Assessment. *Journal of Personality Assessment, 49,* 115–119.

Piotrowski, Z. (1957). *Perceptanalysis.* New York: Macmillan.

Plutchik, R., & Conte, H. R. (1989). Measuring emotions and the derivatives of emotions: Personality traits, ego defenses, and coping styles. In S. Wetzler, & M. M. Katz (Eds.), *Contemporary approaches to psychological assessment.* New York: Brunner/Mazel.

Polyson, J., Norris, D., & Ott, E. (1985). The recent decline in TAT research. *Professional Psychology: Research and Practice, 16,* 26–28.

Ponterotto, J. G., Pace, T. M., & Kaven, M. G. (1989). A counselor's guide to the assessment of depression. *Journal of Counseling and Development, 67,* 301–309.

Popham, W. J. (1981). *Modern educational measurement.* Englewood Cliffs, NJ: Prentice-Hall.

Pound, E. J., & McChesney, S. R. (1982, March). Relationship of the PPVT-R and WISC-R for children referred for evaluation. Paper presented at the annual convention of the National Association of School Psychologists, Toronto, Ontario, Canada.

Power, M., Champion, L., & Aris, S. (1988). The development of a measure of social support: The Significant Others (SOS) Scale. *British Journal of Clinical Psychology, 27,* 349–358.

Prasse, D. P., & Bracken, B. A. (1981). Comparison of the PPVT-R and WISC-R with white and black urban Educable Mentally Retarded students. *Psychology in the Schools, 18,* 174–177.

Prater, G. F. (1957). Cited in Swensen, C. H., Jr. Empirical evaluations of human figure drawings. *Psychological Bulletin, 54,* 431–466.

Pratkanis, A. R., & Greenwald, A. G. (1988). Recent perspectives on unconscious processing: Still no marketing applications. *Psychology & Marketing, 5,* 337–353.

Prelinger, E. (1950). On the reliability of the Szondi Test. *Psychological Service Center Journal* (Brooklyn College), *3,* 227–330.

Prelinger, E. (1952). Kleine studie uber die verlasslichkeit des Szouditests (A note on Szondi validity). *Psychological Abstracts, 26,* No. 5625.

Preston, R. (1961). Improving the item validity of study habits inventories. *Educational and Psychological Measurement, 21,* 129–131.

Price, G., Dunn, R., & Dunn, K. (1982). *Productivity Environmental Survey manual.* Lawrence, KS: Price Systems.

Price, L., Rust, R., & Kumar, V. (1986). Brain-wave analyses of consumer responses to advertising. In J. Olson & K. Sentis (Eds.), *Advertising and consumer psychology* (Vol. 3, pp. 17–34). New York: Praeger.

Primoff, E. S. (1980). The use of self-assessments in examining. *Personnel Psychology, 33,* 283–290.

Prince, R. J., & Guastello, S. J. (1990). The Barnum Effect in a computerized Rorschach interpretation system. *Journal of Psychology: Interdisciplinary and Applied, 124,* 217–222.

Procedures for evaluating specific learning disabilities. (1977). *Federal Register,* December 29, Part III.

Prosser, N., & Crawford, V. V. (1971). Relationship of scores on the WPPSI and the Stanford-Binet Intelligence Scale Form L-M. *Journal of School Psychology, 9,* 278–283.

Prout, H. T., & Phillips, P. D. (1974). A clinical note: The kinetic school drawing. *Psychology in the Schools, 11,* 303–306.

Pulakos, E. D. (1986). The development of training programs to increase accuracy with different rating tasks. *Organizational Behavior and Human Decision Processes, 38,* 76–91.

Puleo, V. T. (1989). IQ differences between the WISC-R and other major tests of cognitive functioning: A review of the literature. Paper presented at the Annual Meeting of the National Association of School Psychologists, Boston, MA.

Pyle, W. H. (1913). *Examination of school children*. New York: Macmillan.

Quay, H. C., & Peterson, C. (1983). *Manual for the Revised Behavior Problem Checklist*. Coral Gables, FL: Authors.

Quay, H. C., & Peterson, D. R. (1967). *Behavior Problem Checklist*. Champaign: University of Illinois Press.

Quinsey, V. L. (1985). Men who have sex with children. In D. Weistubb (Ed.), *Law and mental health: International perspectives* (Vol. 2, pp. 84–121). New York: Pergamon Press.

Quinsey, V. L., Chaplin, T. C., & Upfold, D. (1984). Sexual arousal to nonsexual violence and sadomasochistic themes among rapists and non-sex-offenders. *Journal of Consulting & Clincial Psychology, 52,* 651–657.

Quinsey, V. L., Steinman, C. M., Bergersen, S. G., & Holmes, T. F. (1975). Penile circumference, skin conductance, and ranking responses of child molesters and "normals" to sexual and non-sexual visual stimuli. *Behavior Therapy, 6,* 213–219.

Radloff, L. (1977). The CES-D Scale: A self-report depression scale for research in the general population. *Applied Psychological Measurement, 1,* 385–401.

Ramseyer, G. C., & Cashen, V. M. (1971). The effect of practice sessions on the use of separate answer sheets by first and second graders. *Journal of Educational Measurement, 8,* 177–181.

Randt, C. T., & Brown, E. R. (1983). *Randt Memory Test*. Bayport, NY: Life Science Associates.

Rankin, R. J., & Henderson, R. (1968). Standardized tests and the disadvantaged. *American Psychologist, 76,* 618.

Rapaport, D. (1946–1967). Principles underlying non-projective tests of personality. In M. M. Gill (Ed.), *David Rapaport: Collected papers*. New York: Basic Books.

Rapaport, D., Gill, M. M., & Schafer, R. (1945–1946). *Diagnostic psychological testing*. (2 vols.). Chicago: Year Book Publishers.

Rapaport, D., Gill, M. M., & Schafer, R. (1968). *Diagnostic psychological testing* (Rev. ed.), R. R. Holt (Ed.). New York: International Universities Press.

Rappeport, J. R. (1982). Differences between forensic and general psychiatry. *American Journal of Psychiatry, 139,* 331–334.

Rasbury, W., McCoy, J. G., & Perry, N. W. (1977). Relations of scores on WPPSI and WISC-R at a one year interval. *Perceptual and Motor Skills, 44,* 695–698.

Raskin, D. C., & Yuille, J. C. (1987). Problems of evaluating interviews of children in sexual abuse cases. In S. J. Ceci, M. P. Toglia, & D. F. Ross (Eds.), *New perspectives on the child witness*. New York: Springer-Verlag.

Raskin, L. M., Bloom, A. S., Klee, S. H., & Reese, A. H. (1978). The assessment of developmentally disabled children with the WISC-R, Binet and other tests. *Journal of Clinical Psychology, 34,* 111–116.

Raulin, M. L., & Wee, J. L. (1984). The development and initial validation of a scale to measure social fear. *Journal of Clinical Psychology, 40,* 780–784.

Ray, S. (1979). *An adaptation of the Wechsler Intelligence Scale for Children—Revised for the deaf*. Natchitoches, LA: Steven Ray.

Razran, G. (1961). The observable unconscious and the inferable conscious in current Soviet psychophysiology: Introceptive conditioning, semantic conditioning, and the orienting reflex. *Psychological Review, 68,* 81–147.

Record, R. G., McKeown, T., & Edwards, J. H. (1969). The relationship of measured intelligence to birth order and maternal age. *Annals of Human Genetics, 33,* 61–69.

Reece, R. N., & Groden, M. A. (1985). Recognition of non-accidental injury. *Pediatric Clinics of North America, 32,* 41–60.

Reed, H. B. C., Jr., Reitan, R. M., & Klove, H. (1965). Influence of cerebral lesions on psychological test performances of older children. *Journal of Consulting Psychology, 19,* 247–251.

Reidy, T. J., & Carstens, C. (1990). Stability of the Millon Adolescent Personality Inventory in an incarcerated delinquent population. *Journal of Personality Assessment, 55,* 692–697.

Reinehr, R. C. (1969). Therapist and patient perceptions of hospitalized alcoholics. *Journal of Clinical Psychology, 25,* 443–445.

Reitan, R. M. (1955a). An investigation of the validity of Halstead's measures of biological intelligence. *Archives of Neurology and Psychiatry, 73,* 28–35.

Reitan, R. M. (1955b). Certain differential effects of left and right cerebral lesions in human adults. *Journal of Comparative and Physiological Psychology, 48,* 474–477.

Reitan, R. M. (1969). *Manual for administration of neuro-*

psychological test batteries for adults and children. Indianapolis: Author.

Reitan, R. M., & Davison, L. A. (1974). *Clinical neuropsychology: Current status and applications.* New York: Winston/Wiley.

Remzy, I., & Pickard, P. M. (1949). A study in the reliability of scoring the Rorschach inkblot test. *Journal of General Psychology, 40,* 3–10.

Renzulli, J. S., & Smith, L. H. (1977). Two approaches to identification of gifted students. *Exceptional Children, 43,* 512–518.

Reschly, D. J. (1978). WISC-R factor structures among Anglos, Blacks, Chicanos, and Native-American Papagos. *Journal of Consulting and Clinical Psychology, 46,* 417–422.

Reschly, D. J. (1981). Psychological testing in educational classification and placement. *American Psychologist, 36,* 1094–1102.

Reschly, D. J. (1982). Assessing mild mental retardation: The influence of adaptive behavior, sociocultural status, and prospects for nonbiased assessment. In C. R. Reynolds & T. B. Gutkin (Eds.), *The handbook of school psychology.* New York: Wiley.

Reschly, D. J. (1990). Found: Our intelligences: What do they mean? *Journal of Psychoeducational Assessment, 8,* 259–267.

Reschly, D. J., & Grimes, J. P. (1990). Best practices in intellectual assessment. In A. Thomas & J. Grimes (Eds.), *Best practices in school psychology II* (pp. 425–439). Washington, DC: National Association of School Psychologists.

Reschly, D. J., & Reschly, J. E. (1979). Validity of WISC-R factor scores in predicting achievement and attention for four sociocultural groups. *Journal of School Psychology, 17,* 335–361.

Resnick, P. J. (1988). Malingered psychosis. In R. Rogers (Ed.), *Clinical assessment of malingering and deception* (pp. 34–53). New York: Guilford Press.

Retzlaff, P. D., Sheehan, E. P., & Lorr, M. (1990). MCMI-II scoring: Weighted and unweighted algorithms. *Journal of Personality Assessment, 55,* 219–223.

Reynell, J. (1970). Children with physical handicaps. In P. Mittler (Ed.), *The psychological assessment of mental and physical handicaps* (pp. 443–469). London: Methuen.

Reynolds, C. E., & Brown, R. T. (Eds.), (1984). *Perspectives on bias in mental testing.* New York: Plenum.

Reynolds, C. R. (1985). Review of the System of Multicultural Pluralistic Assessment. In J. V. Mitchell (Ed.), *The ninth mental measurements yearbook* (pp. 1519–1521). Lincoln: University of Nebraska Press.

Reynolds, C. R., & Clark, J. (1983). Assessment of cognitive abilities. In K. Paget & B. Bracken (Eds.), *The psychoeducational assessment of preschool children* (pp. 163–190). New York: Grune & Stratton.

Reynolds, C. R., Gutkin, T. B., Doppen, L., & Wright, D. (1979). Differential validity of the WISC-R for boys and girls referred for psychological services. *Perceptual and Motor Skills, 48,* 868–870.

Reynolds, C. R., & Kaiser, S. M. (1990a). Test bias in psychological assessment. In T. B. Gutkin & C. R. Reynolds (Eds.), *The handbook of school psychology* (2nd ed.; pp. 487–525). New York: Wiley.

Reynolds, C. R., & Kaiser, S. M. (1990b). Bias in assessment of aptitude. In C. R. Reynolds & R. W. Kamphaus (Eds.), *Handbook of psychological and educational assessment of children: Intelligence & achievement* (pp. 611–653). New York: Guilford Press.

Reynolds, C. R., & Kaufman, A. S. (1990). Assessment of children's intelligence with the Wechsler Intelligence Scale for Children—Revised. In C. R. Reynolds & R. W. Kamphaus (Eds.), *Handbook of psychological and educational assessment of children: Intelligence & achievement* (pp. 127–165). New York: Guilford Press.

Reynolds, S. E. (1984). Battle of the experts revisited: 1983 Oregon legislation on the insanity defense. *Willamette Law Review, 20,* 303–317.

Reynolds, W. M. (1985). Review of the Slosson Intelligence Test. In J. V. Mitchell (Ed.), *The ninth mental measurements yearbook.* Lincoln: University of Nebraska Press, 1403–1404.

Reynolds, W. M. (1987). *Reynolds Adolescent Depression Scale: Professional manual.* Odessa, FL: Psychological Assessment Resources.

Reynolds, W. M. (1988). Measurement of academic self-concept in college students. *Journal of Personality Assessment, 52*(2), 223–240.

Rezmovic, V. (1977). The effects of computerized experimentation on response variance. *Behavior Research Methods and Instrumentation, 9,* 144–147.

Reznikoff, M., & Tomblen, D. (1956). The use of human figure drawings in the diagnosis of organic pathology. *Journal of Consulting Psychology, 20,* 467–470.

Richards, J. T. (1969). The effectiveness of the WPPSI in the identification of mentally retarded children. *Dissertation Abstracts, 29,* 3880.

Richardson, M. W., & Kuder, G. F. (1939). The calculation of test reliability based upon the method of rational equivalence. *Journal of Educational Psychology, 30,* 681–687.

Richmond, B. O., Rodrigo, G., & deRodrigo, M. (1988). Factor structure of a Spanish version of the Revised Children's Manifest Anxiety Scale in Uruguay. *Journal of Personality Assessment, 52,* 165–170.

Rierdan, J., & Koff, E. (1981). Sexual ambiguity in children's human figure drawings. *Journal of Personality Assessment, 45,* 256–257.

Rimm, S. B. (1976). *GIFT: Group Inventory for Finding Talent.* Watertown, WI: Educational Assessment Service.

Rimm, S. B. (1981). *PRIDE: Preschool and Kindergarten Interest Descriptor.* Watertown, WI: Educational Assessment Service.

Ritson, B., & Forest, A. (1970). The simulation of psychosis: A contemporary presentation. *British Journal of Medical Psychology, 43,* 31–37.

Roach, R. J., Frazier, L. P., & Bowden, S. R. (1981). The Marital Satisfaction Scale: Development of a measure for intervention research. *Journal of Marriage and the Family, 21,* 251–255.

Roback, A. A. (1961). *History of psychology and psychiatry.* New York: Philosophical Library.

Roberts, R. E., Lewinsohn, P. M., & Seeley, J. R. (1991). Screening for adolescent depression: A comparison of depression scales. *Journal of the American Academy of Child and Adolescent Psychiatry, 30,* 58–66.

Roberts, R. N., & Magrab, P. R. (1991). Psychologists' role in a family-centered approach to practice, training, and research with young children. *American Psychologist, 46,* 144–148.

Robertson, G. J. (1990). A practical model for test development. In C. R. Reynolds & R. W. Kamphaus (Eds.), *Handbook of psychological and educational assessment of children: Intelligence & achievement* (pp. 62–85). New York: Guilford Press.

Robin, A. L., & Foster, S. L. (1989). *Negotiating parent-adolescent conflict: A behavioral family systems approach.* New York: Guilford Press.

Robin, A. L., Koepke, T., & Moye, A. (1990). Multidimensional assessment of parent-adolescent relations. *Psychological Assessment: A Journal of Consulting & Clinical Psychology, 2,* 451–459.

Robinson, J. P., & Shaver, P. R. (1973). *Measures of social psychological attitudes.* Ann Arbor: University of Michigan Press.

Robson, P. J. (1988). Self-esteem: A psychiatric view. *British Journal of Psychiatry, 153,* 6–15.

Rocklin, T. (1987). *Student perceptions of differences among test items.* Poster presentation at the 1987 annual convention of the American Psychological Association, New York.

Rodin, E., & Schmaltz, S. (1984). The Bear-Fedio personality inventory and temporal lobe epilepsy. *Neurology, 34,* 591–596.

Roesch, R., & Golding, S. L. (1980). *Competency to stand trial.* Urbana: University of Illinois Press.

Rogers, C. R. (1959). A theory of therapy, personality, and interpersonal relationships, as developed in the client-centered framework. In S. Koch (Ed.), *Psychology: A study of a science.* (Vol. 3; pp. 184–256). New York: McGraw-Hill.

Rogers, L. S., Knauss, J., & Hammond, K. R. (1951). Predicting continuation in therapy by means of the Rorschach Test. *Journal of Consulting Psychology, 15,* 368–371.

Rogers, R., & Cavanaugh, J. L. (1980). Differences in psychological variables between criminally responsible and insane patients: A preliminary study. *American Journal of Forensic Psychiatry, 1,* 29–37.

Rogers, R., & Cavanaugh, J. L. (1981). Rogers Criminal Responsibility Assessment Scales. *Illinois Medical Journal, 160,* 164–169.

Rogers, R., Dolmetsch, R., & Cavanaugh, J. L. (1981). An empirical approach to insanity evaluations. *Journal of Clinical Psychology, 37,* 683–687.

Rogers, R. (1986). *Structured interview of reported symptoms (SIRS).* Unpublished scale. Toronto: Clarke Institute of Psychiatry.

Rogers, R., Gillis, J. R., Dickens, S. E., & Bagby, R. M. (1991). Standardized assessment of malingering: Validation of the Structured Interview of Reported Symptoms. *Psychological Assessment: A Journal of Consulting and Clinical Psychology, 3,* 89–96.

Rogers, R., Seman, W., & Wasyliw, D. E. (1983). The RCRAS and legal insanity: A cross validation study. *Journal of Clinical Psychology, 39,* 554–559.

Rogers, R., Wasyliw, D. E., & Cavanaugh, J. L. (1984).

Evaluating insanity: A study of construct validity. *Law & Human Behavior, 8,* 293–303.

Rokeach, M. (1973). *The nature of human values.* New York: Free Press.

Rome, H. P., Mataya, P., Pearson, J. S., Swenson, W., & Brannick, T. L. (1965). Automatic personality assessment. In R. W. Stacy & B. Waxman (Eds.), *Computers in biomedical research* (Vol. 1, pp. 505–524). New York: Academic Press.

Rorer, L. G. (1965). The great response-style myth. *Psychological Bulletin, 63,* 129–156.

Rorer, L. G., Hoffman, P. J., LaForge, G. E., & Hsieh, K. (1966). Optimal cutting scores to discriminate groups of unequal size and variance. *Journal of Applied Psychology, 50,* 153–164.

Rorschach, H. (1921/1942). *Psycho-diagnostics: A diagnostic test based on perception* (P. Lemkau & B. Kronenburg, Trans.). Berne: Huber. (First German edition: 1921. Distributed in the United States by Grune & Stratton.).

Rosch, E. R. (1978). Human categorization. In N. Warren (Ed.), *Studies in cross-cultural psychology.* London: Academic Press.

Rosen, J., Silberg, N., & Gross, J. (1988). Eating Attitudes Test and Eating Disorders Inventory: Norms for adolescent girls and boys. *Journal of Consulting and Clinical Psychology, 56,* 305–308.

Rosen, J. C., Srebnik, D., Saltzberg, D & Wendt, S. (1991). Development of a body image avoidance questionnaire. *Psychological Assessment: A Journal of Consulting and Clinical Psychology, 3,* 32–37.

Rosenbach, J. H. (1984). System of Multicultural Pluralistic Assessment. *Test Critiques* (Vol. 1; pp. 648–651). Kansas City, MO: Test Corporation of America.

Rosenman, R. H., Brand, R. J., Jenkins, C. D., Friedman, M., Straus, R., & Wurm, M. (1975). Coronary heart disease in the Western Collaborative Group Study: Final followup experience of 8½ years. *Journal of the American Medical Association, 233,* 872–877.

Rosenzweig, S. (1945). The picture-association method and its application in a study of reactions to frustration. *Journal of Personality, 14,* 3–23.

Rosenzweig, S. (1950). *Revised scoring manual for the Rosenzweig Picture-Frustration Study, Form for Adults.* St. Louis, MO: Author.

Rosenzweig, S. (1978). *The Rosenzweig Picture-Frustration (P-F) Study. Basic manual.* St. Louis, MO: Rana House.

Rosenzweig, S. (1981a). *Adolescent Form Supplement to the basic manual of the Rosenzweig Picture-Frustration (P-F) Study.* St. Louis, MO: Rana House.

Rosenzweig, S. (1981b). *Children's Form Supplement to the basic manual of the Rosenzweig Picture-Frustration (P-F) Study.* St. Louis, MO: Rana House.

Rosenzweig, S. (1988). Revised norms for the Children's Form of the Rosenzweig Picture-Frustration (P-F) Study with updated P-F reference list. *Journal of Clinical Child Psychology, 17,* 326–328.

Rosenzweig, S., Fleming, E. E., & Clarke, H. J. (1947). Revised scoring manual for the Rosenzweig Picture-Frustration Study. *Journal of Psychology, 24,* 165–208.

Rosenzweig, S., Fleming, E. E., & Rosenzweig, L. (1948). The children's form of the Rosenzweig Picture-Frustration Study. *Journal of Psychology, 26,* 141–191.

Rosenzweig, S., & Mirmow, E. L. (1950). The validation of trends in the children's form of the Rosenzweig Picture-Frustration Study. *Journal of Personality, 18,* 306–314.

Roth, M. R., & Hermus, G. P. (1980). *Developmental plan handbook for community skills training* (2nd ed.). New York: Developmental Press.

Rothlisberg, B. A. (1987). Comparing the Stanford-Binet: Fourth Edition to the WISC-R: A concurrent validity study. *Journal of School Psychology, 25,* 193–196.

Rothlisberg, B. A. (1990). The relation of the Stanford-Binet: Fourth Edition to measures of achievement: A concurrent validity study. *Psychology in the Schools, 27,* 120–125.

Rotter, J. B. (1966). Generalized expectancies for internal versus external control of reinforcement. *Psychological Monographs, 80* (Whole Number 609).

Rotter, J. B., & Rafferty, J. E. (1950). *The manual for the Rotter Incomplete Sentences Blank.* New York: Psychological Corporation.

Routh, D. K., & King, K. W. (1972). Social class bias in clinical judgment. *Journal of Consulting and Clinical Psychology, 38,* 202–207.

Rotton, J., & Kelly, I. W. (1985). Much ado about the full moon: A meta-analysis of lunar-lunacy research. *Psychological Bulletin, 97,* 286–306.

Rozensky, R. H., Honor, L. F., Rasinski, K., Tovian, S. M., & Herz, G. I. (1986). Paper-and-pencil versus computer administered MMPIs: A comparison of patients' attitudes. *Computers in Human Behavior, 2,* 111–116.

Rubin, L. S. (1974). The utilization of pupillometry in the differential diagnosis and treatment of psychotic and behavioral disorders. In M. P. Janisse (Ed.), *Pupillary dynamics and behavior* (pp. 75–134). New York: Plenum.

Rubin, S. (1964). A comparison of the Thematic Apperception Test stories of two IQ groups. *Journal of Projective Techniques, 28,* 81–85.

Ruch, L. O., Gartrell, J. W., Amedeo, S. R., & Coyne, B. J. (1991). The Sexual Assault Symptom Scale: Measuring self-reported sexual assault trauma in the emergency room. *Psychological Assessment: A Journal of Consulting and Clinical Psychology, 3,* 3–8.

Ruehlman, L. S., & Karoly, P. (1991). With a little flak from my friends: Development and preliminary validation of the Test of Negative Social Exchange (TENSE). *Psychological Assessment: A Journal of Consulting and Clinical Psychology, 3,* 97–104.

Ruff, G. A., & Barrios, B. A. (1986). Realistic assessment of body image. *Behavioral Assessment, 8,* 237–252.

Rulon, P. J. (1939). A simplified procedure for determining the reliability of a test by split-halves. *Harvard Educational Review, 9,* 99–103.

Runyon, K., & Stewart, D. W. (1987). *Consumer behavior and the practice of marketing.* Columbus, OH: Merrill.

Ruschival, M. L., & Way, J. G. (1971). The WPPSI and the Stanford–Binet Form L-M: A validity and reliability study using gifted preschool children. *Journal of Consulting and Clinical Psychology, 37,* 163.

Russell, E. W., Neuringer, C., & Goldstein, G. (1970). *Assessment of brain damage: A neuropsychological key approach.* New York: Wiley.

Russell, J. S. (1984). A review of fair employment cases in the field of training. *Personnel Psychology, 37,* 261–276.

Rust, J., & Golombok, S. (1985). The Golombok–Rust Inventory of Sexual Satisfaction (GRISS). *British Journal of Clinical Psychology, 24,* 63–64.

Ryan, E. R., & Bell, M. D. (1984). Changes in object relations from psychosis to recovery. *Journal of Abnormal Psychology, 93,* 209–215.

Ryan, E. R., & Cicchetti, D. V. (1985). Predicting quality of alliance in the initial psychotherapy interview. *The Journal of Nervous and Mental Disease, 173,* 717–725.

Ryan, J. J., & Sattler, J. M. (1988). Wechsler Adult Intelligence Scale—Revised. In J. M. Sattler, *Assessment of children* (3rd ed.; pp. 219–244). San Diego, CA: J. M. Sattler.

Sabatelli, R. M. (1984). The Marital Comparison Level Index: A measure for assessing outcomes relative to expectations. *Journal of Marriage and the Family, 46,* 651–662.

Sachs, B. B. (1976). Some views of a deaf Rorschacher on the personality of deaf individuals. *Hearing Rehabilitation Quarterly, 2,* 13–14.

Sackett, P. R., Burris, L. R., & Callahan, C. (1989). Integrity testing for personnel selection: An update. *Personnel Psychology, 42,* 491–529.

Sackett, P. R., & Harris, M. M. (1984). Honesty testing for personnel selection: A review and critique. *Personnel Psychology, 37,* 221–245.

Sacks, E. (1952). Intelligence scores as a function of experimentally established social relationships between the child and examiner. *Journal of Abnormal and Social Psychology, 47,* 354–358.

Salvia, J., & Hritcko, T. (1984). The K-ABC and ability training. *Journal of Special Education, 18,* 345–356.

Salvia, J., & Ysseldyke, J. E. (1981). *Assessment in special and remedial education* (4th ed.). Boston: Houghton Mifflin.

Salvia, J. A., & Ysseldyke, J. E. (1988). *Assessment in special and remedial education* (5th ed.). Boston: Houghton-Mifflin.

Samuda, R. J. (1982). *Psychological testing of American minorities: Issues and consequences.* New York: Harper & Row.

Samuel, W. (1977). Observed IQ as a function of test atmosphere, tester expectation, and race of tester: A replication for female subjects. *Journal of Educational Psychology, 69,* 593–604.

Sampson, J. P., Jr. (1987). "Computer-assisted" or "computerized": What's in a name? *Journal of Counseling and Development, 66,* 116–118.

Sandelands, L. E., & Larson, J. R. (1985). When measurement causes task attitudes: A note from the laboratory. *Journal of Applied Psychology, 70,* 116–121.

Sandoval, J. (1985). Review of the System of Multicultural Pluralistic Assessment. In J. V. Mitchell (Ed.), *The ninth mental measurements yearbook* (pp. 1521–1525). Lincoln: University of Nebraska Press.

Sandoval, J., Sassenrath, J., & Penaloza, M. (1988).

Similarity of WISC-R and WAIS-R scores at age 16. *Psychology in the Schools, 25,* 373–379.

Sanfilippo, J., et al. (1986). Identifying the sexually molested preadolescent girl. *Pediatric Annals, 15,* 621–624.

Sanford, R. N. (1936). The effects of abstinence from food upon imaginal processes: A preliminary experiment. *Journal of Psychology, 2,* 129–136.

Sarnoff, D. (1982). Biofeedback: New uses in counseling. *Personnel and Guidance Journal, 60,* 357–360.

Satinsky, D., & Frerotti, A. (1981). Biofeedback treatment for headache: A two-year follow-up study. *American Journal of Clinical Biofeedback, 4,* 62–65.

Sattler, J. M. (1972). *Intelligence test modifications on handicapped and non-handicapped children.* Washington, DC: Department of Health, Education, and Welfare.

Sattler, J. M. (1974). *Assessment of children's intelligence* (Rev. reprint). Philadelphia: W. B. Saunders.

Sattler, J. M. (1982a). *Assessment of children's intelligence and special abilities.* Boston: Allyn and Bacon.

Sattler, J. M. (1982b). *Assessment of children's intelligence and special abilities* (Rev. ed.). Boston: Allyn & Bacon.

Sattler, J. M. (1988). *Assessment of children* (3rd ed.). San Diego, CA: Author.

Sattler, J. M. (1991). How good are federal judges in detecting differences in item difficulty on intelligence tests for ethnic groups? *Psychological Assessment: A Journal of Consulting and Clinical Psychology, 3,* 125–129.

Sattler, J. M., Andres, J. L., Squire, L. S., Wisely, R., & Maloy, C. F. (1978). Examiner scoring of ambiguous WISC-R responses. *Psychology in the Schools, 15,* 486–489.

Sattler, J. M., & Gwynne, J. (1982). White examiners generally do not impede the intelligence test performance of black children: To debunk a myth. *Journal of Consulting and Clinical Psychology, 50,* 196–208.

Sattler, J. M. & Ryan, J. J. (1981). Relationship between WISC-R and WRAT in children referred for learning difficulties. *Psychology in the Schools, 18,* 290–292.

Sattler, J. M., & Ryan, J. J. (1988). Wechsler Adult Intelligence Scale—Revised. In J. M. Sattler, *Assessment of children* (3rd ed.) (pp. 219–244). San Diego, CA: J. M. Sattler.

Sattler, J. M., Winget, B. M., & Roth, R. J. (1969). Scoring difficulty of WAIS and WISC Compre-hension, Similarities and Vocabulary responses. *Journal of Clinical Psychology, 25,* 175–177.

Satz, P. (1966). A block rotation task: The application of multi-variant and decision theory analysis for the prediction of organic brain disorders. *Psychological Monographs, 80* (21, Whole No. 629).

Saunders, E. A. (1991). Rorschach indicators of chronic childhood sexual abuse in female border-line inpatients. *Bulletin of the Menninger Clinic, 55,* 48–65.

Saunders, S. M., Howard, K., & Orlinsky, D. (1989). The Therapeutic Bond Scales: Psychometric characteristics and relationship to treatment effectiveness. *Psychological Assessment: A Journal of Consulting and Clinical Psychology, 1*(4), 323–330.

Savickas, M. L., Alexander, D. E., Osipow, S. H., & Wolf, F. M. (1985). Measuring specialty indecision among career-decided students. *Journal of Vocational Behavior, 27,* 356–357.

Saxton, J., McGonigle-Gibson, K. L., Swihart, A. A., Miller, V. J., & Boller, F. (1990). Assessment of the severely impaired patient: Description and validation of a new neuropsychological test battery. *Psychological Assessment: A Journal of Consulting and Clinical Psychology, 2,* 298–303.

Saylor, C. F. (1984). Construct validity for measures of childhood depression: Application of multitrait-multimethod methodology. *Journal of Consulting and Clinical Psychology, 52,* 977–985.

Saylor, C. F., Finch, A. J., Spirito, A., & Bennett, B. (1984). The Children's Depression Inventory: A systematic evaluation of psychometric properties. *Journal of Consulting and Clinical Psychology, 52,* 955–967.

Scalise, J. J., Ginter, E. J., & Gerstein, L. H. (1984). A multidimensional loneliness measure: The Loneliness Rating Scale (LRS). *Journal of Personality Assessment, 48,* 525–530.

Schaie, K. W. (1965). A general model for the study of development problems. *Psychological Bulletin, 64,* 92–107.

Schaie, K. W. (1973). Developmental processes and aging. In C. Eisdorfer & M. L. Lawton (Eds.), The psychology of adult development and aging. Washington, D.C.: American Psychological Association.

Schaie, K. W. 1974. Transactions in gerontology—From lab to life. *American Psychologist, 29,* 802–807.

Schaie, K. W. (1978). External validity in the assessment of intellectual development in adulthood. *Journal of Gerontology, 33,* 695–701.

Scherer, K. R. (1986). Vocal affect expression: A review and a model for future research. *Psychological Bulletin, 99,* 143–165.

Schiffman, S. S., Reynolds, M. L., & Young, F. W. (1981). *Introduction to multidimensional scaling: Theory, methods and applications.* New York: Academic Press.

Schlackman, W. A. (1984). A discussion of the use of sensitivity panels in market research: The use of trained respondents in qualitative studies. *Journal of the Market Research Society, 26,* 191–208.

Schloss, I. (1981). Chicken and pickles. *Journal of Advertising Research, 21,* 47–49.

Schmidt, F. L., Gast-Rosenberg, I., & Hunter, J. E. (1980). Validity generalization results for computer programmers. *Journal of Applied Psychology, 65,* 643–661.

Schmidt, F. L., & Hunter, J. E. (1977). Development of a general solution to the problem of validity generalization. *Journal of Applied Psychology, 64,* 609–626.

Schmidt, F. L., Hunter, J. E., McKenzie, R. C., & Muldrow, T. W. (1979). Impact of valid selection procedures on work force productivity. *Journal of Applied Psychology, 64,* 609–626.

Schmidt, F. L., & Hunter, J. E. (1984). A within setting empirical test of the situational specificity hypothesis in personnel selection. *Personnel Psychology, 37,* 317–326.

Schmidt, F. L., Hunter, J. E., Outerbridge, A. N., & Trattner, M. H. (1986). The economic impact of job selection methods on size, productivity, and payroll costs of the federal work force: An empirically based demonstration. *Personnel Psychology, 39,* 1–29.

Schmidt, F. L., Hunter, J. E., & Pearlman, K. (1981). Task differences as moderators of aptitude test validity in selection: A red herring. *Journal of Applied Psychology, 66,* 166–185.

Schmidt, F. L., Hunter, J. E., Pearlman, K., & Shane, G. S. (1979). Further tests of the Schmidt-Hunter Bayesian validity generalization model. *Personnel Psychology, 32,* 257–281.

Schmidt, F. L., Hunter, J. E., & Urry, V. W. (1976). Statistical power in criterion-related validation studies. *Journal of Applied Psychology, 61,* 473–485.

Schmitt, N. (1976). Social and situational determinants of interview decisions: Implications for the employment interview. *Personnel Psychology, 29,* 79–101.

Schneider, M. F. (1989). *Children's Apperceptive Story-telling Test.* Austin, TX: Pro-Ed.

Schneider, M. F., & Perney, J. (1990). Development of the Children's Apperceptive Story-telling Test. *Psychological Assessment: A Journal of Consulting and Clinical Psychology, 2,* 179–185.

Schooler, D. L., Beebe, M. C., & Koepke, T. (1978). Factor analysis of WISC-R scores for children identified as learning disabled, educable mentally impaired, and emotionally impaired. *Psychology in the Schools, 15,* 478–485.

Schuh, A. J. (1978). Contrast effect in the interview. *Bulletin of the Psychonomic Society, 11,* 195–196.

Schultz, D. P. (1969). *A history of modern psychology.* New York: Academic Press.

Schultz, D. P. (1982). *Psychology and industry today* (3rd ed.). New York: Macmillan.

Schwarting, F. G., & Schwarting, K. R. (1977). The relationship of the WISC-R and WRAT: A study based upon a selected population. *Psychology in the Schools, 14,* 431–433.

Schwartz, L. A. (1932). Social situation pictures in the psychiatric interview. *American Journal of Orthopsychiatry, 2,* 124–132.

Schwitzgebel, R. L., & Rugh, J. D. (1975). Of bread, circuses and alpha machines. *American Psychologist, 30,* 363–370.

Sears, R. R. (1977). Sources of life satisfaction of the Terman gifted men. *American Psychologist, 32,* 119–281.

Seashore, C. E. (1938). *Psychology of music.* New York: McGraw-Hill.

Sebold, J. (1987). Indicators of child sexual abuse in males. *Social Casework, 68,* 75–80.

Selby, M. J. (1984). The measurement of generalized self-efficacy: A study of construct validity. *Journal of Personality Assessment, 48,* 531–544.

Select Committee on Equal Educational Opportunity of the United States Senate. (1972). *Environment, intelligence, and scholastic achievement.* Washington, DC: U.S. Government Printing Office.

Selzer, M. L. (1971). The Michigan Alcoholism Screening Test: The quest for a new instrument. *American Journal of Psychiatry, 127,* 1653–1659.

Semrud-Clikeman, M. (1990). Assessment of childhood depression. In C. R. Reynolds & R. W. Kamphaus (Eds.), *Handbook of psychological and* educational assessment of children: Personality, behavior & context (pp. 279–297). New York: Guilford Press.

Serby, M., Corwin, J., Conrad, P., et al. (1985). Olfactory dysfunction in Alzheimer's disease and Parkinson's disease. *American Journal of Psychiatry, 142*, 781–782.

Serby, M., Larson, P., & Kalkstein, D. (1991). The nature and course of olfactory deficits in Alzheimer's disease. *American Journal of Psychiatry, 148*, 357–360.

Seretny, M. L., Dean, R. S., Gray, J. W., & Hartlage, L. C. (1986). The practice of clinical neuropsychology in the United States. *Archives of Clinical Neuropsychology, 1*, 5–12.

Serin, R. C., Peters, R. DeV., & Barbaree, H. E. (1990). Predictors of psychopathy and release outcome in a criminal population. *Psychological Assessment: A Journal of Consulting and Clinical Psychology, 2*, 419–422.

Sewell, T. E. (1977). A comparison of the WPPSI and Stanford-Binet Intelligence Scale among lower SES black children. *Psychology in the Schools, 14*, 158–161.

Seymour, D., & Lessne, G. (1984). Spousal conflict arousal: Scale developments. *Journal of Consumer Research, 11*, 810–821.

Shah, S. A. (1969). Privileged communications, confidentiality, and privacy: Privileged communications. *Professional Psychology, 1*, 56–59.

Shapiro, E. S., & Kratochwill, T. R. (Eds.). (1988). *Behavioral assessment in schools: Conceptual foundation and practical application.* New York: Guilford Press.

Shapiro, E. S., & Skinner, C. H. (1990). Principles of behavior assessment. In C. R. Reynolds & R. W. Kamphaus (Eds.), *Handbook of psychological and educational assessment of children: Personality, behavior & context* (pp. 343–363). New York: Guilford Press.

Share, J., Webb, A., & Koch, R. (1961). A preliminary investigation of the early developmental status of mongoloid infants. *American Journal of Mental Deficiency, 66*, 238.

Sharp, S. E. (1899). Individual psychology. *American Journal of Psychology, 10*, 329–391.

Shavelson, R. J., Webb, N. M., & Rowley, G. L. (1989). Generalizability theory. *American Psychologist, 44*, 922–932.

Sheldon, W. H., Dupertuis, C. W., & McDermott, E.

(1954). *Atlas of men: A guide for somatotyping the adult male of all ages.* New York: Harper & Row.

Sheldon, W. H., & Stevens. S. S. (1942). *The varieties of temperament: A psychology of constitutional differences.* New York: Harper.

Shelton, M. D., & Parsons, O. A. (1987). Alcoholics' self-assessment of their neuropsychology functioning in every day life. *Journal of Clinical Psychology, 43*, 395–403.

Shepard, L. A. (1983). The role of measurement in educational policy: Lessons from the identification of learning disabilities. *The Journal of Special Education, 14*, 79–91.

Sherman, L. J. (1958). The influence of artistic quality on judgments of patient and non-patient status from human figure drawings. *Journal of Projective Techniques, 22*, 338–340.

Sherrets, S., Gard, G., & Langner, H. (1979). Frequency of clerical errors on WISC protocols. *Psychology in the Schools, 16*, 495–496.

Shneidman, E. S. (1952). Manual for the Make a Picture Story Method. *Projective Techniques Monographs, 2.*

Shneidman, E. S. (1958). Some relationships between thematic and drawing materials. In E. F. Hammer (Ed.), *The clinical applications of projective drawings* (pp. 296–307). Springfield, IL: Charles C Thomas.

Shockley, W. (1971). Models, mathematics, and the moral obligation to diagnose the origin of Negro IQ deficits. *Review of Educational Research, 41*, 369–377.

Shuey, A. M. (1966). *The testing of Negro intelligence* (2nd ed.). New York: Social Science Press.

Shurrager, H. C., & Shurrager, P. S. (1964). *Manual for the Haptic Intelligence Scale for Adult Blind.* Chicago: Psychology Research.

Siegel, L. J. (1986). Review of The Children's Depression Inventory. In D. J. Keyser & R. C. Sweetland (Eds.), *Test critiques* (Vol. 5). Kansas City, MO: Test Corporation of America.

Siegler, R. S., & Richards, D. (1980). The development of intelligence. In R. S. Sternberg (Chair), *People's conception of the nature of intelligence.* Symposium presented at the 88th annual convention of the American Psychological Association, Montreal, Canada.

Silverstein, A. B. (1969). An alternative factor analytic solution for Wechsler's Intelligence Scales. *Educational and Psychological Measurement, 29*, 763–767.

Silverstein, A. B. (1977). Alternative factor analytic solutions for the Wechsler Intelligence Scale for Children—Revised. *Educational and Psychological Measurement, 37,* 121–124.

Silverstein, A. B. (1982). Factor structure of the Wechsler Adult Intelligence Scale—Revised. *Journal of Consulting and Clinical Psychology, 50,* 661–664.

Silverstein, A. B. (1990). Short forms of individual intelligence tests. *Psychological Assessment: A Journal of Consulting and Clinical Psychology, 2,* 3–11.

Silverstein, A., Brownlee, L., & Legutki, G. (1980). Reliability of the concept assessment kit—conservations for educable mentally retarded children. *Psychology in the Schools, 17,* 4–6.

Silverstein, A. B., & Fisher, G. M. (1960). Reanalysis of sex differences in the standardization data of the Wechsler Adult Intelligence Scale. *Psychological Reports, 7,* 405–406.

Simon, R. J. (1967). *The jury and the defense of insanity.* Boston: Little, Brown.

Simon, R. J., & Aaronson, D. E. (1988). *The insanity defense.* New York: Praeger.

Simpson, R. (1970). Study of the comparability of the WISC and WAIS. *Journal of Consulting and Clinical Psychology, 2,* 156–158.

Sines, J. O. (1966). Actuarial methods in personality assessment. In B. Maher (Ed.), *Progress in experimental personality research* (Vol. 3; pp. 133–193). New York: Academic Press.

Sines, J. O. (1985). Review of the Roberts Apperception Test for Children. In J. V. Mitchell, Jr. (Ed.), *The ninth mental measurements yearbook* (pp. 1289–1291). Lincoln: Buros Institute of Mental Measurements, University of Nebraska.

Skibbe, A. (1986). Assessing campus needs with nominal groups. *Journal of Counseling and Development, 64,* 532–533.

Skinner, H. A., & Allen, B. A. (1983). Does the computer make a difference? Computerized versus face-to-face versus self-report assessment of alcohol, drug, and tobacco use. *Journal of Consulting and Clinical Psychology, 51,* 267–275.

Skolnick, J. H. (1961). Scientific theory and scientific evidence. An analysis of lie detection. *Yale Law Journal, 70,* 694–728.

Slade, P. D. (1985). A review of body-image studies in anorexia nervosa and bulimia nervosa. *Journal of Psychiatric Research, 19,* 255–265.

Slay, D. K. (1984). A portable Halstead-Reitan Category Test. *Journal of Clinical Psychology, 40,* 1023–1027.

Sloan, W., & Birch, J. W. (1955). A rationale for degrees of retardation. *American Journal of Mental Deficiency, 60,* 258–264.

Slobogin, C. (1985). The guilty but mentally ill verdict: An idea whose time should not have come. *George Washington Law Review, 53,* 494–527.

Slosson, R. L. (1963). *Slosson Intelligence Test (SIT) for children and adults.* New York: Slosson Educational Publications.

Slosson, R. L. (1991). *Slosson Intelligence Test (SIT-R).* East Aurora, NY: Slosson Educational Publications.

Smith, A. (1962). Ambiguities in concepts and studies of "brain damage" and "organicity." *Journal of Nervous and Mental Disease, 135,* 311–326.

Smith, D. E. (1986). Training programs for performance appraisal: A review. *Academy of Management Review, 11,* 22–40.

Smith, D. K. (1985). *Test use and perceived competency: A survey of school psychologists.* Unpublished manuscript, University of Wisconsin-River Falls, School Psychology Program, River Falls, WI.

Smith, D. K., & Bauer, J. J. (1989). Intelligence measures in a preschool sample: S-B:FE and K-ABC relationships. Paper presented at the Annual Meeting of the American Psychological Association, New Orleans, LA. (ERIC Document Reproduction Service No. ED 316 574)

Smith, D. K., Bauer, J. J., & Lyon, M. A. (1987, April). Young children's performance on three measures of ability. Paper presented at the Annual Meeting of American Educational Research Association, Washington, DC. (ERIC Document Reproduction Service No. ED 281 874)

Smith, D. K., Bolin, J. A., & Stovall, D. R. (1988). K-ABC stability in a preschool sample: A longitudinal study. *Journal of Psychoeducational Assessment, 6,* 396–403.

Smith, D. K., & Knudtson, L. S. (1990). K-ABC and S-B:FE relationships in an at-risk preschool sample. Paper presented at the Annual Meeting of the American Psychological Association, Boston.

Smith, D. K., Lasee, M. J., & McCloskey, G. M. (1990). Test-retest reliability of the AGS Early Screening Profiles. Paper presented at the Annual Meeting of the National Association of School Psychologists, San Francisco.

Smith, D. K., Lasee, M. J., Steenson, K. A., & Ouradnik, L. (1991). The Early Screening Profiles: A stability study. Paper presented at the Annual Meeting of the National Association of School Psychologists, Dallas, TX.

Smith, D. K., & Lyon, M. A. (1987). Children with learning difficulties: Differences in ability patterns as a function of placement. Paper presented at the Annual Meeting of the American Educational Research Association, Washington, DC. (ERIC Document Reproduction Service No. ED 285 317)

Smith, D. K., Lyon, M. A., Hunter, E., & Boyd, R. (1988). Relationships between the K-ABC and WISC-R for students referred for severe learning disabilities. *Journal of Learning Disabilities, 21,* 509–513.

Smith, D. K., St. Martin, M. E., & Lyon, M. A. (1989). A validity study of the Stanford-Binet: Fourth Edition with students with learning disabilities. *Journal of Learning Disabilities, 22,* 260–261.

Smith, G. M. (1985). The Collaborative Drawing Technique. *Journal of Personality Assessment, 49,* 582–585.

Smith, M. (1948). Cautions concerning the use of the Taylor-Russell tables in employee selection. *Journal of Applied Psychology, 32,* 595–600.

Smith, M. C., & Thelen, M. H. (1984). Development and validation of a test for bulimia. *Journal of Consulting and Clinical Psychology, 52,* 863–872.

Smith, M. H., May, W. T., & Lebovitz, L. (1966). Testing experience and Stanford-Binet scores. *Journal of Educational Measurement, 3,* 229–233.

Smith, P. C., Kendall, L. M., & Hulin, C. L. (1969). *The measurement of satisfaction in work and retirement.* Chicago: Rand McNally.

Smith, R. E. (1963). Examination by computer. *Behavioral Science, 8,* 76–79.

Smith, S. R., & Meyer, R. G. (1987). *Law, behavior and mental health: Policy and practice.* New York: New York University Press.

Smither, J. W., Reilly, R. R., & Buda, R. (1988). Effect of prior performance information on ratings of present performance: Contrast versus assimilation revisited. *Journal of Applied Psychology, 73,* 487–496.

Smucker, M. R., Craighead, W. E., Craighead, L. W., & Green, B. J. (1986). Normative and reliability data for the Children's Depression Inventory. *Journal of Abnormal Child Psychology, 14,* 25–39.

Snyder, C. R. (1974). Acceptance of personality interpretations as a function of assessment procedures. *Journal of Consulting and Clinical Psychology, 42,* 150.

Snyder, C. R., & Larson, G. R. (1972). A further look at student acceptance of general personality interpretations. *Journal of Consulting and Clinical Psychology, 38,* 384–388.

Snyder, C. R., & Newburg, C. L. (1981). The Barnum effect in a group setting. *Journal of Personality Assessment, 45,* 622–629.

Snyder, C. R., & Shenkel, R. J. (1976). Effects of "favorability," modality, and relevance on acceptance of general personality interpretations prior to and after receiving diagnostician feedback. *Journal of Consulting and Clinical Psychology, 44,* 34–41.

Snyder, C. R., Shenkel, R. J., & Schmidt, A. (1976). Effects of role perspective and client psychiatric history on locus of problem. *Journal of Consulting and Clinical Psychology, 44,* 467–472.

Snyder, C. R., Shenkel, R. J., & Lowery, C. R. (1977). Acceptance of personality interpretations: The "Barnum effect" and beyond. *Journal of Consulting and Clinical Psychology, 45,* 104–114.

Snyder, D. K. (1981). *Marital Satisfaction Inventory (MSI) manual.* Los Angeles: Western Psychological Services.

Snyder, D. K., & Hoover, D. W. (1989, August). *Validity of the computerized interpretive report for the Marital Satisfaction Inventory.* Paper presented at the Annual Convention of the American Psychological Association, New Orleans.

Snyder, D. K., Lachar, D., & Wills, R. M. (1988). Computer-based interpretation of the Marital Satisfaction Inventory: Use in treatment planning. *Journal of Marital and Family Therapy, 14,* 397–409.

Snyder, D. K., Widiger, T. A., & Hoover, D. W. (in press). Methodological considerations in validating computer-based test interpretations: Controlling for response bias. *Journal of Consulting and Clinical Psychology.*

Sokal, M. M. (1991). Psyche Cattell (1893–1989). *American Psychologist, 46,* 72.

Solomon, I. L., & Starr, B. D. (1968). *The School Apperception Method.* New York: Springer.

Sontag, L. W., Baker, C. T., & Nelson, V. L. (1958). Personality as a determinant of performance. *American Journal of Orthopsychiatry, 25,* 555–562.

Spanier, G. (1976). Measuring dyadic adjustment: New scales for assessing the quality of marriage and similar dyads. *Journal of Marriage and the Family, 38*, 15–28.

Spanier, G. B., & Filsinger, E. (1983). The Dyadic Adjustment Scale. In E. Filsinger (Ed.), *Marriage and family assessment*. Beverly Hills, CA: Sage.

Sparrow, S., Balla, D. A., & Cicchetti, D. V. (1984). *Vineland Adaptive Behavior Scale* (Revised). Circle Pines, MN: American Guidance Service.

Spearman, C. (1927). *The abilities of man: Their nature and measurement*. New York: Macmillan.

Spearman, C. S. (1930–1936). Autobiography. In C. Murchison (Ed.), *A history of psychology in autobiography* (3 vols.). Worcester, MA: Clark University Press.

Spence, N. D., Goldney, R. D., & Moffitt, P. F. (1984). Factorial structure of the Aftermath of Suicide Instrument. *Journal of Clinical Psychology, 40*, 1426–1430.

Spielberger, C. D., et al. (1980a). *Preliminary Manual for the State-Trait Anger Scale*. Center for Research in Community Psychology, University of South Florida, Tampa, FL.

Spielberger, C. D., et al. (1980b). *Test Anxiety Inventory-Research Edition*. Palo Alto, CA: Consulting Psychologists Press.

Spielberger, C. D., Edwards, C. D., Montuori, J., & Lushene, R. (1973). *State-Trait Anxiety Inventory for Children*. Palo Alto, CA: Consulting Psychologists Press.

Spielberger, C. D., Gorsuch, R. L., & Lushene, R. E. (1970). *State-Trait Anxiety Inventory*. Palo Alto, CA: Consulting Psychologists Press.

Spielberger, C. D., & Piotrowski, C. (1990). Clinician's attitudes toward computer-based testing. *The Clinical Psychologist, 43*, 60–63.

Spielman, A. J. (1986). Assessment of insomnia. *Clinical Psychology Review, 6*, 11–25.

Spitzer, R. L. (1983). Psychiatric diagnosis: Are clinicians still necessary? *Comprehensive psychiatry, 24*, 399–411.

Spitznagel, E. L., & Helzer, J. E. (1985). A proposed solution to the base rate problem in the kappa statistic. *Archives of General Psychiatry, 42*, 725–728.

Spivack, G., & Spotts, J. (1966). *Devereux Child Behavior Rating Scale Manual*. Devon, PA: Devereux Foundation.

Spivack, G., Spotts, J., & Haimes, P. E. (1967). *Devereux Adolescent Behavior Rating Scale*. Devon, PA: Devereux Foundation Press.

Spranger, E. (1928). *Types of men* (P. J. W. Pigors, Trans.). Halle: Niemeyer.

Spreen, O., & Benton, A. L. (1965). Comparative studies of some psychological tests for cerebral damage. *Journal of Nervous and Mental Disease, 140*, 323–333.

Spreen, O., & Benton, A. L. (1969). *Neurosensory Center Comprehensive Examination for Aphasia*. Victoria, Canada: University of Victoria.

Stambrook, M. (1983). The Luria-Nebraska Neuropsychological Battery: A promise that *may* be partly fulfilled. *Journal of Clinical Neuropsychology, 5*, 247–269.

Standards for educational and psychological tests and manuals. (1966). Washington, DC: American Psychological Association.

Standards for educational and psychological tests and manuals. (1974). Washington, DC: American Psychological Association.

Standards for educational and psychological testing. (1985). Washington, DC: American Psychological Association.

Standing, L. G., & Keays, G. (1986). Computer assessment of personality: A demonstration of gullibility. *Social Behavior and Personality, 14*, 197–202.

Stankov, L., Fogarty, G., & Watt, C. (1989). Competing tasks: Predictors of managerial potential. *Personality and Individual Differences, 10*, 295–302.

Stanley, J. C. (1971). Reliability. In R. L. Thorndike (Ed.), *Educational measurement* (2nd ed.). Washington, DC: American Council on Education.

Starch, D., & Elliot, E. C. (1912). Reliability of grading of high school work in English. *School Review, 20*, 442–457.

Stark-Adamec, C., & Adamec, R. E. (1986). Psychological methodology versus clinical impressions: Different perspectives on psychopathology and seizures. In B. K. Doane & K. E. Livingstone (Eds.), *The limbic system: Functional organization and clinical disorders* (pp. 217–227). New York: Raven Press.

Stehouwer, R. S. (1985). Review of Beck Depression Inventory. In D. J. Keyser & R. C. Sweetland (Eds.), *Test critiques* (Vol. 2; pp. 83–87). Kansas City, MO: Test Corporation of America.

Stephenson, W. (1953). *The study of behavior: Q-*

technique and its methodology. Chicago: University of Chicago Press.

Stephenson, W. (1980). Newton's fifth rule and q-methodology: Application to educational psychology. *American Psychologist, 35*, 882–889.

Stern, W. (1914). *The psychological method of testing intelligence*. Baltimore: Warwick & York.

Sternberg, R. J. (1981). The nature of intelligence. *New York Education Quarterly, 12*(3), 10–17.

Sternberg, R. J. (1982, April). Who's intelligent? *Psychology Today*, pp. 30–33, 35–36, 38–39.

Sternberg, R. J. (1985). *Beyond IQ: A triarchic theory of human intelligence*. Cambridge: Cambridge University Press.

Sternberg, R. J. (1987, September 23). Commentary: The uses and measures of intelligence testing. *Education Week*, pp. 22, 28.

Sternberg, R. J., Conway, B. E., Ketron, J. L., & Bernstein, M. (1981). People's conceptions of intelligence. *Journal of Personality and Social Psychology, 41*, 37–55.

Stevens, G., & Gardner, S. (1982). *The women of psychology: Vol. 2. Expansion and refinement*. Cambridge, MA: Schenkman.

Stevens, M. R., & Reilley, R. R. (1980). MMPI short forms: A literature review. *Journal of Personality Assessment, 44*, 368–376.

Stewart, D. W. (1984). Physiological measurement of advertising effects: An unfulfilled promise. *Psychology & Marketing, 1*, 43–48.

Stewart, D. W., & Furse, D. H. (1982). Applying psychophysiological measures to marketing and advertising research problems (pp. 1–38). *Current issues and research in advertising*. Ann Arbor: University of Michigan.

Stewart, K. D., & Jones, E. L. (1976). Validity of the Slosson Intelligence Test: A ten year review. *Psychology in the Schools, 13*, 372–380.

Stillman, R. (1974). *Assessment of deaf-blind children: The Callier-Azusa Scale*. Paper presented at the Intercom '74, Hyannis, MA.

Stith, M. T. (Ed.). (1989). Psychology, marketing, and the black community (Special issue). *Psychology & Marketing, 6*, 249–347.

Stokes, J. B. (1977). Comment on "Socially reinforced obsessing: Etiology of a disorder in a Christian Scientist." *Journal of Consulting and Clinical Psychology, 45*, 1164–1165.

Stone, A. A. (1986). Vermont adopts *Tarasoff*: A real

barn-burner. *American Journal of Psychiatry, 143*, 352–355.

Stoner, S. (1978). Sex differences in responses of children to the Hand Test. *Perceptual and Motor Skills, 46*, 759–762.

Stotland, S., & Zuroff, D. (1990). A new measure of weight locus of control: The Dieting Beliefs Scale. *Journal of Personality Assessment, 54*, 191–203.

Stott, L. H., & Ball, R. (1965). *Evaluation of infant and preschool mental tests*. Detroit: Merrill-Palmer Institute.

Stoudemire, A., & Hales, R. E. (1991). Psychological and behavioral factors affecting medical conditions and DSM-IV. *Psychosomatics, 32*, 5–13.

Straus, M. A. (1979). Measuring intrafamily conflict and violence: The Conflict Tactics (CT) Scales. *Journal of Marriage and the Family, 41*, 75–85.

Straus, M. A., & Brown, B. (1978). *Family measurement techniques: Abstracts of published instruments, 1935–1974*. Minneapolis: University of Minnesota Press.

Strauss, A. A., & Lehtinen, L. E. (1947). *Psychopathology and education of the brain injured child*. New York: Grune & Stratton.

Streiner, D. L., & Miller, H. R. (1989). The MCMI-II: How much better than the MCMI? *Journal of Personality Assessment, 53*, 81–84.

Stricker, G., & Healey, B. J. (1990). Projective assessment of object relations: A review of the empirical literature. *Psychological Assessment: A Journal of Consulting & Clinical Psychology, 2*, 219–230.

Stricker, L. J., Messick, S., & Jackson, D. N. (1968). Desirability judgments and self-reports as predictors of social behavior. *Journal of Experimental Research in Personality, 3*, 151–167.

Strong, E. K., Jr., Hansen, J. C., & Campbell, D. C. (1985). *Strong Vocational Interest Blank. Revised edition of Form T325, Strong-Campbell Interest Inventory*. Stanford, CA: Stanford University Press (Distributed by Consulting Psychologists Press).

Sturmey, P., Newton, T., & Ghadiali, E. (1988). Psychometric properties of the Pain Assessment Questionnaire. *British Journal of Clinical Psychology, 27*, 183–184.

Subkoviak, M. J. (1980). The reliability of mastery classification decisions. In R. A. Burk (Ed.), *Criterion-referenced measurement: The state of the art*. Baltimore: Johns Hopkins University Press.

Suczek, R. F., & Klopfer, W. G. (1952). Interpretation

of the Bender-Gestalt Test: The associative value of the figures. *American Journal of Orthopsychiatry, 22,* 62–75.

Sugarman, A. (1991). Where's the beef? Putting personality back into personality assessment. *Journal of Personality Assessment, 56,* 130–144.

Sullivan, H. S. (1953). *The interpersonal theory of psychiatry.* New York: Norton.

Sullivan, P. M., & Vernon, M. (1979). Psychological assessment of hearing impaired children. *School Psychology Digest, 8,* 271–287.

Sundberg, N. D. (1955). The acceptability of "fake" versus "bona fide" personality test interpretations. *Journal of Abnormal and Social Psychology, 50,* 145–147.

Sundberg, N. D., Latkin, C. A., Littman, R. A., & Hagan, R. A. (1990). Personality in a religious commune: CPIs in Rajneeshpuram. *Journal of Personality Assessment, 55,* 7–17.

Sundberg, N. D., & Tyler, L. E. (1962). *Clinical psychology.* New York: Appleton-Century-Crofts.

Super, D. E. (1970). *Work Values Inventory.* Boston: Houghton Mifflin.

Supp, G. L., & Sutherland, L. J. (1980). Relationships between intellectual ability, standardized tests and academic achievement. Proceedings from the NASP National Convention, p. 131.

Sutker, P. B., Allain, A. N., Smith, C. J., & Cohen, G. H. (1978). Addict descriptions of therapeutic community, multimodality, and methadone maintenance treatment clients and staff. *Journal of Consulting and Clinical Psychology, 46,* 508–517.

Sutker, P. B., Bugg, F., & Allain, A. N. (1991). Psychometric prediction of PTSD among POW survivors. *Psychological Assessment: A Journal of Consulting and Clinical Psychology, 3,* 105–110.

Sutker, P. B., Winstead, D. K., Galina, Z. H., & Allain, A. N. (1990). Assessment of long-term psychosocial sequelae among POW survivors of the Korean Conflict. *Journal of Personality Assessment, 54,* 170–180.

Sweeney, J. A., Clarkin, J. F., & Fitzgibbon, M. L. (1987). Current practice of psychological assessment. *Professional Psychology: Research and Practice, 18,* 377–380.

Sweetland, R., & Keyser, D. (Eds.) (1986). *Tests* (2nd ed.). Kansas City, MO: Test Corporation of America.

Swensen, C. H. (1968). Empirical evaluations of human figure drawings: 1957–1966. *Psychological Bulletin, 70,* 20–44.

Swenson, W. M., Pearson, J. S., & Osborne, D. (1973). *An MMPI source book: Basic item, scale, and pattern data on 50,000 medical patients.* Minneapolis: University of Minnesota Press.

Swerdlik, M. E. (1985). Review of Brigance Diagnostic Comprehensive Inventory of Basic Skills. In J. V. Mitchell, Jr. (Ed.), *The ninth mental measurements yearbook,* pp. 214–215. Lincoln: The Buros Institute of Mental Measurements, University of Nebraska.

Swerdlik, M. E. (1988). A concurrent validity study of the Stanford-Binet Fourth Edition and three measures of classroom achievement. Paper presented at the Annual Meeting of the National Association of School Psychologists, Chicago.

Swerdlik, M. E. (1991). Review of the Otis–Lennon School Ability Test. In J. J. Kramer & J. C. Conoley (Eds.), *The eleventh mental measurements yearbook.* Lincoln: The Buros Institute of Mental Measurements, University of Nebraska.

Swerdlik, M. E., & Dornback, F. (1988, April). *An interpretation guide to the fourth edition of the Stanford-Binet Intelligence Scale.* Paper presented at the annual meeting of the National Association of School Psychologists, Chicago.

Swerdlik, M. E., & Ryburn, M. (1989). A construct validity study of the Stanford-Binet: Fourth Edition and Wechsler Intelligence Scale for Children—Revised. Paper presented at the Annual Meeting of the National Association of School Psychologists, Boston.

Swift, J. W. (1944). Reliability of Rorschach scoring categories with pre-school children. *Child Development, 15,* 207–216.

Swoboda, J. S., Elwork, A., Sales, B. D., & Levine, D. (1978). Knowledge of and compliance with privileged communication and child-abuse-reporting laws. *Professional Psychology, 9,* 448–457.

Sylvester, R. H. (1913). Clinical psychology adversely criticized. *Psychological Clinic, 7,* 182–188.

Symonds, P. M. (1949). *Adolescent fantasy: An investigation of the picture-story method of personality study.* New York: Columbia University Press.

Synodinos, N. E. (1988). Review and appraisal of subliminal perception within the context of signal detection theory. *Psychology & Marketing, 5,* 317–336.

Szondi, L. (1947). *Experimentelle Triebdiagnostik*. Bern: Hans Huber.

Szondi, L. (1948). *Schicksalsanalyse*. Basel: Benno Schwabe.

Tallent, N. (1958). On individualizing the psychologist's clinical evaluation. *Journal of Clinical Psychology, 14*, 243–244.

Tamkin, A. S., & Kunce, J. T. (1985). A comparison of three neuropsychological tests: The Weigl, Hooper and Benton. *Journal of Clinical Psychology, 41*, 660–664.

Tasto, D. L. (1977). Self-report schedules and inventories. In A. R. Ciminero, K. S. Calhoun, & H. E. Adams (Eds.), *Handbook of behavioral assessment*. New York: Wiley.

Taylor, H. C., & Russell, J. T. (1939). The relationship of validity coefficients to the practical effectiveness of tests in selection. *Journal of Applied Psychology, 23*, 565–578.

Taylor, L. B. (1979). Psychological assessment of neurosurgical patients. In T. Rasmussen & R. Marino (Eds.), *Functional neurosurgery*. New York: Raven Press.

Teague, W. (State Superintendent of Education) (1983). *Basic competency education: Reading, language, mathematics specifications for the Alabama High School Graduation Examination* (Bulletin No. 4). Montgomery: Alabama State Department of Education.

Tellegen, A., et al. (1969). Personality characteristics of members of a serpent-handling religious cult. In J. Butcher (Ed.), *MMPI: Research developments and clinical applications*. New York: McGraw-Hill.

Telzrow, C. F. (1985). Best practices in reducing learning disability qualification. In A. Thomas & J. Grimes (Eds.), *Best practices in school psychology*. Kent, OH: National Association of School Psychologists.

Templer, D. I., King, F. L., Brooner, R. K., & Corgiat, M. D. (1984). Assessment of body elimination attitude. *Journal of Clinical Psychology, 40*, 751–753.

Terman, L. M. (1911). The Binet-Simon scale for measuring intelligence: Impressions gained by its application. *Psychological Clinic, 5*, 199–206.

Terman, L. M. (1916). *The measurement of intelligence*. Boston: Houghton Mifflin.

Terman, L. M., et al. (1925). *The mental and physical traits of a thousand gifted children: Vol. 1. Genetic studies of genius*. Stanford, CA: Stanford University Press.

Terman, L. M., & Childs, H. G. (1912). A tentative revision and extension of the Binet-Simon Measuring Scale of Intelligence. *Journal of Educational Psychology, 3*, 61–74, 133–143, 198–208, 277–289.

Terman, L. M., & Merrill, M. A. (1960). *Stanford-Binet Intelligence Scale Manual for the third revision, Form L-M*. Boston: Houghton Mifflin.

Terman, L. M., & Tyler, L. E. (1954). Psychological sex differences. In L. Carmichael (Ed.), *Manual of child psychology* (2nd ed.; pp. 1004–1114). New York: Wiley.

Tharinger, D. J., & Stark, K. (1990). A qualitative versus quantitative approach to evaluating the Draw-A-Person and Kinetic Family Drawing: A study of mood- and anxiety-disorder children. *Psychological Assessment: A Journal of Consulting and Clinical Psychology, 2*, 365–375.

The College Board Review (1990–91, Winter). Roundtable: The new SAT: Debating its implications. *The College Board Review, 158*, 22–27.

Thelen, M. H., Farmer, J., Wonderlich, S., & Smith, M. (1991). A revision of the Bulimia Test: The BULIT-R. *Psychological Assessment: A Journal of Consulting and Clinical Psychology, 3*, 119–124.

The Psychological Corporation. (1991). *Weschler Intelligence Scale for Children—Third Edition: An update*. San Antonio, TX: Author.

Theron, P. A. (1948). Peripheral vasomotor reactions as indices of basic emotional tension and lability. *Psychosomatic Medicine, 10*, 335–346.

Theye, F. W. (1970). Violation of standard procedure on the Wechsler Scales. *Journal of Clinical Psychology, 26*, 70–71.

Thomas, H. (1970). Psychological assessment instruments for use with human infants. *Merrill-Palmer Quarterly, 10*, 179–223.

Thompson, A. E. (1986). An object relational theory of affect maturity: Applications to the Thematic Apperception Test. In M. Kissen (Ed.), *Assessing object relations phenomena* (pp. 207–224). Madison, CT: International Universities Press.

Thompson, C. (1949). The Thompson modification of the Thematic Apperception Test. *Journal of Projective Techniques, 13*, 469–478.

Thompson, J. K. (1990). *Body image disturbance: Assessment and treatment*. Elmsford, NY: Pergamon Press.

Thompson, J. K., & Spana, R. E. (1988). The adjustable light beam method for the assessment of size estimation accuracy: Description, psychometric, and normative data. *International Journal of Eating Disorders, 7,* 521–526.

Thompson, J. K., & Thompson, C. M. (1986). Body size distortion and self-esteem in asymptomatic, normal weight males and females. *International Journal of Eating Disorders, 5,* 1061–1068.

Thompson, J. M., & Sones, R. (1973). *The Education Apperception Test.* Los Angeles: Western Psychological Services.

Thompson, R. J., & Curry, J. F. (1985). Missouri Children Behavior Checklist profiles with developmentally disabled children: Construct validity. *Journal of Clinical Psychology, 41,* 556–564.

Thompson, T. L., II, & Smith, T. C. (1991). Costumed figures may produce iatrogenic symptoms in delirious patients. *Psychosomatics, 32,* 1–4.

Thorndike, E. L., et al. (1921). Intelligence and its measurement: A symposium. *Journal of Educational Psychology, 12,* 123–147, 195–216.

Thorndike, E. L., Bregman, E. O., Cobb, M. V., Woodward, E., & the staff of the Division of Psychology of the Institute of Educational Research of Teachers College, Columbia University. (1927). *The measurement of intelligence.* New York: Bureau of Publications, Teachers College, Columbia University.

Thorndike, E. L., Lay, W., & Dean, P. R. (1909). The relation of accuracy in sensory discrimination to general intelligence. *American Journal of Psychology, 20,* 364–369.

Thorndike, R. (1985). Reliability. *Journal of Counseling & Development, 63,* 528–530.

Thorndike, R. L., Hagen, E. P., & Sattler, J. P. (1986a). *Guide for administering and scoring the fourth edition of the Stanford-Binet Intelligence Scale.* Chicago: Riverside Publishing.

Thorndike, R. L., Hagen, E. P., & Sattler, J. P. (1986b). *Technical manual for the Stanford-Binet Intelligence Scale, Fourth Edition.* Chicago: Riverside Publishing.

Thorndike, R. L., & Scott, J. (1986). Assessing the pattern and level of cognitive abilities with the fourth edition of the Stanford-Binet. In G. J. Robertson (Chair), *Perspectives on intellectual assessments: 1986.* Symposium presented at the 94th annual convention of the American Psychological Association, Washington, DC.

Thorndike, R. M. (1990). *A century of ability testing.* Chicago: Riverside Publishing.

Thornton, G. C., & Byham, W. C. (1982). *Assessment centers and managerial performance.* New York: Academic Press.

Thurber, S., Snow, M., & Thurber, D. (1990). Psychometric properties of the Child Evaluation Inventory. *Psychological Assessment: A Journal of Consulting and Clinical Psychology, 2,* 206–208.

Thurstone, L. L. (1925). A method of scaling psychological and educational tests. *Journal of Educational Psychology, 16,* 433–451.

Thurstone, L. L. (1926). The mental age concept. *Psychological Review, 33,* 268–278.

Thurstone, L. L. (1927). A law of comparative judgment. *Psychological Review, 34,* 273–286.

Thurstone, L. L. (1929). Theory of attitude measurement. *Psychological Bulletin, 36,* 222–241.

Thurstone, L. L. (1938). Primary mental abilities. *Psychometric Monographs,* No. 1. Chicago: University of Chicago Press.

Thurstone, L. L. (1947). *Multiple factor analysis.* Chicago: University of Chicago Press.

Thurstone, L. L. (1959). *The measurement of values.* Chicago: University of Chicago Press.

Thurstone, L. L., & Chave, E. J. (1929). *The measurement of attitude.* Chicago: University of Chicago Press.

Thurstone, L. L., & Thurstone, T. G. (1962). *Primary Mental Abilities* (Rev. ed.). Chicago: Science Research Associates.

Tillman, M. H. (1973). Intelligence scale for the blind: A review with implications for research. *Journal of School Psychology, 11,* 80–87.

Timex and VALS engineer product launch. (1984, September). *Ad Forum,* 12–14.

Tinsley, H. E., & Tinsley, D. J. (1987). Uses of factor analysis in counseling psychology research. *Journal of Counseling Psychology, 34,* 414–424.

Tittle, C. K. (1975). Review of the Wechsler Intelligence Scale for Children—Revised. *Journal of Educational Measurement, 12,* 140.

Tittle, C. R., & Hill, R. J. (1967). Attitude measurement and prediction of behavior: An evaluation of conditions and measurement techniques. *Sociometry, 30,* 199–213.

Tolor, A., & Brannigan, G. G. (1980). *Research and clinical applications of the Bender-Gestalt test.* Springfield, IL: Charles C Thomas.

Torgerson, W. S. (1958). *Theory and methods of scaling.* New York: Wiley.

Toronto, A. S. (1973). *Screening test of Spanish grammar.* Evanston, IL: Northwestern University Press.

Toronto, A. S. (1976). Developmental assessment of Spanish grammar. *Journal of Speech and Hearing Disorders, 41,* 150–171.

Toronto, A. S., Leverman, D., Hanna, C., et al. (1975). *Del Rio language screening test.* Austin, TX: National Educational Laboratory Publishers.

Torrance, E. P. (1966). *Torrance Tests of Creative Thinking.* Bensenville, IL: Scholastic Testing Service.

Torrance, E. P. (1974). *The Torrance Tests of Creative Thinking: Technical-norms manual.* Bensenville, IL: Scholastic Testing Service.

Torrance, E. P. (1987a). *Guidelines for administration and scoring/comments on using the Torrance Tests of Creative Thinking.* Bensenville, IL: Scholastic Testing Service.

Torrance, E. P. (1987b). *Survey of the uses of the Torrance Tests of Creative Thinking.* Bensenville, IL: Scholastic Testing Service.

Torrance, E. P., Khatena, J., & Cunningham, B. F. (1973). *Thinking Creatively with Sounds and Words.* Bensenville, IL: Scholastic Testing Service.

Tramonta, M. G., Hooper, S. R., & Selzer, S. C. (1988). Research on the preschool prediction of later academic achievement: A review. *Developmental Review, 8,* 89–146.

Trautscholdt, M. (1883). Experimentelle Unterschungen uber die association der vorstellungen. *Philosophesche Studien, 1,* 213–250.

Travin, S., Cullen, K., & Melella, J. T. (1988). The use and abuse of erection measurements: A forensic perspective. *Bulletin of the American Academy of Psychiatry and Law, 16,* 235–250.

Traylor, M. B., & Joseph, W. B. (1984). Measuring consumer involvement in products: Developing a general scale. *Psychology & Marketing, 1,* 65–77.

Trimble, M. R. (Ed.). (1986). *New brain imaging techniques and psychopharmacology.* Oxford: Oxford University Press.

Truscott, D. (1990). Assessment of overcontrolled hostility in adolescence. *Psychological Assessment: A Journal of Consulting & Clinical Psychology, 2,* 145–148.

Trybus, R. J. (1973). Personality assessment of entering hearing-impaired college students using the 16PF, Form E. *Journal of Rehabilitation of the Deaf, 116,* 427–434.

Tryon, R. C. (1957). Reliability and behavior domain validity: Reformulation and historical critique. *Psychological Bulletin, 54,* 229–249.

Tsudzuki, A., Hata, Y., & Kuze, T. (1957). A study of rapport between examiner and subject. *Japanese Journal of Psychology, 27,* 22–28.

Tsujimoto, R. N., Hamilton, M., & Berger, D. E. (1990). Averaging multiple judges to improve validity: Aid to planning cost-effective research. *Psychological Assessment: A Journal of Consulting & Clinical Psychology, 2,* 432–437.

Tuddenham, R. D. (1968). *Psychometricizing Piaget's méthode clinique.* Paper presented at the annual convention of the American Educational Research Association (February), Chicago, IL.

Tukey, J. W. (1977). *Exploratory data analysis.* Reading, MA: Addison-Wesley.

Tulchin, S. H. (1939). The clinical training of psychologists and allied specialists. *Journal of Consulting Psychology, 3,* 105–112.

Turco, T. L. (1989). Review of the Bracken Basic Concept Scale. In J. C. Conoley & J. J. Kramer (Eds.), *The tenth mental measurements yearbook* (pp. 102–104), Lincoln: The Buros Institute of Mental Measurements, University of Nebraska-Lincoln.

Turner, C. (1990). How much alcohol is in a "standard drink"? An analysis of 125 studies. *British Journal of Addiction, 85,* 1171–1175.

Turner, D. R. (1966). Predictive efficiency as a function of amount of information and level of professional experience. *Journal of Projective Techniques and Personality Assessment, 30,* 4–11.

Turner, S., Beidel, D., Dancu, C., & Stanley, M. (1989). An empirically derived inventory to measure social fears and anxiety: The Social Phobic and Anxiety Inventory. *Psychological Assessment: A Journal of Consulting and Clinical Psychology, 1,* 35–40.

Tuttle, F. B., & Becker, A. (1980). *Characteristics and identification of gifted and talented students.* Washington, DC: National Education Association.

Tyler, L. E. (1961). Research explorations in the realm of choice. *Journal of Counseling Psychology, 8,* 195–202.

Tyler, L. E. (1965). *The psychology of human differences* (3rd ed.). New York: Appleton-Century-Crofts.

Tyler, R. W. (1978). *The Florida Accountability program: An evaluation of its educational soundness and implementation.* Washington, DC: National Education Association.

Tziner, A., & Eden, D. (1985). Effects of crew composition on crew performance: Does the whole equal the sum of its parts? *Journal of Applied Psychology, 70,* 85–93.

Udry, J. R. (1981). Marital alternatives and marital disruption. *Journal of Marriage and the Family, 43,* 889–897.

Ulrich, R. E., Stachnik, T. J., & Stainton, N. R. (1963). Student acceptance of generalized personality interpretations. *Psychological Reports, 13,* 831–834.

Umberger, F. G. (1985). Peabody Picture Vocabulary Test—Revised. In D. J. Keyser & R. C. Sweetland (Eds.), *Test Critiques* (Vol. 3). Kansas City, MO: Test Corporation of America.

Undergraduate admissions: The realities of institutional policies, practices and procedures. (1980). American Association of Collegiate Registrars and Admissions Officers and the College Board. New York: College Entrance Examination Board.

Uniform guidelines on employee selection procedures. (1978). *Federal Register, 43*(166), 38296–38309.

United States Department of Labor. (1977). *Dictionary of occupational titles.* Washington, DC: U.S. Government Printing Office.

University of Minnesota (1984). *User's guide for the Minnesota Report: Personnel Selection System.* Minneapolis: National Computer Systems.

Urban, G. L., & Hauser, J. R. (1980). *Design and marketing of new products.* Englewood Cliffs, NJ: Prentice-Hall.

Urbina, S., & Clayton, J. (in press). WPPSI-R / WISC-R: A comparative study. *Journal of Psychoeducational Assessment.*

U.S. Department of Labor. (1977). *Dictionary of occupational titles.* Washington, DC: U.S. Government Printing Office.

Ussher, J. M., & Wilding, J. M. (1991). Performance and state changes during the menstrual cycle, conceptualised within a broadband testing framework. *Social Science and Medicine, 32,* 525–534.

Uzgiris, I. C., & Hunt, J. McV. (1975). Assessment in infancy: Ordinal scales of psychological development. Urbana: University of Illinois Press.

Vaidya, S., & Chansky, N. (1980). Cognitive development and cognitive style as factors in mathematics achievement. *Journal of Educational Psychology, 72,* 326–330.

Vale, C. D., & Keller, L. S. (1987). Developing expert computer systems to interpret psychological tests. In J. N. Butcher (Ed.), *Computerized psychological assessment: A practitioner's guide* (pp. 64–83). New York: Basic Books.

Vale, C. D., & Prestwood, J. S. (1988). *Manual for the Minnesota Clerical Assessment Battery.* St. Paul, MN: Assessment Systems Corporation.

Van der Merwe, A. B., & Theron, P. A. (1947). A new method of measuring emotional stability. *Journal of General Psychology, 37,* 109–124.

Van Hagen, J., & Kaufman, A. S. (1975). Factor analysis of the WISC-R for a group of mentally retarded children and adolescents. *Journal of Consulting and Clinical Psychology, 43,* 661–667.

Vance, H. B., & Wallbrown, F. H. (1978). The structure of intelligence for black children: A hierarchical approach. *The Psychological Record, 28,* 31–39.

Vander Kolk, C. J. (1977). Intelligence testing for visually impaired persons. *Journal of Visual Impairment & Blindness, 71,* 158–163.

Varon, E. J. (1936). Alfred Binet's concept of intelligence. *Psychological Review, 43,* 32–49.

Veldman, D. J., & Sheffield, J. R. (1979). The scaling of sociometric nominations. *Educational and Psychological Measurement, 39,* 99–106.

Veltri, J. J., & Schiffman, L. G. (1984). Fifteen years of consumer lifestyle and value research at AT&T. In R. E. Pitts & A. G. Woodside (Eds.), *Personal values and consumer psychology.* Lexington, MA: Lexington.

Venable, T. C. (1981). Declining SAT scores: Some unpopular hypotheses. *Phi Delta Kappan, 62,* 443–445.

Vernon, M., Blair, R., & Lotz, S. (1979). Psychological evaluation and testing of children who are deaf-blind. *School Psychology Digest, 8,* 291–295.

Vernon, M., & Brown, D. W. (1964). A guide to psychological tests and testing procedures in the evaluation of deaf and hard-of-hearing children. *Journal of Speech and Hearing Disorders, 29,* 414–423.

Vernon, P. E. (1950). *The structure of human abilities.* New York: Wiley.

Vernon, P. E. (1964). *Personality assessment: A critical survey.* New York: Wiley.

Volans, P. J., & Levy, R. (1982). A re-evaluation of an automated tailored test of concept learning with elderly psychiatric patients. *British Journal of Psychology, 21,* 210–214.

Vroom, V. (1964). *Work and motivation.* New York: Wiley.

Wachs, T. D. (1970). Report on the utility of a Piaget based infant scale with older retarded children. *Developmental Psychology, 2,* 449.

Wachs, T. D. (1975). Relation of infants' performance on Piaget scales between twelve and twenty-four months and their Stanford-Binet performance at thirty-one months. *Child Development, 46,* 929–935.

Wachspress, M., Berenberg, A. N., & Jacobson, A. (1953). Simulation of psychosis: A report of three cases. *Psychiatric Quarterly, 27,* 463–473.

Waddell, D. D. (1980). The Stanford-Binet: An evaluation of the technical data available since the 1972 restandardization. *Journal of School Psychology, 18,* 203–209.

Wade, T. C., & Baker, T. B. (1977). Opinions and uses of psychological tests: A survey of clinical psychologists. *American Psychologist, 32,* 874–882.

Wainer, H. (1990). *Computerized adaptive testing: A primer.* Hillsdale, NJ: Erlbaum.

Wald, A. (1947). *Sequential analysis.* New York: Wiley.

Wald, A. (1950). *Statistical decision function.* New York: Wiley.

Walker, H. M. (1976). *Walker Problem Behavior Identification Checklist.* Los Angeles: Western Psychological Services.

Walker, H. M. (1983). *Walker Problem Behavior Identification Checklist.* Los Angeles: Western Psychological Services.

Wall, S. M., & Paradise, L. V. (1981). A comparison of parent and teacher reports of selected adaptive behaviors of children. *Journal of School Psychology, 19,* 73–77.

Wallach, M. A., & Kogan, N. (1965). *Modes of thinking in young children.* New York: Holt, Rinehart & Winston.

Wallbrown, F., Brown, D., & Engin, A. (1978). A factor analysis of reading attitudes along with measures of reading achievement and scholastic aptitude. *Psychology in the Schools, 15,* 160–165.

Wallbrown, F. H., & Fremont, T. (1980). The stability of Koppitz scores on the Bender-Gestalt for reading disabled children. *Psychology in the Schools, 17,* 181–184.

Wallbrown, F. H., Wallbrown, J., & Engin, A. (1976). Test-retest reliability of the Bender-Gestalt for first grade children. *Perceptual and Motor Skills, 42,* 743–746.

Waller, N. G., & Waldman, I. D. (1990). A re-examination of the WAIS-R factor structure. *Psychological Assessment: A Journal of Consulting and Clinical Psychology, 2,* 139–144.

Walsh, T. M. (1966). Responses on the Famous Sayings Test of professional and nonprofessional personnel in a medical population. *Psychological Reports, 18,* 151–157.

Walters, G. D. (in press). Predicting the disciplinary adjustment of maximum and minimum security prison inmates using the Lifestyle Criminality Screening Form. *International Journal of Offender Therapy and Comparitive Criminology.*

Walters, G. D., & White, T. W. (1989). The thinking criminal: A cognitive model of lifestyle criminality. *Criminal Justice Research Bulletin, 4*(4), 1–10.

Walters, G. D., White, T. W., & Denney, D. (in press). The Lifestyle Criminality Screening Form: Preliminary data. *Criminal Justice and Behavior.*

Walters, G. D., Revella, L., & Baltrusaitis, W. J., II. (1990). Predicting parole/probation outcome with the aid of the Lifestyle Criminality Screening Form. *Psychological Assessment: A Journal of Consulting and Clinical Psychology, 2,* 313–316.

Wanderer, Z. W. (1967). *The validity of diagnostic judgments based on "blind" Machover figure drawings.* Unpublished doctoral dissertation, Columbia University, New York.

Wanous, J. P. (1977). Organizational entry: Newcomers moving in from outside to inside. *Psychological Bulletin, 84,* 601–618.

Ward, L. C., & Dillon, E. A. (1990). Psychiatric symptom correlates of the Minnesota Multiphasic Personality Inventory (MMPI) Masculinity-Femininity Scale. *Psychological Assessment: A Journal of Consulting & Clinical Psychology, 2,* 286–288.

Waring, E. M., & Reddon, J. (1983). The measurement of intimacy in marriage: The Waring Questionnaire. *Journal of Clinical Psychology, 39,* 53–57.

Warmke, D. L. (1984). *Successful implementation of the "new" GATB in entry-level selection.* Presentation at the American Society for Personnel Administrators Region 4 Conference, October 15, 1984, Norfolk, VA.

Warren, J. M., & Akert, K. (1964). *The frontal granular cortex and behavior.* New York: McGraw-Hill.

Waters, W. F. (1984). An autonomic nervous system response inventory: Scaling, reliability, and cross-validation. *Journal of Behavioral Medicine, 7,* 315–341.

Watkins, C. E., Jr. (1986). Validity and usefulness

of WAIS-R, WISC-R, and WPPSI short forms. *Professional Psychology: Research and Practice, 17,* 36–43.

Watkins, C. E., Jr., & Campbell, V. L. (1989). Personality assessment and counseling psychology. *Journal of Personality Assessment, 53,* 296–307.

Watkins, C. E., Campbell, V. L., & Manus, M. (1990). Personality assessment training in counseling psychology programs. *Journal of Personality Assessment, 55,* 380–383.

Watkins, C. E., Jr., Campbell, V. L., & McGregor, P. (1988). Counseling psychologists' uses of and opinions about psychological tests: A contemporary perspective. *The Counseling Psychologist, 16,* 476–486.

Watkins, E. O. (1976). *Watkins Bender-Gestalt Scoring System.* Novato, CA: Academic Therapy Publications.

Watson, C. G. (1967). Relationship of distortion to DAP diagnostic accuracy among psychologists at three levels of sophistication. *Journal of Consulting Psychology, 31,* 142–146.

Watson, C. G. (1990). Psychometric posttraumatic stress disorder measurement techniques: A review. *Psychological Assessment: A Journal of Consulting and Clinical Psychology, 2,* 460–469.

Watson, C. G., Felling, J., & Maceacherr, D. G. (1967). Objective draw-a-person scales: An attempted cross-validation. *Journal of Clinical Psychology, 23,* 382–386.

Waxman, S. G., & Geschwind, N. (1975). The interictal behavior syndrome of temporal lobe epilepsy. *Archives of General Psychiatry, 32,* 1580–1586.

Webb, E. J., Campbell, D. T., Schwartz, R. D., & Sechrest, L. (1966). *Unobtrusive measures: Nonreactive research in the social sciences.* Chicago: Rand McNally.

Webb, J. T., Miller, M. L., & Fowler, R. D. (1970). Extending professional time: A computerized MMPI interpretation service. *Journal of Clinical Psychology, 26,* 210–214.

Webb, M. W. (1987). Lipot Szondi (1893–1986). *American Psychologist, 42,* 600.

Webb, W. B., & Hilden, A. H. (1953). Verbal and intellectual ability as factors in projective test results. *Journal of Projective Techniques, 17,* 102–103.

Wechsler, D. (1939). *The measurement of adult intelligence.* Baltimore, MD: Williams & Wilkins.

Wechsler, D. (1955). *Manual for the Wechsler Adult Intelligence Scale.* New York: Psychological Corporation.

Wechsler, D. (1958). *The measurement and appraisal of adult intelligence* (4th ed.). Baltimore, MD: Williams & Wilkins.

Wechsler, D. (1967). *Manual for the Wechsler Preschool and Primary Scale of Intelligence.* New York. Psychological Corporation.

Wechsler, D. (1974). *Manual for the Wechsler Intelligence Scale for Children—Revised.* New York: Psychological Corporation.

Wechsler, D. (1975). Intelligence defined and undefined: A relativistic appraisal. *American Psychologist, 30,* 135–139.

Wechsler, D. (1981). *Manual for the Wechsler Adult Intelligence Scale—Revised.* New York: Psychological Corporation.

Wechsler, D. (1989). *Wechsler Preschool and Primary Scale of Intelligence—Revised.* San Antonio, TX: The Psychological Corporation.

Weeks, D. J. (1985). Conceptual structure in hypochondriasis, arthritis and neurosis. *British Journal of Clinical Psychology, 24,* 125–126.

Weinberger, L. J., & Bradley, L. A. (1980). Effects of "favorability" and type of assessment device upon acceptance of general personality interpretations. *Journal of Personality Assessment, 44,* 44–47.

Weinberger, M., Hiner, E. L., & Tierney, W. M. (1987). In support of hassles as a measure of stress in predicting health outcomes. *Journal of Behavioral Medicine, 10,* 19–31.

Weiner, B. A. (1980). Not guilty by reason of insanity: A sane approach. *Chicago Kent Law Review, 56,* 1057–1085.

Weiner, I. B. (1991). Editor's note: Interscorer agreement in Rorschach research. *Journal of Personality Assessment, 56,* 1.

Weiner, S., & Kaufman, A. S. (1979). WISC-R versus WISC for black children suspected of learning or behavior disorders. *Journal of Learning Disabilities, 12,* 41–46.

Weiss, B., Weisz, J. R., Politano, M., Carey, M., Nelson, W. M., & Finch, A. J. (1991). Developmental differences in the factor structure of the Children's Depression Inventory. *Psychological Assessment: A Journal of Consulting and Clinical Psychology, 3,* 38–45.

Weiss, D. J., & Vale, C. D. (1987). Computerized adaptive testing for measuring abilities and other psychological variables. In J. N. Butcher (Ed.),

Computerized psychological assessment: A practitioner's guide (pp. 325–343). New York: Basic Books.

Weiss, D. J., & Davison, M. L. (1981). Test theory and methods. *Annual Review of Psychology, 32,* 629–658.

Weiss, R., & Summers, K. (1983). Marital Interaction Coding System III. In E. Filsinger (Ed.), *Marriage and family assessment: A sourcebook of family therapy.* Beverly Hills, CA: Sage.

Weisskopf, E. A., & Dieppa, J. J. (1951). Experimentally induced faking of TAT responses. *Journal of Consulting Psychology, 15,* 469–474.

Weissman, H. N. (1991). Forensic psychological examination of the child witness in cases of alleged sexual abuse. *American Journal of Orthopsychiatry, 6,* 48–58.

Weithorn, L. A. (Ed.). (1987). *Psychology and child custody determinations.* Lincoln: University of Nebraska Press.

Welcher, D., Mellitis, E. D., & Hardy, J. B. (1971). A multivariate analysis of factors affecting psychological performance. *The Johns Hopkins Medical Journal, 129,* 19–35.

Wells, W. D. (1975). Psychographics: A critical review. *Journal of Marketing Research, 12,* 195–213.

Welsh, G. S., & Dahlstrom, W. G. (Eds.). (1956). *Basic readings on the MMPI in psychology and medicine.* Minneapolis: University of Minnesota Press.

Wepman, J. M. (1978). *Wepman Auditory Discrimination Test.* Chicago: Language Research Associates.

Werner, E., & Bayley, N. (1966). The reliability of Bayley's Revised Scale of Mental and Motor Development during the first year of life. *Child Development, 37,* 39.

Werner, H., & Strauss, A. A. (1941). Pathology of figure-background relation in the child. *Journal of Abnormal and Social Psychology, 36,* 236–248.

Wertheimer, M. (1923). Untersuchungen zur Lehre von der Gestalt. *Psychologische Forschung* [Studies in the theory of Gestalt Psychology. *Psychology for Schools,*] *4,* 301–303. Translated by Don Cantor in R. J. Herrnstein & E. G. Boring (1965), *A sourcebook in the history of psychology.* Cambridge, MA: Harvard University Press.

Wesman, A. G. (1949). Effect of speed on item-test correlation coefficients. *Educational and Psychological Measurement, 9,* 51–57.

Wesman, A. G. (1968). Intelligent testing. *American Psychologist, 23,* 267–274.

Wessberg, H. W., Mariotto, M. J., Conger, A. J., Conger, J. C., & Farrell, A. D. (1979). The ecological validity of role plays for assessing heterosocial anxiety and skill of male college students. *Journal of Consulting and Clinical Psychology, 47,* 525–535.

Westen, D., Silk, K. R., Lohr, N., & Kerber, K. (1985). *Object relations and social cognition: TAT scoring manual.* Unpublished manuscript. Ann Arbor: University of Michigan.

Westen, D., Barends, A., Leigh, J., Mendel, M., & Silbert, D. (1988). *Manual for coding dimensions of object relations and social cognition from interview data.* Unpublished manuscript. Ann Arbor: University of Michigan.

Wettstein, R. M., Mulvey, E. P., & Rogers, R. (1991). A prospective comparison of four insanity defense standards. *American Journal of Psychiatry, 148,* 21–27.

Wetzler, S. (1990). The Millon Clinical Multiaxial Inventory (MCMI): A review. *Journal of Personality Assessment, 55,* 445–464.

Wexley, K. N., Sanders, R. E., & Yukl, G. A. (1973). Training interviewers to eliminate contrast effects in employment interviews. *Journal of Applied Psychology, 57,* 233–236.

Wexley, K. N., Yukl, G. A., Kovacs, S. Z., & Sanders, R. E. (1972). Importance of contrast effects in employment interviews. *Journal of Applied Psychology, 56,* 45–48.

Wheeler, M. (1977). *Lies, damn lies, and statistics.* New York: Dell.

Whisman, M. A., Strosahl, K., Fruzzetti, A. E., Schmaling, K. B., Jacobson, N. S., & Miller, D. M. (1989). A structured interview version of the Hamilton Rating Scale for Depression: Reliability and validity. *Psychological Assessment: A Journal of Consulting and Clinical Psychology, 1,* 238–241.

White, B. L. (1971). *Human infants: Experience and psychological development.* Englewood Cliffs, NJ: Prentice-Hall.

White, D. M., Clements, C. B., & Fowler, R. D. (1985). A comparison of computer administration with standard administration of the MMPI. *Computers in Human Behavior, 1,* 153–162.

White, L. T. (1984). Attitudinal consequences of the preemployment polygraph examination. *Journal of Applied Social Psychology, 14,* 364–374.

White, S., Santilli, G., & Quinn, K. (1988). Child

evaluator's roles in child sexual abuse assessments. In E. B. Nicholson & J. Bulkley (Eds.), *Sexual abuse allegations in custody and visitation cases: A resource book for judges and court personnel* (pp. 94–105). Washington, DC: American Bar Association.

White, T. H. (1979). Correlations among the WISC-R, PIAT, and DAP. *Psychology in the Schools, 16,* 497–501.

Whitmyre, J. W. (1953). The significance of artistic excellence in the judgment of adjustment inferred from human figure drawings. *Journal of Consulting Psychology, 17,* 421–424.

Whitworth, R. H. (1984). Review of Halstead-Reitan Neuropsychological Battery and allied procedures. In D. J. Keyser & R. C. Sweetland (Eds.), *Test critiques* (Vol. 1; pp. 305–314). Kansas City, MO: Test Corporation of America.

Wicker, A. W. (1969). Attitudes versus actions: The relationship of verbal and overt behavioral responses to attitude objects. *Journal of Social Issues, 25,* 41–78.

Wickes, T. A., Jr. (1956). Examiner influences in a testing situation. *Journal of Consulting Psychology, 20,* 23–26.

Wicklund, R. A., & Koller, M. (1991). Psychological antecedents of consistency in applying traits. *Journal of Research in Personality, 25,* 108–134.

Wiegersma, S. (1951). Een onderzoek naar de gelddigheid van de Szonditest voor de psychologische praktijk. [Investigation of the validity of the Szondi Test for psychological practice.] *Psychological Abstracts, 25,* No. 372.

Wielkiewicz, R. M. (1990). Interpreting low scores on the WISC-R third factor: It's more than distractibility. *Psychological Assessment: A Journal of Consulting and Clinical Psychology, 2,* 91–97.

Wiggins, W. (1966). Individual viewpoints on social desirability. *Psychological Bulletin, 66,* 68–77.

Wiggins, J. S. (1973). *Personality and prediction: Principles of personality assessment.* Reading, MA: Addison-Wesley.

Wikoff, R. L. (1979). The WISC-R as a predictor of achievement. *Psychology in the Schools, 16,* 364–366.

Wilkie, W. L., & Dickson, P. R. (1985). *Shopping for appliances: Consumers' strategies and patterns of information search* (Working paper). Cambridge, MA: Marketing Science Institute.

Wilcox, R., & Krasnoff, A. (1967). Influence of test-taking attitudes on personality inventory scores. *Journal of Consulting Psychology, 31,* 185–194.

Wilkinson, C. Y., & Oakland, T. (1983a, August). *Stability of the SOMPA's sociocultural modalities.* Paper presented at the 90th annual convention of the American Psychological Association, Anaheim, CA.

Wilkinson, C. Y., & Oakland, T. (1983b, August) *Stability of the SOMPA's health history inventory.* Paper presented at the 90th annual convention of the American Psychological Association, Anaheim, CA.

Williams, C. L., Ben-Porath, Y. S., Uchiyama, C., Weed, N. C., & Archer, R. P. (1990). External validity of the new Devereux Adolescent Behavior Rating Scales. *Journal of Personality Assessment, 55,* 73–85.

Williams, R. (1975). The BITCH-100: A culture-specific test. *Journal of Afro-American Issues, 3,* 103–116.

Williams, S. K., Jr. (1978). The Vocational Card Sort: A tool for vocational exploration. *Vocational Guidance Quarterly, 26,* 237–243.

Willson, V. L., Reynolds, C. R., Chatman, S. P., & Kaufman, A. S. (1985). Confirmatory analysis of simultaneous, sequential and achievement factors on the K-ABC at 11 age levels ranging from 2½ to 12½ years. *Journal of School Psychology, 23,* 261–269.

Wilson, S. L., Thompson, J. A., & Wylie, G. (1982). Automated psychological testing for the severely physically handicapped. *International Journal of Man-Machine Studies, 17,* 291–296.

Winslade, W. J. (1986). After Tarasoff: Therapist liability and patient confidentiality. In L. Everstine & D. S. Everstine (Eds.), *Psychotherapy and the law.* Orlando, FL: Grune & Stratton.

Wirt, R. D., Lachar, D., Klinedinst, J. K., & Seat, P. D. (1977/1984). *Multidimensional description of child personality: A manual for the Personality Inventory for Children.* (1984 revision by David Lachar). Los Angeles: Western Psychological Services.

Wirtz, W. (1977). *On further examination: Report on the advisory panel on the Scholastic Aptitude Test score decline.* New York: College Entrance Examination Board.

Wise, S. L. (1985). The development and validation of a scale measuring attitude towards statistics. *Educational & Psychological Measurement, 45,* 401–405.

Wish, J., McCombs, K. F., & Edmonson, B. (1980).

Socio-Sexual Knowledge & Attitudes Test. Chicago: Stoelting.

Witkin, H. A., & Berry, J. W. (1975). Psychological differentiation in cross-cultural perspective. *Journal of Cross-Cultural Psychology, 6,* 4–87.

Witkin, H. A., Dyk, R. B., Faterson, H. F., Goodenough, D. R., & Karp, S. A. (1962). *Psychological differentiation.* New York: Wiley.

Witkin, H. A., & Goodenough, D. R. (1977). Field dependence and interpersonal behavior. *Psychological Bulletin, 84,* 661–689.

Witkin, H. A., & Goodenough, D. R. (1981). *Cognitive styles: Essence and origins* (Psychological Issues Monograph 51). New York: International Universities Press.

Witkin, H. A., Lewis, H. B., Hertzman, M., Machover, K., Meissner, P. B., & Wapner, S. (1954). *Personality through perception: An experimental and clinical study.* New York: Harper.

Witmer, L. (1902). *Analytical psychology: A practical manual for colleges and Normal schools.* Boston: Ginn.

Witmer, L. (1907). Clinical psychology. *Psychological Clinic, 1,* 1–9.

Witmer, L. (1911). *The special class for backward children.* Philadelphia: Psychological Clinic Press.

Witmer, L. (1913). *Progress in education of exceptional children in public schools during the year 1912–13.* Washington, DC: U.S. Bureau of Education.

Witt, J. C., Heffer, R. W., & Pfeiffer, J. (1990). Structural rating scales: A review of self-report and informant rating processes, procedures and issues. In C. R. Reynolds & R. W. Kamphaus (Eds.), *Handbook of psychological and educational assessment of children: Personality, behavior and context* (pp. 364–394). New York: Guilford Press.

Wittenborn, J. R., & Holzberg, J. D. (1951). The Rorschach and descriptive diagnosis. *Journal of Consulting Psychology, 15,* 460–463.

Wittenborn, J. R., et al. (1956). A study of adoptive children. The predictive validity of the Yale development examination of infant behavior. *Psychological Monographs, 70*(1), 59–92.

Wittgenstein, L. (1953). *Philosophical interventions.* New York: Basil Blackwell.

Witty, P. (1940). Some considerations in the education of gifted children. *Educational Administration and Supervision, 26,* 512–521.

Wohlfarth, H. (1982). *International Journal of Biosocial Research, 3,* 35–43.

Wohlfarth, H. (1984). The effect of color-psychodynamic environmental modification on disciplinary incidents in elementary schools over one school year. A controlled study. *International Journal of Biosocial Research, 6,* 44–53.

Wolf, T. M. (1981). Measures of deviant behavior, activity level, and self-concept for educable mentally retarded-emotionally disturbed students. *Psychological Reports, 48,* 903–910.

Wolfe, J., Keane, T. M., Lyons, J. A., & Gerardi, R. J. (1987). Current trends and issues in the assessment of combat-related post-traumatic stress disorder. *Behavior Therapist, 10,* 27–32.

Wolff, C. (1732). *Psychologia empirica.*

Wolff, C. (1734). *Psychologia rationalis.*

Wong, D. L. (1987). False allegations of child abuse: The other side of the tragedy. *Pediatric Nursing, 13,* 329–333.

Woodcock, R. W. (1990). Theoretical foundations of the WJ-R measures of cognitive ability. *Journal of Psychoeducational Assessment, 8,* 231–258.

Woodcock, R. W., & Johnson, M. B. (1989). *Woodcock-Johnson Psycho-Educational Battery—Revised.* Allen, TX: DLM Teaching Resources.

Woodcock, R. W., & Mather, N. (1989). *WJ-R Tests of Cognitive Ability—Standard and Supplemental Batteries: Examiner's Manual.* In R. W. Woodcock & M. B. Johnson, *Woodcock-Johnson Psychoeducational Battery—Revised.* Allen, TX: DLM Teaching Resources.

Woodcock, R. W., & Mather, N. (1989, 1990). *WJ-R Tests of Achievement: Examiner's Manual.* In R. W. Woodcock & M. B. Johnson, *Woodcock-Johnson Psychoeducational Battery—Revised.* Allen, TX: DLM Teaching Resources.

Woodworth, R. S. (1917). *Personal Data Sheet.* Chicago: Stoelting.

Woo-Sam, J. M., & Zimmerman, I. L. (1973). Research with the Wechsler Preschool and Primary Scale of Intelligence (WPPSI): The first five years. *School Psychology Monographs, 1,* 25–50.

Worchel, F. F., & Dupree, J. L. (1990). Projective storytelling techniques. In C. R. Reynolds & R. W. Kamphaus (Eds.), *Handbook of psychological and educational assessment of children: Personality, behavior, & context* (pp. 70–88). New York: Guilford Press.

Worlock, P., et al. (1986). Patterns of fractures in accidental and non-accidental injury in children. *British Medical Journal, 293,* 100–103.

Wright, B. D., & Stone, M. H. (1979). *Best test design: Rasch measurement*. Chicago: Mesa Press.

Wright, M. W., Sister, G. C., & Chylinski, J. (1963). Personality factors in the selection of civilians for isolated northern stations. *Journal of Applied Psychology, 47*, 24–29.

Wylie, R. C. (1974). *The self-concept: 1. A review of the methodological considerations and measuring instruments* (Rev. ed.). Lincoln: University of Nebraska Press.

Wylie, R. C. (1979). *The self-concept: 2. Theory and research on selected topics* (Rev. ed.). Lincoln: University of Nebraska Press.

Yamamoto, J., & Seeman, W. (1960). A psychological study of castrated males. *Psychiatric Research Report, 12*, 97–103.

Yamamoto, K., & Frengel, B. A. (1966). An exploratory component analysis of the Minnesota tests of creative thinking. *California Journal of Educational Research, 17*, 220–229.

Yater, A. C., Barclay, A., & Leskosky, R. (1971). Goodenough-Harris Drawing Test and WPPSI performance of disadvantaged preschool children. *Perceptual and Motor Skills, 33*, 967–970.

Youth, R. (1986, June). Corporate use of polygraphs raises fairness questions. *The New York State Psychologist, 37*, 5, 32.

Yozawitz, A. (1986). Applied neuropsychology in a psychiatric center. In I. Grant & K. M. Adams, (Eds.), *Neuropsychological assessment of neuropsychiatric disorders* (pp. 121–146). New York: Oxford University Press.

Ysseldyke, J. E. (1989). Review of the Bracken Basic Concept Scale. In J. C. Conoley & J. J. Kramer (Eds.), *The tenth mental measurements yearbook* (pp. 104–105). Lincoln: The Buros Institute of Mental Measurements, University of Nebraska-Lincoln.

Ysseldyke, J. E. (1990). Goodness of fit of the Woodcock-Johnson Psycho-Educational Battery —Revised to the Horn Cattell Gf-Gc theory. *Journal of Psychoeducational Assessment, 8*(3), 268–275.

Yule, W., Berger, M., Butler, S., Newham, V., & Tizard, J. (1969). The WPPSI: An empirical evaluation with a British sample. *British Journal of Education Psychology, 39*, 1–13.

Yussen, S. R., & Kane, P. T. (1980). *Children's conception of intelligence*. Madison report for the project on studies of instructional programming for the individual student. University of Wisconsin, Technical Report #546.

Zachary, R. (1984, August). Computer-based test interpretations: Comments and discussion. In J. D. Matarazzo (Chair), *Computer-based test interpretation: Prospects and problems*. Symposium conducted at the Annual Convention of the American Psychological Association, Toronto.

Zaichowsky, J. L. (1985). Measuring the involvement construct. *Journal of Consumer Research, 12*, 281–300.

Zbaracki, J. U., Clark, S. G., & Wolins, L. (1985). Children's Interests Inventory, grades 4–6. *Educational and Psychological Measurement, 45*, 517–521.

Zedeck, S., & Cascio, W. F. (1984). Psychological issues in personnel decisions. *Annual Review of Psychology, 35*, 461–518.

Zeiss, R. A., & Dickman, H. R. (1989). PTSD 40 years later: Incidence and person-situation correlates in former POW's. *Journal of Clinical Psychology, 45*, 80–87.

Zeren, A. S., and Bradley, L. A. (1982). Effects of diagnostician prestige and sex upon subjects' acceptance of genuine personality feedback. *Journal of Personality Assessment, 46*, 169–174.

Zieziula, F. R. (Ed.). (1982). *Assessment of hearing-impaired people*. Washington, DC: Gallaudet College Press.

Zimbardo, P. G., & Ruch, F. L. (1975). *Psychology and life* (9th ed.). Glenview, IL: Scott, Foresman.

Zimmerman, B. J., & Rosenthal, T. C. (1974a). Conserving and retaining equalities and inequalities through observation and correction. *Developmental Psychology, 10*, 260–268.

Zimmerman, B. J., & Rosenthal, T. C. (1974b). Observational learning of rule-governed behavior by children. *Psychological Bulletin, 81*, 29–42.

Zimmerman, I. L., & Woo-Sam, J. (1970). The utility of the WPPSI in the public school. *Journal of Clinical Psychology, 26*, 472.

Zimmerman, I. L., & Woo-Sam, J. M. (1978). Intelligence testing today: Relevance to the school age child. In L. Oettinger (Ed.), *Psychologists and the school age child with MBD/LD*. New York: Grune & Stratton.

Zimmerman, M., & Coryell, W. (1987). The Inventory to Diagnose Depression (IDD): A self-report scale to diagnose major depressive disorder. *Journal of Consulting and Clinical Psychology, 55*, 55–59.

Zimmerman, M., & Coryell, W. (1988). The validity of a self-report questionnaire for diagnosing major depressive disorder. *Archives of General Psychiatry, 45*, 738–740.

Zimmerman, M., Coryell, W., Corenthal, C., & Wilson, S. (1986). A self-report scale to diagnose major depressive disorder. *Archives of General Psychiatry, 43*, 1076–1081.

Zimmerman, W., Michael, J., & Michael, W. (1970). The factored dimensions of the Study Attitudes and Methods Survey test—Experimental form. *Educational and Psychological Measurement, 30*, 433–436.

Zimmerman, W., Parks, H., Gray, K., & Michael, W. (1977). The validity of traditional cognitive measures and of scales of the Study Attitudes and Methods Survey in the prediction of the academic success of Educational Opportunity Program students. *Educational and Psychological Measurement, 37*, 465–470.

Zinberg, N. E. (1985). The private versus the public psychiatric interview. *American Journal of Psychiatry, 142*, 889–894.

Zubin, J., Eron, L. D., & Schumer, F. (1965). *An experimental approach to projective techniques*. New York: Wiley.

Zucker, S. (1985). MSCA-K-ABC with high risk preschoolers. Paper presented at the Annual Meeting of the National Association of School Psychologists, Las Vegas, NV.

Zucker, S., & Copeland, E. P. (1987). K-ABC-McCarthy Scale performance among three groups of "at-risk" preschoolers. Paper presented at the Annual Meeting of the National Association of School Psychologists, Las Vegas, NV.

Zuckerman, M. (1979). Traits, states, situations, and uncertainty. *Journal of Behavioral Assessment, 1*, 43–54.

Zuckerman, M. (1990). Some dubious premises in research and theory on racial differences. *American Psychologist, 45*, 1297–1303.

Zuckerman, M., & Lubin, B. (1965). *Manual for the Multiple Affect Check List*. San Diego, CA: Educational and Industrial Testing Service.

Zuckerman, M., Lubin, B., Vogel, L., & Valerius, E. (1964). Measurement of experimentally induced affects. *Journal of Consulting Psychology, 28*, 418–425.

Zweig, D. R., & Brown, S. M. (1985). Psychometric evaluation of a written stimulus presentation format for the Social Interaction Self-Statement Test. *Cognitive Therapy & Research, 9*, 285–295.

Zybert, P., Stein, Z., & Belmont, L. (1978). Maternal age and children's ability. *Perceptual and Motor Skills, 47*, 815–818.

Name Index

Bryant, S., 468
Brzezinski, E., 710
Buck, J. N., 473
Buck, L., 427
Buckland Heer, K., 645
Buckley, P. D., 603
Bucknam, M. E., 533
Bucofsky, D., 374
Buda, R., 521
Buffaloe, J. D., 720
Bukatman, B. A., 552
Burdick, H., 671
Burdock, E. I., 529
Burgess, A. W., 564
Burisch, M., 406, 407, 417, 435
Burke, M. J., 643, 720
Burks, N., 5
Burnett, J. W., 474
Burnkrant, R. E., 25
Burns, G. L., 505
Burns, R. C., 473
Burns, R. K., 667
Buros, O. K., 22, 30, 49, 53
Burris, L. R., 663
Burstein, A. G., 298
Burt, C., 274
Burwen, L. S., 402
Bush, B., 299
Butcher, J. N., 421, 422, 423, 424,
    425, 709, 735
Butler, N., 268
Butter, E. J., 690
Byers, S., 463
Byham, W. C., 654
Byrne, D., 400

Cabanis, P., 572
Cacioppo, J. T., 700
Cain, L. F., 625
Callahan, C., 663
Calsyn, D. A., 490
Camilli, G., 218
Campbell, D. C., 635
Campbell, D. T., 180, 402, 517
Campbell, D. P., 635, 637, 708
Campbell, J. P., 191
Campbell, L., 533
Campbell, V. L., 449, 526
Campione, J. C., 350
Campo, V., 473

Cancro, R., 497
Canter, A., 604
Cantrell, J. D., 539
Capeli, E., 703
Caputo, G. C., 24
Card, R. D., 511
Carey, M. P., 541
Carlson, V., 562
Carmichael, L., 261
Carr, A. C., 720
Carroll, J. B., 242
Carsrud, A. L., 667
Carstens, C., 539
Carter, E. T., 654
Carver, R. P., 272
Cascio, W. F., 643
Cash, T. F., 19
Cashen V. M., 312
Cassell, R. N., 312, 484
Castiglioni, A., 41
Castonquay, L. G., 511
Cates, J. A., 619, 620
Cattell, J. M., 46, 468
Cattell, P., 46, 381
Cattell, R. B., 46, 240, 269, 273,
    351, 401, 410, 411, 497, 750, 751
Cavanaugh, J. L., 517, 556
Ceci, S. J., 564
Chaille, S. E., 248, 249
Chamberlain, K., 166
Chambless, D. L., 24
Champagne, J. E., 668, 669
Champion, L., 25
Chang, S. S., 535
Chansky, N., 489
Chansky, N. M., 305
Chaplin, T. C., 517
Chapman, L. J., 24
Chatman, S. P., 355
Chatterji, S., 259
Chattin, S. H., 357
Chave, E. J., 197, 678, 679
Chelune, G., 590
Chess, S., 267, 619
Chestnut, R., 699
Chevron, E., 497
Childs, R., 258
Chin, C., 488
Chinoy, E., 268
Chisholm, B., 24

Chissom, B., 284
Choca, J., 539
Chowdri, S., 357
Christenson, S. L. 505
Chun, K., 30
Chylinski, J., 421
Cicchetti, D., 562
Cicchetti, D. V., 498, 627
Cieutat, V. J., 27
Clark, B., 254, 255, 256
Clark, D. H., 268
Clarke, H. J., 476, 478
Clarkin, J. F., 31
Cleckley, H., 558
Clements, N. E., 720
Cleveland, S. E., 527
Clinger, D. I., 571
Clorizio, H. F., 539
Coates, S., 489
Cobb, M. V., 99
Cobb, S., 30
Coble, S. D., 562
Coffman, W. E., 352
Cohen, E., 27
Cohen G. H., 485
Cohen J., 146
Cohen, J. B., 697
Cohen, M. E., 505
Cohen, R., 536
Cohen, R. J., 69, 71, 72, 73, 497,
    509, 536, 671, 677, 694, 696,
    698, 701, 707
Colbus, D., 541
Cole, S. T., 269
Coleman, L., 564
Collard, R. R., 382
Collier, B. R., 258
Colligan, R. C., 421, 422
Collins, B. L., 673, 674
Collins, R. W., 571
Colvin, C. R., 521
Commons, M., 241
Comrey, A. L., 30, 253, 416, 751
Cone, J. D., 521
Conger, A. J., 146, 518
Conger, J. C., 518
Conoley, J. C., 29, 30
Conrad, H. S., 22
Conrad, P., 581
Constantino, G., 464

Huston, T., 547
Hutt, M. L., 602, 605
Hutton, L. H., 25

Ilyin, D., 332
Ingham, J. G., 484
Ingram, E. M., 382
Ingram, R. E., 542
Ishihara, S., 597
Iwata, B. A., 507

Jacklin, C. N., 267, 268
Jackson, D. E., 734
Jackson, G. B., 644
Jackson, D. N., 220, 221, 222, 427, 435, 521, 709, 716, 724
Jacobs, D., 535
Jacobs, J., 254
Jacobson, A., 533
Jacobson, N. S., 541
Jacoby, J., 699
Jaffe, L. T., 539
Jagim, R. D., 67
James, L. R., 643
Janisse, M. P., 517
Jansen, P. G., 175
Janzen, H. L., 287
Jarman, R. F., 243, 351
Jarrett, R. B., 24
Jastak, J. F., 325
Jastak, S., 325
Jay, S. M., 507
Jenkins, C. D., 423
Jensema, C., 620
Jensen, A. R., 54, 193, 217, 218, 262, 269, 270, 272, 299, 354, 389
Jensen, M. R., 350
John, K. L., 604
Johnson, D. L., 27
Johnson, G. S., 620
Johnson, J. H., 734
Johnson, M. B., 365
Johnson, O. G., 30
Johnson, R. C., 263
Jolles, J., 473
Jolley, R. R., 587
Jones, C., 340
Jones, D. P., 564
Jones, E., 545

Jones, E. L., 307
Jones, G., 25
Jones, J. W., 664
Jones, L. V., 197
Jones, M. B., 653
Jordan, B. K., 545
Jorgensen, K., 619
Joseph, W. B., 699
Jung, C. G., 51, 402, 427
Jupp, J. J., 24
Jurgensen, C., 150

Kagan, J., 463
Kahn, J., 387
Kahn, M., 580
Kaiser, H. F., 101, 145, 191
Kales, H. C., 541
Kalhorn, J., 268
Kalkstein, D., 581
Kalkstein, D. S., 19
Kamin, L. J., 263
Kamiya, J., 509
Kamphaus, R. W., 352, 354, 357
Kane, J. S., 374
Kaner, S. T., 533
Kaniel, S., 350
Kanner, A. D., 5
Kantor, J. E., 654
Kaplan, B. J., 542
Kaplan, E., 609
Karasu, T. B., 427
Karchmer, M. A., 621
Karlsson, J., 25
Karnes, F. A., 284
Karoly, P., 25
Karp, S. A., 488, 489
Karplus, R., 389
Karplus, E., 389
Karson, S., 411
Kassarjian, H. H., 697
Katz, E., 623
Katz, L., 357
Kaufman, A. S., 31, 236, 243, 247, 266, 284, 287, 29, 298, 299, 300, 307, 350, 352, 354, 355, 357, 379, 389, 390, 392
Kaufman, N. L., 31, 243, 247, 284, 350, 352, 354, 357, 379, 390
Kauffman, S. H., 473
Kavan, M. G., 539, 540, 541

Kavanaugh, M. J., 671
Kazdin, A., 541
Kazdin, A. E., 24
Kazimour, K. K., 629
Keane, T. M., 550
Keating, J. P., 690
Keegan, J. R., 734
Keenan, P. A., 498
Keilitz, I., 556
Keith, T. Z., 145, 284, 351, 354, 355
Keller, J., 31, 527
Keller, J. W., 449
Keller, L. S., 734
Kelley, M., 395
Kelley, S. J., 562
Kellner, C. H., 587
Kelly, D. H., 511
Kelly, E. J., 403
Kelly, G. A., 497
Kelly, M. D., 607
Kendall, L. M., 671
Kendall, P. C., 492, 542
Kennedy, M. H., 619
Kennedy, O. A., 517
Kennedy, R. S., 653
Kenny, T. J., 604
Kent, N., 268
Kerber, K., 459
Kerlinger, F. N., 82
Kern, J. M., 518
Keyser, D. J., 29, 30
Khaleque, A., 671
Kim, S. P., 497
King, F. L., 24
King, K. W., 480
King, M. A., 564
Kinner, T. C., 688
Kinslinger, H. J., 480
Kinston, W., 549
Kipnis, D., 521
Kirby, J., 243, 351
Kirchner, W. K., 27
Kirk, S. A., 349
Kirkpatrick, E., 50
Kirschenbaum, J., 418
Kissel, R. C., 507
Kitchen, C., 719
Klanderman, J. W., 354
Klee, S. H., 300

McCall, W. A., 101, 258
McCallum, M., 25
McCallum, R. S., 284, 371
McCarthy, D., 389, 390, 391
McCaulley, M. H., 427
McCausland, M. P., 564
McChesney, S. R., 371
McClelland, D. C., 400, 445, 459, 461, 671
McCloskey, G. M., 386
McCloskey, G. W., 357
McClure Butterfield, P., 559
McCombs, K. F., 631
McConaughty, S. H., 505
McCormack, J. K., 539
McCoy, G. F., 621
McCubbin, J. A., 17
McCubbins, H., 547
McCubbins, H. I., 547, 549
McCullough, C. S., 65
McCullough, J., 518
McDermott, E., 403
McFall, M. E., 545
McFarlane, J. W., 378, 381
McGarry, A. L., 552, 555
McGinnies, E., 480
McGonigle Gibson, K. L., 610
McGraw, B., 644
McGraw, J. M., 564
McGregor, P., 526
McGurk, F. J., 269
McHugh, P. R., 533
McIntire, W. G., 545
McKenna, T., 425
McKenzie, R. C., 174, 664
McKeown, T., 268
McKinley, J. C., 417, 418, 421
McKnight, G., 25
McLaughlin, J. D., 423
McLaughlin, R. E., 541
McLean, J. E., 354, 355
McLenore, C. W., 536
McNabb, B., 284
McNeill, J. W., 423
McNemar, Q., 241
McPartland, J. M., 375
McPhee, J. P., 474
McRae, T. D., 533
McReynolds, P., 47
McTurk, R. H.. 383, 384

McWatters, M., 488
Meadow, K. P., 621
Meadows, G., 533
Meagher, R. B., 538
Mealor, D. J
Medlin, W. J., 605
Mednick, S. A., 321, 418
Meehl, P. E., 220, 418, 421, 429, 431
Meeker, M., 253
Meeker, R., 253
Meier, N. C., 646
Meier, S. T., 186
Meissner, P. B., 488
Melella, J. T., 517
Mellitis, E. D., 381
Melman, H., 619
Mendel, M., 459
Mendelson, M., 539
Meng, K., 489
Menninger, K. A., 400
Mercer, J. R., 268, 338
Merikle, P. M., 690
Mermelstein, R. M., 25
Merrens, M. R., 571
Merrill, M. A., 249, 251, 280
Merz, W. R., 352
Messick, S., 198, 220, 222, 434
Metraux, R. W., 445, 446
Metzger, G. D., 686
Meyer, E. C., 25
Meyer, R. G., 69
Meyers, C. E., 313, 374
Meyers, C. J., 69
Meyers, D. V., 474
Miale, F. R., 450
Michael, W. B., 22, 145, 253
Miles, C. C., 279
Miles, M. B., 30
Mill, J., 42
Millard, W., 248
Miller, C., 518
Miller, C. K., 305
Miller, D. A., 505
Miller, D. M., 541
Miller, G. A., 43
Miller, H. R., 422, 539
Miller, J. R., 719
Miller, K. S., 268
Miller, L., 549

Miller, N. E., 509
Miller, P. M., 484
Miller, V. J., 610, 611
Miller, W. R., 2
Millman, J., 150, 715
Millon, T., 538, 539
Milner, B., 591, 608
Milner, J., 24
Mindak, W. A., 693
Minder, C. C., 284
Mirmow, E. L., 478
Misaszek, J., 619
Misaszek, J. G., 619
Mischel, W., 402, 495, 500
Mishlove, M., 24
Mitchel, J. V., Jr., 30, 331
Mitchell, A., 704
Mitchell, J. V., Jr., 734
Mittenberg, W., 455
Mock, J., 539
Moffitt, P. F., 25
Moldofsky, H., 19
Molitor, D. L., 384
Molloy, D. W., 533
Money, J., 595
Monroe, S. M., 5
Montouri, J., 405
Moon, G. W., 295
Mooney, K. C., 505
Mooney, R. L., 409
Moore, M. K., 24
Moos, B. S., 549
Moos, R. H., 548
Moreland, K. L., 61, 707, 733, 734, 735, 736, 737
Morgan, C. D., 459
Morgan, J. N., 686
Moriarty, A., 383
Morrisby, J. R., 258
Morrison, K. L., 518
Morrow, G. R., 507
Morse, S. J., 556
Mosely, E. C., 455
Moses, S., 341
Moskowitz, D. S., 402
Most, R. B., 737
Mostkoff, D. L., 474
Moul, M., 263
Moye, A., 550
Mueser, K. T., 518

Subject Index

(continued)

Association (AERA), 22, 61
American Journal of Psychology, 47
American Law Institute (ALI), 556
American Men of Science, 46, 47
American Psychiatric Association, 80
American Psychological Association
   (APA), 10, 47, 418, 511, 736
   Committee on Ethical Standards
      for Psychology, 59
   Division of Clinical
      Neuropsychology, 590
   Division of Industrial and
      Organizational Psychology, 633
   Ethics Committee, 59
   publications of, 22-23, 30, 55, 59,
      60, 61
   Task Force on the Prediction of
      Dishonesty and Theft in
      Employment Settings, 663
   Testing Committee, 58
American Psychological Foundation,
   51
American Psychologist, 54
American Sign Language (ASL), 617
Americans with Disabilities Act of
   1990, 56
Amnesia, 577
Amusia, 577
Analogue studies, 507-509
*Analysis of the Phenomena of the
   Human Mind* (Mill), 42
Anchoring, 114
Anger, tests to measure, 24
Anhedonia, 24
Animals, attitudes towards treatment
   of, 25
Anomia, 577
Anopia, 577
Anorexia nervosa, 19
Anosmia, 577
Anthropometric Laboratory, 44, 45,
   121
Anxiety
   state-trait, 405
   test, 180, 405
APA. *See* American Psychological
   Association
Aphasia, 577, 595
Application blanks, 650
Applied Ergonomics, 7
Apraxia, 577

Aptitude tests, 333-346
   achievement tests vs., 341
   college level, 343-346
   Differential Aptitude Test, 168,
      169, 170, 254, 638-639
   elementary school level, 336-339
   General Aptitude Test Battery,
      639-645
   intelligence tests vs., 341
   preemployment counseling and,
      638-646
   secondary school level, 339-343,
      344-345
   of specific aptitudes, 645-646
   suppliers of, 761-762, 766
   See also names of specific tests
APTP. *See* Association of Personnel
   Test Publishers
Arithmetic mean, 89
Armed Forces Qualification Test
   (AFQT), 317
Armed Services Vocational Aptitude
   Battery (ASVAB), 315, 317,
   318-320, 645
Army Alpha Test, 314, 315
Arthur Adaptation of Leiter Interna-
   tional Performance Scale, 621
Art tests, 322, 346
ASL. *See* American Sign Language
Assessment
   context of, 568
   defined, 11
   of hearing-impaired people, 248-
      249, 617-622
   of people with cognitive disabili-
      ties, 624-631
   of people with motor disabilities,
      622-624
   process of, 8-19
   testing vs., 9-11, 12-13, 49
   of visually impaired people, 613-
      617, 621-622
   *See also names of specific types of
      assessment*
Assessment centers, 654-656
Assessment data. *See* Data
Assessment of Men (OSS), 11, 51
Assessment tools, 11-19
   behavioral observation, 16-17,
      504, 683
   case study, 16, 17, 535-536

interview, 14-16, 332, 528-535,
   549, 589-590, 651, 683, 694
test, 11-14
Assimilation, 237
Association for Children and Adults
   with Learning Disabilities, 349
Association of American Medical
   Colleges (AAMC), 55
Association of Personnel Test
   Publishers (APTP), 663-664
ASVAB. *See* Armed Services
   Vocational Aptitude Battery
Ataxia, 577
ATQ-N. *See* Automatic Thoughts
   Questionnaire
ATQ-P. *See* Positive Automatic
   Thoughts Questionnaire
At-risk preschool children, 386-387
Attitude measures, 24, 25, 30, 374-
   375, 548, 618, 678-680
"Aunt Fanny" effect, 569
Australia, intelligence tests used in,
   257
Automatic Thoughts Questionnaire
   (ATQ-N), 542
Autonomic Nervous System
   Response Inventory, 25
Average, 91. *See also* Arithmetic
   mean
Average deviation, 93-94
A-V-L. *See* Allport-Vernon-Lindzey
   Study of Values

Bar graph, 85, 86
Barnum effect, 565-571, 734
BAS. *See* British Ability Scales
Basal level, 285
Base rate, 172
Basic English Skills Test (BEST), 331
Basic Inventory of Natural Language
   (BINL), 331
Basic Occupational Literacy Test
   (BOLT), 645
Battelle Developmental Inventory
   (BDI), 384
Batteries. *See* Test batteries
Baugh-Carpenter scale, 475
Bayley Scales of Infant Development,
   381-382
BBCS. *See* Bracken Basic Concept
   Scale

BDI. *See* Battelle Developmental Inventory; Beck Depression Inventory

Beavers-Timberlawn Family Evaluation Scale, 548

Beck Depression Inventory (BDI), 31, 165-166, 539-541

Beck Self-Concept Test (BST), 486-487

Beery-Buktenica Development Test of Visual-Motor Integration, 598

Behavior
adaptive, 31, 625-631
functional analysis of, 507
giftedness and, 255
nervous system and, 573-580
type A and type B, 423

Behavioral assessment, 500-521
behavioral observation, 16-17, 504, 683
behavior rating scales, 504-509
issues in, 519-521
overview of, 500-502
psychophysiological methods of, 509-517
role play, 518-519
self-report measures, 432-435, 517
traditional psychological assessment vs., 502
unobtrusive measures, 517-518

Behavioral checklists, 18

Behavioral observation, 16-17, 504, 683

Behavior Problem Checklist, 505, 621

Behavior Rating Profile, 505

Behn-Rorschach Inkblot Test, 446

Beier-Sternberg Discord Questionnaire, 548

Bell-shaped curve, 85, 88

Bender Visual-Motor Gestalt Test, 31, 580, 599-605, 620
administration of, 600-602
emotional indicators on, 605
modifications of, 604-605
psychometric properties of, 603-604
scoring and interpretation of, 602-603

Benton Test of Visual Retention—

Revised, 591

Berkeley Growth Study, 381

Berkman v. *City of New York,* 662

Bernreuter Personality Inventory, 50

BEST. *See* Basic English Skills Test

Bias, test, 187-193, 217-218

Bilingual Vocational Oral Proficiency Test (BVOPT), 331

Bimodal distribution, 88

Binet-Simon Scale, 48, 231, 248-249, 277-278

Binge-purge syndrome, 19. *See also* Bulimia

BINL. *See* Basic Inventory of Natural Language

Biofeedback, 17, 509-510

Biophysical definitions of personality, 400

Biosocial definitions of personality, 400

BIP Bender, 604

Biserial *r,* 123-124

BIT. *See* British Intelligence Test

Black Intelligence Test of Cultural Homogeneity, 270-271

Blacky Pictures Test, 427, 464

Blake v. *City of Los Angeles,* 661

Blind Learning Aptitude Test, 615

Blindness, 613-617, 621-622

Blood pressure, 17

Blueprinting, 162

Body Image Avoidance Questionnaire, 24

Body image distortion, 19

Body mass, personality types based on, 403, 404

Body temperature, 17

Boehm Test of Basic Concepts— Preschool Version, 393, 395

BOLT. *See* Basic Occupational Literacy Test

Bonding, test to measure, 24

Boyd v. *Ozark Air Lines, Inc.,* 659

Bracken Basic Concept Scale (BBCS), 393

Brain, 573-580
damage to, 577-580, 594
hemispheres of, 575, 577

Brain scan, 586

Brainstem, 573-575

Brain Watchers, The (Gross), 54

Brain wave measurement, 700

Brigance test, 331

British Ability Scales (BAS), 357-358

British Intelligence Test (BIT), 357

Brown v. *Board of Education,* 57

Bruininks-Oseretsky Test of Motor Proficiency, 598, 624

BST. *See* Beck Self-Concept Test

Btu, 3

Bulimia, 19, 24, 186

Burnout, test to measure, 24

Buros Institute of Mental Measurements, 30

Business assessment, 6-7. *See also* Industrial/organizational assessment

BVOPT. *See* Bilingual Vocational Oral Proficiency Test

CAK-C. *See* Concept Assessment Kit—Conservation

California Achievement Tests, 325, 326-327

California Psychological Inventory (CPI), 425-426

California Q-sort, 485

California Test of Mental Maturity, 314

Callery v. *New York City Parks and Recreation Department,* 657

Callier-Azusa Scale (CAS), 622

Canada, intelligence tests used in, 258

CAPA. *See* Computer-assisted psychological assessment

Carat, 3

Career Ability Placement Survey, 645

Career Decision Scale, 638

CAS. *See* Callier-Azusa Scale

Casebook on Ethical Principles of Psychologists, 59, 60-61

Casebook on Ethical Standards of Psychologists, 59

Case history, 16, 17, 535-536

CAST. *See* Children's Apperceptive Story-Telling Test

Castro v. *Beecher,* 657

CAT. *See* Children's Apperception Test

Catalogues, test, 29

Categorical scaling, 201

Cattell Culture Fair Test, 269, 273
Cattell Infant Intelligence Scale (CIIS), 46
Causation vs. correlation, 116
CDI. *See* Children's Depression Inventory
Ceiling effect, 254
Ceiling level, 285
CELT. *See* Comprehensive English Language
CEMSS. *See* Comprehensive Early Memories Scoring System Center for Epidemiological Studies (CES), 541
Central nervous system, 18, 573
Central processing of test data, 720
Central tendency, measures of, 89-92
Central tendency error, 189, 436
Cerebellum, 573, 575
Certification of education, 4
CES-D (Center for Epidemiological Studies depression measure), 541
Character Education Inquiry, 494-495
Chavez v. *Southern Pacific Transportation,* 73
Checklists, behavioral, 18
CHECpoint Systems, Inc., 331
Child
    at-risk, 386-387
    evaluation of, 560-562. *See also* Preschool intelligence and ability assessment; *names of specific tests*
Child abuse and neglect, 24, 562-564
Child Abuse Potential Inventory, 24
Child Behavior Checklist, 505, 621
Child custody, 559-564
Children's Apperception Test (CAT), 464, 498, 561
Children's Apperceptive Story-Telling Test (CAST), 465
Children's Depression Inventory (CDI), 541
Children's Embedded Figures Test, 489
Children's Personality Questionnaire, 416, 498
Children's Self Concept Scale

(CSCS), 487-488, 498
Child's Attitude Toward Father Scale, 548
Child's Attitude Toward Mother Scale, 548
China, proficiency testing in, 39-40
Christensen-Guilford Fluency tests, 321
CIIS. *See* Cattell Infant Intelligence Scale
Civil law, 71-72
Civil Rights Act of 1964, Title VII, 56, 665
CLEP. *See* College Level Examination Program
Clinical and counseling assessment, 4-5, 6, 525-571
    case history, 16, 17, 535-536
    context of, 568
    diagnostic tests, 538-539
    interview, 14-16, 528-535
    marital and family assessment, 25, 177-186, 505, 520, 546-550
    measures of depression, 24, 165-166, 539-542
    measures of values, 542-545
    overview of, 526-527
    posttraumatic stress disorder, 545, 550
    psychological report, 565-571
    psychological tests, 536-538
    special applications
    custody evaluations, 559-564
    forensic psychological assessment, 551-558
    readiness for parole or probation, 558-559
Clinical prediction vs. actuarial prediction, 429-431
Clinical psychology and psychologists, 47
Clinical report. *See* Psychological report; Reports
Cloud Picture Test, 441
Coded Sign English, 619
Code of Fair Testing Practices in Education, 61, 62-63, 108
Coefficient alpha, 144-145
Coefficient of correlation, 117-125
Coefficient of determination, 122

Coefficient of generalizability, 153
Coefficient of regression, 121, 129
Coefficient of reliability, 132, 146-151
Coefficient of stability, 138, 265, 378-380
Coefficient of validity, 166-168
Cognitive Abilities Test, 314
Cognitive development, Piagetian theory of, 236-237, 238
Cognitive disabilities, 624-631
Cognitive functioning, neuro-psychological tests of, 592-595
Cognitive style measures, 488-493
    of field dependence and independence, 488-490
    Group Embedded Figures Test, 489-490
    reflective vs. impulsive cognitive styles, 491-492
College Board, 61, 114, 332
College Board Technical Handbook for the Scholastic Aptitude Test and Achievement Tests (Donlon), 341
College Entrance Examination Board, 330
College Level Examination Program (CLEP), 330
Color blindness, 508
Color-Form Sorting Test, 579, 591, 594
Color Sorting Test, 579
Combat Exposure Scale, 24
Committee on Emotional Fitness, 50
Common factors, 748
Common law, 71
Communality, 752
Communicative Abilities in Daily Living test, 611
Comparative judgment, law of, 197
Comparative scaling, 201
Compensatory damages, 73
Competency
    minimum, 56, 372-373
    social, 616-617, 626
    to stand trial, 552-555
Competency Screening Test, 554-555

Completion item, 205
Comprehensive Early Memories Scoring System (CEMSS), 497-498
Comprehensive English Language (CELT), 331
Computer-assisted psychological assessment (CAPA), 707-738
  access to products of, 737-738
  advantages of, 709-717
  disadvantages of, 717-718
  equivalency issues in, 727-733
  input, 718-722
  interpretive reports, 723-727
  output, 722
  process of, 709
  scoring reports, 722-723
  standards for products of, 736-737
  test administration, 65-66, 450-452, 718-720, 727-733
  test interpretation in, 65-66, 450-452, 733-736
  validity issues in, 733-736
Computer Attitude Scale, 24
Computerized adaptive testing, 709
Computerized axial tomography scan, 586
Concept Assessment Kit—Conservation (CAK-C), 387-388
Conceptualization, test, 195-196
Concrete operations period, 238
Concurrent validity, 164, 165-166
Conditional standards, 23
Confessions (St. Augustine), 41
Confidentiality, 69-70
Conflict Tactics Scales, 548-549
Congressional Office of Technology Assessment, 511
Conners Teacher Rating Scale, 487
Consent, informed, 66
Construct, 175
Constructed-response item format, 205-206
Construction, test, 134, 196-206
  content, 408-410
  by empirical criterion keying, 416-426
  factor-analytic, 410-416
  logical, 408-410
  of oral tests, 225-227

for personality assessment, 408-432
scaling, 196-203
theoretical approach to, 427-432
writing items, 203-206
Construct validity, 10, 175-187
  defined, 175
  evidence of, 176-187
Consultative reports, 727
Consumer assessment, 677-706
  attitude measurement in, 678-680
  literature on, 690
  projective techniques in, 683, 696-697
  psychophysiological methods in, 699-706
  qualitative assessment in, 682-683, 693-696
  surveys and polls in, 682, 685-693
  tools in, 680-685
Content-referenced interpretation, 115
Content sampling, 134
Content test construction, 408-410
Content validity, 161-163
Content validity ratio, 162-163
Continuous scale, 78
Contralateral control, 575, 577
Contrast effect, 520-521
Control, locus of, 492
Controlled Word Association Test, 595
Convenience sample, 107
Convention of the Meter, 3
Convergent evidence, 179-181
Convergent thinking, 317, 320
Convergent validity, 180
Cooperative Achievement Test, 328
Coordination, tests of, 585
Corpus callosum, 573
Correlation, 116-129
  biserial r, 123-124
  causation vs., 116
  coefficient of, 117-125
  concept of, 116-117
  graphic representations of, 125-129
  negative, 117, 127
  nonlinear, 128
  Pearson r, 117-122, 124

phi coefficient, 124-125
point-biserial, 124
positive, 117, 126
Spearman rho, 122, 123, 124
tetrachoric, 124
Cortex, 573
Costa v. Markey, 659-660
Counseling assessment. *See* Clinical and counseling assessment
Couples Interaction Scoring System, 505
Court decisions, 57-58, 657-662
  on bias, 190
  on malpractice, 72-73
  on privacy, 68, 69
CPI. *See* California Psychological Inventory
Cranial nerves, tests of, 588
Create-A-Test program, 710
Creativity, intelligence tests for, 317, 320-321
Criminal law, 71
Criminal responsibility, 555-558
Criterion
  characteristics of, 164-165
  defined, 164
Criterion contamination, 165
Criterion keying, test construction by, 416-417
Criterion-referenced tests
  norm-referenced tests vs., 114-116
  reliability and, 150
Criterion-related validity, 164-175
Critical incidents technique, 667
Critical thinking test, 321
Cross-validation, 219-220
CRUST. *See* Cultural/Regional Uppercrust Savvy Test
Crystallized intelligence, 240, 282
CSCS. *See* Piers-Harris Children's Self Concept Scale
CT scan, 586
Cube Test, 579
Cubit, 1
Cultural loading, 269, 270
Cultural minorities, testing, 61, 64, 249, 268-272, 273, 275, 336-339, 628
Cultural/Regional Uppercrust Savvy

(continued)

Down's syndrome, 18, 383
DQ. *See* Deterioration quotient;
Developmental quotient
Draw-An-Animal procedure, 473
Draw-A-Person Test (DAP), 31,
471-473, 474-475, 547
Driscoll Play Kit, 475-476
Drug abuse, 539
DSM-III. *See* Diagnostic and
*Statistical Manual of Mental
Disorders III*
DTLA-2. *See* Detroit Tests of
Learning Aptitude
Dual-easel test administration format,
377-378
Durham v. United States, 556
Durrell Analysis of Reading Test, 347
Durrel Listening Reading Series, 329
Dusky v. United States, 552
Dynamic characteristics of test, 148-
149
Dysfunctional Attitude Scale, 24

E. T., The Extraterrestrial, 560-561
Early School Personality Question
naire, 416
Early Screening Profiles (ESP), 384-
386
Easel format of test administration,
377-378
Eating disorders, 19, 24, 186
Eating Disorders Inventory, 24
Echoencephalograph, 587
Ecological validity, 10
Ectomorph, 404
*Educational, Psychological and
Personality Tests of 1933 and
1934,* 53
Educational assessment, 3-4, 5, 324-
375
achievement tests, 4, 324-333
aptitude tests, 333-346
diagnostic tests, 346-350
of learning disabilities, 348-350
math tests, 348
minimum competency tests, 372-
373
Peabody Picture Vocabulary
Test—Revised, 369-371
peer appraisal techniques, 371-374

psychoeducational test batteries,
350-369
reading tests, 347
of study habits, interests, and
attitudes, 374-375
See also Assessment
Educational Testing Service, 21, 61,
332
Education Apperception Test, 464
Education for All Handicapped
Children Act of 1975, 3, 56,
349, 613
Edwards Personal Preference
Schedule (EPPS), 50, 427-432,
648-649
EEG. *See* Electroencephalograph
EEOC. *See* Equal Employment
Opportunity Commission
Eigenvalue, 751
Einstellung phenomenon, 492-493
Electrodermal response, 699-700
Electroencephalograph (EEG), 510,
586-587, 700
Electromyograph (EMG), 587, 700
Embedded Figures Test, 489
EMG. *See* Electromyograph
Emotional Factors Inventory, 616
Empirical criterion keying, test
construction by, 416-426
Empiricists, 42
Employee Polygraphy Protection Act
of 1988, 516
Endomorph, 404
Engineering psychology, 672-676
defined, 633
designing environments, 674-676
designing instrumentation and
equipment, 672-674
England, intelligence tests used in,
258-259
English Men of Science (Galton), 261
English proficiency tests, 330, 331-
332
Enhancement, 434
Environment
designing, 674-676
intelligence and, 268
*Environment, Intelligence and
Scholastic Achievement,* 54
EPPS. *See* Edwards Personal

Preference Schedule
Equal-appearing intervals, method of,
199-200
Equal Employment Opportunity Act
of 1964, 56
Equal Employment Opportunity
Commission (EEOC), 58
Equipercentile method, 113
Equipment, designing, 672-674
Equivalency, 727-733
Erg, 7
Ergonomics, 6-7
Error
of central tendency, 189, 436
generosity, 189, 436
leniency, 189, 436
of measurement, 78-79, 154-155
rating, 189-190
severity, 189, 436
standard error of difference
between two scores, 155-157
standard error of measurement,
79, 154-155
Error factors, 748
Error variance, 133, 134-136
ESP. *See* Early Screening Profiles
*Essay Concerning Human Under-
standing, An* (Locke), 42
Essay questions, 206, 333
Estimation, direct and indirect, 200
Eta squared, 125
Ethical considerations
in personnel selection, 666
in testing, 52-74
Ethical Principles of Psychologists,
59, 60, 68
*Ethical Standards for the Distribution of
Psychological Tests and
Diagnostic Aids,* 59-60
Ethical Standards of Psychologists, 59, 60
Event recording, 503
Evidence of construct validity, 176-
187
changes with age, 178
convergent evidence, 179-181
discriminant evidence, 181
from distinct groups, 179
factor analysis, 186-187
homogeneity, 176-178
pretest/posttest changes, 178-179

Item type, 719
Item-validity index, 209-210
Item writing, 203-206
Iverson v. *Frandsen,* 69

Jablonski v. *United States,* 68
JCTP. *See* Joint Committee on Testing Practices
Job Discrimination Index, 671
Job previews, 649
Jobs. *See* Industrial/organizational assessment
Job satisfaction, 671-672
Joint Committee on Testing Practices (JCTP), 61
Journal of Applied Psychology, 171
Journal of Educational Psychology, 197, 233-234
Journal of Personality Assessment, 446, 447
Journal of Phrenology, 572
Journal of the History of the Behavioral Sciences, 51
J-shaped curve, 88

K-ABC. *See* Kaufman Assessment Battery for Children
Kallikak Family, The (Goddard), 263
Kappa statistic, 146
Kaufman Adolescent and Adult Intelligence Scale, 247
Kaufman Assessment Battery for Children (K-ABC), 243, 247, 285, 350-357, 619
  administering, 355
  correlation with Early Screening Profiles, 386
  evaluation of, 357
  preschool assessment and, 378-380, 386, 392, 393, 394
  psychometric properties of, 353-355
  sample test record, 356
  scoring and interpreting, 357
  stability coefficient of, 378-380
  standardization sample, 352
  subtests of, 354
Kendall's tau, 122
Kent-Rosanoff Free Association Test,

469
Key Math Revised: A Diagnostic Inventory of Essential Mathematics, 348
Kinetic Family Drawing (KFD), 473-474
Kuder preference and interest scales, 637
Kuder-Richardson formulas, 143-144, 328, 336
Kuhlmann-Anderson Intelligence Tests, 314
Kurtosis, 97-98

Labeling, 69
"Landmarks in Computer-Assisted Psychological Assessment" (Fowler), 708
Laplace-Gaussian curve, 98
Larry P. v. *Riles,* 57, 190
Latent-trait models, 215-216
Law. *See* Forensic psychological assessment; Legal considerations; Litigation; *names of specific laws*
Law of comparative judgment, 197
Law of initial values, 703
Law School Admission Test (LSAT), 343, 345-346, 646
LCSF. *See* Lifestyle Criminality Screening Form
Leaderless-group situations, 495
Leadership Q-Test, 484
Learning disabilities assessment, 348-350
Legal assessment. *See* Forensic psychological assessment
Legal considerations
  in personnel selection, 666-667
  in testing, 52-74
  concerns of profession, 55-66
  concerns of public, 53-55
  malpractice, 70-74
  rights of test takers, 66-70
Legislation, on psychological testing, 56-58
Leipzig, University of, 45-46
Leiter International Performance Scale, 621
Leniency error, 189, 436

Lesion, 577, 581
Letters from an American Farmer (Crevecoeur), 372
Letters of recommendation, 651
Levelers, 493
Liability, 71, 72
Lie detector tests, 510-511, 513-516
Lifestyle Criminality Screening Form (LCSF), 559
Likert scale, 201-202, 689
Limbic system, 575
Linear transformation of scores, 102-103
Linguistic minorities, testing, 61, 64
Listening Comprehension Test, 272
Litigation, 657-662. *See also* Court decisions
Lobes, 573, 575
Local norms, 113
Local processing of test data, 721-722
Locus of control, 492
Logical test construction, 408-410
Logogram, 697-699
Loneliness Rating Scale, 24
LSAT. *See* Law School Admission Test
Lumbar puncture, 587
Luria Nebraska Neuropsychological Battery, 609
Lying, 512-516

McCarthy Scales of Children's Abilities (MSCA), 389-392, 393, 394
McGraw-Hill Book Company, 331
Machover's Draw-A-Person Test, 31, 471-473, 474-475, 547
Magnetic resonance imaging, 587
Mail surveys, 687-688
Make A Picture Story Method, 465
Make-A-Test program, 710, 711
Malingering, test to measure, 24
Malleus Malificarum, 42
Malpractice, 70-74
Malpractice: A Guide for Mental Health Professionals (Cohen), 73
Management Progress Study (MPS), 654-656

MPS. *See* Management Progress Study

MRT. *See* Metropolitan Readiness Tests

MSCA. *See* McCarthy Scales of Children's Abilities

Multidimensional scaling (MDS), 201, 221, 691-693

Multifactor theory of intelligence, 239-240

Multiple-choice items, 204, 333

Multiple regression, 129, 130-131

Multitrait-multimethod matrix, 180-185

Music listening skills, test for, 321-322, 346

Myers-Briggs Type Indicator, 402-403, 427

NAS. *See* National Academy of Science

NASP. *See* National Association of School Psychologists

National Academy of Neuropsychologists, 590

National Academy of Science (NAS), 644-645

National anchor norms, 112-113

National Association of School Psychologists (NASP), 59, 60

National Council on Measurements in Education (NCME), 22, 55, 61

National Defense Education Act, 53

National Educational Association, 55

National Institute of Mental Health, 271

National norms, 112

Nature/nurture controversy, 263

Nature of Human Values, The (Rokeach), 544

Naylor-Shine tables, 171-172

NCCEA. *See* Neurosensory Center Comprehensive Examination of Aphasia

NCME. *See* National Council on Measurements in Education

Nebraska, University of, 30

Nebraska Test of Learning Aptitude, 621

Needs, hierarchy of, 670

Negative correlation, 117, 127

Negatively skewed distribution, 88

Neglect, of child, 562-564

Negligence, 71

Nelson Reading Skills Test, 329

Nervous system, 18, 25, 573-580

Netherlands, intelligence tests used in, 259

Neuro Developmental Training Balls, 598

Neurological damage, 577-580

Neurology, 573

Neurons, 573

Neuropsychological assessment, 572-611
    examinations, 580-589
    nervous system and, 573-580
    test batteries, 606-611
    tests, 589-605

Neuropsychological examination, 580-589
    history, 582-584
    medical diagnostic aids in, 586-587
    mental status examination, 15, 531-533, 584, 590
    physical examination, 584-589

Neuropsychological Impairment Scale (NIS), 590

Neuropsychological test batteries, 606-611
    flexible, 606
    Halstead-Reitan Neuropsychological Battery, 606-609, 610
    Luria Nebraska Neuropsychological Battery, 609
    Montreal Neurological Institute Battery, 609
    prepackaged, 606-611
    Severe Impairment Battery, 610-611
    Southern California Sensory Integration Tests, 610, 624

Neuropsychological tests, 589-605
    Bender Visual-Motor Gestalt Test, 31, 580, 599-605, 620
    of cognitive functioning, 592-595
    of intellectual ability, 590-591
    interviews, 589-590

of memory, 591-592, 593
    motor, 597-599
    perceptual and perceptual-motor, 597-599
    rating scales, 589-590
    suppliers of, 766
    of verbal functioning, 595-597

Neuropsychology, 573

Neurosensory Center Comprehensive Examination of Aphasia (NCCEA), 595

Newbury House, 332

New Guinea, intelligence tests used in, 259

"New Look at Psychological Testing, A" (Greenspoon and Gersten), 501

New Orleans Medical and Surgical Journal, 248

New Republic, 53

New Zealand, intelligence tests used in, 259

NIS. *See* Neuropsychological Impairment Scale

Nominal scales, 80-81, 198

Nominating technique, 371, 374

Noninvasive procedures, 584

Nonlinear correlation, 128

Nonlinear transformation of scores, 102-103

Normal curve, 85, 88, 98-100
    area under, 99-100

Normalized standard scores, 103-104

Normative sample, 106-108. *See also* Standardization sample

Norm group, 106

Norm-referenced vs. criterion-referenced interpretation, 114-116

Norms, 28-29, 105-116
    age, 109-111
    fixed reference group scoring systems, 113-114
    grade, 111-112
    local, 113
    national, 112
    national anchor, 112-113
    normative or standardization sample, 106-108, 192
    percentiles, 108-109
    race, 644

subgroup, 113

Objective methods of personality assessment. *See* Personality assessment, objective methods
Object Representation Scale for Dreams (ORSD), 498
Object Sorting Test, 579, 594
Observation
behavioral, 16-17, 504, 683
self-observation, 504
Observations on Man, his Frame, his Duty, and his Expectations (Hartley), 42
Occipital lobes, 575
Occupational Preference Inventory, 638
O'Connor Tweezer Dexterity Test, 646
Office of Technology Assessment, 511
Officer Qualifying Test, 315
Officers for Justice v. *Civil Service Commission,* 660
Olfactory nerve, 588
OLSAT. *See* Otis-Lennon School Ability Test
One-dimensional preference scale, 688-689
O'Neill v. *Montefiore Hospital,* 72
One-on-one interviews, 694
On the Origin of Species by Means of Natural Selection (Darwin), 43
Optic nerve, 588
Oral tests, construction of, 225-227
Ordinal scales, 81-82, 198, 689
Ordinal Scales of Psychological Development (OSPD), 387, 388
Organicity, 578, 580
Organizational psychology, 633. *See also* Industrial/organizational assessment
Organization and Pathology of Thought (Rapaport), 537
ORSD. *See* Object Representation Scale for Dreams
OSPD. *See* Ordinal Scales of Psychological Development

OSS. *See* U.S. Office of Strategic Services
Otis-Lennon School Ability Test (OLSAT), 32-37, 254, 314-315, 316
Outlier, 125, 128
PAF. *See* Patient's Assessment of Own Functioning
Pain Assessment Questionnaire, 25
Paired-comparison method, 201, 438
Pantomime, 612
Parallel-forms reliability estimates, 138-140
Paranoia, 419
Parent-Adolescent Relationship Questionnaire, 550
Parents, evaluation of, 548, 550, 559-560
Parents in Action on Special Education (PASE) v. *Joseph P. Hannon,* 190
Parietal lobes, 575
Parole, readiness for, 558-559
PASS model of intellectual functioning, 243
Patient's Assessment of Own Functioning (PAF), 590
Pattern analysis, 590
PCL. *See* Psychopathy Checklist
PDI. *See* Psychomotor Developmental Index
Peabody Individual Achievement Test, 325, 326-327
Peabody Picture Vocabulary Test—Revised (PPVT-R), 369-371
Pearson correlation coefficient, 117-122, 124
Peck v. *Counseling Service of Addison County, Inc.,* 68
Pedagogical Seminary, The, 457
Peer appraisal techniques, 371-374, 667-668
Penile plethysmograph, 17, 511, 517
Pennsylvania, University of, 18-19
Pennsylvania v. *Ritchie,* 69
PEP. *See* Proficiency Examination Program
Percentage, 109
Percentiles, 108-109
Perceptual-motor tests, 597-599

Perceptual tests, 597-599
Performance samples, 651-654
Peripheral nervous system, 573
Perkins Binet intelligence test, 615
Personal Data Sheet, 50, 409
Personality
defining, 399-401
intelligence and, 267
measurement of, 49-51, 405-408
Personality assessment, 399-521
behavioral assessment, 500-521
clinical vs. actuarial prediction in, 429-431
cognitive style measures, 488-493
objective methods, 408-439
California Psychological Inventory, 425-426
Edwards Personal Preference Schedule, 50, 427-432, 648-649
Guilford-Zimmerman Temperament Survey, 410, 647-648
Minnesota Multiphasic Personality Inventory, 13-14, 31, 165, 417-425, 547, 708, 718, 722, 723, 725-726
Mooney Problem Checklist, 50, 409-410
Sixteen Personality Factor Questionnaire, 410-416, 620
Personality Inventory for Children, 498-499, 727, 728-732
preemployment counseling and, 646-649
problems in, 432-439
projective methods, 440-481
assumptions of, 479-480
in custody evaluation, 560, 561
defined, 440-442
figure drawing, 31, 471-475
hand test, 476, 620-621
Holtzman Inkblot Technique, 453-456
Machover's Draw-A-Person Test, 31, 471-473, 474-475, 547
picture-story tests, 456-467
psychometric considerations of, 481
Rorschach Inkblot Test, 13-14, 31, 50, 442-453, 456, 547, 620

Rosenzweig Picture Frustration Study, 476–479, 547

sentence completion tests, 469–470

situational variables in, 480–481

Thematic Apperception Test, 31, 457, 458–464, 547, 615, 620, 671

word association tests, 468–469, 512–513

rating scales and, 435–439

self-concept measures, 483–488

self-report techniques and, 432–435, 517

situational performance measures, 493–497

suppliers of resources, 764–766

test construction and, 408–432

Personality Inventory for Children (PIC), 498–499, 727, 728–732

Personality Projection in the Drawing of the Human Figure: A Method of Personality Investigation (Machover), 471

Personality Research Form (PRF), 220–223, 427

Personality states, 403–405

Personality test battery, 536

Personality traits, 401–402

Personality types, 402–403, 404

Personnel psychology, 649–672
  classification in, 650
  defined, 633
  job satisfaction and, 671–672
  motivation and, 668–671
  placement in, 650
  productivity and, 667–668
  screening in, 649, 650–664
  selection in, 649–650, 664–667

PET scans, 586

Phi coefficient, 124–125

Philosophers, 41–43

Phrenology, 572

Physical concerns, tests to measure, 25

Physical examination
  in job screening, 656–663
  in neurological assessment, 584–589

Physical handicaps. *See* Disabling

conditions

Piagetian scales, 387–389

Piagetian theory of cognitive development, 236–237, 238

PIAT, 31

PIC. *See* Personality Inventory for Children

Pictograms, 672–674

Picture Story Test, 464

Picture-story tests, 456–467

Piers-Harris Children's Self Concept Scale (CSCS), 487–488, 498

Placement, 650

Play Performance Scale for Children, 505

Plethysmography, 17, 511, 517

PMAs. *See* Primary mental abilities

Point-biserial correlation, 124

Polls. *See* Surveys and polls

Polygraphs, 510–511, 513–516

Pond v. *Braniff Airways, Inc.,* 657

Positive Automatic Thoughts Questionnaire (ATQ-P), 542

Positive correlation, 117, 126

Positively skewed distribution, 88

Positron emission tomography (PET) scans, 586

Posttraumatic stress disorder (PTSD), 545, 550

Power tests, and reliability, 149–150

PPVT-R. *See* Peabody Picture Vocabulary Test—Revised

Predeterminism, 260–261

Predictive validity, 164, 166–175, 378–380

Preemployment counseling, 633, 634–649
  aptitude measures and, 638–646
  interest measures and, 634–638
  job previews and, 649
  personality measures and, 646–649

Preformationism, 260–261

Preoperational period, 238

Preschool Embedded Figures Test, 489

Preschool intelligence and ability assessment, 376–395
  at-risk children, 386–387
  Battelle Developmental Inventory, 384

Bayley Scales of Infant Development, 381–382

comparisons of test, 393, 394

Concept Assessment Kit—Conservation, 387–388

Early Screening Profiles, 384–386

Gesell Development Schedules, 383–384

of infants, 46, 244–247, 380–384

McCarthy Scales of Children's Abilities, 389–392, 393, 394

Ordinal Scales of Psychological Development, 387, 388

overview of, 377–380

Piagetian scales, 387–389

predictive validity of, 378–380

of preschool children, 384–395

screening tests, 384–386

stability of, 378–380

Preschool period, defined, 377

Press, 427, 428, 459

Pretest/posttest changes, evidence of, 178–179

PRF. *See* Personality Research Form

PRG Interest Inventory, 617

Primary mental abilities (PMAs), 240, 595

Primary standards, 23

Principles for Professional Ethics, 59, 60

Privacy rights, 67–69

Probation, readiness for, 558–559

Productivity, 667–668

Productivity Environmental Preference Survey, 550

Product-moment correlation, 117–122, 124

Product positioning, 680–681

Professional liability, 71, 72

Proficiency Examination Program (PEP), 330

Proficiency tests, 39–40, 326, 330, 331–332, 598, 624, 651

Prognostic tests. *See* Aptitude tests

Projective hypothesis, 440

Projective methods
  of consumer assessment, 696–697
  of personality assessment. *See* Personality assessment, projective methods

Projective test battery, 536

Regression coefficients, 121, 129
Regression equation, 129-131
Regression line, 121, 129-131
Rehabilitation Act of 1973, 612-613
Reliability, 28, 132-157
    concept of, 133-136
    criterion-referenced tests and, 150
    defined, 132
    generalizability theory, 151, 152-153
    individual scores and, 151-157
    inter-scorer, 145-146
    power tests and, 149-150
    speed tests and, 149-150
    of test items, 210-211
    of Thematic Apperception Test, 459-462
Reliability coefficient, 132, 146-151
Reliability estimates, 136-146
    alternate-forms, 138-140
    for Differential Abilities Scales, 361
    Kuder-Richardson formulas for, 143-144
    parallel-forms, 138-140
    Spearman-Brown formula for, 141-142
    split-half, 140-142
    test-retest, 136-138
Remote Associates Test (RAT), 321
Reports
    in clinical and counseling assessment, 565-571
    consultative, 727
    descriptive, 723, 725
    interpretive, 723-727
    sample, 739-743
    scoring, 722-723, 724-725
    screening, 723-727
    self-reports, 432-435, 517, 550
"Rep Test," 497
Res ipsa loquitur, 73
Resource Development Institute, Inc., 331
Response styles, 434-435
Responsibility, criminal, 555-558
Retardation. See Mental retardation
Reticular formation, 575
Reviews, test, 30-37
Revised Behavior Problem Checklist,
505
Revision, test, 219-220
Rey Auditory Verbal Learning Test, 591
Reynolds Adolescent Depression Scale (RADS), 542
Reznikoff-Tomblen scale, 475
Ripple effect, 613
Riverside Publishing Company, 61
Roberts Apperception Test for Children (RATC), 464-465
Roche Psychiatric Service Institute, 708, 727
Rodriguez v. State, 73
Rogers Criminal Responsibility Assessment Scale (RCRAS), 556-558
Rokeach Value Survey (RVS), 544
Role Construct Repertory Test ("Rep Test"), 497
Role play, 518-519
Rorschach Inkblot Test, 13-14, 31, 50, 442-453, 456, 547, 620
    computerized administration, scoring, and interpretation of, 450-452
    Exner's comprehensive system for administering, scoring, and interpreting, 449, 452-453
    family assessment and, 547
    psychometric properties of, 445-449
Rosenzweig Picture Frustration Study, 476-479, 547
Rotter Incomplete Sentences Blank, 470
RVS. See Rokeach Value Survey

SADS. See Schedule for Affective Disorders and Schizophrenia
Salience, 750
Samms v. Eccles, 73
Sample, normative or standardization, 106-108. See also Standardization sample
Sampling
    appropriate, 199
    content, 134
    domain, 151
incidental, 107
item, 134
purposive, 107
stratified, 107
SAT. See Scholastic Aptitude Test
SATB. See Special Aptitude Test Battery
Satisfaction
    customer, 735
    job, 671-672
    marital, 177-186
    sexual, 25
Satisfaction with Life Scale, 25
Scales, 78-83
    continuous, 78
    defined, 78
    discrete, 78
    interval, 82, 198
    Likert, 201-202, 689
    nominal, 80-81, 198
    one-dimensional preference, 688-689
    ordinal, 81-82, 198, 689
    ratio, 82-83, 198
    summative, 201
    types of, 197-198
Scaling, 196-203
    aggregate, 688-691
    categorical, 201
    comparative, 201
    defined, 196
    Guttman, 202, 691
    methods of, 198-203
    multidimensional, 201, 221, 691-693
    unidimensional, 200
Scatter diagrams, 125-129
Scatterplots, 125-129
Schedule for Affective Disorders and Schizophrenia (SADS), 533
Schema, schemata, 237
Schicksalanalysis, 466
Schizophrenia, 419
Scholastic Aptitude Test (SAT), 4, 101-102, 114, 335, 339, 340-341
School ability test, 3
School Apperception Method, 464
Schools, group intelligence tests in, 54, 313-315, 316

Credits

Chapter 1 Figure 1-1: © 1991 Ronald Jay Cohen. Photo courtesy of The Participatory Theatre Company, Inc. Figure 1-2: Johnny Carson courtesy *The Tonight Show* starring Johnny Carson; Barbara Walters, ABC News; Ed Bradley courtesy CBS News; Joan Rivers courtesy Fox Broadcasting Company, photo by Erik Heinila; Louis Rukeyser courtesy Wall $treet Week with Louis Rukeyser; Oprah Winfrey courtesy Harpo, Inc. Copyright © Paul Natkin; Dan Rather courtesy CBS News; Mike Wallace courtesy CBS News; Dr. Ronald Jay Cohen courtesy Chestnut Ridge Psychological Services. Used by permission. Figure 1-3: © 1991 Ronald Jay Cohen. Figure 1-4: Copyright © 1980 Martin R. Roth and Gary P. Hermus. Chapter 1 Close-up: Reprinted from the *Standards for Educational and Psychological Testing* (1985, p. 79). Copyright 1985 by the American Psychological Association. Reprinted by permission of the publisher. Further reproduction without the express written permission of the American Psychological Association is prohibited. Figure 1-6: Courtesy National Archives.

Chapter 2 Figure 2-1: By Maynard Owen Williams. Copyright © 1927 National Geographic Society. Figure 2-2: Courtesy Staatsbibliothek, Bildarchiv, Berlin. Figure 2-3: National Portrait Gallery, London. Used by permission. Figure 2-4: Photo of James McKeen Cattell from the *Journal of Consulting Psychology*, Vol. 1, Number 1 (1937): In the public domain. Photo of Dr. Psyche Cattell courtesy of Hudson Cattell. Figure 2-5: Photo by Brown Brothers, *Life Magazine*, September 1990. Figure 2-6: Courtesy Henry A. Murray.

Chapter 3 Figure 3-1: © 1987 Ronald Jay Cohen. All rights reserved.

Chapter 4 Figure 4-1: Used by permission of Ronald Jay Cohen. Thanks to Christine D., Christine H., Elise, Susie, Brett, Laurel, Bonnie, Joy, and the two Jennifers. Chapter 4 Close-up photo: University College, London. Figure 4-3: University College, London.

Chapter 5 Table 5-1: COPS/California Occupational Preference Survey Manual. Copyright © 1971 EDITS/Educational and Industrial Testing Service. Reprinted with permission. Chapter 5 Close-up photo: Courtesy Lee J. Cronbach.

Chapter 6 Table 6-1: From Lawshe (1975). Copyright © 1974 Personnel Psychology, Inc. Reprinted by permission. Figure 6-1 and Table 6-2: From the Manual for the Differential Aptitude Tests. Copyright © 1973, 1974 by The Psychological Corporation. All rights reserved. Figure 6-2: *Test Service Bulletin*, "How Effective Are Your Tests?" Copyright © 1949 by The Psychological Corporation. Reproduced by permission. All rights reserved. Chapter 6 Close-up figure: Adapted from Campbell & Fiske, 1959, p. 2. Copyright 1959 by the American Psychological Association. Reprinted by permission.

Chapter 7 Figures 7-2 and 7-3: *From Introduction to Measurement Theory* by M. J. Allen and W. M. Yen. Copyright © 1970 by Wadsworth, Inc. Reprinted by permission of Brooks/Cole Publishers, Pacific Grove, CA. Figure 7-4: From *Measurement Theory for the Behavioral Sciences,* by Edwin E. Ghiselli, John P. Campbell, and Sheldon Zedeck. Copyright © 1981 by W. H. Freeman and Company. Reprinted by permission. Chapter 7 Close-up figure: From Jackson (1970, p. 84). Reprinted by permission of the publisher. Copyright © 1970 Academic Press.

Chapter 8 Figure 8-3: Copyright © McGraw-Hill Book Company. Reproduced by permission. Figure 8-8: Photo courtesy Arthur R. Jensen. Figure 8-9: Sample test items from Cattell, R. B. (1940). A culture-free intelligence test, Part 1. *Journal of Educational Psychology, 31,* 161-179. In the public domain. Figure 8-10: Copyright © 1977 by *Phi Delta Kappan* and reproduced by permission of the author and *Phi Delta Kappan.*

Chapter 9 Figure 9-2: Photo courtesy Stanford University. Figure 9-3: Reprinted with permission of The Riverside Publishing Company from pages 122 of *Stanford-Binet Intelligence Scale Examiner's Handbook: An Expanded Guide for Fourth Edition Users* by E. A. Delaney, and T. F. Hopkins. THE RIVERSIDE PUBLISHING COMPANY, 8420 W. Bryn Mawr Avenue, Chicago, IL 60631. Copyright © 1987. Figure 9-4: Courtesy Mrs. David Wechsler. Figure 9-5: Photo copyright © 1987 Sid Hecker. Figures 9-6 and 9-7: Permission to reprint granted by the Director of Testing, Headquarters, United States Military Entrance Processing Command, North Chicago, IL. Figure 9-8: Copyright © 1940 Meier Art Judgment Test, The University of Iowa, Iowa City, IA. Chapter 9 Close-up table: From Grosswith (1980). Reprinted by permission of *Science Digest.*

Chapter 10 Figure 10-1: Model: Barbara Rich. Courtesy Richard Pavlo Photography and Insurance. Figure 10-2: Copyright © 1985 by PRO-ED, Inc. and used by permission. Table 10-6: Reprinted from Kaufman, A.S., Kaufman, N.L., and Goldsmith, B.Z., Kaufman *Sequential or Simultaneous* (K-SOS) (1984) with modifications. Circle Pines, MN: American Guidance Service. Figures 10-4 and 10-5: Photos courtesy American Guidance Service. Reprinted by permission. Figure 10-7: Reproduced by permission from the Differential Ability Scales. Copyright © 1990 by The Psychological Corporation. All rights reserved. Figure 10-8: Photo courtesy American Guidance Service. Reprinted by permission.

Chapter 11 Figure 11-2: Reproduced by permission of the authors from Powell, *Assessment and Management of Developmental Changes and Problems in Children,* 2nd ed., 1981.

Chapter 12 Figure 12-2: Cartoon by Mario Risso. Narrative Scoring Report copyright © 1967, 1970, 1971, 1986 by the Institute for Personality and Ability Testing, Inc., P.O. Box 188, Champagne,